P9-APE-964

G Volume 8

The World Book Encyclopedia

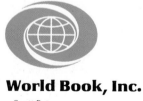

World Book, Inc.
a Scott Fetzer company

Chicago

BRAINERD SCHOOL LIBRARY

The World Book Encyclopedia

© World Book, Inc. All rights reserved. This volume may not be reproduced in whole or in part in any form without prior written permission from the publisher.

World Book, Inc.
233 North Michigan
Chicago, IL 60601

www.worldbook.com

WORLD BOOK and the GLOBE DEVICE are registered trademarks or trademarks of World Book, Inc.

Copyright © 2002, 2001, 2000, 1999, 1998, 1997, 1996, 1995, 1994, 1993, 1992, 1991, 1990, 1989, 1988, 1987, 1986, 1985, 1984, 1983 by World Book, Inc.
Copyright © 1982, 1981, 1980, 1979, 1978 by World Book-Childcraft International, Inc.
Copyright © 1977, 1976, 1975, 1974, 1973, 1972, 1971, 1970, 1969, 1968, 1967, 1966, 1965, 1964, 1963, 1962, 1961, 1960, 1959, 1958, 1957 by Field Enterprises Educational Corporation.
Copyright © 1957, 1956, 1955, 1954, 1953, 1952, 1951, 1950, 1949, 1948 by Field Enterprises, Inc.
Copyright 1948, 1947, 1946, 1945, 1944, 1943, 1942, 1941, 1940, 1939, 1938 by The Quarrie Corporation.
Copyright 1937, 1936, 1935, 1934, 1933, 1931, 1930, 1929 by W. F. Quarrie & Company.
The World Book, Copyright 1928, 1927, 1926, 1925, 1923, 1922, 1921, 1919, 1918, 1917 by W. F. Quarrie & Company.
Copyrights renewed 1990, 1989, 1988, 1987, 1986, 1985, 1984, 1983 by World Book, Inc.
Copyrights renewed 1982, 1981, 1980, 1979, 1978 by World Book-Childcraft International, Inc.
Copyrights renewed 1977, 1976, 1975, 1974, 1973, 1972, 1971, 1970, 1969, 1968, 1967, 1966, 1965, 1964, 1963, 1962, 1961, 1960, 1958 by Field Enterprises Educational Corporation.
Copyrights renewed 1957, 1956, 1955, 1954, 1953, 1952, 1950 by Field Enterprises, Inc.

International Copyright © 2001, 2000, 1999, 1998, 1997, 1996, 1995, 1994, 1993, 1992, 1991, 1990, 1989, 1988, 1987, 1986, 1985, 1984, 1983 by World Book, Inc.
International Copyright © 1982, 1981, 1980, 1979, 1978 by World Book-Childcraft International, Inc.
International Copyright © 1977, 1976, 1975, 1974, 1973, 1972, 1971, 1970, 1969, 1968, 1967, 1966, 1965, 1964, 1963, 1962, 1961, 1960, 1959, 1958, 1957 by Field Enterprises Educational Corporation.
International Copyright © 1957, 1956, 1955, 1954, 1953, 1952, 1951, 1950, 1949, 1948 by Field Enterprises, Inc.
International Copyright 1948, 1947 The Quarrie Corporation.

ISBN 0-7166-0102-8

02 5 4 3 2 1

Library of Congress Control Number: 2001093057

Printed in the United States of America

Gg

G is the seventh letter of our alphabet. Historians believe that it came from an Egyptian *hieroglyphic* (picture symbol) for a boomerang-shaped throwing stick. The Greeks made it the third letter of their alphabet, and used it for the sound of our *g*. The Romans borrowed the letter from the Greeks, and used it for both *g* and *k* sounds. Later, they added a vertical stroke to it, and used the new form for the sound of *g*, and the older form for the *k* sound. See **Alphabet**.

Uses. *G* or *g* is about the 16th most frequently used letter in books, newspapers, and other printed material in English. On a school report card, *G* means *good;* in physics, it indicates *gravity;* in dictionaries and refer-

ence works, it stands for *German.* In geographic abbreviations, *G* may stand for *gulf.* In measuring weight, *g* stands for *gram;* in electricity, it is used to indicate *conductance.*

Pronunciation. In English, a person pronounces hard *g,* as in *gun,* with the tongue back, its sides touching the velum, or soft palate, and with the vocal cords vibrating. *G* can also have the sound of *j,* as in *ginger.* In some English words derived from the French, such as *garage* and *rouge, g* has a *zh* sound. When followed by *h,* in such words as *high* or *bought, g* is silent. In other words, *gh* may have the sound of *f,* as in *rough* and *cough.* See **Pronunciation.**   Marianne Cooley

---

Development of the letter G

The ancient Egyptians, about 3000 B.C., wrote a symbol that represented a boomerang. The letters G and C both developed from this symbol.

The Phoenicians, about 1000 B.C., used a symbol that looked like a hook.

The Greeks wrote the letter as a right angle about 600 B.C. They made it their third letter and called it *gamma.*

The Romans gave the letter G its final form about A.D. 114.

The small letter g appeared during the A.D. 300's. Monks who copied manuscripts reshaped the letter in the 800's. By about 1500, the letter had its present form.

A.D. 300   800   Today

Special ways of expressing the letter G

International
Morse Code

Braille

International
Flag Code

Semaphore Code

Sign Language
Alphabet

Common forms of the letter G

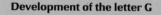

Handwritten letters vary from person to person. *Manuscript* (printed) letters, *left,* have simple curves and straight lines. Cursive letters, *right,* have flowing lines.

Gg Gg

Roman letters have small finishing strokes called *serifs* that extend from the main strokes. The type face shown above is Baskerville. The italic form appears at the right.

Gg Gg

Sans-serif letters are also called *gothic letters.* They have no serifs. The type face shown above is called Futura. The italic form of Futura appears at the right.

G

Computer letters have special shapes. Computers can "read" these letters either optically or by means of the magnetic ink with which the letters may be printed.

G is a symbol used to rate the forces that act on riders in any kind of vehicle, whether an airplane, a spacecraft, or even a Ferris wheel.

The earth's gravitational force acts on people whether they are stationary or moving at a constant speed. Gravity produces a standard *acceleration* (change of speed or direction) of one G. When a vehicle is accelerated, additional forces are observed. For example, a pilot who pulls a plane out of a dive feels an extra weightlike force. If the acceleration is twice the standard amount, it is rated at 2 G's. This means that the pilot's body must support twice as much force as it normally does. At 2 G's, pilots feel that they weigh twice as much as they do normally, at 1 G. After several seconds at 5 G's, a pilot's sight dims and he or she loses consciousness. A pilot can survive a force of 9 G's for only a few seconds.

Gregory Benford

G.A. See Gamblers Anonymous.

Gabardine, *GAB uhr deen,* is a fabric woven in such a way that it has diagonal lines of the yarn raised on one side of the cloth. This is called a *twill* weave. Gabardine may be made of worsted wool, mercerized cotton, spun rayon, or blends of synthetic fibers. It usually comes in widths of 36 inches (91 centimeters) or more in cotton and spun rayon, and 54 inches (137 centimeters) or more in wool. Manufacturers often use cotton and rayon gabardines for curtains, shirts, dresses, slacks, and uniforms. Wool gabardine is frequently used for uniforms, raincoats, and suits. Phyllis Tortora

Gaberones. See Gaborone.

Gable, Clark (1901-1960), was a popular romantic star of American motion pictures. He appeared in about 70 films. Gable was best known for his role as the dashing adventurer Rhett Butler in *Gone with the Wind* (1939). He won the 1934 Academy Award as best actor for his performance in *It Happened One Night.*

Metro-Goldwyn-Mayer Inc.
Clark Gable

Gable, whose full name was William Clark Gable, was born in Cadiz, Ohio. He worked in a tire factory and as a lumberjack before becoming an actor. Gable began his movie career in *The Painted Desert* (1931). His major films included *Red Dust* (1932), *Manhattan Melodrama* (1934), *Mutiny on the Bounty* (1935), *San Francisco* (1936), *Boom Town* (1940), *Command Decision* (1948), and *The Misfits* (1961). Gable served as an aerial gunner in the Army Air Forces from 1942 to 1944, during World War II. Charles Champlin

Gabo, *GAH buh* or *GAH boh,* **Naum,** *nowm* (1890-1977), was a Russian-born sculptor. He is associated with a Soviet art movement of the 1920's called *constructivism.* Gabo settled in the United States in 1946.

Gabo was one of the first sculptors to experiment with plastics, glass, and wire. Using transparent and translucent materials, he tried to integrate space as a positive element of his works. Gabo's later works used curved, transparent, and overlapping surfaces to suggest weightlessness, movement, and space. The clarity and precision of his sculpture seem to refer to mathematical and scientific ideas. Gabo was also an early experimenter in *kinetic* (moving) sculpture.

Gabo was born in Bryansk, Russia. He changed his family name—Pevsner—to avoid confusion with his brother, the sculptor Antoine Pevsner. Gabo was also a painter, designer, and architect. Joseph F. Lamb

Gabon, *ga BOHN,* is a small, heavily forested country that lies on the west coast of Africa. It straddles the equator. Gabon is extremely rich in natural resources. It is noted for its high-quality lumber. It also has some of the world's richest iron and manganese deposits.

Most of Gabon's people are farmers who live in small villages that lie along the coast or along the rivers. One of the inland towns, Lambaréné, became known throughout the world as the home of Albert Schweitzer. This much-honored physician, missionary, and musician built his hospital and leper colony near Lambaréné. See Schweitzer, Albert.

Gabon was a French colony from the early 1900's until it became an independent republic in 1960. Its name in French, the official language, is République Gabonaise (Gabonese Republic). Libreville is the capital.

Government. Gabon is a republic. The people elect a president to a seven-year term. The president is the government's most powerful official. A Council of Ministers appointed by the president carries out the operations of the government. A prime minister heads the Council.

Gabon

	National park (N.P.) or reserve
	International boundary
	Road
	Railroad
⊛	National capital
•	Other city or town
+	Elevation above sea level

WORLD BOOK maps

Gabon's legislature consists of two houses. The National Assembly has 120 members. The members are elected by the people to five-year terms. The president can adjourn the Assembly and rule alone for as long as 18 months. The Senate has 91 members. Senators are elected by regional and local councils to six-year terms.

The Gabonese Democratic Party is Gabon's dominant political party. Other parties include the Gabonese Progress Party and the National Rally of Woodcutters.

People. Gabon is one of the most thinly populated countries in Africa. About half of the people of Gabon live in small villages along the coast, along the rivers, or in the thinly forested parts of the north. They plant bananas, cassava, and yams, their main food crops. The people also raise mangoes, oranges, and pineapples. Some villagers also raise livestock for meat, and many catch fish in the rivers. Libreville is the largest city.

There are many ethnic groups in Gabon. The Fang, the most important group, live in the northern part of the country. They dominate the national government. The Omyéné, a small but important group of related peoples, live along the coast. They were the first to meet and deal with European traders and missionaries. This gave them an early advantage in education and commerce. Small groups of Pygmies live in the thick southern forest, isolated from other people. They hunt and trap animals for food.

The people in most parts of Gabon once lived in houses that had walls made of mud-covered branches and roofs made of woven grass. These houses had reed mats hanging at windows and doors. But now many of the houses have corrugated metal roofs, and Gabonese families now try to save enough money to build houses that have cement walls. Most villages have a meeting place, where the older men of the village gather to visit or to discuss village affairs.

Many Gabonese, especially those in towns, are Christians. Others follow traditional African religions. Music and dancing play a major role in the ceremonies.

About 90 percent of the children go to primary schools, and the number attending secondary schools is increasing rapidly. Over half of the adults can read and write. Since the mid-1900's, the number of schools run by churches and by the government has increased considerably. Gabon has a technical school in Libreville and

Facts in brief

Capital: Libreville.
Official language: French.
Area: 103,347 mi² (267,668 km²). *Coastline*—500 mi (800 km).
Population: *Estimated 2002 population*—1,280,000; density, 12 per mi² (5 per km²); distribution, 73 percent urban, 27 percent rural. *1993 census*—1,014,976.
Chief products: *Agriculture*—bananas, cacao, cassava, coffee, yams. *Forestry*—mahogany, okoumé. *Mining*—gold, iron ore, manganese, petroleum, uranium.
National anthem: "La Concorde" ("Concord").
Flag: Three horizontal stripes, green, yellow, and blue. See **Flag** (picture: Flags of Africa).
Money: *Basic unit*—franc.

an agricultural school in Oyem. For Gabon's literacy rate, see **Literacy** (table: Literacy rates for selected countries).

Land. Gabon lies on the equator and is covered with thick forests. Many palm-lined beaches, lagoons, and swamps lie along the 500 miles (800 kilometers) of coast. Moving inland, the land rises gradually to rolling hills and low mountain ranges that are cut through by valleys of the Ogooué River and its tributaries.

Gabon's climate is hot and humid most of the year. Rainfall is heavy throughout the country, especially along the northern coast. Many regions receive as much as 100 inches (250 centimeters) of rainfall a year. The average annual temperature is about 79 °F (26 °C).

Economy. In natural resources, Gabon is one of the richest countries in Africa. Its forests have been its chief source of wealth. They have provided high-quality lumber for more than a hundred years. Wood from the huge okoumé trees is used for making plywood. Gabonese forests also produce ebony and mahogany. Lumber is the country's main export. On the fertile land of the northwestern region, many farmers grow cacao and coffee for export. But minerals such as iron, manganese, uranium, and petroleum are increasingly important in Gabon's export trade. Gabon is a member of the Organization of Petroleum Exporting Countries (OPEC).

Formerly, most of Gabon's people had a low standard of living. But since the mid-1900's, the development of the country's mineral resources has helped raise living standards by creating new employment opportunities and spreading social services throughout the country.

Shostal

Albert Schweitzer's hospital and leper colony in Lambaréné became famous throughout the world as a haven for the sick. Schweitzer founded the hospital on the bank of the Ogooué River in 1913. It has room for 600 patients and their families.

The Ogooué River is one of Gabon's chief means of transportation. Roads built during the mid-1900's link various parts of the country. The Trans-Gabon Railroad was built in the 1970's and 1980's. It links the port of Owendo and the interior.

History. Portuguese sailors were the first Europeans to reach Gabon. They landed on its coast in the 1470's. Europeans carried on a slave trade with Omyéné people for hundreds of years.

In 1839, France established a naval and trading station near the present site of Libreville. Missionaries arrived and opened schools. In 1849, a group of slaves freed by a French ship landed at the station, which was then named *Libreville* (free town). Later, French explorers paddled up the Ogooué River into the interior of the country. The lumber trade developed around the Ogooué and the Gabon estuary near Libreville.

By 1883, Libreville had become the capital of the new French colony of Gabon, and in 1910, Gabon became a colonial territory within the federation of French Equatorial Africa. French companies acquired much land and gained complete control over Gabon's foreign trade and its forestry products. Much of the country's economy is still controlled by French companies.

Gabon began to move toward independence after World War II. It gained internal self-government in 1957, and the legislature elected by the people chose a Council of Ministers. On Aug. 17, 1960, Gabon became an independent country. Leon Mba, who had been head of government since 1957, became president.

In January 1964, Mba dissolved the National Assembly, and a month later, army rebels arrested Mba in an attempt to overthrow him. But French troops came to Mba's aid, crushed the revolt, and restored Mba to power. Mba was reelected in 1967, but he died the same year. Vice President Bernard-Albert Bongo succeeded Mba. In 1968, Bongo declared Gabon a one-party state and created the Gabonese Democratic Party as the only legal political party. Bongo was elected president in 1973. He changed his name to El Hadj Omar Bongo that year. He was reelected in 1979 and 1986.

Opposition political parties were legalized in Gabon in 1990. Multiparty legislative elections were then held, and Bongo's Gabonese Democratic Party won a majority of the seats. In 1993, facing opposition candidates for the first time, Bongo was reelected president. He was elected president again in 1998.   Samuel Decalo

See also **Libreville; Organization of Petroleum Exporting Countries.**

Gabor, *GAHB awr,* **Dennis** (1900-1979), a Hungarian-born engineer, invented *holography,* a method of three-dimensional photography. He won the 1971 Nobel Prize in physics for his invention. See **Holography.**

Gabor was born in Budapest. His father inspired him with stories about Thomas A. Edison and other inventors. Gabor graduated from the Technical College in Berlin in 1924 and earned a doctor's degree in electrical engineering there in 1927. Gabor left Germany in 1933, after the Nazis rose to power. He arrived in England in 1934 and became a British subject in 1946. Gabor received more than 100 patents for inventions. He wrote *The Mature Society* (1972).   Daniel J. Kevles

Gaborone, *GAHB uh ROH nee* (pop. 96,000), is the capital and largest city of Botswana. Gaborone lies in the southern part of the country. For the location of Gaborone, see **Botswana** (map). The city was formerly called *Gaberones.*

Gaborone is a carefully planned city. Much of it has been built up since 1966, when it became Botswana's capital. Gaborone has many modern government buildings and residential areas. It also has a national museum and art gallery. The University of Botswana and an agricultural college are located in Gaborone. The government is a major employer in the city. An airport and a railroad serve Gaborone.

Gaborone was founded in the 1890's. It was a small village until it became the capital. The presence of the national government in Gaborone has helped the city grow rapidly.   Louis A. Picard

Gadhafi, Muammar Muhammad al-. See Qadhafi, Muammar Muhammad al-.

Gadolinium, *GAD uh LIHN ee um,* is a silver-white metal of the rare-earth group of chemical elements (see **Rare earth**). It was discovered in 1880 by the Swiss scientist Jean de Marignac. Marignac named the element for Johan Gadolin, a Finnish chemist.

Gadolinium is found with other rare earths in the mineral gadolinite. It is sometimes used in control rods of nuclear reactors to absorb neutrons produced inside the reactor. Gadolinium's chemical symbol is Gd. The element's atomic number is 64, and its atomic weight is 157.25. It is strongly magnetic at room temperature, but loses its magnetism when heated slightly. It melts at 1313 °C and boils at 3273 °C. Its density is 7.886 grams per cubic centimeter at 25 °C.   Larry C. Thompson

Gadsden was the family name of two famous South Carolinians, grandfather and grandson.

Christopher Gadsden (1724-1805) was a leader in America's struggle for independence from Britain. He became known as the *Flame of Liberty.* Gadsden served in the Continental Congress, as an officer in the Continental Army, and twice as lieutenant governor of South Carolina. He was born in Charleston.

James Gadsden (1788-1858) arranged the purchase of a strip of border land from Mexico in 1853, while serving as U.S. minister to Mexico. The land became known as the *Gadsden Purchase.* Gadsden was also a railroad executive. He played a key role in Florida's development. He was born in Charleston, and graduated from Yale University.   Robert M. Weir

Gadsden Purchase. The treaty that ended the Mexican War in 1848 left some doubt about the western part of the boundary between Mexico and the United States. To clear up this question, and also to provide the United

WORLD BOOK map

Territory in the Gadsden Purchase

States with a good southern railroad route to the Pacific Coast, the government bought from Mexico a strip of land that included the region south of the Gila River in what is now Arizona and New Mexico. James Gadsden, the U.S. minister to Mexico, conducted the negotiations with Antonio López de Santa Anna, the Mexican president. The treaty of sale was signed on Dec. 30, 1853, and the two countries exchanged ratifications of the treaty on June 30, 1854.

The United States paid $10 million for the 29,640 square miles (76,770 square kilometers) in the purchase. Opposition in Mexico to the sale was one of the reasons for Santa Anna's banishment in 1855.   Norman A. Graebner

Gadwall is a duck found in much of the Northern Hemisphere. During the breeding season in spring, the grayish male gadwall contrasts slightly with the streaked, brownish female. In late summer and fall, the male looks more like the female. The gadwall can be distinguished

© C. C. Lockwood, Animals Animals

The gadwall is a duck that lives in the Northern Hemisphere. In spring, the male, *above,* has grayish feathers.

in flight by the white patch on its wings close to its body. Gadwalls build their nests on dry land near shallow wetlands, where they feed mainly on water vegetation. The female lays from 7 to 12 creamy-white eggs.

Scientific classification. The gadwall is in the family Anatidae. Its scientific name is *Anas strepera.*   Rodger D. Titman

Gaea. See Gaia.

Gaelic language, *GAY lihk,* belongs to the Celtic branch of the Indo-European family of languages. The Gaels introduced it to Ireland from central Europe (see Gaels). Irish colonists took it to Scotland about A.D. 500.

Irish and Scottish Gaelic shared a common written form for centuries. From about A.D. 700 to 1000, Irish authors wrote many poems, romances, sagas, and heroic tales in Gaelic. Beginning in the 900's, Irish and Scottish Gaelic developed as separate spoken languages. Spoken Irish began to split into dialects after 1200, the main ones being Munster, Connacht, and County Donegal. In the 1500's, the first major texts in Scottish Gaelic appeared. Scottish Gaelic literature is rich in poetry.

Invaders from England tried to impose the English language upon the Irish and Scots beginning in the 1100's. By 1800, Gaelic speakers were in the minority in Scotland. By 1851, only about one-fourth of the popula-

tion of Ireland spoke Gaelic. However, since the late 1800's, Irish and Scottish authors have revived the tradition of writing in Gaelic. In 1922, Irish, the Gaelic spoken in Ireland, became the official language of that country. It is the only Celtic language to receive full state recognition and support. Today, both Irish and English are official languages of Ireland. About 30 percent of the people of Ireland can speak Irish. About 80,000 people in Scotland speak Gaelic.   Cailean Spencer

See also **Alphabet** (picture: Gaelic); **Ireland** (Language).

Gaels, *gaylz,* are members of the Goidelic (Gadhelic) branch of the Celtic-speaking peoples. Goidelic Celts originated on the European continent. About 400 B.C., they settled in Ireland and the nearby Isle of Man.

The name *Scotti* was used for the Gaels of northern Ireland in ancient Latin documents. In the A.D. 500's, Irish Scotti settled in Scotland and gave the country their name. The Gaels became the ancestors of the northern Scots. Today, *Gaels* often refers to the people of Scotland's Highland region. Gaelic literature ranges from ancient heroic tales to modern Irish and Scottish poetry and novels.   Malcolm Todd

See also **Celts.**

Gagarin, *gah GAHR ihn,* **Yuri Alekseyevich,** *YOOR ee AH leh KSEH yuh vihch* (1934-1968), a Soviet air force pilot, was the first human to travel in space. Gagarin circled the earth on April 12, 1961, at a speed of more than 17,000 mph (27,400 kph). The trip lasted 1 hour and 48 minutes. His spacecraft Vostok 1 was in orbit for 89.1 minutes. At the highest point, Gagarin was about 203 miles (327 kilometers) above the earth. He was killed in a plane crash in 1968.

Sovfoto

Yuri Gagarin

Gagarin was born near Gzhatsk, west of Moscow. He attended vocational and technical schools and graduated from the Soviet air force cadet training center.   Cathleen S. Lewis

See also **Astronaut**, with picture.

Gage, Thomas (1721-1787), a British general, gave the orders that resulted in the first battle of the Revolutionary War in America. In 1774, he was appointed governor of the province of Massachusetts. Although Gage and his American wife were personally popular, he found the people were increasingly defiant. He knew that some people were collecting military supplies in Concord, and in April 1775, he ordered troops from Boston to seize or destroy the supplies. His soldiers were fired on in Lexington and Concord and suffered heavy losses while returning to Boston. Two months later, Gage ordered the attack on Breed's Hill in the Battle of Bunker Hill, but it was so costly that it led to his recall.

Gage was born in Firle, Sussex. He entered the army in 1741 and came to America with General Edward Braddock in 1755. In 1760, he became governor of Montreal, and from 1763 to 1775, was British commander in chief in North America.   Paul David Nelson

Gaia, *GAY uh,* is the idea that the earth is a living organism which functions as a unified whole to regulate conditions in the air, land, and water. Scientists call Gaia a *hypothesis*—that is, a possible explanation for what they have observed. It was named for Gaia, the ancient Greek goddess of the earth (also spelled *Gaea* or *Ge*).

Scientists have long known that living things alter the environment. Plants, for example, take up carbon dioxide from the air and give off oxygen. The Gaia hypothesis goes further, suggesting that life might actually keep the environment suitable for life. According to the theory, all living things—from the tiniest cells to the largest plants and animals—interact to create the environmental conditions that they need.

An example of how Gaia might work can be found in a tropical rain forest. Trees give off water through their leaves in a process called *transpiration.* By adding humidity to the air, the trees increase the number of rainstorms that occur. As a result, the environment necessary for a rain forest is maintained in two ways. First, the rain keeps the trees watered. Second, rain clouds block the sun to keep the forest from overheating.

The Gaia hypothesis was first presented in 1968 by James E. Lovelock, a British chemist, biologist, and inventor. He and American microbiologist Lynn Margulis have since refined the idea. The theory has aroused skepticism and controversy among scientists, some of whom consider aspects of it unscientific or unoriginal. Other experts think that research on Gaia may add to our understanding of serious environmental problems, such as the greenhouse effect and mass extinctions.

Stephen H. Schneider

Gaillardia, *gay LAHR dee uh,* is a type of flower that looks like a daisy with a dark-colored disk and yellow or red rays. It is also called *blanketflower* and *fire wheel.* Most gaillardias are native to the central and western United States, but they are often raised elsewhere.

The head really consists of two kinds of flowers—the tubular flowers in the disk, and ray flowers with long petals. The plant may be an annual, a biennial, or a perennial. Some types grow 3 feet (91 centimeters) high.

They grow from cuttings or from seeds, depending on the type, and thrive in sunny, open places.

Gaillardias produce many flowers from June to frost in autumn. *Gaillardia aristata* has a head that has yellow petals. The yellow rays of *Gaillardia pulchella* have bases of rose-purple. Other types of gaillardias have canary-yellow petals, and bright crimson or rich maroon disks.

Scientific classification. Gaillardia is in the composite family, Asteraceae or Compositae. The scientific name for a common type is *Gaillardia pulchella.*　　　Robert A. Kennedy

Gainsborough, *GAYNZ buh ruh,* **Thomas** (1727-1788), was one of the greatest British painters. He is famous for his portraits, but he also painted many landscapes. Gainsborough further developed the *conversation piece,* a type of painting that consisted of a group of individuals in a landscape or an interior setting.

Gainsborough was born in Sudbury, Suffolk. His father was a cloth merchant. Thomas showed a talent for drawing and painting and went to London to study under a silversmith at the age of 13. One of his first instructors was the French artist Hubert François Gravelot. The landscapes of the Dutch painters Jacob van Ruisdael and Jan Wynants also influenced him. After Gainsborough married in 1746, he began painting portraits. In 1759, he and his family moved to Bath, a famous resort.

In Bath, Gainsborough won immediate success by painting portraits of the fashionable tourists. As was customary at this time, his portraits intentionally flattered

Oil painting on canvas (1770); Huntington Library and Art Gallery, San Marino, Calif.

The Blue Boy, *above,* ranks as Gainsborough's most famous painting. It reflects his elegant style. Gainsborough posed many of his subjects in idealized landscapes.

WORLD BOOK illustration by Lorraine Epstein

The gaillardia has a disk of dark tubular flowers in the center surrounded by yellow or red ray flowers with long petals.

his subjects. But Gainsborough also possessed a remarkable sensitivity to his subjects, whom he portrayed as charming and graceful. In this respect, he continued the tradition of Sir Anthony Van Dyck, who had painted at the English court from 1632 to 1641.

In 1768, Gainsborough helped found the Royal Academy of Arts, a London-based association of artists. He moved to London in 1774. There he painted portraits of King George III and the royal family. Gainsborough also painted portraits of leading aristocrats, politicians, writers, and actors of the day. His celebrated subjects included the Irish dramatist and politician Richard Brinsley Sheridan and the British prime minister William Pitt.

Gainsborough's early portraits are detailed in style. His later ones are less detailed and more sketchy. Gainsborough's most famous work is *The Blue Boy,* an elegant portrait completed in 1770. It shows the artist's preference for cool blue and green colors, in contrast to the reds, yellows, and browns of his rival portrait painters, Sir Joshua Reynolds and George Romney. At the end of his life, Gainsborough returned to his first love, landscape painting.   Douglas K. S. Hyland

See also **Siddons, Sarah Kemble** (picture).

Galago, *guh LAY goh,* is the name of a group of tree-dwelling African animals known for their ability to leap great distances among branches. Galagos jump with their long hind legs as frogs do. Some galagos can leap 15 feet (4.6 meters). The largest species is about the size of a large squirrel, and the smallest is about as big as a chipmunk. Galagos are sometimes called *bushbabies.* They belong to an order of animals called *primates,* which also includes monkeys, apes, and human beings.

Galagos sleep during the day and become active at night. Their large eyes help them see well in the dark. Galagos feed on many kinds of insects and also eat small birds, eggs, fruits, and lizards. The *needle-clawed galago* has specialized front teeth for removing tree bark so it can feed on tree gum.

A galago has soft, woolly fur and a long tail. Its palms, soles, fingers, and toes have fleshy pads that help it hold tree branches and trunks. Galagos also use their hands to seize prey and to handle objects.   Randall L. Susman

Scientific classification. Galagos are in the loris family,

© Tom McHugh, Photo Researchers

A galago is a small tree-dwelling African animal that is active at night. The animal's large eyes help it see in the dark.

Lorisidae. They make up the genera *Euoticus, Galago, Galagoides,* and *Otolemur.* The needle-clawed galago is *Euoticus elegantulus.*

Galahad, *GAL uh had,* **Sir,** was the noblest and most virtuous knight in the legends of King Arthur's Round Table in medieval England. Galahad first appears in the *Vulgate Cycle,* a group of French prose Arthurian romances dating from about 1215. He is primarily a figure in the quest of the Holy Grail, when he arrives at Arthur's court and sits in the *Siege Perilous.* This seat was reserved for the knight so pure that he would someday find the Holy Grail, often depicted as the cup or dish used by Jesus at the Last Supper. See **Round Table.**

Galahad was the illegitimate son of Sir Lancelot, one of the greatest knights of the Round Table, and King Pelles' daughter, sometimes known as Elaine of Astolat. Galahad was also supposedly the last descendant of Joseph of Arimathea, a follower of Christ.

On the feast of Pentecost, Galahad and other knights of the Round Table saw a brief vision of the Holy Grail. The Grail appeared suspended in the air and covered with a cloth. This vision stirred Galahad and other knights to search for the castle where the Grail was kept. After a number of years and many adventures, Galahad and several other knights found the castle. For the story of their search, see **Holy Grail** (The search for the Grail).

The story of Galahad also appears in Sir Thomas Malory's *Le Morte Darthur* (1470). Galahad became popular in later English literature largely because of his depiction in a poem by Alfred Lord Tennyson. The poem includes the famous lines, "My strength is as the strength of ten/Because my heart is pure."   Edmund Reiss

Galapagos Islands, *guh LAH puh GOHS,* lie in the Pacific Ocean about 600 miles (970 kilometers) west of Ecuador. The islands belong to Ecuador. They are known for their peculiar variety of animal and plant life. Many of these animals and plants exist nowhere else.

The Galapagos cover an area of 3,029 square miles (7,844 square kilometers). They are made up of volcanic peaks, some of which occasionally erupt. Much of the land area of the islands is covered with hardened lava.

The Galapagos are also called the Archipiélago de Colón. There are 13 major islands, 6 smaller ones, and dozens of islets and rocks. They have Spanish and English names. The largest are Isabela (Albemarle), Santa Cruz (Indefatigable), San Cristóbal (Chatham), Fernandina (Narborough), San Salvador (James), and Santa María or Floreana (Charles).

WORLD BOOK map

The Galapagos Islands are part of Ecuador.

Mel Zaloudek from Marilyn Gartman

Marine iguanas inhabit the rocky coastlines of the Galapagos Islands. These unique lizards swim out into the surf to eat seaweed. They are the only lizards known to feed in the ocean.

Many rare creatures live in the Galapagos. They include marine iguanas, which are the only lizards that feed in the sea, and giant tortoises that weigh more than 500 pounds (230 kilograms). The Spanish word for the tortoises, *galápagos,* gave the islands their name. Other peculiar animals include cormorants that cannot fly and the Galapagos penguin, which lives farther north than any other penguin.

The Galapagos became famous after the British naturalist Charles Darwin visited in 1835 and wrote about the unusual wildlife there. His observations helped him form his theory of *evolution*—that is, the idea that living things developed over millions of years. Today, scientists still study the animals and plants of the Galapagos.

The human population of the Galapagos has increased greatly since the 1980's. In 1990, the official estimate was 9,710 people, but recent estimates indicate the population has nearly doubled since then. Also, more than 60,000 tourists visit each year. Many people believe human economic activities, such as fishing, construction, and tourism, are harming the environment of the islands. Human beings have also accidentally and intentionally brought new animals to the islands. These animals, which include cats, dogs, fire ants, goats, pigs, and rats, compete with native animals for food. In some cases, they even feed on the native animals. People also have introduced plants, such as elephant grass and the guava, that threaten the existence of native plants.

In 1959, Ecuador created the Galapagos National Park to help protect the environment there. The park includes over 90 percent of the islands' land area. In 1986, the surrounding waters became a marine reserve. In 1996, the reserve was made part of the national park. In 1998, Ecuador established the Galapagos Marine Reserve, extending the protected waters to 40 miles (65 kilometers) offshore. Laws limit the number of sea cucumbers, lobsters, and other animals that fishing crews can take from this area. Many people in the fishing industry say these limits make it difficult for them to earn a living. Some have disobeyed the limits.   Lynn A. Ebersole

Additional resources

Boyce, Barry. *A Traveler's Guide to the Galapagos Islands.* 2nd ed. Galapagos Travel, 1994.
Litteral, Linda L. *Boobies, Iguanas, and Other Critters: Nature's Story in the Galápagos.* Am. Kestrel, 1994. Younger readers.

Galarza, Ernesto (1905-1984), was a Mexican-American historian and civil rights leader. He worked to end discrimination against his people by teaching, writing, and helping form labor organizations.

Galarza was born near Tepic, in the state of Nayarit, Mexico. He came to the United States with his parents at the age of 6 and went to work as a farm laborer in California. As a young man, Galarza fought for better conditions for Mexican Americans by helping to organize them into labor unions. He graduated from Occidental College and, in 1944, received a Ph.D. degree from Columbia University. Galarza wrote several books, including *Merchants of Labor* (1964), about the problems of Mexican Americans trying to obtain good jobs, housing, and education.   Feliciano M. Ribera

Galatia, *guh LAY shuh* or *guh LAY shee uh,* was a region in central Asia Minor, a region that is now central Turkey. It was named for the Gauls, who were called *Galatai* by the Greeks. The Gauls crossed into Asia from Europe in 278 B.C. and overran parts of Asia Minor. Attalus, king of the Greek city of Pergamum, defeated the Gauls in 239 B.C., and forced them into eastern Phrygia, later named Galatia. Attalus later set up the famous statue of the *Dying Gaul* to celebrate his victory.

The Galatians lived in the countryside and frequently raided the Greek cities near them. The Romans defeated the Galatians in 189 B.C., but allowed them to keep their tribal government.

The emperor Augustus made Galatia a Roman province in 25 B.C. A famous inscription, written by Augustus to describe his deeds, was found in Galatia's capital city, Ancyra (today called Ankara, capital of Turkey). The apostle Paul visited Galatia twice and wrote an *epistle* (letter) to the Christians there.   Arther Ferrill

Galatians, *guh LAY shuhnz,* **Epistle to the,** is the ninth book of the New Testament. It is a letter from the apostle Paul to the churches in the Roman province of Galatia (in what is now central Turkey) and was written in about A.D. 53. Paul wrote the letter to counteract the influence of other apostles who had traveled to Galatia after Paul had left. These apostles taught the Galatians that they should observe the Jewish law. In his letter, Paul strongly rejected this teaching. He did this in part by arguing that he himself was a true apostle, appointed by God. He also argued that the Jewish law was temporary and was intended to come to an end with the arrival of Jesus Christ. See also **Paul, Saint; Bible** (Books of the New Testament).   Terrance D. Callan

Galaxy is a system of stars, dust, and gas held together by gravity. Our solar system is in a galaxy called the Milky Way. Scientists estimate that there are over 100 billion galaxies scattered throughout the visible universe. Astronomers have photographed millions of them through telescopes. The most distant galaxies ever photographed are as far as 10 billion to 13 billion *light-years* away. A light-year is the distance light travels in a vacuum in a year—about 5.88 trillion miles (9.46 trillion kilometers). Galaxies range in diameter from a few thousand to a half-million light-years. Small galaxies have fewer than a billion stars. Large ones have over a trillion.

The Milky Way has a diameter of about 100,000 light-

Galaxy types   Astronomers classify galaxies according to their shape as spirals, ellipticals, and irregulars. A spiral galaxy may have a bar of stars, gas, and dust across its center.

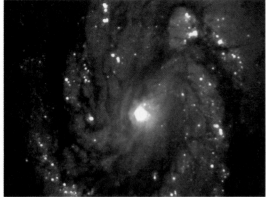

JPL/NASA

A spiral galaxy resembles a pinwheel, with spiral arms coiling out from a central bulge. This photo shows a galaxy known as M100. Our home galaxy, the Milky Way, is also a spiral.

Anglo-Australian Observatory

An elliptical galaxy may be spherical, like the one shown here, or it may resemble a flattened globe. This elliptical galaxy, called M87, is so huge that our galaxy, the Milky Way, could fit inside it.

Anglo-Australian Observatory

An irregular galaxy, Sextans A does not have a simple shape like a spiral or elliptical galaxy. The bright, yellowish stars in the foreground are part of the Milky Way, Earth's "home" galaxy.

Anglo-Australian Observatory

A barred spiral galaxy differs from an ordinary spiral galaxy in having a bar of stars, dust, and gas across its center. Spiral arms project from the bar. The galaxy shown here is called NGC 1365.

years. The solar system lies about 25,000 light-years from the center of the galaxy. There are about 100 billion stars in the Milky Way.

Only three galaxies outside the Milky Way are visible with the unaided eye. People in the Northern Hemisphere can see the Andromeda Galaxy, which is about 2 million light-years away. People in the Southern Hemisphere can see the Large Magellanic Cloud, which is about 160,000 light-years from Earth, and the Small Magellanic Cloud, which is about 180,000 light-years away.

Groups of galaxies. Galaxies are distributed unevenly in space. Some have no close neighbor. Others occur in pairs, with each orbiting the other. But most of them are found in groups called *clusters*. A cluster may contain from a few dozen to several thousand galaxies. It may have a diameter as large as 10 million light-years.

Clusters of galaxies, in turn, are grouped in larger structures called *superclusters*. On even larger scales, galaxies are arranged in huge networks. The networks consist of interconnected *strings* or *filaments* of galaxies surrounding relatively empty regions known as *voids*. One of the largest structures ever mapped is a network

of galaxies known as the Great Wall. This structure is more than 500 million light-years long and 200 million light-years wide.

Shapes of galaxies. Astronomers classify most galaxies by shape as either *spiral galaxies* or *elliptical galaxies*. A spiral galaxy is shaped like a disk with a bulge in the center. The disk resembles a pinwheel, with bright spiral arms that coil out from the central bulge. The Milky Way is a spiral galaxy. Like pinwheels, all spiral galaxies rotate—but slowly. The Milky Way, for example, makes a complete revolution once every 250 million years or so.

New stars are constantly forming out of gas and dust in spiral galaxies. Smaller groups of stars called *globular clusters* often surround spiral galaxies. A typical globular cluster has about 1 million stars.

Elliptical galaxies range in shape from almost perfect spheres to flattened globes. The light from an elliptical galaxy is brightest in the center and gradually becomes fainter toward its outer regions. As far as astronomers can determine, elliptical galaxies rotate much more slowly than spiral galaxies or not at all. The stars within them appear to move in random orbits. Elliptical galaxies have much less dust and gas than spiral galaxies have, and few new stars appear to be forming in them.

Galaxies of a third kind, *irregular galaxies,* lack a simple shape. Some consist mostly of blue stars and puffy clouds of gas, but little dust. The Magellanic Clouds are irregular galaxies of this type. Others are made up mostly of bright young stars along with gas and dust.

Galaxies move relative to one another, and occasionally two galaxies come so close to each other that the gravitational force of each changes the shape of the other. Galaxies can even collide. If two rapidly moving galaxies collide, they may pass right through each other with little or no effect. However, when slow-moving galaxies collide, they can merge into a single galaxy that is bigger than either of the original galaxies. Such mergers can produce spiral filaments of stars that can extend more than 100,000 light-years into space.

Emissions from galaxies. All galaxies *emit* (give off) energy as waves of visible light and other kinds of electromagnetic radiation. In order of decreasing *wavelength* (distance between successive wave crests), electromagnetic radiation consists of radio waves, infrared rays, visible light, ultraviolet rays, X rays, and gamma rays. All these forms of radiation together make up the *electromagnetic spectrum.*

The energy emitted by galaxies comes from various sources. Much of it is due to the heat of the stars and of clouds of dust and gas called *nebulae.* A variety of violent events also provide a great deal of the energy. These events include two kinds of stellar explosions: (1) *nova* explosions, in which one of the two members of a binary star system hurls dust and gas into space; and (2) much more violent *supernova* explosions, in which a star collapses, then throws off most of its matter. One supernova may leave behind a compact, invisible object called a *black hole,* which has such powerful gravitational force that not even light can escape it. Another supernova may leave behind a *neutron star,* which consists mostly of tightly packed *neutrons,* particles that ordinarily occur only in the nuclei of atoms. But some supernovae leave nothing behind.

The intensity of the radiation emitted by a star at various wavelengths depends on the star's surface temperature. For example, the sun, which has a surface temperature of about 5500 °C (10,000 °F) emits most of its radiation in the visible part of the electromagnetic spectrum. Radiation of this type, whose intensity depends on temperature as it does for the sun and other normal stars, is called *thermal radiation.*

A small percentage of galaxies called *active galaxies* emit tremendous amounts of energy. This energy results from violent events occurring in objects at their center. The distribution of the wavelengths of the emissions does not resemble that of normal stars, and so the emissions are known as *nonthermal radiation.* The most powerful such object is a *quasar,* which emits a huge amount of radio, infrared, ultraviolet, X-ray, and gamma-ray energy. Some quasars emit 1,000 times as much energy as the entire Milky Way, yet look like stars in photographs. *Quasar* is short for *quasi-stellar radio source.* The name comes from the fact that the first quasars identified emit mostly radio energy and look much like stars. A *radio galaxy* is related to, but appears larger than, a quasar.

A *Seyfert galaxy* is a spiral galaxy that emits large amounts of infrared rays as well as large amounts of radio waves, X rays, or both radio waves and X rays. Seyfert galaxies get their name from American astronomer Carl K. Seyfert, who in 1943 became the first person to discover one.

Some active galaxies emit jets and blobs of highly energetic, electrically charged particles. These particles include positively charged protons and positrons and negatively charged electrons. Electrons and protons are forms of ordinary matter, but positrons are *antimatter* particles. They are the antimatter opposites of electrons—that is, they have the same *mass* (amount of matter) as electrons, but they carry the opposite charge. See **Antimatter.**

The cause of the intense activity in active galaxies is thought to arise from a colossal black hole at the galactic center. The black hole can be as much as a billion times as massive as the sun. Because the black hole is so massive and compact, its gravitational force is powerful enough to tear apart nearby stars. The resulting dust and gas fall toward the black hole, adding their mass to a disk of matter called an *accretion disk* that orbits the black hole. At the same time, matter from the inner edge of the disk falls into the black hole. As the matter falls, it loses energy, thereby producing the radiation and jets that shoot out of the galaxy.

The Milky Way is not an active galaxy, but it does have a powerful source of radiation called Sagittarius A at its center. The cause of this radiation may be a black hole a million times as massive as the sun.

Origin of galaxies. Scientists have proposed two main kinds of theories of the origin of galaxies: (1) *bottom-up theories* and (2) *top-down theories.* The starting point for both kinds of theories is the *big bang,* the explosion with which the universe began 10 billion to 20 billion years ago. Shortly after the big bang, masses of gas began to gather together or collapse. Gravity then slowly compressed these masses into galaxies.

The two kinds of theories differ concerning how the galaxies evolved. Bottom-up theories state that much smaller objects such as globular clusters formed first. These objects then merged to form galaxies. According to top-down theories, large objects such as galaxies and clusters of galaxies formed first. The smaller groups of stars then formed within them. But all big bang theories of galaxy formation agree that no new galaxies—or very few—have formed since the earliest times.

Astronomers have found evidence of what conditions were like before the galaxies formed. In 1965, American physicists Arno Penzias and Robert Wilson detected faint radio waves throughout the sky. According to the big bang theory, the waves are radiation left over from the initial explosion. The strength of the radio waves appeared to be very nearly the same in every direction. But in 1992, a satellite called the Cosmic Background Explorer (COBE) detected tiny differences in the strength of radio waves coming from different directions. The differences in strength arise from tiny increases in the density of matter in the universe shortly after the big bang. The small regions of increased density had a stronger gravitational force than the surrounding matter. Clumps of matter therefore formed in these regions; and the clumps eventually collapsed into galaxies.

Most astronomical observations made to date support big bang theories. According to these theories, the universe is still expanding. Two kinds of observations strongly support the idea of an expanding universe. These observations indicate that all galaxies are moving away from one another and that the galaxies farthest from the Milky Way are moving away most rapidly. This relationship between speed and distance is known as the Hubble law of *recession* (moving backward). The law was named after American astronomer Edwin P. Hubble, who reported it in 1929.

Astronomers estimate the speed at which a galaxy is moving away by measuring the galaxy's *redshift.* The redshift is an apparent lengthening of electromagnetic waves emitted by an object moving away from the observer. A redshift can be measured when light from a galaxy is broken up and spread out into a band of colors called a *spectrum.* The spectrum of a galaxy contains bright and dark lines that are determined by the galaxy's temperature, density, and chemical composition. These lines are shifted toward the red end of the spectrum if the galaxy is moving away. The greater the amount of redshift, the more rapid the movement. See **Redshift.**

Scientists estimate the distance to galaxies by measuring the galaxies' overall brightness or the brightness of certain kinds of objects within them. These objects include variable stars as well as supernovae.

Evolution of spiral galaxies. Astronomers do not understand clearly how galactic spirals evolved and why they still exist. The mystery arises when one considers how a spiral galaxy rotates. The galaxy spins much like the cream on the surface of a cup of coffee. The inner part of the galaxy rotates somewhat like a solid wheel, and the arms trail behind. Suppose a spiral arm rotated around the center of its galaxy in about 250 million years—as in the Milky Way. After a few rotations, taking perhaps 2 billion years, the arms would "wind up," producing a fairly continuous mass of stars. But almost all spiral galaxies are much older than 2 billion years.

According to one proposed solution to the mystery, differences in gravitational force throughout the galaxy push and pull at the stars, dust, and gas. This activity produces *waves of compression.* A familiar example of waves of compression are ordinary sound waves (see **Sound** [The nature of sound]). Because the galaxy is rotating, the waves seem to travel in a spiral path, leading to the appearance of spiral arms of dense dust and gas. Stars then form in the arms.   Kenneth Brecher

Related articles in *World Book* include:

Andromeda Galaxy	Interstellar medium
Astronomy (Discovering	Maffei galaxies
other galaxies)	Magellanic Clouds
Big bang	Milky Way
Black hole	Nebula
Cosmology	Quasar
Hubble, Edwin Powell	Universe

Additional resources

Clay, Rebecca. *Stars and Galaxies.* 21st Century Bks., 1997. Younger readers.
Elmegreen, Debra M. *Galaxies and Galactic Structure.* Prentice Hall, 1998.
Rubin, Vera C. *Bright Galaxies, Dark Matters.* Am. Inst. of Physics, 1997.

Galbraith, *GAL brayth,* **John Kenneth** (1908-   ), is an American economist whose skillfully written books sparked widespread interest in economic issues. In *American Capitalism* (1952), Galbraith stated that Americans must adjust to new patterns of competition among big industry, big labor, and big government. He argued that strong labor unions and strong buyers, such as chain stores, restrain the power of large producers.

In *The Affluent Society* (1958), Galbraith said that the American economy needs more public goods, such as highways and educational facilities. The public goods that he supports complement, but also come at the expense of, some private goods. Good highways, for example, are necessary for new cars, but the tax money spent on highways leaves less money for people to buy new cars. *The New Industrial State* (1967) analyzes the relationships between industry, the state, and the individual. *The Age of Uncertainty* (1977) traces the history of economic thought. Galbraith also wrote a book of memoirs, *A Life in Our Times* (1981).

Galbraith was born in the Canadian city of Iona Station, near London, Ontario. He became a U.S. citizen in 1937. He became a professor of economics at Harvard University in 1949. Galbraith interrupted his scholarly career to serve from 1961 to 1963 as U.S. ambassador to India. He retired from Harvard in 1975.   Barry W. Poulson

Gale, Zona, *ZOH nuh* (1874-1938), was an American author known for her descriptions of small-town life in the Midwest. Her hometown of Portage, Wisconsin, provided the material for much of her fiction.

Gale's early works were sentimental and romantic. In later works, Gale wrote in a harshly realistic style. Most critics consider these writings her best. These works include the novels *Birth* (1918), *Miss Lulu Bett* (1920), and *Faint Perfume* (1923), and the short stories published in the collections *Yellow Gentians and Blue* (1927) and *Bridal Pond* (1930). Gale won a Pulitzer Prize in 1921 for her dramatization of *Miss Lulu Bett.*   Bert Hitchcock

Galen, *GAY luhn* (A.D. 129-about 210), became one of the most famous and influential physicians in the history of medicine. He discovered that the arteries contain blood, not an airlike substance called *pneuma* as had been believed. Galen performed dissections on monkeys, pigs, and other animals, and established comparative anatomy as a field of anatomy.

Galen developed the first medical theories that were based on scientific experiment. His landmark *Anatomical Procedures* served as the standard anatomy textbook in Western and Middle Eastern civilization until modern times. Galen's ideas about physiology were considered authoritative in Europe until the 1500's. His methods for the treatment of disease continued to influence physicians well into the 1800's.

Galen was born in Pergamum (now Bergama, Turkey), a city of the Roman Empire. He began to study medicine at the age of 14. About A.D. 157, Galen became a physician for trained fighters called *gladiators.* This experience gave him valuable information about surgery and diet. In 161 or 162, Galen went to Rome. There, he presented lectures on anatomy and physiology and soon was hired to be the physician of the household of the Roman emperor, Marcus Aurelius. This position enabled him to write, research, and travel. By 200, he had written many works on medicine and physiology.

As time passed, some of Galen's main theories were proved false. For example, Galen thought that the liver changed digested food into blood, which then flowed to the rest of the body and was absorbed. In 1628, however, the English physician William Harvey showed that blood circulates throughout the body and returns to the heart.   John Scarborough

See also **Color** (Early theories of color vision).

Galena, *guh LEE nuh,* is the chief ore of lead. It is a heavy, brittle, lead-gray mineral with a metallic luster. Galena is a *sulfide* (sulfur compound) of lead and has the chemical formula PbS. In its purest state, it consists of 86.6 percent lead and 13.4 percent sulfur by weight. Galena is found in the form of masses in limestone or as fragments in *sediment* (bits of rock and soil). Some deposits of the mineral contain considerable silver and are refined to obtain lead and silver. Areas where much galena occurs include Australia, Canada, China, Mexico, Peru, and the United States. See also **Lead** (Production); **Mineral** (picture: Galena).   Donald F. Eschman

Galicia, *guh LIHSH ee uh,* is a region that lies on the north slope of the Carpathian Mountains in southeastern Poland and the western part of Ukraine. It extends from the Vistula River Valley in Poland to the Dnestr River Valley in Ukraine and covers about 32,000 square miles (82,900 square kilometers). Kraków, in Poland, and Lvov, in Ukraine, are the principal cities of Galicia.

Galicia has rich deposits of petroleum and natural gas. Other minerals found there include coal, iron, lead, salt, sulfur, and zinc. Farmers in Galicia raise livestock and such crops as barley, oats, potatoes, rye, sugar beets, and wheat. Galicia's forests supply lumber.

Galicia was an independent principality during the Middle Ages. It became part of Poland during the 1300's. Austria took over Galicia during the late 1700's. In 1867, Galicia gained limited self-government under Austrian rule. The region then flourished as a center of Polish culture and education. It served as a source of the movement for Polish independence.

Galicia formed part of the independent nation of Poland that was established after World War I (1914-1918). Germany and the Soviet Union claimed eastern Galicia during World War II (1939-1945). In 1945, a Polish-Soviet treaty united eastern Galicia with the Ukrainian Soviet Socialist Republic. The republic became the independent nation of Ukraine in 1991. Western Galicia remained part of Poland.   Janusz Bugajski

Galilee, *GAL uh lee,* was the northernmost part of Palestine in Roman times. Galilee lay between the Mediterranean Sea on the west and the Jordan River and the Sea of Galilee on the east. The region is now part of Israel. Upper Galilee, the northern part of the region, is mountainous, while Lower Galilee contains broad valleys good for agriculture.

Galilee is first mentioned in the Bible in Joshua 20:7 and 21:32. Its name comes from a Hebrew word that means *circle.* The Bible describes Galilee as the territory of the tribes of Naphtali, Asher, Issachar, and Zebulun, with members of the tribe of Dan settling there later. In 732 B.C., Assyria annexed Galilee and made it a province. Many of its inhabitants were taken into exile. According to the Book of Tobit in the Apocrypha, Tobit was a pious Israelite from Galilee who became an exile in the Assyrian city of Nineveh. Gentiles surrounded Israelites remaining in Galilee.

Galilee has lasting interest for Christians and Jews.

Many Jews settled in Galilee following a revolt led by members of the Maccabean family in the mid-100's B.C. (see **Judah Maccabee**). After the Romans conquered Palestine in 63 B.C., Galilee was made part of the Roman administration of the country. Many of the important events in the life of Jesus Christ took place there. Jesus's home was in Nazareth, a town in southern Galilee. Most of Jesus's apostles came from Capernaum, Bethsaida, and other towns around the Sea of Galilee.

After the Romans destroyed Jerusalem in A.D. 70 and defeated a Jewish revolt in A.D. 132-135, many Jews took refuge in Galilee. The area became famous as a center of learning. There, scholars produced the *Mishnah* (a collection of rabbinic laws) and the Palestinian Talmud, a commentary on the Mishnah.   Carole R. Fontaine

See also **Israel** (The land); **Nazareth; Jesus Christ; Galilee, Sea of.**

Galilee, Sea of, is a small freshwater lake in northern Israel (formerly Palestine). It is often mentioned in the Bible. It is called the *Sea of Chinnereth* and the *Sea of Chinneroth* in the Old Testament. The name Galilee is used in the New Testament. This sea is also called *Gennesaret,* for the plain that lies to the northwest; and *Tiberias,* for a city on its shore. The sea is also known as *Lake Kinneret.*

The Sea of Galilee lies in the Rift Valley in Israel, 30 miles (48 kilometers) from the Mediterranean Sea. It touches the Golan Heights of Syria on the northeast. The

Sea of Galilee

Area: 64 sq. mi. (166 km²)
Elevation: 688 ft. (210 m) below sea level
Deepest point: • 145 ft. (44 m)

Area occupied by Israel in 1967

— Road   ←→ Railroad
o Historic site   ←→ Water carrier

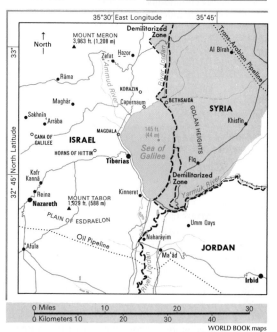

WORLD BOOK maps

River Jordan flows through the Sea of Galilee on its southward course to the Dead Sea. The Sea of Galilee is 14 miles (23 kilometers) long and 8 miles (13 kilometers) across at its broadest point. Many fish live in it. Gently sloping hills lie along the shores, except where the plain of Gennesaret meets the sea. Figs, olives, dates, and pomegranates grow on the southern hills.

The ancient cities of Magdala, Capernaum, and Bethsaida were once situated on the northern shores of Galilee. Today, only ruins of them remain.   Bernard Reich

Galileo, *GAL uh LAY oh* or *GAL uh LEE oh* (1564-1642), an Italian astronomer and physicist, has been called the founder of modern experimental science. Galileo made the first effective use of the refracting telescope to discover important new facts about astronomy. He also discovered the law of falling bodies as well as the law of the pendulum. Galileo designed a variety of scientific instruments. He also developed and improved the refracting telescope, though he did not invent it.

Early life. Galileo Galilei was born in Pisa on Feb. 15, 1564. In the early 1570's, his family moved to Florence, and Galileo began his formal education at a school in a nearby monastery. Galileo's father, determined that his son should be a doctor, sent him to the University of Pisa in 1581. Galileo studied medicine and the philosophy of Aristotle for the next four years.

Early scientific interests. Galileo's years as a student at Pisa marked a turning point for him. Never really interested in medicine, he discovered he had a talent for mathematics. In 1585, he persuaded his father to let him leave the university. Back in Florence with his family, Galileo spent the next four years as a tutor in mathematics. During this time, he began to question Aristotelian philosophy and scientific thought. At the same time, he gained his first public notice with his new hydrostatic balance, an instrument used to find the specific gravity of objects by weighing them in water.

In 1589, Galileo was appointed professor of mathematics at the University of Pisa. This position required him to teach courses in astronomy on the basis of the Greek astronomer Ptolemy's theory that the sun and all the planets revolve around the earth (see **Ptolemy**). Preparing for these courses deepened Galileo's understanding of astronomical theory. In 1592, he took up duties as professor of mathematics at the University of Padua, where he spent the next 18 years. During this time, he became convinced of the truth of the theory, proposed by the Polish astronomer Nicolaus Copernicus, that all planets, including the earth, revolve around the sun (see **Copernicus, Nicolaus**).

Mature scientific career. In 1609, while still at Padua, Galileo built his first telescope. Turning it to the sky, he saw clear evidence that many of Aristotle's and Ptolemy's claims about the heavens were false. Galileo's first discovery was that, far from being perfectly smooth, as Aristotle and Ptolemy had thought, the moon was mountainous and pitted, much like the earth. He made his most sensational discovery in 1610, when he discovered four moons circling Jupiter. He named these moons the "Medicean Planets," in the hope of winning the favor of the Medicis, the ruling family of Florence.

In 1610, Cosimo de Medici, Grand Duke of Tuscany, named Galileo his personal mathematician. This position brought Galileo back to Florence, where he continued

his studies of the heavens. He made observations of sunspots and of Venus, noting that the planet progresses through phases similar to those of the moon. This fact confirmed his doubts about Ptolemaic astronomy and deepened his conviction of the truth of Copernicus' theory that the earth and planets revolve around the sun. Publication of these findings, starting in 1610, brought him wide renown.

Galileo also pursued research on motion—especially the motion of freely falling bodies. The problem, as he saw it, was that the Aristotelian theory of motion, which referred all motion to a stationary earth at the center of the universe, made it impossible to believe the earth actually moves. Galileo went to work to develop a theory of motion consistent with a moving earth.

Among the most important results of this search were the law of the pendulum and the law of freely falling bodies. Galileo observed that pendulums of equal length swing at the same rate whether their arcs are large or small. Modern measuring instruments show that the rate is actually somewhat greater if the arc is large. Galileo's law of falling bodies states that all objects fall at the same speed, regardless of their mass; and that, as they fall, the speed of their descent increases uniformly. See **Pendulum; Falling bodies, Law of.**

Galileo and the Roman Catholic Church. Galileo's quick wit, which he often used to ridicule his opponents, earned him a number of enemies. In 1613, Galileo wrote a letter in which he tried to show that the Copernican theory was consistent with both Catholic doctrine and proper Biblical interpretation. Some of his enemies

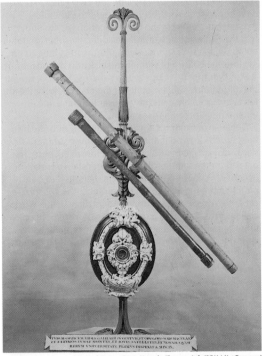

Museo di Fisica e Storia Naturale, Florence, Italy (SCALA/Art Resource)

Galileo's telescopes were larger and more powerful than the telescopes that had been made previously.

Uffizi Gallery, Florence, Italy (Art Resource)

Galileo was a famous astronomer and physicist. Justus Sustermans painted his portrait in 1636, when Galileo was about 72 years old. At that time, the scientist was writing about his life's work on motion, acceleration, and gravity.

sent a copy of this letter to the inquisitors in Rome, who sought out and punished *heretics*—people who opposed church teachings (see **Inquisition**). In early 1616, Galileo was summoned to Rome for a determination on the orthodoxy of his views. Although he was cleared of charges of heresy, he was ordered not "to hold or defend" the Copernican theory. That is, he could treat the theory hypothetically but not treat it as if it were true.

In 1632, Galileo published his first scientific masterpiece, the *Dialogue Concerning the Two Chief World Systems.* In this work, he compared the Ptolemaic-Aristotelian theory to the Copernican theory to show that the Copernican system was logically superior. Once again Galileo was summoned to Rome, this time to answer to the charge of willfully disobeying the order not "to hold or defend" Copernicus's theory. In 1633, the Inquisition found Galileo guilty of the charge, forced him to *recant* (publicly withdraw his statement), and sentenced him to life imprisonment.

Because of Galileo's advanced age and poor health, the church allowed him to serve his imprisonment under house arrest in a villa outside Florence. There, he passed the remainder of his years in relative isolation, eventually becoming blind. But he managed to complete his second scientific masterpiece, the *Discourse on Two New Sciences,* published in 1638. In this work, Galileo provided both a mathematical proof of his new theory of motion and an original study of the tensile strength of materials. In 1979, Pope John Paul II declared that the Roman Catholic Church may have been mistaken in condemning Galileo. He instructed a church commission to study Galileo's case. In 1983, the commission concluded that Galileo should not have been condemned. In 1984, at the commission's recommendation, the church published all documents related to Galileo's trial. In 1992, Pope John Paul II publicly endorsed the commission's finding that the church had made a mistake in condemning Galileo.

Galileo's scientific contribution. Historians disagree about Galileo's role as the "founder of modern experi-

mental science." In fact, some of them doubt that experiment, in the modern sense, played an important part at all in Galileo's scientific development. These historians maintain that Galileo's real originality lay in the way he approached scientific problems. First, Galileo reduced those problems to very simple terms on the basis of everyday experience and common-sense logic. Then he analyzed and resolved the problems according to simple mathematical descriptions. The success with which Galileo applied this technique to the analysis of physics, especially the physics of motion, opened the way for the development of modern mathematical physics.

A. Mark Smith

See also **Light** (The speed of light); **Physics** (The Renaissance; picture); **Science** (Conducting experiments); picture: A pendulum clock; The scientific revolution).

Additional resources

MacLachlan, James. *Galileo Galilei.* Oxford, 1997.
Sharratt, Michael. *Galileo.* 1994. Reprint. Cambridge, 1996.
White, Michael. *Galileo Galilei.* Blackbirch Pr., 1999. Younger readers.

Galileo is a space probe launched by the United States to observe Jupiter, its moons and rings, and the radiation and magnetism in the neighboring space. The National Aeronautics and Space Administration (NASA) launched Galileo on Oct. 18, 1989. The craft went into orbit around Jupiter on Dec. 7, 1995.

NASA designed Galileo to orbit Jupiter for two years, but the craft continued to provide valuable information for years afterward. The Galileo spacecraft was named after Italian astronomer and physicist Galileo, who discovered Jupiter's four largest moons in 1610.

The Galileo craft took an indirect route to Jupiter. First, it made a close approach to Venus, using energy from that planet's gravitational field to increase its speed. It then flew past Earth twice to pick up more speed. On the way to Jupiter, it visited the asteroids Gaspra and Ida. On the day Galileo went into orbit around Jupiter, a

NASA

The Galileo space probe, *upper right,* released a smaller probe that plunged into Jupiter's atmosphere in December 1995. The larger probe continued to explore Jupiter and its moons.

smaller probe that had been released by Galileo five months earlier plunged into the planet's atmosphere. The small probe encountered atmospheric pressures more than 20 times as great as that on Earth. The intense heat of the atmosphere shut down its instruments after 61.4 minutes. Eventually, the entire probe melted and evaporated. One of the probe's major discoveries was that Jupiter's chemical composition resembles what astronomers believe was the original composition of the sun. Jupiter has a higher proportion of heavy elements than the sun. Some of the lighter gases must have been lost during the planet's formation.

Galileo's observations of Jupiter's four largest moons produced many surprises. For example, lava from Io's volcanoes is hotter than lava on Earth. A blanket of dark, smooth material covers the surface of Callisto. Ganymede has a dense core and a *magnetic field* (a region in which magnetism can be detected). Grooves and ridges crisscross the icy surface of Europa. In places, the ice on Europa seems to have broken into blocks—suggesting that there may be an ocean of water underneath.

Andrew P. Ingersoll

Related articles in *World Book* include:

Callisto	Jupiter
Europa	Space exploration (Space
Ganymede	probes)
Io	

Gall (1840-1894) was a leader of the Hunkpapa band of the Teton Sioux Indians. He played an important role in the Indian victory over Lieutenant Colonel George A. Custer in the Battle of the Little Bighorn in 1876. Custer had ordered Major Marcus A. Reno to attack the Indian camp on the Little Bighorn River in what is now Montana. Gall led the Hunkpapa against Reno's troops and forced them to retreat. Gall and his band then helped battle Custer's column.

National Archives, Washington, D.C.
Gall

In late 1876, Gall and other Hunkpapa fled to Canada to avoid being put on a reservation. In 1880, Gall led part of his band back to the United States. After a battle in January 1881, he surrendered and was imprisoned for months. Gall and the Hunkpapa then settled on the Standing Rock reservation in the Dakota Territory.

Gall was born near the Moreau River in what today is South Dakota. His name in the Sioux language was *Pizi*.

Beatrice Medicine

Gall is an abnormal growth on plants that is often seen as a rounded swelling. Galls can form on roots, stems, and leaves, and even on flowers and seed pods. Galls range in size from tiny to enormous.

Most galls are caused by *parasites* (organisms that feed and live on the plant). These parasites include animals, such as certain wasps and worms; fungi, such as smuts and some rusts; plants, including certain mistletoes; and various bacteria and viruses. The gall-causing agents produce chemical substances called *phytohor-*

© Doug Sokell, Tom Stack and Assoc.

Galls can form around the larvae of certain insects. Larvae of the gall wasp produced the galls on this oak leaf. Galls can also be caused by such organisms as bacteria and fungi.

mones, which stimulate plant cells around the agent to multiply and become abnormally enlarged.

Abnormal growths resembling galls also may form as the result of a genetic defect in the plant. Such galls or tumors develop in many plants produced by crossbreeding, including apricot, lily, tobacco, and tomato hybrids. These tumors are thought to result from an imbalance of phytohormones.

Some galls and the agents that cause them can seriously damage plants. For example, a species of worm called the rootknot nematode causes galls in potato, corn, and many other plants. It feeds on the plant roots, and the galls divert nutrients from the rest of the plant.

Other galls benefit plants. For example, galls or nodules formed by *Rhizobium* bacteria on the roots of *legumes* (plants in the pea family) help supply life-giving nitrogen. *Rhizobium* converts nitrogen gas from the air to nitrogen compounds the plant can use.

Studies of *crown gall* have led to the development of improved plants. This gall is caused by *Agrobacterium tumefaciens,* a bacterium that infects many kinds of plants. Upon infection, the bacterium transfers some of its genes to chromosomes of the plant. Using genetic engineering, scientists can alter the bacterium so it transfers genes that give the plant more favorable traits. In this way, researchers have developed disease-resistant varieties of crop plants. Clarence I. Kado

Related articles in *World Book* include:

Bacteria	Fungi	Plant (Diseases)
Eelworm	Nematode	Slime mold

Gallant, Mavis (1922-   ), is a Canadian short-story writer and novelist. Her early stories were collected in *The Other Paris* (1956) and *My Heart Is Broken* (1964). They describe people wandering and lost in a world that lacks meaning. Gallant's first novel, *Green Water, Green Sky* (1959), describes a suffocating mother-daughter relationship. *A Fairly Good Time* (1970) criticizes certain patterns of French behavior and thought.

Gallant has written stories about the continuing influence of authoritarian attitudes in everyday German society after World War II ended in 1945. The stories were collected in *The Pegnitz Junction* (1970) and *From the Fifteenth District* (1979). A number of partially autobiographical stories were collected in *Home Truths* (1981). Several Paris stories were collected in *Overhead in a Balloon* (1985). The stories in *Across the Bridge* (1993) are set in Quebec and Paris. *The Collected Stories of Mavis Gallant* was published in 1996. Her essays were published in *Paris Notebooks* (1986).

Gallant was born in Montreal of English-speaking parents. She traveled to Europe in 1950 and eventually settled in Paris.   Ronald B. Hatch

Gallatin, *GAL uh tihn,* **Albert** (1761-1849), was a prominent American statesman and diplomat. He served as secretary of the treasury under Presidents Thomas Jefferson and James Madison.

Gallatin was born and educated in Geneva, Switzerland. He immigrated to the United States in 1780. In 1790, Gallatin was elected to the Pennsylvania legislature. In 1793, he won election to the U.S. Senate. Gallatin was forced to leave the Senate in 1794 after his political opponents claimed that he had not been a U.S. citizen long enough to qualify for a Senate seat. Later in 1794, Gallatin was elected to the U.S. House of Representatives. He served in the House until 1801, when Jefferson appointed him secretary of the treasury.

As treasury secretary, Gallatin worked to eliminate the national debt. But in 1807, during fighting between Britain and France, Congress halted foreign trade in order to maintain American neutrality. These trade restrictions and—later—the War of 1812 had a disastrous effect on the American economy and thus prevented Gallatin from eliminating the debt. In 1813, Gallatin took a leave of absence as secretary of the treasury to become minister to Russia. He officially resigned as treasury secretary in 1814. Also in 1814, Gallatin helped negotiate the Treaty of Ghent, which ended the War of 1812. He later served as minister to France and as minister to Britain.
        Elliott Robert Barkan

Gallaudet, *GAL uh DEHT,* is the name of three American educators, father and two sons, who pioneered in the education of deaf people in the United States.

Thomas Hopkins Gallaudet (1787-1851) became interested in teaching a 4-year-old deaf girl, Alice Cogswell. He was sent by her father and others to study in Europe. He was discouraged from learning England's oral method, preferring instead the manual, or sign method, that was favored in France. Gallaudet founded the Hartford School for the Deaf in 1817. He wrote many children's books. Gallaudet was born in Philadelphia.

Thomas Gallaudet (1822-1902), the older son, opened a church for the deaf in New York City. **Edward Miner Gallaudet** (1837-1917), the younger son, became president of the Columbia Institution for the Instruction of the Deaf and Dumb and the Blind (now Gallaudet University) in Washington, D.C. Both sons were born in Hartford, Connecticut.   John B. Christiansen

Gallaudet University, *GAL uh DEHT,* in Washington, D.C., is a private, coeducational liberal arts university for deaf students. It also admits some hearing students in areas related to deafness. Courses lead to bachelor's, master's, and doctor's degrees. The university also operates tuition-free demonstration preschool, elementary, and secondary school programs for deaf students. In addition, Gallaudet conducts research programs in deafness and houses both the National Center for Law and the Deaf and the National Information Center on Deafness. Gallaudet has seven regional centers located in major metropolitan areas in the United States.

The school began in 1857 as the Columbia Institution for the Instruction of the Deaf and Dumb and the Blind. In 1864, the United States Congress authorized the institution to grant university degrees. In 1894, the school was renamed in honor of Thomas Hopkins Gallaudet, a pioneer in the education of deaf people.
        Critically reviewed by Gallaudet University

Gallbladder is a small pouch that stores bile. Many, but not all, animals with backbones have gallbladders. In human beings, the gallbladder is a pear-shaped sac that rests on the underside of the right portion of the liver. The gallbladder can hold about $1\frac{1}{2}$ ounces (44 milliliters) of bile at one time.

The neck of the gallbladder connects with the *cystic duct,* which enters the *hepatic duct,* a tube from the liver. Together, these tubes form the *common bile duct.*

During digestion, bile flows from the liver through the hepatic duct into the common bile duct and empties into the *duodenum,* which is the first section of the small intestine. Between meals, the bile is not needed but it continues to flow from the liver into the common bile duct. It is kept out of the duodenum by a small, ring-like muscle called the *sphincter of Oddi,* which tightens around the opening. The fluid then is forced to flow into the gallbladder, where it is concentrated and stored until it is needed for digestion.

The gallbladder is made to contract by action of a hormone called *cholecystokinin* (pronounced *KAHL uh SIHS tuh KY nihn*). This hormone is formed in the upper part of the small intestine.

Gallstones sometimes form within the concentrated

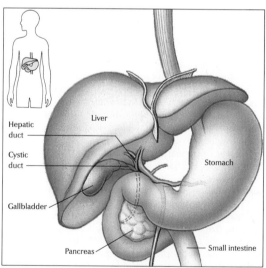

WORLD BOOK illustration by Robert Demarest

The gallbladder is a pouch that stores *bile,* a digestive juice produced by the liver. Bile from the gallbladder and liver empties through the common bile duct into the small intestine.

bile. These small, hard masses may become stuck in the common bile duct, causing severe pain. Blockage of the common bile duct may lead to *jaundice,* a yellowing of the skin resulting from an accumulation of bile in the blood (see **Jaundice**). Doctors commonly treat gallstones by surgically removing the gallbladder. This operation once required a hospital stay of a week or more. Today, the procedure can be done through a *laparoscope,* and the patient often can leave the hospital the next day (see **Laparoscopy**).

Some gallstones can be dissolved by taking a medication. Other gallstones can be treated by using a device called a *lithotripter.* The lithotripter produces shock waves that break the stone into tiny fragments.

Laurence H. Beck

See also **Bile; Digestive system; Hormone; Intestine; Liver.**

Galleon, *GAL ee uhn,* was at first an Italian armed merchant ship. In 1570, the English sea captain John Hawkins developed the galleon into a fighting ship. It was easily maneuvered and swift, compared with other ships of its day. It was the largest ship in the English navy. The early fighting galleon had a heavy *foremast* (front mast). The *mainmast* (mast placed next behind the foremast) was also heavy. Both foremast and mainmast carried deep, square sails. Galleons also had one or two small masts toward the rear of the ship. These masts held three-cornered sails, called *lateen* sails. The *bulwarks* (sides) were usually about 3 to 4 feet (0.9 to 1.2 meters) thick. A long, raised deck, called the *quarterdeck,* ran from the mainmast toward the ship's rear, where a higher deck, called the *poop,* was located. The *forecastle* (raised deck in front of the foremast) was square and low.

The sides of English galleons from the early 1500's were usually pierced for a dozen large guns. A few smaller guns were mounted above the main deck. The Spanish galleon, which appeared about 1550, had a higher and longer poop than the English galleon, and was less manageable. The Spaniards tried the ship for carrying treasure from the Americas in the latter 1500's. But it could not defend itself against pirate ships because it was too hard to maneuver. Nevertheless, by about 1600, the galleon had become the main type of trading vessel in Europe. James C. Bradford

See also **Galley; Ship** (History; picture).

WORLD BOOK illustration by Robert Addison
The galleon helped establish English naval power.

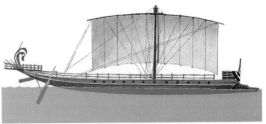

WORLD BOOK illustration by Robert Addison
A Roman galley moved both by oars and by sail. Rowing was used for speed and maneuvering in battle, and in emergencies.

Galley, *GAL ee,* was a long, narrow, wooden warship. It was widely used by the navies of ancient Mediterranean nations. Galleys had an open deck with at least one mast and set of sails. They were also equipped with one or more rows of oars on each side. Galleys traveled under sail when wind permitted. Rowing was used for speed and maneuvering in battle, and also in emergencies.

Two ancient Mediterranean civilizations—the Minoans of Crete and the Mycenaeans of mainland Greece—first built galleys between 2000 and 1000 B.C. A large metal *ram* (point) was fitted to the front of the galleys. The ram was used in battle to punch holes in the sides of enemy vessels. By about 700 B.C., a galley called a *bireme* was developed, probably by the Phoenicians or the Greeks. It featured two *banks* (rows) of oarsmen on each side, one above the other, to provide more speed and ramming power. Until then, all galleys had only a single row of oarsmen on each side. By about 500 B.C., the Greeks had introduced the *trireme,* which had three banks of oars on each side. Each trireme carried a crew of about 200. Later, the Greeks built galleys with four and then five banks of oarsmen.

The Romans used galleys similar to those of the Greeks. The Romans also added a second set of sails to their galleys. The oarsmen of Roman galleys were not slaves, as is often believed. Rather, they were noncitizen subjects of the Roman Empire, mainly from the Balkans and Egypt. As the speed of other types of ships increased, the galleys began to disappear. Mediterranean galleys were probably used for the last time in warfare at the Battle of Matapan in 1717. Octavia N. Cubbins

See also **Navy** (Ancient navies); **Ship** (History).

Gallic wars. See Gaul.

Gallienus, *GAL ee EE nuhs* (A.D. 218?-268), was a Roman emperor. He stopped the persecution of Christians that his father, Valerian, had begun. Gallienus was the first Roman emperor to recognize Christianity as a legal religion. Christians were again persecuted by later emperors. Christianity became permanently legal under Emperor Constantine in 313. Gallienus also prohibited senators from holding military commands, and emphasized the role of cavalry in the Roman army.

Gallienus became co-emperor with his father in 253. He became sole emperor in 260, after his father was captured by the Persians. Gallienus was unable to prevent rebels from taking control of Britain, Gaul, and Spain, but he defeated the Goths in the Balkans in 268. Gallienus was murdered later that year, and Claudius II, a general, succeeded him as emperor. Many historians believe that Claudius helped plan the murder of Gallienus. Thomas W. Africa

Gallinule, *GAL uh nool,* is a water bird that lives in marshes throughout the world. The most widespread species is the *common moorhen,* which nests in North and South America, Europe, Asia, and Africa. It was formerly called the *Florida gallinule* or the *common gallinule* in North America. The common moorhen is sooty-colored or black and looks like a coot, but it has a broad red plate covering its forehead like a shield. Its bill is red instead of white like a coot's. The *purple gallinule* nests from the southern United States to South America. Both birds are about 1 foot (30 centimeters) long.

Gallinules build their nests on rough platforms of reeds and grasses in marshes. Female gallinules lay from 6 to 14 eggs of different colors. Gallinules are excellent swimmers but poor fliers. They stay concealed most of the time in marsh grasses. Peter G. Connors

Scientific classification. Gallinules are in the rail family, Rallidae. The scientific name for the common moorhen is *Gallinula chloropus.* The purple gallinule is *Porphyrula martinica.*

See also **Coot; Rail.**

Gallipoli Peninsula. See **World War I** (The Dardanelles).

Gallium, *GAL ee uhm,* is a soft, silver-white metal found throughout the earth's crust. Its general properties resemble those of aluminum. *Intermetallic compounds* (compounds of two or more metals) with gallium are used as high-temperature rectifiers; as semiconductors in transistors, light-emitting diodes, and semiconductor lasers; and in memory devices in high-speed computers. Gallium remains in liquid form over a larger temperature range than does any other element. It was first used to fill high-temperature thermometers. A mixture of tin, silver, and gallium is used in dental fillings. It is found in various ores, minerals, and rocks, such as diaspore, sphalerite, germanite, bauxite, and coal.

Gallium has the chemical symbol Ga, the atomic number 31, and the atomic weight 69.723. It boils at 2403 °C, and it melts at 29.78 °C. Gallium has a density of 5.907 grams per cubic centimeter at 20 °C. The French chemist Paul Émile Lecoq de Boisbaudran first discovered gallium in 1875. Raymond E. Davis

Gallon, *GAL uhn,* is a unit of volume and capacity used for liquids. It is part of the inch-pound system of measurement customarily used in the United States. A gallon is the amount of liquid that

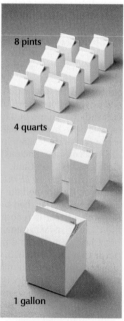

WORLD BOOK photo by Steven Spicer

The standard gallon used in the United States contains 8 pints or 4 quarts.

8 pints

4 quarts

1 gallon

will fill a container of exactly 231 cubic inches. One gallon equals 3.785 liters. A fourth of a gallon is a quart. A half-quart is called a pint.

The *imperial gallon* is sometimes used in the United Kingdom. However, it has been largely replaced by metric units of measurement. The imperial gallon contains 277.420 cubic inches of liquid and is equal to 4.546 liters. Richard S. Davis

See also **Liter; Pint; Quart; Weights and measures.**

Galloway, Joseph (1731-1803), was a prominent Philadelphia lawyer and politician who opposed the Revolutionary War in America (1775-1783). Galloway became a leading spokesman and writer among the Americans who remained loyal to Britain.

Galloway was born in Anne Arundel County, Maryland. He studied law in Philadelphia and became active in politics. Galloway was a Pennsylvania delegate to the Continental Congress in 1774, and he became alarmed at the colonial delegation's support for American independence. Galloway submitted a plan of union aimed at keeping the American Colonies in the British Empire and preserving the colonies' self-governing rights. But the plan was defeated by one vote. Galloway continued to sympathize with the British and moved to Britain in 1778. William Morgan Fowler, Jr.

Gallstone. See **Gallbladder.**

Gallup, New Mexico (pop. 20,209), is called the Indian capital because it is the trading center of Southwest tribes. It is about 135 miles (217 kilometers) west of Albuquerque (see **New Mexico** [political map]). The Navajo, Zuni, and Hopi reservations are nearby. The Inter-Tribal Indian Ceremonial is held in Gallup each August. South of Gallup lie the ancient ruins of Hawikuh, one of the legendary Seven Cities of Cíbola visited by Spanish explorer Francisco Vásquez de Coronado in 1540. Gallup was founded in 1881. The city has a mayor-council government. Important industries include tourism and Indian arts and crafts. Timothy Knowles

Gallup, George Horace (1901-1984), an American statistician, specialized in public opinion and business surveys. His Gallup Poll on political issues and the popularity of politicians became well known. Gallup predicted correctly the outcome of the 1936 presidential election. This success helped boost his reputation for accuracy. Gallup developed a method of measuring reader interest in news features and advertising. In 1935, he founded the American Institute of Public Opinion in Princeton, New Jersey. Gallup was born in Jefferson, Iowa. See also **Public opinion poll** (History).

Joseph W. Dauben

Galsworthy, John (1867-1933), an English novelist and playwright, won the Nobel Prize for literature in 1932. He has an important place in English realistic literature because of his relatively objective descriptions of the society of his time. He was also deeply concerned with the social problems of his day.

Galsworthy's best-known work is *The Forsyte Saga.* It is a *trilogy* (series of three novels) consisting of *The Man of Property* (1906), *In Chancery* (1920), and *To Let* (1921), plus brief connecting interludes. Around the main character of Soames Forsyte, Galsworthy pictured a declining upper middle-class society from the 1880's to the years after World War I (1914-1918). He continued the story in a later trilogy, *A Modern Comedy,* consisting of

The White Monkey (1924), *The Silver Spoon* (1926), and *Swan Song* (1928). Many of the same characters appear in a third trilogy—*Maid in Waiting* (1931), *Flowering Wilderness* (1932), and *One More River* (1933). They were collected as *End of the Chapter*.

In his record of the Forsytes, Galsworthy dealt with the conflict between idealism and love of worldly things. He also captured a sense of time's pitiless passing and of an era's inevitable decay.

Galsworthy's plays brought a new sense of social responsibility to English drama. *The Silver Box* (1906) contrasts the law's treatment of rich and poor people. *Strife* (1909) dramatizes the stubbornness of opposing leaders of a strike. Galsworthy's severe picture of solitary confinement in *Justice* (1910) led to prison reforms. *Loyalties* (1922) deals with social conduct and racial prejudice. Galsworthy's plays pursue these social issues through simple, direct dialogue presented in a naturalistic style. Galsworthy was born in Kingston Hill, Surrey.

Garrett Stewart

Galt, *gawlt,* **Sir Alexander Tilloch,** *TIHL uhk* (1817-1893), was one of Canada's Fathers of Confederation. These individuals were planners of the union of British colonies that formed the Dominion of Canada in 1867. He served as the dominion's first minister of finance.

Galt was born in London. He came to Canada in 1835 to work for a land development company in Quebec. He later became an official of the company. Galt served as finance minister of the Province of Canada from 1858 to 1862 and from 1864 to 1866. In 1859, he sharply raised Canada's tariff on imported manufactured goods. He also supported the development of railroads. Galt was Canada's first high commissioner to Britain. He served in this diplomatic position from 1880 to 1883. Galt was knighted in 1869.   J. M. Bumsted

Galton, *GAWL tuhn,* **Sir Francis** (1822-1911), a British scientist and cousin of Charles Darwin, became known for his research in meteorology, heredity, and anthropology. He spent five years in Sudan and Namibia studying the people there. He suggested important theories in meteorology, published weather charts, and introduced the idea of anticyclones (see **Weather** [Synoptic-scale systems]). His studies of fingerprints led to their use in identification (see **Fingerprinting** [History]).

Galton argued that plants and animals vary according to patterns. He devised new statistical methods and applied them to the study of heredity. He was the first to call the science of human breeding *eugenics*. Galton urged the planned improvement of the human race by selection of superior parents. In his will, he left money to found the Chair of Eugenics at London University.

Galton was born near Birmingham. He was educated at Birmingham General Hospital and Cambridge University. He wrote *Hereditary Genius* (1869), *English Men of Science* (1874), and *Inquiries into the Human Faculty and Its Development* (1883).   Alan R. Rushton

Galvani, *gahl VAH nee,* **Luigi,** *loo EE jee* (1737-1798), an Italian physician and anatomist, discovered that electric currents could cause contractions in muscles and nerves. He demonstrated such contractions in experiments with freshly killed frogs. His work laid the foundation for *neurophysiology,* the branch of physiology that deals with the nervous system.

Galvani won fame for his investigations into animal physiology during the 1770's and 1780's. He inserted brass hooks in the spinal cords of frogs and attached the hooks to an iron railing. When Galvani stimulated the frogs with an electric charge, their legs twitched. He assumed incorrectly that he had proved the existence of a special "animal electricity." But he had unknowingly discovered what is still called *galvanism*—the production of an electric current from two metals in contact with a moist environment. See **Electricity** (Experiments with electric charge).

Galvani was born in Bologna. He became a professor of anatomy and women's health there. Galvani also became well known for his research on bones and on the kidneys and ears of birds.   John Scarborough

Galvanizing, *GAL vuh nyz ihng,* is the process of coating such metals as iron and steel with a thin protective layer of zinc or zinc alloy. This layer protects the metals from *corrosion* (chemical damage). The zinc helps prevent corrosion because it reacts with many chemicals more easily than iron does. For example, when iron reacts with oxygen, it forms *iron oxide* (rust). However, if the iron has been galvanized, the zinc protects the iron by reacting with the oxygen and forming zinc oxide before rust can form.

Steel is the most commonly galvanized metal. One simple and widely used method of applying a zinc coating to steel is called *hot-dip galvanizing*. This method involves dipping steel in a hot bath of liquid zinc. In some cases, steelmakers mix other metals, such as aluminum, antimony, cadmium, and tin, with the zinc. Manufacturers add such metals to improve the appearance or the protective qualities of the coating. Metal pails and similar small objects are dipped in the zinc bath and galvanized one at a time. Steelmakers galvanize huge sheets of steel by passing them continuously through the zinc bath and coiling them up afterward. This method of galvanizing forms coatings that are about $\frac{3}{1,000}$ inch (0.076 millimeter) thick. Sheet steel galvanized in this way may later be stamped or pressed to form such items as automobile body panels and steel roofing and siding. See **Iron and steel** (Finishing; diagram: How steel is shaped and finished).

A less widely used method of galvanizing steel is called *electrogalvanizing*. This process involves placing steel in a solution of zinc sulfate and water. A flow of electric current causes the zinc in the solution to form a thin layer on the surface of the steel. Electrogalvanizing is used chiefly to galvanize a continuous piece of steel. See **Electroplating.**   Gordon H. Geiger

See also **Rust; Zinc.**

Galveston, *GAL vih stuhn,* Texas (pop. 57,247; met. area pop. 250,158), is a seaport on the Gulf of Mexico. The city lies on Galveston Island, about 2 miles (3 kilometers) off the Texas mainland. For the location of Galveston, see **Texas** (political map). Two bridges, a rail line, and a ferry link Galveston Island and the mainland. The Galveston metropolitan area includes Texas City, on the mainland.

The Port of Galveston is the oldest deepwater port on the Gulf of Mexico west of the Mississippi River. It began operating in the 1830's. A channel connects Galveston Harbor with the Gulf of Mexico and the Gulf Intracoastal Waterway, which extends between Brownsville, Texas, and Carrabelle, Florida. Galveston's port handles *bulk* (unpackaged) cargo and acts as a service center for the offshore oil and gas industry.

Galveston is a popular convention and resort city. Galveston Island has 32 miles (51 kilometers) of beaches. Moody Gardens, an entertainment complex, features a re-created rain forest housed in a giant glass pyramid. The Texas Seaport Museum includes a restored 1870's sailing ship and a computerized listing of immigrants who arrived in the United States at Galveston's port.

Galveston is the home of a campus of Texas A&M University, the University of Texas Medical Branch, and Galveston College. Galveston's Rosenberg Library owns an important collection of books and other materials on the history of Texas.

The Karankawa Indians were the first inhabitants of Galveston Island. In 1785, Spanish surveyors named the island for Bernardo de Gálvez, the Spanish governor of Cuba, Louisiana, and Florida. The pirate Jean Laffite ran a smuggling operation there from 1817 to 1821 (see **Laffite, Jean**). Galveston was founded in 1836 and received a city charter in 1839.

Before the Civil War (1861-1865), Galveston was a slave port. It was through an announcement made in Galveston on June 19, 1865, that Texas slaves learned they were free. They marked the event with a festival called *Juneteenth,* which is now celebrated in many states.

By 1880, Galveston was the largest city in Texas. But a hurricane struck the city in 1900 and killed more than 6,000 people. After the hurricane, the people of Galveston built a sea wall to protect the city. Sand dredged from Galveston Bay and the Gulf of Mexico was put in behind the wall and raised the island's elevation. However, Galveston never regained its role as a major port, losing out to nearby Houston.

Galveston is the seat of Galveston County. The city has a council-manager government.   Heber Taylor

Gálvez, *GAHL vays,* **Bernardo de** (1746-1786), was governor of the Spanish colony of Louisiana during most of the Revolutionary War in America (1775-1783). His military efforts against the British helped Spain gain the British colonies of East Florida and West Florida in the Treaty of Paris in 1783, which ended the war.

Gálvez became acting governor of Louisiana in 1777 and soon started aiding American revolutionaries in the area. In 1779, Spain declared war on Britain, and Gálvez was made a brigadier general. He soon engaged in a series of brilliant military expeditions in West Florida. He attacked and captured several British posts along the Mississippi River. In 1780, he took the settlement of Mobile, which was then part of the British colony of West Florida. The British surrendered West Florida to Spain after Gálvez captured the town of Pensacola in 1781.

In 1783, Gálvez went home to Spain a hero. In 1784, he became *captain-general* (governor) of Cuba, Louisiana, and Florida. In 1785, he also became viceroy of New Spain, Spain's empire in the Americas. Gálvez was born in Macharaviaya, Spain, near Málaga.   Paul David Nelson

Galway, *GAWL way* (pop. 47,104), is a port city on the west coast of Ireland. It lies on Galway Bay. For location, see **Ireland** (political map).

Galway serves as the administrative and commercial center for much of western Ireland. Factories in the city make clothing, food products, and electronic and electrical equipment. Tourism contributes to the economy. Salthill, a suburb of Galway, is a popular seaside resort.

St. Nicholas Church in Galway dates from 1320. University College, founded in 1849, is also in the city.

Anglo-Normans founded Galway in the 1200's. The town was chartered as a free port in 1484, and 14 merchant families, or tribes, controlled the town. Thus, Galway is sometimes called the *city of the tribes.* Ireland's potato famine from 1845 to 1848 caused much hardship in Galway. The city expanded greatly during the 1900's. An industrial area and many large residential areas were built.   Desmond A. Gillmor

Gama, Vasco Da. See Da Gama, Vasco.

Gamaliel, *guh MAY lee uhl,* was the name of six great ancient Jewish scholars who lived in Palestine. The first and best known was Gamaliel I, who died about A.D. 50. He was an expert in the Oral Law and a prominent member of the Sanhedrin, the Jewish high court. He was also a Pharisee who belonged to the school of his grandfather, the great Rabbi Hillel I. According to the Acts of the Apostles (5:34-39), Gamaliel I taught Saint Paul. He is also said to have defended the disciples of Jesus before the Sanhedrin. In the Talmud, Gamaliel is known as a famous interpreter of the Jewish law who established rulings favorable to the legal status of women and non-Jews.   Stanley K. Stowers

Gambia is one of the smallest independent countries in Africa. A narrow strip of land in western Africa, Gambia extends inland from the Atlantic Ocean for about 180 miles (290 kilometers). It lies along the banks of the Gambia River. Gambia is only 15 to 30 miles (24 to 48 kilometers) wide. It is a flatland. Mangrove and scrub forests line the areas along the coast and the Gambia River. Elsewhere, sandy soil covers the land. Except for its short coastline, Gambia is entirely surrounded by Senegal. It is officially called the Republic of The Gambia or The Gambia. Banjul, a busy port with about 44,000 people, is the capital and only large town (see **Banjul**).

Gambia is a poor country. It has relatively little fertile soil and no valuable mineral deposits. Tropical crops grow well near the mouth of the river. However, most farmers in Gambia earn a living by raising peanuts. Peanuts account for most of the country's income.

James Island, in the Gambia River, was once a slave trading center from which slaves were shipped to the West Indies and America. All or part of what is now Gambia was controlled by the English from the 1660's to 1965, when Gambia became an independent nation.

Government. In 1996, Gambia adopted a new constitution. The president of Gambia is the head of state and is elected by the people to a five-year term. The president appoints the members of the Cabinet to handle the day to day operations of government. The National Assembly makes the country's laws. The people elect 45 members of the National Assembly to five-year terms. The president appoints an additional 4 Assembly members. All citizens age 18 and over may vote. The Supreme Court is Gambia's highest court.

People. Almost all the people of Gambia are black Africans. The five main ethnic groups, in order of size, are the Mandingo, the Fula (or Fulani), the Wolof, the Serahuli, and the Jola. Most Gambians are Muslims.

About 275,000 Mandingo live throughout Gambia. They are tall, music-loving people who make a meager living as traders and peanut farmers. Most of the 100,000 Fula live in eastern Gambia and raise cattle for a living.

Many of them are nomadic. They move their herds from region to region.

Most of the 90,000 Wolof are either farmers who live near Gambia's northern border or inhabitants of Banjul, where they make up a majority of the population. The Wolof enjoy dancing and music. Wolof women in Banjul often dress elegantly in turbans; high-waisted, full-skirted dresses; and gold ornaments and jewelry.

Most of the 60,000 Serahuli live in eastern Gambia, where the soil is poor and farming is difficult. Every year, people from Senegal called the *strange farmers* come to help the Serahuli plant and harvest the crops. They take an agreed share of the crop and are also given a plot of land on which they raise their own crops.

The 55,000 Jola live south of the Gambia River near the coast. They have lived in Gambia longer than the other ethnic groups, and once were bitter enemies of the Mandingo. The Jola are hard-working farmers who live in small villages surrounded by earthen walls. They raise rice and millet for food. Most Jola follow a traditional African religion practiced by their ancestors.

Almost all children living in and near Banjul attend school, but only about one-third of the children in other parts of Gambia go to school. Most schoolchildren complete a six-year primary course, but only a few go to secondary schools. Gambia has a technical school in Banjul and a teacher-training college in Yundum.

Land. The Gambia River rises in Guinea and winds through Gambia before reaching the Atlantic Ocean. Small oceangoing ships can sail up the river from the Atlantic as far as Kuntaur.

Mangrove swamps line the riverbanks from the coast to the center of the country. Behind the swamps lie the *banto faros*—areas that are firm ground in the dry season, but swamps during the rains. Near the coast, salt water from the tidal reaches of the Gambia River floods the banto faros, ruining the soil. Farther inland, areas that the river floods with fresh water during the wet sea-

Facts in brief

Capital: Banjul.
Official language: English.
Area: 4,361 mi² (11,295 km²).
Population: *Estimated 2002 population*—1,372,000; density, 315 per mi² (121 per km²); distribution, 63 percent rural, 37 percent urban. *1993 census*—1,025,867.
Chief products: *Agriculture*—bananas, cassava, corn, hides and skins, limes, livestock (cattle, goats, sheep), mangoes, millet, oranges, palm kernels, papayas, peanuts, rice, vegetables.
National anthem: "Na Gambia Banko Kamma" ("For Gambia Our Homeland").
Flag: The flag has three horizontal bands (red, blue, and green) divided by two narrow white bands. See **Flag** (picture: Flags of Africa).
Money: *Basic unit*—dalasi. One hundred bututs equal one dalasi.

son are used to raise rice. Beyond the banto faros, sandy plateaus extend from both sides of the river into Senegal. Farmers raise peanuts and rice on the plateaus.

Gambia's summer months (June through October) are hot and humid. Inland temperatures during the summer may reach 110 °F (43 °C). During the winter (November through May), temperatures drop to about 60 °F (16 °C). The *harmattan,* a dry wind, blows from the Sahara during the winter (see **Harmattan**). About 40 inches (100 centimeters) of rain falls near the coast each year. Inland areas get less rainfall.

Economy. Peanuts, which have been exported from Gambia since 1830, make up about 95 percent of the value of the country's exports. Rice is also grown, most of it by Gambian women as food for their families. The only industry in Gambia is peanut processing. The United Kingdom is Gambia's most important trade partner.

The Gambia River is the main transportation route. Oceangoing ships sail upstream to load peanuts for export. Ferries, smaller boats, and large canoes with sails carry passengers on the river. Gambia has no railroads, but there are roads on both sides of the river. The Trans-Gambia Highway, connecting northern and southern Senegal, runs through Gambia. An airport in Yundum, near Banjul, links Gambia with other African countries and the United Kingdom. Radio Gambia, a government service, broadcasts in English and in African languages.

History. The area that is now Gambia was part of the powerful Mali Empire from the 1200's to the 1400's (see **Mali Empire**). The people raised cotton and rice and other foods. Portugal set up trading posts on Gambia's coast in the 1400's. The coast became a center of the English and Portuguese slave trades during the 1500's. England began a settlement on James Island in the Gambia River in 1661. During the next 100 years, England and France fought for control of trade on the river.

In 1765, the British established a colony called Senegambia, which included what are now parts of Gambia and Senegal. In 1783, the British handed over the Senegal territory to France. British merchants founded Bathurst (now Banjul) in 1816. The colony of Gambia was set up in 1888. By 1902, all of what is now Gambia had come under British rule.

Gambia began gaining partial self-government after World War II ended in 1945. It gained complete internal self-government in 1963. David (later Sir Dawda, or Dauda) Jawara, leader of the People's Progressive Party,

Gambia

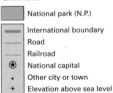

	National park (N.P.)
	International boundary
	Road
	Railroad
✪	National capital
•	Other city or town
+	Elevation above sea level

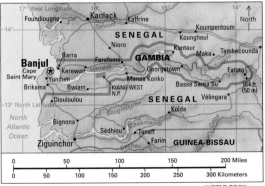

WORLD BOOK maps

Gambian women cultivate a field of rice, *left.* Rice is an important crop in Gambia and is grown mainly by women. Peanuts rank as the country's chief crop and export item.

© Chuck Fishman, De Wys, Inc.

became the first prime minister. Gambia gained complete independence on Feb. 18, 1965. On April 24, 1970, Gambia became a republic. Jawara was elected as the first president.

Under Jawara, the government spent money to improve Gambia's roads and ferries and to modernize Yundum Airport and the harbor at Banjul. Since 1970, tourism in Gambia has grown rapidly. However, since the 1970's, droughts have reduced agricultural production and seriously damaged Gambia's economy.

In 1982, Gambia and Senegal formed a confederation, which—like the earlier colony—was called Senegambia. The confederation strengthened the economic ties between the two countries and united their armed forces. However, disputes between Gambia and Senegal led the two countries to end the confederation in 1989.

In 1994, a group of Gambian military officers led by Yahya Jammeh overthrew Jawara and began to rule Gambia through a military council. In August 1996, Gambia adopted a new constitution. Jammeh won presidential elections later that year. Soon after the elections, Jammeh dissolved the military council. In 1997, Gambia elected a National Assembly.   Harry A. Gailey

Gamblers Anonymous, also called G.A., is a worldwide organization that works to help men and women who suffer from a driving urge to gamble. Members include people who have solved gambling problems. They meet regularly to share their recovery experiences with others whose gambling problem has caused them trouble and misery and who want to do something about it. The only requirement for membership is a desire to stop gambling.

Gamblers Anonymous was founded in Los Angeles in 1957. It now has over 1,000 local groups in the United States and about 15 other nations. The Gamblers Anonymous National Service Office is the center for all G.A. activities. G.A. is headquartered in Los Angeles.

Critically reviewed by Gamblers Anonymous

Gambling is betting on the outcome of a game, event, or chance happening. Gamblers or players usually bet money on the outcome they predict. People bet on such games of chance as lotteries, card games, and dice, or on horse racing, boxing, and other sports events.

The popularity of gambling. Gambling is popular throughout the world. Many people gamble because of the excitement and tensions of uncertainty. Others enjoy

taking risks and the challenge of testing their skill or luck. Some people gamble because they enjoy competing with others. Many people believe gambling is a quick way to make money. In most cases, however, winning is determined by chance. But people can increase their chances of winning by understanding the rules of a game thoroughly and learning which bets offer better chances to win.

In Europe, the Far East, and other parts of the world, gambling usually operates under close government supervision. In the United States, legal and illegal gambling make up a multibillion-dollar industry. Nevada is the only state that permits most forms of gambling, including betting on sports events. Race track betting and lotteries are legal in about three-fourths of the states. Several states allow casino gambling on Indian reservations, on riverboats or cruise ships, or to raise funds for charities or nonprofit organizations. When legal facilities are not available, people often gamble illegally by placing bets with *bookmakers,* also called *bookies.*

Some people oppose gambling because excessive gambling may bring financial ruin to gamblers and their families. Others claim that the gambling industry is influenced by organized crime and that gambling contributes to higher crime rates.

People in favor of legalized gambling claim it encourages economic development through tourism and that tax revenues from gambling benefit the public. They argue that people will always gamble because gambling laws are not fully enforced and probably cannot be. They also claim legalization would end organized crime's influence on gambling.

Casino gambling features four table games: craps, roulette, and the card games baccarat and blackjack. People also play the wheel of fortune game and slot machines. Slot machines, including video poker games, attract more players than any other game and take in about half of all money players bet at casinos. Casinos are found in Australia, Europe, the Far East, and the United States and on several Caribbean islands.

Sports betting involves wagering on such organized sports events as football, baseball, and basketball or on informal games with friends, such as softball or golf. Many people bet on such events through sports pools, private wagers, or bookies.

In the United States, horse racing attracts millions of

racing fans in over 100 race tracks throughout the country. All tracks operate under the *pari-mutuel* wagering system. In this system, the race track, the state, and the owner of the winning horse get a part of each bet. But most of the money is divided among the people who bet on the winning horse.

The payoff on a winning bet is determined by the odds on the horse. If the odds are 5 to 1, people get $6 for every $1 they bet. Harness racing and greyhound racing also operate on the pari-mutuel betting system and produce millions of dollars in gambling revenue.

Dwight Chuman

Related articles in *World Book* include:

Atlantic City	Horse racing	Poker
Dice	Las Vegas	Roulette
Gamblers Anony-	Lottery	Slot machine
mous	Monte Carlo	

Additional resources

Cozic, Charles P., and Winters, P. A., eds. *Gambling.* Greenhaven, 1995.
Sifakis, Carl. *Encyclopedia of Gambling.* Bks. on Demand, 1990.

Game is the name given to most wild animals, especially those sought for the sport of hunting or fishing. Game may be killed to obtain fur, skin, antlers, or horns. People can use game for food, clothing, or trophies. Large wild animals—such as antelopes, bears, deer, lions, and wild sheep—are called *big game.* Smaller animals, such as rabbits and squirrels, are called *small game.* Certain birds, including grouse, pheasants, and quail, are called *upland game.* Doves, waterfowl, and wild pigeons are examples of *migratory game birds. Game fish* range from trout found in lakes and streams to giant marlin that live in the ocean. William R. Quimby

Related articles in *World Book.* See the *Natural resources* section of the province and state articles, such as **Alabama** (Natural resources). See also the following articles:

Animal (How human beings protect animals)	Fur
	Hunting
Bird (Protective laws and treaties)	Poaching
	Safari
Conservation	Spearfishing
Fish (Food and game fish)	Trapping
Fishing	Wildlife conservation
Fox hunting	

Game is a mental or physical contest played according to rules. People have played games since prehistoric times. Games are usually played for fun, but they can also provide excitement, challenge, and relaxation. Many games help develop mental, physical, and social skills. To play a game, players may need a good memory, physical agility, or an understanding of probabilities. Games may also require skill at guessing what players are thinking, or an ability to visualize changing patterns of pieces on a board. Some games, such as the board game chess, are so challenging that people may spend much of their lives practicing and studying to improve their playing skills.

Types of games

There are thousands of different games, and they can be classified in many ways. Games can be grouped according to the kind of people who usually play them, as in *children's games,* or according to the number of players they require, as in *solitaire games.* Games may also be grouped according to the object of the game. For ex-

© David Stone, Berg & Associates

A children's game called musical chairs requires quick reactions. Players walk around a circle of chairs while music plays. When the music stops, players must scramble to find an empty chair. There are always one fewer chairs than players.

ample, in *cooperative games,* players work together toward a common goal instead of competing to win.

Another category of games involves organized competition. These games are usually called sports, especially when they involve physical activity, as in baseball. But even board games such as chess may be thought of as a sport when played in front of spectators, or when the winners receive prizes or titles.

Some games are designed for educational purposes. Such games may teach children reading or arithmetic. They also may teach adults how to do a certain job well.

Games are most commonly grouped by the kind of equipment used to play them. The major game groups are (1) board games, (2) card games, (3) tile games, (4) target games, (5) dice games, (6) table games, (7) paper and pencil games, and (8) electronic games.

Games that do not use any equipment, or that use equipment suitable only for one particular game, are often grouped according to where they are played. These types of games include party games, such as charades; TV game shows, such as *Jeopardy;* casino games, such as roulette; lawn games, such as croquet; and street games, such as hopscotch.

Board games probably have the greatest variety. Each year, hundreds of new board games appear on the market in the United States alone.

One of the oldest known board games was found at Ur, a city of ancient Sumer (now in Iraq). Archaeologists believe the board is about 4,500 years old. The game was probably a race game in which players threw dice and moved pieces around a track. Today, many board games are race games, including Parcheesi and backgammon.

Strategy board games have been played for thousands of years. Most strategy games require two players. The strategy game known as *go* is one of the most difficult, although it has simple rules. Go originated over 2,000 years ago in China, where it is called *weiqi.* Go is played on a board that has 19 horizontal and 19 vertical lines. The object of the game is to capture territory by surrounding it with black and white pieces called "stones." Today, professional go players earn large salaries in Japan and other Asian countries.

Other notable strategy board games include chess, *shogi* (Japanese chess), *xiang qi* (Chinese chess), a variety of different checkers games, and *mancala*. Mancala games are a popular group of ancient mathematical African and Asian games, such as the African game *wari*. They involve strategic moves of pebbles, seeds, or other small objects around pits scooped out of a board.

War games are board games that first gained wide popularity in the United States in the 1960's. Such games offer players opportunities to re-create historical battles in great detail. Other board game categories include trivia games, such as Trivial Pursuit; word games, such as Scrabble Crossword Game; games of logical deduction, such as Clue; and financial games, such as Monopoly. Some board games are based upon a movie, TV show, or fictional character.

Role-playing games make up a relatively new category of games. They may or may not involve a board. Dungeons & Dragons, invented in the 1970's, became the first popular role-playing game. In most role-playing games, one player is named the "gamemaster." The other players each assume the role of a different character with special attributes, such as strength or magical ability. Players lead their characters through imaginary adventures, such as finding treasures in dungeons guarded by monsters. The gamemaster tells the players what happens to them through each stage of the adventure, such as entering a room or meeting a dragon.

Card games probably rank next to board games as having the most variety. Card games have been played for hundreds of years. Most card games use a standard 52-card deck, but some games use only part of a standard deck. Several games are played with a tarot deck, which contains many symbolic face cards. Many card games, such as Uno, use a specially designed deck.

Most card games involve a combination of skill and luck. The most interesting card games, and the ones that remain popular the longest, are the games that require the greatest amount of skill. Card games requiring the most skill include poker, bridge, and the three-player German game Skat.

Tile games use marked tiles made of wood, ivory, bone, stone, or plastic. Several tile games are played with dominoes. Mah-jongg is a Chinese game similar to the popular card game rummy, but it is played with tiles rather than with cards.

Target games involve propelling objects toward a target. Children play many target games with marbles. They may shoot their marbles at those of an opponent, or at another target. In horseshoe pitching, players toss horseshoes at stakes driven into the ground. Darts and bowling are other popular target games.

Dice games are games of chance. They are based on the random roll of objects called *dice*. Most dice games involve gambling. Popular dice games include Yahtzee and liar's dice.

Table games usually involve guiding or striking a ball or disk over a flat surface toward a goal. Billiards is one of the world's most popular table games.

Paper and pencil games developed from board

WORLD BOOK photo by Steinkamp/Ballogg

Mah-jongg players use rectangular tiles engraved with Chinese symbols. Mah-jongg began in China, but the game is now also played in many other parts of the world.

games. One of the oldest and simplest types of paper and pencil games played today is tic-tac-toe.

Electronic games are one of the newest types of games. Most are controlled by a computer and connected to a viewing screen called a *video screen*. Many are based on traditional board games or target games.

R. Wayne Schmittberger

Related articles in *World Book*. See **Sports** and its list of *Related articles*. See also the following articles:

Backgammon	Cribbage	Jacks
Bridge	Crossword puzzle	Mah-jongg
Card game	Darts	Marbles
Checkers	Dice	Pinochle
Chess	Dominoes	Poker
Colonial life in America (Recreation)	Indian, American (Recreation)	Video game

Game theory is a method of studying decision-making situations in which the choices of two or more individuals or groups influence one another. Game theorists refer to these situations as *games* and to the decision makers as *players*. An example of such a situation is one in which the decision of each of several countries about whether to acquire nuclear weapons is affected by the decisions of the other countries. Game theory has become important in economics, international relations, moral philosophy, political science, social psychology, and sociology. Its roots are generally traced back to the book *The Theory of Games and Economic Behavior* (1944), by Hungarian-born mathematician John von Neumann and Austrian economist Oskar Morgenstern.

Game theorists have identified many types of games. In *zero-sum games,* the players have opposite interests. In *nonzero-sum games,* also called *mixed-motive games,* they have some interests in common. When the players can agree on a plan of action, they are in a *cooperative game.* In a *noncooperative game,* the players cannot coordinate their choices. Coordination may be impossible if the players cannot communicate, if no institution exists to enforce an agreement, or if coordination is forbidden by law, as in the case of antitrust laws.

Game theory's most famous game is called Prisoner's Dilemma, a noncooperative game that involves the following imaginary situation: The police arrest two suspects and keep them isolated from each other. Each prisoner is told that if only one of them confesses, the one who confesses will go free but the one who stays silent will get a severe sentence. They are also told that if they both confess, each will get a moderate sentence, and if neither confesses, each will receive an even milder sentence. Under these conditions, each prisoner is better off confessing no matter what the other one does. Yet by pursuing their own advantage and confessing, both get harsher sentences than they would have received if they had trusted each other and kept quiet.

Prisoner's Dilemma highlights and summarizes a conflict between individual and group interests that lies at the heart of many important real-life situations. For example, when farmers maximize their production, prices fall and all the farmers suffer. Collectively, the farmers would be better off restricting the amount they plant. Nonetheless, it is to each farmer's individual advantage to plant as much as possible. Decisions about paying taxes, protecting the environment, or acquiring nuclear weapons may also reflect this tension between what is good for the decision maker and what is good for the group.   Frank C. Zagare

Gamio, Manuel (1883-1960), was a Mexican anthropologist and archaeologist. He was often called the father of Mexican anthropology. He also spent much of his time working to improve the living conditions of American Indians.

Gamio was born in Mexico City. He graduated from the National Preparatory School of San Ildefonso (now part of the National Autonomous University of Mexico) and earned a Ph.D. degree at Columbia University. From 1918 through 1921, he studied the people and environment of the Teotihuacán Valley of Mexico. During that period, he developed the theory of *integral appreciation.* According to this theory, the study of an ancient people, such as the Indians, must include their climate and geography and other social data. These elements, Gamio believed, help shape a people's culture. Gamio's theory first appeared in a book called *The Population of the Valley of Teotihuacán* (1922). Later, some of Gamio's research influenced United States policies on Mexican immigration.   Jesús Chavarría

Gamma globulin is one of the classes of proteins found in blood plasma. Gamma globulins play an important role in the body's disease-fighting immune system, and they are also known as *immune globulins.* Most of the *antibodies* (infection-fighting proteins) in the body fluids are gamma globulins. White blood cells called *lymphocytes* produce antibodies after coming into contact with such harmful substances as bacteria or viruses. The antibodies react with and help destroy the invading germs.

The gamma globulin in a person's plasma consists of the various antibodies produced by that individual. A mixture of plasma from many blood donors contains a wide variety of antibodies because it includes the combined gamma globulin of all the donors.

Drug manufacturers separate the gamma globulin from such a mixture and purify it for medical use. Physicians use gamma globulin injections to prevent or treat certain infectious diseases, including measles and viral hepatitis. In addition, gamma globulin is administered to people who cannot produce enough antibodies and to some patients who have low blood platelet counts be-

cause of autoimmune diseases.   G. David Roodman

See also **Immune system; Plasma; Serum.**

Gamma rays are a form of electromagnetic radiation similar to X rays. Gamma rays have a higher energy and a shorter wavelength than X rays do. However, the dividing line between these two forms of radiation is not clearly defined. Scientists typically apply the term *gamma ray* to electromagnetic radiation with energies above several hundred thousand *electronvolts.* One electronvolt is the amount of energy gained by an electron as it moves freely between two points with a potential difference of 1 volt (see **Volt**).

In 1900, Paul Villard, a scientist working in Paris at the same time as Marie and Pierre Curie, discovered gamma rays through studies of radiation *emitted* (given off) by nuclei of atoms. Uranium and other radioactive elements emit *alpha particles* or *beta particles* from their nuclei when they transform into new elements. An instant later, these nuclei may give off gamma rays.

A nucleus may also emit a gamma ray alone in an *isomeric transition.* In this transition, the emission of the ray does not follow a change in the composition of the nucleus. Rather, the nucleus merely loses a certain amount of energy. See **Radiation.**

Astronomical objects such as pulsars, supernovae, galaxies, and the sun also produce gamma rays. The highest-energy gamma rays ever detected come from a cloud of gas and dust known as the Crab Nebula. These rays have an energy of about 1 trillion electronvolts.

The most energetic event ever detected was a burst of gamma rays that occurred in a distant galaxy. In 1997, two orbiting telescopes detected this burst in a galaxy that is about 12 billion *light-years* from the earth. A light-year is the distance that light travels in a vacuum in a year. This distance equals about 5.88 trillion miles (9.46 trillion kilometers). The burst lasted for about 40 seconds. It released hundreds of times more energy than is released in a supernova explosion. This gamma-ray burst is the highest-energy event known—other than the *big bang,* the explosion that began the universe. Astronomers do not know what caused the burst.

Gamma rays lose energy when they pass through matter. They lose this energy by interacting with electrons or the nuclei of atoms. The electrons absorb energy from the gamma rays, then leave their orbits. This process, called *ionization,* changes electrically neutral atoms into electrically charged atoms. Electrons are negatively charged, and so the atoms become positively charged.

A high-energy gamma ray in the vicinity of a nucleus can change into matter by producing an *electron pair.* One member of this pair is an electron. The other is a positively charged particle known as a *positron.* A positron is an *antiparticle* of an electron. The two particles differ only in their electric charge.

When the opposite process occurs—that is, when an electron and a positron collide—both particles are destroyed. In this *annihilation* process, two gamma rays are almost always formed.

Small amounts of gamma rays bombard our bodies constantly, primarily from naturally occurring radioactive materials in rocks and soil. Some of these materials enter our bodies in the air we breathe, the food we eat, and the water we drink. Gamma rays passing through the body produce ionization in tissue. This process can harm the body's cells. However, gamma rays can also be of benefit. They are helpful in destroying some types of cancers and tumors. They are also used to inspect metal for flaws and to preserve foods.   Cyrus M. Hoffman

See also **Electromagnetic waves; Nuclear energy; Telescope** (Gamma ray telescopes).

Ganda, *GAN duh,* are the largest ethnic group in the African nation of Uganda. They make up about 30 percent of the country's population. Most Ganda live in an area of central and southern Uganda called *Buganda.*

The Ganda, also known as the *Baganda,* have adopted numerous aspects of Western culture while retaining many of their traditions. They speak a language called Luganda, which belongs to the Bantu family of African languages. Many Ganda hold high positions in government or industry. Many other Ganda are farmers who raise such crops as coffee and cotton.

For centuries, Buganda existed as a small independent state. It grew in size and importance in the 1600's and 1700's. By the mid-1800's, it had become one of the richest and most powerful kingdoms in East Africa.

In 1894, Britain made Buganda a British protectorate. In 1896, Britain added several other kingdoms to the protectorate, extending it over most of present-day Uganda. However, the Ganda kept their own *Kabaka* (king) and *Lukiko* (parliament).

Uganda became independent in 1962. The new constitution allowed Buganda to keep its Kabaka and remain partly independent from the central government. Sir Edward Mutesa II, the Kabaka of Buganda, became Uganda's first president. In 1966, Prime Minister A. Milton Obote seized full control of the government, dismissed Mutesa, and ended Buganda's special status. The next year, a new constitution abolished the office of Kabaka.

Ali A. Mazrui and Jessica Musoke

See also **Uganda** (People; History).

Gander. See **Goose.**

Gandhi, *GAHN dee* or *GAN dee,* **Indira,** *ihn DEER uh* (1917-1984), was the first woman prime minister of India. She held the office from 1966 to 1977 and from 1980 until her death in 1984. She was assassinated by two of her security guards, who were members of India's Sikh religious group. Much friction had arisen between the Sikhs and Gandhi's government .

Indira Priyadarshini Gandhi was the only child of Jawaharlal Nehru, who served as India's first prime minister from 1947 to 1964. She was an adviser to her father during his term. Gandhi was first elected to Parliament in 1964. She was minister of information and broadcasting from 1964 until she became prime minister.

In June 1975, a court found Gandhi guilty of using illegal practices during India's 1971 parliamentary election campaign. Gandhi's opponents demanded that she resign from office because of the conviction, but she refused. Criticism of Gandhi grew, and she declared a state of emer-

Embassy of India, Washington, D.C.
Indira Gandhi

gency two weeks after the court ruling. She had her major opponents arrested and imposed press censorship. In November 1975, the Supreme Court of India overturned Gandhi's conviction. In 1977, Gandhi's ruling Congress Party was defeated in India's parliamentary elections. Gandhi lost both her post as prime minister and her seat in Parliament. Following her defeat, she organized the Congress-I Party. The *I* in the party's name stands for *Indira.* In 1980, she won a seat in Parliament, and her party gained control of Parliament. Gandhi again became prime minister.

Gandhi was born in Allahabad. Her maiden name was Indira Priyadarshini Nehru. She attended Santiniketan University in India and Oxford University in England. In 1942, she married Feroze Gandhi (no relation to Mohandas K. Gandhi). Gandhi and her husband were imprisoned for 13 months for their part in India's campaign for independence from Britain. They had two sons, Rajiv and Sanjay. Feroze Gandhi died in 1960. In the 1970's, Sanjay became his mother's chief political adviser and gained much power in Indian politics. He died in an airplane crash in 1980. Rajiv then became a key aide to his mother. When Indira Gandhi was assassinated, the Congress-I Party chose Rajiv as its head. As party head, Rajiv succeeded his mother as prime minister. He held that office until 1989. Rajiv was assassinated while campaigning in parliamentary elections in 1991.   P. P. Karan

See also **India** (India under Indira Gandhi); **Nehru (Jawaharlal); Pandit, Vijaya Lakshmi; Pakistan** (Recent developments); **Sikhism.**

Additional resources

Jayakar, Pupul. *Indira Gandhi.* Pantheon, 1993.
Malhotra, Inder. *Indira Gandhi.* Northeastern Univ. Pr., 1991.

Gandhi, *GAHN dee* or *GAN dee,* **Mohandas Karamchand,** *MOH huhn DAHS KUR uhm CHUHND* (1869-1948), was one of the foremost spiritual and political leaders of the 1900's. He helped free India from British control by a unique method of nonviolent resistance and is honored by the people of India as the father of their nation. Gandhi was slight in build but had limitless physical and moral strength. He was assassinated by an Indian who resented his program of tolerance for all creeds and religions.

Gandhi's beliefs. The people called Gandhi the *Mahatma* (Great Soul). His life was guided by a search for truth. He believed truth could be known only through tolerance and concern for others and that finding a truthful way to solutions required constant testing. He called his autobiography *My Experiments with Truth.* Gandhi overcame fear and taught others to master fear. He believed in nonviolence and taught that to be truly nonviolent required courage. He lived a simple life and thought it was wrong to kill animals for food or for clothing.

Gandhi developed a method of direct social action, based upon principles of courage, nonviolence, and truth, which he called *Satyagraha.* In this method, the way people behave is more important than what they achieve. Satyagraha was used to fight for India's independence and to bring about social change.

Gandhi's early life. Gandhi was born on Oct. 2, 1869, in Porbandar, India. His parents belonged to a *Vaisya* (merchant) caste of Hindus (see **Caste**). Young Gandhi was a shy, serious boy. When he was 13 years old, he married Kasturba, a girl the same age. Their parents had arranged the marriage. The Gandhis had four children.

Gandhi studied law in London. He returned to India in 1891 to practice law, but he met with little success.

In 1893, Gandhi went to South Africa to do some legal work. South Africa was then under British control. Almost immediately, he was abused because he was an Indian who claimed his rights as a British subject. He saw that all Indians suffered from discrimination. His law assignment was for one year, but he stayed in South Africa for 21 years to work for Indian rights.

Gandhi led many campaigns for Indian rights in South Africa and edited a newspaper, *Indian Opinion.* As part of Satyagraha, he promoted civil disobedience campaigns and organized a strike among Indian miners. He was arrested many times by the British, but his efforts brought important reforms. Gandhi also worked for the British when he felt justice was on their side. He was decorated by them for paramedic work in the Boer War (1899-1902) and the Zulu Rebellion (1906).

Gandhi's independence campaigns. In 1914, Gandhi returned to India. Within five years, he became the leader of the Indian nationalist movement.

In 1919, the British imperial government introduced the Rowlatt bills to make it unlawful to organize opposition to the government. Gandhi led a Satyagraha campaign that succeeded in preventing passage of one of these bills. The other was never enforced. Gandhi called off the campaign when riots broke out. He then fasted to impress the people with the need to be nonviolent. His belief in the cruelty of imperial rule was demonstrated by the Amritsar Massacre of April 13, 1919. A British general ordered his men to fire on an unarmed crowd, and almost 400 Indians were killed. This occurrence made Gandhi even more determined to develop Satyagraha and to win independence through nonviolent resistance.

Gandhi began a program of hand spinning and weaving about 1920. He believed the program (1) aided economic freedom by making India self-sufficient in cloth; (2) promoted social freedom through the dignity of labor; and (3) advanced political freedom by challenging the British textile industry and by preparing Indians for self-government.

In 1930, Gandhi led hundreds of followers on a 240-mile (386-kilometer) march to the sea, where they made salt from seawater. This was a protest against the Salt Acts, which made it a crime to possess salt not bought from the government. During World War II (1939-1945), Gandhi continued his struggle for India's freedom through nonviolent disobedience to British rule. He was jailed for the last time in 1942. Altogether, he spent seven years in prison for political activity. He believed that it is honorable to go to jail for a good cause.

Freedom and death. India was granted freedom in 1947. But the partition of India into India and Pakistan grieved Gandhi. He was saddened also by the rioting between Hindus and Muslims that followed. Gandhi had worked for a united country, and he had urged Hindus and Muslims to live together in peace.

On Jan. 13, 1948, at the age of 78, Gandhi began his last fast. His purpose was to end the bloodshed among Hindu, Muslim, and other groups. On January 18, their leaders pledged to stop fighting and Gandhi broke his fast. Twelve days later, in New Delhi, while on his way to a prayer meeting, Gandhi was assassinated. Nathuram Godse, a Hindu fanatic who opposed Gandhi's program of tolerance for all creeds and religions, shot him three times. A shocked India and a saddened world mourned Gandhi's death. The great scientist Albert Einstein said of Gandhi: "Generations to come will scarcely believe that such a one as this walked the earth in flesh and blood."

Raghavan Iyer

See also **Asia** (picture); **India; Nehru.**

Additional resources

Brown, Judith M. *Gandhi.* 1989. Reprint. Yale, 1991.
Dalton, Dennis. *Mahatma Gandhi.* Columbia Univ. Pr., 1993.
Green, Martin. *Gandhi.* Continuum, 1993.
Severance, John B. *Gandhi, Great Soul.* Clarion, 1997.

Gandhi, *GAHN dee* or *GAN dee,* **Rajiv,** *rah jeev* (1944-1991), was India's prime minister from 1984 to 1989. In May 1991, he was assassinated while campaigning to become prime minister again. In 1999, India's Supreme Court convicted four members of the Liberation Tigers of Tamil Eelam (LTTE) for the killing. The LTTE was involved in a civil war in Sri Lanka and had opposed a 1987 peace plan Gandhi had supported.

Rajiv succeeded his mother, Indira Gandhi, as prime minister. Indira had also been assassinated (see **Gandhi, Indira**). As prime minister, Rajiv promoted economic development, population control, and the reduction of tensions among India's ethnic and religious groups.

Rajiv Gandhi was born in Bombay (now Mumbai).

© Baldev, Sygma

Rajiv Gandhi

Government of India

Mahatma Gandhi won freedom for India. He preached nonviolence in his long campaign for freedom and social reform.

From 1962 to 1965, he studied mechanical sciences at Cambridge University and the University of London, in England. After returning to India, Gandhi worked for nine years as a commercial airline pilot.

Gandhi was elected to Parliament in 1981. He then became a close political adviser to his mother. In 1983, she appointed him as a general secretary of the Congress-I Party, which she headed. After Indira was assassinated in October 1984, the party chose Rajiv to succeed her as its head. As party head, Rajiv became prime minister. The Congress-I Party won parliamentary elections held in December, and Gandhi remained prime minister. In 1989 elections, the Congress-I Party lost its majority in Parliament. Vishwanath Pratap Singh replaced Gandhi as prime minister. But Gandhi remained head of his party until his death. In 1998, his widow, Sonia Gandhi, became leader of the Congress Party.   *Robert LaPorte, Jr.*

Gandhi, Sonia (1946-   ), an Italian-born Indian politician, is the president of India's Congress Party. She is the widow of Rajiv Gandhi, a former prime minister of India who was assassinated in 1991.

Sonia Maino was born and grew up near Turin, Italy. She met Rajiv Gandhi while studying at a language school in Cambridge, England. They married in 1968. Sonia Gandhi became an Indian citizen in 1983.

Gandhi had little involvement in politics during her husband's lifetime. However, she joined the Congress Party in 1997 and became its president in 1998. In 1999, she was elected to a seat in the Lok Sabha, the more important of the two houses of the Indian Parliament. Overall, however, Congress won fewer seats in the Lok Sabha than in any previous election. During the campaign, some members of the Congress Party raised questions about having the foreign-born Gandhi lead India and about her inability to speak any Indian language properly. In response, Gandhi resigned as Congress leader, but after an outcry in the party, she returned to the party leadership.   *Vinay Lal*

See also **Gandhi, Rajiv.**

Gang is a group of people who associate with one another for social or criminal reasons. Most gangs consist of teen-agers, though some include children or adults. Reports of gang activity come from around the world. Most gangs are based in low-income city neighborhoods. Gangs have also formed in many prisons.

Nonprison gang members spend much of their time together hanging out on street corners and engaging in other noncriminal behavior. At other times, they may take part in delinquent activities, such as stealing cars and taking them for joy rides, drinking alcohol, using illegal drugs, vandalizing, or engaging in sexual misbehavior or even rape. Some gangs are involved in the illegal drug trade, but many gang members sell drugs only as individuals. Conflict between rival gangs over territory often leads to fighting and sometimes to killing.

Gangs may differ by the age, sex, ethnic group, or neighborhood of their members. Most gangs are made up of males, but there are some female gangs. In the past, most gang members were immigrants from Europe. Today, many gangs consist of people of black, Hispanic, or Asian descent. Some gangs have complex leadership structures, but most are loosely organized.

Sociologists believe that most gang members feel pessimistic about their chances of succeeding in life.

Many members have dropped out of school and lack jobs. Most come from communities with high crime rates, and many come from families with little parental control. Researchers have found that gang activity is most effectively reduced by combining antigang police actions with job programs, recreational activities, and educational support for gang members.

Gangs have existed in the United States since the mid-1800's. Early gangs consisted mostly of adults involved in theft, illegal liquor sales, or political deals. In the 1920's and 1930's, gangs led by Al Capone and other bosses controlled most of the nation's organized crime. Youth gangs of the 1950's and 1960's fought mostly one another in fist, club, or knife fights. Since the 1970's, the increasing use of guns has made gang violence more deadly for members and others.   *John M. Hagedorn*

See also **Juvenile delinquency.**

Ganges River, *GAN jeez,* is the greatest waterway in India and one of the longest in the world. It is most important to the Indians for the part it plays in the Hindu religion. Hindus consider it the most sacred river in India. Each year, thousands of Hindu pilgrims visit such holy cities as Varanasi and Allahabad along the banks of the Ganges to bathe in the river and to take home some of its water. Temples line the riverbank, and *ghats* (stairways) lead down to the water. Some pilgrims come to bathe in the water only to cleanse and purify themselves. The sick and crippled come hoping that the touch of the water will cure their ailments. Others come to die in the river because the Hindus believe that those who die in the Ganges will be carried to Paradise.

The river is an important trade area. Its valley is fertile and densely populated. Some of India's largest cities, such as Calcutta and Kanpur, stand on its banks. But the Ganges is less important commercially than it once was. Irrigation has drained much of its water, and steamers can navigate only in the lower part of the river.

The Ganges has its beginning in an ice cave 10,300 feet (3,139 meters) above sea level in the part of the Himalaya slopes in northern India. The river flows toward the southeast and through Bangladesh for 1,560 miles (2,510 kilometers) to empty into the Bay of Bengal (see

Mischa Scorer, Hutchison Library

The Ganges River in India is sacred to Hindus. Each year thousands of pilgrims bathe there to cleanse and purify themselves.

India [physical map]; **Bangladesh** [map]). Several tributary rivers add to the waters of the Ganges River. The Brahmaputra River joins some branches of the Ganges near its mouth, and together the two rivers form a large delta.　　H. J. McPherson

Ganglion. See **Nervous system** (The cell body).

Gangrene, *GANG green,* is the death of body tissues from lack of oxygen. It is caused by a loss of blood supply to areas of the body, often the hands or feet.

A gradual loss of blood supply causes *dry gangrene.* This is often the result of diabetes, arteriosclerosis, or severe frostbite. The involved area becomes painful and cold. Later, the skin darkens. Then, the dead tissue dries up and drops off. It does not become infected, and complete healing usually occurs at the junction of living and dead tissue. Thus, dry gangrene is not life-threatening.

A far more serious condition, called *moist gangrene,* results from a sudden loss of blood supply. This may follow a crushing injury, a bad burn, or a clot that blocks an artery. The resulting tissue death is irregular, with some cells surviving longer than others. Injured but still living cells leak fluids, making the affected tissues moist. Bacteria flourish in this moist environment. At first, the skin swells and may develop blisters. As the gangrene proceeds, the area becomes foul-smelling. The infection spreads to other parts of the body, and may be fatal.

One form, called *gas gangrene* is particularly deadly. It occurs in wounds infected by bacteria that thrive in a low-oxygen environment. The bacteria release gas and poisons. Gas gangrene causes high fever, brownish pus, and gas bubbles under the skin. The poisons spread, leading to death in days if the person is not treated.

Doctors treat gangrene by improving the blood flow to the affected area. Surgery may be needed to remove or bypass an obstruction in a large artery. Drugs that improve blood flow through smaller arteries may be helpful. Other drugs may be given to combat bacterial infections. In some cases of gas gangrene, the affected limb is put in a pressurized oxygen chamber to prevent the growth of bacteria. When other treatments fail, dead tissue must be removed surgically.　　Giacomo A. DeLaria

Gangster. See **Gang.**

Gannet, *GAN iht,* is a large, white sea bird with black-tipped wings. It often helps fishing crews because it follows schools of herring and other fish and thus shows where the fish are. The gannet dives from the air and plunges under the water for the fish.

Gannets have strong, sharp bills, webbed feet, and a small pouch beneath their throats. They grow to about 3 feet (91 centimeters) long. They make nests of seaweed on rocky cliffs on Bird Rock and Bonaventure in the Gulf of Saint Lawrence, and on islets off the United Kingdom, Iceland, Ireland, and Norway. They are tame. The mother will not move off her one pale, greenish or bluish-white egg when a person comes near. Some tropical relatives are called *boobies* (see **Booby**).　　James J. Dinsmore

Scientific classification. The gannet belongs to the booby family, Sulidae. Its scientific name is *Sula bassanus.*

Ganymede, *GAN uh meed,* was a handsome Trojan prince in Greek mythology. His father was either Tros, the founder of Troy, or Laomedon, the father of the Trojan king Priam. Zeus, ruler of the gods, saw Ganymede on Mount Ida. Zeus admired the young man and, in the form of either a whirlwind or an eagle, swept him away

to Mount Olympus, home of the gods. There, Ganymede served as Zeus's cupbearer.　　Nancy Felson

Ganymede, *GAN uh meed,* a satellite of Jupiter, is the largest moon in the solar system. It is even larger than the planets Mercury and Pluto. The radius of the satellite is 1,636 miles (2,634 kilometers). The upper one-third is ice, except perhaps for a thin ocean of salty water about 105 miles (170 kilometers) beneath the surface. The core is rock and metal. The innermost part of the core is rich in iron. Rock and metal account for about 55 percent of Ganymede's weight, and ice for almost all the remainder. The satellite has an oxygen atmosphere that is only slightly denser than the near-vacuum of outer space.

Ganymede's surface is made up of approximately equal amounts of dark and bright terrain. The dark areas are composed mostly of ice mixed with pieces of dark rock. These areas have many craters and large cracks. The craters are a result of impacts by asteroids and comets. The cracking occurred after Ganymede formed billions of years ago. Forces released by the biggest impacts produced many of the cracks. Other cracks occurred when changes in the satellite's structure and temperature caused it to expand.

The bright terrain is much less cratered. It formed as the surface expanded and cracked. Water, ice, or both flooded the resulting depressions and whatever craters were present. Further cracking and stretching of the new terrain created parallel sets of ridges and valleys.

Ganymede has a *magnetic field* (region in which mag-

NASA

Ganymede, a moon of Jupiter, has craters and cracks on its surface. Asteroids and comets that hit Ganymede made the craters. The cracks are due to expansion and contraction of the surface.

netic force can be detected) that is about 1 percent as strong as Earth's. Ganymede orbits Jupiter every 7.15 days at a distance of 664,900 miles (1,070,000 kilometers). The Italian astronomer Galileo discovered Ganymede in 1610.　　William B. McKinnon

See also **Jupiter** (Satellites); **Satellite** (Recently active satellites).

Gap is a narrow valley or gorge cut by a stream across a ridge or mountain. If the river still occupies a gap, it is a water gap. If the river abandons it, the gap becomes a wind gap. Railroads and highways follow many gaps.

The best-known examples of both types occur in the Appalachian Mountains. Harpers Ferry Gap, cut through the Blue Ridge by the Potomac River, is a water gap. The historic Wilderness Road, scouted by Daniel Boone, passed through Cumberland Gap, a typical wind gap in the Cumberland Mountains. See also **Cumberland Gap; Delaware Water Gap.**   Richard G. Reider

G.A.R. See **Grand Army of the Republic.**

Gar, *gahr,* is a fierce, hungry fish that lives chiefly in freshwater lakes and large rivers. Some gars inhabit marine waters in and around the mouths of coastal rivers. Gars are found in streams along the Atlantic Coast from

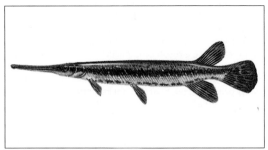

WORLD BOOK illustration by Colin Newman, Linden Artists Ltd.

The longnose gar has long and slender jaws.

Canada to Florida. They also live in the Great Lakes region, throughout the Mississippi River Valley, and as far south as Cuba, Mexico, and Costa Rica.

Gars have long, slender bodies with hard scales. They have beaks armed with large sharp teeth.

The *longnose gar,* or billfish, has extremely long and slender jaws. It grows to about 5 feet (1.5 meters) long. The *shortnose gar* is 2 to 3 feet (61 to 91 centimeters) long. The heavy-set *alligator gar* is the largest gar. It may grow to almost 10 feet (3 meters) long. Historically, only sturgeons had surpassed alligator gars in size in the fresh waters of North America. The flesh of alligator gars can be used for food, but it is not commonly eaten.

The name *gar* is also commonly applied to the marine *needlefishes.* They look like true gars but have soft scales.   Charles H. Hocutt

Scientific classification. Gars are in the gar family, Lepisosteidae. The longnose gar is *Lepisosteus osseus;* the shortnose, *L. platostomus;* and the alligator, *L. spatula.*

See also **Pike.**

Garand rifle, *GAR uhnd,* also called the *M1 rifle,* is a .30-caliber, eight-shot semiautomatic weapon. It was the basic rifle of the United States Army and Marine Corps. The Army used it from 1936 to 1960. The Army now uses the M16. John C. Garand, a government designer, developed the M1 rifle between 1932 and 1934. The M1 replaced the M1903 bolt-action rifle. The Garand rifle is gas operated. The bullet uncovers a small hole before it leaves the barrel. Compressed gases behind the bullet rush through a port to a piston, driving it back against the operating rod. The rod rotates the bolt to unlock it, pushes it back to open the rifle, and ejects the cartridge case. A recoil spring closes the bolt and rams a new cartridge into place to fire when the trigger is pulled. The M1 fires once at each trigger pull.   Frances M. Lussier

See also **Carbine; Machine gun; Rifle.**

Garbage. See **Garbage disposer; Waste disposal.**

Garbage disposer is an electric machine used in many homes and restaurants to get rid of waste food. A disposer, located under the kitchen sink, grinds pieces of food into a semiliquid. Cold water is run from the sink into the disposer while the machine operates.

A disposer enables people to get rid of garbage immediately instead of letting it accumulate. If garbage is left standing too long, it begins to rot. Rotting garbage smells foul and can attract insects and rats.

About a third of the households in the United States have a garbage disposer. After garbage is ground in a disposer, the garbage mixes with the rest of the sewage that comes from a household's sinks and toilets. The use of a disposer increases the amount of solid particles in the household's total sewage by about a fifth. It increases the grease content of the sewage by about a third.

In areas that have a public sewerage system, garbage flows from a disposer to the sewage treatment plant. The ground-up solids settle in the treatment tanks along with other solids in the sewage. In most systems, the settled material is then pumped to other tanks for further treatment. Some homes, especially in rural areas that have no sewerage system, use a concrete, steel, or fiberglass container called a *septic tank* to dispose of sewage. In such homes, the ground garbage flows from the disposer into the tank.

A disposer can be clogged by tough, stringy wastes or by overloading. Most disposers have a device that stops the motor if the grinder gets clogged. The clogged material can then be removed from the machine. The person removing the clogged material should first make sure that the disposer is turned off.

Some cities require that all homes use garbage disposers. These cities no longer collect food waste by truck. Such waste materials as glass bottles, aluminum cans, and paper and plastic products must still be hauled away. But these materials do not decay rapidly, and so they do not have to be collected so frequently as does garbage.   Mary Lynne Bowman

See also **Sewage.**

Garbo, Greta (1905-1990), became one of the most famous actresses in motion-picture history. She was known for her portrayals of mysterious women whose lives ended in tragedy. Garbo played such roles in most of the 27 movies she made from 1922 until her retirement in 1941. She was one of the few stars who gained equal success in both silent and sound films.

Garbo's real name was Greta Lovisa Gustafsson. She was born in Stockholm, Sweden, where she began her career. She first starred in *The Story of Gösta Berling* (1924), a Swedish film. In 1925, Garbo moved to the United States, where she made such silent movies as *Flesh and the Devil* (1927), *Love* (1927), and *A Woman of Affairs* (1928). Garbo's best-known sound films include *Anna Christie* (1930), *Grand Hotel* (1932),

MGM

Greta Garbo

Mata Hari (1932), *Queen Christina* (1933), *Anna Karenina* (1935), and *Camille* (1937). Her first major comedy was *Ninotchka* (1939). Garbo was known for her intense desire for privacy. She retired without explanation at the height of her fame.   Roger Ebert

See also **Steichen, Edward** (picture: *Greta Garbo, 1928*).

García Íñiguez, *gahr SEE ah EE nyee gays,* **Calixto,** *kah LEES toh* (1839-1898), was a Cuban lawyer and revolutionary general. He commanded a Cuban army against Spain during both the Ten Years' War (1868-1878) and in the revolt of 1895 to 1898. Before the Spanish-American War (1898), U.S. Army Lieutenant Andrew S. Rowan carried a message to García asking what aid the United States should send. This inspired Elbert Hubbard's essay, "A Message to Garcia." García was born in Holguín, Cuba.   Louis A. Pérez, Jr.

García Lorca, *gahr THEE ah LAWR kah,* **Federico,** *FAY thay REE koh* (1898-1936), was a great Spanish poet and dramatist. García Lorca and Miguel de Cervantes are the most widely translated Spanish authors.

García Lorca's early poetry, collected in *Libro de poemas* (1921) and *Canciones* (1927), contains delicate, original descriptions of nature. The complex and beautiful *Gypsy Ballads* (1928) is his best-known collection of poetry. One of his finest poems, *Lament for Ignacio Sanchez Mejías,* is an elegy to a bullfighter who was killed in 1934.

García Lorca wrote three stunning rural tragedies: *Blood Wedding* (1933), *Yerma* (1934), and *The House of Bernarda Alba* (completed in 1936 and first performed in 1945). They are filled with violent passion and poetic symbolism. García Lorca was also a skillful writer of comedies and surrealistic farces.

García Lorca was born near Granada. In 1932, he founded a traveling theater that performed plays throughout Spain. He was killed in the Spanish Civil War by followers of Francisco Franco.   David Thatcher Gies

García Márquez, *gahr SEE ah MAHR kayz,* **Gabriel José** (1928-   ), is a Colombian novelist. Many critics consider him one of the most important authors in the history of Latin-American literature. He won the 1982 Nobel Prize for literature.

García Márquez achieved international fame in 1967 with the publication of *One Hundred Years of Solitude.* This novel tells the story of the Buendía family, who live in the isolated jungle town of Macondo. The exploits of the family and the history of the town are often tragic. However, García Márquez describes these events in the form of a humorous tall tale. The novel has been interpreted as a symbolic history of Latin America told with mythical characters and places. *News of a Kidnapping* (1997) is a nonfiction account of several kidnappings in Colombia in 1990 and 1991.

García Márquez' first works were the short novels *Leaf Storm* (1955) and *No One Writes to the Colonel* (1958). Like his major novel, these stories are set in Macondo. A later novel, *The Autumn of the Patriarch* (1975), tells the story of a general who rules his country as a dictator for 100 years. The novel *Chronicle of a Death Foretold* (1983) is a dreamlike story of a brutal murder in a small town. The novel *Love in the Time of Cholera* (1988) is a story of love in an unnamed Latin-American city. *The General In His Labyrinth* (1989) is a fictional biography of the South

American liberator Simón Bolívar. García Márquez has also written short stories, which have been published in *Collected Stories* (1984) and *Strange Pilgrims* (1993).

García Márquez was born in Aracataca, Colombia, near Fundación. In 1954 and 1955, he worked in Paris as a foreign correspondent for a Colombian newspaper. During that period, the newspaper published a series of articles by García Márquez that angered the Colombian government. The government shut down the newspaper, and García Márquez has lived outside of Colombia most of the time since.   David William Foster

García-Sarmiento, Félix Rubén. See Darío, Rubén.

Garden, Mary (1874-1967), a Scottish-born soprano, was considered one of the best singing actresses of her time. While studying in Paris in 1900, she was the understudy for the leading role in Gustave Charpentier's *Louise.* When the star became ill, Garden sang the part and scored a great triumph. In 1902, she created the role of Mélisande in Claude Debussy's opera *Pelléas and Mélisande.*

Garden was born in Aberdeen and came to the United States as a child. She studied voice in Chicago. In 1910, she joined the Chicago Grand Opera Company. Garden was its leading soprano for 20 years. She retired in the early 1930's.   Martin Bernheimer

Garden of Eden. See Eden.

Garden of the Gods is a scenic park near Colorado Springs, Colorado. The park covers an area of over 700 acres (280 hectares) at the eastern base of the Rocky Mountains. It is a region of huge red and white sandstone rock masses that rise in strange shapes. Every year thousands of tourists visit the Garden. Its sunrise church services on Easter Sunday are famous. The heirs of Charles W. Perkins of Burlington, Iowa, gave the eastern half of the park to Colorado Springs. The city purchased the western half in 1932.

The best-known rocks in the Garden of the Gods include the *Cathedral Spires, Balanced Rock,* and *Indian Head.* These formations were created by an upheaval of the rock strata to an almost vertical position. Thousands of years of erosion by wind, rain, and frost followed this upheaval.   John L. Dietz

Gardenia is an evergreen shrub or small tree that bears a fragrant, waxy, white flower. Botanists classify the gardenia with plants of the madder family, which includes the coffee and quinine trees. The gardenia shrub is native to China and Japan. It is very sensitive to temperature. The flower buds form best at temperatures from 60 to 62 °F (16 to 17 °C). The leaves become yellow and unhealthy at lower temperatures. A moist atmosphere is also desirable. Therefore, gardenias are usually raised in greenhouses or conservatories. They are also grown outdoors where winter temperatures do not drop below 10 °F (−12 °C).

The beautiful gardenia blossoms are double. Varieties that are used for corsages are Belmont, Hadley, and McLellans 23. The gardenia is frequently called *Cape jasmine* because it smells like jasmine and was first brought to England from the Cape Colony in Africa. *Veitchiana,* a small-flowered form of gardenia, grows as a potted plant.   Michael A. Dirr

Scientific classification. The gardenia belongs to the madder family, Rubiaceae. Its scientific name is *Gardenia jasminoides.*

Pennsylvania Horticultural Society

A formal flower garden

Paul Meyer

A vegetable and flower garden

People cultivate various kinds of gardens. Some people, for example, beautify their yards with flower gardens. Others cultivate fruits or vegetables. Still others raise house plants indoors. But whatever kind of garden they have, all gardeners take pleasure in seeing living things grow.

Gardening

Gardening is the cultivation of plants, usually in or near the home as a hobby. A home garden may consist of a small plot of ground with flowers, fruits, or vegetables. Or it may consist of individual plants in pots or other containers either indoors or outdoors. Gardening is closely related to the art and science of *horticulture.* This branch of agriculture specializes in growing fruits, vegetables, flowers, shrubs, and trees.

People have gardens for many reasons. Numerous gardeners grow flowers and other ornamental plants to beautify their homes and yards. Many others raise vegetables, fruits, and herbs. They find that home-grown produce is cheaper, fresher, and tastier than that sold in grocery stores. People also like gardening because it provides exercise, relaxation, and the joy of working with living things.

Much information is available to help home gardeners successfully grow the kinds of plants they want. In the United States, the federal and state governments offer free or inexpensive booklets on all aspects of gardening for the amateur gardener. Companies that sell seeds, plants, and garden supplies also provide free

booklets on gardening and on the use of their products. Local garden supply centers can often offer guidance and advice. Many newspapers feature gardening columns, and numerous radio and TV stations broadcast gardening programs. Finally, the number of books and magazines on gardening is increasing yearly.

Many careers are related to gardening. They range from growing produce for the market to managing *botanical gardens,* which specialize in cultivating plants for artistic, educational, or scientific purposes. Many people who like to work with garden plants grow and sell them as florists, garden supply dealers, or nursery operators. *Landscape architects* design and develop yards, gardens, parks, and other land areas. Other gardening-related careers include managing the grounds of recreation areas, museums, national monuments, public buildings, and private estates.

Gardening has become increasingly popular since the late 1940's. In the United States, millions of people are home gardeners. In large part, the popularity of gardening reflects people's growing concern with improving their outdoor and indoor environments.

Home gardens fall into two main groups—outdoor gardens and indoor gardens. This article describes the types of gardens within each group. It also tells how to plan, start, and care for an outdoor and indoor garden.

Kinds of outdoor gardens

Outdoor gardens can be divided into two chief types: (1) ornamental gardens and (2) food gardens.

Jerry Baker, the contributor of this article, is a gardening consultant and the author of Plants Are Like People *and many other books and articles on gardening.*

WORLD BOOK photo

A collection of house plants

Ornamental gardens. There are various kinds of ornamental gardens. They differ in the types of plants grown and in the way the plants are arranged. The most common ornamental gardens include (1) container gardens, (2) formal flower gardens, (3) informal flower gardens, (4) rock gardens, (5) water gardens, and (6) wild flower gardens. Some of these gardens may include grass, shrubs, and trees in addition to the plants mentioned in the following descriptions.

Container gardens. Begonias, geraniums, fuchsias, petunias, and many other plants can be grown outdoors in containers. The choice is almost limitless. But different plants require different amounts of care. The containers themselves may be immovable, such as window boxes, or movable, such as flowerpots. Containers come in a wide range of materials, sizes, shapes, and prices. But many gardeners build their own containers or use items found in the home, such as tubs or crocks. A container garden can thus be as easy to care for and as inexpensive as a gardener wishes.

Formal flower gardens consist of flower beds laid out in balanced and regular patterns. Generally, the edges of the beds are straight or perfectly rounded. The beds contain only a few kinds of flowers, which grow to a similar height and shape. Formal flower gardens need not be expensive to cultivate. But they require the constant care of a skilled gardener to keep them neat and orderly.

Informal flower gardens have one or more beds of flowers laid out in a casual and irregular manner. The edges of the beds may be unevenly curved, and each

bed may have several kinds of flowers, which vary widely in height and shape. A simple flower garden is fairly inexpensive and easy to care for.

Rock gardens consist of plants grown in pockets of soil among rocks. On their property, some people have a natural rock arrangement, which they use to create such a garden. Other people build an artificial rock garden, which can be a costly and difficult project. Any plants that require little soil can be planted in a rock garden. A rock garden may be hard to care for because of its uneven surface.

Water gardens. A water garden consists of a body of water, usually a pool, in which plants that live in water are grown. Some homeowners have a natural body of water on their property and use it to create a water garden. However, most people who want a water garden must either purchase a ready-made pool or build a pool themselves. Construction of a water garden can be expensive and difficult, but a completed garden needs little care.

Wild flower gardens are made up of native wild flowers. Such a garden can be inexpensive and easy to grow. Many gardeners dig up wild flowers or collect the seeds in the countryside for their garden. But such flowers and seeds can also be bought.

Food gardens. There are two kinds of food gardens: (1) herb gardens and (2) vegetable gardens. In addition to herbs or vegetables, each of these gardens may include berry plants and certain types of fruit trees and nut trees.

Herb gardens. Many people cultivate herb gardens for the elaborately patterned beds that they can create with these plants. Many other gardeners raise herbs for the flavor the fresh or dried plants add to food. Herb seeds and seedlings are inexpensive, and the plants require little care. People who do not have enough outdoor space for herb beds can grow most kinds of herbs in containers. Many kinds of herbs can also be raised indoors.

Vegetable gardens help some families reduce their grocery bills. But a vegetable garden requires good planning and considerable care to be productive. Most gardeners plant vegetables in a rectangular plot. But if space is limited, certain vegetables can be grown in small areas. Some vegetables can even be grown in containers.

Cultivating an outdoor garden

The most popular outdoor gardens are the informal flower garden and the vegetable garden. The following discussion explains how a beginning gardener can plan, start, and care for either type. The plants, supplies, and equipment that are needed can be bought at garden supply centers and various other retail outlets. Or they can be ordered from seed and plant companies.

Planning the garden. The main steps in planning a garden are (1) choosing the site, (2) selecting the plants to be grown, (3) sketching a garden plan, and (4) analyzing the soil.

Choosing the site. In choosing a garden site, look for a well-drained area. All plants need water, which they take from the soil through their roots. But few plants grow well in soil that is poorly drained and, therefore, always soggy. In such soil, the roots will rot because of

Some popular garden vegetables

Vegetable	Earliest Planting Time	Space Between Plants	Weeks Until Harvest	Yield per 10-Foot (3-Meter) Row
Beets	Early spring	1 in. (2.5 cm)	8 to 9	5 lbs. (2.3 kg)
Bush snap beans	Early spring	3 in. (7.5 cm)	8	5 lbs. (2.3 kg)
Carrots	Early spring	2 in. (5 cm)	8 to 12	5½ lbs. (2.5 kg)
Leaf lettuce	Early spring	6 to 8 in. (15 to 20 cm)	6 to 7	2 lbs. (0.9 kg)
Onion sets	Spring	2 to 4 in. (5 to 10 cm)	14	10 lbs. (4.5 kg)
Radishes	Early spring	4 to 6 in. (10 to 15 cm)	4 to 8	5 lbs. (2.3 kg)
Spinach	Early spring	3 in. (7.5 cm)	6	3 lbs. (1.4 kg)
Swiss chard	Early spring	4 in. (10 cm)	8	8½ lbs. (3.9 kg)
Tomato plants (staked)	Late spring	2 to 3 ft. (61 to 91 cm)	8 to 12	8 lbs. (3.6 kg) per plant

A vegetable garden plan

The garden plan below shows some popular high-yield vegetables in a small plot. It provides enough growing space for each plant. It also provides for *successive planting,* in which one crop is harvested and then followed by the planting of another.

WORLD BOOK illustrations by Jean Helmer

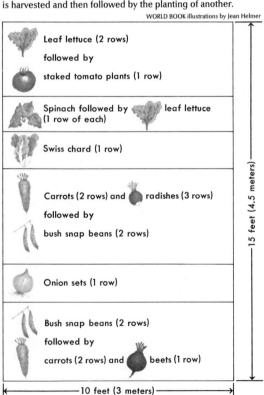

Leaf lettuce (2 rows)

followed by

staked tomato plants (1 row)

Spinach followed by leaf lettuce (1 row of each)

Swiss chard (1 row)

Carrots (2 rows) and radishes (3 rows)

followed by

bush snap beans (2 rows)

Onion sets (1 row)

Bush snap beans (2 rows)

followed by

carrots (2 rows) and beets (1 row)

15 feet (4.5 meters)

10 feet (3 meters)

inadequate air pockets in the soil. The garden site should also be level or gently sloping. A steep slope is difficult to plant and care for. In addition, water running down the slope may carry away topsoil and seeds.

The garden site should also receive the proper amount of light for the plants to grow well. Some kinds of flowers grow best in areas that are shaded for much or most of the day. However, many other flowers and almost all vegetables must receive large amounts of light. You may thus choose either a sunny or shaded area as a flower garden site, and then select the plants accordingly. But to have a successful vegetable garden, you must select a site that receives at least five hours of sunlight a day.

Selecting the plants. As a beginning gardener, select the kinds of plants you like best. But make sure that they are easy to grow and suitable for the climate of your region. You can gain such information by reading gardening books and the catalogs of companies that produce seeds and plants. You can also consult an expert, such as a garden supply dealer. Many people in the United States contact their county agricultural extension agent for help in solving gardening problems (see **County agricultural extension agent**).

Plants differ in how long they live. *Annual* plants grow and die within one year. *Biennial* plants live two years. *Perennial* plants live more than two years. Flower gardens may contain annual, biennial, and perennial plants. Only a few vegetables are perennials. The rest are annuals or biennials. But most biennial vegetables are also grown as annuals—that is, the plants are killed for eating within one year. See **Annual; Biennial; Perennial**. For examples of favorite garden plants, see the tables *Some popular garden flowers* and *Some popular garden vegetables* in this article.

Sketching a garden plan on paper can help you avoid mistakes in planting. After the garden has been planted, the plan will also remind you of what has been planted where. In addition, if you save the dated plans from year to year, they can help you arrange future gardens.

In making your sketch, be sure that all the plants will have enough space around them. Different kinds of plants need different amounts of room to grow well. Plan to grow most kinds of vegetables in straight rows, which are easy to plant and care for. But to make a flower garden look attractively informal, plan to group flowers of the same species in irregularly shaped clusters. If the garden will be backed by a fence, hedge, or wall, plant tall flowers at the back of the bed, medium-sized flowers in the center of the bed, and short flowers in the front of the bed.

To save space in a vegetable garden, you can plan to grow certain spreading vine plants, such as some varieties of tomatoes, on stakes or other supports. You can also make the best use of your garden space by using a planting method called *successive planting.* As soon as you harvest one crop of vegetables, you plant another crop in the same place, providing it will mature by the end of the growing season. Early onions, cabbages, and peas, for example, can be harvested in early summer. They can be followed by plantings of such summer and fall vegetables as beans, eggplants, and peppers. Your sketch for a vegetable garden should provide for successive planting.

Some popular garden flowers

A gardener can choose from a variety of garden flowers. But the selection of flowers should depend largely on the amount of sunlight the garden receives. Some popular garden flowers are listed below. For more information, see the separate *World Book* articles on the specific flowers.

Flowers that bloom in spring

Tall varieties	Light needs
Day lily*	Full sun and partial shade
Gladiolus*	Full sun
Iris	Full sun
Lupine	Full sun or partial shade
Peony	Full sun or partial shade

Medium varieties	
Aster*	Full sun
Bleeding heart	Full sun or partial shade
Columbine	Full sun or partial shade
Daffodil	Full sun or partial shade
Day lily*	Full sun and partial shade
Four-o'clock*	Full sun
Poppy*	Full sun
Tulip	Full sun or partial shade

Short varieties	
Amaryllis	Partial shade
Columbine	Full sun or partial shade
Crocus	Full sun or partial shade
Daisy*	Full sun or partial shade
Forget-me-not*	Partial shade
Hyacinth	Full sun
Iris	Full sun
Lily of the valley*	Partial shade
Pansy	Full sun or partial shade
Snowdrop	Partial shade
Sweet William	Full sun

Flowers that bloom in summer

Tall varieties	Light needs
Clematis	Full sun or partial shade
Cosmos	Full sun or partial shade
Dahlia	Full sun
Foxglove	Full sun or partial shade
Hollyhock	Full sun
Phlox	Full sun or partial shade
Snapdragon	Full sun

Medium varieties	
Bachelor's-button	Full sun
Chrysanthemum	Full sun
Coleus	Full sun or partial shade
Coreopsis	Full sun
Phlox	Full sun or partial shade
Sage	Full sun or partial shade
Zinnia	Full sun

Short varieties	
Ageratum	Full sun
Carnation	Full sun
Feverfew	Full sun or partial shade
Lobelia	Full sun
Marigold	Full sun
Pansy	Full sun or partial shade
Petunia	Full sun or partial shade
Portulaca	Full sun
Sweet alyssum	Full sun or partial shade
Wallflower	Partial shade

Flowers that bloom in fall

Tall varieties	Light needs
Aconite	Full sun or partial shade
Babies'-breath	Full sun
Chrysanthemum	Full sun
Clematis	Full sun or partial shade
Cosmos	Full sun or partial shade
Dahlia	Full sun
Hollyhock	Full sun
Larkspur	Full sun

Medium varieties	
Anemone	Partial shade
Canna	Full sun
Chrysanthemum	Full sun
Dahlia	Full sun
Daisy	Full sun
Lily	Partial shade

Short varieties	
Adonis	Full sun or partial shade
Allwood's pink	Full sun
Begonia	Partial shade
Carnation	Full sun
Cockscomb	Full sun
Colchicum	Full sun or partial shade
Crocus	Full sun or partial shade
Lily	Full sun
Petunia	Full sun or partial shade
Plumbago	Full sun or partial shade
Sage	Full sun or partial shade
Sweet alyssum	Full sun or partial shade

*Blooms in all three seasons.

How to plan a flower garden

A flower garden should be planned according to the height and blooming season of each plant. In the plan below, tall plants are at the back of the garden and shorter ones at the front. Flowers that bloom in different seasons are selected so that the garden will be colorful most of the year.

WORLD BOOK diagram

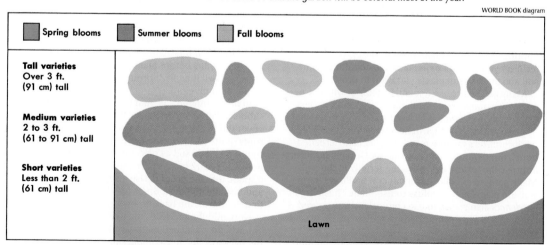

Spring blooms Summer blooms Fall blooms

Tall varieties
Over 3 ft.
(91 cm) tall

Medium varieties
2 to 3 ft.
(61 to 91 cm) tall

Short varieties
Less than 2 ft.
(61 cm) tall

Lawn

How to prepare soil for planting

Preparing the soil is an important step in starting an outdoor garden. If possible, the soil should be prepared several months before planting is to begin. The fertilizer and other added materials will then be thoroughly blended with the soil by planting time.

WORLD BOOK illustrations by David Cunningham

Remove grass and other plants that cover the garden site, using a spade or shovel.

Dig up the soil to a depth of about 8 to 12 inches (20 to 30 centimeters).

Break up the soil, turn it over, and mix in the materials needed to improve it.

Rake the soil thoroughly just before planting until it becomes fine and smooth.

Analyzing the soil. If your garden soil looks and feels either heavy and clayey or light and sandy, the texture needs to be improved. Plan to add to the soil some kind of *organic matter* (decayed plant or animal material). The organic matter will loosen heavy, clayey soil so that air can reach the plant roots. It will make light, sandy soil better able to hold moisture. Many gardeners use a kind of moss called *peat moss* to improve soil texture.

Most garden plants grow best in soil that is slightly acid or *neutral*—that is, neither acid nor its opposite, alkaline. A gardening expert can tell you how acid the soil in your area probably is. But if you want exact information on your soil's acidity, you can buy a soil-testing kit. Many American gardeners take a sample of their soil and send it to their county agricultural extension agent or state agricultural college for testing. If your soil is too acid for the kinds of plants you want to grow, plan to add lime to it. If the soil is too alkaline, plan to add sulfur.

Green plants need certain chemical elements to grow. Some of these elements come from air and water. But the other elements, especially nitrogen, phosphorus, and potassium, must come from soil. Plants absorb these elements from fertile soil through their roots. You should thus check the fertility of your soil. If healthy-looking grass or other plants are growing on the garden site, the soil is probably fertile. But to be certain, you can test the fertility with a soil-testing kit. In the United States, county agents and state agricultural colleges will also run such tests for home gardeners. If your soil lacks important elements, plan to add fertilizer. The type of fertilizer you use will depend on the condition of the soil and the kinds of plants you want to grow.

Many gardeners use mineral fertilizers, which are made from minerals or synthetic compounds. Others use organic fertilizers, which consist of natural animal or plant matter. Some gardeners use both types. Organic fertilizers include manure, *bone meal* (crushed bone), dried blood, and wood ashes. Organic fertilizers improve the texture as well as the fertility of the soil. Many gardeners believe that mineral fertilizers harm soil and plants and so refuse to use them. These *organic gardeners* also refuse to use commercially prepared chemicals to fight plant diseases, garden pests, or weeds.

Both mineral and organic fertilizers can be bought.

But many gardeners make their own organic fertilizer, called *compost.* They pile up several alternate layers of plant matter, soil, and fertilizer mixed with lime, and then allow the heap to decay for several months. The plant matter may include grass clippings, leaves, sawdust, weeds, or wood chips. See **Fertilizer; Compost.**

Starting the garden. Before actually beginning your garden, you should obtain a garden hose, watering can, or sprinkler; a hoe; a rake; a shovel or spade; a spading fork; and a trowel. You will also need the seeds, bulbs, or seedlings that will develop into the plants you want to grow.

Beans, beets, cabbages, carrots, and many other plants are grown from seeds. Certain other plants—especially flowers—are grown from bulbs. Popular flowers grown from bulbs include crocuses, hyacinths, lilies, narcissuses, and tulips. Many gardeners buy seedlings if they want to raise such slow-growing annual flowers and vegetables as petunias and tomatoes. However, seedlings cost more than seeds. To save money, some gardeners purchase seeds, plant them in containers indoors before the growing season begins, and later transplant the seedlings in the garden.

After obtaining the proper gardening equipment and the items to be planted, you are ready to start your garden. This step involves (1) preparing the soil and (2) planting the seeds and bulbs and transplanting the seedlings.

Preparing the soil means breaking it up, adding organic matter or other materials to improve it, and smoothing it. If possible, the soil should be prepared several months before planting is to begin. The added materials will then be thoroughly blended with the soil by planting time.

In preparing the soil, first remove any large stones or rubbish from the garden site. If grass or other plants cover the site, use a spade or shovel to dig under the roots of the plants and remove them. But be careful to remove as little soil as possible. Dig up the soil to a depth of 8 to 12 inches (20 to 30 centimeters) by pushing a spade into the ground. Use a spading fork to break up and turn the soil over. Break up all clods of soil by hitting them with the back of the fork.

Next, add the materials needed to improve the soil. If you use the packaged materials, follow the directions on the package. If you use unpackaged materials, such as manure obtained from a farm, follow the directions of a gardening expert.

After breaking up the soil and adding the materials, leave the surface of the soil rough if planting will not be done for several months. Immediately before planting, rake the soil until it is fine and smooth.

Planting and transplanting. Before planting seeds or bulbs, read the directions on the packages to learn when, how deep, and how far apart to plant. If you have unpackaged bulbs or seedlings, consult a gardening expert or gardening publication for such instructions. The following discussion can serve as a general guide to planting and transplanting.

To plant a group of large or medium-sized seeds in a flower garden, form a hollow in the ground by scraping soil to one side with a hoe or trowel. Then place the seeds in the hollow and cover them with soil. Finally, press the soil down firmly. For extremely small flower seeds, place the seeds on the surface of the ground and sprinkle a light covering of fine soil over them. To plant flower bulbs, use a trowel to dig a separate hole for each bulb. Place the bulbs in the holes. Then cover each bulb with soil and firmly press the soil down. After planting seeds or bulbs, water the soil and keep it moist until tiny plants appear.

Vegetable seeds are planted in rows. For each row, you can use a hoe to make a furrow in the soil. Then drop the seeds in the furrows. You can also use your fingers to walk the length of each row and so make small holes a short distance apart in the soil. Then place the seeds in the holes. Whatever method you use, cover large and medium-sized seeds with soil. Place extremely small vegetable seeds on the ground and cover them with a thin layer of sand, sifted compost, or some other fine material. Then press down on the soil or other covering. Water the soil after planting, and keep it moist until the plants appear.

To transplant seedlings to your garden, dig a hole for each plant. Make the holes deep enough to accommodate the young plants' roots. Gently place the seedlings in the holes. Press soil firmly around the plants and then water them. For additional general information, see the article **Transplanting**.

Caring for the garden after it has been planted involves a number of tasks. In general, the following practices should be observed.

Providing fertilizer and water. Throughout the growing season, you will have to add fertilizer to the soil from time to time. In applying the fertilizer, follow the directions on the fertilizer package or the instructions of an expert.

Your garden will also have to be watered from time to time. How often you should water it will depend on the weather and the kinds of plants you have. Frequent watering, for example, is necessary during a long spell of hot, dry weather. Plants vary in their water needs. But in general, you should water only when the soil looks and feels dry.

The best time to water your garden is in the morning or early afternoon. If you water it in midafternoon, the sun's heat may make the water evaporate too fast. If you water after sunset, the plants and soil will remain wet for so long a time that the plants may become diseased. The fungi that cause most plant diseases need moisture

Some helpful gardening hints

Many gardens need considerable preparation and attention to grow well. The gardening hints illustrated below can help make planning, starting, and caring for a garden easier.

Sow seeds indoors before the growing season begins to give plants an early start.

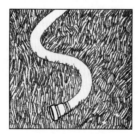

Use a garden hose to lay out a curved, irregular border for an informal flower garden.

To dig with a trowel, push the trowel into the soil and then pull it toward you.

Erect a small fence to protect flower beds and borders from being stepped on.

Spread mulch over the soil to prevent weeds from growing and to keep the soil moist.

Pinch back the main stem to produce a bushier plant or a larger number of flowers.

Cut off the side buds to produce an exceptionally large flower on the main stem.

WORLD BOOK illustrations by David Cunningham

Tie the stem of a plant loosely when staking to protect the stem from injury.

to spread. When you water, soak the soil thoroughly so that the water reaches the plant roots. Also, water with a gentle spray to avoid flattening or uprooting the plants.

Fighting diseases and pests. To reduce the threat of plant disease, select varieties of plants that are disease-resistant. Such varieties are listed in most seed catalogs. You can further reduce the threat of plant diseases and help avoid attacks by insects and other small pests by taking certain preventive measures. In addition to watering before midafternoon, keep your garden free of weeds and of such plant rubbish as dead leaves and stems. Disease-causing bacteria and fungi live in plant rubbish. In addition, pests lay their eggs in weeds and plant rubbish. Watch for damaged leaves and other signs of plant diseases and pests. If a serious disease or pest problem develops, consult a gardening expert for the proper treatment. You can buy chemicals to fight diseases and pests. But experts recommend such products only if no other treatment works.

Removing weeds. Not only do weeds shelter pests, but weeds also take food, water, and space from garden plants. Therefore, begin to remove weeds as soon as your garden plants are large enough to be told apart from the weeds. The weeds may be pulled out by hand or dug out with a hoe. Although you can buy chemical products to kill weeds, many gardening experts do not recommend them. A large number of these weedkillers can also destroy garden plants. Weedkillers must also be applied strictly according to the directions on the package. See **Weed** (Weed control).

Mulching. Many gardeners spread a covering called a *mulch* over the soil among the plants. A mulch helps stop the growth of weeds by depriving them of air and sunlight. It also helps the soil hold moisture. You can make a mulch with such organic materials as chopped leaves, compost, grass clippings, nutshells, peat moss, pine needles, straw, or wood chips. After spreading the mulch, fertilize and water the soil as before. However, you will not need to water so often. A few weeds may come up through the mulch. They should be pulled out by hand. See **Mulch.**

Providing supports. You may need to provide fences or other supports for some plants. For example, such tall flowers as larkspurs and lilies require support to stand gracefully and to show off well. In a vegetable garden,

Soil
Plant matter
Fertilizer and lime
Coarse plant matter

WORLD BOOK diagram

A compost pile consists of several alternate layers of plant matter, soil, and fertilizer and lime. The compost is allowed to decay for several months and then used as fertilizer or mulch.

the main reason for providing supports is to save space that would otherwise be taken by spreading vines. You can make your own supports or buy them.

Obtaining more or larger blossoms. Flowering plants can be forced to produce more or larger blossoms than they normally would. To obtain more blossoms, use a method called *pinching back.* With your fingers, pinch off the tip of a young plant's main stem. The plant's energy will then be used to develop flowering side branches rather than to make the plant grow taller. To obtain larger blossoms, use a method called *disbudding.* Select a plant that has a bud at the top of its main stem as well as side buds. Cut off these side buds and any others that develop later. The plant's energy will then be used to develop the one remaining flower, which will be larger than normal.

Cutting flowers and harvesting vegetables. Most kinds of flowers should be cut before their blossoms have opened completely. Otherwise they will not last long indoors. You can determine when each kind of vegetable will be ready for harvesting by consulting the seed packages or a gardening expert or publication.

Preparing the garden for winter. If you live in a region that does not have a year-round growing season, you must prepare your garden for winter. Many kinds of bulbs, for example, must be dug up in the fall and then stored indoors while the ground is frozen. At the end of the growing season, remove such bulbs from your garden. In the parts of the garden that you will plant in spring, prepare the soil for planting as discussed earlier.

Kinds of indoor gardens

Most indoor gardens contain house plants—that is, ornamental plants especially suited to indoor life. There are two main kinds of indoor gardens: (1) collections of house plants and (2) terrariums.

Collections of house plants. A collection consists of two or more plants grown in open containers. The plants can be potted individually, or several plants can be grown in one open container to form a *dish garden.* There are hundreds of kinds of house plants. They come in many colors, shapes, and sizes. Depending on size and species, house plants can be bought from less than a dollar to several hundred dollars.

Terrariums consist of a group of small house plants grown together in a covered container of clear or lightly tinted glass or plastic. A terrarium may be part of a collection of house plants. If a terrarium has been properly prepared and planted, it will require almost no care. For information on making a terrarium, see **Terrarium.**

Cultivating an indoor garden

The most popular type of indoor garden is probably a collection of a dozen or so assorted house plants in open containers. This section explains how a beginning gardener can plan, start, and care for such a collection. The plants, supplies, and equipment that are needed can be bought at garden supply centers, plant stores, and various other retail outlets. Or they can be ordered from seed and plant companies.

Planning the garden. The first step in planning an indoor garden is to choose the garden's location. It need not be in a sunlit window sill. House plants vary greatly in their light needs. Some require much direct sunlight.

Some popular house plants There are hundreds of kinds of house plants. They come in a wide variety of colors, shapes, and sizes. House plants differ in the type and amount of care they require. As a result, they should be selected carefully. The plants shown below rank among the most popular with indoor gardeners.

WORLD BOOK illustrations by Jean Helmer

Wax begonia

Grows 6 to 14 in. (15 to 36 cm) tall; blooms the year around; has orange, pink, red, white, or yellow flowers; requires direct and indirect sunlight and slightly dry soil.

Boston fern

Grows 1 to over 2 ft. (30 to 61 cm) tall; has light green leaves with yellow markings; often planted in a hanging container; requires indirect sunlight and moist soil.

Bunny ears cactus

Grows 3 to 4 ft. (91 to 122 cm) tall; has green leaves with yellow markings; usually planted in a floor container; requires direct sunlight and dry soil.

Corn plant

Grows 2 to 6 ft. (61 to 183 cm) tall; has green leaves with yellow markings; usually planted in a floor container; requires indirect sunlight and moist soil.

Common coleus

Grows 2 to 3 ft. (61 to 91 cm) tall; has green leaves with pink, red, or yellow markings; usually planted in a floor container; requires direct sunlight and slightly moist soil.

Split-leaved philodendron

Grows over 2 ft. (61 cm) tall; has dark green leaves; usually provided with a stake or trellis to which plant clings; requires indirect sunlight and slightly moist soil.

English ivy

Grows 1 to over 2 ft. (30 to 61 cm) tall; has green leaves with white markings; often planted in a hanging container or staked; requires direct sunlight and moist soil.

Broad-leaved India rubber plant

Grows over 2 ft. (61 cm) tall; has green leaves with brown or red markings; usually planted in a floor container; requires indirect sunlight and slightly moist soil.

African violet

Grows 4 to 6 in. (10 to 15 cm) tall; blooms the year around; has blue, pink, purple, or white flowers; requires indirect sunlight or electric light and slightly moist soil.

Others grow well with a minimum amount of light. If you select a site that receives little or no natural light, you can provide incandescent or fluorescent lamps. But the intensity of such lamps and the hours they must be on will depend on the kinds of plants being grown. Many books on house plants give detailed information on the use of electric lights.

After selecting your garden site, you can decide what kinds of plants to have. Choose plants that you like and that are easy to grow. But also make sure you can provide the right amount of light, the correct temperature, and the proper humidity for each plant. For examples of favorite house plants, see the illustrated table *Some popular house plants* in this article.

Before starting the garden, you should obtain certain equipment. If you plan to grow plants under electric lights, you will need bulbs or tubes and fixtures. Most plants grow best in fairly humid air, and so you should

have equipment to raise the humidity around the plants. You can place the plant containers in saucers or trays that contain moistened pebbles, sand, or bits of charcoal. The moisture will evaporate and make the air more humid. Or you can mist the plants with water as often as once a day. Many stores sell misters, or you can simply use an empty spray-cleaner bottle.

You will also need a watering can, pitcher, or ordinary drinking glass to water your plants. You should also have fertilizer on hand. As your plants grow larger, you will need bigger containers and extra soil.

Starting the garden. Some indoor gardeners raise their own plants from seeds or bulbs. However, most gardeners—especially beginners—buy plants already growing in containers. When buying plants at a store, select bushy ones whose leaves are not brown at the edges, too pale, or yellowed. Also avoid plants that show any signs of disease or pests.

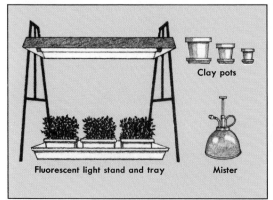

WORLD BOOK illustrations by David Cunningham

Indoor garden equipment may include fluorescent light for areas that get too little sunlight. Many experts recommend spraying plants with a mister and the use of clay pots. Soil dries out quickly in clay pots, reducing the chances of overwatering.

After purchasing new plants, keep them away from any other plants you may have for one or two weeks. During this period, you can make sure that the new plants are free of diseases or pests, which could spread to your other plants. Many newly bought plants should also receive special care for the first week or two. They should be put in a fairly cool place out of direct sunlight, and their soil should be kept slightly more moist than is normally recommended. Such instructions may be attached to the plants or given by the store.

Caring for the garden is something of an art. All house plants require certain basic care. But the ability to grow truly beautiful plants comes only after a great deal of experience and much learning by trial and error.

Basic care. Most indoor gardeners use mineral fertilizers specially made for house plants. In using these fertilizers, you must be especially careful not to overfeed and thus injure your plants. For example, do not fertilize newly purchased plants because professional growers usually give them enough fertilizer to last for a while. Whatever kind of house plant fertilizer you do use, follow the directions on the package.

How often you should water each of your house plants depends largely on each plant's needs. But in general, a plant should be watered only when the soil just below the surface feels dry. Then soak the soil thoroughly with lukewarm water. Do not use cold or hot water, which can harm plants. Watering should be done in the morning. If you mist your plants, it should also be done in the morning with lukewarm water.

Wash your house plants about every two weeks to remove dust and any small pests that may be on them. Again, do the task in the morning, using lukewarm water. Small plants can be sprayed gently in the bathroom shower or in the kitchen sink if the sink has a rinsing hose. You can also wash a small plant by holding the plant upside down and moving it back and forth in a sink filled with water. Plants that are too large to carry can be washed by wiping both sides of each leaf with a damp cloth or sponge. If a plant is particularly dirty, it may be washed with mild soap— not detergent—and then rinsed thoroughly.

If you buy healthy plants and take good care of them,

the plants should have few or no health problems. If a plant becomes diseased or it is attacked by pests, separate it from the healthy plants and consult a gardening expert or publication for methods of treatment.

You can improve the appearance and growth of house plants by removing all dead leaves and flowers from the plants. The appearance of certain plants also can be improved by pinching off the tips of new stems. The plants will then grow bushier and, in the case of flowering plants, produce more blossoms.

Repotting. In time, a plant may wilt between waterings and produce only a few small leaves. Or its roots may show above the soil or stick out of the container's drainage hole. Such a plant has probably outgrown its container and needs to be repotted in a larger one. But to make sure repotting is necessary, remove the plant from its container and examine the roots. To remove the plant, hold the container with one hand. Stretch the other hand across the top of the container so the plant stem is between two fingers. Then turn the container upside down and knock the rim on the edge of a table. The plant and the soil around its roots should slide out in one piece. If a network of roots surrounds the ball of soil, the plant requires repotting.

Set the plant aside. In the bottom of the new container, place a layer of drainage material, such as small pebbles or pieces of broken clay pots. If the container has a drainage hole at the bottom, the layer need be only about 1 inch (2.5 centimeters) thick. If the container has no drainage hole, about twice as much material is needed to make sure that the plant's roots will not stand in water. Next, pour a little *potting soil* (packaged soil specially made for house plants) into the container. Place the plant in the container. The top surface of the old soil ball should be at least $\frac{1}{2}$ inch (1.3 centimeters) below the rim of the container. Add more potting soil a little at a time, pressing it around the old soil, until you reach the top of the old soil ball. Then water the plant thoroughly.

Obtaining new plants from cuttings. Many house plants can be easily *propagated* (reproduced) by taking *cuttings,* or *slips,* from them. Most cuttings consist of stems or leaves. The cuttings are placed in water or

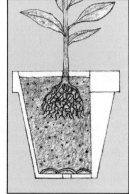

WORLD BOOK illustrations by David Cunningham

Repotting. To repot a plant, hold the container with one hand and stretch the other hand over the top of it. Turn the container upside down and knock the rim on the edge of a table, *above left.* Then place the plant in a larger container, *above right.*

moist sand and, in time, develop roots. The rooted cuttings are then planted in soil and develop into complete new plants. A gardening expert or publication can tell you how to take and care for cuttings from your particular plants.   Jerry Baker

Related articles. See the separate articles on specific garden plants, such as **Petunia; Philodendron; Tomato.** See also the following articles:

Kinds of garden plants

Annual	Perennial
Biennial	Plant
Flower	Shrub
Fruit	Tree
Grass	Vegetable
Herb	Water plant
Nut	

Cultivating a garden

Bird (The importance of birds; Bird watching)	Insecticide
	Lawn
Bonsai	Mulch
Breeding	Peat moss
Bulb	Pest control
Compost	Pollen
Cold frame	Pruning
Corm	Rhizome
Fertilizer	Seed
Fungicide	Soil
Grafting	Terrarium
Greenhouse	Transplanting
Hotbed	Tuber
Hydroponics	Weed
Insect (The importance of insects)	

Other related articles

Arboretum
Botanic Garden, United States
Botanical garden
County agricultural extension agent
Floriculture
Horticulture
Landscape architecture
Nursery
Plant quarantine
Seven Wonders of the Ancient World
Truck farming

Outline

I. Kinds of outdoor gardens
    A. Ornamental gardens   B. Food gardens
II. Cultivating an outdoor garden
    A. Planning the garden
    B. Starting the garden
    C. Caring for the garden
III. Kinds of indoor gardens
    A. Collections of house plants
    B. Terrariums
IV. Cultivating an indoor garden
    A. Planning the garden
    B. Starting the garden
    C. Caring for the garden

Questions

What are the differences between a formal flower garden and an informal flower garden?
What is *successive planting?*
When should a house plant be repotted?
What is an *annual* plant?
What is a *biennial plant?*
What is a *perennial plant?*
What are the main steps in the preparation of outdoor garden soil?

How do organic fertilizers differ from chemical fertilizers? Why do some gardeners prefer organic fertilizers?
What should you look for when buying house plants?
What is *pinching back? Disbudding?*
What rules should be followed in watering an outdoor garden? An indoor garden?
What are two common ways of increasing the humidity around house plants?

Additional resources

Level I
Boring, John K., and others. *Natural Gardening.* Time-Life Bks., 1995.
Rhoades, Diane. *Garden Crafts for Kids.* Sterling Pub., 1995.

Level II
Ball, Liz. *Step-by-Step Garden Basics.* Meredith, 2000.
Bush-Brown, James and Louise. *America's Garden Book.* 4th ed. Ed. by Howard S. Irwin and others. Scribner, 1996.
Taylor's Guides to Gardening. Houghton, 1986-   . Multivolume work. Each volume covers a particular class of plants or aspect of gardening.

Gardner, Erle Stanley (1889-1970), wrote 129 mystery novels that have sold more than 300 million copies throughout the world. In 82 of Gardner's novels, the lawyer Perry Mason brilliantly solves a case. The first Mason story, *The Case of the Velvet Claws* (1933), was Gardner's first novel.

Gardner featured district attorney Douglas Selby in nine novels. Under the pen name A. A. Fair, he wrote 29 novels about the private investigators Bertha Cool and Donald Lam. Gardner also wrote hundreds of mystery, western, and science fiction novelettes and short stories, and several volumes of nonfiction.

AP/Wide World

Erle Stanley Gardner

Gardner was born in Malden, Massachusetts. He studied law in California and was admitted to the bar at the age of 21. He practiced law for more than 20 years, specializing in trial cases.   David Geherin

Gardner, John William (1912-   ), served as United States secretary of health, education, and welfare from 1965 to 1968. He was appointed to the position by President Lyndon B. Johnson. Gardner had been president of the Carnegie Corporation of New York since 1955.

Gardner was born in Los Angeles and graduated from Stanford University in 1935. He received a doctor's degree in psychology from the University of California at Berkeley in 1938. Gardner later taught psychology at several colleges.

In 1942, he became head of the Latin American section of the Foreign Broadcast Intelligence Service. He served in the U.S. Marine Corps from 1943 to 1946, when he joined the Carnegie Corporation. Gardner served as director of the National Urban Coalition (formerly the Urban Coalition) from 1968 to 1970. In 1970, he founded Common Cause, a group that promotes urban and social legislation and government reform (see **Common Cause**). He served as the group's president until 1977.   Steven E. Ambrose

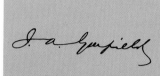

**20th President of
the United States 1881**

Hayes
19th President
1877-1881
Republican

Garfield
20th President
1881
Republican

Arthur
21st President
1881-1885
Republican

**Chester A.
Arthur**
Vice President
1881

Oil painting on canvas (1882) by William T. Mathews; Corcoran Gallery of Art, Washington, D.C.

Garfield, James Abram (1831-1881), was the last President to be born in a log cabin. Nobody knows what kind of President he would have been because he was assassinated only a few months after taking office. Garfield, a Republican, was the fourth President to die in office and the second to be assassinated.

Possibly Garfield accomplished more by his death than if he had lived to complete his term. A major characteristic of national politics in his day was the so-called spoils system, in which thousands of government employees were fired every time a new President took office (see **Spoils system**). Garfield spent most of his short time as President filling these jobs with his political supporters. Although not a reformer, he wrote in his diary shortly before he was shot: "Some civil service reform will come by necessity after the wearisome years of wasted Presidents have paved the way for it." The assassination of Garfield by a disappointed job-seeker shocked the nation into action. Two years later, Congress began civil service reform with the Pendleton Civil Service Act.

Garfield was a big, athletic, handsome man with blond hair and beard. Before becoming President, he was successful as professor, college president, Civil War general, and U.S. congressman. He spoke and wrote well, read widely, and even composed poetry. He occasionally entertained his friends by writing Greek with one hand and at the same time writing Latin with the other. Warmhearted and genial, Garfield wanted to be well liked and generally was. But his eagerness to please everyone sometimes led him into questionable dealings with unscrupulous people.

Early life

Childhood. James Abram Garfield was born in Orange, Cuyahoga County, Ohio, on Nov. 19, 1831. He was the youngest of five children. His parents, Abram and Eliza Ballou Garfield, were pioneers from the East. His fa-

ther died before James was 2 years old. Mrs. Garfield managed to make a fair living on their 30-acre (12-hectare) farm. She became the first woman to attend a son's inauguration as President.

In his early teens, James began to do odd jobs during his vacations from the district school. At 16, inspired by reading adventure stories, he left home with the romantic idea of becoming a sailor on the Great Lakes. He gave up the notion when a ship captain cursed him and drove him away. A cousin then hired him to drive a team of horses that towed a barge along the Ohio Canal. During his six weeks on the canal, he recalled, "I fell into the canal just fourteen times and had fourteen almost miraculous escapes from drowning."

Education and early career. Soon James returned home, ill with malaria. When he recovered, he entered Geauga Seminary in the nearby town of Chester. Following his first term, he supported himself by teaching in the district school. At 20, he enrolled in the Western Reserve Eclectic Institute (now Hiram College) in Hiram, Ohio, near Cleveland. He studied and taught some classes there for three years, then attended Williams College in Williamstown, Massachusetts, for two years. Under the guidance of the president of Williams College, Mark Hopkins, Garfield matured greatly and broadened his interests. He later defined the ideal college as "a simple bench, Mark Hopkins on one end and I on the other ..."

After graduation from Williams in 1856, Garfield returned to Hiram College as a professor of ancient languages and literature. The next year, at the age of 26, he was chosen president of the college. While president, Garfield studied law and occasionally preached sermons for the Disciples of Christ. He had joined that church as a youthful convert.

Garfield's family. On Nov. 11, 1858, Garfield married Lucretia Rudolph (April 19, 1832-March 13, 1918), the daughter of an Ohio farmer. She had been a student of Garfield's at Hiram and taught school while he com-

Garfield was born in a log cabin on a farm in Orange, Ohio, near Cleveland. This painting by James Hope shows Garfield's birthplace as it appeared during his childhood.

The Western Reserve Historical Society

pleted his education. Garfield called her "Crete" and came to rely on her quiet strength. Later, when she was mistress of the White House, he wrote: "Crete grows up to every new emergency with fine tact and faultless taste."

The Garfields had seven children, two of whom died as infants. One son, Harry Augustus Garfield (1863-1942), became president of Williams College and served as fuel administrator under President Woodrow Wilson during World War I. Another son, James Rudolph Garfield (1865-1950), served as secretary of the interior in President Theodore Roosevelt's Cabinet.

Soldier. Shortly after the outbreak of the Civil War, Governor William Dennison commissioned Garfield a lieutenant colonel of Ohio volunteers. The young officer wrote home: "I am cheerful and happy as any one can be in such a fierce business as killing men." Garfield won a minor battle in Middle Creek, Ky., in January 1862. As a reward, he was made a brigadier general, the youngest in the Union Army. He took part in the Battle of Shiloh and in the operations around Corinth. In 1863, as chief of staff under General William S. Rosecrans, Garfield distinguished himself in the Battle of Chickamauga by riding under heavy fire to deliver an important message to General George H. Thomas. He was promoted to major general after the battle.

Political career

Congressman. Garfield had shown an interest in politics as early as 1856, when he campaigned for John C. Frémont, the Republican candidate for President. He was elected to the Ohio state senate three years later. In 1862, while still in the army, Garfield was elected to the

Important dates in Garfield's life

1831 (Nov. 19) Born in Orange, Ohio.
1858 (Nov. 11) Married Lucretia Rudolph.
1862 Became youngest brigadier general in Union Army.
1862 Elected to U.S. House of Representatives.
1880 Elected President of the United States.
1881 (July 2) Shot by Charles Guiteau.
1881 (Sept. 19) Died in Elberon, N.J.

U.S. House of Representatives. However, Garfield did not resign his commission until December 1863.

Garfield won reelection to the House eight times. He served as chairman of the appropriations committee and as a member of the committees on military affairs, ways and means, and banking and currency. He supported the harsh Reconstruction measures of the Radical Republicans, and voted for the impeachment of President Andrew Johnson (see **Reconstruction**).

In 1872, Garfield was one of several congressmen accused of accepting gifts of stock from the Credit Mobilier, a corporation seeking favors from the government (see **Credit Mobilier of America**). He denied the charge, and it was never proved. Garfield was also criticized for accepting a $5,000 fee from a company trying to get a paving contract from the city of Washington, D.C. He ad-

Library of Congress

Lucretia Rudolph Garfield was a student of Garfield's before they married. She won widespread admiration for her quiet strength as her husband fought for his life after being shot.

Garfield's election

Place of nominating convention . .	Chicago
Ballot on which nominated	36th
Democratic opponent	Winfield Scott Hancock
Electoral vote*	214 (Garfield) to
	155 (Hancock)
Popular vote	4,446,158 (Garfield)
	to 4,444,260 (Hancock)
Age at inauguration	49

*For votes by states, see **Electoral College** (table).

mitted taking the fee but contended that his services were not improper.

Garfield served on the commission that settled the disputed Hayes-Tilden election of 1876 (see **Electoral Commission**). He also helped make the arrangements that gave the presidency to Rutherford B. Hayes.

During Hayes' Administration, Garfield became floor leader of the Republicans in the House. The party was divided into two factions: the "Stalwarts," led by Senator Roscoe Conkling of New York, and the "Half-Breeds," led by Senator James G. Blaine of Maine. These groups quarreled over personal differences and government jobs. In general, the Half-Breeds were more interested in modernizing the Republican Party and appealed to younger Republicans. Though closer to the Half-Breeds, Garfield stood between the two factions and kept some of the confidence of both.

Election of 1880. The Ohio legislature elected Garfield to the U.S. Senate in 1880. But before he could take his seat there, he led his state's delegation to the Republican National Convention. The Half-Breeds tried to nominate Blaine for President. The Stalwarts insisted on former President Ulysses S. Grant.

Neither Blaine nor Grant could gather enough votes for the nomination. The Half-Breeds then swung to Garfield, who was a "dark horse," or little-known candidate. The convention finally chose Garfield on the 36th ballot. For Vice President, the convention selected Chester A. Arthur, a Stalwart and Conkling's lieutenant in the New York Republican machine. Garfield defeated his Democratic Party opponent, Winfield Scott Hancock, by 1,898 votes.

Garfield's Administration (1881)

The five Garfield children, ranging in age from 8 to 17, looked forward to moving into the White House. But the President was in a somber mood. He wrote: "I am bidding good-bye to private life and to a long series of happy years which I fear terminate in 1880."

Party quarrels soon confirmed the President's fears. Garfield, who owed his nomination primarily to the Half-Breeds, favored this faction in handing out jobs. He

Vice President and Cabinet

Vice President	* Chester A. Arthur
Secretary of state	* James G. Blaine
Secretary of the treasury	William Windom
Secretary of war	* Robert Todd Lincoln
Attorney general	I. Wayne MacVeagh
Postmaster general	Thomas L. James
Secretary of the Navy	William H. Hunt
Secretary of the interior	* Samuel J. Kirkwood

*Has a separate biography in *World Book.*

made their leader, Blaine, his secretary of state, and appointed several others to important offices. The Stalwarts received only minor positions. Their leader, Conkling, tried to stop the Senate from confirming some key appointments. He failed, and resigned from the Senate. Distracted by these quarrels, Garfield could give little attention to other government business. He did support an investigation by Postmaster General Thomas L. James, who found fraud in the awarding of contracts to transport the mail.

Assassination. On July 2, 1881, Garfield was about to leave Washington to attend the 25th reunion of his class at Williams College. He was walking through a reception room in the railroad station when a stranger fired two pistol shots at him. Garfield fell, and the assassin cried: "I am a Stalwart and Arthur is President now!"

The assassin, Charles J. Guiteau, was arrested immediately. He held a grudge because Garfield had refused to appoint him as United States consul in Paris. At his trial, Guiteau acted like a madman. His attorney argued that he was innocent by reason of insanity, but a jury convicted him. He was hanged in 1882.

Garfield lay near death for 80 days. Although one of the assassin's bullets had merely grazed his arm, the other had lodged in his back. Surgeons could not find it. Alexander Graham Bell tried unsuccessfully to locate the bullet with an electrical device.

Garfield remained calm and cheerful throughout the hot summer in Washington. He performed only one official act, the signing of an extradition paper. The Constitution provides that, in case of a President's "inability to discharge the powers and duties" of his office, "the same shall devolve on the Vice President." But this had never happened, and Arthur did not step in for fear of disturbing Garfield and creating a major political controversy. The Cabinet supported his decision.

If the X ray and modern antiseptics had existed at that time, Garfield's life might have been saved. But infection set in. After being moved to a seaside cottage in Elberon, N.J., he died on Sept. 19, 1881. He was buried in Cleveland. Friends raised a large fund to help Mrs. Garfield and their children.   H. Wayne Morgan

Related articles in *World Book* include:

Arthur, Chester A.	President of the United States
Civil service (History)	Spoils system
Hancock, Winfield Scott	

Outline

I. Early life
  A. Childhood
  B. Education and early career
  C. Garfield's family
  D. Soldier
II. Political career
  A. Congressman   B. Election of 1880
III. Garfield's Administration (1881)
  A. Party quarrels   B. Assassination

Questions

Why did Vice President Arthur not assume the duties of the presidency while Garfield lay dying?

What adventure grew from Garfield's love of reading?

How did Garfield's death affect government reform?

Who were the Stalwarts? The Half-Breeds? How did their rivalry lead to Garfield's nomination?

Why did Garfield never take his Senate seat?

How long did Garfield serve as President?

Additional resources
Brown, Fern G. *James A. Garfield.* Garrett Educational, 1990.
Lillegard, Dee. *James A. Garfield.* Childrens Pr., 1987. Younger readers.
McElroy, Richard L. *James A. Garfield.* Daring Bks., 1986.
Peskin, Allan. *Garfield.* 1978. Reprint. Kent State Univ. Pr., 1999.

Garfunkel, Art. See **Simon, Paul.**

Gargle is a liquid used to soothe sore throats and help prevent the spread of germs. The user puts the liquid in the mouth, throws the head back, and churns the liquid about in the throat. The liquid is not swallowed. Many formulas are used in making gargles. The simplest is 1 teaspoon (4.9 milliliters) of table salt and 1 teaspoon of baking soda in 1 pint (0.5 liter) of water. Often the gargle does not reach far enough down into the throat to relieve the soreness.   Barry L Wenig

Gargoyle, *GAHR goyl,* is a decorated waterspout that projects from the upper part of a building or tower. To protect building walls from rain water running off the roof, ancient Greek architects often attached terra cotta or stone lion heads to building cornices. A hollow channel inside the heads directed the water safely clear of the building.

Haesler Art Publishers/Art Resource

Fanciful gargoyles serve as decorative waterspouts on the side of a medieval cathedral in Amiens, France.

During the Middle Ages, gargoyles became a familiar part of Gothic buildings. Gothic architects adopted the ancient Greek design and created fantastic, carved downspouts. The figures were part animal and part human. The largest ones extended as much as 3 feet (91 centimeters) from the walls of the building.

The term *gargoyle* is sometimes incorrectly used to refer to all sculptures of grotesque beasts on medieval buildings. When not used for drains, such creatures are more properly called *chimeras.*   William J. Hennessey

See also **Chimera.**

Garibaldi, *GAR uh BAWL dee,* **Giuseppe,** *juh SEHP ee* (1807-1882), was a military hero who fought to create an independent, united Italy. He also led military campaigns in Latin America and earned the title "Hero of Two Worlds."

In 1834, Garibaldi took part in a revolt against the king of Sardinia in Piedmont, a region in northern Italy. The revolt failed, and Garibaldi was forced into exile. He went to South America, where he aided the Brazilian province of Rio Grande do Sul in a revolt against the Brazilian government.

Later, Garibaldi fought for Uruguay against Argentina. During this campaign, he formed the Italian Legion, a group of volunteer troops who wore red shirts. In 1848, Garibaldi led this group, which was nicknamed the *red shirts,* to Italy to fight against the country's Austrian rulers. In 1849, Garibaldi's forces defended a republic formed by the Italian patriot Giuseppe Mazzini at Rome. But French and Austrian troops defeated the Italians. Exiled from Italy, Garibaldi went to the United States. He was allowed to return to Italy in 1854.

In 1860, Garibaldi and his famous *red shirts* conquered the Kingdom of the Two Sicilies, which controlled much of southern Italy and the nearby island of Sicily. These areas became part of the Kingdom of Italy, proclaimed in 1861.

During the 1860's, Garibaldi fought to bring Rome into the kingdom by ending the pope's rule there. But Garibaldi's efforts failed. In 1866, Garibaldi helped Italy gain the city of Venice from Austria. During the 1860's and 1870's, he was repeatedly elected to the Italian Parliament. However, he seldom took his seat. Garibaldi was born in Nice, France, which was then part of the Kingdom of Sardinia.   Frank J. Coppa

See also **Italy** (Italy united).

Garland, Hamlin (1860-1940), an American author, was one of the finest writers of regional fiction during the late 1800's. Garland made his literary reputation with short stories about the harsh lives of prairie farmers and their families. Their lives were made hard by loneliness, unproductive land, bad weather, and an economic system that Garland believed was unjust.

The stories in *Main-Travelled Roads* (1891), Garland's best book, established him as an important Midwestern supporter of literary realism. For the next several years, he continued to publish stories about what he called the Middle Border, the recently settled raw farmlands not quite on the edge of the frontier. Ending the first period in his career, Garland wrote his finest novel, *Rose of Dutcher's Coolly* (1895). The work tells the story of a Wisconsin farm girl who becomes a career woman in Chicago. Garland also became active in political reform and the Populist movement (see **Populism**).

In the late 1890's, Garland's enthusiasm for reform and Populism declined. He began writing popular romances set in the Rocky Mountains, starting with *The Spirit of Sweetwater* (1898). These novels lack the literary quality of Garland's earlier work, but they portrayed American Indians with great accuracy. Garland became an important advocate of Indian rights. Garland devoted the final phase of his career to autobiographical writings. *A Son of the Middle Border* (1917) is his best autobiographical volume. *A Daughter of the Middle Border* (1921) won the 1922 Pulitzer Prize for biography.

Hannibal Hamlin Garland was born near West Salem, Wisconsin. He grew up on farms in Wisconsin, Iowa, and what is now South Dakota.   Daniel Mark Fogel

Garland, Judy (1922-1969), was an American singer and motion-picture actress. She won her greatest fame as Dorothy in the musical film *The Wizard of Oz* (1939). Her theme song, "Over the Rainbow," came from this

MGM from the Kobal Collection

Judy Garland gained fame as Dorothy in the movie *The Wizard of Oz.* She starred with Bert Lahr as the Cowardly Lion, Jack Haley as the Tin Man, and Ray Bolger as the Scarecrow.

movie. She became known for her husky and trembling but sweet singing voice.

Garland was born in Grand Rapids, Minnesota. Her real name was Frances Gumm. Her parents were vaudeville performers, and she appeared on stage for the first time at the age of 5. Garland made her motion-picture debut in 1936 in the short film *Every Sunday* and the feature-length film *Pigskin Parade.* During her juvenile period, Garland made nine films with Mickey Rooney. The first one was *Thoroughbreds Don't Cry* (1937). Some of her other movies with him include the comedies *Love Finds Andy Hardy* (1938) and *Andy Hardy Meets Debutante* (1940).

Garland first became famous in the musical film *Broadway Melody of 1938* (1937). Garland later starred in other musicals, several with Rooney, such as *Babes in Arms* (1939) and *Strike Up the Band* (1940). Her other musicals included *For Me and My Gal* (1942), *Meet Me in St. Louis* (1944), and *Easter Parade* (1948).

Garland also appeared in such dramatic films as *The Clock* (1945); *A Star Is Born* (1954), for which she was nominated for an Academy Award; *Judgment at Nuremberg* (1961); and *A Child Is Waiting* (1963). During the 1950's and 1960's, Garland drew large crowds at concerts. She was the mother of the actress and singer Liza Minnelli.   Rachel Gallagher

Additional resources

Coleman, Emily R. *The Complete Judy Garland.* Harper, 1990.
Edwards, Anne. *Judy Garland.* Simon & Schuster, 1975.
Fricke, John. *Judy Garland.* Henry Holt, 1992.
Shipman, David. *Judy Garland.* Hyperion, 1993.

Garlic is a plant grown for its pungently flavored bulb, which is used to season foods. Some plants related to garlic, including the onion, contain the same strong-tasting compound as garlic, but in different amounts. The garlic bulb is made up of parts called *cloves.* The cloves may be eaten, and they are also used for planting. A brittle, papery covering called a *tunic* grows around each clove and around the whole bulb.

Most of the garlic produced commercially in the United States is grown in the state of California. Farmers in California plant the crop in late fall or early winter, and the bulbs mature in the summer. The harvested bulbs are *cured* by drying in the field. After the bulbs are cured, workers braid or remove the tops, and the garlic is ready for market.

WORLD BOOK illustration by John D. Dawson
Garlic bulb

The bulbs can be used in many different ways. They may be sold whole, dehydrated, or ground into powder. Juice from the bulbs also may be extracted and sold. The garlic plant first grew in central Asia and later was widely cultivated in the Mediterranean region.

August A. De Hertogh

Scientific classification. Botanists consider the garlic plant a member of either the amaryllis family, Amaryllidaceae, or the lily family, Liliaceae. The plant's scientific name is *Allium sativum.*

Garment industry. See Clothing.
Garment Workers' Union, International Ladies'. See Union of Needletrades, Industrial and Textile Employees.
Garneau, *gar NOH,* **Marc** (1949-   ), was the first Canadian to travel in space. Garneau, a captain in the Royal Canadian Navy, accompanied six American astronauts on a mission aboard the United States space shuttle Challenger from Oct. 5 to 13, 1984. He did 10 scientific experiments for Canada's government on the flight.

Garneau was born in Quebec City, Quebec. His father, André Garneau, made a career of the Canadian armed forces and became a general. At the age of 16, Marc Garneau enrolled at the Collège militaire royal de

NASA
Marc Garneau

Saint-Jean. He received a bachelor's degree in engineering physics from the Royal Military College of Canada and a doctor's degree in electrical engineering from the Imperial College of Science and Technology in London. Garneau began his naval career in 1965. He became a leading authority on naval communications and warfare systems. Garneau was selected as one of six Canadian astronauts in 1983.   Kendal Windeyer

Garner, John Nance (1868-1967), served as vice president of the United States from 1933 to 1941, during the first two terms of President Franklin D. Roosevelt. Garner, a Conservative Southerner, helped put through Roosevelt's early New Deal program. But he later opposed the president on labor and social welfare reforms (see **New Deal**). He objected to a third term for Roosevelt and ran against him unsuccessfully at the 1940 Democratic National Convention.

Garner was born in Red River County, Texas, and

was often called "Cactus Jack." He served in the United States House of Representatives as a Democrat from Texas from 1903 to 1933. He was elected Speaker of the House in 1931. A shrewd politician, Garner sought the Democratic presidential nomination in 1932. However, he gave his convention votes to Roosevelt and accepted the vice presidential nomination instead.

David E. Kyvig

United Press Int.
John Nance Garner

Garnet is any of a group of hard, glassy minerals. This group of silicate minerals includes six major types: *almandine, andradite, grossularite, pyrope, spessartite,* and *uvarovite.* Garnets are composed of silica and such elements as aluminum, calcium, iron, magnesium, and manganese. They range in color from red, brown, and black to various shades of yellow and green. Crystals of garnet are found in all types of rock, but chiefly in metamorphic varieties (see **Metamorphic rock**).

Some garnet crystals are used in making jewelry. One well-known gemlike type is the red pyrope, which is often sold as an imitation ruby. Most other garnets are used as abrasives for grinding and polishing. Garnets are found throughout the world. Those of gemlike quality are mined chiefly in central Europe, Russia, and South Africa.   Robert Halstead Carpenter

See also **Gem** (picture); **Ruby.**

Garnishment is a legal process by which the credits or property of a debtor, in the hands of a third party, may be held for payment of debts. In the United States, garnishment of wages is limited by federal law. See also **Attachment.**   Joel C. Dobris

Garrett, Pat (1850-1908), an American frontier rancher and sheriff in the West, is best known for killing the outlaw Billy the Kid (see **Billy the Kid**). Garrett was elected sheriff of Lincoln County, New Mexico, in 1880. As sheriff, he captured his one-time friend Billy the Kid, who had been accused of murder. The Kid escaped from jail just before he was to be hanged. In July 1881, Garrett caught up with him in Fort Sumner, a military post near the town of Fort Sumner, New Mexico, and shot him to death from ambush in a darkened house.

After killing Billy the Kid, Garrett operated horse and cattle ranches and worked as a tax collector. He was shot to death by New Mexican rancher Wayne Brazel because of a land dispute. A witness supported Brazel's claim of self-defense, but people generally suspected that Brazel and his associates murdered Garrett.

Patrick Floyd Garrett was born in Chambers County, Alabama. He grew up in Louisiana and worked as a cowboy and buffalo hunter in Texas before moving to New Mexico.   Roger D. McGrath

Garrick, David (1717-1779), ranks among the greatest British actors. He introduced a more natural style of acting and did much to arouse interest in the English playwright William Shakespeare. Garrick excelled as Hamlet and in other Shakespearean roles, and he also organized the popular "Shakespeare Jubilee" of 1769. It was

the first Shakespeare festival held in Stratford-upon-Avon, Shakespeare's birthplace. Garrick also wrote several light comedies, including *The Clandestine Marriage* (1766), written with George Colman the elder.

Garrick was born in Hereford, and went to London in 1737. He won fame in 1741 playing Shakespeare's Richard III. In 1747, he bought a share in the Drury Lane Theatre and began a successful career as a manager. He dominated the English theater as actor and manager for the rest of his life.   Jack D. Durant

See also **Drama** (picture).

Garrison, William Lloyd (1805-1879), was an American journalist and reformer who became famous in the 1830's for his denunciations of slavery. Before his time, abolitionists had made moderate appeals to slaveholders and legislators in behalf of slaves, and hoped that slavery would gradually disappear. Garrison said slavery ought to be ended "immediately," and criticized all who did not entirely agree with him.

Garrison was raised in Newburyport, Massachusetts. A poor boy, he was apprenticed to a printer at 13. By 1827, Garrison was a veteran journalist. He edited the *National Philanthropist,* the world's first temperance paper. In 1828, Garrison met Benjamin Lundy, a Quaker and a pioneer antislavery propagandist and organizer, and became an ardent abolitionist. His attacks on slave dealers in Lundy's newspaper caused Garrison to be jailed for seven months.

In 1831, Garrison began publishing *The Liberator* in Boston. This newspaper had a small circulation, but it was influential and at times aroused violent public reaction. Garrison continued to issue it until 1865, when the 13th Amendment to the Constitution ended slavery.

In 1832, Garrison formed the first society for the immediate abolition of slavery. He attracted such associates as Wendell Phillips, and influenced, among others, Theodore Parker and Henry David Thoreau. In 1835, Garrison's life was endangered by a mob in Boston. His fight to give women equal rights in the American Anti-Slavery Society, formed in 1833, split the abolitionist movement. Garrison believed that the Northern states ought to separate from the South. He refused to vote and opposed the United States government because it permitted slavery. He eventually approved of Abraham Lincoln and sup-

Chicago Historical Society
William Lloyd Garrison

ported his Administration during the Civil War. See also **Abolition movement.**   Michael Emery

Additional resources

Chapman, John J. *William Lloyd Garrison.* 1921. Reprint. Beekman Pubs., 1974.
Garrison, William Lloyd. *The Letters of William Lloyd Garrison.* 6 vols. Harvard Univ. Pr., 1971-1981.
Merrill, Walter M. *Against Wind and Tide: A Biography of Wm. Lloyd Garrison.* Harvard Univ. Pr., 1963.
Stewart, James B. *William Lloyd Garrison and the Challenge of Emancipation.* Harlan Davidson, 1992.

Garrison Dam, about 77 miles (124 kilometers) north of Bismarck, N. Dak., is part of the United States government's Missouri River Basin development program. It is one of the world's largest earth-filled dams. The dam's main section is 12,000 feet (3,658 meters) long and 202 feet (62 meters) high. Construction of the dam started in 1946. The first of the dam's five generating units began to produce power in 1956. The dam has a capacity of 400,000 kilowatts. It forms Lake Sakakawea, which is 178 miles (286 kilometers) long.　　Edward C. Pritchett

Garrote, *guh ROHT* or *guh RAHT,* is an iron collar. It was once used in Spain and Portugal to execute condemned persons. Executioners seated the prisoner in a chair and placed the garrote around the neck. The garrote, attached to an iron post which stood behind the prisoner's chair, was tightened by a screw until the prisoner strangled. Murderers have often used a form of garrote made of loops of wire, or even scarves to strangle their victims.　　Marvin E. Wolfgang

Garter, Order of the, is the highest and oldest order of knighthood in Great Britain. It was founded around 1348 by King Edward III of England. The emblem of the order is a sword belt in the form of a dark blue garter edged in gold, on which are printed the French words *Honi soit qui mal y pense.* In English, the words mean *Dishonored be he who thinks evil of it.* No one knows for certain how this phrase originated. On ceremonial occasions, the garter was worn on the left leg below the knee. On ceremonial occasions today, the item most commonly worn as an emblem of the order is a dark-blue velvet *mantle* (loose cloak).

The Order of the Garter first admitted only 25 members besides the king. In 1831, the order was reorganized, and its membership was increased to include the Prince of Wales, descendants of King George I, and some foreign rulers. The English monarch is always Sovereign of the Order. Women became eligible for membership in the order in 1987. The order has several patron saints, but Saint George was considered its special patron, and the order is sometimes spoken of as "The Order of St. George."

Critically reviewed by the Order of the Garter

Garter snake is one of a group of harmless snakes familiar throughout the United States. The 13 native *species* (kinds) vary greatly in color. Most states have at least one kind of garter snake. These snakes also live in

Her Majesty's Stationery Office

The insignia of the Order of the Garter include the collar, the ribbon, the George Star, and the garter.

southern Canada, Mexico, and Central America.

It is easy to recognize most garter snakes by the three light stripes that run along the body. One runs down the middle of the back, and the others are on each side near the belly. In many species, a pattern like a checkerboard fills the spaces between the stripes. The various kinds of garter snakes differ in size. Grown females are usually 20 to 30 inches (51 to 76 centimeters) long. Males are slightly shorter and much thinner. Two kinds of garter snakes, called *ribbon snakes,* have an extremely slender body. The *red-sided* garter snake lives farther north than any other reptile in the Western Hemisphere. It is found as far north as Canada's Northwest Territories.

Three things make garter snakes different from many other American snakes. (1) They like to live in the parks

WORLD BOOK illustration by John F. Eggert

The garter snake is a graceful, harmless snake of North America and Central America.

of cities and towns. In the spring and warm autumn when snakes are most active, many people in the suburbs find them in backyards and gardens. (2) They bear their young alive instead of laying eggs. The size of a litter varies, but the average is 18. Records show one brood of 80. (3) They catch and eat other cold-blooded animals, such as frogs, salamanders, and fishes. The young of some species of garter snakes eat earthworms.

D. Bruce Means

Scientific classification. Garter snakes are members of the common snake family, Colubridae. The most common garter snake is *Thamnophis sirtalis.*

See also **Snake** (picture).

Garvey, Marcus (1887-1940), was a black leader who started a "Back-to-Africa" movement in the United States. Garvey believed that blacks would never receive justice in countries where most of the people were white. He preached that blacks should consider Africa their homeland and that they should settle there.

Garvey was born in Jamaica. He began his movement there in 1914 and brought it to the United States in 1916, when he moved to New York City. In the early 1920's, Garvey had an estimated 2 million followers, chiefly poor blacks. His supporters sent him thousands of dollars. He used the money to set up some all-black businesses. Business profits were to be used to finance the movement. In 1925, Garvey was convicted of mail fraud in connection with his sale of stock in one of the businesses. The movement then declined. Garvey was released from prison in 1927, and he returned to Jamaica.   Richard Bardolph

Wide World

Marcus Garvey

See also **African Americans** (The Garvey movement; picture).

Additional resources

Clarke, John H., ed. *Marcus Garvey and the Vision of Africa.* Random Hse., 1974.
Cronon, E. David. *Black Moses: The Story of Marcus Garvey and the Universal Negro Improvement Association.* 2nd ed. Univ. of Wis. Pr., 1960. The standard biography.
Lawler, Mary. *Marcus Garvey.* Chelsea Hse., 1988. Younger readers.

Gary, Indiana (pop. 102,746; met. area pop. 631,362), is a leading steel-producing center of the United States. It is often called the *Steel City.* Gary is one of the largest cities in Indiana. Gary lies on Lake Michigan, in the state's northwest corner (see **Indiana** [political map]).

In 1906, the United States Steel Corporation (now USX Corporation) began to build a steel plant on the site of what is now Gary. That same year, the company established a town there for the steelworkers and their families. The firm named the town for Judge Elbert H. Gary, chairman of the board of directors.

Gary covers 52 square miles (135 square kilometers). Indiana University has a campus in Gary. Purdue University has one nearby. The economy of Gary is based on the steel industry. The Gary Works of the USX Corpora-

tion is one of the world's largest steel plants. It can produce 7 million tons (6 million metric tons) of steel a year. Three other large steel plants are in the region. Gary and the nearby cities of East Chicago, Hammond, and Whiting are part of the Calumet region, one of the nation's most highly industrialized areas. Freight railroads and major highways pass through or near Gary. The city has an airport, and harbors on Lake Michigan and on two nearby rivers also serve the area.

Gary has a mayor-council form of government. The voters elect the mayor and the nine council members to four-year terms.

Miami and Potawatomi Indians lived in what is now the Gary area during the 1600's, 1700's, and 1800's. Marshes and sand dunes covered the site, and few whites settled there before 1900. In 1906, the U.S. Steel Corporation filled in the marshes and leveled the dunes. The company built a plant on the site, which lay about midway between eastern coal fields and northern iron ore mines. Coal and iron ore are among the main raw materials used in making steel. Gary was incorporated as a town in 1906. The steel mill began operating in 1909 and attracted other industries and thousands of workers, including blacks, European immigrants, and Hispanic Americans. By 1920, Gary had become an industrial center with about 55,000 people.

During the 1960's, Gary's population dropped because many whites moved to suburbs. By 2000, African Americans made up about 85 percent of the population.

In 1967, Gary voters elected the city's first black mayor, Richard G. Hatcher. He took office in 1968. A Democrat, he was reelected mayor four times and served through 1987. Hatcher's administration improved housing conditions in Gary and helped obtain federal job training programs. See **Hatcher, Richard Gordon.**

During the 1960's and 1970's, the city and its industries worked to reduce air pollution caused by smoke from factories and steel mills. The amount of impurities in Gary's air dropped about 60 percent from 1966 to 1975. However, pollution from steel mills and other industries has continued to be a serious problem. In 1982, the Genesis Convention Center opened in downtown Gary. From 1980 to 1990, the city's population decreased by about one-fourth, a rate of loss larger than that of any other major city in the nation. It fell by 12 percent from 1990 to 2000. In 1996, two gambling casino boats began operating on Gary's Lake Michigan shore. This activity provided many jobs for Gary citizens.   James E. Procter

Gary, Elbert Henry (1846-1927), was an American industrialist and lawyer who helped organize the United States Steel Corporation (now USX Corporation) in 1901. He became the company's chief executive officer and headed the firm until his death. Gary introduced safety and pension reforms for workers. His policies kept U.S. Steel intact at a time when the United States government was breaking up large industrial firms for using unfair business practices. Gary, Indiana, a steelmaking center founded by U.S. Steel in 1906, is named for him.

Gary was born near Wheaton, Illinois. He graduated from Union College of Law and was soon practicing corporate law. He later became a county judge in Illinois and in 1898 helped form the Federal Steel Company.

Bruce E. Seely

See also **USX Corporation.**

Gas is one of the three basic states of matter. The other two states are solid and liquid. These states differ from each other in the way they fill space and change shape. A solid, such as rock, always occupies a fixed *volume* (amount of space) and has a fixed shape. A liquid, such as water, always occupies a fixed volume. But it has no shape of its own, so it takes on the shape of its container. A gas, such as air, has neither a fixed shape nor a fixed volume. It fills any container that holds it and takes on the container's shape. Like solids and liquids, gases have weight. But gases are thinner and lighter than solids and liquids.

Many gases, including the nitrogen and oxygen in air, have no color or odor. They can be identified by their chemical behavior, their weight, their ability to absorb heat, and their other properties. But some gases have a color, or an odor, or both. For example, nitrogen dioxide is brown. Hydrogen sulfide smells like rotten eggs.

Under special conditions, gases change into a fourth state of matter called a *plasma.* Plasmas are formed by heating a gas to an extremely high temperature or by passing an electric current through it. Matter exists in a plasma state in stars and the regions between stars.

How gases behave. The behavior of gases is explained by what scientists call the *kinetic theory.* According to the kinetic theory, all matter is made of constantly moving particles—*atoms* or *molecules.* An atom is one of the basic units of matter, and a molecule is a combination of atoms. The number of atoms or molecules of gas in a container the size of a pin-head is many millions of times as large as the number of people on the earth. But these gas particles are so small that they occupy only about one-thousandth of the space inside the container. The remaining space between the particles is empty.

Gas particles fly around in all directions at about the speed of sound. Their exact speed is determined by their weight and by the temperature of the gas. Gas particles move faster when the gas is hot than when it is cold. But light particles move faster than heavy ones at all temperatures. Each moving gas particle crashes into billions of other particles each second. Gas particles crashing into the walls of their container produce an effect called *pressure.*

A gas *liquefies* (changes to a liquid) when it is cooled to a temperature called its *boiling point.* At this temperature, the gas particles gather together to form a liquid. If the pressure of the gas is increased, it liquefies at a higher temperature. But pressure can raise the liquefying temperature only to a limiting value called the *critical temperature.* For example, oxygen under normal atmospheric pressure liquefies at its boiling point, −183 °C. But under a pressure of 5,171 kilopascals, oxygen liquefies at −119 °C, its critical temperature.

Gas laws. Three laws explain approximately how the pressure, temperature, volume, and the number of particles in a container of gas are related. These laws are *Boyle's law, Charles's law,* and *Avogadro's law.*

Boyle's law says that pressure increases as the volume of gas decreases. According to Boyle's law, the product of the pressure (P) multiplied by the volume (V) remains constant if there is no change in the temperature or in the number of particles inside the container. This law is written:

$$PV = \text{constant.}$$

Boyle's law says that the pressure doubles when a gas is compressed to half its volume at constant temperature.

Boyle's law was first published by the Irish chemist Robert Boyle in 1662. But other chemists had discovered the law earlier. In 1660 and 1661, Richard Towneley and Henry Power of England experimented with air below atmospheric pressure. They found that the product of the air's pressure and volume remained constant. At about the same time, Robert Hooke of England experimented with air above atmospheric pressure. Hooke's findings agreed with those of Towneley and Power. Additional experiments by Boyle confirmed all these findings. In 1679, Edme Mariotte of France published the results of his own experiments with gases. Mariotte's writings became well known in Europe. Thus, the law known today as *Boyle's law* in North America and Great Britain is called *Mariotte's law* in continental Europe.

Charles's law states that a gas expands by the same fraction of its original volume with each degree that its temperature rises. According to Charles's law, the ratio between the volume (V) of a gas and its temperature (T) remains constant if the pressure does not change. The law is written:

$$\frac{V}{T} = \text{constant.}$$

WORLD BOOK photo by Dan Miller

Pressure rises in an air pump's stroke, demonstrating Boyle's law.

Boyle's law

When gas is compressed at a constant temperature, its pressure rises. Squeezing a gas into half its original volume doubles its pressure, as shown below.

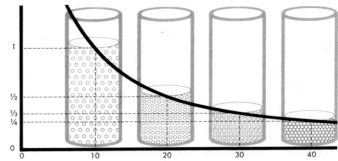

Volume in liters

Pressure in kilograms per square centimeter

In this equation, *T* is the *absolute temperature* of the gas. It is usually measured in *kelvins* (Celsius degrees plus 273.15). Kelvin is abbreviated K. For example, when a gas is heated from 300 K (room temperature) to 600 K, its absolute temperature doubles. Doubling the temperature doubles the gas's volume if the pressure does not change. See **Absolute zero.**

Charles's law was discovered in 1787 by the French chemist Jacques Alexandre César Charles. He found that carbon dioxide, hydrogen, oxygen, and nitrogen all expand at constant rates as their temperatures rise. Charles did not publish his findings, but explained his experiments to the French chemist Joseph Gay-Lussac. Gay-Lussac performed similar experiments and published his results in 1802. As a result, Charles's law is sometimes called *Gay-Lussac's law.*

Avogadro's law was first proposed in 1811 by the Italian scientist and philosopher Amedeo Avogadro. It says that equal volumes of different gases all contain the same number of particles if they all have the same pressure and temperature. It was later discovered that a volume of 22.4 liters of gas at 0 °C and atmospheric pressure contains about 602,000,000,000,000,000,000,000 (602 billion trillion) particles. This number is usually written 6.02×10^{23} and is called the *Avogadro constant.* This number of particles of any substance is called one *mole* of the substance. See **Mole.**

The *universal gas law* combines Boyle's law, Charles's law, and Avogadro's law into a single statement. This law is written:

$$PV = nRT.$$

In this equation, *P* represents the pressure of the gas, *V* represents its volume, *n* represents the number of moles of gas, and *T* represents its absolute temperature. *R* is a constant called the *universal gas constant.* It has a value of 8.314 joules per kelvin per mole. According to the universal gas law, the pressure of a gas can be doubled in three ways: (1) the gas can be squeezed into one-half its original volume, (2) twice as much gas can be forced into the original volume, or (3) the absolute temperature can be doubled.

History. During the early 1600's, scientists began realizing that some matter can exist in a form that is similar to air. The word *gas* was first used to describe this form in the mid-1600's in the writings of the Belgian chemist and physician Jan Baptista van Helmont. He invented the word *gas* by altering the Greek word *chaos,* meaning *space.* In this way, the word describes the ability of a gas to fill any amount of space.

Many gases were discovered and studied during the 1600's and 1700's. These gases include hydrogen, oxygen, and nitrogen.

The first successful attempts to liquefy many gases began in 1823 when the English scientist Michael Faraday liquefied chlorine. After heating chlorine hydrate (chemical formula $Cl_2 \cdot 10H_2O$) in a sealed glass tube, Faraday noticed an oily-looking liquid inside the tube. When he tried to file the end off the tube to examine this liquid, the tube exploded. Faraday repeated the experiment, and concluded that the liquid was chlorine. The chlorine had been freed from the chlorine hydrate during heating, and had condensed under pressure inside the tube. The next day, Faraday liquefied hydrogen chloride in a similar tube. But when he tried to liquefy carbon dioxide by this method, the gas burst the tube without liquefying. Faraday later liquefied carbon dioxide and many other gases by cooling and compressing them. Today, all gases have been solidified as well as liquefied.   Frank C. Andrews

Related articles in *World Book* include:

Biographies

Avogadro, Amedeo	Gay-Lussac, Joseph L.
Boyle, Robert	Lavoisier, Antoine L.
Faraday, Michael	

Gases

Acetylene	Formaldehyde	Nitrogen
Air	Gas (fuel)	Nitrous oxide
Ammonia	Helium	Noble gas
Argon	Hydrogen	Oxygen
Carbon dioxide	Hydrogen iodide	Ozone
Carbon monoxide	Hydrogen sulfide	Radon
Chlorine	Krypton	Steam
Damp	Methane	Vapor
Ethane	Neon	Xenon
Fluorine		

Other related articles

Airship	Evaporation	Matter
Balloon	Expansion	Plasma (physics)
Barometer	Fuel	Pressure
Boiling point	Gas chamber	Solid
Chemistry	Gas mask	Viscosity
Diffusion	Hydraulics	Will-o'-the-wisp
Distillation	Liquid	

Charles's law

When gas is heated at a constant pressure, its volume increases in proportion to its absolute temperature. Doubling the temperature doubles the volume.

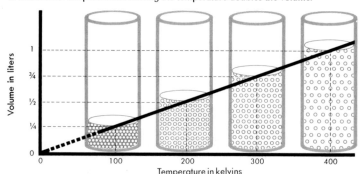

WORLD BOOK photo by Dan Miller

Air expands in a flask when it is heated, proving Charles's law.

Trans-Canada Pipe Lines Ltd.

Industrial use of natural gas accounts for about a third of the gas burned in the United States and Canada. This gas-burning furnace is used to harden gears in an automobile factory.

Gas

Gas (fuel) is one of our most important resources. We burn it to provide heat and to produce energy to run machinery. The chemical industry uses the chemicals in gas to make detergents, drugs, plastics, and many other products.

People sometimes confuse gas with gasoline, which is often called simply *gas*. But gasoline is a liquid. On the other hand, gas fuel—like air and steam—is a *gaseous* form of matter. That is, it does not occupy a fixed amount of space as liquids and solids do. For information on gas as a form of matter, see the **Gas** article just before this article. See also **Gasoline**.

Gas has many uses as a fuel. Millions of people use it to heat their homes, cook meals, burn garbage, heat water, dry laundry, and cool the air. Hotels, restaurants, hospitals, schools, and many other businesses and institutions burn gas for cooking, heating buildings and water, air conditioning, and generating steam. Gas produces little air pollution when it is burned.

Industry has many uses for gas in addition to using it as a raw material in making products. These uses range from burning off the quills of chickens to hardening the nose cones of spacecraft.

There are two kinds of gas—*natural gas* and *manufactured gas*. Almost all the gas used in the United States and Canada is natural gas. Most scientists believe that natural gas has been forming beneath the earth's surface for hundreds of millions of years. The natural forces that created gas also created petroleum. As a result, natural gas is often found with or near oil deposits. The same methods are used to explore and drill into the earth for both fuels. Manufactured gas is produced chiefly from coal or petroleum, using heat and chemical processes.

Manufactured gas costs more than natural gas and is used in regions where large quantities of the natural fuel are not available.

Before its breakup, the Soviet Union was the leading producer of natural gas. The United States was the second largest producer. Until the 1960's, large quantities of natural gas were not available in most European countries, and manufactured gas was used widely. In the 1960's, the development of newly discovered gas fields led to the rapid expansion of Europe's natural gas industry. Expansion was especially rapid in the Soviet Union and the Netherlands. The world's largest known gas field was found in the Soviet Union in 1966. Great Britain began to produce much natural gas from deposits found under the North Sea in the mid-1960's.

The gas industry consists of three main activities: (1) producing gas, either by drilling natural gas wells or by manufacturing gas; (2) transmitting gas, usually by pipeline, to large market areas; and (3) distributing gas to the user. Each part of the gas industry requires its own special skills and equipment. Some gas companies conduct all three activities, but most companies handle only one.

The natural gas industry began in the United States. The industry started to expand rapidly in the late 1920's with the development of improved pipe for transmitting gas great distances economically. By the 1930's, gas produced in Texas was being carried by pipeline to the Midwest. Today, long-distance gas pipelines serve many parts of the world.

In the 1970's and 1980's, the gas industry launched a number of programs to meet an increasing demand for gas. For example, the industry began seeking ways of producing gas from coal.

Gas is best known as a fuel for cooking and heating in homes. But in many countries, industry *consumes* (uses) much more gas than residential users do. Industry consumes about a third of the gas burned in the United States and Canada. Residential users consume only about a fourth. The rest is used by offices, hotels, restaurants, stores, hospitals, schools, and other businesses and institutions.

Gas provides about 25 per cent of the total fuel energy consumed in the United States and about 30 per cent of that used in Canada. Almost all the gas burned in both countries is natural gas. Both countries have large deposits of natural gas and excellent systems for producing, transmitting, and distributing it. Many countries lack either large deposits of natural gas or the systems that are necessary to produce and transport it. These countries consume only small amounts of gas, chiefly manufactured gas.

Gas in the home. Wherever large quantities of natural gas are available, gas is the most popular cooking fuel. One reason for its popularity is that it costs less than most other fuels. In addition, a homemaker can have the desired amount of heat instantly, control the heat easily and even automatically, and shut it off instantly.

Many residential consumers also use gas to heat their homes and water, burn garbage and trash, dry laundry, and operate air conditioners. Some people heat their patios and swimming pools with gas, and many have decorative outdoor gaslights around their homes. Others cook outdoors on gas grills.

Many people who live in mobile homes or in farm areas or other places far from gas pipelines also use gas for cooking and heating. They burn *liquefied petroleum gas* (LPG). LPG is also called *LP gas, propane, butane,* or *bottled gas.* It is produced either from certain compounds in natural gas or from gaseous compounds in petroleum. These compounds become liquid when they are put under pressure. The liquid takes up much less space than the original gas and is easily transported in small pressurized containers. As the fuel is used, normal air pressure changes the liquid back to gas.

Gas in industry has many uses. Companies use gas flames or gas heat in coating, cutting, and shaping metals and other materials. Gas heat is used to harden the nose cones of spacecraft so they do not burn up from the intense heat generated by atmospheric friction. Gas flames are used to remove the bristles from hogs and the fuzz from corduroy. Gas can perform so many industrial operations that it is used to produce or process brick and tile, cement, ceramics, glass, foods, iron and steel, paper, textiles, and countless other products. In-

Northern Illinois Gas Company

Gas service lines distribute gas to millions of home users. Here, lines are being laid in a new development.

S. Roberts, Image Finders

Petrochemical plants use natural gas to produce chemical compounds used in making paints, plastics, and other products.

dustrial scientists find gas extremely useful in the research and development of new products and processes.

The main difference between home cooking with gas and industrial "cooking" with gas is the temperature used. For example, cakes, meats, and pies are baked at temperatures between 300° and 500° F. (150° and 260° C). Temperatures used for industrial "cooking" vary from about 350° F. (177° C) in baking automobile finishes to about 3000° F. (1600° C) in making steel and processing other metals.

An increasing number of factories have *gas total energy systems,* which supply all their power needs. In such systems, gas is the only outside source of energy. It powers a turbine or engine that drives a generator to produce electricity. The exhaust heat from the turbine or engine is used for heating and cooling.

Industry also uses *gas infrared heaters.* The infrared rays from such heaters heat only the objects that they are aimed at, not the air. These types of heaters are especially useful for keeping people warm in large warehouses or other buildings that are difficult to heat. See Infrared rays.

Gas products. Natural gas is an important source of *petrochemicals* (chemicals made from natural gas or pe-

troleum). Petrochemicals serve as building blocks in manufacturing many products, including detergents; drugs; fertilizers; paints; plastics; *synthetic* (man-made) rubber; and acrylic, nylon, polyester, and other synthetic fibers.

Petrochemical production is based on the various compounds of hydrogen and carbon found in crude gas and oil. These compounds include methane, ethane, and propane. They can be removed from the raw material and used alone, or they can be broken apart and restructured to produce compounds that are not present in the raw material. The compounds or their parts are blended with other chemicals in making detergents, drugs, and other products.

All of the compounds found in natural gas are not needed to produce heat. For example, products called *natural gas liquids* (NGL)—a group of chemical compounds that includes ethane, propane, and butane—are usually removed in liquid form before the gas is sent through the pipeline. Many NGL plants and petrochemical factories operate near gas fields so that they can be close to their sources of supply. For additional information about the chemistry of gas, see the section *The chemical story of gas* in this article. See also **Natural gas liquids; Petrochemicals.**

A natural gas total energy system

This diagram shows how a gas total energy system works. The system can meet the power needs of a school, factory, or other building using gas as the only outside source of energy. A turbine drives a generator to produce electricity. Heat from the turbine is used for heating and cooling.

WORLD BOOK diagram by George Suyeoka

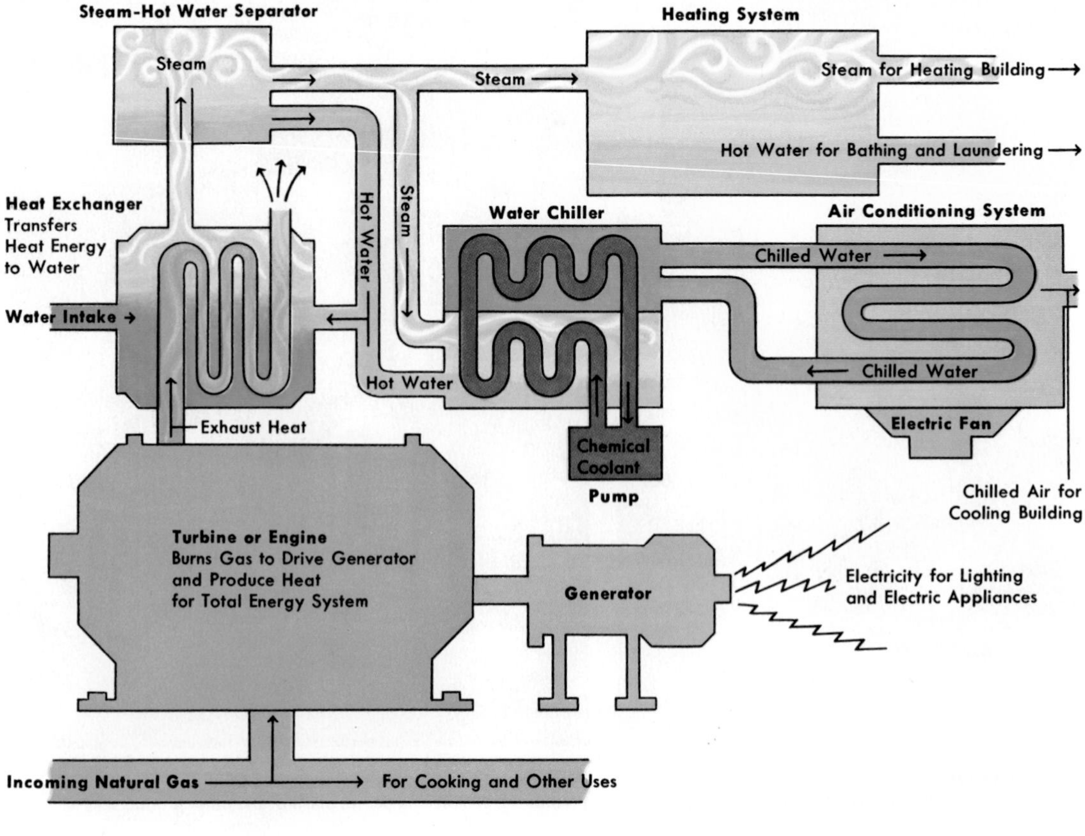

Steam-Hot Water Separator

Heating System

Steam

Steam →

Steam for Heating Building →

Hot Water for Bathing and Laundering →

Heat Exchanger Transfers Heat Energy to Water

Hot Water

Steam

Water Chiller

Air Conditioning System

Chilled Water →

Water Intake →

Chilled Water

Hot Water

Exhaust Heat

Electric Fan

Chemical Coolant

Pump

Chilled Air for Cooling Building

Turbine or Engine Burns Gas to Drive Generator and Produce Heat for Total Energy System

Generator

Electricity for Lighting and Electric Appliances

Incoming Natural Gas ————→ For Cooking and Other Uses

Natural gas is found in the holes of limestone, sandstone, and other rocks that are porous (full of small holes). A dome of nonporous rock forms a cap over the gas-bearing rock, trapping the gas. The gas cannot escape unless well drillers open a hole through the solid rock or unless the earth's surface shifts and cracks the cap. Natural gas is often found on top of oil deposits or dissolved in them, because the same natural forces formed both fuels.

Natural gas can also be also found in *gas hydrates,* solids that resemble wet snow. Gas hydrates, also called *methane hydrates,* are formed when water freezes in the presence of methane in the ocean depths. Under such conditions of extreme cold and pressure, the ice crystals form "cages" with gas molecules trapped inside. Gas hydrates also form readily in the extreme cold that occurs in the Arctic.

The volume of gas stored in gas hydrates may be as great as 5,000 times the amount of conventional gas reserves known to exist in the world today. But retrieving the deposits is difficult because gas hydrates are not stable at normal surface temperatures and pressures. Without special equipment, the gas escapes from the ice when it reaches the surface. No one has yet found a cost-effective way to extract large quantities of fuel from gas hydrates.

Exploring for gas. Modern exploration methods are constantly helping to uncover new reserves of natural gas. These methods show where there are earth formations that could hold gas. However, they cannot indicate the actual presence of gas. The only sure way to find out if an area contains deposits of natural gas is to drill a well.

In *proved areas,* where gas or petroleum has already been found, about 75 percent of new wells bring in one of the two fuels. Drilling in unproved areas is called *wildcatting.* A wildcat well is drilled wherever a prospector believes that gas or oil may be present, in areas far from producing wells.

About 10 percent of the wildcat wells produce some gas or oil. But many fail to produce enough fuel to pay for the cost of drilling them. Prospectors continue to drill in unproved areas because they keep part of the rights to deposits they discover. One successful wildcat well can more than make up for the cost of many unsuccessful ones.

In exploring for gas in unproved areas, prospectors rely on studies made by earth scientists called *geologists* and *geophysicists.* These studies involve maps, drilling records, and measurements.

After selecting a promising site for a well, a geologist studies a detailed map of the features above and below the earth's surface. The map enables the geologist to locate underground formations called *traps,* where natural gas and petroleum can accumulate. In addition, geologists try to determine whether there is *reservoir rock* underground. This type of rock has tiny holes called *pores* through which gas can move. For more information on traps and reservoir rock, see **Petroleum** (How petroleum was formed).

Geologists may also study *well logs.* A well log is a record of the rock formations found in the drilling of a well. Well logs measure such characteristics as the *porosity* (presence of pores) and fluid content of the rock.

Geophysicists commonly use an exploration technique known as *reflection seismology.* In this technique, a loud noise, such as an explosion, is produced at or just below the earth's surface. The sound waves that result travel into the earth and are reflected back to the surface by underground rock layers. In populated areas, a *vibroseis truck,* also called a *thumper truck,* may be used to produce the sound waves. A thumper truck has a huge vibrating pad that repeatedly strikes the earth. In offshore areas, sound waves are produced by sending a compressed-air discharge or electronic pulse from a ship into the water.

Groups of *geophones,* which are similar to microphones, pick up the reflected sound waves. The pattern of the sound waves is recorded on an instrument called a *seismograph* (see **Seismograph**). Sound waves change in *amplitude* (height) when they are reflected from rocks that contain gas. These changes in amplitude appear as irregularities, called *bright spots,* on the seismograph record.

Producing gas. Drilling for gas involves the same methods as those used in drilling for oil. The most common method is *rotary drilling.* It is much like making a hole in wood with a carpenter's drill. Another method, *cable-tool drilling,* is used chiefly to make shallow holes in soft rock. It is similar to punching a hole in wood with a hammer and a nail. For detailed information on drilling and other operations in the production of both gas and oil, see **Petroleum** (Drilling an oil well; Recovering petroleum).

Offshore wells are drilled in water as much as 8,000 feet (2,400 meters) deep. The North Sea and the Gulf Coast waters of the United States are among the richest offshore producing areas. Offshore drilling is usually much more productive than drilling on land, chiefly because much less gas and oil have been taken from beneath the sea. But offshore drilling costs several times more. Instead of simply drilling down from land, offshore drillers must work from a barge, a movable rig, or a fixed platform. See **Petroleum** (pictures: Offshore drilling).

Transmitting and distributing gas. The raw natural gas that flows from a well must be cleaned and treated before it is distributed. A pipe called a *gathering line* carries the gas from the well to an *extraction unit,* which removes such impurities as dust, sulfur, and water. The gas may then flow to nearby processing plants, which remove butane, propane, gasoline, and other substances not needed in the fuel. The processed natural gas is then fed into underground, long-distance *transmission pipelines,* which carry it to communities along their routes.

Gas is sent through transmission pipelines under high pressures—usually about 1,000 pounds per square inch (70 kilograms per square centimeter). The pressure drops along the route because of the friction of the gas against the pipe walls. The pressure in the transmission pipeline also falls when communities remove gas. *Compressor stations* along the line restore high pressure and push the gas on to its farthest destination. Many lines have automatically operated stations that increase or decrease the pressure to meet the demands of various communities.

Gas usually travels through pipelines at about 15

Where natural gas comes from

Natural gas deposits occur throughout the world. The map at right and pictures below show where gas is located and how it is found, transported, and processed for commercial use.

Geo Data Corporation

Exploring for gas may begin with *thumper trucks*. They send sound waves into the earth that aid in locating gas deposits.

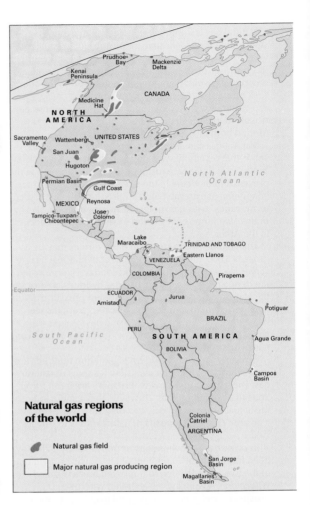

Natural gas regions of the world

Natural gas field

Major natural gas producing region

© Ted Czocowski, Image Finders

Drilling a well is the only sure way to find out if an area has gas. Tall derricks hold the well-drilling equipment.

Northern Illinois Gas Company

Laying underground pipelines requires digging trenches. Pipelines carry gas from producing fields to market areas.

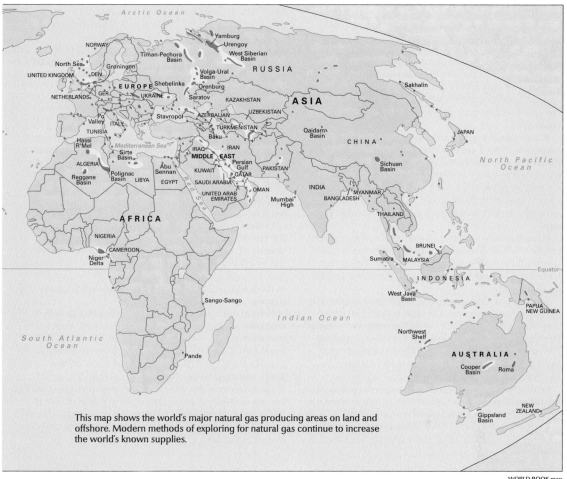

This map shows the world's major natural gas producing areas on land and offshore. Modern methods of exploring for natural gas continue to increase the world's known supplies.

WORLD BOOK map

David R. Frazier

Storing gas assures users of a constant supply. The tank shown above holds natural gas.

Cameramann International, Ltd., from Marilyn Gartman

At a coal gasification plant, coal is converted to *substitute natural gas,* which serves as a fuel to heat homes.

miles (24 kilometers) per hour. If gas produced in Texas starts its journey on a Monday morning, it will reach New York City on Friday afternoon.

Inspectors on foot and in airplanes check continually for conditions that might damage the pipelines. After floods and heavy rains, for example, inspectors check to see whether the earth covering the pipelines has been washed away. In addition, instruments installed along the pipelines automatically report leaks and other faulty conditions.

In cities and towns, *distribution lines* carry the gas to consumers. There are two kinds of distribution lines— *mains* and *individual service lines.* Mains are large pipes connected to the transmission pipelines. Service lines are smaller pipes that branch out from the mains. The service lines carry the fuel sold by gas utility companies to homes, factories, restaurants, hotels, and other buildings.

Gas utility companies add a chemical to the gas that can be smelled. They add this chemical because pure natural gas is odorless and would not be noticed if it leaked out. For more information on pipelines, see the article **Pipeline.**

Storing gas. Consumers use much more natural gas in winter than in summer. On bitterly cold days, they may use six times as much gas as they use on hot days. Pipelines cannot carry enough gas to meet consumer demand for fuel on the coldest days. As a result, gas must be stored when the demand is low for use when the demand is high.

During the summer, many gas companies pump great quantities of natural gas back into the ground. Most underground storage areas are old gas or oil fields that are no longer productive, or other porous rock formations. In Colorado, an abandoned coal mine has been turned

into a gas storage cavern. Ideal storage areas lie near pipelines, compressor stations, and—most important of all—large market areas.

If a gas company selects a nonproductive gas or oil field for storage, it must prepare the site to receive and hold gas. The company may have to repair, clean, or replace the well *casings* (large pipes put down the well to keep it from caving in). The firm also may have to redrill the old well or drill a new one.

To find and prepare underground storage sites, geologists and engineers use methods like those employed in exploring and drilling for gas or oil. After a new storage field has been prepared and tested, huge machines pump in the gas under high pressure. When the company removes the stored gas to meet heavy demand in cold weather, it cleans and treats the fuel before sending it to consumers.

Underground storage reservoirs are also important in the conservation of natural gas. Before the wide use of reservoirs, oil drillers often *flared* (burned) the natural gas found in an oil well to get rid of it during periods of low demand. Some of the great oil-producing countries in the Middle East still waste a large amount of gas in this way.

Natural gas is also stored through *liquefaction*—by changing it into a liquid. Gas becomes liquid when its temperature is lowered to about -260 °F (-162 °C). Raising the temperature returns the fuel to its gaseous form. Liquid natural gas (LNG) requires much less storage space than natural gas. Natural gas takes up about 600 times as much space. LNG can also be shipped overseas. For use in large volumes, LNG is more practical than LP gas or other liquid gases because it has the same chemical makeup as natural gas. As a result, suppliers can easily switch between LNG and natural gas.

Leading natural gas producing countries

Marketed production of gas in a year

Country	Production
Russia	●●●●●●●●●●●●●● 20,168,000,000,000 cu. ft. (571,090,000,000 m³)
United States	●●●●●●●●●●●●● 19,866,000,000,000 cu. ft. (562,540,000,000 m³)
Canada	●●●●◖ 6,504,000,000,000 cu. ft. (184,170,000,000 m³)
United Kingdom	●● 3,141,000,000,000 cu. ft. (88,940,000,000 m³)
Netherlands	●● 2,987,000,000,000 cu. ft. (84,580,000,000 m³)
Algeria	●◖ 2,643,000,000,000 cu. ft. (74,840,000,000 m³)
Indonesia	●◖ 2,422,000,000,000 cu. ft. (68,580,000,000 m³)
Iran	●◖ 1,787,000,000,000 cu. ft. (50,600,000,000 m³)
Uzbekistan	● 1,737,000,000,000 cu. ft. (49,190,000,000 m³)
Norway	● 1,673,000,000,000 cu. ft. (47,370,000,000 m³)

Figures are for 1997.
Source: U.S. Energy Information Administration.

Leading natural gas producing states and provinces

Marketed production of gas in a year

Texas	●●●●●●●●●●●●● 6,319,000,000,000 cu. ft. (178,927,000,000 m³)
Louisiana	●●●●●●●●●●● 5,288,000,000,000 cu. ft. (149,736,000,000 m³)
Alberta	●●●●●●●●◖ 4,727,000,000,000 cu. ft. (133,862,000,000 m³)
Oklahoma	●●●◖ 1,645,000,000,000 cu. ft. (46,568,000,000 m³)
New Mexico	●●● 1,501,000,000,000 cu. ft. (42,506,000,000 m³)
Wyoming	●◖ 761,000,000,000 cu. ft. (21,558,000,000 m³)
British Columbia	●◖ 732,000,000,000 cu. ft. (20,727,000,000 m³)
Colorado	●◖ 696,000,000,000 cu. ft. (19,718,000,000 m³)
Kansas	●◖ 607,000,000,000 cu. ft. (17,177,000,000 m³)
Alabama	●◖ 564,000,000,000 cu. ft. (15,964,000,000 m³)

Figures are for 1998.
Source: U.S. Energy Information Administration; Statistics Canada.

How natural gas was formed. Most scientists believe that natural gas was formed millions of years ago, when water covered much more of the earth's surface than it does today. Down through the ages, tremendous quantities of tiny marine organisms called *plankton* died and settled to the ocean floors (see **Plankton**). There, fine sand and mud drifted down over the plankton. Layer upon layer of these deposits piled up. The great weight of the deposits, plus bacteria, heat, and other natural forces, changed the chemical compounds in the plankton into natural gas and oil. The gas and oil flowed into the holes in limestone, sandstone, and other kinds of porous rocks. Layers of solid rocks formed over the porous rocks and sealed the gas and oil beneath them. Later, movements in the earth's crust caused the ancient seas to draw back, and dry land appeared over many gas and oil deposits.

The composition of natural gas. Pure natural gas is made up of chemical compounds of the elements hydrogen and carbon. These compounds are called *hydrocarbons*. Some hydrocarbons are naturally gaseous, some are liquid, and some are solid. A hydrocarbon's form depends on the number and arrangement of the hydrogen and carbon atoms in the hydrocarbon molecule. See **Hydrocarbon.**

Natural gas is composed chiefly of methane, the lightest hydrocarbon. In a methane molecule, one atom of carbon is bound together with four atoms of hydrogen. Its chemical formula is CH_4. Other gaseous hydrocarbons usually found in natural gas include ethane (C_2H_6), propane (C_3H_8), and butane (C_4H_{10}). Natural gas that is impure may contain such gases as carbon dioxide, helium, and nitrogen. See **Butane and propane; Ethane; Methane.**

When natural gas burns, the hydrocarbon molecules break up into atoms of carbon and hydrogen. The atoms combine with the oxygen in the air and form new substances. The carbon and oxygen form carbon dioxide (CO_2), an odorless, colorless gas. The hydrogen and oxygen produce water vapor (H_2O). As the molecules break up and recombine, heat is released. Heat is measured in *Btu's* (British thermal units) in the customary system of measurement, or in *calories* in the metric system. One cubic foot (28,316 cubic centimeters) of burning gas releases about 1,000 Btu's, or 252,000 calories. See **British thermal unit; Calorie.**

How gas is manufactured. Gas is manufactured for its chemical by-products and for use as fuel. In the United States, manufactured gas accounts for only about 1 per cent of the total amount of gas that is consumed. There are several types of manufactured gas. The most important are coke oven gas, also called coal gas, and acetylene.

Coke oven gas is made by roasting coal. As the coal turns into coke, vapors consisting of many chemicals escape from the coal. The vapors are sent through water, which absorbs some of the unwanted chemicals. The rest of the gas bubbles up through the water. This gas may be further purified by various processes that remove chemical by-products. Coke oven gas has a much lower heating value than natural gas. See **Coke oven gas.**

Acetylene is produced chiefly by dropping water onto calcium carbide, a compound of calcium and carbon. It is also made by breaking apart methane molecules by heating them. Acetylene has a higher heating value than natural gas. It produces a very hot flame. Acetylene is used in welding and cutting metals. See **Acetylene.**

Other manufactured gases include oil gas, producer gas, and water gas. *Oil gas* is produced by breaking apart petroleum molecules by spraying the oil onto hot bricks. *Producer gas* is made by sending air slowly through a deep bed of hot coal or coke. The oxygen in the air combines with the carbon in the coal, forming carbon monoxide. *Water gas* is made by forcing steam through a hot bed of coal or coke, forming carbon monoxide and hydrogen.

How natural gas was formed Ages ago, the remains of tiny marine organisms sank to the sea floors and were buried by sediments, *left.* The decaying matter became gas and oil trapped in porous rock under nonporous rock, *center.* Later, the earth's crust shifted, and dry land appeared over many deposits, *right.*

WORLD BOOK diagram by George Suyeoka

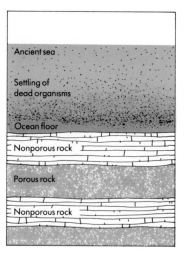 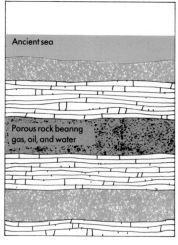 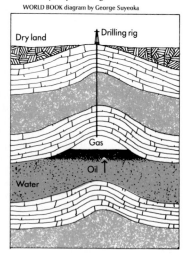

History of the gas industry

Early uses of natural gas. The ancient Chinese were the first people known to use natural gas for industrial purposes. Thousands of years ago, they discovered natural gas deposits and learned to pipe the fuel through bamboo poles. They burned the gas to boil away salty water and collect the salt that remained.

As early as the A.D. 500's, temples with "eternal" fires were built in western Asia, near what is now Baku, Azerbaijan. Worshipers came from as far as Persia and India to see the mysterious, continuous fires and wonder at the power of the temple priests. Secret pipes carried natural gas into the shrines from nearby rock fractures.

First uses of manufactured gas. In 1609, Jan Baptista van Helmont, a Belgian chemist and physician, discovered manufactured gas. He found that a "spirit," which he named *gas,* escaped from heated coal. In the late 1600's, John Clayton, an English clergyman, roasted coal and collected the gas in animal bladders. He then punctured the bladders and lit the escaping gas.

In 1792, William Murdock, a British engineer, lighted his home with gas he made from coal. He lighted the outside of a factory with gaslight in 1802. By 1804, Murdock had installed 900 gaslights in cotton mills. He became known as the father of the gas industry.

The work of Murdock and other experimenters interested Frederick Albert Winsor, a German businessman. Winsor decided to manufacture gas on a large scale. He learned the process from Murdock and obtained a British patent for manufacturing gas in 1804. In 1807, Winsor and his partners staged the first public street lighting with gas—along London's Pall Mall. They formed the first gas company in 1812.

The first gas company in the United States was established in 1817 in Baltimore to light that city's streets. Canada's first gas company, formed in 1836, lighted the streets of Montreal.

Development of the natural gas industry began in the United States. The earliest known discoveries of natural gas in the country occurred in 1775. That year, French missionaries in the Ohio Valley reported seeing "pillars of fire," which probably were caused by seeping gas accidentally set on fire. Also in 1775, George Washington saw a "burning spring"—flames rising from water—near what is now Charleston, West Virginia.

In 1821, mysterious bubbles appeared in a well being drilled for water at Fredonia, New York. The driller gave up his efforts. Soon afterward, on the same site, a gunsmith named William Aaron Hart completed the first natural gas well in the United States. It was 27 feet (8 meters) deep. Hart piped the gas to nearby buildings, and it was burned for lighting. Another shallow natural gas well was drilled near Westfield, New York, in 1826.

The first company known to have distributed natural gas was formed in Fredonia in 1865. By then, about 300 U.S. companies were distributing manufactured gas. Oil was discovered near Titusville, Pennsylvania, in 1859, and natural gas development was nearly forgotten in the oil rush that followed. The gas found in the oil fields lacked both markets and pipeline systems.

The first "long-distance" pipeline was completed in 1872. This 25-mile (40-kilometer) wooden pipeline carried natural gas to hundreds of consumers in Rochester, New York. Also in 1872, the first iron pipeline for natural gas began carrying the fuel 5$\frac{1}{2}$ miles (9 kilometers) to Ti-

Natural gas in the United States

This graph shows proved reserves and marketed production of natural gas in the United States since the early 1900's. Reserves rose rapidly from the 1920's to the 1960's as new deposits were found. But since about 1970, few deposits have been found and reserves have fallen. The production of gas in the United States grew rapidly from the mid-1950's to the mid-1970's.

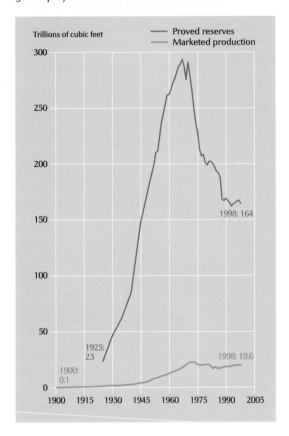

Trillions of cubic feet

— Proved reserves
— Marketed production

1998: 164
1925: 23
1900: 0.1
1998: 19.6

Proved reserves and marketed production

Year	Proved reserves In cubic feet (trillions)	Proved reserves In cubic meters (trillions)	Marketed production In cu. ft. (trillions)	Marketed production In m³ (trillions)
1900	Unknown	Unknown	0.13	0.004
1910	"	"	0.51	0.014
1915	"	"	0.63	0.018
1920	"	"	0.81	0.023
1925	23	0.7	1.20	0.034
1930	46	1.3	2.0	0.056
1935	62	1.8	2.0	0.056
1940	85	2.4	2.7	0.077
1945	147	4.2	4.0	0.11
1950	185	5.2	6.3	0.18
1955	223	6.3	9.4	0.27
1960	262	7.4	12.8	0.36
1965	287	8.1	16.0	0.45
1970	291	8.2	21.9	0.62
1975	228	6.5	20.1	0.57
1980	199	5.6	20.2	0.57
1985	193	5.5	17.2	0.49
1990	169	4.8	18.6	0.53
1995	165	4.7	19.5	0.55
1998	164	4.6	19.6	0.56

Sources: American Gas Association; U.S. Energy Information Administration.

tusville This pipeline delivered 4 million cubic feet (110,000 cubic meters) of gas daily to about 250 consumers.

In 1879, the American inventor Thomas A. Edison developed the first practical incandescent lamp. This development and the introduction of electric lighting nearly destroyed the gas industry. However, the industry started to grow again as more and more consumers turned to manufactured gas for cooking and water heating. Meanwhile, natural gas development remained at a standstill.

However, during the early 1900's, huge gas reserves were discovered in Texas, Louisiana, and Oklahoma. From 1906 to 1920, natural gas production in the United States more than doubled, to 800 billion cubic feet (23 billion cubic meters) a year. The lack of long-distance pipelines held back further growth in the industry. By 1925, there were $3\frac{1}{2}$ million natural gas consumers, but all were within a few hundred miles or kilometers of the gas fields.

The natural gas industry began to expand rapidly in the late 1920's with the introduction of seamless, electrically welded steel pipe. This pipe was stronger than earlier pipe. It could carry gas under higher pressures and, therefore, in greater quantities. With the new pipe, companies could profitably build lines over 1,000 miles (1,600 kilometers) long.

During the 1930's, the first gas came from Texas fields to cities in the Midwest. As more pipelines were built in the United States, more and more cities switched from manufactured gas to the much cheaper natural gas. The fuel became increasingly important for heating as well as for cooking.

The worldwide gas industry. Modern methods of exploring for natural gas have led to the greatest world supply of gas in history. A number of nations that had depended largely or entirely on manufactured gas have discovered large deposits of natural gas and are switching to the cheaper fuel. Producing countries are exporting an increasing amount of natural gas by new pipelines or in liquid form by tanker ships.

Russia produces more natural gas each year than any other country. The United States ranks second in annual production. Texas and Louisiana account for about two-thirds of all production in the United States. Canada is third in yearly production. The Netherlands ranks fourth in production and exports much gas to Germany, France, and Italy.

The gas industry, especially in the United States, is developing more efficient ways to use natural gas. See the *Gas in industry* section of this article for information on these advances. A device under development is a gas fuel cell. It produces electric power chemically, using methane from natural gas.

Natural gas is being used, mostly on an experimental basis, to power some automobiles, trucks, and ships. The growing problem of air pollution has created strong interest in natural gas as a transportation fuel. According to producers of gasoline, natural gas pollutes the air less than gasoline and diesel oil do.

During the late 1960's and early 1970's, consumption of gas in the United States was greater than the amount of newly discovered natural gas reserves. Although the United States has supplies of gas that will last for many years, some people became concerned about the declining reserves. These people feared that the United States was facing an energy crisis in which there would not be enough energy—from gas and other sources—to meet the demand for it. The gas industry has been exploring for additional sources of gas in the United States and throughout the world.

The nation's gas industry has also been seeking ways of producing gas from coal. In 1984, two plants that produce high-quality manufactured gas from coal began operating in the United States. Both of these plants rely heavily on financial support from the federal government (see **Coal** [Coal research]).   Robert C. Laudon

Study aids

Related articles in *World Book* include:

Acetylene	Gas oil
Butane and propane	Gasoline
Carbon monoxide	Hydrocarbon
Coal (Coal as a raw material)	Methane
Coke	Natural gas liquids
Coke oven gas	Petrochemicals
Energy supply	Petroleum
Ethane	Pipeline
Ethylene	Refrigeration
Gas meter	Synthetic fuel

Outline

I. **Uses of gas**
   A. Gas in the home
   B. Gas in industry
   C. Gas products
II. **From well to user**
   A. Exploring for gas
   B. Producing gas
   C. Transmitting and distributing gas
   D. Storing gas
III. **The chemical story of gas**
   A. How natural gas was formed
   B. The composition of natural gas
   C. How gas is manufactured
IV. **History of the gas industry**

Questions

How was natural gas formed?
What percentage of the fuel energy used in the United States and in Canada does natural gas provide?
Where is most gas produced in the United States?
Where was gas first used for street lighting? When?
What is a *bright spot?*
What does it indicate?
Why is storing gas important?
How do geologists and geophysicists help in exploring for natural gas?
With what other fuel is natural gas often found?
Why did the United States gas industry begin to expand rapidly in the late 1920's?
What percentage of wildcat wells strike gas or oil?

Additional resources

Bailey, Donna. *Energy from Oil and Gas.* Steck-Vaughn, 1991. Younger readers.
Cannon, James S. *Paving the Way to Natural Gas Vehicles.* IN-FORM, 1993.
Crowley, William R., ed. *Oil and Gas on the Internet.* Gulf Pub., 1996.
The Natural Gas Yearbook. Wiley, published annually.
Oppenheimer, Ernest J. *Natural Gas: The Best Energy Choice.* Pen & Podium, 1990.
Stevens, Paul, ed. *Oil and Gas Dictionary.* Nichols Pub., 1988.

Gas chamber is a legal means of execution in some states of the United States. The condemned person is strapped in a chair in an airtight chamber. Glass globes containing cyanide drop from beneath the chair and break in a crock containing sulfuric acid. The two chemicals mix and form deadly hydrocyanic acid gas. The person loses consciousness in seconds and usually dies within five minutes. For a list of states that use the gas chamber, see **Capital punishment** (table).

The first execution by lethal gas in the United States took place in Nevada in 1924. During World War II (1939-1945), the Nazis of Germany used huge gas chambers to kill Jews and other minorities in concentration camps. These executions were later classified as war crimes.   George T. Felkenes

Gas mask protects the wearer from breathing harmful gases into the lungs. The mask fits tightly over the face. Air can enter only through special filter pads that purify and filter the air. Activated charcoal purifies the air chemically. Filters remove all small particles of smoke, dust, or chemicals. The purifying materials are in the cheeks of present-day masks, which are often part of an entire protective suit. Older models had a breathing hose attached to a canister.

In World War I (1914-1918), masks were used to protect troops against gas attacks. Gas was not used in World War II (1939-1945), but armies had masks in case gas warfare began. During the Persian

David R. Frazier

Gas mask

Gulf War in 1991, gas masks were issued to troops and civilians in areas where it was feared Iraq would strike with chemical weapons. But Iraq did not use such weapons. Miners, workers in chemical industries, and fire fighters often use gas masks.   Frances M. Lussier

Gas meter is a device for measuring the volume of gas used. It usually is a tight metal box divided through the center into two separate chambers, or *bellows*. Each

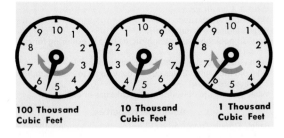

100 Thousand Cubic Feet   **10 Thousand Cubic Feet**   **1 Thousand Cubic Feet**

Reading a gas meter. The meter may have three or four main dials. Begin with the left-hand dial and read the figure at which the hand points on each dial. If the hand rests between two figures, use the lower of the two figures. But on the right-hand dial, use the figure to which the hand is closest. The dials shown here read 5, 4, and 6. You add two ciphers and get 54,600. From this, subtract the meter reading shown on the last gas bill. The result will be the cubic feet of gas used since the last reading.

chamber has a movable partition which divides it into two parts, making four separate chambers in all.

The gas is measured by first filling and then emptying each of these four chambers, and automatically registering the number of times each chamber is filled and emptied. While one chamber is being filled another is being emptied, so that the consumer receives an even flow of gas at all times.

The upper part of the meter contains the mechanism for registering the movement of the various chambers in cubic feet or cubic meters and showing the volume on a set of dials. Gas meters register volumes of gas accurately. State authorities permit their legal use as measuring devices for periods as long as 21 years before requiring rechecking of the meter.   Evan Powell

Gas oil is one of the *fractions* (parts) into which petroleum is divided by distillation. Gas oil comes from about the "middle" of the still. It is heavier than gasoline and kerosene and lighter than *lube distillate* from which lubricating oils and waxes are made. The name *gas oil* comes from the use of this oil in the production of gas fuel. Gas oil is converted into such lighter petroleum fractions as gasoline and chemicals. It is also used for diesel oil and fuel oil. See also **Petroleum** (Refining petroleum).   Donald L. Stinson

Gas poisoning. See **Chemical-Biological-Radiological warfare; First aid** (Inhaled poisons).

Gascoigne, *GAS koyn,* **George** (1525?-1577), was an Elizabethan author who pioneered in many literary forms. His best-known play, *Supposes* (1566), was based on *I Suppositi* (1509) by Ludovico Ariosto, and was the first English adaptation of Italian comedy. *Supposes* was also the first English prose comedy, and brought the classical comedy of romance, disguise, and mistaken identity to English drama. Shakespeare used *Supposes* in the plot of *The Taming of the Shrew.* Gascoigne's poems influenced the work of Edmund Spenser.

Gascoigne's *The Adventures of Master F. J.* (1573) was one of the forerunners of the novel. He also produced courtly entertainments. The most ambitious was *The Princely Pleasures at Kenilworth Castle,* with texts by Gascoigne and others. It was performed before Queen Elizabeth I in 1575. Gascoigne was born in Bedfordshire.
          Stephen Orgel

Gascony, *GAS kuh nee,* an old French province, lies between the Pyrenees Mountains and the Garonne River in southwest France (see **France** [terrain map]). It took its name from the *Vascons,* or Basques, who came from Spain in the 500's. The people grow corn, wheat, and fruits, and raise geese and turkeys. Cities include Auch, Biarritz, and the pilgrimage city of Lourdes.

The Franks conquered Gascony and organized it as a duchy under the late Carolingians. In the 1000's, Gascony became part of the Duchy of Aquitaine, which Henry II of England acquired in the 1100's. Gascony was the scene of constant fighting between French and English forces until the end of the Hundred Years' War. The French finally won the region then. According to tradition, the Gascons are brave and gallant, but somewhat given to boasting. The English word *gasconade* means bragging or blustering talk.   Hugh D. Clout

Gasification. See **Coal** (Coal as a raw material).

Gaskell, *GAS kuhl,* **Elizabeth** (1810-1865), an English writer, is best known for her novel *Cranford* (1853). The book is a lively account of life in the village of Knutsford, where she grew up. Mrs. Gaskell also wrote two novels—*Mary Barton* (1848) and *North and South* (1855)—that show her sympathy for the working class. She created believable characters and realistic backgrounds in her books. Mrs. Gaskell was born Elizabeth Cleghorn Stevenson in London.   Sharon Bassett

Gasoline is one of the most important fuels used for transportation. Most gasoline is used in engines that move automobiles and trucks. Gasoline engines also power such vehicles and machines as airplanes, motorboats, tractors, and lawn mowers. People in the United Kingdom and some other countries call gasoline *petrol* because it is made from petroleum.

The widespread use of gasoline began in the early 1900's, when the mass production of cars started. Gasoline-powered cars made travel easier. People no longer had to live near their jobs, and they could reach remote vacation spots more easily. Gasoline-powered farm machinery allowed for improved crop production.

Through the years, the increasing use of gasoline gave rise to a gigantic industry employing millions of people. However, the use of gasoline has also caused serious problems. For example, transporting petroleum and the manufacture and use of gasoline contribute heavily to air and water pollution. To solve these problems, gasoline manufacturers are developing gasolines that pollute the environment less.

How gasoline is produced

Most gasoline is made by separating and chemically changing the different compounds in petroleum. This process is called *refining*. For information on petroleum refining, see **Petroleum** (Refining petroleum).

Some gasoline comes from the natural gas found with petroleum. Gasoline manufacturers remove this *natural* or *casinghead* gasoline from the natural gas. The refiners then blend the natural gasoline with other gasoline. About 5 percent of the gasoline used in the United States comes from natural gas. Gasoline can be produced by many processes and made from anything containing the elements carbon and hydrogen. One of the most promising sources of gasoline for the future involves processing the oil contained in shale rock. But this source still costs too much for mass production.

Gasoline octane ratings

Gasoline is a blend of hundreds of chemical compounds called *hydrocarbons*. Most of the mixture consists of about 25 of those compounds. Each hydrocarbon in gasoline burns differently in an engine. See **Hydrocarbon.**

Gasolines are made with different combinations of hydrocarbons because all engines cannot run smoothly on the same combination. Engines differ according to how much they *compress* (squeeze) the mixture of evaporated gasoline and air within their cylinders. High-compression engines squeeze the fuel and air more than low-compression engines do. When an engine compresses the gasoline and air, the temperature of the mixture rises. The rise in temperature may ignite the gasoline before the piston is ready to receive the power from the burning gasoline. This process is called *autoignition* or *preignition*. The gasoline mixture may also

explode suddenly when the spark plug fires. These actions waste power and can damage an engine. They cause a "knocking" or "pinging" sound. To operate smoothly, a high-compression engine needs a gasoline more resistant to knocking than does a low-compression engine.

A gasoline's ability to resist knocking is called its *antiknock* quality. The *octane number* of a gasoline indicates the antiknock quality of the fuel. Engineers determine a gasoline's octane number by comparing its resistance to knocking with the antiknock performance of a *reference fuel*. A reference fuel is a mixture of two hydrocarbons called *isooctane* and *normal heptane.*

A gasoline's octane number equals the percentage of isooctane in a reference fuel that has the same antiknock quality as the gasoline. For example, if a gasoline knocks like a reference fuel containing 90 percent isooctane, its octane number is 90. Octane numbers above 100 are measured with a reference fuel containing pure isooctane and chemical antiknock compounds, such as *Methyl-tert-butyl ether* (MTBE). As automobile engines age, microscopic deposits form in the engine. These deposits cause engines to require gasoline with a higher octane number for knock-free operation. Thus, older cars often need higher-octane fuels.

Automobile engineers measure octane number in three ways. Thus, every gasoline has three octane numbers: (1) a *research octane number* (RON), (2) a *motor octane number* (MON), and (3) a *road octane number*. The RON is determined in a special one-cylinder engine in a laboratory. The MON is also determined in a test engine but under conditions more like those found in an ordinary engine. The road octane number is arrived at by comparing the gasoline with various reference fuels in a moving automobile. People generally use either the RON or an average of the RON and the MON to describe a gasoline's antiknock quality.

The RON is the highest octane number, the MON is from 6 to 10 numbers less, and the road octane number is somewhere between the two. For example, a gasoline with an RON of 95 may have an MON of 87 and a road octane of 90. The octane number quoted on the pump at a gas station is usually the average of the RON and the MON.

Gasoline blends and additives

Every brand of gasoline is a blend of different hydrocarbons and additives. The blend changes daily, depending on refinery conditions, so that the gasoline has a constant octane number. Manufacturers also blend gasolines to make engines run better at various altitudes, in different climates, and during different seasons. For example, in summer or in hot climates, gasoline refiners prepare blends containing few hydrocarbons that boil at low temperatures. The heat turns such hydrocarbons into a vapor. If the gasoline contained too many of these hydrocarbons, the resulting vapor could cause *vapor lock*, an interruption in the flow of gasoline to the engine.

Gasolines contain a number of additives. One important group of additives are special oxygen-containing chemicals called *oxygenates*. These chemicals have high octane numbers and may make up as much as 10 percent of a gasoline. Oxygenates include such alcohols as

Amoco Corporation

The octane number on a gasoline pump indicates the quality of the fuel, based on how efficiently it burns. These pumps display the octane number in a yellow square above the handle.

methanol, ethanol, and isopropanol; and a group of compounds called *ethers* that include methyl-tert-butyl ether, ethyl-tert-butyl ether (ETBE), methyl-tert-amyl ether (TAME), and diisopropyl ether (DIPE).

Gasolines also contain smaller amounts of a number of other additives. *Antioxidants* keep the gasoline from becoming gummy. *Anti-icers* prevent ice from clogging gas lines in winter. *Antirust* agents prevent tanks and fuel lines from rusting. *Detergents* and *deposit modifiers* clean off or prevent engine deposits caused by the burning of gasoline. *Metal deactivators* keep small amounts of metal impurities from changing the properties of gasoline.

History

In the early days of the petroleum industry, during the late 1800's, kerosene was by far the leading product of refineries. Refiners considered gasoline a useless by-product. The industry, when refining kerosene from crude oil, produced more gasoline than could possibly be used. Refineries threw away most of the gasoline.

People used only small amounts of gasoline, then called *stove naphtha,* in cookstoves built to burn it.

The mass production of cars, which began in 1908, greatly increased demand for gasoline. In 1913, refiners introduced a process that *cracked* (broke down) heavy fuel oils into the lighter ones that were used in gasoline.

In the early 1970's, U.S. petroleum refiners had difficulty in meeting gasoline demand. As a result, the government allowed increased oil imports and encouraged refiners to increase their capacity. The states reduced highway speed limits, and people were encouraged to use public transportation to save gasoline. Manufacturers began to produce smaller cars with more fuel-efficient engines. For a time, such energy conservation efforts led to a lower demand for gasoline. But gasoline consumption rose again in the 1980's.

Many efforts have been made to control air pollution resulting from the exhaust fumes from gasoline engines. The federal Clean Air Act of 1970 and amendments to the act in 1990 have led to many changes in the design of automobiles and the composition of gasoline.

The 1970 act required sharp reductions of hydrocarbons and carbon monoxide emissions. To meet the emission standards, American automobile manufacturers in 1975 introduced special devices called *catalytic converters* that reduce pollutants in automobile exhaust. At that time, gasoline manufacturers used the antiknock compound *tetraethyl lead* as an additive. Cars with catalytic converters, however, required unleaded gasoline for the converters to function efficiently (see **Catalytic converter**).

By the early 1980's, all new U.S. cars had catalytic converters. Gasoline manufacturers eliminated lead in most gasoline consumed in the United States by the early 1990's and added alcohols and ethers to increase octane ratings.

The 1990 amendments to the Clean Air Act ordered stricter regulations on motor vehicle emissions. It required retailers in areas with the worst carbon monoxide pollution to sell a cleaner-burning type of gasoline. The amendments also encouraged the development of alternative clean fuels, such as liquefied natural gas and pure methanol.

Today, further improvements in the design of car engines and the composition of gasolines are needed to reduce air pollution to acceptable levels. Gasoline manufacturers are working to decrease the amounts of certain hydrocarbons, including compounds called *olefins* and *aromatics* and compounds containing sulfur. Reducing these chemicals lowers the octane number of gasoline, so the use of oxygenates to increase octane has become more important. High levels of oxygenates also help reduce the amount of carbon monoxide produced by burning gasoline, especially in older cars.

In the United States, the Environmental Protection Agency requires gasolines sold in many U.S. cities to contain high levels of oxygenates during cold weather months, when carbon monoxide problems are most serious. Many other countries, including Japan and much of Europe, have made similar changes in the composition of gasoline.   Geoffrey E. Dolbear

See also **Air pollution; Fuel injection; Octane number; Transportation** (Problems of modern transportation); **Vapor lock.**

Gasoline engine is an engine that uses gasoline as a fuel. Inside the engine, the *combustion* (burning) of fuel mixed with air produces hot gases that expand against parts of the engine and cause them to move. For this reason, gasoline engines are called *internal-combustion* engines. The motion inside the engine is transferred outside it to turn wheels and propellers or to operate machines. In this way, a gasoline engine turns heat energy into mechanical work. The rate at which a gasoline engine produces work is usually measured in horsepower or watts (see **Horsepower**).

Gasoline engines are compact and light in weight for the power they produce. This makes them one of the most important types of engines for vehicles. Nearly all automobiles, lawn mowers, motorcycles, motor scooters, snowmobiles, and small tractors have gasoline engines. So do many trucks, buses, airplanes, and small boats. Gasoline engines may also be used as portable power plants—for example, to supply the power to run pumps and other machinery on farms.

Kinds of gasoline engines

There are two main types of gasoline engines, *reciprocating engines* and *rotary engines*. Reciprocating engines have pistons that move up and down or back and forth. A part called a *crankshaft* changes this reciprocating motion into rotary motion. A rotary engine, also known as a *Wankel* engine, uses devices called *rotors* instead of pistons. The rotors produce rotary motion directly. This article discusses reciprocating engines, the more common type. For information on rotary engines, see the *World Book* article on **Rotary engine.**

Reciprocating gasoline engines are classified in a number of ways. These include (1) by the number of piston strokes per cycle, (2) by the type of compression, (3) by the way they are cooled, (4) by their valve arrangement, (5) by their cylinder arrangement, and (6) by the way they are supplied with air and fuel.

Cycle. Most reciprocating gasoline engines operate on either a two-stroke or a four-stroke cycle. *Cycle* means the steps that must be repeated for each combustion of the fuel-air mixture in the cylinders. *Stroke* means the up-and-down or back-and-forth movements of the pistons. A *four-stroke* cycle engine has intake, compression, power, and exhaust strokes. A *two-stroke* cycle engine combines the exhaust and intake steps near the end of the power stroke. Although two-stroke cycle engines are less fuel-efficient than four-stroke cycle engines, they are simpler and cheaper to build. A two-stroke cycle engine is used where low cost is important, as in a power lawn mower. It delivers more power for a given weight and size than does a four-stroke cycle engine. Each cylinder in a two-stroke cycle engine produces a power stroke for every turn of the crankshaft. But in a four-stroke cycle engine, a cylinder produces a power stroke on every other turn.

High and low compression. As a piston moves from the bottom to the top of a cylinder, it compresses the air and gasoline mixture. A number, called the *compression ratio,* tells how much the mixture is compressed. A high-compression engine may have a compression ratio of 10 to 1. Such an engine compresses the mixture to a tenth of its original volume. A low-compression engine may have a ratio of 8 to 1.

High-compression engines burn gasoline more efficiently than do low-compression engines. But high-compression engines require high-octane gasoline (see **Octane number**). Until the 1970's, the octane level of gasoline depended on the amount of lead additives—the more lead, the higher the octane. In the mid-1970's, manufacturers began to equip automobiles with devices called *catalytic converters* that reduce the pollutants in automobile exhausts. Lead was found to interfere with the effectiveness of catalytic converters. Automobiles with catalytic converters had to use low-octane gasoline because high-octane lead-free gasoline was costly to

Leo Burnett Company

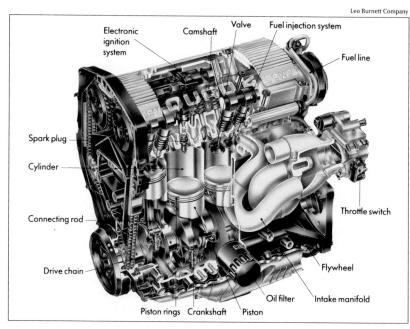

Basic parts of a gasoline engine

Reciprocating gasoline engines have the same basic parts. As the pistons move up and down, connecting rods turn the crankshaft. This cutaway diagram shows the parts of a four-cylinder automobile engine. Like many other engines today, it has an electronic ignition system for easy starting. It also has a fuel injection system instead of a carburetor for better fuel economy.

Electronic ignition system — Camshaft — Valve — Fuel injection system — Fuel line — Spark plug — Cylinder — Connecting rod — Throttle switch — Drive chain — Flywheel — Piston rings — Crankshaft — Piston — Oil filter — Intake manifold

**Gasoline engine
cylinder arrangement**

V-type engines have two rows of cylinders set at an angle. In-line engines have one row of cylinders. The cylinders of horizontal-opposed engines are opposite one another. Those of radial engines are set around the crankshaft. Rotary engines have rotor chambers instead of cylinders.

WORLD BOOK illustration

| **V-type** | **In-line** | **Horizontal opposed** | **Radial** | **Rotary** |

produce. As a result, the automobile industry reduced compression ratios so that engines could burn lower octane lead-free fuels efficiently.

Cooling. The burning fuel-air mixture in a cylinder produces gas temperatures of about 4500° F. (2500° C). Therefore, the metal parts of the engine must be cooled or they would melt. Most automotive gasoline engines are *liquid cooled.* A liquid, usually water, is circulated around the cylinders to cool the metal. The heated liquid is then pumped through a radiator. A fan driven by the engine or by an electric motor draws air through the radiator to cool the liquid.

Most aircraft gasoline engines in small planes are *air cooled* to reduce weight. Air is not as effective a coolant as liquids, so the outside of the cylinders have many metal fins. These fins conduct heat out of the cylinder and offer a large surface area for the air to sweep over.

Valve arrangement. The two most common valve arrangements are (1) L-head and (2) I-head. An *L-head,* or *underhead,* valve engine has the intake and exhaust valves side by side in the cylinder block. The *intake* valve admits the air-fuel mixture into the cylinder and the *exhaust* valve lets out the exhaust gases. An *I-head,* or *overhead,* valve engine has the two valves side by side in the cylinder *head,* the cylinder block's top cover. In some cars, each cylinder has four valves—two intake valves and two exhaust valves.

Cylinder arrangement. Engines are also classified by the number and arrangement of cylinders. The most common types include *in-line, V, radial,* and *horizontal opposed.* Radial engines have an odd number of cylinders, such as 3, 5, 7, or 9. Most other engines have an even number of cylinders—4, 6, 8, or 12.

Air and fuel. Fuel may be *metered,* or sent, to the cylinders by either a carburetor or an injection system. Therefore, reciprocating engines are also classified as *carbureted* or as *fuel-injected* engines (see **Carburetor; Fuel injection**). Because combustion depends upon both air and fuel, the power of an engine is limited by the amount of air reaching the cylinders. To increase power, an engine may be *supercharged* or *turbocharged.* A *supercharger* is an engine-driven pump, and a *turbocharger* is an exhaust-driven pump. Both pumps force extra air into the cylinders, increasing the engine power. The air needed to burn 1 unit of gasoline weighs about 15 times as much as the gasoline.

Parts of a reciprocating gasoline engine

Cylinder block is a rigid frame that holds the cylinders in proper alignment. If the engine is liquid cooled, the block is *jacketed,* or has passages for the liquid

around each cylinder. In automotive engines, the cylinder block and crankcase form a single unit. Most cylinder blocks are made of cast iron or aluminum.

Cylinders are rigid tubes that serve as a bearing for the pistons that move up and down inside them. They have highly polished surfaces. This permits a close fit between piston and cylinder and prevents gases from leaking past the piston. The cylinders in most automobile engines are part of the block. Some engines have a cylinder *sleeve* made of specially hardened steel or cast iron pressed into the cylinder block.

Cylinder head is a casting bolted to the top of the cylinder block. The cylinder head, together with the upper end of the cylinder and the top of the piston, form the *combustion chamber* where the fuel-air mixture burns. A cylinder head and block may be one unit.

Crankcase is a rigid frame that holds the crankshaft and the crankshaft bearings. In small engines, all or part of the crankcase may be part of the cylinder block.

Pistons and connecting rods. When the fuel-air mixture burns, the expanding gases exert a force on the *piston.* This force is then transmitted through a *connecting rod* to the crankshaft. The piston has two to six rings to prevent the gases from escaping past the piston and to keep lubricating oil from getting into the combustion chamber.

Crankshaft changes the reciprocating motion of the pistons into rotary motion. The crankshaft has a number of cranks, or *throws.* These cranks are displaced at angles to each other. For example, in a six-cylinder, in-line, four-stroke cycle engine, the cranks are displaced at 120° angles to each other. As a result, the engine delivers three equally spaced power strokes in each revolution of the crankshaft to assure smooth operation.

Flywheel stores energy during a piston's power stroke and releases it during other strokes. This helps turn the crankshaft at a constant speed (see **Flywheel**).

Valves. In a four-stroke cycle engine, each cylinder has one or two intake valves, to let the air-fuel mixture into the combustion chamber, and one or two exhaust valves, to let the burned gases escape. These are called *poppet valves,* because they pop up and down as they open and close. The opening in the cylinder block or head uncovered by the valve is called the *port.* In many two-stroke cycle engines, the movement of the piston takes the place of separate valves. As the piston moves, it covers and uncovers the ports.

Camshaft runs the length of the engine and has one *cam* (lobe) at each intake and exhaust valve. The cams open and close the valves at the proper point in the engine cycle. In a four-stroke cycle engine, the camshaft is geared to the crankshaft so that it runs at half the crankshaft's speed. The camshaft may be in the head of an overhead valve engine, or in the crankcase.

Fuel system includes (1) a *storage tank* for gasoline, (2) *fuel lines* to carry the gasoline to the carburetor, (3) a *carburetor* to mix the gasoline with air, and (4) an *intake manifold* to distribute the fuel-air mixture to the cylinders. The fuel system also includes a *gasoline filter* to clean dirt out of the fuel and an *air cleaner* to take dirt out of the air that is mixed with the gasoline. In addition, the system may include a *governor* to limit the engine's speed. See **Carburetor; Governor.**

Some gasoline engines have a *fuel injection system* instead of a carburetor. Fuel injection controls and distributes the fuel-air mixture better than a carburetor does. It can improve fuel economy and reduce exhaust emissions. See **Fuel injection.**

Exhaust system consists of one or more parts. It may include (1) an *exhaust manifold* to collect the burned gases from the cylinders, (2) an *exhaust pipe* to carry the burned gases, and (3) a *muffler* to silence the noise of the exhaust gases. See **Muffler.**

Ignition system is the electrical circuit necessary to set fire to, or *ignite,* the fuel-air mixture in the different cylinders at different times. In an automobile a *storage battery* provides electric current, which is increased in voltage by an *induction coil.* The high-voltage current is carried through a *distributor,* which delivers the electricity to each cylinder at about the moment the piston reaches the top of the compression stroke. There the electric current jumps a gap between two terminals and sets fire to the gasoline-air mixture. The terminals are encased in insulating material and called a *spark plug.* See **Battery; Ignition.**

Some automobile engines have an electronic ignition system. These systems use electronic parts, such as capacitors and transistors, to produce the ignition voltage and to control it. Electronic ignition systems may use a

How a two-stroke cycle gasoline engine works

A cycle begins when the piston moves up the cylinder during the intake-compression stroke, *below left.* The piston sucks a fuel-air mixture into the crankcase for the next cycle and compresses the mixture already in the cylinder. When the piston reaches the top, the spark plug ignites the mixture. Burning gases push the piston down for the power-exhaust stroke, *below right.* As the piston uncovers the exhaust port, the gases escape and a fresh mixture enters the cylinder through the intake port.

WORLD BOOK diagram

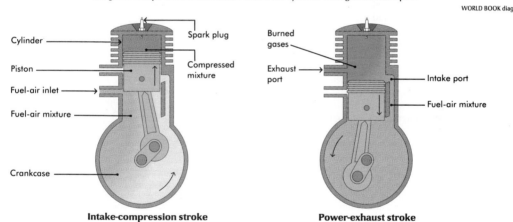

Intake-compression stroke   **Power-exhaust stroke**

How a four-stroke cycle gasoline engine works

A cycle begins with the intake stroke as the piston moves down the cylinder and draws in a fuel-air mixture. Next, the piston compresses the mixture while moving up the cylinder. At the top of the compression stroke, the spark plug ignites the mixture. Burning gases push the piston down for the power stroke. The piston then moves up the cylinder again, pushing the burned gases out during the exhaust stroke.

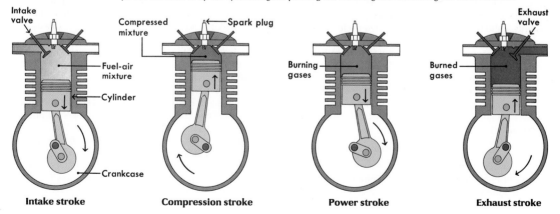

Intake stroke   **Compression stroke**   **Power stroke**   **Exhaust stroke**

distributor to deliver the electricity to each cylinder, or the electricity may be delivered directly to the cylinders. Electronic systems require less maintenance than do ordinary systems and provide better engine performance.

In an airplane engine, the high-voltage electric current may be generated by a *magneto* and carried to the spark plugs. A magneto does not require a battery to operate. See **Magneto**.

Lubrication system provides oil as a film between the moving parts of the engine to prevent wear from friction and to keep the engine cool. The two common types of four-stroke cycle engine lubrication systems are the *wet sump* and the *dry sump*. In the wet-sump engine, the oil supply is contained within the engine, in the bottom of the crankcase. In the dry-sump engine, the oil supply is contained in a separate oil tank.

Some two-stroke cycle engines, such as those used on lawn mowers, motorcycles, and boats, have no separate lubrication system. Users of these engines mix a small amount of lubricating oil with the gasoline. Larger heavy-duty two-stroke cycle engines have lubrication systems that are similar to those on four-stroke cycle engines.

Development of the gasoline engine

Early internal-combustion engines used gases instead of gasoline as fuel. The Reverend W. Cecil read a paper before the Cambridge Philosophical Society in England, in 1820, describing experiments with an engine driven by the explosion of a mixture of hydrogen and air. It is believed to be the earliest working gas engine.

Another English inventor, William Barnett, in 1838 patented a gas engine which compressed the fuel mixture. Barnett's engine had a single up-and-down cylinder with explosions occurring first at the top, then at the bottom, of the piston.

In France, Jean Joseph Étienne Lenoir patented the first practical internal-combustion engine in 1860. It used coke oven gas for fuel. This single-cylinder engine had a storage-battery ignition system. By 1865, about 500 of these engines were being used for such jobs as powering printing presses, lathes, and water pumps. Lenoir also installed one of his engines in a crude motor vehicle.

In 1862, another Frenchman, Beau de Rochas, worked out on paper the idea of the four-cycle engine. But he did not build one. Four years later, Nikolaus August Otto and Eugen Langen of Germany built a successful four-cycle gas engine. In 1876, Otto and Langen obtained patents in the United States on both two-cycle and four-cycle gas engines.

The first successful four-cycle engine to burn gasoline was designed in 1885 by Gottlieb Daimler, a German engineer. In the same year, Karl Benz, another German, also developed a successful gasoline engine. These engines were basically the same as gasoline engines built today. For later development of the gasoline engine, see **Automobile**.

Air pollution controls

Automobile gasoline engines produce certain air pollutants. In 1965, the Congress of the United States amended the Clean Air Act of 1963 to include *emission standards* for automobiles. The 1965 amendment and the Clean Air Act of 1970 with its later amendments established legal limits on the amount of pollutants automobiles may produce. The Environmental Protection Agency (EPA) enforces the Clean Air Act and its amendments.

To meet EPA standards, automakers made a number of modifications in engine design during the 1970's. They began to install catalytic converters on new cars to reduce emissions of pollutants (see **Automobile** [Environmental impact]). Today, automobiles with electronic engine control have a device called an *oxygen sensor* in the exhaust system. The sensor signals the electronic engine control to adjust the fuel-air mixture for the most effective operation of the catalytic converter.

William H. Haverdink

Related articles in *World Book* include:

Parts of a gasoline engine

Battery	Ignition
Carburetor	Induction coil
Flywheel	Magneto
Fuel injection	Starter
Governor	

Other related articles

Airplane (Reciprocating engines)	Free-piston engine
Antifreeze	Gasoline
Automobile	Horsepower
Benz, Karl	Lenoir, Jean Joseph Étienne
Catalytic converter	Rotary engine
Daimler, Gottlieb	Transmission
Diesel engine	Turbine (Gas turbines)
Engine analyzer	Vapor lock

Additional resources

Lumley, John L. *Engines.* Cambridge, 1999.
Roth, Alfred C. *Small Gas Engines.* Rev. ed. Goodheart, 2000.
Stagner, Eugene. *Small Engines.* Prentice Hall, 1998.
Suzuki, Takashi. *The Romance of Engines.* Soc. of Automotive Engineers, 1997.

Gasoline tax is a tax on the purchase of gasoline. This tax, commonly known as a motor fuel tax, is paid chiefly by road and highway users. Off-the-highway users of motor fuel, including the operators of airplanes, some boats, and farm machinery, also pay the tax but get a partial refund. Diesel fuel and other types of fuels are also taxed. The United States government and all the states levy motor fuel taxes. The governments use the revenues to build and improve roads.

Different types of motor fuels are taxed at different rates. In addition, the rates vary among the states. In some cases, the rate depends on the number of axles on the vehicle in which the fuel is used.   Vito Tanzi

See also **Road** (How roads and highways are paid for).

Gaspar. See Magi.

Gaspé Peninsula, *gas PAY,* is the mountainous southeastern part of the province of Quebec. It lies south of the Saint Lawrence River and reaches the Gulf of Saint Lawrence north of Chaleur Bay. For location, see **Quebec** (terrain map).

Gaspé Peninsula is 150 miles (241 kilometers) long and from 70 to 85 miles (113 to 137 kilometers) wide. It has 450 miles (724 kilometers) of coastline and covers over 11,000 square miles (28,500 square kilometers). The highest point is Mount Jacques Cartier (4,160 feet, or 1,268 meters). About 200,000 people live on the peninsula. The area's economic activities include tourism, paper production, and copper mining.   Robin B. Burns

See also **Quebec** (picture).

Gastritis, *gas TRY tihs,* is an inflammation of the stomach. A person with gastritis may suffer from loss of appetite, pain, nausea, vomiting, and bleeding from the stomach. Gastritis may be either *acute* or *chronic.*

Acute gastritis may be caused by chemical or acid injury to the stomach lining. It often occurs because of excessive intake of alcoholic beverages or aspirin. Severe injury to the stomach may result if a person swallows such harmful chemicals as iodine, carbolic acid, or lye. Physicians treat the patient with an antidote or by cleansing the stomach. *Chronic gastritis* may occur during such conditions as stomach cancer, stomach ulcers, and duodenal ulcers. It may also occur after stomach surgery. One form, called *pernicious anemia,* causes *atrophy* (wasting away) of the stomach lining and leads to vitamin B_{12} deficiency.   Andrew G. Plaut

Gastropod. See Mollusk (Gastropods).

Gastroscope, *GAS truh skohp,* is an instrument used by physicians to examine the inside of the stomach. Doctors also use it when examining the esophagus and the upper part of the small intestine.

A gastroscope consists of a long, flexible rubber tube and a rigid metal section that has a lens and various controls. Two bundles of long, thin glass threads called *optical fibers* extend along the inside of the tube.

The physician lowers the tube through the mouth and esophagus and into the stomach. Light travels through one of the bundles of optical fibers and strikes the wall of the stomach. The fibers in the other bundle absorb the light after it is reflected off the stomach wall. They produce an image of the illuminated part of the stomach by transmitting this light to the lens of the gastroscope.

Physicians use a gastroscope to determine the cause of internal bleeding and to help diagnose cancer. A gastroscope can be fitted with various special attachments to photograph tumors and ulcers, to cut out growths called *polyps,* or to remove objects that have been swallowed. A gastroscope can also guide a laser used to destroy tumors in the esophagus or to stop bleeding in the stomach or intestine. Another type of gastroscope has a miniature video camera in its tip.   James L. Franklin

See also **Endoscope** (picture).

Gates, Bill (1955-   ), is a cofounder and the chairman of Microsoft Corporation. From 1975 until 2000, he also served as Microsoft's chief executive officer. Microsoft is the world's largest developer and publisher of software programs for personal computers.

William Henry Gates was born in Seattle. He set up his first software company at age 15 with a schoolmate named Paul Allen. In 1975, he and Allen began to design programs for personal computers, which had just entered the marketplace. The two founded Microsoft that year. In 1980, International Business Machines Corporation (IBM) chose Microsoft to develop the operating system for its first personal computer, the PC. An *operating system* is a special type of program that contains instructions for the operation of the computer. Gates devised the Microsoft Disk Operating System (MS-DOS) for IBM. Millions of copies of MS-DOS were sold for use in IBM and IBM-compatible PC's.

Microsoft continued to grow under Gates's guidance.

In 1985, the company introduced the first of a series of PC programs called Windows. These programs enable users to perform multiple tasks through "windows" on the computer screen and to issue commands by pointing at onscreen symbols rather than by typing instructions. Microsoft has sold millions of copies of Windows.

In 1998, the United States Department of Justice and 20 state attorneys general filed an antitrust suit against Microsoft. The lawsuit charged that Microsoft used unfair practices to destroy its competition in the computer industry. In April 2000, U.S. District Judge Thomas Penfield Jackson ruled that Microsoft had violated U.S. antitrust laws by abusing its monopoly in personal computer operating systems. Microsoft appealed the order.   Keith Ferrell

See also **Gates Foundation.**

Gates, Horatio (1728?-1806), was an American Revolutionary War general. He forced British General John Burgoyne to lay down his arms at Saratoga, New York, in 1777.

Gates was born in England and entered the British Army as a boy. With George Washington, he survived General Edward Braddock's defeat in 1755 and served in America through the French and Indian War (see **French and Indian wars**). In 1761, he served with General Robert Monckton at the conquest of Martinique. Gates retired from the army in 1765.

At the beginning of the Revolutionary War, Congress named Gates adjutant general. He later took command of the Continental Army in the North. After Saratoga, in the winter of 1777-1778, some, including members of the Continental Congress, wanted Gates to replace Washington as commander in chief. But Washington kept his command.

Gates became president of the Board of War, and in 1780 he took command of American troops in the South. British troops under General Charles Cornwallis almost destroyed Gates's army at Camden, South Carolina, in August 1780. General Nathanael Greene replaced Gates in December of that year. Gates again served under Washington and returned to Virginia after the war. Later, he moved to New York.   Paul David Nelson

See also **Revolutionary War in America** (Victory at Saratoga; Camden); **Washington, George** (The Army).

Gates Foundation is the largest charitable foundation in the world. It was established in 1999 by Bill Gates and his wife, Melinda. Bill Gates is the chairman and chief software architect of Microsoft Corporation. Microsoft is the world's largest developer and publisher of software programs for personal computers. The full name of the foundation is the Bill & Melinda Gates Foundation. See also **Gates, Bill.**

The foundation focuses its giving in the areas of global health and learning. It funds programs that are designed to improve the health of people in less developed countries. One such program provides vaccines to protect children from disease. The foundation also makes grants to provide scholarships for minority students, to make technology more accessible to disadvantaged children, and to provide computers and Internet access to public libraries in low-income communities. The foundation has headquarters in Seattle. For assets, see **Foundations** (table).

Critically reviewed by the Bill & Melinda Gates Foundation

Gates of the Arctic National Park is in north-central Alaska. It lies north of the Arctic Circle (see **Alaska** [political map]). Geographical features of the park include part of the Brooks mountain range, treeless areas called *tundra,* winding rivers, broad valleys, and glacial lakes. The park is noted for its scenic wilderness. Its wildlife includes Dall's sheep, grizzly bears, moose, wolves, and great herds of caribou. There is evidence that toolmaking people lived in the area about 7,000 years ago. The area was proclaimed a national monument in 1978 and became a national park in 1980. For the park's area, see **National Park System** (table: National parks).   Critically reviewed by the National Park Service

Gatling, Richard Jordan (1818-1903), was an American inventor. Gatling spent most of his life improving agricultural methods, but he is best known as the inventor of the Gatling gun. His gun was the first practical, quick-firing machine gun developed in the United States. Patented in 1862, the Gatling gun was used only to a limited extent during the American Civil War (1861-1865). But improved models became standard equipment for the U.S. Army and Navy in the Spanish-American War (1898). Gatling also invented agricultural machinery. He was born the son of a planter in North Carolina. See also **Machine gun** (picture: Early machine guns [Gatling gun]).   Merritt Roe Smith

GATT. See **General Agreement on Tariffs and Trade.**

Gatun Lake, *gah TOON,* is an artificial body of water, 85 feet (26 meters) above sea level. It was created in 1912 by damming the Chagres River on the Isthmus of Panama. The Panama Canal crosses Gatun Lake through the Gatun locks on the lake's west side. Gatun Lake covers an area of 163.38 square miles (423.15 square kilometers). A narrow strip of land on the north separates it from the Caribbean Sea. The lake has a rugged coastline and contains many islands. Its water provides part of the route for the Panama Canal and is also used to operate the locks. Gatun Dam, 115 feet (35 meters) high, formed Gatun Lake. See also **Panama Canal** (Gatun Lake).

Gary Brana-Shute

Gaucher's disease, *goh SHAYZ,* is a severe hereditary disorder that affects the spleen, liver, bones, and, in some forms of the disease, the brain and nerves. Gaucher's disease results from the accumulation of a chemical called *glucocerebroside,* which forms as the body replaces worn-out tissues. In most people, this chemical is broken down by an enzyme known as *glucocerebrosidase.* Gaucher's patients do not produce enough glucocerebrosidase. As a result, glucocerebroside builds up in cells called *macrophages* in affected organs. These swollen Gaucher cells damage the organs.

There are three major forms of Gaucher's disease. Type 1, the most common form, can begin at any age. It is characterized by damage to certain bones and joints and by enlargement of the spleen and liver. Many type 1 patients die from complications of the disease, such as pneumonia or blood disorders. Type 1 disease primarily affects Jews of central or eastern European ancestry.

Type 2 and type 3 are rarer. Type 2 generally appears during the first six months of life. It is characterized by mental retardation, loss of muscle control, and enlargement of the spleen and liver. Most patients die by age 2. Type 2 has not been linked to any particular group of people. Type 3 begins during later childhood. It in-

cludes all the symptoms of type 1, plus mental retardation, poor coordination, and muscle weakness. Most patients die from disease-related complications between the ages of 15 and 30. Type 3 occurs mainly among persons of northern Swedish ancestry.

A person inherits two genes—one from each parent—that control production of the enzyme glucocerebrosidase. Gaucher's patients inherit an abnormal gene—called the Gaucher gene—from both parents. A person who inherits one normal gene and one Gaucher gene does not have Gaucher's disease but is a carrier of the disorder. If two carriers have children, each child has 1 chance in 4 of developing the disease. Doctors can usually determine if an unborn baby has Gaucher's disease by testing genes and enzyme levels in both the unborn baby and its parents.

A treatment called *enzyme replacement therapy* has been successful in treating the disorder. In this treatment, a form of glucocerebrosidase is slowly injected into the patient's blood. The enzyme is absorbed into macrophages, where it breaks down accumulated glucocerebroside.   Garret M. Ihler

Gaucho, *GOW choh,* is the cowboy of the South American pampas, or plains. Gauchos played an important part in the development of Argentina and Uruguay. *Peons* (day laborers) have largely replaced the gauchos in these countries.

The gaucho was usually of mixed Spanish and Indian blood. He was a skillful rider and spent most of his time on horseback. His costume was characterized by a wide silver belt, baggy trousers, and a bright scarf. In the early days the gaucho made his living by catching wild cattle and selling their hides in illegal trade on the Brazilian frontier. Sometimes he worked on a cattle ranch, or *estancia.* His tools, which also served as weapons, included the knife and the *bola,* a type of sling. See **Sling.**

The coming of the refrigerator ships led to development of the meat industry. This made cattle raising a big business, and ended the gaucho's way of life. Argentine and Uruguayan writers and musicians have found the gaucho tunes and legends a rich source of material for their works.   Paul B. Goodwin, Jr.

See also **Uruguay** (picture: Uruguayan cowboys); **Latin-American literature** (Romanticism).

Gaudí, *gow DEE,* **Antonio** (1852-1926), was a major Spanish architect. He developed an extremely personal style that featured vivid colors, curved surfaces, and flowing lines and spaces. Gaudí became especially noted for his skillful use of masonry. He often used curved or warped thin masonry shells and diagonal supports that resembled *flying buttresses,* which were external wall supports popular in Gothic architecture.

Gaudí was born in Reus. His full name was Antonio Gaudí i Cornet. Nearly all of Gaudí's buildings were constructed in Barcelona. His early designs reflect the taste in the late 1800's for color and for peasant or folk traditions. In Gaudí's work, this resulted in the use of colorful tiles of the sort used in Moorish architecture. Gaudí's Casa Vicens (1878-1880) began a modern revival in the use of tile in architecture. His best-known designs of the early 1900's include two houses, the Casa Batlló (1905-1907) and the Casa Milá (1905-1910). He also planned a hillside park called the Park Güell (begun in 1900 and unfinished). Gaudí's most famous structure is probably the unfinished Church of the Sagrada Familia. He supervised the construction of the church from 1884 until his death.   Nicholas Adams

Gauge, also called *gage,* is an instrument used for measurement. Gauges are used to measure such quantities as pressure, temperature, water level, and thickness. Two of the most common types of gauges are pressure gauges and water-level gauges. But people working in a great many different fields commonly use other kinds of specialized gauges in their work.

Pressure gauges measure pressure in enclosed vessels or containers, such as boilers or pipes. For pressure greater than that of the atmosphere, most gauges measure in units of pounds per square inch (psi) or kilograms per square centimeter (kg/cm²). Pressures below that of the atmosphere are usually measured in inches or centimeters of mercury.

A pressure gauge consists of a tube with a cross section shaped like an ellipse (see **Ellipse**). This tube is called a *Bourdon tube.* It is bent in a hook-shaped curve. When the pressure inside the tube becomes greater than the pressure outside of it, the elliptical cross section tends to become circular. At the same time, the pressure tends to straighten the Bourdon tube. Levers, gears, or other mechanisms transfer this motion to a pointer, which rotates around a fixed dial calibrated in pressure units.

Vacuum gauges measure pressure below the pressure of the atmosphere. Such gauges are constructed in the same manner as the gauges described above. However, when the pressure inside the Bourdon tube becomes less than the pressure outside the tube, the tube has a tendency to curl. This motion is also transmitted to a pointer that moves across a dial. The dial of a vacuum gauge is calibrated in inches or centimeters of mercury.

Water-level gauges usually consist of a glass tube connected to the side of a container. The level of the water in the container and the level of the water in the tube are the same. Markings on the tube indicate the height of water in the container.

Other types of gauges. *Wire* gauges are used to measure the thickness of wire. *Thickness* gauges are used by automobile mechanics to determine the clearance between the pistons and cylinders of automobile engines.   Gregory Benford

See also **Barometer; Micrometer; Pressure.**

Gauge is the size of certain things. See **Railroad** (Tracks); **Shotgun; Wire** (Sizes).

Gauguin, *goh GAN,* **Paul** (1848-1903), was a French artist. Gauguin developed an original, personal, decorative style of painting. In his best-known works, he emphasized simplified forms and flat planes enclosed by rhythmic lines. He painted with pure, brilliant colors that strongly influenced the Fauves and the expressionists of the early 1900's.

Early career. Eugene Henri Paul Gauguin was born in Paris. From 1865 to 1871, he served as a seaman in the merchant marine and in the French Navy. He then became a stockbroker in Paris, a position he held until he resigned in 1883 to devote himself to painting. Gauguin studied first with impressionist artist Camille Pissarro. He also experimented with the *pointillist* technique developed by the painters Georges Seurat and Paul Signac (see **Seurat, Georges**).

Oil painting on canvas (1889); Albright-Knox Art Gallery, Buffalo, New York

Gauguin's *The Yellow Christ* shows the decorative patterns, simplified forms, and intense color typical of the artist's style.

Historical Pictures Service
Paul Gauguin

Between 1886 and 1890, Gauguin made several visits to Brittany in northwestern France. By 1889, he led a group of artists called the *Pont-Aven school,* named for the Breton village where they first lived. The painters admired the local people for their simple lives and deep, almost superstitious faith. Such qualities, the artists felt, served as a contrast to the sophistication of Paris and helped them move beyond surface appearances to a truth about humanity's basic nature.

During his Pont-Aven period, Gauguin was one of the artists who formulated the philosophy of art called *synthetism.* Synthetism stressed flat planes and intense colors. Gauguin developed this style fully in *The Yellow Christ* (1889), showing three Breton women kneeling to contemplate the Crucifixion. So powerful is their faith that they experience a vision of Christ on the cross. The painting is characteristic of the Pont-Aven school in the simplicity of form, the blue outline around the figure of Jesus, and the apparently arbitrary use of primary colors in the landscape. Gauguin's Pont-Aven painting *The Vision After the Sermon* appears in the **Painting** article.

Gauguin in Tahiti. A trip to Martinique in 1887 sparked a longing in Gauguin for the tropics. In 1891, the French government gave him a grant to observe and paint Tahitian customs. He returned to Paris two years later but moved back to the South Pacific permanently in 1895. He lived in Tahiti and then in the Marquesas Islands, where he died.

Gauguin perceived Tahiti as a land of bright, warm colors and strong, beautiful people, unspoiled by Western civilization. His paintings from this period celebrate that beauty. But Gauguin also injected into his paintings his feelings about art and religion. His painting *Where Do We Come From? What Are We? Where Are We Going?* (1897) shows the human life cycle from infancy to old age. The landscape represents the fertility of nature. In the background, a Maori idol symbolizes the presence of a world beyond the earthly one.

Gauguin also created wood sculptures, ceramics, and prints. He described his early experience in Tahiti in the book *Noa Noa* (1897). A selection from his journals was published in 1918 after his death as *Avant et Après* (translated as *Intimate Journals*).   Ann Friedman

See also **Impressionism; Postimpressionism.**

Additional resources

Howard, Michael. *Gauguin.* Dorling Kindersley, 1992.
Sweetman, David. *Paul Gauguin: A Complete Life.* Simon & Schuster, 1996.

Gaul, *gawl,* is the English name for the region called *Gallia* by the Romans. Gaul occupied the territory that now consists of France, Belgium, Luxembourg, the part of Germany that lies west of the Rhine River, and the section of the Netherlands that lies south of the Rhine. The people of the region, called *Gauls,* spoke forms of Celtic, a language group that includes modern Irish and Welsh. The leaders of their religion were priests called *Druids* (see **Druids**). These priests had great influence in politics. The Romans called some of the Gauls "long haired" because they did not shave their beards or cut their hair.

GAUL
(Transalpine)

Gaul, at the height of the Roman Empire, covered the area shown here.

WORLD BOOK map

In 390 B.C., Gallic tribes crossed the Alps, swept down through Italy, and sacked and burned Rome. The Gauls left the city, but for a time they held the northern part of the Italian peninsula. The region south of the Alps became known to the Romans as *Cisalpine Gaul,* or *Gaul this-side-of-the-Alps.* The Romans called the region north of the Alps *Transalpine* or *beyond-the-Alps* Gaul. During the 200's B.C., Gallic tribes invaded Thrace and Macedonia and finally Asia Minor. There they became known as Galatians (see **Galatia**).

The Gauls were brave and warlike, but they were no match for the well-trained Romans. The Romans defeated the Gauls in Italy in the 200's B.C. and made them subjects of Rome. Then the Roman invasions of Transalpine Gaul began. During the 100's B.C., the Romans gained the strip of Gaul along the Mediterranean Sea. This region is now known as *Provence,* from a Latin word meaning *province.* The Romans did not conquer the rest of Gaul until the time of Julius Caesar, in the 50's B.C.

The emperor Augustus organized Gaul into four provinces for purposes of administration. This form of organization lasted for 400 years. Gaul later suffered heavily through civil wars and barbaric invasions. But it passed on a rich cultural tradition to its new masters. Chief among the invaders were the Franks, who defeated the last Roman governor of Gaul in A.D. 486. From that time, most of Gaul was called *France,* after the Franks.   Herbert M. Howe

See also **Caesar, Julius; French language** (Development).

Gaulle, Charles André Joseph Marie de. See De Gaulle, Charles André Joseph Marie.

Gauntlet was a leather glove covered with steel plates that medieval knights wore as part of their armor. Early gauntlets were made of *chain mail* (metal rings linked together). Later gauntlets had hinges for ease of movement. Gauntlets were used until the 1600's. When a knight threw down his gauntlet in front of an enemy, it was a challenge to combat. The challenge was accepted by picking up the gauntlet. The expression *to throw down the gauntlet* still means *to declare a challenge.* Today, any glove with a long, loose cuff is called a gauntlet. See also **Glove** (picture).   Karin N. Mango

Gaur, *gowr,* is a wild ox of India, Myanmar, and the Malay Peninsula. Adult *bull* (male) gaurs stand 5 to 6 feet (1.5 to 1.8 meters) tall at the shoulder and weigh over 2,000 pounds (910 kilograms). Adult *cows* (females) are slightly smaller. Gaurs have short, dark brown hair. They also have curved horns, a large hump on the back, and a loose fold of skin under the throat. Gaurs live in tropical forests, usually in rocky hill country. These shy animals are usually found in small herds. The gaur faces possible extinction because people have hunted it and destroyed large areas of its forest habitat.   William L. Franklin

Scientific classification. The gaur is in the bovid family, Bovidae. Its scientific name is *Bos gaurus.*

Gauss, *gows,* is a unit used to measure the strength of a magnetic field. It is named for Carl Friedrich Gauss, a German mathematician, who did important work in electromagnetism. The earth's magnetic field is relatively weak. It is only about $\frac{1}{2}$ gauss. The magnetic field of a cyclotron may reach 20,000 gauss.   Lynn W. Hart

Gauss, *gows,* **Carl Friedrich,** *FREE drihk* (1777-1855), was a great German mathematician. His ideas had enormous influence in nearly all areas of mathematics. Gauss proved the fundamental theorem of algebra, which states that certain algebraic equations called *polynomial equations* have at least one root. He also helped bring about the acceptance of *imaginary numbers* (the square roots of negative numbers). He did so by showing how to represent *complex numbers* (combinations of real and imaginary numbers) as points in a plane.

Gauss was born in Brunswick. He attended the University of Göttingen. He later became a professor there and director of the Göttingen Observatory. Gauss contributed to the mathematical theory of electromagnetism. His contributions to astronomy included calculating the orbit of Ceres, the first asteroid discovered.
          Judith V. Grabiner

See also **Ceres** (asteroid); **Gauss.**

Gautama. See Buddha.

Gautier, *goh tee AY,* **Théophile,** *tay oh FEEL* (1811-1872), was a French poet, novelist, and critic. His most famous poetry collection, *Enamels and Cameos* (1852), stresses visual impressions rather than ideas or feelings. One of the poems, "Art," developed the theory of "art for art's sake." It states that art is meant to create only formal beauty and does not depend on moral, intellectual, or emotional values. Gautier opposed the idea of art as imitation and insisted that an artist's creative imagination or "inner vision" is the main source of inspiration. Gautier's novels include *Mademoiselle de Maupin* (1835) and *Captain Fracasse* (1863).

Gautier was born in Tarbes. He was an art and drama critic active in the battle to introduce romantic literature into France. Gautier's *A History of Romanticism* (published in 1874, after his death), is an informative study of French romanticism.   Thomas H. Goetz

Gavial, *GAY vee uhl,* is a reptile that looks like a crocodile. It is one of a group of reptiles called *crocodilians.* The gavial is distinguished from other crocodilians, such as alligators and crocodiles, by its long, narrow snout. It uses its snout to capture fish, its primary food. The gavial grows to 20 feet (6 meters) long or more. It lays 40 or more eggs and buries them in sandbanks. The young are about 15 inches (38 centimeters) long. The gavial is in danger of extinction. It lives only in a few areas of Pakistan, Burma, Bangladesh, India, and Nepal. See also **Crocodile.**

Scientific classification. The gavial makes up the gavial family, Gavialidae. It is *Gavialis gangeticus.*   Laurie J. Vitt

Gawain, *GAH wihn* or *GAH wayn,* **Sir,** was the nephew of the legendary King Arthur of medieval Britain and one of the knights first associated with Arthur's story. Gawain died fighting his treacherous kinsman Modred in the chronicle tradition of Arthurian narratives that developed from Geoffrey of Monmouth's *History of the Kings of Britain* (about 1136).

In medieval French and German accounts, Gawain is identified as both the finest model of chivalry and a prime example of hypocrisy. This confusion over his character continues in Sir Thomas Malory's English prose narrative, *Le Morte Darthur* (about 1470). In this work, Gawain is both a hero and a villain. In English poetic romances, however, he represents the chivalrous ideals of truthfulness and loyalty. He is the only knight of the Round Table to accept the mysterious Green Knight's challenge in one of the most important medieval English verse romances, *Sir Gawain and the Green Knight* (late 1300's). See **Round Table.**   Edmund Reiss

Gay, John (1685-1732), an English playwright and poet, is best known for *The Beggar's Opera* (1728). In the opera, Gay poked fun at Italian opera and satirized politicians by comparing them to criminals. He used English ballads as the music. *Polly* (1729), a sequel to *The Beggar's Opera,* offended the government and was banned from the stage. But it was a success in printed form. Gay also wrote light verse. *The Shepherd's Week* (1714) is a comic pastoral poem of great charm. *Trivia* (1716) paints a vivid picture in verse of London street life.

Gay was born in Barnstaple. He was likeable, friendly, and never serious about life. He held minor public positions and had many friends.   Jack D. Durant

Gay Liberation. See Homosexuality.

Gay-Lussac, *GAY luh SAK,* **Joseph Louis** (1778-1850), was a French chemist and physicist. In 1802, he published the results of his experiments dealing with the effects of temperature on gases. His findings agreed with the earlier unpublished work of French chemist Jacques A. C. Charles and are usually known as *Charles's law* (see **Gas** [Gas laws]). He studied the chemistry of gases and, in 1809, summarized data collected by others in the *law of combining volumes.* This law states that gases form compounds with each other in simple, definite proportions. These proportions can then be expressed in formulas. The formula for water (H_2O) shows it is formed of two parts of hydrogen (H) and one of oxygen (O).

Gay-Lussac investigated the upper atmosphere. In 1804, he rose about 23,000 feet (7,000 meters) above sea level in a hydrogen-filled balloon. He wanted to study the composition, temperature, and moisture of air and the strength of the earth's magnetic pull at high altitudes. Gay-Lussac improved the processes for making sulfuric acid and oxalic acid for industry. He also suggested improved ways of estimating the amount of chlorine in bleaching powder. Gay-Lussac and Louis Jacques Thenard prepared potassium and sodium from potash and soda. The two men also independently isolated boron in the same year (1808) that Sir Humphry Davy of England did (see **Boron**). Gay-Lussac discovered the gas cyanogen in 1815. He was born in Léonard-le-Noblat.   M. J. Nye

Gay Nineties was the period of the 1890's in United States history. Many Americans prospered during those years. But the period included a nationwide depression, much labor unrest, and the Spanish-American War (1898). Largely as a result of these events, few Americans in the 1890's ever regarded the period as gay or lively. The term *Gay Nineties* became widely used during the Great Depression, the worldwide business slump of the 1930's. At that time, people longed for a comfortable past and chose to remember only the prosperous years and heroic events of the 1890's.

Many Americans preferred to recall the gleaming white buildings and the marvelous new Ferris wheel of the World's Columbian Exposition in Chicago in 1893. Others remembered Lieutenant Colonel Theodore Roo-

E. R. Degginger

The gavial is a reptile with a body that resembles that of a crocodile. The gavial uses its long, narrow snout and many teeth to catch fish.

sevelt leading his Rough Rider Regiment against the Spaniards in Cuba three years before he became the nation's 26th President (see **Roosevelt, Theodore** [The Rough Riders]). Still others thought of the charming gas lights and lively vaudeville shows of the 1890's.

Life during the Gay Nineties

The privileges of wealth. In the 1890's about an eighth of the families in the United States controlled about seven-eighths of the nation's income. The wealthy included more than 4,000 millionaires, most of whom had gained their fortune in banking, mining, manufacturing, trade, or transportation.

Wealthy Americans traveled by ocean liner to many parts of the world. Some collected rare books or valuable art objects. The wealthy supported symphony orchestras and operas in Boston, Chicago, New York City, and other large cities. They sent their children to such exclusive colleges as Harvard and Vassar.

Wealthy families lived in elegant mansions or town houses, and many spent the summer in spacious cottages. They furnished their homes with heavily ornamented furniture of the Victorian style. These families often entertained with lavish dinners and parties. Fashionable young women of the 1890's dressed in the Gibson Girl style created by the American artist Charles Dana Gibson (see **Gibson, Charles Dana** [picture]).

The rich often spent leisure time watching horse races, yachting, or playing golf and polo. College men competed in football, rowing, and track. Sports for college women included archery, croquet, and tennis.

Middle-class prosperity. The middle class in America during the 1890's included attorneys, physicians, and other professionals; small-business owners; and skilled workers. Most of them lived in their own homes. Others rented apartments. Like the wealthy, they furnished their

Bettmann Archive

Tea parties, such as this one in a fashionable New England home, were typical of the leisure activities of wealthy Americans during the Gay Nineties.

homes with Victorian furniture. But they had a Persian rug or statuettes instead of expensive art objects.

Some middle-class children went to work after finishing elementary school. But most continued their education at a private or public high school. Only a small number of these children could afford to go to college.

Many people enjoyed plays given by touring theater groups. Leading performers included Maude Adams, John Drew, and Lillian Russell. Popular plays, such as *The Count of Monte Cristo* and *Cyrano de Bergerac,* thrilled audiences across the nation. Outdoor entertainment included professional baseball games, Sunday school picnics, and bicycle rides.

Most middle-class people read daily newspapers and such magazines as *Cosmopolitan, McClure's,* and *Munsey's.* Adults also enjoyed such novels as *The Strange Case of Dr. Jekyll and Mr. Hyde* and *The Red Badge of Courage.* Parents encouraged their children to read Horatio Alger's stories, which stressed the virtues of hard work and honesty, as well as luck. Many children secretly read *dime novels,* adventure stories that cost 10 cents. Many homes had a piano or a phonograph. Popular music included "On the Banks of the Wabash," "Maple Leaf Rag," and marches by John Philip Sousa.

The despair of poverty. Most of the nation's urban poor of the 1890's were unskilled laborers. Many were immigrants who spoke little or no English and who worked about 60 hours a week for less than $10. Millions of unskilled workers lost their jobs during a depression that hit the nation in 1893 and lasted until about 1897. About a fifth of the country's industrial workers had no job during this period, and life became almost unbearable for many of them. Millions of the urban poor lived in crowded tenements that had poor lighting and ventilation. Fire and disease—especially tuberculosis—killed many people. Poor city children left school at an early age, and few attended high school.

Large numbers of rural poor lived in shacks that lacked running water. These people often suffered from disease and had monotonous diets. Rural workers earned only about half the pay that city workers received. Rural children attended one-room schools.

The life of the rural poor was eased by an occasional Saturday night in town and by an annual county fair. In the cities, people could go to a vaudeville show, a baseball game, or a boxing match. Such boxing champions as "Gentleman Jim" Corbett and John L. Sullivan became national heroes.

Economic and political developments

Industrial growth occurred rapidly during the 1890's, except in the depression years. Many large companies bought up smaller ones, and monopolies became common in oil refining and other important industries. The growing power of industrial firms led workers to increase their attempts to organize unions.

Several bloody labor disputes during the 1890's hurt the union movement. In 1892, a strike at the Carnegie Steel Company plant near Homestead, Pa., resulted in several deaths. In 1894, federal troops helped end violence during a strike by railroad workers against the Pullman Company in Chicago. In spite of these setbacks, labor unions gained strength in the prosperous years at the end of the decade.

New types of mechanized equipment enabled farmers to increase production greatly in the 1890's. But they produced more crops than they could sell. Prices fell, and farmers could not earn enough money to pay for their new machines. Many gave up and moved to cities. In the early 1890's, some dissatisfied farmers founded the Populist Party and demanded many economic and political reforms. Above all, they called for unlimited coinage of silver. They believed the so-called *free silver* would raise farm prices by increasing the amount of money in circulation. In 1896, the Democratic presidential candidate, William Jennings Bryan, campaigned for free silver. He lost to Republican William McKinley.

In the mid-1890's, a number of members of Congress believed high import tariffs would help the slumping U.S. economy by reducing competition from products made abroad. In 1897, Congress passed the Dingley Act. It raised tariffs to record levels. People in business and farmers soon began to prosper again.

A growing world power. By 1890, all the chief frontier areas of the United States had been settled. But many Americans wanted the nation to expand further and become a world power. The nation largely accomplished this goal in the Spanish-American War. In February 1898, the battleship U.S.S. *Maine* blew up in the harbor of Havana, Cuba. The actual cause of the explosion was never learned. But most Americans blamed Spain, which ruled Cuba at the time. The United States declared war on Spain in April. American forces defeated the Spaniards in battles in Cuba and the Philippines, which Spain also ruled. Spain asked for peace in August. It granted independence to Cuba and gave Guam, the Philippines, and Puerto Rico to the United States.

Also in 1898, the United States annexed the Hawaiian Islands. In 1899, Filipinos revolted against American forces because the United States had no plan to grant immediate independence to the Philippines.

Rising prosperity and victory in the Spanish-American War unified America during the late 1890's. Most Americans looked forward to the new century with optimism. But many felt uneasy about the nation's growing involvement in foreign affairs.   Ari Hoogenboom

Additional resources

Gale, Robert L. *The Gay Nineties in America.* Greenwood, 1992.
Traxel, David. *1898: The Birth of the American Century.* Knopf, 1998.

Gaza Strip, *GAH zuh* or *GAY zuh,* is a piece of land administered by Palestinians. Israeli troops had occupied it from 1967 to 1994. It lies on the Mediterranean coast, where Egypt and Israel meet. For location, see **Israel** (political map). The Gaza Strip covers 146 square miles (378 square kilometers) and has a population of about 1,215,000. Most of its land is sandy and flat. The vast majority of the people are Palestinian Arabs, including many who became refugees from Israel after the state of Israel was created in 1948. Israeli settlers make up a small percentage of the population. The economy is based on agriculture, including citrus fruit production. Some of the residents commute to jobs in Israel. Gaza, the major city, is overcrowded with refugees.

In ancient times, Egyptian pharaohs ruled the Gaza Strip. Later, at various times, it was ruled by Philistines, Jews, Arabs, and Turks. From 1920 to 1948, it was part of the British-ruled Mandate of Palestine. Egypt gained control of the strip during the Arab-Israeli war of 1948. Israel took control of it after the 1967 Arab-Israeli War.

During the late 1980's, Palestinians in the Gaza Strip and West Bank staged widespread, often violent, demonstrations against Israel's occupation. Israeli forces clashed with protesters, killing many of them. In 1993, Israel and the Palestine Liberation Organization (PLO) signed agreements that led to the withdrawal of Israeli troops from most of the Gaza Strip in 1994. Palestinians then took control of the area. In 1996, Palestinians in the Gaza Strip and parts of the West Bank elected a legislature and a president to make laws and administer these areas. But there is still a large Israeli security presence.

In 1998, Israel and the PLO signed an agreement allowing a Palestinian airport to open in the Gaza Strip. In 2000, Israel and the Palestinians held peace talks but failed to resolve key remaining disagreements. Later that year, violence again broke out between Palestinian demonstrators and Israeli forces in Jerusalem, the West Bank, and the Gaza Strip.   Christine Moss Helms

See also **Arab-Israeli conflict.**

Gazelle, *guh ZEHL,* is a slender antelope that is noted for its beauty, grace, and gentleness. Poets have often written about these qualities of the gazelle. About 15 *species* (kinds) live over a vast area of northern and eastern Africa and Asia. Some gazelles live in mountain ranges, but most of them live on open, sandy plains.

Gazelles have large, soft, black eyes. Both males and females of most species have round black horns. The horns of some types have ringlike ridges around them, but others are smooth. Usually the horns are U-shaped. Gazelles have long, narrow, pointed ears and short tails. Their hair is short and smooth. Some gazelles have tufts of hair on the knees. *Thomson's gazelle* has a light fawn-colored back that deepens to a wide band of dark brown along the flanks. Its underside is pure white.

Gazelles are swift runners. Some gazelles can outrun even the swiftest greyhounds. Some hunters set snares

Gerald Cubitt

Thomson's gazelle is an animal with a light fawn-colored back and white underside separated by a dark band along its flanks.

or build enclosures near watering places to trap the animals when they come to drink.

Gazelles are plant-eating animals. *Loder's gazelle* lives in the northern Sahara and eats berries and leaves. The Arabs believe it never drinks.

The familiar light-brown gazelle, sometimes called the *dorcas,* or *ariel, gazelle,* is less than 2 feet (61 centimeters) tall. It lives in the desert from Morocco east to central India and south to Somalia, where plants are sparse and scrubby. The name *gazelle* comes from an Arabic word that means *to be affectionate.*

Grant's gazelle of eastern Africa has longer horns than any other gazelle. Gazelle horns usually grow 10 to 15 inches (25 to 38 centimeters) long, but those of Grant's gazelle may grow 30 inches (76 centimeters) or longer. This animal stands about 33 inches (84 centimeters) high at the shoulder. It lives in herds of from 6 to as many as 200 animals. It eats grass and the leaves of shrubs. Grant's gazelles often graze with hartebeests and zebras.

About 10 species and subspecies of gazelles, including Loder's gazelle and three kinds of dorcas gazelles, are endangered. Goats and sheep eat most of the *vegetation* (plant life) in the areas where these gazelles graze. The *red gazelle* of Algeria may be extinct. Hunters who ignore game laws kill hundreds of gazelles every year. Conservationists claim that a total ban on gazelle hunting could save some species.   Duane A. Schlitter

Scientific classification. Gazelles belong to the bovid family, Bovidae. They are genus *Gazella.*

Gazelle hound. See Saluki.

Gdańsk, *guh DAHNSK,* or, in German, *Danzig, DAN sihg* (pop. 466,500), a city in northern Poland, is one of the leading ports of central Europe. It lies on the Vistula River, Poland's chief waterway, 4 miles (6 kilometers) from the Baltic Sea (see **Poland** [political map]).

Gdańsk is rich in historical buildings of many styles. One of the best known is the Church of Saint Mary, originally built in the 1300's. Another famous building is the Gothic town hall. Gdańsk serves as the leading cultural center of northern Poland. The University of Gdańsk was founded in 1970. Factories in Gdańsk make chemicals, electrical equipment, food products, machinery, metal products, and textiles.

The Slavs founded Gdańsk in the 900's. It became a rich trading center of the German Hanseatic League during the Middle Ages (see **Hanseatic League**). It became a vassal city of the Polish king in 1466 but had complete self-government. When Russia and Prussia divided Poland in 1793, Gdańsk fell into Prussian hands.

After World War I (1914-1918), Gdańsk became a free city under the supervision of the League of Nations. Poland controlled the city's communications and railroads and the collection of customs duties. Gdańsk had its own assembly, and it was supervised by a commissioner who represented the League of Nations.

In 1939, the Germans demanded that Gdańsk be united with Germany, but Poland refused. Germany invaded Poland in 1939, and Gdańsk fell into German hands. Bombs seriously damaged the city during World War II (1939-1945). After the war, Gdańsk became part of Poland, and the damaged areas were rebuilt. In 1970, Gdańsk was a center of protest against Poland's Communist government. In 1980, strikes in Gdańsk and other cities led to the creation of Solidarity, an organization of trade unions. Solidarity helped bring about free elections in Poland (see **Poland** [Antigovernment protests]).
          Janusz Bugajski

Gê Indians, *zhay,* make up a number of tribes in the dry highland plains of east-central Brazil. The Gê form one of the largest groups of Brazilian Indians. Unlike many other Indian groups, the Gê traditionally did not wear clothes, make pottery, or use canoes.

Gê men hunted many kinds of animals, including deer, anteaters, and armadillos. The women gathered wild plant foods and raised potatoes and yams.

Gê villages had a plaza in the center. In most tribes, the plaza belonged to the men, who also controlled the political and ceremonial life of the village. The houses, which surrounded the plaza, belonged to the women. When a man married, he moved to his wife's house.

In some Gê tribes, men wore wooden plugs in holes cut in their earlobes and lower lip. Both men and women painted their bodies with red and black patterns that indicated each person's social position.

A number of Gê tribes have continued to practice some of their traditional ways. These tribes are the Suyá, Kayapó, Shavante, Sherente, Krahó, Canella, Krikati, Gaviões, and Apinayé.   Roberto DaMatta

Gear is a mechanical device that transfers rotating motion and power from one part of a machine to another. Gears vary greatly in size and use. They range from the tiny gears that drive the hands of a watch to the huge gears that turn the propeller of a supertanker.

A simple gear consists of a metal wheel or disk with slots called *teeth* around the edge. Gears always work in pairs. The teeth of one gear *mesh* (fit together) with the teeth of the other gear. Each gear has a metal axle in its center. The axle of one gear is connected to a power source, such as an electric motor. When the power axle turns, its gear turns and causes the second gear to rotate in the opposite direction. This action powers the axle of the second gear to do useful work.

Most gears are made of steel, but such materials as bronze, or nylon or other plastics are also used. Metal gears are usually lubricated with oil or grease to keep them cool while they rotate.

How gears work. Gears may be used to increase or decrease the speed of rotation. They thus enable various parts of machines to operate at different speeds.

One gear in every pair is smaller than the other. This small gear, called a *pinion,* has fewer teeth than the large gear. The ratio of the number of teeth on the pinion to the number of teeth on the large gear determines the speed at which the pinion rotates and thus the amount of *torque* (rotational force) it transmits. For example, if the pinion has 20 teeth and the large gear has 60, the ratio is 1 to 3, and the large gear will turn once in the time the pinion turns three times. Thus, if the pinion drives the large gear, it reduces the speed of rotation by two-thirds but triples the torque. In such cases, the pinion is known as a *reducing gear.* But when the large gear drives the pinion, it serves as a *multiplying gear.* It increases the speed of rotation but reduces the torque.

Types of gears include *spur gears, helical gears, bevel gears, worm gears, planetary gears,* and *rack-and-pinion gears.* Spur gears have straight teeth and axles that are parallel to each other. Helical gears have teeth set at an angle to the axle. Such gears are quieter at high

Some common types of gears

Gears consist chiefly of an axle and a wheel or disk with slots called *teeth*. They are used in a wide variety of machines. Some of the most common kinds of gears are shown here.

WORLD BOOK illustrations by William Graham

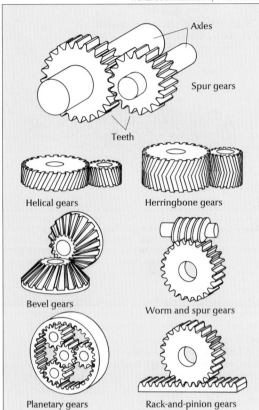

Axles

Spur gears

Teeth

Helical gears

Herringbone gears

Bevel gears

Worm and spur gears

Planetary gears

Rack-and-pinion gears

WORLD BOOK illustration by John F. Eggert

The banded gecko lives in the southwestern United States and northern Mexico. It has prominent striped markings on its body.

closed, transparent eyelids. The toes of most geckos end with pads that have thousands of hairlike bristles. These bristles stick to most surfaces, making the animals good climbers. Some geckos can walk upside down on the underside of a branch or other horizontal surface.

Most female geckos lay eggs. In some species, the temperature at which the eggs are kept before they hatch determines the sex of the offspring. A few species consist only of females. Such geckos can reproduce without mating, but they give birth to female offspring.

Most geckos are active at night, when they hunt insects. If a gecko is attacked, it can distract an enemy by waving its tail. When the enemy attacks the tail, the tail breaks off but keeps wriggling. While the enemy holds the tail, the gecko runs away. It soon grows a new tail.

Geckos are named for the loud call made by one species, the tokay gecko. Most species can make a chirping, squeaking, or barking sound.   Raymond B. Huey

Scientific classification. Geckos belong to the gecko families Gekkonidae, Eublepharidae, and Diplodactylidae. The tokay gecko is *Gekko gecko*.

Geese. See Goose.

Gehrig, Lou (1903-1941), was one of the greatest players in baseball history. He played in 2,130 consecutive games from 1925 to 1939 for the New York Yankees. This total was a major league record for 56 years, until Cal Ripken, Jr., of the Baltimore Orioles broke it in 1995.

Gehrig was born in New York City. His full name was Henry Louis Gehrig. He played his entire major league career—from 1923 to 1939—for the Yankees. Gehrig, a first baseman, had a career batting average of .340. He hit 493 home runs with 40 or more in five seasons. He also hit a major league record of 23 grand slam home runs. But these achievements were overshadowed by those of teammate Babe Ruth. In 1927, when Ruth hit 60 home runs, Gehric hit 47. He batted in 100 or more runs over a record 13 straight seasons. In 1931, he drove in 184 runs, an American League record.

Illness forced Gehrig to retire in 1939. He was suffering from amyotrophic lateral sclerosis, a rare and incurable nerve disease now often called *Lou Gehrig's disease*. He was elected to the Baseball Hall of Fame in 1939.   Jack Lang

Additional resources

Adler, David A. *Lou Gehrig*. Gulliver Bks., 1997. Younger readers.
Bak, Richard. *Lou Gehrig*. Taylor Pub. Co., 1995.

Gehry, *GAYR ee,* **Frank** (1929-   ), is one of the most original and provocative American architects working today. He is known for pushing the limits of architectural design. Many of his buildings resemble free-form sculp-

speeds, but they tend to generate a sideways force, making them less efficient. Helical gears called *herringbone gears* solve this problem. They have two rows of teeth, which generate opposite forces. The forces counteract each other, and the gears run smoothly.

Bevel gears usually mesh at a right angle to transmit power between intersecting axles. Worm gears have a large gear similar to a spur gear, and a pinion that is an endless screw around an axle. The gear and pinion mesh at a right angle to transmit power between axles that are not parallel and do not intersect. Automatic automobile transmissions use planetary gears, also called *epicyclic gears*. These gears are composed of a number of spur gears, called *planet gears,* which rotate around a central gear called a *sun* (see **Transmission** [Planetary gears]). Rack-and-pinion gears used in automobile steering mechanisms consist of a spur gear and a flat rack with teeth on one side. The spur gear runs back and forth along the rack.   Ernest Rabinowicz

Gecko, *GEHK oh,* is the name of certain small, harmless lizards that live in warm climates. They have short, flat bodies covered with small, bumpy scales. Most geckos grow 4 to 6 inches (10 to 15 centimeters) long, including the tail. Many have catlike eyes with permanently

tures constructed with inexpensive materials, such as corrugated metal and chain-link fencing.

Gehry was born Ephraim Owen Goldberg in Toronto, Ontario. In 1947, he moved with his family to Los Angeles. He worked with Austrian architect Victor Gruen while studying architecture at the University of Southern California. Gehry earned his degree in 1954. He began his own practice in Los Angeles in 1962.

Gehry's reconstruction of his home in Santa Monica, California, in the late 1970's drew attention. His commissions include the California Aerospace Museum (1984) in Los Angeles, the University of Toledo Center for the Visual Arts (1992) in Ohio, the Guggenheim Museum (1997) in Bilbao, Spain, and the Experience Music Project rock music museum (2000) in Seattle. In 1989, Gehry was awarded the Pritzker Architecture Prize, often considered the Nobel Prize of architecture.　　Leland M. Roth

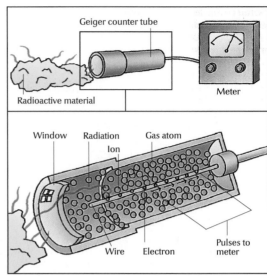

Window　Radiation　Gas atom
Ion
Geiger counter tube
Radioactive material
Meter
Pulses to meter
Wire　Electron

WORLD BOOK illustrations by Oxford Illustrators Limited

How a Geiger counter works. Radiation that enters a Geiger counter tube hits the gas atoms there, causing them to become ionized. The electrons freed by this process spread along the wire, creating electric pulses. These pulses travel along the wire and are amplified and counted by a meter or other device.

© José Fuste Raga, The Stock Market

Frank Gehry's design for the Guggenheim Museum in Bilbao, Spain, gained praise for its sculptural blend of tilting walls and wavelike roofs resembling a giant flower open to the sun.

Geiger counter, also called Geiger-Müller counter, is an instrument that detects forms of ionizing radiation. Such radiation includes gamma rays and alpha and beta particles. Prospectors use Geiger counters to find uranium, thorium, and other radioactive elements. Geiger counters also are used in science and industry, chiefly in studies involving radioactive substances called *radioisotopes* (see **Isotope** [Uses of radioisotopes]).

A typical Geiger counter has a fine wire stretched along the axis of a cylindrical metal tube. This central wire and the metal wall of the tube serve as electrodes. An electronic circuit keeps the wire at a positive voltage of about 1,000 volts, thus creating a strong *electric field* near the wire (see **Electric field**). Most Geiger counter tubes contain a readily ionizable gas, such as argon mixed with a trace amount of ethyl alcohol vapor.

Many Geiger counter tubes have a window of plastic or mica film, through which alpha and beta particles can enter. Unlike gamma rays, these particles cannot penetrate the wall of the metal tube. Radiation that enters the tube collides with a gas atom, causing the atom to become ionized. This process occurs repeatedly, creating

a large number of electrons. The electrons spread along the wire, where together they create an electric pulse. The pulse is amplified electronically and is counted by a meter or some other type of registering device.

A Geiger counter can detect low-energy radiation because even one ionizing particle produces a full pulse on the central wire. However, the instrument cannot measure the energy of a particle because particles of different energies generate pulses of the same size.

Hans Geiger, a German physicist, invented the Geiger counter in 1912. He and the German physicist Walther Müller improved its design in 1928.　　John W. Poston, Sr.

Geisel, Theodor. See Seuss, Dr.

Gelasius I, *juh LAY shee uhs,* **Saint** (? -496), was elected pope in 492. He is most famous for a letter he wrote in 494 to the Byzantine emperor Anastasius I. In the letter, the pope set forth the relationship between spiritual authority and *secular* (nonreligious) power. He wrote that priests and kings ordinarily have separate areas of action and ought not to interfere with one another. But if a conflict should arise between, for example, a pope and an emperor, then the pope must have the last word because, as a priest, he is concerned with immortal souls and not just mortal bodies. Gelasius's letter was based on an earlier dispute with the emperor over the emperor's right to make theological pronouncements. The letter stated Gelasius's belief that the power of the popes was superior to that of secular rulers.

Gelasius was probably born in Rome. He was of North African descent. He was concerned about the poor and often contributed to their welfare.　　Thomas F. X. Noble

Gelatin, *JEHL uh tuhn,* is a protein substance that comes from animal skins and bones. It is hard, tasteless, and odorless. When dry, it appears nearly white. Gelatin dissolved in water is transparent. It forms a stiff jelly after being dissolved in hot water and allowed to cool.

To manufacture gelatin from the bones of animals, the bones must first be freed from grease. They are then soaked in a hydrochloric acid solution to rid them of minerals, and washed repeatedly in plain water. The cleaned bones are heated for several hours in distilled water at about 92 °F (33 °C). The fluid is then run off, and the bones are reheated in fresh distilled water at about 102 °F (39 °C). The fluid that forms must be chemically treated so that the gelatin will be pure. Finally, the gelatin is concentrated, formed into noodlelike strips, and then dried. The final product is usually ground.

Skin gelatin is manufactured in much the same way as bone gelatin, except that the skin gets a different "pre-boiling" treatment. A lime treatment removes the grease and other substances from the skin. Then it is washed in water, and treated with dilute hydrochloric acid.

Gelatin is important as a food. It is particularly benefi-cial for sick people and children because it can be di-gested easily. The photographic industry uses gelatin for making the coating on dry plates, films, and photo-graphic papers. Both soft and hard medicinal capsules are made of gelatin, but the soft capsules, used for oils, have glycerin added. Scientists use gelatin as a medium in which to grow bacteria.   Mary E. Zabik

See also **Dynamite; Glue; Isinglass; Protein.**

Gell-Mann, *GEHL mahn,* **Murray** (1929-   ), an American physicist, won the 1969 Nobel Prize in physics for his work in classifying subatomic particles and their interactions. In the 1950's, physicists found many such particles but had no way to classify them. In 1953, he proposed a theory that explained why certain subatomic particles did not *decay* (change into other particles) as quickly as expected. In 1961, he proposed his *eightfold way,* in which he classified particles into families. An Is-raeli physicist, Yuval Ne'eman, independently had the same idea. Using the theory, Gell-Mann predicted the existence of a particle called *omega-minus.* In 1964, sci-entists at Brookhaven National Laboratory found it.

Gell-Mann received a Ph.D. in 1951 from the Massa-chusetts Institute of Technology. In 1955, he became a physics professor at the California Institute of Technolo-gy. He was born in New York City.   Roger H. Stuewer

Gellée, Claude. See Claude.

Gem is a mineral or other material used in jewelry and other ornaments. Gems include diamonds, emeralds, opals, and rubies, as well as laboratory-grown gems and other artificially created imitations. When mined, most natural gemstones have a rough surface and irregular shape. Skilled gem cutters then cut and polish them.

Most gems are minerals. However, some gems have organic origins. For example, pearls are formed in the shells of living oysters. Amber is a fossil resin from an-cient pine trees. Coral consists of the skeletons of tiny sea animals. Jet is a fossil wood related to coal.

Qualities of gem minerals

Gem minerals are the natural materials made into gemstones for jewelry. To identify such minerals, ex-perts sometimes must use chemical tests or X rays. But gem minerals can usually be identified by such proper-ties as (1) crystal shape, (2) color, (3) index of refraction, (4) cleavage, (5) hardness, and (6) specific gravity.

Crystal shape varies from one type of gem mineral to another. But all the crystals of any one kind of gem mineral have the same type of *symmetry* (balanced arrangement of faces). For example, diamonds crystallize in the *isometric system* and, in most cases, form an *octa-hedron* (double pyramid). See **Crystal.**

Color helps determine the beauty, value, and splen-dor of gems. But color is not an ideal property to use for identifying gems, because different kinds of gems may have similar colors. For example, the blues of some aquamarine and topaz look almost identical. In addition, a single gem mineral may occur in a wide range of col-ors. For instance, varieties of the mineral beryl include goshenite, which is colorless; morganite, which is pink; and emerald, which is green. In general, gem color re-sults from one or more of the following factors: 1) chem-ical impurities in the mineral, (2) defects in the arrange-ment of atoms in the crystal, and (3) the behavior of light passing through the mineral.

Index of refraction indicates the amount that a light ray bends as it passes out of one substance and into an-other. When light passes from air to a denser substance, such as a transparent gem, it slows down. If the light ray enters the gem at any angle except a right angle, the slowing down causes the light ray to bend at the point of entry. This bending is called *refraction.* The ratio of the speed of light in air to its speed in the gem is the gem's index of refraction. The higher a mineral's index of refraction—that is, the more it slows down light rays—the more brilliant the mineral is.

When a ray of white light passes through some gems, it separates into rays of different colors. This is called *dispersion.* The degree of dispersion varies with each type of gem. In most diamonds, dispersion is very dis-tinct. As a result, when light passes through a properly cut diamond, the gem reflects bright flashes of the col-ors of the spectrum. See **Light** (Dispersion).

Cleavage is the tendency of some minerals to split in definite directions, producing a flat surface. Minerals may have one or more cleavage directions. For example, topaz has one prominent cleavage direction, and dia-mond has four. Cleavage differs from *fracture,* which produces uneven gem surfaces. Some minerals have a characteristic fracture.

Hardness is an important quality of gem minerals. Few stones can serve as gems unless they can wear for a long time. Mineralogists use the *Mohs scale* to indi-cate the relative hardness of minerals. The scale num-bers degrees of hardness from 1 to 10. Minerals rated 7 or more wear well as gems. A mineral rated 7, such as quartz, cannot be scratched by a steel knife or by glass. Diamond, the hardest substance in nature, is rated 10. It can scratch any other mineral.

Specific gravity is the ratio of the weight of a given volume of a substance to the weight of an equal volume of pure water. Each type of gem has a certain specific gravity. Amber has a specific gravity of 1.08, about the same as saltwater. Diamond has a specific gravity of 3.52. Thus, a given volume of diamond weighs about $3\frac{1}{2}$ times as much as an equal volume of pure water.

Sources of gems

Gem minerals are found in a variety of geological en-vironments. Some gems, such as peridots and some dia-monds, occur in *igneous* rocks, which are formed by the cooling of hot, melted material. Coarsely grained ig-

Gems

Precious or semiprecious stones cut or polished for use in jewelry are called gems. Most are minerals. Some, such as amber, coral, and pearl, come from living or once-living things. The gems on these two pages were painted for *World Book* by John Langley Howard and Paul D. Turnbaugh.

Agate

natural light   artificial light
Alexandrite

Amber

Amethyst

Aquamarine

Bloodstone

Carnelian

Cat's-eye
(Chrysoberyl)

Coral

Diamond

Diopside

Emerald

Garnet

Goshenite

Jade

Jasper

Jet

Lapis lazuli

Moonstone

Morganite

Onyx

Opal

Pearl

Peridot

Petoskey stone

Rose quartz

Ruby

Sapphire

Sardonyx

Tanzanite

Topaz

Tourmaline

Turquoise

Zircon

neous rocks called *pegmatites* produce most of the world's beryl, spodumene, topaz, and tourmaline. Some rubies and sapphires are found in *metamorphic* rocks, which form under great heat and pressure. Jade is a type of metamorphic rock. Sediments such as sand and gravel may contain such gems as spinel and moonstone and some diamonds, rubies, and sapphires. *Sedimentary* rocks are formed by geologic processes, chiefly from sand and gravel deposited by water, wind, and ice. Opal and turquoise form in sedimentary rocks as a result of mineral-rich water seeping through the rock.

Diamonds are mined mainly in Australia, central and southern Africa, and Russia. The best rubies come from Myanmar, and the best sapphires from Myanmar, Thailand, and Kashmir (a region claimed by India and Pakistan). Brazil produces most of the world's aquamarines. The best emeralds are found in Colombia. Topaz is mined extensively in Brazil. Fine opal comes chiefly from Australia. Turquoise is in the Southwestern United States and in Iran. Pearls are harvested mainly from the Persian Gulf and the gulf between India and Sri Lanka.

Cutting and polishing

Hardness, transparency, and index of refraction determine the way a gem is cut. There are two main styles of cut gems: (1) *faceted gems,* which have many tiny polished sides called *facets,* and (2) *cabochons,* which are rounded, polished stones. A round faceted style called the *brilliant cut* has 58 facets. It is commonly used for diamonds. Such gems as agate, chrysoprase, jasper, and moonstone are often cut in the cabochon style. *Lapidaries* (gem cutters) cut most gems by grinding away material until the desired shape is reached.

To cut and polish a gemstone, lapidaries must use a material that is as hard as, or harder than, the gemstone itself. For example, sapphire and ruby are cut with diamond powder or with *Carborundum powder,* both of which are harder than sapphire and ruby. *Carborundum* is a trade name for silicon carbide. A diamond can be ground and polished only by using diamond dust.

Lapidaries cut most transparent stones into faceted gems. They use the stone's refractive index to determine the proper angle between the top set of facets and the bottom set. If the stone is well proportioned, nearly all the light that enters the stone through the top facets is reflected back up from the bottom facets, giving the stone maximum brilliance.

Value of gems

A gem's value is determined by many factors, including brilliance, color, hardness, rarity, weight, and cut. In general, diamonds are the most prized gems because they surpass all others in hardness and brilliance. But high-quality emeralds can be more valuable than diamonds. Pearls are graded by size, color, and perfection of shape. In general, they should be white or lightly tinted, and round. Opals are valued by the intensity of their color flashes and by their background color. Black opals are the most valuable. They emit bright color flashes from a black, gray, or blue background.

Some famous gems

The most celebrated diamond in the world is probably the Koh-i-noor. Found in India hundreds of years ago, it was presented to Queen Victoria of Britain in 1850 by the British East India Company. The Cullinan diamond, found in South Africa, was the largest diamond ever discovered. It weighed more than 3,100 *carats.* One carat equals 200 milligrams (0.007 ounce). The largest cut diamond in the world came from the Cullinan. It is the 530-carat Star of Africa, set in the royal Scepter with Cross of the British crown jewels. One of the most beautiful pearls ever found is La Pellegrina. Discovered in India, it weighs about 36 carats.

Imitation and synthetic gems

The beauty of natural gems has caused a constant demand for them. But their costliness has prevented many people from owning them. Thus, synthetic and imitation gems have become the foundation of a major industry. The basis of most inexpensive imitations is a soft glass called *paste.* Some high-quality imitation diamonds consist of a synthetic compound called *cubic zirconia.*

Jewelers also sell assembled stones called *doublets* or *triplets.* These stones most often consist of two or three sections fused together or held together by a colorless cement. The most common are opal triplets, which are made of a thin slice of opal sandwiched between a base and a polished quartz or glass top.

In recent years, excellent synthetic gems have been

WORLD BOOK illustrations by Paul D. Turnbaugh

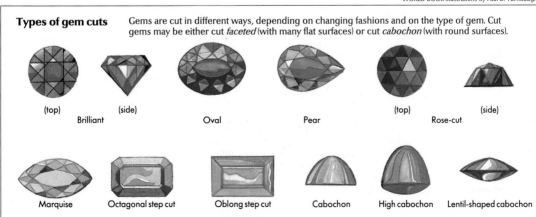

Types of gem cuts Gems are cut in different ways, depending on changing fashions and on the type of gem. Cut gems may be either cut *faceted* (with many flat surfaces) or cut *cabochon* (with round surfaces).

(top) (side)
Brilliant

Oval

Pear

(top) (side)
Rose-cut

Marquise

Octagonal step cut

Oblong step cut

Cabochon

High cabochon

Lentil-shaped cabochon

produced in laboratories. These gems have the same chemical and physical properties that natural gems have. Synthetic rubies and sapphires have been made by melting aluminum oxide in a flame produced by hydrogen and oxygen gases. Other gems created synthetically include emeralds and spinels.　　Robert I. Gait

Related articles in *World Book* include:

Agate	Cat's-eye	Jet	Petoskey stone
Alexandrite	Chalcedony	Jewelry	Ruby
Amber	Coral	Lapidary	Sapphire
Amethyst	Corundum	Lapis lazuli	Sardonyx
Aquamarine	Diamond	Mineral	Tanzanite
Beryl	Diopside	Moonstone	Topaz
Birthstone	Emerald	Onyx	Tourmaline
Cameo	Garnet	Opal	Turquoise
Carat	Jade	Pearl	Zircon
Carnelian	Jasper	Peridot	

Additional resources

Hall, Cally. *Gemstones.* Dorling Kindersley, 1994.
Matlins, Antoinette L., and Bonanno, A. C. *Gem Identification Made Easy.* 2nd ed. Gemstone Pr., 1997.
Schumann, Walter. *Gemstones of the World.* Rev. ed. Sterling Pub., 1997.

Gemini, *JEHM uh ny,* is the third sign of the zodiac. An air sign, it is symbolized by twins. Astrologers believe that Gemini is ruled by the planet Mercury, which is named for the ancient Roman messenger of the gods.

Astrologers regard people born under the sign of Gemini, from May 21 to June 20, as clever, curious, and expressive. Geminis also are witty in conversation. They have a two-sided personality. They often change moods quickly and can see both sides of an argument. Because

Gemini—The Twins

Symbol

Birth dates: May 21–June 20.
Group: Air.
Characteristics: Curious, lively, moody, restless, talkative, witty.

Signs of the Zodiac

Aries
Mar. 21–Apr. 19
Taurus
Apr. 20–May 20
Gemini
May 21–June 20
Cancer
June 21–July 22
Leo
July 23–Aug. 22
Virgo
Aug. 23–Sept. 22
Libra
Sept. 23–Oct. 22
Scorpio
Oct. 23–Nov. 21
Sagittarius
Nov. 22–Dec. 21
Capricorn
Dec. 22–Jan. 19
Aquarius
Jan. 20–Feb. 18
Pisces
Feb. 19–Mar. 20

WORLD BOOK illustration by Robert Keys

of this trait, Geminis can be indecisive.

Geminis are restless and try many activities. They have special talents for communication and language, and so are excellent journalists, politicians, salespeople, and teachers.　　Christopher McIntosh

See also **Astrology; Horoscope; Zodiac.**

Gemini program. See Astronaut.

Gemsbok, *GEHMZ bahk,* also called *gemsbuck,* is a large antelope related to the roan and sable antelopes.

It is a type of long-horned antelope known as an *oryx.* The gemsbok lives in dry regions of southwestern Africa. Other kinds of oryxes live in eastern Africa. The gemsbok stands about 4 feet (1.2 meters) high at the shoulder and weighs about 500 pounds (230 kilograms). The adults of both sexes have nearly straight, sharp horns that sweep backward up to 4 feet.

The gemsbok is mostly gray or tan on top and white beneath, with black markings on the head, sides, legs, and back. Because of its heavy body, it is not a swift runner. It lives in bands of up to 12 animals, feeding on scattered grasses and occasionally digging up juicy roots and bulbs for their moisture.　　Anne Innis Dagg

Scientific classification. The gemsbok belongs to the family Bovidae. Its scientific name is *Oryx gazella.*

See also **Antelope** (with picture).

Gender. In English, living things are classed as male or female, and things without life as neuter, or sexless. In the same way, words are said to belong to the *masculine,* the *feminine,* or the *neuter gender. Neuter* and *gender* are derived from Latin words meaning *neither* and *kind.* The word *animal* may represent either a male or female creature. Such words are said to be of *common* gender. These four classifications cover all nouns and pronouns, and explain all the English genders.

English is the only important language in which gender is largely determined *semantically*—that is, by the sex of the object for which the word stands. Some other languages use gender grammatically. For example, a French feminine hand (*la main*) opens the feminine door (*la porte*) of a feminine house (*la maison*). In German, a neuter girl (*Mädchen*) gazes at a masculine moon (*Mond*) in a feminine night (*Nacht*). Several other modern European languages have this same system of gender. Latin has a similar use of gender.

Personal pronouns are the only pronouns that have different forms to show gender. These forms are in the third person singular—*he, his, him, she, her, hers, it, its.* The gender of others may be assumed for a particular use if one knows that *I, me, my, mine, you* stand for male or female. *It* and *its* are usually neuter, but not always. A young child may be represented by *it* or *its,* as in, "The infant cried for *its* food."

Nouns show the difference between the masculine and feminine gender in three ways.

Some nouns have different forms for the masculine and the feminine. Examples are *man, woman; boy, girl; lad, lass; husband, wife; cock, hen; stallion, mare; gander, goose; buck, doe; beau, belle; wizard, witch.*

Many masculine nouns have been made feminine by adding the suffixes *ess, ine, ina, trix, ne, a,* or *ette.* Sometimes a letter in the masculine is changed or omitted when the suffix is added. Some examples are *actor, actress; waiter, waitress; usher, usherette; heir, heiress; duke, duchess; prior, prioress; prince, princess; Paul, Pauline; Angelo, Angela* or *Angelina; comedian, comedienne; administrator, administratrix; Louis, Louisa; sultan, sultana.* Many such feminine forms are importations from other languages, especially from French.

Many words of common gender are made either masculine or feminine by prefixing a word. Examples are *billy goat, nanny goat; he-bear, she-bear.*

Usage. Grammarians of the 1700's and 1800's recommended that nouns of common gender and indefinite pronouns be followed in English by the masculine pronoun. "Every member of the group has to pay *his* dues." However, usage today increasingly favors avoiding the showing of any sexual preference. Some speakers use *his or her, him or her,* or even *himself or herself.* Others substitute the feminine form or choose plural forms wherever possible.   Patricia A. Moody

See also **Noun** (Gender).

Gene, *jeen,* is part of a cell that determines which characteristics living things inherit from their parents. Genes determine such features as the shape of a leaf or the sex, height, and hair color of a child.

Every cell has tens of thousands of genes, which occur on threadlike structures known as *chromosomes.* Most genes occupy a specific place on a certain chromosome.

Genes produce their effects by influencing chemical and physical processes that control how living things grow, develop, and function. Most genes are encoded within the structure of a chemical called DNA *(de*oxyribo*n*ucleic *a*cid). Each gene is a particular segment of a DNA molecule in a chromosome. However, the genes of some viruses are made up of another chemical called RNA *(r*ibo*n*ucleic *a*cid).   Daniel L. Hartl

For a complete discussion of the role of the gene in heredity, see **Heredity** (Chromosomes and genes) and **Cell** (The code of life). See also **Gene mapping; Genetic engineering; Gene therapy; Races, Human** (How human populations develop and change).

Gene mapping is a method of identifying and locating genes on the chromosomes within cells. Genes carry the chemical instructions that determine an organism's traits. These instructions are stored in DNA (deoxyribonucleic acid), the chief substance of each chromosome. By studying the inheritance of a trait within a family, scientists can map the gene that controls the trait to a position on a particular chromosome.

Modern techniques of gene mapping focus on DNA, unlike previous methods, which involved breeding and crossbreeding plants and animals. Today, scientists construct most chromosome maps by *cleaving* (cutting) a chromosome's DNA into gene-sized fragments. Cleaving is done by means of *restriction enzymes.* Each restriction enzyme cleaves a particular segment of the DNA molecule at a point called the *cleavage site.* By using combinations of restriction enzymes, researchers can isolate a fragment that contains a single gene. The cleavage sites can be used to indicate the location of this fragment in the chromosome, and thus the gene's position on the chromosome map. See **Genetic engineering** (How genes are reintroduced into cells).

Each body cell in a human being contains 23 pairs of chromosomes and an estimated 50,000 to 100,000 genes. Scientists have identified the genes associated with certain hereditary illnesses, including cystic fibrosis and sickle cell anemia. Researchers hope to map the entire human *genome*—that is, all the genes in a human cell. To reach this goal, scientists worldwide share the results of their research in large computerized databases. This cooperative international research effort is called the Human Genome Project. The National Human Genome Research Institute (part of the National Institutes of Health) and the Department of Energy coordinate and fund research on the project in the United States. In

June 2000, the Human Genome Project and Celera Genomics Corporation, a private company, announced that together they had essentially determined the entire sequence of the DNA *bases* in the human genome. Bases are the four chemical compounds found in DNA. Discovering the sequence of the bases was a vital step in mapping the human genome.   Leroy Hood

See also **Heredity** (Hereditary disorders); **Human Genome Project.**

Gene therapy is an experimental technique for treating or preventing diseases by inserting a gene into a patient's cells. Genes are the basic unit of heredity. They carry chemical instructions that determine the form and function of each cell. Through gene therapy, doctors can provide a new set of instructions for treated cells.

Every human cell has an estimated 50,000 to 100,000 genes. Genetic diseases result when a gene is defective or missing, causing affected cells to malfunction. Gene therapy makes it possible to correct such defects in the function of cells. Gene therapy is in the early stages of development but offers hope of treating or preventing genetic diseases that today are incurable. There are thousands of known genetic diseases. They include muscular dystrophy, cystic fibrosis, and hemophilia. Doctors first used gene therapy as a treatment in 1990. The case involved a 4-year-old girl whose deficiency of the enzyme *adenosine deaminase* (ADA) caused defects in her immune system. Scientists at the National Institutes of Health in Bethesda, Maryland, inserted a normal human ADA gene into immune cells taken from the girl's body. They returned the treated cells to her body through a transfusion. The inserted gene instructed the cells to make normal amounts of the missing enzyme, and her defective immune system began to recover. In 2000, a group of French scientists reported that they successfully treated three infants with similar immune system defects using a different gene therapy technique.

Gene therapy also has the potential to treat many nongenetic conditions. By introducing new or modified genes, the cells can be instructed to carry out entirely new functions. For example, researchers have introduced genes into cancerous cells to make cancer therapy more effective or to revert the cells to a nonmalignant state.

The type of gene therapy presently used involves only *somatic cells* (body cells) of the patient, rather than the *reproductive cells* (male sperm and female ova). It is called *somatic cell gene therapy.* Another, theoretical form of gene therapy, called *germline gene therapy,* would introduce genes into the patient's reproductive cells. Thus, patients treated with germline gene therapy would pass along the inserted genes to their offspring. This prospect has aroused concern among both scientists and nonscientists. Many people worry that germline gene therapy could change the basic nature of human beings by altering their genetic makeup.

To provide a forum for concerns about gene therapy and to help monitor its use, all proposals for gene therapy in the United States must be approved by government regulatory groups. These groups include the Food and Drug Administration (FDA) and a special committee at the National Institutes of Health (NIH), where much of the government's work in genetics is done. In 2000, the NIH and FDA began a review of gene therapy research methods following the death in 1999 of a patient in a gene therapy experiment.   R. Michael Blaese

See also **Genetic engineering; Heredity** (Hereditary disorders; The era of genetic engineering).

Genealogy, *JEE nee AHL uh jee* or *JEHN ee AL uh jee,* is the study of family origins based on records of important events in the lives of individuals and their ancestors. Genealogical research is the method used to identify ancestors from written and oral records and to establish their relationships in families.

People engage in genealogical research for various reasons. Some people search for their family roots out of curiosity. Others hope to establish a legal right to inherit property. Still other people seek membership in lineage societies. In addition, some individuals search for parents or children whose identity has been lost to the family through divorce or adoption.

A person begins genealogical research by recording his or her name on a *pedigree chart*—also known as a *family tree*—and continuing with the names of the person's parents, grandparents, great-grandparents, and so on. The family tree is expanded by completing a family group record for each ancestral couple and their children. Each person on the chart is identified by dates and places of birth, marriage, and death.

The best records for establishing the identity of family members are *vital records,* such as birth certificates, marriage licenses, and death certificates. These records are kept by government agencies or church clerks in the area where the family lived. It also may be necessary to search relationship records to place a person in the correct family. These records include census records, land records, probate records, and church surveys.

Genealogical research begins in the home, where there may be copies of vital records and relationship records. Information may also be obtained from family letters, family Bibles, newspaper clippings, obituaries, and printed family histories. The next step is to write the appropriate government or church record keepers or to contact local genealogical societies or libraries.

The world's largest genealogical library is the Family History Library of the Genealogical Society of the Church of Jesus Christ of Latter-day Saints in Salt Lake City, Utah. Its worldwide microfilm collection includes copies of records filmed at government and church record repositories and at other genealogical libraries. Other sources include the Library of Congress in Washington, D.C., Newberry Library in Chicago, Henry E. Huntington Library in San Marino, California, and New England Historical and Genealogical Society in Boston.

Genealogists use computers to prepare lineage-related pedigree charts and family group records and to retrieve information from libraries. People interested in tracing their family tree may hire a genealogical agent or professional genealogist for assistance.   Laureen R. Jaussi

See also **Burke's Peerage.**

Additional resources

Willard, Jim and Terry. *Ancestors: A Beginner's Guide to Family History and Genealogy.* Houghton, 1997.
Wright, Raymond S. *The Genealogist's Handbook.* Am. Lib. Assn., 1995.

General is an officer of the highest rank in the armed forces of many countries. In the United States, the title is used for the highest officers of the Army, Air Force, and Marine Corps. The rank of general entitles an officer to command a force larger than a regiment.

The Army and Air Force have five levels of general, and the Marine Corps has four. The highest level is called *General of the Army* or *General of the Air Force.* An officer holding that rank wears the insignia of five stars. Before 1944, this officer wore four stars. The next rank is called simply *general* and carries four stars. *Lieutenant general* follows with three stars, *major general* with two, and *brigadier general* with one. In most cases, a general commands all ground troops in a continent or other large area of operations. A lieutenant general commands a corps or field army, a major general a division, and a brigadier general a brigade.

Congress created the rank of General of the Army in 1866 and awarded it to Ulysses S. Grant, who led Union troops in the American Civil War (1861-1865). Henry H. Arnold became the first General of the Air Force in 1949.

In 1799, Congress established the nation's highest military title, General of the Armies of the United States. Congress intended the rank for George Washington, commander of the first American army, but he never received it. An act of Congress finally awarded him the title in 1976. The only soldier previously given the rank was John J. Pershing. He received it after leading the American forces in Europe in World War I (1914-1918).

Ann Alexander Warren

General Accounting Office (GAO) is an independent agency in the legislative branch of the United States government. It reviews or *audits* (closely examines) the operations and programs of most federal government agencies and reports its findings to Congress.

The GAO makes investigations to determine whether federal agencies are using public money effectively. It advises Congress on the use of public funds and settles financial disputes between the government and businesses or persons.

The General Accounting Office was established in 1921. It operates under the direction of the comptroller general of the United States.

Critically reviewed by the General Accounting Office

General Agreement on Tariffs and Trade (GATT) is a multilateral treaty that aims to promote trade among its members in manufactured and agricultural goods. About 120 countries subscribe to it. The GATT provides both a forum for discussing trade barriers and trade-related disputes and a code of conduct for its members. The members are called *contracting parties.* The first nations signed the GATT in 1947, and it became the main international agreement on world trade. In 1995, the World Trade Organization (WTO) was set up to administer the GATT and to reduce barriers to trade in services and in other areas not covered by the GATT. The WTO's headquarters are in Geneva, Switzerland.

The GATT's contracting parties meet from time to time to negotiate the removal of barriers to international trade. These meetings have substantially reduced tariffs and other trade obstacles on thousands of products.

The principles of *nondiscrimination* and *transparency* are central to the GATT. Nondiscrimination is reflected in the "most-favored-nation" clause, which specifies that a party granting a trade advantage to one country must grant it to all contracting parties. Transparency means that trade measures should be made known to other contracting parties, preferably in the form of a tariff, which is highly visible. GATT rules work to lessen the use of import quotas and other trade restrictions.

In 1994, GATT officials completed the *Uruguay Round,* a series of trade negotiations that began in Uruguay in 1986. The negotiations resulted in an agreement to further reduce trade barriers among GATT members. The agreement also called for setting up the World Trade Organization (WTO). The agreement went into effect in 1995. Robert M. Stern

See also **Tariff** (United States tariffs); **World Trade Organization.**

General Assembly. See United Nations.

General Electric Company is one of the largest corporations in the United States. Well known for its lamps and other electric appliances, it makes a variety of other products, including locomotives, jet engines, electric motors, power generation equipment, automation systems, medical equipment, and plastics. It also operates General Electric Financial Services, Incorporated, the nation's largest diversified financial services and leasing company. In 1986, General Electric merged with the RCA Corporation, the parent corporation of the National Broadcasting Company.

General Electric, also called GE, has offices in every U.S. state and in Washington, D.C. It has about 170 U.S. manufacturing plants and more than 100 plants in 25 other nations. The Canadian General Electric Company, Limited, makes and sells products in Canada and throughout the world.

GE was founded in 1892, when the Thomas-Houston Electric Company merged with the Edison General Electric Company. Edison General had grown out of several companies, including the Edison Electric Light Company, founded in 1878 by Thomas A. Edison.

GE corporate headquarters are in Fairfield, Connecticut. For sales, assets, and number of employees, see **Manufacturing** (table: 50 leading U.S. manufacturers).

Critically reviewed by the General Electric Company

General Federation of Women's Clubs. See Women's Clubs, General Federation of.

General Motors Corporation is one of the biggest manufacturers, and the largest producer of automobiles, in the world. General Motors (GM) owns more than 250 manufacturing, distribution, and service facilities in the United States. It also operates in about 50 other countries, including Australia, Brazil, Canada, Germany, Mexico, and the United Kingdom. In the United States, dealers sell GM automobiles and trucks under various trade names, including Buick, Cadillac, Chevrolet, GMC, Oldsmobile, Pontiac, and Saturn. Other General Motors products include military vehicles, diesel locomotives, radar equipment, guided missile systems, engines for aircraft, gas turbines for ships, and replacement parts for automobiles and trucks.

GM offers financial services and insurance to dealers and customers. The company also owns Hughes Aircraft Company and the Electronic Data Systems Corporation, a computer services company.

The General Motors Company was organized by American manufacturer William C. Durant in 1908. It was incorporated in Delaware as the General Motors Corporation in 1916. The company became tremendously successful, even turning a profit during the Great Depression years of the 1930's. After World War II (1939-1945), profits soared. But by the 1970's, foreign car makers had begun to make substantial inroads into the United States market. GM's market share slipped during the 1980's, and in 1990 and 1991 it lost more than $6 billion. GM sought to regain profitability by consolidating operations and reducing excess manufacturing capacity. During the 1990's, the company closed a number of plants. It reduced its work force by about 20 percent through layoffs and early retirements, and by not replacing workers who left the company.

GM headquarters are in Detroit. For sales, assets, and number of employees, see **Manufacturing** (table: 50 leading U.S. manufacturers). James Mateja

See also **Durant, William C.**

General Services Administration (GSA) is an independent executive agency of the United States government. It manages federal property and equipment. GSA supervises the construction and operation of government buildings. It obtains and distributes supplies to federal agencies and disposes of surplus property. It stockpiles strategic and critical materials. It also operates government communications and computer systems. GSA was established in 1949, and its headquarters are in Washington, D.C.

In 1978, GSA and U.S. Department of Justice investigations revealed illegal activities by GSA employees and private supply companies. Some of the activities, including bribery and theft, had been going on for nearly 20 years and involved $200 million or more. An additional $200 million may have been lost through wasteful management. The scandal was probably the costliest in the history of the government. To prevent further abuses, GSA officials introduced stricter rules for the awarding of contracts, better inventory systems, and other procedures. Harvey Glickman

Generation is a term that refers to a particular group of animals or plants in a line of descent. Each generation, in turn, produces offspring that make up another generation. For example, parents represent one generation and children represent the next. Each human generation is considered to be about 25 years. Generation may also mean one stage in a person's life cycle, if the stages are markedly different. See also **Alternation of generations; Plant** (How plants reproduce).

George B. Johnson

Generator. See Electric generator.

Genesis, *JEHN uh sihs,* is the first book of the Bible. It is the oldest and most complex of the ancient writings that have been accepted as the Word of God by Western religions. Genesis begins the events of the Bible. It describes the origins of the world, and it introduces the earliest ancestors of the Israelite people. Biblical scholars believe that parts of Genesis began as oral literature, perhaps as early as 2000 to 1500 B.C. The book did not achieve its final form until at least 1,000 years later.

Genesis consists of two main parts. The first part (chapters 1-11), called *primeval history,* describes the origin of life and civilization on earth. It includes the stories of the Creation, Adam and Eve, Cain and Abel, and Noah and the Flood. The primeval history is not history in the traditional sense, but an attempt to provide basic information about the nature of the world and humanity.

Many of the primeval accounts resemble those in other ancient literatures. But the Biblical stories present a unique idea of one benevolent God, an ordered universe, and humanity that has goodness at its core.

The second part of Genesis (chapters 12-50), called *patriarchal history,* focuses on the ancestors of ancient Israel. This section presents stories about Abraham, Isaac, and Jacob, who are considered the *patriarchs* (fathers) of the Israelite people.   Carol L. Meyers

See also **Bible** (Books of the Hebrew Bible); **Pentateuch.**

Genêt, *zhuh NAY,* **Edmond Charles Édouard,** *ehd MAWN sharl ay DWAR* (1763-1834), created the first international crisis for the United States. He came to the United States as minister from France in 1793, during the French Revolution. His mission was to persuade the United States, as an ally of France, to declare war on the United Kingdom. He also wanted to raise an army in America to win Louisiana back from Spain. President George Washington had declared the United States neutral in European quarrels, but Genêt began to arm ships and raise recruits in American ports. These acts violated U.S. neutrality and forced Washington in 1794 to ask France to recall him. Genêt was ordered to France, but Washington saved him from having to return. He settled in New York and became a U.S. citizen.

James H. Hutson

See also **Washington, George** (Relations with France).

Genet, *zhuh NAY,* **Jean,** *zhahn* (1910-1986), a French author, became known for his violent, complex plays. Genet's characters include murderers, thieves, homosexuals, and prostitutes. The underworld they inhabit was well known to Genet, who was a thief as a young man. Genet was sentenced to life imprisonment in 1948 as a habitual criminal, but the sentence was commuted through the intervention of several prominent French writers, notably Jean-Paul Sartre.

The criminal or morally evil actions of Genet's characters have the solemn quality of ritual. Many characters who perform them take on the identity of respectable persons, such as a bishop or a police chief. Genet suggested that the difference between evildoers and admired or ordinary people may be less than it seems.

Genet was born in Paris. His plays include *The Maids* (1947), *Deathwatch* (produced in 1949, but written before *The Maids), The Balcony* (1956), *The Blacks* (1958), and *The Screens* (1961). He also wrote *Our Lady of the Flowers* (1942), a novel; and *The Thief's Journal* (1949), a journal of his early life.   Dora E. Polachek

Genetic counseling is a process in which people seek professional help to diagnose, understand, and cope with inherited conditions. These conditions are passed from one generation to another by *genes.* Genes are microscopic chemical instructions inside every cell that affect how living things develop and function. The importance of genes in determining particular conditions varies. People seek genetic counseling when they know or suspect that genes play a significant role in a condition that affects them or someone in their family.

Techniques of genetic counseling. Genetic counselors review client medical records and interview clients to construct a detailed family medical history. The counseling process may include genetic tests or other evaluations to aid in diagnosis. If a genetic condi-

tion may be present, the counselor interprets the evidence for the client and explains the nature of the condition. The explanation makes clear what is known about the condition, how it is inherited, how it is treated, and how it may affect future generations. Counselors may offer further testing or ongoing medical care, and help clients find additional resources and support.

Understanding and coping with genetic conditions involves medical, moral, and personal challenges. During counseling, clients may confront such difficult issues as understanding the mathematical likelihood that they have inherited a condition or will pass it to their offspring; considering whether they want to know if they have an inherited disorder; learning about current or future health risks and medical care involved in managing a condition; or deciding whether to continue a pregnancy when a genetic condition affects an unborn child.

Genetic counseling is *nondirective*—that is, a counselor does not tell a client what to think or what to do. Counselors aim to provide clients with the information and tools they need to make their own decisions. Counselors also support clients' efforts to maintain confidence and self-worth as they cope with their situation.

Most professionals who offer genetic counseling have special training in the medical and psychological aspects of genetic conditions. Some professionals have a master's degree in genetic counseling. Physicians with certification in a specialty called *medical genetics* may offer counseling. Other counselors have a doctoral degree in genetics or a related academic field. Most counselors work as members of a team that includes other health professionals.

Reasons for seeking genetic counseling. Some common reasons for seeking counseling include obtaining advice before or during pregnancy; diagnosing a child who shows symptoms of an inherited disorder; and testing adult members of a family that has a history of a genetic condition.

Counseling during pregnancy may be offered for many reasons. For example, pregnant women over 35 years old may seek advice because the chance of certain conditions rises as the age of the mother increases.

If analysis of the family medical history or other factors suggest an increased risk of a genetic condition, parents-to-be may be offered one or more tests to help make a diagnosis. Tests commonly offered to pregnant women include: (1) tests of the mother's blood that detect higher than normal levels of chemicals associated with certain abnormalities in the developing baby; and (2) *ultrasound,* which uses sound waves to create an image of the baby within the mother's body. Additional tests may be offered to some women with an unusually high risk of having a baby with a genetic condition. Two tests that provide direct examination of the baby's genetic material are *amniocentesis* and *chorionic villus sampling.* Because these procedures involve minor surgery, they carry a small risk to the developing baby.

Couples considering a future pregnancy may seek counseling to determine their likelihood of having a child with a genetic condition. For example, people who have already had a child with a hereditary disorder may want to know their chances of conceiving another affected child. Also, members of some ethnic groups have an increased chance of being a *carrier* for certain genetic conditions. A carrier is a person who is not affected by a condition, but may pass the condition on to a child if the other parent is also a carrier. One such condition is Tay-Sachs disease, which occurs chiefly in Jews of Eastern European origin. Testing for these conditions usually involves testing the parents' blood for certain chemicals or particular genetic material.

Parents may seek a genetic evaluation to determine if a child has an inherited disorder. Common reasons for seeking evaluation include suspected mental retardation, delayed growth or development, and birth defects.

Some genetic conditions do not become apparent until adulthood. Adults may seek advice when such a condition develops in one or more members of their family, and they want to know if the condition might also affect them. Examples of genetically influenced illnesses that usually appear in adulthood include certain inherited cancers and a fatal neurological disorder called Huntington's disease.   Maureen E. Smith

Related articles in *World Book* include:

Amniocentesis	Heredity
Birth defect	Huntington's disease
Genetic testing	Tay-Sachs disease

Additional resources

Bennett, Robin L. *The Practical Guide to the Genetic Family History.* Wiley, 1999.
Zallen, Doris T. *Does It Run in the Family? A Consumer's Guide to DNA Testing for Genetic Disorders.* Rutgers, 1997.

Genetic engineering is the term applied to techniques that alter the *genes* (hereditary material) or combination of genes in an organism. The cells of all living organisms contain genes. Genes carry chemical information that determines the organism's characteristics. By changing an organism's genes, scientists can give the organism and its descendants different traits.

For thousands of years, breeders of plants and animals have used breeding methods to produce favorable combinations of genes. These "genetic engineers" have produced most of the economically important varieties of flowers, vegetables, grains, cows, horses, dogs, and cats. Beginning in the 1970's, scientists developed ways to reintroduce individual genes into cells or into plants, animals, or other organisms. Such techniques alter the heredity of the cells or organisms.

How genes are reintroduced into cells. Genes lie within cells on tiny, threadlike structures called *chromosomes.* Each chromosome contains a single long molecule of a chemical substance called DNA (deoxyribonucleic acid). A molecule of DNA may contain thousands of genes. DNA stores within its chemical structure the information that determines an organism's hereditary properties.

The physical structure of DNA is much the same in all organisms. The DNA molecule is shaped like a twisted rope ladder, called a *double helix.* The "rungs" of the ladder are made of four chemical compounds called *bases.* A pair of bases forms each rung. Most genes consist of several thousand base pairs. The order of the bases, or the *base sequence,* provides the information necessary for a cell to make a specific protein. The form and function of a cell depend on the proteins it produces. Thus, the base sequences of an organism's DNA make the organism different from all other living things.

In addition to storing information, the DNA molecule's structure allows for easy *replication* (duplication) of the molecule. Before a cell divides, enzymes split the DNA ladder lengthwise, separating the base pairs. Then, the base sequence in each half ladder directs the production of a new matching half. In this way, each of the two new ladders becomes a duplicate of the original ladder. See **Heredity** (Replication).

To alter the genetic makeup of DNA, scientists use a technique called *gene splicing.* In this technique, a gene-sized fragment of DNA is taken from one organism and joined to a DNA molecule from another organism or from the same organism. Gene-sized DNA fragments are isolated by means of *restriction enzymes.* These enzymes react chemically with a specific base sequence in the DNA molecule and break the molecule at that point. This point is called the *cleavage site.* The gene-sized DNA fragment can then be *spliced* (joined) to another DNA molecule by using an enzyme called *ligase.* The hybrid molecule formed is called *recombinant DNA.*

When recombinant DNA is mixed with specially prepared cells, a few of the cells will take up the recombinant DNA in a process called *transformation.* The mixture of cells is then placed on a special culture medium that allows only the "transformed" cells to grow. Each of the transformed cells with the newly added genetic information grows overnight into a colony of millions of cells. This colony represents a *clone*—that is, a group of genetically identical cells.

Uses of genetic engineering. Researchers have found important uses for genetic engineering in such fields as medicine, industry, and agriculture. Many new uses are predicted for the future.

In medicine. A number of human illnesses are caused by the failure of certain genes in the body to make specific proteins. For example, the failure of genes in the pancreas to make insulin causes diabetes. Scientists can produce large quantities of insulin in bacterial "factories" by splicing the insulin gene isolated from human cells to plasmids from cells of *Escherichia coli* bacteria. The insulin is then given to patients who need it. Researchers also have engineered *E. coli* to make proteins called *interferons.* These proteins are normally produced by body cells in response to viral infections. They have been tested against many diseases. See **Interferon.**

Many people suffer from diseases caused by genetic defects. Using recombinant DNA techniques, scientists can test DNA isolated from cells of unborn babies to learn whether the babies will have a disease. Also, researchers have investigated methods of *gene therapy* in an effort to cure diseases.

Doctors first used gene therapy to treat a patient in 1990. The patient suffered from a weak immune system. Since then, many clinical trials using gene therapy on people have been undertaken.

In one approach, the DNA of viruses is modified by replacing disease-causing genes with normal human genes. The modified viruses become vehicles to replace defective genes in patients' cells with normal genes. This method may help doctors treat cystic fibrosis and various liver diseases. In another technique, researchers are introducing genes into cancer cells to make them more vulnerable to drugs that can kill them.

In industry. Genetically engineered microbes have been used to improve the efficiency of food production.

For example, *rennin,* an enzyme used in making cheese, is produced naturally in the stomachs of calves. By means of gene splicing, rennin can be obtained more cheaply. Genetic engineering also has potential in controlling pollution. Researchers are working to develop genetically engineered microorganisms that break down garbage, toxic substances, and other wastes.

Researchers are also developing genetically engineered protein enzymes that can carry out chemical reactions in extremely harsh conditions. For example, these protein enzymes can function at high tempera-

How recombinant DNA is formed

WORLD BOOK diagrams by Zorica Dabich

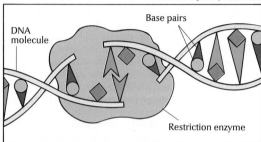

Splitting a DNA molecule. A molecule of DNA is split chemically by means of a *restriction enzyme.* The enzyme separates the molecule lengthwise at a specific sequence of *base pairs.* Base pairs are chemical compounds in the DNA molecule. They contain information that determines the properties of cells.

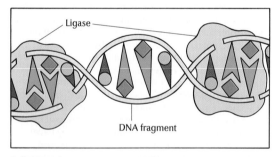

Splicing. A fragment of DNA is isolated from another organism. The bases of the fragment are *spliced* (joined) to the bases of another DNA molecule by using a chemical called *ligase.*

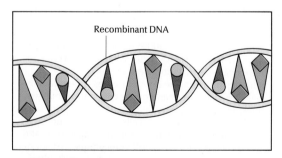

Recombinant DNA. The new hybrid molecule, called *recombinant DNA,* has genetic properties that differ from the original DNA pieces. By inserting recombinant DNA into an organism, scientists can change the organism's physical traits.

tures or in solutions that do not contain water. Such enzymes may become important components in the manufacture of antibiotic drugs and other products.

In agriculture. Scientists have developed numerous genetically engineered plants. Thousands of genetically engineered plant hormones have been safely field tested under conditions approved by the U.S. Department of Agriculture. Special genes have been engineered into tomato plants to enable them to produce tomatoes with increased flavor and shelf life. Small plants have been genetically engineered to produce small amounts of a biodegradable plastic. Such crops as cotton, corn, soybeans, papaya, and squash have been engineered to resist disease or injury from herbicides, insects, or viruses. Other genetically engineered plants are used to produce antibodies, for potential use in medicines.

Large amounts of a growth hormone found in cows have been obtained from genetically engineered bacteria. When treated with this hormone, dairy cows produce more milk, and beef cattle have leaner meat. Similarly, a genetically engineered pig hormone causes hogs to grow faster and decreases fat content in pork.

In 1996, a group of scientists in Scotland, led by British biologist Ian Wilmut, achieved the first successful cloning of a mammal from the cells of an adult animal. They produced a clone of a sheep, which they named Dolly. Cloning may provide numerous benefits for human beings. For example, livestock of superior quality could be cloned for farmers. Such livestock would yield higher quality meat, milk, and wool. People could also clone animals that produce human proteins and other substances used in medical drugs.

History. Genetic engineering is based on genetics, a science begun in the early 1900's but based on experiments done in the mid-1800's by the Austrian monk Gregor Mendel.

Techniques for isolating and altering genes were first developed by American geneticists during the early 1970's. During the late 1970's, researchers used recombinant DNA techniques to engineer bacteria to produce small quantities of insulin and interferon. By the early 1980's, methods of genetic engineering had been adapted to large-scale production of these substances. In 1982, bacterially produced insulin became the first recombinant DNA drug approved by the Food and Drug Administration (FDA) for use on people.

Also in the early 1980's, geneticists made progress in using genetic engineering techniques to add genes to higher organisms. Researchers inserted a human growth-hormone gene into mice, and the mice grew to twice their normal size. In 1982, researchers succeeded in transferring a gene from one species of fruit fly to another. That same year, geneticists proved genes can be transferred between plant species. In 1987, scientists introduced a gene from a bacterial cell into tomato plants, making the plants resistant to caterpillars.

In 1986, the U.S. Patent and Trademark Office issued the first patent on a plant produced through genetic engineering—a variety of corn with increased nutritional value. In 1988, the first U.S. patent on a genetically engineered higher animal was issued. The animal, a type of mouse, was developed for use in cancer research. In 1990, the FDA approved rennin as the first genetically engineered gene product. In 1996, Ian Wilmut and his colleagues pioneered the technique of cloning mammals from the cells of adult animals. The following year, Japanese and American scientists in Hawaii used a similar technique to produce clones of mice.

Concerns about genetic engineering. Despite its many benefits, genetic engineering has caused concern among some people. Some oppose genetic engineering because they fear that harmful, uncontrollable bacteria might be produced accidentally. Others worry about possible environmental damage by the deliberate introduction of organisms whose heredity has been altered. Some people also question the morality of manipulating the genetic material of living creatures. In addition, the successful cloning of mammals has led many to debate the possible benefits and drawbacks of human cloning.

In 1976, the National Institutes of Health (NIH) issued safety guidelines to control laboratory procedures for gene splicing. These guidelines have been gradually relaxed because such research was proved safe. In 1985, the NIH approved experimental guidelines for treatment in which genes are transplanted to correct hereditary defects in human beings. In 1987, a committee of the National Academy of Sciences concluded that transferring genes between species of organisms posed no serious environmental hazards.

In 1997, the USDA amended its regulations on genetically engineered plants. Once plant breeders have shown that a genetically altered plant has no risk for becoming a pest, they can apply to the USDA to obtain nonregulated status for that plant.   Irwin Rubenstein

Related articles in *World Book* include:

Biotechnology	Heredity (The era of genetic
Clone	engineering)
Gene mapping	Medical ethics
Gene therapy	

Additional resources

Aldridge, Susan. *The Thread of Life: The Story of Genes and Genetic Engineering.* Cambridge, 1996.
Darling, David J. *Genetic Engineering: Redrawing the Blueprint of Life.* Dillon Pr., 1995. Younger readers.
Swisher, Clarice. *Genetic Engineering.* Lucent Bks., 1996.

Genetic testing is a medical evaluation that indicates whether a person's cells contain genetic material associated with an inherited disorder. The material consists of a particular form of a *gene.* Genes are chemically coded sets of biological information within every cell. Each form of a gene carries a particular set of instructions.

Genetic testing focuses on identifying disease-related forms of genes and developing methods to detect them. Many such tests are conducted by examining the genetic material inside cells obtained from blood samples, from inside a person's cheeks, or in hair roots. Another approach involves determining whether a gene's product—that is, a protein—is normal. Genetic testing has become an extremely active field of medical research.

How genes carry information. Genes code information in particular lengths of a chemical called DNA (*de*oxyribo*n*ucleic *a*cid). DNA is made up of four types of simpler chemicals called *bases.* The four bases are adenine (A), cytosine (C), guanine (G), and thymine (T). DNA is tightly coiled into microscopic structures called *chromosomes.* People have 23 pairs of chromosomes within the nucleus of every cell except egg and sperm cells, which have only 1 chromosome of each pair. People inherit one chromosome of each pair from their mother and one from their father. Scientists estimate that human chromosomes contain 50,000 to 100,000 genes. The order in which the bases A, C, G, and T are arranged determines the information coded in each gene. The gene's normal position on a chromosome is called its *locus (LOH kuhs),* from the Latin word for *place.*

Any form of a gene that can occur in a particular locus is called an *allele (uh LEEL).* Some genes have as many as several hundred different alleles. In general, people inherit two alleles for each gene—one in the set of chromosomes that they receive from their mother and one from their father. In rare cases, both alleles in a particular locus may come from one parent.

Strictly speaking, genetic testing detects alleles, not genes. Although people commonly refer to "testing for genes," this description is inexact. Everyone has some form of the gene for a particular characteristic at that locus. Genetic tests establish whether an individual carries an abnormal allele associated with a particular disorder. Abnormal alleles arise as a result of *mutation,* a random process that alters the order of bases in a gene.

Scientists often use the example of *hemoglobin,* the molecule in red blood cells that carries oxygen, to illustrate the relationship among genes, alleles, and DNA. Everyone has genes for hemoglobin at the hemoglobin locus, and there are several different alleles for it. One of the hemoglobin alleles, called *hemoglobin S or sickle hemoglobin,* is associated with a disease called *sickle cell anemia.* In this disorder, normally round red blood cells twist into crescent shapes as hemoglobin S releases oxygen. The deformed cells block tiny blood vessels and cause serious symptoms. The allele for hemoglobin S differs from other alleles by only one base in one of the sequences of DNA that codes for hemoglobin.

Genes associated with disease. The importance of genes in determining particular diseases or other characteristics varies. A few thousand disorders occur as a result of one or more abnormal alleles in a single gene. More often, the relationship between genes and disease is complex. Many genetic diseases involve alleles for several genes. In many disorders, environmental factors, such as diet, exercise, or smoking, also play a role.

Single-gene diseases. Most single-gene diseases are rare, and many cause serious disability, severe pain, or even early death. Scientists classify single-gene diseases as *dominant* or *recessive.* Dominant diseases appear in an individual who has inherited an abnormal allele from only one parent. Inheriting a healthy allele from the other parent does not prevent the disease from occurring.

Many dominant diseases are fatal in childhood, so affected individuals do not live long enough to pass the disease on to future generations. But a few dominant diseases do not appear until adulthood, at a time when many affected individuals may have already had children. One such condition is a fatal nerve disorder called Huntington's disease, which typically appears when people are 35 to 40 years old. Children of a person with Huntington's disease have a 50 percent chance of inheriting the affected parent's abnormal allele.

Most single-gene disorders are recessive. These diseases occur only in individuals who have inherited an abnormal allele from both parents. A person who has only one abnormal allele for these diseases is called a *carrier* and usually experiences few or no symptoms. Examples of recessive single-gene diseases in which carriers have few or no symptoms include sickle cell anemia and *cystic fibrosis*, a fatal lung and digestive disorder.

Certain recessive conditions are called *X-linked recessive disorders*. Alleles for these disorders are carried on the X chromosome, one of two chromosomes that determines sex. The other sex-determining chromosome is called the Y chromosome. Males are XY, and females are XX. A male (XY) who inherits an abnormal recessive allele on the X chromosome will lack a normal allele on his Y chromosome and will develop the disorder associated with the abnormality. But females (XX) who inherit an abnormal allele on one X chromosome usually have a normal allele on the other, and so they will not develop the disorder. A blood clotting disorder called *hemophilia* is one example of an X-linked recessive disease.

Single-gene diseases that always occur when people have the one or two alleles involved are called *completely penetrant*. These diseases are also called Mendelian, because they follow predictable patterns of inheritance that Austrian monk Gregor Mendel observed in his experiments with garden peas in the 1800's.

A number of tests are available to detect single-gene, completely penetrant diseases. Such tests can predict conclusively whether a disease will occur. But the tests cannot predict the severity of the condition, which may vary from one person or family to another. For example, blood tests can determine if parents-to-be carry the abnormal allele for cystic fibrosis. If both parents are carriers, their children will have 1 chance in 4 of having cystic fibrosis. Parents who discover that they are both carriers may choose to have further genetic tests performed prior to birth on any children that they conceive. If these tests show that an unborn child has the disorder, the parents may choose to end the pregnancy.

Disorders involving more than one gene. Most genetic diseases involve more than one gene. Many such disorders are also influenced by environmental factors. For example, certain alleles at a locus called BRCA1 greatly increase the likelihood—but do not guarantee—that a woman will develop breast cancer. Such an allele is called *incompletely penetrant*. Inheriting such an allele from one parent is sufficient to increase risk.

Tests are available for some alleles—including those at the BRCA1 locus—that increase the risk of disease. But the results of such a test may be hard to interpret. One difficulty is that not everyone who has one such allele gets the disease. Further, people who have one such allele but have few or no relatives with the disease may get the disease less often than do people who have many family members with the condition.

Promises and challenges of genetic testing. Genetic testing has caused excitement among scientists and patients because it offers the possibility of predicting future health problems. In some cases, knowing that a person carries an abnormal allele may enable the individual to avoid the disorder associated with the allele. Such measures as careful medical supervision and lifestyle changes may help some people escape serious illness. Scientists also hope that future discoveries may enable them to develop treatments that will correct genetic errors directly in abnormal DNA.

But genetic testing also involves medical limitations

and stirs social concerns. One issue is that genetic tests cannot always accurately predict future disease. Further, no treatment yet exists for some of the disorders for which genetic tests are available. Such situations may burden adults with knowledge of future untreatable disease or confront parents of unborn children with difficult choices about whether to end a pregnancy.

Privacy of genetic testing is a social issue that concerns many scientists and policymakers. They fear that insurers will deny health insurance to healthy individuals whose test results indicate a high risk or certainty of future illness. Some states of the United States have enacted laws forbidding discrimination in health insurance based on genetic testing.

Genetic testing also stirs fears that results will be used for purposes that most people find unacceptable, such as *eugenics*. Eugenics is the practice of attempting to control human breeding to encourage "desirable" traits or to prevent "undesirable" ones.

Medical experts urge that genetic tests never be performed without a patient's *informed consent*. Informed consent means that health professionals have clearly explained the risk and benefits, and that the patient has agreed to the procedure.　　Neil A. Holtzman

Related articles in *World Book* include:

Cystic fibrosis	Genetic counsel-	Heredity
Disease (Inherited diseases)	ing	Huntington's disease
	Genetics	
DNA	Hemophilia	Sickle cell anemia

Genetics is the scientific study of *heredity,* the passing on of characteristics of living organisms from one generation to the next. Geneticists investigate the structure, function, and transmission of *genes*. Genes are the basic units of heredity and are present in the cells of all organisms. For example, each of the cells in the human body has from 50,000 to 100,000 genes. They determine overall body build and such traits as eye, hair, and skin color.

Genetics can be divided into three major areas of study. They are (1) molecular genetics, (2) transmission genetics, and (3) population genetics.

Molecular genetics examines the structure of genes and the chemical processes associated with them. Genes are located in cells on threadlike structures called *chromosomes*. Genes are made up of DNA (deoxyribonucleic acid), and most genes carry coded chemical instructions for the production of proteins. Proteins are essential for the repair and replacement of body tissues. Some proteins, called *enzymes,* control the chemical reactions that occur within all living things. The structure of a gene—that is, the instructions that are contained in its DNA—determines which protein it makes and when it makes it.

Molecular geneticists study such processes as *replication* and *mutation*. Replication is the process by which the cell duplicates DNA molecules. DNA replication occurs before cell division. Mutation is a permanent change in a gene's coded chemical instructions. Gene mutations may alter the organism's traits in some way and may be transmitted to future generations.

Some molecular geneticists, called *developmental geneticists,* focus on *gene regulation*. They try to determine the regulatory processes that cause certain genes to become active in some cells and not in others. In the pancreas, for example, some cells produce insulin because a certain gene is active in them. But in all other cells of the human body, this gene is not active even though it is present.

Advances in molecular genetics led to the development of *genetic engineering* (techniques for altering the structure of genes). Genetic engineering has been used to alter genes to increase crop and livestock production. It also has many uses and potential uses in medicine and industry. See **Genetic engineering.**

Transmission genetics is the traditional approach to the study of heredity. Transmission geneticists analyze patterns of inheritance by applying and extending laws discovered by Gregor Mendel, an Austrian botanist and monk. Mendel reported his discoveries in 1866. Transmission geneticists study how genes are transmitted by tracking variations in the patterns of inheritance of a trait over generations.

Transmission geneticists locate and describe where genes are arranged on chromosomes, a process called *gene mapping.* Their work has made it possible to associate certain traits with specific genes.

Discoveries in transmission genetics have many practical applications. For example, the discovery of a gene that is responsible for a hereditary disorder helps identify those who are at risk of developing the condition.

Population genetics focuses on processes that change the relative frequency of genes in a *population* through time. A population is a group of individuals of the same species that live within the same area.

Population geneticists often study how mutations and other processes of evolution, such as natural selection, interact with one another. They try to understand how such interactions affect the frequency with which certain genes occur within a population. Population geneticists believe that an understanding of the processes of evolution and genetic transmission helps explain the diversity of life on the earth—and within our own species.

Irwin Rubenstein

See also **Heredity** and its list of *Related articles.*

Geneva, *juh NEE vuh* (pop. 171,042; met. area pop. 424,028), is a historic city in southwestern Switzerland. It lies at the western end of Lake Geneva, where the Rhône River leaves the lake (see **Switzerland** [political map]). The French spelling for *Geneva* is *Genève,* and the spelling in German is *Genf.* Geneva is the capital of the *canton* (state) of Geneva. It is also a famous international city. Switzerland's neutrality prevents participation in political and military alliances, but it provides an impartial meeting place for other nations. Many international pacts were worked out in Geneva (see **Geneva Accords; Geneva Conventions**).

The Rhône River divides Geneva into two sections. The old section lies south of the river. It has narrow, winding streets. Its landmarks include St. Peter's Cathedral, begun in the 900's; the University of Geneva, founded as a college in 1559 by John Calvin, a leader of the Protestant Reformation; and the town hall, built in the 1500's. Geneva's newer section, north of the Rhône, features many hotels and the Palace of Nations. The palace was headquarters of the League of Nations, an international peacekeeping organization that existed from 1920 to 1946 (see **League of Nations** [picture]).

Many international organizations have their headquarters in Geneva. The Palace of Nations now houses the European headquarters of the United Nations (UN). The International Labour Organization, the Red Cross, and the World Council of Churches also have headquarters in Geneva. Many multinational firms have offices there. The organizations and firms provide many jobs for the city's residents and its *guest workers.* Guest workers come from other nations to work in Geneva and make up about 30 percent of its population. Tourism contributes greatly to the economy. Geneva's products include expensive clocks, watches, and jewelry.

Roman soldiers established a settlement on the site of what is now Geneva in about 50 B.C. During the early Middle Ages, Geneva served as the home of the kings of the region of Burgundy. In the A.D. 1000's, it became a self-governing city of the Holy Roman Empire. During the 1500's, under the leadership of Calvin, Geneva became a center of Protestantism (see **Calvin, John**). In 1815, the Geneva canton joined the union of Swiss cantons called the Swiss Confederation.   Heinz K. Meier

Geneva, Lake. See Lake Geneva.

Geneva Accords, *juh NEE vuh,* were a series of international agreements made on July 20 and 21, 1954. They ended more than $7\frac{1}{2}$ years of war in the former French colony of Indochina. In that war, the forces of France, Cambodia, Laos, and the Associated State of Vietnam had fought Vietminh troops. The Vietminh was a nationalist movement dominated by Communists and led by Ho Chi Minh, ruler of the Democratic Republic of Vietnam. The government of the Associated State of Vietnam was based in southern Vietnam. The government of the Democratic Republic of Vietnam was based in northern Vietnam.

The Geneva Accords, or *Geneva Agreements,* were negotiated at a conference in Geneva, Switzerland. At the conference were representatives of the Associated State of Vietnam, the Democratic Republic of Vietnam, Cambodia, Laos, France, the United States, the United Kingdom, the Soviet Union, and Communist China.

Three of the pacts arranged cease-fires in Cambodia, Laos, and Vietnam. The cease-fires for Cambodia and Laos provided for the withdrawal of foreign troops, both French and North Vietnamese. The Cambodian and Laotian governments were to have full control of their countries. The cease-fire for Vietnam, signed by France and the Vietminh, set up a *provisional* (temporary) boundary at 17° north latitude. The Vietminh was to administer northern Vietnam. The Associated State of Vietnam and France were to administer southern Vietnam. A control commission, composed of representatives of Canada, India, and Poland, was to supervise the cease-fires.

Another agreement called for the major nations of the world to obey the cease-fires and to recognize the independence and neutrality of Cambodia and Laos. A further agreement called for elections to be held in 1956 in Vietnam with the goal of establishing a unified, independent Vietnam. This agreement was orally accepted by all the nations represented at the conference except the United States and the Associated State of Vietnam. They both feared the Communists might win a national election and control all Vietnam. The United States and the Associated State of Vietnam promised only not to use force to oppose the accords.

In 1955, the Associated State of Vietnam became the Republic of Vietnam. Ngo Dinh Diem became president of the republic and refused to permit the proposed elections in South Vietnam. Both sides violated the cease-fire. In 1957, Communist guerrillas called the Viet Cong began the struggle that grew into the Vietnam War (see **Vietnam War**).   Harvey Glickman

Additional resources

Cable, James. *The Geneva Conference of 1954 on Indochina.* St. Martin's, 1986.
Randle, Robert F. *Geneva 1954: The Settlement of the Indochinese War.* Princeton, 1969.

Geneva Conventions, *juh NEE vuh,* provide for the humane treatment of civilians, prisoners, and wounded persons in wartime. The first Geneva Convention, or Treaty, was signed in 1864. It was accepted by all European countries, by the United States, and by some countries in Asia and South America. Agreements in 1906, 1929, 1949, and 1977 added new provisions.

The Geneva Conventions include such provisions as the treatment and care of wounded and sick military personnel in the field; wounded, sick, and shipwrecked members of the armed forces at sea; and the treatment of prisoners of war. They also provide for the protection of civilians and members of militias and volunteer corps during wartime. Methods are provided to identify the dead and wounded, and to send information to their families. The protection of hospitals and medical transports, their proper marking with a red cross, and other provisions and laws for conduct are also set forth in the Geneva Conventions. American codes of conduct for military personnel have adopted these conventions, as have other nations party to them.   Robert J. Pranger

See also **Prisoner of war; Red Cross** (History).

Genghis Khan, *JEHNG gihs KAHN* (1162?-1227), was a Mongol conqueror who founded the largest land empire in history. He ruled an area that stretched across central Asia from the Caspian Sea to the Sea of Japan. His name is also spelled *Chingis* or *Jenghis.*

Genghis Khan was a political and military genius who united Mongol and other nomadic tribes into a disciplined, effective fighting force. The Mongol armies were

also known for their use of terror. When conquered territories resisted, the Mongols slaughtered the population of entire cities.

Genghis Khan was an intelligent man with superior organizational abilities. Although he had little interest in cultural matters, he promoted literacy among his people. He also established the first Mongol code of laws, called the *Yasa* or *Yasak.* The order he created throughout

Drawing (late 1200's or 1300's) by an unknown Chinese artist; National Palace Museum, Taipei, Taiwan

Genghis Khan

his vast empire promoted the growth of trade between China and Europe.

Rise to power. Genghis Khan's original name was Temüjin, which means *ironworker.* His father was the chief of a small but influential Mongol tribe. Temüjin inherited that position at about the age of 13, when members of an enemy tribe poisoned his father. But according to *The Secret History of the Mongols,* a Mongol epic written during the mid-1200's, the members of the tribe abandoned their new chief. For a while, Temüjin and his family lived a harsh, lonely existence. They owned few sheep or other livestock and had to dig roots for food.

Soon, however, Temüjin began to attract followers, form alliances, and build an army. He used harsh training and strict discipline to create a superior fighting force. He also ensured that his troops were well equipped and that they quickly adopted new tactics and weapons. Temüjin appointed officers on the basis of achievement instead of for their family connections, as was customary among the Mongols.

Temüjin used his army to extend his power over neighboring tribes. By 1206, he had become ruler of Mongolia. That year, an assembly of Mongol chieftains proclaimed him *Genghis Khan,* a title that probably

The empire of Genghis Khan

Genghis Khan started his empire from Karakorum in 1206. In 1207, he united the Kyrgyz and other tribes with the Mongols, shown in light yellow on the map. He then conquered the Xi Xia, Kara Kitai, and Khorezm empires. His armies next took over the Kipchaks and then defeated the Russians in 1223 at the Kalka River. The light orange area on the map shows Genghis Khan's empire at the time of his death in 1227.

	Area controlled by Genghis Khan in 1207
	Area controlled by Genghis Khan in 1227

WORLD BOOK map

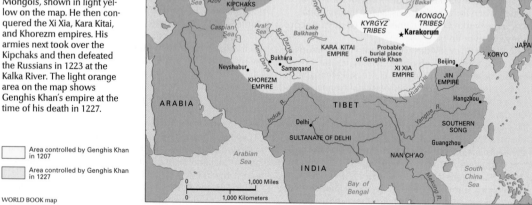

meant either *universal ruler* or *invincible prince.*

Conquests. After becoming the ruler of Mongolia, Genghis Khan set out to conquer China. He first attacked a kingdom in northwestern China called Xi Xia (also spelled Hsi Hsia). He then invaded northeastern China and in 1215 took Beijing (Peking), the capital of the Jin (Chin) Empire.

In 1218, Genghis Khan broke off his assault on China and swept into central Asia. He crushed Khorezm, also spelled *Khwarezm,* a kingdom in what are now Uzbekistan and Turkmenistan. In 1220, he destroyed the cities of Bukhara and Samarqand (Samarkand) in present-day Uzbekistan and Neyshabur (Nishapur) in modern Iran. Two smaller armies invaded the plains north of the Caspian Sea. There, by 1223, they had conquered the Kipchaks, a Turkic people, and had defeated the Russians at the Kalka River.

In 1225, Genghis Khan turned to Xi Xia, which had allied with the Jin Empire. He conquered Xi Xia in 1227, just before he died. His grandson Kublai Khan completed the conquest of China in 1279.   Richard L. Davis

See also **Mongol Empire.**

Additional resources

Marshall, Robert. *Storm from the East: From Genghis Khan to Khubilai Khan.* Univ. of Calif. Pr., 1993.
Ratchnevsky, Paul. *Genghis Khan.* Basil Blackwell, 1992. Translation of 1983 German edition.

Genie is a word often used in English for *jinni* (plural, *jinn),* a type of demon in Arabian mythology. Muslims believed that the jinn were intelligent beings made of air or fire. They were created out of smokeless flame. Human beings, according to Arabian mythology, were made from clay and angels were made from light. Although invisible, jinn could appear as either human beings or animals. They could be either good or bad. Jinn appear in many Eastern fables. They also appear in the *Arabian Nights,* a collection of folk tales. In one story, Aladdin's jinni comes to help him whenever he rubs a magic lamp (see **Aladdin).**   Elaine Fantham

Genital herpes. See Herpes.

Genitive case. See Case.

Genius was a guardian spirit worshiped by the ancient Romans. The Romans believed that every man was born with a genius (plural, *genii*) who protected and guided him throughout his life. A woman's protector was called her *Juno.*

The man gave gifts to his genius on his birthday. After he died, his family honored his genius at his burial site. The emperor's genius was especially sacred and was included in public prayers.   Elaine Fantham

Gennesaret. See Galilee, Sea of.

Genoa, *JEHN oh uh* (pop. 678,771), is Italy's busiest and largest port and a major industrial center. The city's name in Italian is Genova. Christopher Columbus was born in Genoa in 1451. The city is the capital of Liguria, one of Italy's political regions. Genoa lies in northwestern Italy, between the Gulf of Genoa and the Alps and Apennine Mountains (see **Italy** [political map]).

The city lies on a narrow plain along the Gulf of Genoa and on the slopes of the surrounding mountains. The section of the city along the water has many narrow, winding streets and old shops and houses. The newer sections of Genoa are on the mountainsides.

Many beautiful palaces, some dating back to the 1500's, line the main streets of Genoa's old section. Some of these palaces are now art museums. The city has many parks and *piazzas* (public squares). A famous statue of Christopher Columbus by Michele Canzio stands in the Piazza Acquaverde. By the late 1200's, colleges of scholars had been established in Genoa. In 1471, Pope Sixtus IV founded the University of Genoa.

Genoa's port is the city's main source of income. It faces many problems, including old equipment and lack of space. In 1965, a cargo clearing center opened at Rivalta Scrivia, north of Genoa. The center has storage and transportation facilities that help speed the distribution of goods to and from Genoa.

The people of Genoa have been sailors and merchants throughout the city's history. Most Genoese are Roman Catholics, and each year they celebrate the feast of the Madonna della Guardia, the protector of sailors. Genoa has one of Italy's highest standards of living and highest levels of education.

Economy. The port of Genoa serves as northern Italy's chief outlet to the western Mediterranean Sea. Genoa ranks second in size only to Marseille among Mediterranean ports. Ships from Genoa carry farm goods produced in Italy's Po Valley. The port also provides an outlet for the manufactured products of Genoa, Milan, and Turin. These three cities form Italy's Industrial Triangle. This area has the nation's highest concentration of industrial development.

Genoa imports chemicals, coal, crude oil, grain, meat, oil seeds, and ore. The city's chief exports include cotton and silk goods, olive oil, and wine. The industrial area of Genoa extends along the coast west of the harbor. Shipbuilding is a major industry in Genoa, and the city also produces electric, railway, and ship equipment. Genoa has oil refineries, steel mills, and textile factories. The city serves as an important railway center.

History. The Romans settled Genoa in the 200's B.C. The city became the headquarters of the Roman fleet.

The Roman Empire fell during the A.D. 400's, and Genoa had to develop its own defenses against barbarian tribes that invaded the Italian peninsula. By the mid-700's, Genoa was a strong naval power. It became a nearly independent city-state ruled by its nobles. During the 1100's, Genoa joined the Crusades and established trading settlements in Constantinople, Cyprus, Syria, and Tunis. At the height of its power in the 1200's, Genoa controlled the central Mediterranean, including the islands of Corsica and Sardinia.

Genoa fought frequent wars with other Italian naval cities to maintain its power. A series of wars with Venice for control of trade in the eastern Mediterranean ended in 1380 with the defeat of Genoa. The city gradually lost its power. The Turks conquered most of Genoa's eastern possessions. Genoa's last remaining colony, Corsica, was purchased by France in 1768.

Genoa also had many problems at home, including conflicts between the nobles and the people over control of the government. The nobles fought many bloody feuds among themselves as well. In 1339, a revolution overthrew the nobles, and power went to a ruler called a *doge.* The doge, a member of a prominent family, was elected by the people (see **Doge**). In 1528, a new constitution set up a government ruled by the nobles. In 1656, about half of the city's people died in an epidemic.

In 1800, Genoa came under the control of France. After the defeat of Napoleon in 1815, the city was taken over by the Kingdom of Sardinia. In 1861, Genoa became part of the newly formed Kingdom of Italy.

Bombings damaged Genoa during World War II (1939-1945). The damage was repaired, and the city has expanded greatly in area.   David I. Kertzer

Genocide, *JEHN uh syd,* is the deliberate and systematic mistreatment or extermination of a national, racial, political, religious, or cultural group. Genocide is committed by organized groups, usually governments, rather than by individuals. The word *genocide* comes from the Greek word *genos,* which means *race* or *tribe,* and the Latin *-cide,* meaning *killing.*

Throughout history there have been persecutions and atrocities which can be described as cases of genocide. The Russian *pogroms* (persecutions of the Jews) during the late 1800's and early 1900's were an example of genocide. During World War II, the Germans practiced genocide. They killed about 6 million European Jews.

The United Nations drew up an international convention in 1948 that made genocide a crime. Fifty years later, in 1998, the International Criminal Tribunal for Rwanda became the first international court to pass a guilty verdict for the crime of genocide. The verdict related to crimes committed during the 1994 conflict in Rwanda.

Robert J. Pranger

See also **Holocaust; Nuremberg Trials; Racism; Rwanda; War crime.**

Gent. See **Ghent.**

Gentian, *JEHN shuhn,* is a group of wild and cultivated plants that includes about 600 species. The showy flowers are often blue, but may be yellow, white, or red. Gentians grow throughout the world except in Africa. About 20 species thrive in the United States. The best-known species in North America is a type of fringed gentian. Its bright blue, open, bell-shaped flowers appear early in fall. Each stem has one flower. The plants grow from 1 to 3 feet (30 to 91 centimeters) tall and have long, pointed leaves.

The flowers of many gentians never open. These are called *closed,* or *bottle,* gentians. The common closed gentian of the Eastern United States has clusters of blue flowers from August to October.

A large yellow gentian grows in the Alps and the Pyrenees Mountains at elevations from 3,000 to 6,000 feet (900 to 1,800 meters). The plants are about 6 feet (1.8 meters) tall and bear clusters of open yellow flowers. Their yellowish-brown bitter root is used for flavoring in vermouth and as a medicine.   Melinda F. Denton

Scientific classification. Gentians belong to the gentian family, Gentianaceae. The fringed gentian is *Gentianopsis crinita;* the closed gentian is *G. andrewsii;* and the yellow gentian is *G. lutea.*

Gentile, *JEHN tyl,* in ancient times, referred to the people of all nations other than the Jews. Throughout the Bible, the term *gentile* designates any non-Jew. Today, the word is sometimes used to mean *Christian.* In the historical sense, however, this is not a correct use. The earliest Christians were Jews, and not until Saint Paul began his zealous missionary work did gentiles begin to come into the Christian church in large numbers. Both Mormons and Muslims consider all people not of their faith to be gentiles.   H. Darrell Lance

Gentileschi, *jehn tee LEHS kee,* **Artemisia** (1593-1652?), was an Italian painter. She specialized in paintings of strong heroines, especially from the Bible. A favorite subject was Judith, the virtuous Jewish widow who beheaded the Assyrian general Holofernes (see **Judith**).

Gentileschi was one of the most influential followers of the style of the Italian artist Michelangelo Caravaggio. Her emphasis on strong contrasts between light and dark, called *chiaroscuro,* is a main feature of Caravaggio's style. Other notable elements in Gentileschi's style include the realism of her figures and the strength and determination shown by the women in her paintings.

Gentileschi was born in Rome. Her father, Orazio Gentileschi, was also a noted painter. She traveled to England about 1638. There, she undertook some commissions and helped her father with his projects. Her late works were painted in a more classical style and are less admired than her early paintings.   Ann Friedman

Gentlemen's agreement. In the 1890's, many people feared that workers coming to the United States from Japan would take all the jobs and put them out of work. They wanted Congress to pass a law preventing further immigration. Japan protested, and made the *gentlemen's agreement* of 1908 instead. Japan promised to halt unrestricted emigration to the United States. In return, President Theodore Roosevelt promised to discourage any law limiting Japanese immigration. Since then, the term has been applied to any measure agreed upon by a class or group of people, but not made into law, that affects the welfare of another group. See also **Oriental exclusion acts.**   John A. Gable

Genus. See **Classification, Scientific** (Groups in classification).

Geochemistry is a science that applies chemistry to the study of the earth. Geochemists investigate the distribution and quantities of chemical elements, their compounds, and their isotopes throughout the earth, including its crust, waters, and atmosphere. They also seek the natural processes that produced such a distribution.

The principles of geochemistry have many practical uses. *Exploration geochemistry,* also called *geochemical prospecting,* helps locate deposits of ore, natural gas, and petroleum. It involves, for example, sampling and analyzing extremely small amounts of minerals and gases that occur in surface rocks, soil, plants, and ground water. The presence of unusual amounts of certain elements can reveal that large deposits of valuable mineral resources lie below the surface.

A branch of geochemistry called *isotope geology* studies the occurrence of isotopes of various elements. Measurements of lead and strontium isotopes reveal the age of rocks and enable scientists to estimate the age of the earth. Similar measurements of isotopes in lunar rocks and meteorites have contributed to knowledge about the beginnings of the solar system.

Geochemists believe the earth began as part of a huge cloud of dust and gases. The dust and gases collected into a solid mass that grew larger by attracting nearby particles of matter. Various processes occurred within the mass to produce heat, which melted the materials that make up the earth. The heaviest of the molten materials sank to the earth's center and caused the lighter substances to float upward. These materials then settled and formed layers. The earth's elements and compounds became chiefly concentrated in the layers.

Geochemists classify the elements into five groups according to their chemical and physical relationships. The *siderophile* (ironlike) elements, which are found primarily in the earth's core, include cobalt, iron, and nickel. The *chalcophile* (copperlike) elements occur outside the core and consist largely of sulfides of copper, lead, silver, and zinc (see **Sulfide**). The *lithophile* (rocklike) elements, such as aluminum, calcium, magnesium, and silicon, make up most of the rock-forming minerals in the earth's crust. The *atmophile* elements, which include carbon, hydrogen, oxygen, and nitrogen, form the atmospheric gases. They occur alone or in such simple compounds as carbon dioxide and water vapor. The *biophile* elements consist of carbon, hydrogen, oxygen, nitrogen, phosphorus, and sulfur. They form the complex compounds in living matter.   Sherry O. Farwell

Geode, *JEE ohd,* is a hollow, stonelike formation often lined with crystals. Geodes are found in many parts of the world. They average from 2 to 6 inches (5 to 15 centimeters) in diameter. A type of geode called *hydrolite,* or *water stone,* contains quartz crystals left when water that contained silica evaporated.   Kenneth J. De Nault

Geodesic dome. See Fuller, Buckminster.

Geodesy, *jee AHD uh see,* is a science that seeks to determine the size, shape, and gravitational field of the earth. It also monitors variations over time in the earth's rotation, size, and topography. Geodesists use various surveying techniques to measure the distances and directions between points on, under, or above the earth's surface. They calculate the elevation, latitude, and longitude of thousands of places on earth. One major use of geodetic data is the making of a wide variety of maps, from navigational charts to topographical maps.

Since the mid-1960's, space technology has greatly improved the accuracy of geodetic measurements. Geodesists are making measurements with radio waves emitted by *quasars*—extremely luminous objects in distant galaxies—and with laser beams reflected off artificial satellites. Using these tools, geodesists are building a *global reference frame* (a listing of measurements of the locations of various points) that is accurate to 1 centimeter ($\frac{3}{8}$ inch).

Geodesists also use these tools to directly measure the movements of the plates that form the earth's surface with an accuracy of a few millimeters a year. Geodesists map movements of the earth's crust associated with earthquakes and *subsidence,* the sinking of the crust caused by withdrawal of fluid under the surface. In addition, they track variations in the earth's rotation and in the wobble about its axis.   William E. Carter

See also **Surveying.**

Geodetic center of North America, *JEE uh DEHT ihk,* is located at the Meades Ranch Triangulation Station in Osborne County, Kansas. It serves as the point of origin for all governmental mapping in the United States (except Hawaii), Canada, and Mexico. The United States Coast and Geodetic Survey (now National Ocean Survey) chose Meades Ranch as the geodetic center of the United States in 1901. This point was chosen because of its central location. Meades Ranch became the geodetic center of North America in 1913, after Canada and Mexico also adopted it.   Stephen S. Birdsall

Geoduck, *GOO ee duhk,* is the name of a group of large marine clams. The best-known kind, the Pacific geoduck, lives along the Pacific coast of North America. It can weigh as much as 10 pounds (4.5 kilograms), and its open-ended shell may reach 9 inches (23 centimeters) long. The clam's habitat ranges from seacoasts to ocean depths of over 200 feet (61 meters). It lives in burrows that are sometimes over 3 feet (1 meter) deep. A geoduck feeds on tiny plant-like organisms called *phytoplankton.* It uses long, tubelike organs called *siphons* to draw in food and seawater. The animal's large gills then act as a filter to trap the food.

Robert S. Prezant

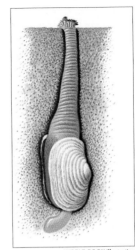

WORLD BOOK illustration by James Teason

Geoduck

Scientific classification. Geoducks are in the family Hiatellidae. The scientific name of the Pacific geoduck is *Panopea abrupta.*

Geoffrey of Monmouth, *JEHF ree, MAHN muhth* (1100?-1155?), was a Welsh historian who wrote the first narrative of the entire life of King Arthur, a legendary ruler of Britain. Geoffrey tells of Arthur in *History of the Kings of Britain* (about 1136). The book is a mythical story of Britain's rulers from its first king, Brut (whom Geoffrey calls Brutus), through the rulers of the A.D. 600's. Geoffrey claimed to have based his work on a chronicle. But most of the tale is probably his own invention. See also **Arthur, King.**   Robert Francis Cook

Geographic center of North America is in Pierce County, North Dakota, just southwest of Rugby. A *cairn* (stone pile) marks the spot. The U.S. Geological Survey defines the geographic center of an area as "that point on which the surface of the area would balance if it were a plane of uniform thickness." For location, see **North Dakota** (physical map).   Stephen S. Birdsall

Geographic center of the United States is in South Dakota, about 17 miles (27 kilometers) west of Castle Rock in Butte County (see **South Dakota** [physical map]). Before Alaska became a state in 1959, the geographic center was in Smith County, Kansas. With the admission of Alaska, it moved to Butte County. When Hawaii became a state later in 1959, it shifted 6 miles (10 kilometers) west-southwest.   Stephen S. Birdsall

Geographic Names, United States Board on, a United States government organization, decides official names of geographic features and places for federal maps and other publications. The board works with officials from U.S. states, the United Nations, and other countries to develop federal standards for both domestic and foreign geographic names. The board works cooperatively with the secretary of the interior and consists of representatives from other executive departments and federal agencies. It was established in 1890.

Critically reviewed by the United States Board on Geographic Names

Geography is the study of the location and distribution of living things and the earth features among which they live. Geographers study where people, animals, and plants live and their relationship with rivers, deserts, and other earth features. Geographers also examine where earth features are located, how they came to be there, and why their location is important. The word *geography* comes from the Greek word *geographia,* which means *earth description.*

Geographers search for patterns in the distribution of features over the earth's surface. They seek to discover the reasons for the patterns. For example, they may study dust storms and why they occur, or they may try to discover why some rivers flood more often than others. Geographers also look for patterns in human economic, political, and social activities and try to find out why these patterns exist. For instance, geographers analyze where cities are located around the world. They also determine the relationship between these locations and the climate, terrain, and other factors.

Geographers want to know about the forces that create and change the landscape. For this reason, they study climate and the alterations caused by such natural forces as wind and water. Geographers are also interested in how human beings change the earth. For example, they may analyze how the expansion of a city affects a nearby river. In addition, geographers examine the ways in which the surface of the earth has changed over time. They may study how a city has grown or how a river valley looked hundreds of years ago.

Geographers use information gathered by scientists in many other fields, including geology, biology, anthropology, economics, physics, and sociology. They combine this material with data from their own research to answer questions about the earth's surface. They often record the results of their research on maps, which serve as their most basic tool. Geographers also rely on such other techniques as travel, photography, surveying, interviewing, and the use of statistics.

What geographers study

Geography considers four principal types of questions. They deal with (1) location; (2) spatial relations; (3) regional characteristics; and (4) the forces that change the earth.

Location. One of the main tasks of geographers is to identify and record the location of places, of earth features, and of human populations and activities. To do this, geographers have marked off the earth's surface with imaginary lines called *meridians* and *parallels.* These lines intersect at right angles to form a grid. Geographers determine the location of features by a process of mathematical measurement called *surveying* (see **Surveying**). The information is transferred to a map, on which the grid has been drawn. Thus, geographers can identify the site of anything on the earth's surface.

Spatial relations are the relations that places, earth features, and groups of people have with one another because of their location. Spatial relations may be important in the development of a place and the activities of its people. For example, many industrial cities have developed along important transportation routes rather than near rich mineral deposits.

Regional characteristics. Few people are satisfied to know only the location of a place. Most also want to know its characteristics. They are interested in the kinds of people who live there, how they build their cities, and how they use their land. They also want to know about its landforms and climate, and the types of animals and plants that are found there.

© Martin Rogers, Stock, Boston   Paul Robert Perry   Runk/Schonenberger from Grant Heilman

Different types of geographers study the earth from different viewpoints. A human geographer, *left,* collects information about peoples around the world. A demographer, *center,* studies births, deaths, and other facts about populations. An oceanographer, *right,* studies sea life.

Forces that change the earth. The earth's surface changes constantly. Human activities cause some changes. For example, people move from one place to another and new homes are built on land that was once farmland. Some changes result from natural forces, such as the water erosion that creates canyons or the ocean currents that alter a coastline. At times, human activities and natural processes combine to cause changes on the earth's surface. For example, the Sahara, a desert in northern Africa, has expanded because farmers have grazed their livestock too heavily on nearby grasslands. Geographers study such processes in order to discover how landscapes developed in the past and how they may change in the future.

Divisions of geography

Geographers organize their study of the earth in several ways. They may divide the field into *regional* or *topical* geography. They also may classify the branches of geography according to whether they deal with the physical environment or with human activity.

Regional and topical geography. Regional geography deals with all or many of the geographic elements of a place or region. For example, geographers studying the character of the Persian Gulf region would examine its climate, landforms, and natural resources. They would also study its populations, religious differences, languages, and political divisions.

Topical geography concentrates on the study of one earth feature or human activity as it occurs throughout the world. The worldwide patterns of soil quality and of railroad transportation are two examples of the topical approach in geography.

Physical geography is concerned with the locations of such earth features as land, water, and climate; their relationship to one another and to human activities; and the forces that create and change them. Physical geography includes geomorphology, climatology, biogeography, oceanography, and soil geography.

Geomorphology is the study of landforms, including their distribution and origin and the forces that change them. For example, geomorphologists study where and why avalanches and earthquakes occur and how glaciers move. They also examine the relationship between landforms and human activities.

Climatology concentrates on patterns of climate. Climatologists study such factors as temperature, precipitation, and humidity. They also study how climate changes and how it is affected by human activity.

Biogeography consists of *plant geography* and *zoogeography*. Plant geographers study patterns of vegetation growth and how changes in climate, soil, and human activity affect such patterns. Plant geography is also called *phytogeography*. Zoogeographers study why certain animals live in one region and others in another. They also investigate the migration of animals and the factors that affect their movements.

Oceanography includes the study of ocean currents, waves, and tides. Oceanographers also explore the geography of the ocean floor.

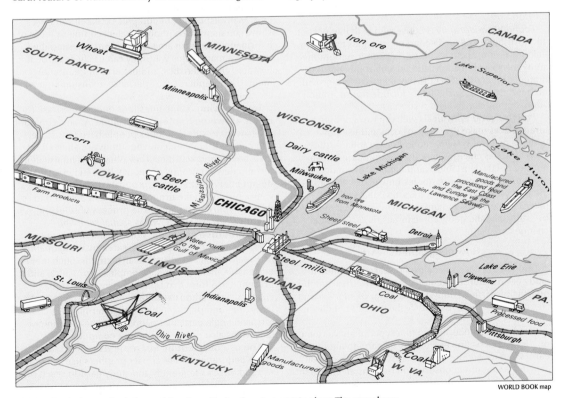

WORLD BOOK map

The study of geography helps explain why a city develops in a certain place. The map above shows that Chicago lies near farmland and areas rich in coal and iron ore. This location, plus nearby lake and river transportation, helped make the city a manufacturing and distribution center.

Soil geography deals with the distribution of various types of soils throughout the world. Soil geographers study how different kinds of soil influence the type and amount of crops produced in an area and how soils are affected by the agricultural methods used in an area.

Human geography concentrates on patterns of human activity and on their relationships with the environment. Specialized fields of human geography include cultural geography, population geography, social geography, urban geography, economic geography, political geography, and historical geography.

Cultural geography examines the location and *diffusion* (spread) of beliefs, customs, and other cultural traits. For example, cultural geographers might study the diffusion of a set of religious beliefs. Or they might explore how a section of the earth has been changed by the cultural practices of the people living there.

Population geography is concerned with patterns of population and the reasons for a change in those patterns. Population geographers deal with birth and death rates, population movements, family size, and other statistical data.

Social geography examines the relationships groups of people have with one another. Social geographers try to analyze how these social relationships affect the places where people live, work, and play.

Urban geography deals with cities and other urban areas. Urban geographers examine how location may be important in the development of cities and other communities. They also may investigate where different groups live within a city or why slums develop where they do.

Economic geography is concerned with the location and distribution of such economic activities as mining, manufacturing, and agriculture. Economic geographers study the spatial relations and the environmental and human factors that affect the development and growth of these activities. Such factors include transportation, labor supply, climate, and resources.

Political geography deals with the ways people in different places make decisions or gain and use power within a political system. Political geographers study such topics as changes in political boundaries, problems of political instability, and patterns of voting.

Historical geography studies how places looked in the past. Historical geographers also deal with how places and patterns of human activity have changed over time and the geographic forces that caused the changes.

How geographers work

Geographers use specialized research methods to study earth features and human activities. These methods include (1) field study, (2) mapping, (3) interviewing, (4) quantitative methods, and (5) the use of scientific instruments.

Field study. Since ancient times, people have relied on direct observation as a means of learning about the earth's surface and the patterns resulting from human activity. Today, direct observation remains an important research method for geographers. They often travel to a region to answer specific questions about that area or to learn about unfamiliar geographic relationships. For example, geographers may study the appearance of an

GECO UK, Science Photo Library

Geomorphologists study surface features of the earth and the forces that change them. These researchers are making a study of earthquakes in Scotland. They are using a *theodolite*, an instrument for measuring angles to calculate distances.

area to help plan new buildings or parks. Or they may observe a farming area suffering from erosion.

Mapping is one of the geographer's most basic activities. Many aspects of geographic research can be shown on maps. Geographers select complex pieces of information about an area and present it in simplified form on a map. In this way, they can easily describe the location, characteristics, and patterns of geographic elements. Geographers who specialize in designing maps are called *cartographers*. See **Map.**

Interviewing. Some questions geographers ask cannot be answered by observation alone. At times, geographers want to study attitudes people have toward certain places or how their surroundings are affected by their beliefs and activities. They obtain this information by interviewing groups of people. Researchers usually do not interview the entire group. Instead, they interview a portion of the group scientifically selected to reflect the entire population. The process of selecting subjects from an area is known as *spatial sampling.*

Quantitative methods. With the aid of computers, geographers often test their research by using *quantitative* (mathematical and statistical) methods. Such methods enable them to simplify complex information and to present it in a form that is more easily understood. Quantitative methods also help geographers find patterns in geographic elements and determine which factors affecting a particular element are the most important. Maps also can be drawn by a computer.

The use of scientific instruments is necessary to much geographic research. Geographers use *remote-sensing devices* to identify and study hard-to-reach or very large physical features. Such devices are instruments that observe and record information from a distance. These devices include aerial and satellite cameras, *infrared* (heat-sensitive) film, and radar. Aerial and

Odyssey Productions

Geographical exploration need not require traveling to distant places. A hike through nearby woods or along a stream can provide curious students with much information about the land features and the animal and plant life of their geographical area.

satellite cameras record information about weather systems, patterns of vegetation growth, and the existence of pollution. Infrared photography reveals information that is invisible to the human eye. For example, infrared photographs show diseased and healthy trees in different colors, even though the trees appear the same to the human eye. Airborne radar can produce photographs similar to aerial photographs, regardless of the weather or time of day (see **Radar** [Pulse radar]).

Some scientific instruments used by geographers measure environmental characteristics. For example, weather gauges measure and record temperature, humidity, wind speed and direction, and air pressure.

Geographers use surveying equipment to identify the precise location of surface features and to measure their distance from other features. Some earth features are so large or change so slowly that geographers can study them best by building a small-scale model of the feature. Geographers use models to study such geographic processes as the flow of rivers, wind erosion, the movements of glaciers, and the effects of tornadoes.

History

Beginnings. Since earliest times, human beings have explored the world around them. Many ancient peoples, including the Egyptians and Phoenicians, traveled through much of Europe and Africa. These ancient explorers journeyed primarily for reasons of trade and conquest. However, as they traveled to unfamiliar areas, they added to what was known about those places. They also became more skilled in mapping. Early maps were simply crude drawings that showed distance and direction. As travel became more common, maps became more accurate and detailed.

The ancient Greeks were the first people of the Western world to study geography in a systematic way. They

attempted to explain how the geographic characteristics of a region affected the activities of the inhabitants. Beginning in the 600's B.C., the Greeks mapped the seacoasts of their own region and sailed throughout the Mediterranean Sea. About 200 B.C., the Greek mathematician Eratosthenes calculated the polar circumference of the earth. His calculation was reasonably close to today's measurement. About two hundred years later, Strabo, a Greek scholar, wrote a 17-volume geography of what was then the known world.

The Romans also contributed to the study of geography during their extensive military campaigns. In the A.D. 100's, the geographer Ptolemy became famous for his mapping skills and his studies of astronomy. Although many of his theories were later proved to be wrong, people believed them for centuries. In fact, his error in estimating the distance between Spain and China encouraged Christopher Columbus to make his famous voyage in 1492. Columbus, an Italian sea captain, sailed from Spain in search of a westward sea route to Asia. Instead, he landed in America.

In the early Middle Ages in Europe, a period that lasted from about the 400's to the 900's, much of the geographic knowledge recorded by the Greeks and Romans was lost. However, the Muslims of the Middle East and North Africa continued to study geography and to make discoveries of their own.

Era of exploration. During the late Middle Ages, which lasted from about the 1000's to the 1500's, Europeans began to travel outside their own region. Many soldiers traveled to the Middle East on the Crusades, a series of expeditions to free the Holy Land from the Muslims. During the 1200's, the Italian trader Marco Polo journeyed to China. He recorded his adventures in a book that includes geographic information about the lands he visited and their inhabitants. However, before about 1400, most Europeans knew little about world geography. Many maps of this period show huge, unknown areas decorated with drawings of dragons, sea serpents, and other imaginary creatures.

During the 1400's and 1500's, the Spaniards and Portuguese began to make long voyages of exploration. In 1492, Columbus landed in America. Vasco da Gama, a Portuguese navigator, sailed around the southern tip of Africa in 1497 and reached India in 1498. In 1519, another Portuguese navigator, Ferdinand Magellan, set out on an expedition to sail around the world. Magellan was killed on the journey, but one of his ships completed the voyage. Also at this time, the Dutch, English, and French began to explore unfamiliar lands. These voyages resulted in an explosion of new information about geography.

From the 1500's to the early 1800's, European explorers mapped many regions of North and South America. Also during the 1800's, Europeans probed the interior of Africa. During the early 1900's, expeditions revealed more information about the Middle East and the North and South poles. Since then, geographers have continued to explore the poles. They also have investigated the ocean floors. For additional information about the exploration of the earth, see **Exploration**.

The growth of geography. Until about the 1820's, geography and geology were considered the same field of study. But then, they each became established as separate fields. Geography achieved such status largely because of the work of the German geographers Alexander von Humboldt and Karl Ritter. The first university geography departments in the United States were established during the early 1900's.

Until about 1920, most geographers were physical geographers. Gradually, geographers began to emphasize the relationships between earth features and human activity. The American geographer Ellen Churchill Semple defined geography as the study of the environment's influence on human history. Carl O. Sauer, also of the United States, studied the diverse ways in which people of different cultures arranged their physical surroundings. During the 1930's, the German geographer Walter Christaller examined the reasons for the growth and distribution of human settlements. In the 1950's, Torsten Hägerstrand of Sweden developed theories for predicting the diffusion of human customs.

Recent developments. Since the 1950's, the study of geography has changed greatly in the United States. Many geographers have chosen to study human geography, especially urban and economic geography, rather than physical geography. Such specialists stress the importance of planning the growth of urban areas and the wise management of natural resources. In addition, geographers have made greater attempts to predict how physical and human processes will affect the earth in the future. To do this, many rely on mathematical and statistical techniques and on the use of computers. Others continue to depend chiefly on field study.

Careers in geography

Geographers work in a variety of jobs. Many geographers teach in high schools and colleges. Others work for state or local governments as planners, land-use specialists, community development experts, and cartographers. The federal government employs geographers in such agencies as the National Park Service, Census Bureau, Forest Service, Geological Survey, and Department of State. Private industry employs economic and population geographers as well as experts in weather forecasting, cartography, land use, and resource management. Most jobs in government and private industry require a bachelor's degree. Higher positions in government and industry, and nearly all academic posts, require a master's or doctor's degree.

Geographers must be knowledgeable on a broad range of subjects. For example, a geographer who wants to study natural resources should also know about such related fields as demography, chemistry, economics, politics, and geology.

Geographers must be able to design and read maps. In addition, they should have a knowledge of statistics and mathematics and be able to work with computers. They should know how to interpret data obtained from remote sensing devices. Geographers must also have the ability to write well so they can communicate their ideas to others.

The major association of geographers in the United States is the Association of American Geographers. It publishes the *Annals* and the *Professional Geographer.* Many geography teachers belong to the National Council for Geographic Education, which publishes the *Journal of Geography.* The American Geographical Society supports research in the field and publishes the *Geographical Review.* People who are interested in geography, even if they are not professional geographers, may belong to the National Geographic Society. It publishes *National Geographic Magazine.*   Stephen S. Birdsall

Related articles in *World Book* include:

Geographers

Grosvenor, Gilbert H.	Ptolemy
Humboldt, Baron von	Strabo
Mercator, Gerardus	

Physical features

See **Desert; Island; Lake; Mountain; Ocean; River; Volcano; Waterfall;** and their lists of *Related articles.*

Other physical geography articles

Climate	Hydrography
Continent	Meteorology
Earth	Season
Ecology	Soil
Geodesy	Weather
Geomorphology	

Human geography

See the various articles on continents, countries, states, and provinces. A complete list of countries appears in the **World** article. See also:

Country	Immigration
Culture	Races, Human
Geopolitics	

Other related articles

Geographic Names, United States Board on	World (Physical features of the world; graphs: Facts about the world's physical features)
National Geographic Society	
Royal Geographical Society	
Seven Natural Wonders of the World	

Additional resources

De Blij, Harm J. *The Earth: An Introduction to Its Physical and Human Geography.* 4th ed. Wiley, 1995.
Demko, George J., and others. *Why in the World: Adventures in Geography.* Anchor, 1992.
Encyclopedia of World Geography. 24 vols. Cavendish, 1994.
Grabham, Sue, ed. *Circling the Globe: A Young People's Guide to Countries and Cultures of the World.* Kingfisher Bks., 1995. Younger readers.
O'Mahony, Kieran. *Geographical Literacy: What Every American Needs to Know About Geography.* Educare Pr., 1992.
Strahler, Alan H. and A. N. *Introducing Physical Geography.* Wiley, 1994. *Modern Physical Geography.* 4th ed. 1992.

Geological Survey is a United States federal agency that conducts studies of public lands and offshore areas. It is part of the U.S. Department of the Interior. Officially known as the United States Geological Survey (USGS), the agency conducts research in geology, geochemistry, geophysics, hydrology, mapmaking, and related sciences. It also studies natural hazards, such as earthquakes and volcanoes, and identifies flood hazard areas. The USGS monitors the quantity, quality, and use of water resources, gathers information on energy and mineral resources, and publishes thousands of technical reports and maps each year. The agency has headquarters in Reston, Virginia, and major facilities in Denver and in Menlo Park, California. The USGS was established in 1879.

The Geological Survey of Canada has duties similar to those of the U.S. agency. It was established in 1842.

Critically reviewed by the United States Geological Survey

Dave Millert, Tom Stack & Assoc.

David Koshman, Earth Images

Kevin Schafer, Tom Stack & Assoc.

Changes in Earth's surface that are studied by geologists include erosion and the effects of volcanoes and glaciers. Moving water can erode soil, *left,* which covers much of the surface. Lava erupting from a volcano, *top right,* flows over the surface and hardens into rock. Glaciers move slowly over the surface, creating lakes and leaving behind rocks and soil, *bottom right.*

Geology is the study of how the planet Earth formed and how it changes. Scientists called *geologists* study rocks, soils, mountains, volcanoes, rivers, oceans, and other parts of the planet. Some geologists study *fossils,* the marks or remains of dead organisms. The study of fossils helps scientists learn how life developed on Earth. Geologists also investigate other objects in the solar system, including Earth's moon, other planets and their satellites, and asteroids and meteorites. The word *geology* comes from Greek words meaning *study of Earth.*

Earth probably formed about $4 \frac{1}{2}$ billion years ago, and it has been changing ever since. Many changes occur slowly, and they will continue to occur as long as the planet exists. Huge land areas rise and shift, creating mountains. Lava flows from volcanoes, then cools and hardens; the resulting crystals grow together into layers of rock. Great rivers of ice called glaciers creep down from mountains, carrying rocks and soil with them. When the glaciers melt, they leave the rocks and soil behind on the lowlands or in the ocean.

Water also changes Earth's surface. Waves strike the shores, gradually washing away the land. Rivers wear down mountains and carry the mud and sand to lowlands. In the lowlands, the mud and sand mix with plant and animal matter, creating rich soil. Rivers also carry soil to the oceans. The movement of water across the ocean floor spreads layers of mud and sand that gradually harden into stone.

There are two main fields of geology: (1) *Physical geology* is the study of the materials that make up Earth and the forces that shape the planet. (2) *Historical geology* deals with Earth's history. Many questions that geologists investigate are a part of both fields.

This article deals with geology as a field of study and as a career. To find out what scientists have learned about the composition of Earth and its history, see the **Earth** article in *World Book.* For information on the geology of other objects in the solar system, see **Satellite** and the articles on individual planets and satellites.

History

The ancient Greeks were the first people to write about Earth's structure and evolution in a scientific manner. But many of their writings were a mixture of facts, superstitions, legends, and guesses. In the 400's B.C., the historian Herodotus observed how water shapes the land. He understood that land at the mouth of the Nile River had formed from sand and mud deposited by the river. He also believed that marine fossils found in Lower Egypt were evidence that the sea had once covered the land.

Empedocles, a philosopher of the 400's B.C., thought that Earth's interior was composed of a hot liquid and that all things came from earth, air, fire, or water. The philosopher Aristotle, who lived in the 300's B.C., believed that Earth's structure was constantly changing. His pupil Theophrastus wrote a short paper called "Concerning Stones," which listed all the rocks and minerals known at the time. Strabo, a geographer and historian, wrote a 17-volume *Geography* about 7 B.C. He recognized that the rising and sinking of lands result partly from volcanic eruptions and earthquakes.

The Romans contributed writings that were more factual than those of the Greeks. But the Roman writings also included much superstition and guessing. Many of those works described mineral ores, mineral trading, and mining in the Roman Empire. In the A.D. 60's, the philosopher Lucius Seneca wrote *Quaestiones naturales,* which provided detailed information on earthquakes, volcanoes, and surface and underground waters. The 37-volume *Historia naturalis* by Pliny the Elder included all Roman knowledge about rocks, minerals, and fossils.

The Roman Empire ended in the A.D. 400's, and little scientific advancement took place for about 600 years. Then, in the early 1020's, the Muslim philosopher Avicenna wrote a book that presented his views of *erosion* (wearing away). The book also discussed the origins of rocks, meteorites, and mountains. Avicenna believed that nature tried to produce living things from nonliving things. He concluded that fossils were unsuccessful attempts by nature to form plants and animals.

The Renaissance, which lasted from about 1300 to 1600, was a period of renewed interest in many fields of learning, including geology. The German physician Georgius Agricola made major contributions to geology in the 1500's. He wrote works on minerals, mining, and *met-*

allurgy (the science of metals). His books included *De natura fossilium* (1546) and *De re metallica* (1556).

About the same time, the Polish astronomer Nicolaus Copernicus accurately described Earth's place in the solar system. Most astronomers had believed that Earth was the center of the universe and did not move. The sun, the moon, and all the other planets supposedly revolved around Earth. In his book *On the Revolutions of the Heavenly Spheres* (1543), Copernicus explained that Earth rotates on its own axis, the moon revolves around Earth, and Earth and all the other planets orbit the sun. In the early 1600's, the Italian astronomer and physicist Galileo supported Copernicus's ideas with discoveries he made with his telescope.

The rock dispute. Nicolaus Steno, a Danish physician, published a key observation in 1669. He discovered that *strata* (layers) of rock in oceans and lakes are always deposited horizontally. Thus, the oldest layers usually lie on the bottom, and the youngest layers sit on the top. This tendency, called the *law of superposition,* helps scientists determine the order in which geologic events occurred.

In the late 1700's and early 1800's, however, a dispute developed concerning the process of rock formation. The German mineralogist Abraham Gottlob Werner believed that an ocean once covered Earth's entire surface. Werner and his followers said that chemicals and sedi-

The branches of geology	Traditionally, geology has been divided into two major fields: (1) physical geology and (2) historical geology. Physical geology is the study of the composition of Earth and the forces that shape the planet. Historical geology is the study of the history of Earth as a physical object. This chart defines 17 important branches of geology. Many of these branches are closely related, and 4 branches are considered part of both physical and historical geology. The chart also shows that geology is related to other sciences.

Physical geology

Economic geology—the study of coal, metals, and other geologic materials useful to industry
Environmental geology—the application of geologic principles to environmental problems
Geochemistry—the study of the substances on and beneath Earth's surface and the chemical changes they undergo
Geophysics—the study of Earth's interior, its magnetic and electrical properties, and the way it transmits energy such as earthquake waves
Hydrology—the study of the movement and distribution of Earth's waters
Mineralogy—the study of minerals
Oceanography—the study of the oceans and life in the oceans
Petrology—the study of igneous, metamorphic, and sedimentary rocks
Planetology—the study of the chemical and physical properties of the planets
Structural geology—the study of the positions and shapes of rocks that are far under the surface, and the causes of changes in these rocks

Physical and historical geology

Geochronology—the study of geologic time
Geomorphology—the study of Earth's surface and the changes that occur there
Glacial geology—the study of glaciers and the way they alter Earth's surface
Sedimentology—the study of sediment and how it is deposited

Historical geology

Paleoecology—the study of the relationship between prehistoric plants and animals and their surroundings
Paleontology—the study of prehistoric plants and animals, based on fossils
Stratigraphy—the study of the layers of rock in Earth's crust

ments in the water slowly settled to the ocean floor, where they formed layers of rock. The oldest, bottom layer was supposedly composed of granite.

According to Werner, all dry land had formed by means of this process. After the layers of rock had formed, water from the global ocean gradually evaporated. The oceans that are present today were left behind in low areas. Werner and his followers also thought that no further changes would occur. Theorists who based their ideas on the notion that all rocks were formed from a global ocean were called *Neptunists*—after Neptune, the Roman god of the sea.

James Hutton, a Scottish geologist, had a different idea. He believed that many rocks form with the aid of heat instead of water. Hutton believed that some rocks form by the cooling of *magma* (melted rock). When magma breaks through the surface, it is known as *lava*. Hutton and his followers said that rocks known as basalt form when lava has cooled. They also believed that magma under the surface cools to form large, irregularly shaped bodies of granite and other kinds of rock. Hutton and his followers were called *Plutonists*—after Pluto, the Roman god of the underworld.

In 1795, in a book called *Theory of the Earth,* Hutton presented what would later be called the *principle of uniformitarianism.* He claimed that Earth was gradually changing in a variety of ways and would continue to change in the same ways. He used his idea of the continuous formation of rocks such as basalt and granite as an example of such a change.

Although some rocks form as particles that settle out of water and do not require heat, Hutton's explanations of the formation of basalt and granite are correct. These findings disproved Werner's idea that all rocks were formed by a global ocean. Hutton died in 1797, before other scientists accepted his ideas. But in 1802, John Playfair, a Scottish mathematician, expanded on Hutton's work in the book *Illustrations of the Huttonian Theory of the Earth.* This book presented Hutton's ideas clearly and with illustrations. It became a leading guide to the development of the field of geology.

Geologists settled the rock dispute largely as a result of the work of Nicolas Desmarest, a French geologist. In the 1760's, Desmarest had shown that the basalt rocks of the Auvergne region of south-central France were created from lava. In the early 1800's, two of Werner's most famous students, Leopold von Buch and Alexander von Humboldt, visited several volcanic areas. Those areas included the Auvergne region and Mount Vesuvius, a volcano in Italy. After studying rocks in those places, the two became Plutonists.

Experimental geology began as a result of the friendship between Hutton and Sir James Hall, a Scottish geologist and physicist. Hall became interested in verifying Hutton's ideas experimentally. He melted rock in large furnaces, much as rock melts far beneath Earth's surface. He found that melted limestone cools to form marble. Hall's work led to the acceptance of Hutton's idea that granite is formed from magma.

William Smith, an English civil engineer, was the first person to use fossils to map rock strata. While surveying and building canals in southern England during the late 1700's, Smith had seen layers of rock that contained fossils. He discovered that the same kinds of fossils occur in the same strata—even in different locations. He then used fossils to trace rocks of the same age across large areas. In 1815, Smith made the first geological maps showing the strata of England.

In 1830, the British geologist Sir Charles Lyell completed the first volume of a three-volume textbook called *Principles of Geology.* Lyell's book greatly influenced other scientists. Lyell supported Hutton's principle of uniformitarianism.

Louis Agassiz, a Swiss-born naturalist, studied European glaciers in the 1830's and 1840's. He suggested that a huge sheet of ice had once extended from the North Pole to Central Europe. Agassiz explained how the slow-moving fields of ice change Earth's surface.

In 1846, Robert Mallet, an Irish-born engineer, began the scientific study of earthquakes. He exploded gunpowder under the ground, then measured how rapidly the resulting vibrations traveled through rock.

The New Zealand-born physicist Ernest Rutherford suggested in 1904 that the *half-life* of radioactive chemical elements in minerals could be used to determine the age of the minerals. The half-life of an element is the length of time needed for half the atoms in a sample of the element to decay. Arthur Holmes, a Scottish geologist, was one of the first scientists to use radioactivity to determine the age of rocks. In 1927, he included a geo-

Dewitt Jones

A petroleum geologist has just set off an explosion in a search for petroleum. Sound waves from the explosion will travel through layers of rock and then bounce back to the surface, where an instrument called a *seismograph* will measure their speed. Sound waves travel at different speeds through different materials. Thus, this measurement will help the geologist determine whether layers of rock that might contain oil lie below.

Ocean Drilling Program, Texas A&M University

Hydrographers use a *sonar transducer* to obtain information about undersea earthquake activity. This instrument uses sound waves to create a diagram of the ocean floor.

logic time scale in the book *The Age of the Earth.*

In 1968, a group of scientists proposed that Earth's outer shell consists of a number of rigid plates that are in continual motion. This theory, called *plate tectonics,* helps support the idea that the continents move about on Earth's surface. It also helps explain the occurrence of mountains, volcanoes, and earthquakes.

Geology of the solar system. Until the late 1950's, scientists could not gather much information about the geology of other objects in the solar system. The only tools available for observing those objects were ground-based telescopes. Earth's atmosphere creates a blurring effect that limits the sharpness of images from such telescopes. In addition, the planet Venus presents another barrier to observation. It is surrounded by thick clouds of sulfuric acid that block views of the planet's surface.

The space age created a new field called *planetary geology,* the study of other objects in the solar system. That age began when the Soviet Union launched the satellite Sputnik in 1957. In 1959, the Soviet space probe Luna 1 flew within 3,700 miles (6,000 kilometers) of the moon. Sensors on the probe gathered scientific data, and radio transmitters sent the data to Earth. Since then, several space probes have orbited the moon or landed there. Astronauts first landed on the moon in 1969, and they brought moon rocks back to Earth. Probes have orbited and landed on Venus and Mars, and a probe has flown past Mercury. In 2000, a space probe made the first close-up observation of an asteroid—an object called 433 Eros.

Space probes have also studied the gas giant planets—Jupiter, Saturn, Uranus, and Neptune—and their major satellites. The planets are not subjects of geological study because they consist mostly of gases and liquids. However, the planets' satellites are made of rock and ice, and so they are of much interest to geologists.

To interpret the information sent to Earth by space probes, geologists use their knowledge of processes that occur on Earth. For example, they apply what they know about volcanoes on Earth to the study of Jupiter's satellite Io, the most geologically active satellite in the solar system. Geologists also apply what they have learned about other objects to the study of Earth. For instance, studies of the moon showed how meteorite impacts helped shape Earth's surface.

Careers

Geologists hold a wide variety of jobs in industry, education, and government. They explore for coal, oil, gas, uranium, and other materials that supply energy. They look for deposits containing such metals as copper, gold, iron, lead, silver, and tin. They also try to find diamonds, emeralds, rubies, and other gems.

Geologists locate building stone, clay, and underground water. They create maps and interpret aerial photographs. They also supply information on how to maintain our supply of water and keep it from becoming polluted. Geologists contribute to space exploration by interpreting images of planetary surfaces, data that indicate the chemical makeup of those surfaces, and rock samples from the moon and other bodies.

Job opportunities. Most geologists work for private companies. Some of the companies explore for oil and gas or for minerals. Other companies work on environmental issues such as water management, waste disposal and cleanup, and land use planning. Geologists also conduct research and teach at colleges and universities.

Areas of specialization in geology are many. *Petroleum geologists* search for oil and gas deposits on land and on or beneath the ocean floor. Their tasks include mapping, fossil studies, and analysis of rock structure.

Barry L. Runk from Grant Heilman

A paleontologist studies fossils found in rocks. The findings provide geologists with information about the age of the rocks and about the land or water in which they were deposited.

Mining geologists look for materials other than gas and oil. They often work in underground or open pit mines, where they examine deposits and direct the removal of ore.

Specialists called *paleontologists* study fossils to learn about life in prehistoric times. *Petrographers* classify rocks. *Stratigraphers* deal with the arrangement of layers of rocks to determine their age and history. *Mineralogists* study and identify minerals. *Geomorphologists* study how Earth's surface was formed and how it changes. *Geophysicists* study Earth's interior using waves from earthquakes or from explosions. In addition, geophysicists investigate Earth's magnetic, electrical, and gravitational properties.   Maria Luisa Crawford

Related articles. For detailed information about Earth, see Earth and its list of *Related articles* and its table: Outline of Earth's history. See also the following articles:

Biographies

Agassiz, Louis	Logan, Sir William E.
Copernicus, Nicolaus	Lyell, Sir Charles
Cuvier, Baron	Pliny the Elder
Dawson, Sir John W.	Silliman, Benjamin
Empedocles	Strabo
Fuchs, Sir Vivian E.	Suess, Eduard
Galileo	Tyrrell, Joseph Burr
Hutton, James	Werner, Abraham G.

Branches

Geochemistry	Petrology
Geodesy	Radiogeology
Geomorphology	Seismology
Geophysics	Speleology
Paleontology	

Other related articles

Basalt	Ocean Drilling Program
Coal	Petroleum
Dinosaur	Plate tectonics
Earthquake	Prehistoric animal
Fossil	Prehistoric people
Gas (fuel)	Prospecting
Geography	Radiation
Geological Survey	Rock
Gravitation	Satellite
Hydrology	Seismograph
Mantle	Soil
Mineral	Space exploration (Space
Mining	probes)
Mountain	Time (Geological time)
Ocean	Volcano

Additional resources

Ellenberger, Francois. *History of Geology.* 2 vols. A. A. Balkema, 1996, 1999.
Gohau, Gabriel. *A History of Geology.* Rev. ed. Rutgers, 1991.
Oldroyd, David. *Sciences of the Earth: Studies in the History in Mineralogy and Geology.* Variorum, 1998.
Petersen, Morris S., and Rigby, J. K. *Interpreting Earth History.* 6th ed. McGraw, 1999.
Spickert, Diane N. *Earthsteps: A Rock's Journey Through Time.* Fulcrum, 2000. Younger readers.
White, George W. *Essays on History of Geology.* 1978.

Geometric style is a term for a number of ancient and modern styles in art. Each style is characterized by distinctive abstract, or geometric, decoration. The geometric style is especially applied to Greek art from 900 to 700 B.C. Early in this period, artists decorated their ceramic vessels with orderly designs of circles, spirals, and angular forms. Later, they used geometric shapes as the basis for human and animal figures in their ceramics

and in bronze statuettes. The ancient Etruscans also worked in a geometric style during this period. American Indians have decorated baskets and other crafts with geometric designs. Modern artists have also used the style. See also **Basket making** (picture: Twining).

Marjorie S. Venit

Geometry, *jee AHM uh tree,* is a branch of mathematics. Geometry involves studying the shape, size, and position of geometric figures. These figures include *plane* (flat) figures, such as circles, triangles, and rectangles, and *solid* (three-dimensional) figures, such as cubes, cones, and spheres.

The name geometry comes from two Greek words meaning *earth* and *to measure.* The earliest uses of geometry included measuring lengths and areas of land. Most scholars believe that the ancient Egyptians were the first people to make extensive use of geometry.

Geometry is important for many reasons. The world is full of geometric shapes. For example, snowflakes are shaped like *hexagons* (six-sided figures), and earthworms are shaped like cylinders. Houses and buildings have rectangular walls, and many bridges have triangular supports. Because geometric shapes are all around us, we can better understand and appreciate our world by knowing something about geometry.

Geometry also has practical applications in many fields. For example, architects and carpenters must understand the properties of geometric objects to construct stable and attractive buildings. Navigators of airplanes, ships, and spacecraft rely on geometric ideas to chart and follow the correct course. Designers, engineers, metalworkers, and photographers also use geometric principles in their jobs.

Geometry as a logical system

Deductive reasoning is important in the study of geometry. Deductive reasoning begins with statements that are already accepted as true. These truths are then combined in a logical way to reach a conclusion. When the original statements are true, correct deductive reasoning always leads to true conclusions.

Here is an example of deductive reasoning: Suppose we wish to prove that the sum of the measures of the angles of a *quadrilateral* (four-sided figure) is 360°. We could begin with two facts that we know are true: (1) Any quadrilateral can be divided into two triangles, and (2) The sum of the measures of the angles of any triangle is 180°. Reasoning deductively, we may conclude that the sum of the measures of the angles of a quadrilateral must equal 2 x 180°—that is, twice the sum of the measures of the angles of a triangle, or 360°. In quadrilateral *ABCD* below, the measure of angle 1 (symbol, $m\angle 1$) + $m\angle 2$ + $m\angle 3$ = 180°, and $m\angle 4$ + $m\angle 5$ + $m\angle 6$ = 180°. Thus, $m\angle 1$ + $m\angle 2$ + $m\angle 3$ + $m\angle 4$ + $m\angle 5$ + $m\angle 6$ = 360°.

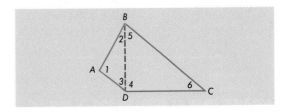

Because we have reasoned logically from known facts, we may be certain that our conclusion is true.

Deductive reasoning is one of two main types of reasoning. The other type is called *inductive reasoning*. For an explanation of inductive reasoning, see **Inductive method.**

Axiomatic organization. Geometry is organized as an *axiomatic system*. Such a system is based on statements that are accepted as true. From these truths, we can reason deductively to prove statements about classes of things. In geometry, those things are geometric figures. Any axiomatic system consists of three sets of elements: (1) terms, (2) axioms, and (3) theorems.

Terms. The terms of geometry fall into two categories: undefined and defined. Undefined terms, such as *point, line,* and *plane,* form the basic building blocks of the axiomatic system of geometry. We consider points, lines, and planes to be exact, but the pictures we draw of these and other figures are only approximate. For example, in geometry, a point has a position in space, but no size at all. A line has length, but no width. On paper, however, a dot representing a point must have some size, and even the finest line has width.

Undefined terms can be used in defining other terms. For example, *line segment AB* (symbol, $\overline{AB}$), shown below, can be defined as the set of points A and B and all points between A and B on line AB ($\overleftrightarrow{AB}$). Similarly, *ray AB* ($\overrightarrow{AB}$) can be defined as the part of line AB that contains point A and all points on the same side of the line as B.

Axioms, also called *postulates,* are statements that are assumed to be true and are therefore accepted without proof. An example of an axiom is the statement *for every pair of distinct points, there is exactly one line that contains them.* The Greek mathematician Euclid developed the first set of geometric axioms about 300 B.C. in his book called the *Elements.* Since then, improved sets of axioms have been developed. Today, the axioms used in most high school geometry textbooks are based on a set introduced in 1932 by G. D. Birkhoff, an American mathematician.

Theorems are statements that can be proved true by using deductive reasoning. A step-by-step procedure is used in proving a theorem. Each step involves a reference to a definition, an axiom, a previously proven theorem, or some other information already given.

An example of a theorem is the statement, discussed previously, that the sum of the measures of the angles of a quadrilateral is 360°. In proving this theorem, a person would refer to the axiom *Any quadrilateral can be divided into two triangles* and to the previously proven theorem *The sum of the measures of the angles of any triangle is 180°.*

Properties of geometric figures

Congruence. Many important axioms and theorems in geometry deal with facts about congruent figures. Congruent figures are figures that have the same size and shape. The notion of congruence is important in many areas of our lives. In the mass production of automobiles, for example, all the front bumpers for a certain model of car must be congruent. If they were not congruent, workers could not efficiently assemble the front of cars of the same model.

The simplest types of congruent figures include congruent line segments and congruent angles. Because all line segments have the same shape, congruent line segments are defined as those that have the same length. Two angles are congruent if they have the same measure. In the illustration below, for example, angle CED is congruent to angle XYZ, since each measures 45°. To express this congruence relationship symbolically, we write $\angle CED \cong \angle XYZ$.

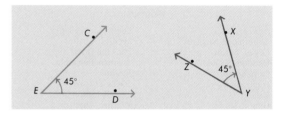

To establish the congruence of two triangles, we must set up a *correspondence* between the triangles' vertices—that is, the points where two sides meet—and between the sides of the triangles. In other words, the vertices and the sides of the two triangles must be paired in such a way that the matched angles and sides are congruent. Suppose we know that in the triangles ABC and EDF below, $\angle B \cong \angle D$, $\angle C \cong \angle F$, $\angle A \cong \angle E$, $\overline{BC} \cong \overline{DF}$, $\overline{AB} \cong \overline{ED}$, and $\overline{AC} \cong \overline{EF}$. We could then conclude that triangles ABC and EDF are congruent ($\triangle ABC \cong \triangle EDF$).

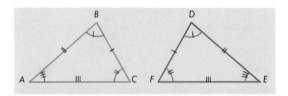

Certain axioms and theorems specify necessary and sufficient conditions for the congruence of triangles. For this reason, it is not always necessary to show that all corresponding angles and sides are congruent in order to prove that two triangles are congruent. For example, the *side-angle-side* (SAS) *axiom* states that if two sides and the angle included between them are congruent to two sides and the included angle of another triangle, then the two triangles are congruent. Although it is possible to define the congruence of figures other than triangles, most work with congruence in geometry focuses on triangles.

Similarity. The triangles ABC and HJK at the top of the next page are examples of similar figures. Notice that $\overline{HJ}$ measures 2 units, and is twice as long as $\overline{AB}$, which measures 1 unit. Symbolically, we write $m(\overline{HJ}) = 2m(\overline{AB})$. Furthermore, $m(\overline{HK}) = 2m(\overline{AC})$ and $m(\overline{JK}) = 2m(\overline{BC})$. Finally, the diagram also shows that $\angle A \cong \angle H$, $\angle C \cong \angle K$, and $\angle B \cong$

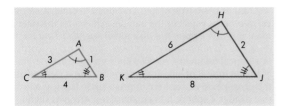

∠J. In other words, the corresponding angles are congruent, and the corresponding sides are *proportional.* The sides of two figures are said to be proportional when the ratios of their corresponding sides are equal. The value of this ratio is called the *constant of proportionality.* For triangles *ABC* and *HJK* above, the constant of proportionality is 2. To express the similarity between triangles *ABC* and *HJK*, we write △ *ABC*∼△*HJK*. Two geometric figures of any kind are said to be similar if their corresponding angles are congruent and their corresponding sides are proportional.

The notion of similarity has many important applications. For example, maps and scale drawings are based on the idea of similarity, as are the reduction and enlargement of drawings and photographs.

Some basic geometric constructions

People have been interested in methods of constructing geometric figures since the time of the ancient Greeks. The Greeks established the practice of using only a compass and a ruler to make geometric constructions. The following constructions can be made by using only those instruments.

Bisecting an angle. Suppose we want to *bisect* (divide into two equal parts) angle *AOC*, below. Place the point of a compass on point *O* and draw an arc that intersects the sides of the angle at points *X* and *Y*. Extend

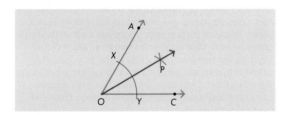

the width of the compass to a length greater than half the distance from *X* to *Y*. Place the compass point on *X* and draw an arc in the interior of ∠*AOC*. Repeat, with the compass point on *Y*. Draw ray *OP*. This ray bisects ∠*AOC*, creating two congruent angles, ∠*POA* and ∠*POC*.

Bisecting a line segment. To bisect line segment *AB*, below, set the compass width at greater than half

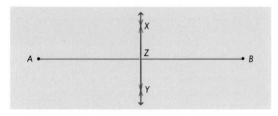

the length of $\overline{AB}$. Put the compass point on point *A* and draw an arc above and below $\overline{AB}$. Move the compass point to point *B* and repeat. Draw line *XY*. The point *Z* bisects $\overline{AB}$. Furthermore, $\overleftrightarrow{XY}$ is perpendicular to $\overline{AB}$.

Drawing a perpendicular to a line. Suppose we want to construct a perpendicular to line *AB* from a point on the line (point *P*) (see the diagram below). Put the compass point on *P* and draw arcs that intersect $\overleftrightarrow{AB}$ on either side of *P* (at points *X* and *Y*). Using *X* and *Y* as end points, bisect $\overline{XY}$ according to the directions given above. The bisecting line, $\overleftrightarrow{MN}$, is perpendicular to $\overleftrightarrow{AB}$ at point *P*.

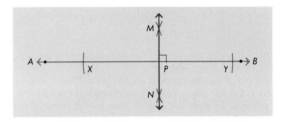

To construct a perpendicular to line *AB* from a point not on $\overleftrightarrow{AB}$ (point *Q*), place the compass point on *Q* and draw an arc that intersects $\overleftrightarrow{AB}$ (see the diagram below). The arc will intersect $\overleftrightarrow{AB}$ at two points (*X* and *Y*). Next,

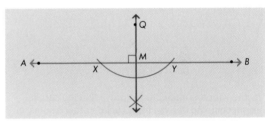

bisect $\overline{XY}$ to find the midpoint (*M*) of $\overline{XY}$. $\overleftrightarrow{QM}$ is perpendicular to $\overleftrightarrow{AB}$.

Types of geometry

The study of geometry can be approached in a number of ways. For example, geometry may be *Euclidean* or *non-Euclidean,* depending on the axioms used in the axiomatic system. *Analytic geometry* uses the same axioms as Euclidean geometry, but it employs algebraic methods in working with geometric figures. All geometries that do not use algebraic methods are called *synthetic geometries.*

Euclidean geometry is based on the axioms developed by Euclid in the *Elements* and on axioms later derived from Euclid's axioms. Euclidean geometry can be divided into plane geometry and solid geometry. *Plane geometry* involves the study of such two-dimensional figures as lines, angles, triangles, quadrilaterals, and circles. *Solid geometry* involves the study of three-dimensional figures, such as those illustrated on the next page.

Topics studied in Euclidean geometry include the congruence and similarity of triangles and other geometric figures, and the properties of parallel and perpendicular lines. Other topics include the properties

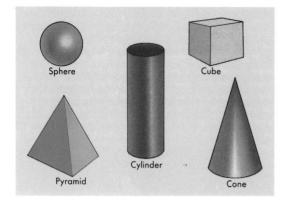

Sphere
Cube
Cylinder
Pyramid
Cone

of circles and spheres and the measurement of the area or volume of figures.

One of the most famous axioms in Euclidean geometry is Euclid's *parallel axiom,* also known as Euclid's *fifth axiom* or the *parallel postulate.* One way of stating the parallel axiom is *through a point not on a given line, only one line can be drawn parallel to the given line.* For example, in the illustration below, line *l* is the only line parallel to line *AB* that can be drawn through point *P.*

During Euclid's time, and for centuries thereafter,

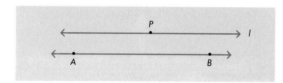

mathematicians attempted to prove that the parallel axiom could be derived from Euclid's other axioms. In the 1800's, however, mathematicians discovered that the parallel axiom cannot be proved from the other axioms. This discovery led to the creation of geometric systems in which the parallel axiom was replaced by other axioms. Such systems are called non-Euclidean.

Non-Euclidean geometry. One basic type of non-Euclidean geometry is called *hyperbolic geometry.* In it, the parallel axiom is replaced by the following axiom: *through a point not on a given line, more than one line may be drawn parallel to the given line.*

In one model of hyperbolic geometry, *plane* is defined as a set of points that lie in the interior of a circle. *Line* is defined as a chord of a circle. And *parallel lines* are defined as lines that never intersect. In the diagram at the right, therefore, lines *L, M,* and *N* are all considered parallel to line *AB,* even though they all pass through the same point, *P.* Hyperbolic geometry is sometimes called *Lobachevskian geometry,* because it was developed—in the early 1800's—by the Russian mathematician Nikolai Lobachevsky.

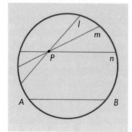

Another basic type of non-Euclidean geometry, *elliptical geometry,* replaces the parallel axiom with the statement *through a point not on a given line, there are no lines that do not intersect the given line.* In other words, in elliptical geometry, parallel lines do not exist.

In one model of elliptical geometry, *line* is defined as the *great circle* of a sphere. A great circle is any circle that divides a sphere into equal halves. Any two such circles on a sphere must intersect. In the sphere at the right, the great circle *ABCD* intersects the great circle *PCQA.* Elliptical geometry is also called *Riemannian geometry.* It was developed in the mid-1800's by the German mathematician Georg Friedrich Bernhard Riemann.

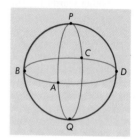

Because one important use of the figures and principles of geometry is to describe the physical world, we might ask which type of geometry, Euclidean or non-Euclidean, provides the best model of reality. Some situations are better described in non-Euclidean terms, such as aspects of Albert Einstein's theory of relativity (see **Relativity** [General relativity theory]). Other situations, such as those related to building, engineering, and surveying, seem better described by Euclidean geometry.

Analytic geometry is a method of studying the properties of geometric figures by using algebraic techniques. Analytic geometry deals with the same subject matter as Euclidean geometry, but provides simpler ways of proving many theorems. It plays an important role in trigonometry and calculus.

Analytic geometry makes use of a *coordinate system,* such as the one illustrated in the figure below. This system, also called the *rectangular system* or *Cartesian system,* consists of two perpendicular number lines in a plane. Points of a geometric figure are located in the plane by assigning each point two *coordinates* (numbers) on the number lines *x* and *y*. The *x*-coordinate, called the *abscissa,* gives the location of the point along the *x*-axis (horizontal number line). The *y*-coordinate, called the *ordinate,* locates the point along the *y*-axis (vertical number line).

For example, the paired coordinates for point *A* in the figure below are (2,1). This means that point *A* is two

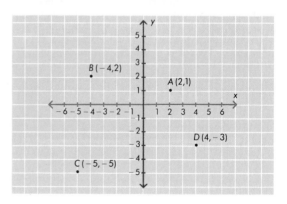

units to the right of the y-axis and one unit directly above the x-axis. In addition, the figure shows several other points—B, C, and D—and their coordinates. There is a one-to-one correspondence between all the points of the plane and ordered pairs of numbers (x,y) on the x- and y-axes.

We can describe geometric figures in terms of coordinates by devising algebraic equations that represent the points that make up the figures. For example, the equation $2x + y = 2$ has many solutions of the form (x,y), such as (−2,6), (−1,4), (0,2), (1,0), and (2,−2). If these points are plotted on a coordinate graph and then connected with a smooth line, they are found to lie on a straight line. A graph of solutions of the equation is shown below. Any point (x,y) that lies on the line has coordinates that satisfy the equation $2x + y = 2$, and any

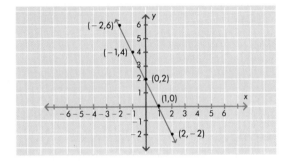

pair of numbers (x,y) that satisfy the equation will be a point on the line. Other plane geometric figures also have their own equations and can be graphed on a coordinate system. These figures include *conic sections.* Conic sections are types of curves formed by the intersection of planes and cones. They include circles, ellipses, and parabolas.

History

Earliest forms of geometry. The exact origins of geometry are not known. However, records of the ancient Egyptians and the Babylonians indicate that they were aware of some geometric principles as long as 5,000 years ago. The Egyptians developed geometric ideas that could be used to reestablish land boundaries after the annual flooding of the Nile River. The Egyptians also used geometry in building the pyramids.

Like the Egyptians, the Babylonians were interested primarily in the practical applications of geometry, such as the methods of measurement needed for building and surveying. The Babylonians also were aware of the ideas later expressed in certain geometric theorems, including the Pythagorean theorem (see **Pythagorean theorem**).

Greek geometry. Two Greek philosophers who lived during the 500's B.C.—Thales and Pythagoras—influenced the later development of geometry. Thales is credited with having created the first deductive proof of a theorem. Pythagoras, often called the father of mathematics, founded a school in which mathematics was studied extensively. He formulated the Pythagorean theorem.

In the 300's B.C., the Greeks became the first people

to study mathematics from a theoretical point of view, and not simply for its practical applications. This change in emphasis was largely due to the influence of the Greek philosopher Plato and the students at his Academy. Plato's most lasting contribution to mathematics was his insistence on the use of deductive reasoning in proving geometric theorems. He argued that because the senses can be fooled, a person should use reason, instead of physical diagrams, to prove geometric theorems. Also during the 300's B.C., the Greek philosopher Aristotle laid out very clearly the foundations for an axiomatic system and deductive reasoning.

The ancient Greek mathematician most often associated with geometry is Euclid. About 300 B.C., Euclid provided in his *Elements* the classic example of an axiomatic system by defining terms, listing axioms, and then using the axioms to prove hundreds of theorems. During the 200's B.C., the Greek mathematician Archimedes discovered methods for finding the area and volume of conic figures.

Beginnings of modern geometry. The beginnings of modern geometry may be traced to the 1600's. At that time, there arose greater communication among mathematicians than there had been since the time of Plato. Two Frenchmen, René Descartes and Pierre de Fermat, began working on what later became known as analytic geometry. Descartes spelled out the foundations of analytic geometry in his book *Géométrie* (1637). Fermat's approach to geometry was more closely related to modern analytic geometry than was the approach of Descartes. However, because Fermat did not publish any of his work, most people have credited Descartes with the discovery of analytic geometry.

Rise of non-Euclidean geometry. In the early 1800's, three mathematicians—Carl Friedrich Gauss of Germany, Janos Bolyai of Hungary, and Nikolai Lobachevsky of Russia—discovered non-Euclidean geometry independently of one another. In attempting to prove Euclid's parallel axiom, each of these mathematicians concluded that no such proof was possible. Each then introduced hyperbolic geometry, the first non-Euclidean geometry. However, Lobachevsky is generally given credit for the discovery because of his published work, especially his article "On the Principles of Geometry" (1829).

Non-Euclidean geometry remained outside traditional geometry until the mid-1800's. At that time, Georg Friedrich Bernhard Riemann began treating non-Euclidean geometry as part of the general subject. In a lecture in 1854, Riemann argued that geometry should be viewed as a study of unspecified objects of any number of dimensions in any number of spaces. His view of geometry as the general study of "curved spaces" made Einstein's theory of relativity possible.

Mathematical findings in the 1800's also led to the development of other approaches to geometry. One of them, *transformation geometry,* investigates properties —of geometric figures—that remain unchanged when the figures undergo certain *transformations* (changes in position). A type of transformation geometry called *topology* involves the study of geometric properties that do not change when figures are deformed by bending, stretching, or molding (see **Topology**). Transformational geometries rank among the most active areas of mathematical research. Mary Kay Corbitt

Additional resources

Banchoff, Thomas F. *Beyond the Third Dimension: Geometry, Computer Graphics, and Higher Dimensions.* 1990. Reprint. W. H. Freeman, 1995.

Holden, Alan. *Shapes, Space, and Symmetry.* 1971. Reprint. Dover, 1991. Younger readers.

Honsberger, Ross. *Episodes in Nineteenth and Twentieth Century Euclidean Geometry.* Mathematical Assn. of Am., 1995.

Kappraff, Jay. *Connections: The Geometric Bridge Between Art and Science.* McGraw, 1990.

Sved, Marta. *Journey into Geometries.* Mathematical Assn. of Am., 1991.

Van Cleave, Janice. *Janice Van Cleave's Geometry for Every Kid.* Wiley, 1994. Younger readers.

Geomorphology, *jee oh mawr FAHL uh jee,* is the study of the earth's surface and the changes that occur there. Geomorphology is a branch of geology or physical geography.

A theory called *plate tectonics* explains the formation of the major surface features of the earth. According to this theory, the earth's outer shell consists of a number of rigid plates. The slow, continual motion of these plates results in such landforms as mountains, plateaus, and islands. See **Plate tectonics.**

Landforms on the earth's surface are changed by the processes of *weathering, erosion,* and *deposition.* Weathering breaks down rocks into small pieces. Erosion carries off these pieces (see **Erosion**). Through deposition, the pieces accumulate elsewhere. For example, rivers and glaciers carve valleys and deposit the eroded material in plains and deltas. In desert regions, winds can wear away rock and build huge sand dunes. Waves erode rocky shorelines and create sandy beaches.

Geomorphology can aid us in controlling such natural hazards as avalanches, river flooding, and coastal erosion. It can also help reduce the environmental damage caused by poor farming practices, mining, and other human activities.   Robin G. D. Davidson-Arnott

See also **Earth** (How the earth changes).

Geophysics is the study of the earth and its atmosphere and waters by means of the science of physics. Geophysics is an extremely broad field that combines numerous narrower fields of study. For example, it includes *seismology,* the study of earthquakes; *hydrology,* the study of the movement and distribution of water; and *meteorology,* the study of the atmosphere and weather.

Geophysicists measure the earth's shape, temperature, gravity, electricity, and magnetism. They attempt to answer questions about the origin and history of the earth. They also study volcanoes, oceans, and the forces and processes in the earth's interior.

Geophysics has led to a better understanding of earthquakes and other forces that shape the earth. According to the theory of *plate tectonics,* the earth's outer shell, called the *lithosphere,* consists of a number of rigid plates (see **Plate tectonics**). Geophysicists have found that the majority of earthquakes occur at the edges of these plates. The plates are continually in motion, and an earthquake occurs when two plates suddenly slip past each other. Geophysicists are developing methods of predicting when and where earthquakes will occur (see **Earthquake**).

Scientists called *oceanographers* use geophysical techniques to study the ocean and the land beneath it. Geologists use geophysical methods to search for underground deposits of minerals, natural gas, and oil. For example, geologists measure the slight variations in gravity that occur from place to place. By using such measurements, they can locate rock formations where oil is likely to be found.

One of the newest branches of geophysics, *planetary exploration,* involves the study of other planets, especially Jupiter, Mars, and Venus. Geophysicists compare the earth with other planets to understand the earth and its origin better. A geophysical topic of worldwide concern is the decrease in the ozone layer in the upper atmosphere (see **Ozone**).   Robert E. Horita

Geopolitics, *JEE oh PAHL uh tihks,* attempts to explain world political developments in terms of geographic space. According to this theory, the world contains a limited amount of space, and all countries struggle among themselves to get enough to survive. Geopolitics tries to describe the relationship between geographic space and foreign policy. A Swedish scholar, Rudolf Kjellen, first used the term. Geographers, historians, and political scientists study the influence of geography on foreign policy. But the term *geopolitics* is rarely used today because it seems to emphasize only one factor in explaining the power of great nations.

In the early 1900's, Sir Halford Mackinder, an English geographer, advanced a theory of geopolitics that emphasized the importance in world politics of nations that controlled great land areas. He called the great land mass of Europe, Asia, and Africa, the *World Island.* All other areas were only satellites. The central land of

Europe and Asia, including Germany and Russia, was the *Heartland*. Control of the Heartland was supposed to be the key to world power. Nicholas Spykman, an American scholar, argued that it was also important to control what he called the *Rimland*. The Rimland consisted of Western Europe, the Middle East, and southern and eastern Asia.

German geopoliticians, especially Karl Haushofer (1869-1946), combined Mackinder's theory with some of their own theories and developed geopolitics into a pseudoscience. Haushofer and others argued that oceanic countries would have to grant *lebensraum* (living space) to the newer, more dynamic continental countries. German dictator Adolf Hitler tried to put these theories of geopolitics into practice.   Michael P. Sullivan

George I (1660-1727) of Britain became king when his distant cousin Queen Anne died in 1714. After Anne's last surviving child had died in 1700, many people claimed that only her half brother James Francis Edward Stuart, a Roman Catholic and son of King James II, had the right to succeed her. In 1701, however, Parliament passed an Act of Settlement that made sure that no Catholic would become monarch. The act provided that Princess Sophia, a Protestant, would succeed Anne as ruler of England unless Anne had another child. Sophia was a granddaughter of King James I of England and electress of the German territory of Hanover (see **Hanover**). Sophia's son George became heir to the throne after her death in June 1714 and became king after Anne's death in August. George was born in the city of Hanover. He became elector of the territory of Hanover in 1698.

George was ignorant of British politics and did not speak English well. But he kept in close touch with his ministers, of whom the most famous was Sir Robert Walpole (see **Walpole, Sir Robert**). The two most dramatic events of George's reign were the Jacobite rebellion of 1715, which attempted to restore the Stuart family as rulers of Britain, and the bursting of the "South Sea Bubble," a great financial scandal, in 1720.

J. C. D. Clark

George I (1845-1913) was king of Greece from 1863 to 1913. During George's reign, Greece expanded its territories. It received the Ionian Islands from Britain in 1864 and acquired the Thessaly region and other territory from the Ottoman Empire in 1881. George supported a movement to revive the Olympic Games, which had been abolished in A.D. 393. The first modern Olympic Games were held in Athens in 1896.

George was born in Copenhagen, Denmark. His father became King Christian IX of Denmark. George's full given name was Christian William Ferdinand Adolphus George. In Denmark, he was known as Prince William. The Greek Parliament elected George king in 1863 after King Otto of Greece had been overthrown in 1862. George was assassinated on March 18, 1913. George's oldest son, Constantine I, succeeded him as king.

John A. Koumoulides
See also **Greece** (History).

George II (1683-1760) of Britain succeeded his father, George I, in 1727. George II was a brave man and ambitious for military prestige. He saw himself as a warrior-prince and was the last British ruler to lead troops on the battlefield.

Great changes marked the reign of George II. Military triumphs, especially during the Seven Years' War (1756-1763), laid the foundations of empire in India and Canada and increased British prestige throughout Europe. Britain also experienced growing commercial prosperity and, eventually, increasing political stability. In 1745, George put down the last serious attempt by Charles Edward Stuart to regain the British throne for the Stuart family.

Detail of an oil portrait (1744) by Thomas Hudson; National Portrait Gallery, London

George II

During the first part of George's reign, his chief advisers were his wife—Queen Caroline—and Sir Robert Walpole. Later, his chief ministers, Henry Pelham and William Pitt, helped him greatly. George II was born in Herrenhausen, near what is now Oldenburg, Germany.

J. C. D. Clark

George II (1890-1947) was king of Greece from 1922 to 1923 and from 1935 to 1947. George succeeded his father, King Constantine I, who was deposed in 1922 after a Greek invasion of the Ottoman Empire in 1921 was crushed. A military revolt forced George from the throne in 1923. In 1924, Greece became a republic. George was recalled to the throne in 1935 when the republic ended. In 1936, he permitted General John Metaxas to establish a military dictatorship. In 1941, during World War II, an invasion by Germany drove George and his government into exile. After his return to the throne in 1946, a civil war broke out between Greek Communists and people who supported the monarchy. George was born at Tatoi, near Athens. He was succeeded as king by his brother, Paul I. See **Greece** (History).

John A. Koumoulides

George III (1738-1820) of Britain was king during one of the most critical periods in the country's history. He succeeded his grandfather George II in 1760. During the following 60 years, several revolutions modified every aspect of British life. The French Revolution led to a war between Britain and France that threatened Britain's existence. The American Revolution cost Britain its American Colonies. The Industrial Revolution created a new society and more than doubled the British population. Britain also acquired new territories in southern Africa, southern Asia, and Australia during

Detail of a portrait (about 1775) from the studio of Allan Ramsay; National Portrait Gallery, London

George III

the reign of George III. The Act of Union, which became effective in 1801, brought Ireland into the kingdom. The kingdom then became the United Kingdom of Great Britain and Ireland.

George III took a far greater part in governing the

country than did George II. He tried to destroy the power of the Whig aristocrats, who had held control for many years under Sir Robert Walpole, Henry Pelham, and the Duke of Newcastle. George chose his ministers, especially Lord North and William Pitt the Younger, with this in mind (see **North, Lord**).

George was born in London. He probably suffered from a disease now known as *porphyria.* The sickness struck at various times and made him appear to be mentally ill. By 1810, he had become incapable of logical acts and was thought to be insane.　James J. Sack

Additional resources

Ayling, Stanley. *George the Third.* Knopf, 1972.
Brooke, John. *King George III.* McGraw, 1972.
George III, King of Great Britain. *The Later Correspondence of George III.* Ed. by A. Aspinall. 5 vols. Cambridge, 1962-1970.
Green, Robert. *King George III.* Watts, 1997. Younger readers.

George IV (1762-1830) of the United Kingdom became king in 1820. He had served as regent for his father, George III, from 1811 to 1820.

George IV lacked his father's ambition to govern and, with his brothers, lowered the prestige of the royal family. His private life was disgraceful, and he had no share in the important reforms of his reign. Among these were the reform of criminal law and of the police, the freeing of trade, and the grant of increased toleration to Roman Catholics and Protestant dissenters from the Church of England. However, George IV was a man of taste, and he commissioned many beautiful buildings. In addition, George helped persuade the government to buy paintings that formed part of the original collection of the United Kingdom's National Gallery. George was born in London.　James J. Sack

George V (1865-1936) of the United Kingdom became king in 1910. He was the second son of Edward VII and became heir to the throne when his older brother, the Duke of Clarence, died in 1892. Meanwhile, he had been trained for the navy and became a vice admiral in 1903. He married Princess Victoria Mary of Teck in 1893.

George was born in London. After he succeeded his father in 1910, he and his queen gained lasting popularity by their courage and devotion during World War I (1914-1918). George was also admired for his conscien-

Brown Brothers
George V

tious attention to his duties. George was fair-minded and devoted much time to strengthening the United Kingdom's links with its vast empire. George was succeeded by his oldest son, Edward VIII.　Denis Judd

George VI (1895-1952) of the United Kingdom became king in December 1936, after his older brother, Edward VIII, abdicated. George VI, second son of George V, reigned during one of the country's most troubled eras. He was a popular monarch because of his devotion to royal duty and due to his ordinary, modest personality.

George was born in Sandringham, England, and was known as Prince Albert. He studied under private tutors

and then went to Osborne and Dartmouth naval schools. He served in World War I (1914-1918) and fought in the Battle of Jutland in 1916. In 1918, he joined the Royal Flying Corps and became a wing commander. In 1919, he studied at Cambridge University. In 1920, he became Duke of York. In 1923, he married Lady Elizabeth Bowes-Lyon.

Karsh, Ottawa
George VI

King George and Elizabeth toured Canada and South Africa, and became the first British monarchs to visit North America. During World War II (1939-1945), the royal family endeared itself to the people by sharing dangers and hardships with them. Welfare measures enacted following the war included socialized medicine and the nationalization of the Bank of England, the railways, and other industries. India gained independence in 1947, and the words "Emperor of India" were dropped from the king's title.

George VI had two daughters, Elizabeth and Margaret. He was succeeded by the older daughter, who became Elizabeth II.　Denis Judd

George, David Lloyd. See Lloyd George, David.

George, Francis Cardinal (1937-　), was appointed a cardinal of the Roman Catholic Church in 1998 by Pope John Paul II. In 1997, the pope had appointed him archbishop of Chicago. George holds doctor's degrees in philosophy and theology. He is known as a traditionalist in theology and a progressive on issues of social justice.

Francis Eugene George was born in Chicago. In 1957, he graduated from St. Henry Preparatory Seminary in Belleville, Illinois, and entered the Missionary Oblates of Mary Immaculate. He was ordained a priest in 1963. George was appointed bishop of Yakima, Washington, in 1990 and became archbishop of Portland, Oregon, in 1996. He was appointed archbishop of Chicago following the death of the previous archbishop, Joseph Cardinal Bernardin.　Robert P. Imbelli

George, Henry (1839-1897), an American social reformer, originated the *single tax.* The basic principle of this plan was that land is a free gift of nature; that all men have an equal right to use the land; and that it is unfair for a few to acquire great wealth by holding land that increases in value. George proposed to make this *unearned increment* (increase in value) the source of all taxation (see **Single tax**). His theories were first published in 1871 in a pamphlet called *Our Land and Land Policy.* He stated his theory more completely in *Progress and Poverty* (1879). George was born in Philadelphia.

H. W. Spiegel

George, James Zachariah (1826-1897), was an American soldier, jurist, and politician. He fought in the Mexican War (1846-1848) and the Civil War (1861-1865). From 1879 to 1881, George served as chief justice of the Mississippi Supreme Court. He then represented Mississippi in the United States Senate from 1881 until his death. He was the only Democrat who helped write the Sherman Antitrust Act of 1890 (see **Antitrust laws**).

George was born in Monroe County, Georgia. A statue of George represents Mississippi in the United States Capitol in Washington, D.C.   Edward A. Lukes-Lukaszewski

George, Saint, is the patron saint of England. He became the subject of many legends in the Middle East and Europe. The best-known legend tells how he slew a dragon with a lance, thus saving the king's daughter, who was being sacrificed to the monster.

Little is known about Saint George's life. He probably either was born or died in Diospolis, which is now the city of Lod in Israel. According to tradition, Saint George became a soldier in the Roman army and rose to high rank. But his open profession of Christianity led to his arrest and execution, perhaps about A.D. 303, during the persecution of the Christians by the Roman emperor Diocletian.

During the Middle Ages, Saint George became a favorite saint of the crusaders. The crusaders believed that Saint George could protect them in battle. King Edward III of England chose Saint George to be patron saint of the Order of the Garter, the highest order of English knighthood. For many years, English soldiers wore a badge that displayed Saint George's symbol—a red cross on a white background. The symbol, called St. George's cross, still appears on the British Union Flag. Saint George's feast day is celebrated on April 23.

William J. Courtenay

See also **Donatello** (picture); **Flag** (picture: Historical flags of the world); **Garter, Order of the; Painting** (pictures: Tempera paintings).

George, *gay OHR guh,* **Stefan,** *SHTEH fahn* (1868-1933), was a major German representative of the European *symbolism* movement in poetry. He was the intellectual leader of a group of poets, philosophers, and scholars who insisted on a noble poetic language, classical forms, and the detachment of literature and art from everyday reality. George rejected realism and naturalism, movements designed to make art and literature reflect life. George supported the principle of *art for art's sake.* He regarded the poet, especially himself, as a seer and priestlike figure.

Most of George's poems appear in groups called *cycles.* They express an aristocratic concept of life, a cult of beauty, and a preference for mythological, historical, and legendary subject matter. His works include *Algabal* (1892), *The Year of the Soul* (1897), *The Star of the League* (1914), and *The New Kingdom* (1928).

George was born in Büdesheim, Hesse. He traveled widely in Europe during most of his life.

Werner Hoffmeister

George Town (pop. 219,603) is the capital of the state of Penang in northwestern Malaysia. The city lies on the island of Penang in the Strait of Malacca. For location, see **Malaysia** (map).

George Town, one of Malaysia's busiest ports, serves as the commercial center of northwestern Malaysia. Two of the world's largest tin refineries are located in the George Town metropolitan area. The city is the home of the University of Science, Penang. George Town's beaches, historic buildings, inexpensive shopping, and fine restaurants attract many tourists. Chinese make up most of the population, but the city has many Europeans, Indians, and Malays.

British traders founded George Town in 1786. Britain ruled it until 1957, when Penang joined Malaya (now part of Malaysia).   David P. Chandler

George Washington Birthplace National Monument, in Virginia, contains the site of the house where George Washington was born. The Memorial Mansion, which is not a replica of the original structure, was erected on the site of Washington's birthplace. The national monument was established in 1930. For the area of the monument, see **National Park System** (table: National monuments). For the monument's location, see **Virginia** (political map [Westmoreland County]).

Critically reviewed by the National Park Service

See also **Washington, George** (picture: A memorial mansion).

George Washington Bridge over the Hudson River connects New York City at 178th Street with Fort Lee, New Jersey. The bridge's span is 3,500 feet (1,100 meters) long. Four huge cables hold up this suspension bridge. Each cable is 36 inches (91 centimeters) in diameter and consists of 26,474 steel wires, which are woven tightly together. The cables holding up the central portion of the bridge contain 107,000 miles (172,000 kilometers) of wire. Two towers that rise 604 feet (184 meters) above the water support the cables. The bridge measures 119 feet (36 meters) in width. It has two levels, an original section with eight traffic lanes and a lower deck with six. The bridge was the world's first 14-lane suspension bridge.

The first eight lanes opened to traffic in 1931. The lower deck, which lies 15 feet (4.6 meters) below the top level, opened in 1962. It offers new outlets to major interstate highways and new approaches to the bridge.

Fred F. Videon

George Washington Carver National Monument, in southwestern Missouri, marks the birthplace of this famous scientist. He was born of slave parents in a cabin on the farm of Moses Carver. The monument was established in 1951. For the area of the monument, see **National Park System** (table: National monuments).

Critically reviewed by the National Park Service

See also **National Park System** (picture).

Georgetown (pop. 72,049; met. area pop. 188,000) is the capital and chief city of Guyana. It lies on the east bank of the Demerara River, facing the Atlantic Ocean. For the location of Georgetown, see **Guyana** (map). Georgetown is built on low land. A sea wall and a system of dikes protect the city from ocean tides. Georgetown is the main outlet for the exports of Guyana.

Anthony P. Maingot

Georgetown University is a coeducational institution in Washington, D.C. It is the oldest Roman Catholic university in the United States. It was founded in 1789 by Bishop John Carroll and is affiliated with the Jesuit religious order.

Georgetown University has five undergraduate schools: the College of Arts and Sciences, the School of Business, the School of Nursing, the School of Languages and Linguistics, and the Edmund A. Walsh School of Foreign Service. The university also has a graduate school as well as professional schools of law and medicine. The university's facilities include the Kennedy Institute of Ethics, the Center for the Advanced Study of Ethics, and the Women's Law and Public Policy Program.   Critically reviewed by Georgetown University

Georgia is a country in the Caucasus Mountains at the eastern end of the Black Sea. It lies mostly in southwestern Asia, but part of northern Georgia is located in Europe. Tbilisi is the capital and largest city. Georgia became independent in 1991 after nearly 200 years of Russian and Soviet rule.

Government. Georgia's legislature consists of one house called Parliament, which has 235 members. The members of Parliament serve four-year terms.

A president is Georgia's head of state. The president is elected by the people to a five-year term. A Council of Ministers acts as an advisory body to the president. The president chooses the council members, with the consent of Parliament.

People. About 70 percent of the people are ethnic Georgians. The population also includes Armenians, Abkhazians, Azerbaijanis, Ossetians, and Russians.

Most people of Georgia are Christians who belong to the Georgian Orthodox Church. Some people are Muslims. The primary language is Georgian. The Georgian language is not related to any other languages in the region. It is written in its own alphabet.

Many of the houses in Georgia's urban areas are closely grouped one- or two-story structures. Large public buildings erected while Georgia was under Soviet control also stand in some of the cities. In the villages and small towns, many people build large, spacious, two-story homes. People who live in these areas often keep gardens or orchards.

The Georgian people are known for their strong family ties. Family gatherings and celebrations are important occasions. A wide variety of food is often served at these gatherings. Popular foods include *shashlik,* a type of shish kebab, and *chicken tabaka,* which is pressed fried chicken. Georgia is also famous for its wines.

Georgia's children must attend school through the 10th grade. Tbilisi University is the most important university in the country. The Georgian Academy of Sciences has its headquarters in Tbilisi.

Georgia has a rich literary tradition. Music and poetry are especially popular among the Georgian people. Shota Rustaveli, one of the country's greatest poets, wrote around 1200.

Facts in brief

Capital: Tbilisi.
Official language: Georgian.
Area: 26,911 mi² (69,700 km²). *Greatest distances*—north-south, 175 mi (280 km); east-west, 350 mi (565 km).
Elevation: *Highest*—Mount Shkhara, 17,163 ft (5,201 m) above sea level. *Lowest*—sea level along the coast.
Population: *Estimated 2002 population*—4,969,000; density, 185 per mi² (71 per km²); distribution, 56 percent urban, 44 percent rural. *1989 census*—5,400,841.
Chief products: *Agriculture*—citrus fruit, corn, grapes, silk, tea, tobacco, tung nut, wheat. *Manufacturing and processing*—food products. *Mining*—barite, coal, copper, manganese.
Flag: The flag has a red field. A canton in the upper left corner is divided into two horizontal stripes of black and white. See Flag (picture: Flags of Europe).
Money: *Basic unit*—lari. One hundred tetri equal one lari.

Land and climate. Much of Georgia has a rugged landscape. The Caucasus Mountains cover the northern part of Georgia, and the Little Caucasus Mountains extend over much of the south. The lower mountain slopes that are close to and facing the Black Sea have a mild, wet climate. Mountains farther inland and slopes facing away from the sea have colder, drier climates. The highest areas are permanently snow covered. Forests cover many of the mountains and hills. Evergreen, beech, and oak trees are common.

Mount Shkhara, in the Caucasus Mountains, is Georgia's highest peak. It rises 17,163 feet (5,201 meters) above sea level.

Western Georgia includes the Rioni Valley and other lowlands near the Black Sea. This region has a warm, humid climate. Rainfall is heavy, and temperatures rarely drop below freezing. Much of western Georgia is productive farmland.

Eastern Georgia includes part of the upper Kur Valley, which extends into Azerbaijan. This region has a much drier climate than does western Georgia. The lack of rainfall requires farmers to irrigate some crops. Eastern Georgia has cold winters and warm summers.

Economy. Georgia's greatest natural resources are its fertile soil and mild climate, which make farming a ma-

Georgia

	International boundary
	Road
	Railroad
⊛	National capital
•	Other city or town
+	Elevation above sea level

WORLD BOOK maps

SCR Photo Library

Tbilisi, Georgia's capital, lies on the banks of the Kur River. Part of the city is modern, but the older section has buildings that date from hundreds of years ago.

jor economic activity. In western Georgia, farmers produce citrus fruit, tea, and tung oil. Farther inland, farmers grow tobacco and wheat as well as grapes, corn, and a variety of other fruits and vegetables. Georgia also produces silk. Farmers in the mountainous regions raise sheep and cattle.

Food processing is Georgia's chief industry, and food products are its main export. Mining is another important industry in Georgia. Mines in Georgia yield *barite* (barium ore), coal, copper, and manganese. In addition, tourism ranks as an important economic activity in some parts of the country. Health resorts along the coast of the Black Sea attract thousands of vacationers every year. Georgia's swift rivers and rugged terrain provide many good sites for hydroelectric power plants. Georgia's most important trading partners include Armenia, Azerbaijan, Russia, Turkey, and Ukraine.

Transportation across the Caucasus Mountains is limited. The major highway crossing the mountains is often closed in winter. Railroads along the Black Sea skirt the mountains.

History. People have lived in what is now Georgia for thousands of years. The first Georgian state was established in the 500's B.C. In the 200's B.C., most of what is now Georgia was united as one kingdom. But for almost all of its history, Georgia was divided, and powerful empires fought over it. From the 60's B.C. until the A.D. 1000's, Georgia was invaded by Romans, Persians, Byzantines, Arabs, and Seljuk Turks. The first Christian state appeared in Georgia in the A.D. 300's.

During the 1000's and 1100's, a series of Georgian rulers gradually freed Georgia of foreign control and centralized its government. These efforts eventually produced Georgia's "Golden Age" during the reign of Queen Tamara (1184-1212), when Georgians made great advances in culture, science, and art.

Beginning in the early 1200's, however, other nations again attacked Georgia. Mongol armies, including those of Asian conquerors Genghis Khan and Timur (also called Tamerlane), raided Georgian lands from the 1220's to the early 1400's. These attacks sent Georgia into a period of decline. From the 1500's to the 1700's, the Ottoman Empire and Iran fought over Georgian territory.

In the late 1700's, the ruler of one of the kingdoms in east Georgia accepted partial Russian rule in exchange for military protection. By the early 1800's, all of Georgia became part of the Russian Empire.

A socialist republic was established in Georgia after World War I (1914-1918). But Russian Communist forces invaded Georgia in 1921 and proclaimed it a Communist republic. In early 1922, Georgia, Armenia, and Azerbaijan joined to make up the Transcaucasian republic. This republic was one of the four original republics that combined to form the Soviet Union in late 1922. Joseph Stalin, who ruled the Soviet Union as a dictator from 1929 to 1953, was a Georgian. In 1936, Georgia, Armenia, and Azerbaijan became separate Soviet republics.

In the late 1980's, a strong independence movement emerged in Georgia. Until 1990, Georgia's Communist Party controlled the republic's government. Elections were held in 1990, and non-Communist candidates won a majority of seats in Parliament. The members of Parliament elected Zviad K. Gamsakhurdia, leader of the non-Communist majority, as president.

Independence. In April 1991, Parliament declared Georgia independent. The people elected Gamsakhurdia president the next month. Opposition leaders soon accused Gamsakhurdia of moving toward dictatorship. He jailed political opponents and censored the press. In December 1991, the Soviet Union formally dissolved. Eleven former republics formed an association called the Commonwealth of Independent States. Georgia did not join at that time but became a member in 1993.

Opposition to Gamsakhurdia grew after the Soviet Union broke up. In January 1992, opposition forces formed an alternate government, and Gamsakhurdia fled the country. In March, Eduard A. Shevardnadze became head of the State Council that ruled Georgia until elections were held in October 1992. Shevardnadze was then elected to serve as chairman of parliament.

Ethnic conflict. During the early 1990's, tensions between Georgians and other ethnic groups erupted into violence. In 1990, South Ossetia, an *autonomous* (self-governing) region in north-central Georgia inhabited by Ossetians, declared itself independent. The Georgian government ruled the declaration invalid, and fighting broke out between Ossetians and Georgians. Both sides agreed to a cease-fire in 1992.

Ethnic violence also occurred in the autonomous region of Abkhazia, in northwestern Georgia, during the early 1990's. In 1992, Abkhazia declared that its laws took precedence over those of Georgia. Fighting between Abkhazians and Georgians increased. The Abkhazians drove the Georgian forces from Abkhazia by late 1993. But disagreement over Abkhazia's status continued.

Recent developments. In 1995, a new constitution became effective, and voters elected Shevardnadze president. In 2000, voters reelected Shevardnadze as president.   Jaroslaw Bilocerkowycz

See also **Tbilisi; Caucasus; Shevardnadze, Eduard A.**

Fred Whitehead, Southern Light

Cumberland Island National Seashore lies off the Georgia coast. The interior of the island is forested with live oaks and other trees. The scenery and wildlife attract many nature lovers.

Georgia   *The Empire State of the South*

Georgia has the largest land area of any state of the United States that lies east of the Mississippi River. It also is one of the leading manufacturing states of the Southern States. Georgia's large size and thriving industries have given it one of its nicknames, the *Empire State of the South*. Atlanta is Georgia's capital and largest city. It is also the state's chief industrial and transportation center.

For many years, almost all the people of Georgia grew cotton for a living. During the early 1900's, many Georgia farmers began growing more of such crops as corn, fruits, and tobacco. Manufacturing expanded, and the weaving of cotton soon became more important than growing it. Today, service industries are Georgia's chief source of income. Manufacturing is also an important

source of income. Georgia's leading manufactured goods include chemicals, food products, textiles, and transportation equipment.

But farming is still important to Georgia. The state is a leading producer of pecans and tobacco. It also ranks high in growing peaches and is sometimes called the *Peach State*. No other state produces more peanuts—often called *goobers* in the South—and Georgia is also known as the *Goober State*.

Mountains and ridges along Georgia's northern border slope southward to a wide belt of gently rolling hills. Flat coastal plains, extending to the Atlantic Ocean, form the southern half of the state. Pine and hardwood forests cover large parts of Georgia. The state is one of the nation's leading producers of forest products. The towering pine trees led to the expression "tall as a Georgia pine." From beneath the land have come some of the largest blocks of marble, including two weighing about 90 short tons (82 metric tons) each. Georgia marble was used in building the Lincoln Memorial in Washington, D.C., and the capitols of several states.

The contributors of this article are Dan T. Carter, William Rand Kenan, Jr., Professor in the Humanities at Emory University; and James O. Wheeler, Professor of Geography at the University of Georgia.

John Scowen, FPG

Downtown Atlanta includes the 73-story Peachtree Center Plaza Hotel, which towers above the city's Peachtree Street.

Interesting facts about Georgia

WORLD BOOK illustrations by Kevin Chadwick

The Girl Scouts of the U.S.A. originated in Georgia. Juliette Gordon Low, of Savannah, founded the group on March 12, 1912. Low's childhood home is now the Girl Scout National Center and one of Savannah's National Historical Landmarks.

The first successful use of ether in surgery took place in Georgia in 1842. Crawford W. Long anesthetized his patient, James Venable, with ether, and painlessly removed a tumor from Venable's neck.

Juliette Gordon Low

The Rock Eagle Effigy, near Eatonton, is a 10-foot (3-meter) high mound of milky white quartz shaped like a great prone bird with wings spread and head turned eastward. The bird is 102 feet (31 meters) from head to tail and 120 feet (37 meters) from wingtip to wingtip. Archaeologists estimate that the monument is more than 6,000 years old, and believe it was used by ancient Indians for religious ceremonials.

A double-barreled cannon stands on the lawn of the City Hall of Athens. Cast in Athens and first fired in 1863, it is believed to be the world's only double-barreled cannon.

The first known newspaper to use an Indian language in the United States was the bilingual *Cherokee Phoenix,* first printed in New Echota in 1828. The newspaper was printed in both English and the Cherokee *syllabary* (system of writing using syllables) developed by the Cherokee Indian Sequoyah.

Double-barreled cannon

Much of Georgia is a mild, sunny land of pines, magnolias and moss-draped trees. The state's natural beauty has inspired many songs and stories. The Suwannee River, which rises near Waycross, was made famous by Stephen Foster's song, "Old Folks at Home." Tales from Georgia include the Uncle Remus stories of Joel Chandler Harris. Other noted writers from Georgia include the poet Sidney Lanier and novelists Erskine Caldwell, Margaret Mitchell, Carson McCullers, and Flannery O'Connor.

Of the 13 colonies that fought in the Revolutionary War in America (1775-1783), Georgia was the last one founded. The colony was named for King George II of England. The University of Georgia, founded in 1785, was one of the first state universities in the United States to receive a charter.

Many bloody Civil War battles were fought on Georgia soil. In 1922, Rebecca L. Felton of Georgia became the first woman to serve in the United States Senate. In 1943, Georgia became the first state to allow 18-year-olds to vote.

C. A. Heitger, Southern Stock

The Savannah riverfront is a restored area of the historic city with nine blocks of restaurants, shops, and museums. Savannah, founded in 1733, was Georgia's first colonial settlement.

Georgia in brief

Symbols of Georgia

The state flag, adopted in 2001, displays one side of the state seal surrounded by 13 stars representing the original 13 states. The state seal was adopted in 1914. Below the seal is a scroll with five flags on it. The flags, from left to right, are (1) a 13-star U.S. flag, (2) a Georgia military banner from the 1800's, (3) the flag that served as the Georgia state flag from 1914 to 1956, (4) the state flag from 1956 to 2001, and (5) the 50-star U.S. flag.

State flag

State seal

Georgia (brown) ranks 21st in size among all the states and is the largest of the Southern States (yellow).

General information

Statehood: Jan. 2, 1788, the fourth state.
State abbreviations: Ga. (traditional); GA (postal).
State motto: *Wisdom, Justice, and Moderation.*
State song: "Georgia on My Mind." Words by Stuart Gorrell; music by Hoagy Carmichael.

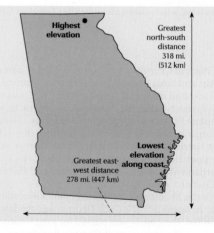

Atlanta has housed the State Capitol since 1868. Earlier capitals included Savannah (1733-1782), Augusta (1786-1795), Louisville (1796-1806), and Milledgeville (1807-1868).

Land and climate

Area: 58,930 sq. mi. (152,627 km²), including 1,011 sq. mi. (2,618 km²) of inland water but excluding 47 sq. mi. (123 km²) of coastal water.
Elevation: *Highest*—Brasstown Bald Mountain, 4,784 ft. (1,458 m) above sea level. *Lowest*—sea level along the Atlantic coast.
Coastline: 100 mi. (161 km).
Record high temperature: 112 °F (44 °C) at Greenville on Aug. 20, 1983.
Record low temperature: −17 °F (−27 °C) in Floyd County on Jan. 27, 1940.
Average July temperature: 80 °F (27 °C).
Average January temperature: 47 °F (8 °C).
Average yearly precipitation: 50 in. (127 cm).

Highest elevation

Greatest north-south distance 318 mi. (512 km)

Lowest elevation along coast

Greatest east-west distance 278 mi. (447 km)

Important dates

James Oglethorpe brought the first English settlers to Georgia.

Georgia adopted its first constitution.

| 1540 | 1733 | 1754 | 1777 |

The Spanish explorer Hernando de Soto passed through the Georgia region.

Georgia became a British royal province.

State bird
Brown thrasher

State flower
Cherokee rose

State tree
Live oak

People

Population: 8,186,453 (2000 census)
Rank among the states: 10th
Density: 139 per mi² (54 per km²), U.S. average 78 per mi² (30 per km²)
Distribution*: 63 percent urban, 37 percent rural

Largest cities in Georgia

Atlanta	416,474
Augusta	199,775
Columbus	186,291
Savannah	131,510
Athens	101,489
Macon	97,255

Source: 2000 census, except for *, where figures are for 1990.

Population trend

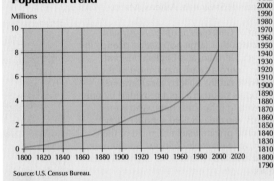

Millions

Source: U.S. Census Bureau.

Year	Population
2000	8,186,453
1990	6,508,419
1980	5,463,087
1970	4,587,930
1960	3,943,116
1950	3,444,578
1940	3,123,723
1930	2,908,506
1920	2,895,832
1910	2,609,121
1900	2,216,331
1890	1,837,353
1880	1,542,180
1870	1,184,109
1860	1,057,286
1850	906,185
1840	691,392
1830	340,989
1810	252,433
1800	162,686
1790	82,548

Economy

Chief products

Agriculture: broilers, peanuts, cotton, eggs, beef cattle, hogs, milk.
Manufacturing: food products, transportation equipment, chemicals, textiles, paper products.
Mining: clays, crushed stone.

Gross state product

Value of goods and services produced in 1998: $253,771,000,000. *Services* include community, business, and personal services; finance; government; trade; and transportation, communication, and utilities. *Industry* includes construction, manufacturing, and mining. *Agriculture* includes agriculture, fishing, and forestry.

Source: U.S. Bureau of Economic Analysis

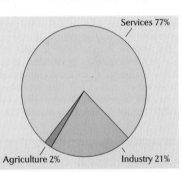

Services 77%

Agriculture 2%

Industry 21%

Government

State government

Governor: 4-year term
State senators: 56; 2-year terms
State representatives: 180; 2-year terms
Counties: 159

Federal government

United States senators: 2
United States representatives*: 11 (13)
Electoral votes*: 13 (15)

*Figures in parentheses are for January 2003 and beyond.

Sources of information

For information about tourism, write to: Georgia Department of Industry, Trade & Tourism, 285 Peachtree Center Avenue, NE, Suites 1000 & 1100, Atlanta, GA 30303-1230. The Web site at 209.144.138.98/tourism/index.html also provides information.
For information on the economy, write to: Georgia Department of Industry, Trade & Tourism, Strategic Planning and Research Division, 285 Peachtree Center Avenue, NE, Suites 1000 & 1100, Atlanta, GA 30303-1230.
The state's official Web site at www.state.ga.us also provides a gateway to information on the economy and government.

Georgia became the first state
to allow 18-year-olds to vote.

A new state constitution
went into effect.

1788	1943	1973	1983

Georgia became the
4th state on January 2.

Maynard H. Jackson, Jr., elected mayor of Atlanta,
became the first black mayor of a large Southern city.

Population. The 2000 United States census reported that Georgia had 8,186,453 people. The state's population had increased about 26 percent over the 1990 census figure of 6,478,216. According to the 2000 census, Georgia ranks 10th in population among the 50 states.

About 70 percent of Georgia's people live in metropolitan areas. About half of all Georgians live in the metropolitan area of Atlanta, Georgia's largest city. The state has eight metropolitan areas (see **Metropolitan area**). For the names and populations of these areas, see the *Index* to the political map of Georgia.

Georgia has 28 cities with populations of more than 20,000. Eight of these cities have more than 70,000 people each. Following Atlanta in order of size, these cities are Augusta, Columbus, Savannah, Athens, Macon, Roswell, and Albany.

About 29 percent of Georgia's people are African Americans. The state's other large population groups include people of Irish, German, and English descent.

Schools. During Georgia's early days, most of the school buildings were cabins built by local farmers. These *old field schools* stood in a field provided by one of the farmers. Traveling schoolteachers, who were hired by the parents, ran the old field schools. Rich Georgia planters hired private teachers, most of them from New England, to teach their children. Sometimes children who lived at nearby plantations attended these *plantation schools.*

The state began paying teachers' fees for some needy children during the early 1800's, and built some public schools. But the schools received little or no state support after they had opened, and they had to charge tuition. At some *manual-labor schools,* students could pay part of their expenses by working on the schools' farms. A few of Georgia's cities and counties provided public funds for education, but most schooling was private.

In 1870, Georgia legislators created the state's first public school system. They closely followed the recommendations of Gustavus Orr, who became the state commissioner of schools in 1872. Orr is known as the father of Georgia's public school system. Some cities and towns had high schools, but the state did not support high schools until 1912. Today, Georgia has about 1,800 public elementary, middle, and high schools.

The state superintendent of schools, elected to a four-year term, directs the school program. The superintendent is the executive officer of the State Board of Educa-

Population density

The Atlanta metropolitan area is Georgia's most densely populated region. About half of the state's people live there. Much of the southern two-thirds of the state is thinly populated.

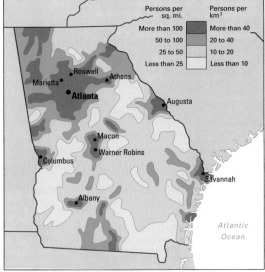

Persons per sq. mi.	Persons per km²
More than 100	More than 40
50 to 100	20 to 40
25 to 50	10 to 20
Less than 25	Less than 10

WORLD BOOK map based on U.S. Census Bureau data.

George Hall

Central City Park, in downtown Atlanta, is a favorite gathering place for people in the city. Atlanta is the capital and largest city of Georgia. It ranks as the leading center for finance and transportation in the southeastern United States.

Ezra Stoller/ESTO from High Museum of Art

The High Museum of Art, in Atlanta, is a striking white structure located in the Robert W. Woodruff Arts Center. The museum is one of the largest art museums in the United States.

tion, the policymaking agency. Georgia law requires children from ages 7 through 16 to attend school. For the number of students and teachers in Georgia, see **Education** (table).

The University of Georgia, which was founded in 1785, was one of the first state universities in the United States to receive a charter. The university did not open until 1801. Many of its branches were established in the state and run by boards of trustees. In 1931, the legislature put the branches under a single board of regents. Today, the system has about 35 state-supported universities and colleges. Georgia also has 33 technical institutes and 17 satellite-TV campuses, all run by the Technical and Adult Education Department.

Libraries. The leaders of the Georgia colony established a library in Savannah in 1736. In 1888, Francis T. Willis, a physician of Richmond, Virginia, gave Georgia its first free library, the Mary Willis Free Library in

University of Georgia

The University of Georgia is located in Athens. Facilities at the Boyd Graduate Research Center, *shown here,* include the university's computer center and a science library.

Universities and colleges

This table lists the universities and colleges in Georgia that grant bachelor's or advanced degrees and are accredited by the Southern Association of Colleges and Schools.

Name	Mailing address
Agnes Scott College	Decatur
Albany State University	Albany
American InterContinental University	Atlanta
Armstrong Atlantic State University	Savannah
Art Institute of Atlanta	Atlanta
Atlanta Christian College	East Point
Atlanta College of Art	Atlanta
Augusta State University	Augusta
Berry College	Mount Berry
Brenau University	Gainesville
Brewton-Parker College	Mount Vernon
Clark Atlanta University	Atlanta
Clayton College and State University	Morrow
Columbia Theological Seminary	Decatur
Columbus State University	Columbus
Covenant College	Lookout Mountain
Dalton State College	Dalton
DeVry Institute of Technology	*
Emmanuel College	Franklin Springs
Emory University	Atlanta
Fort Valley State University	Fort Valley
Georgia, Medical College of	Augusta
Georgia, University of	Athens
Georgia Baptist College of Nursing	Atlanta
Georgia College and State University	Milledgeville
Georgia Institute of Technology	Atlanta
Georgia School of Professional Psychology	Atlanta
Georgia Southern University	Statesboro
Georgia Southwestern State University	Americus
Georgia State University	Atlanta
Interdenominational Theological Center	Atlanta
Kennesaw State University	Kennesaw
LaGrange College	La Grange
Life University	Marietta
Macon State College	Macon
Medical College of Georgia	Augusta
Mercer University	Macon
Morehouse College	Atlanta
Morehouse School of Medicine	Atlanta
Morris Brown College	Atlanta
North Georgia College and State University	Dahlonega
Oglethorpe University	Atlanta
Paine College	Augusta
Paper Science and Technology, Institute of	Atlanta
Piedmont College	Demorest
Reinhardt College	Waleska
Savannah College of Art and Design	Savannah
Savannah State University	Savannah
Shorter College	Rome
South College	Savannah
Southern Polytechnic State University	Marietta
Spelman College	Atlanta
Thomas College	Thomasville
Toccoa Falls College	Toccoa Falls
Valdosta State University	Valdosta
Wesleyan College	Macon
West Georgia, State University of	Carrollton

*Campuses at Alpharetta and Decatur.

Washington. The Young Men's Library Association established one of the first libraries in Atlanta in 1867. This library was opened to the public in 1902, and today is the Atlanta-Fulton Public Library, the largest in Georgia.

Museums. The museum at Ocmulgee National Monument, near Macon, is one of the largest museums of Indian history in the United States. It has exhibits that explain nearby Indian burial grounds. The Fernbank Museum of Natural History, in Atlanta, is one of the largest museums of natural history in the Southeast. The High Museum of Art, in Atlanta, is one of the largest art museums in the United States. Other art museums include the Telfair Museum of Art in Savannah and the Georgia Museum of Art at the University of Georgia in Athens.

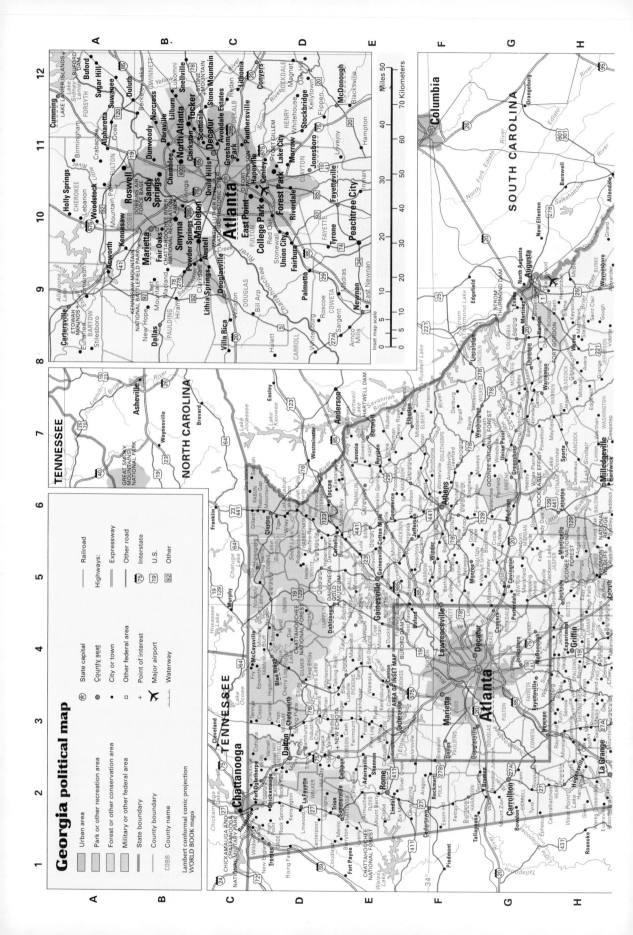

Georgia political map

Urban area

Park or other recreation area

Forest or other conservation area

Military or other federal area

State boundary

County boundary

COBB   County name

Lambert conformal conic projection
WORLD BOOK maps

State capital

County seat

City or town

Other federal area

Point of interest

Major airport

Waterway

Highways:
    Expressway
    Other road
    Interstate
    U.S.
    Other

Railroad

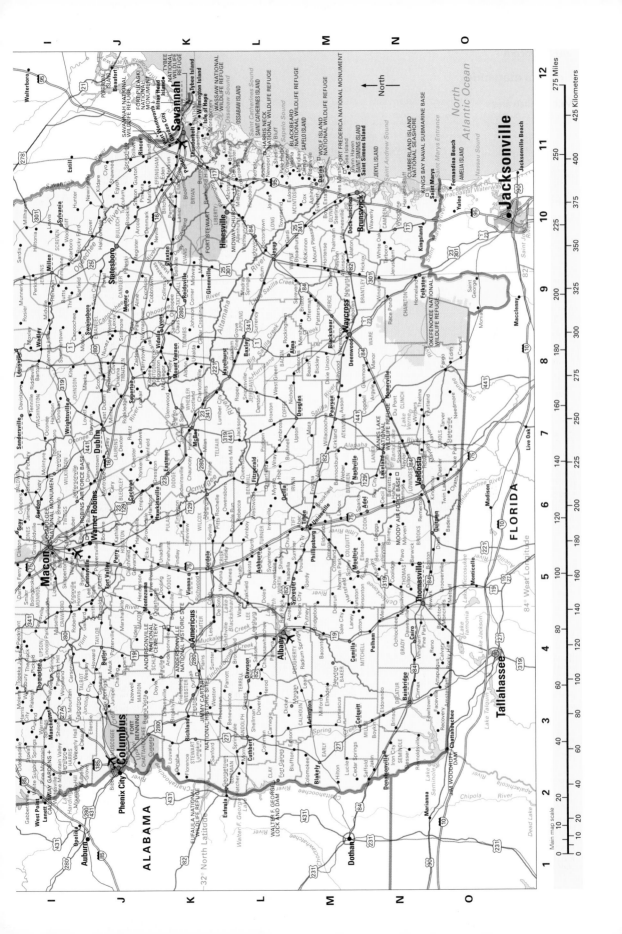

Georgia map index

Hahira	1,626	N 6
Hamilton°	307	I 3
Hampton	3,857	E 11
Hapeville	6,180	C 10
Haralson	144	H 3
Hardwick		H 6
Harlem	1,814	G 8
Harris City		I 3
Harrison	509	I 7
Harrisonville		H 2
Hartford		J 6
Hartwell°	4,188	E 7
Hatley		K 5
Hawkinsville°	3,280	K 6
Hazlehurst°	3,787	L 8
Helen	430	D 5
Helena	2,307	K 7
Hemp		D 4
Henderson		J 5
Hephzibah	3,880	H 9
Herod		L 4
Hiawassee°	808	C 5
Hickox		M 9
Higdon		D 4
Higgston	316	K 8
Hill City		D 2
Hillsboro		H 5
Hilltonia	421	I 10
Hilton		M 2
Hinesville°	30,392	L 10
Hinsonton		M 5
Hiram	1,361	B 9
Hoboken	463	M 9
Hogansville	2,774	H 3
Holly Springs	3,195	A 10
Hollywood		D 6
Homeland	765	N 9
Homer°	950	E 6
Homerville°	2,803	N 7
Hortense		M 9
Hoschton	1,070	F 5
Howard		J 4
Howell		N 7
Huber		I 6
Hulett		D 8
Hull	160	F 6
Ideal	518	J 4
Ila	328	E 6
Indian Springs†	1,982	H 5
Industrial City		D 3
Inman		E 10
Iron City	321	N 3
Irondale*†	7,727	D 11
Irwinton°	587	I 6
Irwinville		L 6
Isle of Hope [-Dutch Island]†	2,605	K 11
Ivey	1,100	I 6
Jackson°	3,934	H 5
Jacksonville	118	L 7
Jakin	157	N 2
James		I 6
Jasper°	2,167	E 4
Jefferson°	3,825	F 6
Jeffersonville°	1,209	I 6
Jenkinsburg	203	H 5
Jersey	163	G 5
Jerusalem		N 10
Jesup°	9,279	L 9
Jonesboro°	3,829	G 4
Juliette		H 5
Junction City	179	J 4
Juniper		J 3
Kathleen		J 5
Kellytown		D 12
Kennesaw	21,675	A 10
Keysville	180	H 9
Kinderlou		N 6
Kings Bay Base*†	2,599	N 10
Kingsland	10,506	N 10
Kingston	659	E 3
Kirkland		M 7
Kite	241	I 8
Knoxville°		I 5
La Fayette°	6,702	D 2
La Grange°	25,998	H 2
Lake City	2,886	D 11
Lake Park	549	O 6
Lakeland°	2,730	N 7
Lakemont		D 6
Lakeview*†	4,820	C 2
Lakeview Estates*†	2,637	G 5
Lavonia	1,827	E 7
Lawrenceville°	22,397	F 5
Leary	666	M 3
Lebanon		A 10
Lee Pope		J 5
Leesburg°	2,633	L 4
Lenox	889	M 6
Leslie	455	K 4
Lexington°	239	F 7
Lifsey		H 4
Lilburn	11,307	B 12
Lilly	221	K 5
Lincoln Park†	1,122	I 4
Lincolnton°	1,595	F 8
Lindale†	4,088	E 2
Linwood		D 2
Lithia Springs†	2,072	C 9
Lithonia	2,187	C 12
Lizella		I 5
Locust Grove	2,322	H 4
Loganville	5,435	F 5
Lone Oak	104	H 3
Lookout Mountain*	1,617	C 2
Lost Mountain		B 9
Louisville°	2,712	I 8
Louvale		K 3
Lovejoy	2,495	E 11
Lovett		J 7
Ludowici°	1,440	L 10
Ludville		E 3
Luella		H 4
Lula	1,438	E 5
Lumber City	1,247	K 8
Lumpkin°	1,369	K 3
Luthersville	783	H 3
Luxomni		B 12
Lyerly	488	E 1
Lyons°	4,169	K 8
Mableton†	29,733	B 10
Macland		B 9
Macon°	97,255	I 5
Madison°	3,636	G 6
Madras		E 9
Magnet		D 12
Manassas	100	K 9
Manchester	3,988	I 3
Manor		N 8
Mansfield	392	G 5
Marblehill		E 4
Marietta°	58,748	F 3
Marlow		J 10
Marshallville	1,335	J 5
Martin	311	E 6
Martinez†	27,749	G 9
Matthews		H 8
Maxeys	210	G 6
Mayday		N 7
Maysville	1,247	E 6
McAfee, see Candler-McAfee		
McCaysville	1,071	C 4
McDonough°	8,493	G 4
McIntosh		L 10
McIntyre	718	I 6
McRae°	2,682	K 7
Meansville	192	H 4
Meigs	1,090	N 4
Meldrim		K 11
Mendes		K 9
Menlo	485	E 1
Meridian		M 11
Merrillville		N 5
Mershon		M 9
Mesena		G 8
Metasville		G 8
Metcalf		O 5
Metter°	3,879	J 9
Middleton		F 7
Midville	457	I 9
Midway	1,100	L 10
Midway-Hardwick*†	5,135	H 6
Milan	1,012	K 7
Milledgeville°	18,757	H 6
Millen°	3,492	I 9
Milner	522	H 4
Milstead		G 5
Mineral Bluff		C 4
Minter		J 7
Mitchell	173	H 8
Modoc		I 8
Molena	475	I 3
Moncriefs		O 4
Monroe°	11,407	F 5
Montezuma	3,999	J 5
Montgomery†	4,134	K 11
Monticello°	2,428	H 5
Montrose	154	J 6
Moody AFB†	993	N 6
Moreland	393	H 3
Morgan°	1,464	L 3
Morganton	299	D 4
Morris		L 2
Morrow	4,882	D 11
Morven	634	N 6
Moultrie°	14,387	M 5
Mount Airy	604	D 6
Mount Berry		E 2
Mount Vernon°	2,082	K 8
Mount Vernon		D 2
Mount Zion	1,275	G 2
Mountain City	829	C 6
Mountain Hill		I 2
Mountain Park	506	A 10
Mountain Park*†	11,753	B 12
Mountville		H 3
Murrayville		E 5
Mystic		L 6
Nahunta°	930	M 9
Nashville°	4,697	M 6
Naylor		N 7
Nelson	626	E 4
Nevils		J 10
New England		C 1
New Hope		B 9
Newborn	520	G 5
Newington	322	J 10
Newnan°	16,242	H 3
Newton°	851	M 4
Nicholls	1,008	L 8
Nicholson	1,247	F 6
Norcross	8,410	B 11
Norman Park	849	M 5
Normantown		J 8
Norristown		J 8
North Atlanta†	38,579	B 11
North Canton		E 3
North Decatur*†	15,270	C 11
North Druid Hills*†	18,852	C 11
North High Shoals*	439	F 6
Norwood	299	G 7
Nunez	131	J 8
Oak Hill		D 12
Oak Park	366	J 8
Oak Mountain		I 3
Oakfield		L 5
Oakman		D 3
Oakwood	2,689	E 5
Ocee		A 11
Ochlocknee	605	N 4
Ocilla°	3,270	L 6
Oconee	280	I 7
Odessadale		I 3
Odum	414	L 9
Offerman	403	M 9
Oglethorpe°	1,200	J 4
Ohoopee		K 9
Oliver	253	J 10
Omaha		K 2
Omega	1,340	M 6
Orchard Hill	230	H 4
Osierfield		L 7
Oxford	1,892	G 5
Palmetto	3,400	D 9
Palmyra		L 4
Panthersville†	11,791	C 11
Parrott	156	L 3
Patterson	627	M 9
Pavo	711	N 5
Payne	178	I 5
Peachtree City	31,580	E 11
Pearson°	1,805	M 7
Pelham	4,126	N 4
Pembroke°	2,379	K 10
Pendergrass	431	E 5
Penfield		G 6
Perkins		I 9
Perry°	9,602	J 5
Phillipsburg†	887	M 6
Philomath		G 7
Pine Harbor		L 11
Pine Lake*	621	C 11
Pine Log		E 3
Pine Mountain	1,141	I 3
Pine Mountain Valley		I 3
Pine Park		N 4
Pinehurst	307	K 5
Pineora		J 10
Pineview	532	K 6
Pitts	308	K 6
Plainfield		J 7
Plains	637	K 4
Plainville	257	E 2
Pocotalago		E 6
Pomona		H 4
Pooler	6,239	K 11
Port Wentworth	3,276	K 11
Portal	597	J 9
Porterdale	1,278	G 5
Potterville		J 4
Poulan	946	M 5
Powder Springs	12,481	B 9
Powersville		J 5
Preston°	453	K 3
Primrose		H 3
Pulaski	261	J 9
Pumpkin Center		G 8
Putney†	2,998	M 4
Queensland		L 6
Quitman°	4,638	O 6
Rabun Gap		C 6
Race Pond		N 9
Radium Springs		M 4
Raines		L 5
Raleigh		I 3
Raoul*†	1,816	E 6
Ramhurst		D 3
Ranger	85	E 3
Ray City	746	N 6
Raybon		M 9
Rayle	139	F 7
Raymond		H 3
Rebecca	246	L 6
Red Oak		C 10
Redan†	33,841	C 12
Reed Creek†	2,148	E 7
Register	164	J 9
Reidsville°	2,235	K 9
Remerton	847	N 6
Reno		O 4
Rentz	304	J 7
Resaca	815	D 3
Rest Haven	151	F 5
Reynolds	1,036	J 4
Rhine	422	K 6
Riceboro	736	L 10
Richland	1,794	K 3
Richmond Hill	6,959	K 11
Richwood		K 5
Riddleville	124	I 8
Ridgeville		M 11
Rincon	4,376	J 11
Ringgold°	2,422	C 2
Rising Fawn		D 1
Riverdale	12,478	D 10
Riverside	57	M 5
Roberta	808	I 5
Robertstown		D 5
Robins AFB†	3,949	J 6
Rochelle	1,415	K 6
Rock, The		I 4
Rock Spring		D 2
Rockledge		J 8
Rockmart	3,870	F 2
Rocky Face		D 2
Rocky Ford	186	I 10
Rocky Mount		H 3
Rome°	34,980	E 2
Roopville	177	G 2
Roscoe		D 9
Rossville	3,511	C 2
Roswell	79,334	A 11
Round Oak		H 5
Royston	2,493	E 7
Ruckersville		E 7
Russell		F 5
Rutledge	707	G 5
St. George		O 9
St. Marks		H 3
St. Marys	13,761	O 10
St. Simons Island†	13,381	M 11
Sale City	319	M 5
Sandersville°	6,144	I 7
Sandfly		K 11
Sandy Springs†	85,781	B 11
Santa Claus	237	K 8
Sardis	1,171	I 10
Sargent		E 8
Sasser	393	L 4
Sautee-Nacoochee		D 5
Savannah°	131,510	K 11
Scotland	300	K 7
Scott		J 8
Scottdale†	9,803	C 11
Screven	702	M 9
Sea Island		M 11
Senoia	1,738	H 3
Seville		K 6
Shady Dale	242	H 6
Shannon†	1,682	E 2
Sharon	105	G 7
Sharpsburg	316	H 3
Shawnee		J 10
Shellman	1,166	L 3
Shellman Bluff		L 11
Shiloh	423	I 3
Siloam	331	G 7
Silver Creek		E 2
Six Mile		E 2
Skidaway Island*†	6,914	K 11
Skipperton		I 5
Sky Valley	221	C 6
Smithonia		F 6
Smithville	774	K 4
Smyrna	40,999	B 10
Snellville	15,351	B 12
Social Circle	3,379	G 5
Sofkee		I 5
Soperton°	2,824	J 8
South Augusta*		G 9
South Newport		L 11
Sparks	1,755	M 6
Sparta°	1,522	H 7
Spring Place		D 3
Springfield°	1,821	J 11
Springvale		L 3
Stapleton	318	H 8
Stantenville°		O 7
Statesboro°	22,698	J 10
Statham	2,040	F 6
Stephens		F 6
Sterling		M 10
Stevens Pottery		I 6
Stilesboro		A 8
Stillmore	730	J 9
Stilson		J 10
Stockbridge	9,853	D 11
Stockton		N 7
Stone Mountain	7,145	C 12
Stonewall		D 10
Stovall		I 3
Subligna		D 2
Sugar Hill	11,399	A 12
Sugar Valley		D 2
Summertown	140	I 8
Summerville°	4,456	E 2
Sumner	309	M 5
Sumter		K 4
Sunny Side	142	H 4
Sunnyside*†	1,385	M 8
Surrency	237	L 9
Suwanee	8,725	A 12
Swainsboro°	6,943	J 8
Sycamore	496	L 5
Sylvania°	2,675	I 10
Sylvester	5,990	M 5
Talbotton°	1,019	I 3
Talking Rock	49	E 3
Tallapoosa	2,789	G 2
Tallulah Falls	164	D 6
Talmo	477	E 5
Tarboro		N 10
Tarrytown	100	J 8
Tate		E 4
Taylorsville	229	F 2
Tazewell		J 4
Temple	2,383	G 2
Tennga		C 3
Tennille	1,505	I 7
Thomaston°	9,411	I 4
Thomasville°	18,162	N 5
Thomson°	6,828	G 8
Thunderbolt	2,340	K 11
Tifton°	15,060	M 6
Tiger	316	D 6
Tignall	653	F 7
Tilton		D 3
Toccoa°	9,323	D 6
Toccoa Falls		D 6
Toomsboro	622	I 7
Towns		K 7
Townsend		L 10
Trenton°	1,942	D 1
Trion	1,993	D 2
Tucker†	26,532	B 11
Tunnel Hill	1,209	D 2
Turin	165	H 3
Turnerville		D 6
Twin City	1,752	J 9
Twin Lakes		O 6
Ty Ty	716	M 5
Tybee Island	3,392	K 12
Tyrone	3,916	D 10
Unadilla	2,772	K 5
Union City	11,621	D 10
Union Point	1,669	G 7
Unionville†	2,074	M 6
Uvalda	530	K 8
Valdosta°	43,724	N 6
Vanna		E 7
Varnell	1,491	D 2
Vaughn		H 4
Vernonburg	138	K 11
Vidalia	10,491	K 8
Vidette	112	H 9
Vienna°	2,973	K 5
Villa Rica	4,134	C 8
Vinings†	9,677	B 10
Waco	469	G 2
Wadley	2,088	I 8
Waleska	616	E 3
Walnut Grove	1,241	G 5
Walthourville	4,030	L 10
Waresboro		M 8
Warm Springs	485	I 3
Warner Robins	48,804	J 5
Warrenton°	2,013	G 8
Warthen		H 7
Warwick	430	L 5
Washington°	4,295	G 7
Watkinsville°	2,097	F 6
Waverly		N 10
Waverly Hall	709	I 3
Waycross°	15,333	M 8
Waynesboro°	5,813	H 9
Wenona		K 5
Wesley		J 8
West Augusta*		G 9
West Green		L 7
West Point	3,382	I 2
Weston	75	K 3
Westside*		E 5
Whigham	631	N 4
White	693	E 3
White Oak		N 10
White Plains	283	G 7
White Sulphur Springs		I 3
Whitehall		F 6
Whitehouse		D 12
Whitesburg	596	D 8
Whitemarsh Island*†	5,824	K 11
Whitestone		D 4
Whitesville		I 2
Wildwood		C 1
Wiley		D 6
Willacoochee	1,434	M 7
Williamson	297	H 4
Wilmington Island†	14,213	K 11
Winder°	10,201	F 5
Winokur		N 9
Winston		C 9
Winterville	1,068	F 6
Woodbine°	1,218	N 10
Woodbury	1,184	I 3
Woodcliff		I 10
Woodland	432	I 3
Woodstock	10,050	A 10
Woodville	400	G 7
Woolsey	175	H 4
Wrens	2,314	H 8
Wrightsville°	2,223	I 7
Yatesville	408	I 4
Young Harris	604	C 5
Zebulon°	1,181	H 4

*Does not appear on map; key shows general location.
†Census designated place—unincorporated, but recognized as a significant settled community by the U.S. Census Bureau.

°County seat.
Places without population figures are unincorporated areas.
Source: 2000 census.

The natural beauty and famous resorts of Georgia attract visitors from all parts of the United States. Vacationers enjoy the water sports and luxury hotels of Sea Island and the other *Golden Isles* along Georgia's coast. People fish for bass, flounder, mullet, and trout at the seashore or in Georgia's many lakes and streams. Hunters trail deer, fox, and quail in the thick forests.

Since Indian days, physically disabled people have found relief in the soothing waters of Warm Springs. President Franklin D. Roosevelt, who was a victim of polio, established a summer home there called the Little

White House. Tourists can visit Roosevelt's home.

Many beautiful monuments and parks—including reminders of important Civil War battles and heroes—dot the Georgia landscape. Stone Mountain, near Atlanta, has huge figures of Confederate leaders carved on its face (see **Stone Mountain**).

The most famous annual event in Georgia is probably the Masters golf tournament. It is held the second week in April at the Augusta National Golf Course. Top golfers from the United States and other countries compete in this tournament.

Places to visit

Antebellum Trail features historic buildings of the South. The trail passes through Athens, Watkinsville, Madison, Eatonton, Milledgeville, Old Clinton, and Macon.

Atlanta History Center, in Atlanta, is on a beautiful 32-acre (13-hectare) site that includes gardens, wooded trails, and the Atlanta History Museum. The site includes a farm that dates from the 1840's and Swan House, an elegant mansion built in 1928.

Callaway Gardens, near Pine Mountain, include 2,500 acres (1,010 hectares) of meadows, hills, lakes, flowers, and woodlands. Visitors can view live butterflies from all over the world at the Day Butterfly Center. The Callaway Gardens also offer boating, dining, fishing, golfing, and swimming.

Dahlonega Gold Museum is at the site of the first major U.S. gold rush, in 1828. It contains maps, pictures, and relics from the gold rush days. Visitors can pan for gold nearby and keep all they find.

Etowah Mounds, near Cartersville, were built by prehistoric Indians. There, one of the nation's largest Indian mounds rises 53 feet (16 meters) and covers 3 acres (1.2 hectares). A museum displays flint blades, pottery, sculptured images, and other objects found there.

First African Baptist Church, in Savannah, is believed to be the first black church in the United States. It was organized in 1788. The present church building was built in 1859.

Helen is a town that was designed to re-create the atmosphere of a village in the Bavarian Alps in Germany. It has cobblestone streets, old-style buildings, and arts and crafts shops. Helen was built on the site of an old lumber mill village.

Historic Savannah, the nation's largest national landmark district, includes museums, restaurants, galleries, arts and crafts shops, and historic homes and churches. A restored riverfront area stands near the district along the Savannah River. The riverfront once consisted of a row of warehouses for the cotton trade.

Lake Lanier Islands, near Buford, is a 1,200-acre (486-hectare) resort. Attractions include camping, swimming, tennis, golf, sailing, and horseback riding.

Okefenokee Swamp, in southeastern Georgia, includes the Okefenokee National Wildlife Refuge. Visitors may explore its water trails on guided boat tours.

National parklands. Jimmy Carter National Historic Site, in Plains, includes the past and present homes of the former President. Recreation areas managed by the National Park Service in Georgia include Chickamauga and Chattanooga National Military Park and the Chattahoochee River National Recreation Area. The park, which includes several famous Civil War battlefields, is in northwestern Georgia and southern Tennessee. Georgia also has three national monuments—Fort Frederica, Fort Pulaski, and Ocmulgee—and other national parklands. For information on these areas, see **National Park System**.

National forests. Georgia has two national forests—Chattahoochee and Oconee.

State parks. Georgia has 58 state parks and 79 wildlife management areas. For information on the state parks of Georgia, write to Director, Department of Natural Resources, 270 Washington St. S.W., Atlanta, GA 30334.

M. Timothy O'Keefe, Southern Stock

Callaway Gardens near Pine Mountain

Little White House Historic Site

The Little White House in Warm Springs

E. A. McGee, FPG

Sculpture of Confederate leaders on Stone Mountain

Annual events

January-March
Fasching Karnival in Helen (mid-January); Georgia Day in Sa-
vannah (early February); Rattlesnake Roundup in Claxton (early
March); Cherry Blossom Festival in Macon (mid-March); State-
wide Tours of Homes and Gardens (late March and early
April).

April-June
Dogwood Festival in Atlanta (early April); Thomasville Rose
Festival (late April); Georgia Renaissance Festival in Fairburn
and Peachtree City (late April); Stay and See Georgia, Stone
Mountain Park, Atlanta (early May); Blessing of the Shrimp
Fleet in Brunswick (May); Vidalia Onion Festival (mid-May).

July-September
Georgia Shakespeare Festival in Atlanta (early July); Georgia
Mountain Fair in Hiawassee (August); Beach Music Festival on
Jekyll Island (mid-August); Powers Crossroads Arts and Crafts
Festival in Newnan (Labor Day Weekend); Arts Festival of At-
lanta (mid-September).

October-December
Andersonville Historic Fair in Andersonville (October); Geor-
gia National Fair in Perry (October); Gold Rush Days in Dah-
lonega (October); Oktoberfest Celebration in Helen (October);
Prater's Mill Country Fair near Dalton (October and May);
Christmas on Jekyll Island (December); Marietta Pilgrimage in
Marietta (December).

Helen Area Chamber of Commerce

Oktoberfest Celebration in Helen

Masters golf tournament in Augusta

Runk/Schoenberger from Grant Heilman

Okefenokee Swamp in southeastern Georgia

Land regions. Georgia has six main land regions. The three northernmost regions form part of the Appalachian Mountains. They are (1) the Appalachian Plateau, (2) the Appalachian Ridge and Valley Region, and (3) the Blue Ridge. See **Appalachian Mountains.**

The other three land regions of Georgia are (4) the Piedmont, (5) the Atlantic Coastal Plain, and (6) the East Gulf Coastal Plain. The Piedmont is a wide belt of hilly and rolling land that lies along the eastern edge of the central and southern Appalachians. It reaches across most of the northern half of Georgia, just south of the Appalachian areas (see **Piedmont Region**). Georgia's two coastal plains form part of the great lowland that lies along the Atlantic Ocean and Gulf of Mexico from Massachusetts to Central America.

The Appalachian Plateau covers the northwestern corner of Georgia. It ranges from 1,800 to 2,000 feet (550 to 610 meters) above sea level. Narrow valleys separate wooded ridges on the plateau. Thin, sandy soil makes this region the state's poorest farming area.

The Appalachian Ridge and Valley Region, also in northwestern Georgia, has several broad, fertile valleys separated by long, parallel ridges of sandstone rocks. Pine and hardwood forests once covered these valleys. Today, the rich soils produce fruits, grains, and vegetables, though much of the area is still forested. Beef cattle graze in the valley pastures.

The Blue Ridge rises in the northeastern part of the state. The peaks vary from 2,000 to nearly 5,000 feet (610 to nearly 1,500 meters) above sea level. Hardwoods and pine trees cover the slopes of these mountains. The region's rivers provide much of the state's hydroelectric power.

The Piedmont has gently rolling hills. The northern edge of the region meets the Appalachian areas at about 1,500 feet (457 meters) above sea level. The Piedmont gradually slopes down toward the south, where it meets the coastal plains at an elevation of less than 400 feet (120 meters). Such large cities as Atlanta and Athens help make the region the most heavily populated section of Georgia. Three other large cities, Augusta, Columbus, and Macon, lie at the southern boundary of the Piedmont, which is known as the *Fall Line* (see **Fall line**). These cities grew at water power sites, where rivers flow from the Piedmont to the softer ground of the coastal plains and form falls and rapids.

The Atlantic Coastal Plain spreads across more than a fourth of the state in the southeast. This flatland has a light, sandy loam soil that is good for growing onions, peanuts, sweet potatoes, tobacco, and watermelons. The rivers follow the slope of the plains and flow into the Atlantic Ocean. Okefenokee Swamp lies in the southern part of the Atlantic Coastal Plain and extends into the East Gulf Coastal Plain.

The East Gulf Coastal Plain covers almost a fourth of Georgia in the southwest. Its flat surface resembles that of the Atlantic Coastal Plain, but it has much richer soils and more land in crops. Soybeans, peanuts, and tobacco

Michael Phillip Manheim, Southern Light

Providence Canyon State Park, near Lumpkin, has beautiful gullies formed by erosion, some as deep as 150 feet (45 meters). The park is part of Georgia's East Gulf Coastal Plain region.

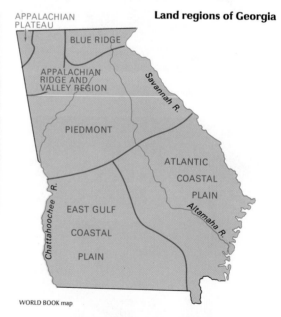

Land regions of Georgia

WORLD BOOK map

Map index

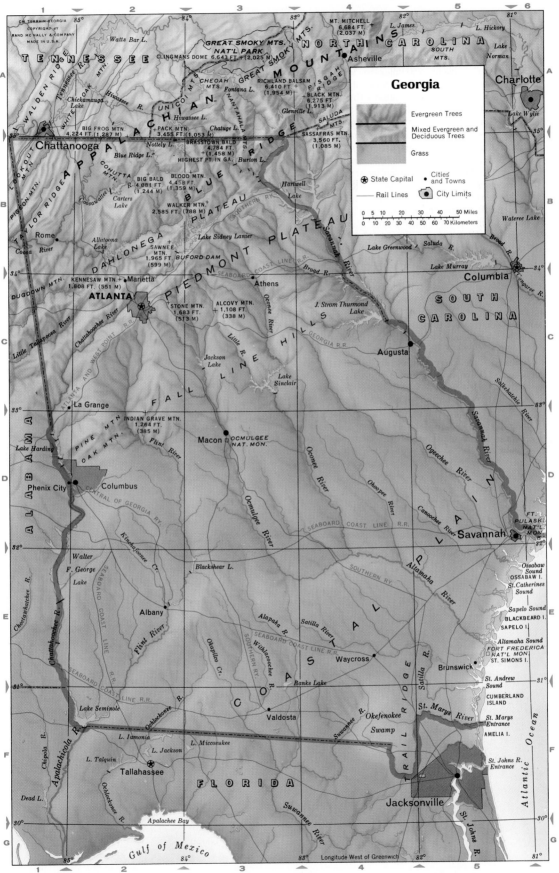

Specially created for *The World Book Encyclopedia* by Rand McNally and World Book editors

are its leading crops. The rivers draining the region flow to the Gulf of Mexico.

Coastline. Georgia has 100 miles (161 kilometers) of general coastline on the Atlantic Ocean. If bays, offshore islands, and river mouths are included, the coastline measures 2,344 miles (3,772 kilometers). The principal ports are Savannah and Brunswick. Several islands along the coast are popular vacation resorts.

Mountains. The Appalachian Mountains in Georgia cover about 1,850 square miles (4,971 square kilometers). The Blue Ridge is the main range of these mountains. Travelers can easily cross the Blue Ridge at Rabun Gap in the northeastern corner of the state and at Ellijay Valley in north-central Georgia. A steep climb is necessary to cross the range at other places. More than 20 Georgia mountains rise more than 4,000 feet (1,200 meters) above sea level. The state's highest peak is 4,784-foot (1,458-meter) Brasstown Bald Mountain, also called Mount Enotah, near Young Harris.

Rivers, lakes, and waterfalls. Georgia has several large rivers that flow from the higher elevations in the north down toward the Gulf of Mexico or the Atlantic Ocean. These rivers include the Altamaha, Chattahoochee, Flint, and Savannah. Some streams of northwestern Georgia empty into the Tennessee River.

Hydroelectric power dams form beautiful lakes on many rivers. These lakes include Allatoona Lake on the Etowah River, Hartwell and J. Strom Thurmond lakes on the Savannah, Lake Sidney Lanier on the Chattahoochee, Lake Seminole on the Flint and Chattahoochee, and Lake Sinclair and Lake Oconee on the Oconee.

The most beautiful waterfalls in the state are Amicalola and Toccoa. Amicalola Falls on Amicalola Creek plunges 729 feet (222 meters) near Dawsonville. Toccoa Falls, formed by Toccoa Creek near Toccoa, drops 186 feet (57 meters).

Plant and animal life. Forests cover about 65 percent of Georgia. Pine and hardwood trees cover northern Georgia. The southern half of the state has chiefly pines and live oaks. Laurels and rhododendrons grow in the mountains. Beneath the tall trees of the coastal area is a thick undergrowth of grass, small shrubs, palmettos, and vines. Wild flowers add their beauty throughout the state. They include Cherokee roses, daisies, Japanese honeysuckles, and violets.

Animal life in Georgia includes bears, beavers, deer, foxes, opossums, rabbits, raccoons, and squirrels. The state has such game birds as doves, marsh hens, quail, ruffed grouse, wild turkeys, and many kinds of ducks. Such songbirds as brown thrashers, mockingbirds, and wood thrushes add their melodies to Georgia's landscape. One of the largest natural bird refuges in the country is Okefenokee Swamp, which covers 700 square miles (1,813 square kilometers) in southeastern Georgia.

Average monthly weather

	Atlanta						Savannah				
	Temperatures				Days of rain or snow		Temperatures				Days of rain or snow
	F°		C°				F°		C°		
	High	Low	High	Low			High	Low	High	Low	
Jan.	53	36	12	2	12	Jan.	62	41	17	5	9
Feb.	56	37	13	3	11	Feb.	64	43	18	6	9
Mar.	63	42	17	6	12	Mar.	70	48	21	9	9
Apr.	73	51	23	11	10	Apr.	77	54	25	12	7
May	81	59	27	15	9	May	84	62	29	17	9
June	88	67	31	19	11	June	90	69	32	21	12
July	89	70	32	21	12	July	91	72	33	22	14
Aug.	89	69	32	21	11	Aug.	90	71	32	22	13
Sept.	84	64	29	18	8	Sept.	86	67	30	19	10
Oct.	74	53	23	12	7	Oct.	78	56	26	13	7
Nov.	62	42	17	6	8	Nov.	69	46	21	8	6
Dec.	54	37	12	3	11	Dec.	63	41	17	5	9

Average January temperatures

Georgia has short, mild winters. Only the mountainous northern section has fairly cold temperatures in wintertime.

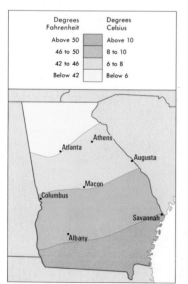

Degrees Fahrenheit	Degrees Celsius
Above 50	Above 10
46 to 50	8 to 10
42 to 46	6 to 8
Below 42	Below 6

Average July temperatures

The state has warm, humid summers. Southern Georgia has the hottest temperatures. The northeast is coolest.

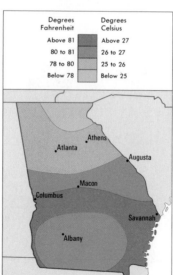

Degrees Fahrenheit	Degrees Celsius
Above 81	Above 27
80 to 81	26 to 27
78 to 80	25 to 26
Below 78	Below 25

Average yearly precipitation

The state receives its greatest amount of precipitation in midsummer. The dry season comes in October and November.

WORLD BOOK maps

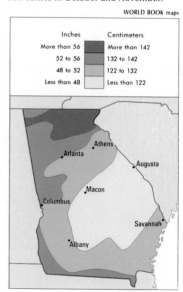

Inches	Centimeters
More than 56	More than 142
52 to 56	132 to 142
48 to 52	122 to 132
Less than 48	Less than 122

The state's inland waters are the home of bass, bream, catfish, eels, rainbow trout, and shad. Alligators, crabs, oysters, turtles, and shrimp are plentiful in the coastal waters.

Climate. Georgia has a mild climate, with an average annual temperature of 65 °F (18 °C). Most of the state has warm, humid summers and short, mild winters. The mountainous north has cool summers and fairly cold winters. January temperatures average 54 °F (12 °C) in the south, and 45 °F (7 °C) in the north. In July, southern temperatures average 82 °F (28 °C), while temperatures in the north average 78 °F (26 °C). The state's highest recorded temperature, 112 °F (44 °C), occurred at Greenville on Aug. 20, 1983. The lowest, −17 °F (−27 °C), occurred in Floyd County on Jan. 27, 1940.

Georgia's *precipitation* (rain, melted snow, and other forms of moisture) averages 50 inches (127 centimeters) a year. The rainiest months are July and August, and the driest are October and November. About 1 inch (2.5 centimeters) of snow falls yearly.

Economy

Georgia's economy has kept pace with its rapidly growing population. Service industries, taken together, make up the largest part of Georgia's *gross state product*—the total value of all goods and services produced in a state in a year. The state's leading industries include finance, manufacturing, services, and trade.

The Atlanta area has had one of the highest economic growth rates of any place in the United States since 1960. Atlanta is one of the nation's leading centers of finance, trade, and transportation. Such major companies as Coca-Cola, Georgia-Pacific, United Parcel Service, and Delta Air Lines are headquartered in the city.

Outside of the Atlanta area, important economic activities include textile and paper manufacturing, chicken and peanut farming, and clay mining. Retail trade and education also employ many people.

Natural resources of Georgia include various mined products, great forests, and plentiful water supplies.

Soils. Fertile soils occur in the valleys of mountainous northern Georgia, especially in the Appalachian Ridge and Valley Region. Ridges in this region have coarse, sandy soil, with low fertility. Thin, sandy soils cover the Appalachian Plateau. Clay loams with red clay subsoils cover the Piedmont, and give many of the hillsides a red color. The soils of the coastal plains are reddish-brown, sandy loams of medium fertility.

Minerals. Clays are the state's most important mined product. Clays and large deposits of granite lie along the southern edge of the Piedmont. Georgia's chief marble deposits are in Pickens County. The north-central Piedmont has rich deposits of feldspar and granite, and some gold. Most of the nation's gold once came from the Dahlonega area, where the nation's first major gold rush took place in 1829. The gold mining ended in 1849, after larger deposits were discovered in California.

Mined resources of the coastal plains include bauxite, fuller's earth, kaolin, and claylike materials called *bentonites,* used in oil drilling. Deposits of barite and manganese occur near Cartersville. The state's coal deposits are in the Appalachian Plateau. Other mined products include kyanite, limestone, mica, peat, slate, and talc.

Forests cover more than 60 percent of Georgia. The state has about 250 kinds of trees, including black tupelos, cedars, hickories, oaks, pines, sweet gums, yellow-poplars, tupelos, and walnuts. Pine and hardwood trees cover the northern half of the state. The southern half has chiefly pine trees and magnificent live oaks, the state tree. Beech, birch, hickory, maple, and oak trees cover parts of the Blue Ridge.

Service industries account for the largest portion of

Production and workers by economic activities

Economic activities	Percent of GSP* produced	Employed workers Number of people	Employed workers Percent of total
Community, business, & personal services	19	1,302,700	28
Wholesale & retail trade	18	1,050,900	23
Manufacturing	17	608,700	13
Finance, insurance, & real estate	16	307,000	7
Government	12	679,400	14
Transportation, communication, & utilities	12	272,200	6
Construction	4	270,400	6
Agriculture	2	123,500	3
Mining	†	9,400	†
Total	100	4,624,200	100

*GSP = gross state product, the total value of goods and services produced in a year.
†Less than one-half of 1 percent.
Figures are for 1998.
Sources: *World Book* estimates based on data from U.S. Bureau of Economic Analysis and U.S. Bureau of Labor Statistics.

Georgia's gross state product. The majority of the service industries in the state are located in the Atlanta metropolitan area.

Community, business, and personal services is Georgia's leading service industry in terms of the gross state product. This group also employs more people than any other economic activity in the state. This industry includes such businesses as private health care, hotels, law firms, information technology companies, and repair shops.

Wholesale and retail trade, also a major employer in Georgia, ranks second. The wholesale trade of food products, petroleum products, and transportation equipment is important in Georgia. Retail businesses include automobile dealerships, discount stores, grocery stores, and restaurants. Home Depot, one of the nation's largest retailers, has its headquarters in Atlanta.

Finance, insurance, and real estate rank next among the state's service industries. Real estate is the most important part of this industry group. The development of many homes and office buildings has made the Atlanta area a center of real estate activity. Atlanta is also one of the nation's major banking centers. Atlanta, Columbus, and Macon have large insurance companies.

Both (1) government and (2) transportation, communication, and utilities contribute about the same amount to Georgia's gross state product.

Government services include the operation of public schools, public hospitals, and military bases. The state's military bases include the U.S. Army Signal Center near Augusta, a U.S. Navy submarine base, and several Army forts and Air Force bases.

Some of the nation's largest companies in the transportation, communication, and utilities sector are based in Georgia. Atlanta is the home of Delta, a major airline, and BellSouth, one of the nation's major telephone companies. Turner Broadcasting System, Inc., and Cable News Network were established in Atlanta by business executive Ted Turner in the late 1970's and early 1980's. They strengthened the city's position as a major communications center. Many shipping companies are based in Savannah. Southern Company, Georgia's largest utility, is headquartered in Atlanta. More information about these industries can be found later in this section.

Manufacturing. Goods manufactured in Georgia have an annual *value added by manufacture* of about $59 billion. This figure represents the increase in value of raw materials after they become finished products.

Processed foods and beverages are Georgia's leading manufactured product in terms of value added by manufacture. The state's major food products are baked goods, beer, packaged chicken, and peanut butter. Atlanta, Augusta, Columbus, and Macon have large bakeries. Albany and Cartersville have breweries. Plants in Cornelia, Douglas, and Gainesville process chicken. Peanut butter is made in Chamblee. Other food products include candy, cooking oil, sauces, and soft drinks.

Transportation equipment ranks second among Georgia's manufactured products. Motor vehicle and aerospace companies lead the state's transportation equipment industries. Atlanta and Doraville have large car assembly plants. Factories in the Atlanta area also produce aircraft parts, military aircraft, and missiles.

Chemicals rank third among Georgia's manufactured products. The Augusta and Atlanta areas are the chief centers of chemical production in the state. Georgia's leading chemical products are cleaning compounds and pharmaceuticals. Other important chemical products include adhesives, paints, and plastics resins.

Textile products rank fourth among Georgia's manufactures. Only North Carolina produces more textiles than Georgia. Carpet is Georgia's leading textile product. Dalton manufactures more carpeting than any other city in the nation. Calhoun, Cartersville, and La Grange also have large carpet mills. Other textile products include cotton and synthetic fabrics, tire cord, and yarn.

Other products made in Georgia include electrical equipment, machinery, paper products, and plastics and rubber products. Factories near Atlanta make radio communication systems and other electrical equipment. Important types of machinery include farm equipment, metalworking machinery, and refrigeration equipment. Brunswick and Jesup have pulp mills. Augusta, Macon, Rome, and St. Mary's have paperboard mills, and Albany has a factory that makes bathroom tissue. Plastic sheeting, polystyrene foam, and tires are key products of the plastics and rubber industry.

Agriculture. Farms cover about a third of Georgia's land area. The state has approximately 50,000 farms.

Georgia ranks among the leading states in producing eggs and *broilers* (chickens 5 to 12 weeks old). Broilers

Economy of Georgia

This map shows the economic uses of land in Georgia and where the state's leading farm, mineral, and fishing products are produced. The major urban areas (shown on the map in red) are the state's important manufacturing centers.

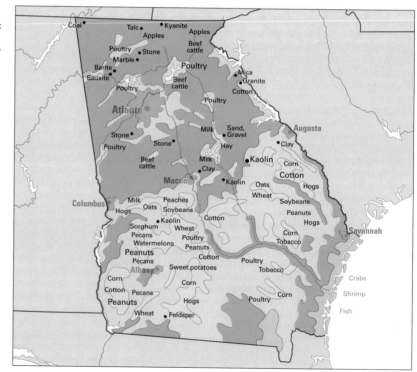

Mostly cropland

Cropland and woodland

Forest land

Marsh and swamp land

Urban area

•   Manufacturing center

•   Mineral deposit

Clyde H. Smith, FPG

Beef cattle graze on a pasture in a valley in northern Georgia. Livestock raised in the state includes beef cattle and chickens. In addition, purebred dairy cows produce much milk.

are the state's leading farm product. Georgia's broiler and egg production is heaviest in the region that lies northeast of Atlanta.

Beef cattle, hogs, and milk are also important sources of farm income in Georgia. Southeastern Georgia is the leading area for hog farming, and northeastern Georgia is the leading area for beef-cattle farming. North-central Georgia is the leading area for dairy farming.

Peanuts are Georgia's most valuable crop. Georgia leads the nation in total nut production and in peanut production. Farmers throughout the southwestern part of the state raise peanuts. Georgia also ranks first in pecan production. The Albany area is one of the nation's centers for the production of paper-shell pecans.

Cotton ranks second among Georgia's crops. It is grown primarily in the southern, eastern, and northeastern parts of the state. Georgia ranks among the leading states in cotton production.

Another of the state's important field crops is tobacco, which is grown primarily in the southeastern part of the state. Soybeans and corn are also valuable crops. Other crops include hay, oats, sorghum grain, and wheat. Sweet potatoes are Georgia's most valuable vegetable.

Georgia is a leading peach producer, and one of its nicknames is the *Peach State*. Peach County is the center of Georgia's peach-growing belt. Many famous varieties of peaches grow there. Apples thrive in Fannin, Gilmer, Habersham, and Rabun counties. The state is also among the leaders in growing watermelons.

Mining. Clays are Georgia's most valuable mined product, and the state leads the United States in clay production. Georgia is the leading producer of kaolin, a clay used in coating paper to give it a glossy finish. One of the nation's greatest kaolin belts lies across Georgia, just south of Augusta and Columbus. Georgia is a leading producer of fuller's earth, an absorbent clay used on factory floors and in pet litter boxes.

Georgia ranks among the leading states in the production of crushed stone and building stone. Granite is the most important type of stone quarried in the state,

and Georgia ranks first in granite production. Crushed granite is produced in the north-central and northeastern parts of the state. Building granite is produced in northeastern Georgia, primarily in Elbert County. Limestone and marble are also quarried in Georgia.

Sand and gravel are also important mined products in Georgia. Sand and gravel production is centered in the Piedmont. The state also mines barite, bauxite, feldspar, kyanite, mica, and talc.

Fishing industry in Georgia has an annual catch worth about $21 million. Shrimp are by far the most valuable type of catch for the state's fishing industry. Crabs rank second. Ports in McIntosh County handle most of Georgia's commercial fish catch.

Electric power. Power plants that burn coal supply about 65 percent of the electric power generated in Georgia. Nuclear plants supply about 30 percent. Most of the rest comes from hydroelectric plants.

Transportation. Hartsfield International Airport in Atlanta is Georgia's busiest airport. It ranks among the world's leading airports in aircraft take-offs and landings and in passenger arrivals and departures. Savannah has Georgia's second busiest commercial airport.

Georgia began building state highways during the early 1900's, and paving county roads after World War II (1939-1945). Today, the state has about 112,000 miles (180,000 kilometers) of roads.

Development of an extensive system of railroads began in Georgia before the Civil War. Today, two major railroads provide freight service. Passenger trains serve five Georgia cities and towns. Atlanta is the chief railroad center of the Southeast.

Savannah handles more waterborne cargo than any other port in Georgia. The State Port of Savannah is one of the most modern United States ports. Brunswick is the state's other major port. Barges can travel to Georgia ports via the Atlantic Intracoastal Waterway. Barges also can travel along the state's rivers. The Flint River is navigable to Bainbridge, and the Chattahoochee River to Columbus.

Communication. The state's first newspaper, the *Georgia Gazette,* was founded in Savannah in 1763. The *Cherokee Phoenix,* the first-known newspaper in the United States to be published using an Indian language, was established in New Echota in 1828. It was printed in English and in the Cherokee writing system invented by Sequoyah, a Cherokee (see **Sequoyah**). The *Augusta Chronicle,* Georgia's oldest newspaper still being published, first appeared in 1785.

About 250 newspapers, including about 25 dailies, are published in the state today. *The Atlanta Journal-Constitution, The Augusta Chronicle, The Macon Telegraph,* and the *Savannah Morning News* are the largest newspapers. Georgia publishers also print about 190 periodicals.

The Atlanta Journal established the South's first radio station, WSB, in 1922. WSB became the first radio station in the United States to have regular nightly programs and a slogan, "The Voice of the South." WSB also originated the use of musical notes for station identification. The South's first television station, WSB-TV, began broadcasting in Atlanta in 1948. Georgia now has about 275 radio stations and 35 TV stations. Cable TV systems and Internet providers serve communities statewide.

Constitution of Georgia was adopted in 1982 and went into effect in 1983. Earlier constitutions had been adopted in 1777, 1789, 1798, 1861, 1865, 1868, 1877, 1945, and 1976. An *amendment* (change) to the Constitution can be proposed by the legislature, or by a constitutional convention called by the legislature. An amendment must be approved by a majority of the people voting on it in a general election.

Executive. The governor of Georgia is elected to a four-year term. A person can serve only two terms as governor. The governor is the director of the budget and has great control of state finances. The governor also appoints more than 1,000 state officers and members of boards and commissions, in most cases with the approval of the state Senate.

Other elected state officials include the lieutenant governor, attorney general, commissioner of agriculture, commissioner of labor, insurance commissioner, secretary of state, and superintendent of schools. All serve four-year terms. The voters also elect the five members of the Public Service Commission to six-year terms. The commissioners control the rates and services of transportation companies and of public utilities such as electric and telephone companies.

Legislature of Georgia is called the General Assembly. It consists of a Senate of 56 members and a House of Representatives of 180 members, all elected to two-year terms. The legislature meets each year on the second Monday in January. Regular sessions last 40 days.

In 1962, the legislature *reapportioned* (redivided) the Senate to provide equal representation based on population. The House was reapportioned in 1965. By 1968, for the first time, the number of representatives and senators from urban areas exceeded that from rural areas.

Courts. The highest court in Georgia is the state Supreme Court. It has a chief justice and six associate justices, elected to six-year terms. The justices elect one of their number to be chief justice for a four-year term. The Supreme Court is the state's highest appeals court. There is also a lower nine-judge court of appeals. The judges of this court are elected to six-year terms. The chief trial courts are the 45 superior courts. Each of

The state governors of Georgia

	Party	Term		Party	Term
John A. Treutlen	Whig	1777-1778	Charles J. Jenkins	Democratic	1865-1868
John Houstoun	Whig	1778-1779	Brig. Gen. Thomas	U.S. Military	
John Wereat	Whig	1779-1780	H. Ruger	Governor	1868
George Walton	Whig	1779-1780	Rufus B. Bullock	Republican	1868-1871
Richard Howley	Whig	1780	Benjamin Conley	Republican	1871-1872
Stephen Heard	Whig	1780	James M. Smith	Democratic	1872-1877
Myrick Davies	Whig	1780-1781	Alfred H. Colquitt	Democratic	1877-1882
Nathan Brownson	Whig	1781-1782	Alexander H. Stephens	Democratic	1882-1883
John Martin	Whig	1782-1783	James S. Boynton	Democratic	1883
Lyman Hall	None	1783-1784	Henry D. McDaniel	Democratic	1883-1886
John Houstoun	None	1784-1785	John B. Gordon	Democratic	1886-1890
Samuel Elbert	None	1785-1786	William J. Northen	Democratic	1890-1894
Edward Telfair	None	1786-1787	William Y. Atkinson	Democratic	1894-1898
George Mathews	None	1787-1788	Allen D. Candler	Democratic	1898-1902
George Handley	None	1788-1789	Joseph M. Terrell	Democratic	1902-1907
George Walton	None	1789-1790	Hoke Smith	Democratic	1907-1909
Edward Telfair	None	1790-1793	Joseph M. Brown	Democratic	1909-1911
George Mathews	None	1793-1796	Hoke Smith	Democratic	1911
Jared Irwin	None	1796-1798	John M. Slaton	Democratic	1911-1912
James Jackson	*Jeff.-Rep.	1798-1801	Joseph M. Brown	Democratic	1912-1913
David Emanuel	Jeff.-Rep.	1801	John M. Slaton	Democratic	1913-1915
Josiah Tattnall, Jr.	Jeff.-Rep.	1801-1802	Nathaniel E. Harris	Democratic	1915-1917
John Milledge	Jeff.-Rep.	1802-1806	Hugh M. Dorsey	Democratic	1917-1921
Jared Irwin	Jeff.-Rep.	1806-1809	Thomas W. Hardwick	Democratic	1921-1923
David B. Mitchell	Jeff.-Rep.	1809-1813	Clifford Walker	Democratic	1923-1927
Peter Early	Jeff.-Rep.	1813-1815	Lamartine G. Hardman	Democratic	1927-1931
David B. Mitchell	Jeff.-Rep.	1815-1817	Richard B. Russell, Jr.	Democratic	1931-1933
William Rabun	Jeff.-Rep.	1817-1819	Eugene Talmadge	Democratic	1933-1937
Matthew Talbot	Jeff.-Rep.	1819	Eurith D. Rivers	Democratic	1937-1941
John Clark	Jeff.-Rep.	1819-1823	Eugene Talmadge	Democratic	1941-1943
George M. Troup	Jeff.-Rep.	1823-1827	Ellis Arnall	Democratic	1943-1947
John Forsyth	Jeff.-Rep.	1827-1829	Melvin E. Thompson	Democratic	1947-1948
George R. Gilmer	Unknown	1829-1831	Herman E. Talmadge	Democratic	1948-1955
Wilson Lumpkin	Democratic	1831-1835	Marvin Griffin	Democratic	1955-1959
William Schley	Democratic	1835-1837	Ernest Vandiver	Democratic	1959-1963
George R. Gilmer	Whig	1837-1839	Carl E. Sanders	Democratic	1963-1967
Charles J. McDonald	Democratic	1839-1843	Lester G. Maddox	Democratic	1967-1971
George W. Crawford	Whig	1843-1847	Jimmy Carter	Democratic	1971-1975
George W. Towns	Democratic	1847-1851	George D. Busbee	Democratic	1975-1983
Howell Cobb	Union (Democratic)	1851-1853	Joe Frank Harris	Democratic	1983-1991
Herschel V. Johnson	Union (Democratic)	1853-1857	Zell Miller	Democratic	1991-1999
Joseph E. Brown	Democratic	1857-1865	Roy Barnes	Democratic	1999-
James Johnson	Democratic	1865			

*Jeffersonian-Republican, sometimes called Democratic-Republican.

these courts has from 1 to 12 judges, depending on the population of the district from which the judges are elected. Most of these judges are elected to four-year terms. The judges in the Atlanta circuit are elected to eight-year terms. Most judges of the lower appeals and trial courts are elected. The governor, with the Senate's approval, appoints judges of county courts and some city courts.

Local government. Of Georgia's 159 counties, 149 are governed by boards of commissioners. These boards consist of from 3 to 11 members, depending on special acts of the legislature. Georgia's other 10 counties are governed by one commissioner instead of a board. All commissioners are elected. Most of them serve four-year terms, but one county has a two-year term and two counties have six-year terms. Many counties also have a county manager or administrator. Muscogee County has a joint council-manager government with the city of Columbus, as does Clarke County with Athens and Richmond County with Augusta.

Georgia has 536 cities, towns, and villages. Their charters are drawn up and amended by special acts of the legislature. However, in 1965, the legislature passed a *home-rule* law giving local governments the power to deal with many administrative and service matters without needing amendments to their charters. No charter or amendment may conflict with state laws. Most of Georgia's cities have mayor-council governments. Many have city managers.

Revenue. Taxation provides over half of the state government's *general revenue* (income). Most of the rest comes from federal grants and other U.S. government programs. A personal income tax and a general sales tax are the main sources of tax money. Other taxes include those on corporate income, insurance premiums, motor vehicle licenses, and on sales of alcohol, gasoline, and tobacco.

Politics. The Democratic Party has controlled Georgia politics throughout most of the state's history. Since 1872, when the state had a Republican governor during the Reconstruction period, all Georgia governors have been Democrats. In 1964, Georgia elected its first Republican U.S. representative since 1872. Also in 1964, Barry M. Goldwater of Arizona became the first Republican presidential candidate ever to win the electoral votes of Georgia. George C. Wallace of the American Independent Party carried Georgia in 1968. Since then,

Georgia State Senate

The Georgia State Senate meets in the State Capitol in Atlanta. The members of the Senate, as well as the state's House of Representatives, are elected to two-year terms.

the Republican candidate has won the state's electoral votes in more than half of the presidential elections. For Georgia's voting record in presidential elections since 1804, see **Electoral College** (table).

The Democrats are also powerful in local elections. Until the 1960's, Republicans were strong only in several rural north-central and northeastern counties. Political contests generally took place between rival Democratic groups. Republican strength has increased, beginning in the 1960's. But the Republican gains have been partially offset because black Georgians have become more active in Georgia politics and have strongly supported the Democratic Party. The growing influence of African American voters within Georgia's Democratic Party has led to a sharp increase in the number of black elected state and local officials.

Until 1962, Democratic candidates for state offices and the U.S. House of Representatives and Senate were nominated under the *county-unit* system. The nominations went to those candidates who won primary elections in the most counties, regardless of the total number of popular votes. In 1962, a United States district court ruled the county-unit system unconstitutional. Later that year, primary election results were determined by popular vote for the first time. As a result, voters in heavily populated counties gained much greater power to nominate candidates.

History

Indian days. The first people to live in what is now Georgia were prehistoric Indians called *Mound Builders.* Before white people came to the Georgia region, the Creek Indians had settled in the south and the Cherokee in the north. See **Mound Builders.**

Exploration. In 1526, Lucas Vásquez de Ayllón, a judge from Hispaniola, founded the first European settlement in what is now the United States. Historians believe the settlement, San Miguel de Gualdape, may have been on the coast of present-day Georgia or South Carolina. Disease and bad weather forced the settlers to return to Hispaniola after about six months. In 1540, Hernando de Soto of Spain crossed the Georgia area on his

way from Florida to the Mississippi River. In 1564, French settlers established a colony in Florida. The formation of this colony angered King Philip II of Spain, who claimed all of what is now the southeastern United States. In 1565, he sent Pedro Menéndez de Avilés to drive out the French. Menéndez defeated the French and then built forts along the Atlantic coast. In 1566, Menéndez built a fort on St. Catherines Island in what is now Georgia.

In 1629, the Georgia region became part of a colonial land grant made by England's King Charles I. The English built a fort on the Altamaha River in 1721. They abandoned the fort in 1727 because of its expense.

Colonial period. In 1730, a few Englishmen made plans to establish a separate colony in the region, which was to be named Georgia for King George II. The group included James Oglethorpe, who planned to send imprisoned or released debtors to the colony. But this plan was abandoned, and few debtors went to Georgia.

In 1732, King George granted a 21-year charter for the new colony to a corporation called Trustees for Establishing the Colony of Georgia in America. Spain, which had claimed the area, protested to England. Nevertheless, Oglethorpe and the first band of about 120 colonists sailed from England on Nov. 17, 1732. They arrived at Yamacraw Bluff, the site of present-day Savannah, on Feb. 12, 1733. Tomochichi, a Creek chief whose tribe lived nearby, aided the colonists. He helped persuade other Creek tribes to allow the colonists to settle in the area. In the 21 years that the trustees controlled Georgia, more than 4,000 settlers arrived. About half came at the trustees' expense.

During this period, many English ships smuggled merchandise to Spanish colonies in the West Indies. The illegal trading, plus disagreement over the Georgia-Florida boundary, led to war between England and Spain in 1739. Oglethorpe tried to capture Florida, but failed. In 1742, his troops crushed a Spanish landing in the Battle of Bloody Marsh on St. Simons Island. This victory ended the war in America, but it continued in Europe without settling the original disputes.

The Revolutionary War. The Georgia trustees gave up their 21-year charter in 1752, and King George reorganized the colony as a royal province in 1754. Georgia's farmers prospered, and the colony might have continued quietly under this rule if left to itself. But a desire for independence that was growing in the other Atlantic colonies spread to Georgia. Many of the colonists wanted to be free of British rule. After the Revolutionary War began in Massachusetts in 1775, many Georgians who had been neutral joined the movement for freedom. The patriots seized power, and James Wright, the royal governor, fled to a British warship off the Georgia coast.

The first fighting between Georgians and the British occurred in March 1776. A British warship tried to seize 11 rice boats in the harbor of Savannah, but got only 2 of them. On July 24, 1778, Georgia *ratified* (approved) the Articles of Confederation, which was the forerunner of the United States Constitution.

Georgia did not become a major battleground until December 1778, when British troops captured Savannah. An American army supported by a French naval force laid siege to the city in September 1779. After three weeks, the Americans and their allies attacked the city. They were driven back with a loss of about 250 lives. By the end of 1779, British troops had seized all Georgia except Wilkes County. They were driven out of Savannah and the rest of Georgia in 1782.

Early statehood. The Revolutionary War ended in 1783. On Jan. 2, 1788, Georgia became the fourth state in the Union to ratify the United States Constitution.

Eli Whitney invented the toothed cotton gin near Savannah in 1793. This machine, which separated the seed from the fiber, saved much work and led to a great expansion in cotton farming.

Settlers and land companies began developing Geor-

gia rapidly during the 1790's. In 1795, land companies bribed state legislators to sell them Georgia land for about $1\frac{1}{2}$ cents per acre (4 cents per hectare). The companies planned to sell the land, which covered much of present-day Alabama and Mississippi, at great profit. This scheme came to be known as the Yazoo Fraud, because the Yazoo River flowed through part of the land. Later in 1795, angry Georgians elected a new legislature that repealed the sale the next year. But many buyers refused to give up their purchases.

In 1802, Georgia sold its lands west of the Chattahoochee River to the federal government. The United States promised to settle the land claims of the Yazoo companies. In 1810, the Supreme Court of the United States ruled that the sales were legal. Congress voted in 1814 to pay more than $4,200,000 to settle the Yazoo claims. See **Fletcher v. Peck; Yazoo Fraud.**

The federal government also promised to remove the Indians from Georgia. By 1827, the Creek Indians had sold all their land in Georgia to the United States and moved to the Arkansas Territory. In 1838, federal troops rounded up the last of the Cherokee Indians in Georgia and forced them to move to the Indian Territory in present-day Oklahoma. As the Indians left, settlers quickly cleared the former Indian land and planted cotton. By 1840, Georgia had begun developing an extensive railway system.

The Civil War. Georgia's economy was based on raising cotton, and many Georgians depended on slave labor. After Abraham Lincoln was elected President in 1860, Governor Joseph E. Brown led the movement for Georgia's *secession* (withdrawal) from the Union. Opposition to the movement was led by Alexander H. Stephens, a former congressman. Stephens later became Vice President of the Confederacy. On Jan. 19, 1861, Georgia became the fifth southern state to secede.

Early in the Civil War (1861-1865), the Union navy raided the Georgia coast and closed the port of Savannah. Confederate troops won the first great battle in Georgia—at Chickamauga in September 1863. The following May, General William T. Sherman's Union forces advanced on Atlanta from Chattanooga, Tenn. Sherman captured the city in September. In November, he burned Atlanta and began his famous march to the sea. As Sherman's troops marched almost unopposed across Georgia to Savannah, they destroyed about $100 million worth of property. The Union soldiers cut a path 60 miles (97 kilometers) wide, destroying all factories, mills, public buildings, and railroads. The troops carried few supplies and lived off the land. They looted the countryside, stealing food and other property from the plantations and towns. Sherman captured Savannah in December 1864. See **Civil War** (Battle of Chickamauga; The Atlanta Campaign; Sherman's March).

Reconstruction and recovery. Georgia suffered hard times during the Reconstruction period that followed the Civil War. Congress set up military rule in Georgia, and it lasted off and on until 1870.

Georgia was readmitted to the Union in 1868. But it was expelled in 1869 because it refused to ratify Amendment 15 of the U.S. Constitution. This amendment made it illegal to deny the right to vote on the basis of race. Georgia ratified the amendment in 1870 and was permanently readmitted to the Union on July 15.

Historic Georgia

British troops captured Savannah during the Revolutionary War in December 1778. The British occupied most of Georgia until colonial forces drove them out in 1782.

Julian Bond, a black civil rights leader, graduated from Morehouse College in Atlanta. He has served in both the Georgia House of Representatives and the Georgia Senate.

The cotton gin that Eli Whitney invented near Savannah in 1793 helped make cotton the South's leading crop.

Confederate troops won the first great Civil War battle fought in Georgia—at Chickamauga in September 1863.

James Oglethorpe and a band of about 120 colonists established Georgia's first permanent white settlement at the site of present-day Savannah in 1733.

Important dates in Georgia

WORLD BOOK illustrations by Kevin Chadwick

1540 The Spanish explorer Hernando de Soto passed through what is now Georgia.

1732 King George II of England granted a 21-year charter to establish the Georgia colony.

1733 James Oglethorpe brought the first English settlers to Georgia.

1742 Oglethorpe defeated a Spanish landing force on St. Simons Island.

1754 Georgia became a British royal province.

1777 Georgia adopted its first Constitution.

1778 British troops captured Savannah during the Revolutionary War.

1788 Georgia ratified the U.S. Constitution on January 2 and became the fourth state.

1793 Eli Whitney invented his cotton gin near Savannah.

1838 The last Indians in Georgia, the Cherokee, were forced to leave the state.

1861 Georgia seceded from the Union.

1863 Confederate troops defeated Union forces in the Battle of Chickamauga.

1864 Union General William T. Sherman burned Atlanta and marched to the sea.

1870 Georgia was permanently readmitted as a state in the Union.

1920's and 1930's Georgia suffered an economic depression.

1943 Georgia became the first state to allow 18-year-olds to vote.

1962 Georgia abolished its county-unit voting system.

1977 Former Georgia governor Jimmy Carter became the 39th President of the United States.

1977 A new state constitution went into effect.

1983 Another new state constitution went into effect in Georgia.

1994 Floods caused 31 deaths and much property damage in central and southern Georgia.

Manufacturing and trade began expanding in Georgia in the 1870's. Railway construction resumed, banking activities increased, and cities grew. In the 1890's, the state legislature increased funds for schools and social services, and set up programs to help farmers.

The early 1900's. Industry continued to grow after 1900, and farmers began depending less on cotton. The production of corn, fruits, livestock, and tobacco gained in importance. After the United States entered World War I in 1917, Georgia's factory and farm production expanded still further.

In 1922, Rebecca L. Felton became the first woman U.S. senator. She was appointed by Governor Thomas W. Hardwick after Senator Thomas E. Watson died. Felton served only one day while Congress was in session. Walter F. George, who had been elected to complete Watson's term, took her place.

Beetles called boll weevils caused great damage to Georgia's cotton crops during the early 1920's. As a result, many farmers lost their crops and could not afford to keep their farms. In 1929, the Great Depression hit the state. Many factories had to close down. Federal programs began to create jobs in 1933. The programs included construction of highways, public buildings, and sewerage and drainage systems. Federal soil conservation programs helped many farmers.

The mid-1900's. Manufacturing activity in Georgia increased again during World War II (1939-1945). Many Georgians worked in various defense industries during the war. Large numbers of farmworkers left rural areas to take defense jobs in cities, and many of them stayed in the cities after the war. In 1943, Georgia became the first state to allow 18-year-olds to vote.

After World War II, many companies from outside the state opened factories and offices in Georgia. Georgians continued to move into the cities to fill jobs created by the industrial expansion. The 1950 United States census reported that, for the first time, more Georgians worked in manufacturing than in agriculture. In 1960, for the first time, the census reported that more Georgians lived in urban areas than in rural areas.

Political changes accompanied the growth of the urban areas. Since the 1960's, Georgia has *reapportioned* (redivided) its state legislative districts several times. It has also reapportioned its congressional districts. These changes were designed to provide more equal representation based on population and to give urban residents more say in government. Georgia's cities also gained political power when the state abolished its *county-unit system* in 1962. Under this system of nominating candidates, voters in thinly populated rural areas had controlled primary elections. For more on this system, see the *Politics* section of this article.

Julian Bond, a black civil rights leader and a Democrat, won election to the Georgia House of Representatives in 1965. At first, the other Georgia House members refused to let Bond be seated. They said they objected to his statements opposing U.S. involvement in the Vietnam War. But in 1966, the Supreme Court of the United States ruled that the House had denied Bond his freedom of speech and must seat him.

Until the 1960's, the Democratic Party controlled Georgia politics almost completely. Then, many Georgians became dissatisfied with some policies of the national Democratic Party, especially its support of civil rights legislation. In 1964, Georgia elected a Republican to the U.S. House of Representatives for the first time since 1872. The 1964 election also marked the first time in Georgia's history that voters backed a Republican presidential candidate—Barry M. Goldwater. George C. Wallace, the candidate of the American Independent Party, carried Georgia in the 1968 presidential election. Republican Richard M. Nixon carried the state in 1972. However, in 1976 and 1980, Democrat Jimmy Carter, a former Georgia governor, carried the state. Since then, the Republican candidate has carried the state most of the time.

Like many other states, Georgia has had serious racial problems. In 1954, the Supreme Court of the United States ruled that compulsory segregation in public schools was unconstitutional. Early in 1960, Georgia had to integrate its public schools under federal court orders or close them. A special committee appointed by the state legislature held public hearings on the issue throughout the state. The legislature then passed laws prohibiting compulsory segregation.

In 1961, black children attended all-white schools in Georgia for the first time. By the mid-1960's, several school districts and colleges had been integrated. However, in August 1969, the U.S. Department of Justice filed a suit against Georgia calling for complete integration of the state's public schools.

Integration also took place in other areas of Georgia life, including libraries and restaurants. Some white people in Georgia resisted the change. In 1964, for example, Lester G. Maddox closed his Atlanta restaurant rather than obey a federal court order to serve blacks.

In 1966, Maddox, a Democrat, became a candidate for governor. None of the candidates received 50 percent of the votes, and Georgia law provided that the state legislature choose a winner. The legislature elected Maddox governor in January 1967.

In November 1968, Georgia voters approved a constitutional amendment providing that elections that do not give any candidate at least half the votes be decided by a runoff election. The two candidates who received the most votes in the first election would oppose one another in the runoff.

Recent developments. The growth of industry helped Georgia's economy, but it also created problems. Parts of the state's cities became crowded and slums developed. The increased industrial activity and population in the state caused air and water pollution.

Georgia's population continues to shift from rural to urban areas. The state has difficulty keeping the correct balance between urban and rural representation in the General Assembly. Cities and towns won long-sought powers in the mid-1970's, when the state government authorized them to levy new local taxes. The state continues to seek ways to redevelop rural areas and, thereby, slow the shift of people to the cities.

Racial tension has eased, though school integration remains a major concern in Atlanta and other Georgia cities. White families have been moving from heavily black school districts in Atlanta, and blacks now outnumber whites in the city. In 1973, Maynard H. Jackson, Jr., was elected mayor of Atlanta. He became the first black mayor of a large Southern city.

In 1976, Georgia voters approved a new state constitution. The constitution went into effect in 1977. In 1981, the General Assembly passed another new constitution. It was approved by the voters in 1982 and went into effect on July 1, 1983. In July 1994, heavy rains caused disastrous flooding in central and southern Georgia, resulting in 31 deaths and millions of dollars in damage.

Dan T. Carter and James O. Wheeler

Study aids

Related articles in *World Book* include:

Biographies

Baldwin, Abraham	Long, Crawford W.
Bond, Julian	Low, Juliette Gordon
Carter, Jimmy	Menéndez de
Crawford, William H.	Avilés, Pedro
Gibson, Josh	Mitchell, Margaret
Gingrich, Newt	O'Connor, Flannery
Grady, Henry W.	Oglethorpe, James E.
Gwinnett, Button	Rusk, Dean
Hall, Lyman	Russell, Richard B.
Harris, Joel C.	Stephens, Alexander H.
Johnson, Herschel V.	Toombs, Robert A.
King, Martin Luther, Jr.	Walton, George
Lanier, Sidney	Young, Andrew J., Jr.

Cities

Atlanta	Augusta	Columbus	Macon	Savannah

History

Cherokee Indians	Creek Indians
Civil War	Reconstruction
Colonial life in America	Revolutionary War in America
Confederate States of America	Yazoo Fraud

Other related articles

Appalachian Mountains	Martin Luther King, Jr.,
Blue Ridge Mountains	National Historic Site
Coca-Cola Company	Ocmulgee National
Fall line	Monument
Fort Benning	Okefenokee Swamp
Fort Gordon	Piedmont Region
Fort Pulaski National	Savannah River
Monument	Stone Mountain

Outline

I. People
  A. Population
  B. Schools
  C. Libraries
  D. Museums

II. Visitor's guide
  A. Places to visit
  B. Annual events

III. Land and climate
  A. Land regions
  B. Coastline
  C. Mountains
  D. Rivers, lakes, and waterfalls
  E. Plant and animal life
  F. Climate

IV. Economy
  A. Natural resources
  B. Service industries
  C. Manufacturing
  D. Agriculture
  E. Mining
  F. Fishing industry
  G. Electric power
  H. Transportation
  I. Communication

V. Government
  A. Constitution
  B. Executive
  C. Legislature
  D. Courts
  E. Local government
  F. Revenue
  G. Politics

VI. History

Questions

Who brought the first English settlers to Georgia?
How did abolishing the county-unit voting system affect primary elections in Georgia?
What are Georgia's largest cities?
What is Georgia's most important economic activity?
Which mountains extend into northern Georgia?

Why is Georgia called the *Empire State of the South*?
What is Georgia's most important farm product?
What famous Civil War battles took place in Georgia?
Which nuts grow plentifully in Georgia?
Where and when did the nation's first major gold rush take place?

Additional resources

Level I
Coleman, Brooke. *The Colony of Georgia.* PowerKids Pr., 2000.
Kent, Deborah. *Atlanta.* Children's Pr., 2000.
Lommel, Cookie. *James Oglethorpe.* Chelsea Hse., 2001.
Otfinoski, Steven. *Georgia.* Benchmark Bks. 2001.
Robinson Masters, Nancy. *Georgia.* Children's Pr., 1999.
Wills, Charles A. *A Historical Album of Georgia.* Millbrook, 1996.

Level II
Atlanta. Time-Life Bks., 1999.
Bartley, Numan V. *The Creation of Modern Georgia.* 2nd ed. Univ. of Ga. Pr., 1990.
Coleman, Kenneth, ed. *A History of Georgia.* 2nd ed. Univ. of Ga. Pr., 1991.
Hepburn, Lawrence R., ed. *Contemporary Georgia.* Univ. of Ga., Carl Vinson Inst. of Government, 1987.
Hodler, Thomas W., and Schretter, H. A. *The Atlas of Georgia.* Univ. of Ga., Inst. of Community & Area Development, 1986.
McMurry, Richard M. *Atlanta 1864: Last Chance for the Confederacy.* Univ. of Neb. Pr., 2000.
Ruppersburg, Hugh. *Georgia Voices. Vol. 2: Nonfiction.* Univ. of Ga. Pr., 1994. Collection of writings by Georgia residents.
Stann, Kap. *Georgia Handbook.* 3rd ed. Moon Pubns., 1999. A travel guide.
Williams, David. *The Georgia Gold Rush: Twenty-Niners, Cherokees, and Gold Fever.* 1993. Reprint. Univ. of S. C. Pr., 1995.

Georgia, University of, is a coeducational state-assisted institution in Athens, Georgia. It has colleges of agriculture, arts and sciences, business administration, education, home economics, journalism, pharmacy, and veterinary medicine; schools of environmental design, forestry, law, and social work; and a graduate school.

In 1785, the institution became the first state-chartered university in the United States. It opened in 1801.

Critically reviewed by the University of Georgia

Georgia Institute of Technology is a state-assisted coeducational university in Atlanta. It has colleges of architecture; computing; engineering; sciences; and management, policy, and international affairs. The institute, often called Georgia Tech, grants bachelor's, master's, and doctor's degrees in 32 fields of study. Georgia Tech's College of Engineering is one of the largest in the United States. It offers degrees in materials, aerospace, ceramic, chemical, civil, electrical, environmental, industrial, mechanical, nuclear, and textile engineering, and in engineering science. Georgia Tech also operates the Georgia Tech Research Institute, one of the largest university research organizations in the nation. Georgia Tech was founded in 1885.

Critically reviewed by the Georgia Institute of Technology

Georgian architecture was the chief architectural style of England during the reigns of Kings George I, II, III, and IV. The kings reigned from 1714 to 1830. Georgian architecture also strongly influenced buildings in the American Colonies and the Eastern United States during the 1700's and early 1800's.

The character of Georgian architecture was primarily influenced by classical Roman architecture and its revival by the Italian architect Andrea Palladio in the 1500's. A typical Georgian design emphasized simplicity, symmetry, classical details, and columns that featured classical *orders.* For a description of these orders, see **Architecture** (Architectural terms).

Georgian architecture had a bold formality that made buildings in the style both monumental and symbolic. As a result, it was often used for important civic buildings, churches, and college structures, as well as for large residences. Examples include the original Bank of England building in London, Queen's College at Oxford University, Saint Martin-in-the-Fields church in London, and Blenheim Palace in Oxfordshire.

Georgian architecture was extensively used in the development of many English communities during the 1700's. An especially significant example of Georgian city planning appears in the fine houses, squares, and terraces of Bath, a fashionable resort.   J. William Rudd

See also **Palladio, Andrea.**

Georgian Bay is a northeastern arm of Lake Huron. It lies within the Canadian province of Ontario. The bay is about 120 miles (193 kilometers) long and 50 miles (80 kilometers) wide. Bruce Peninsula and a chain of islands shut off the bay almost entirely from the main part of Lake Huron. For location, see **Ontario** (physical map). See also **Ontario** (picture).

Geothermal power. See Energy supply (Geothermal power); Volcano (Benefits of volcanoes).

Gephardt, Richard Andrew (1941-   ), a Democrat from Missouri, became minority leader of the United States House of Representatives in 1995. He served as majority leader of the House from 1989 to 1995. Gephardt was an unsuccessful candidate for the 1988 Democratic presidential nomination.

Gephardt was born in St. Louis, Missouri. He received a B.S. degree from Northwestern University in 1962 and a law degree from the University of Michigan in 1965. He served on the St. Louis city council from 1971 to 1976.

Gephardt was first elected to the U.S. House of Representatives in 1976. He has served on two important House committees, the Budget Committee and the Ways and Means Committee. He was elected chairman of the House Democratic Caucus in 1984 and again in 1986. As a congressman, Gephardt has promoted tax reform, expansion of national health care, and arms control. He has also supported legislation to penalize nations that restricted the importation of goods from the United States.   Guy Halverson

Geranium is a plant native to temperate regions throughout the world. Geraniums are widely grown in the United States and Canada. Wild geraniums are popularly called *crane's-bill* and *heron's-bill* because of the shape of their fruit. Cultivated and indoor geraniums are varieties of another plant group, commonly called storksbill.

Many forms of geraniums have been commercially developed. They vary in the size and color of their flowers and in the markings and texture of their leaves. In California and areas with a similar climate, the plants

WORLD BOOK illustration by Robert Hynes

The rose geranium has clusters of fragrant scarlet blossoms. Geraniums are often grown in gardens and in window boxes.

may grow to the size of a bush. Common groups are *ivy; scented leaf; zonal,* or *horseshoe;* and *Lady Washington,* or *showy pelargonium.*

Geraniums are widely grown in homes and gardens. They grow easily from *slips,* or stems cut from the plants. Slips for summer blooming are taken from plants in the early spring, and those for winter flowering are taken in fall. Geraniums potted for winter growth must be cut back and shaped. This prevents the plants from becoming too tall and ragged looking. Commercially, geraniums are also grown from seeds. The plants do not need rich soil, but they must have plenty of sunshine and enough water to keep the roots moist.

Cooks often use leaves of the rose geranium to flavor jellies. A wild geranium, called *herb Robert* or *red robin,* has been used in medicine. Another wild geranium, known as *alfilaria* or *red-stem filaree,* is grown for *forage* (food for cattle) in the Western and Southwestern United States.

Scientific classification. Geraniums make up the geranium family, Geraniaceae. Cultivated forms are *Pelargonium.* The scientific name for the rose geranium is *P. graveolens;* Lady Washington is *P. domesticum.* Herb Robert is *Geranium Robertianum.* Alfilaria is *Erodium cicutarium.*   August A. De Hertogh

See also **Flower** (picture: Flowers of the tropics and subtropics).

Gerbil, *JUR buhl,* is any of a group of furry, ratlike rodents, most of which have long hind legs and a long, hairy tail. There are about 100 species of gerbils, and they live in dry regions of Africa and Asia. The Mongolian gerbil, also called the *clawed jird,* is the best-known type. Its curiosity, gentle nature, and interesting behavior make it a popular pet. It is also used for many types of medical and other scientific research.

The Mongolian gerbil weighs about 3 ounces (85 grams) and measures about 8 inches (20 centimeters) long, including its tail. The tail has a tuft of black hair at the tip. The animal usually walks on all four legs, but it occasionally hops like a kangaroo, using only its hind legs. Its color ranges from yellowish to grayish or

WORLD BOOK photo

Mongolian gerbils are lively animals that make excellent pets. They can be fed a mixture of fruits, seeds, and vegetables. Their enclosure should be lined with wood shavings or sawdust.

brownish. The underparts of the Mongolian gerbil are white, dull yellow, or pale gray. The feet have strong, dark brown or black claws.

Wild Mongolian gerbils live in parts of China and Russia and throughout most of Mongolia. Groups of them form colonies and dig burrows for shelter. Mongolian gerbils are active day and night. They eat bulbs, leaves, roots, seeds, and stems.

Mongolian gerbils can breed when they are 10 to 12 weeks old. The female carries her young in her body for 24 to 26 days. She gives birth to an average of 4 or 5 young at a time but may have as many as 12.

Gerbils are popular pets in the United States and some other countries. They are clean, practically odorless, and easy to care for. All pet gerbils are the descendants of gerbils captured in eastern Mongolia in 1935. In 1954, a Japanese laboratory sent 22 gerbils to the United States for use in scientific research. These animals became the ancestors of pet gerbils in the United States.

The floor of a gerbil cage should be covered with wood shavings, sawdust, or some other material that the animals can sleep on. Gerbils can be fed food pellets manufactured for pet rats and mice, or a mixture of fruits, small seeds, and raw vegetables. Water should be available, though gerbils seldom drink. They obtain water from the moisture in the food they eat. Pet Mongolian gerbils live up to four years or longer.

Clark E. Adams

Scientific classification. Gerbils belong to the family Cricetidae. The scientific name for the Mongolian gerbil is *Meriones unguiculatus.*

Additional resources

Field, Karl, and Sibold, A. L. *The Laboratory Hamster & Gerbil.* CRC Pr., 1998.
Siino, Betsy S. *Gerbil: An Owner's Guide to a Happy Healthy Pet.* Hungry Minds, 2000.

Geriatrics, *JEHR ee AT rihks,* is the branch of medicine that deals with old age and its diseases. Doctors who are involved in geriatrics diagnose and treat diseases of the aged. In order to do this, doctors must also understand the changes that take place in the human body during middle age that could possibly lead to diseases later in life.

The problems of aging have become increasingly important because more people are living to old age (see **Old age**). Scientists in several fields work with physicians to deal with geriatric problems. Biologists doing research in *gerontology* study body processes involved in *senescence* (aging). Psychologists investigate changes that occur in mental reactions in older people. Sociologists study the role of an aging person in a changing world.

Hospitals and universities in many cities have clinics for treating older people. Medical schools are expanding the study of old-age problems and are training doctors to deal with them. The United States Department of Health and Human Services supports research in aging. Foundations, insurance firms, industries, labor unions, and individuals are giving funds to study the problems of aging. Edward L. Schneider

See also **Aging; Senility.**

Géricault, *ZHAY ree KOH,* **Théodore,** *tay aw DAWR* (1791-1824), a French artist, was one of the first romantic painters. His most famous work, *The Raft of the Medusa* (1819), depicts the survivors of an actual shipwreck who were left adrift on a raft at sea, where most of them died. The painting appears in **Painting** (Romanticism).

Géricault was fascinated by the strength and spirit of the horse, especially when the animal fought against restraining ropes and bridles. He painted several versions of *The Race of the Riderless Horses.* His *Epsom Downs Derby* (1821) imitates English sporting paintings and prints. Géricault's last great works were a series of portraits of insane people. They give their subjects a new sympathetic air of calm seriousness and dignity.

Géricault was born in Rouen. His full name was Jean Louis André Théodore Géricault. He died at the age of 32 because of complications from a riding accident.

Ann Friedman

Germ. See **Bacteria; Disease** (Infectious diseases); **Virus.**

Germ cell. See **Cell** (Meiosis).

Germ warfare. See **Chemical-biological-radiological warfare.**

German Democratic Republic. See **Germany** (History [East Germany]).

German language is the official language of Germany, Austria, and Liechtenstein, and one of the official languages of Switzerland and Luxembourg. Estimates of the number of German speakers worldwide range from 100 million to 120 million. German is the fourth most widely used European language, following English, Spanish, and Russian.

German and English are related languages. Both developed from an ancient language called Proto-Germanic. Language scholars believe this language was spoken by the people of northern and central Europe long before recorded history. The similarity between many basic German and English vocabulary words shows that the two languages share a common origin. Examples of similar German and English words include *light* and *Licht, house* and *Haus,* and *cat* and *Katze.* A number of English words have come directly from German, such as *flak, hinterland,* and *kindergarten.* Some

German words have come directly from English, including *fair, Filmstar, Manager,* and *Toast.*

German grammar

Nouns. In German, all nouns are capitalized. Nouns may be masculine, feminine, or neuter, but the grammatical gender generally does not indicate the sexual nature of the thing named. For example, *pencil (der Bleistift)* is masculine, *pen (die Feder)* is feminine, and *paper (das Papier)* is neuter.

In German, articles and adjectives have a variety of forms. A noun's grammatical gender and function determine which form of the adjective or article is used. For example, compare the following two sentences: (1) *Die Frau gibt dem Mann einen Hut* (The woman gives the man a hat) and (2) *Der Mann gibt der Frau einen Hut* (The man gives the woman a hat). These two sentences show how the German word meaning *the* changes to show the gender and function of the noun described. *Die Frau* in the first sentence becomes *der Frau* in the second sentence to show that *Frau* is a subject in the first sentence but an indirect object in the second. Also, *die* before *Frau* in the first sentence changes to *der* at the beginning of the second sentence to show that the noun it now describes, *Mann,* is masculine, not feminine.

Verbs. German verbs also have a variety of forms. The subject of the sentence determines, in part, which form of the verb is used. For example, the verb *kaufen* (to buy) would have the following forms in the present tense: *ich kaufe* (I buy), *du kaufst* (you [singular] buy), *er kauft* (he buys), *wir kaufen* (we buy), *ihr kauft* (you [plural] buy), and *sie kaufen* (they buy). The form for the verb used with singular *you* is also determined by how well the speaker knows the person addressed as *you.* For example, to a close friend one would say *Du kaufst ein schönes Haus* (You are buying a fine house), but to an acquaintance one would say *Sie kaufen ein schönes Haus* (You are buying a fine house).

Word order. The rules for German word order are particularly difficult for English speakers to master. The sentence *At two o'clock we came home in a taxicab* would have this word order in German: *At two o'clock came we in a taxicab home.* Word placement follows fairly definite rules. The verb normally comes in the second position in the sentence. If the subject does not begin the sentence, it immediately follows the verb. But in a dependent clause, the verb comes at the very end, as in : *Our parents were not angry, though we at two o'clock in a taxicab returned.*

Pronunciation. German pronunciation follows German spelling more closely than English pronunciation follows English spelling. German has few letters pronounced in more than one way and has almost no silent letters. The language contains a number of sounds that do not exist in English, such as the *ch* in *Nacht* (night), the *ö* in *König* (king), and *ü* in *Hüte* (hats). Other sounds, such as the German *r* and *l,* are pronounced differently, and English speakers who use the English sounds for the German *r* and *l* will have a noticeable accent.

German dialects

As a spoken language, German includes a large number of dialects. In general, spoken German consists of two principal forms—*High German* and *Low German.*

High German. High German developed through four stages. They are (1) Old High German, used from about A.D. 750 to 1050; (2) Middle High German, used from about 1050 to 1350; (3) Early New High German, used from about 1350 to 1600; and (4) New High German, used after 1600. New High German was greatly influenced by Martin Luther, the leader of the Reformation. In the early 1500's, he translated the Bible into German, using the dialect of east-central Germany, then called Saxony. This dialect thus became important in the development of New High German.

Today, High German or *Hochdeutsch* is spoken in the "high," mountainous regions of central and southern Germany. High German also serves as the base for *Standard German.* Standard German is spoken in schools and on radio and television. Standard German is also the written language of Germany.

Low German. Low German or *Plattdeutsch* is spoken in the lowlands of northern Germany. Low German differs from High German chiefly in the sounds of its vowels and consonants. It sounds more like English and Dutch than High German does. For example, the Low German *eten* and *twe* are closer to the English *eat* and *two* than to the High German *essen* and *zwei.* Low German served as both the spoken and literary language of northern Germany until the 1550's, when it lost its importance as a written language.   Lois Marion Huffines

See also **German literature; Language** (Indo-European).

German literature is the literature of the German-speaking peoples of central Europe. It includes works from Germany, Austria, Switzerland, and such neighboring regions as Alsace, Bohemia, and Silesia.

Almost all German literature is written in *High German,* the language of the various regions of southern and central Germany. Few important works have appeared in *Low German,* the language of northern Germany. German literature can be divided into four periods, based on changes in the language: Old High German, A.D. 750 to 1050; Middle High German, about 1050 to 1350; Early New High German 1350 to 1600; and New High German, after 1600.

The history of German literature has been marked by high peaks and low periods. Its first flowering came in the Middle High German period, around 1200. It enjoyed a second golden age around 1800, during the lifetime of one of its greatest authors, Goethe.

Characteristics of German literature

German literature is decentralized and often regional. This came about because for hundreds of years the German-speaking peoples had no capital or center of culture such as the French had in Paris.

German writers and poets developed as individuals. They had little concern for the conventions of polished society. They were equally uninterested in smoothness, elegance, or regularity of form for their own sake. Literary academies and rule-books, which served as supreme umpires in literary matters for the French and Italians, never succeeded in Germany.

German authors have constantly sought to evaluate human beings' relationship to God and nature. Their unquenchable thirst for knowledge is best exemplified in the legend of Faust, a magician who made a pact with the devil in order to gain his ends. The story of *Dr. Faust* was first published anonymously in Frankfurt (am Main) in 1587. The Faust theme continued to appear in German plays, stories, and poems. Goethe used it for his great drama, *Faust.* More recently, it was the basis of Thomas Mann's profound novel, *Dr. Faustus.* See **Faust.**

In their individual ponderings about life, German authors are apt to become philosophical and involved. Answering weighty questions is far more important to them than mere beauty or elegance of expression. German poets have found lyric poetry the ideal expression for their personal, and at times musical, genius. German novelists often use a cumbersome and tortured style to express their involved and problematical thoughts. In the field of drama, German tragedies outnumber comedies by at least five to one.

Early German literature

The early Germanic tribes that migrated to western Europe composed ballads and stories about their gods and heroes. They passed these on by word of mouth from one generation to the next. About A.D. 800, at the end of the migrations, monasteries became centers of learning and literature. Monks spread Christian teachings through poems and stories based on the Bible and Christian legends. Otfried von Weissenburg, a monk who became the first German author known by name, wrote *The Book of Gospels* in rhyme. *Der Heliand (The Savior),* an anonymous epic in Low German, pictured Jesus as a Saxon chief and His disciples as warriors.

The monks also began to record some of the old heroic sagas and to compose new ones to glorify the feudal lords of their time. One of the few heroic poems to survive is the anonymous *Lay of Hildebrand,* the story of a battle between a father and son. Charlemagne and his successors encouraged Latin learning. About 930, Ekkehard, a monk at the Swiss monastery of St. Gallen, put the Germanic tale of *Walther with the Strong Hand* into the form of a Latin epic. Notker, another monk at St. Gallen, translated Boethius and some of Aristotle's works.

The first golden age (1150-1250)

German literature burst into sudden bloom during the Crusades in the 1100's. Knights became the culture bearers of the period. They wrote *epics* (narrative poems) on love and chivalry (see **Epic**). German minstrels called *minnesingers* wandered from court to court composing lyrical poems of love and adventure (see **Minnesinger**). The elegance and grace of French court literature strongly influenced German poetry.

Epic poetry was a major contribution of Middle High German literature. Anonymous authors recorded such old Germanic tales as the *Song of the Nibelungs* and *Gudrun* (see **Nibelungenlied**). They added a thin coating of Christian chivalry to these popular epics. But basically the poems remained monuments to the period of old Germanic valor and loyalty.

Court epics showed the influence of French form. Many were based on tales of King Arthur that had come to Germany by way of France (see **Arthur, King**). The Crusades also offered a rich lore of fairylike adventures in distant lands. Hartmann von Aue, born about 1170, was the first major German poet to use Arthurian

themes. But he gained his greatest fame with the epic, *Poor Henry,* the story of a stricken Swabian knight. In his *Parzival,* the greatest work of the Middle Ages in Germany, Wolfram von Eschenbach combined a glittering tale of a knight-errant with an earnest description of a search for God. Gottfried von Strassburg, who lived in the early 1200's, imitated French grace in his version of *Tristan and Isolde.*

The minnesingers became popular in the 1100's and 1200's. Many of their lyric poems imitated the songs of the French troubadours (see **Troubadour**). The most famous minnesinger was Walther von der Vogelweide. He transformed the often insincere poems of the troubadours into warm and genuine expressions of love. Walther was the first great German poet to glorify nature, and to write political verse in defense of the Empire against the Papacy.

The interim period (1250-1750)

Popular literature. The period from 1250 to 1600 witnessed the decline of knighthood within the Holy Roman Empire (see **Holy Roman Empire**). People of the middle class emerged as the next cultural leaders. The romantic idealism of the 1200's gave way to middle-class realism, sobriety, and satire. Epics such as *Meier Helmbrecht* by Wernher the Gardener described the degeneracy of the knighthood. Fables became popular as a means of teaching practical lessons. The mocking epic of *Reynard the Fox* and the merry pranks of *Till Eulenspiegel* won wide acclaim. Religious plays, such as the *Redentin Easter Play* and the *Oberammergau Passion Play,* originally combined religious fervor with realistic coarseness and laughter.

In the 1400's and 1500's, *meistersingers* (mastersingers) attempted to revive the lyric poetry of the minnesinger (see **Meistersinger**). The poems and plays of Hans Sachs, a shoemaker and uninspired meistersinger from Nuremberg, are examples of the homespun effort of the German middle class to produce literature.

The Renaissance in Germany took the form of a spiritual rebirth during the 1500's. There was no major revival of letters similar to that of the Italian Renaissance (see **Renaissance**). But two outstanding features of the Renaissance achieved greatness in German-speaking regions. They were humanism and the Reformation (see **Humanism; Reformation**).

German humanism began in Bohemia about 1350 with the establishment of universities. The best-known work of this period is *The Plowman of Bohemia,* written by Johannes von Saaz about 1400. Humanism reached its height from 1480 to 1530. The humanists delved into the philosophy and history of ancient Greece and Rome in their search for a new ideal of humanity. They wrote most of their works in Latin and Greek. Desiderius Erasmus ranked as the foremost humanist of the northern Renaissance. Other outstanding humanists included Johannes Reuchlin, a leading scholar of Hebrew; Philipp Melanchthon, a close friend of Martin Luther; and Ulrich von Hutten, an ardent nationalist and enemy of the Roman Catholic Church.

The Reformation, which began in 1517, left a lasting mark on German life and culture. Most of the literature produced during the Reformation was in the form of religious essays and pamphlets. Martin Luther translated the Bible into German, thus preparing the way for a standard German language. He wrote treatises to support his program of religious reform. Thomas Murner was Luther's most bitter religious and literary opponent.

Baroque literature. The religious wars that grew out of the Reformation produced a strongly pessimistic and despairing literature in the 1600's. Often called *baroque literature,* it was bombastic and highly emotional. Powerful and imploring church hymns thrived as never before. Andreas Gryphius, the greatest poet and dramatist of the age, wrote moving religious poetry that preached steadfastness to God. In *Simplicius Simplicissimus,* Hans Jakob von Grimmelshausen told the story of a hero who found his way to God in spite of the horrors and crimes of the Thirty Years' War.

French classicism exerted a strong influence on German literature from about 1680 to 1750. Rigid classical rules stifled German creativity, and much of the writing seems a poor imitation of French literature.

The second golden age (1750-1830)

All the arts in Germany flourished from the second half of the 1700's through the early 1800's. Artists and scholars such as Goethe in literature, Immanuel Kant in philosophy, and Ludwig van Beethoven in music created the richest cultural period in German history. For the first time, German literature won fame and prestige throughout Europe and the Americas.

The enlightenment came to Germany during the second half of the 1700's. German writers were caught up in the spirit of reform that swept across Europe. In literature, the enlightenment took the form of a resurgence of national pride and a rejection of French influence. Gotthold Ephraim Lessing, Germany's first important literary critic, laid the basis for a German national literature of true greatness. Lessing turned from French classical models to ancient Greek ones. His dramas tried to blend Greek restraint with Shakespearean greatness. One of the best-known of Lessing's plays, *Nathan the Wise,* preached religious tolerance.

The spirit of the enlightenment also appeared in the writings of Christoph Martin Wieland. Through his novels and verse epics, Wieland did more to enrich the German language than any previous poet.

The Storm and Stress movement, called *Sturm und Drang* in German, began about 1770. It represented a powerful reaction against French formalism and rationalism. The new writers, sometimes called *Pre-Romantics,* clamored for nature instead of civilization, originality instead of imitation, religion instead of irony, and passion instead of etiquette.

Friedrich Gottlieb Klopstock was a forerunner of the movement. His religious epic *The Messiah,* published from 1748 through 1773, used ecstatic language to describe the life of Christ. Johann Gottfried von Herder, the most celebrated student of folklore of his time, became the philosophical leader of the movement. He defended German national tastes against the conventions of French classicism.

Herder's work had a profound influence on the young

German literature

Masters of German literature from the 1100's to the present rank among the world's greatest literary figures. This table lists leading German writers in chronological order. The table also includes a number of works that have played a major part in the history of German literature.

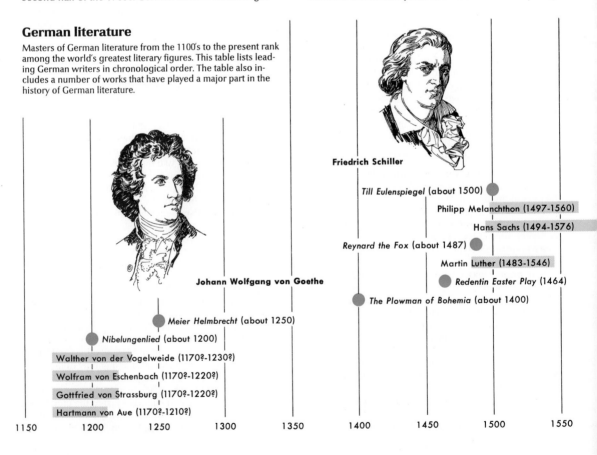

Friedrich Schiller

Johann Wolfgang von Goethe

Till Eulenspiegel (about 1500)

Philipp Melanchthon (1497-1560)

Hans Sachs (1494-1576)

Reynard the Fox (about 1487)

Martin Luther (1483-1546)

Redentin Easter Play (1464)

The Plowman of Bohemia (about 1400)

Meier Helmbrecht (about 1250)

Nibelungenlied (about 1200)

Walther von der Vogelweide (1170?-1230?)

Wolfram von Eschenbach (1170?-1220?)

Gottfried von Strassburg (1170?-1220?)

Hartmann von Aue (1170?-1210?)

1150   1200   1250   1300   1350   1400   1450   1500   1550

Goethe. Both Goethe and the dramatist Friedrich Schiller began their careers as Storm and Stress writers. Their early romantic works include Goethe's *The Sorrows of Young Werther* and the first part of *Faust* (begun about 1770, but not published until 1808), and Schiller's play *The Robbers*. Later, both writers turned to the noble simplicity and quiet grandeur of Greek literature. Their classical period, from 1787 to 1805, produced such works as Goethe's *Iphigenia* and *Hermann and Dorothea*, and Schiller's *Wallenstein* and *William Tell*. Goethe's later writing became more philosophical and symbolic. The second part of *Faust* (1832) was the major production of his old age.

Romanticism in Germany grew out of the Storm and Stress movement. It dominated German literature from 1790 to 1830. Goethe had introduced the feeling of *Weltschmerz* (world-grief) in *The Sorrows of Young Werther*. Napoleon's conquest of Germany helped turn German poets to the pessimism and disillusionment of *Weltschmerz*. These poets expressed themselves through emotional, highly subjective writings. Many turned from their society to the glories of their national past, particularly the Middle Ages. The color and fantasy of fables and fairy tales also attracted many romantics.

The publication of Goethe's *Werther* brought international fame to German literature. Early translators of German works included the English writers Sir Walter Scott and Thomas Carlyle. Although German romanticism had run its course by 1830, it continued to influence world literature for many years.

The list of romantic writers includes some of the greatest names in German literature. The brothers August Wilhelm Schlegel and Friedrich Schlegel led the movement and won international recognition for their literary criticism. Melancholy poets such as Novalis, whose real name was Friedrich von Hardenberg, and Nikolaus Lenau expressed the pessimism and despair of the romantics. Joseph von Eichendorff was one of the finest nature poets of the 1800's. Heinrich von Kleist and Franz Grillparzer were the foremost dramatists of the romantic age. E. T. A. Hoffmann wrote novels and stories based on fantasy and horror.

Clemens Brentano and Achim von Arnim made important contributions in the field of folklore. Their book *The Boy's Magic Horn* (*Des Knaben Wunderhorn*, 1805-1818) was the first systematic collection of German folk songs. Also in the early 1800's, the German scholars Jakob Grimm and Wilhelm Grimm collected their famous *Fairy Tales*.

German literature from 1830-1890

The Young Germans were a group of radical writers who became active in the 1830's. These writers strongly opposed the reactionary policies of Prince von Metternich. They wrote angry political dramas and stories directed against the government. They also took an active part in the revolutions of 1830 and 1848. The most important leader of the Young Germans was Heinrich Heine. He bitterly attacked the government in such works as *Germany, A Winter Tale*. Heine was also one of

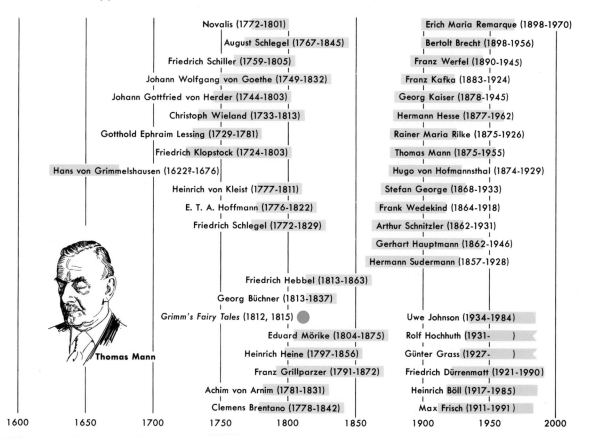

Novalis (1772-1801)
August Schlegel (1767-1845)
Friedrich Schiller (1759-1805)
Johann Wolfgang von Goethe (1749-1832)
Johann Gottfried von Herder (1744-1803)
Christoph Wieland (1733-1813)
Gotthold Ephraim Lessing (1729-1781)
Friedrich Klopstock (1724-1803)
Hans von Grimmelshausen (1622?-1676)
Heinrich von Kleist (1777-1811)
E. T. A. Hoffmann (1776-1822)
Friedrich Schlegel (1772-1829)

Erich Maria Remarque (1898-1970)
Bertolt Brecht (1898-1956)
Franz Werfel (1890-1945)
Franz Kafka (1883-1924)
Georg Kaiser (1878-1945)
Hermann Hesse (1877-1962)
Rainer Maria Rilke (1875-1926)
Thomas Mann (1875-1955)
Hugo von Hofmannsthal (1874-1929)
Stefan George (1868-1933)
Frank Wedekind (1864-1918)
Arthur Schnitzler (1862-1931)
Gerhart Hauptmann (1862-1946)
Hermann Sudermann (1857-1928)

Friedrich Hebbel (1813-1863)
Georg Büchner (1813-1837)
Grimm's Fairy Tales (1812, 1815)
Eduard Mörike (1804-1875)
Heinrich Heine (1797-1856)
Franz Grillparzer (1791-1872)
Achim von Arnim (1781-1831)
Clemens Brentano (1778-1842)

Uwe Johnson (1934-1984)
Rolf Hochhuth (1931-   )
Günter Grass (1927-   )
Friedrich Dürrenmatt (1921-1990)
Heinrich Böll (1917-1985)
Max Frisch (1911-1991)

Thomas Mann

1600   1650   1700   1750   1800   1850   1900   1950   2000

Germany's greatest lyric poets. Such poems as "The Lorelei" and "Du bist wie eine Blume" gained fame.

The realists had far greater importance as a literary movement than the Young Germans had (see **Realism**). The realists revolted against the emotionalism and exaggerations of the romantics and turned to objective descriptions of life. Regionalism became an important factor. Theodor Storm wrote about his community on the North Sea shore. The Moldau River region served as the setting for the works of Adalbert Stifter. Fritz Reuter wrote in the Low German of northeastern Germany, and Gottfried Keller made his native Switzerland the backdrop for his stories and novels. Friedrich Hebbel ranked as the leading realist dramatist.

German literature from 1890 to 1945

Naturalism. After 1890, objective realism gave way to naturalism, a literary movement that emphasized social injustice, crime, slum conditions, and the role of heredity in human development. *The Weavers* (1893), by Gerhart Hauptmann, is the finest example of naturalistic drama. It describes a revolt by oppressed textile workers against their employers. See **Naturalism**.

Impressionism. In contrast to the "bleeding slice of life" presented by the naturalists, the impressionists reemphasized aesthetic and idealistic literature. Thomas Mann, the outstanding German impressionist writer, portrayed sensitive characters in *The Magic Mountain* (1924) and other novels. Other important writers include Hermann Hesse and Arthur Schnitzler. Hesse, an imaginative romantic writer, is best known for his philosophical novel *Steppenwolf* (1927). Schnitzler became famous for analyses of human emotions in short stories and plays dealing with imperial Old Vienna. Hugo von Hofmannsthal, Rainer Maria Rilke, and Stefan George rank among the major German poets of the early 1900's.

Expressionism. Expressionist literature developed during World War I. Much of it had a nightmarish quality, but it had much in common with naturalism's goal of social progress. Expressionist novels and plays cried out against social and political injustice.

The greatest expressionist author was Franz Kafka, a Czech who wrote in German. Kafka wrote about humanity's search for God and justice in short stories and in such novels as *The Castle* (1926). The leading expressionist dramatists included Georg Kaiser, Ernst Toller, and Bertolt Brecht. Kaiser and Toller called for a revolt by workers against the abuses of the industrial system. Brecht wrote several satirical plays, including *The Threepenny Opera* (1928). See **Expressionism**.

Literature under the Nazis. The rule of Adolf Hitler and the Nazi Party from 1933 to 1945 produced much Nazi propaganda but no great literature. Many leading writers left Germany in protest against Nazism. Other writers were driven out of the country or died in concentration camps. Writers supporting the Nazis were extremely nationalistic and anti-intellectual. These writers glorified the German state, often by praising the life of the peasant tilling the German soil.

German literature after 1945

Postwar German literature largely dealt with experiences under Nazism and in World War II (1939-1945). Carl Zuckmayer's play *The Devil's General* (1946) focused on the Nazi past, analyzing conflict between conscience and obedience to a morally corrupt state. Wolfgang Borchert showed a returning German soldier as a social outcast in his play *The Man Outside* (1947).

The leading German-language dramatists of the 1950's were the Swiss writers Friedrich Dürrenmatt and Max Frisch. Both showed the influence of Bertolt Brecht's social criticism. In the 1960's, Rolf Hochhuth wrote the controversial play *The Deputy* (1963). The drama accuses Pope Pius XII of tolerating the Nazi extermination of the Jews. Peter Weiss wrote *Marat/Sade* (1964), an unconventional play that mixes psychology with political ideas.

The leading postwar novelists in West Germany included Heinrich Böll, Günter Grass, Siegfried Lenz, and Martin Walser. Much of their fiction deals with the spiritual and physical damage inflicted on Germany by the Nazis, the lost war, and the turmoil of reconstruction. Böll traced the life of an innocent, humane heroine from prewar times to 1970 in his novel *Group Portrait with Lady* (1971). Grass gained fame for *The Tin Drum* (1959), a satirical account of Nazi rule in a German-Polish city and life in prosperous postwar West Germany. Grass used innovative narrative techniques to critically examine feminism in his novel *The Flounder* (1977).

East German novelists also contributed to postwar German literature. Uwe Johnson and Christa Wolf examined the anxieties of a politically divided Germany. Ulrich Plenzdorf's prose tale and play *The New Sufferings of Young W.* (1973) dealt with the relationship between the individual and the state. Thomas Bernhard and Peter Handke, two Austrian novelists and playwrights, rejected political themes in their works. Instead, they have concentrated on the inner lives of their characters.

German literature today. In 1990, East and West Germany were unified. After unification, East German writers began dealing, often self-critically, with their lives and attitudes under East Germany's Communist society and government. Such authors as Wolfgang Hilbig, Erich Loest, Monika Maron, and Christa Wolf have struggled to come to terms with the past in autobiographies, essays, and novels. West German authors, including Günter Grass and Martin Walser, have also significantly contributed to the ongoing discussion of problems relating to Germany's division, its unification, and the aftermath.   Werner P. Friederich

Related articles in *World Book* include:

Dramatists

Brecht, Bertolt	Kaiser, Georg
Büchner, Georg	Kleist, Heinrich von
Dürrenmatt, Friedrich	Lessing, Gotthold E.
Frisch, Max	Schiller, Johann Christoph
Goethe, Johann W. von	Friedrich von
Hauptmann, Gerhart	Sudermann, Hermann
Hochhuth, Rolf	Wedekind, Frank

Fiction writers

Böll, Heinrich	Grimmelshausen,	Mann, Thomas
Fontane, Theodor	Hans von	Remarque, Erich
Grass, Günter	Hesse, Hermann	Maria
Grimm	Hoffmann, E. T. A.	Schnitzler, Arthur
	Kafka, Franz	Wyss family
		Zweig, Stefan

Poets

George, Stefan	Hartmann von Aue
Gottfried von Strassburg	Heine, Heinrich

Additional resources

Demetz, Peter. *After the Fires: Recent Writing in the Germanies, Austria, and Switzerland.* 1986. Reprint. Harcourt, 1992.
Furness, Raymond, and Humble, Malcomb, eds., *A Companion to Twentieth-Century German Literature.* 2nd ed. Routledge, 1997.
Garland, Henry and Mary. *The Oxford Companion to German Literature.* 3rd ed. Oxford, 1997.
Lange, Victor. *The Classical Age of German Literature, 1740-1815.* Holmes & Meier, 1982.
Vivian, Kim, ed. *A Concise History of German Literature to 1900.* Camden Hse., 1992.
Watanabe-O'Kelly, Helen, ed. *The Cambridge History of German Literature.* Cambridge, 1997.

German measles. See Rubella.

German shepherd dog is one of the most useful dog breeds. It possesses a loyal, courageous, and intelligent personality. Originally developed in Germany as a herding dog, the breed now often serves as a police dog and as a dog guide for the blind. People around the world also keep German shepherds as pets.

The German shepherd dog stands about 24 inches (61 centimeters) high at the shoulder. It somewhat resembles a wolf in shape and has erect ears and a long, wedge-shaped muzzle. The dogs vary in color from black and tan to light brown. See also **Dog** (picture: Herding dogs); **Dog guide.**

Critically reviewed by the American Kennel Club

© Reynolds Photography

The German shepherd dog was bred as a herding dog.

German shorthaired pointer is a dog often used to hunt game birds. It works well as a pointer on land and as a retriever on land and in the water. It has an unusually keen sense of smell.

The German shorthaired pointer is a little larger than most pointers. It stands about 21 to 25 inches (53 to 64 centimeters) high and weighs 45 to 70 pounds (20 to 32 kilograms). The dog's coat is liver-colored or liver and white.

Critically reviewed by the German Shorthaired Pointer Club of America

See also **Dog** (picture: Sporting dogs).

German wirehaired pointer is a hunting dog that was developed by crossing German shorthaired pointers and "poodle-pointers." It is an all-purpose hunter and a good retriever on land or in water. The dog

Ralph A. Reinhold, Animals Animals

The German wirehaired pointer is a hunting dog.

weighs from 55 to 65 pounds (25 to 29 kilograms) and stands 24 to 26 inches (61 to 66 centimeters) high. Its color varies from brown to brown-and-white with liver-colored spots.

Critically reviewed by the German Wirehaired Pointer Club of America

Germanium, *juhr MAY nee uhm,* is a hard, brittle, grayish-white metallic element. It is obtained during the refining of copper, zinc, and lead ores.

Germanium is one of the most widely used materials known as semiconductors (see **Semiconductor**). Germanium is a good semiconductor because it does not have strong metallic properties. Industry uses germanium in such semiconducting devices as diodes and solar batteries. It is also a component of various infrared optics devices that are used in telephone lines, data transmission lines, and computer cables.

The addition of trace amounts of germanium to a lead-acid storage battery can help the battery last longer. Germanium oxide, a germanium compound, is used in medicine. Germanium has the chemical symbol Ge. Its atomic number is 32, and it has an atomic weight of 72.61. It melts at 937.4 °C and boils at 2830 °C. The German chemist Clemens Winkler discovered germanium in 1886.   Raymond E. Davis

Germantown, Battle of. See Revolutionary War in America (Brandywine and Germantown; table: Major battles of the Revolutionary War).

Picture Finders from Bavaria

The beautiful Rhine River, made famous in song and legend, has come to symbolize Germany. Picturesque towns line the river, which is also one of Europe's most important waterways.

Germany

Germany is a large country in central Europe. It has more people than any other European country except Russia. Berlin, Germany's capital and largest city, is a cultural, economic, and political center of Europe.

Germany's land ranges from a low, flat plain in the north to mountainous regions in the south. The country has a number of world-famous scenic areas. The Bavarian Alps, along Germany's southern border, are a favorite winter sports region. The Black Forest, a mountainous area in southwest Germany, is known for its mineral springs and health resorts. In western Germany, many people enjoy boat rides on the beautiful Rhine River.

James J. Sheehan, the contributor of this article, is Dickason Professor of Humanities at Stanford University.

The Rhine winds through valleys where grand castles overlook the river.

Germans have made important contributions to culture. For example, Johann Sebastian Bach and Ludwig van Beethoven composed some of the world's greatest music. Johann Wolfgang von Goethe and Thomas Mann wrote masterpieces of literature. German scientists have made breakthroughs in the areas of chemistry, medicine, and physics.

For hundreds of years, Germans lived in many separate states, one of the most powerful of which was the kingdom of Prussia. During the late 1800's, Otto von Bismarck, the prime minister of Prussia, united most of these states and cities under Prussian leadership. After Bismarck, German leaders tried to expand their influence in Europe and overseas. These policies helped trigger World War I in 1914. When the war ended in 1918, Germany had been defeated, and a period of political and economic crises followed.

In 1933, Adolf Hitler—leader of the Nazi Party, an extremely militaristic and nationalistic political movement—established his dictatorship and began to rebuild Germany's military power. In 1939, Hitler started World War II. Germany was defeated in 1945 and was divided into zones that, in 1949, became West Germany and East Germany. Berlin was also divided. West Germany became a parliamentary democracy with strong ties to Western Europe and the United States. East Germany became a Communist dictatorship closely associated with the Soviet Union.

After World War II, the West Germans and East Germans rebuilt their shattered industries and made them more productive than ever. West Germany became one of the leading industrial nations. Although East Germany's economic development was not as rapid, the country ranked as one of the most economically advanced of the nations that adopted Communism. Yet dissatisfaction led millions of East Germans to flee to West Germany in the mid-1900's. In 1961, however, East Germany built a wall through the city of Berlin. The purpose of the Berlin Wall was to prevent East Germans from emigrating to the West.

In 1989, reform movements swept through the Communist nations of Europe. In East Germany, political protests and massive emigration set in motion the chain of events that ended in the unification of East and West Germany. In November 1989—in response to the protests—the East German government allowed its citi-

© David Pollack, The Stock Market

Neuschwanstein Castle in Bavaria was begun in 1869 by King Ludwig II, known as Mad King Ludwig. The "fairy-tale" castle is one of Germany's popular tourist attractions.

Kappelmeyer, Bavaria

The Brandenburg Gate stands in the downtown section of Berlin, Germany's capital and largest city. The gate, completed in 1791, has become a symbol of Berlin and Germany.

Carl Zeiss, Inc.

Manufacturing is the basis of Germany's economic strength. The country produces many finely crafted products. The worker above is employed in grinding and polishing optical lenses.

Germany in brief

General information

Capital: Berlin.
Official language: German.
Official name: Bundesrepublik Deutschland (Federal Republic of Germany).
National anthem: Third stanza of "Deutschland-Lied" ("Song of Germany").
Largest cities: (1990 official estimate)

Berlin (3,433,695)
Hamburg (1,652,363)
Munich (1,299,026)
Cologne (953,551)
Frankfurt am Main (644,865)

Essen (626,973)
Dortmund (599,055)
Stuttgart (579,988)
Düsseldorf (575,794)
Bremen (551,219)

H. E. Harris & Co.

The German flag has stripes of black, red, and gold—colors that have been associated with German unity since the 1800's.

Coat of arms. The eagle emblem has been used since the ancient Romans introduced it into Germany.

Land and climate

Land: Germany lies in central Europe. It borders France, Switzerland, Austria, Czech Republic, Poland, Denmark, Netherlands, Belgium, and Luxembourg, and it has a short coastline on the North and Baltic seas. The northern part of the country is mostly flat; the terrain is hilly in central and southern Germany. The Alps run along the border with Austria; the rugged Black Forest lies in the southwest; the Bohemian Forest is along the Czech border. Major rivers include Rhine in the west, Danube in the south, Elbe and Weser in the north, and Oder in the east.

Area: 137,735 mi² (356,733 km²). *Greatest distances*—north-south, 540 mi (869 km); east-west, 390 mi (628 km). *Coastline*—574 mi (924 km).
Elevation: *Highest*—9,721 ft (2,963 m) at Zugspitze, in the Alps. *Lowest*—sea level along the coast.
Climate: Mild summers, cool winters. Typical summer daytime highs are in low 70's °F (20's °C). In winter, typical daytime high is a few degrees above freezing. The Rhine Valley is generally the warmest part of the country; the coastal areas are usually milder than the inland areas. Moderate rainfall in all seasons.

Government

Head of state: Federal president.
Head of government: Federal chancellor.
Legislature: Parliament of two houses—the Bundestag (669 members) and the Bundesrat (up to 68 members). The Bundestag is more powerful than the Bundesrat.
Executive: Federal chancellor (elected by Bundestag). Chancellor selects Cabinet ministers.
Judiciary: Highest court is the Federal Constitutional Court.
Political subdivisions: 16 states.

People

Population: *2002 estimate*—82,286,000. *1995 census*—81,538,603.
Population density: 597 persons per mi² (231 per km²).
Distribution: 86 percent urban, 14 percent rural.
Major ethnic/national groups: 95 percent German, 5 percent other Europeans.
Major religions: 38 percent Protestant (chiefly Lutheran); 34 percent Roman Catholic; 2 percent Muslim.

Population trend

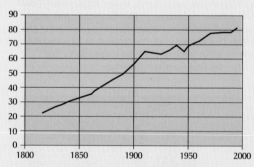

Year	Population	Year	Population	
1816	22,377,000	1946	46,560,000	W. Ger.
1828	26,646,000		18,488,000	E. Ger.
1840	30,382,000		65,048,000	Total
1852	33,413,000	1960	55,423,000	W. Ger.
1861	35,567,000		17,058,000	E. Ger.
1871	41,059,000		72,481,000	Total
1880	45,234,000	1970-71	60,651,000	W. Ger.
1890	49,428,000		17,068,000	E. Ger.
1900	56,367,000		77,739,000	Total
1910	64,926,000	1981	61,666,000	W. Ger.
1925	63,181,000		16,732,000	E. Ger.
1933	66,030,000		78,398,000	Total
		1995	81,538,603	

Economy

Chief products: *Agriculture*—barley, beef cattle, hogs, milk, potatoes, sugar beets, wheat. *Manufacturing*—chemicals and pharmaceuticals, electrical equipment, machinery, motor vehicles, processed foods and beverages, steel. *Mining*—coal.
Money: *Basic unit*—euro. One hundred cents equal one euro. The Deutsche mark was scheduled to be taken out of circulation in 2002.
Foreign trade: *Major exports*—chemicals, electrical equipment, machinery, motor vehicles. *Major imports*—clothing, electrical machinery, food products, petroleum and petroleum products. *Major trading partners*—Belgium, France, Italy, Netherlands, United Kingdom.

zens to travel freely for the first time. The end of travel restrictions included the opening of the Berlin Wall. Also for the first time, non-Communist political parties were permitted to organize. In March 1990, East Germany held free parliamentary elections, and non-Communists gained control of the government.

With the end of Communist control in East Germany, many Germans in East and West Germany began considering unification. In July 1990, East Germany and West Germany united their economies into one system. In August, both nations signed a treaty to finalize unification. The treaty took effect on October 3. That December, the first national elections after unification were held.

For Germany's population and other key statistics, see the *Germany in brief* feature that appears in this article.

Government

Germany is a federal republic. The government's main bodies and offices include a Parliament, a federal chancellor, and a Cabinet.

The government was established after the unification of East and West Germany in 1990. It was based on the democratic system of West Germany. East Germany had operated under a dictatorial Communist government until shortly before unification, when a democratic system was established.

Parliament of Germany has two houses, the *Bundestag* (Federal Diet) and the *Bundesrat* (Federal Council). The Bundestag, which is the more powerful of the two houses, passes the laws and chooses the head of government. The Bundestag has 669 deputies elected by the voters to four-year terms.

The Bundesrat is the house in which Germany's states are represented. Each state has three to six votes in the Bundesrat, depending on the population of the state. Each state government may appoint up to as many delegates to the Bundesrat as the state has votes. The maximum membership of the Bundesrat is 68.

Some laws passed by the Bundestag require approval of the Bundesrat. They include laws that relate directly to the states' responsibilities, such as matters dealing with education and local government. The Bundesrat can raise objections to other laws. Its objections can be overridden by a majority vote of the Bundestag.

Executive. The federal chancellor is the head of Germany's government. The chancellor is elected by a majority of the Bundestag. The Bundestag can remove the chancellor from office by electing a replacement. The chancellor selects the ministers who make up the Cabinet and head government departments.

The federal president is the head of state, but the powers of the office are largely ceremonial. Bundestag deputies and an equal number of electors selected by the German state legislatures elect the president to a five-year term.

State government. Germany has 16 states. Each state has a legislature. Members of most of the legislatures are elected to four-year terms. In most states, the legislature elects a minister president to head the state government. In Berlin, Bremen, and Hamburg, which are cities as well as states, a mayor heads the government.

Politics. The Christian Democratic Union (CDU) and the Social Democratic Party are Germany's largest political parties. The CDU's branch in Bavaria is the Christian Social Union. Traditionally, both large parties support close ties to other Western nations. The CDU has conservative economic and social policies. The Social Democratic Party supports more social welfare programs and greater regulation of the economy.

In most national elections, neither of the major parties gains enough votes to control the Bundestag. In such cases, the political party that has the most votes must form a *coalition* (alliance) to gain a majority of seats in the Bundestag.

Germany also has several smaller political parties. They include the Free Democratic Party, which is a liberal party, and the Green Party, which represents environmental causes. They also include the Party of Democratic Socialism, which is the Communist party that formerly controlled East Germany, and the Republican Party, a very small, extremely conservative party. Germans must be at least 18 years old to vote.

Courts. Germany's highest court is the Federal Constitutional Court. It interprets the Constitution and settles disputes between the executive and the legislature and between federal and state governments. Its 16 judges are appointed for 12-year terms. Half of the judges are appointed by the Bundestag and half by the Bundesrat.

The regular court system tries civil and criminal cases, which can be reviewed by regional and national appellate courts. Judges in all these courts are appointed for life. Administrative courts decide disputes between individuals and government agencies. There are special courts for disputes about labor issues, taxes, and social security payments.

Armed forces. After World War II, the Allies—the countries that had defeated Germany and its partners—planned to keep Germany disarmed. But by the 1950's, the Western Allies wanted West Germany's help against possible Communist expansion. West Germany joined the North Atlantic Treaty Organization (NATO) in 1955, and began to build up its armed forces under NATO command. After unification, Germany remained in NATO. The East German armed forces were dissolved, but some of the personnel joined the unified German armed forces.

The German armed forces have about 330,000 troops. German men are required to serve a term in the military after reaching age 18. In 2001, Germany began allowing women to serve as combat troops.

People

Germany ranks second in population among the countries of Europe. Only Russia has more people. Berlin, the country's capital, is also its largest city.

Ancestry. Germans are descended from many ancient tribes, including the Cimbri, Franks, Goths, and Teutons. A small group of Slavic people called Sorbs live in eastern Germany.

Most of the people living in Germany were born there. Most non-Germans who live in the country moved there with their families as guest workers. They came mostly from Turkey, Yugoslavia, and Italy to work in western Germany.

The largest population movement in German history took place from 1944 to 1947. Millions of Germans poured into Germany from throughout Eastern Europe. During the 1950's, many East Germans fled to West

Germany map index

States

Name	Population	Area In sq. mi.	Area In km²	Capital	Map key
Baden-Württemberg	9,822,000	13,804	35,751	Stuttgart	I 3
Bavaria	11,449,000	27,238	70,546	Munich	H 5
Berlin	3,434,000	341	883	Berlin	D 6
Brandenburg	2,578,000	11,219	29,056	Potsdam	E 6
Bremen	682,000	156	404	Bremen	C 3
Hamburg	1,652,000	289	748	Hamburg	C 4
Hesse	5,763,000	8,152	21,113	Wiesbaden	G 3
Lower Saxony	7,387,000	18,308	47,418	Hanover	D 3
Mecklenburg-Western Pomerania	1,924,000	9,189	23,800	Schwerin	C 5
North Rhine-Westphalia	17,350,000	13,154	34,069	Düsseldorf	E 2
Rhineland-Palatinate	3,764,000	7,660	19,839	Mainz	G 1
Saar	1,073,000	994	2,574	Saarbrücken	H 1
Saxony	4,764,000	7,066	18,300	Dresden	F 6
Saxony-Anhalt	2,874,000	7,876	20,400	Magdeburg	E 5
Schleswig-Holstein	2,626,000	6,065	15,709	Kiel	B 3
Thuringia	2,611,000	6,255	16,200	Erfurt	F 5

Cities and towns

Aachen	238,587	F 1
Aalen	63,195	I 4
Ahlen	52,405	E 2
Albstadt	45,870	I 3
Alfeld	22,453	E 4
Alsdorf*	45,896	F 1
Altenburg	54,659	F 6
Amberg	43,523	H 5
Andernach	26.520	G 2
Anklam	20,202	C 6
Annaberg-Buchholz	26,211	G 6
Ansbach	37,395	H 4
Apolda	28,535	F 5
Arnsberg	74,970	F 2
Arnstadt	29,830	F 4
Aschaffenburg	59,240	G 3
Aschersleben	34,231	E 5
Aue	28,398	G 6
Augsburg	245,193	I 5
Aurich	35,005	C 2
Bad Homburg	50,905	G 3
Bad Kreuznach	39,813	G 2
Bad Oeynhausen	43,207	E 3
Bad Salzuflen	50,819	E 3
Baden-Baden	48,684	I 2
Balingen	29,917	I 3
Bamberg	69,920	G 4
Bautzen	51,615	F 7
Bayreuth	71,848	G 5
Bensheim	33,311	H 3
Berchtesgaden	8,345	J 6
Bergheim*	54,061	F 1
Bergisch Gladbach	104,037	F 2
Bergkamen*	47,747	E 2
Berlin	3,433,695	D 6
Bernau	19,173	D 6
Bernburg	40,826	E 5
Bielefeld	319,037	E 3
Bingen	22,138	G 2
Bitburg	10,309	G 1
Bitterfeld	21,068	E 5
Bocholt	66,105	E 1
Bochum	396,486	E 2
Bonn	292,234	F 2
Borna*	23,384	F 6
Bottrop	118,936	E 2
Brandenburg	95,021	D 6
Braunschweig	258,833	E 4
Bremen	551,219	D 3
Bremerhaven	130,446	C 3
Bruchsal	36,602	H 3
Brühl*	40,723	F 1
Burg	28,633	E 5
Buxtehude	32,453	C 3
Castrop-Rauxel*	76,430	E 2
Celle	70,482	D 4
Chemnitz	294,244	F 6
Coburg	44,244	G 5
Coesfeld	31,508	E 2
Cologne	953,551	F 1
Coswig	28,209	E 6
Cottbus	125,891	E 7
Crimmitschau*	24,881	F 5
Cuxhaven	56,504	C 3
Dachau	32,682	I 5
Darmstadt	138,920	G 3
Delitzsch	28,094	E 5
Delmenhorst	70,546	D 3
Dessau	103,748	E 5
Detmold	66,403	E 3
Dinslaken*	61,032	E 1
Döbeln	27,115	F 6
Dormagen*	57,293	F 1
Dorsten*	72,945	E 2
Dortmund	599,055	E 2
Dreieich*	37,936	G 3
Dresden	490,571	F 6
Duisburg	535,447	E 1
Düren	84,272	F 1
Düsseldorf	575,794	F 1
Eberswalde	54,032	D 6
Einbeck	27,440	E 4
Eisenach	50,949	F 4
Eisenhüttenstadt	48,463	E 7
Eisleben*	26,869	F 5
Elmshorn	41,192	C 3
Emden	49,686	C 2
Erding	24,555	I 5
Erftstadt*	44,738	F 1
Erfurt	208,989	F 5
Erkrath*	44,626	E 1
Erlangen	102,440	H 5
Eschweiler	52,786	F 1
Essen	626,973	F 2
Esslingen	87,467	I 3
Euskirchen*	45,309	F 1
Falkensee	23,471	D 6
Finsterwalde	23,965	E 6
Flensburg	86,779	B 3
Forst	26,331	E 7
Frankenthal	43,941	H 2
Frankfurt [am Main]	644,865	G 3
Frankfurt [an der Oder]	85,185	D 7
Frechen*	42,424	F 1
Freiberg	50,008	F 6
Freiburg	191,029	J 2
Freising	36,061	I 5
Freital	43,968	F 6
Freudenstadt	20,058	I 2
Friedrichshafen	51,665	J 3
Fulda	54,780	G 3
Fürstenfeldbruck	31,476	I 5
Fürstenwalde	35,083	D 7
Fürth	103,362	H 5
Garbsen	57,249	D 3
Gelsenkirchen	293,714	E 2
Gera	129,037	F 5
Giessen	71,104	G 3
Gifhorn	34,133	D 4
Gladbeck*	76,592	E 2
Glauchau	29,095	F 6
Göppingen	51,471	I 4
Görlitz	79,506	F 7
Goslar	49,636	E 4
Gotha	57,583	F 4
Göttingen	121,831	E 4
Greifswald	64,661	B 6
Greiz	35,601	F 5
Grevenbroich	57,049	F 1
Gronau	39,769	E 2
Guben	34,594	E 7
Gummersbach*	48,373	F 2
Gustrow	39,065	C 5
Gütersloh	79,001	E 2
Hagen	214,449	F 2
Halberstadt	46,915	E 4
Halle	310,234	E 5
Halle-Neustadt	92,168	E 5
Hamburg	1,652,363	C 4
Hameln	55,580	E 3
Hamm	179,639	E 2
Hanau	84,672	G 3
Hanover	513,010	D 4
Hattingen*	55,051	F 2
Heidelberg	137,796	H 3
Heidenheim	47,584	I 4
Heilbronn	115,843	H 3
Hennigsdorf	27,254	D 6
Herford	59,640	E 3
Herne	178,132	E 2
Herten*	69,004	E 2
Herzogenrath*	43,274	F 1
Hilden*	53,413	F 2
Hildesheim	105,291	E 4
Hof	51,035	G 5
Homburg	41,295	H 2
Höxter	31,579	E 3
Hoyerswerda	69,969	F 7
Hürth	50,741	F 1
Ibbenbueren	42,447	E 2
Idar-Oberstein	34,258	H 2
Ilmenau	29,504	F 4
Ingolstadt	105,489	I 5
Iserlohn	89,539	F 2
Itzehoe	32,072	C 3
Jena	102,518	F 5
Kaiserslautern	97,664	H 2
Kamen*	44,393	E 2
Karlsruhe	275,061	H 2
Kassel	194,268	F 3
Kaufbeuren	41,365	J 4
Kempten	56,705	J 4
Kerpen*	54,769	F 1
Kiel	245,567	B 4
Kleve	44,548	E 1
Koblenz	108,733	G 2
Köln, see Cologne		
Konstanz	69,852	J 3
Köthen	34,507	E 5
Krefeld	244,020	F 1
Kreuztal	28,989	F 2
Lahr	34,594	I 2
Landau	35,482	H 2
Langenfeld*	48,357	F 1
Langenhagen	46,520	D 4
Lauchhammer	24,304	E 6
Lauf	22,217	H 5
Leer	30,075	C 2
Leipzig	511,079	F 6
Leverkusen	160,919	F 1
Limbach-Oberfrohna*	22,247	F 6
Limburg	28,905	G 2
Lingen	45,433	D 2
Lippstadt	60,032	E 3
Lörrach	40,862	J 2
Lübbenau	21,256	E 7
Lübeck	210,318	C 4
Luckenwalde	26,845	E 6
Lüdenscheid	73,292	F 2
Ludwigsburg	76,973	I 3
Ludwigshafen	162,173	H 2
Lüneburg	59,645	C 4
Lünen*	84,532	E 2
Magdeburg	278,807	E 5
Mainz	179,486	G 2
Mannheim	294,984	H 3
Marburg	75,092	F 3
Marl*	87,449	E 2
Meerane*	21,134	F 5
Meerbusch*	49,037	F 1
Meiningen	25,890	G 4
Meissen	38,137	F 6
Memmingen	37,370	J 4
Menden*	52,082	F 2
Merseburg	48,002	F 5
Merzig	29,228	H 1
Minden	75,511	E 3
Moers*	104,595	E 1
Mönchengladbach	259,436	F 1
Mühlhausen	43,403	F 4
Mülheim	177,681	F 1
München, see Munich		
Munich	1,229,026	I 5
Münster	259,438	E 2
Naumburg	32,491	F 5
Neubrandenburg	84,017	C 6
Neumarkt	31,780	H 5
Neumünster	78,280	B 4
Neunkirchen	49,759	H 1
Neuruppin	26,755	D 6
Neuss	147,019	F 1
Neustadt [am Rübenberge]	37,918	D 3
Neustadt [an der Weinstrasse]	48,463	H 2
Neustrelitz	27,276	C 6
Neu-Ulm	46,253	I 4
Neuwied	58,471	G 2
Norderstedt	67,232	C 4
Nordhausen	47,219	F 4
Nordhorn	47,921	D 2
Northeim	31,033	E 4
Nuremberg	465,255	H 5
Nürnberg, see Nuremberg		
Nürtingen	35,681	I 3
Oberammergau	4,664	J 4
Oberhausen	223,840	E 1
Oberursel	38,857	G 3
Offenbach	114,992	G 3
Offenburg	50,207	I 2
Oldenburg	143,131	D 2
Oranienburg	28,443	D 6
Osnabrück	163,168	E 2
Osterode	26,990	E 4
Paderborn	120,680	E 3
Parchim	23,350	C 5
Pasewalk	15,883	C 7
Passau	52,523	I 6
Peine	45,707	E 4
Pforzheim	112,944	I 3
Pinneberg	35,326	C 4
Pirmasens	46,526	H 2
Pirna	47,387	F 7
Plauen	77,733	G 5
Potsdam	138,737	D 6
Prenzlau	23,797	C 6
Pulheim*	47,353	F 1
Quedlinburg	29,488	E 5
Radebeul	34,356	F 6
Radolfzell	25,016	J 3
Rastatt	37,337	I 2
Rathenow	31,630	D 5
Ratingen*	88,718	F 1
Ravensburg	42,911	J 3
Recklinghausen*	125,060	E 2
Regensburg	121,691	H 5
Reichenbach*	24,855	G 5
Remscheid	123,155	F 2
Rendsburg	30,970	B 3
Reutlingen	103,687	I 3
Rheine	70,662	E 2
Riesa	49,744	F 6
Rosenheim	52,743	J 5
Rostock	242,729	B 5
Rottenburg	32,934	I 3
Rudolstadt	32,485	F 5
Rüsselsheim	57,579	G 3
Saalfeld	33,592	G 5
Saarbrücken	191,694	H 1
Salzgitter	114,355	E 4
Salzwedel	23,201	D 5
Sangerhausen	33,388	F 5
Schmallenberg	24,429	F 2
Schönebeck	45,093	E 5
Schwabach	35,437	H 5
Schwäbisch Gmünd	56,117	I 4
Schwäbisch Hall	30,913	H 4
Schwedt	51,700	D 7
Schweinfurt	51,016	G 4
Schwerin	127,065	C 5
Schwerte*	48,138	F 2
Senftenberg	32,211	E 7
Siegen	109,174	F 2
Sindelfingen	55,501	I 3
Singen	41,531	J 3
Sinsheim	27,716	H 3
Solingen	165,401	F 2
Sömmerda	23,417	F 5
Sondershausen	23,807	F 4
Sonnerberg	28,368	G 5
Sonthofen	20,781	J 4
Speyer	43,923	H 2
Spremberg	24,460	E 7
Stade	42,988	C 3
Stadtallendorf	20,412	F 3
Stassfurt	27,302	E 5
Stendal	46,380	D 5
Stolberg	56,435	F 1
Stralsund	75,408	B 6
Straubing	41,632	I 6
Strausberg	26,727	D 7
Stuttgart	579,988	I 3
Suhl	53,933	G 4
Templin	14,500	D 6
Torgau	21,717	E 6
Trier	93,472	H 1
Troisdorf	60,981	F 2
Tübingen	75,825	I 3
Uelzen	35,518	D 4
Ulm	110,529	I 4
Unna*	58,778	E 2
Varel	23,859	C 2
Velbert*	88,403	F 2
Viersen*	78,489	F 1
Villingen-Schwenningen	76,303	J 3
Völklingen	43,413	H 1
Waiblingen	44,570	I 3
Waren	24,300	C 6
Weiden	42,073	H 5
Weimar	63,438	F 5
Weinheim	40,655	H 3
Weissenfels	36,606	F 5
Weisswasser	35,341	E 7
Wernigerode	36,168	E 4
Wesel	54,791	E 1
Wetzlar	50,063	F 3
Wiesbaden	266,623	G 2
Wilhelmshaven	95,570	C 2
Wismar	57,662	C 5
Witten*	105,403	F 2
Wittenberg	54,190	E 6
Wittenberge	30,675	D 5
Wittstock	14,400	D 6
Wolfen	42,414	E 5
Wolfenbüttel	48,641	E 4
Wolfsburg	128,510	D 4
Wolgast	16,923	B 6
Worms	71,827	H 2
Wunstorf	37,368	D 3
Wuppertal	383,660	F 2
Würzburg	127,777	G 4
Zeitz	43,467	F 5
Zittau	40,040	F 7
Zweibrücken	33,018	H 2
Zwickau	114,632	F 6

*Does not appear on map; key shows general location.
Sources: 1990 official estimates for states and largest cities; 1988 and earlier official estimates for other places.

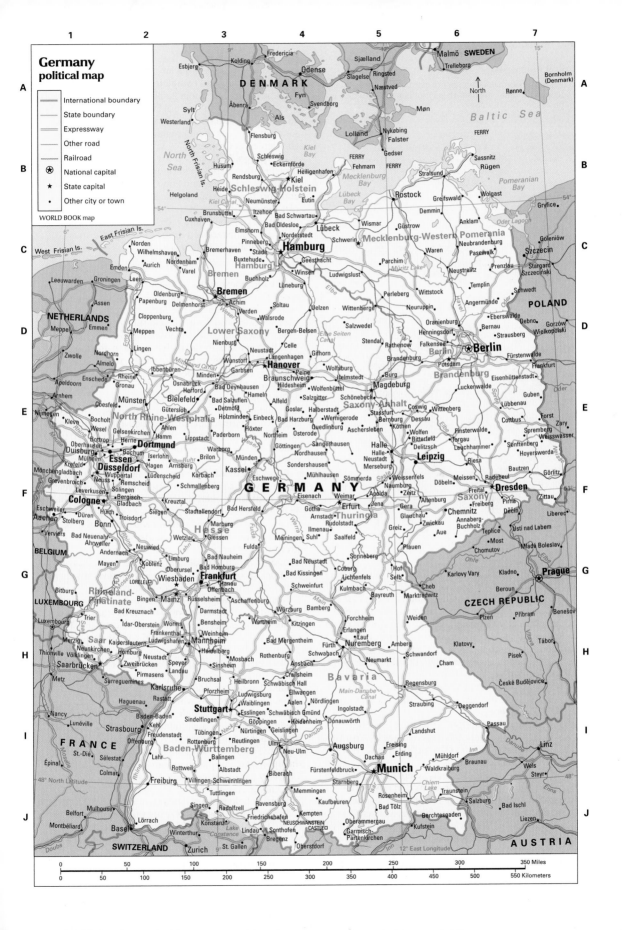

Germany
political map

International boundary
State boundary
Expressway
Other road
Railroad
National capital
State capital
Other city or town

WORLD BOOK map

1   2   3   4   5   6   7

DENMARK

Esbjerg   Kolding   Fredericia   Sjælland   Ringsted   Malmö   SWEDEN
Odense   Slagelse   Næstved   Trelleborg
Åbenrå   Fyn   Svendborg   Møn   Bornholm (Denmark)
Sylt   Als   Nykøbing   Rønne
Westerland   Flensburg   Lolland   Falster

North Frisian Is.   Schleswig   Heiligenhafen   Gedser   Baltic Sea
Husum   Eckernförde   Fehmarn   FERRY   Sassnitz
North Sea   Rendsburg   Kiel   Rügen   Pomeranian Bay
Helgoland   Heide   Neumünster   Eutin   Lübeck Bay   Rostock   Greifswald   Wolgast   Gryfice
East Frisian Is.   Brunsbüttel   Itzehoe   Bad Schwartau   Wismar   Güstrow   Anklam   Szczecin
Norden   Cuxhaven   Elmshorn   Norderstedt   Schwerin   Waren   Neubrandenburg   Pasewalk
West Frisian Is.   Wilhelmshaven   Bremerhaven   Pinneberg   Stade   Hamburg   Schleswig-Holstein   Mecklenburg-Western Pomerania   Prenzlau   Stargard Szczeciński
Leeuwarden   Groningen   Nordenham   Buxtehude   Geesthacht   Parchim   Müritz Lake   Neustrelitz   Schwedt
Emden   Aurich   Varel   Buchholz   Winsen   Ludwigslust   Perleberg   Wittstock   Templin   Angermünde
Meppel   Emmen   Oldenburg   Delmenhorst   Bremen   Lüneburg   Wittenberge   Neuruppin   Oranienburg   Eberswalde   Debno   Gorzów Wielkopolski
Assen   Papenburg   Achim   Soltau   Uelzen   Salzwedel   Rathenow   Henningsdorf   Bernau   Strausberg   POLAND
Cloppenburg   Verden   Walsrode   Bergen-Belsen   Stendal   Falkensee   Berlin
Vechta   Nienburg   Celle   Gifhorn   Brandenburg   Potsdam   Fürstenwalde
Nordhorn   Lingen   Neustadt   Wunstorf   Garbsen   Peine   Wolfsburg   Helmstedt   Burg   Magdeburg   Luckenwalde   Eisenhüttenstadt   Frankfurt
Zwolle   Almelo   Rheine   Ibbenbüren   Minden   Hanover   Braunschweig   Hildesheim   Wolfenbüttel   Schönebeck   Brandenburg   Guben
Apeldoorn   Enschede   Gronau   Osnabrück   Herford   Bad Oeynhausen   Hameln   Alfeld   Salzgitter   Saxony-Anhalt   Coswig   Wittenberg   Lübbenau
Arnhem   Coesfeld   Münster   Bielefeld   Bad Salzuflen   Detmold   Holzminden   Einbeck   Bad Harzburg   Wernigerode   Stassfurt   Dessau   Köthen   Wolfen   Finsterwalde   Cottbus   Forst
Nijmegen   Kleve   Bocholt   Gütersloh   Ahlen   Lippstadt   Paderborn   Höxter   Northeim   Göttingen   Goslar   Halberstadt   Bernburg   Bitterfeld   Delitzsch   Torgau   Lauchhammer   Spremberg   Weisswasser
Wesel   Gelsenkirchen   Herne   Dortmund   Iserlohn   Warburg   Brilon   Münden   Sangerhausen   Quedlinburg   Aschersleben   Halle   Wolfen   Senftenberg   Hoyerswerda
Oberhausen   Bottrop   Bochum   Hagen   Arnsberg   Korbach   Kassel   Nordhausen   Sömmerda   Halle   Merseburg   Riesa   Bautzen
Duisburg   Mülheim   Essen   Lüdenscheid   Schmallenberg   Eschwege   Mühlhausen   Weissenfels   Naumburg   Leipzig   Meissen   Radebeul   Görlitz
Mönchengladbach   Düsseldorf   Wuppertal   Remscheid   GERMANY   Sondershausen   Zeitz   Döbeln   Freital   Dresden
Grevenbroich   Neuss   Solingen   Kreuztal   Stadtallendorf   Bad Hersfeld   Eisenach   Weimar   Erfurt   Apolda   Jena   Gera   Altenburg   Freiberg   Pirna   Zittau
Eschweiler   Cologne   Bergisch Gladbach   Siegen   Gotha   Arnstadt   Saxony   Liberec
Leverkusen   Hürth   Troisdorf   Marburg   Wetzlar   Rudolstadt   Thuringia   Glauchau   Chemnitz   Annaberg-Buchholz   Děčín
Aachen   Düren   Bonn   Giessen   Fulda   Meiningen   Suhl   Ilmenau   Saalfeld   Greiz   Zwickau   Aue   Teplice   Ústí nad Labem
BELGIUM   Stolberg   Bad Neuenahr-Ahrweiler   Neuwied   Limburg   Bad Nauheim   Sonneberg   Hof   Plauen   Most   Chomutov   Mladá Boleslav
Verviers   Mayen   Oberursel   Bad Homburg   Bad Neustadt   Coburg   Selb   Marktredwitz   Karlovy Vary   Kladno   Prague
Bitburg   Andernach   Koblenz   LORELEI   Wiesbaden   Frankfurt   Hanau   Bad Kissingen   Lichtenfels   Cheb   Beroun   CZECH REPUBLIC
LUXEMBOURG   Rhineland-Palatinate   Bingen   Mainz   Rüsselsheim   Aschaffenburg   Schweinfurt   Kulmbach   Bayreuth   Weiden   Benešov
Trier   Bad Kreuznach   Worms   Darmstadt   Bensheim   Wertheim   Würzburg   Bamberg   Forchheim   Příbram
Luxembourg   Idar-Oberstein   Frankenthal   Weinheim   Bad Mergentheim   Kitzingen   Erlangen   Lauf   Amberg   Plzeň
Merzig   Saar   Kaiserslautern   Ludwigshafen   Mannheim   Heidelberg   Rothenburg   Fürth   Nuremberg   Schwandorf   Klatovy
Thionville   Völklingen   Neunkirchen   Homburg   Neustadt   Speyer   Mosbach   Schwäbisch Hall   Schwabach   Neumarkt   Cham   České Budějovice
Saarbrücken   Zweibrücken   Landau   Sinsheim   Crailsheim   Ansbach   Bavaria   Regensburg   Pisek
Metz   Pirmasens   Bruchsal   Heilbronn   Ellwangen   Nördlingen   Ingolstadt   Straubing   Deggendorf
Sarreguemines   Karlsruhe   Pforzheim   Ludwigsburg   Schwäbisch Gmünd   Aalen   Donauwörth   Landshut   Passau   Linz
Nancy   Rastatt   Waiblingen   Heidenheim   Augsburg   Freising   Erding   Mühldorf   Wels
Lunéville   Baden-Baden   Kehl   Stuttgart   Sindelfingen   Esslingen   Göppingen   Geislingen   Dachau   Waldkraiburg   Braunau   Steyr
FRANCE   Strasbourg   Offenburg   Freudenstadt   Tübingen   Nürtingen   Ulm   Neu-Ulm   Fürstenfeldbruck   Munich   Salzburg   Bad Ischl
St-Dié   Sélestat   Lahr   Rottenburg   Reutlingen   Biberach   Memmingen   Starnberg   Chiem Lake   Berchtesgaden   Liezen
Épinal   Baden-Württemberg   Rottweil   Balingen   Villingen-Schwenningen   Ravensburg   Kaufbeuren   Rosenheim   Bad Tölz   Bad Ischl
Colmar   Freiburg   Tuttlingen   Singen   Radolfzell   Friedrichshafen   Kempten   Oberammergau   Garmisch-Partenkirchen   Kufstein
Belfort   Mulhouse   Lörrach   Konstanz   Lindau   Sonthofen   NEUSCHWANSTEIN CASTLE   Traunstein
Montbéliard   Basel   Winterthur   Bregenz   Oberstdorf   AUSTRIA
SWITZERLAND   Zurich   St. Gallen   Lake Constance

North Sea   Kiel Bay   Mecklenburg Bay   Lübeck Bay   Elbe   Havel   Spree   Oder   Weser   Rhine   Main   Danube   Neckar   Inn   Isar   Lech

0   50   100   150   200   250   300   350 Miles
0   50   100   150   200   250   300   350   400   450   500   550 Kilometers

Population density

A majority of Germany's people live in urban areas. The area surrounding the Rhine and Ruhr rivers is one of the most densely
populated parts of Europe.

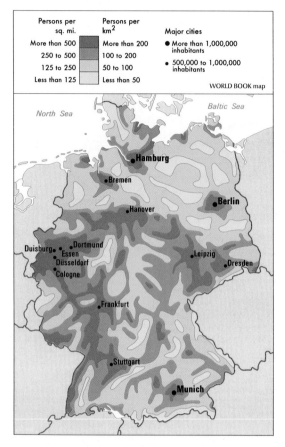

Persons per sq. mi.	Persons per km²	Major cities
More than 500	More than 200	● More than 1,000,000 inhabitants
250 to 500	100 to 200	
125 to 250	50 to 100	● 500,000 to 1,000,000 inhabitants
Less than 125	Less than 50	

WORLD BOOK map

Germany, through Berlin. At the time, the German people were divided by the heavily guarded 858-mile (1,381-
kilometer) border that split their land between East and
West. Relatives and friends were separated from one
another. The East German government restricted travel
between East and West Germany. In August 1961, the
Communist government of East Germany closed off the
escape route in Berlin by building the high, heavily
guarded Berlin Wall between eastern and western sectors of the city. Although some East Germans were allowed to resettle in West Germany, most people could
not even visit there.

It was during the mid-1900's that the many guest
workers from other countries came to live in West Germany. The West Germans recruited them to work in the
country's booming industries.

In 1989, as reform movements swept through Eastern
Europe, thousands of East Germans fled to West Germany by way of neighboring countries. In response to
these departures and popular protests, the East German
government lifted all restrictions on travel. The Berlin
Wall was opened and later torn down. East Germans
were permitted to travel to West Germany or any other
country. In addition, West Germans were permitted to

visit East Germany without any restrictions. After unification, all Germans had complete freedom of travel.

In the late 1900's, about 2 million ethnic Germans
from the countries of Eastern Europe and the former Soviet Union immigrated to Germany. Hundreds of thousands of refugees of other ethnic backgrounds have
also settled in Germany.

Language. Two main forms of the German language
have long been spoken in Germany—High German in
the south and center and Low German in the north. In
addition, there are many dialects associated with particular regions or cities. In Germany today, schools, businesses, newspapers, and radio and television broadcasts use a standardized form of the High German
language called Standard German.

Way of life

City life. Most of the people of Germany live in urban
areas. German cities face the problems of pollution and
congestion that affect urban areas everywhere. Many
German cities also have housing shortages.

Many German cities were destroyed during World
War II. In some of them, such as Munich, the old city
center has been restored. Most cities, however, have
buildings dating from the postwar construction of the
1950's and 1960's.

Rural life. In western Germany, most farms are small
and owned by families that live on them. In eastern Germany, most farms were large collective farms formerly
controlled by the East German government. Since unification, the German government has returned most of
this land to private ownership.

Food and drink. Germans usually eat their main meal
of the day at noon. This main meal often features veal,
pork, beef, or chicken. It also includes such vegetables
as beets, carrots, onions, potatoes, or turnips. Breakfast
usually consists of rolls and jam with coffee or milk. In
the afternoon, especially on Sunday, many Germans enjoy a snack of fancy pastries. They generally eat a light
supper of bread, cheese, and sausage. Beer and wine
are popular beverages. German beer and wine are internationally famous for their high quality.

Many world-famous German dishes were created
hundreds of years ago to prevent foods from spoiling.
Sauerkraut was developed to preserve cabbage. To preserve meat, German cooks soaked it in vinegar and
spices—and created sauerbraten. The Germans also preserved meats by making such sausages as bratwurst and
frankfurters. They developed many kinds of cheeses, including Limburger, Münster, and Tilsiter, which were
named for the regions where they were first made.

Recreation. The people of Germany enjoy hiking,
reading, gardening, swimming, and watching television.
Many young people take bicycling, hiking, or hitchhik-
ing trips. They carry knapsacks and spend the night in
the open or at inexpensive inns called youth hostels.
Germany has many lakes and rivers for canoeing, rowing, sailing, and swimming. The high, snow-covered
mountains help make skiing a favorite winter sport.

Soccer is the most popular organized sport in Germany. There are thousands of soccer teams, most of
which represent various towns or cities. Gymnastics,
tennis, and track are also popular. Some Germans belong to sharpshooting clubs.

© Owen Franken, German Information Center

Shopping malls in German cities carry a great variety of goods. The mall shown in this photograph is in Stuttgart.

© Lois Wille

Picturesque old buildings are preserved in many towns. This photograph shows Wernigerode, in central Germany.

Religion. The religious movement called the Reformation started in Germany. It began in 1517 when Martin Luther, a German monk, protested certain practices of the Roman Catholic Church. The Reformation brought about the establishment of Protestantism. By 1600, most of the people in northern and central Germany had become Protestants. Most of those in the south remained Roman Catholics.

Today, about 38 percent of Germans are Protestants, mostly Lutherans. About 33 percent of the people are Roman Catholics. About 2 percent are Muslims.

About 560,000 Jews lived in Germany when the Nazis came to power in 1933. By the end of World War II, most Jews had been killed by the Nazis or had fled the country. Today, about 100,000 Jews live in Germany.

Education. The German states were among the first in the world to set up a public education system for all children. Prussia established a system during the early 1800's. The other German states developed their own public education systems by the mid-1800's. By the 1900's, almost all Germans over the age of 15 could read and write.

Germany also developed one of the finest university systems in the world. In the late 1800's and early 1900's, students came from many countries to study in Germany. Such German universities as the University of Berlin (now Humboldt University) and the University of Leipzig (called Karl Marx University from 1953 to 1991)

© Messerschmidt, Bavaria-Verlag

Oktoberfest is a lively festival held in Munich each autumn. People fill beerhalls for food, beer, and music. Oktoberfest began in the 1800's after a royal wedding celebration.

The Telegraph from Bavaria-Verlag

Shops and cafes line the Kurfürstendamm, a famous boulevard in Berlin. At its east end, the bombed-out Kaiser Wilhelm Memorial Church, *left,* serves as a reminder of World War II.

Picture Finders from Bavaria-Verlag

Picturesque Heidelberg includes the ruins of Heidelberg Castle, *center background.* The castle dates from the Middle Ages and overlooks the old city and a square called the *Kornmarkt.*

were especially famous for scientific research. Between 1900 and 1933, German scientists won more Nobel Prizes than scientists from any other country.

Education in Germany is controlled by the individual states. All children must go to school full-time for at least 9 or 10 years, starting at age 6. But the length of time children spend in elementary and other types of schools varies from state to state.

In most German states, children attend elementary school for four years. Children may then go to one of several types of schools. A *gymnasium* is a traditional junior and senior high school. This type of school prepares students for entrance into a university. There are also intermediate schools. They provide students with academic subjects as well as some job training. Other schools are *hauptschulen* (vocational schools). These have fewer academic subjects than the other types of

© Bruno Widen, TSW Click/Chicago

Swimmers crowd the beaches on Germany's seacoast during the warm summer months.

© Muhlberger, Bavaria-Verlag

Soccer is the most popular organized sport in Germany. Thousands of teams represent towns and cities. This photograph shows a game between clubs from Munich and Stuttgart.

schools but offer much job training. *Comprehensive schools* combine all three types of junior and senior high levels of education.

Germany has about 60 universities and many specialized and technical colleges. The University of Heidelberg, founded in 1386, is Germany's oldest university.

Arts

Many of the world's greatest artists, musicians, writers, and thinkers have been German. During the Middle Ages and the Renaissance, German architects, painters, and sculptors produced great works, mostly with religious subjects. During the 1700's, many German writers and thinkers were part of the European Enlightenment, which focused on rational thinking and the order of nature. In the late 1700's and early 1800's, Germans helped create the Romantic movement. More recently, Ger-

© Owen Franken, German Information Center

Schools in Germany are famous for the quality of their education. Students must attend school for at least 9 or 10 years. These students are watching their teacher conduct an experiment.

mans were among the pioneers in modern art, motion pictures, literature, and music.

This section mentions only some of the most important German contributions to the arts. For more detailed information, see the separate articles on **Architecture; Classical music; Drama; German literature; Motion picture; Opera; Painting; Sculpture;** and **Theater.**

Literature and philosophy. The greatest period of German literature lasted from about 1750 to 1830. During these years, Johann Wolfgang von Goethe, Gotthold Ephraim Lessing, Friedrich Schiller, Friedrich Hölderlin, Heinrich von Kleist, and many other German novelists, poets, and dramatists produced works of lasting importance. The most important German philosopher during this period was Immanuel Kant, who wrote three influential works in the 1780's.

During the early 1800's, Georg Wilhelm Friedrich Hegel produced a philosophy of history that would have a lasting impact on Western thought. Hegel's work greatly influenced Karl Marx, the philosopher, social scientist, and professional revolutionary who was the chief founder of the two powerful movements of democratic socialism and revolutionary communism. Marx used Hegelian ideas as the basis for his theories.

From the mid-1800's on, German writers and philosophers often focused on the political and cultural situations in their own land. Poet Heinrich Heine produced works that were critical of the German political establishment. Theodor Fontane wrote gently ironic novels about Prussian society in the late 1800's. Friedrich Nietzsche wrote a series of poetic philosophical works on the nature of language and culture. Between 1890 and 1920, Max Weber created a series of studies about modern society. During the 1900's, novelist Thomas Mann and dramatist Bertolt Brecht wrote about the problems of German politics and culture.

After World War II and the collapse of Nazi Germany, Günter Grass, Heinrich Böll, Paul Celan, and many other writers tried to come to terms with the burden of the Nazi past. In East Germany, a number of novelists explored the problems of a socialist society, sometimes with a muted criticism of government policies.

Music. The great tradition of German music was established during the early 1700's by Johann Sebastian Bach and George Frideric Handel. Later in the 1700's, one of the greatest musical geniuses of all time, Wolfgang Amadeus Mozart, carried on this tradition in Austria, which was historically connected to the other German states.

In the early 1800's, Ludwig van Beethoven invented new and powerful forms of symphonic expression and then reached new heights of creative power with his last quartets. Felix Mendelssohn became the most famous composer of his time, with his own classical works and by reviving interest in the works of Bach. Franz Schubert and Robert Schumann achieved greatness by composing the romantic German art songs called *lieder.*

In the mid-1800's, Richard Wagner established a new style in opera with his *music dramas,* which sought to combine music, poetry, and theatrical design. In the late 1800's and early 1900's, Richard Strauss and Arnold Schoenberg wrote important music in different styles. During the 1920's, Kurt Weill broke new musical ground with his innovative music for the stage.

Saint James the Greater (1510);
Öffentliche Kunstsammlung
Basel, Kunstmuseum (© Color-
photo Hans Hinz)

Porcelain figurine (1746) by Johann Kändler; Wadsworth Atheneum, Francis G. Mayer Art Color
Slides, Inc.

Sculpture and ceramics have long traditions in German art. A
carving by Tilman Riemenschneider, *left,* is a masterpiece of late
medieval sculpture. The Meissen factory created beautiful ceramic figurines, *right,* in the 1700's.

© Wilhelm Rauh, Bayreuther Festspiele

Richard Wagner's opera *Lohengrin,* first performed in 1850,
is based on a medieval German legend. Wagner's music dramas
established a new style in opera and influenced many composers. His operas are performed each year at a special festival in
Bayreuth, *above.*

Film Stills Archive, The Museum of Modern Art

German filmmaking has excelled in portraying psychological
themes. The silent film *Metropolis* (1926), *above,* was directed
by the famous German director Fritz Lang. The film depicts a city
of the future that has been corrupted by mad scientists.

Giraudon/Art Resource

The interior of the Wies church near Oberammergau is a
masterpiece of rococo decoration. The interior was intended to
give visitors a vision of heaven. The church, designed by
Dominkus Zimmermann, was built between 1745 and 1754.

Oil painting on canvas (1911); Collection Walker Art Center,
Minneapolis, gift of the T. B. Walker Foundation, Gilbert M. Walker Fund, 1942

German expressionism was one of the most important art movements of the 1900's. In 1911,
Franz Marc helped found a school of expressionism in Munich called *Der Blaue Reiter* (The Blue
Rider). Marc's *The Large Blue Horses, shown here,* is one of his best-known paintings.

Painting and sculpture. German artists created some outstanding works during the Renaissance. Albrecht Dürer and Hans Holbein the Younger produced great paintings and engravings. They are especially famous for their portraits. Matthias Grünewald painted masterpieces of religious art, and sculptor Tilman Riemenschneider made beautiful woodcarvings.

In the early 1800's, Caspar David Friedrich was an important romantic painter. In the late 1800's and early 1900's, Max Beckmann and other German painters developed the expressionist style. They sought to express unconscious emotions and dreamlike states. In the late 1900's, Anselm Kiefer and other painters created monumental works that tried to capture the painful memories of the Nazi past. Their paintings came to be referred to as *neoexpressionism.*

© Scholz, Bavaria-Verlag

The Dresden Opera House was built between 1871 and 1878. The building shows the influence of the baroque architectural style of the 1700's. It was damaged by bombs in 1945, during World War II. But it was restored to its original appearance.

© F. Karsten, London from Bauhaus-Archive, Berlin

The Bauhaus was an internationally important school of design founded by German architect Walter Gropius in Weimar in 1919. This photograph shows the buildings Gropius designed for the school when it moved from Weimar to Dessau in 1925.

Architecture. During the Middle Ages, magnificent cathedrals in the Romanesque and Gothic styles were built in such cities as Bamberg, Cologne, Regensberg, Ulm, and Worms. In the 1700's, German princes built palaces modeled on the magnificent French palace at Versailles. At the same time, Germans built great baroque and rococo churches, especially in the predominantly Roman Catholic southern German states. During the 1800's, such German architects as Friedrich Schinkel built museums and other public buildings in the neoclassical style. In the early 1900's, Walter Gropius and his famous Bauhaus group developed a basic style of modern architecture.

Motion pictures. The German film industry achieved its first period of success from the end of World War I in 1918 to the rise of the Nazi dictatorship in 1933. During the 1920's and early 1930's, German filmmakers stressed fantasy and legend, and also an intense psychological realism. The Germans often treated themes in a style called *Expressionism.*

Expressionist films used nonrealistic sets and unusual camera angles to represent a character's inner feelings. One artistic approach stressed lighting and camera movement. German filmmakers created a threatening visual mood to accompany their tales of the supernatural. The leading German directors of the time included Fritz Lang, F. W. Murnau, G. W. Pabst, and Robert Wiene.

German cinema produced chiefly propaganda films during the Nazi years. The major movies included the documentaries *Triumph of the Will* (1935) and *Olympia* (1938), directed by Leni Riefenstahl. Many German film artists fled the country with the rise of the Nazis and moved to the United States. There they had a major influence on American movies.

The German film industry did not gain international recognition again until the 1960's and 1970's, primarily through the work of directors Rainer Werner Fassbinder, Werner Herzog, Wolfgang Petersen, Volker Schlöndorff, and Wim Wenders. By the end of the 1900's, German filmmakers were struggling to gain a larger share in an industry heavily dominated by American motion pictures.

The land

Germany has a varied landscape made up of five main regions. From north to south, they are (1) the North German Plain, (2) the Central Highlands, (3) the South German Hills, (4) the Black Forest, and (5) the Bavarian Alps.

The North German Plain, the largest land region in Germany, is low and nearly flat. Almost the entire plain lies less than 300 feet (91 meters) above sea level. The region is drained by broad rivers that flow northward into the North Sea or the Baltic Sea. These rivers include the Elbe, Ems, Oder, Rhine, and Weser, all of which are important commercial waterways. Large ports and industrial centers are located on them.

The wide river valleys, as well as land along the seacoasts, have soft, fertile soil. Between the river valleys are large areas covered with sand and gravel. These areas are called *heathlands.* The sand and gravel were deposited by glaciers that moved across much of Europe thousands of years ago. The glaciers also formed many small lakes in the North German Plain. The soil of the heathlands is not suitable for farming, and trees

have been planted in many of them to provide timber.

The southern edge of the North German Plain has highly fertile, dustlike soil called *loess.* This area is heavily cultivated and thickly populated. Many of Germany's oldest cities, including Bonn and Cologne, are located in this area.

The Central Highlands are a series of plateaus that range from nearly flat to mountainous. They are covered with rock and poor soil. Most of the plateaus lie from 1,000 to 2,500 feet (300 to 760 meters) above sea level. Two of them—the Harz Mountains and the Thuringian Forest—have peaks that rise more than 3,000 feet (910 meters).

Rivers in the Central Highlands have cut steep, narrow valleys. These rugged gorges, especially that of the Rhine River, are among the most beautiful sights in Germany. In some areas, the valleys broaden into small, fertile basins.

The South German Hills include a series of long, parallel ridges, called *escarpments,* that extend from southwest to northeast. Sheep are raised on these rocky ridges. Lowlands between the ridges have fertile clay soil. Some of these lowlands are among the best farmlands in Germany.

Along the southern edge of the hill region are large areas covered with sand and gravel. This soil was deposited by ancient glaciers that spread northward from the Alps. Most of the South German Hills rise from 500 to 2,500 feet (150 to 762 meters).

Much of the region is drained by the Rhine River and two of its branches, the Main and Neckar rivers. The Danube River drains the southern part. The Danube is the only major river in Germany that flows eastward.

The Black Forest is a mountainous region. Its name comes from the thick forests of dark fir and spruce trees that cover the mountainsides.

© K. W. Gruber, Bavaria-Verlag

The North German Plain is a low, flat region that covers all of northern Germany. Fertile lands are found in the river valleys and along the seacoast of the plain.

The region consists of granite and sandstone uplands with deep, narrow valleys. It averages between 2,500 and 3,000 feet (762 and 910 meters) above sea level. Some peaks rise more than 4,000 feet (1,200 meters).

The Black Forest is the scene of many old German legends and fairy tales. It is also known for its mineral springs. Many famous health resorts are located near the springs.

The Bavarian Alps are part of the Alps, the largest mountain system in Europe. The majestic, snow-capped Bavarian Alps rise more than 6,000 feet (1,800 meters). The highest point in Germany, the 9,721-foot (2,963-meter) peak Zugspitze, is in this region.

The beauty of the Bavarian Alps has made them a year-round vacationland. The region has many lakes formed by the ancient glaciers from the Alps. It is

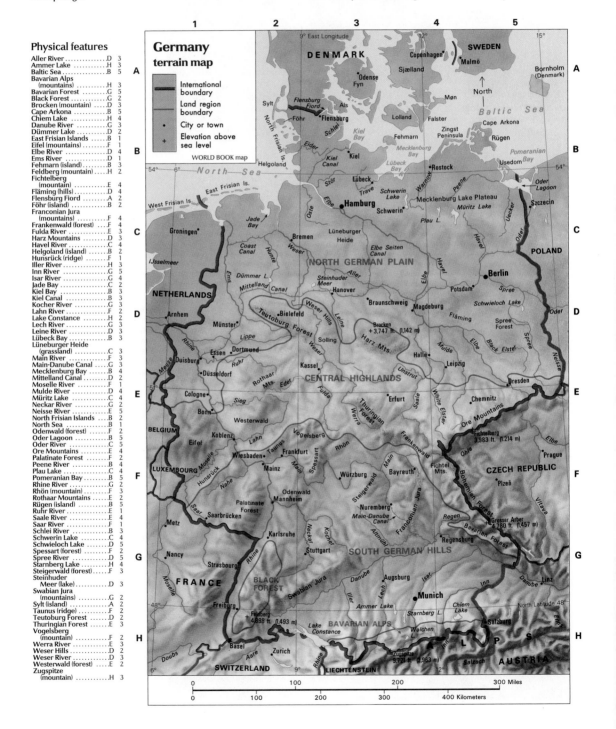

© Marvullo, The Stock Market

The Central Highlands are a series of flat to mountainous plateaus. Many rivers, including the Rhine, *left,* one of Europe's most important rivers, flow through the region.

© M. u. H., Bavaria-Verlag

The Black Forest is a mountainous region of southwestern Germany. It is named for the dark fir and spruce trees that cover its slopes. Many German legends are set in the Black Forest.

© L. H. Mantell, The Stock Market

The Bavarian Alps, forming part of Germany's southern boundary, are part of Europe's highest mountain chain. Their scenic beauty makes them a popular year-round vacation destination.

drained by mountain streams that flow into the Danube River.

Climate

Germany has a mild climate, largely because the land is near the sea. In winter, the sea is not as cold as the land. In summer, it is not as warm. As a result, west winds from the sea help warm Germany in winter and cool it in summer. Away from the sea, in southern areas, winters are colder and summers are warmer.

The average temperature in January, the coldest month in Germany, is above 30 °F (-1 °C). Cold winds from eastern Europe sometimes reach Germany in winter, and the temperature may drop sharply for short periods. In July, the hottest month in Germany, the temperature averages about 64 °F (18 °C).

Most of Germany receives from 20 to 40 inches (50 to 100 centimeters) of *precipitation* (rain, melted snow, and other forms of moisture) a year. Some hilly and mountainous areas receive more precipitation.

The moisture-bearing west winds first reach Germany in the northwest. In that area, rain falls almost evenly throughout the year, with a little more in autumn and winter than in spring and summer. Inland, most rain falls in summer, often in heavy thunderstorms. Deep snow covers some mountainous areas throughout the winter.

Economy

In 1945, at the end of World War II, Germany's economy lay almost in total ruin. Both West and East Germany had to be rebuilt by the controlling Allied powers. The West German economy recovered at an amazing rate in the 1950's. This recovery is described as West Germany's "economic miracle."

In East Germany, the Soviet Union set up a strong Communist state where the government controlled the economy, including production, distribution, and pricing of almost all goods. Under this system, East Germany grew to be one of the wealthiest Communist countries, though it lagged well behind West Germany.

In 1989, popular protests forced the government of East Germany to make political and economic reforms. As part of these reforms, free, multiparty elections were held in 1990. East German voters elected officials who favored unification with West Germany.

One of the first steps toward the unification of East Germany and West Germany was the union of the two

Average monthly weather

	Berlin						Munich				
	Temperatures F° High Low		C° High Low		Days of rain or snow		Temperatures F° High Low		C° High Low		Days of rain or snow
Jan.	35	26	2	−3	10	Jan.	33	23	1	−5	10
Feb.	38	27	3	−3	8	Feb.	37	25	3	−4	9
Mar.	46	32	8	0	9	Mar.	45	31	7	−1	10
Apr.	55	38	13	3	9	Apr.	54	37	12	3	13
May	65	46	18	8	8	May	63	45	17	7	13
June	70	51	21	11	9	June	69	51	21	11	14
July	74	55	23	13	10	July	72	54	22	12	14
Aug.	72	54	22	12	10	Aug.	71	53	22	12	13
Sept.	66	48	19	9	8	Sept.	64	48	18	9	11
Oct.	55	41	13	5	8	Oct.	53	40	12	4	10
Nov.	43	33	6	1	8	Nov.	42	31	6	−1	9
Dec.	37	29	3	−2	11	Dec.	36	26	2	−3	11

Average January temperatures
January is Germany's coldest month. Winds from the sea warm the northern part of Germany during winter.

Average July temperatures
July is Germany's hottest month. But German summers are mild, thanks to sea winds that cool the land.

Average yearly precipitation
Precipitation levels vary throughout Germany. Mountainous areas in the south receive the most rain and snow.

WORLD BOOK maps

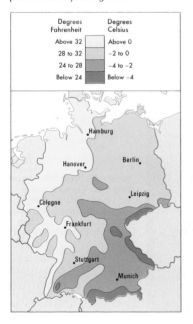

Degrees Fahrenheit	Degrees Celsius
Above 32	Above 0
28 to 32	−2 to 0
24 to 28	−4 to −2
Below 24	Below −4

Degrees Fahrenheit	Degrees Celsius
Above 68	Above 20
64 to 68	18 to 20
60 to 64	16 to 18
Below 60	Below 16

Inches	Centimeters
More than 40	More than 100
32 to 40	80 to 100
24 to 32	60 to 80
Less than 24	Less than 60

economies. Economic unification began on July 1, 1990. East Germany adopted West Germany's currency and began to operate under a free enterprise system.

After unification, Germany remained a member of the European Community (EC), an economic association of European nations. In the 1950's, West Germany had helped found several European economic groups that had become the basis for the EC. The EC helped strengthen Germany's economy through increased trade with other member nations of the association. In 1993, the EC became incorporated into the European Union (EU), which works for both economic and political cooperation among its member nations.

Manufacturing is the foundation of Germany's economic strength. Germany has several major manufacturing regions, and there are factories almost everywhere. The Ruhr is the most important industrial region and one of the busiest in the world. It includes such manufacturing centers as Dortmund, Duisburg, and Düsseldorf. This region has more than 8 million people. It produces most of the nation's iron and steel and has important chemical and textile industries.

Much of Germany's steel is used to make automobiles and trucks, industrial and agricultural machinery, ships, and tools. Germany is the world's third largest manufacturer of automobiles, after Japan and the United States. The country also produces large quantities of cement, clothing, electrical equipment, and processed foods and metals. The chemical industry produces large quantities of drugs, fertilizer, plastics, sulfuric acid, and artificial rubber and fibers. Other important products that are manufactured in Germany include cameras, computers, leather goods, scientific instruments, toys, and wood pulp and paper.

Service industries are those economic activities that produce services, not goods. Service industries account for a large share of Germany's economic production.

The most important group of service industries in Germany is community, government, and personal services. Community services include such economic activities as education and health care. Personal services consist of such activities as advertising and data processing, and the operation of cleaning establishments, repair shops, and beauty salons. Government includes both public administration and defense. Other service indus-

Germany's gross domestic product

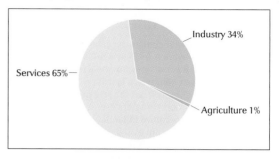

Germany's gross domestic product (GDP) was $2,346,452,000,000 in 1995. The GDP is the total value of goods and services produced within a country in a year. *Services* include community, government, and personal services; finance, insurance, and real estate; wholesale and retail trade; and transportation and communication. *Industry* includes mining and utilities; manufacturing; and construction. *Agriculture* includes agriculture, forestry, and fishing.

Production and workers by economic activities

Economic activities	Percent of GDP produced	Employed workers	
		Number of people	Percent of total
Community, government, & personal services	34	10,232,000	28
Manufacturing	24	8,945,000	25
Finance, insurance, & real estate	16	3,454,000	10
Wholesale & retail trade	9	6,188,000	17
Construction	7	3,379,000	9
Transportation & communication	6	2,031,000	6
Mining & utilities	3	621,000	2
Agriculture, forestry, & fishing	1	1,163,000	3
Total	100	36,013,000	100

Figures are for 1995.
Sources: International Labour Office; *World Book* estimates based on data from the International Monetary Fund.

tries are finance and insurance, trade, transportation and communication, and utilities.

Agriculture. About a third of Germany's food must be imported. Germany is one of the world's largest importers of agricultural goods.

© Cameramann International, Ltd.

Steel mills in the Ruhr region help make Germany one of the world's leading steel producers. Most of the country's steel is used to manufacture automobiles, machinery, and ships.

The chief grains grown by German farmers include barley, oats, rye, and wheat. Sugar beets, vegetables, apples, grapes, and other fruits are also important crops. Fine wines are made from grapes grown in vineyards along the Rhine and Moselle (or Mosel) rivers. Livestock and livestock products are important sources of farm income. Large numbers of farmers raise beef and dairy cattle, hogs, horses, poultry, and sheep.

Many German farms are 25 acres (10 hectares) or less in size. Most of these small farms are operated part-time by farmers who have other jobs. In eastern Germany, most of the large farms that were formerly controlled by the East German government have been broken up and sold to individuals.

Mining. Germany has large supplies of potash and rock salt. It also has some copper, lead, petroleum, tin, uranium, and zinc. In the 1800's, coal deposits near the Ruhr River helped German industries grow. But by the 1970's, most of the high-quality deposits had been exhausted. Eastern Germany produces large quantities of a low-quality coal called *lignite.*

International trade. Germany is one of the world's leading trading nations. It imports great amounts of food, fuel, manufactured goods, and industrial raw materials. The country's major exports include automobiles,

BMW of North America, Inc.

Automobiles built in Germany are shipped worldwide, making motor vehicles one of the nation's chief exports. Germany is the world's third largest producer of cars.

chemicals, iron and steel products, and machinery.

Germany trades with countries in all parts of the world. More than half its trade is with European Union nations. Switzerland and the United States are also important trading partners.

Energy sources. Coal is still a major source of electrical power in Germany, but its use has declined since 1970 as oil-burning and nuclear-powered generating plants have become more common. In southern Ger-

Economy of Germany

This map shows the economic uses of land in Germany. It also shows the main farm and mineral products, and it includes German cities that are important manufacturing centers.

Mostly cropland

Grazing land mixed with cropland

Mostly forest land

Major urban-industrial area

Fishing

● Major manufacturing center

• Mineral deposit

WORLD BOOK map

© Müller-Güll, Bavaria-Verlag

Farms in western Germany are mostly small. German farmers produce only about two-thirds of the nation's food. Germany is one of the world's largest importers of agricultural goods.

many, mountain streams are used to generate hydro-electric power. Germany has some gas fields, but it must import most of its natural gas. The nation also depends on imported oil, mainly from the Middle East.

Transportation. Railroads and highways connect all parts of Germany. Germany has one of the most extensive railroad networks in the world, providing excellent passenger and freight service. Its fine highway system includes about 6,500 miles (10,500 kilometers) of four-lane highways called autobahns. Adolf Hitler began building the *autobahns* in the 1930's. Today, Germany has one of the world's highest rates of private automobile ownership.

The Rhine River and its branches carry more traffic than any other European river system. Canals connect the major rivers of Germany. The chief seaports are Bremen, Hamburg, and Wilhelmshaven.

Germany's largest airline, Deutsche Lufthansa, flies to all parts of the world. Major airports operate at many cities, including Berlin, Düsseldorf, Frankfurt am Main, Hamburg, Leipzig, and Munich.

Communication. Germany has about 400 daily newspapers. The largest is the *Bild Zeitung* of Hamburg. Several other large newspapers circulate throughout the country. The press is free from government censorship.

Germany has public and private broadcasting corporations that offer radio and television programming. On the public channels, commercials may be broadcast at only a few times a day. The public broadcasting corporations receive money from license fees paid by owners of radios and TV sets. Private broadcasting companies finance their operations with advertising revenues.

History

Ancient times. Fossils discovered in what is now Germany indicate that the area was home to primitive human beings as early as 500,000 years ago. The Neanderthal people, who lived throughout Europe between about 130,000 and 35,000 years ago, are named for a fossil that was discovered in Germany's Neander Valley, near Düsseldorf.

But the history of the German people really began sometime after 1000 B.C., when warlike tribes began to

migrate from northern Europe into what is now Germany. These tribes wandered the area and lived by hunting and farming. In the 100's B.C., they moved south to the Rhine and Danube rivers, the northern frontiers of the Roman Empire. The Romans called the tribes *Germani,* though that was the name of only one tribe. Other tribes included the Cimbri, Franks, Goths, and Vandals. The Romans called the land of the tribes *Germania.*

In A.D. 9, the Romans tried to conquer the tribes, but Germanic warriors crushed the Roman armies in a decisive battle at the Teutoburg Forest. The Romans built a wall, called the *limes,* between the Rhine and Danube rivers to protect their lands to the south from attacks. By the late A.D. 300's, Roman power had begun to collapse. In the 400's, Germanic tribes moved south, plundered Rome, and eventually broke up the western portion of the empire into tribal kingdoms. The kingdom of the Franks became the largest and most important.

Kingdom of the Franks. In 486, Clovis, a Frankish king, defeated the independent Roman governor of Gaul (now mainly France). Clovis extended the boundaries of his territory by defeating other Germanic tribes in Gaul and parts of what is now western Germany. He became an orthodox Christian and also introduced other Roman ways of life into his kingdom. The greatest Frankish ruler, Charlemagne, came to power in 768. He established his capital in Aachen. Charlemagne expanded his kingdom east to the Elbe River and, in some places, beyond the river. In 800, Pope Leo III crowned him emperor of the Romans.

The breakup of Charlemagne's empire. In 843, the Treaty of Verdun divided Charlemagne's empire into three kingdoms, one for each of his grandsons. Louis II (called the German) received lands east of the Rhine River, most of which later became what is now Germany. The western part, later called France, went to Charles II (the Bald). Lothair I received the middle kingdom, a narrow strip that extended from the North Sea to central Italy. He also kept the title of emperor.

In 911, the German branch of the Frankish royal family died out. By then, the German kingdom had been divided into five powerful *duchies* (territories ruled by a duke)—Bavaria, Lorraine, Franconia, Saxony, and Swabia. The dukes elected Conrad I of Franconia as king. In 919, Conrad was succeeded by Henry I (the Fowler) of Saxony, whose family ruled until 1024. With the founding of the Saxon *dynasty* (a series of rulers from the same family), the lands given to Louis II became permanently separated from the French parts of Charlemagne's empire.

Henry's son, Otto I (the Great), drove invading Hungarians out of southern Germany in 955, and extended the German frontier in the north. Otto also won control over most of the old middle Frankish kingdom, including Italy. This gave him the right to claim the title of emperor. In 962, Otto was crowned emperor in Rome. This marked the beginning of what later was called the Holy Roman Empire.

The Holy Roman Empire. Under the Saxon emperors, the Holy Roman Empire was a powerful combination of territories, each with a separate ruler. The Salian dynasty (1024-1125) included several strong emperors. In 1075, Pope Gregory VII disputed the right of Emperor Henry IV to appoint bishops. Many German princes sided with the pope and a series of civil wars began.

The Hohenstaufen emperors (1138-1254) reestablished order. But after the dynasty died out, disorder returned. By the 1300's, the emperors were almost powerless. The last Hohenstaufen died in 1254. The German princes did not elect another emperor until 1273. He was Rudolf I of Habsburg (or Hapsburg). Rudolf seized Austria and made it his main duchy. After Rudolf, emperors of various families reigned. Starting in 1438, the Habsburgs reigned almost continuously until 1806.

The Holy Roman Empire was never fully a German territory. Some Germans lived outside its borders, while some non-German areas were part of the empire. For a time, the empire included parts of Italy, as well as Slavic areas in eastern Europe, and part of what are now Belgium and the Netherlands. The empire also was made up of independent territories. A strong emperor could make their rulers cooperate. But often the emperor could not force them to do what he wanted.

The rise of cities. Before the fall of the West Roman Empire in 476, Roman towns stood along and near the Rhine and Danube rivers. These towns were centers of trade. They included what are now Bonn, Cologne, Regensburg, Trier, and Vienna. After the fall of Rome, these towns almost disappeared. Trade gradually resumed under the Saxon and Salian emperors. Some of the old towns grew again, and new ones appeared around the castles of princes and bishops. Many cities became so large and rich that they gained self-rule.

When the emperors began losing power, the cities could not rely on outside help in case of attack. The more prosperous cities banded together into leagues and formed their own armies for protection. The strongest league was the Hanseatic League, which began to develop in the late 1100's. It included Cologne, Dortmund, and the major ports of Bremen, Hamburg, and Lübeck. It became a great commercial and naval power in the North and Baltic seas during the 1300's.

Drawing (1457) by Hektor Muelich; Archiv für Kunst und Geschichte

Otto I (the Great) drove the Hungarians out of southern Germany in the battle of the Lech River in A.D. 955. In 962 he was crowned emperor of what became the Holy Roman Empire.

Serfdom in Germany. By the 700's, most peasant farmers in western Germany had become serfs. Each serf worked on land that was owned by a powerful person or by the church. In return for their work, the serfs received protection and a share of the harvest. Generally, serfs were not free to leave the land they worked. Beginning in the 1100's, some serfs gained their freedom by escaping to towns. In the western parts of Germany, serfdom gradually died out as peasants were allowed to substitute monetary payments for labor. In eastern Germany, serfdom did not begin to develop until the 1300's. It lasted until the early 1800's.

Important dates in Germany

c. 1000 B.C. Tribes from northern Europe began to arrive in what is now Germany.

A.D. 486 Clovis, a Germanic king, defeated the Roman governor of Gaul (now mainly France).

800 Charlemagne's empire was established.

843 The Treaty of Verdun divided Charlemagne's empire.

962 Otto I was crowned emperor of what later became the Holy Roman Empire.

1438 The Habsburg family of Austria began almost continuous rule of the Holy Roman Empire.

1517 The Reformation began in Germany.

1618-1648 The Thirty Years' War devastated much of Germany.

1740-1786 Frederick the Great made Prussia a great power.

1806 The Holy Roman Empire came to an end.

1815 The German Confederation was established at the Congress of Vienna.

1848 Revolution broke out, but it failed.

1866 Prussia forced Austria out of German affairs.

1867 Prussia established the North German Confederation.

1870-1871 Germany defeated France in the Franco-Prussian War, and the German Empire was founded.

1914-1918 The Allies defeated Germany in World War I, and the German Empire ended.

1919 The Weimar Republic was established.

1933 Adolf Hitler began to create a Nazi dictatorship.

1939-1945 The Allies defeated Germany in World War II, ending Hitler's dictatorship. They divided Germany into four military occupation zones in 1945.

1948-1949 A Soviet blockade failed to force the Western Allies out of Berlin.

1949 East and West Germany were established.

1953 The Soviet Union crushed an East German revolt.

1955 East and West Germany were declared independent, and joined opposing Cold War military alliances.

1961 The East German Communists built the Berlin Wall to prevent East Germans from escaping to West Berlin.

1973 East and West Germany ratified a treaty calling for closer relations between the two nations. Both nations joined the United Nations (UN).

1989 East Germany opened the Berlin Wall and other border barriers, and allowed its citizens to travel freely to West Germany.

1990 East Germany held free elections in March, resulting in the end of Communist rule there. In October, East and West Germany were unified and became the single nation of Germany.

The Reformation. In 1517, Martin Luther, a German monk, began to attack many teachings and practices of the Roman Catholic Church. Nobles, peasants, and townspeople joined this movement, called the Reformation, and it spread quickly. Its followers became known as *Protestants,* meaning *those who protest.*

Some princes were sincere reformers, but others became Protestants in order to gain church property. Many peasants hoped the Protestant movement would free them from their lord's control. The peasants revolted against the lords in the Peasants' War of 1524-1525, but were brutally crushed.

Neither the pope nor Emperor Charles V could stop the Protestant movement. In 1555, Protestant princes forced Charles to accept the Peace of Augsburg. This treaty gave each Lutheran and Roman Catholic prince the right to choose the religion for his own land. It also established a division of church lands between the two religions.

During the 1500's and 1600's, the Roman Catholic Church underwent its own reform, called the *Counter Reformation* or *Catholic Reformation.* In this movement, the church won back many Protestants by peaceful means or by force. By 1600, relatively few Protestants were left in Austria, Bavaria, and parts of Bohemia and the Rhineland. The rest of Germany remained chiefly Lutheran.

The Thirty Years' War. By 1600, the German lands were divided by many political and religious rivalries. In 1618, a Protestant revolt in Bohemia set off a series of wars that lasted for 30 years. The wars were partially religious struggles between Protestants and Catholics, but they were also political struggles between certain princes and the emperor. In addition, the kings of Denmark, Sweden, and France entered the wars to gain German lands and to reduce the Habsburgs's power.

The Peace of Westphalia ended the Thirty Years' War in 1648. Under this treaty, France and Sweden received some German lands. The wars had been hard on German trade and farming. Large parts of Germany were ru-ined, and some of the towns had nearly disappeared. The emperor's already limited power had been further weakened by the wars. Germany was a collection of free cities and hundreds of states.

The rise of Prussia. During the 1600's, the Hohenzollern family began to expand its power in eastern Germany. The Hohenzollerns ruled the state of Brandenburg. Berlin was their capital. In 1618, the ruler of Brandenburg inherited the duchy of Prussia. The Peace of Westphalia added part of Pomerania and some territories on the lower Rhine River to the Hohenzollern holdings.

The Hohenzollerns's rise to power began with Frederick William (the Great Elector), who became ruler of Brandenburg in 1640. He began to unite and expand his lands after the Thirty Years' War. In 1701, his son Frederick became the first king of Prussia. The Hohenzollerns's power continued to grow under the next two kings, Frederick William I and Frederick II (the Great).

The Hohenzollerns built a large, well-trained professional army and a strong civil service to defend and rule their scattered territories. Through their civil service, they improved farming and industry, and filled their treasury with tax money. They built canals, schools, and roads, and promoted the arts and learning.

After Frederick the Great became king in 1740, he seized Silesia, a rich province of Austria. This invasion led to fighting between Prussia and Austria in two wars, the War of the Austrian Succession (1740-1748) and the Seven Years' War (1756-1763). Many other nations fought in these wars. Some sided with Frederick, and others with his enemy, Empress Maria Theresa of Austria. Under the final peace treaty, Silesia remained under Prussian rule. Prussia was now recognized as a great power.

During the 1770's, Prussia, along with Austria and Russia, began to seize parts of Poland. By the end of 1795, Poland had been divided among these states.

Conflicts with France. The French Revolution, which began in 1789, caused many changes throughout Europe. France built huge armies made up of citizens in-

German Information Center

Martin Luther was the leader of the Reformation, a religious movement that led to the birth of Protantism. He was summoned before the emperor in the city of Worms in 1521. There, Luther was urged to retract his teachings, but he refused to so so.

spired by patriotism. Germany's old-fashioned professional armies were not prepared for the new age.

From 1792 until 1815, France was almost continually at war with other European states. Much of the fighting involved German states and took place on German soil. By the end of 1806, Napoleon—who had seized control of France in 1799—had taken parts of western Germany, set up dependent states, and destroyed the Holy Roman Empire. Some German states became members of the Confederation of the Rhine, which Napoleon had established in 1806 and which was allied with France.

Between 1795 and 1806, Prussia stayed out of the wars. But Napoleon's threats became too great. In 1806, Prussia declared war on France. Napoleon crushed the Prussian army at the battles of Jena and Auerstädt that same year. As a result, Prussia lost its territories west of the Elbe River and had to pay war damages to France. To recover from this defeat, the Prussian government introduced reforms, including laws that freed the serfs and gave some self-government to the cities. In the army, reformers fired incompetent officers and improved military training.

After the failure of Napoleon's Russian campaign in 1812, Austria, Britain, Prussia, and Russia joined against him. The reformed Prussian army helped defeat Napoleon at Leipzig in 1813 and at Waterloo in 1815.

The Congress of Vienna. The victorious powers met in Vienna from late 1814 to early 1815 to restore order to Europe. They left intact most of the middle-sized states created in the Confederation of the Rhine. But their treaty divided the rest of Napoleon's lands among themselves. Prussia received lands including the Rhineland, Westphalia, and much of Saxony, greatly increasing its power in northern and western Germany. Austria gave up its territories in southern Germany and the lands that are now Belgium and Luxembourg, and it took territories in Italy. Austria, Prussia, and Russia again divided Poland.

The German Confederation. The Congress of Vienna also set up the German Confederation, a union of 39 independent states. An assembly called the *Bundestag* was established. Members of the Bundestag were appointed by the rulers of the states. Austria appointed the president.

Except for four self-governing cities, the German states were ruled by kings or princes. Each state had its own laws, collected its own taxes, and was responsible for its own defense. Several states had constitutions and parliaments, but even in these states the people had little voice in their government. Although the king of Prussia had promised to grant a constitution during the war against Napoleon, he did not keep his word.

During the early 1800's, the German population was growing faster than the economy. Some regions prospered, but most areas were still poor. Cities were small, and most people still lived by farming. In the 1840's, popular discontent increased. Business and professional people wanted more opportunities for political involvement. Farmers and craftworkers suffered from poor harvests and economic depression.

The revolution of 1848. In February 1848, the people of Paris rebelled against their king. When this news reached the Germans, they also rebelled. In Austria, rioting and demonstrations forced the chancellor to resign.

In Berlin, people defied the army and forced the Prussian king to appoint new ministers and to promise a constitution. Similar rebellions occurred in most other German capitals. Many Germans hoped that they could replace the Confederation with a more unified nation. In May, an elected assembly met in Frankfurt to write a new constitution.

However, some people began to lose interest in the revolution. Others disagreed about its goals. Meanwhile, the governments began to recover. In October 1848, Austrian troops recaptured Vienna. In December, the new Prussian assembly was dissolved by troops.

The Frankfurt Assembly was divided on many issues, especially on whether Catholic Austria or Protestant Prussia should be the leading power in the new German nation. In March 1849, members compromised on a constitution that called for an emperor and a two-house parliament. The Prussian king Frederick William IV was invited to be emperor but he refused. The assembly then broke up. The revolution was defeated in the spring of 1849. The German Confederation of 1815 was reestablished.

The unification of Germany. In the early 1860's, a conflict about army reforms caused a constitutional crisis in Prussia. The Prussian king, Wilhelm I, appointed Otto von Bismarck prime minister in 1862. Bismarck hoped he could resolve the constitutional crisis with foreign triumphs. He also wanted to establish Prussia as the leading German power.

Between 1864 and 1870, Bismarck had the German states fight three short, victorious wars. In the first, Austria and Prussia, in the name of the German Confederation, took the duchies of Schleswig and Holstein from Denmark. In 1866, Bismarck picked a quarrel with Austria. His army easily defeated Austria at Königgrätz in what was called the Seven Weeks' War. Bismarck then dissolved the German Confederation, annexed some territory to Prussia, and established the North German Confederation under Prussian leadership. The four German states south of the Main River remained independent, but made military alliances with Prussia. Austria's defeat left it greatly weakened. In 1867, the Austrian emperor was forced to give equal status to his Hungarian holdings, creating the Dual Monarchy of Austria-Hungary. Austria was never again a power in Germany.

To complete the unification of Germany, Bismarck knew that he needed to overcome the opposition of France. In 1870, he encouraged a Hohenzollern prince to accept the throne of Spain. As Bismarck expected, France objected. Although the prince withdrew as a candidate, Bismarck used the dispute to start the Franco-Prussian War. This conflict pitted France against the North German Confederation and its south German allies. After several battles, the Germans defeated the main French armies at Sedan in September 1870. The German army captured Paris in January 1871. Under the peace treaty, France gave up almost all of Alsace and part of Lorraine.

During the Franco-Prussian War, the four south German states agreed to join a united German nation under Prussian leadership. On Jan. 18, 1871, Wilhelm I was crowned the first kaiser (emperor) of the new German Empire. Wilhelm appointed Bismarck chancellor and head of government.

The German Empire. The German constitution provided for a two-house parliament. Members of one house, the Reichstag, were elected by the people. Members of the other house, the Bundesrat, were appointed by the state governments. The empire had 26 member states. Most states were very small, and several were completely surrounded by Prussia. The emperor, who was also the king of Prussia, controlled foreign policy, commanded the army, and appointed the chancellor. The parliament approved all laws and taxes, but could not force the chancellor to resign.

Bismarck allowed all men over 25 to vote, thinking that most Germans would support the government. He won support from the growing class of business people and the traditional Prussian landowners and nobles. But Bismarck faced opposition from Roman Catholics and Socialists. Catholics did not trust the Protestant-led empire and organized their own political party. Socialism was growing popular among city dwellers and the workers in the developing industries. Bismarck tried to wreck the Catholic and Socialist parties, but failed.

Foreign policy. After 1871, Bismarck tried to avoid conflicts so the newly united empire could develop. He particularly feared a combined attack from east and west. He tried to keep Germany allied with Russia and Austria-Hungary so they would not form alliances with France. But Russia and Austria-Hungary had opposing interests in the Balkans, a group of countries in the southeast corner of Europe, and that made it difficult to keep an alliance with both of them.

Germany, Austria-Hungary, and Russia formed a loose alliance in 1873, but it soon broke up over the Balkan problem. In 1879, Bismarck established a military and political alliance with Austria-Hungary. Italy joined in 1882, and the alliance became known as the Triple Alliance. During the 1880's, Germany also established colonies in Africa and on islands in the Pacific Ocean.

In 1888, Wilhelm I died. He was succeeded by his terminally ill son Frederick III, whose reign lasted only 99 days. The crown then passed to Frederick's son, Wilhelm II, who was eager to establish his own authority. In 1890, he forced Bismarck to resign. Wilhelm demanded that Germany have influence throughout the world. He also wanted to build a modern navy to defend German interests and challenge British naval supremacy.

Wilhelm's ambitions, which he often expressed in an aggressive manner, frightened other powers. In 1894, Russia allied itself with France. Britain felt its control of the seas threatened and established the Entente Cordiale (cordial understanding) with France in 1904. In 1907, Britain and Russia signed a similar agreement. Under these agreements, the three countries formed the Triple Entente. Europe was divided into two armed camps, with the Triple Alliance on one side and the Triple Entente on the other.

World War I started in the Balkans. On June 28, 1914, Archduke Franz Ferdinand of Austria-Hungary and his wife were murdered in Sarajevo, Bosnia-Herzegovina. Bosnia-Herzegovina was an Austrian territory claimed by Serbia, a little Balkan country where the murder had been planned. Austria-Hungary decided to punish Serbia, and Germany promised to support these efforts. Austria-Hungary declared war on Serbia on July 28, 1914. Russia prepared for war to support Serbia. Germany then declared war on Russia. After France called up its troops to support Russia, Germany went to war against France. In an effort to reach Paris quickly, German troops invaded neutral Belgium. Britain then declared war on Germany.

Germany won the opening battles of the war, but Britain, France, and Russia continued to fight. Germany, Austria-Hungary, and their allies were called the Central Powers. The nations opposing them were called the Allies. As the war dragged on, other countries became in-

German unification was completed in 1871 under the leadership of Otto von Bismarck, prime minister of Prussia. By maneuvering the German states to fight three wars, Bismarck unified them to form the German Empire.

Boundary of Germany in 1871

Kingdom of Prussia

Other German states

Areas gained 1864-1871

WORLD BOOK map

volved. Almost all of them joined the Allies. In 1915, Italy joined the Allies, hoping to gain Austrian land. In 1917, the United States entered the war on the Allied side.

Despite the size and strength of the Allies, Germany seemed close to winning the war. After 1914, German troops held Luxembourg, most of Belgium, and part of northern France. In 1917, Germany won on the Eastern Front as the Russian war effort collapsed. But by 1918, Germany's armies were exhausted. Supplies were running low and there was social unrest at home. Meanwhile, an increasing number of fresh American troops were arriving to reinforce the Allies. In the summer of 1918, American troops helped stop the last great German offensive in the west. On November 11, Germany signed an armistice.

Under the Treaty of Versailles, which was signed after World War I, Germany lost its colonies and some of its European territory. Alsace and the German part of Lorraine were returned to France. Poland was reestablished, and it received Posen (now Poznan), some of Silesia, and part of West Prussia. France got control of the Saar region for 15 years. The treaty also placed the Rhineland under Allied occupation for 15 years. Germany's army was reduced to 100,000 men, and the nation was forbidden from having an air force. Germany was also required to pay the Allies *reparations* (payments for war damages), which were later set at about $33 billion.

The Weimar Republic. Before the armistice was signed in November 1918, German workers and troops had revolted in protest against continuing the war. This revolution began in Kiel, and spread quickly from city to city. On November 9, Germany was declared a republic. Emperor Wilhelm II fled to safety in the Netherlands.

In January 1919, the German voters, including women for the first time, elected a national assembly to write a constitution. The assembly met in Weimar, and the new republic became known as the Weimar Republic. The constitution established a democratic federal republic in August 1919. It provided for a parliament of two houses—the Reichstag and the Reichsrat—and a president elected by the people. The chancellor and the cabinet members were appointed by the president, but they

Germany in World War I drove deep into eastern Europe, overwhelming the old-fashioned Russian army. But continued battles along the Western Front eventually defeated the Germans. Germany gave up some territory in the peace agreement.

could be removed from office by the Reichstag.

The Weimar Republic was weak from the start. Many important Germans remained loyal to the empire. German army officers claimed that Germany had been defeated by the revolution, not by Allied armies. The terms of the Treaty of Versailles were harsher than the Germans had expected.

In 1922 and 1923, the economy collapsed when inflation ruined the value of German money. By 1923, the republic appeared doomed. Communists rebelled in some areas. In Munich, the National Socialist German Workers Party—better known as the Nazi Party—attempted an armed rebellion under its leader, Adolf Hitler. But despite these events, the republic survived.

Gustav Stresemann became chancellor and then foreign minister. Under his leadership, order was restored. A new money system was set up to end the inflation. In 1924, the Allies made it easier for Germany to pay its reparations. At the Locarno Conference in 1925, Stresemann signed a security pact with France and Belgium. The pact was also guaranteed by Britain and Italy.

The republic's prospects looked much brighter by the late 1920's. But in 1929, a worldwide economic depression began. Millions of Germans lost their jobs. The government appeared powerless and political violence increased. The voters increasingly supported groups that promised a new system of government. After the 1930 elections, political parties in the Reichstag failed to agree on a program. Between 1930 and 1933, President Paul von Hindenburg and his chancellors ruled largely by issuing laws without the approval of parliament.

Nazi Germany. During the political confusion of the early 1930's, the Nazi Party made rapid gains in German elections. The party had been founded in 1919. After its 1923 revolt failed, party leader Adolf Hitler decided to gain power by lawful means rather than by revolution. From 1924 to 1929, the republic was prosperous and stable, so the Nazis attracted few voters. After the Great Depression struck, more Germans were attracted to Hitler's

Bettmann Archive
The powerful German army won early victories in World War I. These German forces fought Russian troops in trenches along the Eastern Front during 1914.

Bettmann Archive

Burning money for fuel became a symbolic gesture in Germany in the 1920's. Runaway inflation in 1922 and 1923 made German money almost worthless and ruined the economy.

promises to improve the economy, defy the hated Treaty of Versailles, and rebuild Germany's military power. In 1932, the Nazi Party emerged as the Reichstag's strongest party. In 1933, Hindenburg appointed Hitler chancellor.

Soon after he became chancellor, Hitler began to destroy the constitution and build a dictatorship. He permitted only one political party—the Nazis. The party seized control of the nation's courts, newspapers, police, and schools. People who opposed the government were murdered, imprisoned in concentration camps, forced to leave Germany, or beaten up by the Nazis' private army called *storm troopers.* After Hindenburg died in 1934, Hitler declared himself *der Führer* (the leader) of Germany. The Nazis called their government the *Third Reich* (Third Empire). The first was the Holy Roman Empire, and the second was the German Empire.

Many Germans approved of Nazism. Many others objected to some features of Nazi rule, but supported Hitler's efforts to improve the economy and rebuild the military. Some Germans opposed Hitler but remained silent. Only a very few resisted.

Hitler pursued two goals. He wanted to assert German superiority over what he believed to be inferior races, including Jews, Slavs, and other non-German peoples. He also wanted to gain territory—*lebensraum* (living space)—for Germany, especially in eastern Europe. In 1933, Hitler removed all German Jews from government jobs. In 1935, he took away the rights of Jewish citizens. Faced with this persecution, more than half of Germany's 500,000 Jews left the country. On the night of Nov. 9-10, 1938, Nazi crowds burned down synagogues

and broke the windows of Jewish businesses in an event later called *Kristallnacht* (Crystal Night). In English, the event is known as the Night of Broken Glass.

At the same time Hitler was acting against the Jews, he was also preparing for war. In 1936, German troops reoccupied the Rhineland. Also in 1936, Germany formed an alliance with Italy and signed an anti-Communist agreement with Japan. The three countries became known as the *Axis* powers. In March 1938, Germany occupied Austria and made it part of the Third Reich. In September, Britain and France consented to Hitler's demands to take over the German-speaking areas of Czechoslovakia. The next year, Germany seized the rest of Czechoslovakia.

In August 1939, Germany and the Soviet Union (which had been formed under Russia's leadership in 1922 and existed until 1991) agreed to remain neutral if the other became involved in a war. They also secretly planned to divide Poland and much of the rest of eastern Europe between themselves. On September 1, Germany invaded Poland and World War II began.

World War II. On Sept. 3, 1939, Britain and France responded to the invasion of Poland by declaring war on Germany. Poland fell quickly under the German, and later, Soviet attacks. In the spring of 1940, German forces captured Denmark, Norway, the Netherlands, Belgium, and Luxembourg. The Allied forces that opposed the Germans had been unprepared for Germany's *blitzkrieg* (lightning war) methods. Hitler used fast-moving tanks and infantry supported by dive bombers.

In May 1940, the German army moved around France's eastern defenses and overwhelmed the French army. France fell by the end of June.

The German advance stopped at the English Channel.

Bettmann Archive

Adolf Hitler's Nazi Party controlled most aspects of German life from 1933 to 1945. Large rallies, like this one at Nuremberg, glorified Hitler and encouraged loyalty to the Nazi cause.

After a series of desperate air battles over Britain in the summer and fall of 1940, the Germans failed to gain the air superiority they needed to invade England. Hitler now turned to the east and the south. He conquered the Balkans, occupied Crete, and sent an army to northern Africa. In June 1941, a huge German force invaded the Soviet Union and drove deep into Soviet territory.

At the end of 1941, Nazi Germany dominated the continent. Hitler used his power as proof of his theory that the Germans belonged to a "master race." The Nazis ruthlessly murdered about 6 million European Jews and about 5 million Poles, Gypsies, and others. Many of these people died in the Nazi concentration camps.

Despite his army's initial success, Hitler could not defeat the Soviet Union. The Soviets continued to resist and slowly pushed the invaders back. Japan's attack on Pearl Harbor on Dec. 7, 1941, brought the United States into the war. The tide turned against Germany in 1943. The Soviets counterattacked in the east. American and British troops drove the Germans out of North Africa and invaded Italy from the south. In June 1944, the Allies invaded France. After the failure of the last German offensive in December 1944, Allied troops poured into Germany. As Soviet troops closed in on Berlin from the east, Hitler committed suicide on April 30, 1945. Germany surrendered on May 7.

Occupied Germany. The war left most of Germany in ruins. The Allied bombing and invasion had destroyed cities, farms, industries, and transportation. Supplies of food, fuel, and water were very low. People were half starved, and many lived in ruined buildings.

In June 1945, the Allied Big Four—Britain, France, the Soviet Union and the United States—officially took over supreme authority in Germany. The country was divided into four zones of military occupation, with each power occupying a zone. Berlin, located deep in the Soviet zone, was also divided into four sectors.

In July and August 1945, leaders of Britain, the Soviet Union, and the United States met in Potsdam, Germany. They agreed to govern Germany together and to rebuild it as a democracy. They also agreed to stamp out Nazism and to settle German refugees from Eastern Europe in Germany. Under the agreement, the Soviet Union also was granted northern East Prussia, which it claimed. The rest of that region, and German territory east of the Oder and Neisse rivers, were placed under Polish control. As a result, Germany lost about a fourth of its land.

Many of the most important Nazi leaders had committed suicide or had disappeared. The Allies brought to trial those remaining. A number of these Nazis were hanged or imprisoned. The most important trials took place in Nuremberg.

The division of Germany. Almost immediately after their victory, the Allies began to quarrel among themselves. The Soviet Union began to establish Communist governments in the Eastern European countries its army had occupied at the end of the war. The Western powers tried to block Communist expansion in the areas under their control. The Soviets imposed barriers against communication, trade, and travel between East and West. Extreme mistrust and tension grew on each side, a condition that came to be called the Cold War.

The outbreak of the Cold War affected Germany immediately. When the Soviet Union and the Western Al-

UPI/Bettmann Newsphotos

Nuremberg, like cities throughout Germany, lay in ruins after the Nazis's defeat in World War II.

lies could not agree on a common policy in Germany, each side began to organize its own occupation zones in Germany overall and in Berlin. The Western Allies occupied western Germany, and the Soviet Union occupied the east. Berlin, located in the east, was divided into Allied-occupied West Berlin and Soviet-occupied East Berlin. Britain, France, and the United States combined the economies of the zones they controlled and prepared to unite the zones politically. The Soviet Union imposed Communist rule on its zone.

In June 1948, the Western Allies moved to rebuild the economy of their occupation zones in Germany. They reorganized the German monetary system and issued new money, replacing the virtually worthless existing currency. Under the aid program known as the Marshall Plan, U.S. aid began to pour into the Western Allied zones, and economic recovery got underway. The Soviets responded by stopping all highway, rail, and water travel between Berlin and western Germany. The Soviets

WORLD BOOK map

After World War II, Germany was divided into zones occupied by the victors—Britain, France, the Soviet Union, and the United States. These zones later became East and West Germany. Other German lands were lost to Poland and the Soviet Union.

hoped to force the Allies out of Berlin. However, the Allies set up the huge Berlin Airlift and flew about 8,000 short tons (7,300 metric tons) of supplies into the city every day. The Soviet Union lifted the blockade in May 1949, realizing that the blockade had failed.

West Germany. The Western Allies turned over more authority to German officials. As the division between the Eastern and Western zones grew, the Allies arranged for a German council to write a constitution. The Allies approved the written constitution in May 1949. On Sept. 21, 1949, the Western zones were officially combined as the Federal Republic of Germany (also called West Germany). The military occupation ended, and the Allied High Commission, a civilian agency, replaced the military governors. On May 5, 1955, the Allied High Commission was dissolved, and West Germany became completely independent. Military occupation continued in West Berlin because treaties uniting Germany had not been signed.

The new West German parliament met for the first time in Bonn, the country's capital, in September 1949. It elected Konrad Adenauer chancellor. Under Adenauer, West Germany helped found the Council of Europe and several organizations that eventually became the European Community (EC), an economic association. The EC was later incorporated into the European Union. In 1955, West Germany joined the North Atlantic Treaty Organization (NATO) and began to establish its armed forces.

By 1955, West Germany had made an amazing economic recovery. The value of goods produced there was greater than that for all Germany in 1936. This "economic miracle" helped West Germany absorb more than 10 million refugees from Eastern Europe and more than a million workers from the rest of Europe.

West Germany's prosperity helped the republic gain the support of its citizens. Also, Adenauer was a strong leader, though he was criticized in his later years for ignoring the views of others. Adenauer retired in 1963. Ludwig Erhard succeeded Adenauer as chancellor and served until 1966. Kurt Georg Kiesinger was chancellor from 1966 to 1969. Adenauer, Erhard, and Kiesinger were members of a political party called the Christian Democratic Union.

Willy Brandt of the Social Democratic Party, who had been vice chancellor since 1966, became chancellor in 1969. He resigned in 1974 after it was discovered that one of his aides was an East German spy. Helmut Schmidt, also a Social Democrat, succeeded Brandt. In 1982, Schmidt was forced from office by a vote of no confidence from the Bundestag. The small Free Democratic Party, which had supported the Social Democrats, switched its parliamentary support to the Christian Democratic Union. The Bundestag elected as chancellor Helmut Kohl, the leader of the Christian Democratic Union. Kohl remained chancellor following the 1983 and 1987 elections. In both of those elections, the Christian Democratic coalition with the Free Democrats won majorities in the Bundestag.

In the 1980's, many Germans, especially the country's young people, expressed concern for the environment and opposition to the placement of U.S. missiles in West Germany. Mass protests occurred. The Green Party, an organization devoted to environmental issues, gained popularity.

East Germany. After World War II, the Soviet Union appointed German Communists to local offices and set up a system much like that of the Soviet Union. Banks, farms, and industries were seized and reorganized. People suspected of opposing Communism were thrown into prison camps. In 1946, the Communists forced the Social Democratic Party to join them in forming the Socialist Unity Party. The party came under control of the Communist leader Walter Ulbricht. Ulbricht became first secretary, or head, of the Socialist Unity Party. The first secretary (later general secretary) was the most powerful leader in East Germany.

A Communist-prepared constitution was adopted in May 1949. On October 7, the Soviet zone became the German Democratic Republic (commonly called East Germany), with East Berlin as its capital. Ulbricht held the real power, though he did not head the government. In October 1955, East Germany became officially independent, but Soviet influence continued. Also in 1955, East Germany joined the Warsaw Pact, an Eastern European military alliance under Soviet command. East Germany's armed forces were established officially in 1956, though special "police" units had been given tanks and other heavy weapons as early as 1952.

The East German economy recovered gradually after 1945, but the standard of living remained much lower than West Germany's. In 1953, Ulbricht tried to increase working hours without raising wages. Strikes and riots broke out in East Berlin and other cities. Soviet tanks and troops crushed the revolt. Living and working conditions slowly improved, but many people remained dissatisfied. Every week, thousands of East Germans fled to West Germany. Almost 3 million East Germans left, and the labor force fell sharply. Most refugees fled through Berlin because the Communists had sealed off the East-West border.

In August 1961, the Communists built the Berlin Wall between East and West Berlin. They also strengthened barriers around the rest of West Berlin and along the border between East and West Germany. From 1961 to 1989, when the borders were opened, hundreds died trying to escape from East Germany, including many who tried to cross the Berlin Wall.

In 1971, Ulbricht resigned as head of the Socialist Unity Party. Erich Honecker, a member of the party's Central Committee, succeeded him. Under Honecker, East Germany improved its relations with many non-Communist nations. Before 1960, only the Soviet Union and several other Communist countries had diplomatic relations with East Germany. But eventually, East Germany established relations with other nations.

East Germany experienced major changes in 1989. In many Eastern European nations, people demonstrated against their Communist governments. Communist Hungary removed its barriers on its border with non-Communist Austria. Thousands of East Germans went to Hungary, crossed into Austria, and then moved to West Germany. Throughout East Germany, citizens protested for more freedom. In October, the growing pressure forced Honecker to resign as head of the party and from his government positions. He was succeeded in all his positions by another Communist, Egon Krenz. In November 1990, the German government charged Honecker with manslaughter for ordering border guards to shoot

© B. Bisson, Sygma

Unification of East Germany and West Germany took place on Oct. 3, 1990. Millions of Germans celebrated throughout the country, including these people at Berlin's Brandenburg Gate.

East Germans trying to escape to West Germany during his leadership. Honecker became ill and died in 1994 while in exile in Chile.

In a dramatic change in policy, the East German government announced on Nov. 9, 1989, that it would open its borders and permit its citizens to travel freely. The opening of the Berlin Wall, long a symbol of the East German government's control of its citizens, was part of this policy change. Thousands more East Germans moved to West Germany. During this time, protests continued. Non-Communist political parties and organizations were started. In December, Krenz resigned as party head and from his government positions. Hans Modrow, chairman of East Germany's cabinet, took control of the government, though he was not a party head.

On March 18, 1990, East Germans voted in free parliamentary elections for the first time. The Christian Democratic Union, a non-Communist party, won the most seats in parliament. Together with the Social Democrats and some smaller parties, the Christian Democratic Union formed a government with CDU leader Lothar de Maizière as its head. The Socialist Unity Party, which had been renamed the Party of Democratic Socialism, won only about 17 percent of the seats in the legislature.

East-West relations. Throughout the 1950's and 1960's, relations between East Germany and West Germany were strained. Little travel was permitted between the two nations. Neither one recognized the other as a legitimate state. In the 1970's, their relations improved a little. West Germany began to provide loans and credits to East Germany in return for eased travel restrictions and other concessions.

The unification of East and West Germany. With the move toward a more democratic government in East Germany, many people began to consider the idea of a

unified Germany. In February 1990, East German leader Modrow announced that he favored unification. In their March elections, most East Germans voted for candidates who favored rapid unification. Most West Germans also supported unification.

In mid-1990, East Germany began selling many government-owned businesses. In May, East Germany and West Germany signed a treaty providing for close economic cooperation. In July, the economies of East Germany and West Germany were united.

Economic unification had several results. Goods that had been scarce in East Germany became readily available. But the cost of many goods in the free market was higher than they had been when the government controlled prices. Many East German businesses were not able to continue to operate without the government's financial support. They closed or operated on shorter hours, which caused increased unemployment.

Between May and September, talks about unification were held among the foreign ministers of the two German states and the four Allied powers of World War II—Britain, France, the Soviet Union, and the United States. The Allied powers still held some occupation rights in Berlin and in East and West Germany, including certain rights to oversee Berlin and to approve Germany's borders. In a treaty signed on September 12, the Allied powers agreed to give up these rights. The treaty, called the Treaty on the Final Settlement With Respect to Germany, made it possible for the Germans to complete the unification of East and West Germany.

On August 31, representatives of East and West Germany signed their own treaty for unification. The treaty detailed the major aspects of unification, including the merging of the social and legal systems. It took effect on Oct. 3, 1990, marking the official date for the unification of East and West Germany. Berlin was also unified and named the country's capital.

The government of unified Germany continued selling businesses formerly owned by the East German government. Some of the largest East German companies were closed because they damaged the environment with air and soil pollution.

West German Chancellor Helmut Kohl continued to serve as chancellor of Germany. The first national elections of unified Germany were held in December 1990. As a result of the elections, Kohl remained chancellor, and his coalition of Christian Democrats and Free Democrats remained in power. Kohl's coalition also won again in 1994. In spite of Kohl's election victories, however, dissatisfaction with his policies increased.

In the former East Germany, people were disappointed at the slow rate of progress toward an improved economy. In the former West Germany, some people resented the cost of unification. Germany also faced the problem of growing unemployment, particularly in its industrial regions. Many Germans feared they would not have the resources to support the country's large social welfare budget.

Germany also experienced a wave of social unrest in the early 1990's. Large numbers of immigrants had entered the country. Neo-Nazis and other right-wing Germans began to protest the increased immigration. Some of them made attacks against foreigners, resulting in a number of deaths. Large numbers of Germans took part in public demonstrations that protested the attacks. Germany had had a policy of allowing any people who said they were fleeing persecution to enter the country. In 1993, the German parliament amended the Constitution to reduce the flow of immigrants into Germany.

Recent developments. In the election of 1998, Kohl's coalition was defeated after 16 years in power. Gerhard Schröder, the leader of the Social Democratic Party, became Germany's chancellor. He formed a new coalition, consisting of the Social Democratic and Green parties. The election marked the first time since 1945 that a government had been voted out of office. It also marked the first time that one of the preceding coalition partners did not remain in the new coalition.

In 1999, Germany and most other members of the European Union formally adopted a common currency called the euro. These countries agreed that euro coins and notes would go into circulation at the beginning of 2002 and their own currencies would be phased out by mid-2002.   James J. Sheehan

Related articles in *World Book* include:

Rulers

Charles V (Holy Roman emperor)	Henry III (of Germany)
	Henry IV (of Germany)
Charles VII (Holy Roman emperor)	Henry VI (of Germany)
	Louise of Mecklenburg-Strelitz
Frederick I (Holy Roman emperor)	Ludwig II
Frederick II (of Prussia)	Otto I, the Great
Frederick III (of Prussia)	Otto II (Holy Roman emperor)
Frederick William	Wilhelm (emperors)
Frederick William I (of Prussia)	

Political and military leaders

Adenauer, Konrad	Jodl, Alfred
Bismarck, Otto von	Kohl, Helmut
Blücher, Gebhard von	Ludendorff, Erich F. W.
Bormann, Martin	Luxemburg, Rosa
Brandt, Willy	Mengele, Josef
Clausewitz, Karl von	Moltke, Helmuth Karl von
Doenitz, Karl	Papen, Franz von
Eichmann, Adolf	Ribbentrop, Joachim von
Goebbels, Joseph	Rommel, Erwin
Goering, Hermann W.	Rosenberg, Alfred
Hess, Rudolf	Schmidt, Helmut
Heydrich, Reinhard	Schröder, Gerhard
Himmler, Heinrich	Speer, Albert
Hindenburg, Paul von	Virchow, Rudolf
Hitler, Adolf	Wallenstein, Albrecht
Honecker, Erich	

Cities and towns

Aachen	Cologne	Heidelberg	Oberammergau
Augsburg	Dresden	Leipzig	gau
Baden-Baden	Duisburg	Lübeck	Potsdam
Bayreuth	Düsseldorf	Mainz	Rostock
Berlin	Essen	Mannheim	Stuttgart
Bonn	Frankfurt	Munich	Trier
Bremen	Hamburg	Nuremberg	Wiesbaden
Chemnitz	Hanover		Worms

History

Alsace-Lorraine	Europe, Council of
Augsburg Confession	European Union
Axis	Feudalism
Berlin, Congress of	Franco-Prussian War
Berlin Airlift	Franks
Berlin Wall	Free city
Brunswick (family)	Guelphs and Ghibellines
Cold War	Habsburg, House of
Dawes Plan	Hanseatic League

Hohenstaufen	Rome, Ancient (Decline and fall)
Hohenzollern	
Holy Alliance	Schmalkaldic League
Holy Roman Empire	Seven Weeks' War
Kaiser	Seven Years' War
Kristallnacht	Succession wars
Krupp	Teutonic Knights
Locarno Conference	Teutons
Munich Agreement	Thirty Years' War
Nazism	Vandals
Nuremberg Trials	Verdun, Treaty of
Peasants' War	Versailles, Treaty of
Potsdam Conference	Vienna, Congress of
Prussia	Warsaw Pact
Reformation	World War I
Revolution of 1848	World War II
Rhineland	

Physical features

Alps	Elbe River	Lake Constance	Oder River
Black Forest	Helgoland	stance	Rhine River
Danube River	Kiel Canal	Moselle River	Weser River

States and regions

Bavaria	Hanover	Ruhr
Brandenburg	Palatinate	Saar

Other related articles

Air force (the German Air Force; History)	Heidelberg, University of
	Lieder
Christmas (In Germany)	Volkswagen
Deutschland über Alles	Wine (Where wine comes from)
Doll (The history of dolls)	
German language	

Outline

I. Government

II. People
  A. Ancestry   B. Language

III. Way of life
  A. City life   D. Recreation
  B. Rural life   E. Religion
  C. Food and drink   F. Education

IV. Arts
  A. Literature and   C. Painting and sculpture
     philosophy   D. Architecture
  B. Music   E. Film

V. The land
  A. The North German Plain
  B. The Central Highlands
  C. The South German Hills
  D. The Black Forest
  E. The Bavarian Alps

VI. Climate

VII. Economy
  A. Manufacturing   E. International trade
  B. Service industries F. Energy sources
  C. Agriculture   G. Transportation
  D. Mining   H. Communication

VIII. History

Questions

Who were some important writers during the greatest period of German literature?

What conditions led to the rise of Adolf Hitler and the Nazis?

What is Germany's leading industrial region?

What events in East Germany helped bring about the unification of East and West Germany?

Why did German cooks create sauerbraten?

What nations occupied Germany after World War II?

Which of Germany's land regions is the scene of many old German legends and fairy tales?

Why did the Communists build the Berlin Wall in 1961?

What was the cause of the Franco-Prussian War?

When did Germany establish its current system of government?

Additional resources

Balfour, Michael. *Germany: The Tides of Power.* Routledge, 1992.
Fulbrook, Mary. *A Concise History of Germany.* Cambridge, 1991.
Insight Guide to Germany. Houghton, 1996.
Kitchen, Martin. *The Cambridge Illustrated History of Germany.* Cambridge, 1996.
Spencer, William. *Germany Then and Now.* Watts, 1994.

Germination, JUR muh NAY shuhn, is the sprouting of a seed. All seeds need moisture, oxygen, and warmth to germinate. These requirements, especially the need for warmth, vary from species to species.

The seeds of many kinds of tropical plants germinate within a few days if the proper conditions are present. Among most other plants, the seeds go through a period of *dormancy* (inactivity). Dormant seeds do not germinate for weeks or months, even if the conditions for sprouting seem ideal. Some dormant seeds must have their outer layer broken before they can germinate. Others require a period of cold temperatures or of additional daylight. Dormancy delays germination until conditions become favorable for growth. For example, it prevents germination during the fall, thus protecting the plants from being killed during winter.

Most seed-producing plants are flowering plants. Each seed of a flowering plant is covered by a dense protective coat. A layer of tissue called the *endosperm* lies inside the coat. The endosperm stores the food necessary for germination. The seed also includes the *embryo,* which develops into the mature plant. The embryo has a long structure called the *axis,* to which one or two seed leaves, known as *cotyledons,* are attached. The portion of the axis above the cotyledons, the *epicotyl,* consists of a young shoot with undeveloped leaves and stem. The portion below the cotyledons is called the *hypocotyl.* The lower end of the hypocotyl, called the *radicle,* develops into the plant's first root.

Seeds become dehydrated during dormancy. When germination begins, they absorb great amounts of water from the soil. The water triggers chemical changes that enable the embryo to convert the stored food into energy needed for growth. The absorption of water also causes the embryo to swell and split open the seed coat. The radicle emerges and grows down into the soil, forming the first root. In some species of plants, the upper portion of the hypocotyl lengthens. It arches upward and pulls the cotyledons above the ground. In other plants, the cotyledons remain underground.

Among both groups of plants, the epicotyl grows upward above the ground. It produces stem growth and the plant's first fully developed leaves. Germination is now complete because the young plant can gather water and minerals through its root and make food in its leaves.　　　Richard C. Keating

See also **Cotyledon; Plant** (Germination); **Seed** (How seeds sprout).

Geronimo, juh RAHN uh moh (1829-1909), was a warrior of the Chiricahua Apache Indians. He led attacks on settlers and soldiers in Mexico and the Southwestern United States during the 1870's and 1880's.

Geronimo was born in what is now western New Mexico. He grew up among the Nednais, a southern band of Chiricahua Apache, in the Mexican state of Chi-

National Archives, Washington, D.C.

Geronimo led Indian attacks on troops and settlers in the Southwestern States and Mexico during the 1870's and 1880's.

huahua. His Apache name was *Goyaale,* which means *the smart one.* The Mexicans gave him the name *Geronimo,* which means *Jerome* in Spanish.

About 1877, the U.S. government rounded up the Apache whom Geronimo had joined and moved them to the San Carlos Reservation in Arizona. This action resulted from increasing conflicts between the Indians and white settlers. The Apache became known as brave fighters. Geronimo escaped from the reservation and fought U.S. troops in the Southwest and in Chihuahua. He was returned to the reservation in 1880.

In 1882, Geronimo and other Apache fled to the Sierra Madre in Mexico. He and his followers founded hidden camps from which they made many bloody raids on both sides of the United States-Mexican border. General George Crook then led U.S. forces in attacks on the Apache camps in the Sierra Madre. In 1883, Geronimo and his band surrendered. They moved to the White Mountain Reservation north of San Carlos, Arizona, in 1884. Geronimo and other Chiricahua Apache escaped again in 1885 but surrendered the next year.

The U.S. government moved Geronimo to Fort Sill in Oklahoma in 1894. He lived there for the rest of his life and was a celebrity at many fairs.　　　Edgar Perry

See also **Indian wars.**

Additional resources

Aleshire, Peter. *The Fox and the Whirlwind: Gen. George Crook and Geronimo, a Paired Biography.* Wiley, 2000.
Hermann, Spring. *Geronimo.* Enslow, 1997. Younger readers.
Roberts, David. *Once They Moved Like the Wind: Cochise, Geronimo, and the Apache Wars.* Simon & Schuster, 1993.

Gerontology. See Aging; Geriatrics.

Gerry, *GEHR ee,* **Elbridge** (1744-1814), served as vice president of the United States under President James Madison from 1813 until his death. Gerry had served as governor of Massachusetts from 1810 to 1812. While he was governor, his political opponents claimed his party created unfair voting districts. They invented the word *gerrymander* for the division of districts to help a political party keep power (see **Gerrymander**).

Gerry attended the Constitutional Convention of 1787 as a delegate, but he refused to sign the Constitution of the United States. He said that it allowed the federal government too much control over the states. In 1797, President John Adams sent Gerry to France to smooth relations between the countries (see **XYZ Affair**).

Gerry was born in Marblehead, Massachusetts, and graduated from Harvard University in 1762. He signed the Declaration of Independence in 1776. Gerry represented Massachusetts in the U.S. House of Representatives from 1789 to 1793.   Jack N. Rakove

See also **Vice President of the United States** (picture).

Gerrymander, *JEHR ee MAN duhr,* is the practice of dividing a city, state, or country into voting districts to favor the party in power or some other group. The word *gerrymander* comes from the name of Governor Elbridge Gerry of Massachusetts. In 1812, the Massachusetts legislature passed a bill that divided the state into state senatorial districts. The bill was designed to defeat the Federalist Party and grouped certain counties that had large Federalist majorities. Thus, the Federalists could win a few seats by huge majorities, while their opponents could win many more seats by small majorities.

One of the new districts had a shape much like that of a mythical animal. Some people said it looked like a salamander, but a guest at a dinner party suggested that it

Wide World

Gerrymander was a word that came into use in 1812 when Massachusetts was divided into election districts to defeat the Federalist Party. Some people said one of the districts shown above looked like a salamander. It was finally called a *gerrymander* after Elbridge Gerry, then governor of Massachusetts.

should be called a *gerrymander.* The word became popular with Federalists and later became part of the American language. Some state constitutions forbid gerrymandering. The Supreme Court of the United States ruled in 1962 *(Baker v. Carr)* that citizens may challenge in the federal courts unequal distribution of seats in state legislatures. In 1964, it ruled that U.S. congressional districts *(Wesberry v. Sanders)* must be as equal in population as possible, and that state legislative districts *(Reynolds v. Sims)* must meet the same requirement. The court also said that both houses of a state legislature must follow the principle known as "one-person, one-vote." Gerrymandering still takes place but now must produce districts of equal population. Computers are used to produce such districts.

In the late 1900's, gerrymandering was used to create voting districts in which certain minority groups made up the majority of the voters. But in the 1990's, the U.S. Supreme Court ruled that race could not be used as the chief factor in creating U.S. congressional districts.

Charles O. Jones

Gershwin, George (1898-1937), an American composer, became famous for his musical comedies, popular songs, symphonic works, and the opera *Porgy and Bess.* His *Rhapsody in Blue* is probably the best-known orchestral piece by an American.

Gershwin was born in the Brooklyn section of New York City, of Russian immigrant parents. He began writing popular songs at 15, but he studied composition and orchestration all his life. He wanted to be a successful popular composer and to follow in the footsteps of the great masters.

In 1919, Gershwin wrote his first successful popular song, "Swanee." This was a tremendous hit as sung by Al Jolson. In the same year, Gershwin worked on a string quartet with a blues theme called *Lullaby.*

Gershwin rose to fame on Broadway in the 1920's. His sparkling musical comedies include *Lady, Be Good* (1924), *Tip-Toes* (1925), *Oh, Kay!* (1926), *Funny Face* (1927), and *Girl Crazy* (1930). He then turned to political satire with the musical comedies *Strike Up the Band* (1930); *Of Thee I Sing* (1931), a spoof on presidential elections; and *Let 'Em Eat Cake* (1933). *Of Thee I Sing* was the first musical comedy to win a Pulitzer Prize. All of Gershwin's musicals had tunes of lasting fame. Examples include "Embraceable You," "I Got Rhythm," "Love Walked In," "Soon," and "'S Wonderful." The words for most of his songs were written by his brother Ira.

Meanwhile, Gershwin was writing successful concert hall music, beginning with *Rhapsody in Blue* (1924). This piece was written for piano and jazz band and arranged by American composer Ferde Grofé. Grofé later arranged the piece for symphony orchestra. It combined jazz elements with the romantic tradition in classical music. The *Concerto in F* for piano and orchestra (1925), a larger work in three movements, also used blues and jazzlike effects. Gershwin, an excellent pianist, was the soloist in the first performance of both works.

Gershwin continued to display his varied talents with *An American in Paris* (1928). This symphonic poem is tuneful, rhythmically exciting, effectively orchestrated, and thoroughly American. Gershwin's last symphonic work consists of variations on "I Got Rhythm" for piano and orchestra. In 1935, Gershwin completed the black "folk opera" *Porgy and Bess,* the most popular opera ever written by an American.   Richard Jackson

See also **Heyward, DuBose; Gershwin, Ira; Grofé, Ferde.**

Additional resources

Gilbert, Steven E. *The Music of Gershwin.* Yale, 1995.
Jablonski, Edward. *Gershwin.* 1988. Reprint. Da Capo, 1998.
Vernon, Roland. *Introducing Gershwin.* Silver Burdett, 1996. Younger readers.

Gershwin, Ira (1896-1983), became famous for the sparkling, witty lyrics he wrote for musical comedies and motion pictures. His lyrics are noted for their unique rhyming, an infectious sense of fun, and a depth of emotion rare in popular song. Most of his lyrics were written to music composed by his brother George. Ira's hit songs include "Someone to Watch over Me," "The Man That Got Away," "A Foggy Day," "They Can't Take That Away from Me," and "It Ain't Necessarily So."

Gershwin was born in New York City. By the mid-1920's, he was writing lyrics that brought a jazz influence to musical comedy writing. He collaborated on a series of shows with his brother. Their greatest artistic success on Broadway was *Porgy and Bess* (1935), written with DuBose Heyward. The brothers then concentrated on movie musicals. After George's unexpected death in 1937, Ira stopped working out of grief. In the 1940's, he returned to work on Broadway and then on movies, collaborating with Harold Arlen, Jerome Kern, Harry Warren, and other composers.   Ken Bloom

See also **Gershwin, George; Musical comedy; Opera** *(Porgy and Bess).*

Gestalt psychology, *guh SHTAHLT,* is a school of psychology that emphasizes the study of experience as a unified whole. Gestalt psychologists believe that *pattern,* or *form,* is the most important part of experience. The whole pattern gives meaning to each individual element of experience. In other words, the whole is more important than the sum of its parts. *Gestalt* is a German word that means *pattern, form,* or *shape.*

Gestalt psychology was founded about 1912 by Max Wertheimer, a German psychologist. Experiments performed by Wertheimer and his two colleagues, Kurt Koffka and Wolfgang Köhler, helped spread Gestalt ideas throughout Europe and the United States. These ideas were a revolt against *structuralism,* the most common psychological view of the early 1900's. Structural psychologists believed the best way to study experience was to analyze its separate elements, such as feelings, images, and sensations. The Gestalt viewpoint also differed from *behaviorism,* which called for the study of only observable aspects of behavior.

Gestalt psychology greatly influenced the study of human perception, and psychologists used Gestalt ideas in developing several principles. For example, the principle of *closure* states that people tend to see incomplete patterns as complete or unified wholes. According to this principle, a fragmented circle is often perceived as a complete circle. The principle of *figure-ground perception* states that people tend to regard any kind of pattern as a figure against a background. Examples include pictures on a wall and words on a page. Gestalt psychology no longer exists as a separate school, but psychologists still use its ideas.   William M. Smith

See also **Köhler, Wolfgang; Psychology** (Gestalt psychology); **Psychotherapy.**

Gestapo, *guh STAH poh,* was the secret police force of Nazi Germany. The name is a short form of *Geheime Staatspolizei* (Secret State Police). Nazi Party officials first used the Gestapo, noted for its brutality, to smash opposition within the party. The Gestapo, created in 1933, combined with Germany's regular police force in 1936. Heinrich Himmler became head of the organization. During World War II (1939-1945), the Gestapo helped control conquered areas of Europe. See also **Himmler, Heinrich; Nazism.**   Otis C. Mitchell

Gestation. See Pregnancy.

Gethsemane, *gehth SEHM uh nee,* is a garden spoken of in the New Testament. *Gethsemane* is a Greek word that means *oil press.* The garden was located east of Jerusalem, above the brook Kidron, on the side of the Mount of Olives (see **Mount of Olives**). Jesus went there to pray on the night before His arrest and Crucifixion.

The exact location of the garden is not now known. The Latins built a wall around a plot of ground just across the Kidron from Jerusalem. They arranged it as a European garden and kept it as a sacred spot, "the Garden." The Greeks, however, thought that Gethsemane was a little to the southeast of this garden. A third possible location was thought to be a short way north of both these places, beside the Virgin's tomb. There is a cave to the right of the Church of the Tomb of the Virgin, called "the Grotto of the Agony." Friars of the Franciscan order have controlled the Grotto since 1392, and the Garden since 1681.   Stanley K. Stowers

Getty, J. Paul (1892-1976), an American business executive, became one of the richest people in the world. Getty made his fortune, which may have totaled as much as $4 billion, in the petroleum business. His financial empire included the Getty Oil Company, Skelly Oil Company, and many smaller firms.

Jean Paul Getty was born in Minneapolis, Minnesota. He began his career in 1909 as a worker in the oil fields near Bartlesville, Oklahoma. After graduating from Oxford University in England in 1913, he started to invest in oil wells with money borrowed from his father, who was a wealthy Oklahoma oilman. He made his first million dollars when he was 23 years old.

Getty was a noted art collector and wrote two books on the subject, *Collector's Choice* (1955) and *The Joys of Collecting* (1965). He also wrote *History of the Oil Business of George F. and J. Paul Getty* (1941), *As I See It: The Autobiography of J. Paul Getty* (1976), and other books. Getty was a United States citizen, but he lived near London.   Leonard S. Silk

Getty Center is a complex of six buildings devoted to the fine arts and humanities. The center stands on a 110-acre (44.5-hectare) campus on a hill in the Los Angeles suburb of Brentwood. The largest building is the J. Paul Getty Museum, which has a distinguished collection of Western European paintings, drawings, sculpture, decorative arts, illuminated manuscripts, and photographs.

The J. Paul Getty Trust oversees all the components of the Getty Center, which include the Getty Conservation and Education Institutes. The center is also home to the Getty Research Institute for the History of Art and the Humanities. The institute features an extensive library that is an important resource for scholars. The center sponsors a wide range of exhibitions and public and professional programs.

American architect Richard Meier designed the Getty Center, which opened in 1997. It immediately became one of the most popular tourist attractions in the Los Angeles area.   Critically reviewed by the Getty Trust

See also **Getty Trust, J. Paul; Meier, Richard** (picture).

Getty Museum, J. Paul, houses a distinguished collection of western European art. The museum, which opened in 1997, is located in the Getty Center in Los Angeles. Its collection includes paintings, drawings, sculpture, decorative arts, *illuminated* (illustrated) manuscripts, and photographs. The Getty Villa in Malibu, California, is a center for the study of comparative archaeology and cultures. The villa is a re-creation of an ancient Roman country house and exhibits an outstanding collection of Greek and Roman antiquities. The villa was closed to the public for remodeling in 1997 and will reopen in 2002. The museum and villa are operated by the J. Paul Getty Trust, a foundation devoted to the visual arts.   Critically reviewed by the Getty Trust

See also **Getty Center; Getty Trust, J. Paul.**

Getty Trust, J. Paul, is a private foundation that promotes education, conservation, and scholarship in the visual arts and related humanities. The trust is one of the largest foundations in the United States. It was established by American business executive J. Paul Getty in 1953. The Getty Center in the Los Angeles area of Brentwood is the home of most of the programs sponsored by the trust. The most popular attraction at the center is the J. Paul Getty Museum, with its extensive art collections, and an elaborate central garden.

The trust also operates an art museum in Malibu, California, that closed for renovation in 1997. The museum building is a re-creation of an ancient Roman country house with gardens. When it reopens in the early 2000's, the museum will exhibit art from ancient Greece and Rome.   Critically reviewed by the Getty Trust

See also **Getty, J. Paul; Getty Center.**

Gettysburg, *GEHT eez BUHRG* or *GEHT ihz BUHRG* (pop. 7,490), is a community in southern Pennsylvania that is famous as the site of the Battle of Gettysburg, one of the most important battles of the American Civil War (1861-1865). The battle is described in the article **Gettysburg, Battle of.** Gettysburg is one of Pennsylvania's small municipal communities that are classed as boroughs. For location, see **Pennsylvania** (political map).

Gettysburg's economy is based on tourism. The town's rich history attracts more than 1 million tourists each year. The Civil War battlefield, just outside Gettysburg, is maintained by the National Park Service as the Gettysburg National Military Park and the Gettysburg National Cemetery. Commercial orchards near the town produce large quantities of apples and peaches. Gettysburg is the home of Gettysburg College and the Lutheran Theological Seminary at Gettysburg.

Gettysburg was founded about 1786 by James Gettys, a local tavern owner. The town is the seat of Adams County and has a mayor-council form of government.

William C. Rense

See also **Gettysburg Address.**

Gettysburg, Battle of, fought from July 1 through July 3, 1863, marked a turning point in the American Civil War in the North's favor. General George G. Meade led a Northern army of about 90,000 men to victory against General Robert E. Lee's Southern army of about 75,000. The shooting began when the two forces met accidentally in Gettysburg, Pennsylvania, on July 1.

That day, Southern forces took the town. But Union troops took a strong position on high ground south of town. On July 2, Lee tried but failed to break the North's line at points known as Culp's Hill, Cemetery Ridge, the Peach Orchard, the Wheatfield, Devil's Den, and Little Round Top. Early on July 3, fighting resumed at Culp's Hill, on the Union's right. Lee also attacked the Union's center, on Cemetery Ridge. Following an artillery duel, about 13,000 troops organized and in part led by General George E. Pickett advanced across an open field and up Cemetery Ridge in what became known as "Pickett's charge." Facing impossible odds, only a few of the Southern troops reached the top of the ridge. On July 4, Lee began to withdraw to Virginia.

About 4,000 Southerners and more than 3,000 Northerners were killed in the battle. The total number of casualties—those killed, wounded, missing, or captured—was about 23,000 for the North and from 25,000 to 28,000 for the South.   Gabor S. Boritt

See also **Civil War** (Battle of Gettysburg; table; Major battles; picture: The Battle of Gettysburg).

Gettysburg Address is a short speech that United States President Abraham Lincoln delivered during the American Civil War at the site of the Battle of Gettysburg in Pennsylvania. He delivered the address on Nov. 19, 1863, at ceremonies to dedicate a part of the battlefield as a cemetery for those who had lost their lives in the battle. Lincoln wrote the address to help ensure that the battle would be seen as a great Union triumph and to define for the people of the Northern States the purpose in fighting the war. Some historians think his simple and inspired words, among the best remembered in American history, reshaped the nation by defining it as one people dedicated to one principle—that of equality.

Lincoln wrote five different versions of the speech. He wrote most of the first version in Washington, D.C., and probably completed it at Gettysburg. He probably wrote the second version at Gettysburg on the evening before he delivered his address. He held this second version in his hand during the address. But he made several changes as he spoke. The most important change was to add the phrase "under God" after the word "nation" in the last sentence. Lincoln also added that phrase to the three versions of the address that he wrote after the ceremonies at Gettysburg.

Lincoln wrote the final version of the address—the fifth written version—in 1864. This version also differed somewhat from the speech he actually gave, but it was the only copy he signed. It is carved on a stone plaque in the Lincoln Memorial.

Many false stories have grown up about this famous speech. One story says that the people of Lincoln's time did not appreciate the speech. However, the reaction of the nation's newspapers largely followed party lines. Most of the newspapers that backed the Republican Party, the party to which Lincoln belonged, liked the speech. A majority of the newspapers that supported the Democratic Party did not. Edward Everett, the principal speaker at the dedication, wrote to Lincoln: "I should be glad if I could flatter myself that I came as near to the

Two versions of the Gettysburg Address

Lincoln wrote five different versions of his famous Gettysburg Address. The fifth version, *below left*, is the only one he signed. The version at the right differs slightly from all five of the written versions but is probably closer to what Lincoln actually said at Gettysburg. It is based on the shorthand notes of a reporter who heard Lincoln deliver the speech.

Four score and seven years ago our fathers brought forth on this continent, a new nation, conceived in Liberty, and dedicated to the proposition that all men are created equal.

Now we are engaged in a great civil war, testing whether that nation, or any nation so conceived and so dedicated, can long endure. We are met on a great battlefield of that war. We have come to dedicate a portion of that field, as a final resting place for those who here gave their lives that that nation might live. It is altogether fitting and proper that we should do this.

But, in a larger sense, we can not dedicate—we can not consecrate—we can not hallow—this ground. The brave men, living and dead, who struggled here, have consecrated it, far above our poor power to add or detract. The world will little note, nor long remember what we say here, but it can never forget what they did here. It is for us the living, rather, to be dedicated here to the unfinished work which they who fought here have thus far so nobly advanced. It is rather for us to be here dedicated to the great task remaining before us—that from these honored dead we take increased devotion to that cause for which they here gave the last full measure of devotion—that we here highly resolve that these dead shall not have died in vain—that this nation, under God, shall have a new birth of freedom—and that government of the people, by the people, for the people, shall not perish from the earth.

Four score and seven years ago our fathers brought forth upon this continent a new nation, conceived in Liberty, and dedicated to the proposition that all men are created equal.

Now we are engaged in a great civil war, testing whether that nation or any nation so conceived and so dedicated can long endure. We are met on a great battlefield of that war. We are met to dedicate a portion of it as the final resting place of those who here gave their lives that that nation might live. It is altogether fitting and proper that we should do this.

But in a larger sense we cannot dedicate—we cannot consecrate—we cannot hallow this ground. The brave men living and dead who struggled here have consecrated it far above our poor power to add or detract. The world will little note nor long remember what we say here, but it can never forget what they did here. It is for us, the living, rather to be dedicated here to the unfinished work that they have thus far so nobly carried on. It is rather for us to be here dedicated to the great task remaining before us—that from these honored dead we take increased devotion to that cause for which they here gave the last full measure of devotion—that we here highly resolve that the dead shall not have died in vain—that the nation shall, under God, have a new birth of freedom—and that governments of the people, by the people, and for the people, shall not perish from the earth.

---

central idea of the occasion in two hours as you did in two minutes."   Gabor S. Boritt

Additional resources

Richards, Kenneth G. *The Gettysburg Address*. Rev. ed. Childrens Pr., 1992. Younger readers.
Wills, Garry. *Lincoln at Gettysburg*. 1992. Reprint. Simon & Schuster, 1993.

Getz, Stan (1927-1991), was an American jazz tenor saxophonist known for his light, smooth tone and lyrical approach to improvisation. Getz rose to fame in the late 1940's, playing a style known as *cool jazz* (see **Jazz** [Cool jazz]). In the early 1960's, he helped to popularize the style called *bossa nova,* which blends the melodies and rhythms of Brazilian sambas with the improvisations and harmonies of American jazz.

Stanley Getz was born in Philadelphia. He began his career with the Jack Teagarden band in 1943 and earned recognition with Woody Herman's orchestra from 1947 to 1949. He recorded his first famous solo, "Early Autumn," with Herman's orchestra in 1948. Getz formed a quartet in 1949. He made his first bossa nova recording in 1962. Getz continued to lead a successful combo during the 1970's and 1980's.   Gary Giddins

Geyser, *GY zuhr,* is a spring that throws up hot water with explosive force from time to time. Often, the water shoots up in great columns, cloudy with steam.

"Old Faithful" in Yellowstone National Park is probably the world's most famous geyser. In most years, it erupts about every 76 minutes. The actual intervals between eruptions vary from about 30 to 120 minutes. Most eruptions are 120 to 150 feet (37 to 46 meters) high. "Old Faithful" has not missed an eruption in over 80 years.

Most other geysers erupt at irregular intervals, and no one knows when they will go off. Some geysers erupt several times during an hour. Other geysers do not go off for hours, days, weeks, or even months. In some, the water only bubbles above the ground. In others, water soars more than 100 feet (30 meters) high.

Where geysers are found. There are at least 200 active geysers in Yellowstone Park. Two other noted geyser groups are found in lands that are extremely different from each other. One group of geysers lies in Iceland 70 miles (110 kilometers) from Reykjavík in the midst of barren lava fields. Here, dozens of geysers appear within a circle of 10 miles (16 kilometers). The other group of geysers is located far to the south in New Zealand, a country that is green with plant life.

How geysers form. Geysers form in areas where water drains through the earth deep below the surface. A deep channel reaches from the surface far into the earth. Cold water seeps down this channel until it reaches rocks that are hot. Then it fills the channel. The water at the bottom is heated by the rocks. But the water cannot boil because of the weight of the column of water above it. Gradually, the heat at the bottom of the column rises far above the boiling point. Steam begins to form. The rising bubbles lift the water column a little, pushing some of the water onto the earth's surface. That makes the column of water lighter, and more water is able to turn into steam. This process, in turn, lifts

Comstock

A geyser sends a blast of steaming hot water high into the air. Geysers may erupt frequently or at irregular times.

How geysers erupt

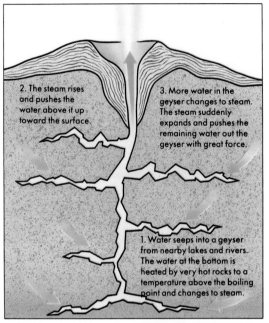

2. The steam rises and pushes the water above it up toward the surface.

3. More water in the geyser changes to steam. The steam suddenly expands and pushes the remaining water out the geyser with great force.

1. Water seeps into a geyser from nearby lakes and rivers. The water at the bottom is heated by very hot rocks to a temperature above the boiling point and changes to steam.

WORLD BOOK diagram by Sarah Woodward

the column still more, until suddenly all the water near the bottom of the channel expands into steam and forces out the rest in a steam explosion. After the water and steam settle back on the earth, some of the water seeps back into the earth and fills up the channel again. The crevices that feed the channel usually contain constrictions or sharp bends. This prevents convections that cause the water to mix to a uniform temperature. This mixing would keep the water from becoming superheated enough to explode into steam.

Geysers have often been compared with volcanoes, for they act similarly. But volcanoes shoot forth melted rock, while geysers erupt water containing dissolved mineral matter. After the eruption, the water evaporates or seeps back into the earth, leaving deposits of silica or lime carbonate. These deposits may form castlelike figures, towers, or other curious shapes. Many of them form cones. Some, such as the "Giantess" in Yellowstone Park, form craters that fill with clear water between eruptions. Very little water is left after the eruption of a geyser that has a cone. One exception is the tiny "Model" in Yellowstone Park. All the water from this geyser falls back into its cuplike cone.   Nicholas C. Crawford

See also Iceland (The land); Silica; Yellowstone National Park; Wyoming (picture: Old Faithful geyser).

Ghali, Boutros Boutros-. See Boutros-Ghali, Boutros.

Ghana, *GAH nuh,* is a tropical country in western Africa. Ghana lies on the Gulf of Guinea, where Africa bulges westward into the Atlantic Ocean. *Cacao seeds,* which are used to make chocolate, are the country's most important crop and its leading export. Ghana's forests yield valuable tropical hardwoods. Ghana has important deposits of bauxite, diamonds, gold, and manganese.

Portuguese explorers landed in what is now Ghana in 1471. They found so much gold there that they called it the *Gold Coast.* Later, European merchants came to compete for profits in the gold and slave trades. In the late 1800's, the Gold Coast became a British colony.

The Gold Coast gained its independence in 1957. It took the name *Ghana,* the name of an ancient African kingdom. Its official name is the Republic of Ghana. Accra is the capital and largest city.

Government. A president heads the government. The people elect the president to a four-year term. The president cannot serve more than two terms. The president appoints a cabinet to help carry out the functions of the government. A 200-member parliament makes the country's laws. Its members are elected by the people to four-year terms. Ghana is divided into 10 regions for purposes of local government.

People. About 99 percent of Ghana's people are black Africans. The population also includes small groups of people of Asian and European descent. Ghana's black Africans belong to about 100 different ethnic groups. The Ashanti and the Fante, two closely related ethnic groups, make up much of the population. They belong to a larger group of African peoples called the Akan. Other important ethnic groups in Ghana include the Ewe, the Ga, and the Moshi (Mossi)-Dagomba. Most Ghanaians speak African languages. But a large number also speak English, the official language.

A majority of Ghana's people live in rural areas. Most rural Ghanaians are farmers. In the forest regions, many men raise cacao on small farms. Many women raise food for their families on small plots of ground. Most of the people who live in Ghana's cities and towns hold jobs in the government or operate small businesses.

Ghana's cities have many modern buildings. But some people in the cities live in houses that have mud walls and tin roofs. In central and southern Ghana, many of the people live in rectangular houses with mud or concrete walls, thatched or tin roofs, and often courtyards. Many of the people in northern Ghana live in round houses with mud walls and cone-shaped, thatched roofs.

The national dress in Ghana is made from brightly colored cloth. Men wrap the cloth around them. Women make blouses and narrow skirts from it. Many of the people also wear clothing similar to that worn in Europe and North America.

Facts in brief

Capital: Accra.
Official language: English.
Area: 92,098 mi² (238,533 km²). *Greatest distances*—north-south, 445 mi (716 km); east-west, 310 mi (499 km). *Coastline*—335 mi (539 km).
Population: *Estimated 2002 population*—21,318,000; density, 231 persons per mi² (89 per km²); distribution, 63 percent rural, 37 percent urban. *1984 census*—12,296,081.
Chief products: *Agriculture*—cacao, cassava, coconuts, palm oil and kernels, yams. *Mining*—bauxite, diamonds, gold, manganese. *Forestry*—mahogany.
Flag: The flag has horizontal red, yellow, and green stripes with a black star symbolizing African freedom in the center. See Flag (picture: Flags of Africa).
Money: *Basic unit*—new cedi.

About 40 percent of the people practice traditional African religions. About 40 percent are Christians, and about 20 percent are Muslims.

Primary, secondary, and technical education is free in Ghana. Most children attend school until they are about 12 years old. Ghana has three universities. Most of the nation's adults can read and write. For Ghana's literacy rate, see **Literacy** (table: Literacy rates).

Land. Ghana rises from a heavily populated plain along the Gulf of Guinea to the Kwahu Plateau. The plateau runs from the northwest to the southeast across central Ghana. It forms a divide between the White Volta and the Black Volta rivers in the north and east, and the Ankobra, the Pra, and the Tano rivers in the south and west. A thick forest covers southwestern Ghana. North of the plateau, the land gradually becomes a *savanna* (grassy, thinly wooded plain), and then grasslands. Lake Volta, one of the world's largest artificially created lakes, is located in east-central Ghana.

Ghana has a tropical climate. Accra, in the south, has an average temperature of 80 °F (27 °C). Northern Ghana has higher temperatures. Most of Ghana receives 40 to 60 inches (100 to 150 centimeters) of rain a year, with the heaviest rains in the southwest. Axim, a town on the Gulf of Guinea, receives over 80 inches (200 centimeters) of rain a year. Northern and eastern Ghana have severe dry spells from November to March.

Economy. Ghana is an agricultural country, but it has important mineral deposits. Cacao is the most important crop and the country's chief export. Other important crops include coffee, coconuts, kola nuts, and *kernels* (seeds) from palm trees. Valuable tropical hardwood trees, such as mahogany, grow in Ghana's forests. The country also produces such minerals as bauxite, diamonds, gold, and manganese. Besides cacao, Ghana exports diamonds, gold, manganese, and timber.

Most of Ghana's factories are small plants that process agricultural products or timber. Manufactured products include beverages, cement, and clothing. An aluminum smelter at Tema is Ghana's largest factory. Hydroelectric power plants at the southern end of Lake Volta produce electric power for much of Ghana and the nearby countries of Togo and Benin.

Few Ghanaians own an automobile. Many people travel on buses or flat-bed trucks. Others must walk.

History. People from African kingdoms to the northwest probably settled in what is now Ghana in the 1200's. Portuguese explorers landed on the coast in 1471 and named the area the Gold Coast. Later, the Dutch came to compete with the Portuguese for gold. By 1642, the Dutch had seized all the Portuguese forts, and ended Portuguese control in the Gold Coast.

A large slave trade developed in the 1600's, and the Danes and English competed with the Dutch for profits. The slave trade ended in the 1860's, and by 1872, the British had gained control of the Dutch and Danish forts.

In 1874, the United Kingdom made the lands from the coast to the inland Ashanti empire a British colony. By 1901, the United Kingdom had made the Ashanti lands a

Ghana

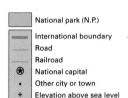

	National park (N.P.)
	International boundary
	Road
	Railroad
⊛	National capital
•	Other city or town
+	Elevation above sea level

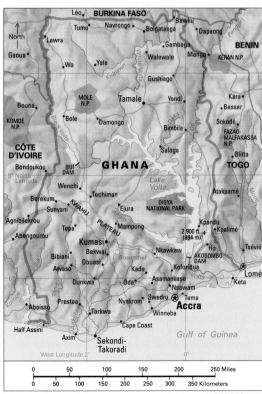

WORLD BOOK maps

© John Elk III, Wheeler Pictures

Life in rural Ghana centers mainly around small villages. In the marketplace in central Ghana, villagers buy and sell goods.

© John Elk III, Wheeler Pictures

Downtown Accra bustles with activity. Accra is Ghana's capital, largest city, and leading business center.

colony and had started a protectorate over what is now northern Ghana.

The cacao industry prospered in the Gold Coast during the early 1900's. The British extended roads and railways, built hospitals, and developed the schools.

In the late 1940's and in the 1950's, the British gradually granted the Africans more power. In 1946, a majority in parliament were Africans elected to represent the people. But the British governor and Cabinet kept most of the power. In 1951, Kwame Nkrumah was asked to form a Cabinet, and in 1952, he became prime minister. By 1954, the people ran their own government, except in the areas of external affairs, defense, and the police.

The Gold Coast finally achieved its independence in 1957. British Togoland became part of the new nation, which was named Ghana (see **Togo** [History]).

In 1960, the people of Ghana voted to become a republic and elected Nkrumah president. He made his Convention People's Party (CPP) the only legal political party and increased his personal power through the mid-1960's. But government debt and corruption combined with the falling price of cacao to greatly weaken the economy. In 1966, a military council seized the government and ousted Nkrumah.

In 1969, Brigadier Akwasi Amankwa Afrifa became head of the military council. Also in 1969, Ghana adopted a new constitution and returned to civilian rule. Kofi Busia, leader of the Progressive Party, became prime minister. Busia served until 1972, when military leaders took control of the government. Colonel I. K. Acheampong became head of the new military government. In 1978, he was forced to resign by other military leaders. General Frederick William Kwasi Akuffo replaced him. In June 1979, still other military leaders overthrew Akuffo. Lieutenant Jerry Rawlings, who led the revolt against Akuffo, became head of the government. The new government executed Afrifa, Acheampong, and Akuffo. In September 1979, a civilian government was elected. In 1981, Rawlings led another revolt and regained control of the government.

During the 1970's and early 1980's, Ghana suffered se-

vere economic problems. Many people left Ghana to work in Nigeria. But Nigeria also experienced economic difficulties. In 1983, Nigeria forced about 1 million people to return to Ghana. The return of the people created shortages of food, housing, water, and jobs in Ghana.

In 1992, Ghana's voters approved a constitution designed to make Ghana a multiparty democracy. Political parties, banned since 1981, were again allowed. Elections for a president and legislature were held in late 1992. Rawlings was elected president, and his party, the National Democratic Congress, won a vast majority of the seats in parliament. Rawlings was reelected president in 1996. In a vote held in December 2000, John A. Kufuor of the opposition New Patriotic Party was elected president. Ghana's constitution prohibited Rawlings from seeking another term. Kufuor took office in January 2001.   Barbara E. McDade

Related articles in World Book include:

Accra	Ashanti	Nkrumah, Kwame
Africa (pictures)	Clothing (picture)	Rawlings, Jerry
Annan, Kofi Atta	Lake Volta	John

Ghana Empire, *GAH nuh,* was an important black trading state in West Africa from about the A.D. 300's to the mid-1000's. Arab camel caravans brought salt and copper from mines in the Sahara and dried fruits from North Africa to Ghana's markets. There the products were traded for gold, ivory, and slaves from regions south of Ghana. Ghanaian jewelry and leather goods were sold and traded for textiles, clothing, and fine tools from Arabia and Europe. Kumbi Saleh, the capital, and Audagost were probably the largest cities in West Af-

The Ghana Empire about 1050

This map shows the location of the Ghana Empire, in dark gray, as it existed about 1050. Ghana ruled an area in West Africa now occupied by Mauritania and Mali. The current boundaries are shown as white lines. The Ghanaians traded salt, copper, gold, and ivory with the Songhai, Sosso, Wangara, and other tribes.

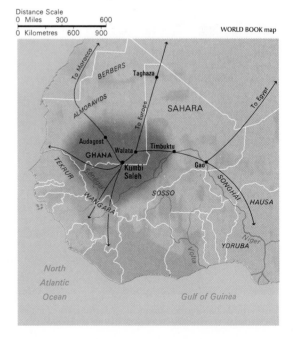

rica. Each of them may have had over 15,000 people.

The Ghana Empire lay in what is now southeastern Mauritania and western Mali. During Ghana's early period, Berbers from the north ruled the native Soninke people. Ghana's greatest period began in the 700's, soon after the Soninkes gained control, and lasted until the mid-1000's. The king of Ghana charged import and export taxes, which were paid in gold. He also claimed all gold nuggets found in his kingdom. With this wealth, the king maintained an efficient government and an army that kept the trade routes to Ghana safe. Skilled ironworkers produced weapons that contributed to Ghana's strength. Moroccan Berbers called *Almoravids* conquered Ghana in the mid-1000's. The Soninkes retook Kumbi Saleh in the late 1000's, but the outer parts of the empire had declared their freedom. Ghana never regained its power and fell to the Sosso in the early 1200's.　　Leo Spitzer

Ghent, *gehnt* (pop. 228,490), is a Belgian city 31 miles (50 kilometers) northwest of Brussels. The city is in the Dutch-speaking part of Belgium. Its Dutch name is Gent. Its name in French is Gand. Ghent lies at the fork of the Schelde and Leie rivers, and is an important seaport (see **Belgium** [political map]). A ship canal built in 1886 connects the city with the North Sea. Ghent is known for its chemical products, cotton mills, flax, and flowers and bulbs. More than 200 bridges span the waterways that crisscross the city. The town hall, built in the 1500's, is a fine example of Gothic architecture.

The first buildings at Ghent were two monasteries built in the 600's. Ghent became important during the Middle Ages and reached its height in the 1400's. For many years afterward, Ghent was torn by revolutions and war. It was held by the Spanish, French, and Austrians at various times before Belgium became independent. Ghent was occupied by German forces in World Wars I and II.　　Aristide R. Zolberg

Ghent, *gehnt,* **Treaty of,** ended the War of 1812 between the United Kingdom and the United States. The two countries signed the treaty at Ghent, Belgium, on Dec. 24, 1814, and then ratified it on Feb. 17, 1815. The American negotiators were John Quincy Adams, James A. Bayard, Henry Clay, Jonathan Russell, and Albert Gallatin. The British representatives were Sir James Gambier, Henry Goulburn, and William Adams. The treaty settled none of the disputes that caused the war. It merely restored the situation that had existed before the war. The treaty did not even mention the fact that American seamen had been forced to serve on British ships. This omission was less important than it seemed because the British had no reason to continue the practice after the final defeat of Napoleon in 1815.

The Treaty of Ghent marked the start of a period in which the United Kingdom and the United States chose to settle their disputes peacefully. The troublesome fisheries question, the problem of payment for slaves seized by the British during the war, and the disagreement over the northwestern boundary of the United States were all worked out in later negotiations.

The Rush-Bagot Agreement of 1817 provided for naval disarmament on the Great Lakes. It also paved the way for an unfortified frontier between Canada and the United States.　　Philip Dwight Jones

Gherkin. See Cucumber.

Ghetto, *GEHT oh,* is a section of a city settled by a minority ethnic, religious, or nationality group. The term *ghetto* originally referred to sections of European cities where Jews settled or were forced to live. Today, the term is applied to poverty-stricken areas where blacks and other minority groups are forced to live because of social and economic pressure.

Early ghettos. Ghettos appeared in Europe as early as A.D. 70, when the Romans reconquered Palestine after a revolt by the Jews. Many Jews moved to Europe then. At first, they voluntarily settled in separate communities so they could more easily continue their cultural traditions. It was easier to prepare their food according to traditional laws, to live closer to the synagogue, and to have a closer community life. In some places, Jews lived together because they feared other groups.

However, other people later forced Jews to live in ghettos. Religious or political leaders demanded segregation of Jews, and ghettos became more common. Persecution of the Jews increased about 1100, when the Crusades began. The term *ghetto* is thought to have been derived from the medieval Venetian word *gèto,* which meant *foundry.* The term was probably first used in 1516, when Venice expelled its Jews to an island within the city, on which a foundry was located. In 1555, Pope Paul IV decreed that Jews in the *Papal States,* the area around Rome governed by the Roman Catholic Church, had to live in separate quarters. Authorities in the Christian world followed the pope's example. Crowded ghettos developed that were usually surrounded by walls. The gates were locked at night.

During the 1700's and 1800's, most enforced segregation of Jews ended. But Nazi Germany revived the practice of forcing Jews to live in ghettos during World War II (1939-1945). See **Warsaw** (History).

Ghettos today. The term *ghetto* now refers mostly to large settlements of blacks in United States cities. Groups of Mexicans, Puerto Ricans, and other Spanish-speaking Americans also live in ghettos.

Before World War I (1914-1918), most African Americans lived in the rural South. But industrial jobs during World Wars I and II drew hundreds of thousands of blacks to cities in the North. Almost all of these people were poor, unskilled workers. They settled in slum areas near the factories where they worked in the inner city. As slums grew, ghetto conditions worsened. Prejudice and discrimination have made it difficult for African Americans and other minorities to improve these conditions. Legislation has been used to try to eliminate ghetto conditions in the United States. But segregation remains a serious problem.　　James W. Vander Zanden

See also **African Americans** (Unrest in the cities); **Jews** (Jews in Christian Europe); **Open housing; Segregation.**

Additional resources

Goldsmith, William W., and Blakely, E. J. *Separate Societies: Poverty and Inequality in U.S. Cities.* Temple Univ. Pr., 1992.
Vergara, Camilo J. *The New American Ghetto.* Rutgers, 1995.
Wilson, William J. *When Work Disappears: The World of the New Urban Poor.* Knopf, 1996.

Ghibellines. See Guelphs and Ghibellines.

Ghiberti, *gee BEHR tee,* **Lorenzo** (1378-1455), was an Italian sculptor and goldsmith. He is best known for two sets of bronze doors he created for the *baptistery* (a building used for baptisms) in his native Florence. The doors have 28 panels, decorated with *reliefs* (raised designs). Each is composed within a Gothic frame of a shape called *quatrefoil,* which restricts the freedom of the designer. Yet Ghiberti created striking variations of many important traditional themes.

Ghiberti worked on these doors from 1403 to 1424. Then he produced another set, often called the *Gates of Paradise.* These doors have 10 large panels. This gave Ghiberti freedom to compose his reliefs like pictures. The panels depict episodes from the Old Testament.

Ghiberti worked on the doors for about 50 years. He also created many other works and trained dozens of artists who were his assistants.   Roger Ward

See also **Florence** (picture: Bronze doors); **Relief** (picture: High-relief figures).

Ghirlandajo, *geer lahn DAH yoh,* **Domenico,** *doh MAY nee koh* (1449-1494), also spelled Ghirlandaio, was the most successful Italian painter of his time in Florence. He painted frescoes and altarpieces in a direct, sober, and detailed manner. His style differed greatly from the more lyrical and complex style of other major Florentine artists of his time. Michelangelo was one of his apprentices. Ghirlandajo was born Domenico di Tommaso Bigordi in Florence.   Vernon Hyde Minor

Ghost, according to tradition, is a spirit of a dead person that visits the living. Most people do not believe in ghosts, but some do. Reports of seeing or hearing ghosts have been common throughout history—more so in ancient and medieval times than today. There have been many stories, books, motion pictures, and plays about ghosts. In most stories and reports about ghosts, the ghost resembles its living form. Many ghosts are transparent or shadowy. Some ghosts are pictured as white sheets shaped somewhat like a body.

Many ghosts are *malevolent.* That is, they try to do harm. But some ghosts are friendly. A malevolent ghost is usually the spirit of a person who was murdered or otherwise harmed by relatives or friends. Most malevolent ghosts haunt the place where, in their real form, they died or were buried. A ghost that haunts a place by making strange noises and causing furniture and other objects to move by themselves is sometimes called a *poltergeist.* Friendly ghosts include Marley in Charles Dickens's *A Christmas Carol.* Marley helps Ebenezer Scrooge, the main character, become a better person.

In many stories and reports, a ghost returns from the dead without being contacted by anyone. In others, a *medium* (a person with special powers) calls the ghost back to earth. Ghosts—which are associated with darkness and night—usually end their visits by dawn. Some ghosts refuse to leave. Methods used to get rid of them include reburying the corpse, piercing the corpse or its grave with a stake, and praying.

Ghosts play an important role in some religions. Many American Indians and tribespeople in Africa and the Pacific Islands believe in spirits that influence the living world. They perform rites to please the spirits in order to assure success. Many peoples fear the dead and observe special funeral customs to make sure that ghosts do not return.   Alan Dundes

See also **Ghost story; Mythology; Spiritualism.**

Ghost Dance was a religious movement among American Indians of the Western United States in the late 1800's. It offered the Indians hope of spiritual renewal and a return to their old way of living. The religion promised that dead Indian ancestors and game animals would come back to life. It was first adopted by Indians in what is now Nevada in the late 1860's. The religion was revived in 1889 and by 1890 was rapidly spreading among the Indians of the Great Plains. Plains Indians who adopted the religion had been forced onto reservations and were suffering from hunger and disease. Whites had wiped out the buffalo herds, leaving the Indians without their chief source of food.

The religion centered on a ceremony called the *ghost dance,* which differed somewhat from one tribe to another. Among Western Sioux in 1890, believers danced around a pole or tree decorated with sacred objects. The dancers wore special clothing called *ghost shirts,* which were painted with sacred symbols, including moons, stars, and eagles. The Sioux believed the shirts would protect them from enemy bullets. Some dancers fell into trances and saw visions of the promised world.

The religion was nonviolent, but U.S. Army leaders feared it would lead to a Sioux uprising in what is now South Dakota. The dance was largely abandoned by the Sioux after the U.S. Army massacred Sioux followers of the religion in 1890 at Wounded Knee Creek in South Dakota. The dance declined among other tribes when its promises were never fulfilled.   Jerome A. Greene

See also **Wounded Knee; Wovoka.**

Ghost story is a supernatural tale in which the spirit of a dead person haunts the living. Many ghost stories play on the readers' fear of death and their dread of uncomfortable, strange places, such as deserted mansions or medieval castles. But many stories tease and often frighten readers by making a ghost's disruptive behavior happen in normal or even in civilized settings. See **Ghost.**

Many ghosts are evil or unpleasant, but some may be helpful. A restless ghost may return from the dead for many reasons. The spirit may right a wrong, take revenge, expose a crime that had gone unpunished, reveal the location of a lost will or hidden treasure, or teach someone an important lesson. Although most ghost stories try to frighten readers, some are amusing.

Writers since ancient times have used ghosts in their stories. But the golden age of ghost stories is considered to be the 1800's in England. The inventor of the modern ghost story was the Irish author Joseph Sheridan Le Fanu, who wrote his first ghost story in 1838. Other notable authors of ghost stories included British authors Algernon Blackwood and M. R. James, and American writers August Derleth and Henry James.   William A. Kumbier

Ghost town is the name given to the ruins of a town that has been abandoned. Numerous ghost towns exist in the Western United States, including Alaska, and in Canada. Many are the ruins of towns that sprang up after 1850 around mines or, later, oil fields. The residents abandoned the towns as the mines or fields were worked out. See also **Idaho** (Places to visit); **Western frontier life in America** (Frontier towns).   Dan L. Flores

GI is a common term for members of the United States Army. It was first applied to the men in the ranks of the Army during World War II (1939-1945) and the Korean War (1950-1953). *GI* is an abbreviation for *general issue,* a term for clothing or equipment issued to U.S. soldiers.

GI Bill of Rights. See Veterans' Affairs, Department of.

Giacometti, *JAH kuh MEHT ee,* **Alberto** (1901-1966), was a Swiss-born sculptor. Much of his work is small and created in bronze. Until 1935, Giacometti was closely associated with the surrealism movement. Works such as *The Palace at 4 A.M.* (1932-1933) have a dream-

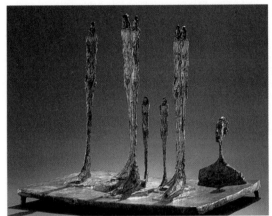

Composition with Seven Figures and a Head (The Forest) (1950), painted bronze; Lee Boltin

Giacometti's sculpture emphasizes human figures as they might appear from a distance. His gaunt, elongated figures seem anonymous and isolated. These qualities made Giacometti the leading sculptor of the art movement called *surrealism.*

like quality often found in surrealism and deal with the anxieties and aloneness he saw in modern urban life. *The Palace at 4 A.M.* is shown in the **Sculpture** article.

After the end of World War II in 1945, Giacometti concentrated on human figures, to which he tried to give spiritual qualities. These figures are small, thin, and elongated, with rough surfaces and blank, expressionless faces. Whether single figures or in groups, the sculptures are arranged to suggest a sense of loneliness and isolation.

Giacometti was born in Stampa, Switzerland. He moved to Paris in 1922. He was also a painter, graphic artist, and poet.   Joseph F. Lamb

Giant is a person who grows abnormally tall because of a disorder in the pituitary gland. This condition, called *gigantism,* can cause people to grow as tall as 9 feet (274 centimeters). Many individuals are excessively tall because of an inherited trait, but physicians do not consider them giants.

The growth of human bones is regulated by a hormone called *growth hormone* (GH), which is secreted by the pituitary. During childhood, GH causes a thickening of the *epiphyseal cartilage,* a plate of soft tissue near the ends of the bones. This cartilage develops through the years and is absorbed by new layers of bone tissue. The continued absorption of cartilage increases the length of the bones. Gigantism occurs when the pituitary secretes excessive GH, increasing the growth of epiphyseal cartilage. In some cases, this malfunction is caused by a pituitary tumor.

A person stops growing after all epiphyseal cartilage has been absorbed by the bones—usually between the ages of 18 and 24. When this occurs, GH can no longer

increase height, but excessive amounts of it may cause *acromegaly.* This condition produces overgrowths in the bones of the face, feet, and hands. Many cases of acromegaly are caused by a pituitary tumor and occur in people of normal height.

If treatment begins during childhood, gigantism can be controlled by decreasing the activity of the pituitary gland with radiation treatment. In some cases, pituitary tumors are removed surgically. The surgeon may reach the tumor through the nasal cavity, cutting through the floor of the cranium to get to the pituitary. The patient has no apparent scar after such surgery.   Russel J. Reiter

See also **Pituitary gland.**

Giant, in Greek and Roman mythology, belonged to a race of beings that looked like people, but were much bigger. The ancient Greeks and Romans believed people had grown smaller as time passed. They thought their ancestors had been huge individuals of great strength and power.

Giants, in Greek legend, represented the elements of nature, such as earth, air, and water. They were said to have been born from the blood of Uranus (Heaven) which fell into the lap of Gaea (Earth).

Giants appear in every country's mythology. For example, Welsh giants are well known through the story of Jack the Giant Killer.

Races of giants are first spoken of in the Bible in Genesis 6: 4. One giant, King Og of Bashan, had a bed 9 cubits long. A Hebrew cubit is 17.58 inches (44.7 centimeters), and 9 cubits is over 13 feet (396 centimeters). Goliath, who was killed by David with a stone from a

Khurram Amroha

A giant is abnormally tall because of a disorder in the pituitary gland. The giant shown in this photograph with two average-sized men is 7 feet 10 inches (239 centimeters) tall.

sling, is the best-known giant in the Bible. According to the Bible story, Goliath stood about 9 $\frac{1}{4}$ feet (282 centimeters) tall.   Ellen J. Stekert

Giant schnauzer, *SHNOW zuhr,* is the largest of the three schnauzer dog breeds. It was developed in southern Germany in the 1700's by people who needed dogs that could drive cattle to market. Besides being a pet, its jobs today include police and guard duties. The giant schnauzer was bred by crossing *standard* (medium-sized) schnauzers with large German sheepdogs. Later the new breed was crossed with Great Danes and, perhaps, with Bouviers des Flandres.

The giant schnauzer has a blunt, powerful mouth and stubby whiskers. Its black or black-and-white coat is hard and wiry. The giant schnauzer stands about 26 inches (66 centimeters) high and weighs about 75 pounds (34 kilograms).

Critically reviewed by the Giant Schnauzer Club of America

Giant squid is a huge sea creature that lives in many parts of the world's oceans, probably at depths of 1,000 to 3,300 feet (300 to 1,000 meters). The giant squid often appears in sea monster stories. However, no one has ever seen a living giant squid, and so little is known about it. Scientists have learned about the animals by studying dead ones found in fishing nets or washed up on shores. They have also studied body parts of giant squid found in the stomachs of sperm whales.

Giant squid belong to a group of animals called *mollusks,* which have soft, boneless bodies. The squid's body is long and shaped like a bullet. An adult can grow about 60 feet (18 meters) in length and weigh more than 1,000 pounds (454 kilograms). The giant squid has two huge eyes about 10 inches (25 centimeters) wide, the largest eyes in the animal kingdom. Its flesh contains ammonium, which is lighter than water, enabling the animal to hover in deep water. A long body part called the *mantle* extends from one side of the head and tapers toward a wide tail with two rounded fins. Eight arms and two long tentacles extend from the other side of the head. Each arm and tentacle is lined with rows of round sucking disks. The animal uses its tentacles to seize prey and draw it to a large, beaklike structure near its mouth. Inside this structure is a toothed *radula* (tongue), which

shreds the prey. Giant squid eat fish, octopus, and smaller squid.   Brian Hartwick

Scientific classification. Giant squids make up the giant squid family, Architeuthidae.

See also **Mollusk; Squid.**

Giant's Causeway is an unusual formation of rock columns along the north coast of Northern Ireland. It gets its name from an old legend that the causeway was built by Finn MacCool, or Fingal, to bridge the channel

Manley Photo from Shostal

The Giant's Causeway is a natural wonder in Northern Ireland. It is formed by about 40,000 columns of basalt.

from Ireland to Scotland so that giants could pass over it. The causeway is formed of about 40,000 separate basalt columns, quite close together. Some pillars are up to 20 feet (6 meters) high. They are from 15 to 20 inches (38 to 51 centimeters) in diameter. Geologists believe the causeway resulted from the contracting of a lava flow. See also **Basalt.**   A. T. Q. Stewart

Giardiasis, *JEE ahr DY uh sihs,* is an intestinal disease caused by a *protozoan* (one-celled organism) that lives as a parasite in human beings and animals. The scientific name for this parasite is *Giardia lamblia.* Symptoms of giardiasis include mild to severe diarrhea, abdominal swelling, cramps, nausea, and weight loss. The infection commonly lasts several weeks, but some cases become chronic and may last for years.

People become infected with *G. lamblia* by drinking contaminated water or from close contact with an infect-

National Museum of Natural History © Smithsonian Institution

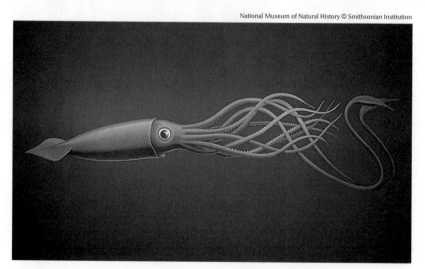

The giant squid has a bullet-shaped body with eight arms and two long tentacles. Sucking disks that line each arm and each tentacle help the animal catch prey. The giant squid's huge eyes, the largest in the animal kingdom, measure about 10 inches (25 centimeters) wide.

ed person. The parasite moves through the digestive system and attaches to the inner surface of the small intestine. There, it interferes with the body's ability to absorb fat and vitamins, leading to diarrhea. The parasite eventually leaves the body in *feces* (solid body waste).

Giardiasis occurs throughout the world in areas with contaminated water supplies. Animals can spread the parasite. For example, beavers can contaminate water upstream from areas where outbreaks of giardiasis have occurred. Each year in the United States, many people become infected by drinking water directly from mountain streams. Physicians use the drugs quinacrine and metronidazole to treat the disease.   James L. Franklin

Gibberellin, *JIHB uh REHL ihn,* also called GA, is any of a group of hormones that regulate plant growth. Gibberellins occur naturally in green plants and fungi. They also can be produced from green plants and fungi by laboratory methods. Scientists have discovered more than 60 types of gibberellins. Of these, *gibberellic acid* is the best known.

Preparations of GA may be sprayed on certain plants to promote growth. When GA is applied to a plant, the stem of the plant may grow faster and taller than it normally would. GA may also speed up the rate at which a plant sprouts, flowers, and fruits. Gibberellins have many commercial uses. For example, a grapevine treated with GA produces larger grapes. Growers use GA to increase the yield of grapes.   Richard C. Keating

Gibbon is the smallest of the apes. It also ranges over a wider area than the other members of the ape family—the bonobo, chimpanzee, gorilla, and orangutan. The gibbon lives in the forests of the Indian state of Assam, and in Myanmar, Thailand, Malaysia, Indonesia, and elsewhere in Southeast Asia. There are several species of gibbons. All have long arms and legs, but no tail. A gibbon weighs about 15 pounds (7 kilograms) and stands about 3 feet (91 centimeters) high. It ranges from black to pale brown.

Gibbons live in the tops of trees and rarely come to the ground. They eat fruits and leaves. Gibbons use their arms to swing from branch to branch. They also walk on top of tree branches using only their legs. This way of

© Giuseppe Mazza

The gibbon is the smallest member of the ape family. It has long arms and legs. It grows about 3 feet (91 centimeters) tall.

walking is similar to the way human beings walk on the ground. Gibbons live in family groups that usually consist of a male, a female, and one or two of their young. A gibbon family claims an area called a *territory* and uses loud calls and songs to warn other families to stay away.

Two species, *Kloss's gibbon* and the *pileated gibbon,* have become endangered. The destruction of their forest homes and the capture of young animals for food or for sale as pets threaten these species with extinction.
Randall L. Susman

Scientific classification. Gibbons make up the lesser ape family, Hylobatidae.

See also **Animal** (pictures); **Ape.**

Gibbon, Edward (1737-1794), was a British scholar who wrote the *History of the Decline and Fall of the Roman Empire,* a masterpiece of historical writing. The *Decline and Fall,* as it is sometimes called, was published in six volumes between 1776 and 1788 and made Gibbon the most famous historian of his day. Today, historians still admire the work's careful scholarship, powerful narration, vast range, and ironic wit. The book became controversial because it argued that Christianity was a major cause of the fall of the Roman Empire.

Gibbon was born in Surrey, England. A sickly child, he spent much of his time reading. He enrolled in Oxford University, but hated the 14 months he spent there. In 1753, after he converted to Roman Catholicism, Gibbon was forced to leave Oxford. At that time, only Anglicans were permitted to study at Oxford. Gibbon's father, a wealthy country gentleman, then sent his disgraced son to Lausanne, Switzerland, to live with a Calvinist minister. While there, Gibbon mastered Latin, Greek, and French, and he laid the foundations of his enormous learning. He was virtually self-educated.

A visit to Rome in 1764 inspired Gibbon to write the *Decline and Fall.* He settled in London in 1772. He served in the British Parliament but devoted most of his time to scholarship and literature. He spent his last years in Lausanne.   David P. Jordan

Gibbons, Orlando (1583-1625), was an English composer and musician. He is primarily known for his church music, which consists of anthems, psalms, and entire worship services, all written in English. His madrigal *The Silver Swan* (1612) is perhaps his best-known nonreligious composition.

Gibbons was born in Oxford and grew up in Cambridge. From 1605 until his death, he was organist at the Chapel Royal. Gibbons was a fine keyboard performer, and composed works for two keyboard instruments, the organ and the virginal. Some of his works for the virginal appeared in a famous collection called *Parthenia* (1611). Gibbons also wrote more music for strings than most composers of his time. This music consists of works for the viola da gamba, a stringed instrument popular in the 1500's and 1600's.   Joscelyn Godwin

Gibbons v. Ogden, an 1824 Supreme Court case, marked the first time the Supreme Court of the United States dealt with the powers of Congress to regulate *interstate commerce* (trade between states). The court ruled that federal powers were superior to those of the states in all matters of interstate commerce. The court broadly defined commerce to include the means and routes of transportation. See **Interstate commerce** (The commerce clause).

Aaron Ogden had a monopoly, which was granted by New York state, to operate steamboats on the Hudson River between New York and New Jersey. Thomas Gibbons, however, had a federal license to use the same waters. The Supreme Court ruled in favor of Gibbons, declaring the federal license superior to the state grant. This decision led to widespread federal regulation of the economy.   Stanley I. Kutler

Gibbs, Josiah Willard (1839-1903), was an American mathematical physicist who contributed to the basic theories of *thermodynamics* and *statistical mechanics.* Thermodynamics is the study of various forms of energy, such as heat and work, and of the conversion of energy from one form into another. Statistical mechanics is the study of temperature, pressure, and related phenomena by a mathematical analysis of movements of molecules that are assumed to obey the laws of mechanics. Gibbs published *Elementary Principles in Statistical Mechanics* (1902), a pioneering textbook. Gibbs also developed the *phase rule,* which explains physical relationships among the solid, liquid, and gaseous *phases* (states) of matter.

Gibbs was born in New Haven, Connecticut. He received a Ph.D. degree from Yale University in 1863 and taught there from 1871 until his death. He won many distinguished science awards, including the Rumford Medal from the American Academy of Arts and Sciences in 1880 and the Copley Medal from the Royal Society in England in 1901.   Albert E. Moyer

Gibraltar, *juh BRAWL tuhr,* is an overseas territory of the United Kingdom on Spain's southern coast. It lies on a narrow peninsula near the entrance to the Mediterranean Sea. The Rock of Gibraltar, a huge limestone mass 1,398 feet (426 meters) at its highest point, occupies most of Gibraltar's 2.5 square miles (6.5 square kilometers). Until recently, its location made Gibraltar militarily important.

Government. A governor, appointed by the United Kingdom, heads Gibraltar's government. The Gibraltar Council, made up of five leading officials and four members of the House of Assembly, assists the governor.

© Superstock

Gibraltar lies on a narrow peninsula that juts out into the Mediterranean Sea off the southern coast of Spain.

The 15 members of the House of Assembly are elected by the people to four-year terms. Eight members make up a Council of Ministers that advises the House. The Supreme Court is Gibraltar's highest court.

People. Gibraltar has a population of about 30,000. The major ethnic groups—British, Italian, Maltese, Portuguese, and Spanish—reflect the history of the region. Many Moroccans live and work in Gibraltar.

Almost all the people live in apartments in the town of Gibraltar. English is the official language, but many families speak Spanish at home. Over three-quarters of the people are Roman Catholics. Gibraltar imports all its food because it has no farmland. It has a mild climate.

Most workers are employed by the Gibraltar government, a dockyard, or in the tourist industry. Financial services became an important industry in the late 1900's.

History. Moors from North Africa settled in Gibraltar in A.D. 711 and held it for almost 600 years. The Spanish conquered Gibraltar in 1309 but lost it to the Moors again in 1333. The Spanish reconquered the peninsula in 1462 and held it until 1704, when a British naval force captured it. The Treaty of Utrecht, signed in 1713, gave Gibraltar to the United Kingdom. According to the

Gibraltar

Gibraltar, a British overseas territory, lies on a peninsula of Spain near the entrance to the Mediterranean Sea.

- City or town

----- Road

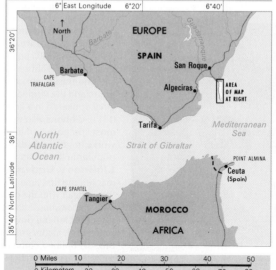

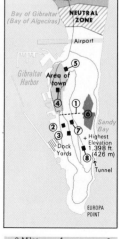

treaty, the United Kingdom must offer Gibraltar to Spain if the United Kingdom decides to give up the territory.

In 1964, the United Kingdom considered granting independence to Gibraltar. Spain objected and began a campaign to force the United Kingdom to return it to Spain. In 1965, the United Nations supported Spain's claim to Gibraltar. But the United Kingdom decided in 1967 to keep the territory after the people of Gibraltar voted for continued British control.

In the past, Gibraltar had great military value to the British because of its location. In the early 1700's, the United Kingdom established a military base there. The British used Gibraltar to keep enemy ships from entering or leaving the Mediterranean Sea. In 1942, during World War II, the Allies launched an attack from Gibraltar against German and Italian forces in North Africa. After the war, Gibraltar's military importance declined gradually. In 1991, the United Kingdom withdrew its military forces from Gibraltar. However, Gibraltar remained a British overseas territory.   Maurice Harvey

See also **Barbary ape; Gibraltar, Strait of; Utrecht, Peace of.**

Gibraltar, *juh BRAWL tuhr,* **Strait of,** is a narrow body of water that connects the Mediterranean Sea and the Atlantic Ocean. It is one of the world's most important sea lanes. The strait is about 32 miles (51 kilometers) long and 8 to 23 miles (13 to 37 kilometers) wide. It separates southernmost Spain from the northern coast of Africa. Cape Trafalgar in Spain and Cape Spartel in Tangier mark its western limits; its eastern limits are the British overseas territory of Gibraltar and Point Almina in North Africa (see **Spain** [political map]).

On each side of the Strait of Gibraltar at its eastern end is a huge rock. These rocks are called Pillars of Hercules. The Mediterranean receives waters that flow east from the Atlantic through the strait. The sea has little tide, and its surplus waters are carried west by an undercurrent that flows through the strait into the Atlantic.

Edward Malefakis

See also **Gibraltar.**

Gibraltar of America. See **Quebec** (city).

Gibran, *jih BRAHN,* **Kahlil,** *kah LEEL* (1883-1931), was a Lebanese writer. His first name is sometimes spelled Khalil. Gibran's writings teach a philosophy of universal peace and religious tolerance based on a spirit of love that transcends cultural differences. He wrote in Arabic until 1918, when he began writing in English. The publication of *The Prophet* (1923) established his fame in English-speaking countries. It is a mystical poem that explores the importance of love. Gibran also wrote fiction and nonfiction. Many of his works are collected in *Treasury of Writings of Kahlil Gibran* (1989).

Gibran was born in the village of Bsharri in Maronite Christian Lebanon. His given and family name was Gibran Khalil Gibran. In 1895, he and his mother immigrated to Boston, where Gibran studied English. In 1898, he returned to Lebanon and, at 15 years of age, entered the Maronite school in Beirut. Later, he studied painting in Paris. In 1912, Gibran moved to New York, where he lived until his death. Gibran's multicultural upbringing greatly influenced his writing.   Dick Davis

Gibson, Althea, *al THEE uh* (1927-   ), became the first important African American tennis player. She was one of the leading women amateur players from 1950 to 1958, and dominated women's tennis in 1957 and 1958. Gibson won singles titles in the United States National Championships (now the U.S. Open) and the All-England (Wimbledon) Championships in 1957 and 1958. She also played on the winning U.S. teams in the Wightman Cup meets for American and British women both years.

Gibson was born in Silver, South Carolina, and grew up in New York City. She began playing amateur tennis in the early 1940's. She retired from tennis in 1958, and became a professional golfer.   Arthur Ashe

Gibson, Charles Dana, *DAY nuh* (1867-1944), an American illustrator, drew the famous "Gibson girl." She was intended to represent a typical society woman and to be the image of ideal American femininity. Gibson portrayed her in pen and ink drawings as an attractive, athletic, outdoor type who was poised and intelligent. The "Gibson girl" became a favorite in the United States and many other countries during the 1890's and early 1900's. Gibson was born in Roxbury, Massachusetts.

Charles P. Green

Culver

"The Gibson girl" was created by the American artist Charles Dana Gibson.

Gibson, Josh (1911-1947), was one of the greatest hitters in baseball history. Gibson played in the Negro leagues between 1930 and 1946, before African Americans were allowed to play in the major leagues. Gibson, a catcher, led his league in home runs nine times and in batting twice. His batting average of .517 in 1943 was the second highest in the history of the Negro leagues. Gibson also gained fame for the length of many of his home runs.

Joshua Gibson was born in Buena Vista, Georgia. He began his professional baseball career with the Homestead (Pennsylvania) Grays in 1930. He played for the Pittsburgh Crawfords from 1932 to 1936 and returned to the Grays in 1937. In winter, he played baseball for various teams outside the United States, including teams in Mexico, Puerto Rico, and the Dominican Republic. Gibson died of a brain tumor at age 35. He was elected to the National Baseball Hall of Fame in 1972.   Larry Lester

Gide, *zheed,* **André,** *ahn DRAY* (1869-1951), a French author, won the 1947 Nobel Prize for literature. He had a strong impact on literature in France and other countries because of his many friendships with writers and his work as cofounder in 1909 of *The New French Revue,* an influential literary magazine.

Gide was born in Paris and was raised in a rigid Protestant environment. During a trip to North Africa when he was 24, Gide discovered that he had leanings toward homosexuality. From then on, the themes of his works alternated between the extremes of his puritanical upbringing and his sensual feelings. For example, his story *The Immoralist* (1902) stresses total individual freedom, and *Strait Is the Gate* (1909) emphasizes suppression of physical desire.

Influenced by the novels of the Russian author Fyodor Dostoevsky and the ideas of the German philosopher Friedrich Nietzsche, Gide created characters who express individual choices despite society's moral constraints. The *gratuitous act,* which is seemingly without motivation, is one example of free will. But Gide recognized that all acts are psychologically motivated.

Gide's style is noted for its simplicity, clarity, and occasional irony. He referred to his fiction as *récits* (tales), with the exception of *The Counterfeiters* (1926), which he called a novel. The central character of this work is a novelist writing a novel about a novelist who is writing a novel and theorizing about his art. Gide's récits include *The Pastoral Symphony* (1919) and *Theseus* (1946), his last work, which sums up his life and beliefs. Gide's *Journals* (1889-1949) and correspondence also provide insight into his life and work. Gide wrote several plays, including *Oedipus* (1931).   Elaine D. Cancalon

See also **French literature** (The four masters).

Gideon, *GIHD ee uhn,* in the Old Testament, was a hero of Israel who saved his people from the Midianites. Gideon and 300 followers, each carrying a trumpet and a jar with a torch inside it, surrounded the Midianite army at night. At Gideon's signal, they smashed their jars, blew their trumpets, and shouted. The Midianites fled in terror, and the Israelites slaughtered them. The story is told in Judges 6-8.   J. Maxwell Miller

Gideon v. Wainwright, *GIHD ee uhn,* was a landmark decision of the Supreme Court of the United States concerning the rights of accused persons. The court ruled that a state must provide legal counsel for anyone who is accused of a felony and cannot afford a lawyer. This 1963 decision overruled the 1942 ruling in *Betts v. Brady.* At that time, the court had decided that the right to a lawyer was not essential to a fair trial.

In 1961, Clarence Gideon, a penniless Florida resident, was accused of breaking into a poolroom. He claimed in a Florida court that he was too poor to hire a lawyer and that the state should provide one for him. The state refused, on the basis of the Betts case, and Gideon was convicted.

While in prison, Gideon asked the Supreme Court to review the Florida decision. The court assigned a prominent attorney, Abe Fortas, to plead Gideon's right to counsel. The court ruled that the guarantee of a lawyer, set forth in the Sixth Amendment to the U.S. Constitution, applied in state as well as federal cases. The state provided Gideon with a lawyer, his case was retried, and he was acquitted.

The 1972 case of *Argersinger v. Hamlin* expanded on the Gideon decision. The court ruled that states must provide counsel in any case involving possible imprisonment, however minor the offense.   Stanley I. Kutler

Gideons International, *GIHD ee uhnz,* is an association of Christian business and professional men. It promotes the Christian gospel and the acceptance of Jesus Christ as each individual's personal Saviour.

Gideons International was formed in Janesville, Wisconsin, in 1899. In 1908, the association began placing Bibles in hotel rooms. Since then, the Gideons have distributed more than 500 million Bibles and New Testaments with Psalms and Proverbs to hotels, motels, hospitals, and prisons, and to students, public nurses, and military personnel. The association is active in more than 130 countries. It publishes a monthly magazine, *The Gideon.* The international headquarters are in Nashville.
        Critically reviewed by the Gideons International

Gielgud, *GEEL gud,* **John** (1904-2000), was a leading English actor and director. He became famous for his performances in the plays of William Shakespeare, particularly the title role in *Hamlet.* Gielgud played Hamlet more than 500 times. He directed many of the plays in which he performed. In the late 1950's, Gielgud achieved worldwide recognition when he toured with his one-man show of Shakespearean readings, *Ages of Man.* He won the 1981 Academy Award for best supporting actor for his role in the motion picture *Arthur.*

Keith Butler, Gamma-Liaison
John Gielgud

Gielgud made his stage debut in 1921 in Shakespeare's *Henry V.* He made his screen debut in 1924 in the film *Who Is the Man?* Gielgud also appeared in the films *The Secret Agent* (1936), *Julius Caesar* (1953), *Becket* (1964), *Murder on the Orient Express* (1974), and *Plenty* (1985).

Arthur John Gielgud was born in London. He was knighted in 1953. He wrote two autobiographical works, *Early Stages* (1939) and *An Actor and His Time* (1979). His essays and speeches on acting and directing were published as *Stage Directions* (1963).   John F. Mariani

Gifted children are young people who have extremely high intelligence or exceptional creative ability—or both—in one or more areas. These areas can include art, drama, leadership, mathematics, music, and science. Gifted children need special programs to develop their abilities fully. Such programs encourage creativity, independent thinking, and the use of individual talents, while providing a well-rounded education.

Educators identify gifted children in two chief ways. The youngsters may perform well on tests that measure creativity, intelligence, or a specific skill. Or, they may distinguish themselves through outstanding achievements noticed by their teachers, friends, or parents. Gifted children may be identified at any age, from infancy through young adulthood.

Many schools offer programs that encourage gifted children to develop at their own rate in regular classrooms. For example, a teacher may provide learning materials and individual instruction to help a student investigate a subject beyond the point reached by his or her classmates. Some schools promote gifted children to a higher grade as quickly as they learn the required subjects at each one. In other cases, an exceptional child may be grouped with students at the same level of ability for specific subjects. The gifted child's pace may be accelerated only in that area in which he or she excels. For example, a third-grader with an aptitude for mathematics may take a fifth-grade mathematics course.

Some schools also arrange special activities outside the classroom for gifted children. In addition, the gifted child may be paired with a specialist who coaches the child.   A. Harry Passow

See also **Special education**.

Gigantism. See Giant.

Gikuyu. See Kikuyu.

Gila Cliff Dwellings National Monument, *HEE luh,* lies in southwestern New Mexico, in the Gila Wilderness Area. The monument was established in 1907. It contains ruins of dwellings built by early Indians. The dwellings are about 150 feet (46 meters) up in the sheer walls of a small, wooded canyon. They are made of stone, mud, and timbers. The Indians who lived there farmed the rich bottom lands in the canyon. For the monument's area, see **National Park System** (table: National monuments). See also **Anasazi**.

Critically reviewed by the National Park Service

Gila monster, *HEE luh,* is a large, poisonous lizard. It lives in deserts of the southwestern United States and northern Mexico. This reptile and the Mexican beaded

© Tom Brakefield, Bruce Coleman Inc.

The Gila monster is a poisonous lizard found in deserts of the Southwest. This Gila monster is feeding on quail eggs.

lizard are the only poisonous lizards known.

The Gila monster usually grows to a length of about 16 inches (41 centimeters). It has a stout body, broad blunt head, and stumpy tail. The head and body have areas of black or brown, and of orange or salmon. Fat is stored in its thick tail. The Gila monster can live on this stored-up fat for months without eating.

Gila monsters come out at night during summer and during the day in spring and fall. They eat bird and reptile eggs and young mammals. Gila monsters move slowly, but they can travel long distances.

The Gila monster has a powerful *venom* (poison). It uses the venom mainly to defend itself against creatures. The venom is secreted along the grooves in the teeth at the base of the lower jaw. When the lizard bites a victim, these grooves carry venom into the wound. The bites are painful but not deadly to people.   Raymond B. Huey

Scientific classification. The Gila monster is in the poisonous lizard family, Helodermatidae. Its scientific name is *Heloderma suspectum.*

Gila River, *HEE luh,* rises in the Mogollon Mountains of New Mexico and flows west across Arizona to empty into the Colorado River near Yuma (see **Arizona** [physical map]). The Gila River is 630 miles (1,014 kilometers) long. The river generates hydroelectric power. Since 1928, when Coolidge Dam was completed, farmers have used the river to irrigate large areas of land. Irrigation uses so much water that the river's flow between Coolidge Dam and the Colorado River is disrupted. During years of especially low rainfall, this section often dries up.   Lay James Gibson

See also **Gadsden Purchase**.

Gilbert, Sir Humphrey (1539?-1583), an English scholar and soldier, became famous as a navigator and explorer. He believed there was a northwest passage by water across the North American continent that would lead to the East Indies. He wrote an essay about his theory in 1576. In 1578, Queen Elizabeth I gave him permission to sail in search of a passage. Little is known about the voyage. Gilbert returned to England after losing one of his best ships and one of his bravest captains.

He set sail again in 1583 in command of another expedition. His half brother, Sir Walter Raleigh, started with him. Raleigh and his crew turned back two days after they left Plymouth, but Gilbert went on. He landed in Newfoundland and took possession of the land in the queen's name. On the way back to England, Gilbert and his crew were lost in a severe storm.   Barry M. Gough

See also **Northwest Passage**.

Gilbert, Sir William Schwenck (1836-1911), was one of the most eminent playwrights in Victorian England. He wrote both serious and comic plays, but he became best known for a series of comic operettas he wrote with the English composer Sir Arthur Sullivan.

Gilbert was born in London. He began his literary career in 1861 by contributing articles, a column, and drawings to a periodical called *Fun*. In 1867, the magazine began publishing his comic ballads. They were collected in *Bab Ballads* (1869) and *More Bab Ballads* (1873). The poems provided material for several Gilbert and Sullivan operettas. Gilbert's first work for the theater was a satire on Italian opera staged in 1866. He quickly wrote a number of other successful operatic burlesques. Gilbert and Sullivan began collaborating in 1871. For information about their collaboration, see **Gilbert and Sullivan**.   Katherine K. Preston

Gilbert and Sullivan wrote the most popular operettas in the history of the English theater. Their works are often called *comic operas*. **Sir William Schwenck Gilbert** (1836-1911) and **Sir Arthur Seymour Sullivan** (1842-1900) collaborated on 14 operettas. Most of their works are light-hearted satires on Victorian behavior and the British Empire. Gilbert wrote the charming and witty words; Sullivan, the clear and dramatic music.

Gilbert and Sullivan had contrasting personalities. Gilbert had a sharp, biting wit and Sullivan had a sensitive nature. These differences sometimes led to severe quarrels between them. Despite frequent arguments, they worked together from 1871 to 1896. Their satirical operettas include *The Sorcerer* (1877, rev. 1884), *H.M.S. Pinafore* (1878), *The Pirates of Penzance* (1879), *Patience* (1881), *Iolanthe* (1882), *Princess Ida* (1884), *The Mikado* (1885), *Ruddigore* (1887), *The Gondoliers* (1889), *Utopia Limited* (1893), and *The Grand Duke* (1896). For *The Yeomen of the Guard* (1888), they used a more serious story set in medieval England.

Gilbert and Sullivan's first operetta, *Thespis* (1871), was only moderately successful. They gained popularity with their second work, *Trial by Jury* (1875), which was produced by Richard D'Oyly Carte. D'Oyly Carte also produced the other 12 Gilbert and Sullivan operettas and formed a company to perform the team's works. See **D'Oyly Carte, Richard.**

Gilbert and Sullivan also had independent careers. Gilbert was a noted journalist, humorist, and playwright. His humorous ballads in *Bab Ballads* (1869, 1873) provided material for operettas. He was born in London. Sullivan, one of the most famous English composers of his day, composed the music for the hymn "Onward, Christian Soldiers" (1871) and the song "The Lost Chord" (1877). He was born in London.   Charles H. Webb

See also **Sullivan, Sir Arthur S.**

Additional resources

Bradley, Ian, ed. *The Complete Annotated Gilbert and Sullivan.* Oxford, 1996.
Eden, David. *Gilbert & Sullivan.* Fairleigh Dickinson, 1986.
Stedman, Jane W. *W. S. Gilbert: A Classic Victorian and His Theatre.* Oxford, 1996.

Gilbert Islands are a group of 16 small *atolls* (coral reefs) in the central Pacific Ocean. They lie northeast of Australia and form part of the island country of Kiribati. For location, see **Kiribati** (map). The Gilberts have a total land area of about 105 square miles (272 square kilometers) and a population of about 65,000.

During the 1890's, the United Kingdom took control of the Gilbert Islands and the neighboring Ellice Islands (now Tuvalu). In 1916, the United Kingdom combined the two groups of islands, plus Ocean Island (now called Banaba), to form the Gilbert and Ellice Islands Colony. In 1979, the Gilberts and other islands became the country of Kiribati.   Robert C. Kiste

See also **Kiribati; Tarawa; Tuvalu.**

Gilbreth, Frank and Lillian, were American industrial engineers and were husband and wife. They pioneered in the field of scientific management and improved a technique called *time and motion study.* Such a study analyzes how tasks are done, with the goal of eliminating wasted motion, thus saving time and energy. The Gilbreths wrote a number of books, including *Fatigue Study* (1916) and *Applied Motion Study* (1917).

Frank Bunker Gilbreth (1868-1924) was born in Fairfield, Maine. He started an internationally successful contracting business in 1895. He married Lillian E. Moller in 1904, and they founded a management consulting firm in 1911.

Lillian Evelyn Moller Gilbreth (1878-1972) was born in Oakland, California. She graduated from the University of California and earned a master's degree there. In 1915, she earned a Ph.D. degree at Brown University. After her husband's death, she took over their business and became a leading engineer.   Robert E. Schofield

Gilgamesh, *GIHL guh mehsh,* **Epic of,** a Middle Eastern poem, is one of the oldest epics in world literature. The earliest verses were composed in southern Mesopotamia before 2000 B.C. The most complete text comes from the library of the Assyrian king Ashurbanipal (668-627 B.C.). Fragments of copies were found in Syria and Turkey, showing it was popular throughout the ancient Middle East.

The epic centers around Gilgamesh, a powerful king in ancient Sumeria who oppresses his people. When the people pray for help, the gods create a champion, Enkidu, to meet Gilgamesh in battle. But Enkidu and Gilgamesh become friends and share many adventures until Enkidu dies. Gilgamesh then becomes afraid of death and searches for the secret of immortality. The epic includes an account of a great flood, which has parallels to the Biblical story of Noah.   Carl Lindahl

Gill. See **Fish** (Respiratory system).

Gillespie, *guh LEHS pee,* **Dizzy** (1917-1993), was an American trumpet player, composer, and bandleader. With Charlie Parker and Thelonious Monk, he cofounded the *bebop* or *bop* jazz movement. This movement revitalized the harmonic, melodic, and rhythmic character of jazz. Gillespie pioneered in the development of Afro-Cuban jazz, which combines bop improvisations with Latin rhythms. Many of his compositions are jazz standards, including "A Night in Tunisia," "Groovin' High," "Con Alma," "Salt Peanuts," "Blue 'n Boogie," "Woody 'n You," and "Birks Works."

Gillespie was born in Cheraw, South Carolina. His full name was John Birks Gillespie. From 1937 to 1944, he played in the big bands of Cab Calloway, Earl Hines, Billy Eckstine, and others. Gillespie was a leading figure in the small groups that helped develop bop in the early 1940's. In 1946, Gillespie formed a big band. His original style and brilliant technique established him as a vital new force in music. In 1956, his band was the first to be sponsored on an international tour by the United States Department of State.   Gary Giddins

Gillette, *jih LEHT,* **William** (1855-1937), was a leading American playwright and actor. His 25 plays are filled with swift-moving action and realistic detail, specifically indicated in his elaborate stage directions. Gillette's reputation rests mainly on two plays. *Secret Service* (1895) is a Civil War spy drama. He adapted *Sherlock Holmes* (1899) from the Conan Doyle stories. His performance as Holmes became the model for later actors. His other plays include the Civil War drama *Held by the Enemy* (1886) and the comedy *Too Much Johnson* (1894). He was born in Hartford, Connecticut.   Frederick C. Wilkins

Gillyflower. See **Wallflower.**

Gilman, Charlotte Perkins (1860-1935), was a leading writer on women's rights in the United States. Her writings and lectures influenced the women's movement in the early 1900's. Her best-known book, *Women and Economics* (1898), urged women to work outside the home to gain economic independence.

Gilman attacked traditional marriage, in which the wife takes care of the home and the husband works outside the home. In *Concerning Children* (1900) and *The Home* (1903), she called for the establishment of cooperative apartments where a professional staff could cook, clean, and care for children. Women would then be free to hold jobs. In her novel *Herland* (1915), Gilman described what happened when three men discovered a race of females who had lived without men for 2,000 years. From 1909 to 1916, she published the *Forerunner,* a monthly magazine devoted to improving the position of women in society.

Gilman was born in Hartford, Connecticut. She was largely self-educated.   Carl N. Degler

Gilman, Nicholas (1755-1814), was a New Hampshire signer of the Constitution of the United States. He also helped win *ratification* (approval) of the Constitution by New Hampshire.

Gilman was born in Exeter, New Hampshire. His family was influential in New Hampshire politics. Gilman was a delegate to the Congress of the Confederation from 1787 to 1789. He served four terms in the U.S. House of Representatives, from 1789 to 1797. After a period of service in various New Hampshire state offices, he served as a United States senator from 1805 until his death. Gilman followed more than he led during his long political career and remained a figure of only minor influence. Jere Daniell

Gilmore, Patrick Sarsfield (1829-1892), was the best-known American bandmaster of the 1800's. He developed the first great American band, which became known as Gilmore's Band. It created a sensation during a European tour in 1878. The instrumentation of this band set the basic pattern for modern bands. Gilmore introduced and probably composed the American Civil War song "When Johnny Comes Marching Home" (1863).

Gilmore was born in Ballygar, Ireland, near Dublin. He settled in Salem, Massachusetts, in 1848. He organized two huge music festivals, called Peace Jubilees, in Boston in 1869 and 1872. These festivals raised American performance standards and helped improve American professional bands. Stewart L. Ross

Gin. See Alcoholic beverage (Gin; History).

Gin, Cotton. See Cotton gin.

Ginastera, *HEE nuh STEHR uh,* **Alberto** (1916-1983), was an Argentine composer. Ginastera's most notable works include the highly dramatic and violent operas *Don Rodrigo* (1964), *Bomarzo* (1967), and *Beatrix Cenci* (1971). These operas reflect the influence of motion-picture techniques such as flashbacks and quickly alternating scenes, as well as the *expressionism* of Alban Berg's operas. Until the mid-1940's, Ginastera based his works on Argentine folk music, as in his ballet *Estancia* (1941). His nontheatrical works include a piano sonata (1952), *Variaciones Concertantes* for orchestra (1953), String Quartet No. 2 (1958), and Violin Concerto (1963). Ginastera was born in Buenos Aires. Stephen Jaffe

Ginger is a tangy spice most commonly used in baking, in cooking, and in flavoring beverages. It comes from the *rhizome* (underground stem) of the ginger plant, which is grown throughout tropical Asia, Japan, the West Indies, South America, and western Africa. The finest ginger comes from India and Jamaica.

The long stems and grasslike leaves of the ginger plant sprout directly from the knotty, root-bearing rhizome. Conelike yellowish-green flowers, streaked with purple, grow on the stems. There are four main varieties of the spice: (1) dried, (2) black, (3) white, and (4) preserved. Dried ginger is made by washing and drying the rhizomes. Black ginger is prepared by scalding the rhizomes with water and drying them. In making white ginger, the outer layers of the rhizomes are peeled off before being washed and dried. Preserved ginger is made by peeling the rhizomes and boiling them in syrup. Most preserved ginger is made in China.

Ginger spice is used to flavor such baked goods as biscuits, cookies, gingerbread, and pies, and to season meat and vegetable dishes. It is also an ingredient of ginger ale, ginger tea, and other beverages. The fresh rhizome, called *ginger root,* is used in many dishes, especially in Asian and African cooking. Oil of ginger is used in making perfumes and as a medicine for certain ailments, including stomachache and toothache.

Wild ginger, a plant in the birthwort family, is unrelated to true ginger. It grows in shady woodlands of the Northern United States. It has heart-shaped leaves and one bell-shaped, brownish-purple blossom. Its root is used as a stimulant and a spice. Lyle E. Craker

Scientific classification. Ginger belongs to the family Zingiberaceae. Its scientific name is *Zingiber officinale.* Wild ginger belongs to the family Aristolochiaceae. It is *Asarum canadense.*

Gingerbread tree. See Doum palm.

Gingham is a cloth used to make clothes, curtains, and furniture covers. It is made of colored yarns in a plain weave that has a checked design. Gingham fabrics include chambray, shirting, madras, cheviot shirting, apron check, tissue gingham, and fine Scotch-type gingham. Keith Slater

Gingrich, Newt (1943-   ), a Georgia Republican, served as speaker of the United States House of Representatives from 1995 to 1999. He was a member of the House from 1979 until he resigned in 1999. He was minority whip (assistant leader) from 1989 until 1995.

During the 1994 congressional elections, Gingrich led a Republican movement that included calls for cuts in government spending to balance the federal budget. The goals were outlined in a statement called the *Contract with America.* Under Gingrich's leadership, the Republicans gained their first House majority in 40 years.

In 1997, the House voted to reprimand Gingrich and fine him $300,000. It marked the first time the House had reprimanded a speaker. The action was based on House Ethics Committee findings (1) that Gingrich had used tax-exempt foundation money to promote Republican goals in a televised course he taught and in televised town meetings, and (2) that he gave the committee untrue information during its investigation.

AP/Wide World
Newt Gingrich

Most Republican leaders believed their party would gain seats in the 1998 House elections. However, they lost seats, and dissatisfaction with Gingrich's leadership grew. He resigned as speaker and from Congress in early 1999.

Gingrich was born in Harrisburg, Pennsylvania. His given and family name was Newton Leroy McPherson. When he was a child, his mother divorced his father and married Robert Bruce Gingrich, who adopted him. He earned a bachelor's degree from Emory University in 1965 and a Ph.D. in history from Tulane University in 1971. Gingrich taught history at West Georgia College from 1970 to 1978. His writings include *To Renew America* (1995). Barbara A. Reynolds

Ginkgo, *GIHNG koh,* also called the *maidenhair tree,* is the only surviving member of a group of plants that lived millions of years ago. It served as food for dinosaurs during the Mesozoic Era, which lasted from 248 million to 65 million years ago. For many centuries, the ginkgo has been planted as a sacred tree in Chinese and Japanese Buddhist temple gardens. It is resistant to disease and air pollution.

Ginkgo leaves are fan-shaped and grow in bunches at

Atoz

The ginkgo is a slender ornamental tree with fan-shaped, fern-like leaves. The ginkgo is also called the maidenhair tree.

the end of short stalks. The tree usually stands 60 to 80 feet (18 to 24 meters) tall at maturity. Some ginkgoes are believed to be over 1,000 years old.

Ginkgoes are female or male, carrying either *ovules* (eggs) or pollen on the same short stalks as the leaves. The ovules mature into round seeds covered by yellow to orange flesh. People roast and eat the nutlike meat inside the seeds. However, the flesh is foul-smelling and is irritating to the skin of some people. The pollen-bearing (male) form does not produce seeds. It is planted as a decorative street tree in many countries, including the United States.   Bruce H. Tiffney

Scientific classification. The ginkgo makes up the division Ginkgophyta and the ginkgo family, Ginkgoaceae. Its scientific name is *Ginkgo biloba.*

See also **Gymnosperm; Tree** (Ginkgo trees).

Ginnie Mae. See **Government National Mortgage Association.**

Ginsberg, Allen (1926-1997), was an American poet. He became known as a leader of the *beat* literary movement of the 1950's and also of the cultural and political protests of the 1960's. Critics praised him as a prophetic poet in the tradition of William Blake of England and Walt Whitman of the United States.

Ginsberg's writing combines the spiritual and rhythmic qualities of certain Eastern and Western religious texts with the language, imagery, and subject matter of modern life. Many critics see him as representing a struggle for spiritual survival in a dehumanized, repressive society. Ginsberg's long poem "Howl" (1956) attacks the forces of conformity and mechanization that he believed destroyed the best minds of his generation.

Ginsberg was born in Newark, New Jersey. The death of his mother in 1956 inspired his famous elegy "Kaddish" (1961). His other works include *Reality Sandwiches* (1963), *The Fall of America: Poems of These States* (1972), and *Mind Breaths* (1978). His *Selected Poems 1947-1995 was published in 1997.*   Bonnie Costello

See also **Beat movement.**

Ginsburg, Ruth Bader (1933-   ), became an associate justice of the Supreme Court of the United States

in 1993. She is the second woman to serve on the court. Sandra Day O'Connor became the first. Ginsburg was appointed to the Surpeme Court by President Bill Clinton.

Ginsburg was born in New York City. She graduated from Cornell University in 1954 and earned a law degree from Columbia University in 1959. She taught law at Rutgers The State University of New Jersey from 1963 to 1972 and at Columbia University from 1972 to 1980. During the 1970's, Ginsburg served as general counsel to the American Civil Liberties Union. In this position, she argued and won before the Supreme Court a number of cases involving equality between the sexes. She has been an active supporter of women's rights.

In 1980, President Jimmy Carter appointed Ginsburg, a Democrat, to the United States Court of Appeals for the District of Columbia. During her 13 years as a member of this court, Ginsburg became known as a moderate who worked to bring about agreement between her liberal and conservative colleagues.   Sheldon Goldman

See also **Supreme Court of the United States** (picture).

Ginseng, *JIHN sehng,* is a perennial herb of eastern Asia and eastern North America. It is a low plant with three to five leaves on top. Each leaf has five leaflets. Ginseng has a long, fleshy root whose shape somewhat resembles that of a human body. The plant's name comes from Chinese words meaning *likeness of a man.*

The ginseng root is used as a medicine in a number of countries. However, its medical value has not been proven. Manufacturers may add ginseng to such products as hair tonics, shampoos, skin creams, and soft drinks. The root is dried, sold whole, and then ground into a powder or processed into tablets.

Wild ginseng has almost disappeared, and the plant is grown chiefly in China, Korea, and the United States. Most American ginseng is exported to China.

Lyle E. Craker

Scientific classification. Ginseng is in the family Araliaceae. The scientific name for the American species is *Panax quinquefolius.* The Asian species is *P. ginseng.*

WORLD BOOK illustration by John D. Dawson

American ginseng has tiny flowers and berries. The Chinese use the long, fleshy roots of this plant for medicine.

Giorgione, *jawr JAW neh* (1478?-1510), was an Italian artist who helped make Venice a center of painting during the Italian Renaissance. His richly colored pictures influenced Venetian artists in the 1500's.

Unlike other Italian painters of his time, Giorgione did not emphasize religious themes. Instead, he used non-religious subjects set in rural landscapes. He achieved a moody, shadowy feeling by applying paint in a loose, sketchy manner. Giorgione's *Concert Champêtre* (about 1510) illustrates his style. This painting features five figures, including two nude women, in a landscape setting. Giorgione's hazy light gives the figures a dreamy, romantic appearance. The rich colors, soft flesh tones, and merging of the figures into the background are typical of his style.

Giorgione was born in the village of Castelfranco, near Venice, and died of the plague in his early 30's. He did not sign his paintings, and so scholars still dispute which works are entirely his. Only six paintings are accepted as his own, including *The Tempest,* which appears in the **Painting** article.　　Donald Rabiner

Giotto, *JAH toh* (1267?-1337), was the most important painter of the 1300's. His realistic style revolutionized painting in Italy and became a strong influence on the Renaissance masters of the 1400's.

Giotto's works. At the time of Giotto's birth, Italian painters followed the medieval Byzantine style, which portrayed subjects in a flat, unrealistic manner. Giotto, on the other hand, painted solid, natural-looking forms. For example, to show how light shines on an object in nature, he illuminated one side of the object while painting the other side of it in shadow.

Giotto's *Madonna Enthroned with Saints* shows some of the natural, lifelike qualities he introduced into the art of his time. Giotto painted the throne of the *Madonna* (Virgin Mary) with open sides. He showed two bearded men looking through the openings. In this way, Giotto increased the feeling that the scene is not flat but realistically recedes into space. However, Giotto followed the medieval tradition of making the Madonna larger than the saints and angels who surround her.

Giotto's greatest achievement was the series of frescoes he painted inside the Scrovegni, or Arena, Chapel in Padua. Most of these are scenes from the lives of Jesus and the Virgin Mary. They show Giotto's genius at painting natural and simple compositions that express deep human emotions in a moving but restrained way. For pictures of Giotto's work, see **Jesus Christ; Mural; Painting** (picture: *Joachim with the Shepherds*).

Giotto's last great surviving paintings are frescoes in the Church of Santa Croce in Florence. In these works, Giotto used more complicated compositions than he did in the Scrovegni frescoes.

Giotto was also an architect. In 1334, he became chief architect of the Cathedral of Florence. Giotto designed the *campanile* (bell tower) that still stands beside it.

His life. Giotto, the son of a poor shepherd, was born in a village near Florence. His real name was Giotto di Bondone. Scholars know little about Giotto's early life or his beginnings as an artist. According to one legend, Giotto was watching his father's sheep and sketching pictures of them on a rock with a sharp stone. The famous Italian painter Giovanni Cimabue happened to be passing by and saw him. The youth's talent impressed

Tempera and gold painting on wood (about 1310) from the Church of the Ognissanti, Florence, Italy; Uffizi Gallery, Florence (SCALA/Art Resource)

Giotto's Madonna and Child Enthroned reflects a new sense of realism that appeared in Italian art in the 1300's through the solid quality of the Virgin Mary, Christ Child, and other figures.

Cimabue so much that he made Giotto his apprentice.

The earliest surviving works definitely attributed to Giotto are the Scrovegni frescoes (about 1305 to 1310). But he had become famous much earlier. In the late 1200's, a cathedral was built at Assisi to honor Saint Francis. The leading Italian artists were asked to paint frescoes in the cathedral. There is no definite evidence that Giotto worked on the project. But many scholars believe he was commissioned to paint the most important frescoes—those portraying scenes from the life of Saint Francis.　　Donald Rabiner

Giovanni, Nikki (1943-　), is an American poet, essayist, and children's writer. She is known for her writings about the experiences of black people, particularly women, living in American cities. Many of Giovanni's early poems deal with social revolution and the possibility of violence. Her later work is more personal, dealing with childhood and family experiences and love relationships, often with humor. Many of Giovanni's poems effectively use jazz and blues rhythms. She became a leader in the revival of oral and performance art and often gives readings of her works.

Giovanni's collections of poems include *Black Feeling, Black Talk* (1968); *Black Judgement* (1968); *Re: Creation* (1970); *My House* (1972); *The Women and the Men* (1975);

Cotton Candy on a Rainy Day (1978); and *Those Who Ride the Night Winds* (1983). Many of her children's poems are in *Ego Tripping and Other Poems for Young People* (1973). Her essays are in *Gemini* (1971) and *Sacred Cows ... and Other Edibles* (1988).

Giovanni was born in Knoxville, Tennessee. Her full name is Yolande Cornelia Giovanni, Jr.

Linda Wagner-Martin

Giraffe is the tallest of all animals. Male giraffes may grow more than 18 feet (5.5 meters) tall—5 feet (1.5 meters) taller than the African elephant, the second tallest animal. Most adult male giraffes stand about 17 feet (5.2 meters) tall, and most females grow to about 14 feet (4.3 meters) in height. The giraffe gets its great height from its legs, which are 6 feet (1.8 meters) long, and a neck that may be even longer. But even though giraffes tower over other animals, most adult males weigh only about 2,600 pounds (1,200 kilograms). A male African elephant may weigh more than five times as much.

Giraffes live in Africa south of the Sahara in open woodlands. They feed on the leaves, twigs, and fruit of trees and bushes. A giraffe, like a cow, chews a *cud,* which is food that has entered the stomach but is returned to the mouth for a second chewing. Giraffes can go without drinking water for many weeks.

The body of a giraffe. A giraffe's coat has patchlike markings of *tawny* (light brownish-yellow) to chestnut-brown. The lines that separate the patches are lighter tawny or white. This color pattern helps protect giraffes by making them hard to see when they stand among trees. Each individual giraffe has its own distinct coat pattern.

Two bony "horns" grow from a giraffe's skull. These horns, which are covered by skin and hair, resemble a deer's antlers before the antlers develop branches. They are not true horns because they do not have a horny covering. Some giraffes also have one or more short

Where giraffes live

The yellow areas of this map show where giraffes live. Most giraffes live in national parks or game preserves in Africa.

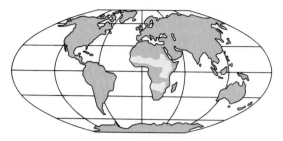

hornlike bumps on the forehead. The horns of the female are smaller than those of the male.

A giraffe can close its nostrils completely to keep out sand and dust. It uses its long upper lip and its tongue, which is about 21 inches (53 centimeters) long, to gather food from tree branches. Giraffes have good vision and hearing. A giraffe seldom uses its voice, though it can utter a variety of soft sounds.

Despite the length of its neck, a giraffe has only seven neck bones—the same number that human beings and most other mammals have. A short mane grows along the back of the neck from the head to the shoulders. The sloping back measures about 5 feet (1.5 meters) from the base of the neck to the base of the tail. The tail, which is about 3 feet (91 centimeters) long, ends in a tuft of long, black hairs. A giraffe's hoofs are split into two parts. Each part consists of the hardened tip of one toe. A giraffe's closest relative—and the only other member of the giraffe family—is the okapi (see **Okapi**).

The life of a giraffe. A female giraffe carries her young inside her body for about 15 months before giving birth. Giraffes bear one baby at a time, except for rare cases of twins. At birth, a *calf* (baby giraffe) may stand as tall as 6 feet (1.8 meters) and weigh as much as 150 pounds (68 kilograms). It can stand up within an hour. The *cow* (female giraffe) nurses its young with milk for 9 or 10 months, though the baby eats small amounts of green plants from the age of 2 weeks. A female can bear her first baby when she is 5 years old. In the wild, giraffes may live as long as 28 years.

Giraffes walk by moving both legs on one side of the body forward almost together and then both legs on the other side. When they gallop, both hind feet swing forward and land outside and in front of the front feet. Giraffes can gallop up to 35 miles (56 kilometers) per hour.

To drink, a giraffe spreads its forelegs far apart, or bends them forward, so that its mouth can reach down to the water. A giraffe usually sleeps standing up. When lying down, it holds its neck upright or rests it on one of its hips or on a low tree limb.

Female giraffes and their young often form small, loosely organized groups. They are joined from time to time by an adult male. Giraffes stay in the same general area for most of their lives. This area often covers about 29 square miles (75 square kilometers). A *bull* (male giraffe) fights with another bull by butting its head against the chest or neck of its opponent. If a fight becomes serious, the powerful blows may be heard at a distance of 100 yards (91 meters). However, the animals rarely injure

A. Myers, De Wys, Inc.

Giraffes live in small groups on African grasslands. They feed on leaves, twigs, and fruit from trees that grow in scattered groves. Every giraffe has its own distinct coat pattern.

The skeleton of a giraffe

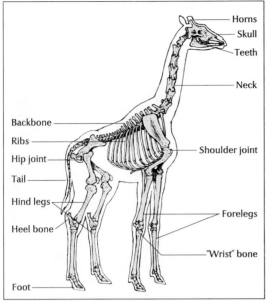

WORLD BOOK illustration by John D. Dawson

Giraffe tracks

Hind feet

Front feet

Norman Myers, Bruce Coleman Inc.

To bend down, a giraffe spreads its forelegs and then lowers its head. This animal is licking salt from a natural salt deposit.

each other. Female giraffes do not fight.

Lions are the only animals that attack adult giraffes. A lion may kill a giraffe if it catches the victim lying down or if it springs onto the giraffe's back from ambush. Giraffes defend themselves by kicking with their feet. Their kicks are sometimes powerful enough to kill a lion. Young giraffes may be killed by lions, leopards, cheetahs, hyenas, and crocodiles.

Giraffes and people. People have greatly reduced the number of giraffes by hunting them and by changing lands once occupied by giraffes into farms. Today, most giraffes live in national parks or game preserves.

People use giraffes for many purposes. For example, some African tribes use the tail hairs for bracelets and string. They use the hides for shields and twist shredded *tendons* (cords of tissue that connect muscle to bone) to make bowstrings.

A few African ranches raise giraffes for meat. Some experts have urged that greater use be made of such animals as giraffes, hippopotamuses, and African antelope for this purpose. The meat provided by such animals could improve the diet of millions of Africans who eat little meat. These animals gain weight more quickly on a diet of tropical plants than do cattle or sheep. In addition, giraffes eat food that grows so high in trees that it cannot be reached by other kinds of animals eaten by people.   Anne Innis Dagg

Scientific classification. The giraffe belongs to the giraffe family, Giraffidae. It is *Giraffa camelopardalis.*

Giraudoux, ZHEER oh DOO, **Jean,** zhahn (1882-1944), was a prominent French playwright. His work was especially noted for its stylistic elegance and poetic fantasy. Giraudoux's dominant theme is the relationship between men and women. In many of his plays, a young woman must choose between a man who represents an impossible romantic ideal and one who can provide an unexciting but stable existence.

Giraudoux was born in Bellac, near Limoges. He had distinguished careers in the French foreign service and as a novelist before he began writing plays. His love for German culture inspired his first play, *Siegfried* (1928), as well as *Ondine* (1939). Giraudoux drew upon classical Greek sources for *Amphitryon 38* (1929), *Tiger at the Gates* (1935), and *Electra* (1937). The Bible inspired his dramas *Judith* (1931) and *Sodom and Gomorrah* (1943). Three popular plays were staged after Giraudoux's death, *The Madwoman of Chaillot* (1945), *The Apollo of Bellac* (1946), and *Duel of Angels* (1953).

Felicia Hardison Londré

Girl Guides is an international organization for girls between the ages of 6 and 18. The Girl Guides movement began in England soon after Lord Baden-Powell introduced the Boy Scout movement there. In 1909, Baden-Powell officially recognized the Guides and published the pamphlet *Scheme of Training for Girl Guides.*

His sister, Agnes Baden-Powell, served as first commissioner of the Girl Guides and helped organize the Girl Guides Association. By 1910, the movement had spread to Canada and many other parts of the British Commonwealth and also to other countries. The organization is called Girl Scouts in the United States and its possessions. For a fuller discussion of Girl Guides, see the **Girl Scouts** article. See also **Baden-Powell, Lord.**

Critically reviewed by the Girl Guides of Canada

Girl Scouts of the USA

Girl Scouts is an organization that helps girls of different ages learn personal values and useful skills. These Cadette, Brownie, and Senior Girl Scouts represent different levels of Girl Scouts.

Girl Scouts

Girl Scouts is an organization dedicated to helping girls build character and develop skills for success. Through Girl Scout activities, girls discover the fun, friendship, and power of working together. In partnership with committed adults, they develop strong values, social conscience, and conviction about their own potential and self-worth.

In the United States, the official name of the organization is Girl Scouts of the USA. In Canada and many other countries, members of similar organizations are known as Girl Guides. The organizations of Girl Scouts and Girl Guides throughout the world make up the World Association of Girl Guides and Girl Scouts.

All Girl Scouts and Girl Guides have a pledge called a Promise and a set of standards called a Law. The exact wording of the Promise and the Law varies from country to country. In the United States, the Girl Scout Promise is:

On my honor, I will try:
To serve God and my country,
To help people at all times,
And to live by the Girl Scout Law.

In the United States, the Girl Scout Law is:

I will do my best to be
Honest and fair,
Friendly and helpful,
Considerate and caring,
Courageous and strong, and
Responsible for what I say and do,

And to
Respect myself and others,
Respect authority,
Use resources wisely,
Make the world a better place, and
Be a sister to every Girl Scout.

The emblem of the Girl Scouts and Girl Guides is a *trefoil,* or three-leaf clover. It stands for the three parts of the Promise. The symbol of Girl Scouts of the USA has the profiles of three young women. The Girl Scout and Girl Guide motto is *Be Prepared.*

Girl Scouts of the USA

Girls from 5 to 17 years old may become Girl Scouts. The Girl Scout program has five levels: (1) Daisy Girl Scouts, (2) Brownie Girl Scouts, (3) Junior Girl Scouts, (4) Cadette Girl Scouts, and (5) Senior Girl Scouts. Girls may enter the program at any level appropriate to their age. For example, a girl can become a Junior Girl Scout even if she has not been a Brownie. Girls from all walks of life are encouraged to take part in Girl Scouting, regardless of race, religion, or ability. Girl Scouts are organized into

Girl Scouts of the USA

Girl Scout emblem

troops, which include girls of the same age level, and *groups,* which include girls from various age levels. Adult volunteers supervise Girl Scout activities. These men and women may serve as advisers, troop committee members, leaders, or council or national board members.

Every member of the Girl Scouts pays dues to the national organization and her troop or group. The national organization publishes handbooks and *Leader Magazine* for adult volunteers. It also maintains two national centers that serve as meeting places for Girl Scouts and visitors from other countries. The centers are in Savannah, Georgia, and in Briarcliff Manor, New York. The Girl Scouts' national headquarters are in New York City.

Daisy Girl Scouts are 5 to 6 years old or in kindergarten. To become a Daisy Girl Scout, a girl attends meetings and learns the Promise and the Law. She then takes part in an *investiture* (formal enrollment) ceremony and receives a membership pin and certificate.

Adult volunteers and teen-age Girl Scouts organize Daisy Girl Scout activities. Typical activities include storytelling, playing games, and performing service projects. The Daisy Girl Scout level originated in 1984. It is named after Girl Scout founder Juliette Gordon Low, whose nickname was Daisy. Daisy Girl Scouts wear blue *tunics* (shirtlike garments extending below the waist).

Brownie Girl Scouts are 6 to 8 years old or in the first, second, or third grade. To become a Brownie, a girl who has been a Daisy Girl Scout participates in a *bridging* (graduation) ceremony. She receives a Brownie Girl Scout pin and a certificate marking the completion of her year as a Daisy Girl Scout. A girl who has not been a Daisy Girl Scout makes the Promise and receives a Brownie Girl Scout pin at an investiture ceremony.

Brownie activities may include computer projects on the World Wide Web, mathematics and science experiments, and community service. The girls practice hospitality and service at home and in their communities. They can earn awards called Try-Its by completing activities in different areas. During their last year as Brownie Girl Scouts, girls may work in groups to learn more about Junior Girl Scouting. They may also visit Junior Girl Scout troop meetings. Brownie Girl Scouts wear brown uniforms.

Junior Girl Scouts are 8 to 11 years old or in the third, fourth, fifth, or sixth grades. To become a Junior Girl Scout, a girl who has been a Brownie Girl Scout participates in a *fly-up* ceremony. At this ceremony, she receives the Brownie Girl Scout wings emblem and a Girl Scout pin. She also renews the Girl Scout Promise. A girl who has not been a Brownie Girl Scout makes the Promise and receives her Girl Scout pin at an investiture ceremony.

Junior Girl Scouting explores careers and enables girls to investigate particular fields of interest. Junior Girl Scouts can earn a wide variety of badges and other emblems called *signs* in such areas as science and technology, the arts, health and fitness, sports, and global awareness. They may also earn the Junior Aide Award for assisting Brownie Girl Scouts who are bridging to become Junior Girl Scouts. Girls can also receive a Bridge to Cadette Girl Scout Award after completing activities in preparation for becoming a Cadette Girl Scout. Junior Girl Scouts wear green.

Girl Scouts of the USA

Adult volunteers supervise Girl Scout activities. These Daisy Girl Scouts are learning about science and nature, under the guidance of their adult leader.

Cadette Girl Scouts are 11 to 14 years old or in the sixth, seventh, eighth, or ninth grades. Cadette Girl Scouting stresses the exploration of career opportunities in many areas, such as the arts, business, health, science, and social services. Cadette Girl Scouts learn what abilities, values, training, and education are required for different jobs.

Senior Girl Scouts are 14 to 17 years old or in the 9th, 10th, 11th, or 12th grades. Senior Girl Scouting offers further opportunities for career exploration, self-improvement, community service, and fun. Senior Girl Scouts evaluate their interests and participate in such career experiences as volunteer work and paying jobs. Both Cadette and Senior Girl Scouts wear khaki.

Cadette and Senior Girl Scouts may earn awards for projects in such areas as automobile mechanics, fashion, energy conservation, and money management. Adult leaders help the girls plan projects and gather necessary resources. Cadette and Senior Girl Scouts may earn volunteer service bars, recognition for activities in career exploration, and leadership awards.

Cadette and Senior Girl Scouts may also work on two

Girl Scouts of the USA

Outdoor activities, such as camping and hiking, are an important part of the Girl Scout program. Girl Scouts learn to respect and protect the environment through such activities.

Junior Girl Scout badges

Girl Scouts earn badges by learning skills in various fields. Junior Girl Scouts choose from among a wide range of badges on different subjects, each with its own set of requirements. Ten of the most popular badges are shown here. Girl Scouts wear their badges on the uniform sash.

Girl Scouts of the USA

Girl Scouting in the USA   Fun and Fit   Global Awareness   Ms. Fix-It   Sports Sampler

Science Sleuth   Discovering Technology   Healthy Relationships   Horse Fan   Troop Camper

challenges called the Challenge of Being a Girl Scout and the Challenge of Living the Promise and Law. The challenges are steps toward the Girl Scout Silver Award and the Girl Scout Gold Award. The Girl Scout Gold Award is the highest achievement in Girl Scouting. Both awards require hard work and a special commitment to assisting the community and the world.

Uniforms are not required for participation in Girl Scouting. However, many girls and adults choose to wear uniforms to be recognized and to show their pride. Many girls wear the awards they have earned, such as pins and badges, on a sash or a vest.

Uniforms for the different Girl Scout levels vary in style and color. They can involve skirts, blouses, dresses, jumpers, pants, culottes, shorts, T-shirts, and sweaters. Adults in Girl Scouting wear forest-green uniforms. Uniform designs change about every seven years to keep pace with the changing tastes of Girl Scout members. Often, when girls or adults are representing the Girl Scout organization, they simply wear a Girl Scout membership pin and regular clothes.

Annual events. Girl Scouts of the USA observes special days throughout the year. On Founders Day, October 31, Girl Scouts honor the birthday of Girl Scout founder Juliette Gordon Low. They also celebrate Girl Scout Week during the week in which March 12 falls. Girl Scout Week honors the first Girl Scout group meeting in the United States, which was held on March 12, 1912. During Girl Scout Week, members perform volunteer work in their communities and learn more about the Girl Scout organization. On Thinking Day, February 22, they celebrate the birthday of Lord Baden-Powell, who started the Boy Scout movement and organized the Girl Guides in England. Girl Scouts and Girl Guides throughout the world observe Thinking Day by thinking about international friendship.

Troops, groups, and councils. Girls and adults participate in Girl Scouting through activities in official

troops and in less formal groups. Girl Scout troops and groups have adult leaders. Members of each troop elect a leader, a scribe, and a treasurer. These officers and the troop or group leader make up the Court of Honor, which meets before or after every meeting to organize activities. A troop committee, which consists of parents of troop members and other interested adults, supports and assists in troop activities.

Girl Scout troops and groups are organized by Girl Scout *councils*. Councils are local units established by the national organization to administer and develop Girl Scouting in a specific geographical region. Local Girl Scout councils are responsible for recruiting girls and leaders. Girl Scout councils must meet strict standards to maintain their charter from the national organization. Each local Girl Scout council sends delegates to the Girl Scout National Council. The National Council meets every three years to review Girl Scout policy and to elect a board of directors. The directors set goals and policy for the organization.

Girl Guides of Canada-Guides du Canada

The activities and organization of Girl Guides of Canada are similar to those of Girl Scouts of the USA. The Canadian organization's official name appears in both English and French: Girl Guides of Canada-Guides du Canada.

The Girl Guide program is designed to enrich a girl's life and to benefit the lives of the people around her. It challenges girls to reach their potential and empowers them to give leadership and service as responsible citizens of the world. Girl Guides of Canada-Guides du Canada is an all-female organization in which women provide role models for girls. Guiding for girls is divided into five age groups. These groups are (1) Sparks, (2) Brownies, (3) Guides, (4) Pathfinders, and (5) Senior Branches.

The Girl Guide program is based on their Mission and

their Principles of Guiding, which outline the organization's philosophy and goals. Each girl must make the Promise to become a member. The Guides' main paths of discovery include camping, the home, the community, the outdoors, and the world.

Girl Guides pay an annual fee to the national organization and sometimes a small weekly fee to cover unit expenses. Girl Guides of Canada-Guides du Canada publishes *The Canadian Guider* magazine for adult leaders and several Girl Guide handbooks. National headquarters are in Toronto.

Sparks are 5 and 6 years old. They enjoy a program of playing, singing, listening to stories, outdoor fun, and creative activities in a relaxed and caring atmosphere. By promising to "share and be a friend," Sparks learn interpersonal skills and the value of friendship. They wear a pink T-shirt or sweatshirt.

Brownies are 7 and 8 years old. In any Brownie unit, there are at least two adult Brownie Guiders. One of them is called Brown Owl. The others have different owl names, such as Tawny Owl or Snowy Owl. Brownie units are divided into smaller groups called *circles,* which consist of up to six girls each. Brownies take part in a program that has three areas of focus, called Windows: (1) My Window on People, (2) My Window on the Outdoors, and (3) My Window on Today and Tomorrow.

Brownies learn cooperation through group activities and games. Activities, such as hiking and camping, encourage development of individual talents, friendships, and concern for others. Brownies wear a brown dress with a brown and orange belt, or a T-shirt or sweatshirt with brown pants. They may also wear an orange tie, a brown badge sash, and the official Brownie pin, which is in the shape of an elf.

Guides may be 9 to 12 years old. They are formed into *patrols* of about six girls each, and four or five patrols make up a unit. Each patrol has a Patrol Leader. The adult leaders are called Guiders. The Unit Council is the decision-making body of the Guide unit.

Guides attend weekly meetings where they work in small groups to plan activities. Guides enjoy the excitement of camping, the satisfaction of connecting with their communities, and a variety of activities that help develop initiative and resourcefulness. Guides wear a blue dress with a blue-and-red belt, or a T-shirt or sweatshirt with blue pants. They also wear a white tie, a blue badge sash, and a gold enrollment pin.

Pathfinders are 12 to 15 years old. Pathfinder units have about 15 girls and at least 2 Guiders. Every member of a Pathfinder unit has an equal voice in all decisions. Everyone discusses and decides on group activities. A chairwoman may be selected by the unit to guide discussions and to help the group arrive at decisions.

Pathfinders explore the community, the outdoors, the home, and the world. Community service projects and camping are important in the Pathfinder program. Pathfinders wear a navy-blue skirt or pants with a blue-and-white striped blouse, a T-shirt, or a sweatshirt. They wear a green tie, green emblem sash, and green enrollment pin.

Pathfinders may earn any of several emblems: the Be Prepared Emblem, the Camping Emblem, the Community Emblem, the Home Emblem, the Leadership Emblem, the Outdoor Emblem, and the World Emblem. Girls may also earn the Religion in Life Emblem. By earning emblems, each girl can further her interests and work at her own pace.

Senior Branches are for young women 15 to 17 years old and older. There are three Senior Branch programs: (1) Cadets, (2) Junior Leaders, and (3) Rangers. Cadets gain practical experience in different branches of Guiding. Cadets meet as a unit to exchange ideas and plan activities. Junior Leaders work individually in Spark, Brownie, or Guide units, helping the adult leaders. Rangers plan and lead their own activities based on the program's interest areas. They enjoy a wide variety of activities designed to help them understand their community, their roles as women and citizens, and the world as a global village. Camping is popular with members of all three Senior Branches.

Members of the Senior Branches wear navy-blue pants or a skirt, with a blue-and-white striped blouse or polo shirt or a navy-blue sweatshirt. Cadets wear a yellow tie and a white trefoil pin. Junior Leaders wear a navy-blue tie and a navy-blue trefoil pin. Rangers wear a red tie and a red trefoil pin.

Lones. Girls who are unable to attend regular meetings because of distance, health, work, or studies can become members of Lone units. Lones carry out the program of their branch through correspondence and often take part in camps and events with active units. Girls interested in becoming Lones should contact the nearest Girl Guide office or the national headquarters.

In other countries

The World Association of Girl Guides and Girl Scouts represents national organizations in more than 140

Pathfinder emblems

Pathfinders may earn several different emblems representing the Girl Guides' paths of discovery. The Be Prepared Emblem combines safety awareness elements of the different paths.

Girl Guides of Canada

Outdoor

World

Camping

Home

Community

Be Prepared

Craig Pryce, Girl Guides of Canada

Girl Guides of Canada helps girls learn about the world by developing skills in many areas. These Girl Guides are building a bird feeder to earn their woodworking badge.

countries throughout the world. More than 10 million girls and adult leaders belong to the World Association. The association aims to provide girls with opportunities for individual development, responsible citizenship, and community service. It maintains four centers: Pax Lodge in London; Our Chalet near Adelboden, Switzerland; Our Cabaña in Cuernavaca, Mexico; and Sangam in Pune, India. The centers provide accommodations and meeting places for visiting Girl Scouts and Girl Guides at international Girl Scout and Girl Guide events.

History

Robert Baden-Powell, a British Army officer, began the Boy Scouts in 1907 to give boys training in citizenship. Many girls wanted to belong to a similar group, so he helped work out the principles for a separate organization. The Girl Guides program began in England in 1909. The movement quickly spread to other lands.

The first registered Canadian Guide Company was formed in 1910 in St. Catharines, Ontario. The same year, companies began elsewhere in Canada, including Toronto, Saskatchewan, Manitoba, and Newfoundland. In 1917, the Canadian Parliament granted a charter to the Canadian Council of the Girl Guides Association.

In 1920, Baden-Powell's wife, Olave, called the first international conference. Members from 15 countries met in the United Kingdom. World conferences are now held every three years for representatives from all the member countries of the World Association.

Juliette Gordon Low established Girl Guiding in the United States in 1912. She soon changed the name to Girl Scouting. Low held the first group meeting in her home in Savannah, Georgia, on March 12, 1912. The organization opened its national headquarters in Washington, D.C., in 1913. The headquarters later were moved to New York City. The national organization was incorpo-

rated in 1915, and Low became the first president. In 1950, the U.S. Congress issued a charter to Girl Scouts of the USA.

Girl Scouts of the USA was a founding member of the World Association of Girl Guides and Girl Scouts. It has been active in international programs throughout its history, especially since the mid-1900's. The Juliette Low World Friendship Fund, made up of voluntary contributions from Girl Scouts in the United States, provides partial financing for international exchange visits of Girl Guides and Girl Scouts. The fund also helps develop Girl Guiding on all continents by preparing training materials in other languages and by providing equipment.

Critically reviewed by Girl Scouts of the USA and Girl Guides of Canada-Guides du Canada

See also **Baden-Powell, Lord; Boy Scouts; Girl Guides; Low, Juliette Gordon; Scouts Canada.**

Outline

I. Girl Scouts of the USA
 A. Daisy Girl Scouts
 B. Brownie Girl Scouts
 C. Junior Girl Scouts
 D. Cadette Girl Scouts
 E. Senior Girl Scouts
 F. Uniforms
 G. Annual events
 H. Troops, groups, and councils
II. Girl Guides of Canada-Guides du Canada
 A. Sparks
 B. Brownies
 C. Guides
 D. Pathfinders
 E. Senior Branches
 F. Lones
III. In other countries
IV. History

Questions

What is the Girl Scout Promise?
What is the Court of Honor?
What is an *investiture* ceremony?
Who was Juliette Gordon Low?
What roles do adults play in Girl Scout activities?
What is a *fly-up* ceremony?
What is a *patrol*? A *troop*? The National Council?
What is the Girl Scout Law?
Who was Robert Baden-Powell?
What is the World Association of Girl Guides and Girl Scouts?

Additional resources

Kudlinski, Kathleen V. *Juliette Gordon Low: America's First Girl Scout.* Viking, 1988. Younger readers.
Soto, Carolyn. *The Girl Scouts.* Exeter Bks., 1987. Younger readers.
Trefoil Round the World: Girl Guiding and Girl Scouting in Many Lands. Rev. ed. World Assn. of Girl Guides and Girl Scouts, 1992. Younger readers.
The Wide World of Girl Guiding and Girl Scouting. Girl Scouts of the USA, 1980. Younger readers.
Handbooks and other publications for each level of scouting are available from the Girl Scouts of the USA.

Girls and Boys Town is a private institution for homeless, abused, neglected, and disabled children of every race and religion. It is near Omaha, Nebraska. The town includes housing, recreational facilities, a grade school, high school, and career center. It cares for thousands of boys and girls each year. Girls and Boys Town also runs youth centers throughout the country and an institute for children with communication disorders.

The institution was established as Boys Town in 1917 by Edward J. Flanagan, a Roman Catholic priest. It was also known as Father Flanagan's Boys' Home. Flanagan believed that if boys received the best possible home, education, and training, they would grow up to be productive members of society. Flanagan borrowed $90 to rent an old house in Omaha to care for five boys. As more boys moved into the house, it became necessary to move to larger quarters. In 1921, Flanagan bought a 160-acre (65-hectare) farm.

Over the years, the farm was enlarged. Today, it covers 900 acres (364 hectares), including about 500 acres (200 hectares) of farmland. Boys Town was incorporated as a village in 1936. The institution first admitted girls in 1979. In 2000, the national program headquartered at Boys Town, Nebraska, changed its name to Girls and Boys Town. Critically reviewed by Girls and Boys Town

See also **Flanagan, Edward Joseph; Nebraska** (picture: Boys Town Hall of History).

Girls Incorporated is an organization of community clubs in the United States for girls age 6 through 18. The organization helps girls reach their potential through programs that promote self-reliance, responsibility, leadership, and teamwork. It also encourages them to set realistic, constructive life goals.

About 250,000 girls belong to more than 200 Girls Incorporated centers in approximately 120 U.S. cities. About half the members are from minority groups, and about half come from families headed by a single parent. Most Girls Incorporated clubs are in low-income areas.

The clubs provide activities after school, on weekends, and during the summer. They offer programs and services in health care; family life; sports and physical fitness; youth leadership; and the prevention of teen-age pregnancy, drug abuse, and the disease AIDS. The clubs also offer programs in job training and career development. Many of these programs focus on math, science, and modern technology.

Each club has at least one professional administrator who serves as its executive director, plus other paid and volunteer workers. Local clubs are managed by a board of directors who represent many segments of the community. Girls Incorporated is supported by United Way campaigns in many communities and by funds from corporations, foundations, and individuals.

Girls Incorporated was formed in 1945 as Girls Clubs of America, Inc. The group changed its name to Girls Incorporated in 1990. Headquarters are in New York City. Critically reviewed by Girls Incorporated

See also **Boys Clubs of America.**

Girls State is a program for training girls in democratic leadership, sponsored by the American Legion Auxiliary. Girls who have completed their third year in high school take part in statewide training courses called *Girls States.* The girls practice operating the machinery of democratic government. They hold political party conventions and nominate candidates for state office. They wage political campaigns and hold elections. The winners are installed in office. Legislative, executive, and judicial branches of these miniature state governments carry out their work.

Girls States are usually held on college campuses for one week in June or July. Girls who attend are selected for potential leadership ability. Activities are directed and counseled by Auxiliary members and college faculty members. State officials give lectures during visits by the girls to state capitols. Each Girls State selects two girls to serve as senators at *Girls Nation,* held every year in Washington, D.C. These delegates study and practice the processes of the national government.

In 1937, the American Legion Auxiliary first proposed the establishment of Girls States, modeling them after the Boys States conducted by the American Legion. Girls State programs were tried in the District of Columbia and in Delaware in 1938. The first weeklong Girls States were held in Kansas and Nebraska in 1939. Headquarters for the Girls State are in Indianapolis. Critically reviewed by the American Legion Auxiliary

See also **American Legion Auxiliary; Boys State.**

Girondists, *juh RAHN dihsts,* were members of a French political group that began during the French Revolution (1789-1799). The name came from the fact that some of the party's leading orators were from a *department* (district) called the Gironde. The Girondists were republicans inspired by the new United States government. They represented the middle class and believed in a person's right to own property. They favored doing away with the monarchy in France and establishing a federal republic. They feared that Paris would dominate France and that radical groups centered there would take away private ownership of property. Two important Girondists were Jacques-Pierre Brissot de Warville and Madame Marie Jeanne Roland de la Platière.

The Girondists came to power under the Constitution of 1791. In June 1793, a Paris mob forced the National Convention to expel and persecute a group of prominent Girondist deputies. The government came under control of the *Jacobins,* republicans who favored domination by Paris. Many Girondist leaders were guillotined during the Reign of Terror. Eric A. Arnold, Jr.

See also **French Revolution; Jacobins; Roland de la Platière, Marie Jeanne; Corday, Charlotte.**

Girty, Simon (1741-1818), was an American pioneer who fought with the Indians against white settlers. His parents were white, but he was an American Indian by training, sentiment, and choice. Seneca Indians captured Girty and his family when he was 15. He spent three years with the Seneca and learned Indian languages and customs. He then worked as an interpreter around Fort Pitt, Pennsylvania, until 1774. Girty sided with the British during the Revolutionary War in America (1775-1783). He led Indians in many raids against colonists.

After the war, Girty helped Indian tribes attack pioneers moving west. But he sometimes persuaded the Indians to spare the lives of the people they captured. He fled to Canada in 1796, after the British gave up Detroit, their last outpost in the United States. Girty was born near Harrisburg, Pennsylvania. Frank Goodwyn

Giscard d'Estaing, *zhee SKAHR dehs TANG,* **Valéry** (1926-   ), served as president of France from 1974 until 1981. In 1981, he was defeated in a presidential election by François Mitterrand. Giscard, as he is usually called, founded the Independent Republican Party in 1962. Under Giscard, the party was allied with the Gaullist Party, a major French political party.

Under Giscard, the French Parliament passed laws that raised old age pensions and the minimum wage.

Parliament also lowered the voting age from 21 to 18.

During the mid-1970's, France experienced poor economic conditions, including rising prices and unemployment. Giscard took several steps to improve the economy. For example, he signed agreements to sell more French goods to some foreign nations, hoping that the resulting increase in exports would boost the economy. Giscard also changed the country's foreign policy by stressing the importance of cooperation with other nations. Previously, French foreign policy had emphasized self-reliance more than cooperation.

Giscard was born of French parents in Koblenz, Germany. In 1951, he graduated from the National School of Administration. In 1952, he joined the staff of the French government's Ministry of Finance. Giscard was elected to the National Assembly as a member of the Gaullist Party in 1956. He resigned from the Assembly in 1959 to become secretary of state for finance. In 1962, President Charles de Gaulle named him finance minister. Giscard was dismissed from this post in 1966.

In 1967, Giscard was elected to the Assembly as a member of the Independent Republican Party. President Georges Pompidou appointed him finance minister in 1969. Giscard then resigned from the National Assembly. In 1984, three years after his term as president, he again won a seat in the Assembly.   Michael M. Harrison

Gish, Dorothy (1898-1968), was an American star of silent motion pictures. She was noted for her roles as light-hearted, mischievous young women. Perhaps her best films were *Hearts of the World* (1918) and *Orphans of the Storm* (1922), both directed by D. W. Griffith.

Gish was born in Dayton, Ohio. She began acting on the stage at the age of 4 and made her movie debut in 1912 in a Griffith film. With the arrival of sound films in the late 1920's, Gish concentrated on stage acting, starring in a number of Broadway plays. However, she did appear in five sound films, including *Our Hearts Were Young and Gay* (1944). Gish's sister, Lillian, was an even more famous silent film star.   James MacKillop

American Film Institute

The Gish sisters, Lillian, *left,* and Dorothy, *right,* starred in the silent film *Orphans of the Storm* (1922). The actresses played sisters caught up in the turmoil of the French Revolution.

Gish, Lillian (1893-1993), was one of the leading stars of silent motion pictures in the United States. Gish's fragile beauty conveyed a spiritual quality that made her especially effective as an innocent heroine. She gained her greatest fame in films directed by D. W. Griffith. Gish starred in Griffith's American Civil War epic *The Birth of a Nation* (1915). Her other films for Griffith included *Intolerance* (1916), *Broken Blossoms* (1919), *Way Down East* (1920), and *Orphans of the Storm* (1922). She also appeared in a few sound films, notably *Night of the Hunter* (1955) and *The Whales of August* (1987).

Gish was born in Springfield, Ohio. She began acting on the stage at age 6 and made her film debut in 1912. Gish wrote an autobiography, *The Movies, Mr. Griffith, and Me* (1969). During the 1970's and 1980's, she appeared in many TV dramas. Her sister, Dorothy, was also a star of silent films.   James MacKillop

Gissing, George Robert (1857-1903), was an English novelist. His books are noted for realism and for clear psychological portraits of people. Gissing's novels reflect his own miserable life, which was dominated by poverty and tuberculosis. Gissing's best novel, *New Grub Street* (1891), describes how struggling writers try to maintain their literary standards when their work is rejected by society. *The Odd Women* (1893) is a sympathetic portrayal of the economic struggles of several middle-class women in Victorian England. Gissing also wrote a warm, charming autobiographical novel, *The Private Papers of Henry Ryecroft* (1903).

Gissing was born in Wakefield. His early writing shows the influence of Charles Dickens. Gissing wrote one of the first important studies of Dickens: *Charles Dickens, A Critical Study* (1898).   Sharon Bassett

Gist, *gihst,* **Christopher** (1706?-1759), was an American frontier guide and a friend of future United States President George Washington. Gist was the first to survey the Ohio River Valley, in 1751. In 1755, during the French and Indian War, he fought under British General Edward Braddock at Fort Duquesne (now Pittsburgh, Pennsylvania). Later, Gist served as captain of a company of scouts and as an Indian agent in Tennessee. Gist was born in Maryland.   Fred W. Anderson

Giza, *GEE zuh* (pop. 2,144,000), is a suburb of Cairo and Egypt's third largest city. Only Cairo and Alexandria are larger. Giza is the site of the most famous remains of ancient Egypt—the Great Sphinx and the three largest pyramids (see **Pyramids; Sphinx**). Its name in Arabic is Al Jizah. Giza lies on the Nile River, opposite Cairo (see **Egypt** [political map]).

Bridges connect Giza with Cairo and the island of Roda, in the Nile. Along the river, the Silver Coast section of Giza includes luxurious apartment buildings, large homes, and embassies of foreign governments. These structures contrast sharply with many small shacks occupied by the city's unskilled workers.

Many wealthy Egyptians, and business people and diplomats from other nations, live in Giza. Large numbers of unskilled workers arrive yearly in search of jobs in factories. Giza's population rose from about 260,000 in 1960 to more than 900,000 in the mid-1970's and to more than 2 million in the early 1990's.

Factories in Giza manufacture such products as bricks, chemicals, cigarettes, and machine tools. Egypt's motion-picture industry makes dozens of films annually in the city. Giza is the home of the main campus of Cairo University. Robert L. Tignor

Gizzard is a muscular organ of the digestive system of birds and a few other animals. It breaks up and grinds hard, solid foods. The gizzard in birds is associated with the stomach and is lined with thick, tough plates. The breakdown of food in the gizzard is aided by gravel that the bird has swallowed. Food enters a pouch of the gullet called the *crop* and is moistened there. It passes from the crop to the glandular part of the stomach, where it is mixed with gastric juices. The food then passes into the gizzard, where it is crushed by the movements of the muscular walls and the gravel. Gizzards of grain-eating birds are well developed, and those of fruit-eating birds are often poorly developed.

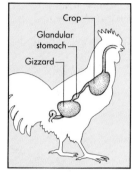

Crop

Glandular
stomach

Gizzard

WORLD BOOK illustration
by Patricia Wynne

Gizzard

G. J. Kenagy

Glaciation. See Ice Age.

Glacier is a large mass of ice that flows slowly over land in the cold polar regions and in high mountain valleys. The low temperatures in these places enable large amounts of snow to build up and turn into ice. Most glaciers range in thickness from about 300 to 10,000 feet (91 to 3,000 meters).

Kinds of glaciers. There are two main kinds of glaciers, *continental glaciers* and *valley glaciers*. They differ in shape, size, and location.

Continental glaciers, also called *icecaps,* are broad, extremely thick ice sheets that cover vast areas of land near the earth's polar regions. The continental glaciers on Greenland and Antarctica bury plateaus and conceal the entire landscape except for the highest peaks. Glaciers of this type build up at the center and slope outward to flow toward the sea in all directions.

Valley glaciers are long, narrow bodies of ice that fill high mountain valleys. Many of them move down sloping valleys from a *cirque,* a bowl-shaped hollow with steep walls located among the peaks. In mountains near the equator, such as the northern Andes of South America, valley glaciers occur at elevations above 15,000 feet (4,570 meters) or higher. They occur at lower elevations in the European Alps, the Southern Alps of New Zealand, and other mountain ranges nearer the poles.

How glaciers form. Glaciers begin to form when more snow falls during the winter than melts and evaporates in summer. The excess snow gradually builds up in layers. Its increasing weight causes the snow crystals under the surface to become compact, grainlike pellets called *firn.* At depths of 50 feet (15 meters) or more, the firn is further compressed into dense crystals of glacial ice. The ice eventually becomes so thick that it moves under the pressure of its own great weight.

Glaciers are affected by seasonal variations in snowfall and temperature. Most glaciers increase slightly in size during the winter because snow falls over much of

Bob and Ira Spring

A valley glacier flows down this mountain valley in Alaska. Dark strips of rock debris called *moraines* run through the ice. Melting ice forms a lake, *foreground,* at the end of the glacier.

John R. T. Molholm

A continental glacier covers most of Antarctica. The Ross Ice Shelf, *above,* forms part of the huge ice sheet. Its edge rises above the Ross Sea along the western edge of the continent.

A sectional view of a valley glacier

A valley glacier moves downslope from a *cirque,* a bowl-shaped hollow near a mountain peak. As the glacier travels over uneven terrain or changes its velocity, its surface forms cracks called *crevasses.* The glacier picks up rocks and other materials and piles them up in ridges called *moraines.*

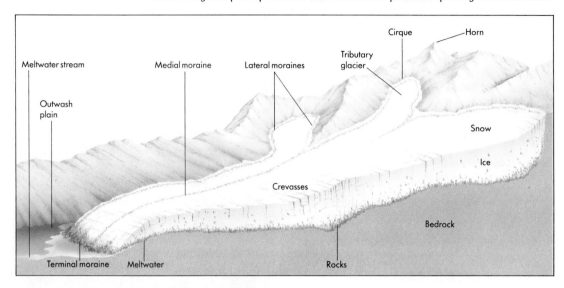

their surface. The cold temperatures slow the melting of snow. They also limit the melting of the lower parts of the glaciers as the ice masses move downslope. In areas away from the poles, rising temperatures in summer cause surface parts of a glacier to melt. As the size of the glacier decreases, the glacier is said to *retreat.* In the always frigid polar regions, glaciers shrink for other reasons. When glaciers reach the sea, for example, huge chunks of ice break away from them. These chunks fall into the water and become icebergs (see **Iceberg**).

Glaciers may also increase or decrease in size as a result of changes in climate that occur over long periods of time. For example, the ice sheet that covers much of Greenland is growing smaller because of a gradual rise in temperature in the area since the early 1900's.

The movement of glaciers. A glacier flows downslope because of the pull of gravity. The ice crystals deep within the glacier change their shapes and regroup as a result of the pressure of the surface layers. These small changes in the individual crystals cause the entire ice mass to move. The melting and refreezing of the ice crystals along the base of a glacier also help it slide downslope. Heat from friction and from the earth's interior melts some of the crystals of the glacier's bottom layer. The water from the dissolved crystals flows down into cracks in the rock underneath. As the water refreezes, it expands and breaks away pieces of rock, which then become part of the glacier.

The surface of a glacier is stiff and rigid, unlike the mass of ice below. It often fractures and forms deep cracks called *crevasses* as the glacier flows over uneven or steep terrain or changes its velocity. Crevasses also develop because the upper layers of a glacier move more rapidly than its lower layers.

Most glaciers flow slowly and move less than a foot (30 centimeters) per day. But sometimes a glacier may travel much faster for several years. Some glaciers at times flow more than 100 feet (30 meters) per day. The

Land forms created by a glacier

As a glacier melts, it leaves behind humps of hard bedrock, and rounded hills and narrow ridges of rock debris. Hollows in the loose rocks trap water from the melting glacier, forming lakes.

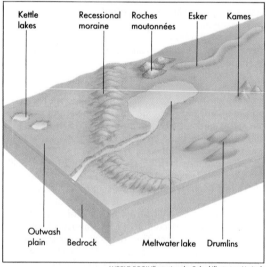

WORLD BOOK illustrations by Oxford Illustrators Limited; adapted from a drawing by Janet Allin

various parts of a glacier move at different speeds. The center and upper areas of a valley glacier flow the fastest. The sides and bottom move more slowly because they rub against the walls and floor of the valley. Scientists measure a glacier's speed by driving stakes into the ice and recording the changes in their position.

How glaciers shape the land. As glaciers pass over an area, they help shape its features. They create a variety of land forms by means of erosion and by transporting and depositing rock debris. Glaciers greatly altered the surface of large parts of Europe, Asia, and North America during the Pleistocene Ice Age, which ended about 10,000 years ago (see **Ice age**).

Glacial erosion occurs when an advancing ice mass scoops up rock fragments and drags them along its base. In doing so, the glacier grinds the *bedrock* (layer of solid rock beneath the loose rock fragments), producing a polished but often scratched or furrowed surface. When a glacier retreats, it often leaves behind broad humps of bedrock called *roches moutonnées.* One side of this kind of land form is smoothly rounded and polished, while the other side is rough and irregular.

A glacier in a mountain valley may produce a cirque near the peak of the mountain. A cirque forms when the upper part of a glacier removes blocks of rock from the surrounding cliffs. A glacier also can gouge out a U-shaped depression in a river valley. Such a depression that is flooded by the ocean is called a *fiord* (see **Fiord**).

Glacial deposits consist of clay, silt, sand, and rocks of various sizes. Glaciers pile up these materials, forming uneven ridges called *moraines.* The ridges along the sides of a valley glacier are known as *lateral moraines.* When two valley glaciers come together, the lateral moraines between them merge to form a *medial moraine* along the center of the combined ice mass. The hilly ridge at the lower end of a valley glacier is called a *terminal moraine.* Such a moraine also develops around the edge of a continental glacier. A *recessional moraine* forms when a glacier pauses for a long time during its retreat. See **Moraine**.

Other land forms associated with glacial deposits include *drumlins* and *eskers.* A drumlin is an oval-shaped hill that usually consists of rock debris. Most drumlins occur in groups. An esker is a long, narrow ridge of sand and gravel deposited by a stream of water that flowed in a tunnel beneath a melting glacier.

Famous glaciers. Many of the world's most notable glaciers are in Europe. The best-known ones are those in the French and Swiss Alps. These glaciers include the Mer de Glace on Mont Blanc and the Aletsch Glacier near the Jungfrau. The Jostedal Glacier in Norway is the largest on the European continent. It covers about 300 square miles (780 square kilometers).

Major glaciers also cover regions of northwestern North America. The largest and most famous of these glaciers is the 840-square-mile (2,176-square-kilometer) Malaspina Glacier on Yakutat Bay in Alaska. Other glaciers include those in Banff National Park in Alberta, in Glacier National Park in Montana, and on Mount Rainier in Washington.   William C. Mahaney

Related articles in *World Book* include:

Alaska (Glaciers)	Great Lakes (How the lakes
Alberta (picture)	were formed)
Alps (How the Alps were	Iceland (The inland plateau)
formed)	River (picture: A melting gla-
Climate (Determining past cli-	cier)
mates)	

Additional resources

Erickson, Jon. *Glacial Geology.* Facts on File, 1996.
Hambrey, Michael J., and Alean, Jürg. *Glaciers.* Cambridge, 1992.
Sharp, Robert P. *Living Ice.* Cambridge, 1988.

Glacier Bay National Park lies in southeastern Alaska, about 100 miles (160 kilometers) west of Juneau. For location, see **Alaska** (political map). More than 100,000 people visit the park each year. As recently as 200 years ago, the park was entirely covered by glacial ice. The park's glaciers have been retreating rapidly, uncovering new land and sea areas. Visitors can see whales in offshore waters and watch icebergs break from glaciers and fall into the water. Wildlife of the park includes Alaskan brown bears, mountain goats, wolves, and about 200 species of birds. The area was declared a national monument in 1925 and became a national park in 1980. For the area of Glacier Bay National Park, see **National Park System** (table: National parks).

Critically reviewed by the National Park Service

Glacier National Park lies in northern Montana on the boundary between the United States and Canada. Part of the Rocky Mountain chain, called the *Great Divide* or *Continental Divide,* runs north and south through the park. The park was established in 1910. Its eastern half was once part of the Blackfeet Indian Reservation. A Canadian preserve, Waterton Lakes National Park, lies north of Glacier National Park. In 1932, the two parks were united by the U.S. and Canadian governments. Together they are called the Waterton-Glacier International Peace Park, but they are under separate administrations. For the area of Glacier National Park, see **National Park System** (table: National parks).

Glaciers. The park was named for the more than 50 glaciers found there. These beds of ice are the remains of a large system of mountain glaciers that once covered the entire area. Some of the glaciers are small, but others are very large. Grinnell Glacier, the park's largest, is $1\frac{1}{2}$ miles (2.4 kilometers) long and 1 mile (1.6 kilometers) wide. It covers 298 acres (121 hectares) and is up to 500 feet (150 meters) thick in some places. It lies on the northeastern slopes of Mount Gould, high above Many Glacier Valley in the northeastern section of the park.

Mountains. Glacier National Park is also noted for its beautiful mountains, whose peaks form picturelike designs. The summits of some of these mountains have never been reached by climbers. The highest peak in the area is Mount Cleveland (10,466 feet, or 3,190 meters), which lies in the northern part of the park. Other mountains higher than 10,000 feet (3,000 meters) include Kintla Peak, Mount Siyeh, and Mount Stimson.

Lewis Overthrust is a high ridge visited by thousands of tourists. Colorful layers of rock may be seen along the sides of the ridge, much like the layers found in the Grand Canyon of Arizona. This overthrust was made in ancient times when a disturbance inside the earth caused the earth's surface to crack. One area was pushed, or thrust, up and over another area.

Lakes. The park has about 250 lakes. Some lie high in the mountains, and others nestle deep in the valleys.

WORLD BOOK map

Location of Glacier National Park

One of the most beautiful of these lakes is St. Mary Lake. It is about 10 miles (16 kilometers) long and is surrounded by mountains, except at the point where it meets the St. Mary River. Lake McDonald, the largest in the park, measures 11 miles (18 kilometers) long and has an average width of 1½ miles (2.4 kilometers). Swiftcurrent Lake, one of the smallest lakes in the park, is also one of the most famous because it lies in a region of great beauty. Iceberg Lake, only ½ mile (0.8 kilometer) long, lies on such high ground (6,000 feet, or 1,800 meters) that it contains icebergs even in summer.

Animal life in Glacier National Park is protected by law, and hunting is never allowed. Among the wildlife found there are Rocky Mountain goat and sheep, bear, moose, elk, deer, coyote, wolves, and lynx. Game birds, such as geese and ducks, nest in the park. The streams are abundant with fish, especially cutthroat trout. Eastern brook trout and mountain whitefish are also found in the streams.   Critically reviewed by Glacier National Park

See also **Montana** (picture).

Glackens, William James (1870-1938), was an American painter and illustrator. His illustrations are sympathetic commentaries on life in city streets and crowded tenements. As a painter, Glackens preferred subjects reflecting fashionable life in cafes and parks. Glackens' style of painting shows the influence of the French impressionists. His early works are in the dark manner of Edouard Manet. The paintings of his most productive years reflect the lighter colors of Pierre Auguste Renoir.

Glackens was born in Philadelphia, and studied art there and in Paris. Early in his career, he worked as an illustrator for newspapers, magazines, and books. His most memorable early work is a series of drawings he produced as an artist-war correspondent in Cuba during the Spanish-American War in 1898. Glackens became one of the original members of a group of realistic artists called *The Eight* (later the *Ashcan School*).

Charles C. Eldredge

See also **Ashcan School.**

Gladiator, *GLAD ee AY tuhr,* was a trained warrior who fought bloody battles to entertain the ancient Romans. Gladiators used many different types of weapons. Some of the warriors used an oblong shield, a visored helmet, and a stabbing sword about 2 feet (61 centimeters) long. Some used a small, round shield called a *buckler* and a *sica* (short, curved sword). Others used only a net and a three-pronged spear called a *trident.* Gladiators usually fought until one was killed. However, the life of the loser could be spared if the spectators waved handkerchiefs.

Most gladiators were prisoners of war, slaves, or criminals condemned to fight in these contests. However, some freemen fought for money and fame, and knights, senators, and even women occasionally fought. One emperor, Commodus, also fought in the arena. Successful gladiators became famous in Rome. The comment "the girls' delight" is scratched after the name of one gladiator on a Pompeian wall. One of the most famous gladiators was Spartacus, a slave from Thrace who led an unsuccessful rebellion of gladiators and slaves (see **Spartacus**). Gladiators were carefully fed, and they received medical care. They were generally housed in barracks.

The first gladiator games were held in a Roman cattle market in 264 B.C. at the funeral of an aristocrat. Most of the contests after that were held at funerals or celebrations, and were under state control. At the Colosseum, wild beasts fought in the morning, and the gladiators fought in the afternoon. Contests were also held in provincial amphitheaters. Many Greek theaters were converted to house the popular contests. These cruel battles were justified as hardening Roman citizens to the sight of human bloodshed, so they could endure war better. The battles were finally banned about A.D. 404 by Emperor Honorius.   D. Brendan Nagle

See also **Colosseum; Rome, Ancient** (picture).

Gladiolus, *GLAD ee OH luhs* or *gluh DY uh luhs,* is a garden plant with spikes of large silky blossoms that are popular as cut flowers. It is also called *sword lily.* Many gladioli are grown in the United States and Europe. A common type is the *garden gladiolus.*

The flowers of gladioli are of many different colors, through all the shades of red and orange to white. There is even a blue gladiolus, which comes mainly from South Africa. The tube-shaped flowers grow above one another in long clusters along one side of the stem. A lower blossom opens first. If the lower flowers are the only ones in bloom when a spike is cut, the buds above them will open one after another.

Gladioli have tall, slender stems like an iris, and long sword-shaped leaves. Their name is the Latin word for *little dagger.* They grow from bulblike underground stems called *corms,* and new corms develop above the old ones. Each fall the corms should be dug out of the garden, cleaned, and stored indoors at a temperature of 40° F. (4° C). Gladioli grow well when they have a rich, soft soil, sunlight, and plenty of water. The gladiolus thrips, a tiny insect, feeds upon gladioli. The gladiolus is one of the special flowers of the month of August.

Scientific classification. Gladioli belong to the iris family, Iridaceae. They are classified as genus *Gladiolus.* The garden gladiolus is *G. hortulanus.*   August A. De Hertogh

See also **Corm; Flower** (picture: Garden perennials [Bulbs]).

Gladstone, William Ewart *YOO uhrt* (1809-1898), was one of the most respected British political leaders of the 1800's. He served as prime minister of Britain four times: from 1868 to 1874, from 1880 to 1885, in 1886, and from 1892 to 1894. As a statesman, Gladstone had boundless energy and, in later life, a strong desire to aid oppressed people. He helped pass many laws that strengthened democratic institutions in Britain.

Gladstone also had many other interests besides politics. He was a lay leader of the Church of England, and he wrote several books on religion and the culture of ancient Greece.

Gladstone was born in Liverpool, England. He studied at Eton College and Oxford University. In 1832, he was elected to the House of Commons as a member of the Tory Party (later called the Conservative Party). During the 1840's and 1850's, Glad-

Chicago Historical Society

William E. Gladstone

stone gradually switched to the Liberal Party. Gladstone served in mixed-party and Liberal cabinets as chancellor of the exchequer, the official who prepares the annual budget.

By 1865, Gladstone had become a brilliant orator and a firm liberal. In that year, he was named leader of the Liberal Party in the Commons. Gladstone helped amend the Conservative government's Reform Act of 1867 so that it doubled the number of men able to vote in national elections. At that time, the right to vote was limited to adult males who owned property. The act gave the vote to many small farmers and city workers.

Gladstone's first term as prime minister began in 1868. He was determined to correct abuses in the administration of Ireland, which was then under British control as part of the United Kingdom. Gladstone sponsored an 1869 act that released the Irish, many of whom were Roman Catholic, from paying taxes to the Church of England. He also pushed through legislation in 1870 that made it harder to evict Irish tenants from the lands they rented. Another important act that year gave England, for the first time, a system of elementary schools open to all children. When the Conservatives, under Benjamin Disraeli, returned to power in 1874, Gladstone resigned as leader of the Liberal Party.

Later political career. Gladstone ended a temporary retirement in 1879 when he became morally outraged by Disraeli's foreign and colonial policies. Angered by Ottoman cruelty in the Balkan region of Europe, then controlled by the Ottoman Empire, he attacked Disraeli's pro-Ottoman policies. In the election of 1880, Gladstone led the Liberals to victory and again became prime minister. In 1882, he ordered a British invasion of Egypt to protect British interests there. In 1884, Gladstone won Parliament's approval of a reform act that gave the vote to almost all adult males.

The Liberals won the 1885 election, and Gladstone became prime minister for a third time in February 1886. But his term ended in July of that year, after he tried to give Ireland more self-government through his Home Rule Bill. The bill was defeated in the House of Commons and resulted in a deep split in the Liberal Party.

In 1892, Gladstone again became prime minister. He made a final attempt to win home rule for Ireland, but Parliament's House of Lords defeated his bill. Gladstone retired from office in 1894.   Denis Judd

See also **Disraeli, Benjamin; Liberal Democrats; Victoria.**

Gland is a tissue or organ that produces and releases a useful chemical substance. Glands are located in various places throughout the bodies of human beings and most other animals. The substances released by glands perform various functions. For example, some of these secretions help keep the skin moist. Others promote digestion. Still others regulate the growth and development of the body.

Human beings have two chief kinds of glands—*endocrine glands* and *exocrine glands*. These glands differ in their method of secretion. Endocrine glands release secretions into the blood. Exocrine glands discharge secretions into small *ducts* (tubes). The ducts lead to the outer surface of the skin and eyes or to the interior surfaces of such organs as the stomach and small intestine.

Endocrine glands, also called *ductless glands,* help

the nervous system regulate various body activities. These glands produce and secrete chemical substances called *hormones,* which travel through the blood to all parts of the body. After a hormone arrives at its *target—* that is, the organ or tissue it affects—it causes certain actions to occur.

Hormones regulate such body processes as growth and development, and reproduction. They also coordinate the body's responses to stress and help keep the chemical composition of the blood within normal range. In addition, hormones regulate the process by which the body changes food into energy and living tissue.

Most endocrine glands are organs and produce one or more hormones. Some of these glands consist of two or more parts, each of which secretes different hormones. Each of the two *adrenal glands,* for example, has two parts—the *cortex,* or outer layer, and the *medulla,* or inner layer. The cortex produces the hormones *cortisol* and *aldosterone.* The medulla secretes the hormones *epinephrine* and *norepinephrine.* Some endocrine glands are simply made up of tissue that forms part of another organ, such as the kidneys, pancreas, small intestine, and stomach.

The *pituitary gland* is one of the most important endocrine glands. It consists of two parts, the *anterior lobe* and the *posterior lobe.* The anterior lobe releases hormones that regulate the secretions of many other endocrine glands. For this reason, the pituitary is sometimes called the *master gland.* The anterior lobe of the pitu-

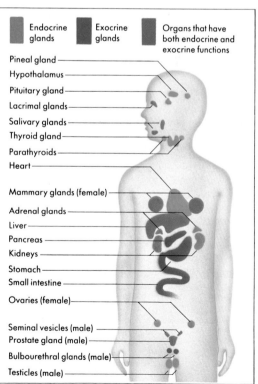

| Endocrine glands | Exocrine glands | Organs that have both endocrine and exocrine functions |

Pineal gland
Hypothalamus
Pituitary gland
Lacrimal glands
Salivary glands
Thyroid gland
Parathyroids
Heart

Mammary glands (female)
Adrenal glands
Liver
Pancreas
Kidneys
Stomach
Small intestine
Ovaries (female)

Seminal vesicles (male)
Prostate gland (male)
Bulbourethral glands (male)
Testicles (male)

WORLD BOOK illustration by Charles Wellek

Some major glands of the human body. The human body has two kinds of glands—*endocrine* and *exocrine.* Some organs have both types. This diagram shows some of the major glands.

itary is controlled by a part of the brain known as the *hypothalamus.* The hypothalamus secretes *releasing hormones,* which cause the anterior lobe to discharge its hormones. The hypothalamus consists of nervous tissue. It forms the main link between the body's endocrine and nervous systems.

Some endocrine glands are not controlled by the pituitary or the nervous system. These glands, such as those that help maintain the normal chemical composition of the blood, respond to changes in the amounts of various chemicals. For example, the *parathyroid glands* secrete *parathormone* when the amount of calcium in the blood drops below the normal level. Parathormone causes a rise in the calcium level of the blood.

Diseases of the endocrine glands may cause them to secrete too much or too little of a hormone. Most cases of excess secretion result from tumors. Insufficient secretion occurs if a gland has been partly destroyed. This destruction may be caused by cancer, a decrease in the blood supply to the gland, or, in rare cases, infection. In many instances, the partial destruction of a gland results when the body's disease-fighting cells mistakenly attack healthy tissue.

Exocrine glands, unlike endocrine glands, do not empty their secretions into the blood. Instead, their products are carried by ducts to the surface of the skin or other organs. The secretions perform various functions. The *sweat glands,* for example, secrete fluids that help cool the skin. The *sebaceous glands* supply oil that lubricates the skin. The *lacrimal glands* produce tears, which moisten the eyes. Other exocrine glands secrete substances that moisten and lubricate surfaces of organs within the body. Other glands that lie in the mouth, the stomach, and the intestine help digest food.

Certain exocrine glands secrete scents known as *pheromones,* which play a role in communication among individuals in many animal species. The role in human behavior is more limited. See **Pheromone.**

Some exocrine glands consist of single cells. Others are made up of groups of tubes and *sacs* (baglike structures). Most exocrine glands release their secretions in response to stimulation of local nerve endings. But the secretions of some exocrine glands are controlled by hormones. For example, *gastrin,* a hormone secreted by the stomach, stimulates certain exocrine glands to release digestive juices. Exocrine glands, like endocrine

Major glands of the human body
Endocrine glands

Gland	Secretion	Function of secretion
Adrenal gland, cortex of	Glucocorticoids, particularly cortisol	Help regulate *metabolism,* the process by which the body turns food into energy and living tissue. Help the body adjust to stress.
	Mineralocorticoids, particularly aldosterone	Stimulate kidneys to retain sodium and excrete potassium.
	Sex hormones, particularly androgens	Stimulate development of sexual characteristics, particularly in males.
Adrenal gland, medulla of	Epinephrine, also called adrenalin	Prepares the body to deal with stress. Increases amount of sugar in the blood. Increases heart rate and blood pressure.
	Norepinephrine, also called noradrenalin	Helps coordinate the body's response to stress. Causes blood vessels to contract and increases blood pressure.
Heart	Atrial natriuretic factor	Stimulates kidneys to excrete salt.
Hypothalamus	Adrenocorticotropin-releasing hormone	Stimulates secretion of ACTH by anterior pituitary.
	Growth hormone-releasing hormone	Stimulates secretion of growth hormone by anterior pituitary.
	Gonadotropin-releasing hormone	Stimulates secretion of FSH and LH by anterior pituitary.
	Thyrotropin-releasing hormone	Stimulates secretion of thyrotropin by anterior pituitary.
	Prolactin-inhibiting hormone	Controls secretion of prolactin by anterior pituitary.
	Oxytocin, Vasopressin	See *Pituitary gland, posterior lobe of,* in this table.
	Somatostatin	Inhibits secretion of growth hormone by anterior pituitary.
Kidneys	Erythropoietin	Stimulates production of red blood cells.
	Renin	Reacts with a protein in the blood to produce *angiotensin,* a hormone that increases blood pressure.
Ovaries (females only)	Estrogens	Stimulate development of female sex organs and sexual characteristics. Stimulate female sexual behavior and regulate menstruation.
	Progesterone	Acts with estrogens to regulate menstruation.
	Relaxin	Causes birth canal to widen.
Pancreas (islets of Langerhans)	Insulin	Decreases amount of sugar in the blood.
	Glucagon	Increases amount of sugar in the blood.
Parathyroid glands	Parathormone	Increases amount of calcium in the blood. Decreases amount of phosphate in the blood.
Pineal gland	Melatonin	Lightens skin color in some animals. Function in human beings uncertain. May help regulate sexual development and menstruation.
Pituitary gland, anterior lobe of	Adrenocorticotropic hormone (ACTH)	Stimulates secretion of various hormones by adrenal cortex.
	Follicle-stimulating hormone (FSH)	Stimulates growth of ovarian follicles in females and semeniferous tubules in males.
	Luteinizing hormone (LH)	Stimulates secretion of sex hormones by ovaries and testes.
	Thyrotropin or thyroid-stimulating hormone (TSH)	Stimulates secretion of thyroxine by thyroid gland.
	Prolactin	Stimulates production of milk by mammary glands.
	Growth hormone (GH)	Stimulates general body growth. Helps regulate metabolism.
	Endorphins	Act on the central nervous system.
	Melanocyte-stimulating hormone (MSH)	Regulates amount of pigment in skin of certain animals. Function in human beings unknown.

glands, may be affected by various diseases that disrupt their secretions.

Glandlike structures. The *thymus,* an organ in the chest, is often called a gland. This organ helps protect the body against disease. Some scientists believe the thymus produces and releases one or more hormones, but researchers have not identified these secretions. Certain groups of *lymph nodes,* particularly those of the neck and armpit, are also called glands. But these structures do not produce secretions. Like the thymus, lymph nodes form part of the body's system of defense against disease.　　　Nandalal Bagchi

Related articles in *World Book* include:

Glands

Adrenal gland	Parathyroid gland
Hypothalamus	Pineal gland
Kidney	Pituitary gland
Liver	Prostate gland
Mammary glands	Testicle
Pancreas	Thyroid gland

Diseases of glands

Addison's disease	Goiter
Cretinism	Graves' disease
Diabetes	Hypoglycemia

Other related articles

ACTH	Insulin
Dwarf	Perspiration
Epinephrine	Saliva
Giant	Skin (Hair, nails, and glands)
Hormone	Stomach
Hormone replacement therapy	Tears
	Thymus

Additional resources

Creager, Joan G. *Human Anatomy and Physiology.* 2nd ed. Wm. C. Brown Pubs., 1992. One of five major sections discusses glands and hormones.
Little, Marjorie. *The Endocrine System.* Chelsea Hse., 1990. Younger readers.
Whitfield, Philip, ed. *The Human Body Explained.* Henry Holt, 1995. Discusses glands and hormones.
Young, John K. *Hormones.* Watts, 1994. Younger readers.

Endocrine glands (continued)

Gland	Secretion	Function of secretion
Pituitary gland, posterior lobe of (stores and releases oxytocin and vasopressin, which are produced by the hypothalamus)	Oxytocin	Stimulates muscles of uterus to contract during labor. Stimulates release of milk by mammary glands.
	Vasopressin or antidiuretic hormone	Stimulates kidneys to retain water. Causes blood vessels to contract.
Placenta (pregnant females only)	Chorionic gonadotropin	Acts with other hormones to maintain lining of uterus during pregnancy.
	Placental lactogen	Stimulates changes in breasts of pregnant women. Stimulates growth of embryo.
Small intestine	Secretin	Stimulates secretion of digestive enzymes by pancreas.
	Cholecystokinin (pancreozymin)	Stimulates release of bile by gallbladder and of digestive enzymes by pancreas.
	Gastric inhibitory peptide	Inhibits secretion of gastric juices and contraction of stomach.
	Vasoactive intestinal peptide	Stimulates secretion of water and electrolytes by the intestine. Causes blood vessels to dilate.
Stomach	Gastrin	Stimulates secretion of digestive enzymes and hydrochloric acid by stomach.
Testicles (males only)	Androgens, particularly testosterone	Stimulate development of male sex organs and sexual characteristics. Stimulates male sexual behavior.
Thyroid gland	Thyroxine	Increases rate of metabolism.
	Triiodothyronine	Increases rate of metabolism.
	Calcitonin	Decreases amount of calcium in the blood.

Exocrine glands

Gland	Secretion	Function
Lacrimal glands	Tears	Moisten the eyes.
Liver	Bile	Aids digestion and absorption of fats.
Mammary glands (function in females only)	Milk	Nourishes nursing babies.
Mucus glands	Mucus	Moistens and lubricates mucous membranes.
Pancreas	Amylase	Helps digest starches.
	Lipase	Helps digest fats.
	Trypsin	Helps digest proteins.
Salivary glands	Saliva	Moistens and softens food and begins chemical breakdown of starches.
Sebaceous glands	Sebum	Lubricates skin and hair.
Seminal vesicles, bulbo-urethrals, and prostate gland (males only)	Seminal fluid	Nourishes sperm and promotes movement of sperm through urethra.
Stomach and intestine	Digestive enzymes	Help digest food.
Sweat glands	Sweat	Helps cool skin.

Glanders is a severe disease of horses and mules. It also occurs in dogs, cats, goats, and sheep, and occasionally in people. Cattle and hogs seem to be immune to it. Glanders is caused by the bacillus *Pseudomonas mallei.* This bacillus may lodge in almost any organ of the body. It spreads through nasal discharges and cuts or scrapes in the skin.

Glanders causes fever, weight loss, a nasal discharge containing pus, and ulcers in the skin and nose. The disease is especially dangerous when many animals are together, such as in stables. Few infected animals recover from glanders. Physicians usually prescribe antibiotics to treat the disease in people. In its early stages, glanders in animals is also called *farcy.*

Infected animals usually can be detected by the *mallein test.* In this test, products of the bacillus that causes glanders are injected into the eye. A pus-containing discharge from the eye indicates the presence of glanders.

Lawrence D. McGill

Glandular fever. See Mononucleosis.

Glasgow, *GLAS goh* (pop. 654,542), is the largest city in Scotland and a center of industry and commerce. It lies on both sides of the River Clyde, in the Central Lowlands of Scotland. For the location of Glasgow, see **Scotland** (political map).

The River Clyde leads into the Atlantic Ocean near Glasgow, and the city serves as a port for oceangoing vessels. Glasgow is a center of engineering activities. Its manufactured goods include computers and other electronic products. Major Scotch whisky firms have their headquarters in the city. Glasgow is a center for Scottish television broadcasting, and some filmmaking takes place there.

The River Clyde runs through the center of Glasgow, and Highland hills are visible on the city's outskirts. Glasgow has many parks and wide streets. Its major landmark is its medieval cathedral. The city also has many impressive stone buildings that were constructed in the 1800's, as well as numerous modern buildings. Rich in culture, Glasgow is the home of the Scottish Opera, the Scottish National Orchestra, and the Citizens Theatre. The city has two major museums—the Burrell Collection and the Kelvingrove Museum. It has several schools of higher education, including the University of Glasgow and the University of Strathclyde.

The residents of Glasgow are called *Glaswegians.* Glasgow is close to Ireland, and the city has always had a large population of Irish immigrants.

Glasgow's history can be traced back to the founding of a church in the 500's on the city's present site by Saint Kentigern. The name *Glasgow* is said to be derived from a Gaelic word that means *dear green place.* The city was officially founded about 1180, and received the rights of a royal burgh in 1636.

In 1707, the Act of Union united Scotland with England. This act allowed Scottish ports to trade directly with North America. The resulting commerce helped establish Glasgow as an important port, and contributed to its early prosperity. Glasgow was one of the first cities to become involved in the Industrial Revolution, which began in the 1700's. James Watt developed his steam engine near Glasgow. Plentiful deposits of coal and iron ore in hills near the city helped make Glasgow a center for steel mills and the building of steamships and railroad locomotives. Glasgow's industrial success attracted large numbers of workers from other areas. By the late 1800's, Glasgow was the second largest city in the British Empire, after London.

Partly because of a depressed shipbuilding industry, Glasgow suffered serious economic problems from the end of World War I in 1918 until the 1950's. Housing conditions worsened, and slums became widespread. In the late 1950's, the city government began building multistory apartment buildings to replace run-down buildings. Since then, many other new buildings have been constructed in Glasgow, and many old ones have been rehabilitated. Richard Rose

Glasgow, *GLAS goh,* **Ellen** (1873-1945), was an American author known for her novels about the South. Glasgow criticized the Southern fiction of her time as too romantic and sentimental. She believed the South needed a more realistic awareness of itself. Many of Glasgow's novels examine life and values in Virginia from 1850 to the 1900's. She described the great social and political changes that took place during this period, when the South was changing from an agricultural to a more industrial society. Many of her novels deal with the role of women in the changing Southern social structure.

Ellen Anderson Gholson Glasgow was born into an aristocratic family in Richmond, Va., and her fiction strongly reflects her Southern heritage. The first of Glasgow's 19 novels was *The Descendant* (1897). She began her long series of novels on Virginia society with her next work, *The Voice of the People* (1900). Glasgow's other major novels include *Barren Ground* (1925), *The Romantic Comedians* (1926), *The Sheltered Life* (1932), and *Vein of Iron* (1935). She won the 1942 Pulitzer Prize for fiction for *In This Our Life* (1941). Her essays on the art of writing fiction were collected in *A Certain Measure* (1943). Her autobiography, *The Woman Within,* was published in 1954, after her death. Bert Hitchcock

Glasgow, *GLAS goh,* **University of,** is the second oldest university in Scotland. It has faculties in arts, divinity, engineering, law, medicine, social sciences, science, and veterinary medicine. The enrollment is about 13,000. The university was founded in 1451 by William Turnbull, bishop of Glasgow. P. A. McGinley

Glaspell, *GLAS pehl,* **Susan** (1882-1948), was an American playwright. With her husband, George Cram Cook, she was cofounder of the Provincetown Players and a prominent playwright for them. This influential theatrical organization, formed in 1915, produced Eugene O'Neill's first plays. It became the Playwrights Theater, which produced Broadway plays during the 1920's.

Susan Glaspell was born in Davenport, Ia. She gained recognition with two excellent one-act plays. In *Trifles* (1916), several women accompany their husbands on an investigation of a farmer's death. The women spot trifles that show why the wife was driven to kill the farmer. *Suppressed Desires* (1915) is a lively satire on psychoanalysis and freedom of expression and action. Glaspell won a Pulitzer Prize for *Alison's House* (1930). This play tells of a struggle in the family of a dead poet over whether to publish the poet's poems. The poet represents Emily Dickinson. During later years, Glaspell turned to writing short stories and novels, maintaining her truthful portrayals of life with its psychological tensions. Frank R. Cunningham

Milt and Joan Mann
Window glass

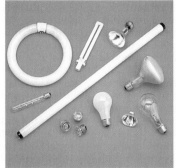
WORLD BOOK photo by Ralph J. Brunke
Glass electrical products

NASA
Fiberglass textiles

WORLD BOOK photo by Ralph J. Brunke
Glass containers

Pontiac Division, GMC
Windshield safety glass

Corning Incorporated
Glass-ceramic cookware

Milt and Joan Mann
Laboratory glassware

WORLD BOOK photo by Fred Weituschat
Optical glass

The Spirit of Glass by Dominick Labino
Art glass

Glass is used in making hundreds of products that are part of modern everyday life. These photographs show some of the many uses of this valuable material.

Glass

Glass is one of the most useful materials in the world. Few manufactured substances add as much to modern living as does glass. Yet few products are made of such inexpensive raw materials. Glass is made chiefly from *silica sand* (silica, also called silicon dioxide), *soda ash*

Steve W. Martin, the contributor of this article, is Professor of Materials Science and Engineering at Iowa State University of Science and Technology.

(sodium carbonate), and *limestone* (calcium carbonate).

Glass has countless uses. Food is preserved in glass jars. People drink from glass containers called glasses. Windows in homes, schools, and office buildings are glass. Motor vehicles have glass windshields and windows. People with vision problems wear eyeglasses. Scientists use glass test tubes, and microscopes and telescopes with glass lenses. Glass optical fibers carry data all over the world at the speed of light over the Internet, the worldwide network of computers.

Besides being useful, glass is also ornamental. Ever since people learned how to make glass, they have used it as an art material.

Glass can take many different forms. It can be spun finer than a spider web. Or it can be molded into a disk for a telescope lens or mirror weighing many tons. Glass can be stronger than steel, or more fragile than paper. Most glass is transparent, but glass can also be colored to any desired shade.

Most countries of the world have glass industries. For many years, Germany was the major world source for optical glass, laboratory glassware, and glass Christmas tree ornaments. Today, glass manufacturers in many countries produce such objects on a large scale. Beautiful art glassware is made in many countries, including the Czech Republic, France, Ireland, Italy, and Sweden.

Major glass companies spend millions of dollars each year on research to discover ways to make better glass and to develop new uses for glass. Many of the revolutionary developments in glass during the 1900's have come from the laboratories of glass manufacturers.

Kinds of glass

When people speak of glass, they ordinarily mean a transparent, shiny substance that breaks rather easily. They may think of the glass in windows and the glass used in eyeglasses as being the same material. Actually, they are not. There are many kinds of glass. Several important kinds of glass are discussed in this article.

Flat glass is used chiefly in windows. It is also used in mirrors, room dividers, and some kinds of furniture. All flat glass is made in the form of flat sheets. But some of it, such as that used in automobile windshields, is reheated and *sagged* (curved) over molds.

Glass containers are used for packaging food, beverages, medicines, chemicals, and cosmetics. Glass jars and bottles are made in a wide variety of shapes, sizes, and colors. Many are for common uses, such as soft-drink bottles or jars for home canning. Others are made from special glass formulas to make sure there will be no contamination or deterioration of blood plasma, serums, and chemicals stored in them. See **Bottle.**

Optical glass is used in eyeglasses, microscopes, telescopes, camera lenses, and many instruments for factories and laboratories. The raw materials must be pure so that the glass can be made almost flawless. The care required for producing optical glass makes it expensive compared with other kinds of glass. See **Glasses; Lens; Microscope; Telescope.**

Fiberglass consists of fine but solid rods of glass, each of which may be less than one-twentieth the width of a human hair. These tiny glass fibers can be loosely packed together in a woollike mass that can serve as heat insulation. They also can be used like wool or cotton fibers to make glass yarn, tape, cloth, and mats. Fiberglass has many other uses. It is used for electrical insulation, chemical filtration, and firefighters' suits. Combined with plastics, fiberglass can be used for airplane wings and bodies, automobile bodies, and boat hulls. Fiberglass is a popular curtain material because it is fire-resistant and washable. See **Fiberglass.**

Specialty glasses are all other types of glass besides flat glass, glass containers, optical glass, and fiberglass. Below are descriptions of 22 important specialty glasses.

Laminated safety glass is a "sandwich" made by combining alternate layers of flat glass and plastics. The outside layer of glass may break when struck by an object, but the plastic layer is elastic and so it stretches. The plastic holds the broken pieces of glass together and keeps them from flying in all directions. Laminated glass is used where broken glass might cause serious injuries, as in automobile windshields.

Bullet-resisting glass is thick, multilayer laminated glass. This glass can stop even heavy-caliber bullets at close range. Bullet-resisting glass is heavy enough to absorb the energy of the bullet, and the several plastic layers hold the shattered fragments together. Such glass is used in bank teller windows and in windshields for military tanks, aircraft, and special automobiles.

Tempered safety glass, unlike laminated glass, is a single piece that has been given a special heat treatment. It looks, feels, and weighs the same as ordinary glass. But it can be several times stronger. Tempered glass is used widely for all-glass doors in stores, side and rear windows of automobiles, and basketball backboards, and for other special purposes. It is hard to break even when hit with a hammer. When it does break, the whole piece of glass collapses into small, dull-edged fragments.

Colored structural glass is a heavy plate glass, available in many colors. It is used in buildings as an exterior facing, and for interior walls, partitions, and tabletops.

Opal glass has small particles in the body of the glass that disperse the light passing through it, making the glass appear milky. The ingredients necessary to produce opal glass include *fluorides* (chemical compounds containing fluorine). This glass is widely used in lighting fixtures and for tableware.

Foam glass, when it is cut, looks like a black honeycomb. It is filled with many tiny cells of gas. Each cell is surrounded and sealed off from the others by thin walls of glass. Foam glass is so light that it floats on water. It is widely used as a heat insulator in buildings, on steam pipes, and on chemical equipment. Foam glass can be cut into various shapes with a saw.

Glass building blocks are made from two hollow half-sections sealed together at a high temperature. Glass building blocks are good insulators against heat or cold because of the dead-air space inside. The blocks are laid like bricks to make walls and other structures.

Heat-resistant glass is high in silica and usually contains boric oxide. It expands little when heated, so it can withstand great temperature changes without cracking. This quality is necessary in cookware and other household equipment, and in many types of industrial gear.

Laboratory glassware includes beakers, flasks, test tubes, and special chemical apparatus. It is made from heat-resistant glass to withstand severe *heat shock* (rapid change in temperature). This glass is also much more resistant to chemical attack than ordinary glass.

Glass for electrical uses. Glass has properties that make it useful in electrical applications: ability to resist heat, resistance to the flow of electric current, and ability to seal tightly to metals without cracking. Because of these properties, glass is used in electric light bulbs and for picture tubes in television sets.

Glass optical fibers are glass fibers used to transmit information as pulses of light. Thin, extremely pure optical fibers are used to carry telephone and television signals and *digital* (numeric) data over long distances. Glass optical fibers are also used in control board displays and in medical instruments. See **Fiber optics.**

Glass tubing is used to make fluorescent lights, neon signs, glass piping, and chemical apparatus. Glass tubing is made from many kinds of glass and in many sizes.

Glass-ceramics are strong materials made by heating glass to rearrange some of its atoms into regular patterns. These partially crystalline materials can withstand high temperatures, sudden changes in temperature, and chemical attacks better than ordinary glass can. They are used in a variety of products, including heat-resistant cookware, turbine engines, electronic equipment, and nose cones of guided missiles. Glass-ceramics have such trade names as Pyroceram, Cervit, and Hercuvit.

Radiation-absorbing and radiation-transmitting glass can transmit, modify, or block heat, light, X rays, and other types of radiant energy. For example, ultraviolet glass absorbs the ultraviolet rays of the sun but transmits visible light. Other glass transmits heat rays freely but passes little visible light. Polarized glass cuts out the glare of brilliant light. One-way glass is specially coated so that a person can look through a window without being seen from the other side. See **Polarized light.**

Laser glass is an optical glass containing small amounts of substances that enable the glass to generate laser beams efficiently. Such glass is used as the active medium in *solid-state lasers,* a type of laser that sends light out through crystals or glass (see **Laser** (Solid-state lasers). One substance commonly used in laser glass is the element neodymium. Researchers are using glass lasers in an attempt to harness *nuclear fusion* (the joining of atomic nuclei) as a source of commercially useful amounts of energy. In their experiments, powerful glass lasers heat hydrogen atoms until hydrogen nuclei fuse, releasing large amounts of energy.

"Invisible glass" is used principally for coated camera lenses and eyeglasses. The coating is a chemical film that decreases the normal loss of light by reflection. This allows more light to pass through the glass.

Photochromic glass darkens when exposed to ultraviolet rays and clears up when the rays are removed. Photochromic glass is used for windows, sunglasses, and instrument controls.

Photosensitive glass can be exposed to ultraviolet light and to heat so that any pattern or photograph can be reproduced within the body of the glass itself. Because the photographic print then becomes an actual part of the glass, it will last as long as the glass itself.

Photochemical glass is a special composition of photosensitive glass that can be cut by acid. Any design can be reproduced on the glass from a photographic film. Then when the glass is dipped in acid, the exposed areas are eaten away, leaving the design in the glass in three dimensions. By this means, lacelike glass patterns can be made.

Heavy metal fluoride glass is an extremely transparent glass being developed for use in optical fibers that transmit infrared rays. Infrared rays are much like light waves but are invisible to the human eye. In optical fibers, infrared light transmits better over distance than visible light does.

Chalcogenide glass is made up of elements from the chalcogen group, including selenium, sulfur, and tellurium. The glass is transparent to infrared light and is useful as a semiconductor in some electronic devices.

Chalcogenide glass fibers are a component of devices used to perform laser surgery.

Sol-Gel glass can be used as a protective coating on certain solar collectors or as an insulating material. It is also used to make short, thick tubes that are drawn into optical fibers. To make Sol-Gel glass, workers dissolve the ingredients in a liquid. They then heat the liquid. The liquid evaporates, leaving behind small particles of glass. Heating these particles *fuses* (joins) them to form a solid piece of glass. The temperatures involved in Sol-Gel processes are often lower than those needed to make ordinary glass.

Composition of glass

Glass can be generally divided into two groups: oxide glass and non-oxide glass. The ingredients of oxide glasses include *oxides* (chemical compounds that include oxygen). Non-oxide glasses are made from compounds that contain no oxides, and which often instead contain sulfides or metals. Oxide glasses are much more widely used commercially. The common types of glass discussed below are all oxide glasses.

Soda-lime glass is the kind of glass used for flat glass, most containers and electric light bulbs, and many other industrial and art objects. More than 90 percent of all glass is soda-lime glass. It has been made of almost the same materials for hundreds of years. The composition is about 72 percent silica (from sand), about 13 percent sodium oxide (from soda ash), about 11 percent calcium oxide (from limestone), and about 4 percent minor ingredients. Soda-lime glass is inexpensive, easy to melt and shape, and reasonably strong.

All glass container manufacturers use the same basic soda-lime composition, making the containers easy to recycle. Manufacturers sort the glass by color and then later reuse it in the production of new containers.

Soda-lead glass, commonly called *crystal* or *lead glass,* is made by substituting lead oxide for calcium oxide and often for part of the silica used in soda-lime glass. Soda-lead glass is easy to melt. It is much more expensive than soda-lime glass. Soda-lead glass has such beautiful optical properties that it is widely used for the finest tableware and art objects. In addition, lead oxide improves the electrical properties of glass.

Borosilicate glass is heat-shock resistant and better known by such trade names as Pyrex and Kimax. It contains about 80 percent silica, 4 percent sodium oxide, 2 percent alumina, and 13 percent boric oxide. Such glass is about three times as heat-shock resistant as soda-lime glass and is excellent for chemical and electrical uses. This glass makes possible such products as ovenware, beakers, test tubes, and other laboratory equipment.

Fused silica glass is a highly heat-shock resistant glass that consists entirely of silica. It can be heated to extremely high temperatures and then plunged into ice-cold water without cracking. Fused silica is expensive because exceptionally high temperatures must be maintained during production. It is used in laboratory glassware and optical fibers.

96 percent silica glass resists heat almost as well as fused silica, but it is less expensive to produce. It consists of a special borosilicate composition that has been made porous by chemical treatment. The pores shrink when the glass is heated, leaving a smooth, transparent

Making glass by machine

The raw materials used to make glass are mixed together and then melted in huge furnaces. The molten glass is shaped by various methods, depending on the type of product being made. This diagram shows the (1) blowing, (2) pressing, and (3) drawing methods. The shaped pieces are put into an annealing oven, where they are reheated and then cooled to strengthen the glass.

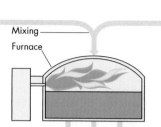

Sand, soda, and lime are the chief raw materials used in making glass.

Cullet is waste glass or recycled glass that is added to aid the melting process.

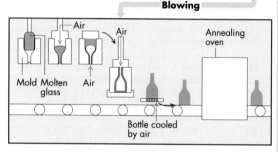

Blowing glass bottles. Gobs of molten glass are dropped into molds. Air blows the glass into a bottlelike shape. Next, the glass is flipped over and blown into its final shape. The bottle is then cooled slightly on a plate and annealed.

Pressing glass dishes. Gobs of molten glass are dropped into molds. A plunger presses down on the glass, forcing it to spread and fill the mold. The dish is cooled slightly, removed from the mold by suction, and moved into the annealing oven.

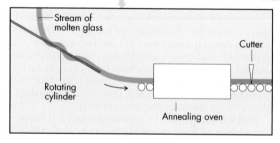

WORLD BOOK diagrams by Precision Graphics

Drawing glass tubing. A stream of molten glass is drawn around a rotating cylinder. Air blown through the cylinder causes the glass to form a continuous tube. The finished tubing passes through the annealing oven and is then cut into pieces.

Drawing flat glass. Sheets of molten glass are drawn into a float bath containing molten tin. Imperfections are melted out of the glass as it floats in an even layer on the tin. The finished sheet is then annealed and cut into smaller sheets.

surface. The glass is sold under the trade name Vycor.

Colored glass gets its coloring from certain oxides that are added to the glass. For example, 1 part of nickel oxide in 50,000 produces a tint that may range from yellow to purple, depending on the base glass. One part of cobalt oxide in 10,000 gives an intense blue. Red glasses are made with gold, copper, or selenium oxides. Other colors can be produced in glass with other chemicals.

How glass is made

No other kind of factory looks like a glass plant. Huge bins called *silos* hold the raw materials for glassmaking.

These materials are powders that look much alike but can produce greatly different results. Giant roof ventilators and huge stacks release the terrific heat required to melt these powders to a white-hot liquid. At the *hot end* of the plant are the furnaces.

Mixing. The principal raw materials come to the glass plant in railroad cars and are stored in large silos. The materials are carefully weighed and mechanically mixed in the proper proportions. The mix of ingredients is called the *batch.* The manufacturer then adds *cullet* to the batch. Cullet is either recycled glass or waste glass from a previous melt of the same kind of glass. Adding cullet to the batch uses materials that otherwise would be wasted. It also reduces the amount of heat needed to melt the new batch of raw materials. Sometimes, glassmakers produce a new batch entirely from cullet. After mixing, the batch goes to the furnaces in batch cars, in hoppers, or on conveyor belts.

Melting. The mixture melts at 2600 to 2900 °F (1425 to 1600 °C), depending on its composition. In early times, the batch was melted in *refractory pots* (small clay pots) that were generally heated by wood fires. Special refractory pots today hold up to 3,000 pounds (1,400 kilograms) of glass. They are heated by gas or oil, and a single furnace may contain 6 to 12 pots. Small quantities of optical glass, art glass, and specialty glass still are made in refractory pots.

Larger quantities of glass are made in furnaces that are called *day tanks* because the process that goes on in them takes about 24 hours. The day tank is filled with raw materials, the glass is melted, and all the glass is used before the furnace is filled again. Day tanks can hold 1 to 4 tons (0.9 to 3.6 metric tons) of glass.

Most glass is melted in large furnaces called *continuous tanks*. The largest continuous tanks can melt 400 to 600 tons (360 to 540 metric tons) a day for production of flat glass. From 50 to 300 tons (45 to 270 metric tons) of container glass can be melted daily. Smaller continuous tanks are used to produce most other glass products. The operation is continuous. Raw materials are fed into the loading end as rapidly as molten glass is removed from the working end. Loading, melting, and working go on from when the fires are first lighted until they are extinguished at the end of a period called a *campaign*. A campaign may last as long as 10 years. The length of a campaign is almost always determined by the time it takes the refractory brick walls of the furnace to wear out from the constant heat and friction of the glass.

How glass is shaped and finished

There are four main methods of shaping glass: *blowing, pressing, drawing,* and *casting*. After the shaping process, *annealing* is used to increase the strength of the glass. *Tempering* and other finishing techniques may also be used to further strengthen the glass. At the *cold end* of the plant, finished glass products are inspected and boxed for sale. The glass may also be decorated before packaging. See the section *How glass is decorated* later in this article.

Blowing. *Offhand glass blowing* (blowing glass without the use of molds) is an art about 2,000 years old. A hollow iron *blowpipe*, 4 to 5 feet (1.2 to 1.5 meters) long, is dipped in molten glass, some of which sticks to the pear-shaped end of the pipe. A worker blows gently into the pipe until the glass bulges out and forms a hollow bulb. The bulb can be squeezed, stretched, twirled, and cut. From time to time, the worker reheats the glass to keep it soft. When the red-hot glass has been given its final shape, it is removed from the pipe. Glass can also be blown into iron molds—by hand or by machine.

Pressing is accomplished by dropping a hot gob of glass into a mold, then pressing it with a plunger until it spreads and fills the inside of the mold. To be pressed, an article must be of such a shape that the plunger can be withdrawn. Baking dishes, glass blocks, and lenses are often pressed. As with blowing, pressing can be done by hand or by machine, and with single or multiple molds. Press-and-blow machines use a combination of the pressing and the blowing methods to form the article. Such machines can produce hundreds of glass containers per hour.

Drawing is the method used for shaping flat glass, glass rod, glass tubing, and fiberglass. Almost all flat glass produced today is float glass. It is shaped by drawing a wide sheet of molten glass into a furnace containing a bath of molten tin. This furnace is called a *float bath* because the glass "floats" in an even layer on the perfectly smooth surface of the molten tin. Heating in the float bath is carefully controlled to melt out any roughness in the glass. Because glass turns solid at a higher temperature than tin, it can be moved from the molten tin for further cooling. When flat glass is shaped in a float bath, both sides come out with a brilliant finish that requires no grinding or polishing.

Owens-Illinois

Blown glass bottles move from the blowing machine onto a conveyor belt, which carries them to an annealing oven. There, the bottles are cooled and reheated to strengthen the glass.

Corning Glass Works

Pressing machines shape fairly flat glass products, such as the roasting pans shown here. Molten glass has been dropped into molds and is being pressed into shape by plungers.

Libbey-Owens-Ford Company

Drawing glass is the method used to shape flat glass and glass tubing. The sheet of flat glass shown above has been shaped in a tank of molten tin and then annealed. The finished sheet is being moved to a machine that will cut it into smaller sheets. In the scene shown on the right, a stream of molten glass is being drawn from the furnace onto a rotating cylinder that shapes glass tubing.

Corning Glass Works

Glass rod is made by drawing a stream of molten glass out of the furnace. Tubing is made by drawing the molten glass around a rotating cylinder or cone called a *mandrel.* Air blowing through the mandrel causes the glass to form a continuous tube. Fiberglass is made by drawing the molten glass through tiny holes in the bottom of the furnace.

Casting involves filling molds with molten glass. The glass may be poured either from ladles or directly from the furnace, or drained from the bottom of the furnace. Casting is used in the production of architectural glass pieces, art glass, laser glass, and telescope mirrors.

Lampworking is a method of reshaping solid glass into new forms by reheating it. Lampworkers reheat various kinds and sizes of glass tubing and rod over a blowtorch fired by gas and oxygen. Then they can bend, twist, stretch, and seal the softened glass into a variety of objects. In this way, lampworkers make miniature animals, vases, sailing ships, beads, scientific equipment, and parts for incandescent lamps and various kinds of industrial equipment. Lampworkers produce many small parts for the electrical, chemical, and medical industries on high-speed automatic machines by reworking the softened glass.

Annealing is a process that removes the stresses and strains remaining in glass after shaping. Most glassware is annealed just after it has been formed. If it is not annealed, glass may shatter from tension caused by un-

Steuben Glass (Henry Groskinsky)

Blowing glass without the use of molds involves several steps. First, a worker blows gently into an iron blowpipe that has been dipped in molten glass, *left.* This piece is being blown into the shape of a bowl. The rim of the bowl is shaped by cutting the molten glass as the pipe is turned, *center.* The glass blower works the bowl into its final shape, *right.*

even cooling. Annealing is done by reheating the glass and gradually cooling it according to a planned time-and-temperature schedule. See **Annealing**.

Tempering is a process in which a glass article that is already formed is reheated until almost soft. Then, under carefully controlled conditions, it is chilled suddenly by blasts of cold air or by plunging it in oil or certain chemicals in a liquid state. This tempering treatment makes the glass much stronger than ordinary glass. Glass articles can also be tempered with chemicals.

Inspection. In almost every glass plant, engineers take frequent samples directly from the furnace and test them for quality and desired properties. Samples of finished glass products also are tested for size, proper annealing, and other qualities.

How glass is decorated

Several preliminary finishing operations are often necessary before glass articles can be decorated. Excess glass must be removed from blown items. In hand operations, the glass is cut off while it is still soft. Sometimes the glass piece is revolved in front of an intensely hot gas flame. The sudden expansion of the hot, narrow band of glass revolving opposite the flame makes it break off from the cooler glass next to it. In other cases, the item may be supported upside down while even hotter flames are applied until the glass melts and separates. The weight of the extra glass makes it drop into a cullet bin, from which it is returned to the furnace to be used again. The extra glass also can be cut off by *scoring* (cutting) the glass piece with a diamond or steel wheel, and then snapping off the excess glass with sudden pressure. If the *severed* (cut) edges of the glass article are not smooth enough, they may be polished with fine abrasives, or by flames in a fire-polishing machine.

Etching. Hydrofluoric acid and some of its compounds readily dissolve glass. Glass articles dipped in, or sprayed with, these chemicals are said to be *etched*. The finish of an etched-glass surface depends on the glass composition, concentration of fluorides, and time. The surface may be rough, frosted, and almost opaque; or it may have a translucent, soft, satiny-smooth appearance. The interiors of electric light bulbs are frosted with this satiny finish. Pitchers, water tumblers, and art glass often are etched with intricate designs. They are first painted with a *resist* (acid-resistant chemical) to protect the parts of the glass outside the desired pattern. Then acid eats away the unpainted surface of the glass, leaving the pattern. A brilliant acid polish can be made by combining hydrofluoric and sulfuric acid.

Sandblasting gives glass a translucent surface, which is usually rougher than that obtained by etching. Compressed air blows coarse, rough-grained sand against the glass, often through a rubber stencil, to form a design. The labels on glass laboratory equipment are often sandblasted. Lighting devices, ovenware, and plate and window glass are frequently decorated or made translucent by sandblasting.

Cutting involves wearing away considerable quantities of the original glass by holding it against revolving sandstone or carborundum wheels. The worker follows a design previously marked on the article. The cuts may be quite deep. The original luster is restored to the cut surfaces by etching or by polishing with fine abrasives.

James L. Amos, Corbis

Lampworking involves heating finished glass and reshaping it by hand. This lampworker shapes heat-resistant borosilicate glass into a container that will be used as laboratory glassware.

Copper-wheel engraving can be used to create delicate, detailed, and flowing designs, faithfully reproduced in three dimensions. Many masterpieces in glass are engraved. The process involves the careful cutting of glass with dozens of abrasive-fed copper wheels.

Fired decorations. Colored enamels and lusters can be applied to glass by hand painting, by *decalomania* (the process of transferring decals), or by the silk-screen printing process. When these decorations are heated to the proper temperature, they fuse to the glass and thus become part of the article. Tumblers, jugs, pitchers, lighting devices, novelties, and many other glass products are decorated in this way. See **Decal; Enamel; Screen printing**.

History of glass

Early times. Before people learned to make glass, they had found two forms of natural glass. When light-

Milt and Joan Mann

Copper-wheel engraving, *shown here,* can produce ornate three-dimensional designs in glass. Glass engravers cut into the surface of the glass with rotating copper wheels of various sizes.

Important dates in glass development

c. 3000 B.C. The first manufactured glass was made in the form of a glaze on ceramic vessels.
c. 1500 B.C. The first vessels entirely of glass were made.
c. 30 B.C. The blowpipe for blowing glass was invented.
c. A.D. 50 The first window glass was manufactured.
c. 900 Glass industries flourished in Persia and Iraq.
c. 1300 Venetians began to dominate glassmaking.
1535 The first glass produced in the Western Hemisphere was made at Puebla de los Angeles in Mexico.
1674 George Ravenscroft in England patented lead glass.
1688 Plate glass was produced by casting by Louis Lucas in France. This led to the wide use of mirrors.
1790 Good optical glass was made by Pierre-Louis Guinand in France, by stirring glass in melting pots.
1879 The bulb for Thomas Edison's electric light was blown by Fred Douerlein, Corning Glass Works in New York.
1902 A machine to draw a continuous sheet of glass was developed by Émile Fourcault of Belgium.
1903 Laminated glass was invented by Edouard Benedictus in France.
1904 An automatic bottle-making machine was invented by Michael J. Owens in Toledo, Ohio.
1908-1917 A sheet window-glass drawing machine was invented by I. W. Colburn and developed by Libbey-Owens Sheet Glass Company in Charleston, West Virginia.
1912-1915 Heat-shock resistant borosilicate glass (trademark Pyrex) was developed by Eugene C. Sullivan and William C. Taylor of Corning Glass Works.
1920 Polarized glass was invented by Lewis W. Chubb of Westinghouse Electric Company, East Pittsburgh, Pennsylvania.
1926 A fully automatic machine to blow electric-light bulbs was developed by Corning Glass Works.
1926 Mass production of safety glass was developed by Libbey-Owens Glass Company.
1926 A machine to draw sheet glass directly from the furnace was developed by Pittsburgh Plate Glass Company (now PPG Industries, Inc.).
1930 Insulated window glass (trademark Thermopane) was invented by C. D. Haven in the United States.

1931-1938 Fiberglass was developed by the Owens-Illinois Glass Company (now Owens-Illinois, Inc.) and Corning Glass Works.
1939 96 percent silica glass was developed by Harrison Hood and Martin Nordberg of Corning Glass Works.
1942 Foam glass was developed by Pittsburgh Corning Corp.
1947 Photosensitive glass was developed by S. D. Stookey of Corning Glass Works.
1951 Photochemical glass was developed by Corning Glass Works.
1955 Lightweight glass solder was developed by Owens-Illinois Glass Company (now Owens-Illinois, Inc.).
1957 Glass-ceramic crystalline materials (trademark Pyroceram) were developed by S. D. Stookey of Corning Glass Works.
1959 Float process for continuous production of flat glass was developed by Pilkington Brothers, Ltd., in St. Helens, England.
1961 Laser glass was invented by Elias Snitzer of the American Optical Corp.
1962 Chemically tempered glass was developed by Corning Glass Works.
1964 Photochromic glass was developed by W. H. Armistead and S. D. Stookey of Corning Glass Works.
1967 High-strength laminated sheet glass for dinnerware (trademark Corelle) was developed by James W. Giffen of the Corning Glass Works.
1970 Optical fibers suitable for communications were developed by D. B. Keck, R. D. Maurer, and P. C. Schultz of Corning Glass Works.
1974 Heavy metal fluoride glass was discovered by Michel Poulain of the University of Rennes, France.
1978 Scientists in Marcoule, France, incorporated nuclear waste into special glass for storage.
1980 Transparent glass-ceramic cookware was introduced by Corning Glass Works.
1990 Optical amplifier to boost signals for optical fiber transmissions was developed by Bell Laboratories (now part of Lucent Technologies).

ning strikes sand, the heat sometimes fuses the sand into long, slender glass tubes called *fulgurites,* which are commonly called *petrified lightning.* The terrific heat of a volcanic eruption also sometimes fuses rocks and sand into a glass called *obsidian.* In early times, people shaped obsidian into knives, arrowheads, jewelry, and money. See **Obsidian.**

We do not know exactly when, where, or how people first learned to make glass. It is generally believed that the first manufactured glass was in the form of a glaze on ceramic vessels, about 3000 B.C. The first glass vessels were produced about 1500 B.C. in Egypt and Mesopotamia. The glass industry was extremely successful for the next 300 years, and then declined. It was revived in Mesopotamia in the 700's B.C. and in Egypt in the 500's B.C. For the next 500 years, Egypt, Syria, and the other countries along the eastern shore of the Mediterranean Sea were glassmaking centers.

Early glassmaking was slow and costly, and it required hard work. Glass blowing and glass pressing were unknown, furnaces were small, the clay pots were of poor quality, and the heat was hardly sufficient for melting. But glassmakers eventually learned how to make colored glass jewelry, cosmetics cases, and tiny jugs and jars. People who could afford them—the priests and the ruling classes—considered glass objects as valuable as jewels. Soon merchants learned that wines, honey, and oils could be carried and preserved far better in

glass than in wood or clay containers.

The blowpipe was invented about 30 B.C., probably along the eastern Mediterranean coast. This invention made glass production easier, faster, and cheaper. As a result, glass became available to the common people for the first time. Glass manufacture became important in all countries under Roman rule. In fact, the first four centuries of the Christian Era may justly be called the *First Golden Age of Glass.* The glassmakers of this time knew how to make a transparent glass, and they did offhand glass blowing, painting, and *gilding* (application of gold leaf). They knew how to build up layers of glass of different colors and then cut out designs in high relief. The celebrated Portland vase, which was probably made in Rome about the beginning of the Christian Era, is an excellent example of this art. This vase is considered one of the most valuable glass art objects in the world.

The Middle Ages. Little is known about the glass industry between the decline of the Roman Empire and the 1200's. Glass manufacture had developed in Venice by the time of the Crusades (A.D. 1096-1270), and by the 1290's an elaborate guild system of glassworkers had been set up. Equipment was transferred to the Venetian island of Murano, and the *Second Golden Age of Glass* began. Venetian glass blowers created some of the most delicate and graceful glass the world has ever seen. They perfected *Cristallo* glass, a nearly colorless, transparent glass, which could be blown to extreme thinness

The Art Institute of Chicago,
Gift of Theodore W. Robinson

An Egyptian glass bottle of the 18th dynasty (1570-1300 B.C.) was shaped by winding glass rods of various colors around a sand mold.

The Corning Museum of Glass,
Corning, New York

The Corning Ewer is a fine example of Islamic glassware. The vessel, probably made during the A.D. 900's, has elaborate designs carved in relief.

British Museum

The famous Portland Vase is one of the most valuable glass art objects in the world. It was probably made in Rome at the beginning of the Christian Era.

in almost any shape. From Cristallo, they made intricate lacework patterns in goblets, jars, bowls, cups, and vases. In the 1100's and 1200's, the art of making stained-glass windows reached its height throughout Europe.

By the late 1400's and early 1500's, glassmaking had become important in Germany and other northern European countries. Manufacturers there chiefly produced containers and drinking vessels. Northern forms were heavier, sturdier, and less clear than Venice's Cristallo. During the late 1500's, many Venetians went to northern Europe, hoping to earn a better living. They established factories there and made glass in the Venetian fashion. A new type of glass that worked well for copper-wheel engraving was perfected in Bohemia (now part of the Czech Republic) and Germany in the mid-1600's, and a flourishing industry developed.

Glassmaking became important in England during the 1500's. By 1575, English glassmakers were producing Venetian-style glass. In 1674, an English glassmaker named George Ravenscroft patented a new type of glass

(*text continued on page 222*)

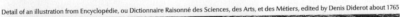

Detail of an illustration from Encyclopédie, ou Dictionnaire Raisonné des Sciences, des Arts, et des Métiers, edited by Denis Diderot about 1765

Glassmakers of the 1700's worked around a furnace that held pots of molten glass. Workers in the factory shown here are gathering molten glass onto pipes and blowing it into shape.

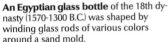

Types of art glass

Art glass is glassware made solely or partly for its beauty. Numerous people collect such glassware because it is beautiful and, in many cases, because it also is old or rare. This section describes some of the kinds of art glass valued by collectors.

Cylindrical drinking glass with enamel decoration; Corning Museum of Glass, Corning, N.Y.

Bohemian tumbler from 1574

Corning Museum of Glass, Corning, N.Y.

Burmese lamp from the late 1800's

The Art Institute of Chicago, Gift of Julius and Augusta N. Rosenwald

Winged goblet from about 1600

Amberina glass is colored by adding gold to the glass. It ranges in color from pale amber-yellow to rich ruby-red. It was patented in 1883 by Joseph Locke of Massachusetts.

Amelung glass includes bowls, bottles, and goblets that were made by John Frederick Amelung at his New Bremen Glass Manufactory in Frederick County, Maryland, from 1784 to 1795. His glassware was engraved with mottoes, monograms, crests, and flower wreaths.

Baccarat glass. The glass works at Baccarat, France, produced some of the best cut glass made in Europe in the 1800's. It also made paperweights with *millefiori* (floral) ornaments and other designs embedded in clear glass. Baccarat glass is still being produced. Today, it includes specially designed crystal sculptures, as well as bowls, table service, and vases.

Bohemian glass. Beginning in the mid-1500's, large amounts of decorative glassware were produced in Bohemia and Silesia, which are regions of Eastern Europe. The glassware often was ornamented with enameled castles, people, and animals. Casper Lehmann, a gem cutter in Prague, is credited with starting glass engraving in Bohemia in 1609.

Burmese glass was produced by the Mount Washington Glass Company of New Bedford, Mass., beginning in 1885. The surface of some of the glass is glossy. The surface of other pieces was given a dull satin finish by treating it with acid. Burmese glass is translucent and ranges in color from salmon-pink to lemon-yellow.

Cristallo glass was the typical clear, thin glass the Venetians developed in the mid-1400's or early 1500's. Its beauty depended on the blower's shaping skills. The glass is slightly gray.

Crystal glass contains a high percentage of lead oxide, which causes light rays to *refract* (bend). For this reason, crystal glass is widely used in optical instruments. But it is also used in making tableware and art objects. The first crystal glass was patented in England by George Ravenscroft in 1674.

Daum glass. The Daum company of Nancy, France, is an important producer of modern art glass. Daum glass includes table services, bowls, vases, lamps, and crystal sculptures. Most of the pieces are of clear crystal. Some of them are decorated with applied, lightly colored crystal.

Gallé glass was produced by the French glassmaker Emile Gallé in the late 1800's and early 1900's. Gallé made decorative items, including vases and bowls, out of colored or uncolored glass. He created raised animal, floral, and other designs on these objects by carving through an outer layer of glass to one of another color.

Kew-Blas glass, also spelled *Kewblas,* is an iridescent glass made in the 1890's by W. S. Blake at the Union Glass Works of Somerville, Mass.

Lace glass, or latticinio, is a Venetian type of glass made in the 1500's. It has fine lacelike patterns of white glass contained in a body of clear glass.

Leerdam glass is the best-known glass made today in the Netherlands. The Royal Leerdam company, located in Leerdam, near Gorinchem, produces a fine crystal and a clear, colored glass in shades of blue, gray, green, purple, and yellow. The company also makes one-of-a-kind pieces called *Unica* that are of especially high quality. The Leerdam factory maintains a school for the training of glass designers and craftworkers.

Goblet by George Ravenscroft; Corning Museum of Glass, Corning, N.Y.

English goblet from the 1670's

Nailsea glass was made in the late 1700's and in the 1800's at Nailsea, England. It was often decorated with loops and stripes of colored glass. The best-known type was the *witch ball*. Witch balls were used as stoppers on pitchers and jars. Superstitious people sometimes hung them in windows to ward off witches.

Orrefors glass is produced in Orrefors, Sweden. The Orrefors Company is a major producer of modern art glass. Some Orrefors designers have emphasized engraving in their designs. Orrefors glass includes *Ariel glass*, in which air bubbles form a design in layers of colored or uncolored glass.

Pomona glass was patented in 1885 by Joseph Locke of Massachusetts. It is a tinted, clear glass that was blown into a mold. Then its surface was decorated with etching.

Sandwich glass was made by the Boston and Sandwich Glass Company of Sandwich, Mass., from 1825 to 1888. The company produced many kinds of glassware but is best known for its pressed glass. Some people mistakenly believe that all pressed glassware of the 1800's was Sandwich glass. But in reality, many companies made pressed glass in large quantities.

Satin glass was made by many companies in the late 1800's. Its surface has a satiny appearance. This appearance is caused by treating the glass with the fumes of hydrofluoric acid.

Steuben glass is the most famous art glass made in the United States today. The Steuben Glass Company was founded in 1903 at Corning, N.Y., by an Englishman named Frederick Carder. The only glass used by the company today is a heavy lead crystal that is sparkling, transparent, and almost free from imperfection. Most Steuben pieces are entirely handmade and are either completely unadorned or copper-wheel engraved.

Stiegel glass was made by Henry William Stiegel from 1763 to 1774 in Lancaster County, Pennsylvania. He made good colorless glassware, as well as glass objects in a wide variety of colors. Stiegel applied patterns to the glass by molding, enameling, and engraving.

Tiffany Favrile glass was made by Louis Comfort Tiffany from 1893 to 1933 in Corona, Long Island (now part of New York City). This glass is iridescent with rich colors that range from deep blue to purple and from green to yellow-gold. Some pieces were decorated by carving through one layer down to that of another color. The surface has a silky appearance.

Waterford glass, which is famous for its fine crystal, is made in Waterford, Ireland. It was made from 1783 to 1851, when production ended. Production was resumed in 1952.

Wistar glass, or South Jersey glass. In 1739, Caspar Wistar built a glassworks in Salem County, New Jersey. The county later became a center of production for many small glass factories, and it remained so for a number of years. Wistar glass is green or amber, of the type used in common bottles. It is decorated with bands, swirls, and threads of applied glass.

Corning Museum of Glass, Corning, N.Y.

Gallé glass with dragonfly design

Mercury glass, or silvered glass, was made in the United States from the 1850's to the 1880's. The glass was given a silvery appearance by pouring a mercury alloy between the thin inside and outside walls of a piece of glassware. The opening then was sealed to make the piece airtight.

Milk glass, or opal glass, is an opaque white glass widely used for tableware. Milk glass pieces include covered dishes that have a statue of a chicken, rabbit, or other animal on the lid.

Millefiori glass, which means *glass of a thousand flowers,* was first made by the early Egyptians and Romans, and still is produced today. Tiny colored glass rods are arranged in bundles and then fused together with heat. When the piece of glass is cut across, it has a design like that of many small flowers. This type of glassware frequently has been used for paperweights.

Steuben Glass

Steuben bowl with swan design

WORLD BOOK photo by Steven Spicer

Waterford crystal jar

Corning Museum of Glass, Corning, N.Y.

Wistar sugar bowl

The Corning Museum of Glass, Corning, New York

Stained-glass windows have been used for decoration since the 1000's. This window was created by Louis C. Tiffany, who became a leading American glassware designer in the late 1800's.

(text continued from page 219)

in which he had changed the usual ingredients. This glass, called *lead glass,* contains a large amount of lead oxide. Lead glass, which is especially suitable for optical instruments, caused English glassmaking to prosper.

Early American glass. The first factory in what is now the United States was a glass plant built at Jamestown, Virginia, in 1608. The venture failed within a year because of a famine that took the lives of many

Glass terms

Bait is the tool dipped into molten glass to start any drawing operation.

Blister is a large gas bubble that is an imperfection in the glass.

Blow-over is a thin-walled bubble formed above a hand-blown mold to make it easier to crack off.

Checks are cracks, imperfections in the glass.

Cord is an imperfection that appears as long strings of a different composition from the main body of the glass.

Doghouse is the place where the batch is fed into a furnace.

Feeder is a mechanical device for producing and delivering gobs to a glass-forming unit.

Fire-over is to allow a melting unit to idle at operating temperature.

Gaffer is the person in charge of a shop of glass blowers.

Gather is a gob, or blob, of glass collected on the end of a blowpipe.

Glory hole is an opening in a small furnace used to reheat glass in handworking.

Marver is a flat plate, usually metal, on which a gather of glass is rolled, shaped, and cooled.

Moil is the glass remaining on a punty or blowpipe after a gob has been cut off for pressing, or after a piece of ware has been blown and cracked off.

Pontil, or **Punty,** is a solid iron rod, about the size of a blowpipe, used to carry and manipulate small amounts of glass.

Seed is a small gas bubble that is an imperfection in the glass.

Stone is any nonglassy material imbedded in the glass. It is an imperfection.

Teaser is a worker who regulates the fires and the loading of the batch into a furnace.

colonists. The Jamestown colonists tried glassmaking again in 1621, but an Indian attack in 1622 and the scarcity of workers ended this attempt in 1624. The industry was reestablished in America in 1739, when Caspar Wistar built a glassmaking plant in what is now Salem County, New Jersey. This plant operated until 1780.

Wistar is one of the great names of early American glass. The second great American glassmaker was Henry William Stiegel, also known by his nickname, "Baron" Stiegel. Stiegel made clear and colored glass, engraved and enameled glass, and the first lead glass produced in North America. A third important American glassmaker was John F. Amelung, who became best known for his elegant engraved glass.

Another important early American glass, *Sandwich glass,* was made by the Boston and Sandwich Glass Company, founded by Deming Jarves in 1825. It was long believed to be the first company in America to produce pressed glass. But the first was actually the Bakewell, Page, and Bakewell Company of Pittsburgh, Pennsylvania, which began to make pressed glass earlier in 1825. These two companies and many others soon made large quantities of inexpensive glass, both pressed and blown. Every effort was made to produce a "poor man's cut glass." In lacy Sandwich, for example, glassmakers decorated molds with elaborate designs to give the objects a complex, lacelike effect.

In the early 1800's, the type of glass in greatest demand was window glass. At that time, window glass was called *crown glass.* Glassmakers made it by blowing a bubble of glass, then spinning it until it was flat. This process left a sheet of glass with a bump called a *crown* in the center. By 1825, the *cylinder* process had replaced the crown method. In this process, molten glass was blown into the shape of a cylinder. After the cylinder cooled, it was sliced down one side. When reheated, it opened up to form a large sheet of thin, clear window glass. In the 1850's, plate glass was developed for mirrors and other products requiring a high quality of flat glass. This glass was made by casting a large quantity of molten glass onto a round or square plate. After the glass was cooled, it was polished on both sides.

Bottles and flasks were first used chiefly for whiskey, but the patent-medicine industry soon used large numbers of bottles. The screw-top Mason jar for home canning appeared in 1858. By 1880, commercial food packers began to use glass containers. Glass tableware was used in steadily increasing quantities. The discovery of petroleum and the appearance of the kerosene lamp in the early 1860's led to a demand for millions of glass lamp chimneys. All these developments helped to expand the market for glass.

Modern glassmaking. Changes in the fuel used by the glass industry affected the location of glass factories. In the early days when wood was used as fuel, glassworks were built near forests. By 1880, coal had become the most widely used fuel for glassmaking, and glassmaking operations were near large coal deposits. After 1880, natural gas became accepted as the perfect fuel for melting glass. Today, most glass manufacturing plants are near the major sales markets. Pipelines carry petroleum and natural gas to the glass plants.

After 1890, the development, manufacture, and use of glass increased rapidly. The science and engineering of glass as a material are now so much better understood that glass can be tailored to meet an exact need. Any one of thousands of compositions may be used. Machinery has been developed for precise, continuous manufacture of sheet glass, tubing, containers, bulbs, and a host of other products.

New methods of cutting, welding, sealing, and tempering, as well as better glass at lower cost, have led to new uses of glass. Glass is now used to make pipelines, cookware, building blocks, and heat insulation.

Ordinary glass turns brown when exposed to nuclear radiation, so glass companies developed a special non-browning glass for use in observation windows in nuclear power plants. More than 10 tons (9 metric tons) of this glass are used in windows in one nuclear power plant. In 1953, automobile manufacturers introduced fiberglass-plastic bodies. Today, such materials are used in architectural panels to sheathe the walls of buildings. They are also used to make boat hulls and such products as missile *radomes* (housings for radar antennas). Other types of glass have been developed that turn dark when exposed to light and clear up when the light source is removed. These *photochromic glasses* are used in eyeglasses that change from clear glasses to sunglasses when worn in sunlight.

During the late 1960's, glass manufacturers established collection centers where people could return empty bottles, jars, and other types of glass containers. The used containers are *recycled*—that is, broken up and then melted with silica sand, limestone, and soda ash to make glass for new containers. Glass can be recycled easily because it does not deteriorate with use or age. In addition to the collection centers, some communities have set up systems to sort glass and other reusable materials from regular waste pickups.

In the 1970's, optical fibers were developed for use as "light pipes" in laser communication systems. These pipes maintain the brightness and intensity of light being transmitted over long distances. Types of glass that can store radioactive wastes safely for thousands of years were also developed during the 1970's.

The late 1900's brought important new specialty glasses. Among the new specialty glasses were transparent glass ceramics, which are used to make cookware, and chalcogenide glass, an infrared-transmitting glass that can be used to make lenses for night vision goggles.

Steve W. Martin

Related articles in *World Book* include:

Annealing	Etching	Stiegel, Henry W.
Antique	Fiberglass	Telescope
Binoculars	Glasses	Tempering
Bottle	Microscope	Tiffany, Louis C.
Cameo	Mirror	West Virginia (pic-
Ductility	Sand	ture: A glass-
Enamel	Stained glass	maker)
		Window

Outline

I. **Kinds of glass**
　A. Flat glass
　B. Glass containers
　C. Optical glass
　D. Fiberglass
　E. Specialty glasses

II. **The composition of glass**
　A. Soda-lime glass
　B. Soda-lead glass
　C. Borosilicate glass
　D. Fused silica glass
　E. 96 percent silica glass
　F. Colored glass

III. **How glass is made**
　A. Mixing
　B. Melting

IV. **How glass is shaped and finished**
　A. Blowing
　B. Pressing
　C. Drawing
　D. Casting
　E. Lampworking
　F. Annealing
　G. Tempering
　H. Inspection

V. **How glass is decorated**
　A. Etching
　B. Sandblasting
　C. Cutting
　D. Copper-wheel engraving
　E. Fired decorations

VI. **History of glass**

Questions

How is glass etched?
How is glass colored?
What is lampworking?
What is the difference between annealing and tempering glass?
In what different ways can glass be decorated?
Who made the first good optical glass?
What is radiation-absorbing glass? Invisible glass?
What ingredients make up soda-lime glass?
How is glass blown?
What is sandblasting?
What is fiberglass? How was glass first made?

Additional resources

Battie, David, and Cottle, Simon, eds. *Sotheby's Concise Encyclopedia of Glass.* 1991. Reprint. Conran Octopus, 1995.
Bray, Charles. *Dictionary of Glass Materials and Techniques.* Univ. of Penn. Pr., 1995.
Doremus, R. H. *Glass Science.* 2nd ed. Wiley, 1994.
Ellis, William S. *Glass.* 1998. Reprint. Avon, 1999.
Fisher, Leonard E. *The Glassmakers.* 1964. Reprint. Benchmark Bks., 1997. Younger readers.
Tait, Hugh, ed. *Glass: 5,000 Years.* Abrams, 1991.

Glass, Carter (1858-1946), was a leading American statesman. A Virginia Democrat, Glass served in the U.S. House of Representatives from 1902 until 1918, and in the U.S. Senate from 1920 until his death. He was president *pro tempore* of the Senate from 1941 to 1945. He served as secretary of the treasury under President

© Donald S. Heintzelman, Photo Researchers

Used glass containers can be recycled to make new glass products. Manufacturers break up the used glass and then melt it with silica sand, limestone, and soda ash to make new glass.

Woodrow Wilson between 1918 and 1920. An advocate of banking reforms, Glass sponsored the Federal Reserve Act of 1913. The act set up the Federal Reserve System. He co-sponsored the Glass-Steagall Banking Act of 1933. This act created the Federal Deposit Insurance Corporation (see **Federal Deposit Insurance Corporation**). He was born in Lynchburg, Virginia.   Brent Tarter

Glass, Philip (1937-   ), is an American composer. His works combine elements of rock music, the music of Africa and India, and classical Western music. In the late 1960's, Glass and fellow American composers Steve Reich, La Monte Young, and Terry Riley began to compose in a style called *minimalism,* which uses repeated short patterns of music with simple harmonies and occasional variation. Typical is Glass's repetitious, hypnotic *Music in 12 Parts* (1974), which lasts four hours.

In 1968, Glass formed a chamber music group, the Philip Glass Ensemble, consisting of amplified instruments. Glass himself performs on electronic keyboards.

Glass frequently collaborates with artists in dance, film, and drama. With playwright and director Robert Wilson, he created the opera *Einstein on the Beach* (1976), loosely based on the life of scientist Albert Einstein, and the nearly abstract *The Civil Wars: A Tree Is Best Measured When It's Down* (1983). Glass provided music for only the fifth and final act of this 12-hour work. Glass collaborated with choreographer Jerome Robbins in *Glass Pieces* (1983).

The Glass opera *Akhanaten* (1984) deals with an Egyptian pharaoh and religious reformer of the 1300's B.C. The opera *The Voyage* (1992) commemorates Christopher Columbus's accidental discovery of the New World. *Orphée* (1993) is an opera based on a 1950 French motion picture. Glass composed three operas based on motion pictures by the French writer and director Jean Cocteau. These operas were *Orphée* (1993), *La Belle et la Bête* (1994), and *Les Enfants Terribles* (1996).

Glass was born in Baltimore. While living in Paris, he worked briefly with Indian musician Ravi Shankar, who strongly influenced his music.   Richard Jackson

Glass lizard is the name of certain legless lizards. Glass lizards are found in the southeastern and central parts of the United States and in Mexico, Europe, Asia, and Africa. They grow about 2 feet (60 centimeters) long, not including their tail, which can be twice as long as their body. The tail is very fragile and can easily be bro-

ken off by animals that prey on the lizards. The broken tail wriggles and may attract the attacker's attention, allowing the lizard to escape. After its tail breaks off, the lizard can grow a new one.

Glass lizards resemble snakes and are sometimes called *glass snakes.* But unlike snakes, glass lizards have movable eyelids, external ear openings, and breakable tails. They eat insects, snails, and other lizards.

Raymond B. Huey

Scientific classification. Glass lizards belong to the genus *Ophisaurus* in the family Anguidae.

Glasses are a pair of lenses held in place in front of the eyes by a frame. People wear glasses primarily to correct faulty vision. Most corrective glasses are prescribed by an eye specialist and are called *prescription glasses.* People also wear *nonprescription glasses,* which include sunglasses and safety glasses. Such glasses can be purchased without consulting an eye specialist.

No one knows when or where people first wore glasses. Europeans probably began wearing them in the 1200's. Marco Polo, an Italian trader and traveler, reported that he saw people wearing glasses in China about 1275. The demand for glasses used for reading increased after printed books started to become available in the late 1400's. During the 1500's, people also began using glasses for clearer distance vision. In 1784, the American scientist and statesman Benjamin Franklin invented *bifocals.* Bifocals have two-part lenses—one part for reading and one for distance vision.

Prescription glasses help the eye focus light rays correctly. To form a clear image, the eye must focus light rays on the *retina,* the area at the back of the eyeball. If light rays do not focus on the retina, a blurred image results. Common focusing problems that can be corrected by glasses include *nearsightedness, farsightedness, presbyopia, strabismus,* and *astigmatism.*

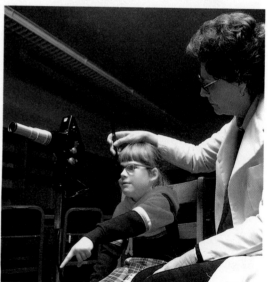
© Billy E. Barnes, Miller Services
An eye examination determines whether a person needs glasses. By testing how well this girl can see letters of different sizes on a screen, this public health worker can advise whether she should see an eye specialist for a new prescription.

Z. Leszczynski, Animals Animals
The glass lizard has no legs. Like many other kinds of lizards, it can shed its tail when attacked and grow a new one.

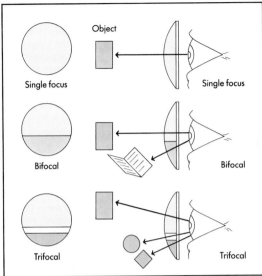

Single focus
Single focus
Object

Bifocal
Bifocal

Trifocal
Trifocal

WORLD BOOK diagram by Zorica Dabich

Glasses have *single-focus, bifocal,* or *trifocal* lenses. A single-focus lens has one focal point. A bifocal lens has two focal points—one for distance vision and one for near vision. A trifocal lens adds a third focal point, for middle-distance vision.

Nearsightedness, also called *myopia,* results if the light rays reflected from distant objects focus before they reach the retina. Nearsighted people can see nearby objects clearly, but distant ones are blurred. *Concave lenses,* which are thinner in the middle than at the edges, correct myopia. See **Nearsightedness.**

In farsightedness, also known as *hyperopia,* the light rays reflected from nearby objects reach the retina before focusing. Farsighted people generally can see distant objects clearly, but nearby ones appear blurred. *Convex lenses,* which are thicker in the middle than at the edges, correct hyperopia. See **Farsightedness.**

Nearly all people develop presbyopia sometime during their 40's. This condition results in the loss of the ability to focus on near objects. People with presbyopia require convex lenses for reading and for other close work.

Some children develop strabismus, commonly called *cross-eye.* In strabismus, the eyes look in different directions. Some cases of strabismus are associated with extreme farsightedness. In such cases, glasses that correct the farsightedness enable the eyes to look in the same direction. Without the help of glasses, the vision in one eye may grow poorer and poorer. See **Strabismus.**

Astigmatism results when light rays meet in two places within the eye, producing blurred, misshapen images. In most cases, astigmatism occurs because the *cornea,* the transparent covering at the front of the eye, has an uneven shape. Cylindrical lenses correct astigmatism. See **Astigmatism.**

Glasses may have *single-focus, bifocal,* or *trifocal* lenses. A single-focus lens has one *focal point*—that is, all light rays that pass through the lens meet at one point. In a bifocal lens, the top of the lens has a different focal point than the bottom. The top part is used for distance vision and the bottom part for near vision. A trifo-

cal lens has a third focal point in the middle of the lens. This part of the lens enables a person to see objects at in-between distances.

How glasses are prescribed and made. Glasses are prescribed on the basis of an eye examination made by an *ophthalmologist* or an *optometrist.* An ophthalmologist is a physician who specializes in treating eye problems. An optometrist examines the eye, diagnoses problems, and prescribes glasses. Optometrists are not physicians.

As light rays enter the eye, they are *refracted* (bent). During a part of the examination called the *refraction,* the ophthalmologist or optometrist measures how much more or less each eye needs to refract light rays to focus them on the retina. The patient looks through different lenses, and the examiner then writes a prescription for those that provide the best vision.

The lenses for glasses are made by an *optician,* a specialist who shapes them according to the prescription. The optician fits the lenses into a frame chosen by the patient and also adjusts the frame to fit the patient properly and comfortably. Lenses are made of glass or plastic. In the United States, the Food and Drug Administration, an agency of the federal government, requires lenses to be impact resistant. Such glasses do not shatter from moderately sharp blows.

Nonprescription glasses may be purchased without an eye examination and are sold by many stores. Sunglasses have tinted glass or plastic lenses that reduce eye discomfort from sunlight and glare. Dark gray lenses work best, but green and brown lenses are also effective. Many sunglasses contain polarized plastic lenses, which filter out glaring light reflected from flat surfaces (see **Polarized light**). Some have special filters that block out ultraviolet rays, which can harm the eyes. Safety glasses are made of extremely strong glass or plastic. They prevent eye injuries from chemicals or from fragments of metal and other materials. Many industries require workers to wear such glasses. People also wear safety glasses while playing such sports as basketball, squash, and tennis. Some people buy nonprescription glasses that have magnifying lenses. These glasses are used for reading. 	Ron Klein

See also **Contact lens; Lens.**

Glasswort is the name of several species of plants found worldwide. Glassworts grow from 4 to 24 inches (10 to 61 centimeters) high. Their small leaves look like scales on the fleshy green stems. Small flowers are concealed in groups of three between the leaves and the stems. A kind of glasswort called the *samphire* grows along seacoasts in temperate regions of the Northern Hemisphere.

Scientific classification. Glassworts belong to the goosefoot family, Chenopodiaceae. The scientific name for the samphire is *Salicornia europaea.* 	Melinda F. Denton

Glastonbury, *GLAS tuhn BEHR ee,* an English town, is famous in history and in the legends of King Arthur. It lies in southwestern England. For location, see **England** (political map). Glastonbury is the largest town in the district of Sedgemoor, which has a population of about 93,000. It is an important center of service and light industry. According to tradition, Joseph of Arimathea founded England's first Christian Church in Glastonbury. The ruins of an abbey, founded in the A.D. 700's, lie in

the town. The town's history makes it popular with tourists. See also **Arthur, King; Joseph of Arimathea.**
D. A. Pinder

Glaucoma, *glaw KOH muh,* is an eye disease characterized by increased pressure of the fluid within the eye. Glaucoma is a leading cause of blindness in the United States and worldwide.

The clear, watery fluid inside the eye is produced by cells behind the iris. The fluid circulates between the lens and the cornea, providing nourishment to these tissues. Normally, the fluid drains through tiny channels into the blood vessels leading away from the eye. If a blockage occurs at any point in the fluid's pathway, pressure within the eye increases, producing glaucoma. Blindness results when this pressure destroys the *optic nerve,* which connects the eye to the brain.

The most common type of glaucoma is *primary open-angle glaucoma,* also known as *chronic simple glaucoma.* It occurs mainly in people over 40 years old and may be inherited. It often advances unnoticed because it does not cause pain or other obvious symptoms. The person's vision may slowly narrow until he or she is blind. There is no cure for this type of glaucoma, but most cases can be controlled with drugs. A doctor may also form a new drainage pathway for the eye's fluid through surgery or by using a high-energy light from a *laser.* In addition, doctors have used *ultrasound* (high-frequency sound waves) to treat primary open-angle glaucoma. Such treatment reduces the amount of fluid produced in the eye.

Another type of glaucoma, known as *primary narrow-angle glaucoma* or *acute glaucoma,* may occur suddenly and at any age. Symptoms include seeing rainbowlike rings around lights, redness of the eye, and severe pain in the eyes and forehead. Blindness results unless the person is immediately treated with drugs, surgery, or laser therapy.

Glaucoma sometimes occurs as a result of other disorders or conditions. These include internal inflammation of the eye, diseases of the lens of the eye, injury to the eye, or complications of eye surgery. A doctor can usually cure such *secondary glaucomas* by treating the underlying disorder. Ramesh C. Tripathi and Brenda Tripathi

See also **Eye** (Glaucoma); **Julian, Percy Lavon.**

Glauconite, *GLAW kuh nyt,* is a bright green mineral that looks like tiny flakes of the mineral mica, or small lumps of clay. Nearly pure glauconite, called *greensand,* is used as a water softener. Glauconite deposits occur in Colorado, New Jersey, and Wisconsin. Chemically, glauconite is a *hydrous* (water-containing) silicate of potassium and iron. It may have been formed originally from *biotite* (a dark-colored mica), but other minerals, and even organic matter, may change into glauconite. Glauconite is slowly forming from seawater.

Glauconite is valuable to geologists for dating rocks and fossils because it contains potassium. Natural potassium always contains a number of radioactive atoms. Radioactive potassium breaks down at a known and constant rate to a gas called argon. By measuring the ratio of potassium to argon in a glauconite sample, geologists can determine the sample's age. David F. Hess

Glen Canyon Dam, in northern Arizona near the Utah border, helps control the flow of the Colorado River. One of the world's highest dams, it is 710 feet (216 me-

ters) high. The dam traps water in Glen Canyon and forms Lake Powell, one of the world's largest artificially created lakes. Glen Canyon Dam was completed in 1964. It is one of four major dams to be built in the Upper Colorado River Basin. It supplies water and electric power to a large section of the Rocky Mountain States. See also **Lake Powell; Arizona** (picture). Larry W. Mays

Glenn, John Herschel, Jr. (1921–   ), was the first American to orbit the earth. On Feb. 20, 1962, he circled the earth three times in less than five hours. Millions of people watched on television as an Atlas rocket carried the spacecraft Friendship 7 into the sky.

The success of Glenn's flight helped overcome fears that the United States lagged behind the Soviet Union in the race for space. In 1961, two Soviet cosmonauts made the first orbital flights around the earth.

Glenn resigned from the astronaut program in 1964. He was elected to the U.S. Senate from Ohio in 1974. He was reelected in 1980, 1986, and 1992. Glenn tried to win the 1984 Democratic presidential nomination, but failed. He did not run for reelection to the Senate in 1998.

Early life. John Herschel Glenn, Jr., was born on July 18, 1921, in Cambridge, Ohio. He grew up in New Concord, Ohio. In 1939, Glenn entered Muskingum College in New Concord. He left college in 1942—during his junior year—to become a U.S. Marine Corps pilot in World War II. Later, Glenn attended classes at the University of Maryland. As a result of credits from these courses and work in the space program, he received a Bachelor of Science degree in chemistry from Muskingum College in 1962.

Soon after Glenn received his commission in the Marine Corps, he married Anna Castor, his hometown sweetheart. They had two children, John David and Carolyn Ann.

During World War II, Glenn was a pilot in the Pacific Theater. He flew 59 missions supporting ground troops. During the Korean War (1950–1953), Glenn flew 90 combat missions and shot down three enemy planes. He earned a total of five Distinguished Flying Crosses and 19 Air Medals. After the Korean War, Glenn became a test pilot. He made headlines in 1957 when he set a transcontinental speed record, flying from Los Angeles to New York City in 3 hours 23 minutes.

In 1959, Glenn and six other men were chosen from 110 test pilot volunteers for the Mercury program. This program had the goal of putting an American into space. Glenn, the oldest member of the group, served as "backup pilot" in 1961 when fellow astronauts Alan B. Shepard, Jr., and Virgil I. Grissom each made suborbital flights.

Glenn's historic flight lasted 4 hours 55 minutes from launch to landing. His spacecraft lifted off from Cape Canaveral, Florida, at 9:47 a.m. (EST) on Feb. 20, 1962. It made three orbits of the earth, each about $1\frac{1}{2}$ hours long, and traveled 80,966 statute miles (130,302 kilometers). During the flight, the spacecraft's altitude varied from 98.9 to 162.5 miles (159.2 to 261.5 kilometers).

After crossing the Atlantic Ocean, Friendship 7 flew over Africa, the Indian Ocean, and Australia. Then the spacecraft sped over the Pacific Ocean, the West Coast of the United States, and back again over Florida. Eighteen radar stations around the world kept track of the spacecraft. Because he was circling the earth, Glenn

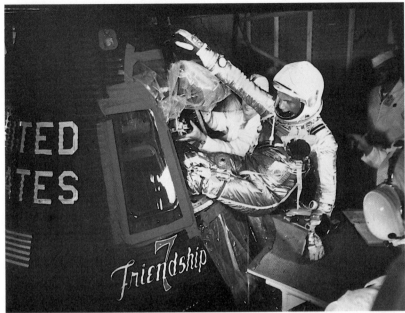

Office of Senator John H. Glenn, Jr.

Astronaut and senator. Astronaut John H. Glenn, Jr., became the first American to orbit the earth. On Feb. 20, 1962, Glenn circled the earth three times in less than five hours. He made his historic flight in a spacecraft named Friendship 7. Glenn resigned from the astronaut program in 1964. From 1975 to 1999, he served as a United States senator from Ohio.

NASA

traveled from daylight to darkness and back in less than two hours.

Trouble occurred near the end of the first orbit when the spacecraft passed over the tracking station in Guaymas, Mexico. Up to this point, the spacecraft's *attitude* (position in space) had been controlled automatically. Friendship 7 began to swing to the right. During the rest of the flight, Glenn held the spacecraft in its proper position using the vehicle's manual controls. He was probably the first human being to "fly" a spacecraft manually for any length of time.

At 2:20 p.m., $4\frac{1}{2}$ hours after the launch, the spacecraft's retrorockets fired, slowing the vehicle so that it would drop out of orbit and plunge into the atmosphere. At about 2:30 p.m., the spacecraft's main parachute opened. Five minutes later, the parachute lowered Friendship 7 into the Atlantic Ocean, near the West Indies. The spacecraft landed at 2:43 p.m. About 15 minutes later, the U.S. destroyer *Noa* picked up the spacecraft with Glenn still inside. At 3:24 p.m., he crawled out of Friendship 7.

Later career. In January 1964, Glenn resigned from the astronaut program, and he entered the Ohio primary as a Democratic candidate for U.S. senator. But he withdrew after injuring his inner ear in a fall. Glenn became a colonel in 1964. He left the Marines in 1965 and entered private business. He also became a consultant for the National Aeronautics and Space Administration (NASA). In 1970, Glenn again entered the Democratic primary for the U.S. Senate, but lost. In 1974, however, Glenn won election to the Senate from Ohio.

In the Senate, Glenn has opposed the *proliferation* (spread) of nuclear weapons. He is the author of the Nuclear Nonproliferation Act of 1978, which prohibits the sale of nuclear equipment to nations that do not yet possess nuclear weapons. Glenn favors increased federal aid for education and new federal training programs that prepare people for jobs requiring certain skills. He also has backed federal aid to such industries suffering

from financial problems as the steel and automobile industries.

Glenn criticized many of President Ronald Reagan's foreign and domestic policies. In April 1983, Glenn became a candidate for the 1984 Democratic presidential nomination. But he quit the race after failing to win any early primary or caucus elections. Glenn was chairman of the Senate Governmental Affairs Committee from 1987 to 1995.

Glenn made his return to space in October 1998 aboard the space shuttle Discovery. He took part in experiments dealing with physical problems experienced by astronauts in space and elderly people on the earth. Glenn was 77 years old at the time of the flight, making him the oldest person ever to travel in space.

Lillian D. Kozloski

See also **Astronaut** (picture).

Glenview Naval Air Station served as headquarters of the naval and marine air reserve training commands of the United States from 1942 to 1995. It covered 1,120 acres (453 hectares) and was located about 18 miles (29 kilometers) northwest of Chicago. The station was closed in 1995.   W .W. Reid

Glick, George Washington (1827-1911), was the first Democrat to be elected governor of Kansas. Born in Ohio, he studied law in the office of Rutherford B. Hayes and practiced in Ohio from 1850 to 1858, when he moved to Atchison, Kansas.

Glick was an attorney for the Union Pacific Railroad and served eight terms in the Kansas state Legislature. He was governor from 1883 to 1885. Later, he served on the state board of agriculture. A statue of Glick represents Kansas in the United States Capitol in Washington, D.C.   Edward A. Lukes-Lukaszewski

Glidden, Carlos (1834-1877), an American inventor, is best known for his share in the invention of the Remington typewriter. He met his co-inventors, Christopher Latham Sholes and Samuel W. Soulé, while in Milwau-

Schweizer Aircraft Corporation

A glider has long, narrow wings that enable it to fly great distances without an engine. The glider shown above is a high-performance aircraft, with wings more than 20 times as long as they are wide. It can be used for recreational flying or for competition.

kee, where he was working on the development of a spading machine for agricultural use. Glidden suggested that the three of them work together to produce a type-writing machine. They patented the typewriter in 1868. In 1873, the rights to the patent were sold to E. Remington and Sons (see **Typewriter**). Glidden was born in Scioto, Ohio.   George H. Daniels

Glider is an aircraft that resembles an airplane but has no engine. It flies in air currents as silently and gracefully as a bird. Gliders are sometimes called *sailplanes.*

Airplanes and gliders remain aloft by flying fast enough for the pressure of the air moving around their wings to produce an upward force. An airplane's engine or propellers provide the thrust that gives the plane enough speed to take off and fly. A glider has no power, and so it must rely on other means for flight.

Gliders are usually launched by being towed into the air by an airplane and then released. Level flight cannot be sustained without a motor. Therefore, the glider pilot keeps the nose of the aircraft pointed just below the horizon and glides downward through the air. In this way, the force of gravity produces the speed necessary for the glider to remain airborne.

Gliders can soar upward, even though they are always pointed slightly downward. They can gain altitude rapid-ly by flying in air currents that rise faster than the plane sinks. Glider pilots use these rising air currents, called *updrafts,* to remain aloft for long periods. Flights of more than 70 hours have been made. But most flights range from one to five hours.

Gliders are used chiefly for recreation and sport. The Soaring Society of America (SSA), founded in 1932, has about 120 gliding clubs. There are about 20,000 licensed glider pilots in the United States. The sport is popular in Australia, Canada, New Zealand, and South Africa, and in many European and South American countries.

Parts of a glider

Most gliders have three main parts: (1) wings, (2) body, and (3) tail assembly. All these parts have a streamlined design that enables a glider to knife through the air with minimum *drag* (air resistance).

The reduction of drag gives a glider a high *glide ratio.* Glide ratio is the relationship between forward and downward motion. A typical glider used for recreation has a glide ratio of about 30—that is, for every mile or kilometer of altitude lost, it can fly 30 times as far for-ward. A high-performance glider has a glide ratio of more than 30. A glider made for competitive flying has a glide ratio of more than 40.

The wings of a glider are much narrower in relation to their length than the wings of an airplane. This nar-rowness reduces the drag at the glider's wing tips.

As a glider or airplane flies, air tends to flow in oppo-site directions along the length of the wings. Air along the bottom of each wing tends to flow outward, and air along the top tends to flow inward. This opposite flow causes a swirling stream of air, called a *vortex,* to form behind each wing tip and hold the aircraft back.

Long, narrow wings reduce the strength of the vortex-es and play the most important part in decreasing drag. A typical glider used for recreation has wings about 50 feet (15 meters) long and about 3 feet (1 meter) wide. A sailplane made for competition may have wings 70 feet (21 meters) long and only $2\frac{1}{3}$ feet (71 centimeters) wide. Some competition gliders also have *winglets,* vertical ex-tensions at the wing tips that further reduce drag.

The wings of a glider also produce *lift,* the upward force that enables aircraft to fly. A glider's wings provide lift by the same principles as the wings of an airplane. See **Aerodynamics**.

Each wing has a set of flight controls called *ailerons.* The wings of some gliders also have controls called *flaps.* Ailerons and flaps are hinged panels located along the *trailing* (rear) edge of the wings. The ailerons are nearest the wing tips. The pilot moves them up or down to make the glider *bank* (tip) to the right or left for a turn. If one aileron is raised, the other is lowered automatical-ly. The flaps are nearer the body. The pilot can lower them slightly and increase lift at low speeds when flying in updrafts. Raising them slightly enables the glider to fly at a shallow angle at high speeds.

The body, or *fuselage,* of a glider extends from the nose to the tail and gradually narrows toward the rear. In high-performance gliders, the fuselage has an extremely slim design that reduces drag. Such a design does not provide enough room for pilots to sit up, and so they must lie back while flying. In gliders used for flight training, the fuselage is less streamlined, and so the trainee pilot and instructor can sit up. Training gliders have two seats and dual controls, enabling the instructor to watch as the student pilots the plane. Some high-performance gliders also seat two people.

Gliders are made of materials with a smooth finish, such as aluminum, fiberglass, or wood. A glider may also contain some steel parts. Most gliders have only one wheel, located on the undersurface of the aircraft, between the wings. The landing gear of most high-performance gliders can be *retracted* (folded up) into the body after take-off to reduce drag.

The tail assembly, or *empennage,* of most gliders consists of a horizontal *stabilizer* and *elevator* and a vertical *fin* and *rudder.* The elevator is hinged to the stabilizer and is raised or lowered by means of a control stick in the cockpit. The position of the elevator tilts the glider to the angle desired by the pilot and helps control its speed. The rudder is hinged to the fin. The pilot moves the rudder to the right or left by means of pedals. The rudder helps control the glider during a turn.

The stabilizer of a sailplane may be attached to the top or the bottom of the fin, or it may be connected to the fuselage. Some glider designers believe that two movable surfaces in a V-shaped tail assembly improve the performance of certain planes.

Flying a glider

A glider pilot uses four main instruments when launching, soaring, or landing. The Federal Aviation Administration (FAA) requires all gliders sold in the United States to be equipped with three of these devices. The required instruments are an air-speed indicator; an *altimeter,* which shows the altitude; and a compass. The fourth instrument, a *variometer,* shows the rate at which the plane rises or sinks. It helps the pilot detect upward air currents. In addition, pilots of competition gliders use computers to calculate glide angles precisely.

Launching. In the United States, most gliders are launched by an airplane that tows them into the air. The plane pulls the glider with a rope that measures from 150 to 200 feet (46 to 61 meters) long. One end of the rope is connected to a towhook near the tail wheel of the plane. The other end is fastened to a similar hook near the nose of the glider. A helper runs alongside the glider during the first moments of take-off and holds the wings level. Once airborne, the glider pilot releases the glider from the rope by means of a knob in the cockpit. The pilot generally cuts loose at an altitude of 2,000 to 3,000 feet (610 to 910 meters).

In Europe, gliders are usually pulled into the air like kites by an automobile or by a hauling device called a *winch* that stands on the ground. A few gliders have an engine-driven propeller that is used to take off. The pilot turns the engine off after the craft is airborne.

Soaring. Most gliders fly with their best glide angle at 50 to 60 miles per hour (80 to 95 kilometers per hour). To gain altitude, the pilot searches for updrafts. There are four main kinds: (1) slope winds, (2) thermals, (3) mountain waves, and (4) shear lines.

Slope winds blow against a hill and are deflected upward. A glider can fly back and forth along the windward side of a slope as long as a strong wind is present. Skilled pilots have used the slope winds of a mountain range to make flights of nearly 1,000 miles (1,600 kilometers). Birds drifting along a slope without flapping their wings indicate the presence of slope winds.

Thermals consist of air that rises in a column or a bubble after being warmed by contact with heated areas of the ground. Dry surfaces that are dark or flat, such as blacktop roads, deserts, plowed fields, and roofs, generally absorb much heat from the sun. The air immediately above these surfaces becomes warm and rises until it mixes with cooler air high in the atmosphere. Thermals may be present from late morning to late afternoon on sunny days. As a result, this type of updraft is the one that is most widely used by glider pilots. The heat given off by cities can also produce thermals. The development of a puffy, white *cumulus* cloud may indicate the top of a thermal. Other signs include rising dust and birds soaring upward without flapping their wings.

Mountain waves occur on the *lee side*—the side away from the wind—of steep mountains. Generally, the lee side of a mountain produces downward air currents. Certain weather conditions, however, may produce a powerful upward air current that may reach an altitude of 80,000 feet (24,000 meters) or more. *Lenticular* clouds, which curve upward on top and are flat on the bottom, often indicate the presence of mountain waves.

Shear lines, or *convergence zones,* occur when a mass of cool, heavy air moves into an area and forces warmer, lighter air upwards. Some shear lines can be flown for hundreds of miles or kilometers.

Landing. The pilot usually glides toward a landing area at a steep angle and levels off just before touching down. Many gliders have plates called *spoilers* that can be extended from the wings to control the angle of the glide during landing. If a glider has flaps instead of spoilers, the pilot approaches the landing area with the flaps tilted down sharply.

A pilot who flies far from the gliderport and cannot find enough updrafts to get back must make an off-field landing. Gliders can land on any large, flat surface. The

E. R. Degginger

A glider, *lower right,* is launched by an airplane that tows it into the air. At the desired height, the glider pilot cuts free from the towing rope by means of a knob in the cockpit.

aircraft can then be dismantled, put on a trailer, and returned to the gliderport or taken home.

Gliding regulations

In the United States, the FAA regulates both glider pilots and gliders. A person must be at least 14 years old and in good health to be eligible for a glider pilot certificate. This certificate permits the individual to make solo flights in a glider. Other requirements include a course of study and flight training under an instructor certified by the FAA. The instruction may be given at a flight school or a gliding club. A pilot must be at least 16 and pass written and flying tests of the FAA to obtain a private glider pilot certificate, which permits the person to carry nonpaying passengers. A pilot must be at least 18 to qualify for a commercial glider pilot certificate, which allows the pilot to fly paying passengers.

Gliders must be tested and approved by the FAA before they can be manufactured and sold. Some pilots build gliders from kits. This procedure lowers the cost of the aircraft by a half to two-thirds. Such gliders also must be approved by an FAA inspector.

History

Early days. In 1809, Sir George Cayley, an English inventor, built the first successful full-sized glider. In 1853, Cayley built a crude glider that carried his coachman across a small valley. Historians regard the coachman's flight as the first human glider flight, though he had no control over the aircraft. Otto Lilienthal, a German engineer, became the first person to pilot a glider in flight. From 1891 to 1896, he made about 2,500 glider flights. In 1897, a Scottish engineer named Percy S. Pilcher first used a towing technique to launch a glider. Both Lilienthal and Pilcher died in glider crashes.

Wilbur and Orville Wright experimented with gliders near Kitty Hawk, North Carolina, from 1900 to 1902 before their first successful powered flight in 1903. In 1911,

U.S. National Air and Space Museum, Smithsonian Institution

An early glider, built by Otto Lilienthal, a German engineer, was the first such aircraft to be controlled in flight. Lilienthal steered the glider by swinging his body from side to side.

Orville Wright made the first documented soaring flight in a glider. He used slope winds on a flight that lasted almost 10 minutes. Interest in gliders declined after the Wright brothers developed the powered airplane.

After World War I ended in 1918, Germany was prohibited from developing powered aircraft. As a result, many German engineers turned to *aerodonetics,* the study of glider flight. By the early 1920's, they had developed gliders with advanced designs. The variometer was invented in Germany in 1928. The next year, German pilots established the first U.S. gliding school at South Wellfleet, Massachusetts. In 1930, the first U.S. gliding championship took place at Elmira, New York.

During World War II, large gliders towed by airplanes were used to transport soldiers and artillery. In 1940, during its invasion of Belgium, Germany became

WORLD BOOK diagram by Jean Helmer

A glider flies in air currents. The glider shown in the above diagram soars in an upcurrent that is deflected from a hill. It then sinks as it flies into a downdraft produced by a cool lake. Next, a field gives off rising warm air that sends the glider up again. The aircraft loses altitude in the downdraft of a cool forest. It then rises in an upcurrent produced by the heat of a city.

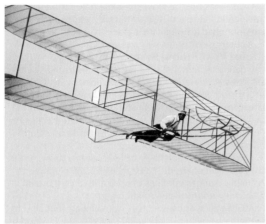

Brown Bros.

The Wright brothers experimented with gliders before making their first successful powered flight in 1903. They used gliders in solving many problems of flight control.

Focus on Sports

Hang gliding has been a popular sport in the United States since the early 1970's. The pilot hangs from a harness and steers the glider with a control bar that shifts the aircraft's framework.

the first country to use such military transport gliders.

Gliding today is a competitive sport supervised in the United States by the Soaring Society of America (SSA). The Soaring Society of America oversees the awarding of badges for flights of specified distance, duration, and height. It also regulates national and regional gliding contests. The top pilots in the national contest represent the United States in world competition. The worldwide competition is held every two years. The headquarters of the SSA is in Hobbs, New Mexico.

The most common event in gliding contests consists of races against time. In a race, the contestants follow a course around three or more predetermined markers. Contestants fly as far as 620 miles (1,000 kilometers). Gliders have crossed the finish line at speeds of more than 150 miles per hour (241 kilometers per hour). Germany ranks as the chief producer of high-performance competition sailplanes. German aircraft have been used almost exclusively in U.S. national gliding contests.

Hang gliding is a form of gliding that became popular in the United States in the early 1970's. It is now practiced throughout the world. Most hang gliders consist of a triangular sail of synthetic fabric attached to an aluminum frame that is 32 feet (9.8 meters) wide. The pilot

hangs from a harness and steers the glider and regulates its speed with a *control bar.* Pilots make adjustments with the control bar by shifting their body weight.

There are three basic launching methods in hang gliding. In *foot-launched gliding,* the pilot holds the glider and runs down the windward side of a hill until the glider is airborne. In *kiting,* or *tow-launched gliding,* a pickup truck or a boat pulls the glider by a rope until the glider reaches an altitude of 400 to 500 feet (120 to 150 meters). Then the pilot releases the tow rope. In *motorized hang gliding,* which is also called *ultralight flying,* a small engine that is fitted on the glider is used for launching and landing.

The United States Hang Gliding Association, located in Los Angeles, offers licenses and insurance to pilots. It also certifies instructors and appoints safety officers.

Howard Banks

See also **Airplane; Cayley, Sir George; Wright brothers.**

Additional resources

Ayres, Carter M. *Soaring.* Lerner, 1986. Younger readers.
Conway, Carle. *Joy of Soaring.* Rev. ed. Soaring Soc. of Am., 1993.
Coombs, Charles I. *Soaring.* Holt, 1988. Younger readers.
Piggott, Derek. *Gliding.* 6th ed., Barnes & Noble, 1990.

Glider world records*

Event	Record	Year	Pilot	Country
Altitude above sea level	49,009 feet (14,938 meters)	1986	Robert Harris	United States
Distance in a straight line	907.70 miles (1,460.80 kilometers)	1972	Hans Werner Grosse	West Germany
Distance to a goal	859.35 miles (1,383.00 kilometers)	1992	Gerard Herbaud, Jean Noel Herbaud	France
Distance to a goal and return	1,023.19 miles (1,646.68 kilometers)	1983	Thomas Knauff	United States
Speed over a measured triangular course				
100 kilometers	135.09 mph (217.41 kph)	1997	James M. Payne	United States
300 kilometers	106.19 mph (170.90 kph)	1988	Hans Werner Grosse, Karin Grosse	West Germany
500 kilometers	105.67 mph (170.06 kph)	1988	Beat Bunzli	Switzerland
750 kilometers	100.24 mph (161.33 kph)	1988	Hans Werner Grosse, Karin Grosse	West Germany
1,000 kilometers	105.45 mph (169.72 kph)	1995	Helmut H. Fischer	Germany

*Records listing more than one pilot are for multi-place aircraft.
Source: National Aeronautic Association.

Glider is a type of possum that lives in forests in New Guinea and northern and eastern Australia. Gliders can glide through the air from branch to branch or from tree to tree. A fold of furry skin connects the front and rear legs on each side of the animal's body. When the glider extends its legs, the skin serves as "wings" for gliding. The animal's long tail helps steer during the glide. A glider's fur is grayish on the back and gray, orange, yellow, creamy white, or white on the belly. Gliders are also called *gliding possums.*

Gliders are *marsupials.* Female marsupials bear tiny, poorly developed young. Most gliders give birth to one or two young. The young are carried in a pouch on the

©Jean-Paul Ferrero, AUSCAPE International

A glider sails through the air from tree to tree.

mother's belly until they develop more fully. Gliders eat mainly leaves, blossoms, and sap. They nest in the hollows of trees and are active mainly at night.

The largest glider, which is known as the *greater glider,* weighs as much as $3 \frac{3}{4}$ pounds (1.7 kilograms) and travels as far as 350 feet (105 meters) in one glide. The smallest glider, the *pygmy glider,* weighs as little as $\frac{1}{3}$ ounce (10 grams). It glides as far as 65 feet (20 meters).

Michael L. Augee

Scientific classification. Most gliders belong to the family Petauridae. The greater glider is *Petauroides volans.* The pygmy glider belongs to the family Burramyidae. It is *Acrobates pygmaeus.*

See also **Marsupial; Possum.**

Glinka, *GLIHNG kuh,* **Mikhail Ivanovich,** *mih kah EEL ih VAH nuh vihch* (1804-1857), was the first important Russian composer of the 1800's. His music, which uses characteristics of folk songs and Russian Orthodox choral themes, launched a major national school of Russian music in the second half of the 1800's.

Glinka's first opera, *A Life for the Tsar* (1836; now retitled *Ivan Susanin),* was based on an incident from Russian history from the early 1600's. It inspired other composers, especially Modest Mussorgsky and Alexander Borodin, to compose works based on Russian historical and patriotic subjects. For his second opera, *Ruslan and Lyudmila* (1842), Glinka used a fairy tale written by his friend, the poet Alexander Pushkin. The work inspired a number of Russian fantasy operas by Nikolai Rimsky-Korsakov and Peter Ilich Tchaikovsky.

Glinka's orchestral works include two Spanish overtures (1850, 1852) and the *Valse-fantaisie* (1845). His folksong fantasy *Kamarinskaya* (1850) is considered the beginning of the Russian symphonic school.

Glinka was born at Novospasskoe near Smolensk. He traveled in Italy from 1830 to 1833. His exposure to Italian opera had a significant impact on his development as a composer. Edward V. Williams

Global Positioning System, or GPS, is a worldwide navigation system that uses radio signals broadcast by satellites. A computerized radio receiver in an airplane, ship, or other vehicle uses the satellite signals to calculate its own location. Hikers and other people on foot may use small, portable receivers. The United States Air Force operates the satellites, but the system has both military and civilian users.

The GPS has 24 satellites, called Navstars, in six orbits with a height of about 12,500 miles (20,200 kilometers). As many as eight satellites may be above the horizon when viewed from any point on earth.

A GPS receiver uses signals from at least four, and often more, satellites. Each signal indicates the location of the satellite that sent the signal, and the broadcast time. The receiver can determine its latitude and longitude using only three satellites if its altitude is known.

GPS users can normally determine their location within 10 meters (33 feet). A technique called *carrier phase GPS* can be accurate to within 1 centimeter (0.4 inch). The U.S. armed forces began developing the GPS in the early 1970's. It became fully operational in 1995.

Alison K. Brown

See also **Navigation.**

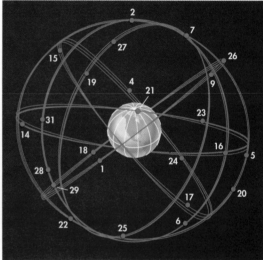

WORLD BOOK illustration by Precision Graphics

Global Positioning System satellites, each identified by a number, *shown here,* broadcast radio signals. Aircraft and surface vehicles can use these signals to determine their own locations.

Global warming is an increase in the average temperature of the earth's surface. Since the late 1800's, the average temperature has increased about 0.9 to 1.6 Fahrenheit degrees (0.5 to 0.9 Celsius degree). Many experts estimate that the average temperature will rise between 2.5 to 10.4 additional Fahrenheit degrees (1.4 to 5.8 Celsius degrees) by 2100. This rate of increase would be several times faster than global rates that typically occurred over long periods in the past.

Scientists disagree about the importance of various causes and potential impacts of the warming trend. Most *climatologists* (scientists who study climate) believe that human activities have contributed to the trend by enhancing the earth's natural *greenhouse effect*. This effect warms the surface through a complex process involving sunlight, gases, and particles in the atmosphere.

Since the mid-1800's, human activities—chiefly the burning of *fossil fuels* (coal, oil, and natural gas) and the clearing of land—have increased the amounts of heat-trapping atmospheric gases, called *greenhouse gases*. The burning of fossil fuels produces the greenhouse gas carbon dioxide. Most of this burning occurs in buildings, automobiles, electric power plants, and factories. The clearing of land reduces the amount of carbon dioxide that trees and other plants remove from the atmosphere in a process called *photosynthesis*.

Although researchers have not yet fully proved that the increase in greenhouse gases has raised the surface temperature, many climatologists consider such a relationship likely. A much smaller number of scientists argue that the increase in greenhouse gases has not made a measurable difference in the climate. These scientists say that the warming trend is a normal change in the climate system. They argue that natural processes, such as increases in the energy *emitted* (given off) by the sun, could have caused global warming. But the greater weight of evidence suggests that an unusual climate change is occurring and that human activities are mostly responsible for it.

The impact of continued global warming. Global warming affects many aspects of the environment, including sea levels, coastlines, agriculture, forestry, and wildlife. Continued global warming could have a beneficial impact in some areas and a harmful impact in others. For example, people could begin to farm in regions where it is currently too cold to raise crops. At the same time, sea levels could rise, increasing the threat of flooding in low-lying coastal regions.

Conference on global warming. Delegates from more than 160 countries met in December 1997 to draft an agreement to limit global warming. The meeting, called the United Nations Framework Convention on Climate Change, took place in Kyoto, Japan. The resulting agreement, known as the Kyoto Protocol, calls for decreases in the emission of greenhouse gases. Thirty-eight industrialized nations would have to cut their emissions of carbon dioxide and five other gases. The cuts would occur during the years from 2008 through 2012. The cuts would average from 6 percent to 8 percent of the 38 nations' 1990 emissions levels. Developing countries would limit emissions voluntarily or by cooperating with nations that would be subject to limitations.

In addition, the Kyoto Protocol would allow industrialized nations to buy or sell *emissions permits*. Suppose such a nation cut its emissions more than required by the agreement. That country could sell other industrialized nations permits allowing those nations to emit the remaining amounts.

An industrialized nation could also earn credit toward meeting its requirement by helping a developing country reduce emissions. For example, the industrialized nation might help the developing country replace fossil fuels in some applications. One replacement might be solar-energy devices that generate electric power.

The protocol would take effect if two requirements were met: (1) Fifty-five or more countries *ratified* (approved) it, and (2) the ratifying countries' emissions were equal to or greater than 55 percent of the 1990 emissions of the 38 industrialized nations. By early 2001, 33 countries had ratified the protocol. No industrialized country had yet ratified it, but several such nations had announced plans to curb their emissions sharply.

In March 2001, the United States rejected the agreement. U.S. President George W. Bush said that the United States would work with its allies to reduce greenhouse gases, but that the Kyoto Protocol could harm the U.S. economy.   Stephen H. Schneider

See also **Greenhouse effect; Solar energy.**

Globe is a hollow sphere with a world map on it. In most cases, the map is printed on paper that is then pasted onto the sphere. The paper consists of one or more tapered strips called gores. The gores are then pasted on cardboard half-spheres, which are glued together into a globe. In other cases, the map is printed on flat pieces of plastic pulled into half-spheres and glued together.

Globes of the earth are known as *terrestrial globes*. They are used in the study of geography and can be found in classrooms and libraries. They are also helpful in planning air and sea routes and in establishing satellite communications. Globes of the moon and other planets have also been produced. A globe that is a map of the sky is called a *celestial globe*. The earth itself is often referred to as *the globe*.

Only a globe can give a correct picture of the earth as a whole. Because the surface of a globe is rounded like the earth's surface, a globe represents all parts of the earth's surface true to scale. Distances, areas, and directions can be observed without the distortion caused by projections used for flat maps. The proportions and positions of the earth's land features and oceans in relation to each other are seen on a globe exactly as they are on the earth. The shortest distance between two points on the earth or globe is defined by what is called a *great circle*. Navigators make use of a great-circle route in planning ship and air lanes (see **Great-circle route**).

Globes may be mounted on a center axis to show how the earth rotates, or they may be placed in a cradle without attachment. With special accessories, relationships between the earth and the sun can be demonstrated on a globe. Such relationships include the length of daylight, time differences, and satellite paths.

Martin Behaim made one of the first terrestrial globes in Nuremberg, Germany, in 1492. Few globes are more than 22 inches (56 centimeters) in diameter. The Langlois Globe, produced in France in 1824, measures 128 feet (39 meters) in diameter and is probably the largest globe in the world. Other large globes, which measure up to 30 feet (9 meters) in diameter, have been made for newspapers and museums.   Stephen S. Birdsall

See also **Hemisphere; Map.**

Globe Theatre was an early English theater in London. Most of William Shakespeare's plays were first presented at the Globe. The brothers Cuthbert and Richard Burbage constructed the theater in 1599 from the timbers of London's first playhouse, called The Theatre. They erected the Globe in the area known as the Bankside on the south side of the River Thames in the suburb of Southwark.

Little is known about the Globe's design except what can be learned from maps and evidence from the plays presented there. The Globe was round or polygonal on the outside and probably round on the inside. It may have held as many as 3,000 spectators. In 1613, the Globe burned down. It was rebuilt on the same foundation and reopened in 1614. The Globe was torn down in 1644.

A reconstruction of the theater was completed in London in 1996. The new Globe opened officially in 1997.

Albert Wertheim

See also **Drama** (Elizabethan theaters); **Shakespeare, William** (The Elizabethan theater).

Globulin, *GLAHB yuh lihn,* is a protein component of the *plasma* (watery) part of the blood. Scientists classify globulin as alpha, beta, and gamma globulin. Each group, particularly gamma, contains *antibodies,* which give protection against specific infections (see **Immune system**). When additional antibodies are needed, as during infections, gamma globulin content increases.

G. David Roodman

See also **Gamma globulin.**

Glockenspiel, *GLAHK uhn SPEEL* or *GLAHK uhn SHPEEL,* is a percussion instrument that consists of two rows of metal bars on a frame. The musician strikes the bars with one or two mallets.

There are two main types of glockenspiels, the *bell-lyra* and the *orchestra bells.* A bell-lyra has aluminum bars on a lyre-shaped frame. The player holds the instrument with one hand and strikes the bars with a hard, plastic mallet held in the other hand. The bell-lyra is used mainly in marching bands and drum and bugle corps. Most bell-lyras have a range of two octaves. Orchestra bells have steel bars arranged in a case. The case, which amplifies the sound, rests on a flat horizontal surface. The player strikes the bars with two hard mallets made of plastic, rubber, brass, or steel. The characteristic sound is bright and metallic. Orchestra bells are used primarily in concert bands, orchestras, and chamber music groups.

Northwestern University (WORLD BOOK photo by Ted Nielsen)
The glockenspiel produces a clear, bell-like sound. It can be placed on a stand, *shown here,* or held upright on an arm.

Almost every culture has developed a version of the glockenspiel. Bell makers in the Netherlands created the present-day instrument between 1650 and 1700. The bell-lyra was first played in a royal fife and drum corps in England during the 1850's.   John H. Beck

Glomerulonephritis. See Nephritis.

Glooscap. See Micmac Indians; New Brunswick (Interesting facts about New Brunswick); **Prince Edward Island** (introduction).

Glorious Revolution of 1688 ended the rule of King James II of England and brought William III and Mary II to the throne. It established Parliament's right to control succession to the throne and to limit the monarch's power. In 1689, Parliament passed the Bill of Rights, which banned Roman Catholics from the throne and made it illegal for a monarch to suspend laws, keep an army in peacetime, or levy taxes without Parliament's consent.

James, a Roman Catholic, became king in 1685. He favored Catholics in his appointments and policies. Many people in England disliked his policies. But they put up with James because they expected Mary, his Protestant daughter, to succeed him. However, the birth of a son to James's wife in June 1688 raised the prospect of continued Catholic rule. Leading politicians then invited William of Orange, Mary's husband and ruler of the Netherlands, to invade England with Dutch forces. The English wanted William to help restore their liberties. William invaded England in November, and James fled to France. William and Mary were crowned co-rulers of England in February 1689. William and Mary accepted the crown of Scotland several months later. The revolution met with little resistance in England. However, William had to put down resistance in Scotland and Ireland.

Roger Howell, Jr.

See also **Monmouth, Duke of.**

Gloucester, *GLAHS tuhr,* Massachusetts (pop. 30,273), has been an important fishing center since colonial days. Gloucester lies in northeastern Massachusetts near the tip of Cape Ann, about 30 miles (48 kilometers) from Boston (see **Massachusetts** [political map]). A statue, *Fishermen's Memorial,* overlooks the small, well-protected harbor of Gloucester. The city constructed it as a tribute to the many people from Gloucester who have lost their lives in fishing accidents.

The processing of fish and manufacture of fish products rank as the city's chief industries. Gloucester is a famous summer resort. Its whale-watching trips attract many tourists.

Gloucester was settled in 1623. It was incorporated as a city in 1873.   Laurence A. Lewis

Glove is a protective or decorative covering for the hand. It has a separate sheath for each finger. The word glove comes from an Anglo-Saxon term that means *palm of the hand.*

Archaeologists claim that prehistoric cave dwellers wore crude gloves. Workers in ancient Egypt, Greece, and Rome wore gloves to protect their hands during rough work.

During the Middle Ages, most Europeans wore mittens. Only the wealthy wore gloves, which were often decorated with embroidery and jewels. Armored knights wore *gauntlets,* or gloves made of heavy leather covered with plates of steel or iron. Knights often

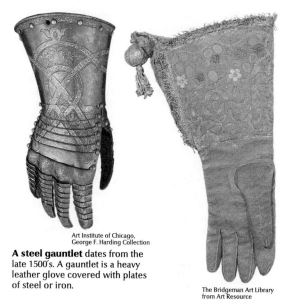

Art Institute of Chicago,
George F. Harding Collection

A steel gauntlet dates from the late 1500's. A gauntlet is a heavy leather glove covered with plates of steel or iron.

The Bridgeman Art Library
from Art Resource

Gold and silver threads decorate the cuff of this fancy leather hawking glove. It was made in France in the early 1600's.

Rawlings Sporting Goods Company, SHER-WOOD

Gloves in sports. A fielder's glove, *left,* is used by baseball players to catch the ball. A hockey player wears a heavily padded glove, *right,* to protect the hands and wrists.

fastened ladies' gloves to their helmets to show love or devotion.

Gloves of fine leather and silk were a symbol of rank in the 1800's. The spotlessly clean gloves of people in the upper class showed that they did not have to do manual labor. Women were expected to wear white gloves for formal dress until the mid-1960's.

Today, gloves are woven or knit from many types of materials. Such natural materials as leather, fur, silk, cotton, rubber, and wool continue to be used. Gloves are also made from various types of manufactured fibers, including nylon, acrylic, polyester, polypropylene, and spandex.

Insulated gloves protect the hands of workers from extreme heat or cold. Gloves treated with special plastics protect laboratory workers from harmful chemicals. Gloves with padded palms cushion the hands of baseball players and long-distance bikers. Medical profes-

sionals use smooth, tight-fitting gloves of latex rubber that allow flexibility while preventing contact with viruses.   Rachel K. Pannabecker

See also **Baseball** (Equipment; pictures); **Gauntlet.**

Glowworm. See Firefly.

Gloxinia, *glahk SIHN ee uh,* is a plant remarkable for its richly colored velvety leaves and large bell-shaped flowers. It is native to tropical America, but is grown as a house plant and in greenhouses. Gloxinias should not be exposed to direct sunlight or constant high humidity. The soil should be kept slightly moist. The plant grows from tubers, seeds, or cuttings from stems or leaves.

WORLD BOOK illustration by Robert Hynes

The gloxinia is a popular tropical American plant. It has large bell-shaped flowers and richly colored velvety leaves.

Scientific classification. The gloxinia belongs to the gesneria family, Gesneriaceae. Its scientific name is *Sinningia speciosa.*   Michael J. Tanabe

See also **Flower** (picture: Flowers of the tropics and subtropics).

Gluck, Christoph Willibald, *VIHL ih BAHLT* (1714-1787), a German composer, reformed opera in the 1700's. Gluck eliminated the mere display of brilliant singing that previously had dominated opera. He tried to achieve a balance between the musical and the dramatic aspects of opera. Gluck enriched the orchestral component of opera and gave more emphasis to choral and ensemble singing. The enhanced orchestra provided more opportunity to develop an opera's dramatic qualities.

Gluck was born in Erasbach in Bavaria. His important operatic work began in Vienna. There he collaborated with an Italian poet, Ranieri di Calzabigi, on three operas—*Orpheus and Eurydice* (1762), also known as *Orfeo; Alceste* (1767); and *Paris and Helen* (1770). Like all of Gluck's best operas, these works were based on ancient Greek themes. Gluck's next opera, *Iphigenia in Aulis,* opened in Paris in 1774. He achieved another reform with this work by insisting on six months of rehearsal instead of the usual few weeks. Gluck also stressed the importance of the composer's wishes, rather than the whims of the star singers, in deciding how an opera should be performed. His greatest opera, *Iphigenia in Tauris,* was presented in Paris in 1779.

Carolyn Abbate

See also **Opera** (Classical opera).

Glucose, *GLOO kohs,* is a type of sugar. It is sometimes called *grape sugar* or *blood sugar.* Glucose is a product of photosynthesis in green plants and is the chief source of energy for most living organisms, including human beings. Honey and such fruits as grapes and figs contain large amounts of glucose. Pure glucose is a white crystal. It is about three-fourths as sweet as *sucrose* (table sugar). Its chemical formula is $C_6H_{12}O_6$.

Glucose belongs to a class of foods called *carbohydrates*. It is the most abundant of the *monosaccharides,* which are the simplest carbohydrates. Because of its simple chemical structure, glucose can be absorbed directly into the blood from the intestine. Most complex carbohydrates, such as sucrose and starch, must be broken down into monosaccharides before they can be absorbed into the blood.

The blood normally is about 0.1 per cent glucose. After a meal rich in carbohydrates, the amount of glucose in the blood rises and remains higher than normal for a brief period. The extra glucose is rapidly removed from the blood and stored in the liver and muscles as a complex carbohydrate called *glycogen*. When quick energy is needed, stored glycogen is converted back into glucose. If the glycogen storage areas are full, excess glucose may be converted into fat.

In the disease *diabetes mellitus,* glucose is not efficiently used by the body cells, and the amount of glucose in the blood remains abnormally high. As the blood moves through the kidneys, some excess glucose passes into the urine. Urine is analyzed for the presence of glucose as a test for diabetes mellitus.

Glucose is made commercially from starch by treating the starch with acid under steam pressure. If all the starch is converted into glucose, the product is sold under the name *dextrose.* If the conversion is not complete, and a mixture of glucose and other sugars results, the product is sold as *corn syrup.* Manufacturers use dextrose and corn syrup in a wide variety of foods and beverages, including baked goods, candy, canned fruits, and soft drinks.   Dorothy M. Feigl

See also **Corn syrup; Hypoglycemia.**

Glue is an adhesive made from the skins, connective tissues, or bones of animals. Many people use the term *glue* for all types of adhesives, including those made from plants or plastics. This article deals only with glues made from animal tissues. For information on other types of bonding substances, see **Adhesive.**

Glue is an impure form of *gelatin,* a protein substance obtained by boiling bones or other animal parts. Glue makes objects stick together by penetrating pores in their surfaces and then drying to form a hard bond. People have made glue for many centuries, and it is one of the most widely used adhesives today.

Types of glue. There are three types of glue: (1) hide glue, (2) bone glue, and (3) fish glue. Most hide and bone glues are sold in the form of powder or small grains and must be dissolved in hot water before they can be used. These glues can be stored for any length of time if they are kept dry. Fish glue is a concentrated liquid that contains about 45 per cent solids. If unused, fish glue begins to lose its strength as an adhesive about two years after it is made.

How glue is made. Manufacturers obtain glue from animal parts by cooking them in water. Cooking breaks down the protein in the animal tissue and dissolves it. The resulting solution may be filtered and concentrated before being sold as glue. The preparations for cooking and the final manufacturing steps vary with the type of glue.

Manufacturers of hide or bone glue obtain their raw materials from meat packing houses or tanning factories. Hide glue is made by first washing the hides in water. The skins are then soaked in water containing lime to remove nonglue proteins. Next, they are treated with a mild acid and rinsed with water. The rinsed hides are cooked in water in large kettles or tubs. The resulting glue is drained off, filtered, and evaporated. The glue then cools and, in most cases, turns solid. Machines grind the solid glue into grains or powder and then package it for shipping. If the glue is to be sold as a liquid, substances called *antigelling agents* are added while it is still hot. The antigelling agents keep the glue from solidifying as it cools.

Bone glue is made by first washing the bones in water or dilute acids and crushing them. Next, the bones are cooked in water. The rest of the process resembles that used for hide glues.

Most fish glue is made from washed fish skins. The skins are cooked to form a concentrated broth, which is then cooled and packaged.

Uses of glue. Industries consume most glue. Many manufacturers of wood products use glue to hold together such items as furniture, toys, and musical instruments. Other manufacturers coat paper, cloth, or plastic with glue to make adhesive tape. Makers of sandpaper use glue to hold the scratchy particles to the paper backing. In the textile and paper industries, glue serves as *sizing,* a preparation used to stiffen cloth and glaze paper. Many book manufacturers hold pages to bindings with glue.   James Nelson Rieck

See also **Gelatin.**

Gluon, *GLOO ahn,* is a subatomic particle that carries a powerful force which holds together the components of protons and neutrons. This force is called the *strong interaction.* Gluons are *elementary particles*—that is, they are not made up of smaller objects. Gluons have no mass. They travel at the speed of light.

Gluons are created and absorbed only by other gluons and by elementary particles known as *quarks* and *antiquarks.* Gluons act as messengers, carrying bundles of energy between elementary particles. This exchange of energy binds the particles to one another in a group called a *hadron.* Some hadrons contain a quark and an antiquark, but they are extremely unstable and disintegrate in a fraction of a second. The only hadrons found in ordinary matter are protons and neutrons, which have only quarks. Each proton and neutron also contains a swarm of gluons, which travel between the quarks, holding them together.

Gluons rapidly multiply themselves and are just as rapidly absorbed by other particles. The multiplication of gluons intensifies the strong interaction holding the particles together. This force is so strong that no gluon—or quark or antiquark—can be separated from a hadron long enough to be directly observed.

The modern theory of gluons was proposed in 1974 by United States physicists H. David Politzer, David J. Gross, and Frank A. Wilczek. The theory is called *quan-*

tum chromodynamics, or *QCD.* Researchers obtained the first direct evidence for the existence of gluons in 1979 at the German Electron Synchrotron Laboratory (DESY) in Hamburg. Robert H. March

Gluten, *GLOOT uhn,* is the sticky, elastic substance in bread dough. Gluten forms and develops when wheat flour is mixed with water and the dough is kneaded. The word *gluten* comes from a Latin word meaning *glue.*

Gluten consists chiefly of two proteins, *gliadins* and *glutenins.* Wheat and some other cereal grains contain varying proportions of these proteins. The type and quality of cereal grains used to make a flour determine the amount and strength of its gluten.

In breadmaking, bakers add yeast to the dough to produce carbon dioxide gas by means of a process called *fermentation.* The gluten in the dough traps the carbon dioxide. As the gas expands, it stretches the gluten, causing the bread to rise.

Commercial bread bakers often add gluten to dough if the proteins in the flour would not provide enough strength and elasticity. Some food companies add gluten to bread to increase the protein content of the bread. Helen C. Brittin

See also **Flour** (Types of flour); **Yeast** (How yeast is used).

Glycerin. See Glycerol.

Glycerol, *GLIHS uh rohl,* also called glycerin, *GLIHS uhr ihn,* is a thick, sweet-tasting liquid used in the manufacture of many products for homes and industry. Its name comes from the Greek word *glykys,* which means *sweet.* Glycerol forms a part of all fats. Swedish chemist Carl Wilhelm Scheele made the first glycerol from olive oil in 1783.

Uses. Glycerol is used to make synthetic *resins* that harden paints. Cellophane and special papers are treated with glycerol to make them flexible and tough. Processors spray glycerol on tobacco leaves to prevent them from crumbling during treatment.

Glycerol is used to make ice cream, candy, and icings smooth and creamy. It also makes toothpaste and cosmetics smooth. Numerous medicines contain glycerol.

The chemical industry uses glycerol in the manufacture of sealing compounds and antifreeze. Glycerol is a major ingredient of *nitroglycerin,* also called *nitroglycerol,* a powerful explosive that is used to make dynamite and gunpowder (see **Nitroglycerin**). Air brakes, electrical equipment, and oil-refining machinery are lubricated with glycerol.

Production. Most glycerol is a by-product of soap-making (see **Detergent and soap** [How soap is made]). However, large amounts of synthetic glycerol are made from a hydrocarbon gas called *propylene.* Crude glycerol is purified to make various grades, such as *dynamite grade, yellow distilled,* and *chemically pure* glycerol. Only the highest grades of glycerol are used in foods and medicines.

Properties. Glycerol is a clear, colorless liquid that has no odor. It is an alcohol with the formula C_3H_5 (OH)$_3$. At low temperatures, glycerol sometimes forms crystals. These melt at 17.9 °C. Liquid glycerol boils at 290 °C. Its specific gravity is 1.26. It dissolves in water and in alcohols, but not in liquid hydrocarbons. Glycerol draws water from its surroundings. Heat produced by the absorption makes glycerol feel warm. Myron E. Feinstein

Glycogen, *GLY kuh juhn,* is a tasteless, odorless white powder. Glycogen is a carbohydrate (see **Carbohydrate**). It is made up of units of a simple sugar called *glucose,* linked together in branched chains.

Glycogen is formed and stored in the liver and muscles. It is made from excess starch and sugars in the body. The starch and sugars are first converted to glucose. Excess glucose is then changed into glycogen. Glycogen is often called *animal starch.* It is a reserve food and is easily reconverted to glucose. Liver glycogen regulates the sugar level in the blood. In the muscles, liver glycogen is converted to glucose when the body needs energy. André Dubois

Glycol, *GLY kohl* or *GLY kahl,* is a type of organic compound. Glycols are also called *diols.* They make up a class of alcohols. The simplest glycol is ethylene glycol, a poisonous liquid that is thick and colorless. Its chemical formula is $CH_2OH \cdot CH_2OH$. Ethylene glycol has a high boiling point (197.6 °C) and is very soluble in water. It is used in hydraulic brake fluids and as a permanent antifreeze in automobiles. Manufacturers use ethylene glycol as a *humectant* (moistening agent), as a solvent in paint and plastic products, and as a chemical intermediate in the production of alkyd resins, synthetic fibers, and plasticizers.

Polymers—that is, molecular chains—of ethylene glycol range from transparent, *viscous* (thick) liquids to waxlike solids. They are used as lubricants, solvents, and chemical intermediates. The nonpoisonous propylene glycol is used in pharmaceuticals, cosmetics, and even foods. David C. Armbruster

Gnat, *nat,* is a general name given to a wide variety of small flies. Some types of gnats feed on the blood of animals, including human beings, and have a surprisingly painful bite. Other types of gnats do not bite. A gnat has mouthparts that form a snout called a *proboscis.* A biting gnat uses the proboscis to pierce the skin of the animal on which it feeds.

Some gnats, such as *black flies,* lay their eggs on water. The eggs float for one to several days and then hatch. The *larvae* (young) cling to rocks in fast-flowing streams. Black flies live in most parts of the world, from the polar regions to the tropics. In some tropical and subtropical regions, black flies spread a disease called *onchocerciasis* or *river blindness.* This disease may cause blindness.

Other types of gnats, including *wood gnats* and *fungus gnats,* lay eggs in decaying plant material, on moist foliage, and in mushroom gardens. Gnats called *biting midges, punkies,* or *no-see-ums* lay eggs in or near sand, mud, tree holes, and wet plant debris. These tiny gnats have a fierce bite and are serious pests throughout the United States. Certain gnats lay their eggs in plant tissue, causing *galls* (swellings) in the plant. The *Hessian fly,* which attacks wheat, is among the most

WORLD BOOK illustration by Shirley Hooper, Oxford Illustrators Limited

Gnat

harmful of these gnats. See **Midge; Hessian fly.**

There are a great variety of nonbiting gnats. Most of them are types of midges or fruit flies.

Scientific classification. Gnats consist of several families in the order Diptera.   Sandra J. Glover

See also **Fruit fly; Sand fly.**

Gnatcatcher, *NAT кAсH uhr,* is the name of several small songbirds native to the Western Hemisphere. The best-known species is the *blue-gray gnatcatcher,* which ranges from the north-central United States to Guatemala. It is 4 to 5 inches (10 to 13 centimeters) long, with a bluish-gray back and white breast. This bird covers its

WORLD BOOK illustration by John F. Eggert

The blue-gray gnatcatcher is a North American songbird.

nest with lichens and uses spider webs to bind it to the limb of a tree. The female lays four or five pale blue eggs. The name *gnatcatcher* comes from the bird's habit of darting after flying insects.

Scientific classification. Gnatcatchers are in the subfamily Sylviinae of the family Muscicapidae. The blue-gray gnatcatcher is classified as *Polioptila caerulea.*   Martha Hatch Balph

Gneiss, *nys,* is a banded, coarse-grained rock. In most forms of gneiss, the banding results from the arrangement of dark- and light-colored minerals into alternating layers. In some, it is produced by the parallel alignment

© Breck P. Kent, Earth Scenes

Gneiss is a coarse-grained rock formed by heat and pressure deep within the earth's crust. Most forms of gneiss have alternating layers of dark- and light-colored minerals.

of platelike or needle-shaped crystals. Unlike schist and various other banded rocks, gneiss does not readily break along its layers.

Gneiss is a common variety of *metamorphic rock,* one of the major kinds of rocks. It is formed during the *regional metamorphism* of the two other main types of rocks, *igneous* and *sedimentary.* In this process, heat and pressure alter the original rock deep within the earth's crust. Gneiss that has been formed from igneous rock is called *orthogneiss.* It consists of feldspar, quartz, and *ferromagnesian silicates* (see **Silicate**). Gneiss that originates from sedimentary rock is called *paragneiss.* Paragneiss consists of feldspar, quartz, and such other minerals as graphite and biotite.   Mary Emma Wagner

GNMA. See **Government National Mortgage Association.**

Gnome, *nohm,* is a dwarflike creature in European folklore. Most gnomes are said to look like small, misshapen men with long beards. They live underground and are thought to guard fabulous treasures of precious metals and jewels. Gnomes are associated with mines and mining activities. Gnomes are sometimes said to have the magic ability to make people feel sad.

Paracelsus, a Swiss physician of the 1500's, helped make the idea of gnomes well known. He wrote that gnomes could move through solid earth as easily as fish swim through water.   C. Scott Littleton

Gnosticism, *NAHS tuh sihz uhm,* was a religious and philosophical movement in Europe and the Middle East that flourished from about the A.D. 100's to the 700's. There were many Christian and non-Christian Gnostic sects. However, they all believed they had secret knowledge about the nature of the universe and the origin and destiny of humanity.

Gnostics believed that people could attain salvation only by acquiring *gnosis,* a Greek word meaning *knowledge.* Most Gnostics believed in an unknown and remote Supreme Being. An evil and subordinate supernatural being called the Demiurge created the world, which was ruled by evil spirits. Gnostics generally taught that selected individuals had a divine spark imprisoned in their material body. Through gnosis, that divine spark would be liberated from the basically evil world and united with the Supreme Being.

Most Christian Gnostics believed that Jesus was a divine messenger who brought gnosis to ordinary Christians. They claimed Jesus only inhabited a human body temporarily. They thus denied His death on the cross and Resurrection as described in the New Testament.

Many philosophies and religions of the ancient world contributed to the origin of Gnosticism. Such early Christian leaders as Saint Irenaeus attacked the movement for heresy. These attacks stressed the pagan elements in Gnosticism and the Gnostics' unorthodox views about the nature of Jesus.   Richard R. Ring

See also **Irenaeus, Saint.**

Gnotobiotics, *NOH toh by AHT ihks,* is the scientific study of animals or other organisms raised in environments that are free of germs or that contain only specifically known germs. Scientists compare gnotobiotic animals with ordinary animals whose bodies carry many bacteria, viruses, and parasites. In this way, scientists can determine more precisely how specific germs affect the body. Gnotobiotics has aided the study of metabolism and other body functions, of the interaction of various germs in the body, of organ and tissue transplantation, and of the effects of radiation on the body.

Gnotobiotic animals are obtained by removing unborn animals from their mother's womb and putting them into a sterilized cage called an *isolator.* Rats and mice are two types of animals frequently used. Rubber gloves built into the isolator enable scientists to handle and care for the animals without contaminating them. All food, water, and other supplies are sterilized before being put into the isolator.

Gnotobiotic animals look like ordinary animals and are fully capable of normal life functions, such as survival, growth, and reproduction. However, they differ from ordinary animals in some ways. The major differences in gnotobiotic animals are in the size of organs that come in direct contact with germs, such as organs of the digestive tract and respiratory system. For example, the small intestine of gnotobiotic animals is generally shorter and thinner and the *cecum* (part of the large intestine) generally much larger than those of ordinary animals. Gnotobiotic animals also have lower rates of metabolism, heartbeat, and blood flow than do ordinary animals. In addition, gnotobiotic animals are less resistant to disease.   J. Derrell Clark

Gnu, *noo,* also called *wildebeest, WIHL duh BEEST,* is a large African antelope. Its high, massive shoulders and thick neck support a large head with long, curved horns. The gnu has thin legs and a horselike tail. It eats leaves, twigs, and grass. *Gnu* is an African name.

There are two kinds of gnu. The *brindled gnu* stands about 4½ feet (137 centimeters) high and has a long, sad-looking face. It ranges from yellowish-brown to gray in color, and has dark vertical stripes on its shoulders and neck. Brindled gnu graze in herds between northern

Kenya and northern South Africa and Namibia. The *white-tailed gnu* lives only in South Africa. It stands about 3½ feet (107 centimeters) high and has a fierce-looking, hairy face. It ranges from brown to black and has a yellowish-white tail.

Scientific classification. Gnu belong to the bovid family, Bovidae. They make up the genus *Connochaetes.* The scientific name for the brindled gnu is *C. taurinus.* The white-tailed gnu is *C. gnou.*   Duane A. Schlitter

Go-kart. See Kart racing.

Goat is an animal that has provided people with milk, meat, and wool since prehistoric times. Goats were probably first tamed more than 9,000 years ago by peoples in Asia and in the Eastern Mediterranean region. Today, *domestic* (tame) goats are important farm animals throughout the world, especially in mountainous areas and in dry or semitropical climates. Unlike most other kinds of livestock, goats thrive in these harsh environments.

Various terms are used to classify goats according to their sex and age. An adult male goat is called a *buck* or a *billy goat,* and an adult female is a *doe* or a *nanny goat.* A goat less than a year old is called a *kid.*

Kinds of goats

Wild goats can survive in almost any kind of environment. However, they thrive in rocky and mountainous areas. The does and kids travel in herds of up to about 50 animals. Bucks live alone or in separate groups except during the mating season, when they join the herd. Wild goats eat almost any kind of vegetation, including bushes, leaves, and tree bark.

There are several species of wild goats, and most of them live in Asia. The true wild goat, or *bezoar goat,* is found in the Near East and on the Greek islands. Another species, the ibex, lives in the mountainous areas of Sudan and Siberia, and in the Alps and Caucasus Mountains.

The Rocky Mountain goat, which lives in parts of Canada and the United States, is not a true goat. Rather, it is classified as a *goat antelope.* See **Mountain goat.**

Domestic goats probably descended from the wild goats of the Near East. There are about 600 breeds of domestic goats, many of which are commercially important. Domestic goats produce great quantities of milk and meat yearly. They also provide large quantities of leather and wool.

The major breeds of dairy goats are the Saanen, Toggenburg, and Alpine, all of which were developed in Switzerland. The Anglo-Nubian goat, also called the Nubian goat, is the most popular milk-producing goat in Canada and the United States. It was developed by breeding British dairy goats with goats imported from Africa and India.

Goats raised for meat include the Boer of South Africa and the Red Sokoto of Nigeria. The Red Sokoto is also raised for leather. Pygmy goats are used for meat in West Africa, and they are also kept as pets in the United States.

Major breeds of wool-producing goats include the Angora and the Cashmere. The Angora goat originated in the Turkish province of Ankara (formerly Angora). From the Angora's outer coat of soft, shaggy, white wool comes mohair wool. The Cashmere goat originated in

© Giuseppe Mazza

The brindled gnu is one of the fastest animals in southern Africa. It has a large head and long curved horns and is marked by dark vertical stripes on its head and neck.

the Himalaya and supplies cashmere wool. The wool is taken from the Cashmere goat's fine, silky undercoat.

How people use goats

Products. Goat meat, sometimes known as *chevon* (pronounced *CHEHV uhn*), is a popular food in Greece, Italy, the Caribbean, Latin America, and many African and Asian nations. It is often used in *curries* (dishes with a spicy sauce).

In North America and western Europe, people often raise goats for dairy products, rather than meat. Goat's milk differs only slightly in composition from cow's milk. It has a higher content of vitamin A than does cow's milk, but it has smaller quantities of vitamin C and certain B vitamins. Goat's milk is easier to digest than cow's milk. It is, therefore, an important source of milk for many babies, elderly people, and people with stomach ailments. People who are allergic to the protein in cow's milk may be able to safely drink goat's milk. However, people who are allergic to the *lactose* in cow's milk cannot drink goat's milk, because this milk sugar is the same in milk from both animals.

Goat's milk cheese has become quite popular. These cheeses have a creamy consistency and a wide range of flavors. They are widely used in gourmet cooking. Popular cheeses made from goat's milk include blue, chèvre, feta, and riccota.

Another important goat product is wool. Mohair wool is used to make clothes, draperies, upholstery, and other articles. Cashmere wool is used to make warm, soft garments, including sweaters, dresses, and scarves. Other goat products include leather, fertilizer, goat's milk soap, goat's milk fudge, and *cajeta,* a goat's milk caramel that is popular in Mexico.

Other uses. Although goats are raised chiefly for the products they provide, people also keep goats for other purposes. Goats are popular pets because of their curious and friendly nature and their ability to produce family-sized quantities of milk. In some African and Asian cultures, people own large herds of goats as an indication of wealth. Scientists use goats as laboratory test animals, because they are easy to manage, smaller and less

expensive than cows, and similar in body size to human beings. Cattle and sheep ranchers use goats to clear brush and other unwanted plants from their pastures. However, goats can destroy all plant life in an area if they are not carefully controlled.

The bodies of goats

Size and general appearance. Goats vary greatly in size. Pakistani dwarf goats weigh as little as 20 pounds (9 kilograms) and stand only about $1\frac{1}{2}$ feet (46 centimeters) tall. But some ibexes weigh about 300 pounds (135 kilograms) and stand about 4 feet (1.2 meters) tall. Modern dairy breeds weigh between 130 and 200 pounds (60 and 90 kilograms).

A goat's body is covered with wool. The wool can be of one color or a combination of colors. Common colors include black, brown, gray, red, and white. Goats have *cloven hoofs*—that is, hoofs that are divided into two toes. The animals have short tails that usually stand straight up. The ears are long and drooping in most Indian and African goats, but short and erect in the European breeds. Most goats have horns, which they use in fighting. Some horns curve backwards, but others are straight and spiral like a corkscrew. Both sexes may have beards.

Digestive system. Goats are grazing animals with specialized teeth and digestive organs. On the front of its upper jaw, the animal has a hard pad instead of teeth. Eight *incisors* (biting teeth) on the goat's lower jaw bite and cut food against the pad. A goat chews its food with its *molars* (back teeth). The animal has 12 pairs of upper and lower molars.

A goat's stomach system has four chambers for digesting food. The first three stomach chambers have bacteria and other microorganisms that help break down the tough plant matter that makes up a goat's diet. After the animal swallows, the slightly chewed food is temporarily stored in the first stomach. Later, the food passes into the second stomach. There, it softens and forms a ball-like mass called *cud,* which then returns to the mouth. After the goat chews and swallows the cud, it goes to the other two stomachs and to the intestines

Wild Most wild goats live in the rocky and mountainous areas of Asia. Species of wild goats include the
goats ibex and the true wild goat, or *bezoar goat.* Wild goats eat almost any kind of vegetation.

V. Renaud, Jacana

Ibex

© Photo Duscher from Bruce Coleman Inc.

True wild goat, or *bezoar goat*

for further digestion. Animals that digest their food in this way are called *ruminants.*

Unlike other ruminants, such as cows and sheep, goats can eat a wide variety of plants and select from them the most nourishing parts. They use their small mouths and flexible lips, which are adapted to grasping, to pick off leaves, flowers, fruits, and other plant parts. Goats actively hunt for food, and they can cover a wide area in search of scarce plant materials.

Raising dairy goats

Dairy goats can be raised on a small number of acres. The animals need an exercise area and a well-built shelter, without drafts. Goats are clever and will continually try to escape from fencing and enclosures. The best way to prevent them from escaping is to use solid board fencing or electric fencing.

Adult dairy goats should be fed good quality hay and grain. Abundant, clean water and salt must be available at all times. Does should be milked two times a day on a regular schedule. Good dairy goats produce a maximum of 3 to 8 quarts (2.8 to 7.6 liters) of milk a day, with an average of 2 quarts (1.9 liters) a day over 10 months. Most dairy goats live from 8 to 10 years.

Breeding. The mating season of a goat depends on where it lives. In the hot, tropical areas near the equator, goats mate throughout the year, while in the temperate regions, they breed only from late summer to late winter. They begin breeding as the days become shorter. During the mating season, glands on the buck produce an oily substance whose odor attracts the does. A doe gives birth to two or three kids about five months after mating.

Feeding kids. Kids can either get milk from their mothers or be raised by hand using a bottle or pan. They should be fed 1 to 2 quarts (0.95 to 1.9 liters) a day of goat's milk, cow's milk, or goat- or sheep-milk replacer. They need milk three to four times per day the first week and then two times a day for six weeks to three or four months. Kids should be offered leafy hay and grain starting at a week of age. After weaning, kids should get 1 pound (0.45 kilogram) of grain a day and all the hay they will eat.

Disease. Most goat keepers vaccinate their animals against two serious diseases—tetanus, which affects the muscles, and enterotoxemia, which affects the intestine. Goats receive selenium shots in areas where there is a lack of this mineral. Worms cause many problems in

Domestic goats Domestic goats are important farm animals throughout the world. Saanen, Toggenburg, and Nubian goats are major milk producers. The Angora is raised for its wool, called *mohair.*

Agri-Graphics, Ltd.

Saanen goat

Grant Heilman

Toggenburg goat

Daniel Considine, Sunshine Farms

Nubian goat

Grant Heilman

Angora goats

goat herds, so regular worming is usually necessary. Several contagious diseases are widespread in the United States goat population. Sore mouth is a highly contagious disease that causes ugly sores on the mouth area of goats. Caprine arthritic encephalitis (CAE) is a virus that causes arthritis in goats of all ages. It can cause paralysis in goat kids and may reduce milk production among does. About 80 percent of the goats tested within the United States have CAE, though many show no symptoms.

Scientific classification. Goats belong to the family Bovidae. They make up the genus *Capra*. The scientific name for the true wild goat is *C. aegagrus*. Domestic goats are *C. hircus*.

Beth McCammon Feldman

Related articles in *World Book* include:

Angora	Leather	Sheep
Cashmere goat	Mohair	Wool
Ibex	Prion	

Goatsucker, or *nightjar,* is one of a widespread family of birds that largely fly at night. The nighthawk and the whippoorwill also belong to this family.

Goatsuckers are 8 to 15 inches (20 to 38 centimeters) long. Their dull coloring, gray and brown mottled with white, acts as effective camouflage. The wings of goatsuckers are long and slender, and their extremely short bills have bristles at the base. Goatsuckers catch their

WORLD BOOK illustration by John Rignall, Linden Artists Ltd.
The goatsucker has gray, brown, and white coloring that serves as effective camouflage. The bird is most active at night.

chief foods, which are insects, while in flight.

The name goatsucker comes from the old fable that the birds milk goats. This arose because of the birds' wide, soft mouths and because they feed at twilight near grazing animals. The name *nightjar* comes from the birds' habit of flying at night and their jarring cries.

Scientific classification. The goatsucker belongs to the family Caprimulgidae. The scientific name for the common goatsucker of Europe is *Caprimulgus europaeus*.

Bertin W. Anderson

See also **Nighthawk; Whippoorwill**.

Gobi, *GOH bee,* is a windswept, nearly treeless desert that stretches across part of southern Mongolia and northern China. The Gobi covers more than 500,000 square miles (1,300,000 square kilometers). It extends about 1,200 miles (1,930 kilometers) from east to west and about 600 miles (970 kilometers) from north to

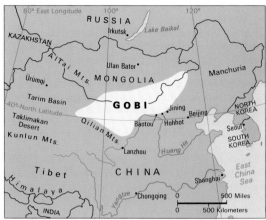

WORLD BOOK map
The Gobi is a huge desert that stretches across part of southern Mongolia and northern China. It covers more than 500,000 square miles (1,300,000 square kilometers).

south. The Gobi lies in a basin on a high plateau. Elevations in the desert range from 3,000 to 5,000 feet (910 to 1,500 meters) above sea level.

The center of the Gobi consists largely of dry, rocklike or sandy soil. *Steppes* (dry grasslands) surround this central area. Sand dunes are not common in the Gobi. They cover only about 5 percent of the desert.

The Gobi often has long heat waves in summer and cold periods in winter. The temperature averages 70 °F (21 °C) in July and 10 °F (−12 °C) in January. The climate is very dry. Most of the desert receives less than 10 inches (25 centimeters) of precipitation annually.

Animals of the Gobi include donkeys, goitered—or longtailed—gazelles, desert hamsters, sand rats, and eagles, hawks, and vultures. The chief economic activities in the desert are raising animals and processing animal products. For centuries, nomads have roamed the Gobi with herds of sheep, cattle, and goats in search of vegetation for their animals. Beginning in the mid-1900's, the governments of China and Mongolia established many farms in the Gobi. People in the wetter areas of the Gobi grow spring wheat, millet, oats, and a tall cereal grass called *gaoliang*. The desert provides small amounts of coal, oil shale, salt, and various compounds known as *soda*.

The interior part of the Gobi has no major cities. However, two cities on its southern edge, Hohhot and Baotou, serve as commercial centers for the Chinese part of the desert. A railroad crosses the Gobi between the Chinese city of Jining and the capital of Mongolia, Ulan Bator. In summer, trucks and camel caravans carry cargo across the desert.

Archaeologists have found evidence of ancient civilizations in the Gobi. During the Middle Ages, the armies of the Mongol leaders Genghis Khan and Kublai Khan roamed the desert. The Chinese built the Great Wall of China near the Gobi to guard against attacks from the north. But in the 1200's, forces led by Genghis Khan swept across the wall and conquered much of China (see **Great Wall of China**). George J. Demko

See also **Andrews, Roy Chapman; Camel** (picture).

Goblin. See Fairy.

The **Gobi** is the coldest, most northern desert in the world. Low mountains rise along an area of sandy soil, *left*. The chief economic activities in the desert are raising animals and processing the products obtained from them.

© Brian Vikander, West Light

Goby, *GOH bee,* is the name of about 2,000 kinds of fish that live in the shallow parts of warm oceans. A few species also live in cool ocean waters and enter freshwater rivers, streams, and lakes. Gobies have a pair of pelvic fins that join on the underside of the body to form a cup. This cup can create suction, which enables the fish to attach itself to rocks, coral, or other fish.

Most gobies are only about 1 to 5 inches (2.5 to 13 centimeters) long. One kind found in the Indian Ocean, the dwarf goby, is the world's tiniest fish and smallest *vertebrate* (animal with a backbone). It measures about $\frac{2}{5}$ inch (1 centimeter) long. However, a few gobies grow to 1 foot (30 centimeters) in length.

Different gobies eat different foods, including crabs,

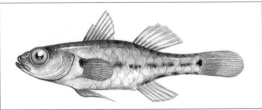

WORLD BOOK illustration by John F. Eggert
A goby lives in shallow ocean waters.

mussels, shrimp, worms, and small fish. Certain kinds of gobies undergo a process called *sex reversal.* They are born as females and become males later in life. Some gobies burrow into sand or mud, while others live with shrimp in coral reef burrows. A few species of gobies are kept in home aquariums.

In the 1980's, gobies were accidentally introduced into the Great Lakes of North America. They reproduced quickly and became so abundant that they threatened the survival of many fish native to those waters.

John E. McCosker

Scientific classification. Gobies belong to the goby family, Gobiidae. The scientific name for the dwarf goby is *Trimmatom nanus.*

God is a religious term for the "supreme reality." In many religions, God is the creator of the universe and the ultimate source of knowledge, power, and love.

God is sometimes portrayed as a humanlike male with supernatural powers. However, most religions teach that God has many different forms. Christians believe that God appears in three ways: as Father and Creator, as His Son Jesus Christ, and as the Holy Spirit. Hindus refer to the ultimate reality as Brahman, but they think that God is also revealed in more than 1,000 other gods and goddesses. Although Buddhists do not accept the idea of God as Creator, the role Buddha plays in their religion is similar to that of God in other religions. In the Hebrew Bible, or Old Testament, God is called by a variety of names, such as Yahweh (Jehovah), Elohim, and Adonai. Muslims call God Allah, as well as 99 other names that describe perfect qualities.

Cosmic Gods. Some early religions came to associate a sky god with the entire expanse of the universe. The Greeks' Zeus and the Romans' Jupiter, for example, emerged as supergods. In other religions, such as Judaism and Islam, the cosmic God has been thought to be the sole creator and sustainer of life.

Personal Gods. In many religions, people believe that a supreme God has been revealed as a friendly human being. For example, most Christians believe that God is seen through the person of Jesus Christ. In Hindu tradition, the god Krishna is portrayed as a lovable and intimate human being, especially in stories about his childhood. In some traditions, intermediary spirits, such as the Buddhists' Bodhisattva, bridge the gap between humanity and a remote and distant God. In other traditions, even the distant, cosmic God is sometimes believed to interact in a personal and loving way with His followers. For example, in the Hebrew Bible, God forms a covenant with the Jewish people and promises to bless them if they stay faithful to the divine laws. Muslim mystics, known as *sufis,* also claim to have a special and intimate relationship with God.

Gods of nature. In the Shinto religion of Japan, gods are thought to reside in particular trees, rocks, and streams. In other societies where natural forces are an important part of life, gods have also been identified with nature. For example, a major god in the Yoruba religion of Africa is the god of iron. In the religion of the Hopi Indian tribe, divine spirits are identified with eagles, foxes, and buffaloes. In ancient Mesopotamia, there were gods of the sky, water, and wind, and in ancient Egypt the central god was Re, god of the sun.

Ideas about God. There are many ways of thinking about God. *Agnostics* question the existence of God. *Atheists* deny the existence of God. *Theists* believe that a Supreme Being exists. *Theology* is the study of ideas about God. Experts in this study are called *theologians.*

Many theologians have used rational arguments to defend the existence of God. Some have developed *cosmological arguments,* which state that a first cause must have begun the process of creation, a cause that must be God. Others have set forth *teleological arguments* based on belief in a grand design or purpose for the world that only a supreme God could have created.

Some Christian theologians in the 1960's suggested that "God is dead." They argued that the traditional image of God as a father figure with supernatural powers does not reflect the modern world's scientific view of reality. Other theologians have kept the idea of God but used names that are not personalized or limited, such as "the unconditioned ultimate" and "the wholly other."

Mark Juergensmeyer

Related articles in *World Book.* For the way God is viewed in major religions, see **Christianity, Hinduism, Islam,** and **Judaism.** See also the following articles:

Agnosticism	Elohim	Odin	Theology
Allah	Jehovah	Pantheism	Trinity
Atheism	Jesus Christ	Polytheism	Zeus
Brahman	Jupiter	Religion	Zoroastrian-
Buddha	Mythology	Theism	ism
Deism			

Additional resources

Armstrong, Karen. *A History of God.* Knopf, 1993.
Eliade, Mircea, and others, eds. *The Encyclopedia of Religion.* 16 vols. Macmillan, 1987. Includes articles on each religion's concept of God.
Paterson, John and Katherine. *Images of God.* Clarion, 1998. Younger readers.
Miles, Jack. *God.* Knopf, 1995.

God Bless America is a popular American patriotic song composed by Irving Berlin. Although written in 1918, it remained unknown until 1938, when singer Kate Smith asked Berlin for a patriotic song to perform on the radio on Armistice Day (now Veterans Day). It became one of the most popular songs of that year. As an expression of gratitude to his country, Berlin donated his earnings from the song to the Boy Scouts and Girl Scouts of America. Because it is effective, sincere, and easy to sing, and because an American wrote it, some people have suggested that the song replace "The Star-Spangled Banner" as the American national anthem. "The Star-Spangled Banner" is based on a British melody.   Katherine K. Preston

God Save the Queen, or "God Save the King," is the national anthem of the United Kingdom. It is also the royal anthem in Australia, Canada, and New Zealand for official occasions when the queen or her representative is present. The song is a prayer for the glory and happiness of the British monarch, who is also the head of the

Commonwealth of Nations. In the United States, the music is used for the song "America," and other nations also have adopted the tune. The origin of the words and music is unknown. Henry Carey, a British composer, may have composed the tune in the early 1700's. The words were printed in London as early as 1744. The words of "God Save the Queen" are changed when a king reigns.   Valerie Woodring Goertzen

Godard, *gaw DAHR,* **Jean-Luc,** *zhahn look* (1930-), is a radical experiments with camera work, subject matter, and scripts have won both praise and criticism. Some critics commend him for opening the way for other directors to experiment. But others complain that his films are needlessly difficult to understand.

Many of Godard's films give the impression that they are semidocumentaries. The actors exist as real people playing roles and also as the characters of a story. In the middle of a scene, for example, the actors may begin talking about the characters they are playing.

Godard was born in Paris. His first film, *Breathless* (1960), launched his career. In *Breathless,* the performers sometimes improvised their lines. This film became famous for its short, jerky changes of scenes. *A Woman Is a Woman* (1961) was Godard's first comedy.

Since 1965, political and social discussions, often stressing left wing philosophy, have dominated many of Godard's films. *La Chinoise* (1967) tells about a group of young French Marxists. *Alphaville* (1965) and *Weekend* (1969) present different views of individuals trapped in a meaningless existence. Godard's other major works include *Le Petit Soldat* (1960), *Contempt* (1963), and *Sympathy for the Devil* (1970).   Gene D. Phillips

Goddard, *GAHD uhrd,* **Mary Katherine** (1736-1816), helped publish and print three newspapers in the American Colonies—*The Providence Gazette, The Pennsylvania Chronicle,* and *The Maryland Journal.* All three were founded and then abandoned by her brother William.

From 1774 to 1784, Goddard was publisher of the *Journal,* a widely read revolutionary paper. On Jan. 18, 1777, she became the first person to publish the Declaration of Independence with the names of all its signers. In March 1782, the *Journal* reprinted Thomas Paine's revolutionary pamphlet *Common Sense.* Goddard ran various businesses together with the *Journal,* including a bookstore and a paper mill. She also was postmistress of Baltimore from 1775 to 1789. Goddard was born in New London, Connecticut.   Lee B. Jolliffe

See also **Goddard, William.**

Goddard, Robert Hutchings (1882-1945), was an American pioneer of rocket science. His experiments with solid- and liquid-propellant rockets between 1909 and 1945 led to the development of powerful boosters for intercontinental missiles and for spacecraft. Goddard's achievements in the field of rocketry were not fully appreciated until after his death.

Goddard was born in Worcester, Massachusetts. While a student at Worcester Polytechnic Institute, he began to analyze the possibilities of rocket flight. Goddard received a Ph.D. degree from Clark University in 1911. He joined the physics faculty at Clark in 1914.

Goddard received modest support for his research from the Smithsonian Institution. In 1919, his classic report, ""A Method of Reaching Extreme Altitudes," was published in the *Smithsonian Miscellaneous Collections*. In the article, Goddard described the kind of rocket flight necessary to reach the moon. The article met with skeptical comments by the press, and as a result, Goddard avoided further publicity, continuing his work in relative anonymity. But he received enough research funding to design and build the world's first liquid-propellant rocket. He launched it from the farm of a relative, near Auburn, Massachusetts, in 1926. This success brought Goddard additional funding.

In the 1930's, Goddard successfully launched larger liquid-fueled rockets. He also made fundamental contributions to developments in propellant pumps, gyroscopic controls, and gimbal systems. During World War II (1939-1945), he conducted research for the U.S. Navy on rocket motors for *jet-assisted takeoff* of aircraft.

After his death, Goddard was given many awards and honors. They included the Congressional Gold Medal and the Langley Gold Medal.   Roger E. Bilstein

See also **Rocket** (Rockets of the early 1900's; picture: Robert H. Goddard).

Additional resources

Farley, Karin C. *Robert H. Goddard.* Silver Burdett, 1992.
Maurer, Richard. *Rocket!: How a Toy Launched the Space Age.* Crown, 1995. Younger readers.
Streissguth, Thomas. *Rocket Man: The Story of Robert Goddard.* Carolrhoda, 1995. Younger readers.

Goddard, *GAHD uhrd,* **William** (1740-1817), was an American publisher, editor, and printer. He and his mother, Sarah Updike Goddard, and his sister, Mary Katherine Goddard, were among the first newspaper publishers in the American Colonies. Goddard also developed a private mail-carrying business in 1774. His business was incorporated into the national postal service established by the Continental Congress in 1775.

Goddard founded three major newspapers—*The Providence Gazette* (1762); *The Pennsylvania Chronicle* in Philadelphia (1767); and Baltimore's first newspaper, *The Maryland Journal,* (1773). An active revolutionary, he used his papers to support the patriot cause. Goddard returned to the *Journal* in 1776 and retired in 1793. He was born in New London, Connecticut.   Lee B. Jolliffe

See also **Goddard, Mary Katherine.**

Goddess. See Mythology (Mythical beings).

Godetia, *goh DEE shuh,* is the name of a group of popular garden flowers. About 40 kinds grow wild in western North America. Godetias are also called *farewell-to-spring.* A popular type is the *satin flower.* Most satin flowers grow from 12 to 30 inches (30 to 76 centimeters) tall and have leaves 1 to 2 inches (2.5 to 5 centimeters) long. The flowers are about 2 inches (5 centimeters) wide. They have four broad, satiny petals that may be white, pink, lavender, or red. Godeitas are *annuals*—that is, they grow and die in one year. The plant was named for Swiss botanist Charles H. Godet.   William G. D'Arcy

Scientific classification. Godetias make up the genus *Clarkia* in the family Onagraceae. The scientific name for the satin flower is *C. amoena.*

Godey, *GOH dee,* **Louis Antoine,** *AN twahn* (1804-1878), in 1830 founded *Godey's Lady's Book,* the first women's magazine in the United States. It was edited by Sarah Josepha Hale. Noted writers of the day wrote for it, including Emerson, Longfellow, Poe, and Hawthorne.

Godey was born in New York City. He had little formal education. He started work at the age of 15 as a clerk on a Philadelphia newspaper.   Michael Emery

See also **Hale, Sarah Josepha.**

Godiva, *guh DY vuh,* **Lady,** lived in England during the 1000's. She was the wife of Earl Leofric of Mercia. According to legend, she asked her husband to reduce the heavy taxes he imposed as lord of Coventry. He agreed to do so if she would ride naked through the town. She asked all the townspeople to remain indoors, and, clothed only in her long hair, she mounted a horse and rode through the streets. According to a later story, a tailor named Tom peeped through a shutter and was struck blind. This traditional incident is the origin of the phrase "Peeping Tom." Until the late 1800's, a procession was held at intervals to celebrate Lady Godiva's courage.   Ralph A. Griffiths

Godkin, Edward Lawrence (1831-1902), founded *The Nation* and edited it from 1865 to 1901. This liberal weekly newspaper became one of the most influential periodicals in America. In 1881, *The Nation* became the weekly edition of the *New York Evening Post.* Within two years, Godkin was the *Post's* editor. He carried on a successful campaign against the corrupt politicians of New York City's Tammany Hall. Godkin was born in County Wicklow, Ireland.   John Tebbel

Gods. See Mythology; Polytheism; Religion.

Godthåb, *GAWT hawp* (pop. 11,957), is the capital of Greenland. The Greenlandic name for Godthåb is Nuuk. Godthåb lies on Davis Strait, near the entrance of Godthåb Fiord (see **Greenland** [map]). It has a harbor that is ice-free all year. Godthåb is the seat of the Provincial Council, Greenland's legislature. It also has a teachers college. Hunting, fishing, and sheep raising are the chief occupations of the people.

A Danish-Norwegian missionary, Hans Egede, set up a mission at this site in 1721. The town was founded in 1728. When World War II (1939-1945) cut communications between Greenland and its mother country, Denmark, Greenland was administered from Godthåb.   M. Donald Hancock

WORLD BOOK illustration by Christabel King
The godetia is a popular garden flower. It is a slender branching plant that produces numerous colorful satiny blossoms.

Godwin, William (1756-1836), was an English author and philosopher. His major work is *An Enquiry Concerning Political Justice, and Its Influence on General Virtue and Happiness* (1793). It discusses the individual's relationship to the government and to society.

Godwin believed that all monarchies were "unavoidably corrupt." He felt that no individual should hold power over another. He objected to the accumulating of private property and opposed most existing social institutions, including marriage. According to Godwin, human beings were naturally reasonable and capable of perfection, and society's problems could be solved by rational discussion. Godwin's belief that reason could and should rule over our lives reflected the influence of French philosophers of the 1700's called Philosophes (see **Philosophes**).

Godwin was born in Wisbech, near Cambridge. In 1797, he married Mary Wollstonecraft, an important early feminist. Their daughter, Mary, wrote the horror novel *Frankenstein* (1818). Godwin's ideas influenced such English romantic writers of the early 1800's as the poet Percy Bysshe Shelley. In 1816, Shelley married Godwin's daughter, Mary.   James Douglas Merritt

See also **Shelley, Mary W.; Wollstonecraft, Mary**.

Godwin Austen, Mount. See K2.

Godwit, *GAHD wiht,* is the name of four species of wading birds. Godwits measure 16 to 21 inches (41 to 53 centimeters) in length. Their long bills curve slightly upward. The birds have grayish or brownish feathers marked with spots and streaks. Godwits nest in marshes or grassy areas in northern Europe and in Canada and the northern part of the United States. They fly south to warmer climates in winter.

Scientific classification. Godwits make up the genus *Limosa* in the family Scolopacidae.   Fritz L. Knopf

Goebbels, *GEHR buhls,* **Joseph,** *YOH zehf* (1897-1945), was the official propagandist of Nazi Germany. As minister of popular enlightenment and propaganda, he tried to persuade both the Germans and the outside world to believe what the Nazis wanted them to believe. Goebbels controlled publications, radio programs, motion pictures, and the arts in Germany, and in German-dominated Europe.

Paul Joseph Goebbels was born in Rheydt into a working-class family. Appointed propaganda leader of the Nazi Party in 1929, Goebbels helped Hitler bring the Nazis to power in 1933. During Nazi rule, Goebbels worked at persuading the German public to support the Hitler regime. When Germany fell, Goebbels and his wife, Magda, poisoned their six children. Then, at Goebbels' request, a Nazi attendant shot Goebbels and his wife to death.   Otis C. Mitchell

See also **World War II** (Propaganda).

Goeduck. See Geoduck.

Goeppert Mayer, Maria. See Mayer, Maria Goeppert.

Goering, *GEHR ihng,* **Hermann Wilhelm,** *HEHR mahn VIHL hehlm* (1893-1946), was second to Adolf Hitler as a leader of Nazi Germany. He became reich marshal and commanded the German air force. He also directed the build-up of Germany's war industry before the outbreak of World War II in 1939. Goering had earned a distinguished record in World War I (1914-1918). In that war, he served as the last commander of

the famous squadron of fighter aircraft previously led by Baron Manfred von Richthofen.

Goering was born at Rosenheim and became one of Hitler's followers in the early 1920's. Elected to the Reichstag (German legislature) in 1928, he became its president. This enabled him to frustrate democratic procedures and help Hitler gain unlimited power in 1933. At the

United Press Int.

Hermann Goering

start of World War II, Hitler chose Goering as his chief aide. But Goering's influence declined when the air force failed to subdue England or stop the invasion of the European continent or the bombing of Germany.

Goering loved extravagant entertainment, lavish uniforms, and unusual military decorations. But although he was jovial, he was ruthless with opponents and rivals. Goering was judged guilty of war crimes at Nuremberg. He committed suicide by taking poison just before he was to be hanged.   Otis C. Mitchell

Goes, Hugo Van der. See Van der Goes, Hugo.

Goethals, *GOH thuhlz,* **George Washington** (1858-1928), an American civil engineer and Army officer, directed the completion of the Panama Canal. In 1907, after two civilian engineers had resigned from the job, President Theodore Roosevelt appointed Goethals as chief of the Army engineers supervising construction of the canal.

Goethals overcame many problems of organization, supply, sanitation, and health; and the canal was ready ahead of schedule. In 1914, Goethals retired from the Army to serve as the first civilian governor of the Panama Canal Zone. Goethals resigned in 1916. See **Panama Canal**.

Early life. Goethals was born in Brooklyn, N.Y. He attended the College of the City of New York, and was graduated in 1880 from the U.S. Military Academy. He served as a second lieutenant with the corps of engineers until 1885, and then taught civil and military engineering at West Point until 1889. From 1889 to 1894, Goethals supervised the construction and operation of the canal, locks, and dams of the Muscle Shoals project on the Tennessee River.

During the Spanish-American War in 1898, Goethals served as a lieutenant colonel and as chief of engineers in the First Army Corps. He was assigned to the General Staff of the United States Army from 1903 to 1907.

Engineer and supply officer. After his work on the Panama Canal, Goethals helped administer the Adamson Eight-Hour law, which established the eight-hour day for railroad workers engaged in interstate commerce. He also worked as a highway engineer for the state of New Jersey. In 1917, Goethals was recalled to active duty as general manager of the U.S. Shipping Board Emergency Fleet Corporation. He also served as acting quartermaster general of the Army and as assistant chief of staff and director of the Army's Division of Purchase, Storage, and Traffic. He was one of the greatest supply officers of World War I (1914-1918).

Goethals retired from the Army in 1919 and established a firm of consulting engineers. His company acted as consultant in developing the inner harbor of New Orleans, and on the Columbia Basin irrigation project. Goethals served as chief consulting engineer for the Port Authority of New York and New Jersey. Goethals received many honors, and state and national governments frequently called upon him to serve as an adviser.

Terry S. Reynolds

Goethe, *GUR tuh,* **Johann Wolfgang von,** *YOH hahn VOHLF gahng fuhn* (1749-1832), was a German poet, novelist, and playwright. He ranks among the most important and influential writers of modern European literature. His masterpiece is the verse play *Faust* (see **Faust**). Goethe was also a leading thinker and scientist. The scope and originality of his literary works and the diversity of his intellectual pursuits make him the central figure of German classical and romantic literature.

Early years. Goethe was born in Frankfurt (am Main) into a well-to-do family. He received an excellent education, which stressed foreign languages, literature, and fine arts. While studying law in Leipzig from 1765 to 1768, Goethe wrote gallant and playful poems. A physical breakdown forced him to return to Frankfurt in 1768. After his recovery, he completed his law studies in Strasbourg in 1770 and 1771. While in Strasbourg, he wrote the *Sesenheimer Lieder,* his first significant poetry. This collection of highly personal and unconventional love lyrics was inspired by his love for a pastor's daughter from nearby Sesenheim.

Goethe met the philosopher Johann Gottfried Herder at Strasbourg. Goethe was deeply impressed by Herder's enthusiasm for nature, his understanding of history, and his opposition to rationalism and artificiality in literature. Herder stimulated Goethe's interest in ballads and *Volkslieder* (folk poetry), and in Homer, Shakespeare, and Gothic architecture. Under Herder's influence, Goethe came to regard naturalness, sincerity, and simplicity as the prime virtues of all art.

After Goethe returned to Frankfurt, he wrote his first successful play, *Götz von Berlichingen* (1771, revised 1773). The play describes a nobleman's tragic fight for freedom and justice within a corrupt social system during the Reformation. The young German writers of the *Storm and Stress* movement praised it, and used it as a model for their own works. See **German literature** (The Storm and Stress movement).

The Sorrows of Young Werther (1774) made young Goethe famous throughout Europe. It is a novel written in the form of letters. The work is the story of a sensitive and uncompromising youth who commits suicide after being torn by uncontrollable passions.

During these fruitful years in Frankfurt, Goethe also produced the original form of *Faust,* the so-called *Urfaust.* In addition, he wrote several satires, plays, and love poems. He also wrote philosophic hymns on art, nature, and the mission of the poetic genius.

Middle years. In 1775, Goethe moved to the Duchy of Weimar, southwest of Leipzig, to assume an administrative post in the government of Duke Karl August. Weimar was Goethe's home for the rest of his life. His work there involved such diverse fields as agriculture, mining, military affairs, and finance. In addition, Goethe took an increasing interest in scientific studies, especially in

geology, mineralogy, botany, and zoology.

The outstanding achievement of Goethe's early Weimar years consists of several nature and love poems. The calm and serene beauty of these poems contrasts with the irrational tone of his earlier works. Influenced by the intellectual companionship of Charlotte von Stein, Goethe learned to discipline his passions and he developed a greater balance between emotion and reason.

To free himself from routine chores and find fresh artistic stimulation, Goethe lived in Italy from 1786 to 1788. While studying ancient art, he searched for his own classical ideal of art and life. To Goethe, this ideal became a combination of clarity and expressiveness, form and feeling. His autobiographical *Italian Journey* (1816-1817) mirrors this maturing process. In the *Roman Elegies* (1788-1790), Goethe's expression of sensuality and joy in life is controlled by a strict poetic form.

In Rome, Goethe completed *Egmont* (1788), a play that takes place during the conflict between Spain and the Netherlands in the 1500's. It tells the tragic story of a trusting, self-confident, and freedom-loving young aristocrat who falls victim to the political scheming of his tyrannical opponents. *Iphigenia in Tauris* (1787) is a modern version of a Greek myth based on a play by Euripides. It expresses Goethe's belief in people's inborn goodness. Human guilt and failure are redeemed through the heroine's noble character.

After his return to Weimar, Goethe finished *Torquato Tasso* (1790), a tragedy about a poet who fails to come to terms with his surroundings because of his lack of self-discipline. The novel *Wilhelm Meister's Apprenticeship* (1795-1796) shows the gradual, sometimes painful, process by which a young man interested in the arts gains maturity, self-knowledge, and a sense of social responsibility. It is a typical *Bildungsroman* (a novel about an individual's educational development). It holds a central position in German fiction, and was much imitated. Goethe emphasized middle-class values in *Hermann and Dorothea* (1797), an idyllic epic poem set during the French Revolution.

Goethe's friendship with the dramatist and philosopher Friedrich Schiller, which began in 1794, proved to be extremely stimulating for both writers. They worked together on several projects and exchanged views on life and art in their correspondence. Schiller encouraged Goethe to complete Part I of *Faust* (1808).

Late years. By the early 1800's, Goethe had become Europe's most celebrated writer. After Schiller died in 1805, Goethe deeply felt a lack of intellectual companionship. In 1807, he married Christiane Vulpius, a girl who had lived in his house since his return from Italy. He spent much of his time on scientific projects. He became director of the Weimar theater.

In 1809, Goethe created *Elective Affinities*, one of his finest prose works. This

Goethe by J. H. Lips. Goethe-Nationalmuseum, Weimar, Germany (New York Public Library)

Johann Wolfgang von Goethe

novel is a study of the tragic relationship between a married couple and their two friends. Three parts of Goethe's autobiography, *Dichtung und Wahrheit* (*Poetry and Truth*), appeared between 1811 and 1814. The fourth part was published in 1833, after his death. The autobiography vividly describes his life up to 1775. In *Wilhelm Meister's Journeyman Years* (1821-1829), Goethe only loosely continued the plot of the earlier Wilhelm Meister novel. The second work primarily conveys the author's views on education, social ethics, and the problems of the coming industrial age.

Goethe completed *Faust* a few months before his death. Faust is a man who desires complete knowledge, unlimited experience of life, and self-perfection. Guided by Mephistopheles, the devil, he moves from one realm of human experience to another without ever attaining full satisfaction. At the end of Part II, Faust is saved by God's grace in spite of his guilt and pride. The devil loses a wager for Faust's soul because Faust continually sought perfection.   Klaus L. Berghahn

See also **Color** (Newton and Goethe); **Faust; Mephistopheles.**

Additional resources

Atkins, Stuart. *Essays on Goethe*. Camden Hse., 1995.
Boyle, Nicholas. *Goethe: The Poet and the Age*. Oxford, 1991-.
   Multivolume work.
Wagner, Irmgard. *Goethe*. Twayne, 1999.
Williams, John R. *The Life of Goethe*. Blackwell, 1998.

Gogh, Vincent Van. See Van Gogh, Vincent.

Gogol, *GAW guhl,* **Nikolai,** *nih kah LY* (1809-1852), was a major Russian playwright, novelist, and short story writer. In the West, his writing is admired for its ornamental use of language, its romantic treatment of theme, and its use of the fantastic, the grotesque, and caricature. In Russia, he is best loved as a humorist.

Nikolai Vasilievich Gogol was born in Ukraine. In 1828, Gogol went to St. Petersburg to become an actor but decided on a literary career. In 1832, he won attention for *Evenings on a Farm near Dikanka,* a collection of Ukrainian tales.

Gogol's most important contribution to Russian drama was *The Inspector-General* (1836), a satire on corruption among provincial government officials. The play was so harshly criticized that Gogol decided to live abroad. He spent most of the years from 1836 to 1844 in Rome, and returned to Russia in 1848. In 1842, he published the first part of *Dead Souls,* a novel about a swindler who creates a scheme to cheat the government by using the names of dead serfs. That year, he also published his most famous short story, "The Overcoat," a tale about a pathetic clerk.

As years passed, Gogol worried increasingly about the moral influence of his works on the Russians. He felt he had failed to express the positive essence of the Russian soul in his characters. As he worked on the second part of *Dead Souls,* he grew melancholy. While living in Rome, he fell under the influence of a fanatic priest. The priest convinced him that his second novel was evil and demanded that he destroy it. Gogol burned the novel on Feb. 24, 1852, and died several days later.

Anna Lisa Crone

See also **Russian literature** (Late romanticism).

Goiter is a condition in which the thyroid gland becomes enlarged. The gland is located toward the front of the neck between the Adam's apple and the top of the breastbone. In most cases, a goiter appears as a smooth swelling at the front of the neck.

In healthy individuals, the thyroid gland takes up iodine from the blood to form a hormone called *thyroxine.* This hormone regulates growth and *metabolism,* the process by which the body turns food into energy and living tissue. Another hormone, called *thyroid-stimulating hormone* (TSH), causes the thyroid to release the thyroxine. TSH is produced by the pituitary gland, which lies near the center of the skull.

Goiters develop because the thyroid gland is not active enough or because it is too active. When the thyroid is not active enough, the condition is called *hypothyroidism.* In this condition, the pituitary gland responds to the low level of thyroid activity by producing more TSH. This excess TSH causes the thyroid to swell. Patients suffering from hypothyroidism become physically and mentally sluggish. Their skin becomes thick and dry, and they may gain weight.

Hypothyroidism may have any of several causes. In the past, a lack of iodine in the diet led to many cases of hypothyroidism. However, the use of iodized salt has virtually eliminated this type of hypothyroidism in developed countries. Hypothyroidism also may occur because of defects in the enzymes that produce the thyroxine. Another form of hypothyroidism develops when certain substances in the blood called *antibodies* attack the thyroid. Antibodies normally protect the body from infection.

When the thyroid is too active, a disorder called *hyperthyroidism* results. In this disorder, the thyroid cells produce too much thyroxine, and the thyroid may enlarge to form a goiter. Common symptoms of hyperthyroidism include nervousness, more rapid heartbeat, and weight loss. Another symptom is *exophthalmos,* a condition in which the eyeballs protrude.

Doctors treat goiter in a variety of ways, depending on its cause. For example, they may give pills containing small amounts of thyroxine to patients suffering from hypothyroidism. Doctors treat hyperthyroidism with drugs, surgery, or *radioactive iodine,* a form of iodine that slows down the thyroid's activity.   Don H. Nelson

See also **Cretinism; Iodine** (Uses of iodine); **Thyroid gland.**

Golan. See Cities of refuge.

Golan Heights, *GOH lahn,* is a hilly area in the southwestern corner of Syria. Its steep western slopes overlook the Sea of Galilee and the Jordan River in Israel. For location, see **Syria** (map). The Golan Heights covers 454 square miles (1,176 square kilometers). Most of its land is rocky, but a small part of it is fertile and supports agriculture. About 14,500 Arabic-speaking people called Druses and about 14,000 Israelis live in the area.

The Golan Heights has been a part of Syria since ancient times. In 1948, Israelis started farming settlements in disputed territory near their border with Syria, and Syrians began firing on the settlements from the Golan Heights. Since the 1967 Arab-Israeli war, Israeli troops have occupied the Golan Heights. Israel has set up military and agricultural operations there. In 1981, Israel claimed legal and political authority in the Golan Heights. But Syria rejects this claim, and many other countries do not recognize it.   Malcolm C. Peck

WORLD BOOK photo courtesy Tiffany & Co.

The beauty of gold makes it a favorite metal for such delicately designed jewelry as bracelets, earrings, and clips.

The value of gold makes it a major form of money for payment of international debts. The Federal Reserve Bank of New York, *right,* stores the gold reserves of many nations.

Federal Reserve Bank of New York

Gold is a metal prized for its beauty, usefulness, and scarcity. Throughout history, people have sought gold more eagerly than any other metal.

Gold has a lovely yellow color and a metallic glow. It is one of the easiest metals to shape. It can be beaten into thinner sheets than any other metal. Gold does not rust or tarnish. Gold deposits rich enough to mine profitably are found in many locations. But mining such deposits yields only small amounts of gold.

Gold was one of the first metals discovered. People have used gold for jewelry and money for thousands of years. Today, gold mining is an important industry in many parts of the world.

Properties of gold

Gold has valuable physical and chemical properties.

Physical properties. Gold is one of the most *lustrous* (shiny) metals. Its chemical symbol, *Au,* comes from *aurum,* the Latin word for *shining dawn.* Gold is a soft metal. It is the most *malleable* of all metals. Malleability is a metal's ability to be beaten or pressed into various shapes without breaking. Gold can be beaten into extremely thin, transparent sheets. Gold also has the greatest *ductility* of all metals. A metal's ductility is its ability to be drawn into fine wires without breaking. One troy ounce of gold (31.1035 grams) can be drawn into a

thin wire about 50 miles (80 kilometers) long. Gold is one of the densest metals. Gold weighs about 19 times as much as an equal volume of water at 20 °C (68 °F).

Gold *conducts* (carries) electric current better than all other metals except silver and copper. Gold also conducts heat well. In addition, gold reflects *infrared* (heat) rays better than any other metal.

Chemical properties. Gold is a *stable* metal. It does not dissolve or *corrode* (wear away due to chemical action) in simple acids, such as sulfuric acid or hydrochloric acid, or in simple bases, such as sodium hydroxide or lime. Gold does not rust like iron because it is unaffected by water or oxygen in air. Gold does not tarnish

Properties of pure gold

Au **Chemical symbol**	Atomic number Atomic weight Density (at 20° C) Melting point Boiling point Class Radioactive isotopes	79 196.967 19.32 (g/cm³) 1064° C 2808° C Transition metal 20

How gold is removed from ore

The diagrams below show the carbon-in-pulp process, a widely used method of separating gold from ore. The process produces bars that are at least 99.9 percent gold.

WORLD BOOK diagrams by Oxford Illustrators Limited

Crushing and grinding reduce chunks of gold ore to the fineness of sand or flour. First, a crusher breaks the ore into fragments the size of road gravel. Next, a cyanide solution is mixed with the fragments. A rotating ball mill then reduces the fragments, forming a pulp. A cyclone classifier returns any coarse particles in the pulp to the mill for regrinding.

Leaching dissolves the gold out of the ground ore. Pulp from the mill flows to a tank, where air is blown in. Oxygen in the air and cyanide in the pulp react with the gold so that the gold can dissolve. Carbon grains then collect the gold, and screens separate the grains from the pulp. In another tank, a special solution strips gold and other metals from the grains, which are recycled.

Electrowinning and smelting separate gold from the solution and from all impurities except silver. In electrowinning, an electric current passes through the solution, causing the metal to be deposited onto steel wool cathodes. In smelting, the steel wool is melted with a chemical mixture called flux. The flux combines with the steel and all impurities except silver.

Refining the ingots involves one or more electroplating processes that remove the silver. These processes produce gold that is at least 99.9 percent pure. The pure gold is then melted and cast into bars.

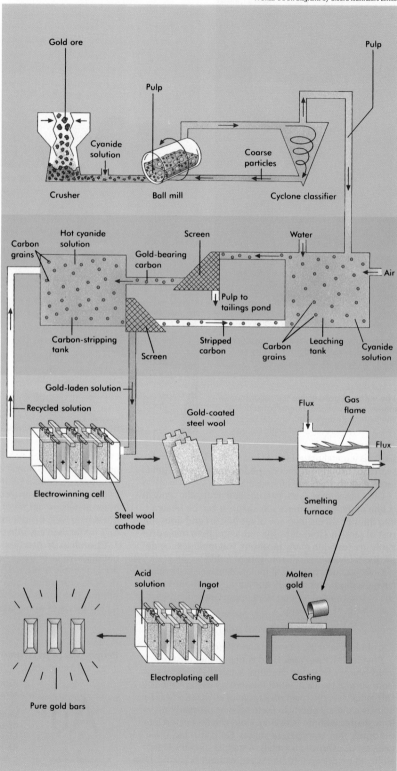

Gold ore

Pulp

Pulp

Cyanide solution

Coarse particles

Crusher

Ball mill

Cyclone classifier

Carbon grains

Hot cyanide solution

Screen

Water

Gold-bearing carbon

Air

Pulp to tailings pond

Carbon-stripping tank

Screen

Stripped carbon

Carbon grains

Leaching tank

Cyanide solution

Gold-laden solution

Recycled solution

Gold-coated steel wool

Flux

Gas flame

Flux

Electrowinning cell

Steel wool cathode

Smelting furnace

Acid solution

Ingot

Molten gold

Electroplating cell

Casting

Pure gold bars

like silver because it is unaffected by sulfur compounds in air. However, gold dissolves in *aqua regia,* a mixture of hydrochloric acid and nitric acid. In addition, gold dissolves in *cyanide* solutions when oxygen is present. Cyanide is a chemical compound of the elements carbon and nitrogen.

Gold alloys

Gold is rarely used in pure form. It is usually combined with one or more other metals to form an *alloy.* Gold alloy is less expensive than pure gold, yet the alloy retains the valuable properties of the gold. Copper is the metal most commonly alloyed with gold.

Manufacturers express the proportion of gold in an alloy by: (1) *karats,* or (2) *fineness.* The karat system, which is usually used for jewelry and ornaments, divides the alloy into 24 parts. One karat (sometimes spelled *carat*) is equal to one 24th part. Thus, 24-karat gold is pure gold. Jewelry made of 14-karat gold consists of 14 parts gold and 10 parts of some other metal or metals.

The fineness scale, used mostly for industrial products, expresses the proportion of gold in parts per thousand. Thus, *500 fine gold* means the alloy consists of 500 parts gold and 500 parts other metal.

Uses of gold

Throughout history, people have used gold mostly as money and for jewelry. Today, gold also has many other uses.

Money. All countries accept gold in payment for international debts, though such payments are not common. The world's governments hold about 42,000 short tons (38,000 metric tons or 38 million kilograms) of gold in their official stocks. Almost all this gold is in bricklike bars, which are also called *ingots.* The United States government stores its gold mainly at the Federal Reserve Bank in New York City and at a depository in Fort Knox, Kentucky. Gold bars are a form of *bullion*—that is, metal held for its value as a metal rather than as money.

Since the 1930's, few gold coins have circulated as money. However, some countries continue to make gold coins for collectors and investors. Individuals and corporations hold more than 55,000 short tons (50,000 metric tons) of gold, mostly as bullion, coins in collections, and jewelry.

Jewelry accounts for about two-thirds of the gold used commercially each year. Gold jewelry can be various colors, depending on the metals used in the gold alloy. For example, *white gold* is a silver colored alloy of gold, copper, and such metals as nickel, palladium, silver, and zinc. In *yellow gold,* about equal amounts of copper and silver are mixed with a greater amount of gold, so that the alloy retains the color of pure gold.

In the United States, the metal in *solid gold* jewelry is mostly 10-karat to 21-karat gold. *Gold-filled* and *gold-plated* items consist of silver or another metal coated with gold. In gold-filled items, 5 percent or more of the object's weight comes from gold. Gold-plated items contain less gold.

Other uses. Many electrical and electronic devices, including computers, radios, and television sets have parts made with gold. Gold makes excellent electrical contacts because of its ability to conduct electric current, its high resistance to corrosion, and its ductility.

Thin gold films on spacecraft reflect infrared rays from the sun, which can harm both people and equipment. A transparent gold film in windows of large office buildings also reflects infrared rays, helping to keep the buildings cool in summer. Dentists use gold for crowns because gold is easy to shape and will not corrode in the mouth. Artists use *gold leaf,* thin sheets of gold, for decoration and lettering.

Pure colloidal gold, a powder of extremely fine parti-

Royal Bank of Canada

Gold reflects *infrared* (heat) rays better than any other metal, so it can be used to filter sunlight. Gold mixed into window glass, *above,* helps keep an office building cool in summer. Gold film in an astronaut's visor, *below,* protects the eyes and face without interfering with vision.

NASA

cles of gold, appears black. *Colloids* of gold, consisting of particles of pure or coated colloidal gold mixed with one or more other substances, produce various colors. For example, pure colloidal gold mixed into normally clear glass produces a deep red color. A colloid that has gold particles coated with tin oxide is known as *purple of Cassius* for its rich color.

Recycling. Because gold is so valuable, the gold used in many objects has been recycled throughout history. Today, gold refineries recover gold from discarded jewelry, dental materials, and other scrap that contains small amounts of gold.

Gold deposits

Gold is present in almost all rocks and soil. In addition, all the oceans contain dissolved gold. But most gold is too scarcely distributed to recover profitably. People recover gold only where nature has concentrated the metal in the earth's crust.

Scientists known as *prospectors* or *explorationists* search for deposits of gold for mining companies. Explorationists have extensive training in geology, physics, and mining. They use a variety of instruments to analyze the chemical makeup of topsoil, water, and plants, and the rocks beneath the earth's surface.

Types of deposits. There are two main types of gold deposits: (1) *lode deposits,* and (2) *placer* (pronounced *PLAS ur)* deposits.

Lode deposits, also called *vein deposits,* are concentrations of gold and other metals in cracks in rocks. The *ore* (metal-bearing rock) may be at or near the surface of the earth, or deep in the ground. Lode deposits provide most of the gold produced today.

Many scientists believe lode deposits form from hot water solutions that rise from far beneath the earth's surface. Volcanic activity heats the underground water. As the water rises through cracks in rock, it dissolves gold and other metals in the rock. Rocks near the surface cool the water. Then, the gold and other metals come out of the solution, forming solid deposits.

Deposits of pure gold—also known as *native gold*—are rare. In nature, gold is usually combined with silver in an alloy called *electrum,* or with one or more other metals. In addition, traces of gold often occur in the ore deposits of *sulfides* (sulfur compounds) of such metals

as iron, copper, nickel, lead, and zinc.

In some cases, the sulfides and gold were once too scarcely distributed to be of commercial value, but the action of water has concentrated them. Water concentrates these materials by dissolving other substances and carrying them to lower levels under the ground. The water can do this because it is acidic. Before reaching the ground as rain or snow, the water dissolves carbon dioxide, which is always present in the atmosphere, forming carbonic acid. When the water soaks into the ground, it becomes more acidic by reacting with iron sulfide to form sulfuric acid.

Placer deposits are accumulations of loose gold in sand, gravel, or rock, usually in the bottom of a valley. Placer deposits form when a lode deposit at the earth's surface is *eroded* (worn away) by wind and water. Rain washes the eroded material downhill, in some cases into a stream. Gold in a stream sinks to the bottom, while the stream's current carries particles of lighter materials away. Over millions of years, placer deposits may become buried and compressed into rocks. Much native gold is found in placer deposits.

Mining. Lode deposits require *hard-rock mining,* in which miners drill and blast the rock to remove it from the ground. The exact method used depends on the location of the deposit. *Open-pit mining* recovers ore deposited at or near the surface of the earth. *Underground mining* recovers ore from deep beneath the surface. Trucks haul the mined ore to a mill.

To mine placer deposits, miners use machines to scoop up rock, sand, and gravel from the valley bottom. The miners then usually sift the ore at the site of the deposit. They place the ore in a container and wash it with water. The gold sinks faster than the other materials and collects at the bottom. Amateur miners use the sifting method when they *pan* for gold by hand.

In the United States, open-pit mines produce about 80 percent of the gold, underground mines about 8 percent, and placer mines about 2 percent. About 10 percent is a by-product of mining other metals.

Extracting gold from the ore

There are several methods of *extracting* (removing) gold from ores. The method used depends on the type of ore. However, all the methods are designed to ex-

Leading gold-mining countries

Amount of gold produced in a year	
South Africa	●●●●●●●●●●●●● 15,998,000 troy ounces (498,000 kilograms)
United States	●●●●●●●● 10,224,000 troy ounces (318,000 kilograms)
Australia	●●●●●●● 9,292,000 troy ounces (289,000 kilograms)
Canada	●●●● 5,277,000 troy ounces (164,000 kilograms)
China	●●●(4,662,000 troy ounces (145,000 kilograms)

Figures are for 1996.
Source: U. S. Bureau of Mines.

Leading gold-mining states and provinces

Amount of gold produced in a year	
Nevada	●●●●●●●●●●● 6,752,000 troy ounces (210,000 kilograms)
Ontario	●●●●(2,388,000 troy ounces (74,000 kilograms)
Quebec	●●(1,343,000 troy ounces (42,000 kilograms)
California	●(823,000 troy ounces (26,000 kilograms)
British Columbia	● 573,000 troy ounces (18,000 kilograms)

Figures are for 1996.
Source: U. S. Bureau of Mines; Statistics Canada.

pose valuable minerals to the surface of the ore, to extract gold and any other metals that may be in the resulting mixture, and to purify the metals that are extracted. Processing about 10 tons (9 metric tons) of ore yields as much as 1 troy ounce of gold.

Exposing the gold beneath the ore's surface is necessary so that the gold can be dissolved out of the ore. At the mill, machines called crushers reduce large chunks of ore to the size of road gravel. Then, *ball mills* grind the ore—mixed with water or a solution of cyanide and water—to the fineness of sand or flour. A ball mill is a rotating drum partially filled with metal balls about the size of baseballs.

Leaching dissolves the exposed gold out of the ground ore using a chemical solvent. Today, most gold leaching processes use cyanide and oxygen. The most common process is known as *carbon-in-pulp.*

In this process, the ore from the crusher is mixed with a cyanide solution, then ground in the ball mill. The resulting pulp flows to a tank. Air is blown into the tank to supply oxygen. The cyanide and oxygen react chemically with the gold in the ore so that the gold can dissolve. Carbon grains the size of wheat or rice grains are added to the pulp to *adsorb* (collect) the gold as it dissolves. Filtering the pulp through screens removes the gold-bearing carbon. Treating the carbon with a hot solution of sodium hydroxide and cyanide releases the gold and any adsorbed silver or other metals. Screens remove the carbon grains.

Electrowinning is a method of electroplating used to recover the metal from the leaching solution. First, the metallic solution is placed in a container called a *cell.* Also in the cell are a group of *anodes* (positive electric terminals) and a group of *cathodes* (negative electric terminals). Chemical reactions cause the metal to be deposited on the cathodes. The cathodes are made of steel wool. This material exposes a great deal of surface area to the solution, so the electrowinning step proceeds more rapidly than it would if the cathodes were steel plates. See **Electrolysis; Electroplating.**

Smelting removes the gold from the steel wool cathodes. The steel wool is melted in a furnace with a chemical mixture called *flux.* The flux combines with the steel wool and all impurities except silver. The flux floats on top of the gold. Workers pour off the flux and then pour the molten gold into molds to make bars called *ingots.*

Refining. The ingots are purified by one or more electroplating processes. The processes used depend on the amount of silver in the ingots. After refining, the gold is at least 99.9 percent pure. Workers then melt the gold and cast it into bars.

World gold production

South Africa is by far the leading gold-producing country. The United States is the second largest producer of gold, followed by Australia.

In the United States, Nevada supplies the most gold. In Canada, Ontario provides the most gold.

The biggest gold field in the world is in the *Witwatersrand,* a district that is located in the Gauteng Province of South Africa. In Australia, the largest gold deposit is in Kalgoorlie in Western Australia. In North America, the biggest gold deposit is located in Lead, South Dakota.

Throughout history, about 123,000 tons (112,000 metric tons) of gold have been produced. Since about 1980, world gold production has sharply increased. The increase is due in part to a rise in the price of gold. At current rates, more gold will be produced in the next 50 years than in all of history.

History of gold

No one knows when people first discovered gold. Archaeologists have dug up gold jewelry dating from about 4000 B.C. near Varna, Bulgaria, on the coast of the Black Sea. Coins made of electrum were produced in Lydia, a country in what is now western Turkey, during the 500's B.C.

In the 1500's, Spanish conquerors sought gold in Mexico and Peru. A legend grew about a land rich in gold called El Dorado, meaning *the gilded.* In that land, gold was supposed to be as common as sand. Through the centuries, many explorers set out to find El Dorado. The rich gold discoveries in California, Australia, Alaska, and South Africa were all believed by many people to be El Dorado at first, and each discovery began a gold rush. Probably the most famous gold rush was the one to California in 1849. The largest U.S. gold strike of the 1900's was made near Carlin, Nevada, in the early 1960's. An open-pit mine began operating there in 1965. The Carlin mine added about 10 percent to the annual gold production of the United States.

During the late 1800's and early 1900's, monetary systems of the United States and many other Western countries followed a *gold standard.* Under such a standard, a nation agrees to buy and sell gold at a fixed price and to exchange its paper money for gold on demand. The United States went off and on the gold standard several times and finally abandoned it in 1971. Since the 1930's, gold has played a smaller and smaller role in world monetary systems. The United States has not minted gold coins as legal currency since 1933.

John Gerlach and Sara Steck Melford

Related articles in *World Book* include:

Alchemy	Element, Chemical	Mining
Alloy	Forty-Niners	Money
Aqua regia	Gold leaf	South Africa (picture)
California (The gold rush)	Gold rush	
	Gold standard	South Dakota (picture)
El Dorado	Jewelry	

Additional resources

Fodor, R. V. *Gold, Copper, Iron: How Metals Are Formed, Found, and Used.* Enslow, 1989.
Klein, James. *Gold Rush! The Young Prospector's Guide to Striking It Rich.* Tricycle, 1998. Younger readers.
Meltzer, Milton. *Gold.* HarperCollins, 1993. Younger readers.
Trytell, Sue. *The Glory of Gold: A Contemporary Approach to Gilding.* Sally Milner, 1995.

Gold Coast. See Ghana.

Gold Cup race. See Motorboat racing (Types of racing).

Gold leaf is gold metal that has been beaten into very thin sheets or leaves. It is often used to decorate the surface of picture frames and furniture and to letter signs on windows. Gold is preferred to other metals because it is not brittle and does not rust or tarnish. Gold leaf is applied to a previously smoothed surface by a process called *gilding.* First, an adhesive material called *gold size* is applied to the surface. Then, the gilder places the leaf on the surface with a wide, soft-hair brush called a *gilder's tip*. When the gold size dries, the gold leaf sticks permanently to the surface and makes it look like solid gold.

Gold leaf was used in ancient times in Greece, Rome, the Middle East, and Asia. From the Middle Ages to the early Renaissance, artists in Europe and the Byzantine Empire often covered the background of their pictures with it. Today, artists rarely use gold leaf.　　Roger Ward

See also **Gold** (Other uses).

Gold rush is a rapid movement of people to a site where gold has been discovered. The discovery of gold fields has long attracted large numbers of prospectors and other people because of the traditionally high value of gold. Towns developed overnight, transportation networks were hacked out of the wilderness, and new territories were born within months.

Gold rushes in the United States. The greatest gold rush in United States history began with the discovery of gold by James Marshall at Sutter's Mill in California on Jan. 24, 1848. By 1849, a large-scale gold rush was underway. San Francisco, the nearest port, grew from a small town to a city of 25,000 in a year's time as people arrived from all over the world. By 1850, California had enough people to be admitted to the Union as a state.

California set the pattern for other gold rushes throughout the West. The Pikes Peak gold rush in 1859 opened Colorado, launched the city of Denver, and started a great mining industry. Gold rushes also brought people to Alaska, Arizona, Idaho, Montana, Nevada, New Mexico, South Dakota, Utah, and Wyoming. Some mining districts and camps died within a year, but others lasted more than a hundred years. These districts include several mining areas in Colorado and the Homestake Mine near Lead, South Dakota.

Gold rushes played an important role in the development of the West. They led to clashes between white settlers and Indians, and to permanent cities, states, transportation systems, and varied economies. Many sites of gold rushes also have become important tourist attractions in the western United States.

Gold rushes in other countries also have had important effects. Gold was discovered in Australia in 1851, and Australia's population almost tripled in the next nine years. An 1861 gold rush in New Zealand doubled that country's population in six years. The city of Johannesburg, South Africa, was founded as a result of a gold rush in 1886. Another great gold rush sparked development in the Klondike region of Canada's Yukon Territory during 1897 and 1898.　　Duane A. Smith

Related articles in *World Book* include:

Alaska (The gold rush)
Asian Americans (History of Asian immigration)
Australia (The Australian gold rush)
California (The gold rush)
Colorado (The gold rush)
Fargo, William George
Forty-Niners

Gold
Klondike
Murieta, Joaquín
Western frontier life in America (The search for gold and silver)
Westward movement in America (California)

Additional resources

Blumberg, Rhoda. *The Great American Gold Rush.* Bradbury, 1989. Younger readers.
Ketchum, Liza. *The Gold Rush.* Little, Brown, 1996. Younger readers.
MacMillan, Gordon. *At the End of the Rainbow? Gold, Land, and People in the Brazilian Amazon.* Columbia Univ. Pr., 1995.
Rohrbough, Malcolm J. *Days of Gold: The California Gold Rush and the American Nation.* Univ. of Calif. Pr., 1997.

Gold standard is the use of gold as the standard of value for the money of a country. A country is *on the gold standard* when it will redeem any of its money in gold and when it agrees to buy and sell gold at a fixed price. Advantages of following the gold standard are that it checks inflation, restrains government spending, and stabilizes currency exchange rates among countries that use it. The disadvantages are that it prevents necessary adjustments in domestic currency supplies and international exchange rates.

The United States and many other Western countries followed the gold standard or a form of it during the late 1800's and early 1900's. Since the 1930's, gold has played an increasingly smaller role in world monetary systems. Over the years, the United States went off and on the gold standard several times before abandoning it in 1971. By the late 1970's, gold played almost no role in national or international monetary systems. A small number of experts strongly favor a return to the gold standard. But most economists consider it unlikely that the United States or other countries will ever return to it.

Irving Morrissett

See also **Money** (The rebirth of paper money).

Goldberg, Arthur Joseph (1908-1990), served as secretary of labor, Supreme Court justice, and United States ambassador to the United Nations (UN). President John F. Kennedy named him secretary of labor in January 1961, and appointed him to the Supreme Court of the United States in 1962. At the request of President Lyndon B. Johnson, Goldberg left the court in 1965 to become ambassador to the United Nations. He resigned as ambassador to the UN in 1968. In 1970, in his first attempt to win an elective office, Goldberg became the Democratic nominee for governor of New York. He lost to Republican Governor Nelson A. Rockefeller.

Until 1961, Goldberg was noted mainly for his skill

Historical Pictures Service

Gold rush prospectors often used a *cradle* to separate gold from worthless stone. They rocked gravel and water in the cradle, sifting out lighter materials and leaving the gold.

in mediating labor-management disputes. He became general counsel of the Congress of Industrial Organizations (CIO) and of the United Steelworkers of America in 1948. He helped negotiate the merger of the CIO and the American Federation of Labor (AFL) in 1955. Born in Chicago, Goldberg graduated from Northwestern University Law School in 1929.   Eric Sevareid

Goldberger, Joseph (1874-1929), was an American physician known for his work on pellagra. He proved the disease was caused by a deficiency of a specific nutrient, which he called *P-P factor,* for *pellagra preventive.* This nutrient, found in such foods as milk, meat, and yeast, is today recognized as niacin (see **Pellagra; Vitamin** [Vitamin B complex]). Goldberger's studies of pellagra in isolated villages pioneered efforts to relate occurrences of disease to social and economic factors. Goldberger also contributed to the control of yellow fever, typhus, measles, and other diseases.

Goldberger was born in Giralt, Hungary. He received his M.D. degree in 1895 from Bellevue Hospital Medical College in New York City. From 1899 to 1929, Goldberger served in the United States Public Health Service.

Dale C. Smith

Golden Age is a term used by the Greek poet Homer to describe a remote period of the past that he considered more civilized and enlightened than his own. Homer had no written records of such a period. But he might have been acquainted with the traditions of the wonderful Mycenaean and Minoan civilizations that had flourished hundreds of years before his time.

Many historians have applied the phrase *Golden Age* to the period when a nation reaches its highest peak of development, particularly in art, architecture, literature, or science. For example, most historians maintain that the Golden Age of Greece actually lasted from 477 to 431 B.C., long after Homer's time. During that period, Athens reached great heights in sculpture, architecture, and drama. Many other nations also enjoyed eras that have been described as their Golden Age. Historians would probably agree on the following:

Egypt, the Golden Age of Literature, 2200-2050 B.C.; the Golden Age of Wealth and Empire, 1500-1375 B.C.

Rome, 27 B.C.-A.D. 14, the Age of Augustus.

Mexico, 1440-1520, the reign of the Montezumas.

Spain, the Golden Age of Art and Literature, mid-1500's to late 1600's.

England, 1558-1603, the reign of Elizabeth I.

France, 1640-1740, the reigns of Louis XIV and Louis XV.   Robert F. Berkhofer, Jr.

See also **Greece, Ancient** (The rivalry between Athens and Sparta; illustrations: Greece in the Golden Age); **India** (The golden age); **Netherlands** (Prosperity and power); **Tang dynasty; Spanish literature** (The Golden Age).

Golden Fleece, in Greek mythology, was the golden wool of a flying ram. The fleece was the object of a famous quest by the Greek hero Jason and a band of men called the Argonauts.

The story of the Golden Fleece began in the Greek kingdom of Thessaly, which was ruled by King Athamas. The king had two wives. Athamas and his first wife, Nephele, had a son named Phrixus and a daughter named Helle. Ino, the king's second wife, hated the children. She persuaded Phrixus and Helle to eat all the seeds that the Greek farmers had intended to plant. Ino

convinced them that their action would please the gods. Thus, no crops grew, and a terrible famine occurred.

Athamas sent a messenger to the oracle at Delphi to learn how to end the famine (see **Oracle**). After the messenger returned, Ino bribed him to give the king a false report. The messenger told Athamas that the famine would end only if Phrixus and Helle were sacrificed to the gods. The king sadly agreed to sacrifice his children. However, Nephele saved them. She sent them to a distant land called Colchis on a flying ram that had a golden fleece.

On the way to Colchis, the ram flew over the Dardanelles, a strait between Europe and Asia. Helle fell off the ram's back and drowned. In her memory, the strait was called the Hellespont in ancient times. Phrixus arrived safely in Colchis, where he sacrificed the ram to the god Zeus and hung its fleece in a grove of trees. Jason later captured the Golden Fleece and brought it back to Greece.   John Hamilton

See also **Argonauts; Jason; Medea.**

Golden Gate Bridge is one of the largest and most spectacular suspension bridges in the world. It spans the Golden Gate, a strait at the entrance of San Francisco Bay. The bridge, which has a total length of 8,981 feet (2,737 meters), connects northern California to the peninsula of San Francisco. It contains about 88,000 tons (75,000 metric tons) of steel, 390,000 cubic yards (300,000 cubic meters) of concrete, and 160,000 miles (260,000 kilometers) of wire in its two main cables.

Towers stand on either side of the bridge, about 1,120 feet (340 meters) from the ends. They hold up the two steel cables, $36 \frac{3}{8}$ inches (92 centimeters) in diameter, from which the bridge hangs. The section between the towers is 4,200 feet (1,280 meters) long, one of the world's longest spans. The floor is 220 feet (67 meters) above the water and 90 feet (27 meters) wide. It has a six-lane road and sidewalks.

The idea for a bridge across the Golden Gate was popularized in 1916 by James H. Wilkins, a San Francisco journalist. The United States War Department, which owned the land around the strait, approved the project in 1924. The Golden Gate Bridge and Highway District was formed in 1928. Joseph B. Strauss was appointed chief engineer of the project and designed the bridge. The bridge was planned and constructed to withstand strong tidal forces, wind, and earthquakes. Irving F. Morrow, an architect hired by Strauss, designed the towers and selected the bridge's distinctive rust color.

Construction of the Golden Gate Bridge began in 1933. The bridge was completed in 1937 at a cost of $35 \frac{1}{2}$ million.   Fred F. Videon

See also **Bridge** (picture); **California** (picture); **San Francisco** (map).

Golden Gloves Tournament. See Boxing (Amateur boxing).

Golden retriever is a medium-sized hunting dog. It has won recognition in the United Kingdom and the United States as an intelligent, hard-working gun dog and as a guide for the blind. For dog shows, the American Kennel Club requires that golden retrievers stand $21 \frac{1}{2}$ to 24 inches (55 to 61 centimeters) high at the shoulder and weigh from 55 to 75 pounds (25 to 34 kilograms). The dog has a thick, double coat of flat, gold-colored hair. It has a good-natured personality that makes it a popular pet. Golden retrievers were first bred in Scotland about 1870.

Critically reviewed by the Golden Retriever Club of America

See also **Dog** (picture: Sporting dogs); **Dog guide**.

Golden rule is the principle that people should treat others as they would like to be treated themselves. The rule is called *golden* to indicate that it is the finest or highest rule of life.

There are both positive and negative versions of the golden rule. One positive version is found in Christianity, in the Sermon on the Mount. During the sermon, Jesus Christ said, "So whatever you wish that men would do to you, do so to them" (Matthew 7:12, Revised Standard Version). A similar version appears in Luke 6:31.

The golden rule in a negative form states that people should not treat others the way they do not want to be treated themselves. Several ancient Greek and Jewish thinkers taught the negative form. The Chinese philosopher Confucius taught both the positive and negative versions of the golden rule.

The golden rule is sometimes identified with the idea of *altruism*. Altruism is the notion that one should value the welfare of others more highly than one's own self-interest.   Mark Juergensmeyer

See also **Religion** (A code of conduct).

Golden section, also called the *divine proportion,* is the division of a line segment in such a way that the ratio of the whole segment to the larger part is equal to the ratio of the larger part to the smaller part. The ratio is approximately 1.61803 to 1.

A rectangle whose length and width correspond to this ratio is called a *golden rectangle*. Rectangles that look like a golden rectangle are more pleasing to the eye than other rectangles, though no one knows why.

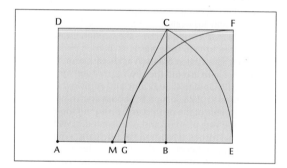

Many golden sections and golden rectangles appear in famous paintings, sculpture, and architecture. Buildings that incorporate golden sections and rectangles include the Parthenon, constructed in Athens in the 400's B.C., and buildings designed in the 1900's by the French architect Le Corbusier.

The figure with this article shows how to construct a golden rectangle and a golden section. First draw a square *ABCD*. Then, locate the midpoint *M* of side *AB*. Next, use a compass to extend *AB* to a point *E* so that *ME=MC*. Rectangle *AEFD* is a golden rectangle. To divide *AB* according to the golden section, use a compass to find a point *G* on *AE* so that *EF=EG*.

George E. Martin

Golden State. See California.

Goldenrod is a common wildflower. About 100 kinds of goldenrods grow in North America, and a few grow in Europe. Goldenrods grow along dry roadsides, in moist woods, in swamps and peat bogs, and in prairies and fields. They are also cultivated. The most common kinds include the *early goldenrod,* the large, handsome *Canada goldenrod,* the *wreath,* the *showy,* and the *sweet goldenrod.*

The goldenrod has a slender stem like a wand. The leaves and stem may be smooth or hairy. The leaves may also have toothed, or jagged, edges. The bright yellow, or deep golden, flowers grow in thick, graceful clusters at the top of the stem. The flowers bloom in the summer and the autumn. Many people incorrectly believe goldenrod pollen causes hay fever and similar allergies. Its pollen is too moist and sticky to float freely through the air. The pollen of ragweed and several other plants with light pollen, easily carried by the wind, is the real cause.

The goldenrod is a favorite flower in America. Kentucky and Nebraska have adopted the goldenrod as their state emblem. People often dry the early goldenrod for floral interior decoration. Some brew the leaves of the sweet goldenrod to make tea. These leaves also produce an oil, used as a tonic. Thomas A. Edison developed a method for extracting natural rubber from the goldenrod, but the process proved to be too expensive for commercial use.   Anton A. Reznicek

Scientific classification. Goldenrod belongs to the composite family, Compositae. The scientific name for the early goldenrod is *Solidago juncea;* the Canada goldenrod, *S. canadensis;* the wreath, *S. caesia.* The showy goldenrod is *S. speciosa* and the sweet is *S. odora.*

See also **Flower** (picture: Flowers of woodlands and forests).

Goldfield, Nevada, was the scene of one of the greatest gold rushes in the history of the United States. It lies on a plateau about 26 miles (42 kilometers) south of Tonopah (see **Nevada** [political map]). It is the seat of Esmeralda County.

The gold rush began when rich gold deposits were discovered in 1903. By 1907, Goldfield had a population of about 15,000 and was the state's largest city. Its mines yielded $11 million in gold and other metals in 1910, their peak year of production. But intensive operations soon exhausted the richest ore. Some mining activity was resumed in the area in the 1930's. Since then, there has been only occasional mining activity. Only a few hundred people now live in Goldfield.   Eric N. Moody

Goldfinch is the name of several kinds of small, short-tailed birds. The *American goldfinch* is found in southern Canada and in the northern and central United States. It is often called the *wild canary* because of its yellow color and lovely song. This goldfinch is the state bird of Iowa, New Jersey, and Washington.

The American goldfinch measures about 5 inches (13 centimeters) long. The male has a bright yellow body and a patch of black on the top of its head. In winter, the male loses its feathers and grows new feathers that are olive-brown with some yellow. The female is olive-brown all year. Both the male and female have a black tail and black wings with white markings.

The American goldfinch nests from July through September. It weaves a tight, cup-shaped nest of plant fibers, thistle fuzz, and spider silk. The female lays from four to six bluish-white eggs and sits on them almost constantly until they hatch. The male feeds the female and provides most of the food for the chicks.

Other North American goldfinches include the *lesser goldfinch* and *Lawrence's goldfinch.* The lesser goldfinch lives from the southwestern part of the United States through Central America. Lawrence's goldfinch is found in parts of California, southern Arizona, and northern Mexico. The *European goldfinch,* which lives throughout Europe, was introduced to New York in the late 1800's but is no longer found wild in North America.

Edward H. Burtt, Jr.

Scientific classification. Goldfinches are genus *Carduelis* in the finch family, Fringillidae.

American goldfinch
Carduelis tristis
Found in North America
from southern Canada to
Florida and Baja California
Body length: 5 inches
(13 centimeters)

Male

Female

WORLD BOOK
illustrations
by Albert Gilbert

European goldfinch
Carduelis carduelis
Found in Europe, western
Asia, and northwest Africa
Body length: 5 $\frac{1}{2}$ inches
(14 centimeters)

See also **Bird** (picture: Birds' eggs); **Finch.**

Goldfish, also called *golden carp,* is a fish in the carp family. Young goldfish do not have bright colors, but many develop brilliant hues. They are all called goldfish, though their colors range from red, gold, and orange to bronze, brown, gray, black, and white. Multicolored goldfish are produced by selective breeding from plain-colored goldfish. Goldfish are widely used in many lands as an ornamental fish.

Kinds of goldfish. Although 100 fancy varieties exist, only about 20 kinds of goldfish are sold today. They have such names as *comet, lionhead, fantail,* and *veiltail.* Some have scales so thin that they can hardly be seen. They are called *scaleless.* These have deep red colors and may have spots of blue, purple, lavender, or calico. Some grow only 2 or 3 inches (5 or 8 centimeters) long, and others grow to more than 1 foot (30 centimeters) in length.

Goldfish can live to be very old. Some are known to have lived over 50 years. Wild goldfish usually do not live longer than 15 years, and most goldfish in homes live less than 5 years.

Their care. Goldfish require little care compared with many pets. A container with straight sides is better than a curved bowl, because it gives more surface for the absorption of air. The water should be about 65 °F (18 °C) and must be clean and free of toxic chemicals, such as chlorine. Chlorine is used to purify tap water in many cities. If chlorinated tap water is left to stand for 24 hours, the chlorine will leave the water and the goldfish can safely be added. Extreme changes of water temperature are harmful to goldfish. Goldfish should be fed once a day. They eat worms, bread crumbs, water fleas, and plants. Shade must be provided in the tank because goldfish have no eyelids. See **Aquarium, Home.**

Their beginnings. The ancestor of the goldfish is a plain-colored fish of China and Japan. Goldfish placed in bodies of flowing water, such as lakes and rivers, soon lose their striking appearance and look like their plain-colored ancestors. Centuries ago, the Chinese bred goldfish to produce beautiful colorings and unusual fins and body forms. The Japanese helped create many of the strange kinds seen today. Goldfish were first bred in

Jane Burton, Bruce Coleman Inc.

The common goldfish is a popular aquarium pet.

Treat Davidson, NAS
John H. Tashjian

Goldfish differ widely in color and shape. Popular varieties include the fringetail, *top left,* and, from left to right, the calico, popeye, and lionhead, *top right.*

the United States in 1878. Today there are goldfish farms in many parts of the United States. Leighton R. Taylor, Jr.

Scientific classification. Goldfish belong to the family Cyprinidae. They are *Carassius auratus.*

See also **Carp.**

Additional resources

Goldfish Society of America. *The Official Guide to Goldfish.* Rev. ed. T. F. H., 1996.
Glass, Spencer. *Goldfish.* Chelsea Hse., 1998.

Golding, William (1911-1993), was an English novelist whose exciting adventure stories deal with the conflict between mind and instinct. His novels are moral fables that reveal how dangerous and destructive human beings may be unless they are restrained by conscience. Golding won the 1983 Nobel Prize for literature.

Golding's most famous book, *Lord of the Flies* (1954), tells of a group of boys stranded on an island. The boys gradually lose all moral purpose and develop savage ways. They try to save themselves through planning—a renewal of civilized behavior. They divide into hunters (doers) and fire-keepers (thinkers). But the two groups soon begin to fight. The story implies that civilization is merely a covering for people's natural violence.

Golding's novels have varied settings. *The Inheritors* (1955) is set in prehistoric times. The Napoleonic era of the early 1800's forms the setting for the sea-adventure trilogy consisting of *Rites of Passage* (1980), *Close Quarters* (1987), and *Fire Down Below* (1989). Golding's other novels include *Pincher Martin* (1956), *Free Fall* (1959), *The Spire* (1964), *The Pyramid* (1967), and *Darkness Visible* (1979). His essays were collected in *The Hot Gates* (1965).

William Gerald Golding was born in St. Columb Minor, in Cornwall. Queen Elizabeth II knighted him in 1988, and he became known as Sir William Golding.

Michael Seidel

Goldman, Edwin Franko (1878-1956), was a leading American bandmaster. In 1911, he organized the New York Military Band, which was renamed the Goldman Band in 1918. The band became famous for its skill and its unusual programs, which included both symphonic music and traditional band numbers. Many classical composers, including Henry Cowell, Darius Milhaud, and Ottorino Respighi, wrote works especially for the band. Goldman himself wrote 109 marches and 3 books

on music. His best-known march is *On the Mall* (1923).

Goldman was born in Louisville, Kentucky. As a teenager, he studied composition in New York City with the Czech composer Antonín Dvořák. From 1895 to 1905, Goldman played solo cornet at the Metropolitan Opera. His visits to schools and colleges toward the end of his life helped raise the standards of bands and band music. After he died, his son, Richard Franko Goldman, became leader of the Goldman Band. Stewart L. Ross

Goldman, Emma (1869-1940), was a revolutionary who came to the United States from Russia in 1885. In 1889, she joined a group of *anarchists.* These revolutionaries opposed all forms of government.

During the Homestead Strike of 1892, guards of the Carnegie Steel Company shot several strikers (see **Homestead Strike**). Goldman and another anarchist, Alexander Berkman, blamed the company president, Henry Clay Frick, for the shootings. They plotted to kill Frick, but Berkman's attempt failed. In 1893, Goldman was imprisoned for a year for urging unemployed people to steal bread if they were starving. Goldman later came to generally oppose violence.

Goldman lectured in favor of anarchism, birth control, and women's

Library of Congress
Emma Goldman

rights. She and Berkman edited a monthly magazine, *Mother Earth,* from 1906 to 1917. In 1916, she was imprisoned for distributing birth control information. In 1917, during World War I, she and Berkman were imprisoned for two years for opposing the draft. After their release, they were deported to Russia. Goldman was born in Kovno (now Kaunas), Lithuania. Miriam Schneir

Goldoni, Carlo (1707-1793), was an Italian playwright. Almost all his plays deal with light and humorous subjects, though he often questioned the values and conduct of the aristocracy and the middle class. Unlike other dramatists of his day, who let the actors improvise on a plot outline, Goldoni insisted on writing the entire play. He gradually abandoned the use of stock characters and created realistic roles instead. His best plays include *The Servant of Two Masters* (1745), *The Family of the Antique Dealer* (1750), *The Liar* (1750), and *The Mistress of the Inn* (1753).

Goldoni was born in Venice. He studied law in several universities before deciding in 1748 to become a playwright. He wrote more than 150 comedies in Italian, in the Venetian dialect, and in French. He also wrote an *Autobiography* (1787) in French.   Richard H. Lansing

Goldsmith, Oliver (1730?-1774), was an Irish-born writer who produced a variety of works marked by a charming, lively style. His play *She Stoops to Conquer* (1773) ranks among the finest comedies ever written. Its hero is a bashful young man who mistakes a country mansion for an inn. He treats the master of the house as an innkeeper and the master's beautiful daughter as a servant. The most amusing character is the daughter's brother Tony Lumpkin, a prankster whose antics add to the confusion. Goldsmith's comedy *The Good-Natur'd Man* (1768) was less successful.

Goldsmith believed that comedy should make people laugh. He attacked the tearful comedies then popular on the London stage in the essay "A Comparison Between Laughing and Sentimental Comedy" (1773).

The Vicar of Wakefield (1766), Goldsmith's only novel, is a charming story about the simple life of the Primrose family and their misfortunes. The father, a *vicar* (country clergyman), is an idealized figure with a wise philosophy. The novel is filled with kindly emotions, and it teaches the value of humility and courage.

The Deserted Village (1770) is a long poem about the English countryside. It shows the evil that results when people place too much importance on money and luxury. It also paints a tender picture of a happy farm village before commercial considerations destroyed it.

The Citizen of the World (1762) is a collection of Goldsmith's essays. In it, Goldsmith adopted the then-common practice among English writers of having a visitor to England write home about the strange customs he noticed. Goldsmith thus exposed the shortcomings he saw in the English people of his time.

Goldsmith was born in Ballymahon, Ireland. He studied medicine in Scotland but was never a serious student. In 1756, after traveling for two years in Europe, he went to London and tried unsuccessfully to establish himself as a doctor. He began writing for magazines to support himself. Goldsmith won his first recognition for *The Traveller* (1764), a philosophical poem. He became a successful author, but he was careless with money and owed many debts when he died. He belonged to the famous Literary Club, which gathered around Samuel Johnson.   Jack D. Durant

See also **English literature** (picture: Samuel Johnson); **Newbery, John.**

Goldwater, Barry Morris (1909-1998), an American statesman, was the Republican presidential candidate in 1964. He and his running mate, Representative William E. Miller of New York, lost to their Democratic opponents, President Lyndon B. Johnson and Senator Hubert H. Humphrey.

When Goldwater ran for president, he was completing his second term as a United States senator from Arizona. During the 1964 campaign, Goldwater called for fewer powers for the federal government and a stronger stand against Communism. He declared that the government had no powers except those clearly set forth in the Constitution of the United States. He said other powers belonged to the states.

Barry M. Goldwater

Early life. Barry Goldwater was born on New Year's Day, 1909, in Phoenix. His grandfather had been an immigrant peddler in the Western gold camps. By 1909, the Goldwaters were prosperous department store owners. Barry's father died in 1929, and the boy left the University of Arizona after his freshman year to work in the family store. He became company president in 1937.

In 1934, Goldwater married Margaret "Peggy" Johnson of Muncie, Indiana. They had two sons and two daughters. In World War II (1939-1945), Goldwater was an Army Air Forces pilot overseas. After the war, he helped organize the Arizona Air National Guard. He stayed active in the Air Force Reserve and became a major general in 1962.

Political career. In 1949, Goldwater was elected to the Phoenix city council. He resigned in 1952 to run for the U.S. Senate. Goldwater defeated Senate Majority Leader Ernest W. McFarland by a narrow margin and was reelected in 1958.

Goldwater became the leader of the Republican conservatives after a 1957 Senate speech in which he attacked President Dwight D. Eisenhower's 1958 budget as too high. He outlined his political ideas in *The Conscience of a Conservative* (1960).

In 1960, Goldwater was a candidate for the presidential nomination. But he withdrew and urged conservatives to work for control of the Republican Party. In 1964, the Republican National Convention nominated him on the first ballot. Goldwater held no political office from the time of the election until 1968, when Arizonans elected him to the Senate again. He was reelected in 1974 and 1980. Goldwater served as chairman of the Senate's Intelligence Committee from 1981 until 1987, when he retired from politics.   Stephen E. Ambrose

Goldwyn, Samuel (1882-1974), was one of the first and most successful American motion-picture producers. Such stars as Gary Cooper, Danny Kaye, Merle Oberon, and Lucille Ball gained fame in Goldwyn movies. His best-known films include *Dead End* (1937), *Wuthering Heights* (1939), *The Little Foxes* (1941), *The Best Years of Our Lives* (1946), and *Guys and Dolls* (1955).

Goldwyn was born in Warsaw, Poland. His given and family name was Samuel Goldfish. At 13, he traveled alone to the United States. He helped produce Hollywood's first full-length film, *The Squaw Man*, in 1913. In 1917, he and the Selwyn brothers, two Broadway producers, formed Goldwyn Pictures. He soon changed his name to Goldwyn. In 1922, the company merged with Metro Pictures to form Metro-Goldwyn-Mayer (MGM). Goldwyn left MGM, and in 1923, formed Samuel Goldwyn Productions.   Rachel Gallagher

Golf Digest

Golf is an exciting sport and a popular form of recreation. A golf tournament may attract thousands of fans who watch skilled professionals or amateurs play. Many people enjoy the exercise and friendly competition of playing golf with friends on a beautifully landscaped course.

Golf

Golf is an outdoor sport in which a player attempts to hit a small, hard ball into a hole in as few swings as possible. Players hit the ball with one of several kinds of long, slender golf clubs. Golf is played on a course that normally is divided into 18 units, also called *holes,* of varying lengths and difficulty.

Golf is one of the most popular outdoor sports in the world. Millions of men, women, and children play golf as an individual or team sport, and in high school and college competition. Millions more enjoy golf as a form of recreation and exercise. Golf is also a popular spectator sport, attracting thousands of fans to tournaments. Millions more may watch tournaments on television.

More than 26 million Americans play golf every year. About a fourth of them are women. The United States has more than 16,000 golf courses. About 4,700 are private courses—country clubs and golf clubs available to members only. Another 11,300 are *daily fee courses,* which are privately owned facilities that admit the public for a fee. About 2,500 of these are publicly owned. The remainder are privately owned.

The course

Golf courses have no regulation length or shape, but most consist of 18 holes numbered 1 to 18. Playing all 18 holes makes up a *round* of golf. Some courses have only nine holes. Each hole is played twice for a round.

An 18-hole course averages about 140 acres (57 hectares). Each hole includes a *tee,* a *fairway,* a *green,* and often one or more *hazards.* For the layout of a typical golf course, see the diagram in this article. Courses for men generally range from about 6,500 to more than 7,000 yards (5,900 to 6,400 meters) in length. This distance is the total length from the tees to all 18 holes. Courses are shortened for women, senior golfers, and young people by positioning the *forward tee* closer to the hole.

A golf course contains a mixture of par 3, par 4, and par 5 holes. A player shoots par by hitting the ball from the tee into the hole in a certain number of strokes, usually 3, 4, or 5. A typical par 3 hole measures up to 250 yards (229 meters), a par 4 from 251 to 470 yards (230 to 430 meters), and a par 5 at least 471 yards (431 meters).

Most courses are laid out in a loop that brings the golfer back to a point near the first tee at the end of each nine holes. The holes are arranged so that players are relatively safe from balls hit by players on another hole. Golfers shout the traditional warning "Fore!" to alert other golfers that a shot is about to be hit or that a ball has been hit in their direction.

The tee. Each golf hole begins at the tee, a small flat area from which the golfer takes the first *stroke,* or *shot.* This stroke is sometimes called a *drive.* Before hitting

Golf terms

Birdie. A score of one under par on a hole.
Bogey, *BOH gee.* A score of one above par on a hole. A *double bogey* is two over par and a *triple bogey* is three over par.
Eagle. A score of two under par on a hole.
Handicap. A method of equalizing competition by allowing a certain number of strokes to a golfer competing against a more skillful player. The handicap is computed from a golfer's previous scores.
Hole-in-one, also called an *ace.* This rare score occurs when the golfer's tee shot goes into the hole.
Lie is the position in which the ball lies on the course after a stroke. An *unplayable lie* exists when the ball's position makes it impossible to hit.

the ball, the golfer places it on a wooden or plastic peg that is also called a *tee.* The peg may only be used on the tee. After the tee shot, the golfer must hit the ball as it lies on the course.

The fairway is a stretch of closely mowed grass that extends from the tee to the green. The fairway may be a straight path to the green or it may be laid out at an angle, called a *dogleg.* The fairway is designed to give the golfer the clearest route to the green. Golfers who hit their ball outside the fairway land in the *rough.* This area borders each side of the fairway. It has higher grass and may include bushes and trees.

The green is an area at the end of the fairway. The green is covered with special grass that is mowed very closely. It contains a hole $4\frac{1}{4}$ inches (10.8 centimeters) in diameter and at least 4 inches (10 centimeters) in depth.

A movable marker called the *flagstick* or *pin* is placed in the hole to show its location.

Play on the hole is completed when the golfer hits the ball into the hole. The number of strokes the player takes to hit the ball into the hole becomes the player's score for that hole. The player normally takes progressively shorter shots from the tee to the green. Once on the green, the golfer *putts* (rolls) the ball into the hole with a club called the *putter.* The surface of the green is usually gently sloped, and the golfer should allow for the slope when putting.

Hazards are obstacles placed throughout the course to make play more difficult. Golfers try to avoid them. Hazards include *bunkers* and *water hazards.* Bunkers are depressions in the ground. If they contain sand they are called *sand traps.* Water hazards include ponds and streams. If the ball lands in a water hazard, the golfer may hit it out if the ball is playable. Otherwise, the golfer lifts it out by hand or plays another ball, adding an extra stroke to the score as a penalty.

The equipment

A golfer's main equipment consists of the ball and a set of clubs. Each club is designed to play a particular type of stroke or to hit the ball a certain distance.

Golf balls used in competition throughout the world can weigh no less than 1.62 ounces (45.9 grams) and must measure at least 1.68 inches (4.27 centimeters) in diameter.

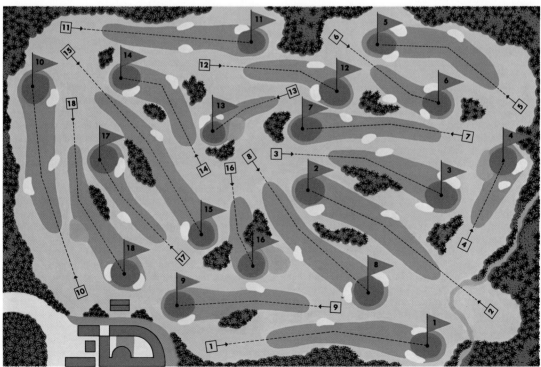

WORLD BOOK illustration by George Suyeoka

An 18-hole golf course might be designed as shown in the above diagram. Play at each hole begins at the tee, indicated above by a number in a square. A fairway leads to the green, marked with a number in a flag. Obstacles include sand traps, shown in yellow, and water hazards, in blue.

WORLD BOOK illustrations by J. Harlan Hunt

A golf ball has a dimpled cover to add accuracy and distance to its flight. Two types of balls are manufactured—*two-piece, left,* and *wound, right.*

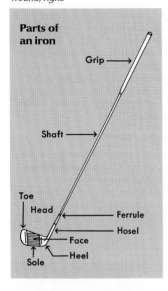

Basic golf clubs

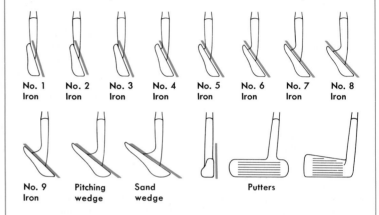

No. 1 Wood (Driver)   No. 2 Wood   No. 3 Wood   No. 4 Wood

Woods are used by golfers when they want to hit the ball a long distance. Golfers use the *driver* to tee off. They use the other woods for shots from the fairway.

No. 1 Iron   No. 2 Iron   No. 3 Iron   No. 4 Iron   No. 5 Iron   No. 6 Iron   No. 7 Iron   No. 8 Iron

No. 9 Iron   Pitching wedge   Sand wedge   Putters

The greater *loft* (angle of the clubface) gives iron shots more height but less distance than wood shots. The greater the loft, the higher and shorter the shot. Skillful golfers can put backspin on iron shots, which stops the ball when it lands on the green. Golfers then tap the ball with the putter to roll it into the hole.

WORLD BOOK illustrations

There are two types of balls, *wound* and *two-piece.* Wound balls are made of thin rubber thread wound tightly around a core. The core may be solid rubber, or a sac filled with water or another liquid. Wound balls are softer and take more spin, allowing skillful golfers more control of the ball's flight. Two-piece balls have a solid core with no rubber thread. They are harder and more popular with less skillful golfers. Both types can be covered with rubber or synthetic material. The cover has numerous tiny depressions called *dimples* that increase the ball's distance and accuracy.

Golf clubs are slender tubes, usually of steel, with a *grip* at one end for the golfer to hold and a *head* at the other for striking the ball. There are two types of clubs: *woods* and *irons.* Both underwent major changes during the late 1900's. Woods got their name from their large, bulky head made of solid wood. However, beginning in the early 1980's, most woods had hollow heads made of various metals, such as stainless steel and titanium. Irons have much thinner bladelike heads. They were first made of iron, then steel, and finally various other metals. Players use woods for the longest shots and irons for shorter shots requiring greater accuracy. Most club shafts are made of steel. Shafts made of graphite or graphite and another material are also popular. In golf's early days, shafts were made of ash and then hickory.

Woods and irons are usually numbered from 1 to 9. The higher the number of the club, the greater is the *loft* (slope) on the *face* (front of the head). Each club has a dif-

ferent vertically angled loft. The greater the loft, the higher and shorter the ball will travel.

The No. 1 wood, also called the *driver,* has the least amount of loft of any club except the putter. It also hits the ball the farthest. The driver is used off the tee. Professional golfers and top amateurs will average about 250 yards (229 meters) on a drive. Other woods, called *fairway woods,* are used for long shots off the fairway. Fairway woods include the No. 2 (rarely used today), No. 3, No. 4, and No. 5 woods. Professional golfers usually do not carry woods beyond No. 5.

Lofts on irons range from the No. 1, which has the least amount, to No. 9, which has the most. Other irons include the *pitching wedge* for short, accurate shots; the *sand wedge,* for shots from sand traps; and other specialty wedges. Some golfers carry three wedges.

Golfers may carry a maximum of 14 clubs during a round. Golfers are free to choose their own set. By the mid-1980's, the set used by professional or top amateur golfers consisted of a driver, a No. 3 wood, and either a No. 4 or No. 5 wood, No. 2 iron through No. 9 iron, the two wedges, and a putter. When a No. 1 iron is included, one of the fairway woods is usually left out.

Golf competition

Golf is played in two basic ways—*match* and *stroke.*

Match play. In match play, one golfer or team plays against one or more others. The player or team hitting the ball into the hole in the fewest number of strokes

Some principles of golf

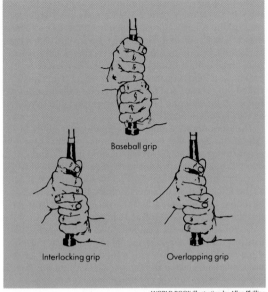

WORLD BOOK illustration by Allan Phillips

The grip is an important golf technique. Nearly all golfers use one of three grips—the overlapping grip, the interlocking grip, or the baseball grip. The overlapping grip is the most popular, but a golfer should choose the most comfortable one.

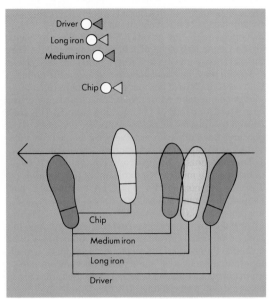

WORLD BOOK diagram by Mas Nakagawa

A proper stance is necessary for an accurate swing. The above drawing shows the position of the feet for right-handed golfers. To maintain balance, a golfer should use a wide stance for long-distance shots and a narrower stance for shorter shots.

WORLD BOOK illustration by Allan Phillips

A correct swing requires proper body coordination. First the golfer lines up the club head with the ball. Then he makes his backswing, shifting his weight to his rear leg. As he starts his downswing, he shifts his weight forward. He snaps the club into the ball and follows through.

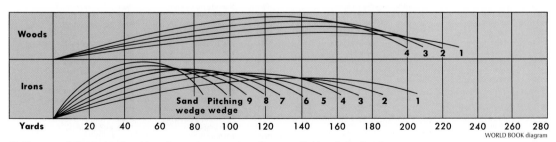

WORLD BOOK diagram

A diagram of distances shows how far an average male golfer normally hits a ball using the basic woods and irons. In planning a shot, the golfer should consider the condition of the golf course and such weather factors as wind direction and velocity.

wins that hole. The player or team winning the most holes wins the match. The score is determined by the number of holes won. A match is decided when a golfer leads by more holes than there are holes left to play. If both golfers or teams make the same score on a hole, that hole is said to be *halved.* If the two golfers or teams are tied at the end of the match, play may continue. Then the player or team who first wins a hole wins the match.

Stroke play. In stroke play, the winner is the golfer who takes the fewest number of total strokes to complete a competition. Most professional tournaments use stroke play for a total of 72 holes (four rounds). Ties are broken by a playoff. In most playoffs, the tied golfers play until one golfer scores lower on a single hole. In some cases, ties are settled using an 18-hole playoff.

Tournaments. A group of four competitions is recognized as the modern "Grand Slam" of golf for men. The tournaments, in order of play, are the Masters Tournament, the United States Open, the British Open, and the Professional Golfers' Association of America (PGA) Championship. The two *open* tournaments are open to both professional and amateur golfers. Both may also be invited to the Masters Tournament. No man has won all four tournaments in the same year. Important women's tournaments include the U.S. Open and the Ladies Professional Golf Association (LPGA) Championship.

The original "Grand Slam" for men consisted of the U.S. Amateur, U.S. Open, British Amateur, and British Open. It was won only once in a single year, by American amateur golfer Bobby Jones in 1930. American golfer Tiger Woods won the modern "Grand Slam" over two years, in 2000 and 2001.

Most countries have amateur competitions for youths and adults. Many countries also compete in international team competitions. In the Walker Cup tournament for amateur men, a U.S. team competes against a team from the United Kingdom and Ireland every two years. The Curtis Cup is a similar tournament for amateur women. In the Ryder Cup, U.S. professional men golfers compete against a team from the United Kingdom and Europe every two years. In the Presidents Cup, every two years a team of U.S. professional men golfers plays a team from the rest of the world excluding Europe. United States professional women golfers play British and European women in the Solheim Cup every two years.

History

Beginnings. Some authorities trace golf back to a Roman game called *paganica.* The Romans, who occupied most of the island of Great Britain from the A.D. 40's to the early 400's, played paganica in the streets with a bent stick and a leather ball stuffed with feathers. Other historians trace golf to a Dutch game called *het kolven,* a French and Belgian game called *chole,* a French game called *jeu de mail,* and an English game called *cambuca.* But most believe golf probably developed into the game as we know it in Scotland.

The Honourable Company of Edinburgh Golfers in Edinburgh, Scotland, is often recognized as the first organized golf club. It was established in 1744 and set down the first written rules of the game. The Royal and Ancient Golf Club of St. Andrews was founded in 1754 as the Society of St. Andrews Golfers. It was the leader in setting golf's rules and standards. For example, it set the standard round of golf at 18 holes.

Golfers played with a leather-covered ball stuffed with feathers, called the *feathery,* until the *gutty* was introduced in 1848. The gutty was a solid ball made of a rubbery substance called *gutta-percha.* The gutty was later replaced by the rubber-cored ball invented in 1898 by U.S. golfer Coburn Haskell.

The popularity of golf spread from Scotland and England to parts of the British Commonwealth. The first North American golf club was the Royal Montreal, organized in 1873.

Historians disagree over which existing golf club in the United States was founded first. Among the oldest American clubs are the Dorset Field Club in Dorset, Vermont; the Foxburg Country Club in Foxburg, Pennsylvania; and the St. Andrews Golf Club in Hastings-on-Hudson, New York. All three clubs claim founding dates in the 1880's. The Amateur Golf Association of the United States (now the United States Golf Association) was founded in 1894 to serve as the governing body for golf in the United States. In 1951, the USGA and the United Kingdom's Royal and Ancient Golf Club of St. Andrews agreed to jointly interpret the rules and standards that now govern golf throughout the world.

Major tournament champions

British Open

Year		Year		Year		Year	
1914	Harry Vardon	1939	Richard Burton	1965	Peter Thomson	1986	Greg Norman
1915-19	No tournaments	1940-45	No tournaments	1966	Jack Nicklaus	1987	Nick Faldo
1920	George Duncan	1946	Sam Snead	1967	Roberto de Vicenzo	1988	Severiano Ballesteros
1921	Jock Hutchison	1947	Fred Daly	1968	Gary Player	1989	Mark Calcavecchia
1922	Walter Hagen	1948	Henry Cotton	1969	Tony Jacklin	1990	Nick Faldo
1923	Arthur G. Havers	1949	Bobby Locke	1970	Jack Nicklaus	1991	Ian Baker-Finch
1924	Walter Hagen	1950	Bobby Locke	1971	Lee Trevino	1992	Nick Faldo
1925	James M. Barnes	1951	Max Faulkner	1972	Lee Trevino	1993	Greg Norman
1926	Bobby Jones	1952	Bobby Locke	1973	Tom Weiskopf	1994	Nick Price
1927	Bobby Jones	1953	Ben Hogan	1974	Gary Player	1995	John Daly
1928	Walter Hagen	1954	Peter Thomson	1975	Tom Watson	1996	Tom Lehman
1929	Walter Hagen	1955	Peter Thomson	1976	Johnny Miller	1997	Justin Leonard
1930	Bobby Jones	1956	Peter Thomson	1977	Tom Watson	1998	Mark O'Meara
1931	Tommy Armour	1957	Bobby Locke	1978	Jack Nicklaus	1999	Paul Lawrie
1932	Gene Sarazen	1958	Peter Thomson	1979	Severiano Ballesteros	2000	Tiger Woods
1933	Denny Shute	1959	Gary Player	1980	Tom Watson	2001	David Duval
1934	Henry Cotton	1960	Kel Nagle	1981	Bill Rogers		
1935	Alf Perry	1961	Arnold Palmer	1982	Tom Watson		
1936	Alfred Padgham	1962	Arnold Palmer	1983	Tom Watson		
1937	Henry Cotton	1963	Bob Charles	1984	Severiano Ballesteros		
1938	R. A. Whitcombe	1964	Tony Lema	1985	Sandy Lyle		

U.S. Open

Year		Year		Year		Year	
1914	Walter Hagen	1936	Tony Manero	1960	Arnold Palmer	1981	David Graham
1915	Jerome Travers	1937	Ralph Guldahl	1961	Gene Littler	1982	Tom Watson
1916	Charles Evans, Jr.	1938	Ralph Guldahl	1962	Jack Nicklaus	1983	Larry Nelson
1917-18	No tournaments	1939	Byron Nelson	1963	Julius Boros	1984	Fuzzy Zoeller
1919	Walter Hagen	1940	Lawson Little, Jr.	1964	Ken Venturi	1985	Andy North
1920	Edward Ray	1941	Craig Wood	1965	Gary Player	1986	Ray Floyd
1921	James M. Barnes	1942-45	No tournaments	1966	Billy Casper, Jr.	1987	Scott Simpson
1922	Gene Sarazen	1946	Lloyd Mangrum	1967	Jack Nicklaus	1988	Curtis Strange
1923	Bobby Jones	1947	Lew Worsham	1968	Lee Trevino	1989	Curtis Strange
1924	Cyril Walker	1948	Ben Hogan	1969	Orville Moody	1990	Hale Irwin
1925	Willie Macfarlane	1949	Cary Middlecoff	1970	Tony Jacklin	1991	Payne Stewart
1926	Bobby Jones	1950	Ben Hogan	1971	Lee Trevino	1992	Tom Kite
1927	Tommy Armour	1951	Ben Hogan	1972	Jack Nicklaus	1993	Lee Janzen
1928	Johnny Farrell	1952	Julius Boros	1973	Johnny Miller	1994	Ernie Els
1929	Bobby Jones	1953	Ben Hogan	1974	Hale Irwin	1995	Corey Pavin
1930	Bobby Jones	1954	Ed Furgol	1975	Lou Graham	1996	Steve Jones
1931	Billy Burke	1955	Jack Fleck	1976	Jerry Pate	1997	Ernie Els
1932	Gene Sarazen	1956	Cary Middlecoff	1977	Hubert Green	1998	Lee Janzen
1933	John Goodman	1957	Dick Mayer	1978	Andy North	1999	Payne Stewart
1934	Olin Dutra	1958	Tommy Bolt	1979	Hale Irwin	2000	Tiger Woods
1935	Sam Parks, Jr.	1959	Billy Casper, Jr.	1980	Jack Nicklaus	2001	Retief Goosen

Masters Tournament

Year		Year		Year		Year	
1934	Horton Smith	1953	Ben Hogan	1970	Billy Casper, Jr.	1987	Larry Mize
1935	Gene Sarazen	1954	Sam Snead	1971	Charles Coody	1988	Sandy Lyle
1936	Horton Smith	1955	Cary Middlecoff	1972	Jack Nicklaus	1989	Nick Faldo
1937	Byron Nelson	1956	Jack Burke	1973	Tommy Aaron	1990	Nick Faldo
1938	Henry Picard	1957	Doug Ford	1974	Gary Player	1991	Ian Woosnam
1939	Ralph Guldahl	1958	Arnold Palmer	1975	Jack Nicklaus	1992	Fred Couples
1940	Jimmy Demaret	1959	Art Wall, Jr.	1976	Ray Floyd	1993	Bernhard Langer
1941	Craig Wood	1960	Arnold Palmer	1977	Tom Watson	1994	Jose Maria Olazabal
1942	Byron Nelson	1961	Gary Player	1978	Gary Player	1995	Ben Crenshaw
1943-45	No tournaments	1962	Arnold Palmer	1979	Fuzzy Zoeller	1996	Nick Faldo
1946	Herman Keiser	1963	Jack Nicklaus	1980	Severiano Ballesteros	1997	Tiger Woods
1947	Jimmy Demaret	1964	Arnold Palmer	1981	Tom Watson	1998	Mark O'Meara
1948	Claude Harmon	1965	Jack Nicklaus	1982	Craig Stadler	1999	Jose Maria Olazabal
1949	Sam Snead	1966	Jack Nicklaus	1983	Severiano Ballesteros	2000	Vijay Singh
1950	Jimmy Demaret	1967	Gay Brewer	1984	Ben Crenshaw	2001	Tiger Woods
1951	Ben Hogan	1968	Bob Goalby	1985	Bernhard Langer		
1952	Sam Snead	1969	George Archer	1986	Jack Nicklaus		

PGA Championship

Year		Year		Year		Year	
1916	Jim Barnes	1939	Henry Picard	1961	Jerry Barber	1983	Hal Sutton
1917-18	No tournaments	1940	Byron Nelson	1962	Gary Player	1984	Lee Trevino
1919	Jim Barnes	1941	Vic Ghezzi	1963	Jack Nicklaus	1985	Hubert Green
1920	Jock Hutchison	1942	Sam Snead	1964	Bob Nichols	1986	Bob Tway
1921	Walter Hagen	1943	No tournament	1965	Dave Marr	1987	Larry Nelson
1922	Gene Sarazen	1944	Bob Hamilton	1966	Al Geiberger	1988	Jeff Sluman
1923	Gene Sarazen	1945	Byron Nelson	1967	Don January	1989	Payne Stewart
1924	Walter Hagen	1946	Ben Hogan	1968	Julius Boros	1990	Wayne Grady
1925	Walter Hagen	1947	Jim Ferrier	1969	Ray Floyd	1991	John Daly
1926	Walter Hagen	1948	Ben Hogan	1970	Dave Stockton	1992	Nick Price
1927	Walter Hagen	1949	Sam Snead	1971	Jack Nicklaus	1993	Paul Azinger
1928	Leo Diegel	1950	Chandler Harper	1972	Gary Player	1994	Nick Price
1929	Leo Diegel	1951	Sam Snead	1973	Jack Nicklaus	1995	Steve Elkington
1930	Tommy Armour	1952	Jim Turnesa	1974	Lee Trevino	1996	Mark Brooks
1931	Tom Creavy	1953	Walter Burkemo	1975	Jack Nicklaus	1997	Davis Love III
1932	Olin Dutra	1954	Chick Harbert	1976	Dave Stockton	1998	Vijay Singh
1933	Gene Sarazen	1955	Doug Ford	1977	Lanny Wadkins	1999	Tiger Woods
1934	Paul Runyan	1956	Jack Burke	1978	John Mahaffey	2000	Tiger Woods
1935	Johnny Revolta	1957	Lionel Hebert	1979	David Graham	2001	David Toms
1936	Denny Shute	1958	Dow Finsterwald	1980	Jack Nicklaus		
1937	Denny Shute	1959	Bob Rosburg	1981	Larry Nelson		
1938	Paul Runyan	1960	Jay Hebert	1982	Ray Floyd		

U.S. Women's Open

Year		Year		Year		Year	
1946	Patty Berg	1960	Betsy Rawls	1974	Sandra Haynie	1988	Liselotte Neumann
1947	Betty Jameson	1961	Mickey Wright	1975	Sandra Palmer	1989	Betsy King
1948	Babe Zaharias	1962	Murie Lindstrom	1976	JoAnne Carner	1990	Betsy King
1949	Louise Suggs	1963	Mary Mills	1977	Hollis Stacy	1991	Meg Mallon
1950	Babe Zaharias	1964	Mickey Wright	1978	Hollis Stacy	1992	Patty Sheehan
1951	Betsy Rawls	1965	Carol Mann	1979	Jerilyn Britz	1993	Lauri Merten
1952	Louise Suggs	1966	Sandra Spuzich	1980	Amy Alcott	1994	Patty Sheehan
1953	Betsy Rawls	1967	Catherine Lacoste	1981	Pat Bradley	1995	Annika Sorenstam
1954	Babe Zaharias	1968	Susie Berning	1982	Janet Alex	1996	Annika Sorenstam
1955	Fay Crocker	1969	Donna Caponi	1983	Jan Stephenson	1997	Alison Nicholas
1956	Kathy Cornelius	1970	Donna Caponi	1984	Hollis Stacy	1998	Se Ri Pak
1957	Betsy Rawls	1971	JoAnne Carner	1985	Kathy Baker	1999	Juli Inkster
1958	Mickey Wright	1972	Susie Berning	1986	Jane Geddes	2000	Karrie Webb
1959	Mickey Wright	1973	Susie Berning	1987	Laura Davies	2001	Karrie Webb

AP/Wide World · AP/Wide World · AP/Wide World

Golf stars of the 1950's and 1960's helped make the sport popular throughout the world. Patty Berg, *left,* was the leading woman golfer of her time. Well-known men golfers included Ben Hogan, *center;* and at the right, *from left to right,* Gary Player, Arnold Palmer, and Sam Snead.

The rise of professional golf. In 1916, American professional golfers formed the PGA. Until then, amateur golfers dominated the sport. Bobby Jones, who retired in 1930, was the finest amateur golfer of his day. But outstanding professionals, notably Walter Hagen, were beginning to establish golf as a major sport. Hagen was a superb golfer who won additional fame in the 1920's for his showmanship and flamboyant style.

Some of the first tournaments on the American professional tour began in the early 1920's, and the tour became established in the 1930's. It was led by such golfers as Ben Hogan, Byron Nelson, and Sam Snead. Prize money averaged less than $10,000 per tournament until after World War II ended in 1945. Hogan and Snead dominated the sport in the 1950's along with Jimmy Demaret, Lloyd Mangrum, and Cary Middlecoff. Top professionals of the 1960's and early 1970's included Americans Arnold Palmer, Jack Nicklaus, and Billy Casper, along with Gary Player of South Africa.

The U.S. PGA Tour is the biggest and richest in the world. It ovesees about 50 tournaments, each offering several million dollars in prize money.

Women's golf has enjoyed a growth similar to that of men's golf. From about 1900 through the 1920's, British amateurs dominated women's golf. Joyce Wethered was the top British golfer during the 1920's, and some experts consider her the greatest woman golfer in history. By the 1930's, United States women golfers had become important. Top U.S. golfers included Patty Berg, Babe Didrikson Zaharias, and Betty Jameson.

Widespread interest in women's professional golf developed after World War II. Berg and Zaharias turned professional and became leaders of the LPGA. The LPGA Tour began in 1950 with 11 tournaments. In the early 2000's, it had more than 40 tournaments. Stars of the late 1900's and early 2000's included Nancy Lopez, Juli Inkster, and Betsy King of the United States; Laura Davies of the United Kingdom; Annika Sorenstam of Sweden; Se Ri Pak of South Korea; and Karrie Webb of Australia.

Golf today. United States golfers dominated golf internationally until the late 1970's, when golfers from oth-

AP/Wide World · AP/Wide World · AP/Wide World · AP/Wide World

Golf stars of today include, *from left to right,* Tiger Woods of the United States, Vijay Singh of Fiji, Annika Sorenstam of Sweden, and Phil Mickelson of the United States. All four rank among the leading tournament winners in professional golf.

er countries began to emerge. These golfers included Greg Norman of Australia, Severiano Ballesteros of Spain, Bernhard Langer of West Germany, Isao Aoki of Japan, and Sandy Lyle and Nick Faldo of the United Kingdom. Several professional tours also flourished outside the United States. The most important were the European tour, based in the United Kingdom; the South African tour; the Japanese tour; the Asian tour; and the Australia/New Zealand tour. Among the top U.S. golfers of the 1970's and 1980's were Tom Watson, Lee Trevino, Ray Floyd, and Fuzzy Zoeller.

In 1980, the PGA Tour started the PGA Senior Tour for players at least 50 years old. Many prominent players from the PGA tour moved to the Senior Tour, extending their careers as competitive professional golfers. In 1990, a developmental tour, largely for younger players, was established. It is now known as the Buy.com Tour. The World Golf Championships consist of four tournaments, three of which have purses of about $5 million. The fourth tournament has a $3-million purse. The Championships are a cooperative effort of the six major tours—the U.S. PGA Tour and those of Europe, Japan, Australia, South Africa, and Asia.

In 2000, Tiger Woods won the PGA Championship, the U.S. Open, and the British Open. He also won the Masters Tournament in 2001. Woods thus became the first professional golfer to hold all four major titles at the same time.   Marino A. Parascenzo

Related articles in *World Book* include:

Hagen, Walter	Ryder Cup	Snead, Sam
Hogan, Ben	Scotland (picture:	Trevino, Lee
Jones, Bobby	The Royal and	Woods, Tiger
Lopez, Nancy	Ancient Golf	Zaharias, Babe
Nicklaus, Jack	Club)	Didrikson
Palmer, Arnold		

Outline

I. **The course**
   A. The tee   C. The green
   B. The fairway   D. Hazards
II. **The equipment**
   A. Golf balls   B. Golf clubs
III. **Golf competition**
   A. Match play   B. Stroke play   C. Tournaments
IV. **History**

Questions

What is the *professional tour?*
How long is a typical par 3 hole?
When does a golfer use a *wood?* An *iron?* A *putter?*
What is a *birdie?* A *bogey?* A *hole-in-one?*
Who was Joyce Wethered? Bobby Jones?
How do match play and stroke play differ?
Why does a golf ball have "dimples"?
What is the fairway?
Who competes for the Ryder Cup?
How many clubs may a player carry during a round?

Additional resources

Golf Magazine's Encyclopedia of Golf. 2nd ed. HarperCollins, 1993.
Krause, Peter. *Fundamental Golf.* Lerner, 1995. Younger readers.
Ruthenberg, Stephen J. *Golf Fore!! Beginners.* RGS Pub., 1992.
U.S. Golf Assn. *Golf Rules in Pictures.* Rev. ed. Perigee, 1993.

Golgi, *GAWL jee,* **Camillo,** *kah MEEL loh* (1844-1926), an Italian anatomist and pathologist, shared the 1906 Nobel Prize for physiology or medicine for his studies on the structure of the nervous system. In 1873, he developed a method of staining tissues with silver nitrate for microscopic study. He later discovered the "Golgi cells"—nerve cells with long or short *axons* (nerve fibers)—and described the nerve endings in tendons and muscles. Golgi was born in what is now Córteno Golgi, Italy, near Sondrio.   Dale C. Smith

Golgotha. See Calvary.

Goliath, *guh LY uhth,* in the Old Testament, was a Philistine warrior almost 10 feet (300 centimeters) tall. He defied the Israelite army to send a champion to fight him. Young David, armed with only a sling and five stones, volunteered. David, confident that he upheld God's honor, shot his first stone into Goliath's forehead, killing the giant. The story is told in I Samuel 17. In II Samuel 21:19, Goliath is said to have been killed by Elhanan, one of David's soldiers.   J. Maxwell Miller

Gomorrah. See Sodom and Gomorrah.

Gompers, Samuel (1850-1924), an American labor leader, was the first president of the American Federation of Labor. From 1886 until his death, he missed only one year, 1895, as president. His was perhaps the most important personal influence in shaping the federation.

Gompers insisted that unions should rely on bargaining with employers, and avoid ties with government and political parties. He campaigned vigorously to get rid of the labor injunction issued by courts to curb strikes. He worked hard for provisions in the Clayton Antitrust Act of 1914, which he hailed as labor's "Magna Carta" (see **Antitrust laws**). Gompers supported labor laws aimed at regulating the conditions and hours of work of women and minors. He was influential in the national legislation that established the U.S. Department of Labor.

Gompers was born in London. He moved to the United States when he was 13. A year later he became the first registered member of the Cigar-Makers' International Union. He made this organization one of the most successful trade unions.   Jack Barbash

Additional resources

Gompers, Samuel. *Seventy Years of Life and Labor: An Autobiography.* Ed. by Nick Salvatore. 1925. Reprint. ILR Pr., 1984. An abridged version.
Livesay, Harold C. *Samuel Gompers and Organized Labor in America.* 1978. Reprint. Waveland Pr., 1993.

Goncourt, *gawn KOOR,* was the family name of two French brothers who had an important influence on literature. Edmond de Goncourt (1822-1896) and Jules de Goncourt (1830-1870) wrote novels that provided the basis for the Realist and Naturalist literary movements in France. In their writings, they presented life among the lowest classes of society with rigid Realism. Their novel *Germinie Lacerteux* (1864) ranks among the earliest examples of Naturalism in fiction (see **Naturalism**). The brothers were also historians and art critics.

Edmond was born in Nancy, and Jules in Paris. Their home in Paris became a meeting place for writers, artists, and intellectuals. The brothers left a huge collection of anecdotes, incidents, and gossip about the literary world of their time. Called the *Journal,* it is an important aid to scholars studying that period.   Thomas H. Goetz

Gondola, *GAHN duh luh,* is a long, slender boat used on the canals of Venice, Italy. An old law requires that all gondolas, except those belonging to high officials, be painted black. The *gondolier* pushes the boat through the water with a long *sweep* (narrow-bladed oar). Today in Venice, gasoline launches have replaced gondolas for

Fritz Prenzel, Bruce Coleman Ltd.

Gondolas carry passengers up and down the canals of Venice, Italy. However, motorboats have replaced gondolas as the chief means of transportation in the city.

light freight transportation. Tourists now prefer motorboat taxis to gondolas for sightseeing in the city. See also **Venice.**   Joseph A. Gutierrez, Jr.

Gong is a metal percussion instrument shaped like a circular plate. It hangs on a stand and is played by striking it with a mallet. There are two types of gongs. One type, called a *tuned gong,* has a fixed pitch. The other, called an *untuned gong* or *tam-tam,* has no fixed pitch.

A gong produces a deep, rich sound that varies with the type of mallet used. Most mallets are made of rubber or wood and covered with felt or wool. Gongs vary in size, and no two sound alike. Gongs originated in the Far East and were introduced into Europe during the late Middle Ages. Gongs are used in bands, orchestras, and small musical groups. In many cultures, they are also used for religious purposes.   John H. Beck

Góngora, *GAWNG goh rah,* **Luis de,** *loo EES day* (1561-1627), was the greatest poet of the Spanish baroque period. He led a poetic movement known as *gongorismo,* or *culteranismo.* He believed the creation of beauty is an end in itself, and that art need not be concerned with ethical and spiritual values. But modern criticism shows that much of his poetry dealt with social issues. Góngora used an ornate style, featuring elaborate figures of speech, involved sentence structures, obscure terms, and references to classical mythology. His ballads and *epigrams* (sayings) show wit and satiric talent. But he is best known for three poems that idealize rural life: *Soledades* (1613), *Polifemo and Galatea* (1612), and *Pyramus and Thisbe* (1618).

Born in Córdoba, Góngora became a priest in 1611 and honorary chaplain to King Philip III of Spain in 1612. However, Góngora devoted himself almost entirely to literature and the courtly life.   Harry Sieber

Gonorrhea, *gahn uh REE uh,* is a sexually transmitted disease caused by a bacterium found only in human beings. The scientific name for this bacterium is *Neisseria*

gonorrhoeae. The bacterium is nearly always spread from person to person through intimate sexual contact. If left untreated, gonorrhea can have serious health consequences, particularly in women.

In men, gonorrhea bacteria usually infect the *urethra* (urinary tube), just inside the opening at the tip of the penis. About 1 to 14 days after infection, most men develop a burning sensation when urinating, accompanied by a discharge from the penis. The discharge may at first be thin and watery, but it soon becomes heavy, thick, and yellowish. Some men experience few or no symptoms.

In women, the infection usually starts in the *cervix* (neck of the uterus) inside the vagina. Symptoms include discharge from the vagina and painful urination. These symptoms may be mild, and they frequently go unnoticed. Without prompt treatment, the bacteria may spread through the uterus to the fallopian tubes, causing *pelvic inflammatory disease* (PID). This condition may lead to sterility or even death.

Babies born to women with gonorrhea may become infected during the birthing process. In most such cases, the bacteria infect the infant's eyes. If not treated promptly, the infant may become blind. Routine treatment of newborns with eyedrops containing silver nitrate or with antibiotic ointment prevents eye infection from gonorrhea.

Doctors treat gonorrhea with antibiotics. Through the years, some strains of gonorrhea bacteria have become resistant to many antibiotics. However, new antibiotics have been developed that effectively fight the disease. Individuals may reduce their risk of infection with gonorrhea by using condoms or other protective measures during sexual activity.   Ronald K. St. John

See also **Pelvic inflammatory disease; Sexually transmitted disease.**

Gonzales, *guhn ZAH lihs,* **Rodolfo,** *roh DOHL foh* (1928-   ), is a leader of the Chicano movement, a civil rights campaign by Mexican Americans. In 1965, he founded and became director of the Crusade for Justice, based in Denver. This group provides medical and legal aid to needy Mexican Americans and works for better housing and job opportunities.

Gonzales encourages Mexican Americans to take pride in their history, customs, and accomplishments. He favors organizing independent communities where Mexican Americans can control their own businesses, schools, and other local institutions.

Gonzales, the son of a migrant worker, was born in Denver. He has had the nickname "Corky" since boyhood. His poem "I Am Joaquín" (1967) traces the injustices suffered by people of Mexican descent. The poem was popular among Chicanos.   Feliciano M. Ribera

Gonzalez, *guhn ZAH lihs,* **Pancho,** *PAHN choh* (1928-1995), became one of the greatest players in tennis history. He won the United States amateur singles championship in 1948 and 1949, and played on the United States Davis Cup team that defeated Australia in 1949. Gonzalez quit amateur tennis in 1949 and became an outstanding professional player.

Richard Alonzo Gonzalez was born in Los Angeles. He also spelled his name Gonzales. He got his start in tennis by accident when he was 12. He had been pestering his mother to buy him a bicycle, but she bought him a 51-

cent tennis racket instead. At first, Gonzalez did not want to play tennis, but he soon changed his mind. By 1948, he was the top-ranked amateur in the United States.

Arthur Ashe

Goober. See Peanut.

Good Friday is the Friday before Easter Sunday, the central festival of the Christian year. Good Friday is usually observed as a day for mourning the death of Jesus. Some churches hold a three-hour worship service. In some churches, Good Friday marks the beginning of the *Paschal Triduum,* the three days of Easter.

The earliest records from the A.D. 100's show that Good Friday had no connection with mourning Jesus's death. It was simply a day of fasting before Easter. By the late 300's, however, Christians observed Good Friday with a long series of readings and prayers that focused on the death of Jesus on the cross. This service was held from noon to 3 p.m. David G. Truemper

See also **Easter** (Good Friday); **Holy Week.**

Good Hope, Cape of. See Cape of Good Hope.

Good Templars, International Organization of, is an organization founded in Utica, New York, in 1851, to promote temperance, peace, and brotherhood. It has chapters and groups in the United States and 40 other countries. Membership is open to all people, regardless of ethnic origin or religious beliefs. The organization publishes *The Globe,* a magazine on alcohol and drug problems. International headquarters are in Cambridge, England. The U.S. national division, with headquarters in Minneapolis, Minnesota, publishes the *National Good Templar* magazine.

Critically reviewed by the International Organization of Good Templars

Goodall, Jane (1934-), is an English zoologist who studies the behavior of animals. She became known for her work with chimpanzees and her efforts to ensure their survival in the wild. Goodall began her research in 1960 at what is now Gombe Stream National Park in northwestern Tanzania. She won the trust of many chimpanzees through daily contact with them. She observed them at close range and wrote detailed reports.

Before Goodall's research, scientists believed that chimpanzees ate chiefly fruits and vegetables and, occasionally, insects and small rodents. But Goodall found that chimpanzees also hunt and eat larger animals, in-

Breese, Gamma/Liaison

Jane Goodall uncovered many similarities between human beings and chimpanzees through years of observation.

cluding young monkeys and pigs. She also discovered that they make and use tools more than any other animal except human beings. Goodall observed them stripping tree twigs and using the twigs as tools for catching termites. She also observed the first known instance where one group of chimpanzees systematically killed off another group for no obvious survival reason. Goodall's research surprised most naturalists because it suggests that such behaviors as hunting, tool use, and "warfare" are not unique to human beings.

Goodall was born in London. She earned a Ph.D. from Cambridge University. Her writings include *My Friends, the Wild Chimpanzees* (1967), *In the Shadow of Man* (1971), *The Chimpanzees of Gombe* (1986), and *Through a Window* (1990). She has also produced numerous films on the Gombe chimpanzees. Randall L. Susman

Goodman, Benny (1909-1986), was an American clarinet player and bandleader. He became the symbol of the "swing era" in jazz in the mid-1930's and remained "The King of Swing" until his death. Goodman was the first jazz musician to achieve a reputation as a soloist with symphony orchestras. He collaborated with and commissioned works from many classical composers. He pioneered in the public presentation of interracial music groups, introducing Teddy Wilson, Lionel Hampton, and other African American musicians who gained fame.

Benjamin David Goodman was born into a large, poor family in Chicago. A child prodigy, he played on the stage at the age of 12. At 16, he became a member of Ben Pollack's touring band. In 1962, Goodman's orchestra became the first jazz band to tour the Soviet Union since the 1920's. Frank Tirro

See also **Jazz** (The swing era; picture).

Goodrich, Benjamin Franklin (1841-1888), founded the rubber industry in Akron, Ohio. A real estate transaction in 1869 made him part-owner of a small rubber factory in Hastings-on-Hudson, New York. It was unsuccessful, but he had confidence in the future of rubber. He moved to Akron in 1870, and set up a new company that produced such items as fire hose and billiard cushions. By 1880, the company was in sound financial condition, and was incorporated as the B. F. Goodrich Company. Goodrich was born in Ripley, New York. He studied medicine and was an army surgeon during the Civil War (1861-1865). David F. Channell

Goodwill Industries are nonprofit organizations that provide disabled and socially disadvantaged individuals with such work-related services as employment, job placement, training, and vocational evaluation. Goodwill Industries are financed partly through the sale of clothing and household items donated by the public. Additional funds are raised by processing salvage and providing services to the government and the public. The organizations use the income to pay their workers and to help other disabled people find jobs. They also perform vocational rehabilitation services for businesses and government agencies. Each organization is directed by local volunteers and operated by a professional staff. There are about 180 local Goodwill Industries in the United States and Canada and 45 affiliated groups in other nations. The international organization is Goodwill Industries of America, Inc. Goodwill was founded in 1902. Headquarters are in Bethesda, Maryland.

Critically reviewed by Goodwill Industries of America, Inc.

Goodyear, Charles (1800-1860), was an American inventor. He developed *vulcanization,* a method of making rubber strong and resistant to heat and cold.

Goodyear was born in New Haven, Conn. In 1832, he began experimenting with a crude form of rubber, called *India rubber,* to find a way to make the substance useful for manufacturing. India rubber becomes brittle when cold and sticky when hot. After many experiments, Goodyear learned that sulfur helps to make rubber less sticky. One day in 1839, Goodyear accidentally spilled a mixture of rubber and sulfur onto a hot stove. To his surprise, the mixture did not melt. Goodyear realized that heat is needed to *cure* (strengthen) a rubber-sulfur mixture. He spent five years improving this curing process. In 1844, he received the patent for it.

Goodyear licensed the process, later called vulcanization, to many people. But he failed to become wealthy. He spent all his money on unsuccessful businesses, costly experiments, and attempts to promote his process. He died a poor man.   David L. Lewis

See also **Rubber** (Discovery of vulcanization; Vulcanization).

Goodyear, Miles (1817-1849), an American pioneer and fur trader, built the first settled homestead in Utah in about 1845. He was born in Connecticut, and spent his boyhood there. He then moved to the frontier, where Marcus Whitman found him in a destitute condition (see **Whitman, Marcus**). He later became associated with mountain fur traders and explored the territory around Salt Lake. The Mormons bought Goodyear's property in 1848.   John Elgin Foster

Googol, *GOO gahl,* is the number written as 1 followed by 100 zeros, or 10^{100}. A *googolplex* is an even larger number than a googol. It is 10 to the googol power, or 10 multiplied by itself a googol number of times. The term *googol* was introduced by the American mathematician Edward Kasner. His 9-year-old nephew is said to have invented it.

Goose is a water bird closely related to the duck and swan. Like ducks and swans, geese have a flattened bill; a long neck; water-repellent feathers; long, pointed wings; a short tail; short legs; and webbed feet. But geese are larger than ducks and smaller than swans, and they honk rather than quack or whistle. Male geese are called *ganders.*

Their webbed feet make geese good swimmers, but they are as much at home on land as in the water. All geese are *migratory* birds, flying north in spring and south in fall. They are graceful in flight and have great endurance. Some kinds of geese can fly more than 1,000 miles (1,600 kilometers) without stopping to rest.

There are more than 40 species of wild geese, found chiefly in Asia, Europe, and North America. Domestic geese are probably descended from two wild species— the *graylag goose* and the *swan goose.* Geese were first domesticated in Asia thousands of years ago. People raise geese for their rich, tasty meat and for their *down* (soft feathers). Goose down is widely used as stuffing in pillows and mattresses and as a lightweight, insulating material in sleeping bags and outdoor clothing.

The body of a goose. Adult geese range in weight from about $3\frac{1}{4}$ pounds to $8\frac{3}{4}$ pounds (1.5 kilograms to 4.0 kilograms). Feathers cover most of the body of a goose, except for the legs and feet. The largest feathers

are the long, stiff *flight feathers* of the wings and tail. The goose has a thick coat of down underneath its outer feathers. Scales cover the goose's legs. The four clawed toes on each foot are connected by flaps of skin.

The goose has eyes on the sides of its head, and must turn its head to see objects in front of it clearly. The inner surface of the goose's bill is very sensitive, enabling the goose to find its food by touch as well as sight. Geese have a long *esophagus* (tube leading to the stomach), but the rest of their internal organs are similar to those of other birds. The *uropygial gland,* at the base of the tail, produces an oily substance the goose uses to *preen* (smooth) and waterproof its feathers.

Kinds of geese. The *Canada goose* is one of the most common wild geese of North America. It has a brownish body with gray underparts and a black head, bill, and neck. A white band stretches across its throat and cheeks. During the summer, Canada geese nest throughout Canada and Alaska. They spend the winter as far south as northern Florida and northern Mexico.

The graylag goose has grayish-brown feathers, an orange bill, and pink legs and feet. It nests in Iceland and throughout northern Europe and northern Asia. Its wintering grounds stretch across southern Europe and southern Asia. The swan goose has its nesting grounds in northeastern Asia. Its winter range extends south to Korea, Japan, and China. The swan goose is brown, with a black bill and orange legs. Other wild geese include the *snow goose* and the saltwater *brant.*

Breeders have developed many varieties of domestic geese. The *Embden* is a graceful white goose with a rounded breast. The *Toulouse* is a stocky gray bird. It has a flap of skin, called a *dewlap,* that hangs beneath its jaw. The *Chinese goose* and the *African goose* both

WORLD BOOK illustration by Trevor Boyer, Linden Artists Ltd.

Wild geese live chiefly in Asia, Europe, and North America. There are more than 40 species. Three of the best-known species of North American wild geese are shown above.

WORLD BOOK illustration by Trevor Boyer, Linden Artists Ltd.

Domestic geese are raised on farms, particularly in Europe and Asia. Three common types are shown above.

have a large knob on the bill. Other domestic geese include the *Sebastopol* and the *American buff*.

The life of a wild goose. Wild geese feed chiefly on water plants, grasses, corn, and wheat. During fall migrations, they may hunt for food in cropland stubble. Migrating geese fly in large groups, often in a V-shaped formation. Some naturalists believe geese use this formation because air currents created by the birds in front make flying easier for the rest of the birds. Others believe that the V-shaped formation enables the geese to follow one leader, helping them to stay together.

Geese arrive at their northern nesting grounds in early spring. Young adult geese select mates at this time, and will stay with the same mate for life. The mating pair chooses a nesting site on the ground, away from the rest of the flock. The female then fashions a nest from twigs, grass, weeds, and moss, and lines the nest with down. The female may lay several eggs, not more than one a day. She stays on the nest almost continuously, frequently turning the eggs with her bill. While the female tends the eggs, the male defends the site.

The eggs generally hatch in 28 to 32 days. The *goslings* (young geese) are covered with fine, fluffy down. They are able to hunt for food as soon as they hatch, but must be protected from the cold for at least the first few days. Goslings learn to swim a few days after hatching. They grow rapidly during the summer and develop sturdy feathers for flying. They begin to fly after about two months. Young geese stay with their parents for at least a year. As fall approaches, the adult geese shed their feathers and grow a new set. The geese gather into large groups to feed and fatten themselves in preparation for the migration to warmer wintering grounds.

Geese have many natural enemies, including foxes, wolves, and coyotes. Small mammals and gulls and

other sea birds may steal goose eggs and attack goslings. Geese defend themselves by hissing and biting, and by striking with their wings. They have long lives and sometimes reach over 30 years of age in captivity.

Raising geese. Goose farming is common in Europe and Asia. Many geese are also raised on large farms in Canada and the United States. Most geese are raised outdoors in pens or in fenced fields where they can graze. Goose farmers use special poultry feed to promote rapid growth. The feed consists of such ingredients as corn or another grain, soybean meal, meat by-products, vitamins, and minerals. Geese are slaughtered for meat when they are several months old. In Europe, a delicately flavored pastelike food called *pâté de foie gras* is made from the livers of specially fattened geese. A large, extra fatty liver is produced by forcing the goose to eat more food than it ordinarily would. This feeding practice is illegal in the United States.

Scientific classification. Geese are in the class Aves. They belong to the family Anatidae. The Canada goose is *Branta canadensis*. The graylag goose is *Anser anser*. The swan goose is *A. cygnoides*.   Richard E. Austic

See also **Bird; Brant; Canada goose; Feather; Swan.**

Gooseberry is an oval, tart fruit or berry that is closely related to the currant. Gooseberries are commonly used in jams, jellies, preserves, and pies. The fruit may be white, yellow, green, or red, and may have a prickly, hairy, or smooth surface. The gooseberry shrub grows in Europe and North America. In the United States, it grows chiefly in the Great Lakes region and the Pacific Northwest. Gooseberry shrubs grow well in light shade in cool, moist regions. The shrubs can be grown from cuttings. They grow best in soil that drains excess moisture well and is rich in *nutrients* (nourishing substances). Shrubs should be planted 4 to 5 feet (1.2 to 1.5 meters) apart in rows. The rows may be 8 feet (2.4 meters) apart. Gooseberry shrubs are host plants for *white pine blister rust fungus,* a disease harmful to white pine trees. Thus, they should not be planted close to white pines. See also **Currant; Saxifrage.**

WORLD BOOK illustration by Stuart Lafford, Linden Artists Ltd.

Gooseberries

Scientific classification. Gooseberries belong to the saxifrage family, Saxifragaceae. The scientific name for the American gooseberry is *Ribes hirtellum*. The European is *R. grossularia*.
          Max E. Austin

G.O.P. See Republican Party.

Gopher is a small mammal that lives in long, underground tunnels. Gophers dig the tunnels with the large claws of the front feet, and with their front teeth. They move slowly and spend most of their time alone in the dark tunnels, which may be as long as 800 feet (240 meters). They usually keep other gophers from entering the tunnels, except in the breeding season.

Gophers live in all regions of North America, except the far north and the east. They are also called *pocket gophers* because they have fur-lined pouches on the

© Tom McHugh, Photo Researchers
The pocket gopher is native to North America.

outsides of their cheeks. Pocket gophers grow about 10 inches (25 centimeters) long. They have short legs, a broad, blunt head, small ears and eyes, and a short tail. The nearly hairless tail is *tactile*—that is, it serves as an organ of touch. Gophers feel their way with the tail when they back up in a tunnel. Gophers vary in color from reddish-brown to slate gray. They eat buds, farm vegetables, grass, nuts, and roots. They carry food in their cheek pouches. Their digging breaks up tightly packed soil and thus can help promote the growth of plants. Gophers are rodents and belong to the same order as beavers, mice, and squirrels.   James L. Patton

Scientific classification. Pocket gophers are in the pocket gopher family, Geomyidae.

Gorbachev, *gawr buh CHAWF,* **Mikhail Sergeye-vich,** *mih KYL suhr GAY uh vihch* (1931-   ), was the leader of the Soviet Union from 1985 to 1991. He gained worldwide fame for his efforts to make changes in his country and its rela-
tions with other nations. In 1990, Gorbachev received the Nobel Peace Prize for his contributions to world peace.

On Aug. 19, 1991, sever-
al conservative Soviet Communist officials tried to overthrow Gorbachev as president of the Soviet Union. The coup quickly collapsed in the face of widespread opposition, and Gorbachev retained his leadership, although his government was weakened by the attempt. Soon afterward, most of the 15 republics that made up the Soviet Union declared independence but indicated their will-
ingness to become part of a loose confederation of for-
mer Soviet republics. Three republics—Estonia, Latvia, and Lithuania—became independent nations.

Gorbachev tried to prevent the complete breakup of the Soviet Union. However, on Dec. 8, 1991, the republics of Russia, Ukraine, and Byelorussia broke away completely from the Soviet Union and formed the Commonwealth of Independent States. They were soon

© R. Maiman, Sygma
Mikhail Gorbachev

joined by all the remaining republics except Georgia. On December 25, Gorbachev resigned as president, and the Soviet Union formally ceased to exist.

Domestic policies. Gorbachev became Soviet leader as the country's economy was beginning to decline. In 1985, he announced that the country was facing a major crisis and that drastic changes were needed. The most important job, he said, was to modernize the economy and make it more productive. He proposed changes to move from the Communist system—in which the government controls the economy—to a more decentral-
ized system with less government control.

Gorbachev also made many proposals to change the Soviet political system to make it and other parts of the social system more open and democratic. He called for a reduction in the power of the Communist Party—
which controlled the country—and increased power for elected bodies. His program of economic and political reform was called *perestroika* (restructuring). His call for more openness was known as *glasnost.*

Most of Gorbachev's most important reform proposals were approved in 1988 and 1990. But officials op-
posed to changes that might reduce their power and privileges tried to prevent the reforms from being car-
ried out. Other Soviet officials and citizens called for greater democracy than Gorbachev proposed. Also, in spite of Gorbachev's reforms, the country continued to face severe economic problems. Many Soviet citizens blamed Gorbachev for the hardships they faced.

Gorbachev's domestic reforms had influence outside the Soviet Union. Following the Soviet actions, people in other Eastern European Communist countries increased their demands for more freedom and for an end to rule by their Communist parties. In 1989, most of the Communist governments were overthrown and replaced by more democratic governments.

International policies. Gorbachev worked to im-
prove Soviet relations with the Western countries and to reduce tension and conflicts worldwide. In 1987, Gor-
bachev and President Ronald Reagan of the United States signed a treaty that called for the elimination of all intermediate-range nuclear missiles of the two nations. In July 1991, Gorbachev and President George Bush of the United States signed the Strategic Arms Reduction Treaty. This treaty was designed to reduce U.S. and Soviet long-range nuclear missiles and bombers by about a third. See **Strategic Arms Reduction Treaty.**

In 1988 and 1989, Gorbachev withdrew all Soviet mili-
tary forces from Afghanistan. Since 1979, Soviet troops had been fighting there to support an unpopular Communist government against Afghan rebels.

Early life and political rise and fall. Gorbachev was born on March 2, 1931, in the village of Privolnoye, near the city of Stavropol. His parents were peasant farmers. Gorbachev entered Moscow State University in 1950 and joined the Communist Party in 1952. He graduated in 1955 with a law degree and then began a career in the Communist Party organization in Stavropol.

Gorbachev rose through the ranks and became the head of the Stavropol regional Communist Party Com-
mittee in 1970. He attracted the attention of some of the top Soviet leaders, including Yuri Andropov. Gorbachev became a member of the Communist Party's Central Committee in 1971. In 1978, he was brought to Moscow

and made party secretary in charge of agriculture.

In 1980, Gorbachev became a full member of the Politburo, which was the Communist Party's chief policymaking body. Andropov became the Communist Party head in 1982. At that time, the head of the party was the most powerful Soviet leader. Andropov put Gorbachev in charge of the country's economic policy. Andropov died in 1984 and was followed briefly by Konstantin U. Chernenko as party leader. When Chernenko died in March 1985, Gorbachev was chosen party head.

In October 1988, Gorbachev also became chairman of the Presidium of the Supreme Soviet, which was then a largely ceremonial post. Under Gorbachev, the powers of the office were greatly strengthened. The post came to be called the chairmanship of the Supreme Soviet.

In March 1990, the Soviet Union created a new office of president of the U.S.S.R. Gorbachev was chosen for this office. The office replaced that of Communist Party head as the country's most powerful position. Gorbachev remained as party head. However, in 1991, following the failed coup, Gorbachev resigned from the Communist Party. Soon afterward, the Soviet parliament suspended Communist Party activities. In December, after the formation of the Commonwealth of Independent States, Gorbachev resigned as president and the Soviet Union ceased to exist. Gorbachev became the head of a political research group in Moscow and remained active in Russian politics.　　Stuart D. Goldman

See also **Communism** (The decline of Communism); **Union of Soviet Socialist Republics** (Gorbachev's reforms).

Gordian knot, *GAWR dee uhn,* in Greek mythology, was a skillfully tied knot. A Phrygian peasant named Gordius used it to tie the ox yoke to his chariot. According to the myth, Gordius became king of Phrygia because an oracle advised it. A legend said whoever could loosen the knot would rule Asia. Many tried and failed. Finally Alexander the Great cut it with his sword and claimed he had fulfilled the prophecy. The expression *cutting the Gordian knot* means solving a hard problem easily. Gordius was the father of Midas, whose touch turned everything to gold.　　Mary R. Lefkowitz

Gordimer, Nadine (1923-　　), a South African writer, won the 1991 Nobel Prize for literature, the first South African author to receive the award. Her novels and short stories portray the impact of South Africa's restrictive social policies upon individuals and their relationships with one another. She conveys her opposition to racial segregation and injustice in South Africa through precise characterization and irony. Gordimer's works express her conviction that the life of the individual cannot be separated from the problems of society.

Gordimer's first published works were collections of short stories, *Face to Face* (1949) and *The Soft Voice of the Serpent* (1952). Her first novel was *The Lying Days* (1953). Her other novels include *Occasion for Loving* (1963), *A Guest of Honor* (1970), *The Conservationist* (1974), *Burger's Daughter* (1979), *July's People* (1981), *A Sport of Nature* (1987), *My Son's Story* (1990), and *None to Accompany Me* (1994). Gordimer was born in Springs, a mining town near Johannesburg.　　Linda Wagner-Martin

Gordon, Charles George (1833-1885), a British soldier, was called Chinese Gordon and Gordon Pasha because of his distinguished service in China and Egypt.

Gordon was born at Woolwich and educated at the Royal Military Academy. He fought in the Crimean War (1853-1856). He took part in an expedition to China in 1860 and helped capture Beijing. He later won victories as commander of the Chinese who fought the Taiping rebels (see China [The Taiping rebellion]).

In 1873, the *khedive* (ruler) of Egypt made Gordon governor of southern Sudan. Gordon was governor general of the Sudan from 1877 to 1880, and spent the next four years in England. Britain then sent him to Sudan to help the khedive put down a revolt. He defended Khartoum against troops led by Muslim leader Muhammad Ahmed. Gordon held the city for 317 days but was killed two days before a British relief party came within sight of the city.　　Philip Dwight Jones

Gordon, Charles William (1860-1937), was a Canadian novelist and clergyman who wrote under the pen name of Ralph Connor. Gordon's most valued works are the series of novels he wrote about the eastern Ontario county of Glengarry, where he was born. *The Man from Glengarry* (1901) is the most notable work in the series. It combines dialect speech and accurate descriptions of local environment with a Christian vision of life. Gordon presented the title character, Ranald Macdonald, as the ideal Canadian hero. Gordon's other novels include *Black Rock* (1898) and *The Sky Pilot* (1899).

Gordon was ordained a Presbyterian minister in 1890 and became active in national church affairs. He helped form the United Church of Canada in 1925. His autobiography, *Postscript to Adventure,* was published in 1938, after his death.　　Sherrill E. Grace

Gordon, Jeff (1971-　　), is one of the most successful drivers in American automobile racing. In 1995, Gordon became the youngest driver to win the National Association for Stock Car Auto Racing (NASCAR) Winston Cup Championship during the modern era of the series, which began in 1972. Gordon won the Winston Cup series again in 1997 and 1998. He is the youngest NASCAR driver to win three driving championships. See **Automobile racing** (Stock car racing).

In 1998, Gordon won 13 NASCAR races, tying Richard Petty's 13 victories in 1975 for the most races won in a season during the modern era of this racing series. Gordon was the first NASCAR driver to win at least 10 races in three consecutive seasons. In 1998, Gordon won the Southern 500 race in Darlington, South Carolina, becoming the first driver in modern stock car history to win this superspeedway event four years in a row.

Jeffrey Michael Gordon was born in Vallejo, California. He was the United States Auto Club (USAC) midget car Rookie of the Year in 1989. Gordon won the midget national championship in 1990 and the USAC dirt track title in 1991.　　Sylvia Wilkinson

Gordon, John Campbell Hamilton-. See **Aberdeen and Temair, Marquess of.**

Gordon setter is a black-and-tan hunting dog that was well known as early as 1620. The dog was named for Alexander Gordon, a Scottish nobleman. It points with its nose to locate game. Gordon setters stand about 23 to 27 inches (58 to 69 centimeters) high and weigh from 45 to 80 pounds (20 to 36 kilograms). The dog has a long, flat coat with a slight wave. It has long hairs on its ears, legs, and tail. See also **Dog** (picture: Sporting dogs).

Critically reviewed by the American Kennel Club

Gore, Al (1948-   ),
served as vice president of
the United States from
1993 to 2001. He was the
Democratic nominee for
president of the United
States in 2000 but lost to
his Republican opponent,
Texas Governor George
W. Bush, in an extremely
close race. Although Gore
won more popular votes,
Bush won more votes in
the Electoral College (see
Election of 2000).

Democratic National Committee
Al Gore

Early life. Albert Gore, Jr., was born on March 31,
1948, in Washington, D.C. His father, Albert Gore, Sr.,
served in the U.S. House of Representatives and U.S.
Senate as a Democrat from Tennessee.

Gore graduated from Harvard University in 1969 with
a bachelor's degree in government. He opposed U.S. involvement in the Vietnam War but enlisted in the U.S.
Army in 1969 and served until 1971. He spent about six
months of his service as an Army journalist in Vietnam.

From 1971 to 1976, Gore was a reporter and editorial
writer for *The Tennessean,* a Nashville paper. He also
operated a small farm and worked as a real estate developer. He attended Vanderbilt University, where he studied at the Divinity School in 1971 and 1972 and in the
School of Law from 1974 to 1976.

In 1970, Gore married Mary Elizabeth (Tipper) Aitche-
son. The Gores had four children—Karenna, Kristin,
Sarah, and Albert III.

Political career. Gore was elected to the U.S. House
of Representatives in 1976. He won reelection in 1978,
1980, and 1982. In Congress, Gore gained a reputation as
a moderate liberal. He also became known as an expert
on nuclear arms control, public health, and the environment. Gore won election to the United States Senate in
1984 and was reelected in 1990.

In 1988, Gore campaigned for the Democratic presidential nomination. He did not win, but he received
widespread support in a number of Southern States.

In June 1992, Gore led a Senate delegation to the
United Nations Conference on Environment and Devel-
opment, also known as the Earth Summit, in Rio de
Janeiro, Brazil. He is the author of *Earth in the Balance:
Ecology and the Human Spirit* (1992).

In July 1992, the Democratic National Convention
nominated Arkansas Governor Bill Clinton for president.
At Clinton's request, the delegates nominated Gore for
vice president. In the November election, Clinton and
Gore defeated their Republican opponents, President
George H. W. Bush and Vice President Dan Quayle.

In 1996, Clinton and Gore were reelected. Their Republican foes were former Kansas Senator Robert Dole,
the presidential candidate, and former New York Representative Jack Kemp, the vice presidential candidate.

As vice president, Gore was President Clinton's closest adviser on most major issues. He played a leading
role in foreign affairs, trade policy, environmental protection, and efforts to improve U.S. communications
technology. In 1993, Gore became head of the National
Performance Review (now called the National Partner-

ship for Reinventing Government), a panel that recommends ways to increase the federal government's efficiency and reduce its costs.

In 1999, Gore began campaigning for the Democratic
presidential nomination for the 2000 election. By March
2000, victories in primary elections had given him
enough delegates to secure the nomination. In August,
at the Democratic National Convention in Los Angeles,
the delegates nominated Gore for president. At Gore's
request, they nominated Senator Joseph I. Lieberman of
Connecticut for vice president. Lieberman became the
first Jewish vice presidential candidate of a major American political party. The Republicans nominated George
W. Bush, governor of Texas, for president and Richard B.
Cheney, a former congressman and U.S. secretary of defense, for vice president.

In his campaign, Gore emphasized his extensive experience, and he pledged to maintain the nation's economic prosperity. In the election of 2000, Bush and Cheney
defeated Gore and Lieberman.   Bill Turque

Gorée, *gaw RAY,* is an African island off the coast of
Dakar, Senegal, that played a key role in the Atlantic
slave trade. In the early years of this slave trade, beginning in the 1400's, the principal source of African slaves
was Senegambia, the mainland area near Gorée. Blacks
captured in Africa were brought to Gorée and other
points along the coast for examination, storage, and
shipment overseas as slaves. Many of the slaves were
sent to work on sugar plantations on Mediterranean islands and in Latin America.

By the late 1600's, regions farther south in Africa had
overtaken Senegambia as the most important sources
for slaves. But Gorée remained an important holding site
for captives before their export to the Americas. Trading
companies based on Gorée shifted their focus to dealing in material goods after many countries abolished the
slave trade in the 1800's.

Today, the Senegalese government maintains Gorée
as a historic landmark. A building called the *House of
Slaves* with its *Door of No Return* bears tribute to the
millions of Africans sold into slavery.   Zayde G. Antrim

Gorgas, *GAWR guhs,* **William Crawford** (1854-
1920), an American physician, became known as the
world's leading public health expert. He helped make
possible construction of the Panama Canal by destroying mosquitoes that carried yellow fever and malaria.

In 1880, Gorgas was appointed first lieutenant in the
medical department of the United States Army. In 1898,
he became chief sanitary officer in Havana, Cuba, and
worked to improve health conditions there. However, an
epidemic of yellow fever broke out in 1900. In 1901, a
commission headed by Walter Reed, an Army doctor,
proved that certain mosquitoes transmitted the disease
(see **Reed, Walter**). Gorgas ordered the elimination of
the mosquitoes' breeding areas and quickly rid Havana
of yellow fever. In 1904, Gorgas became chief sanitary
officer of the Panama Canal Commission. He began to
control yellow fever and malaria in the Canal Zone by
eliminating mosquitoes there.

In 1914, Gorgas became surgeon general of the U.S.
Army. Gorgas was born in Toulminville, Alabama. He
graduated from Bellevue Hospital Medical College in
New York City.   Dale C. Smith

See also **Panama Canal** (Victory over disease).

Gorgons, *GAWR guhnz,* were three sisters in Greek mythology. Most ancient sources describe them as monstrous creatures whose ugliness could turn a viewer to stone. Their hair was a mass of living snakes. They had bronze hands and golden wings. The Greeks carved images of a Gorgon's head on their armor to terrify their enemies in battle and used images of a Gorgon head as a charm to protect them from evil spells.

According to most accounts, the Gorgons were the daughters of Phorcys, a sea god, and his sister Ceto, a sea monster. The Gorgons were named *Stheno,* meaning *strength; Euryale,* meaning *wide-leaping;* and *Medusa,* meaning *queen* or *ruler.* Stheno and Euryale were immortal, but Medusa was slain by the hero Perseus with the aid of the goddess Athena.   Nancy Felson

See also **Medusa; Pegasus; Perseus.**

Gorham, Nathaniel (1738-1796), was a Massachusetts signer of the Constitution of the United States. He favored a strong central government at the Constitutional Convention in 1787. Gorham later helped win ratification of the U.S. Constitution by Massachusetts.

Gorham was born in Charlestown, Massachusetts. He became a prosperous merchant there and took an active part in public affairs. In 1780, Gorham was a member of the Massachusetts Senate. He served in the state House of Representatives from 1781 to 1787 and held the position of speaker in 1781, 1782, and 1785. Gorham represented his state in the Congress of the Confederation almost continuously from 1782 to 1787. He served as president of the congress in 1786 and 1787. From 1785 to 1796, Gorham served as a judge of the Middlesex County Court of Common Pleas. He died in poverty due to unsuccessful investments.   William Morgan Fowler, Jr.

Gorilla is the largest of the apes. It has huge shoulders, a broad chest, long arms, and short legs. A large male gorilla in the wild may weigh 450 pounds (204 kilograms). Standing up on its legs, it may be 6 feet (1.8 meters) tall. Females usually weigh about 200 pounds (91

Where gorillas live

The yellow areas on the map below show the regions of the world inhabited by gorillas. Most gorillas live in central Africa.

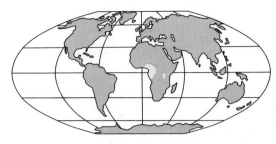

kilograms) and are shorter than males. Gorillas, chimpanzees, and bonobos make up the group known as African apes, the closest relatives of humans. There are three kinds of gorillas: the *western lowland gorilla,* the *eastern lowland gorilla,* and the *mountain gorilla.*

A gorilla looks fierce. It has a shiny black face, large canine teeth, and a thick ridge of bone above its eyes. Black or brownish hair covers all of its body, except its face, chest, palms, and the soles of its feet. The adult male gorilla has a hairy crest on its head and a grayish back. When a gorilla is excited or wants to drive off intruders, it stands up and slaps its hands against its chest. This produces a loud, threatening sound.

Actually, a gorilla is not as fierce as it looks. It will not

Facts in brief

Gestation period: From 8 to 9 months.
Number of newborn: 1.
Length of life: Up to 50 years in captivity; in the wild, unknown.
Where found: East-central and west Africa.
Scientific classification: Gorillas belong to the great ape family, Pongidae. They are genus *Gorilla,* species *G. gorilla.*

San Diego Zoo

The gorilla is the largest ape. Powerful male gorillas, such as the one shown here, may weigh as much as 450 pounds (204 kilograms). Gorillas can walk a few steps using only their legs. But they generally use their knuckles to support the upper part of their body.

The skeleton of a gorilla

WORLD BOOK illustration by John D. Dawson

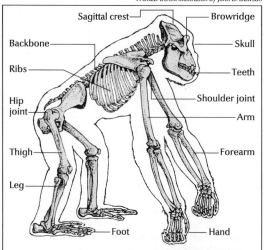

Sagittal crest — Browridge
Backbone — Skull
Ribs — Teeth
Hip joint — Shoulder joint
Thigh — Arm
Leg — Forearm
Foot — Hand

Hand

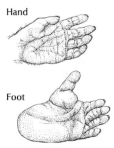

Foot

A gorilla's foot has a "thumb" and resembles the hand. Such feet help the gorilla climb trees.

Ben McCall, FPG

A gorilla's head has a ridge of bone called a *sagittal crest* on top of the skull. A *browridge* lies above the eyes.

hurt a human being unless it is threatened or attacked. Gorillas are shy, friendly animals that seem to need companionship and attention. Gorillas are not as outgoing as chimpanzees, and are less eager to do tricks.

A gorilla usually walks on all fours, with its feet flat on the ground and its upper body supported on the knuckles of its hands. African apes are the only animals that walk exactly this way. A gorilla often stands up on its legs, but it travels only a few steps in this position. It sometimes climbs into trees to sit or eat.

Gorillas are quiet animals, though they can make about 20 different sounds. Angry males produce a startling roar. Babies whimper when distressed and scream if frightened. Adults grumble softly when contented. Gorillas have no enemies except human beings. People hunt gorillas for food and body parts, capture them for zoos, and cut down their forests. As a result, gorillas have become rare, and their survival is threatened. Today, fewer than 1,000 mountain gorillas remain in the wild, and the numbers of western lowland gorillas and eastern lowland gorillas are decreasing.

The gorilla's home lies in the rain forests of Africa near the equator. The western lowland gorilla lives in the forests of western Africa, from Nigeria south to the Congo River. The eastern lowland gorilla lives in the lowlands of eastern Congo (Kinshasa). The mountain gorilla inhabits upland regions in Rwanda, the Virunga Mountains of Congo (Kinshasa), and mountain forests in Uganda. It lives at altitudes of up to 13,000 feet (3,960 meters), where the temperature is freezing at night.

Gorillas lead a peaceful life, although males occasionally may kill infants of other males. The apes travel through forests in groups of from 2 to 34. A group may be made up of one or more males, two or more females, and several young gorillas. An adult male always leads the group. He makes all the decisions, such as where to go and when to rest. This male also protects the group against danger. The extra males sometimes leave the group and wander alone. A new group forms when one or more females leave the group of their birth to join another group or a lone male.

Each group wanders around in its own home range, which is from 2 to 15 square miles (5 to 39 square kilometers). Gorillas never spend more than one night in the same place. Several groups may live in the same area of a forest, but they usually avoid one another.

The gorilla's day usually begins about an hour after sunrise. In the early morning, the apes feed on leaves, buds, barks, and fruits. Mountain gorillas eat herbs near the ground. Western lowland gorillas climb more to find ripe fruit. Only gorillas living in captivity eat meat.

From mid-morning to mid-afternoon is nap time. The adults rest while the younger apes wrestle with each other, play games, and swing on vines. After the rest period, all the gorillas eat again. Every evening just before dark, the gorillas build a simple nest where they sleep at night. They break or bend branches to make a crude platform, either on the ground or in trees.

Life cycle. The gorilla's pregnancy lasts for from 8 to 9 months. The newborn gorilla is helpless. It weighs from 3 to 5 pounds (1.4 to 2.3 kilograms) at birth and remains with its mother for about $3\frac{1}{2}$ years. At first, the mother carries her baby by holding it to her chest. After about three months, the baby is strong enough to hold on by itself. It is able to crawl by the age of 3 months and walk by 5 months. But it usually rides "piggyback" until it is almost 3 years old. Then it travels by itself.

Females usually mate when about 8 years old. Males reach full adulthood at about 12 years old. No one knows how long wild gorillas live. Gorillas in captivity have lived up to 50 years. Most wild gorillas probably die younger. They suffer from diseases, especially those caused by parasites in the blood and intestines. They also may suffer from respiratory disorders and colds.

Gorillas in captivity. The gorilla was not discovered until 1847. In 1911, the first gorilla was exhibited in a U.S. zoo. In 1956, Colo, the first gorilla born in captivity, was born in a zoo in Columbus, Ohio.

Gorillas rank among the most intelligent animals. In 1972, researchers at Stanford University began to teach sign language to a female gorilla named Koko. Koko learned several hundred signs and used them to communicate.   Randall L. Susman

See also **Ape; Chimpanzee; Fossey, Dian.**

Additional resources

Freedman, Suzanne. *Dian Fossey: Befriending the Gorillas*. Raintree Steck-Vaughn, 1997.

Rock, Maxine. *Kishina: A True Story of Gorilla Survival.* Peachtree, 1996. Younger readers.

Gorki. See Nizhniy Novgorod.

Gorki, *GAWR kee,* **Maxim,** *mahk SEEM* (1868-1936), was a Russian novelist, playwright, and short-story writer. He vividly portrayed the poverty of peasants and workers, as well as the decay and narrow-mindedness of the middle class before the Communist Revolution of 1917. *The Lower Depths* (1902), Gorki's most popular play, describes the miserable lives of the inhabitants of a cheap boarding house. His most famous novel, *The Mother* (1907), tells the story of an old peasant woman who is converted to the revolutionary cause.

Gorki was born in Nizhny Novgorod, later renamed Gorki in his honor. His real name was Alexey Maximovich Peshkov. He took the pen name *Gorki,* a Russian word meaning *bitter,* to express his criticism of the Russian political and social order. Gorki had only a few months of schooling and was largely self-educated. He roamed throughout Russia, going from job to job. He described his wanderings masterfully in his three-volume autobiography—*Childhood* (1913), *In the World* (1916), and *My Universities* (1923). During his travels, he wrote stories based on his experiences and the people he met. In the early 1930's, he helped institute the Soviet doctrine of literature and art called *socialist realism.*

Gorki died unexpectedly while undergoing medical treatment. The Soviet authorities accused his doctors of poisoning him. But the true circumstances of his death remain unknown.   Anna Lisa Crone

See **Russian literature** (Late realism; The period of socialist realism; picture).

Gorky, *GAWR kee,* **Arshile,** *AHR sheel* (1904-1948), an American artist, was a leading member of the abstract expressionist movement. He developed an individual style in which living things, such as blades of grass and human figures, are the basis for imaginative abstract compositions. His linear details show his skill as a draftsman. Gorky was also a master in the use of color.

Gorky applied paint thinly in his works to preserve each color's radiance. Hints of the human body, such as heart and bone shapes, are combined with elements from nature in his paintings. These shapes and elements prompted critics to describe his style as "biomorphic." Gorky has been called a surrealist, but his artistic style eludes precise definition. See **Abstract expressionism.**

Gorky was born in what is now eastern Turkey. His real name was Vosdanig Manoog Adoian. Gorky moved to the United States in 1920 and later settled in New York City. He committed suicide in 1948.   Dore Ashton

Gorrie, John. See Air conditioning (History); **Food preservation** (Modern food preservation).

Goshawk. See Hawk (North American hawks).

Gosnold, *GAHZ nohld,* **Bartholomew** (? -1607), was an English navigator. In 1602, he explored much of the coast of New England and was the first European known to reach Martha's Vineyard (see **Martha's Vineyard**). In 1606, Gosnold helped secure grants of American charters for the Virginia companies of London and Plymouth. He belonged to the first governing council of the English colony in Jamestown, Virginia, in 1607.   James Axtell

Gospels are the first four books of the New Testament. They are the primary source of information about the life and teachings of Jesus Christ. The Gospels are named for the four men who are said to have written them: Matthew, Mark, Luke, and John. But many scholars today doubt that these men actually wrote the Gospels. The word *gospel* comes from *godspell,* an Old English word meaning *good news.*

None of the Gospels gives a complete story of the life of Jesus. Each is a collection of His acts and words, written as an expression of the faith of a particular Christian community. All four Gospels describe the teachings and miracles of Jesus's ministry. They also describe Jesus's betrayal, arrest, Crucifixion, and Resurrection.

The Gospels of Matthew, Mark, and Luke agree on additional details of Jesus's career. These Gospels are so similar that they can be arranged side by side in parallel columns. Such an arrangement is called a *synopsis.* Matthew, Mark, and Luke are called *Synoptic Gospels* because they can be arranged in this way. Most scholars explain the similarity of the Synoptic Gospels by assuming that Mark was the first Gospel written, and was used as a source for Matthew and Luke. Scholars also suggest that Matthew and Luke used a second source, called Q. But no copy has been found.   Terrance D. Callan

See also **Bible** (Books of the New Testament); **Beatitudes; Lord's Prayer.**

Göteborg, *YUH tuh BAWR yuh,* also called Gothenburg, *GAHTH uhn buhrg* (pop. 437,313), is Sweden's second largest city and its most important port. It lies on the southwestern coast of Sweden at the mouth of the Göta River. The Göta Canal links the city with Stockholm, 150 miles (241 kilometers) northeast. For Göteborg's location, see **Sweden** (political map).

Göteborg is a center of commerce and transportation, with direct ferry links to Denmark, Norway, and Germany. Its main industries include food processing and the manufacture of motor vehicles and textiles. The city is the home of Göteborg University. Major attractions include the Göteborg Maritime Museum and Liseberg, an amusement park. Avenyn (Avenue) is a popular street of shops and restaurants. In front of the art museum at Avenyn's south end stands a fountain and statue of the Greek god Poseidon, created by Swedish-born sculptor Carl Milles. Göteborg was founded by King Gustavus Adolphus in 1619.   M. Donald Hancock

The Museum of Modern Art, A. Conger Goodyear Fund, New York City

Arshile Gorky's *Agony* shows the artist's imaginative use of line in his compositions. Gorky painted this picture in 1947.

Gothenburg. See Göteborg.

Gothic art is the name given to the art of the later Middle Ages, especially from the mid-1100's to about 1400. The term *Gothic* originated with Italian Renaissance scholars called humanists. It refers to the Germanic Goths who invaded Italy in the A.D. 400's. Humanists considered medieval art so barbaric that they thought it was created by the uncivilized Goths.

Early Gothic architecture. Gothic art is one of the few artistic styles whose precise date of creation is known. The style was first introduced at the Abbey of St.-Denis, the burial place of French kings, just north of Paris. Abbot Suger supervised the rebuilding of the west and east ends of the church in this new style, which were completed in 1144. The Gothic style was an immediate success, and by about 1250, it had spread through Europe. During the 1200's and the 1300's, many regions in Europe developed distinctive variations.

The Gothic style is associated with the age of cathedral construction in northern Europe. The style often is identified with such constructional devices as pointed arches, ribbed vaults, and flying buttresses (see **Architecture** [Architectural terms]). But both pointed arches and ribbed vaults were present in the Romanesque style, which thrived during the 1000's and the early 1100's. The difference between Romanesque and Gothic styles is the way in which space is conceived. Space in a Romanesque building is achieved by adding bays, unit by unit, to create the total space. But a Gothic building is conceived as a total space that is subdivided into units.

Early Gothic architecture was noted for its huge size and height. These two elements were first combined in the design of the Cathedral of Notre Dame in Paris. The flying buttress, introduced about 1175, reduced the amount of solid wall space needed for support, allowing the walls to be opened with stained glass windows.

High Gothic architecture. A style called High Gothic was created at the end of the 1100's. Chartres Cathedral and the cathedrals at Bourges, Reims, and Amiens in France represent some of the finest examples of the High Gothic style. All are significant for their enormous height. For pictures of these cathedrals, see **Amiens; Cathedral; Chartres;** and **Reims**.

By the mid-1200's, the taste for gigantic structure had passed. At the same time, the skill of designers and the technical ability of carvers led to a new elegance and a desire for more elaborate decorations, particularly in window tracery (see **Tracery**).

A new style known as *Rayonnant* also became popular during the High Gothic period. It was named for the radiating geometric patterns of large rose windows. The most brilliant example of the style is the Ste.-Chapelle in Paris, which was built by King Louis IX. Rayonnant helped spread the Gothic style across Europe partly because many kings wanted to imitate the style of Louis IX.

Gothic architecture in England began with the rebuilding of the choir of Canterbury Cathedral in 1174 by a French builder, William of Sens. The English developed a distinctive, thoroughly native style, first in St. Hugh's choir at Lincoln Cathedral and then in cathedrals at Wells and Salisbury. The *Decorated* style, the English version of Rayonnant and characterized by flowing curves, appeared in cathedrals at York, Exeter, and Wells. This style continued well into the 1300's. It pre-

Art Resource

Gothic architecture produced many huge cathedrals throughout western Europe. Inside Amiens Cathedral in France, *shown here*, architects arranged arches, pillars, and stained-glass windows to achieve a feeling of harmony and soaring height.

ceded and coexisted with another English variation, called the *Perpendicular*, named for the complex vertical tracery patterns on walls and vaults. An example can be found in King's College Chapel at Cambridge.

Gothic sculpture and painting. Gothic sculpture first appeared at St.-Denis and at Chartres. Romanesque sculpture was vigorous, dramatic, and abstract. In comparison, Gothic sculpture was calmer, grander, and more humane. Most of the early Gothic sculpture was created to decorate cathedral entrances. Some of the finest examples decorate the west facade of Chartres Cathedral. They probably portray figures from the Old Testament. Later sculptors created a freer style, inspired by ancient Greek and Roman art. This can be seen in the figures on the west facade of the cathedral at Reims.

The late Gothic of the 1400's is best known for the development of oil painting in Flanders. Jan van Eyck, Robert Campin, and Rogier van der Weyden perfected this new technique.   William W. Clark

See also **Architecture** (Gothic architecture); **Cathedral; Painting** (Medieval painting); **Sculpture** (Medieval sculpture); **Stained glass**.

Additional resources

Camille, Michael. *Gothic Art*. Abrams, 1996.
Toman, Rolf, ed. *The Art of Gothic: Architecture, Sculpture, Painting*. Konemann, 1999.

Gothic novel was a type of fiction that became popular in England during the late 1700's and early 1800's.

The plots of Gothic novels included mysterious and supernatural events intended to frighten the reader. The stories were called *Gothic* because most of them took place in gloomy, medieval castles built in the Gothic style of architecture. Such buildings had many secret passageways, dungeons, and towers that provided ideal settings for strange happenings. Most Gothic novels were set in Italy or Spain because those countries seemed remote and mysterious to the English.

The first Gothic novel was *The Castle of Otranto* (1754) by Horace Walpole. The best-known Gothic novels include *The Mysteries of Udolpho* (1794) and *The Italian* (1797) by Ann Radcliffe, *The Monk* (1796) by Matthew G. Lewis, and *Melmouth the Wanderer* (1820) by Charles Maturin. In *Northanger Abbey* (1818), Jane Austen satirized Gothic novels and their effect on readers.

In the 1800's, elements of the Gothic novel appeared in other forms of fiction that shared its interest in the terrible and the exotic. Such novels as *Frankenstein* (1818) by Mary Shelley and *Wuthering Heights* (1847) by Emily Brontë reflect a relationship with earlier Gothic novels, as do many historical romances of the time. The Gothic novel also influenced such American writers as Nathaniel Hawthorne, Herman Melville, and Edgar Allan Poe. In the 1900's, romantic adventure stories were called Gothic novels, but they placed more emphasis on love than on terror.   Richard J. Dunn

Goths, *gahths,* were a confederation of Germanic tribes who attacked the Roman Empire beginning in the

Illumination (about 1230) by an unknown French painter; the Pierpont Morgan Library, New York City

Gothic painting is best known for beautifully colored illuminated manuscripts. This illumination from a Bible shows King Louis IX of France and his mother, Blanche of Castile.

A.D. 200's. The Goths, along with other Germanic peoples, helped destroy the West Roman Empire in the A.D. 400's. They were the first Germanic peoples to become Christians.

The Goths probably originated in what is now southern Scandinavia. They migrated to what is now Poland and to the region north of the Black Sea. During the A.D. 200's, they invaded eastern provinces of the Roman Empire. In the 300's, the Goths split into two groups. The Goths north of the lower Danube became the Visigoths, and those north of the Black Sea became the Ostrogoths.

After A.D. 370, both Gothic kingdoms were attacked by the nomadic Huns of western Asia. The Ostrogoths were overrun and absorbed into the Hun empire. Many Visigoths fled to the Roman province of Thrace but soon revolted against the Roman commanders. They destroyed a Roman army at Adrianople (now Edirne, Turkey) in 378 and killed the Roman emperor Valens. Under their king, Alaric, the Visigoths invaded Italy during the early 400's and looted Rome in 410 (see **Alaric**). Alaric's successors took the people into Gaul (now France) and Spain. In 507, the Visigoths in France were defeated by the Franks. Most of the Visigoths in France then withdrew to Spain. The Visigoths' Spanish kingdom was destroyed after the Arab invasion of 711.

The Ostrogoths gained their freedom from Hun control soon after the death in 453 of Attila, the powerful king of the Huns. Under their king Theodoric, the Ostrogoths invaded northern Italy in 489 and took control of the region. They remained in Italy until they were overthrown by armies of the Byzantine (East Roman) Empire during the mid-500's.   Malcolm Todd

Gottfried von Strassburg (1170?-1220?) was a medieval German poet. His unfinished poem *Tristan and Isolde* is a masterpiece of German literature. In the poem, Tristan travels to Ireland to escort Isolde back to England where she will marry his uncle, King Mark. On the journey, Tristan and Isolde drink a magic love potion by mistake and fall in love. Isolde marries the king but continues her love affair with Tristan. The affair ends with the death of the lovers.

In describing the tragic results of their passion, Gottfried gave sensitive psychological portraits of the lovers. While he did not excuse the lovers' guilt, he exposed the hypocrisy of their enemies. Richard Wagner based his opera *Tristan and Isolde* on the poem.

Little is known about Gottfried except that he was a learned clergyman. He adapted his poem from a French tale by Thomas of Brittany.   James F. Poag

Gottlieb, *GAHT leeb,* **Adolph** (1903-1974), was a leading American Abstract Expressionist artist. He became especially well known for a series of paintings that he called "bursts." Most of these paintings feature a moonlike or sunlike globe above a jagged, harsh-looking mass of bold paint strokes. Gottlieb varied the colors in his series of "bursts," but the content of the paintings remained much the same.

Gottlieb was born in New York City. During the 1930's, he painted American scenes that incorporated designs based on American Indian *petroglyphs* (rock carvings) and *totems* (emblems). By the 1940's, Gottlieb had turned to painting what he called "pictographs." These paintings contained images that were sometimes identifiable but

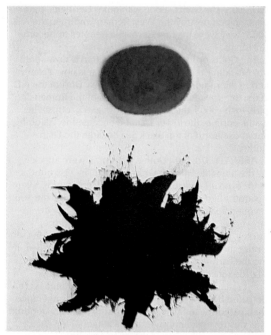

Metropolitan Museum of Art, New York City, George A. Hearn Fund, 1959

Adolph Gottlieb's *Thrust,* completed in 1959, is one of his "burst" paintings. It shows a sunlike form over a jagged shape.

not necessarily related in a logical way. Gottlieb began to paint his series of "bursts" in 1957.   Dore Ashton

Gottschalk, *GAHTS chawk,* **Louis Moreau,** *moh ROH* (1829-1869), was the first internationally famous American musical artist. He was best known during his lifetime as a pianist. Since his death, his reputation has grown as a composer, especially of piano pieces.

Gottschalk toured widely as a concert pianist. He was probably the first North American pianist to perform in Central and South America. He used elements of Latin American, Spanish, and Caribbean music in his compositions. Gottschalk was born in New Orleans, and many of his works reflect the Creole and black folk music heritage of that city. Particularly notable is his "Louisiana Trilogy" for piano—*Bamboula, Le bananier,* and *La savane* (all composed during the 1840's). A number of his piano compositions have distinctly American themes, such as *The Banjo* (about 1855), *Columbia* (1859), *The Union* (1862), and *The Battle Cry of Freedom* (1863). He also wrote such popular sentimental piano pieces as *The Last Hope* (1854).   Richard Jackson

Goudy, *GOW dee,* **Frederic William** (1865-1947), was an American type designer and printer. He created more than 100 designs for type faces, including Village, Goudy Old Style, and Forum.

Goudy was born in Bloomington, Illinois. He became a full-time designer of letters and books in 1899. In 1903, he and his wife set up the Village Press, a printing company. A fire in 1908 forced the press to close for two years. After the fire, Goudy concentrated on the design, production, and selling of type. He taught lettering at the Art Students League in New York City from 1916 to 1924, and graphic arts at New York University from 1927 to 1929.   Peter M. VanWingen

Gould, *goold,* **Glenn** (1932-1982), was a famous Canadian pianist. His performances emphasized compositions from the 1700's, early 1800's, and 1900's. Gould's best-known recordings were of Johann Sebastian Bach's *Goldberg Variations.* He also wrote about music.

Glenn Herbert Gould was born in Toronto. His mother began teaching him to play the piano at the age of 3. At 10, he entered the Royal Conservatory of Music of Toronto. In 1947, he made his debut with the Toronto Symphony. Gould made his debut in the United States in 1955, and he performed on tour in Europe in 1957. He was probably the first North American pianist to tour the Soviet Union. At the age of 32, he retired from the concert stage to concentrate on recordings. He often performed on radio and TV.   Lydia Hailparn Ledeen

Gould, *goold,* **Jay** (1836-1892), was an American financier who became the leading railroad owner of the late 1800's. By 1882, he controlled more than 15,000 miles (24,000 kilometers) of track in the United States. Gould acquired his fortune and power largely through the use of questionable business practices.

Gould was born near Roxbury in Delaware County, New York. He began his railroad career in the early 1860's, by purchasing stock in small rail lines. Gould soon gained control of the Rutland & Washington Railroad and combined it with the Rensselaer & Saratoga Railroad. He later sold these two lines at a profit. In 1867, Gould joined two of his associates, James Fisk and Daniel Drew, on the board of directors of the Erie Railroad. In 1868, they illegally issued new stock to prevent financier Cornelius Vanderbilt from taking over the line. Gould made millions by manipulating Erie stock. But lawsuits forced him to give up control of the Erie in 1872 and to return several million dollars to the railroad.

In 1869, Gould conspired with Fisk and others to gain control of the gold market by buying up all the gold available in New York City. Their actions caused the Black Friday panic of September 24, in which thousands of investors suffered losses. Gould, however, made a fortune on his gold transactions. See **Black Friday.**

In 1873, Gould began to buy shares in Western railroads. Among the Western railroads he eventually owned or controlled were the Denver Pacific, Kansas Pacific, Missouri Pacific, and Union Pacific. During the 1880's, Gould gained control of the Western Union Telegraph Company and of several elevated railroads in New York City.   Robert Sobel

Gould, *goold,* **Morton** (1913-1996), was an American composer. Much of his music concerns American subjects and emphasizes blues, jazz, and folk music. These elements appear in his orchestral composition *Stringmusic* (1994). Gould won the 1995 Pulitzer Prize for this work.

Gould included elements of jazz in *Chorale and Fugue in Jazz* (1934), his first large work for orchestra, and in *Boogie-Woogie Étude* (1943), a piano composition. His interest in American themes appears in several works, including *Spirituals for String Choir and Orchestra* (1941), *American Salute* (1943), and the ballet score *Fall River Legend* (1947). Gould based *American Salute* on the folk song "When Johnny Comes Marching Home." Gould displayed his talent for creating colorful instrumental sounds in *Homespun Overture* (1938) for banjo and orchestra; *Latin American Symphonette*

(1941); and *Venice* (1967) for double orchestra and brass band. He also wrote *Of Time and the River* (1946), a choral work; and the novelty piece *Concerto for Tap Dancer and Orchestra* (1952).

Gould tried to improve the quality of music available to student groups. He wrote *Folk Suite* (1941) for high school orchestras and *Symphony for Band* (1952) for the United States Military Academy band. Gould was born in New York City.　　　Richard Jackson

Gould, *goold,* **Stephen Jay** (1941-　　　), is an American scientist and educator. He has written widely on *paleontology,* the scientific study of animals, plants, and other organisms that lived in prehistoric times. Gould is best known for his writings on the *evolution* (development) of life on earth. He has questioned the traditional idea that evolution is a gradual and continuous process. He has suggested that evolution occurs in rapid, irregular spurts, a process called "punctuated equilibrium."

Gould has done much to make scientific subjects understandable to nonscientists. He has done this largely through essays, including some on such topics as baseball and Mickey Mouse. Many of these essays have appeared in his books *Ever Since Darwin* (1977), *The Panda's Thumb* (1980), *Hen's Teeth and Horse's Toes* (1983), *The Flamingo's Smile* (1985), *Bully for Brontosaurus* (1991), *Dinosaur in a Haystack* (1995), and *The Lying Stones of Marrakech* (2000). Other books by Gould include *The Mismeasure of Man* (1981), *Wonderful Life* (1990), *Full House* (1996), and *Rocks of Ages* (1999).

Gould was born in New York City. He graduated from Antioch College and earned a Ph.D. degree in geology from Columbia University. Gould has taught at Harvard University since 1967.　　　Patricia H. Kelley

Gounod, *GOO noh* or *goo NOH,* **Charles** (1818-1893), was a French composer best known for his opera *Faust* (1859, revised and expanded 1869). This opera is loosely based on Johann Wolfgang von Goethe's play *Faust,* about a scholar who sells his soul to the devil. Gounod's opera emphasizes the love story between Faust and Marguerite. It is noted for its beautiful *arias* (solos) and its familiar "Soldiers' Chorus."

Gounod's music includes elements of seriousness and sensuality, though some of his works lapse into melodrama and sentimentality. He was a skillful craftsman, and some of his shorter works, including his songs, are impressive. His orchestrations are rich and colorful, and reflect the style of the French composer Hector Berlioz.

Charles François Gounod was born in Paris. He entered the Paris Conservatory in 1836 and won the *Grand Prix de Rome* after only three years of study. He then studied for three years in Rome, where he learned the great choral works of Italian composer Giovanni Palestrina. About 1850, Gounod began to write operas, of which relatively few were successful. Other than *Faust,* his successful operas included *Romeo and Juliet* (1867) and *Mireille* (1864, revised and abridged 1876). He was also a choir director and wrote several masses and other sacred works.　　　Stewart L. Ross

Gourd is the name of a group of ornamental trailing or climbing plants. Gourds are vegetables closely related to squashes and pumpkins. They grow wild in America, Africa, and the Pacific Islands. Gourds bear fruits of many colors and shapes. The leaves are large with point-

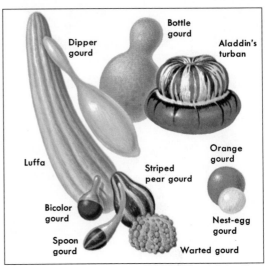

WORLD BOOK illustration by James Teason

Gourds bear attractive fruits of many colors and shapes. This illustration shows some of the most popular ornamental gourds.

ed lobes, and the flowers are usually yellow.

Some of the smaller and more attractive gourds include *salt-and-pepper gourds, nest-egg gourds,* and *dishcloth gourds.* The dishcloth gourd, also called the *luffa* or *loofah,* has become popular in America. The inside of the dried fruit is full of fibers that make a dishcloth or bath sponge which smells sweet. Very young dishcloth gourds are among the few that can be eaten.

Bottle gourds bear large fruits used mainly as novelties and ornaments. Other popular gourds include the *dipper; pipe gourd* or *calabash; apple, orange,* and *pear-shaped gourds; powder horn;* and *Hercules's-club.*

Gourds are easy to grow. The seeds need only be planted in a sunny area after danger of frost has passed.
Jerry M. Baskin

Scientific classification. Gourds belong to the family Cucurbitaceae. Bottle gourds make up the genus *Lagenaria.* The dishcloth gourd found in North America is *Luffa cylindrica.*

Related articles in *World Book* include:

Calabash	Cucumber	Pumpkin
Casaba	Melon	Squash
Chayote	Muskmelon	Watermelon

Gout is a chronic disease that can produce severe swelling of the joints. It is caused by a defect in the body's natural action of breaking down nitrogen-containing compounds called *purines.* This action results in the production of too much uric acid, which accumulates in the blood (see **Uric acid**). Crystals of uric acid are deposited in tissues around the joints. These deposits cause sudden attacks of swelling, most often in the feet. This is called *gouty arthritis.* The tendency to gout is hereditary.

The treatment of gout consists of limiting the amount of protein in the diet, and taking drugs such as probenecid and sulfinpyrazone to hasten the elimination of uric acid. The drug allopurinol may be prescribed to reduce uric acid production. Colchicine is a drug that relieves acute gouty attacks. Gout is not curable, but it is controlled by proper treatment.　　　William J. Kane

U.S. Army

Steve Smith, Wheeler Pictures

Judith Selsor, Wheeler Pictures

Frank Siteman from Marilyn Gartman

Government services cover a wide range of activities. They include national defense, *top left;* recreation, *top right;* education, *bottom left;* and road construction, *bottom right.*

Government

Government is one of humanity's oldest and most important institutions. From earliest times, some kind of government has been a vital part of every society. This is because every society needs some people to make and enforce decisions that affect conduct within the group. The term *government* also refers to the process of exercising power in a group.

Any formal or informal group—a family, a church, a baseball team, a club, a corporation, a labor union—may be said to have government. But when we speak of government, we generally mean public government, such as that of a nation, a state, a province, a city, or a village. This article mainly discusses the nature and powers of public governments.

Government of some kind affects every human activity in important ways. For that reason, most *political scientists* (specialists in the study of government) believe that government should not be studied by itself. They urge that when we study government we should also know something about anthropology, economics, history, philosophy, science, and sociology. Therefore, the *World Book* articles on these subjects should be read in connection with the **Government** article.

Elements of government

A number of basic elements are common to all governments. These elements are (1) rules of conduct, (2) sovereignty, (3) legitimacy, (4) jurisdiction, and (5) enforcement.

Gerald Benjamin, the contributor of this article, is Director of the Center for New York State and Local Government Studies, Rockefeller Institute of Government, and Professor of Political Science, State University of New York at New Paltz.

Rules of conduct. Every group of people—from a family to a nation—has rules of conduct to govern the lives of its members. For example, a family may have a rule that all its members be on time for meals. This rule makes it possible for the family members to eat together and then go about their own business. It is meant to keep life running smoothly for group members.

The rules made by a group are really decisions about matters that affect the group as a whole. The decisions are designed to encourage or require certain kinds of behavior, or to discourage or forbid other kinds of behavior by individual members.

Sovereignty is supreme power or authority. A sovereign government has the authority to use force within its boundaries. Through the years, different ideas about the source of a public government's sovereignty have developed. An early idea was that a government ruled by *divine right.* This idea suggested that authority flowed to the government from God and was unlimited. Today, the people are regarded as the chief source of the government's authority in democratic countries.

Legitimacy is the acceptance by the people of the government's authority to exercise power. No political system can exist unless its government has such acceptance. The legitimacy of a government depends in part on the *socialization* of its people. Socialization is a learning process in which the people come to accept the standards of their society. Most countries promote socialization through educational systems that teach people to have positive views about their government. In this way, people develop loyalty to such symbols of the government as a flag or national anthem.

Jurisdiction means the right or power of making and enforcing rules or laws. The jurisdiction of a public government extends over all the people who live in a certain area. The only way a person can escape such jurisdiction is to move out of its area.

Public governments have broad *functional jurisdiction*—the range of activities to which their rules or laws apply. Public governments in the United States govern behavior that affects national defense, social welfare, the economy, marriage and divorce, public health, education, taxation, and transportation. In addition, these public governments regulate most businesses, professions, and trades.

Law enforcement. Rules of conduct are not likely to have much effect unless people obey them. If the members of a group were permitted to ignore or disobey its rules, a society could not operate. Soon there would be no law or order.

Most people obey the decisions of their group willingly. But some must be forced to obey by the threat of punishment. Clubs, corporations, and labor unions have officers who enforce their regulations. Cities, states, provinces, and nations have police officers, judges, and soldiers who enforce their laws. Enforcement usually means some kind of punishment for people found guilty of disobedience. Those who have the power to control behavior by making and enforcing the rules of a group are often called a *power structure.*

Probably the most important difference between private and public governments lies in how they enforce their rules or laws. Only public governments have the right to define certain acts as crimes or to use physical force against disobedient people. A private government may fine or even expel a disobedient member. But only a public government can legally imprison or execute a person.

The scope of government

Many questions about government concern the relations between public and private governments. How far, and over what kinds of activities, should the functional jurisdiction of public governments extend? Should the goods and services needed by the people be produced and provided entirely by private governments? Or should some industries and services be owned and operated by public governments? Should corporations and labor unions settle their disputes by themselves? Or should some public government step in to iron out labor-management disagreements? Who should establish educational standards for schools and colleges—public or private governments? Should public governments manage the way news is reported in newspapers or on radio or television? Or should all news reporting be controlled only by private governments?

Anarchism. Some people believe that public governments should have little or no functional jurisdiction. The most extreme belief of this kind is called *anarchism.* Anarchists believe that all public governments conflict with personal liberty and are unnecessary. Thus, anarchists would eliminate all public governments and let only individuals and private groups govern the activities of a country. Anarchism has few followers today.

Totalitarianism. At the other extreme from anarchism is *totalitarianism.* Totalitarian governments demand total loyalty. They seek to regulate, or even destroy, such institutions as the family, church, corporation, or labor union. There are no limits on the functional jurisdiction of such governments. Totalitarian countries are usually governed by a small group of people. They put down all opposition and try to socialize citizens to believe the state is all-important. Individual free-

Levels and functions of government

WORLD BOOK illustrations by David Cunningham

Most public government systems consist of many governments. These governments operate on various levels, such as local, state, and national, and each performs certain functions.

Local governments serve such areas as counties, cities, towns, townships, villages, and park and school districts. Their chief responsibilities include safety functions, which they provide through local police forces, courts, and fire departments. Local governments also provide libraries and mass transportation.

Law enforcement

Fire protection

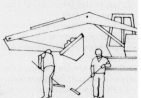

State governments have broad jurisdiction. In the United States, they generally may take any action that does not conflict with the U.S. Constitution, acts of Congress, or treaties. State services include education, public safety, public works, recreation, welfare, and conservation. States also license and regulate most occupations, professions, and businesses.

Road construction

Park regulation

Federal governments, such as the national government of the United States, carry out functions that mainly affect all the people in the country. The U.S. Constitution gives the federal government the right to collect taxes, coin money, declare war, regulate commerce, and provide for the common defense and general welfare.

Mail delivery

National defense

Important terms in government

Abdication is giving up the right to rule.

Amendment is a change made in a law, a constitution, or a legislative bill.

Amnesty means forgiveness granted by a government.

Anarchism is a belief that every form of government regulation is wrong and that public governments should be destroyed.

Aristocracy is a form of government controlled by a few people, usually wealthy members of the nobility.

Authoritarianism is a form of government in which the governing power is used without the consent of the governed. It is undemocratic, but it is generally not so extreme as totalitarianism.

Authority is the right and duty to make decisions, and the power to enforce them.

Autocracy is rule by one person who has complete control of all branches of the government.

Autonomy means self-government and usually refers to a political unit that is not completely independent. Each state of the United States has some autonomy.

Bill of rights is a document that describes the basic liberties of the people and forbids the government to violate those rights. The U.S. Bill of Rights consists of the first 10 amendments to the Constitution.

Bureaucracy is the system of officials who carry out the functions of a government.

Cabinet is a group of advisers, including the heads of major government departments and other high officials.

Capitalism is an economic system in which individuals or private businesses own most of a nation's means of producing goods and services.

Checks and balances are limitations on the powers of any branch of government. Checks and balances are created by giving each branch some powers that offset those of the other branches.

Civil rights are the freedoms that people may have as members of a community, particularly a nation. In most countries, law and custom guarantee civil rights.

Civil service includes most civilian government employees who are appointed rather than elected.

Colonialism is a term that refers to the rule of a group of people by a foreign power.

Common law is the body of rules found in the written records of judges' decisions. It is law made by courts, rather than by legislatures.

Communism is a form of government, an economic system, a revolutionary movement, and a philosophy. Communism calls for government control of economic activity and for government ownership of factories, machines, and other means of production.

Conservatism is a political belief in making changes in line with proven values of the past. Most American conservatives, for example, want to hold public governments strictly within the limits of their powers as set forth in the Constitution.

Constitution is the written or unwritten collection of rules and principles followed by governments.

Democracy means rule by the people. It may refer to a form of government, or to a way of life.

Despotism is a form of government in which the ruler has unlimited power over the people.

Dictator is any ruler whose power is not limited by law or by the acts of any official body, such as a legislature.

Due process of law consists of the legal steps that must be taken whenever a person is charged with breaking the law. Every American citizen is guaranteed *due process* by the U.S. Constitution.

Executive is the branch of government that oversees the carrying out of laws. The U.S. Constitution separates the work of government into three branches: *legislative, judicial,* and *executive.* Although power is shared, Congress has most legislative duties, the courts have most judicial duties, and the President is the chief executive.

Fascism is a strongly nationalistic movement favoring government control of economic and social activity but private ownership of property.

Federalism is a union of two or more sovereign political units, such as states or provinces, under a single government of limited powers.

Filibustering is a method sometimes used by lawmakers to block or delay passage of a proposed bill. One legislator, or a group of legislators, makes long speeches or demands unnecessary roll calls to use up time and keep the bill from coming to a vote.

Habeas corpus refers usually to a *writ of habeas corpus,* an order by a judge requiring the police to bring an arrested person into court. The court then decides if there is good reason to hold the prisoner.

Impeachment is an official charge by a legislative body accusing a government official of being unworthy of office.

Imperialism is the policy or action by which one country controls another country or territory.

Initiative and referendum are actions that allow voters a certain amount of direct control over lawmaking. Through the *initiative,* the voters can introduce a law. Through the *referendum,* a proposed law is put up to the voters for approval or disapproval.

Judiciary is the branch of government made up of courts and judges.

Law is a set of rules that public governments make and enforce.

Left wing is a group of people and parties holding radical views. Many left wing groups support socialist or Communist views.

Legislature is the lawmaking branch of a government.

Legitimacy is the widespread acceptance of the authority of a public government.

Liberalism is a political philosophy that favors rapid social change as a means of correcting economic and social inequality.

Monarchy is a form of government in which a ruler, such as an emperor, king, or queen, holds power, either actually or ceremonially, for life.

Nationalism is a people's sense of belonging together as a nation.

Oligarchy is a form of government in which a small group of people holds the ruling power.

Parliamentary system of government consists of a legislature (parliament) and a Cabinet. A *prime minister* or *premier* heads the Cabinet, which is chosen from the parliament and stays in office as long as it is supported by a majority of the representatives.

Plebiscite is a vote of the people. The term has come to mean the vote of the people of a certain place to choose the nation that will govern them.

Political party is an organized group of people who control or seek to control a government.

Presidential system of government consists of separate legislative and executive branches. A president, who is elected for a fixed term, heads the executive branch.

Radicalism is a political philosophy that emphasizes the need to find and eliminate the basic injustices of society.

Republic is a form of government in which the citizens elect representatives to manage the government.

Right wing is a group of people and parties holding conservative or reactionary views.

Socialism is an economic system and also a way of life. Socialists believe that a country's principal means of production should be owned or controlled by public governments or by cooperatives.

Socialization is the process of learning or being taught the standards of a group or society.

Sovereignty is the supreme power of a country over its own affairs.

Totalitarianism is a form of government in which the state claims control of all the activities of the people.

Tyranny is a term used throughout history to describe various forms of government by rulers who have unrestricted power.

Welfare state is a term sometimes applied to a country in which the government assumes major responsibility for the social welfare of the people.

doms are given little importance. Some totalitarian systems require total loyalty to a particular leader. These systems include military dictatorships that have been common in some Latin-American countries. Other totalitarian systems require citizens to believe in a certain system of ideas. All types of totalitarian governments use force, the threat of force, or terrorism to maintain control of the people.

The basic idea of totalitarianism exists today—in varying degrees—in such Communist countries as China, Cuba, and North Korea. In practice, however, few governments have been able to extend their functional jurisdiction to every kind of group or individual behavior. Some private groups, such as families and churches, continue to make some rules for their members.

Pluralism. Most nations have both public and private governments to make and enforce rules of behavior. These countries are called *pluralistic* because public and private groups have legitimacy and can affect the way the country is run. Groups representing the interests of business, farming, labor, ethnic, or racial segments of society work with public government to develop public policy. Each group exerts pressure on the others and on public government. Together, they produce balancing pressures that keep a single group from taking over. In pluralistic societies, interaction among interest groups is a way of forming public opinion.

Freedom for the individual is the most important value in a pluralistic system. People in pluralistic countries, such as the United States and Canada, place firm limits on government powers that affect the rights of individuals. Private individuals and groups generally accept the procedure of working out their conflicts in the judicial and legislative systems of public government. The rules for resolving conflicts are found in a constitution and laws, and are an important part of a pluralistic society. Preserving these rules thus becomes a primary goal of the political system.

The public governments of some pluralistic countries, including the Scandinavian nations and the United Kingdom, base some of their economic policies on the principles of *socialism.* These public governments own or operate certain basic industries or services. Other pluralistic countries, such as the United States and Canada, base their economies on the principles of *capitalism,* also called *free enterprise.* In these countries, almost all industries and services are controlled by individuals or private groups, under government regulation.

Who governs?

The ancient Greek philosopher Aristotle classified governments by the number of rulers and by certain principles under which they operated. Today, various forms of government, including democracy and communism, differ mainly by the degree in which the people participate in them.

Aristotle's categories. Aristotle, sometimes called the *father of political science,* suggested that all governments fall into one of three categories: (1) rule by one person, (2) rule by a few people, and (3) rule by many people. Within each category, rule could be exercised for the benefit of all and be "virtuous," or for the benefit of only the rulers and be "corrupt."

When one person ruled for the good of all, Aristotle taught, the government was a *monarchy.* A corrupt monarchy was a *tyranny,* whose leader ruled to satisfy an appetite for power or wealth. Government by a few people, for the good of all, was an *aristocracy.* When a small group of people ruled to increase their own power or wealth, the government was an *oligarchy.* Rule by many people, for the good of all, was called *polity* by Aristotle. In a polity, a large number of citizens could rule for the benefit of the rest. *Democracy* was Aristotle's name for corrupt rule by the majority, and it was to be feared as a dangerous kind of mob rule.

Democracy. Since the late 1600's, the idea that a nation's people are the most legitimate source of authority for public government has won increasing acceptance. United States President Abraham Lincoln emphasized this idea in 1863 in his Gettysburg Address, in which he referred to the nation's democracy as a government "of the people, by the people, for the people, ..."

In a *direct democracy,* the people govern themselves, making the laws for their community together. But direct democracy can work only in small communities, where the people can all meet in one place. All the people of large communities—cities, states, provinces, or countries—cannot meet in one place. Instead, they elect a certain number of their fellow citizens to represent them in making laws. An assembly of representatives may be a council, a legislature, a congress, or a parliament. Each permits the people to make the laws indirectly—through their representatives.

Representative government is the chief feature of a *republic.* The republican form of government achieves self-government, the goal of modern democracy, for large communities, such as cities or countries. In democratic countries, the people have almost unlimited opportunities to make the government truly representative. They vote in secret, may seek public office, and may demand the removal of public officials who behave improperly. The basic laws of democratic countries guarantee many rights, including freedom of speech and of the press.

If people can take an actual part in the process of their government, the government may be called democratic. Under such a system of government, the people have *political democracy.* Many people in a democracy take part in government by supporting a political party. Such organizations are vital to a democracy. They compete to capture control of public government and give it direction. They also recruit candidates, adopt policies, and work to form public opinion on important issues.

Some scholars suggest that capitalism, in which the means of production are mostly privately owned, is also a necessary condition for democracy. But political democracy exists in such countries as Sweden and Israel, where Socialist parties have spent many years in power.

The term *democracy* can be confusing because some nations that have kept the forms of monarchy and aristocracy, such as the United Kingdom and Japan, actually function as democracies. On the other hand, some nations calling themselves democracies or republics are not democratic at all.

Communism. In traditional Communist societies, the process of government is tightly controlled by a small group—the members of the Communist Party. Few other people have any voice in the government. Voting consists of casting ballots for Communist candidates only. Rival political parties cannot be organized. The government controls all publications, radio, and television, and strongly restricts what may be said or written.

Leaders in most Communist nations call their systems democratic because the systems are designed to eliminate extremes of wealth and poverty. Such countries provide programs that bring education, medical care, housing, culture, and employment to the mass of the people. The programs focus on groups or classes, not on individuals. Communist Party members say that individual liberty is sacrificed for the good of the whole of society. But in spite of being troubled by continuing poverty, democracies with capitalistic or mixed economies have provided greater prosperity for more people than has any other system of government. In addition, such prosperity has been achieved without major sacrifices of personal liberty.

Constitutional government

Every major country has a constitution—the basic set of laws by which the people are governed. But the force and meaning of the constitution may vary widely among the various countries.

The United Kingdom, one of the oldest constitutional monarchies, has no single, written constitution. The British constitution is made up of certain documents and basic traditions of freedom, justice, and human rights that date back hundreds of years. British laws and processes of government uphold these rights and traditions as strongly as if they were all in writing.

The U.S. Constitution, *ratified* (approved) in 1788, is the oldest written national constitution still in force. In fact, one of the country's major contributions to the world is the idea that a written constitution is necessary and desirable. The Constitution establishes the form of the United States government and the rights and liberties of the American people. Probably the most important part of the Constitution is a declaration of the government's goals and purposes. They form the nation's *constitutional principles.*

The constitutional principles of the United States are declared in the Preamble to the Constitution:

"We the people of the United States, in order to *form a more perfect Union, establish justice, insure domestic tranquility, provide for the common defense, promote the general welfare,* and *secure the blessings of liberty to ourselves and our posterity,* do ordain and establish this Constitution for the United States of America."

(The phrases printed in italics do not appear in italics in the Constitution. All words have been given their modern spelling.)

The Constitution of the United States gives the federal government certain powers to be used in reaching the goals stated in the Preamble. Most of these powers are defined in Articles I, II, and III of the Constitution. Those articles give some powers to Congress, some to the President, and some to the Supreme Court.

Important powers given to Congress include the right to collect taxes, coin money, declare war, regulate commerce, and provide for the common defense and general welfare. The President is made the chief executive officer of the nation and commander in chief of the armed forces. The President is authorized to appoint and direct other executive officers to see that "the laws be faithfully executed." The President has the power to appoint the justices of the Supreme Court and judges of certain other courts "by and with the advice and consent of the Senate." The powers given to the Supreme Court are quite general. They extend to "all cases, in law and equity, arising under this Constitution, the laws of the United States, and treaties . . ."

The Supreme Court's most important power is that of *judicial review.* That is, the court may decide whether any federal or state law, when challenged, is *constitutional.* If the court finds the law conflicts with the Constitution of the United States, the law is unconstitutional and therefore illegal. Judicial review is not clearly granted in the Constitution, but it is implied.

Constitutional questions. The powers granted to Congress, the President, and the Supreme Court provide broad jurisdiction. But the definitions of these powers are not always clearly stated in the Constitution. Some are defined in general terms or in terms that could have more than one meaning. As a result, questions arise over the meaning of certain phrases. For example, the phrase "to regulate commerce with foreign nations, and among the several states" is frequently questioned. What does "among the several states" mean? Does it mean from state to state or *within* the states? Does "regulate" mean only to promote and encourage, or also to discourage or even prohibit certain forms of commerce?

The questions raised about the meaning of the Constitution are answered during the actual process of government. Congress and the President try to answer the questions when they adopt laws or issue orders. If the laws or orders are challenged as unconstitutional, the question may be decided by the Supreme Court.

Sometimes, when a law or order is challenged, the Supreme Court does not decide the issue. In other cases, its decision may be challenged. At such times, the matter may be settled in one of four ways: (1) the law may be *amended* (changed), (2) the law may be *repealed* (eliminated), (3) the Constitution may be amended, or (4) the court may change its decision.

Individual rights of every person are protected by the U.S. Constitution. The Constitution describes the basic human liberties, and forbids governmental actions that would weaken personal freedom. As a result, the protection of individual rights is one of the most important duties of the U.S. government.

The Constitution originally guaranteed only a few personal freedoms. Some states refused to approve it until amendments guaranteeing more freedoms were promised. The first 10 amendments to the Constitution became known as the Bill of Rights. The liberties they safeguard include freedom of religion, of speech, and of the press, and the right of people to assemble peacefully. The Bill of Rights also protects the rights of people accused of breaking the law and guarantees them a fair trial. The extent of personal liberty under the Bill of Rights is constantly being defined by the courts as questions arise in specific cases.

Most pluralistic countries have bills of rights. The Canadian Charter of Rights and Freedoms is part of Canada's constitution. The English Bill of Rights is a declaration made by the English Parliament. The French

Declaration of the Rights of Man is included in the French constitution. For the texts of both the United States and Canadian bills of rights, see the *World Book* article on **Bill of rights.**

Systems of government

In most countries, the public government system consists of many governments, each with certain jurisdiction. These governments include a central, or national, government, and the governments of states, provinces, counties, cities, towns, and villages. All these governments operate according to some orderly plan. Most countries have either a *unitary* or *federal* system of government.

The unitary system gives the principal powers to the central government. The state, provincial, and local governments are created by the central government. They have only those powers that the central government gives them. France, Italy, the United Kingdom, and many other pluralistic countries have unitary systems. China, North Korea, and other Communist nations have unitary systems.

The federal system develops when a number of states or provinces *federate* (form a union) in order to establish a nation. The powers of government are shared between the central government and the state or provincial governments. Both national and regional governments have direct ties to the people, who are the source of the government's authority. The United States and Canada have federal systems. Other nations with federal systems include Argentina, Australia, Austria, Brazil, India, Mexico, and Switzerland. Because true federalism requires decentralization, it cannot coexist with totalitarianism.

The U.S. federal system

The role of state government. The federal system of the United States is set forth in the United States Constitution and its amendments. The role of state government in the federal system extends to several areas. Elections for all national offices are conducted by the states. The Electoral College, used to select the President, is organized on the basis of the states and their populations. Both the Senate and the House of Representatives are made up of people who represent the states' interests. The 10th Amendment states, "The powers not delegated to the United States by the Constitution, nor prohibited by it to the states, are reserved to the states respectively, or to the people."

The Constitution also limits the role of the states. Section 10 of Article I, for example, has a provision that bars states from making treaties, coining money, maintaining an army or navy, engaging in war, or taxing imports and exports. Other restrictions on state powers are contained in the 14th Amendment. This amendment says: "… No state shall make or enforce any law which shall abridge the privileges or immunities of citizens of the United States; nor shall any state deprive any person of life, liberty, or property without due process of law; nor deny to any person within its jurisdiction the equal protection of the laws."

Interpreting the states' rights. Like some other parts of the Constitution, the 14th Amendment uses several words or terms that are not clear. For example, what

are "the privileges or immunities of citizens"? What is "liberty"? What does "due process of law" really mean? And what is "equal protection of the laws"? The Supreme Court has tried to define these terms in its decisions.

The term "equal protection of the laws" has received special attention because many laws actually do not apply to everybody. They affect only certain groups of people. In general, the Supreme Court has permitted state governments to make and enforce such laws if the basis for classifying people is reasonable. The court has ruled that it is reasonable—for tax purposes—to classify people according to the size of their income. A state law also may classify people according to their occupation or profession for educational or welfare purposes. But the court has decided that a state government may not classify people according to their race or religion for any purpose. The court has ruled as unconstitutional state laws that required blacks and whites to attend separate schools. Such laws, the Supreme Court has decided, denied people "equal protection of the laws" on a basis that was not reasonable.

The Supreme Court has decided many cases that arose over the meaning of "liberty" as the word is used in the 14th Amendment. The Bill of Rights forbids Congress to make any law that would deprive citizens of certain liberties. But the Bill of Rights does not forbid state governments from making such laws. For many years, the Supreme Court ruled that the Bill of Rights applied only to the federal government. But a number of decisions of the Supreme Court since 1925 have ruled that most guarantees of the Bill of Rights do apply to the states.

Government at work

The people of most countries depend on public governments to make the laws that keep life running smoothly. These laws regulate many important functions. Some functions belong to the national government, and others come under the jurisdiction of state, provincial, or local governments.

In a constitutional democracy, the function of the national government must be specifically provided for in the constitution. To meet unexpected needs, the legislature and courts must sometimes interpret a constitution broadly. In the United States, such interpretations are based on the Constitution's *elastic clause.* This clause allows Congress to pass all laws "necessary and proper" to carry out the functions of government.

Defense. Probably the most important function of a national government is to make and enforce laws for the nation's defense. The United States government spends hundreds of billions of dollars every year to maintain the armed forces at home and in other lands. Expenses also include billions of dollars annually in aid to developing countries. In fact, most of the U.S. foreign aid program is conducted under the government's power to "provide for the common defense."

Commerce. The broad power of the federal government to regulate interstate commerce is used to make laws that have a far-reaching effect on the nation's economy. Many federal agencies enforce the commerce laws. These agencies include the Environmental Protection Agency (EPA), Equal Employment Opportunity Commission (EEOC), Federal Communications Commission (FCC), Federal Trade Commission (FTC), National Labor Relations Board (NLRB), Occupational Safety and Health Administration (OSHA), and Securities and Exchange Commission (SEC). Other federal agencies regulate farm production and the prices of many farm products. In addition, the United States government enforces the Civil Rights Act of 1964 under the commerce power. The Civil Rights Act forbids racial discrimination in such public places as restaurants, hotels, and theaters.

Taxation. The broad federal powers "to lay and collect taxes" and to provide for the "general welfare" are used for many activities. Under these powers, the U.S. government has tried to stabilize the economy, to avoid inflation and depression, and to provide full employment.

Some tax funds support the functions of the federal government under its defense and commerce powers. Other tax money supports the huge social security program, including unemployment insurance, old-age pensions, and aid to families with dependent children. General welfare functions include programs that fight poverty, finance public housing, assist in slum clearance, and maintain national parks. None of these programs, or the agencies that conduct them, is mentioned by name in the Constitution.

State services. Federal responsibilities have increased through the years, but state and local governments continue to be a vital part of public government. They have the major responsibility for providing most of the services needed by the people. These services include education, community health, police and fire protection, street and highway maintenance, and sewage disposal. State and local governments make and enforce laws that deal with most crimes, with most kinds of contracts, and with marriage and divorce. They also license and regulate most occupations, professions, and businesses. Each state has a constitution that defines and limits the powers of the state.

Relationships among public governments. The federal government has used its taxing and general welfare powers to make *grants-in-aid* to state, and sometimes local, governments. These grants may support the delivery of traditional state or local services or provide incentives for these governments to enter into new areas. Through grants-in-aid, the federal government becomes a partner of the state. Together, the federal and state governments provide public services that the state alone could not support.

The federal government has also developed a common market shared by the people of all the states. In this common market, goods and services move freely among the states. They are not burdened by state tariffs or by different systems of money or credit.

The organization of government

A variety of forms of national government organization are possible in democracies. Two widely used arrangements are the *presidential* and the *parliamentary* models.

Presidential government. The United States uses the presidential form. The U.S. Constitution provides for a government with three separate branches: (1) the executive, represented by the President; (2) the legislative, represented by Congress; and (3) the judicial, represented by the Supreme Court.

The U.S. presidential system is based on the principle of *separation of powers.* Under this principle, governing powers are divided among the President, Congress, and the federal courts. The purpose of separating the powers is to prevent any single branch of government from becoming too powerful. The separation principle is not meant to keep the three branches of government completely apart. Actually, the President, Congress, and the Supreme Court often blend their powers. For example, the President may make a treaty with the government of another country, but it must have the advice and consent of the Senate in order for the treaty to take effect. The Senate also must approve presidential appointments of ambassadors, federal judges, and certain other high officials.

The President, in turn, checks the power of the legislature. The President may *veto* (refuse to consent to) any law passed by Congress and may also request Congress to pass new laws. The President's messages to Congress serve largely to shape its legislative program. On the other hand, Congress strongly influences many of the President's activities. Congress may grant or withhold funds the President needs for the operation of the various executive departments.

This form of government is called presidential partly because the President is given considerable authority under it. Another reason is because the President is elected separately from, and independent of, the legislative branch. The presidential system can also be found in such countries as France and Mexico.

Parliamentary government. Canada and most democratic countries of Europe, Africa, and Asia have governments modeled on that of the United Kingdom. Unlike the U.S. system, the British government unites its executive and legislative branches. The prime minister and members of the Cabinet are the top executives. But they are also members of Parliament, function under its direct control, and are collectively responsible to it. The British system is called *parliamentary government* or *cabinet government.*

In both presidential and parliamentary governments, the judicial branch functions independently. But the powers of the judiciary differ under the two systems. The Supreme Court of the United States may, in some cases, declare an action of the President or Congress unconstitutional. But no British court can overrule the prime minister or Parliament.

The head of government and the head of state are different people in parliamentary systems. Generally, the prime minister is the head of government, and a monarch is the head of state. In most presidential governments, however, the president has both these roles. Another major difference between presidential and parliamentary governments is the method of choosing the chief executive. The U.S. President is elected for a fixed term of four years. The British prime minister, usually the majority party leader in the House of Commons, holds office for as long as Parliament supports his or her policies, but for no longer than five years without a general election. See **United Kingdom** (Government).

Party systems. Differences in government structure lead to variations in party systems in democratic coun-

Presidential and parliamentary forms of government

Two widely used forms of national government organization in democracies are the presidential and the parliamentary models. A president heads most presidential forms, and a prime minister is the chief executive in the parliamentary system. This diagram shows other comparisons.

WORLD BOOK diagram by David Cunningham

Presidential Government (United States)

The President is elected to a term of four years. The President has the power to appoint many high federal officials and may veto laws passed by Congress. The President is also the leader of a major political party.

The Legislature, or Congress, consists of two houses—the Senate and the House of Representatives. Members serve for fixed terms. They have the power to pass laws and to override presidential vetoes.

The U.S. Supreme Court is the highest court in the nation. The President appoints its members, subject to Senate consent, for life or until retirement. The court may decide whether laws and some executive actions are constitutional.

Other Nations That Use a Presidential System or forms of it include France, Mexico, and many republics in South America.

Parliamentary Government (Great Britain)

The Prime Minister is usually the majority party leader in the House of Commons, one of the two houses of Parliament. The prime minister holds office for as long as Parliament supports his or her policies.

The Legislature, or Parliament, consists of the House of Commons and the House of Lords. Its members directly control the actions of the prime minister and the Cabinet. Elections may be held at any time.

The Highest Court for most lawsuits in Great Britain consists of a group of members of the House of Lords. These judges serve for life or until retirement. They may not review the constitutionality of any laws.

Other Nations That Use a Parliamentary System include Australia, Canada, and many other democracies.

Sources of Authority

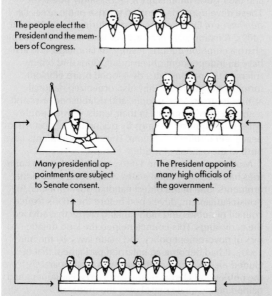

The people elect the President and the members of Congress.

Many presidential appointments are subject to Senate consent.

The President appoints many high officials of the government.

The Supreme Court, in some cases, may declare an action of the President or Congress unconstitutional, or illegal.

Sources of Authority

The people elect the members of the House of Commons.

The prime minister is determined by the makeup of the House of Commons.

The prime minister selects most high officials of the government.

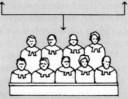

The judicial branch functions independently, but no British court can overrule the prime minister or actions of the Parliament.

tries. Two-party systems are common in countries with a presidential structure, legislative districts with only one representative, and a *plurality rule* for winning elections. A plurality rule states that the candidate who receives the most votes wins an election, even if no one receives a *majority* (more than half) of the votes. The United States has a two-party system.

Some democratic countries have a *multiparty system,* with more than two major parties. There is a greater chance for small parties to gain seats in the legislature in a country with a multiparty system, especially in one with a parliamentary system and legislative districts with more than one representative. Israel and Japan have multiparty systems.

When candidates from several major parties run for office, it is sometimes difficult for one person to get a majority of votes. Two or more parties may then join to form a *coalition government.* In this type of government, the legislative or Cabinet seats are divided among the parties and responsibility for governing is shared.

In most presidential systems, compromise on issues and positions to form a broad governing coalition takes place within parties and before the election. In most parliamentary systems, compromise occurs among parties and follows the election. But in all democracies, competition for power to govern keeps parties accountable to the people.

History of government

The practice of government is thousands of years old. Some types of government that exist today have been in use for hundreds of years. Others have emerged only since 1900.

Beginnings. The earliest forms of government were those of primitive groups or tribes. Each of these groups consisted of several families and had at least one leader. Custom and superstition determined how decisions were made and disputes were settled. About 10,000 years ago, various groups of people began to establish villages. These early communities had few government officials. Someone probably took care of the surplus food, and there may have been a chief planner for defense against outsiders.

Ancient times. By about 3500 B.C., some villages had developed into small cities. The city governments took on a greater role in managing community affairs and providing services for the people.

Many rulers during ancient times were also religious leaders. The people believed the authority of these rulers came from gods. As communities developed, emperors, kings, and other nonreligious rulers took over the power to govern. These rulers established laws that were enforced by military and police power.

The first democratic governments were established in the Greek *city-states* (independent cities and their outlying areas) by the 400's B.C. During the 300's B.C., such Greek political thinkers as Aristotle and Plato stressed the idea of rule by laws. Greek democracy, as it developed in Athens, was a *direct democracy* rather than a representative one. Each male citizen had the duty to serve permanently in the assembly, which passed the laws and decided all important government policies. This assembly was the supreme authority of the city-state. Neither slaves nor women could vote, but more

people took part in government in Greek democracies than in any other earlier civilization.

The Roman Empire became the major world power when it defeated Carthage during the 200's B.C. The Romans were the first to impose central authority upon a large area while preserving local government. Ancient Roman political thinkers taught that political power comes from the consent of the people. The Roman statesman Cicero contributed the idea of a universal law of reason that is binding on all people and governments everywhere. He suggested that people have natural rights that every state must respect.

The Middle Ages. After the fall of the Roman Empire during the A.D. 400's, barbarian invasions divided the huge Roman Empire into many kingdoms. The strong central and local governments of the Romans disappeared, and during the A.D. 700's, the feudal system emerged.

Feudalism was a political and military arrangement between a lord and his vassals. The lord gave vassals land in exchange for military and other services. Differences among vassals were settled at the lord's *court,* consisting of all the vassals. Many of the customs that developed in these courts continue today in American and British courts of law. The lords' courts also led to kings' councils, representative assemblies, and modern parliaments. See **Feudalism** (Justice under feudalism).

The Roman Catholic Church affected political life greatly during the Middle Ages. Christian theologians described government in terms of divine law and human law. The conflict between divine law and human governments helped lay the foundations for constitutional government (see **Constitution**).

During the 1200's, the feudal system of lords and vassals entered a period of major decline, and ruling kings and their governments grew increasingly powerful. These developments signaled the rise of the great *nation-states* of England and France during the 1300's and 1400's. A nation-state is an area of land where the people share a common culture, history, or language, and also have an independent government. Kings and other rulers of the nation-states developed more efficient forms of government. They also organized national armies to protect the people, and established laws and courts to provide justice in their lands. Townspeople agreed to support the kings by paying taxes in return for peace and good government. These developments gave birth to the nations of modern Europe.

Modern times. By the 1700's, several European countries had become nation-states with strong central governments. One of the oldest national governments, the British Parliament, developed before the 1000's from a council of nobles and high-ranking clergy that advised the early kings. This council helped the king decide matters of government policy and made laws. By the mid-1300's, it had become an enlarged parliament that included elected representatives who met separately from the nobles and clergy. By the late 1700's, Parliament had gained nearly total control over the monarch.

Government in the American Colonies during the early 1700's resembled that of Britain. Each colony had a governor and a legislature with two houses. By the end of the 1700's, the United States had a two-house Congress and a Constitution that was the supreme law of the land. The Constitution provided for a presidential system of government. By the late 1800's, nearly every European nation had a constitution.

Democracy, however, did not develop throughout the world at this time. The development of modern totalitarianism has been traced to Napoleon I, who ruled France as a dictator during the early 1800's. Napoleon established one of the first modern secret police systems. He also controlled the French press, and used propaganda and strict censorship to win support of his programs. Modern dictators, such as Benito Mussolini of Italy and Adolf Hitler of Germany, adopted many of Napoleon's methods. Mussolini developed Fascism in Italy during the 1920's, and Hitler brought Nazism to power in Germany during the 1930's. See **Fascism; Nazism.**

The word *communism* comes from the Latin word *communis,* which means *common* or *belong to all.* The idea of *communal* property dates at least from the time of the ancient Greeks. The ancient Greek philosopher Plato expressed communal ideas in his book *The Republic.* Plato proposed that a ruling class own everything in common, putting the welfare of the state above all personal desires. A number of early Christian groups had some form of community ownership of property.

Modern communism is based on the theories of the German social philosopher Karl Marx. Marx's basic ideas were first expressed in the *Communist Manifesto* (1848), which he wrote with Friedrich Engels, a German economist. Marx believed the only way to ensure a happy, harmonious society was to have the workers in control. Marx was convinced that the triumph of communism was inevitable. The first Communist government was established in Russia in 1917. This government collapsed in 1991. Today, Russia and most countries of the world have democratic forms of government.

Careers in government

Government service is a major field of employment in most countries. Although elected officials are responsible for making policy, most of the day-to-day work is done by career public service employees. In the United States, government service includes several thousand occupations—from accountant to zoologist.

The work of government employees—whether federal, state, or local—affects the health, welfare, and security of every person. Government workers represent a nation's interests in other countries, and provide many of the supplies that keep the armed forces strong. They inspect food and drugs, collect taxes, mint money, maintain law and order, and administer social security. They explore space, forecast the weather, control the airways, and protect parks and forests. They enforce environmental protection standards and carry on many scientific research projects.

Services provided by government require many highly trained professionals—doctors, educators, engineers, lawyers, scientists, and administrators. Government service also needs clerks, mechanics, stenographers, and administrative assistants. In the United States, about 22 million people, or about a seventh of the civilian workers, have government jobs. About 3 million are federal employees, not counting members of the armed forces. Most are employed in the executive branch. The U.S. government is the nation's largest employer.

Rewards in government service. Many young people choose government service because they take pride in serving people and helping the progress of their nation, state, or city. Salaries generally are comparable to those paid by private firms. Prospects of salary increases and promotions are good for employees who show they are ready for more responsible tasks. Job benefits in government service include liberal vacations and generous retirement programs. The U.S. government and many state and local governments sponsor low-cost health and life insurance plans for their employees.

Preparation for a government job is generally the same as for a similar job in private employment. Some knowledge of government organization and processes is helpful. This knowledge may be gained by taking civics courses in high school and political science courses in college. For many jobs, training continues after employment begins.

Many agencies offer college students a chance to try government service before graduation. The student alternates between work periods in a government office and study periods on the campus, sometimes spending a semester or a year working in a federal agency.

Obtaining a government job. The best method of starting in government service in the United States is to take a civil service examination. The civil service system, operated by state and local commissions and the federal Office of Personnel Management, covers most government jobs. It seeks to guarantee that a person will keep the job on the basis of good performance, not on allegiance to a political party. See **Civil service.**

For information about federal jobs, contact the U.S. Office of Personnel Management in Washington, D.C. Many cities also have a Federal Job Information Center. For addresses, consult the *United States Government* listing in the telephone directory. For information about state or city jobs, contact the civil service commission in the state capital or inquire at the city hall.

The political route to government service. Many people aim for careers in government through political activity. Government service includes all public officials who are elected to office, plus all those whom they appoint to office. Public officials who are elected to government service include the president and vice president, lawmakers, governors, mayors, judges, state legislators, and city council members.

Political candidates need many people to help them get votes. Successful candidates often reward their chief supporters by appointing them to government jobs under their control. Such jobs are not included in the civil service system. They range from important positions in the executive departments of government to part-time jobs in city services.   Gerald Benjamin

Related articles in *World Book.* See the *Government* section of each state, province, and country article. See also the separate articles **United States, Government of the; Canada, Government of; State government; City government; Local government.** See also the following articles:

Political philosophers and writers

Aquinas, Saint Thomas	Jefferson, Thomas	Marx, Karl
Aristotle	Locke, John	Milton, John
Engels, Friedrich	Machiavelli, Niccolò	Montesquieu
Hobbes, Thomas		Paine, Thomas
		Plato

Plekhanov, Georgi V.
Proudhon, Pierre J.
Rousseau, Jean-Jacques

Suárez, Francisco
Thomas, Norman M.
Tocqueville, Alexis de

Kinds of government

Absolutism
Aristocracy
Authoritarian-
  ism
Autocracy
Bureaucracy

Communism
Democracy
Despotism
Dictatorship
Fascism
Federalism

Monarchy
Nazism
Oligarchy
Police state
Provisional
  government

Republic
Socialism
Theocracy
Totalitarianism
Tyranny

Rulers and political leaders

Czar
Emperor
Governor
Governor general
Kaiser
King
Lieutenant gov-
  ernor

Pharaoh
President
President of the
  United States
Prime minister
Prince
Queen
Rajah

Regent
Sultan
Vice President of
  the United
  States
Viceroy
Vizier

Judicial systems

Attorney general
Chief justice
Court
District attorney

Judge
Law
Supreme Court of the United
  States

Legislatures

Congress of the
  United States
Duma
House of
  Burgesses

House of Com-
  mons
House of Lords
House of Repre-
  sentatives

Legislature
Parliament
Senate

Civil rights

Attainder
Bill of rights
Censorship
Civil rights
Fifth Amendment
Freedom
Freedom of
  assembly

Freedom of
  religion
Freedom of
  speech
Freedom of the
  press
Habeas corpus

Privacy, Right of
Rights of Man,
  Declaration of
  the
Second Amend-
  ment

Political units

Borough
City-state
Colony
Commonwealth
Country

Empire
Enclave
Mandated ter-
  ritory
Nation

Province
Territory
Trust territory

Symbols

Columbia
Crown
Fasces
Flag
Fleur-de-lis
Great Seal of the United
  States

John Bull
Mace
Seal
Swastika
Symbol
Uncle Sam

Other related articles

Anarchism
Checks and bal-
  ances
Civics
Colonialism
Conflict of interest
Conservatism
Constitution
Coup d'état
Election
Foreign policy
Geopolitics
Graft

Home rule
Imperialism
International rela-
  tions
Junta
Liberalism
Martial law
Nationalism
Ombudsman
Philosophy
Political action
  committee

Political party
Political science
Radicalism
Revolution
Sovereignty
Sunshine laws
Term limits
Town meeting
United Nations
Welfare state

Outline

I. Elements of government
  A. Rules of conduct
  B. Sovereignty
  C. Legitimacy
  D. Jurisdiction
  E. Law enforcement
II. The scope of government
  A. Anarchism
  B. Totalitarianism
  C. Pluralism
III. Who governs?
  A. Aristotle's categories
  B. Democracy
  C. Communism
IV. Constitutional government
  A. The U.S. Constitution
  B. Constitutional questions
  C. Individual rights
V. Systems of government
  A. The unitary system
  B. The federal system
VI. The U.S. federal system
  A. The role of state government
  B. Interpreting the states' rights
VII. Government at work
  A. Defense
  B. Commerce
  C. Taxation
  D. State services
  E. Relationships among public governments
VIII. The organization of government
  A. Presidential government
  B. Parliamentary government
  C. Party systems
IX. History of government
X. Careers in government

Questions

What is a private government?
What purpose is served by the Preamble of the United States
  Constitution?
How does a democracy differ from a republic?
What is a coalition government?
What are the chief differences between a presidential govern-
  ment and a parliamentary government?
How do the federal and unitary systems differ?
What purpose is served by a bill of rights?
How do the branches of the United States government check
  one another's power?
What is the *elastic clause* of the Constitution of the United
  States?
What are grants-in-aid?

Additional resources

Level I
Bernotas, Bob. *The Federal Government: How It Works.* Chelsea
  Hse., 1990.
Feinberg, Barbara S. *The National Government.* Watts, 1993.
  State Governments. 1993.
Maestro, Betsy. *The Voice of the People: American Democracy in
  Action.* Lothrop, 1996.

Level II
Bejermi, John Z. *Canadian Parliamentary Handbook.* Borealis Pr.
  Published annually.
Burns, James M. *Government by the People: National, State, and
  Local.* 16th ed. Prentice Hall, 1994.
CQ Guide to Current American Government. Congressional
  Quarterly. Published semiannually.
Lauber, Daniel. *Government Job Finder.* 2nd ed. Planning Com-
  munications, 1994.
Taylor, Peter J., ed. *World Government.* Rev. ed. Oxford, 1995.
Wilson, James Q., and Dilulio, J. J., Jr. *American Government: In-
  stitutions and Policies.* 6th ed. Heath, 1995.

Government National Mortgage Association is a corporation owned by the United States government. It works to make housing more affordable in the United States. It is also known by its initials, GNMA, or by the nickname *Ginnie Mae.* The corporation is part of the Department of Housing and Urban Development.

The GNMA tries to increase the affordability of housing by attracting new investors to the home mortgage market. To attract investors, it guarantees mortgage-backed securities that have been issued by private financial institutions. The GNMA operates the single most important program for financing home loans that are assisted by the federal government. The program has helped finance millions of home purchases. The GNMA especially tries to help low- and moderate-income families who have difficulty finding decent, affordable housing. The corporation was created in 1968.

Critically reviewed by the Government National Mortgage Association

Government ownership, also called *public ownership,* is the ownership and operation of a service, business, or industry by a government. In the United States, most government-owned projects provide vital public services that private companies cannot provide. For example, sometimes the amount of money needed to start a project is more than a private business can afford to spend. This was the case in the development of the Tennessee River Valley (see **Tennessee Valley Authority**). Sometimes a needed service must be provided at such low rates that a private company could not operate at a profit.

State government ownership includes toll roads, bridges, historic sites, and recreational facilities. Local government ownership in the United States includes some public utilities, such as water systems.

The transportation and communication systems of most countries are government-owned. So are manufacturing plants in some European countries. In China and North Korea, the government owns nearly all means of production and distribution.   Richard C. Wiles

See also **Communism; Economics** (Kinds of economies); **Public utility; Socialism.**

Government Printing Office (GPO) is the largest multipurpose printing plant in the world. It prints and binds publications for the United States government, supplies paper and ink for government offices, and distributes publications for them. It sells copies of government publications to the public, if their content is not confidential. An official called the public printer directs the GPO. An assistant public printer, also called the superintendent of documents, supervises sales.

In one year, the Government Printing Office may produce or administer the printing of over $1\frac{3}{4}$ billion copies of various publications, including more than $4\frac{1}{2}$ million copies of the *Congressional Record* (see **Congressional Record**). The Documents Sales Service may handle the sale of more than $32\frac{3}{4}$ million documents in one year. Congress created the GPO in 1860, and it began operations the following year.

Critically reviewed by Government Printing Office

Government regulation is the supervision of privately owned businesses by government agencies to serve the public interest. Such agencies control prices, health and safety standards, standards of service, and other aspects of business. In the United States, nearly all industries are subject to some regulation at the federal, state, and local government levels. This article discusses federal regulation.

Regulation by the federal government began in 1887, when Congress established the Interstate Commerce Commission (ICC) to oversee the nation's railroads. During the 1930's, the government set up a number of regulatory agencies under New Deal legislation. The New Deal was President Franklin D. Roosevelt's program for economic recovery from the Great Depression. New Deal agencies included the Federal Communications Commission (FCC), the Federal Deposit Insurance Corporation (FDIC), and the Securities and Exchange Commission (SEC).

A new wave of government regulation occurred during the 1970's. For example, public interest in controlling pollution spurred the establishment of the Environmental Protection Agency (EPA). Concern for industrial and public safety led to the formation of the Occupational Safety and Health Administration (OSHA) and the Consumer Product Safety Commission.

Until about 1980, most of the older government agencies regulated a wide range of activities within a specific industry. For example, the ICC regulated the fares, freight rates, and standards of service of the railroad and trucking industries. Some people claimed that this kind of government regulation resulted in too close a relationship between an agency and the industry it regulated. Others charged that it reduced competition within an industry and caused higher prices. Since the late 1970's, government reforms have reduced or eliminated the regulation of financial services and the telecommunications, transportation, and petroleum and natural gas industries.

Most of the agencies formed during the 1970's each regulate only one aspect of the activities of many industries. For example, OSHA sets job safety and health standards for numerous industries. OSHA and similar agencies have been criticized for setting standards without regard for their economic impact on the industries involved.   Richard H. K. Vietor

Related articles. See the separate articles on each regulatory agency. See also the following articles:

Advertising (Regulation of advertising)	Industry (Government regulation)
Bank (Regulation of U.S. banks)	Insurance (Government regulation)
Business (Government regulation of business)	Public utility
Coal (Government regulation)	Pure food and drug laws
Consumerism	Television (Regulating U.S. television)
Fishing industry (Government regulation)	Transportation (Government and transportation)
	Truck (Regulation of trucks)

Governor is a device that keeps machines running at desired speeds. Cruise control mechanisms in some automobiles and trucks use governors to keep the vehicles moving at a constant speed. They are also used to keep industrial machinery and some electric motors running at proper speeds. Most governors regulate the speed of a machine by controlling the flow of electric current or of a fluid, such as fuel or steam. There are three main types of governors: mechanical, electronic, and fluid.

The illustration with this article shows a simple mechanical governor. The large disk and the flyweights of

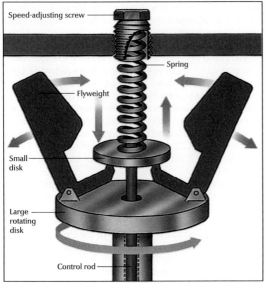

Speed-adjusting screw

Spring

Flyweight

Small disk

Large rotating disk

Control rod

WORLD BOOK illustration by Sarah Woodward

A mechanical governor controls machine speed. Levers, weights, and a spring regulate the flow of fluid or electricity.

the governor rotate with the machine. If the machine runs too fast, the flyweights tip outward. Then the levers raise the small disk, compressing the spring and lifting the control rod. This motion of the control rod decreases the machine's speed by reducing its supply of fluid or electricity. If the machine runs too slowly, the flyweights tip inward. Then the levers lower the control rod. This motion raises the machine's speed by increasing the supply of fluid or electric power. The desired speed is set on this governor by adjusting the force that the spring exerts on the small disk.

Electronic governors, such as the *direct current tach generator* and the *timed-pulse transducer,* regulate machine speed by supplying a certain voltage or pulse signal. Fluid governors may use air or liquids. Some fluid governors work like small rotating pumps. As they spin, their pressure regulates the machine speed.

On a steam turbine or conventional gasoline engine, the governor regulates the machine's speed by operating a throttle valve. In a jet or diesel engine, the governor controls the fuel valve.   David E. Foster

Governor, in the United States, is the chief executive of a state. Governors serve for four years in most states, and for two years in a few states. Their duties, like those of the president of the United States, are partly executive, partly legislative, and partly judicial.

As chief executives, governors have broad powers of supervision over administrative agencies. They can appoint people to many government positions, or remove them. They have the state militia and state police at their disposal. They prepare the budget for the legislature and supervise its administration.

As chief legislator, the governor recommends a program to the legislature and may veto the body's actions. In most states, the governor may veto specific items in appropriation bills. The governor also may call the legislature into special sessions. The legislature gives the governor the power to detail general statutes.

The governor's judicial powers include the granting of pardons, reprieves, and commutations. The governor may return to other states fugitives who have escaped from justice. The governor may fill judicial vacancies.

A governor may be impeached and tried by the legislature. In some states, the governor can be recalled from office in special elections.

In early state constitutions, the governorship was a weak position. Experience with royal governors made the people wary of giving the office too much power. But the governorship has become a powerful post, often leading to higher political office.   David R. Berman

See the tables of governors in the state articles. See also **Address, Forms of; Lieutenant governor.**

Governor general is an executive official who directs the activities of deputy or lieutenant governors. The chief executive officer of a territorial possession is often known as a governor general. The governor general directly represents the head of the government that controls the possession. Governors general administer the possessions of the Netherlands, Portugal, Spain, and the United Kingdom. They also administer the overseas departments and territories of France.

The powers of the governor general vary according to the laws of different countries. For example, the governor general of Canada has no real authority. But in some possessions or colonies, a governor general has almost the power of an absolute monarch.

At times, governors general have asserted themselves more firmly than would be proper for a monarch to do. In 1926, Lord Byng, the governor general of Canada,

Governors general of Canada

Name	Served
Viscount Monck (Charles Stanley Monck)	1867-1868
Baron Lisgar (John Young)	1869-1872
Marquess of Dufferin and Ava (Frederick Blackwood)	1872-1878
Marquess of Lorne (John Campbell)	1878-1883
Marquess of Lansdowne (Henry Petty-Fitzmaurice)	1883-1888
Baron Stanley of Preston (Frederick Stanley)	1888-1893
Marquess of Aberdeen and Temair (John Gordon)	1893-1898
Earl of Minto (Gilbert John Murray Kynynmond Elliot)	1898-1904
Earl Grey (Albert Grey)	1904-1911
Duke of Connaught and Strathearn (Arthur Albert)	1911-1916
Duke of Devonshire (Victor Cavendish)	1916-1921
Julian H. G. Byng (Viscount Byng of Vimy)	1921-1926
Marquess of Willingdon (Freeman Freeman-Thomas)	1926-1931
Earl of Bessborough (Vere Ponsonby)	1931-1935
John Buchan (Baron Tweedsmuir)	1935-1940
Earl of Athlone (Alexander Cambridge)	1940-1946
Earl Alexander of Tunis (Harold R. L. G. Alexander)	1946-1952
Vincent Massey	1952-1959
Georges-Philias Vanier	1959-1967
Roland Michener	1967-1974
Jules Léger	1974-1979
Edward Richard Schreyer	1979-1984
Jeanne Mathilde Sauvé	1984-1990
Ramon John Hnatyshyn	1990-1995
Roméo LeBlanc	1995-1999
Adrienne Clarkson	1999-

Each governor general has a biography in *World Book.*

provoked a grave constitutional crisis. He refused to dissolve Parliament when the prime minister, W. L. Mackenzie King, asked him to do so. Byng's decision caused a dispute that resulted in British approval of a proposal limiting the governor general's influence over local affairs. The dispute also contributed to British recognition of Canada as a voluntary partner in the Commonwealth of Nations. See **Byng, Julian H. G.**

Most governors general are citizens of the country or colony they govern. Some are selected by the people in the colony, and others by the government of the mother country. Governors general often work with councils or legislatures elected by the people. Under the more centralized French system, governors and governors general have extensive powers. Under the French constitution of 1958, the positions of governors and governors general were modified in most French possessions. Governors general of Portuguese colonies still rule in absolute fashion. They are holdovers of classical colonialism.

Robert G. Neumann

Governor General's Literary Awards are the highest national prizes given to Canadian authors. Fourteen awards are presented annually for works published in Canada in the previous calendar year.

Awards are given in seven categories—fiction, nonfiction, poetry, text for a children's book, illustration for a children's book, translation, and drama. Seven awards go to authors or artists whose works are in English, and seven to those whose works are in French. A committee chosen by the Canada Council, a government agency, selects the winners, each of whom gets $5,000.

The Governor General's Literary Awards were established in 1937 under an agreement between the Canadian Authors Association and the then governor general of Canada, John Buchan, a historian and novelist. At first, the awards were given only for works written in English. Each winner received a medal. The Canada Council began to sponsor the awards in 1959. It replaced the medal with a cash prize and also created awards for works written in French. Rosemary Sullivan

Goya, *GOY uh,* **Francisco** (1746-1828), a leading Spanish painter, was one of the first masters of modern art. His free brushwork and brilliant colors suggest to some critics the impressionist movement of the late 1800's. Goya's skill in capturing a dramatic moment and his fantastic imagination influenced the romantics of the early 1800's. His bitter satire on human nature and his search for a deeper reality in human emotions and subconscious inspired expressionism and surrealism, two major art movements of the 1900's.

Goya was born near Saragossa. His full name was Francisco José de Goya y Lucientes. He studied painting in Madrid. In 1774, he was appointed painter to the Royal Tapestry Factory. His tapestry designs are typical of the late rococo style in their elegance of line and color. But their recording of daily events anticipates the realism of the 1800's. Goya was admitted to the Royal Academy of Fine Arts in 1780. His paintings of the 1780's seem rich and optimistic.

In 1792, Goya became ill and gradually lost his hearing. His art became more personal and more imaginative. In the 1790's, he produced religious paintings, plus a series of biting social satires in his etchings *The Caprices.* His large portrait *The Family of Charles IV*

(1800) is considered one of the most brilliant, revealing portraits of all time. The two *Majas* (ladies), one dressed and the other nude, created a sensation. Napoleon I's invasion and occupation of Spain from 1808 to 1813 inspired Goya's most powerful paintings—*The Uprising of 2nd May* and *The Executions of 3rd May, 1808*—and his prints—*The Disasters of War.* These works depict the horrors of war.

In 1820, isolated by his deafness, Goya retired to his country house near Madrid. He filled the house with nightmarish paintings. Unlike his war paintings, the fantastic horrors of these pictures are relieved by touches of morbid humor, delicate beauty, and realistic observation. In 1824, Goya moved to France to escape the harsh rule of King Ferdinand VII. His last paintings are again characterized by brilliant color and dazzling technique.

Marilyn Stokstad

See also **Painting** (Romanticism; picture).

Additional resources

Tomlinson, Janis A. *Goya.* 1994. Reprint. Phaidon, 1999.
Wilson-Bareau, Juliet. *Goya.* Yale, 1994. An exhibition catalog.

GPS. See Global Positioning System.

Gracchus family, *GRAK uhs,* was a family of high nobility in ancient Rome. Two brothers, Tiberius and Gaius Gracchus, became famous as officials who tried to reform the political and economic system of the Roman

Oil painting on canvas (1797); The Hispanic Society of America, New York City

Francisco Goya was noted for his portraits. He painted a famous portrait, *shown here,* of the Duchess of Alba, his friend and supporter. The duchess points to an inscription in the sand, "Solo Goya," which is Spanish for "Only Goya."

Republic. The two are sometimes called the *Gracchi.*

Tiberius Sempronius Gracchus, *ty BEER ee uhs sehm PROH nee uhs* (163-133 B.C.), was elected *tribune of the people* (protector of the people's rights) in 133 B.C. One of his chief goals was land reform. He planned to enforce a law that limited the size of estates. In this way, he would recover land from the wealthy and distribute it to the poor. This plan would also qualify the new landholders for military service and strengthen the army. The Roman Senate opposed the plan because many senators had illegally occupied public land and would stand to lose. The Senate got another tribune to veto the law. But Tiberius persuaded the Popular Assembly to dismiss the rival tribune, even though such removal was illegal. The law then passed the assembly. Tiberius further alarmed the Senate when he sought reelection, which also was illegal. During the campaign, Tiberius was seized by enemies and killed.

Gaius Sempronius Gracchus, *GAY uhs sehm PROH nee uhs* (153-121 B.C.), served as a tribune in 123 and 122 B.C. Like Tiberius, Gaius worked to resettle landless farmers. He did this partly by sponsoring the establishment of Roman colonies. Gaius also worked to help the poor by lowering the price of grain. Tribunes could be reelected during Gaius's time, and he won a second term in spite of bitter Senate opposition. However, Gaius lost a bid for a third term in 121 B.C. After he left office, the Senate tried to arrest him. Gaius died during a riot that broke out when he refused the Senate order to surrender. Historians are not certain whether Gaius's enemies killed him or whether he committed suicide by ordering one of his slaves to kill him.   William G. Sinnigen

Grace, in Christianity, is the term for God's action in forgiving, sanctifying, or strengthening people. The term also refers to God's freely given love for all individuals. Christian churches teach that people need grace because they cannot overcome the effects of sin by themselves. According to Christian belief, people need grace to receive salvation and to live according to God's will. In both Christianity and Judaism, *grace* also refers to prayers of thanksgiving said before or after meals.

Christians regard Jesus Christ as the primary bearer of grace. However, they disagree about the exact nature and effects of grace and the ways of receiving grace. In Calvinist churches, for example, *grace* refers mainly to God's will, especially in *predestining* (choosing beforehand) certain people for salvation. The Roman Catholic Church teaches that grace pours faith, hope, and love into the human soul. Eastern Orthodox Churches regard grace as the communication of divine energy.

Christianity teaches that grace cannot be earned but only accepted as a gift. Most Protestants believe that people respond to it by expressing their faith through the sacraments of baptism and the Lord's Supper and through reading or hearing the Bible. Roman Catholics think of grace in terms of prayer, good works, and the seven sacraments of the church.   Jerry A. Irish

See also **Predestination.**

Graceland, in Memphis, Tennessee, is the former home of rock music star Elvis Presley, who died there in 1977. The 23-room mansion is one of the most visited buildings in the United States.

Visitors to Graceland may tour its main floor and lower level as well as the grounds of the estate, which covers about 14 acres (5.7 hectares). Presley and members of his family are buried in a garden on the estate. Presley's film and stage costumes and other mementos of his life are exhibited in a building next to the house. The estate's other attractions include Presley's private jet airplane and a number of his automobiles.

Presley bought Graceland in 1957 for about $100,000. He died there on Aug. 16, 1977, at the age of 42. Presley's former wife, Priscilla, an executor of his estate, opened Graceland to the public in 1982.   David Rubel

See also **Presley, Elvis.**

Graces, in Greek mythology, were daughters of Zeus, king of the gods, and the nymph Eurynome. The Graces served as patron goddesses of the arts and were the favored companions of the goddess Aphrodite. They were keepers of oaths of loyalty that young men often made in their name. The Graces also bestowed beauty on girls and gentleness or "grace" on poetry. The number of Graces varied among ancient sources, but there were usually three: Aglaia, Euphrosyne, and Thalia.

In art, the Graces are portrayed embracing or holding hands, and clothed in flowing garments. They stand in the foreground of Sandro Botticelli's famous Renaissance painting *La Primavera.*   Nancy Felson

Detail of *La Primavera* (1477-1478), a tempera painting on wood panel by Sandro Botticelli; Uffizi Gallery, Florence, Italy (SCALA/Art Resource)

The Graces in Greek mythology were goddesses of the arts. There were usually three: Aglaia, Euphrosyne, and Thalia.

Grackle is the name of several species of blackbirds that live in North and South America. The best-known species, the *common grackle,* measures about 12 inches (30 centimeters) long. It is black all over, with yellow eyes. The male has a sheen of purple or blue-green on its head and neck. Common grackles are found east of the Rocky Mountains, from Canada to the Gulf Coast.

WORLD BOOK illustration by Trevor Boyer, Linden Artists Ltd.
The common grackle lives east of the Rockies.

Two other widespread species are the *boat-tailed grackle* and the *great-tailed grackle*. In both species, the males grow about 16 inches (41 centimeters) long and are black with a purple or blue sheen. The females are brown and much smaller. The boat-tailed grackle lives along the Atlantic and Gulf coasts and in Florida. The great-tailed grackle is found in the south-central and southwestern parts of the United States and in Mexico, Central America, and northern South America.

Grackles live in flocks. They build bulky nests of mud and grass. The female lays three to six eggs that are greenish- or bluish-white with dark spots.

Martha Hatch Balph

Scientific classification. Grackles belong to the sub-family Icterinae of the emberizid family, Emberizidae. They make up the genus *Quiscalus*. The common grackle is *Q. quiscula;* the boat-tailed grackle, *Q. major;* and the great-tailed grackle, *Q. mexicanus.*

See also **Blackbird.**

Grade school. See Elementary school.

Grading is a method used by teachers to evaluate, record, and report student achievement. Most grades are given in the form of a number or letter. The most common numerical system uses percentages, with 100 as the highest mark and 65 or 70 as the lowest passing grade. The most widely used system of letter grades consists of the letters A, B, C, D, and E or F. The grade of A represents the highest achievement, and E or F means failure. Some schools use the numbers 4 for A, 3 for B, 2 for C, 1 for D, and 0 for E or F. Another system consists of the letters P (for pass) and F (for fail). Some schools use the letters O (outstanding), S (satisfactory), and NI (needs improvement).

Grades serve a number of purposes. They help teachers determine how well students have learned from their instruction. They help students learn about their strengths and weaknesses. Grades also inform parents about their children's progress and alert them to problems. Colleges use transcripts of grades to help decide whether to admit a student. Some employers use transcripts to help determine which applicants to hire.

Other factors besides achievement also influence grades. They include neatness in written work, willingness to work, and effort put forth. Some schools give separate grades for achievement and for effort.

Some schools supplement grades with other forms of reporting. Many elementary schools provide conferences at which parents discuss their child's progress with the teacher. Few high schools have such conferences because no teacher knows about a student's work in all subjects. However, most schools provide opportunities for parents to discuss their child's work with individual instructors. The teachers at some institutions write comments on report cards or send detailed letters to the parents. A few schools give no grades at all but use other methods to report student achievement.

Many educators and others believe grades are stressed too much, and some propose that grades be abolished. Many people object to grading because it forces a teacher to summarize many achievements with a single symbol. Other critics argue that grades result from personal judgment and vary from teacher to teacher.

People who favor grading point out that grades are the quickest and most efficient way to report student progress. They also argue that many students want such evaluations of their achievement. Most educators accept the necessity for grading and urge that present systems be improved.   Richard M. Wolf

Graduation. Schools and colleges usually award a diploma or certificate in recognition of achievement to students who satisfactorily complete a regular course. Most institutions present their diplomas at special ceremonies, called graduation exercises.

Graduation exercises were first held by European universities of the Middle Ages. American educational institutions still have many of the European graduation customs. Usually there are two special graduation ceremonies—baccalaureate and commencement. The *baccalaureate* service is a religious service, usually held on the Sunday before commencement. The diplomas are given out in the *commencement* exercise.

In most colleges, graduates wear academic gowns and caps to the ceremonies. By tradition, gowns are long and black. The tasseled, flat black caps are called *mortarboards.* Both cap and gown are patterned after European academic dress. The color of the tassel shows the kind of degree the graduate is receiving. Graduates may wear colored hoods on their backs to show the highest degree they already hold, and the institution which conferred it. In some colleges, they wear colored caps and gowns as well as hoods.

It is a custom at many high schools and some colleges for the valedictorian and salutatorian of the graduating class to make speeches. The *valedictorian* is the graduate with the highest marks. The *salutatorian* is the graduate with the second highest marks.   Gerald L. Gutek

See also **Degree, College.**

Grady, *GRAY dee,* **Henry Woodfin** (1850-1889), was a journalist and orator of the southern United States. He edited *The Atlanta Constitution* from 1879 until his death. Through editorials and speeches, he helped promote the rebuilding of the South after the Civil War. He delivered one of his most famous speeches, "The New South," in New York City in 1886. His works, published after his death, include *The New South and Other Ad-*

dresses (1904) and *Complete Orations and Speeches* (1910). Grady was born in Athens, Georgia, and attended the University of Georgia.   I. W. Cole

Graf, Steffi (1969-   ), a German tennis player, became one of the most dominant champions in women's professional tennis in the late 1980's and 1990's. In 1988, Graf won the *grand slam* of tennis—the Australian Open, French Open, All-England (Wimbledon) Championship, and United States Open titles. She also won the gold medal in women's singles in the 1988 Olympic Summer Games. In 1989, Graf won the Australian, Wimbledon, and U.S. championships but lost in the French Open finals. She again won the Australian Open in 1990 and 1994; Wimbledon in 1991, 1992, 1993, 1995, and 1996; the U.S. Open in 1993, 1995, and 1996; and the French Open in 1987, 1993, 1995, 1996, and 1999. She won a record 22 grand slam titles and was the only player to win each grand slam championship at least four times.

Stefanie Maria Graf was born in Mannheim and grew up in Brühl. She became a professional player in 1982, and was the top-ranked player in the world by 1987. She held the ranking a record 377 weeks. Graf announced her retirement from tennis in 1999.   J. Norman Arey

See also **Tennis** (picture: Modern women stars).

Graf Spee, *grahf shpay,* was one of three German *pocket battleships* (swift, heavily armed cruisers) that preyed on British merchant ships in the Atlantic Ocean early in World War II. In 1939, after a battle with three smaller British ships, the *Graf Spee* was cornered in the neutral port of Montevideo, Uruguay. Hitler ordered it scuttled, probably to prevent the British from learning the secrets of its construction and weapons. It was named *Admiral Graf Spee* after the German commander who went down with his ship in the World War I Battle of the Falkland Islands.   William A. Jenks

Graft in American politics refers to the acquisition of money or position through dishonest means. Examples of graft by an officeholder include accepting money for political favors and awarding government contracts to firms in which the officeholder has an interest. Some officials place unqualified relatives and friends on the government payroll in exchange for part of their salary or their campaign support. Corrupt big-city parties, commonly called *machines,* are sometimes associated with graft on a large scale.   Charles O. Jones

Grafting. See **Skin grafting; Plastic surgery.**

Grafting is the process of uniting parts of two plants to form a single plant. Plant growers reproduce many trees and bushes by means of grafting. They also use grafting to improve and repair plants.

Grafting requires two plant pieces: a *scion* (*SY uhn*) and a *stock.* The scion consists of a bud, branch, or cutting from a stem. The stock, or *rootstock,* is the piece to which the scion is grafted. The stock provides the root system and may also include part of a stem. For grafting to succeed, the scion and stock should belong to the same or related species. Each part contributes its own characteristics to the graft. The scion determines the kind and quality of fruit, nut, or flower that will be produced by the grafted plant. The stock nourishes the grafted plant and affects its size and productivity.

Uses of grafting

The primary use of grafting is to *propagate* (repro-

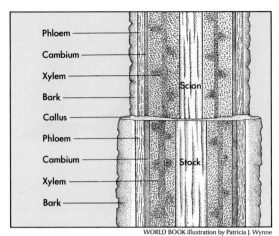

WORLD BOOK illustration by Patricia J. Wynne

Grafting involves joining a *scion*—a bud or cutting from one plant—to a *stock*—the root system of another plant. A *callus* then develops, forming the *cambium* of a new plant. The cambium produces the *phloem* and *xylem,* which carry food and water.

duce) existing varieties of plants. Most fruit trees, including nut trees, are propagated by grafting. Grapevines and rose bushes may also be grafted. In addition, rare varieties of such flowers as magnolias, dahlias, and peonies may be propagated by grafting.

Grafting can propagate hybrids, which do not grow true to variety if raised from seed. For example, seeds from McIntosh apples almost never produce trees with typical McIntosh fruit. However, a McIntosh scion will produce apples with the same characteristics as its parent. Grafting can also propagate seedless fruit, such as navel oranges and seedless grapefruit.

Grafting can be used to change the variety of fruit a plant produces. For example, a grower can graft different apple scions to one stock and thus make a single tree bear many kinds of apples. However, grafting does not create new kinds of fruit or flowers, even when the scion and stock belong to different species. For example, a Bartlett pear scion grafted to quince stock will produce Bartlett pears.

Grafting can change a plant's growing habits. A graft using established roots as the stock saves growing time. Orange and lemon trees, among others, grow faster and bear fruit earlier when they have been grafted.

Grafting can also produce hardier, disease-resistant plants. Stocks that grow in poor soils or survive low temperatures can support scions that suffer under those conditions. Pear varieties that are attacked by a disease called fire blight can be grafted to quince stock to reduce the chance of infection.

Grafting can change the shape or size of a plant. For example, vigorous scions grafted to less vigorous roots will produce dwarfs. Dwarf trees bear fruit sooner than standard trees and are easier to care for and harvest because of their smaller size. Plant growers also use grafting to repair injured parts of trees. For example, scions can be grafted in place of broken branches.

Kinds of grafting

Commonly used grafting methods include *whip grafting, cleft grafting,* and *bark grafting.* In all methods, the

Some methods of grafting

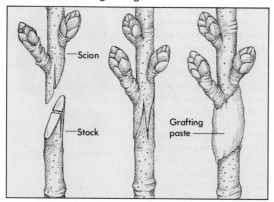

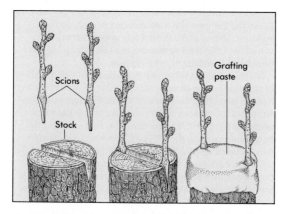

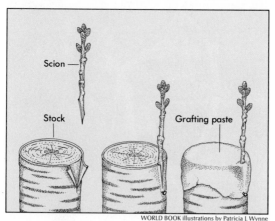

In **whip grafting,** a scion and a stock of about the same diameter are joined. The scion and stock are cut diagonally, and then a notch is made in each piece. The pieces are fitted together and sealed with grafting paste to keep them from drying out.

In **cleft grafting,** a cut is made in the top of the stock. The bottoms of two smaller scions are trimmed, and a scion is wedged into each end of the opening. The exposed areas of the stock and scions are then covered with grafting paste.

WORLD BOOK illustrations by Patricia J. Wynne

In **bark grafting,** the bark of the stock is slit and peeled back. The scion is trimmed, fitted in place, and secured with a nail. The exposed surfaces are then covered with grafting paste. Several scions can be grafted around the stock in this way.

cambium of the scion and the stock must touch. The cambium is a thin layer of growing tissue between the bark and the wood.

Scion and stock unite as new cells grow from their cambium. While these cells form, the scion and stock must remain firmly in place. Gardeners wrap most graft joints with tape or rubber bands, or they use a nail to hold the graft in place. For a successful graft, the plant tissues must not dry out. If scions are cut more than a day before they are to be used, they should be kept cold and moist. After joining the scion and stock, the gardener spreads a preparation called grafting paste over the joint to prevent drying.

Whip grafting is used when the scion and stock have about the same diameter. To make a whip graft, cut scions in winter and graft them as soon as possible. Slice off the bottom of the scion and the top of the stock on a slant. Make a slash about $\frac{1}{2}$ inch (1.3 centimeters) deep in each piece. The projecting tongue on one piece should fit snugly into the slash on the other, with the cambium meeting. Tie the joint and cover it with grafting paste. When the scion begins to grow after about a month, cut away the tying materials.

Cleft grafting is done in midwinter, when the plant is dormant. This type of graft is used when the scion has a smaller diameter than the stock. To make a cleft graft, saw the stock straight across. Split the sawed-off stock across the center to a depth of a few inches. Smooth the surface with a sharp knife. Trim two scions to a wedge shape at the bottom. On each side of the split or cleft, insert a scion so that its cambium touches the cambium of the stock. Spread grafting paste over the exposed surfaces.

Bark grafting takes place in spring when the stock begins to grow and the bark peels more easily. Cut several scions in winter and store them until spring. When you are ready to graft, saw the stock straight across and peel back its bark in several places just enough to make room for a scion. Pare the bottom of each scion diagonally for about $1\frac{1}{4}$ inches (3.2 centimeters) on one side and about $\frac{1}{2}$ inch (1.3 centimeters) on the opposite side. Insert each piece between the bark and wood of the stock with its long cut against the wood. Drive a nail through the bark and bottom of the scion and into the wood. Cover the graft with grafting paste.

Other kinds of grafting include *bud grafting, bridge grafting,* and *inarching.* Bud grafting, or *budding,* uses a bud rather than a stem cutting for a scion. The grower makes a T-shaped cut in the bark of the stock to receive the bud. The bark is peeled back and the bud inserted and pressed down into the cut. Bridge grafting is used to repair injuries in which large sections of bark have been destroyed. Scions are joined to the stock above and below the damaged area. Inarching is the grafting of two complete plants side by side. The gardener removes a small area of bark on each plant and ties the two together. After the plants have joined, the root and lower stem of one is cut away.   William H. Carlson

See also **Pear** (How pears are grown); **Quince.**

Grafton, Sue (1940-   ), is an American author of detective novels. Her novels feature Kinsey Millhone, a tough and humorous female *private eye* (private investigator) based in a fictional city in southern California. Grafton was one of the first writers to feature a woman in the realistic style of such male detective story writers as Raymond Chandler and Ross Macdonald.

Millhone first appeared in *"A" Is for Alibi* in 1982. *"B" Is for Burglar* followed in 1985. Grafton has since regularly published Millhone novels that follow an alphabetical title pattern. Other novels in the series include *"C" Is for Corpse* (1986), *"D" Is for Deadbeat* (1987), *"E" Is for Evidence*

Michael Goldman
Sue Grafton

(1988), *"F" Is for Fugitive* (1989), *"G" Is for Gumshoe* (1990), *"H" Is for Homicide* (1991), *"I" Is for Innocent* (1992), *"J" Is for Judgment* (1993), *"K" Is for Killer* (1994), *"L" Is for Lawless* (1995), *"M" Is for Malice* (1996), *"N" Is for Noose* (1998), *"O" Is for Outlaw* (1999), and *"P" Is for Peril* (2001). Grafton was born in Louisville, Kentucky.   Jon L. Breen

Graham, Billy (1918-   ), of the United States, became a world-famous evangelist. His early work in the United States and England for the "Youth for Christ Crusade" led him and his colleagues to conduct a large-scale evangelistic campaign in Los Angeles in 1949. His success there influenced him to engage solely in large-scale evangelism. Graham has conducted evangelistic campaigns throughout the world. He started a radio program, "The Hour of Decision," in 1950. He wrote *Peace with God* (1954), *Secret of Happiness* (1955), *My Answer* (1960), and *How to Be Born Again* (1977). Graham also wrote an autobiography, *Just As I Am* (1997).

Russ Busby
Billy Graham

Born near Charlotte, North Carolina, William Franklin Graham graduated from Wheaton (Illinois) College. He was ordained in 1940.   Henry Warner Bowden

Graham, Katharine (1917-2001), was an influential American journalist. From 1973 to 1993, she served as chairman of the board of the Washington Post Company, which owns *The Washington Post* newspaper, *Newsweek* magazine, and several television stations. Graham's position at the *Post* gave her entry into circles of power, both political and corporate, that were normally closed to women at the time. She thus ranked as one of the most powerful women in the United States.

Graham was born Katharine Meyer in New York City. Her father, Eugene Meyer, bought *The Washington Post* in 1933. Katharine graduated from the University of Chicago in 1938 and worked briefly as a reporter for the *San Francisco News*. She worked in the *Post's* editorial and circulation departments from 1939 to 1945. In 1940, she married Philip L. Graham, who succeeded her father as president of the Washington Post Company in 1946.

Katharine assumed the company's presidency after her husband's death in 1963 and became its chairman

and chief executive officer (CEO) in 1973. She served as the *Post's* publisher from 1969 to 1979, heading the influential paper when it led the U.S. press in uncovering the Watergate scandal (see **Watergate**). Her son Donald E. Graham succeeded her as publisher and, later, as CEO and chairman of the board. Her memoir, *Personal History* (1997), won the 1998 Pulitzer Prize for biography or autobiography.

Bill King, *The Washington Post*
Katharine Graham

Catherine Cassara

Graham, Martha (1894-1991), became a leading American dancer and *choreographer* (creator of dances). She pioneered a movement called *modern dance*. She defined dance as "making visible the interior landscape," and she used the entire body in dance movement to reveal the inner, true feelings of the characters she portrayed. Her movements were not always "pretty," because the feelings she tried to express included fear, jealousy, anger, and hatred. Early in her career, she sometimes shocked audiences with her sharp, angular poses and her abrupt, jerky actions.

Martha Graham was born in a suburb of Pittsburgh, Pennsylvania. She danced with the Denishawn company from 1916 to 1923. In the early 1930's, Graham began to choreograph dances for her own company based on primitive ritual and on American life. In the 1940's, she began interpreting the feelings of women. Graham's dances were inspired by the lives of Emily Dickinson, the Brontë sisters, and the great figures of Greek mythology as interpreted by the psychoanalytic theories of Swiss psychiatrist Carl Jung. Perhaps the greatest of her

Martha Swope
Martha Graham created dances expressing her psychological interpretation of Greek myths. She starred in *Alcestis* in 1960.

Greek dances was *Clytemnestra* (1958), a study of guilt and redemption. But along with such tragedies, she also created the joyous *Appalachian Spring* (1944) and the sparkling comment on dancers and their discipline, *Acrobats of God* (1960). Graham wrote an autobiography, *Blood Memory* (1991). Selma Landen Odom

See also **United States** (The arts [picture]).

Grahame, Kenneth (1859-1932), a Scottish author, wrote *The Wind in the Willows* (1908), a children's classic. The story tells about the adventures of Toad, Rat, Mole, Badger, and other small animals in the woods, rivers, and fields of England. Grahame created some of these adventures in a series of letters to his little son Alastair, who was known as "Mouse."

Grahame's first book was *Pagan Papers* (1893). He also wrote *The Golden Age* (1895), containing studies of childhood which were read throughout the English-speaking world. In 1898, he published *Dream Days,* a sequel to *The Golden Age,* which included the tale of "The Reluctant Dragon." Grahame was born in Edinburgh. He studied at Oxford University. Jill P. May

Grain is any of several cereal plants that rank among the most important food crops. These plants include corn, wheat, rice, and other grasses commonly called *cereals* or *cereal grains.* Their high starch content makes them an excellent source of energy for people and animals. The term *grain* also refers to the seed produced by the cereals.

Kinds. The most important grains, in order of world production, are wheat, corn, rice, barley, sorghum, oats, rye, and millet. Corn, wheat, and sorghum—in that order—occupy the largest acreage in the United States. Farmers and scientists have developed many varieties of each grain crop.

Uses. People use grain for two chief purposes—as food for themselves and as livestock feed.

As food. Some kinds of grain are eaten after simply being cooked. But grains generally are milled and then further processed into flour, meal, syrup, oil, starch, or some other form. These substances serve as important ingredients of such food products as bread, breakfast food, and cooking oil.

Wheat ranks as the world's chief food grain. Most wheat is ground into flour and used for making bread, other baked goods, and pasta. The use and importance of various grains differ from one part of the world to another. For example, rice is the main food of about half the world's people, including most Asians. But Americans and Canadians eat little rice in comparison.

As livestock feed. Any grain can be processed into feed. Those used most widely as feed in the United States include, in order of importance, corn, sorghum, oats, and barley. Farmers use about 60 percent of the U.S. corn crop as livestock feed. Most farmers feed their livestock both farm-grown grain and commercially prepared *mixed feed.* A feed manufacturer makes mixed feed by combining grain or grain by-products with vitamins, drugs, proteins, and other ingredients.

People indirectly eat grain fed to livestock because they drink milk and eat meat, eggs, and other foods produced by those animals. In the United States and other developed countries, people eat by far the greatest amount of grain indirectly. But most of the world's people eat grain directly because they do not have enough food to feed grain to animals.

Other uses. Many alcoholic beverages are made from grain by a process called *fermentation.* In this process, yeast or bacteria change grain starch into alcohol. Manufacturers also make a food product called *malt* by special processing of barley and other grains. Brewers use malt in making beer. In addition, malt is used as a food flavoring.

Hundreds of industrial products contain grain by-products or parts of grain. For example, manufacturers prepare starch from grain and use this material to stiffen paper and fabrics. They also use starch in making cosmetics, drugs, explosives, and pastes. Chemical companies mix grain parts with acid to make *furfural.* Furfural is a chemical used in making plastics and in refining certain petroleum products (see **Furfural**).

History. The origin of some cereal grains is more fully understood than that of others. Some developed from wild plants that grew long before history began. Scientists believe people in the Middle East and Asia Minor (now Turkey) started to domesticate some of these plants for use as food about 9000 B.C.

Various grains probably were developed in different parts of the world. For example, scientists believe wheat and barley may first have been cultivated in the Fertile Crescent region of the Middle East. Corn probably originated in what is now Mexico. Robert D. Wych

Related articles in *World Book* include:

Kinds of grain

Barley	Millet	Rice	Triticale
Corn	Oats	Rye	Wheat
Grain sorghum	Quinoa		

Other related articles

Bread	Commodity ex-	Grain weevil
Carbohydrate	change	Grass
Cereal	Flour	Malt
Combine	Grain elevator	

Grain elevator is a tall building equipped with machinery for loading, unloading, cleaning, mixing, and storing grain. These buildings are familiar sights in farm areas and in ports where grain is stored before shipment.

The term *grain elevator* is also used to mean the machine that lifts grain from a train or a ship to the storage bins. Some of these machines consist of systems of buckets that can unload the largest grain-carrying ships in a matter of hours.

Kinds of grain elevators. There are two general types of grain elevators—country elevators and terminal elevators.

Country elevators are found in nearly every town in grain-producing areas. These smaller elevators receive grain from farmers and generally store it for only short periods. The grain is cleaned in country elevators, and then graded before it is loaded in railroad cars and shipped to the large markets. Country elevators may be owned by independent business people, by farm cooperatives, or by grain elevator companies.

Terminal elevators stand at large grain markets and shipping centers such as Chicago; Duluth, Minnesota; Kansas City, Missouri; Minneapolis, Minnesota; and New Orleans. Most terminal elevators are larger than country elevators. In these elevators, grain is stored for the use of millers or to await shipment on the Great Lakes or overseas. Nearly all terminal elevators hold over 1 million bushels (35,000 cubic meters) of grain. One elevator in Wichita, Kansas, can hold 30 $\frac{1}{2}$ million bushels (1.1 million cubic meters).

How grain elevators operate. Grain elevators were once made of wood. Today, country elevators are often concrete or steel, and terminal elevators are concrete. Most grain elevators are over 100 feet (30 meters) high. Weighing and cleaning occur above the storage bins. This area is called the *cupola* or *headhouse.*

Railroad cars are unloaded at grain elevators by means of devices that tip a boxcar so that the grain runs out of the doors. Elevators for loading and unloading ships have *marine legs* on the dock side. To unload a vessel, the hatches are first removed, and the marine legs are lowered into the holds. Electrically operated buckets in the legs quickly raise the grain to the top of the cupola. From there, the grain goes through a *scale hopper* that weighs it, and then through a cleaner to the storage bins. A huge shipping port elevator can load vessels at the rate of 100,000 bushels (3,500 cubic meters) per hour.   Martin L. Hellickson

See also **Wheat** (Transporting and storing wheat; picture: A country elevator).

Grain sorghum, *SAWR guhm,* is a cereal plant grown mainly as food for livestock. Grain sorghum is also sometimes used as human food in Africa and Asia. People grind seeds of the grain sorghum plant into flour for making bread or porridge, or roast or pop the seeds whole. In many parts of Africa, beer is made from grain sorghum.

A grain sorghum plant bears small, round, starchy seeds in several compact clusters at the end of each stem. The plant grows from about 2 feet (61 centimeters) to more than 6 feet (183 centimeters) tall. Grain sorghum resists heat and drought well and requires less water for growth than most other cereal grains.

Grain sorghum is native to Africa. It was introduced into the United States during the late 1800's. Today, the United States is the world's leading producer of grain sorghum.   Robert D. Wych

Scientific classification. Grain sorghum belongs to the grass family, Poaceae or Gramineae. Its scientific name is *Sorghum bicolor.*

See also **Sorghum** (picture); **Kafir.**

Grain weevil is a small, dark beetle that destroys grain. The best-known *species* (kinds) of grain weevils are the granary weevil, which usually attacks grain stored in granaries; and the rice weevil, which often attacks rice and other grains in the field.

Grain weevils belong to a large group of beetles known as the *snout beetles.* Grain weevils measure about $\frac{1}{8}$ inch (3 millimeters), including their long snouts. Granary weevils do not have wings and cannot fly. But rice weevils have well-developed wings and can fly.

The female grain weevil punctures grains with her snout and lays one egg in each hole. She may lay 200 to 400 eggs over a period of several months. The eggs hatch into tiny, legless *grubs* (wormlike animals). The grubs eat the inside of the grains and become adults in about a month (longer in cold weather).

Storing grain in clean, dry, tight bins helps control grain weevils. Bins should be cleaned and sprayed be-fore new harvests are stored. Infested grain should be fumigated with a gas that is poisonous to grain weevils.

Ellis W. Huddleston

Scientific classification. Grain weevils belong to the order Coleoptera and the weevil family, Curculionidae. The scientific name for the granary weevil is *Sitophilus granarius.* The rice weevil is *S. oryzae.*

See also **Weevil** (picture: Weevils).

WORLD BOOK illustration by Shirley Hooper, Oxford Illustrators Limited

Grain weevil

Grainger, Percy Aldridge (1882-1961), was an Australian-born composer and pianist. His best-known compositions are based on the folk music of England, Scotland, and Ireland. Among these is *Molly on the Shore* in versions for orchestra, small orchestra, strings, and piano. His choral works include *Green Bushes, Marching Song of Democracy,* and *Tribute to Foster.* Grainger was also a music experimenter. For example, his *Free Music for Theremin* uses one of the earliest electronic instruments. Grainger's music has become popular with wind bands.

Grainger was born in Melbourne. In 1906, Grainger met the Norwegian composer Edvard Grieg. Grainger became a leading interpreter of Grieg's piano music. Grieg inspired Grainger to collect British folk songs and dances. Grainger moved to the United States in 1914 and he became a United States citizen in 1919.

Stewart L. Ross

Gram is a unit of *mass* (quantity of matter) in the metric system. One gram contains about as much mass as 1 cubic centimeter of water whose temperature is 4 °C (39.2 °F) at sea level. The gram is commonly used to measure weight. One gram equals 0.035 avoirdupois ounce, and 1 avoirdupois ounce equals 28.350 grams. The gram is used to weigh light articles, especially drugs and medicines. There are 1,000 grams in a kilogram. The symbol for gram is *g.*   Richard S. Davis

See also **Kilogram; Metric system** (Structure of the metric system); **Weights and measures.**

Gramm, Phil (1942-   ), a Texas Republican, is one of the most prominent members of the United States Senate. A conservative, he supports reduced federal spending on welfare and other social programs, strict limits on taxation, and a constitutional amendment to balance the federal budget. Gramm ran for the Republican nomination for president in 1996 but attracted little support in primary elections.

Gramm was born in Fort Benning, Georgia. His full name is William Philip Gramm. Gramm earned a Ph.D. in economics from the University of Georgia in 1967. From 1967 to 1978, he taught economics at Texas A&M University. Gramm

U.S. Senate

Phil Gramm

won election to the U.S. House of Representatives as a Democrat in 1978. In 1983, he resigned his seat, switched parties, and won reelection as a Republican. Gramm was elected to the Senate in 1984. In 1985, he coauthored the Gramm-Rudman-Hollings Act, which required federal spending cuts if deficit reduction targets were not met. Jackie Koszczuk

Grammar is the system by which a language functions. The description of that system is also called a *grammar.* Children study grammar in school to improve understanding of their language, and of other languages.

All languages do not function in the same way. Latin depends heavily on changes in the forms of words. Chinese stresses the pitch of the speaker's voice. English emphasizes the order of words. However, many languages include all these features to some degree.

Many grammarians believe that babies begin to learn basic grammar during their first year. By the age of 4 or 5, children have absorbed enough of it to communicate their thoughts. By the time they start school, they have used grammar continually for several years.

Anyone who understands how a language functions can identify that language even if most of the words are nonsense. For example, the major features of English grammar appear in the nonsense sentence *The plomic basinkers pirked the lampix at the simter ciptically.*

The above combination of words begins with a capital letter and ends with a period. It also has the rhythm of an English sentence. But more important, the words function like an English sentence. The word *basinkers* is a noun because it has a plural ending, *-s.* It also is marked by the article *the.* In the same way, *lampix* and *simter* are nouns because both are marked by the article *the.* The two words probably are singular nouns because they do not have a plural ending.

The word *plomic* is probably an adjective because it appears between an article and a noun. *Pirked* is probably a verb because *-ed* is a characteristic past tense ending of verbs. The word also has a position in the sentence typical of a verb. *Pirked* is a transitive verb because it has an object, *lampix. At the simter* can be identified as a phrase that modifies *pirked,* telling where. *At* is a preposition often followed by an object. *Ciptically* is probably an adverb because it ends in *-ly.* It may modify *pirked,* telling how or when.

Not all grammarians describe the system by which language functions in the same way. Various grammarians have formulated their own descriptions of how English grammar functions. The best-known descriptions are called *traditional grammar, structural grammar,* and *generative grammar* (also known as *transformational grammar*). Traditional grammar defines parts of speech by their meaning and function. Structural grammar defines them primarily by their order in a sentence. Generative grammar shifts the emphasis from analysis of parts of speech to the way people produce all of the possible sentences of the language.

Principles of English grammar

Words must be arranged in an orderly pattern to create a meaningful sentence structure. In English grammar, such a structure depends on three features: (1) word order, (2) inflection, and (3) function words.

Word order ranks as the most important feature of English grammar. Changing the order of the words in a sentence can change the meaning of the sentence. For example, the words in the sentence *John teased Joe* are reversed in *Joe teased John.* The second sentence also has the reverse meaning. Word order shows which word in a sentence is the subject and which is the object. Word order also indicates which words modify other words.

Inflection is a change in the form of a word. It shows a change in meaning or in the relationship between one word and another word or group of words.

The inflection of adjectives or adverbs is called *comparison.* The inflectional endings *-er* and *-est* are used to compare adjectives and adverbs, as in *near, nearer, nearest.* The ending *-ly* identifies many adverbs, such as *nicely* and *tenderly.* The listing of the different case forms of a noun or pronoun is called *declension.* English nouns have only two case forms: a *common* case for subject and object and a *possessive* case. The pronouns *I, he, she, we, they,* and *who* show three case forms—subjective (also called nominative), objective, and possessive. The pronouns *it* and *you* show only two case forms, common and possessive. *Conjugation* is the listing of the forms of a verb by mood, number, person, tense, and voice. For a summary of these forms, see the *World Book* article on **Conjugation.**

English also has the inflectional endings *-s* and *-es* to show most plurals: *town, towns; church, churches.* The endings *-'s* and *-s'* show possession: *man's, boys'.*

Function words primarily express relationships between various other words in a sentence or specify grammatical meanings. The most important function words, such as prepositions and conjunctions, show relationships. For example, the sentence *He walked over the bridge* includes the preposition *over,* and the sentence *Tom and Jim went home* has the conjunction *and.* Other function words include the articles *a, an,* and *the.* They identify nouns, as in A *boy ran away* or The *boy ran away.* The meaning of the main verb in a sentence can be affected by an auxiliary verb—for example, *He* must *go now* and *He* might *return later.*

Suprasegmentals express meanings and show contrasts in spoken English. By using variations of sounds and pauses, a speaker can indicate exclamations, questions, and statements. The speaker can also express the difference in meaning between *a lighthouse keeper* and *a light housekeeper.* A writer must use punctuation marks and typography to show such differences.

Grammatical relationships

English has various grammatical relationships. They can be classified into: (1) the actor-action-goal relationship, (2) coordination, and (3) subordination.

The actor-action-goal relationship, or *subject-verb-complement relationship,* is the basic grammatical relationship. It is the core of a sentence. This relationship expresses the idea that somebody or something does something, or is somebody or something. It is shown mainly by word order, as in *John visited the twins.*

Coordination is a relationship which shows that two or more ideas should be considered equal. Their equality can be illustrated by expressing the ideas in parallel form. In the sentence *She had been to Japan and had also traveled to Europe,* the verbs *had been* and *had traveled* are parallel. Function words, such as *and* or *or,* are used to express coordination—for example, *The farmer planted in March and harvested in August.*

Subordination, the third main grammatical relationship, indicates that one thing depends on another. The subordinate parts of most sentences serve as modifiers. They change in some way the meaning of the passage to which they are subordinate.

In most sentences, word order and function words show subordination, as in *After the apples ripened, the farmer sent them to the local market.* The clause *the farmer sent them* forms the actor-action-goal core of the sentence. The rest is subordination. The phrase *after the apples ripened* modifies the main action by telling when. The phrase *to the local market* modifies the action by telling where. The article *the* is a marker, and the adjective *local* modifies *market* by telling which one.

Grammar and usage

Grammar is the system of a language, and usage is the way people use that system. Usage thus reflects attitudes toward language, and what is regarded as "standard." Grammar and usage may differ in everyday life. Just as some people drive cars better than others do, some speak and write "better" than others. However, usage means more than following or not following standard practices. A language develops through usage. A language that does not change becomes a dead language. Latin is a dead language because it exists almost exclusively as literature written centuries ago. To change, a language must be used by many people in everyday life.

Standard usage is basically determined by the majority of the educated people of a country. This group includes government leaders, teachers and other educators, and men and women who write for newspapers, magazines, television, and radio.

All language habits do not result from standard usage. For example, most people who live in the United States speak English, but they use certain forms of speech heard in their region. These forms of speech are called *dialects.* A person's use of language also may depend on the situation. For example, an individual may speak formal English at a dinner party but use informal English at a sports event. Language habits can be influenced by a person's occupation as well. People who work in an automobile plant may use slang that outsiders cannot understand. At other times, those same workers use standard English.

Many people want to know what is "correct" or "incorrect" English. A sentence may be grammatical or ungrammatical, but no absolute agreement exists about all usage and standard practices. The best guide to usage of English is what is appropriate or inappropriate at any particular time or place. Dictionaries and grammar handbooks can provide guidelines for appropriate usage.

Most disagreement about grammar and usage occurs when a certain usage begins to undergo change. For example, usage is gradually eliminating the distinction between the words *who* and *whom.* Because usage seems to favor *who, whom* may someday disappear.

Patricia A. Moody

Related articles. See the separate articles on various languages, such as **English language** and **Latin language.** See also the following *World Book* articles:

Adjective	Conjunction	Number
Adverb	Declension	Paragraph
Antecedent	Etymology	Participle
Apposition	Gender	Parts of speech
Article	Inflection	Person
Capitalization	Interjection	Preposition
Case	Language	Pronoun
Clause	Linguistics (De-	Punctuation
Communication	scriptive lin-	Sentence
Comparison	guistics)	Tense
Composition	Mood	Verb
Conjugation	Noun	Voice

Additional resources

Fine, Edith, and Josephson, Judith. *Nitty Gritty Grammar.* Ten Speed, 1998.
Maizels, Jennie, and Petty, Kate. *The Amazing Pop-Up Grammar Book.* Dutton, 1996. Younger readers.
O'Conner, Patricia T. *Woe Is I: The Grammarphobe's Guide to Better English in Plain English.* Putnam, 1996.
Venolia, Jan. *Write Right!* 3rd ed. Ten Speed, 1995.

Grammar school. See Elementary school.

Gramophone, *GRAM uh fohn,* is the term used in Britain and the Commonwealth nations for phonograph. See Phonograph.

Gran Chaco, *grahn CHAH koh,* is a great, low-lying plain in South America. It covers more than 200,000 square miles (520,000 square kilometers) west of the Paraguay and Paraná rivers. Most of the Chaco lies in northern Argentina and western Paraguay, but it also extends into southern Bolivia. Over half of the Chaco is in Paraguay. The boundary between Paraguay and Bolivia was settled in 1938 after the Chaco War (1932-1935). The Chaco has great swamps, thorny brush jungles, and grassy plains. Its chief rivers are the Pilcomayo and Bermejo, which flow into the Paraguay River. Products of the Chaco include cattle, cotton, and quebracho.

Jerry R. Williams

See also **Argentina** (The land); **Paraguay** (Land regions; Military ruin); **Bolivia** (Territorial losses).

Granada, *gruh NAH duh* (pop. 96,966), a port on Lake Nicaragua, is an important commercial center in Nicaragua (see **Nicaragua** [map]). From Granada, merchants ship sugar, coffee, cacao, alcohol, hides, cotton, and indigo to the Pacific Coast. Granada is the oldest city in Nicaragua. It was founded in 1524. William Walker, an American military adventurer, burned Granada in 1856, but it was soon rebuilt (see **Walker, William**). Many beautiful buildings still are standing.   Gary S. Elbow

Granada, *gruh NAH duh* (pop. 254,034), in southeastern Spain, is the site of the Alhambra palace and fortress (see **Alhambra**). It is also the capital of Granada province. The tombs of the Spanish monarchs Ferdinand and Isabella lie in the Royal Chapel of Granada's cathedral. Granada factories produce textiles, leather, macaroni, and chocolate. For the location of Granada, see **Spain** (political map).

The Moors founded Granada about A.D. 750. In the 1200's, the city served as the center of Moorish wealth and culture. In 1492, when the armies of Ferdinand and Isabella conquered Granada, it was the last Moorish stronghold in Europe.   Stanley G. Payne

Granada, *gruh NAH duh,* was once a Moorish kingdom in southern Spain. The name may have come

Granada is a historic region in southern Spain.

from the Spanish word *granada* (pomegranate) or from the Arabic word *Karnattah* (Hill of Strangers).

Granada lay on the southern coast of Spain, and had an area of about 12,000 square miles (31,100 square kilometers). In the 700's, Moorish invaders conquered Granada and most of the rest of Spain. Granada became an independent kingdom in 1238. It remained a center of Muslim learning and civilization after the Moorish strongholds in other parts of Spain had fallen.

The downfall of Granada came when Moorish rulers began to quarrel among themselves. The armies of Ferdinand and Isabella gained possession of the kingdom of Granada in 1492. During the 1800's, the area was divided into three provinces called Granada, Málaga, and Almería. The province of Granada has an area of 4,838 square miles (12,530 square kilometers) and a population of 790,515. The capital of the province is also called *Granada.*   Stanley G. Payne

See also **Boabdil; Moors.**

Grand Alliance was the name of three unions of European countries formed to curb the military power of France under King Louis XIV. Each checked French expansion and maintained a balance of power in Europe.

In the first alliance, from 1673 to 1679, the Netherlands, the Holy Roman Empire, Prussia, and several German states opposed France in the Franco-Dutch War. In the second alliance, from 1689 to 1697, the Netherlands, England, Spain, the Holy Roman Empire, and many German states fought France in the War of the League of Augsburg. In the third alliance, from 1701 to 1714, the Netherlands, England, Austria, Prussia, and several German states fought France in the War of the Spanish Succession.   Claude C. Sturgill

See also **Succession wars.**

Grand Army of the Republic (G.A.R.) was a society of veterans who fought for the North in the Civil War (1861-1865). The G.A.R. was founded by Benjamin F. Stephenson in Decatur, Ill., on April 6, 1866.

The society was founded to strengthen fellowship among men who fought to preserve the Union, to honor those killed in the war, to provide care for their dependents, and to uphold the Constitution. Membership was open to honorably discharged soldiers, sailors, or marines of the Union armed forces who served between April 12, 1861, and April 9, 1865. The Grand Army had 409,489 members in 1890. In the 1870's and 1880's, it was an important political force in the North, especially in the Republican Party. It had one woman member, Sarah Edmonds. She had served in the Civil War disguised as a man. The last member of the Grand Army of the Republic, Albert H. Woolson, died in 1956, and the organization was discontinued.

Milwaukee Public Museum

The G.A.R. badge was a bronze star hung on a ribbon. The star shows a soldier and sailor shaking hands in front of a figure of Liberty.

The G.A.R. founded soldiers' homes, and was active in relief work and pension legislation. It started the celebration of Memorial Day in the North by a general order issued by John A. Logan. The Woman's Relief Corps began as a G.A.R. auxiliary.   Gabor S. Boritt

See also **Edmonds, Sarah E. E.; Memorial Day; Unknown Soldier; Woman's Relief Corps, National.**

Grand Banks is one of the world's richest fishing grounds. It covers about 139,000 square miles (360,000 square kilometers) off the southeast coast of the Canadian province of Newfoundland. The Grand Banks gets its name from being part of a system of underwater plateaus called *banks.*

There are millions of fish at the Grand Banks because the area has excellent sources of food for fish. This food

Parward, Hutchison Library

The Alhambra is a palace and fortress in Granada, Spain. Granada lies at the foot of the Sierra Nevada mountains in southern Spain. It was founded by the Moors about A.D. 750.

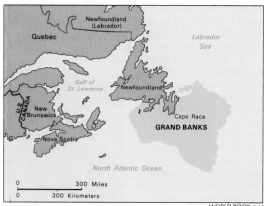

WORLD BOOK map

Location of the Grand Banks

consists of masses of tiny aquatic organisms called *plankton*. Plankton thrives on nutrients that are brought up to the surface from deep in the ocean by strongly circulating waters. The peak fishing season lasts from spring until fall. The fish catch has traditionally consisted mostly of cod. Other fishes caught in the area include flounder, haddock, halibut, herring, and redfish.

During the early 1500's, the fishing resources of the Grand Banks attracted large numbers of European fishing vessels, especially from France. By the late 1500's, English fishing crews established permanent stations on what is now the island of Newfoundland. Through the years, fishing fleets came from many countries, including France, Portugal, Spain, the Soviet Union, and the United States, as well as from Canada.

Due to the intense competition, the fish stocks of the

Grand Banks had declined greatly by the 1960's. In 1977, Canada extended its authority to cover all areas within 200 nautical miles (370 kilometers) of its coastline. All vessels—including foreign ones—now must have a license from Canada to fish in this zone, which includes most of the Grand Banks. Canada also prohibits ships from catching more than a certain number of fish of various species in the Grand Banks. In 1992, the Canadian government banned cod fishing indefinitely. The annual fish catch in the Grand Banks declined significantly during the 1990's.

Also during the late 1970's, surveys showed that deposits of petroleum and natural gas lie under the Grand Banks. In 1997, oil production began on a section of the Grand Banks called *Hibernia*. Whether offshore oil wells can be successfully managed without endangering the fish stocks remains a concern.   Simon M. Evans

Grand Canyon is one of the most spectacular canyons in the world. It cuts through northwestern Arizona in Grand Canyon National Park (see **Grand Canyon National Park** [map]). The Grand Canyon extends 277 miles (446 kilometers). It is about 1 mile (1.6 kilometers) deep. The canyon varies in width from less than 1 mile to 18 miles (29 kilometers).

The Colorado River flows through the canyon. The river formed the canyon over millions of years by cutting through layers of limestone, sandstone, shale, and other rocks. The rock layers vary in shade and color, and the tones seem to change during the day. At sunset, the red and brown layers in the walls of the canyon are especially brilliant.

Climate. Temperatures at the bottom of the canyon may be as much as 25 Fahrenheit degrees (14 Celsius degrees) higher than at the top. The average annual rainfall varies from 7 inches (18 centimeters) at the bottom of the canyon to 26 inches (66 centimeters) on the highest

Josef Muench

The Grand Canyon is one of the most famous scenic wonders in the United States. It makes up almost the entire area of Grand Canyon National Park. At Mohave Point on the canyon's South Rim, shown here, walls of brown and red rock rise above shadowy gorges.

part of the rim. The variations in elevation and climate create several different zones, which have a wide variety of wildlife.

Wildlife. About 300 species of birds are found in the Grand Canyon area. The area also has about 120 other kinds of animals, including beavers, bighorn sheep, elk, lizards, mountain lions, mule deer, pronghorns, and snakes. White-tailed Kaibab squirrels and pink Grand Canyon rattlesnakes live only in the area.

Vegetation. Ponderosa pine trees thrive on the canyon's rim. On the south side, juniper and piñon pines grow in lower areas. Aspen, fir, and spruce live at the highest elevations in the north. Cactuses grow throughout the canyon area, especially in low areas.

History. Some rocks in the deepest part of the Grand Canyon date back 2 billion years. The Colorado River began to form the Grand Canyon about 6 million years ago. Through the centuries, the water eroded the layers of rock, forming the canyon. Fossils found in the canyon walls indicate that animals and plants lived in the area millions of years ago.

Various Indian tribes have lived in the Grand Canyon during the last 4,000 years. Today, about 300 members of the Havasupai tribe live on a reservation in a side canyon called Havasu Canyon.

In 1540, a group of Spanish explorers led by García López de Cárdenas became the first Europeans to see the Grand Canyon. They were part of Francisco Vásquez de Coronado's expedition to the area. In 1869, the American geologist John Wesley Powell became the first white person to lead a river expedition through the vast canyon, which he named the Grand Canyon.

In 1919, Grand Canyon National Park was established. The park consists almost entirely of the Grand Canyon.

Lay James Gibson

See also **Grand Canyon National Park; Colorado River; Fossil** (picture; diagram: Tracing the history of life); **Seven Natural Wonders of the World.**

Additional resources

Aitchison, Stewart. *A Wilderness Called Grand Canyon.* 1991. Reprint. Voyageur Pr., 1993.
Anderson, Peter. *A Grand Canyon Journey.* Watts, 1997. Younger readers.
Pyne, Stephen J. *How the Canyon Became Grand.* Viking, 1998.

Grand Canyon National Park, in northwest Arizona, consists almost entirely of the spectacular Grand Canyon. The canyon, with the Colorado River running through it, extends 277 miles (446 kilometers). It is about 1 mile (1.6 kilometers) deep and varies in width from less than 1 mile to 18 miles (29 kilometers). The park also includes steep hills, tall spires of rock, and other scenic attractions. It covers nearly $1\frac{1}{4}$ million acres (500,000 hectares). The park, established in 1919, is one of the country's most popular national parks.

Viewing the Grand Canyon. The majority of visitors drive along park roads and stop at the scenic viewing points about the Grand Canyon. Visitors may also walk along the rim of the canyon. Many tourists hike along trails in the park. Some people ride mules into the canyon, and others enter by boat or raft on the Colorado River.

The South Rim of the Grand Canyon is the most developed part of Grand Canyon National Park. About 90 percent of the visitors view the canyon from this area. The more remote North Rim begins about 10 miles (16 kilometers) away on the other side of the canyon. However, the Grand Canyon is a natural barrier to rapid travel between the South and North rims. Visitors may drive around the canyon or hike across it. The distance around the canyon to the North Rim by road is 214 miles (344 kilometers). The hiking distance by trail across the canyon is almost 21 miles (34 kilometers). The trail takes most visitors at least two days to hike.

The headquarters of the park are at Grand Canyon Village, on the South Rim of the canyon. Major viewing points along the South Rim include Desert View, Mather Point, and Hermit's Rest. Among those on the North Rim are Bright Angel Point, Cape Royal, and Point Imperial. The South Rim is open to visitors throughout the year. The North Rim is closed from late October to mid-May because of heavy snow.

Recreational activities. Grand Canyon National Park has 38 hiking trails. They cover a total of about 400

Grand Canyon National Park

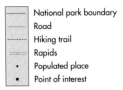

National park boundary
Road
Hiking trail
Rapids
• Populated place
■ Point of interest

WORLD BOOK maps

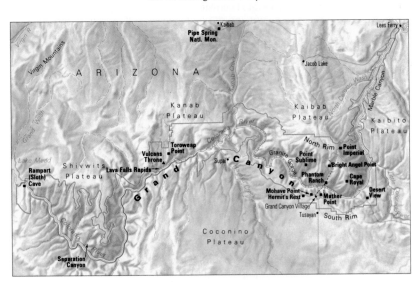

miles (640 kilometers). The three main trails into the canyon are Bright Angel and South Kaibab, which begin on the South Rim, and North Kaibab, starting on the North Rim. These trails connect on the bottom of the canyon at Phantom Ranch, which has cabins, a dining hall, and a campground. Reservations are required for Phantom Ranch. One-day trips by mule into the Grand Canyon begin on both the North and South rims. Two-day trips begin only on the South Rim. Visitors who take the two-day trip spend the night at Phantom Ranch.

Visitors may travel by boat or raft down the Colorado River as it flows east to west through the Grand Canyon. Private companies provide most of the river trips, but visitors with the proper skill and equipment may obtain permits to travel the river on their own.

The park also offers horseback riding and fishing, but hunting is prohibited. Reservations or permits are required for all overnight hikes, mule trips, and river tours. Applications should be made far in advance.

Critically reviewed by Grand Canyon National Park

See also **Arizona** (picture); **Grand Canyon.**

Grand Coulee Dam is the largest concrete dam and the greatest single source of water power in the United States. It stands across the Columbia River about 90 miles (140 kilometers) northwest of Spokane, Washington. The dam is near the head of the Grand Coulee, a steep-walled chasm where the Columbia once flowed.

The dam is the chief engineering feature of the Columbia Basin Project. The U.S. Bureau of Reclamation designed and built the dam, which was completed in 1942. It took less than eight years to build. Since then, the dam has had additional construction. Grand Coulee Dam is 5,223 feet (1,592 meters) long, 500 feet (152 meters) thick at the base, and 550 feet (168 meters) high, or about as high as a 46-story building. It contains about 12 million cubic yards (9 million cubic meters) of concrete.

Grand Coulee Dam has three power plants. The first plant began operation in 1941, and the second was completed in 1951. The third plant began partial operation in 1975 and was completed in 1980. The three plants house 24 main generators and 3 smaller generators.

Behind Grand Coulee Dam is Franklin D. Roosevelt Lake. This reservoir is 151 miles (243 kilometers) long. A pumping facility houses six pumps and six pump-generators. A pump-generator is a reversible unit capable of generating electric power and pumping water. The dam's total generating capacity is 6,494,000 kilowatts.

The pumps raise water from the lake 280 feet (85 meters) to a canal that flows into a reservoir in the Grand Coulee. From the reservoir, which is 27 miles (43 kilometers) long, the water enters the Grand Coulee irrigation system. Large-scale irrigation began in 1952. Eventually, the system will provide water for more than 1 million acres (400,000 hectares) of land. Edward C. Pritchett

See also **Columbia River** (Hydroelectric power and irrigation; map).

Grand jury is a group of citizens who decide whether there is sufficient evidence of a crime to try a person in court. Most grand juries have from 16 to 23 members, a majority of whom must agree on a decision.

In many states of the United States, there are two types of grand juries, *charging* and *investigatory.* Both meet in secret. Charging grand juries hear evidence presented by a prosecutor against a person suspected of a crime. The grand jury then decides if sufficient evidence exists to issue a formal charge, called an *indictment,* against the person. Investigatory grand juries examine (1) suspected dishonesty by public officials and (2) possible crime, especially organized crime. Many investigatory grand juries work with *special prosecutors,* who are appointed specifically for the investigation. Investigatory grand juries also issue indictments if they discover evidence of crime. In certain other states and in the federal court system, a single jury may function as both a charging and an investigatory grand jury.

The grand jury system is opposed by many people. Some claim it is too slow and costs taxpayers too much money. Some also charge that grand juries too often follow the prosecutor's wishes without considering the evidence. Supporters of the system believe it protects people from unjustified prosecution. Jack M. Kress

Grand National is the most famous steeplechase horse race in the world. It is run each year at the Aintree race course near Liverpool, England. Horses must be at least 6 years old to enter this grueling race of 4 miles, 856 yards (7.2 kilometers). The course has 16 jumps, 14 of which must be taken twice. Most of the jumps consist of sturdy thorn fences up to 5 feet (1.5 meters) high. The course also has several water hazards. Often, only a few horses finish the race. The first Grand National was held on Feb. 12, 1839, although it was not called by that name. William F. Reed

Grand Old Party. See Republican Party.

Grand Ole Opry is a radio program that has been a popular showcase for music since 1925. The "Opry" is the world's longest running live radio broadcast.

The "Grand Ole Opry" is broadcast on WSM, based in Nashville, Tennessee. The program was conceived by radio announcer George D. Hay. It was originally called the "WSM Barn Dance," but the name was changed to "Grand Ole Opry" in 1927. The name referred to a program of grand opera that preceded the country music show on Saturday nights.

The "Grand Ole Opry" had no studio audience at first, but its immediate popularity led WSM to build a studio. The show's following increased after WSM increased the power of its transmitters in 1932, carrying the station's signal throughout the South and Midwest. As the show's popularity spread, the "Opry" moved out of the studio in 1934 to a number of theaters in Nashville, notably the Ryman Auditorium, the show's home from 1943 to 1974. The "Opry" became a national institution after it began broadcasting over the NBC radio network in 1939. The "Grand Ole Opry" also appeared on network television in 1955 and 1956, and on cable television as the "Grand Ole Opry Live" beginning in 1983. In 1974, the "Opry" moved to its own 4,000-seat theater in the Opryland entertainment complex in Nashville.

The "Opry" originally emphasized folk performers from Tennessee. However, by 1938, the show featured a broader range of country singers and instrumentalists, such as Roy Acuff, Eddie Arnold, Red Foley, Lester Flatt and Earl Scruggs, Ernest Tubb, and Hank Williams. Another popular "Opry" performer was comedian Minnie Pearl. Today, the "Opry" has a 70-member roster that includes such entertainers as Garth Brooks, Dolly Parton, Reba McEntire, Vince Gill, Patty Loveless, and Trisha Yearwood. Critically reviewed by the Grand Ole Opry

Grand Portage National Monument marks the site of a famous trail crossing and fur-trading center during the 1700's. It is in the town of Grand Portage, Minnesota, just south of the United States-Canadian boundary, on the shore of Lake Superior. The monument was established in 1958. See **National Park System** (table: National monuments).

In the 1700's, fur traders and *voyageurs* (canoeists) carried their canoes and goods overland at this point to avoid falls and rapids in the Pigeon River. This 9-mile (14-kilometer) portage was the longest in the canoe route from Montreal to the Rocky Mountains.

The North West Company established a headquarters in Grand Portage in the 1780's. Each summer, brigades of canoes brought goods and supplies from Montreal. Fur traders brought their collection of pelts from the Canadian wilderness. Grand Portage remained an important canoe route and fur-trading center until the United States took possession of the territory in the early 1800's.

Critically reviewed by the National Park Service

Grand Pré, *gran pray,* is a historic village on Minas Basin in Nova Scotia. It was one of the largest communities in Acadia, a region in what is now eastern Canada and northern Maine that became the site of the first French colony in North America (see **Acadia** [map]). French colonists settled in Acadia in 1604 and founded Grand Pré about 1680. The French developed Grand Pré into a successful agricultural district that exported goods to nearby French and English towns.

In 1713, Britain gained control of the part of Acadia that is now the mainland of Nova Scotia. The British wanted the French-speaking peoples of Acadia to swear unconditional loyalty to Britain or leave Acadia, but the Acadians refused to do so. The power struggle in Acadia brought disaster to Grand Pré. The Acadians made a final refusal of the British oath of allegiance in 1755. In response, the governor of Nova Scotia had Grand Pré burned and sent more than 2,000 people from the Grand Pré area into exile. The poet Henry Wadsworth Longfellow described this tragic event in his poem *Evangeline.* Today, Grand Pré contains a national historical park in memory of Acadian history. D. A. Sutherland

Grand Prix. See **Automobile racing** (Formula One racing).

Grand Rapids (pop. 197,800) is the chief manufacturing, distribution, financial, and transportation center of western Michigan. It is the state's second largest city, after Detroit. Grand Rapids lies along the Grand River (see **Michigan** [political map]). It was named for the Grand River's rapids. Grand Rapids, Muskegon, and Holland form a metropolitan area with a population of 1,088,514.

The city center includes the Grand Center convention and entertainment complex, the Monroe Center shopping area, and the Van Andel Arena. In the plaza of the Vandenberg Center, a cluster of office buildings, stands a 43-foot (13-meter) steel sculpture by the American artist Alexander Calder. Part of another large sculpture extends into the river. It includes a series of steps up which trout and salmon leap. The Heritage Hill district has many restored houses of the 1800's and early 1900's.

Former United States President Gerald R. Ford grew up in Grand Rapids, and the Gerald R. Ford Museum is located in the city. Other attractions include the Grand Rapids Public Museum, the Grand Rapids Art Museum,

the John Ball Park and Zoo, and the Frederik Meijer Botanical Gardens. The Calder Arts Festival is held each year in the spring. The city has a symphony orchestra, opera and ballet companies, several theater groups, and several minor league sports teams.

Grand Rapids is the home of Aquinas College, Calvin College, Cornerstone University, Davenport College, Grace Bible College, Kendall College of Art and Design, and a campus of Grand Valley State University. The Van Andel Institute for Medical Research is in Grand Rapids. The Christian Reformed Church in North America has headquarters in the city.

About 2,400 manufacturing firms operate in the metropolitan area. Chief products include aircraft equipment, automobile parts, machinery, and office and home furniture. Other leading industries include the convention trade, fruit-growing, printing, publishing, and the production of cleaning and home-care goods. The Gerald R. Ford International Airport serves the area.

Ottawa Indians were living in what is now the Grand Rapids area before European missionaries arrived in 1825. Louis Campau, a fur trader, founded Grand Rapids in 1826. Grand Rapids was incorporated as a city in 1850. Its early growth resulted partly from its location on the southern edge of Michigan's great pine forest. Grand Rapids became a lumber center in the 1860's.

Many Dutch and Polish craftworkers settled in the area during the mid-1800's and helped develop the city's furniture-manufacturing industry. Grand Rapids grew into a major center of furniture production and became known as the *Furniture Capital of America.* Beginning in the 1920's, the city's furniture industry declined as many manufacturers moved to Southern states, where production costs were lower. Many new industries were later developed in the city. However, Grand Rapids still produces much furniture, and it is sometimes called the *Furniture City.*

Grand Rapids is the seat of Kent County. It has a commission-manager government. Joseph P. Crawford

Grand Teton National Park, *TEE tahn,* is an area of mountains, lakes, and forests in northwestern Wyoming, 7 miles (11 kilometers) south of Yellowstone National Park. For the area of Grand Teton National Park, see **National Park System** (table: National parks). The Teton Mountains rise 7,000 feet (2,100 meters) from the level floor of Jackson Hole, a valley in the park. Many people consider them to be the most majestic mountains in North America. The highest peak is Grand Teton (13,770 feet, or 4,197 meters, above sea level). More than 20 mountain peaks rise higher than 10,000 feet (3,000 meters) above sea level.

The Teton Mountains were formed when underground pressure caused two blocks of the earth's crust to shift. One block pushed upward to form the Teton Range, while the other block sank to form Jackson Hole. This shifting took place over millions of years. Because of the way the mountains formed, no foothills hide the jagged peaks and broad canyons of the Tetons.

At the eastern base of the Teton Range, melting glaciers formed a series of large lakes. Jackson Lake, the largest of these lakes, was partially artificially created. A dam at the place where the Snake River flows out of the lake has raised its level. Water from Jackson Lake is used for irrigation in Idaho. Other lakes in the park include

Grand Teton National Park, in northwestern Wyoming, contains the majestic Teton Mountains. The mountains rise sharply from the level floor of the Jackson Hole valley.

C. Douglass, Wyoming Division of Tourism

Phelps, Taggart, Bradley, Jenny, and Leigh.

Most of the trees in Grand Teton National Park are evergreens. Elk, moose, mule deer, and black bear live in the forests. Buffaloes and coyotes roam Jackson Hole. Beaver live in the Snake River. The river also contains several species of trout, including cutthroat trout and steelhead. The park also provides shelter for ospreys and rare bald eagles.

Grand Teton National Park was created in 1929, after efforts to incorporate the area in Yellowstone National Park had failed. It was enlarged in 1950. In that year, Congress abolished Jackson Hole National Monument, and most of its area was included in Grand Teton National Park.   Critically reviewed by the National Park Service

See also **Teton Range; Wyoming** (picture).

Grandfather clause, in modern law, refers to any legal provision that excuses an individual or corporation from a requirement or prohibition because the person or corporation has enjoyed a certain privilege or right at some time in the past. For example, a law that requires teachers to be certified may include a grandfather clause that allows teachers working when the law was passed to continue teaching without certification.

In United States history, *grandfather clause* also refers to a legal provision used by some Southern states after 1890 to deny voting rights to African Americans. To keep African Americans from voting, these states adopted strict literacy tests for all people who wanted to vote. Most blacks failed the tests. But so did many whites. As a result, the states adopted grandfather clauses. These clauses set aside the literacy requirement for certain groups—groups that included almost no blacks. For example, Louisiana's clause gave voting rights to people who were eligible to vote, or whose direct ancestors were eligible, on Jan. 1, 1867. At that time, few of the state's blacks could vote. The U.S. Supreme Court declared such grandfather clauses unconstitutional in 1915 and 1939.   James E. Sefton

See also **Fifteenth Amendment.**

Grandfather clock. See **Colonial life in America** (Furnishings).

Grandma Moses. See **Moses, Grandma.**

Grange, National, officially called the Patrons of Husbandry, is a major farm and rural community service organization in the United States. The Grange is a fraternal order. It has about 4,000 local groups in more than 37 states. Most members live in the Northeastern, Northwestern, and Middle Atlantic states. The organization provides community service and education programs for its members. Many of the local groups, called *Granges,* build their own halls, which serve as meeting and recreation centers. The Grange works with the U.S. Department of Agriculture and other federal and state agencies. It helps farmers and rural groups promote laws that benefit people in rural areas.

The Grange was founded in 1867 by a government clerk named Oliver Hudson Kelley, and six of his associates. Kelley had toured the South for the Bureau of Agriculture. He had found the farmers poor, discouraged, and uninformed. He believed a fraternal order would attract members and give the farmers a chance to learn advanced farming methods.

In 1868, Kelley went to Minnesota, his home state, and began organizing local Granges. The movement spread rapidly, and soon the Grange became an agricultural force in the Midwest. By 1875, there were over 21,000 Granges with a total of 850,000 members. Farmers used the Grange to organize opposition to the unfair practices of the railroads. Freight charges remained high, though farm prices had dropped. The Grange secured the passage of state laws to limit railroad rates. The Grange also worked for an income tax, laws against trusts, and other measures which later became law.

Some of these projects failed, and the Grange lost many of its members in the 1880's. The Grange began to grow again in the 1890's and built a large membership on the basis of its legislative, educational, and community service programs. Its headquarters are in Washington, D.C.   Critically reviewed by the National Grange

See also **Cooperative; Granger cases; Iowa** (The coming of the railroads); **Waite, Morrison Remick.**

Grange, Red (1903-1991), was one of the greatest running backs in football history. He won all-American honors in 1923, 1924, and 1925 while playing for the University of Illinois. His speed and elusive running style earned him the nickname "the Galloping Ghost." Grange's most spectacular performance came against the University of Michigan in 1924, when he scored five touchdowns, four on long runs during the first 12 minutes of the game.

In 1925, Grange joined the Chicago Bears of the National Football League (NFL). He traveled coast to coast with the team as it played a series of specially arranged games. These games drew huge crowds, who came mainly to see Grange, and played an important part in the growth of professional football. Grange played with the New York Yankees football team in 1926 and 1927 and again with the Bears from 1929 to 1934. From 1947 to 1963, he was a sports commentator on radio and television. Harold Edward Grange was born in Forksville, Pa., and raised in Wheaton, Ill.   Bob Carroll

See also **Football** (The rise of professional football).

Granger cases were five cases decided by the Supreme Court of the United States in 1877. The Supreme Court ruled that within their own boundaries states could regulate property affecting the public interest. These rulings of the court led to state regulation of many industries.

After the Civil War, Midwestern farmers faced rising transportation and storage costs and declining profits. The farmers formed clubs called *Granges,* through which they appealed to the states to regulate the railroads and storehouses. Some states with large farm populations, such as Illinois and Wisconsin, passed acts setting maximum transportation and grain storage rates.

Owners of railroads and grain elevators denounced the laws as interference with *interstate commerce* (trade between states), and violation of property rights. In *Munn v. Illinois,* the most important Granger case, the Supreme Court upheld the Illinois law. The court ruled that property which affected the community at large "must submit to be controlled by the public for the common good."   Stanley I. Kutler

Granite is a hard, coarse-grained rock that makes up a large part of every continent. Granite consists chiefly of three minerals—quartz, alkali feldspar, and plagioclase feldspar. These minerals make granite white, pink, or light gray. Granite also contains small amounts of dark-brown, dark-green, or black minerals, such as hornblende and biotite mica. The grains of the minerals in granite are so large that they can easily be distinguished. Many grains measure more than $\frac{1}{5}$ inch (0.5 centimeter) wide.

The minerals in granite are interlocked like the pieces of a jigsaw puzzle. As a result, granite is a strong, durable rock useful in the construction of buildings. Most granite can withstand weathering for centuries and can be polished smooth, making it especially suitable for columns, tombstones, and monuments.

Geologists classify granite as an *igneous rock* (see **Igneous rock**). They have concluded most granite is formed by the slow cooling and crystallization of molten material called *magma.* This magma has the same chemical composition as granite. It forms from rocks that melt 16 to 25 miles (25 to 40 kilometers) below the surface of the continents. These rocks melt at temperatures between 1200° and 1650° F. (650° and 900° C). The magma rises because it is lighter than the surrounding solid rocks. As the magma rises, it cools. Most granite magma cools slowly enough to form coarse crystals, and it solidifies below the earth's surface.

Sometimes granitic magma erupts from volcanoes and cools too quickly to form large crystals. The resulting rock, called *rhyolite,* has the same mineral composition as granite but is fine grained.

Experiments have shown that many kinds of rocks

yield granite when they melt. Rocks melt in stages, and the minerals that form granite melt first. One of the reasons that granite is so abundant may be the ease with which granitic magma forms.

North America consists largely of granite buried under *sedimentary rock* (see **Sedimentary rock**). Most granite appears where deeply buried rocks are brought to the surface of the earth by mountain-building movements in the earth's crust. Erosion removes the upper parts of the mountains, exposing the granite underneath. Large amounts of granite occur in such North American mountain ranges as the Appalachians, the Sierra Nevada, and the Rockies.   Maria Luisa Crawford

Related articles in *World Book* include:

Building stone	Mica	Quartz
Feldspar	Porphyry	Vermont (picture)
Hornblende	Quarrying	

Grant, Cary (1904-1986), was an American motion-picture actor. He became famous for his good looks and his suave, sophisticated screen personality. Grant appeared in many comedies, including *The Awful Truth* (1937), *Topper* (1937), *Bringing Up Baby* (1938), *Holiday* (1938), *The Philadelphia Story* (1940), *His Girl Friday* (1940), *Operation Petticoat* (1959), and *Father Goose* (1964). He also starred in the thrillers *Notorious* (1946), *To Catch a Thief* (1955), and *North by Northwest* (1959), all directed by Alfred Hitchcock.

Grant was born in Bristol, England. His real name was Alexander Archibald Leach. He moved to the United States in 1920 and became a singer in stage musical comedies. Grant made his film debut in 1932 and appeared in over 70 movies. He achieved his first major success in *She Done Him Wrong* (1933), in

Universal Pictures

Cary Grant

which he starred with Mae West. Grant became a U.S. citizen in 1942 and retired from films in 1966.

Rachel Gallagher

Grant, George Monro (1835-1902), was a Canadian educator, minister, and writer. He became best known as principal of Queen's University, in Kingston, Ont. Grant raised the educational standards of the university during his term, from 1877 until his death.

Grant was born in Albion Mines (now Stellarton), N.S. He attended Pictou Academy and West River Seminary, both in Nova Scotia, and Glasgow University in Scotland. In 1860, Grant was ordained as a Presbyterian minister in the Church of Scotland. He served as minister of St. Matthew's Church in Halifax, N.S., from 1863 to 1877.

In 1872, Grant traveled across Canada with Sandford Fleming, a civil engineer who was searching for a route for a transcontinental railroad (see **Fleming, Sir Sandford**). Grant wrote an account of the trip, *Ocean to Ocean* (1873). From 1889 to 1891, Grant lectured and wrote in favor of Imperial Federation. Supporters of this philosophy believed that Canada and other members of the British Empire should formally agree to trade with and defend one another.   P. B. Waite

**18th President of
the United States 1869-1877**

Johnson
17th President
1865-1869
Union

Grant
18th President
1869-1877
Republican

Hayes
19th President
1877-1881
Republican

Schuyler Colfax
Vice President
1869-1873

Henry Wilson
Vice President
1873-1875

Detail of an oil painting (1880) by Thomas Le Clear; National Portrait Gallery, Smithsonian Institution, Washington, D.C.

Grant, Ulysses S. (1822-1885), commanded the victorious Union armies at the close of the Civil War in 1865. His success and fame as a general led to his election as President in 1868. During his military career, Grant led his troops with energy and determination. He developed great confidence in his own judgment, and an ability to learn from experience. These traits also characterized Grant's political career. But the qualities that had brought him military glory were not enough to solve the nation's problems in the 1870's. Grant's enemies called him a poor President. Historians have generally agreed.

Grant was the first West Point graduate to become President. A quiet, unassuming man, he had an almost shy manner and did not look like a leader. Grant's presidency was clouded by disgrace and dishonesty. Congressional investigations revealed widespread corruption in both state and local governments. Grant was slow to realize that some persons who pretended to be his friends could not be trusted. Several of his major appointees became involved in scandals. But Grant himself was so honest that few historians believe he could have been involved personally.

Grant remembered that black soldiers had fought to defend the Union. He tried to protect the rights of former slaves to vote, hold property, and have other privileges of citizenship. He also sought to correct injustices suffered by American Indians. But Grant lacked the political skills to achieve these goals of justice and reform.

Two months after Grant became President in 1869, the nation's first transcontinental railroad was completed. In October 1871, the great Chicago fire killed about 300 persons and left more than 90,000 homeless. In 1872, Congress established Yellowstone National Park, the first national park in the United States. Alexander Graham Bell patented the telephone in 1876. That same year, in the Battle of the Little Bighorn, Sioux and Cheyenne warriors massacred about 210 men under Lieutenant Colonel George A. Custer.

Early life

Boyhood. Ulysses Grant was born on April 27, 1822, in Point Pleasant, Ohio, a village on the Ohio River southeast of Cincinnati. He was the first child of Jesse and Hannah Simpson Grant. They named their son Hiram Ulysses Grant but always called him Ulysses or 'Lyss. In 1823, the family moved to nearby Georgetown, Ohio, where Ulysses' father owned a tannery and some farmland. Grant's two brothers and three sisters were born in Georgetown.

Important dates in Grant's life

1822	(April 27) Born in Point Pleasant, Ohio.
1843	Graduated from West Point.
1848	(Aug. 22) Married Julia Dent.
1854	Resigned from the army.
1861	Appointed a colonel of Illinois volunteers.
1863	Led Union troops to victory at Vicksburg, Miss.
1864	Named commander of all Union forces.
1865	(April 9) Accepted the surrender of Confederate forces under General Robert E. Lee.
1868	Elected President of the United States.
1872	Reelected President.
1880	Defeated for presidential nomination.
1885	(July 23) Died in Mount McGregor, N.Y.

John Y. Simon, the contributor of this article, is Associate Professor of History at Southern Illinois University and Executive Director of the Ulysses S. Grant Association.

Colorado became a state in 1876, making a total of 38 states in the Union. No new territories were created by Congress during Grant's Administration.

The world of President Grant

The first transcontinental railroad system was completed in 1869. The tracks of the Union Pacific and Central Pacific railroads met at Promontory, Utah.

The Suez Canal, joining the Mediterranean and the Red seas, opened in 1869.

The National Woman Suffrage Association was founded in 1869 by Susan B. Anthony and Elizabeth Cady Stanton. That same year, the Territory of Wyoming gave women the right to vote.

Amendment 15 to the Constitution, which states that citizens cannot be denied the right to vote because of race, was adopted in 1870.

Canada increased its territory in 1870 by adding Rupert's Land, part of which became the province of Manitoba in 1870. British Columbia became a province in 1871.

Yellowstone National Park, the first national park in the United States, was established by Congress in 1872.

The first commercially successful barbed wire was designed by Joseph Glidden in 1873. Barbed wire brought an end to the open range of the West and made possible the settlement of the frontier by small farmers.

The Battle of the Little Bighorn, also known as "Custer's Last Stand," took place in 1876. During the battle, Indians massacred Lieutenant Colonel George A. Custer and about 210 of his troops.

New inventions included the telephone, patented by Alexander Graham Bell in 1876, and the electric light, developed by Thomas Edison in 1879.

WORLD BOOK map

Jesse Grant prospered in his tannery. The shy and retiring Ulysses disliked working in the tannery but enjoyed farm work and managing horses. He became an excellent horseman. Ulysses was trustworthy, and his father often sent him on business trips.

Education. Ulysses attended school in Georgetown until he was 14. He then spent one year at an academy in Maysville, Ky., and in 1838, he entered an academy in nearby Ripley, Ohio. Early in 1839, his father learned that a neighbor's son had been dismissed from the U.S. Military Academy. Jesse asked his congressman to appoint Ulysses as a replacement. The congressman made a mistake in Grant's name. He thought that Ulysses was the youth's first name, and his middle name that of his mother's family. He made out the appointment to Ulysses S. Grant. Ulysses never corrected the mistake. He thought he might be teased about his real initials, "H.U.G."

Grant was an average student at West Point. He spent much time reading novels and little time studying. But he ranked high in mathematics and made a fine record in horsemanship. Ulysses disliked military life and had no intention of making the Army his career. He considered teaching mathematics in a college.

Early Army career. Grant graduated from West Point in 1843 and was commissioned a second lieutenant. He was assigned to the Fourth Infantry Regiment, then stationed near St. Louis. There he met Julia Dent (Jan. 26, 1826-Dec. 14, 1902), the sister of a classmate. They fell in love and soon became engaged. The threat of war with Mexico delayed their wedding.

Grant's regiment went to Louisiana in 1844 and to Texas in 1845. He was in an area claimed by both Mexico and the United States when the Mexican War began in 1846. Grant became regimental quartermaster, in charge

of supplies. At Monterrey, he volunteered to carry a message through streets lined with enemy snipers. In 1847, Grant took part in the capture of Mexico City and won praise and promotion for his skill and bravery. He reached the rank of first lieutenant by the end of the war. Grant's experiences taught him lessons that later helped him during the Civil War.

Grant's family. Grant returned to St. Louis as soon as he could leave Mexico. On Aug. 22, 1848, he was married to Julia Dent. She was a devoted wife and gave Grant constant encouragement. Their life together

Ohio Office of Travel and Tourism

Grant's birthplace still stands in Point Pleasant, Ohio, near Cincinnati. When Grant was about one year old, he and his family moved to nearby Georgetown, Ohio.

Library of Congress

Julia Dent Grant met her future husband when he was a second lieutenant with the Fourth Infantry Regiment near St. Louis.

brought them great happiness. The Grants had four children: Frederick Dent, Ulysses S., Jr., Ellen (Nellie) Wrenshall, and Jesse Root, Jr.

Army resignation. Grant remained in the Army after his marriage. He was stationed in Detroit and in Sackets Harbor, N.Y. Then in 1852, he was ordered to Fort Vancouver in the Oregon Territory. Grant did not take his wife and infant son on the journey because his Army pay would not support a family in the West, where living costs were high. Mrs. Grant and Frederick went to live with Grant's parents in Ohio.

Fort Vancouver was a lonely post. Grant won promotion to captain in 1853 and was transferred to Fort Humboldt in California. But even a captain's pay was too small to support a family in the West. Separated from his family, Grant became depressed. Some Army officers gossiped that he had started to drink heavily. Several times in later years, Grant's critics charged that he drank too much. But no formal proof was ever offered. In 1854, Grant resigned from the Army and settled with his family in St. Louis.

Business failures. For the next six years, Grant's life was one of failure. Mrs. Grant's father gave her a farm near St. Louis, and Grant built a cabin there that he named *Hardscrabble.* Grant liked farming, but he failed because crop prices were low and his health was poor. He sometimes peddled firewood in St. Louis.

In 1859, Grant sold the farm and moved to St. Louis. A relative gave him a job in a real estate office, but Grant could not collect rents. He next obtained, and then lost, a job in the U.S. Customs House. Grant's father had opened a leather goods store in Galena, Ill. Ulysses' two younger brothers operated the store. In 1860, Grant's father offered Ulysses a $50-a-month job as a clerk. Ulysses accepted, but he showed no interest in becoming a storekeeper.

Civil War general

Return to the Army. Grant was almost 39 years old when the Civil War began in 1861. He had freed his only slave in 1859 and strongly opposed secession. As soon

as the war broke out, Grant knew he had a duty to fight for the Union.

After President Abraham Lincoln called for Army volunteers, Grant helped drill a company that was formed in Galena. Then he went to Springfield, the state capital, and worked for the Illinois adjutant general. Grant asked the federal government for a commission as colonel, but his request was ignored. Two months later, Governor Richard Yates appointed him colonel of a regiment that became the 21st Illinois Volunteers. Grant led these troops on a campaign against Confederates in Missouri.

During two months of campaigning, Grant refreshed his memory about handling troops and supplies. Upon the recommendation of Elihu B. Washburne, an Illinois congressman, President Lincoln appointed Grant a brigadier general in August 1861. Grant selected a young Galena lawyer, John A. Rawlins, to serve on his staff. Rawlins soon became Grant's closest adviser, critic, friend, and defender.

"Unconditional Surrender" Grant. Steadily, Grant revealed the qualities of a great military commander. He took the initiative, fought aggressively, and made quick decisions. Grant established his headquarters at Cairo, Ill., in September 1861. He soon learned that Confederate forces planned to seize Paducah, Ky. Grant ruined this plan by occupying the city. On Nov. 7, 1861, his troops drove the Confederates from Belmont, Mo., but the enemy rallied and retook the position.

In January 1862, Grant persuaded his commanding officer, General Henry W. Halleck, to allow him to attack Fort Henry, on the Tennessee River. As Grant's army approached Fort Henry, most of the Confederates withdrew. A Union gunboat fleet, sent ahead to aid Grant, captured the fort easily. On his own initiative, Grant then lay siege to nearby Fort Donelson. When the fort commander asked for terms of surrender, Grant replied: "No terms except an unconditional and immediate surrender can be accepted." The Confederate commander realized he had no choice but to accept what he called Grant's "ungenerous and unchivalrous" demand. Northerners joyfully declared that Grant's initials, U. S., stood for "Unconditional Surrender." Grant was promoted to major general.

Grant learned from his mistakes. On April 6, 1862, the Confederates opened the Battle of Shiloh by launching a surprise attack on Grant's forces at Pittsburg Landing, Tenn. The Union troops barely held off the enemy until reinforcements arrived. Grant was never again surprised in battle.

Grant was severely criticized for the heavy Union losses at Shiloh. Many congressmen urged Lincoln to replace him. Lincoln answered their criticism by declaring: "I can't spare this man—he fights!"

Persistence brought Grant a great victory at Vicksburg, Miss. All through the winter of 1862-1863, his troops advanced against this key Confederate stronghold on the Mississippi River. In May 1863, Grant defeated a Confederate army and then besieged Vicksburg. On July 4, 1863, the Confederates surrendered.

Grant's willingness to make decisions saved the Union forces that were under siege at Chattanooga, Tenn. Grant was given command of all Union forces in the West in October 1863. He immediately went to Chattanooga and found that plans had been made for breaking the siege. He put the plans into effect at once. On November 25, 1863, Grant's troops won a sweeping victory.

Grant in command. Grant succeeded consistently in the West while Union generals in the East were failing. Early in 1864, Lincoln promoted Grant to lieutenant general and put him in command of all Union armies. Grant went to Virginia and began a campaign against the forces of General Robert E. Lee.

Grant's troops suffered severe losses in several battles as he forced Lee to retreat slowly toward Richmond, Va., the Confederate capital. Many critics in the North called Grant a "butcher" because he lost so many men. During a bloody battle at Spotsylvania Court House on May 8-12, 1864, Grant declared: "I . . . purpose to fight it out on this line if it takes all summer." Actually, it took all summer, fall, and winter.

The fierce pressure of the Union Army forced Lee to abandon Richmond early in April 1865. Grant quickly pursued him, and Lee surrendered on April 9, 1865, at Appomattox Court House, Va. Grant released Lee and his soldiers on their honor and allowed the men to keep their horses "for the spring plowing."

National hero. Grant's victory won him great popularity in the North. Southerners appreciated his generous terms to Lee. After the Civil War, a bitter conflict developed between President Andrew Johnson and a group of Republicans in Congress. This group, called the Radical Republicans, demanded harsh treatment of the former enemy and strict protection of the civil rights of blacks. President Johnson favored a mild Reconstruction program. He was more concerned with the constitutional rights of states than with the rights of former slaves.

At first, Grant sided with Johnson. But Grant soon began to believe that Johnson's policies permitted the Southern States to restrict the rights of blacks. Grant was also disturbed by what he felt was Johnson's interference with military commanders sent into the South to carry out Reconstruction policies.

Library of Congress

As a Civil War general, Grant won several major Union victories and became commander of all Union forces in 1864. Grant is seated at the left in this photograph.

In 1867, Johnson removed Secretary of War Edwin M. Stanton and appointed Grant to replace him. But the Senate refused to approve the dismissal of Stanton. Grant gave up the office to Stanton and broke with Johnson publicly. Grant then gave his full support to the Republicans.

Election of 1868. The Republicans badly needed a popular hero for their presidential candidate in 1868. The Democratic Party still controlled many large Northern states that had a great percentage of the electoral votes. Delegates to the Republican National Convention nominated Grant unanimously on the first ballot. They chose Speaker of the House Schuyler Colfax of Indiana for Vice President. The Democrats nominated former Governor Horatio Seymour of New York for President and former Representative Francis P. Blair, Jr., of Missouri as his running mate. Grant defeated Seymour by a decisive majority of the electoral votes.

Grant's first Administration (1869-1873)

Inauguration. In his inaugural address on March 4, 1869, Grant admitted that he had no political experience. But he promised that he would not be ruled by professional politicians. "The office has come to me unsought," he said. "I commence its duties untrammeled." Grant's selections for his Cabinet showed his independence from the Republican Party. He did not consult party leaders about his appointments. For other government offices, Grant chose personal friends and army officers. He also appointed some relatives.

Reconstruction policies. Grant's Administration worked to bring the North and South closer together. It helped persuade Congress to pardon many former Confederate leaders and tried to limit the use of federal troops stationed in the South.

Grant also tried to maintain the rights of Southern blacks. He used federal troops to protect blacks from the Ku Klux Klan and other white groups that organized in the South to keep blacks from voting. In 1870 and 1871, Congress passed three *force bills* to enforce the voting rights of blacks (see **Force bill**).

Political corruption continued at all levels of government during Grant's terms in office. In the South, blacks and Northern adventurers known as *carpetbaggers* controlled some state governments (see **Carpetbaggers**). Some of these state governments were corrupt. In Northern cities, political machines such as the Tweed Ring in New York City made huge profits from graft on city contracts. Scandals came to light even in the federal government. President Grant himself was honest, but some of his appointees were men of low standards.

Part of the reason for the low state of public morality was the spoils system, which gave great power to politicians. Under this system, successful political candidates rewarded their supporters by giving them government jobs. Many incapable or dishonest persons received high government positions. Grant tried to change the system and urged Congress to adopt measures that would bring a merit system into government service. But Congress refused to appropriate money for a civil service commission that would regulate government jobs. The scandals that soon developed showed the need for civil service reform.

Detail of an oil painting on canvas; National Museum
of American History, Smithsonian Institution, Washington, D.C.

The Grant family posed for this portrait by American artist William F. Cogswell in 1867. From left to right are Grant's son Jesse; Grant's daughter Ellen, nicknamed Nellie; his sons Ulysses, Jr., and Frederick; his wife, Julia; and Grant himself.

Grant's first election

Place of nominating convention	Chicago
Ballot on which nominated	1st
Democratic opponent	Horatio Seymour
Electoral vote*	214 (Grant) to 80 (Seymour)
Popular vote	3,013,650 (Grant) to 2,708,744 (Seymour)
Age at inauguration	46

*For votes by states, see **Electoral College** (table).

One scandal began during the summer of 1869. Jay Gould, James Fisk, and other financial speculators tried to *corner* (gain control of) the gold market by buying all the gold available in New York City. They planned to force bankers and businessmen to buy gold from them at highly inflated prices. The only way this corner on the gold market could be broken was by having the federal government sell some of its own gold. But Grant's brother-in-law, Abel R. Corbin, assured the speculators that he could persuade the President not to permit the sale of government gold. Corbin had no position in the government, but Gould and Fisk accepted his word.

On September 24, which became known as Black Friday, Secretary of the Treasury George S. Boutwell told Grant that the plotters had created a financial panic. Grant then ordered Boutwell to sell government gold, and the panic ended. See **Black Friday.**

Foreign relations. In 1869, the president of the Dominican Republic offered to sell his country to the United States. Grant's secretary, General Orville Babcock, signed a treaty of annexation with the black republic. Senator Charles Sumner of Massachusetts, chairman of the Senate Foreign Relations Committee, attacked the

Vice Presidents and Cabinet

Vice President	* Schuyler Colfax
	* Henry Wilson (1873)
Secretary of state	Elihu B. Washburne
	* Hamilton Fish (1869)
Secretary of the treasury	George S. Boutwell
	William A. Richardson (1873)
	Benjamin H. Bristow (1874)
	Lot M. Morrill (1876)
Secretary of war	John A. Rawlins
	William W. Belknap (1869)
	Alphonso Taft (1876)
	James D. Cameron (1876)
Attorney general	E. Rockwood Hoar
	Amos T. Akerman (1870)
	George H. Williams (1871)
	Edwards Pierrepont (1875)
	Alphonso Taft (1876)
Postmaster general	John A. J. Creswell
	James W. Marshall (1874)
	Marshall Jewell (1874)
	James N. Tyner (1876)
Secretary of the Navy	Adolph E. Borie
	George M. Robeson (1869)
Secretary of the interior	Jacob D. Cox
	Columbus Delano (1870)
	* Zachariah Chandler (1875)

*Has a separate biography in WORLD BOOK.

treaty and denounced Grant. Sumner, a supporter of political rights for blacks, was angered at the thought of a black republic losing its independence. The Senate rejected the treaty. From then on, Grant regarded Sumner, Carl Schurz of Missouri, and other senators who had opposed him as enemies.

The government had more success in its relations with Great Britain. The *Alabama* and other Confederate warships built in Britain had destroyed much Northern shipping during the Civil War. The United States claimed that Britain should pay for this damage. On May 8, 1871, the two countries signed the Treaty of Washington. They agreed to submit the claims to an arbitration commission in Switzerland. The Geneva Tribunal of 1872 ruled that Great Britain should pay the United States $15,500,000. See **Alabama** (the ship).

Life in the White House. Grant took little part in Washington social life except for official appearances. The shy, retiring President reserved warmth and affection for his family. Grant followed a simple daily routine. He arose early and read the newspapers until breakfast. After a short walk, he went to his office, where he carried on official business until 3 p.m. He took a carriage ride or another stroll, ate dinner, and then read newspapers or visited with friends until 10 or 11 o'clock.

In 1874, Grant's daughter Nellie married Algernon Sartoris, an Englishman. Their wedding in the White House attracted international attention.

Election of 1872. Grant's first Administration achieved some real success. The national debt was reduced, and the dispute with Great Britain over war claims was settled. But Grant offended some politicians and disappointed others who wanted civil service reform. In addition, people who favored free trade opposed the high tariff then in effect.

Discontented Republicans held a convention of their own. They called themselves Liberal Republicans. Senator Schurz and a group of journalists controlled the con-

Quotations from Grant

The following quotations come from some of Ulysses S. Grant's speeches and writings.

No terms except an unconditional and immediate surrender can be accepted.
Message to General Simon Bolivar Buckner at Fort Donelson, Tenn., Feb. 16, 1862

I . . . purpose to fight it out on this line if it takes all summer.
Dispatch from Spotsylvania Court House, Va., May 11, 1864

The war is over—the rebels are our countrymen again.
Remarks at the surrender of General Robert E. Lee at Appomattox Court House, Va., April 9, 1865

Let no guilty man escape, if it can be avoided. . . . No personal considerations should stand in the way of performing a public duty.
Comment written on a letter about the Whiskey Ring political scandal, July 29, 1875

Now, the right of revolution is an inherent one. . . . But any people or part of a people who resort to this remedy, stake their lives, their property, and every claim for protection given by citizenship—on the issue. Victory, or the conditions imposed by the conqueror—must be the result.
Personal Memoirs of U. S. Grant (1885)

vention. They nominated Horace Greeley, editor of the *New York Tribune,* for President.

The Democrats also nominated Greeley for President. They hoped, by combining with the Liberal Republicans, to overthrow the corrupt Republican Administration. But the Democrats were also corrupt. Their political machines in several big cities had swindled millions of dollars from taxpayers. Also, Greeley had been an ardent Republican and a supporter of the high tariff, which many Democrats opposed. As a result, the Democrats and Liberal Republicans found it hard to cooperate.

Grant's Republicans presented a united front. Experienced politicians led the party's campaign. Also, the Republicans knew that they could count on the black vote of the South. The party renominated Grant for President and named Senator Henry Wilson of Massachusetts as his running mate. Grant won reelection by a greater majority than he had received in 1868.

Grant's second Administration (1873-1877)

Grant's second term got off to a bad start as Congress investigated the Credit Mobilier, a construction company owned by leading stockholders of the Union Pacific Railroad. The investigation revealed that many congressmen had taken bribes from the firm to do favors for the Union Pacific. Congress reprimanded several men involved in the scandal. See **Credit Mobilier of America.**

Grant's second election

Place of nominating convention	Philadelphia
Ballot on which nominated	1st
Democratic-Liberal Republican opponent	Horace Greeley
Electoral vote*	286 (Grant) to 3 (Greeley)†
Popular vote	3,598,235 (Grant) to 2,834,761 (Greeley)
Age at inauguration	50

*For votes by states, see **Electoral College** (table).
†Greeley died three weeks after the election, and the Democratic presidential electors split their 63 votes among a number of persons. The three votes cast for Greeley were not actually counted.

The Panic of 1873. In September 1873, several important Eastern banks failed, and a financial panic swept the country. Hardest hit by the panic were bankers, manufacturers, and farmers of the South and West. In an attempt to gain relief, many farmers joined the Greenback Party. This party and other groups demanded an inflation of the nation's currency to ease the depression. See **Greenback Party.**

Under such pressure, Congress passed an inflation bill that would have added $18 million to the paper currency in circulation. But Grant vetoed the bill.

Government frauds. The voters reacted strongly to the panic and to continued evidence of corruption in government. Grant himself showed poor judgment by accepting personal gifts. The Democrats won a sweeping victory in the congressional elections of 1874. The new Congress investigated the Whiskey Ring, which Secretary of the Treasury Benjamin H. Bristow had uncovered. The investigators found that whiskey distillers in St. Louis and other cities had conspired with tax officials to rob the government of excise taxes. The investigators also charged that Grant's secretary, General Babcock, had protected the ring from exposure. Grant stoutly defended Babcock, who was cleared of the charges. Many other officials were convicted of defrauding the government. See **Whiskey Ring.**

In 1876, another investigation revealed that Secretary of War William W. Belknap had accepted bribes from a trader at an Indian post. Belknap resigned, but the House of Representatives impeached him anyway. He was acquitted on a technicality. Just before the Republican National Convention of 1876, rumors arose of suspicious connections between the Union Pacific Railroad and James G. Blaine, former Speaker of the House.

In spite of the growing list of scandals, many Republican leaders wanted to nominate Grant for a third term as President. But Grant refused to run again. In June 1876, the Republicans nominated Governor Rutherford B. Hayes of Ohio for President. Hayes won the presidency by a margin of only one electoral vote.

Later years

Grant and his family traveled in Europe and the Far East for more than two years after he left office. He received enthusiastic welcomes wherever he went. When Grant returned home in 1879, he was still highly popular. He rarely occupied a house in Galena, Ill., that had been given to him by the people of Galena after the Civil War. In 1881, Grant moved to New York City.

At the Republican National Convention of 1880, Grant received strong support. More than 300 delegates voted for him through 36 ballots. Senator-elect James A. Garfield of Ohio won the nomination on the 36th ballot. When Grant learned of Garfield's nomination, he said: "I feel a great responsibility lifted from my shoulders."

Grant retired to private life with savings of about $100,000. He invested all his money in the banking firm of Grant & Ward. His son, Ulysses, Jr., was a partner in this company. Grant knew nothing about banking, but his son assured him that Ferdinand Ward was a financial genius. Ward turned out to be dishonest, and the company failed in 1884. The collapse of the company left Grant almost penniless.

To make a living, Grant began writing magazine articles about his war experiences. Soon he announced he would write his memoirs. Mark Twain, the famous American author, became his publisher. The memoirs were a great success and earned Grant's family about $500,000.

Grant knew he was dying of cancer when he wrote his memoirs. But he was cheered by the good wishes of the American people. In 1885, he moved to Mount Mc-Gregor, New York, near Saratoga. Grant died on July 23, 1885, soon after completing his memoirs. His body lies in a tomb in New York City that is officially named the General Grant National Memorial. Mrs. Grant died in 1902 and was buried at his side.   John Y. Simon

Related articles in World Book include:

Civil War	President of the
Colfax, Schuyler	United States
Lee, Robert Edward	Reconstruction
Mexican War	Wilson, Henry
Parker, Ely Samuel	

Outline

I. Early life
   A. Boyhood
   B. Education
   C. Early Army career
   D. Grant's family
   E. Army resignation
   F. Business failures

©Jim Anderson

Grant's tomb stands on Riverside Drive in New York City. More than 90,000 people donated money to build the monument.

II. Civil War general
   A. Return to the Army
   B. "Unconditional Surrender" Grant
   C. Grant in command
   D. National hero
   E. Election of 1868

III. Grant's first administration (1869-1873)
   A. Inauguration   E. Life in the White House
   B. Reconstruction   F. Election of 1872
      policies
   C. Political corruption
   D. Foreign relations

IV. Grant's second administration (1873-1877)
   A. The Panic of 1873
   B. Government frauds

V. Later years

©Doris De Witt, Atoz Images

Grant's home in Galena, Illinois, was given to him by the town shortly after the Civil War. It is now a state memorial.

Questions

Why did Grant not use his real first name?
Why did the Democrats combine with the Liberal Republicans in 1872?
When did Grant start writing magazine articles? Why?
What nickname was given to Grant after the capture of Fort Donelson? Why?
In what subject did Grant excel at West Point?
Why did the Senate oppose Grant's plan to annex the Dominican Republic?
Why did President Lincoln make Grant commander of all Union forces?
Why did the Republicans nominate Grant in 1868?
Why did many of Grant's critics in the North call him a "butcher"?
What did Grant's first Administration accomplish?

Additional resources

Catton, Bruce. *Grant Moves South, 1861-1863.* 1960. Reprint. Little, Brown, 1990. *Grant Takes Command, 1863-1865.* 1969. Reprint. 1990. *U. S. Grant and the American Military Tradition.* 1954. Reprint. Harper, 1987.
Perret, Geoffrey. *Ulysses S. Grant.* 1997. Reprint. Modern Lib., 1998.
Simpson, Brooks D. *Ulysses S. Grant.* Houghton, 2000.

Library of Congress

Grant visited an Egyptian pyramid in 1877 during a world tour after he left office. He is shown in the white circle.

Granville-Barker, Harley (1877-1946), was an English playwright, actor, producer, and critic. He managed the Royal Court Theatre in London with J. E. Vedrenne from 1904 to 1907. During that time, he made theatrical history by pioneering realistic acting and by introducing the plays of George Bernard Shaw, Henrik Ibsen, and other classical and modern dramatists. From 1912 to 1914, he helped revolutionize the staging of William Shakespeare's plays through productions that featured an open stage, continuous action, and natural speech.

Granville-Barker's plays include *The Voysey Inheritance* (1905), *Waste* (1907), and *The Madras House* (1910). They reflect Shaw's influence in their form and in their emphasis on politics, money-making, and marriage. Granville-Barker also wrote *Prefaces to Shakespeare* (1927-1947). In this series of essays, he interpreted Shakespeare's plays both as literary masterpieces and as works for the stage. Granville-Barker was born in London.   Charles A. Berst

Grape is a juicy, smooth-skinned berry that grows on a woody vine. Grapes grow in clusters of as few as 6 to as many as 300 berries. The berries may be black, blue, golden, green, purple, red, or white, depending on the variety of the plant.

About 66 million short tons (60 million metric tons) of grapes are harvested annually throughout the world. About 80 per cent is used in making wine. About 13 per cent is sold as table grapes, which people eat fresh. The rest is used, in order of importance, for drying into raisins, in making juice or jelly, and in canning with other fruits. Grapes have a high sugar content, which makes them a good source of energy.

Most grapes are grown in Europe, especially in the vineyards of France, Italy, and Spain. California produces about 90 per cent of the grape crop of the United States. About a fifth of the world's raisins and a tenth of its table grapes come from California vineyards. Other leading grape-producing states include, in order of rank, Washington, New York, and Pennsylvania. Ontario is Canada's leading grape-producing province.

Fossils of grape leaves and seeds indicate that human beings have eaten grapes since prehistoric times. The cultivation of grapes appears in ancient Egyptian tomb paintings that date back to 2440 B.C.

Kinds of grapes

There are two main kinds of grapes: (1) European, or Old World; and (2) North American.

European grapes were brought to Mexico by Spanish adventurers of the A.D. 1500's. By the late 1700's, Franciscan missionaries had taken grapevines north into the area that is now California.

About 95 per cent of all the grapes grown in the world are European grapes. In the United States, these grapes are raised mainly in California. Growers classify the varieties as wine, table, or raisin grapes.

Wine grapes contain the proper amounts of natural fruit acids and sugars required to produce a quality wine. Leading wine grape varieties grown in California include the Colombard, Chenin Blanc, and Thompson Seedless, also called the Sultana. They are used in making white wines. The Carignane and Zinfandel varieties are used in making red table wines. Premium wine grapes, such as the Cabernet Sauvignon, Chardonnay, and Pinot Noir, are also grown in California.

Table grapes are large and tasty and have a brilliant

Taylor Wine Company

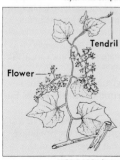
WORLD BOOK diagram

Thomas Nebbia, DPI

Grapes are grown in many parts of the world. In the photograph at the right above, workers are harvesting grapes in the Burgundy region of France. Seibel grapes, grown in the Finger Lakes area of New York, are shown in the upper left. The diagram shows the parts of a grapevine.

color. The chief varieties include the Emperor and the Tokay, which grow in large clusters consisting of red berries. Other table grapes include the greenish-white, seedless Perlette, the red Flame Seedless, and the black Ribier.

Most raisin grapes are seedless, and they have a soft texture when dried. The most important variety is the Thompson Seedless, which has greenish-white to light golden berries. It also ranks as a leading table grape and accounts for about 40 percent of the grape production of California. Other raisin grapes include the Black Corinth and the Muscat of Alexandria.

North American grapes consist of two main species: (1) *fox grapes* and (2) *muscadine grapes.* Both species can be eaten fresh or made into jelly or wine. They are not used for raisins. A third class of North American grapes includes the many hybrids developed from other grape species. These varieties are descended from crosses between North American species or between European and North American species. Most hybrids are eaten fresh or are used for wine.

Fox grapes are grown chiefly in the Northeastern States; along the eastern and southern shores of Lakes Erie, Michigan, and Ontario; and in Washington. The Concord ranks as the most important variety of fox grape. It has large purple berries. Most U.S. grape juice and grape jelly come from Concord grapes. Other fox grapes include the Catawba and the Delaware, which are red; and the Niagara, which is white.

Muscadine grapes grow throughout the Southeastern United States, from North Carolina to eastern Texas. Their natural resistance to insects, disease, and heat stress makes them well adapted to this area. The berries grow in small clusters and fall off singly as they ripen. The best-known variety, the Scuppernong, has medium-sized, bronze-colored berries. Muscadine grapes are widely planted, but mostly in home vineyards.

Growing grapes

European grapevines grow well in climates that have warm to hot, dry summers and winter temperatures no lower than 10 °F (−12 °C). North American grapevines can withstand greater humidity and temperatures as low as −10 °F (−23 °C).

Leading grape-growing countries

Tons of grapes produced in a year

Italy	●●●●●●●●●●●●●●	9,920,000 tons (8,999,000 metric tons)
France	●●●●●●●●●●●◖	8,159,000 tons (7,402,000 metric tons)
United States	●●●●●●●●●	6,583,000 tons (5,972,000 metric tons)
Spain	●●●●●●●◖	5,651,000 tons (5,126,000 metric tons)
Turkey	●●●●●	4,042,000 tons (3,667,000 metric tons)
China	●●●◖	2,616,000 tons (2,373,000 metric tons)

Figures are for a three-year average, 1997-1999.
Source: Food and Agriculture Organization of the United Nations.

Planting and cultivating. Grapevines reproduce by a process called *propagation,* in which a part of the plant grows into a complete new plant. In winter, growers cut branchlike growths called *canes* from the vine. The canes are cut into sections that are from 12 to 18 inches (30 to 46 centimeters) long. The sections, called *cuttings,* are buried in moist sand and then stored in a cool place until early spring. At that time, workers plant the cuttings in nurseries, leaving one bud aboveground. The cuttings grow roots and are replanted in the vineyard the following spring, where they develop into vines.

A year later, workers build supports for the young vines by stringing wires between posts placed next to each plant. The vines fasten themselves to the wires by means of coiled growths called *tendrils.* Every winter, the growers prune the vines to regulate the amount of fruit produced. Grapevines produce a partial crop the third and fourth years in the vineyard and a full crop thereafter. With proper care, a vine may bear from 15 to 80 pounds (7 to 36 kilograms) of grapes yearly for as long as 100 years.

Harvesting. European grapes are harvested in California from June to October, about 60 to 120 days after blossoming. North American grapes are harvested in September and October, about 90 to 120 days after blossoming. Workers harvest table grapes by carefully cutting each cluster by its main stem and removing any damaged berries. Wine grapes and raisin grapes may be harvested by hand or by machine. Wine grapes are taken directly to a winery for crushing. Table grapes are packed in the vineyard or in specially equipped buildings located nearby. Workers place raisin grapes on sheets of heavy paper and leave them in the vineyard to dry in the sun.

Packing and shipping. Workers pack table grapes in wide, shallow boxes that are padded to prevent the fruit from being bruised. The grapes are then precooled to about 40 °F (4 °C) and treated with sulfur dioxide gas to retard decay. The boxes are put into refrigerated trucks or railroad cars for shipment to market.

Diseases and pests. Major grape diseases in the Eastern United States include downy mildew and black rot. Grapevines throughout the country may be destroyed by powdery mildew or virus diseases. All of these diseases attack both the vine and berries, but they can be controlled with chemical dusts and sprays. Roots of European grapevines may be destroyed by insects called *grape phylloxera* and roundworms called *nematodes.* Growers control such pests by *grafting* (attaching) vines to the roots of various North American species, which resist phylloxera and nematodes.   Bruce I. Reisch

Scientific classification. Grapes belong to the family Vitaceae. European grapes are *Vitis vinifera.* Fox grapes are *V. labrusca.* Muscadine grapes are *V. rotundifolia.*

See also **Fruit** (table: Leading fruits in the United States); **Grafting; Phylloxera; Pruning; Raisin; Wine; Europe** (picture: Grapes).

Grapefruit is a large, round citrus fruit. People in many parts of the world enjoy grapefruit for breakfast. They also drink the tart, somewhat bitter juice of the fruit. Grapefruit probably got its name because some varieties produce fruit in clusters, like grapes.

A grapefruit measures 4 to 6 inches (10 to 15 centimeters) in diameter. It consists of 10 to 14 segments sur-

Graph 321

rounded by a soft white inner rind and a leathery yellow outer rind. The segments contain pulp, juice, and seeds, though most commercial varieties of grapefruit have few or no seeds. The fruit is rich in vitamin C.

The pulp and juice of grapefruit range in color from white to pink or red. The white-fleshed, seedless *Marsh* grapefruit is the most important white variety. A well-known pink variety is the seedless *Thompson,* also known as the *Pink Marsh.* An important red grapefruit is the seedless *Redblush,* also known as the *Ruby.* The flesh and, in some cases, the rind of pink and red varieties have a pink tinge. All varieties of grapefruit have a similar taste and texture.

The United States produces about half of the world's grapefruit. Cuba, Israel, and Mexico rank next in production. Growers in the United States harvest about 5 $\frac{1}{2}$ billion pounds (2 $\frac{1}{2}$ billion kilograms) of the fruit yearly. Florida produces over 80 percent of the nation's grapefruit. About half of the United States crop is processed into juice or fruit sections to be canned or frozen.

Growing grapefruit. The grapefruit tree can grow to a height of about 30 feet (9 meters). It has dark green leaves and white flowers. The trees are grown from the buds of other grapefruit trees that produce the variety of grapefruit desired (see **Grafting** [Other kinds of grafting]). The fruit, which appears in 3 to 4 years, develops from the ovaries of the blossoms. It is harvested 8 to 14 months after the flowers bloom.

Grapefruit trees and fruit may be severely damaged by frost and cold temperatures. The trees also may be attacked by such pests as mites, aphids, and scale insects. Growers control these pests by spraying the trees with insecticides. In addition, they spray with fungicides to protect the leaves and fruit from fungus diseases, including greasy spot, melanose, and scab.

In the United States, federal and state laws establish standards of maturity for grapefruit. As grapefruit matures, the sugar and juice in the fruit increase, and the

Leading grapefruit-growing states

Amount of grapefruit produced in a year

Florida	●●●●●●●●●●●●●●
	4,642,400,000 pounds (2,105,800,000 kilograms)
California	●●◖
	571,700,000 pounds (259,300,000 kilograms)
Texas	●◖
	386,700,000 pounds (175,400,000 kilograms)
Arizona	◖
	78,200,000 pounds (35,500,000 kilograms)

Figures are for a three-year average, 1995-1997.
Source: U.S. Department of Agriculture.

acid decreases. The fruit does not mature further after being harvested. Therefore, growers pick grapefruit when it contains the required amounts of sugar, juice, and acid.

History. Grapefruit probably originated in the West Indies in the early 1700's. Scientists believe it developed as a natural hybrid of the *shaddock,* or *pummelo,* a citrus fruit of Southeast Asia. The first grapefruit trees in Florida were planted about 1820. By 1900, the fruit was being shipped throughout the United States.

Wilfred F. Wardowski

Scientific classification. Grapefruit belongs to the rue family, Rutaceae. Its scientific name is *Citrus paradisi.*

See also **Citrus; Fruit** (table: Leading fruits in the United States); **Tangelo.**

Graph is a drawing that shows the relative sizes of numerical quantities. It is used to present facts in picture form so that they will be clearer and easier to understand. For example, suppose there is a record of the number of pupils present in a classroom on the first day of each of five months. On September 1, 24 pupils were

WORLD BOOK illustration by Kate Lloyd-Jones, Linden Artists Ltd.

Florida Department of Citrus

Grapefruit is a large citrus fruit that has a tart flavor and is frequently eaten for breakfast. The ripe fruit is picked by hand. It stays fresh on the tree for several months and can be harvested at any time during that period.

Number of pupils present

Graph 1

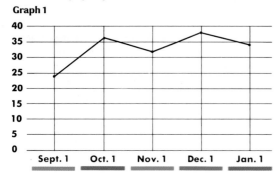

Graph 2

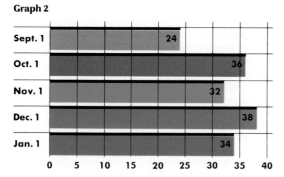

Graph 3

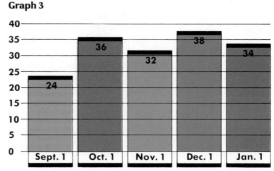

Graph 4

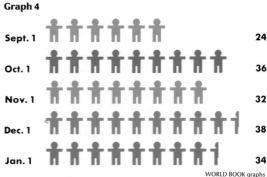

WORLD BOOK graphs

Each symbol represents 4 pupils present.

present; on the first of October, 36; and on November 1, 32. On December 1, 38 were present; and on the first of January, 34. Graphs 1 through 4 show four different ways of representing these facts.

Line graphs are the simplest type of graph. They are also one of the easiest ways to compare numbers. A line graph is illustrated in Graph 1.

Line graphs are made using a grid. The vertical *axis* (scale) indicates frequency, and the horizontal axis shows the categories being considered. In this case, the frequency is the number of pupils present, and the categories are dates. Points on the graph indicate how many pupils were present on each date. Straight lines connect these points in order to highlight trends and patterns.

Line graphs can be used to present many kinds of data, such as the grades a pupil achieves on certain days, or the production level of factories or farms at a given time. They can illustrate statistics of income, taxes, and wealth, as well as athletics, trade, and population.

Bar graphs are a good way to compare increases and decreases in quantity over a period of time. There are two kinds of bar graphs—*horizontal bar graphs* and *vertical bar graphs*. Graph 2 is a horizontal bar graph of the number of pupils present on these dates. Graph 3 is a vertical bar graph that shows the same information.

Picture graphs convey information through symbols instead of lines or bars. The pictorial form of these graphs helps readers understand the meaning of data without having to examine lists of figures. Picture graphs are most often used in magazines and newspapers. This type of graph originated in the pictographs used by primitive people and was the earliest form of writing.

Graph 4 is an example of a picture graph. In this case, each symbol represents the presence of four pupils.

Circle graphs show the relation of parts to the whole. For example, suppose the cost of education in a country was $2 billion and this sum was divided as follows: general control, 3.4 per cent; instruction, 61.9 per cent; operation, maintenance, and auxiliary agencies, 19.1 per cent; capital outlay, 8.8 per cent; interest, 6.8 per cent. If a circle graph is constructed, as in Graph 5, these percentages appear as wedges that look like pieces of pie. For this reason, such graphs are often called *pie charts*.

Graph 5

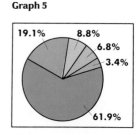

Graphs can be used to illustrate many types of data and are not limited to the simpler types shown here. They should be used to make facts clearer and more understandable.　Doris F. Hertsgaard

See also **Algebra** (Functions); **Pictograph**; **Statistics**.

Graphic arts is a general term for drawing and other techniques used to reproduce words and pictures. The techniques include block printing, engraving, etching, lithography, and silk-screen printing. Painting was once considered one of the graphic arts, but today it is generally considered a separate art form.

The graphic arts are used both commercially and in the fine arts. Commercially, the graphic arts are used in advertising to prepare newspaper and magazine illustrations, posters, and brochures and pamphlets. Other commercial uses include art reproduction, bookmaking, and fashion design. In the fine arts, many artists have created masterpieces of engraving, etching, and other graphic arts. These artists include Albrecht Dürer of Germany, Francisco Goya and Pablo Picasso of Spain, and Rembrandt of the Netherlands.

Until the 1400's, manuscripts and illustrations had to be copied by hand, a laborious and often inaccurate process. After Johannes Gutenberg invented movable type in Europe about 1440, it became possible to print identical copies of books quickly. As more books were made available, the level of education increased. This increase helped bring about the growth of art, literature, and science during the Renaissance. By the end of the Middle Ages, block printing and engraving had become known in Europe. These and other techniques were sometimes used to make reproductions of artworks, especially before the beginning of photography in the early 1800's. These graphic reproductions provided many people with their only exposure to fine art.

Elizabeth Broun

Related articles in *World Book* include:

Advertising	Etching	Printing
Block printing	Lithography	Screen printing
Commercial art	Manuscript	Woodcut
Engraving	Photography	

Graphite is a soft black mineral that is greasy to the touch. It is a form of the chemical element carbon.

Manufacturers use graphite in making a variety of products. For example, they harden graphite with clay to produce the material in pencils that we call "lead." At one time, graphite was mistaken for lead. But lead is much denser than graphite. The name *graphite* comes from a Greek word meaning *to write*. The German geologist Abraham Werner named the mineral in 1789.

Natural graphite is widely distributed in the United States and in other countries. However, the United States has only one active graphite mine, in Texas. The country imports most of its natural graphite from Mexico. Graphite can be manufactured from coke by heating the coke in an electric furnace. The American inventor Edward Acheson developed the process for making graphite from coke in 1896. Manufactured graphite is purer and more dense than natural graphite. It also costs more. But manufactured graphite makes up about 80 percent of the graphite used in the United States.

Graphite has many uses in addition to its use in pencils. It conducts electric current and is difficult to burn. For these reasons, *electrodes* (electric contact points) made of graphite work under conditions that would destroy metal electrodes. Graphite conducts heat and does not combine with other chemicals except at very high temperatures. Therefore, many *crucibles* (melting pots for metals) are made from graphite. Graphite is not easily dissolved, and so it is built into tanks that hold strong acids. Bricks of graphite form the cores of some nuclear reactors. The graphite slows down *neutrons* (atomic particles) in the reactors to keep the reactors operating properly. Graphite's slipperiness makes it a good lubricant for clocks, door locks, and other machines with small parts. Graphite is also the major raw material for synthetic diamonds.

Both graphite and diamond are made from pure carbon. But diamond is extremely hard and transparent. Diamond also is much denser than an equal amount of graphite. Graphite and diamond have different *crystal structures*—that is, the carbon atoms are arranged differently in the two minerals. Graphite contains carbon atoms arranged in flat layers that slide easily over each other. Thus, graphite is soft and slippery. In diamond, the atoms are arranged in a strong three-dimensional pattern that prevents the atoms from slipping over each other. Finley C. Bishop

See also **Carbon; Mineral** (picture); **Pencil; Powder metallurgy.**

Graphology, *gra FAHL uh jee,* is the study of a person's handwriting to obtain information about his or her personality. Although most scientists classify graphology as a *pseudoscience* (false science), its practice is widespread in Europe. Many American business firms consult graphologists for advice about which people to hire. In the United States, instruction in graphology is available through various correspondence courses.

Some principles of graphology are true. For example, handwriting is affected by illness, old age, and tension. But most of the broader claims of graphology lack scientific proof. For example, graphologists claim that lines slanting upward indicate enthusiasm, and that lines slanting downward indicate discouragement. A few scientific researchers have studied the relationship between handwriting and personality. It is important to distinguish their work from that of most graphologists with whom the public comes into contact. Many of these "graphoanalysis graduates" earned their degrees from schools with no official standing.

The serious psychological study of handwriting has been more widespread in Europe than in the United States. In the late 1800's, the French psychologist Alfred Binet tested seven graphologists. He asked them to distinguish writing samples of very intelligent men from samples of average men. All the graphologists performed better than chance would allow, and one scored correctly on 92 percent of the cases. In the 1940's, the Soviet psychologist Alexander R. Luria studied the use of handwriting to determine the location of brain injuries. Most other studies examining the exact relationships between personality and handwriting that graphologists claim exist have produced negative results.

Despite the lack of evidence for the claims of graphology, many psychologists consider the study of handwriting a useful diagnostic tool. Several psychology textbooks on *projective techniques* include discussions of graphology. Such techniques are testing methods that obtain information about a patient's personality without asking direct questions about it.

Official licensing in graphology exists in Europe, and several universities there teach graphology courses. The subject has little academic standing in the United States. Many scholars have called for thorough scientific studies of graphology. But research indicates that graphology probably has limited value for the study of character, health, and personality.

The term *graphology* also refers to scientific examination of handwriting to detect forgery. Handwriting experts who testify in court perform this type of graphology. Marcello Truzzi

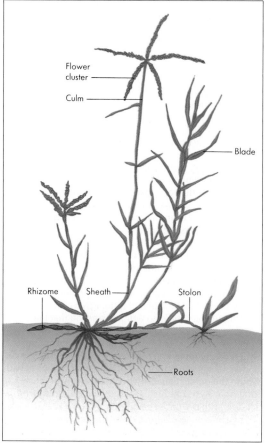

Flower cluster

Culm

Blade

Rhizome

Sheath

Stolon

Roots

WORLD BOOK illustration by Paul D. Turnbaugh

The parts of a Bermuda grass plant include two types of creeping stems, *stolons* and *rhizomes*. Stolons develop above the ground, and rhizomes grow below the ground.

Grass is one of the largest and most varied families in the plant kingdom. Some kind of grass can be found on almost all the land surfaces of the earth. Grasses grow in swamps and deserts; in subzero polar regions and hot tropical areas; on rocky land; and on cold, snowy mountains. Grasses range from the short kinds found in lawns to woody, tall bamboos from which cane fishing poles and furniture are made. Cereal grasses such as wheat, oats, barley, and corn are used to make bread, pastes, plastics, and many other products. Most sugar we eat comes from a grass plant called *sugar cane*. Brewers and *distillers* (liquor makers) use corn and barley in making alcoholic beverages. Paper can be made from the leaves and stems of some grasses.

Grass also beautifies the landscape and plays an important part in conservation. It forms an attractive surface for lawns, parks, and playgrounds. It also helps to save the fertile topsoil from *erosion* (wearing away). Grass covers the surface of the soil, and its roots hold the soil particles together so that wind cannot easily blow them away and water cannot wash them away.

Grass, like other plants, is usually green because it contains a green-colored substance called *chlorophyll.* Through a process called *photosynthesis*, this material helps change sunlight into energy that plants—and the animals that eat plants—can use.

The grass plant

A grass plant has two main parts—the *vegetative organs* and the *floral organs.* The vegetative organs include the roots, stems, and leaves. They keep the plant growing. The floral organs are the parts from which the flowers develop. They include the *stamens* (male floral parts), the *pistil* (female floral parts), and two or three delicate little scales called *lodicules.* The floral organs, which are grouped together in flower clusters, produce the seeds from which new plants grow.

Grass has *fibrous* (threadlike) roots and stems called *culms* above ground from which the leaves grow. These are made up of *nodes* (joints) and *internodes* (the areas between the nodes). The nodes are always solid, but the internodes in some grasses such as wheat are hollow. Some grasses, such as smooth brome grass, have creeping stems called *rhizomes* that grow below the ground. Others, such as buffalo grass, have creeping stems called *stolons* that grow above the ground. Still others, including Bermuda grass and Japanese lawngrass, have both rhizomes and stolons. Rhizomes and stolons spread out from the plant to start new plants.

Grass leaves are called *two-ranked,* because each leaf grows on the opposite side of the culm from the leaf below it. Each leaf is made up of a *sheath, blade, ligule,* and *auricle.* The sheath wraps around the culm above each node. The blade, which is sometimes incorrectly called the leaf, is usually flat and narrow. It is fastened to the top of the sheath. The ligule grows where the blade and the sheath meet. It may form a thin sheet or look like a row of eyelashes. The auricle grows on the back of the leaf where the blade meets the sheath.

Grasses may be either *annual* or *perennial.* Annual grasses die at the end of the growing season, and new seed must be planted at the beginning of the next season. Perennial grasses live through the winter, however, and grow again each year.

Kinds of grasses

Grasses may be classified in six main groups: (1) grazing and forage grasses, (2) turfgrasses, (3) ornamental grasses, (4) cereals, (5) sugar cane, and (6) woody grasses.

Grazing and forage grasses provide most of the feed that animals eat. Grass is the principal source of food for such grazing animals as cattle, goats, horses, and sheep. In winter, these animals eat grass in the form of hay, straw, and *silage* (cut grasses and grains that are stored in a silo). Some important grazing and forage grasses are described in the table in this article.

Turfgrasses are used to cover athletic fields, golf courses, lawns, and playgrounds. Some turfgrasses, such as colonial bent, creeping bent, Kentucky bluegrass, and ryegrass, grow better in colder climates. Bahia grass, Bermuda grass, carpet grass, centipede grass, St. Augustine grass, and zoysia grass are grown in warmer climates. Buffalo grass, blue grama, and crested wheatgrass are used for lawns and turfgrass in dry areas that are not watered because they withstand hot, dry weather best. The putting greens on golf courses are usually covered with bent or Bermuda grass.

Common grasses

This table shows and describes ten kinds of grass plants and their flower clusters. The plant is shown in green and the flower in black.

Bermuda grass
Cynodon dactylon

Bermuda grass is used for hay, lawns, general-purpose turf, and erosion control. It grows best in the fertile soils of the Southern United States. The plant has rhizomes and stolons from 2 inches (5 centimeters) to more than 20 feet (6 meters) long. The grass generally grows from 6 to 12 inches (15 to 30 centimeters) tall.

Blue grama
Bouteloua gracilis

Blue grama is commonly found in the Great Plains of the United States. It can withstand drought and is used for grazing and erosion control. The plant grows from 1 to 2 feet (30 to 61 centimeters) high and is very leafy at the base. It has narrow blades.

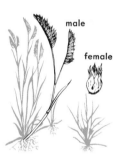

Buffalo grass
Buchloe dactyloides

Buffalo grass forms a thick gray-green sod and spreads by stolons. It grows from 4 to 6 inches (10 to 15 centimeters) high and can be identified by its burrlike female flower cluster. Buffalo grass is found throughout the Great Plains region. It can withstand heavy grazing.

Crested wheatgrass
Agropyron desertorum

Crested wheatgrass is widely used for grazing on rangelands in the western United States. It can withstand drought and thrives in cool weather. It grows in bunches with culms from 10 to 40 inches (25 to 100 centimeters) high. The blades are from 6 to 10 inches (15 to 25 centimeters) long. The flower clusters grow from 2 to 3 inches (5 to 8 centimeters) long.

Kentucky bluegrass
Poa pratensis

Kentucky bluegrass is a valuable and widely grown pasture and lawn grass. It grows from 1 to 2½ feet (30 to 76 centimeters) high. The tip of the blade is curved in the shape of a bow of a boat. Rhizomes spread out from the plant to start new plants.

Little bluestem
Andropogon scoparius

Little bluestem is distributed throughout the United States. But it is especially abundant in Kansas and Oklahoma. It grows from 2 to 4 feet (0.6 to 1.2 meters) high and has narrow flat leaves 4 to 8 inches (10 to 20 centimeters) long. The blades are green when young, but turn reddish-brown when the plant matures.

Orchard grass
Dactylis glomerata

Orchard grass is grown for hay and pasture. It is one of the first grasses to turn green in the spring, providing early grazing. It grows in bunches with stems 2 to 4 feet (0.6 to 1.2 meters) high. It can be identified by its tightly clustered flowers.

Smooth brome
Bromus inermis

Smooth brome is used for hay and pasture. It spreads by rhizomes and grows from 3 to 4 feet (0.9 to 1.2 meters) high. The blades are from 6 to 12 inches (15 to 30 centimeters) long and about ½ inch (13 millimeters) wide. The plant is very leafy and has a loose, spreading flower cluster.

Sudan grass
Sorghum vulgare sudanense

Sudan grass makes good hay, pasture grass, and silage because it grows fast and can withstand dry weather. It has many fine stems and grows from 4 to 7 feet (1.2 to 2 meters) high. It has many narrow blades, and its flower clusters range from 6 to 18 inches (15 to 46 centimeters) long. Under certain conditions, sudan grass may be toxic to livestock.

Timothy
Phleum pratense

Timothy is an important kind of grass used for hay. It grows from 20 to 40 inches (51 to 100 centimeters) high. It thrives in cool, humid weather. Its many stems make up large bunches of grass. Timothy flower clusters have a cylindrical shape.

Ornamental grasses have beautiful, plumelike flower clusters. They are used in flower gardens, parks, and other landscaped areas. Common varieties of ornamental grasses include Chinese silver grass, pampas grass, and uva grass.

Cereals are one of the world's most important food crops. The seeds of the cereals provide grain that is ground into flour. The cereal grasses—wheat, rice, corn, oats, sorghum, and millet—are sometimes called *grains* or *cereal grains.*

Wheat is a major source of food. Young wheat plants are used for grazing or are fed to livestock as hay and silage. Wheat kernels can be ground into flour. The flour is used to make many kinds of food, such as bread, rolls, noodles, and breakfast cereals. Wheat germ, bran, and malt also come from wheat. Wheat kernels contain a protein called *gluten.* This substance enables dough with yeast to rise by forming small pockets of carbon dioxide in the dough. Most wheat is called "bread wheat." Bread wheat may be brownish-red or white. Wheat is an annual, and it grows from 2 to 5 feet (0.6 to 1.5 meters) high. It has spikelike flower clusters. Durum wheat is also called *macaroni wheat* because it makes good macaroni, spaghetti, and other kinds of noodles. It may be yellow or brownish-red.

Rice has been a basic food for millions of people throughout the world for hundreds of years. The two major types of rice are *lowland rice* and *upland rice.* Lowland rice grows best on flooded land, while upland rice depends on rain to supply the moisture.

People eat rice in many forms. The white cooked rice we eat has been milled to remove the covering. It is made up mainly of starch, an important food. Rice and rice flour are both used in making many kinds of breakfast foods. Rice is also used in making alcohol, candy, cosmetics, glue, laundry starch, paste, and vinegar. Rice stalks provide straw that is used in making brooms, hats, mats, rope, sacks, and sandals. In some parts of the world, rice straw is burned to heat houses. The rice plant grows from 2 to 6 feet (0.6 to 1.8 meters) high and has a tight flower cluster. It is an annual.

Corn is called *maize* in some countries. Most of the crop in the United States is fed to livestock, particularly beef cattle. Corn provides about half the grain fed to livestock and poultry. Many people like to eat sweet corn and popcorn. Corn is also made into meal, oil, and flour. Corn is an annual that grows from about 3 to 20 feet (0.9 to 6 meters) high. At the top of its stalk, it has a spikelike *tassel,* the male flowering structure. The *ears,* or female flowering structures, are on the stalk's side branches.

Oats are grown mainly for feeding livestock. Livestock feed on oats in pastures or, during winter months, the oats are fed in hay and silage. Industry uses about one-fourth of the oats crop in the United States. Of this amount, only about 4 percent is used to produce oatmeal. The oat plant is an annual that grows from 2 to 4 feet (0.6 to 1.2 meters) high. An open seed cluster grows at the tip of the stem.

Other cereal grains include grain sorghums and millets. In the United States, they are grown mainly for livestock feed. In many other nations, people eat them.

Sugar cane provides more than half of the world's sugar supply. Sugar cane also produces a fiber called

bagasse that is used in making wallboard, plastics, and fuel to heat homes. The sugar cane plant is a perennial that grows from 7 to 15 feet (2 to 4.6 meters) tall.

Woody grasses include the bamboos. Bamboos have strong, woodlike stems that are used for building houses, rafts, bridges, and furniture. The stems can be used to make boards that are 1 foot (30 centimeters) or more wide. Bamboo stems also can serve as water pipe when the solid nodes have been removed. Bamboo is a perennial that may grow as high as 120 feet (37 meters) and measure 6 to 12 inches (15 to 30 centimeters) thick at the bottom.   Kay H. Asay

Scientific classification. Grasses are in the grass family, Poaceae or Gramineae. Wheat makes up the genus *Triticum.* The scientific name for rice is *Oryza sativa.* Corn is *Zea mays.* Oats makes up the genus *Avena.* The common cultivated oats is *A. sativa.* Sugar cane is *Saccharum officinarum.* Bamboos include the genera *Phyllostachys, Arundinaria, Bambusa,* and *Dendrocalamus.*

Related articles in *World Book.* For lawn grasses and their care, see the **Lawn** article. See also:

Kinds of grass

Artificial turf	Oats
Bamboo	Reed
Barley	Rice
Bentgrass	Rye
Bluegrass	Sandbur
Brome	Sorghum
Corn	Spartina
Fescue	Sudan grass
Foxtail barley	Sugar cane
Kafir	Timothy
Millet	Wheat

Other related articles

Grain	Hay	Sedge
Grassland	Herb	Weed

Grass, *grahs,* **Günter,** *GUN tuhr* (1927-   ), is a German novelist, poet, playwright, artist, and essayist. He has played a key role in German literary and intellectual life since the late 1950's. Grass was a prominent member of the "Group 47," an association of writers who helped restore substance and integrity to German literature after the Nazi period. Grass won the 1999 Nobel Prize for literature.

Grass is internationally known for his innovative novels, which often combine raw realism with fantasy and grotesque narrative situations. His writing is predominantly devoted to social and political issues, and advocates the values of democratic socialism. His best-known novel, *The Tin Drum* (1959), as well as *Cat and Mouse* (1961) and *Dog Years* (1963), critically analyzes fascism as a social disease. In his later writings, Grass criticizes, often satirically, German society following World War II (1939-1945). These works include *Local Anaesthetic* (1969), *From the Diary of a Snail* (1972), *The Flounder* (1977), *Headbirths, or the Germans Are Dying Out* (1980), and the play *The Plebeians Rehearse the Uprising* (1966). *The Rat* (1986), Grass's gloomiest novel, confronts the possibility of human self-destruction by nuclear war.

Grass was born in Danzig (now Gdańsk, Poland). This area is the setting for several of his novels.

Werner Hoffmeister

Grasse, François Joseph Paul. See De Grasse, François Joseph Paul.

Alexander B. Klots

Lubber grasshopper, *above and below,* is a short-horned grasshopper. Fingerlike parts under the insect's powerful jaws contain "taste buds." The lubber has a large body and short wings, and cannot fly. Its ears are on its body under the wings.

John H. Gerard

Shaw, APF

Narrow-winged katydid is one of the best known long-horned grasshoppers. Katydids are named for the "songs" of certain males, which sound like "Katy did, Katy she did." The oval-shaped hole below the right front knee joint of this katydid is one of its ears.

Grasshopper is an insect that can leap about 20 times as far as the length of its body. If a human being had that same leaping ability, he or she could jump about 120 feet (37 meters). Grasshoppers are either short-horned, with short *antennae* (feelers), or long-horned, with long antennae.

Grasshoppers live in most parts of the world, except near the North and South poles. Short-horned grasshoppers feed on plants. Many live in fields and meadows where there are plenty of leaves to eat. Some eat only certain kinds of plants. Others eat any plants they can find. They may destroy whole crops of alfalfa, cotton, and corn and other grains. Most long-horned grasshoppers also eat plants. Some, however, eat the remains of animals. A few capture and eat other insects.

Many animals prey on grasshoppers, including beetles, birds, lizards, mice, snakes, and spiders. Several types of spiders and wasps capture and paralyze grasshoppers and use them to feed their young. Certain kinds of flies lay eggs in or near grasshopper eggs. After the fly eggs hatch, the newborn flies eat the grasshopper eggs. Other flies lay their eggs on a grasshopper's body. The newborn flies then eat the grasshopper.

Grasshoppers can sometimes escape from their enemies by jumping up and flying away, by biting the enemy with their strong jaws, or by hiding. Their coloring often resembles their surroundings so closely that the grasshopper cannot be seen unless it moves. Grasshoppers that live among green leaves are green, those that live near the ground are brownish, and those that live near the beach are sand-colored. When grasshop-

pers are handled, they "spit" a brown liquid that many people call "tobacco juice." This liquid may also help protect grasshoppers from attacks by other insects.

The body of a grasshopper has three main sections: (1) the head, (2) the thorax, and (3) the abdomen. A stiff shell called an *exoskeleton* covers the body.

The head. Two antennae grow forward and curve upward from the head. They function as the grasshopper's nose. Two lips and jaws that move from side to side form the main parts of the mouth. Thin, fingerlike parts called *palpi* grow on both sides of the mouth and on the lower lip. They contain the insect's "taste buds."

A grasshopper has five eyes. A large *compound eye,* consisting of thousands of single lenses, is on each side of the head. With these eyes, the insect can see to the front, to the side, and to the back. A grasshopper also has three small single eyes—one above the base of each antenna, and one below and midway between the two antennae. No one knows what these small eyes do.

The thorax. A grasshopper's wings and legs are attached to its thorax. Grasshoppers have six legs, and most have two pairs of wings. Some species have short, useless wings, and others have no wings at all.

A grasshopper's front wings are narrow and tough. They cover and protect the large, thin hind wings, which are the main wings used for flying. When the insect rests, its hind wings fold up like fans under its front wings. When a grasshopper flies, the downstroke of the wings gives the insect "lift" and moves it forward. The upstroke helps keep the insect moving until the wings reach the downstroke position.

The body of a grasshopper

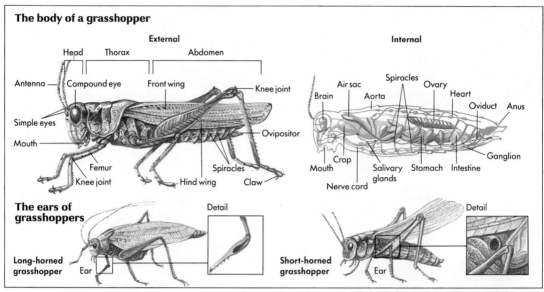

External

Head Thorax Abdomen

Antenna — Compound eye Front wing
Knee joint
Simple eyes
Mouth
Ovipositor
Femur
Spiracles
Knee joint Hind wing Claw

Internal

Spiracles
Air sac Ovary
Brain Aorta Heart
Oviduct Anus

Crop
Mouth Salivary Stomach Intestine
glands
Nerve cord
Ganglion

The ears of grasshoppers

Detail

Long-horned grasshopper Ear

Short-horned grasshopper Ear

Detail

WORLD BOOK illustrations by Tony Gibbons, Bernard Thornton Artists

A grasshopper uses all six legs when it walks. The front legs hold food when the animal eats. Powerful muscles in the hind legs supply the force that pushes the insect forward in a leap, or shoots it into the air to fly.

The abdomen of a grasshopper expands and contracts to pump air in and out of 10 pairs of breathing holes. These holes, called *spiracles,* are along the sides of the abdomen and the thorax. Tubes branch out from the spiracles and carry air to all parts of the body.

Most of a grasshopper's digestive tract is located within the abdomen. In addition, female grasshoppers have a strong, sharp part called an *ovipositor,* or *egg placer,* at the rear of the abdomen. Eggs pass out of the female's body through the ovipositor.

Young. Female grasshoppers lay as few as 2 or as many as 120 eggs at a time. The eggs, held together by a sticky substance made by the female's body, are packed into holes dug by her ovipositor. She sprays more of the sticky material over the eggs, and it hardens into a waterproof covering. The mass of eggs is called a *pod.*

Most kinds of grasshoppers begin to lay their eggs in late summer and continue into autumn. The eggs hatch the following spring. Newborn grasshoppers look like adults except they have no wings. It takes 40 to 60 days for a young grasshopper to become an adult. During this time, the insect must shed its exoskeleton in order

How a grasshopper lays eggs

A female grasshopper digs a hole in the ground with her ovipositor. She lays her eggs and covers them with soil.

WORLD BOOK illustration by Tony Gibbons, Bernard Thornton Artists

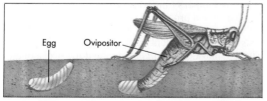

Egg Ovipositor

to grow. This process is called *molting.* The young grasshopper molts five or six times, growing a new exoskeleton each time. Wings are present after the last molt, when the insect reaches adulthood.

Long-horned grasshoppers have threadlike antennae that may grow longer than the insect's body. These grasshoppers include *katydids* and *Mormon crickets.*

Many kinds of long-horned grasshoppers are green, but some are black, brown, or gray. Although most kinds live on the ground, katydids usually live in trees. Male long-horned grasshoppers "sing" to attract their mates. They rub the bases of their front wings together, which vibrate and make a loud sound. Different species have their own special songs. Long-horned grasshoppers hear by means of organs on their front legs.

Short-horned grasshoppers have shorter, thicker antennae than the long-horned kinds. They include *lubber grasshoppers* and *migratory locusts.* Lubber grasshoppers are especially large. Two common North American species are the *lubber grasshopper* of the western United States and the *eastern lubber grasshopper.* The western lubber grasshopper is brown or grayish-green. Its short, pink front wings have black dots. The eastern lubber is yellow and black with small red and black hind wings. Both species may become pests.

Migratory locusts sometimes greatly increase in number, form large swarms, and migrate—but no one knows exactly why. These swarms damage crops and other plants. Many people catch and eat the swarming locusts, especially in the Middle East and parts of Africa. They remove the wings and legs before eating them.

Like long-horned grasshoppers, male short-horned grasshoppers "sing" to their mates. Most species make sounds by rubbing their hind legs against their front wings. Short-horned grasshoppers have hearing organs on their abdomen just above the base of their hind legs.

Scientific classification. Long-horned grasshoppers belong to the family Tettigoniidae. Short-horned grasshoppers belong to the family Acrididae.   Betty Lane Faber

See also **Cricket; Katydid; Locust.**

© Jim Brandenburg

Grassland is one of the main kinds of natural vegetation. The grassland shown above is a prairie in northwestern Iowa.

Grassland is one of the four chief kinds of natural vegetation. The other three types are forest, desert shrub, and tundra. Most grasslands lie between very arid lands, or deserts, and humid lands covered with forests. Some grasslands occur in humid climates.

The two types of grasslands are (1) steppes with short grasses, and (2) prairies with tall grasses. Some biologists consider tropical savannas, which have coarse grasses and scattered trees, to be a third type of grassland. The word *steppe* refers to semiarid grasslands. Well-known steppes include the Great Plains of North America, the western part of the Pampa of Argentina, and the Veld of South Africa. In the driest parts of the steppes, grasses are short and occur as scattered bunches. On the humid edges of steppes, grasses grow taller and are more closely spaced. See **Pampa; Steppe.**

Prairies are grasslands in more humid climates. Prairies have a thick cover of grasses and often occur with patches of forests. Large prairies include much of the American Midwest, the Pampa of eastern Argentina, and parts of Hungary and northeastern China. Much of the prairie grasslands have been turned into farms and ranches. In some areas, overgrazing by livestock has killed many of the taller grasses. See **Prairie.**

Tropical savanna areas have a dry season in winter and a rainy summer. Most grasses in these areas grow in clumps. Tropical savannas include the Llanos of Venezuela; the Campos of southern Brazil; much of central, southern, and eastern Africa; the northwestern part of the Deccan of India; and parts of eastern Australia. See **Savanna.**   René W. Barendregt

See also **Animal** (Animals of the grasslands); **Plant** (Where plants live; picture: Plants of the grasslands).

Grasso, Ella Tambussi (1919-1981), served as governor of Connecticut from 1975 to 1980. She was the first woman elected governor in the United States who did not succeed her husband in the office.

Grasso was born in Windsor Locks, Connecticut. Her parents were Italian immigrants. She graduated from Mount Holyoke College in 1940 and received a master's degree from Mount Holyoke in 1942. During World War II (1939-1945), Grasso held the position of assistant director of research for the War Manpower Commission of Connecticut.

Wide World

Ella T. Grasso

Grasso, a Democrat, was elected to the Connecticut House of Representatives in 1952 and served there until 1959. In 1955, she became the Democratic floor leader in the state legislature. The floor leader directs debates on legislation. Grasso was the first woman to hold that position. From 1959 to 1970, she served as Connecticut secretary of state. Grasso was floor leader at the Connecticut Constitutional Convention in 1965.

Grasso won election to the U.S. House of Representatives in 1970. She was reelected in 1972 and served until she became governor of Connecticut. She resigned as governor in 1980 because of illness.   Guy Halverson

Grateful Dead was one of the most popular and longest-lasting American bands in rock music history. The band's music combined elements of country, blues, folk, rhythm and blues, and rock, with extended instrumental

© Jay Blakesberg, Retna, Ltd.

The Grateful Dead was one of rock's most popular bands. It was formed in San Francisco in the mid-1960's. The group was known for its live performances, which included extended instrumental improvisations and drew thousands of devoted fans. Lead guitarist and founding member Jerry Garcia appears second from the right in this photo of a 1990's concert.

improvisations that are more common to jazz.

The Grateful Dead was known primarily for its musically spontaneous concerts, rather than for its recordings. Its live performances created a large number of devoted fans known as *Deadheads*. Fans followed the group from concert to concert, helping to make the Dead one of the most popular touring acts in rock. The Dead's only hit single, "Touch of Gray," came in 1987.

The group formed in San Francisco in 1965 as the Warlocks, but changed its name within a year to the Grateful Dead. Members included guitarists and vocalists Jerry Garcia (1942-1995) and Bob Weir (1947-   ), bassist and vocalist Phil Lesh (1940-   ), and drummers Bill Kreutzmann (1946-   ) and Mickey Hart (1950?-   ). Garcia, Weir, Lesh, and Kreutzmann were original members, along with keyboardist and vocalist Ron "Pigpen" McKernan (1945-1973). In 1995, after Garcia's death, the group disbanded.   Don McLeese

Grattan, Henry (1746-1820), an Irish politician, led a movement that temporarily freed Ireland's Parliament from British control. He was an eloquent orator and a distinguished spokesman for Irish independence.

Grattan studied law at Trinity College in Dublin and in 1775 became a member of the Irish Parliament. In 1782, he led a successful effort to overturn the British government's Declaratory Act of 1720, a law that affirmed the supremacy of the British Parliament over the Parliament of Ireland. Although a Protestant, Grattan also condemned longstanding laws that prohibited Roman Catholics from voting and holding political office. Three-fourths of Ireland's people were Catholics.

After the Declaratory Act was repealed, people called the independent Irish legislature "Grattan's parliament." British fears of Irish rebellion, however, caused Britain to pass the Act of Union in 1800. This act ended the Irish Parliament and merged Ireland with Britain to form the United Kingdom of Great Britain and Ireland. Grattan was born in Dublin.   Thomas E. Hachey

See also **Ireland** (Union with Britain).

Gravel is a mixture of loose pieces of rock and particles of sand and clay. At least 30 percent of gravel consists of pieces of rock that are *coarser,* or larger, than sand—that is, they measure more than $\frac{1}{12}$ inch (2 millimeters) across. Sand and clay make up the rest of gravel, often forming 50 to 70 percent of the gravel's total mass.

Most of the useful deposits of gravel were laid down by rivers and glaciers or were formed in lakes and oceans. In preparation for industrial use, gravel is dug up from pits and washed. Screens are then used to sort the chunks of rock according to size.

Taken together, gravel and sand are one of the largest products by volume in the construction industry. Gravel is used to build roads, railroad embankments, and airfield landing strips. Paved surfaces are made with gravel mixed with cement or *asphalt,* a dark tarlike substance. Gravel mixed with sand, water, and cement makes concrete.   Finley C. Bishop

See also **Cement and concrete** (How concrete is made); **Rock.**

Gravenhage, 'S. See Hague, The.

Graves, Michael (1934-   ), an American architect, is a leader of the movement in architecture known as *Postmodernism*. Postmodern architects feature elements from earlier architectural styles in their designs. For example, in Graves's 1977 design for the Fargo-Moorhead (North Dakota-Minnesota) Cultural Center, he used bold geometric forms that recalled classical arches. The references to classical architecture increased in Graves's work, leading to his design for the Portland Building (1982) in Portland, Oregon. This was the first major application of Postmodern historic references in an important public building. See **Architecture** (picture: Postmodernism).

In his design for the San Juan Capistrano, California, Public Library (1984), Graves incorporated subtle references to Spanish and mission architecture. Later projects include the Humana Building (1985) in Louisville, Kentucky, and designs for a proposed expansion of the Whitney Museum of American Art in New York City. He designed buildings for Disney, including hotels at the Walt Disney World Resort near Orlando, Florida, and Disneyland Paris Theme Park (1992) near Paris. Graves was born in Indianapolis.   Leland M. Roth

See also **Postmodernism.**

Graves, Morris (1910-2001), was an American artist who became known for his paintings and water colors that show the influence of oriental mysticism. Graves tended to work in themes and in series, such as his "moonlight paintings" or his "leaf series." He frequently painted pictures of animals, especially birds. Graves was influenced by the American artist Mark Tobey and the oriental philosophy of Zen Buddhism. See **Tobey, Mark.**

Graves was born in Fox Valley, Oregon. A self-taught artist, Graves traveled widely and lived chiefly in

Dolphin Hotel (1992); © Steven Brooke

A Michael Graves hotel in the Walt Disney World Resort is a colorful structure facing a lagoon. The hotel is part of a convention center Graves designed near Orlando, Florida. The hotel is crowned by two huge sculptures of dolphins that contribute to a playful appearance the architect felt was appropriate to the Walt Disney image.

Bird Singing in the Moonlight (1938-1939), a tempera and water color painting on mulberry paper; Museum of Modern Art, New York City

A Morris Graves painting shows the personal interpretation of bird images that is typical of the artist's work. Graves's style reflects the influence of Oriental mysticism.

the American Northwest. Graves's first significant recognition came in 1939 when his work was included in an exhibit at the Museum of Modern Art in New York City.
Charles C. Eldredge

Graves, Robert (1895-1985), was an English author. His fiction includes two historical novels of imperial Rome—*I, Claudius* (1934) and *Claudius the God* (1935). He wrote *The White Goddess* (1948), a study of myth and the source of poetry in mythology. *The Crowning Privilege* (1955) is an informal commentary on modern poetry and poets. Graves's early autobiography, *Goodbye to All That* (1929), ranks among his most popular works.

Graves's most impressive poetry includes some realistic verses about World War I and his later love poems. At its best, his poetry achieves the "shining" that he speaks of in his poem "To Juan at the Winter Solstice":

> There is one story and one story only
> That will prove worth your telling,
> Whether as learned bard or gifted child;
> To it all lines or lesser gauds belong
> That startle with their shining
> Such common stories as they stray into.

Reprinted by permission of Curtis Brown, Ltd.
Copyright © 1945 by Robert Graves, renewed 1973.

Graves was born in Wimbledon. He traveled widely and lived for many years in Majorca. But he said his poems ". . . have never adopted a foreign accent or colouring; they remain true to the Anglo-Irish poetic tradition into which I was born." William Harmon

Graves' disease is a disorder that causes the thyroid gland to become overactive. Excessive activity of the thyroid gland is referred to as *hyperthyroidism*. Graves' disease is the most common cause of hyperthyroidism. It can occur at any age and in either sex, but it is most common in women from 20 to 40 years of age.

Enlargement of the thyroid gland usually accompanies the hyperthyroidism caused by Graves' disease. Symptoms of the disease that are caused by hyperthy-

roidism include nervousness, weight loss, sweating, and an irregular or rapid heartbeat. Less common symptoms of Graves' disease include redness and irritation of the eyes and *exophthalmos* (bulging of the eyeballs).

The cause of Graves' disease is related to a disturbance in the immune system of the body. Most patients have antibodies in the bloodstream that react with thyroid tissue, stimulating it to grow and to produce extra amounts of thyroid hormone. The cause of the eye problems is unknown.

Graves' disease is commonly treated with drugs that decrease the secretion of thyroid hormone. In some cases, a solution containing radioactive iodine is administered to destroy most of the thyroid gland. After successful treatment, most patients have no symptoms of the disorder. In patients with exophthalmos, however, some bulging of the eye may remain. Theodore Mazzone

Gravitation is the force of attraction that acts between all objects because of their *mass*—that is, the amount of matter they are made of. Because of gravitation, objects that are on or near the earth are pulled toward it. Gravitation holds together the hot gases in the sun. It keeps the planets in their orbits around the sun, and it keeps all the stars in our galaxy in their orbits about its center. The gravitational attraction that an object has for objects near it is called the *force of gravity.*

Although the effects of gravity are easy to see, an explanation for gravitational force has puzzled people for centuries. The ancient Greek philosopher Aristotle taught that heavy objects fall faster than light ones. This view was accepted for centuries. But in the early 1600's, the Italian scientist Galileo introduced a different view of gravity. According to Galileo, all objects fall with the same *acceleration* (rate of change of velocity), unless air resistance or some other force slows them down.

Ancient astronomers studied the motions of the moon and the planets. But these motions were not correctly explained until the late 1600's, when the English scientist Sir Isaac Newton showed that there is a connection between the force that attracts objects to the earth and the way the planets move. Newton based his work on the careful study of planetary motions by two astronomers of the late 1500's and early 1600's—Tycho Brahe, a Dane, and Johannes Kepler, a German. When Newton was 23 years old, a falling apple caused him to question how far the force of gravity reaches. He realized that the same force that pulled the apple from the tree could hold the moon in its orbit around the earth. From laws discovered by Kepler, Newton showed how the sun's gravitational attraction must decrease with distance. He assumed that the gravity of the earth behaves the same way. Newton calculated what the force that attracts the moon toward the earth would be at the earth's surface. This force proved to be the same as the force that gave the apple its acceleration.

Newton's theory of gravitation says that the gravitational force between two objects is *proportional* (related directly) to the size of their masses. That is, the larger either mass is, the larger the force is between the two objects. The theory refers to mass rather than weight because the weight of an object on the earth is really the strength of the earth's gravity on that object. On different planets, the same object would have different weights, but its mass would always be the same.

Gravitational force

The diagram at the right shows how an object's *weight* (the strength of the gravitational force pulling on it) decreases as the object moves away from the earth. At some point between the earth and the moon, the object is pulled equally by both bodies and, therefore, weighs nothing. This point varies with the distance between the two bodies. The object's weight then increases until it reaches the moon's surface. The diagram below shows that an object does not weigh the same at all places on the earth's surface because (1) the earth is not perfectly round and (2) it is rotating. An object would weigh nothing at the earth's center because the earth's matter pulls on it equally from all directions.

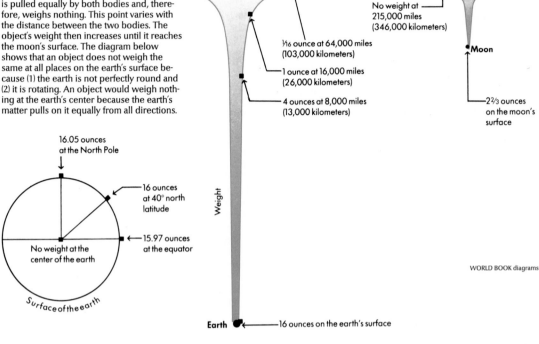

Distance from the center of the earth

50,000 100,000 150,000 200,000 250,000 miles

100,000 200,000 300,000 400,000 kilometers

No weight at 215,000 miles (346,000 kilometers)

Moon

1/16 ounce at 64,000 miles (103,000 kilometers)

1 ounce at 16,000 miles (26,000 kilometers)

4 ounces at 8,000 miles (13,000 kilometers)

2 2/3 ounces on the moon's surface

16.05 ounces at the North Pole

16 ounces at 40° north latitude

15.97 ounces at the equator

No weight at the center of the earth

Surface of the earth

Weight

Earth — 16 ounces on the earth's surface

WORLD BOOK diagrams

Also, the gravitational force is *inversely* (oppositely) proportional to the distance between the centers of gravity of the two objects *squared* (multiplied by itself). For example, if the distance between the two objects doubles, the force between them becomes a fourth of its original strength.

Newton's theory of gravitation appeared in a work published in 1687. Until the early 1900's, scientists observed only one phenomenon that disagreed with the predictions of the theory. This was the motion of the planet Mercury, and the disagreement was very small.

Einstein's theory of gravitation. In 1915, the German-born physicist Albert Einstein announced his theory of gravitation, the *general theory of relativity.* A key idea of general relativity is that gravitation is an effect of the curvature of space and time.

Although Einstein's theory involved a complete change in ideas about gravitation, it expanded upon rather than contradicted Newton's theory. In most circumstances, it produced results that differed only slightly from those calculated with Newton's theory. When Einstein's theory was used to calculate the motion of Mercury, the calculations agreed exactly with the observed motions of the planet. This was the first confirmation of his theory.

The general theory of relativity is based on two assumptions. The first assumption is that space and time are curved wherever matter or energy is present. Einstein provided equations that describe this curvature precisely. The second assumption, known as the *Principle of Equivalence,* states that the effects of gravity are

equivalent to acceleration. To understand this principle, suppose you are in a rocket ship at rest in space—that is, without gravity or acceleration. If you drop a ball, it floats and does not fall. If the rocket accelerates upward, the ball will appear to you to fall to the floor exactly as if gravity had acted upon it. Thus, acceleration produces the same effect as gravity.

The Principle of Equivalence predicts that gravity must cause the path of a light ray to bend as the ray passes near massive bodies, such as the sun, that curve space. This prediction was first confirmed in 1919 during a total eclipse of the sun. The sun also bends and delays radio waves. This delay was measured by sending radio signals between the earth and the Viking space probes that reached Mars in 1976, providing the most precise confirmation yet of general relativity.

Predictions of general relativity. According to general relativity, massive bodies that orbit one another emit gravitational waves. This prediction was indirectly confirmed in 1978 by observations of a *binary pulsar,* which is a rapidly rotating neutron star that orbits a companion star. The observations indicated that the orbital period of the pulsar is decreasing. The amount of this decrease agrees with predictions by general relativity of the energy that the stars would lose by emitting gravity waves.

General relativity has been applied to *cosmology,* the study of the universe as a whole. The theory predicted that the universe must either expand or contract. Such observations as a shift in the wavelength of light from distant stars indicate that the stars are moving away from us and that the universe is expanding. Accurate measurement of the rate of expansion of the universe and the amount of matter may indicate whether the universe will expand forever, or whether the universe will contract.   Joel R. Primack

Related articles in *World Book* include:

Antigravity	Hooke, Robert
Earth (Earth's size and shape)	Newton, Sir Isaac
Einstein, Albert	Pendulum
Force (Kinds of force)	Relativity
Fourth dimension	Space exploration (Overcom-
G (symbol)	ing gravity; Microgravity)
Galileo	String theory
Gravity, Center of	Torsion balance
Hawking, Stephen W.	Weight

Additional resources

Bergmann, Peter G. *The Riddle of Gravitation.* Rev. ed. 1987. Reprint. Dover, 1992.
Blair, David, and McNamara, Geoff. *Ripples on a Cosmic Sea: The Search for Gravitational Waves.* Addison Wesley Longman, 1997.
Wheeler, John A. *A Journey into Gravity and Spacetime.* Scientific Am. Lib., 1990.

Gravity, Center of, is the point in an object where the force of gravity appears to act. If an object is suspended from any point on the vertical line passing through its center of gravity, the object will remain stationary. But if the center of gravity is to one side of a point around which the object can pivot, the object will turn in that direction.

The center of gravity of a child's seesaw is at the center of the board when no one sits on it. If the seesaw is pivoted at its center, it will remain balanced. When two children of different weights get on opposite ends of the seesaw, the force of gravity will be greater on one end. The center of gravity will then be between the center of the board and the end where the greater force is acting—that is, where the heavier child is sitting. The seesaw will tilt toward that end. If the heavier child moves toward the center of the seesaw, the center of gravity also moves toward the center of the board and it will again balance.

The force of gravity acts on all points in an object where there is *mass* (material), not simply at the center of gravity. Physicists explain how gravity acts on objects in terms of *moments*. The moment of the gravitational force acting on any point is found by multiplying the force times the horizontal distance to the pivot point being used. The moment has a size and a direction. That is,

the moments of forces acting on one side of a seesaw tend to make it turn up or down, and the moments acting on the opposite side tend to make it turn in the opposite direction. Moments of the same size but opposite direction cancel one another, and so the seesaw does not move.

Thus, in terms of moments, the center of gravity of any object is the point where the moments of the gravitational forces cancel one another. The center of gravity of a seesaw is at the center of the board because the moments cancel one another there.

An object pivoted so that it is not balanced will turn until its center of gravity is at *stable equilibrium* (the lowest position possible). If the object is balanced with its center of gravity directly above the pivot, the slightest turn will cause the object to become unstable. An object balanced in this way is said to be in a position of *unstable equilibrium.*

When an object moves, the center of gravity moves as if all the mass of the object were concentrated there. The motion of an object moving under the force of gravity is described as the sum of the motion of the object's center of gravity and the object's rotation around its center of gravity. An object's *center of mass* is located at the same point as the object's center of gravity. The center of mass is used to calculate the motion of objects due to all kinds of forces, not only gravitational forces.

Joel R. Primack

Gravity, Specific. See Density.

Gravure. See Printing (Recess printing).

Gray, Asa (1810-1888), was the leading authority of his time on plant life in the United States. Gray specialized in the classification and description of plants and gained fame for interpreting the plant life of past geological ages. Gray's *Manual of Botany,* which was first published in 1848, helped to increase knowledge of plants growing in the northeastern United States and to popularize botany.

He believed that each plant species originated in one place, and that physical means, such as wind, spread a plant species from its point of origin. In his own studies, Gray found evidence that supported Charles Darwin's principles of evolution, and he vigorously defended Darwin's ideas. See **Darwin, Charles R.**

Gray was born in Sauquoit, New York. He became interested in botany while studying medicine and spent his spare time in the countryside searching for plants. He earned an M.D. degree from Fairfield Medical Col-

Center of gravity and stability

To find the center of gravity of a flat object, suspend the object and a plumb bob from one point. Draw a line along the plumb line. Then repeat from a second point. The center of gravity is where the two lines cross. The object will be unstable if a plumb line from its center of gravity falls outside the object's base.

WORLD BOOK diagram

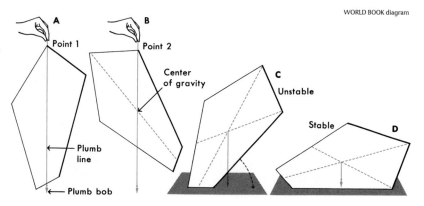

lege in Herkimer County, New York, in 1831 but never practiced. He taught science in Utica, N.Y., and in 1836, he became curator at the New York Lyceum of Natural History. Two years later he was appointed professor of natural history at the University of Michigan. In 1842, he became professor of natural history at Harvard University, and stayed there until his death. His library and herbarium formed the nucleus of the present Harvard University Herbarium, one of the largest and most noted in the world.   Keith R. Benson

Gray, Elisha (1835-1901), was an American inventor who—were it not for a few hours—might have become known as the inventor of the telephone. On Feb. 14, 1876, he went to the United States Patent Office (now the Patent and Trademark Office) and filed a *caveat*—a warning to other inventors—that he was working on a device to transmit speech. However, a few hours earlier, Gardiner G. Hubbard, a partner of American inventor Alexander Graham Bell, had filed a patent application for the telephone on Bell's behalf.

The Western Union Telegraph Company later bought Gray's patents and unsuccessfully challenged Bell's claim. A firm Gray had cofounded, Western Electric Manufacturing Company, made telephone equipment for Western Union. Gray made a fortune from other inventions. He was born in Barnesville, Ohio.

Arthur R. Brodsky

Gray, Robert (1755-1806), was the first person to sail around the world under the United States flag. His voyage established an important trade route for U.S. merchants. Gray sailed from Boston in 1787 bound for the North Pacific by way of Cape Horn. He visited China, and returned by way of the Cape of Good Hope in 1790. Gray set out again on the same route and sailed into the mouth of the Columbia River in 1792. He named the river after his ship. Gray's entrance into the river became a basis for U.S. claims to the Oregon Territory. Gray was born in Tiverton, R.I.   Michael J. Crawford

Gray, Simon (1936-   ), is an English dramatist known for his plays with academic and publishing set-tings. Gray's dramas explore modern British life, showing the secret frustrations and unhappiness that hide beneath a seemingly successful surface.

Gray's first popular play was *Butley* (1971). It concerns a university teacher who loses faith in his subject at the same time his personal life is crumbling. *Otherwise Engaged* (1975) shows a publisher so absorbed in himself that he hardly notices the problems and suffering of his friends and family. In *Close of Play* (1979), a family reunion is the occasion for characters to reveal their unhappiness. *Quartermaine's Terms* (1981) is about another university teacher—a man so insignificant, even to himself, that he is barely aware of the emptiness of his life. *The Common Pursuit* (1984) follows a group of college friends after graduation, as they experience the small compromises and betrayals of life in the real world. Gray's other plays include *Wise Child* (1967), his first; *The Rear Column* (1978); and *Melon* (1987).

Gray was born on Hayling Island, northeast of the Isle of Wight, England. He taught English literature at the University of London from 1965 to 1985. Gray wrote about his experiences writing and rehearsing his plays in *An Unnatural Pursuit* (1985) and *How's That for Telling 'Em, Fat Lady* (1988).   Gerald M. Berkowitz

Gray, Thomas (1716-1771), was an English poet. His masterpiece, "Elegy Written in a Country Churchyard" (1751), is one of the best-known poems in the English language. Its theme is the common fate of common people, who live and die unnoticed and unremembered. The poem includes the famous line "The paths of glory lead but to the grave."

Gray was born in London and attended Eton College and Cambridge University. He spent much of his life as a scholar at Cambridge. Gray traveled through France and Italy from 1739 to 1741, and later made many trips through Scotland and the English Lake District. His journals of these travels reveal Gray's appreciation of nature.

Gray's first published poem was "Ode on a Distant Prospect of Eton College" (1747). It includes the famous line ". . . where ignorance is bliss/'Tis folly to be wise."

© Ian Berry, Magnum

Detail of an oil portrait (mid-1700's) by J. G. Eccardt; National Portrait Gallery, London

Thomas Gray, *above,* was an English poet best known for his "Elegy Written in a Country Churchyard" (1751). The setting of the poem is a churchyard, *left,* in the English village of Stoke Poges, his mother's home. Gray is buried there.

Other major early poems are "Hymn to Adversity" and a sonnet on the death of a friend, Richard West. All were written at his mother's home in Stoke Poges, the village of the churchyard depicted in his famous elegy. The language reflects Gray's fondness for the artificial diction typical of poetry of his time. But he illustrated a new trend toward romanticism in his mood of melancholy moralizing. A romantic feeling appears in his odes "The Bard" (1757) and "The Progress of Poesy" (1757), written in the style of the Greek poet Pindar.

Although a shy man, Gray carried on a large correspondence. His letters to such friends as the author-politician Horace Walpole, are themselves examples of a minor art form of the period.   Gary A. Stringer

Gray Panthers is a national organization that fights age discrimination. It has about 85 local chapters throughout the United States and about 70,000 members and supporters of all ages. The Gray Panthers works to end age discrimination in employment and housing and negative portrayals of older people by the media. It supports the establishment of a national health care service and programs to increase the supply of affordable housing. The organization publishes a bimonthly newspaper called *The Network.* The Gray Panthers was founded in 1970. The organization's headquarters are located in Philadelphia.

Critically reviewed by the Gray Panthers

Gray whale is a medium-sized whale that lives in the Pacific Ocean. It reaches up to 43 feet (13 meters) in length. The gray whale has a low hump at the beginning of the lower third of its back and a series of fleshy knobs between this hump and the tail. The skin is gray with whitish blotches. *Barnacles* and other invertebrates cling to the skin and can alter its appearance.

Gray whales are *baleen* whales. Instead of teeth, they have 130 to 180 coarse, thin plates, called *baleen,* on each side of the mouth. Gray whales feed mainly on tiny invertebrates that live in mud on the ocean floor. Using their tongue, the whales suck mud, sand, and water into their mouth. They then use the baleen to filter out the food as they force the water from their mouth.

Gray whales have one of the longest annual migrations of any mammal. They spend summers in seas near Russia and Alaska, then migrate south to spend winters in and around lagoons along the coast of Baja California in Mexico. Because most of their migration occurs close to shore, whale watching has become a popular pastime along the Pacific coast. Gray whales were nearly hunted to extinction in the 1800's and early 1900's. But whale hunting declined in the late 1930's, and there are now about 20,000 to 22,000 gray whales.

Scientific classification. The gray whale belongs to the family Eschrichtiidae in the suborder Mysticeti, order Cetacea. Its scientific name is *Eschrichtius robustus.*   Bernd Würsig

Grayling is a game fish related to trout. The four known species live in the rivers and lakes of cool or Arctic regions. The European grayling may weigh as much as 5 pounds (2.3 kilograms). The Arctic grayling of North America may weigh up to 6 pounds (2.7 kilograms).

Graylings resemble trout in their habits, but graylings are more slender, graceful, and active. The grayling's scales also are larger than those of trout. Its beauty lies largely in its colorful fins. Arctic graylings are found from the Arctic region to Canada's southern border and

WORLD BOOK illustration by Colin Newman, Linden Artists Ltd.
A grayling has a slender body with colorful fins.

in the United States, mainly in Montana. They also live in eastern Siberia. Graylings are considered a delicacy.

Scientific classification. Graylings belong to the trout family, Salmonidae. The scientific name for the Arctic grayling is *Thymallus arcticus.*   David W. Greenfield

Graz, *grahts* (pop. 237,810), is the second largest city in Austria. Only Vienna is larger. Graz is the capital of the province of Styria. It lies on the Mur River in southeastern Austria (see **Austria** [political map]). Products include chemicals, hats, iron and steel products, leather, lithographic work, mathematical instruments, and paper. Charles Francis University dates from 1586. The city has a cathedral that was built in the 1400's; the Joanneum, a museum; and the Schlossberg, a castle. Bavarian Germans settled Graz during the Middle Ages.

William J. McGrath

Greasewood is a scraggly, thorny bush with stiff, dense, gray-barked branches and narrow, fleshy leaves. Greasewood grows over vast areas in the desert valleys of Nevada, Utah, and other states of the Great Basin. It particularly thrives in areas that have standing water or that periodically become flooded. The bush is a valuable food for livestock, but it may be poisonous to sheep when eaten as their only food in the spring.

Scientific classification. Greasewood belongs to the goosefoot family, Chenopodiaceae. Its scientific name is *Sarcobatus vermiculatus.*   Philip W. Rundel

Great Awakening is the name given to a series of religious revivals in the American Colonies during the mid-1700's. The movements began in the Middle Colonies in the 1730's and spread to New England and to some areas of the South. Leaders of the Great Awakening included Jonathan Edwards, a Congregational pastor in Massachusetts; Theodore J. Frelinghuysen, a Dutch Reformed pastor in New Jersey; Gilbert Tennent, a Presbyterian pastor in New Jersey; and George Whitefield, a traveling Methodist preacher from England.

The Great Awakening had a strong influence on American religious life. It produced a new, excited form of preaching. The structure of worship services changed to permit increased participation by the laity. Elements of *revivalism* also became widely accepted as a means of converting people to a particular church. Revivalism emphasizes individual religious experience rather than the doctrines of a specific church. The issue of personal experience divided many congregations and denominations. Supporters insisted that such an experience was necessary as a test of membership in a church. Opponents declared that a person could belong to a church without having such an experience.   Charles H. Lippy

See also **Edwards, Jonathan; Revivalism; Tennent,**

Gilbert; Whitefield, George; Colonial life in America (Religion).

Great Barrier Reef is the largest group of coral reefs in the world. A coral reef is a limestone formation that lies under or just above the surface of the sea. The Great Barrier Reef, famous for its beauty, extends in broken chains of reefs for about 1,250 miles (2,010 kilometers) along the northeast coast of Australia (see **Australia** [terrain map]). Parts of the reef are more than 100 miles (160 kilometers) from the coast. The closest parts lie about 10 miles (16 kilometers) from the coast.

The coral that forms the Great Barrier Reef is made of the hardened skeletons of dead water animals called *polyps*. Billions of living coral polyps are attached to the reef. They range in diameter from much less than 1 inch (2.5 centimeters) to 1 foot (30 centimeters). The colors of these polyps include blue, green, purple, red, and yellow. These colors, and the colors of many animals living in the Great Barrier Reef, give the reef an appearance of a lovely sea garden. Many small islands are scattered throughout the reef.

The reef supports a fascinating variety of life. About 400 species of polyps, about 1,500 species of fish, and many kinds of birds live there. Other animals that live on the reef include crabs, giant clams, and sea turtles.

Scientists believe the Great Barrier Reef began forming about 500,000 years ago. Today, large numbers of tourists visit the reef, and petroleum companies want to drill in the area for oil. Conservationists are concerned about possible damage to the reef from these and other sources. Australia has made most of the reef a national park. The Great Barrier Reef Marine Park Authority, an Australian government agency, works to protect the reef. The government has made it illegal to collect any of the coral. Conservationists have prevented petroleum companies from drilling in the area. Since the 1960's, some parts of the reef have been invaded by crown-of-thorns starfish, which feed on living polyps. During the 1980's and 1990's, scientists conducted studies of these

periodic starfish invasions. But they still do not know what causes the problem.   Garry R. LeDuff

See also **National park** (picture); **Seven Natural Wonders of the World.**

Great Basin is a large desert region in the western United States. It has several lakes and streams. Water in the streams either dries up or empties into one of the lakes, where it evaporates. The Great Basin is a region of *interior drainage* because its streams drain inside the

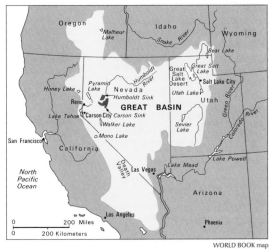

WORLD BOOK map

Location of the Great Basin

area rather than into bodies of water outside the area.

The basin covers about 200,000 square miles (520,000 square kilometers) in California, Idaho, Nevada, Oregon, Utah, and Wyoming. Desert shrubs cover the area. Trees are limited to the high mountains that encircle the area and to mountain ranges that rise within it. *Sinks* (low areas that may hold water) lie in some valleys. The largest are the Great Salt Lake, Carson and Humboldt sinks, and Pyramid Lake. The basin's deepest depression is Death Valley in California.   Christopher H. Exline

Great Basin National Park is in eastern Nevada. It lies entirely within the Great Basin region. Established in 1986, the park was created out of land that formerly made up Lehman Caves National Monument and part of Humboldt National Forest. The terrain of Great Basin National Park ranges from high desert to mountain peaks. Wheeler Peak, the park's highest mountain, rises 13,063 feet (3,982 meters) above sea level. Bristlecone pines, some more than 3,000 years old, grow in the park. Animals include bighorn sheep, bobcats, eagles, hawks, mountain lions, and mule deer. For the area of the park, see **National Park System** (table: National parks).

Critically reviewed by Great Basin National Park

Great Bear Lake is the largest lake in Canada and the fourth largest in the Americas. Only Lakes Superior, Huron, and Michigan are larger. Great Bear Lake covers 12,096 square miles (31,328 square kilometers) in the Northwest Territories. The lake spreads across parts of two of Canada's major land regions, the Canadian Shield and the northern Interior Plains. Part of the lake also lies within the Arctic Circle. Ice covers the lake for about three-fourths of the year. The lake's Dease Arm and Mc-

Chuck Nicklin

The Great Barrier Reef, along the northeast coast of Australia, includes coral formations such as those shown above.

Great Bear Lake

Area: 12,096 sq. mi.
(31,328 km²)

Elevation: 512 ft. (156 m)
above sea level

Deepest point: • 1,299 ft.
(396 m)

—— Road

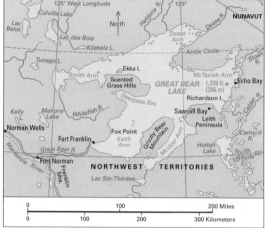

WORLD BOOK maps

comes part of Canada's longest navigable river system.

Great Bear Lake contains many fish, including trout, whitefish, and northern pike. The region around the lake has abundant wildlife. Residents from Fort Franklin, on the southwest side of the lake, trap many animals for the fur market. The lake probably got its name because of its size and because of the bears that lived on its shores.

From the 1930's to 1960, large quantities of pitchblende were mined near Echo Bay on the east side of the lake. Uranium taken from pitchblende that was mined in this area helped make atomic bombs used in 1945 during World War II.   G. Peter Kershaw

Great Britain is an island located off the northwest coast of the mainland of Europe. It is separated from the mainland by the English Channel to the south and the North Sea to the east. Great Britain is the largest island in Europe and the eighth largest island in the world. It covers 88,764 square miles (229,898 square kilometers). The landscape of Great Britain varies from mountainous terrain in Wales and northern Scotland to gently rolling hills and plains in central and southeastern England. Much of the island's coast is rocky and has deep bays and other inlets.

Politically, the island of Great Britain consists of three of the four political divisions of the country of the United Kingdom. The divisions are England, which covers most of the southern two-thirds of the island; Scotland, which covers the northern third; and Wales, a small division in the southwest. The fourth political division of the United Kingdom—Northern Ireland—lies just west of Great Britain, in the northeast corner of the island of Ireland.

Tavish Arm extend north into the *tundra,* which is a dry, cold, treeless region. Forests of small trees line the shores of the rest of Great Bear Lake. The Great Bear River drains the lake into the Mackenzie River and be-

Tom Bean, DRK

Great Basin National Park includes mountainous areas of natural beauty, *shown here,* and desert areas. The park lies in eastern Nevada in a large region called the Great Basin.

The name *Great Britain* is also sometimes used to mean the country of the United Kingdom. For location and detailed information on the country and the island, see **United Kingdom.**   Peter R. Mounfield

Great-circle route is the shortest, most direct route between two points on the earth's surface. A *great circle* is any circle that divides the globe into equal halves. Its length is the same as that of the equator. On most flat maps, a straight line appears to be the shortest distance between two places. A great-circle route often appears as a longer curve. But maps are not true pictures of the surface of the earth. Maps are flat, but the earth is a sphere. The shortest distance between any two points on the earth can be found easily only on a globe. The shortest distance lies along the great circle passing through the two points. A special kind of map called a *gnomonic projection* shows a great-circle route as a straight line.

To follow a great-circle route exactly, a ship must constantly change the compass direction in which it is heading. A ship's navigator would find it hard to follow a rapidly changing course. Instead, the navigator can plot a course with a series of connected lines, each line following a constant direction. These lines, called *rhumb lines,* join selected points along the great-circle route. By following the compass directions that are indicated by the rhumb lines, the ship can sail a course that is close to the shortest possible route. Airplanes can follow great-circle routes more easily than can ships. Many airplanes use a method of navigation known as *inertial guidance,* which allows aircraft to follow great-circle routes accurately. Ballistic missiles also use inertial guidance systems to follow great-circle routes (see **Inertial guidance**).

In 1537, Pedro Nunes, a Portuguese navigator, wrote about the advantages of great-circle-route navigation. Most ships did not sail great-circle routes until the 1800's, when navigation improved. Since the 1900's, great-circle routes have determined the major air routes.   Judy M. Olson

Great Dane is a breed of large dog. Great Danes are strong, elegant, courageous, and friendly. They weigh from 120 to 175 pounds (54 to 79 kilograms). Males stand about 34 inches (86 centimeters) high at the shoulder and females about 30 inches (76 centimeters) high. The Great Dane's short, dense coat may be tan, brown with black stripes, black, blue, or white with black patches.

The Great Dane was developed in Germany during the 1500's. It was first used in hunting boars and as a guard dog. Today, Great Danes make gentle, devoted, protective family dogs.

Critically reviewed by the Great Dane Club of America

E. R. Degginger

A Great Dane makes a good guard dog and family pet.

Great Depression was a worldwide business slump of the 1930's. It ranked as the worst and longest period of high unemployment and low business activity in modern times. The Great Depression began in October 1929, when stock values in the United States dropped rapidly. Thousands of stockholders lost large sums of money. Many of these stockholders were even wiped out. Banks, factories, and stores closed and left millions of Americans jobless and penniless. Many people had to depend on the government or charity to provide them with food.

President Herbert Hoover held office when the Great Depression began. The voters elected Franklin D. Roosevelt President in 1932. Roosevelt's reforms gave the government more power and helped ease the depression.

The Great Depression affected almost every nation. It caused a sharp decrease in world trade because each country tried to help its own industries by raising tariffs on imported goods. The depression caused some nations to change their leader and their type of government. The poor economic conditions of these times led to the rise of the German dictator Adolf Hitler and to the Japanese invasion of China. The German people supported Hitler because his plans to make Germany a world leader gave them hope for improved conditions.

WORLD BOOK maps

A great-circle route is the shortest distance between two points on the earth's surface. A kind of map called a *gnomonic projection, top,* shows a great-circle route as a straight line. Any other map, including the Mercator map, *bottom,* does not.

The Japanese developed industries and mines in Manchuria, a region of China, and claimed this economic growth would relieve the depression in Japan. The militarism of the Germans and the Japanese helped bring on World War II (1939-1945).

The Great Depression ended after nations increased their production of war materials at the start of World War II. This increased level of production provided many jobs and put large amounts of money back into circulation.

The depression had lasting effects on the United States government and on many Americans. For example, the government took more responsibility than ever before for strengthening the nation's economy. In addition, many Americans who lived during the depression stressed the importance in later years of acquiring such material comforts as household appliances and an automobile.

UPI/Bettmann

Rural poverty rose sharply during the Great Depression. The homeless farm families shown above are traveling from Missouri to Arkansas in 1939 in search of food, shelter, and jobs.

Causes of the Great Depression

Many causes contributed to making the Great Depression as severe as it was. During the 1920's, many bank failures, together with low incomes among farmers and factory workers, helped set the stage for the depression. Uneven distribution of income among workers also contributed to the slump. Most economists agree that the stock market crash of 1929 started the depression.

The farm depression of the 1920's. Although the 1920's were a prosperous period for business, most farmers did not prosper. Prices of farm products fell about 40 percent in 1920 and 1921, and they remained low through the 1920's. As a result, some farmers lost so much money that they could not pay the mortgage on their farm. These farmers then had to either rent their land or move.

Bank failures increased during the 1920's. Most of them occurred in agricultural areas because farmers experienced such poor conditions. About 550 banks went out of business from July 1, 1928, to June 30, 1929, the period of greatest prosperity in the 1920's.

Uneven distribution of income. In addition to the farmers, workers in the coal, railroad, and textile industries failed to share in the prosperity of the 1920's. Industrial production increased about 50 percent, but the wages of industrial workers rose far more slowly. As a result, these workers could not buy goods so fast as industry produced them. Many people had to buy on credit. After a while, workers reduced their spending to hold down their debts. Then the amount of money in circulation decreased, and business became even worse.

The stock market crash. From 1925 to 1929, the average price of common stocks on the New York Stock Exchange more than doubled. Rising stock values encouraged many people to *speculate*—that is, buy stocks in hope of making large profits following future price increases.

Stock values dropped rapidly on Oct. 24, 1929, now known as Black Thursday. Most stock prices remained steady on Friday and Saturday. But the next Monday, stock prices fell again. Then, on Tuesday, October 29, stockholders panicked and sold a record 16,410,030 shares of stock. Thousands of people lost huge sums of money as stock values fell far below the prices paid for the stock. Banks and businesses had also bought stock,

UPI/Bettmann

Rough shacks sprang up in vacant areas of many cities after thousands of people lost their homes during the Great Depression. Groups of shacks, such as these in New York City in 1932, became known as *Hoovervilles*. The name was a scornful reference to Herbert Hoover, who was President when the depression struck.

Wide World

Bank failures wiped out the savings of millions of people during the Great Depression. Depositors crowded around the American Union Bank in New York City, *left,* after it failed in 1931. About 9,000 banks in the United States closed from January 1930 to March 1933.

and many lost so much that they had to close. Stock values fell almost steadily for the next three years.

The deepening depression

The Great Depression differed in both length and harshness from previous depressions in the United States. In earlier depressions, business activity had started to pick up after one or two years. But from October 1929 until Franklin D. Roosevelt became President in March 1933 the economy slumped almost every month. Business failures increased rapidly among banks, factories, and stores, and unemployment soared. Millions of people lost their job, savings, and home.

Economic breakdown. From 1930 to 1933, prices of industrial stocks fell about 80 percent. Banks and individuals with investments in the stock market lost large sums. Banks had also loaned money to many people who could not repay it. The deepening depression forced large numbers of people to withdraw their savings. Banks had great difficulty meeting the withdrawals, which came at a time when the banks were unable to collect on many loans. Between January 1930 and March 1933, about 9,000 banks failed. The bank failures wiped out the savings of millions of people.

Ben Isaacs, who lived in Chicago during the depression, described what happened to him: "I was in business for myself, selling clothes on credit. . . . But . . . banks closed down overnight. We lost everything. . . . I couldn't pay the rent. . . . I sold it [the car] for $15 in order to buy some food for the family. . . . I would bend my head low [in the relief line] so nobody would recognize me. . . ." (The quotations in this article are from *Hard Times: An Oral History of the Great Depression* © 1970 by Studs Terkel, published by Pantheon Books, a Division of Random House, Inc.)

Bank failures made less money available for loans to industry. The decline in available money caused a drop in production and a further rise in unemployment. From 1929 to 1933, the total value of goods and services produced annually in the United States fell from about $104 billion to about $56 billion. In 1932, the number of business closings was almost a third higher than the 1929 level.

In 1925, about 3 percent of the nation's workers were unemployed. The unemployment rate reached about 9 percent in 1930 and about 25 percent—or about 13 million persons—in 1933. Many people who kept or found jobs had to take salary cuts. In 1932, wage cuts averaged about 18 percent. Many people, including college graduates, felt lucky to find any job. In 1932, the New York City Police Department estimated that 7,000 persons over the age of 17 shined shoes for a living. A popular song of the 1930's called "Brother, Can You Spare a Dime?" expressed the nationwide despair.

Foreign trade also fell greatly during the Great Depression. The Smoot-Hawley Tariff Act of 1930 contributed to the drop. This law greatly increased a number of tariffs. President Hoover signed the law because he thought it would reduce competition from foreign products. But tariffs rose so high that other nations reacted by raising tariffs on U.S. goods.

From 1929 to 1933, prices of farm goods fell about 50 percent. This drop occurred partly because high tariffs made exports unprofitable. In addition, farmers produced a surplus of crops. The surplus pushed prices down because there was more food than people could buy.

Human suffering became a reality for millions of Americans as the depression continued. Many died of disease resulting from malnutrition. Thousands lost their home because they could not pay the mortgage. In 1932, at least 25,000 families and more than 200,000 young people wandered through the country seeking food, clothing, shelter, and a job. Many youths traveled in freight trains and lived near train yards in camps called *hobo jungles.*

The homeless, jobless travelers obtained food from welfare agencies or religious missions in towns along the way. Most of their meals consisted of soup, beans, or stew and had little nourishment. The travelers begged for food or stole it if they could not get something to eat in any other way. Sometimes they ate scraps of food from garbage cans.

The ragged travelers found clothing harder to obtain than food. Missions gave most of the clothing they had to needy local people. Some of the travelers became ill because they did not have proper food and clothing. Even the sick wanderers had trouble getting help because hospitals aided local residents first.

Many people who lost their home remained in the community. Some crowded into the home of a relative. Others moved to a shabby section of town and built shacks from flattened tin cans and old crates. Groups of these shacks were called *Hoovervilles,* a name that reflected the people's anger and disappointment at President Hoover's failure to end the depression.

Peggy Terry, who grew up in Oklahoma during the depression, recalled a visit to a Hooverville in Oklahoma City: "Here were all these people living in old rusted-out car bodies. ... One family ... [was] living in a piano box. This wasn't just a little section, this was maybe 10 miles wide and 10 miles long. People living in whatever they could junk together. ..."

In 1932, many farmers refused to ship their products to market. They hoped a reduced supply of farm products would help raise the price of these goods. Such farmers' strikes occurred throughout the country, but they centered in Iowa and the surrounding states.

Harry Terrell, who lived in Iowa during the depression, described the conditions among farmers: "Corn was going for 8 cents a bushel. One county insisted on using corn to heat the courthouse, 'cause it was cheaper than coal. ... The people were desperate. ... [Farmers] stopped milk wagons, dumped milk. ..."

Severe droughts and dust storms hit parts of the Midwest and Southwest during the 1930's. The afflicted region became known as the *Dust Bowl,* and thousands of farm families there were wiped out. Many farmers went to the fertile agricultural areas of California to look for work. Most who found jobs had to work as fruit or vegetable pickers for extremely low wages. The migrant families crowded into shacks near the fields or camped outdoors. John Steinbeck's famous novel *The Grapes of Wrath* (1939) describes the hardships some migrant families faced during the depression. See **Dust Bowl**.

Hoover's policies. President Hoover believed that business, if left alone to operate without government supervision, would correct the economic conditions. He vetoed several bills aimed at relieving the depression because he felt they gave the federal government too much power.

Hoover declared that state and local governments should provide relief to the needy. But those governments did not have enough money to do so. In 1932, Congress approved Hoover's most successful antidepression measure, the Reconstruction Finance Corpora-

tion (RFC). This government agency provided some relief by lending money to banks, railroads, and other large institutions whose failure would have made the depression even worse. However, most Americans felt that Hoover did not do enough to fight the depression. They elected Franklin D. Roosevelt President in 1932. See **Hoover, Herbert Clark** (Hoover's Administration).

The New Deal. Roosevelt believed the federal government had the chief responsibility of fighting the depression. He called Congress into a special session, now called the *Hundred Days,* to pass laws to relieve the depression. Roosevelt called his program the *New Deal.*

The laws established by the New Deal had three main purposes. First, they provided relief for the needy. Second, they aided nationwide recovery by providing jobs and encouraging business. Third, the laws tried to reform business and government so that such a severe depression would never happen in the United States again.

Congress created several agencies to manage relief programs. The Civilian Conservation Corps (CCC), established in 1933, employed thousands of young men in conservation projects. The Federal Emergency Relief Administration (FERA), founded in 1933, gave the states money for the needy. The Works Progress Administration (WPA), created in 1935, provided jobs in building such public projects as highways and parks. In 1939, this agency was renamed the Work Projects Administration.

Some New Deal agencies established and managed recovery programs. The Agricultural Adjustment Administration (AAA), set up in 1933, helped regulate farm production. The National Recovery Administration (NRA), established in 1933, set up and enforced rules of fair practice for business and industry. The Public Works Administration (PWA), founded in 1933, provided jobs in the construction of bridges, dams, and schools.

The government also aided recovery by spending large sums of money. This spending gave business leaders the confidence to also begin spending. The economy improved after money began to circulate. The government also increased trade by lowering tariffs on some imported goods. In return, other nations lowered tariffs on some United States products they imported.

Congress created several agencies to supervise banking and labor reforms. The Federal Deposit Insurance

UPI/Bettmann

The Civilian Conservation Corps (CCC) was founded in 1933 to provide jobs for the unemployed. In this photograph, CCC workers help U.S. Forest Service employees in Oregon in 1939.

Corporation (FDIC), founded in 1933, insured bank deposits. The National Labor Relations Board (NLRB), established in 1935, worked to prevent unfair labor practices and aid the development of labor unions. The Securities and Exchange Commission (SEC), created in 1934, tried to protect investors from buying unsafe stocks and bonds. In 1935, Congress passed the Social Security Act to provide money for retired and unemployed people.

Some Americans who kept their jobs during the Great Depression managed to live comfortably. Many of those who had a steady income could afford to buy an automobile, clothes, and other products that were out of reach for most people. Steak cost about 29 cents a pound, and gasoline about 18 cents a gallon. People who had enough money found that, because of low prices, conditions were better during the depression than they had been in the 1920's.

The New Deal programs not only helped relieve the depression but also renewed the confidence of Americans in the government. But about 15 percent of the nation's working force still did not have a job in 1940. The Great Depression did not end in the United States until 1942, after the country had entered World War II. The great increase in production of war materials provided so many jobs that the U.S. unemployment rate fell to about 1 percent in 1944. See **New Deal; Roosevelt, Franklin Delano** (Roosevelt's first Administration).

In Canada, the economy depended on the export of grain and raw materials. Farmers and exporters suffered huge losses after other countries increased tariffs on imported products. Many Canadian companies closed, and the unemployment rate rose from about 3 percent of the labor force in 1929 to about 23 percent in 1933.

Richard B. Bennett, who served as prime minister from 1930 to 1935, had little success in his efforts to relieve the depression in Canada. W. L. Mackenzie King succeeded Bennett and adopted programs similar to those of Roosevelt to fight the depression. See **Bennett, Richard Bedford; King, William Lyon Mackenzie; Canada, History of** (The Great Depression).

Effects of the depression

The Great Depression caused many changes in the United States. It brought new laws that gave the government far more power than at any previous time in the nation's history. It also changed the attitudes of countless Americans toward various aspects of life.

New government policies that resulted from the New Deal increased federal control over banks and the stock market. Laws of the New Deal also gave the government more power to provide money for the needy. Ever since the depression, both Democratic and Republican administrations have broadened the powers of the federal government. For example, the government now provides hospital and medical insurance for the aged. The government may also regulate price and wage increases to try to keep the cost of living from rising.

The depression also changed the basic philosophy of the United States government in spending money. Before the depression, the government tried to spend the same amount of money it collected. But to support the New Deal, the government used *deficit spending*—that is, it spent more money than it collected. This policy greatly increased the national debt. The government has

Brown Bros.

Apple peddlers lined the streets of many large cities during the Great Depression. Thousands of men who had lost their jobs sold apples to earn enough money for food and clothing.

continued to rely on deficit spending during most years since World War II ended in 1945.

New public attitudes. The depression changed the attitudes of many Americans toward business and the federal government. Before the depression, most people regarded bankers and business executives as the nation's leaders. After the stock market crashed and these leaders could not relieve the depression, Americans lost faith in them. The government finally succeeded in improving conditions. As a result, many Americans decided that the government—not business—had the responsibility to maintain the national economy.

Many people changed their basic attitudes toward life because of the suffering they experienced during the depression. They previously had believed they would have a reasonably happy life if they worked hard, saved money, and treated others well. The depression shattered that belief. The situation seemed especially hard to understand because there appeared to be no reason for so many of the things that happened.

The depression probably affected young adults more than any other group from a psychological viewpoint. These men and women encountered great difficulty in finding a job and starting a career. If they did find a position, they had little chance for promotion because employers eliminated jobs throughout the depression. Consequently, many young adults lost confidence in themselves and lowered their ambitions.

Some people who lived through the Great Depression became more concerned with material possessions than did people born after that era. The depression forced people to worry about such necessities as food, clothing, and shelter. After the economy improved, many people wanted material comforts they had lost or they had never owned before, including appliances, a car, and a house. Other people sought financial security.

They stressed the importance of having a job and saving money as a precaution against hard times in the future.

The importance of material comforts and financial security that developed among many people of the depression generation affected their relationship with their children. Most people who grew up during the 1950's and 1960's did not know the experience of being wiped out. They knew nothing about having to struggle for money and a job. They did not understand why their parents so desired material possessions and financial security. Many young people criticized such attitudes of their parents. A lack of both understanding and communication helped create what became known as the "generation gap" of the 1960's and early 1970's.   Robert Sobel

Related articles in *World Book* include:

African Americans (The Great Depression)	Depression	Unemployment
	Economics (New solutions for old problems)	United States, History of the (The Great Depression)
Bank holiday		
Capitalism	Hopkins, Harry L.	

Additional resources

McElvaine, Robert S. *The Great Depression*. Times Bks., 1984. Reprint. 1993.
Stein, R. Conrad. *The Great Depression*. Childrens Pr., 1993. Younger readers.

Great Divide, also called Continental Divide, is the high ground in North America that separates streams flowing into the Pacific Ocean from those flowing into the Atlantic Ocean, Gulf of Mexico, and Arctic Ocean. The northern section of the Great Divide is in the United States, in the Seward Peninsula and Brooks Range of Alaska. The divide twists through Canada's Yukon Territory, then curves across British Columbia and forms part of that province's boundary with Alberta. It reenters the United States in western Montana.

The divide forms part of Montana's boundary with Idaho, and then winds through Wyoming, Colorado, and New Mexico. It then enters Mexico. It passes through the plateau between Mexico's Sierra Madre ranges. In Central America, it lies roughly along the mountains near the Pacific Ocean.   John Edwin Coffman

See also **Continental divide; Divide.**

Great Falls (pop. 56,690; met. area pop. 80,357) is an industrial and trade center in north-central Montana (see **Montana** [political map]). It is also an important regional medical center. The city lies near a series of falls of the Missouri River and was named for them. The falls furnish power for hydroelectric plants.

The city's industries include flour milling, meat packing, noodle making, petroleum processing, printing and publishing, and tourism. Giant Springs State Park in Great Falls has one of the world's largest freshwater springs. The city is the home of the University of Great Falls. Malmstrom Air Force Base lies near the city.

Paris Gibson, an American pioneer, founded Great Falls in 1884, and it became a city in 1888. The seat of Cascade County, Great Falls has a commission-manager form of government. For the monthly weather in Great Falls, see **Montana** (Climate).   Tom Kotynski

Great Irish Famine of 1845-1850 killed about 1 million Irish people and caused millions more to leave Ireland. The famine began after a plant disease called *blight* destroyed potato crops, the chief food of the poor. Most historians agree, though, that British mishan-

From *The Illustrated London News,* 1849
During the Great Irish Famine, Irish peasants evicted from their rented lands lived in hovels or by the roadsides. The potato crop was wiped out by disease, and many peasants starved.

dling of the food shortage turned it into a tragedy.

England had dominated Ireland for centuries. In the 1500's and 1600's, the English monarchy fought to eliminate Roman Catholicism from Ireland. In what is known as the *plantation of Ireland*, the government took land from the Irish, who were mostly Catholic, and gave it to English and Scottish Protestants. The Penal Laws tried to force Catholics to renounce their faith. The laws later decreed that no Catholic, and therefore few Irish people, could purchase land, vote, or hold public office. In 1800, the British passed the Act of Union, ending Ireland's parliament and making Ireland part of the United Kingdom.

As a result of the plantation and the Penal Laws, Protestants owned most of the land in Ireland. Some of the Irish were tenant farmers, who paid as rent most of the crops and animals they raised. But many of the Irish were landless laborers who worked the fields in exchange for a small plot on which to grow potatoes. Most Irish families lived on potatoes and little else.

The potato blight struck in 1845, but with limited effect. It struck harder in 1846, and many of the poor sold their animals and other possessions to buy food. When the blight returned in 1847, farmers and laborers could no longer feed themselves. Landlords evicted hundreds of thousands of people. Some paid for their tenants' passage on "coffin ships" bound for England, Canada, or the United States. Thousands of passengers perished from disease, either on board ship or soon after arrival.

Despite the blight, other crops thrived in Ireland. However, the food was shipped elsewhere to be sold. In 1847, the worst year of the starvation, nearly 4,000 shiploads of food left famine-stricken areas in Ireland for English and Scottish ports.

The British government set up public works to employ people so they could buy food. But the wages were too low to feed a family. Charity- and government-operated soup kitchens could not feed all the starving. Diseases, including typhus and cholera, overwhelmed the malnourished people and wiped out large numbers. Many died by the roads or in ramshackle huts. Many of the dead were buried without coffins in mass graves.

The potato blight began to disappear in 1848, and by 1850 the harvest was good in most of Ireland. But rates of death and disease remained high for several years. By 1900, continued emigration reduced the country's population to about 4 million, half its size before the famine. Many left Ireland full of bitterness, blaming the British government for their suffering.   James V. Mullin

Great Lakes. Lakes Superior, Michigan, Huron, Erie, and Ontario—the five Great Lakes—are the world's largest group of freshwater lakes. They contain 18 percent of the world's fresh surface water. The Great Lakes also form the most important inland waterway in North America. They were the chief route used by early explorers and settlers of the Midwestern States and Ontario. Later, the cheap transportation offered by the lakes turned this region into a major industrial area.

Of the five Great Lakes, only Lake Michigan lies entirely in the United States. The other four are shared by the United States and Canada and form part of the boundary between the nations. The Boundary Waters Treaty of 1909 provides joint control of the lakes by the two countries.

Among the most important lake ports are Chicago, Milwaukee, and Gary on Lake Michigan; Buffalo, Cleveland, Toledo, and Ashtabula on Lake Erie; and Duluth, Superior, and Thunder Bay on Lake Superior. Other major ports in the Great Lakes region include Detroit, which lies on a river connecting Lake St. Clair and Lake Erie; and Toronto, on Lake Ontario.

How the lakes were formed. In the last 2 million years, glaciers repeatedly advanced south over the land that is now the Great Lakes region. The glaciers were about 6,600 feet (2,000 meters) thick, and they dug out deep depressions and pushed along great amounts of earth and rocks during their advance. The last advance took place about 25,000 years ago. The last withdrawal, or melting, of the glaciers occurred about 11,000 to 15,000 years ago. Earth and rocks that had piled up blocked the natural drainage of the depressions. Water gradually filled in the depressions and formed thousands of lakes, including the Great Lakes.

Size and elevation. The Great Lakes have a combined area of 94,230 square miles (244,060 square kilometers). Lake Superior, the largest of the lakes, covers 31,700 square miles (82,100 square kilometers). Lake Huron, the second largest, has an area of 23,000 square miles (59,570 square kilometers). The third largest lake is

The Great Lakes region

Canada

AREA OF MAP AT RIGHT

United States

Depth of the Great Lakes

0 to 328 ft. (0 to 100 m)

328 to 656 ft. (100 to 200 m)

656 to 984 ft. (200 to 300 m)

Deeper than 984 ft. (300 m)

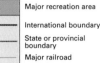

Major recreation area

International boundary

State or provincial boundary

Major railroad

Major highway

Canal

⊛ National capital

⊛ State or provincial capital

• City or town

■ Point of interest

▽ Deepest point

WORLD BOOK map

[Map of the Great Lakes region showing states Minnesota, Wisconsin, Iowa, Illinois, Indiana, Ohio, Michigan, and the Canadian province of Ontario, with Lakes Superior, Michigan, Huron, and Erie. Labeled cities include Thunder Bay, Marathon, Timmins, Duluth, Superior, St. Paul, Eau Claire, Madison, Milwaukee, Green Bay, Chicago, Gary, Detroit, Toledo, Cleveland, Sault Ste. Marie, Sudbury, and others. Scales shown at bottom in miles (0 to 500) and kilometers (0 to 800).]

Lake Michigan, which covers 22,300 square miles (57,760 square kilometers). Lake Erie ranks fourth, with an area of 9,910 square miles (25,670 square kilometers). The smallest of the lakes is Lake Ontario, with an area of 7,320 square miles (18,960 square kilometers).

The elevation of the lakes varies greatly. Lake Superior lies 600 feet (183 meters) above sea level, and Lake Ontario lies 243 feet (74 meters) above sea level. The greatest change in water levels between one lake and the next one is the 326-foot (99-meter) drop from Lake Erie to Lake Ontario. Part of this difference in water levels can be seen at Niagara Falls.

Drainage. Many small streams empty into the Great Lakes, but the lakes drain a comparatively small land area. The Great Lakes can be thought of as a series of deep pools connected by narrow channels. From Lake Superior to Lake Ontario, the elevations drop. The waterflow follows that same general direction, from Lake Superior southeastward. Also, each lake gains water from rain, snow, and runoff from the land.

Each of the Great Lakes loses water by evaporation and flow to a downstream lake or a connecting river. If rainfall is much greater than evaporation, lake levels rise. All the water in the lakes drains into the St. Lawrence River except for a small amount that goes down the Chicago River. The course of the Chicago River was turned away from Lake Michigan in 1900 when the Chicago Sanitary and Ship Canal was opened.

Water routes to the sea. Some Great Lakes ports lie over 1,000 miles (1,600 kilometers) inland, but ships can sail from any of these ports to any other port in the world. This was made possible by three great sets of canals and locks built by the governments of the United States and Canada. These canals and locks compensate for differences in the water levels of the lakes.

One set of canals and locks is the St. Lawrence Seaway. The seaway extends about 450 miles (724 kilometers) from Montreal to Lake Erie. Its canals and locks enable oceangoing ships to sail from the Atlantic Ocean to Lake Superior. The seaway includes a set of canals and locks called the Welland Ship Canal. This section of the seaway lies a little west of the Niagara River, and connects Lake Erie and Lake Ontario. The Welland Ship Canal allows ships to pass around Niagara Falls.

Another set of canals and locks is called the *Soo Canals.* They are on the St. Marys River, which connects Lake Superior and Lake Huron. The Soo Canals were built around rapids that occur at a 20-foot (6-meter) drop in the St. Marys River. The route to the sea goes from Lake Huron to Lake Erie, to Lake Ontario, down the St. Lawrence to the Atlantic.

Smaller craft may reach the sea by two other routes. One is by the New York State Barge Canal System from Buffalo, New York, to Albany, New York, connecting Lake Erie with the Hudson River and the Atlantic Ocean. Another takes ships from Lake Michigan to the Gulf of Mexico by way of the Chicago Sanitary and Ship Canal, through the Illinois River, and down the Mississippi.

Commerce. The Soo Canals and the St. Lawrence Seaway are among the busiest canal systems in the world. The Great Lakes have greatly aided the industrial development of the United States and central Canada, especially in the steel industry. These waterways provide a quick route for ships that carry iron ore from the ports of Duluth and Two Harbors, Minnesota; Superior and Ashland, Wisconsin; and Escanaba and Marquette, Michigan, to the steelmaking centers that are located in northern Indiana, Ohio, and Pennsylvania.

The Great Lakes also offer the best means for the shipment of the huge wheat crops of western Canada and the northern United States to milling centers in eastern Canada and in Buffalo. Other ships carry coal, copper, flour, and manufactured goods on the lakes.

The most common type of ship on the lakes is the *ore carrier,* a vessel built for lake trade. This long craft lies low in the water when fully loaded. Its surface is covered with openings called *hatches.* The ship pulls alongside a dock, and ore is poured into the *hold* (ship's body) from automatic chutes or conveyors. The hatches are then closed. A large ore carrier is loaded within 8 to 10 hours, and can carry as much as 70,000 tons (64,000 metric tons) of ore in one trip. Most carriers unload their own cargo by means of an on-board conveyor system. On their return trips on the Great Lakes, the carriers often carry coal and limestone.

Changes in lake levels. In the early 1960's, water levels were low. However, several wet years resulted in record high levels in the early 1970's and again in 1985 and 1986. By the late 1980's, water levels had returned to

Profile of the Great Lakes

This diagram of the Great Lakes shows the depth of each of the bodies of water in profile. See the larger map in this article for the geographic location of the lakes.

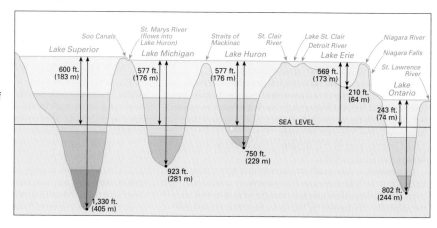

Depth of the Great Lakes

	0 to 328 ft. (0 to 100 m)
	328 to 656 ft. (100 to 200 m)
	656 to 984 ft. (200 to 300 m)
	Deeper than 984 ft. (300 m)

WORLD BOOK illustration

a near-normal range. High water levels, combined with high waves during storms, cause flooding and erosion of the shoreline. Low water levels create problems for wildlife, ships, and hydroelectric power production.

Water quality. Industrial wastes, sewage, and other wastes have polluted the Great Lakes since the mid-1800's. To remedy pollution and to control water use, the United States and Canada set up the International Joint Commission (IJC) in 1909. See **International Joint Commission.**

In the late 1960's, concern grew about pollution, particularly in Lake Erie. In 1972, the two governments signed the Great Lakes Water Quality Agreement. Improvements resulted, especially a reduction in phosphorus dumped into the lake. Phosphorus, sewage, and fertilizer wastes had caused algae growth that made beaches messy and smelly. But less visible pollutants, such as toxic chemicals and metals, are still a problem. Much of these substances reaches the Great Lakes by air from such sources as the spraying of insecticides and the burning of wastes and fuels. These pollutants may have caused diseases seen in some Great Lakes fish. As a result, the Great Lakes states and Ontario have suggested that people avoid eating certain fish and limit consumption of others. Further efforts have been planned to make waters comply with safe standards for drinking, swimming, and fishing.   A. P. Lino Grima

Related articles in *World Book* include:

Buffalo (Economy)	Icebreaker	Niagara River
Chicago (Economy)	Lake Erie	Saint Lawrence River
Cleveland	Lake Huron	Saint Lawrence Seaway
Detroit	Lake Michigan	Saint Lawrence Seaway
Detroit River	Lake Ontario	Soo Canals
Duluth	Lake Superior	Welland Ship Canal
Erie Canal	New York State Barge Canal	Zebra mussel
Ice age	System	

Additional resources

Ashworth, William. *The Late, Great Lakes: An Environmental History.* 1986. Reprint. Wayne State Univ. Pr., 1987.
Great Lakes. 3rd ed. Environment Canada, 1995.

Great Lakes Naval Training Center, Illinois, is the site of the United States Navy's largest recruit training command. It occupies 1,568 acres (635 hectares) along Lake Michigan, 40 miles (64 kilometers) north of Chicago. The center houses a Naval Hospital and a Naval Supply Depot. The training command provides basic naval

training and advanced training in various technical schools. Leading Chicago merchants bought the land in 1905 and gave it to the government. The Navy commissioned the center in 1911.   W. W. Reid

Great Lakes–Saint Lawrence Seaway. See Saint Lawrence Seaway.

Great Plains is a vast, dry grassland in North America. It is an important agricultural and mining region. The Great Plains extends for about 2,500 miles (4,020 kilometers) from northern Canada into New Mexico and Texas in the United States. It stretches eastward for about 400 miles (640 kilometers), from the Rocky Mountains to western Saskatchewan in Canada; and to eastern South Dakota, Nebraska, Kansas, and Oklahoma in the United States. The western boundary along the mountain front is from 4,500 to 6,500 feet (1,370 to 1,980 meters) high. The eastern boundary is from 1,500 to 2,000 feet (457 to 610 meters) high. Major rivers include the Arkansas, Canadian, Missouri, Platte, and Saskatchewan.

Relatively few people live in the western Great Plains. The region's population increases toward the east.

The Great Plains supports much plant and animal life. It has a variety of grasses, including blue grama, buffalo grass, crested wheatgrass, and little bluestem. Animals of the region include lizards, opossums, prairie dogs, weasels, raccoons, rattlesnakes, and skunks.

WORLD BOOK map

The Great Plains, shown in yellow, is an important agricultural and mining region of Canada and the United States.

Agriculture and mining dominate the economy. The Great Plains is one of the world's chief wheat-growing areas. Other farm products include alfalfa, barley, oats, and rye. Cattle, goats, and sheep graze there. The Great Plains yields more oil than any other area of the United States or Canada. The north has huge coal deposits.

Indians were the first inhabitants of the Great Plains. Spaniards became the first Europeans to explore the area, in the 1500's. The French began a fur trade with Indians of the region in the 1700's. After the Civil War in the United States (1861-1865), railroads that were built westward across the Great Plains led to the establishment of new towns and farming and ranching areas. Large deposits of petroleum and natural gas were discovered in the region in the 1920's. Since World War II (1939-1945), petroleum and coal mining have contributed to the region's prosperity.   John Edwin Coffman

Great Purge. See **Stalin, Joseph** (Rule by terror); **Saint Petersburg** (History).

Great Pyrenees is a large breed of dog developed in the Pyrenees Mountains of southwestern Europe. For centuries, it has served people there by guarding sheep. The dog stands 27 to 32 inches (69 to 81 centimeters) high at the shoulder. It has a thick, primarily white coat, a heavy head, and a rolling walk. See also **Dog** (picture: Working dogs).   Critically reviewed by the American Kennel Club

Great Rift Valley is a series of valleys that cuts through much of eastern Africa and part of southwestern Asia. It extends about 4,500 miles (7,200 kilometers) from Syria in southwestern Asia to Mozambique in southeastern Africa. Its steep walls rise about 6,600 feet (2,000 meters) high in some places. Most parts of the valley are from 18 to 60 miles (30 to 100 kilometers) wide. It has some of Africa's most spectacular scenery, including lakes and volcanoes.

A western branch of the valley runs along the eastern border of Congo (Kinshasa). Two of the earth's deepest lakes, Lake Tanganyika and Lake Nyasa, cover most of this section. The valley's eastern branch runs through Eritrea, Ethiopia, Kenya, and Tanzania. Some of the earliest-known human remains have been found there.

Scientists explain the formation of the Great Rift Valley with the *plate tectonics theory*. According to this theory, the earth's outer shell consists of about 30 rigid sections of rock called *plates*. Movement along the boundary between two plates is generally about $\frac{1}{2}$ to 4 inches (1 to 10 centimeters) a year. As plates move, their boundaries may collide, spread apart, or slide alongside one another. Such movements have formed most parts of the valley. Erosion and volcanic activity have also helped form the valley.   Hartmut S. Walter

Great Salt Lake, a saltwater lake in northwestern Utah, is the largest lake in the western United States. It is three to eight times as salty as the ocean. The Great Salt Lake is fed by precipitation and by inflowing streams. It has no outflowing streams. The inflowing streams carry salts, which are left behind when the water evaporates.

At its deepest point, the Great Salt Lake is only 33 feet (10 meters) deep. Because it is so shallow, it varies in size according to climate conditions. On average, the lake covers about 1,600 square miles (4,200 square kilometers). It averages about 75 miles (120 kilometers) long and about 35 miles (48 kilometers) wide. During warm, dry weather, reduced inflows of water and increased

evaporation shrink the lake's size. In the early 1960's, for example, it covered only 970 square miles (2,500 square kilometers). On the other hand, heavy snowfall in the nearby mountains leads to an increase in the water flowing into the lake. In the mid-1980's, the lake grew to one of its largest sizes, about 2,300 square miles (6,000 square kilometers). It expanded across public and private lands and caused millions of dollars of damage.

The concentration of salt varies, depending on the amount of water in the lake at any given time. The saltiness also varies from one end of the lake to the other. An earthen railroad causeway, constructed in 1959, divides the lake into north and south sections. The salt content of the south end ranges from about 5 to 14 percent. The north end, which has fewer inflows than the south end, ranges from about 16 to 28 percent salt.

The salt in the Great Salt Lake comes from minerals dissolved in the creeks and rivers that flow into the lake. Sodium and chloride—which make up salt—account for about 80 percent of the lake's mineral content. Other minerals include magnesium, potassium, and sulfate.

Bathers and boaters enjoy using the lake. Swimmers float easily in the salty water. Many visitors go to Antelope Island, which is the lake's largest island and a state park. A herd of wild buffalo lives there.

The wetlands around the lake make it an important stopover for migrating birds. The birds feed on the lake's small brine shrimp and on the tiny brine flies that live in the lake during their grub stage. Carp and some Utah chub live near the lake's freshwater inflows. In the salty waters at the north end, only salt-loving bacteria

Great Salt Lake

Area: 1,616 sq. mi. (4,184 km²)

Elevation: 4,200 ft. (1,280 m) above sea level

Deepest point: ● 33 ft. (10 m)

——— Road   ——— Railroad

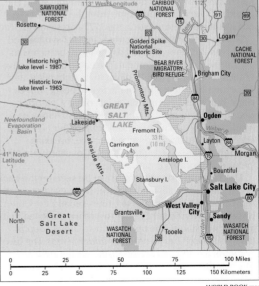

WORLD BOOK map

can live. At certain times of the year, these organisms give the lake a pinkish-purple color.

Scientists believe a lake has existed on the Great Salt Lake's site for millions of years. The Great Salt Lake was once part of an ancient freshwater lake called Lake Bonneville. The lake drained away thousands of years ago in a great flood, leaving a few isolated lakes. The Great Salt Lake is the largest of these lakes.   Katrina A. Moser

See also **Bridger, Jim; Great Basin; Utah** (picture).

Great Salt Lake Desert is a low, flat, arid region in northwestern Utah, just west of Salt Lake City. It extends south for about 110 miles (177 kilometers) from the Grouse Creek Mountains, and borders on Nevada (see Utah [physical map]). The desert covers about 4,000 square miles (10,000 square kilometers).

The Bonneville Salt Flats occupy about 70 square miles (180 square kilometers) of extremely level salt beds in the desert near Wendover, close to the Nevada border. The Bonneville Salt Flats International Speedway is on the Bonneville Salt Flats. These salt beds are usually hard enough to allow automobile racing on them. But rises in the water level of the Great Salt Lake near the desert sometimes make the surface of the salt beds soft and wet. Automobile-racing drivers have set international speed records on the Speedway.   Christopher H. Exline

See also **Utah** (picture).

Great Schism. See Pope (The troubles of the papacy); Roman Catholic Church (The Great Schism); Sigismund.

Great Seal of the United States, also called Seal of the United States, symbolizes the sovereignty of the United States. The government adopted it on June 20, 1782. It uses the seal to authenticate important documents. European countries had long used seals, and the new nation signified its equal rank by adopting its own seal. William Barton, a specialist in heraldry, advised the committee that designed the seal. He designed most of the seal's reverse side. Charles Thomson, secretary of the Congress, prepared the design used on the face.

The face bears the design used on official documents. The American eagle, with an *escutcheon,* or shield, on its breast, symbolizes self-reliance. Its pose is rather stiff because it is displayed in heraldic style. The shield's 13 vertical stripes came from the flag of 1777, but seven are white, while in the 1777 flag seven are red.

The blue *chief* above the stripes in 1782 symbolized Congress. But since 1789, it has meant all branches of the United States government. The eagle holds an olive branch of 13 leaves and 13 olives in its right talon, and 13 arrows in its left. It prefers to live in peace, but can wage war. In its beak is a scroll inscribed *E pluribus unum,* or *One* (nation) *out of many* (states). Above its head is the 13-star "new constellation" of the 1777 flag, enclosed in a *glory,* or golden radiance, breaking through a cloud. See United States, Government of the (picture); E pluribus unum.

The reverse side of the seal can be seen on the back of the one-dollar bill, but has never been used as a seal. A pyramid of 13 stone courses, representing the Union, is watched over by the Eye of Providence enclosed in its traditional triangle. The upper motto, *Annuit coeptis,* means *He* (God) *has favored our undertakings.* The lower motto, *Novus ordo seclorum,* means the *new order of the ages* that began in 1776, the date on the pyramid's base. The present official drawing of the seal was made

in 1885, when a fourth die was cut. The fifth die, which replaced it in 1904, still is used. This die is on permanent exhibition in the Department of State Building in Washington, D.C.   Critically reviewed by the Department of the Treasury

Great Slave Lake is one of the largest lakes in the Americas. It covers 11,030 square miles (28,568 square kilometers) in Canada's Northwest Territories. It ranks second behind Great Bear Lake among the largest lakes lying entirely within Canada. Great Slave Lake is fed chiefly by the Slave River, which combines the waters of the Peace and Athabasca systems. Its outlet forms the beginning of the great Mackenzie River.

Yellowknife, the capital and largest city of the Northwest Territories, and several small settlements lie on or near the lake's shores. Yellowknife is a gold-mining cen-

Great Slave Lake

Area: 11,030 sq. mi.
(28,568 km^2)

Elevation: 512 ft. (156 m)
above sea level

Deepest point: ● 2,015 ft.
(614 m)

─── Road   ─── Railroad

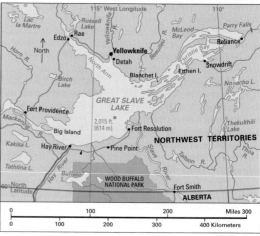

WORLD BOOK map

ter. Commercial fishing and good timber on the southern shore provide other sources of income in the area. Great Slave Lake is famous for severe and unpredictable storms. Ice covers Great Slave Lake eight months a year.

In 1771, the English explorer Samuel Hearne became the first white person to reach the lake. Several fur-trading posts were established in the area and later became permanent settlements. The lake was named for the Slavey Indians, who lived in the area.   G. Peter Kershaw

Great Smoky Mountains, a range of the Blue Ridge Mountains, are so named because they are usually covered by a smoky mist or haze. They are among the highest and most rugged mountains in the Appalachian system. They are thickly forested with more than 200 species of trees. The trees help create a dense, humid atmosphere that looks from afar like a smoky mist.

The Great Smokies form the boundary between Tennessee and North Carolina (see **Tennessee** [physical map]). The highest peak is Clingmans Dome (6,643 feet, or 2,025 meters). Other peaks that are about 6,000 feet

(1,800 meters) high include Mount Collins, Mount Le Conte, Mount Kephart, Mount Chapman, Tricorner Knob, Mount Guyot, and Sam Knob.

Hardwood and evergreen forests on the slopes of the Great Smokies supply valuable timber. Minerals include a little gold and copper. Agriculture is limited to a few small mountain valleys and basins. Much of the area was made a national park in 1930.   Charles S. Aiken

See also **Blue Ridge Mountains; Clingmans Dome; Tennessee** (picture).

Great Smoky Mountains National Park contains the most extensive virgin hardwood and red spruce forests in the United States. It lies in the Great Smoky Mountains, on the boundary between North Carolina and Tennessee (see **Tennessee** [physical map]). Sixteen peaks in the park are more than 6,000 feet (1,800 meters) high. The highest is Clingmans Dome, which towers 6,643 feet (2,025 meters) in southeastern Tennessee. See **Great Smoky Mountains; Clingmans Dome.**

Peter Beney, FPG

Great Smoky Mountains National Park, named for the smoky blue of its peaks, lies in North Carolina and Tennessee.

There are about 150 kinds of trees in the park. Spruce, fir, and hemlock cover the highest mountains and slopes. Many kinds of shrubs and flowering plants grow in the park area. There are about 600 miles (970 kilometers) of clear, spring-fed streams. Many of the streams have roaring falls. These streams are full of trout. The Appalachian National Scenic Trail winds through the park for over 70 miles (110 kilometers).

Cherokee Indians were the region's first settlers. The National Park Service maintains several pioneer homes in the park. In 1926, Congress passed a bill to create the Great Smoky Mountains National Park. The park area was donated to the U.S. government by North Carolina and Tennessee, and the park was established in 1930. Federal financial aid and a gift from John D. Rockefeller, Jr., also helped establish the park. For the area of the park, see **National Park System** (table: National parks).

Critically reviewed by the National Park Service

Great Society is the name given to the domestic program of United States President Lyndon B. Johnson, who served from 1963 to 1969. During his presidency, Johnson proposed, and pushed through Congress, many laws designed to help the poor and to add to the economic security of other Americans. Many people rank the Great Society with President Franklin D. Roosevelt's New Deal of the 1930's as the two most liberal programs ever established by the U.S. government. Johnson first used the term *Great Society* to describe his program in a speech in 1964. The name quickly caught on.

Development. Johnson entered politics in the 1930's and was influenced by the New Deal. The Great Society incorporated the New Deal's faith in the ability of government to bring about beneficial changes in society.

The strength of American liberalism declined in the late 1940's and the 1950's. But Democrat John F. Kennedy became president in 1961, with Johnson as his vice president. Kennedy proposed liberal legislation, much of which remained stalled in Congress when he was assassinated in November 1963. The assassination created sympathy for Kennedy and enabled Johnson, the new president, to get many of the measures approved by Congress. Johnson also proposed much more of his own legislation. A former Senate leader, he had legislative skill that helped him get the proposals approved.

Other factors also helped win passage of Great Society plans. A booming economy in the early 1960's contributed to public acceptance of laws designed to help the poor. The civil rights movement of the period gained support for laws promoting racial justice. Finally, Johnson defeated conservative Republican Barry M. Goldwater by a landslide in the 1964 presidential election. At the same time, numerous Democrats who were prepared to support Johnson were elected to Congress.

Legislation. During 1964 and 1965, a wave of Great Society legislation cleared Congress. Much of it provided financial aid to the poor. Johnson called these efforts the "War on Poverty." The Medicare and Medicaid programs of 1965 provided health-care funding for the nation's senior citizens and for the needy. The Higher Education Act and the Elementary and Secondary Education Act of 1965 provided much federal aid to schools.

Great Society legislation also dealt with civil rights. The Civil Rights Act of 1964 is considered one of the strongest antidiscrimination laws in U.S. history. The Voting Rights Act of 1965 broke down many restrictions that had been used to keep African Americans from voting. The Great Society program also included a wide range of efforts to improve the environment.

Johnson continued to promote liberal legislation throughout his presidency. But by the end of 1966, congressional acceptance of his ideas had slowed. Also, the country's increasing participation in the Vietnam War had moved attention away from domestic reforms.

Influence and controversy. The impact of the Great Society has been enormous, and also controversial. The program's defenders point out that the percentage of Americans living below the poverty level dropped from 22 percent in 1960 to 12 percent in 1969. They say people of higher economic classes also benefited from Great Society aid to education and health care. Conservative critics claim tax cuts passed under Johnson did more to reduce poverty than any Great Society initiatives. They say the program's spending contributed to a large government budget deficit and to other problems. They call for cuts in the government's spending and in its involvement in the people's lives.   Lewis L. Gould

See also **Civil Rights Act of 1964; Elementary and Secondary Education Act; Johnson, Lyndon B.; Medicaid; Medicare.**

Great Victoria Desert, an area of shifting sand dunes, stretches for about 800 miles (1,300 kilometers) across southwestern Australia (see **Australia** [terrain map]). The desert covers an area of about 250,000 square miles (647,000 square kilometers). Because it merges on the north into the Gibson Desert, its area is not sharply defined. The desert lies north of the Nullarbor Plain. At some points, the Great Victoria Desert spreads southward, to an area about 20 miles (32 kilometers) from the southern coast of Australia. Several small salt lakes lie in the center of this area.   D. N. Jeans

Great Wall of China is the longest structure ever built. Its length is about 4,500 miles (7,240 kilometers), and it was erected entirely by hand. The wall crosses northern China between the east coast and north-central China (see **China** [political map]).

Over the centuries, various rulers built walls to protect their northern border against invaders. Some of the walls stood on or near the site of the Great Wall. Most of what is now called the Great Wall dates from the Ming dynasty (1368-1644). The eastern end of the surviving Ming wall is at Shahaiguan, a town near Qinhuangdao on the coast of the Bo Gulf. In the west, the wall ends in the Lop Nur region of the Xinjiang province. But during some periods, the wall reached as far east as Dandong and as far west as Dunhuang, near Anxi.

Description. Parts of the Great Wall have crumbled through the years. However, much of it remains, and some sections have been restored. The main part of the wall is about 2,500 miles (4,020 kilometers) long. Additional branches make up the rest of its length.

One of the highest sections of the Great Wall, on Mount Badaling, near Beijing, rises to about 35 feet (11 meters) high. This section is about 25 feet (7.6 meters) wide at its base and nearly 20 feet (6 meters) at the top. Watchtowers stand about 100 to 200 yards (91 to 180 meters) apart along the wall. The towers, about 40 feet (12 meters) high, once served as lookout posts.

In the east, the wall winds through the mountainous Mongolian Border Uplands. This part of the wall has a foundation of granite blocks. It has sides of stone or brick, and the inside of the wall is filled with earth. The top is paved with bricks set in mortar. The bricks form a road that was used by the workers who built the wall and by the soldiers who defended it.

Farther west, the Great Wall runs through hilly areas and along the borders of deserts. Stone and brick were scarce in these hilly and desert areas, and so the workers used earth to build this section of the wall. They moistened the earth and pounded it to make it solid.

History. Written records indicate that the Chinese built walls along their borders as early as the 600's B.C. Emperor Shi Huangdi of the Qin dynasty (221-206 B.C.) is traditionally regarded as the first ruler to conceive of, and build, a Great Wall. Most of the Qin wall was north of the present-day wall. Shi Huangdi had the wall built by connecting new walls with older ones. Building continued during later dynasties, including the Han (202 B.C.-A.D. 220) and the Sui (581-618).

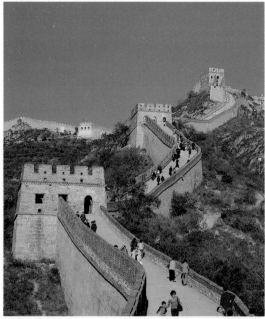

© Dallas & John Heaton, Stock, Boston

The Great Wall of China is the longest structure ever built. It was constructed to keep out invaders. The Great Wall, which is made mostly of stone and brick, extends for about 4,500 miles (7,240 kilometers). It follows a winding course that stretches over mountains and hills and along the borders of deserts.

By the time the Ming dynasty began in 1368, much of the wall had fallen into ruin. In response to the growing threat of a Mongol invasion, the Ming government began building a major wall in the late 1400's. This wall included most of what remains today. Like earlier ones, it protected China from minor attacks but provided little defense against a major invasion.

Through the centuries, much of the Great Wall again collapsed. However, the Chinese Communists have done restoration work since 1949, when they began to rule the nation. The wall no longer serves the purpose of defense, but it attracts many visitors. Tourists from around the world come to see the wall. Historians study writing and objects found in fortifications and tombs along the structure. Scientists study earthquakes by examining parts of the wall that have been affected by these earth movements.   Kai-wing Chow

Additional resources

Mann, Elizabeth. *The Great Wall.* Mikaya, 1997. Younger readers.
McNeese, Tim. *The Great Wall of China.* Lucent Bks., 1997.
Waldron, Arthur. *The Great Wall of China.* Cambridge, 1990.

Greater Swiss mountain dog is a breed of dog developed in Switzerland. Its short, thick fur is mostly black, but the dog has white and brown markings on its face, chest, legs, and tail. It weighs 90 to 140 pounds (41 to 64 kilograms) and grows 23 to 29 inches (58 to 74 centimeters) high. Roman soldiers brought the ancestors of these dogs to Switzerland more than 2,000 years ago. For centuries, people used the dogs to pull carts and to herd livestock.

Critically reviewed by the Greater Swiss Mountain Dog Club of America

Grebe, *greeb,* is a kind of diving bird. Grebes dive underwater to catch such food as small fish, insects, snails, and shrimp. About 19 species of grebes live throughout the world. Six species live in North America. They are the *western,* the *red-necked,* the *pied-billed,* the *horned,* the *eared,* and the *least.*

Grebes have flattened bodies that are thickly covered with waterproof feathers. They do not have webbed feet like most other diving birds, but each long toe has several flaplike lobes. Grebes have small wings and a short tail. Their legs are far back on their bodies. For this reason, grebes have poor balance for standing or walking and are almost helpless on land. But they dive and swim with such ease that they have been called *hell-divers* and *water witches.* Grebes have great difficulty taking flight. But once they are airborne, they can fly long distances.

Grebes make nests of decaying plants and water-soaked grasses. They build them in shallow marshes or ponds, usually in rushes. Some nests float like rafts on the water. Grebe eggs are white, pale green, or blue. They hatch in 20 to 30 days. The young can swim as soon as they hatch, though they often rest on their parents' backs or under their wings. Scientists believe grebes are the only birds that dive while carrying their young.

Grebes were once killed for their feathers, which were used to make women's hats. The birds are now protected by law.   Milton W. Weller

Scientific classification. Grebes make up the grebe family, Podicipedidae.

See also **Bird** (picture: Birds of inland waters and marshes).

Greco, *GREHK oh,* **El,** *ehl* (1541?-1614), was one of the world's great painters. He was born Domenikos Theotokopoulos in Candia (now Iraklion), Crete, but did most of his work in Spain. The Spaniards called him *El Greco* (the Greek).

El Greco was a master draftsman whose works combine courtly elegance with religious fervor. He intentionally elongated and distorted forms to emphasize the spiritual quality of a figure or event. His saints are ghostly creations of his imagination. However, El Greco's por-

Oil painting on canvas (early 1600's); Metropolitan Museum of Art, New York City, Bequest of Mrs. H. O. Havemeyer, 1929. The H. O. Havemeyer Collection

El Greco's *View of Toledo* is one of the most famous landscapes ever painted. The contrasts between light and dark areas are typical of his dramatic and individual style.

traits of nobles are elegant and realistic.

In 1559 or 1560, El Greco left Crete to study in Venice. He studied there for 10 years and then in Rome for 7 years. His mature work is based on the Venetian version of the style called *mannerism* practiced by such artists as Tintoretto. El Greco's version of this style is characterized by graceful, elongated forms and metallic colors with white highlights.

Seeking patronage, El Greco went to Spain in 1577, where King Philip II was hiring artists to work on the palace and monastery of the Escorial. Unfortunately for El Greco, the king disliked his great painting of the *Martyrdom of St. Maurice,* and the painter never gained royal favor. He settled in Toledo, the religious center of Spain. There, he created many great paintings and portraits. El Greco painted his masterpiece, *The Burial of Count Orgaz,* for the Church of Santo Tomé in Toledo, in 1586. In this painting, the realistic drawing and color of the lower, earthly portion of the painting contrasts with the abstract forms in the upper, heavenly section of the work. El Greco's son is the boy in the lower left side of the painting.

After 1600, El Greco's style involved more distortion of light, space, and form. His painting *View of Toledo* is not a realistic view of the city but rather an expression of his feelings about his adopted home. This dramatic landscape and other late paintings, such as *Laocoon,* had a profound influence on the expressionist painters of the 1900's.   Marilyn Stokstad

See also pictures in **Art and the arts; Resurrection.**

Additional resources

Bronstein, Leo. *El Greco.* 1950. Reprint. Abrams, 1990.
El Greco of Toledo. N. Y. Graphic Soc., 1982.

© Henry Ausloos, Animals Animals

The Greater Swiss mountain dog has a sturdy body.

© J. Pavlovsky, Sygma

Athens, Greece's capital and largest city, contains many reminders of ancient Greek civilization. The Parthenon, *left center,* and other historic structures stand among the modern buildings of downtown Athens.

Greece

Greece is a small country where Western civilization started about 2,500 years ago. In those days, Greece controlled much of the land bordering the Mediterranean and Black seas. Athens is the capital and the largest city of Greece. In Athens and many other parts of Greece, magnificent ruins stand as monuments to the nation's glorious past.

About one-fifth of the workers in Greece earn their living by farming, and agriculture is an important economic activity. But mountains cover most of Greece, and the land is rocky with little fertile soil. A Greek legend tells that God sifted the earth through a strainer while making the world. He made one country after another with the good soil that sifted through, and threw away the stones left in the strainer. According to the legend, these stones became Greece.

No part of Greece is more than 85 miles (137 kilometers) from the sea. The Greeks have always been seafaring people. About a fifth of Greece consists of islands. The mainland makes up the southern tip of the Balkan Peninsula, extending into the Mediterranean Sea. Many ancient Greek legends, including those about Odysseus and Jason, center on sea voyages. Today, Greece has one of the largest merchant fleets in the world.

The Greeks came under the control of invaders for more than 2,000 years. They lost their independence to the Macedonians in 338 B.C. The Greeks did not regain their independence until A.D. 1829, from the Ottoman

Empire. Until recently, Greece has had many serious political problems, largely because of weak or undemocratic governments.

In ancient times, the Greeks established the traditions of justice and individual freedom that are basic to democracy. Their arts, philosophy, and science became foundations of Western thought and culture. See the *World Book* article on **Greece, Ancient.**

Government

National government. Greece adopted its present constitution in 1975. This document officially eliminated the monarchy that had ruled Greece, and it made the nation a parliamentary republic headed by a president.

Facts in brief

Capital: Athens.
Official language: Greek.
Official name: *Elliniki dimokratia* (Hellenic Republic).
Area: 50,949 mi² (131,957 km²). *Greatest mainland distances—* north-south, 365 mi (587 km); east-west, 345 mi (555 km). *Coastline* (including islands)—9,333 mi (15,020 km).
Elevation: *Highest—*Mount Olympus, 9,570 ft (2,917 m) above sea level. *Lowest—*sea level along the coasts.
Population: *Estimated 2002 population—*10,647,000; density, 209 per mi² (81 per km²); distribution, 59 percent urban, 41 percent rural. *1991 census—*10,259,900.
Chief products: *Agriculture—*corn, cotton, grapes and raisins, olives, poultry, sheep, sugar beets, tobacco, wheat. *Manufacturing—*cement, chemicals, cigarettes, clothing, fabricated metal products, petrochemicals, processed foods, textiles. *Mining—*bauxite, chromite, iron ore, lignite, magnesite.
National anthem: *"Ethnikos Hymnos"* ("National Anthem").
Money: *Basic unit—*euro. One hundred cents equal one euro. Circulation of the drachma was scheduled to end in 2002.

The contributor of this article is John J. Baxevanis, Chairperson of the Geography Department at East Stroudsburg University and the author of Economy and Population Movements in the Peloponnesos of Greece *and* The Port of Thessaloniki.

The constitution was amended in 1986 to limit the powers of the president. The president serves as head of state but mainly performs ceremonial duties. The prime minister, who serves as head of government, holds the real power. The president is elected by the parliament to a five-year term. The president appoints the prime minister, who must then win a vote of confidence from the parliament. The prime minister is usually the leader of the party with the most seats in the parliament.

Executive power is exercised by the Cabinet, which consists of the prime minister and various departmental ministers. The Cabinet forms and directs general governmental policy. The president appoints the departmental ministers on the advice of the prime minister.

The parliament, Greece's lawmaking body, is called the *Vouli.* It consists of a single house of 300 members, called deputies. Deputies are elected to four-year terms.

Local government. Greece is divided into 51 *nomoi* (departments) and Mount Athos, a self-governing community of monks. Each of the nomoi is headed by a *nomarch* (governor) appointed by the national government to a three-year term. Nomarchs maintain public order, administer the civil service, and collect taxes. Nomoi, in turn, are subdivided into 147 *eparchie,* or smaller administrative districts. City, town, and village governments consist of an elected chief executive—either a mayor or a president—and an elected council.

Politics. Greece has two major political parties: the Panhellenic Socialist Movement (PASOK) and the New Democracy Party. PASOK supports social welfare programs and government intervention in the economy to protect workers. The party has been critical of the North Atlantic Treaty Organization (NATO) for its handling of conflicts in the nearby Balkan region. Greece is a member of NATO, which is a military alliance of Western nations. PASOK also opposes the continuing presence of United States military bases in Greece.

The New Democracy Party favors a free market economy with limited government interference in private business. The party approves of the presence of U.S. military bases on Greek soil.

Greece also has a number of smaller political parties, including the Communist Party of Greece. Greeks who are at least 18 years old can vote.

Courts. The Special Supreme Tribunal is the highest court in Greece. It has 11 members. The court rules on the constitutionality of laws in some cases, and it decides election and referendum disputes. The regular court system consists of administrative, civil, and criminal courts; appellate courts; and a Supreme Court. Judges are appointed for life by the president.

Armed forces. Because of tensions with its neighbors—particularly Turkey—Greece devotes a substantial portion of its national budget to defense. Greece's army, navy, and air force have a total of about 165,000 troops. Greek men are required to serve up to 21 months on active duty in the armed forces and are eligible for the draft at age 21. Greek women are required to serve four days per year in support roles, and they may volunteer for regular service.

People

Population. Greece's capital, Athens, is also its largest city. About 30 percent of all Greeks live in Athens

The Greek flag and national emblem have a white cross symbolizing the Greek Orthodox religion. The flag's blue stripes represent the sea and sky. The white stripes stand for the purity of the struggle for independence. The laurel wreath on the emblem is another symbol of Greece. The flag was adopted in 1822 and readopted in 1978. The emblem was adopted in 1975.

WORLD BOOK map

Greece lies in southeastern Europe on the Mediterranean Sea. It covers part of the Balkan Peninsula and also many islands.

or its suburbs. Thessaloniki is the country's second largest city. The most densely populated areas of Greece are the coastal and interior plains. The mountainous areas are lightly populated, as are many of the Aegean Islands.

Ethnic Greeks make up about 98 percent of Greece's population. Turks form the largest ethnic minority, but they comprise only about 1 percent of the country's population.

Ancestry. Greeks are descendants of the ancient Indo-Europeans. Various groups of people invaded Greece and settled there. As a result, some segments of the population have been influenced by such ethnic groups as the Italians, Slavs, and Turks.

Language. Greek is the official language of Greece. The people use a modern form of Greek called *demotic.* It includes words and phrases borrowed from many languages, especially English, French, Italian, Slavic, and Turkish. See **Greek language.**

Way of life

City life. The majority of Greece's people reside in urban areas. Most Greek cities consist of both old and modern sections. The old section of a Greek city has low buildings, narrow streets, and few sidewalks. The modern section usually has tall apartment buildings, wide streets, and modern shopping areas. Urban lifestyles in Greece are similar to those in other Western nations. Greek cities boast modern mass transit systems and an abundance of shopping centers and drive-in restaurants. Most city dwellers work in tourism, commerce, or shipping.

Although Greek cities are remarkably free of slums, population growth has led to housing shortages in many Greek cities. Industrial growth and the increased use of automobiles have led to problems of urban pollution. In Athens, air pollution poses a health hazard and

has damaged the city's ancient ruins. Athens has tried to ease this problem by tightening controls on industry, by banning automobiles from certain sections of the city, and by limiting the number of automobiles moving through the city each day.

Rural life. Since the 1960's, the population has declined in rural areas—especially in the mountains—as people have left farms to seek jobs in the cities. As a result, many small farms in the mountains have been abandoned. Today, the largest Greek farms lie in the coastal and interior plains, where irrigation produces high crop yields. These profitable farms have led to an improved

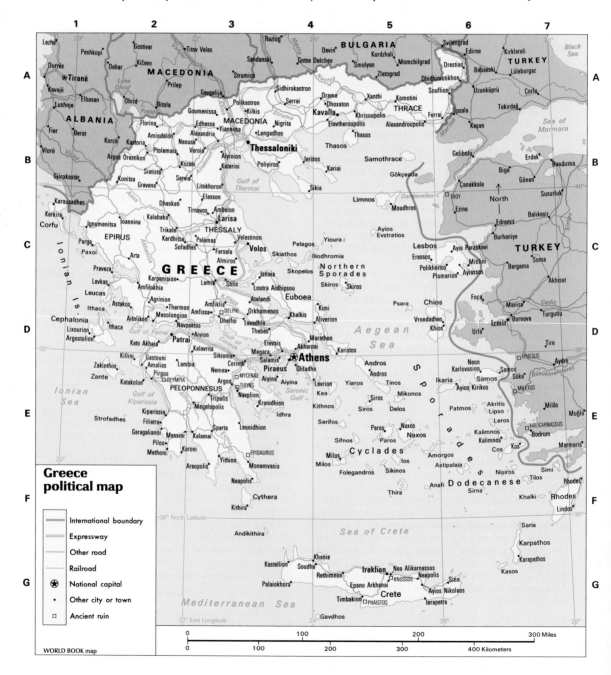

Greece political map

| International boundary |
| Expressway |
| Other road |
| Railroad |
| ✪ National capital |
| • Other city or town |
| ◻ Ancient ruin |

WORLD BOOK map

0   100   200   300 Miles
0   100   200   300   400 Kilometers

Population density

The most densely populated areas of Greece are the coastal and interior plains. The mountainous areas and many of the Aegean Islands are lightly populated.

WORLD BOOK map

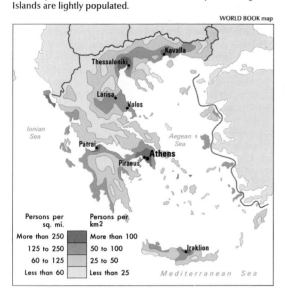

Persons per sq. mi.	Persons per km2
More than 250	More than 100
125 to 250	50 to 100
60 to 125	25 to 50
Less than 60	Less than 25

Margot Granitsas, Photo Researchers

Outdoor marketplaces in Greek cities offer a wide variety of merchandise. In the photograph above, shoppers examine baskets and other items at a market in Thessaloniki.

quality of rural life. Houses are centrally heated and have indoor plumbing and electricity. Modern, paved roads link rural settlements to cities and towns.

Rural Greeks are strongly attached to their communities. Many Greeks who have migrated to the cities own land and a summer house in their rural village.

Clothing. Today, Greeks wear Western-style clothing. Traditional dress, such as braided jackets and pleated kilts for men, are worn only during public social events or celebrations. Traditional dress varies from region to region. See **Clothing** (picture: Traditional costumes).

Food and drink. The Greek diet includes a variety of meats, such as lamb, chicken, pork, and beef, and many fresh vegetables, such as tomatoes, eggplant, and beans. Meats and vegetables are often combined in stews. Greeks enjoy many different cheeses, some of which are regional specialties.

The Greeks eat more lamb than any other meat. They also serve a wide variety of fish and other seafood from the Mediterranean Sea. They almost always cook food in olive oil and often use olive oil for flavoring. Greek cooking also uses oregano, garlic, onions, and *fennel* (an herb related to parsley) as seasonings.

Popular Greek dishes include *soupa avgolemono* (lemon-flavored chicken soup), *dolmathes* (vine leaves filled with rice and ground meat), *moussaka* (layers of eggplant and ground meat), and *souvlaki* (meat cooked

Greece map index

*Not on map; key shows general location.
†Population of metropolitan area, including suburbs.

Source: 1991 census.

© Starfoto from Zefa

Greek coffee houses are popular gathering places. Most of these cafes have tables outdoors as well as indoors.

on a long spit, usually with onions and tomatoes). Also popular are olives and *feta* (a cheese made from sheep's or goat's milk). Fresh fruit is a common dessert. Greeks also enjoy a wide variety of sweet pastries.

Popular beverages include beer and *retsina* (a white wine flavored with pine resin). Greeks like to drink *ouzo* (a strong, anise-flavored liquor) and brandy. Favorite hot beverages include tea and dark, thick coffee.

Recreation. Greeks enjoy sports, particularly soccer, basketball, and swimming. They also enjoy socializing in outdoor theaters, cafes, and restaurants. On weekends and holidays, Greeks like to travel to visit with friends and relatives in other parts of the country.

Religion. About 98 percent of Greece's people belong to the Greek Orthodox Church. Greek Orthodoxy is

© Joe Viesti

Easter is the most important Greek religious holiday. Members of the Greek Orthodox Church—to which most Greeks belong—celebrate Easter with processions, services, and feasting.

the nation's official religion, but everyone has freedom of worship. The Greek Orthodox Church is a self-governing member of the Eastern Orthodox Churches. It is headed by the archbishop of Athens, who is called the *primate* of Greece (see **Eastern Orthodox Churches**). But Crete, the Dodecanese Islands, and the communities of monks on Mount Athos are under the spiritual jurisdiction of the ecumenical patriarch of Constantinople. The Greek government pays the salaries of Greek Orthodox clergy. Other religious groups in Greece include Roman Catholics, Jews, Protestants, and Muslims. Muslims live mainly in Thrace.

Most Greeks attend church during such events as baptisms, weddings, and funerals, and during the major religious holidays of Easter and Christmas. Easter is the most important religious holiday in Greece. The people serve lamb feasts on Easter Sunday. Instead of giving presents on Christmas, many Greeks do so on St. Basil's Day, which falls on New Year's Day. See **Basil, Saint.**

Greek Orthodox festivals help to maintain religious influence throughout the country. Every major settlement has a patron saint. The people may go to church on the evening before the saint's yearly feast day, as well as on the feast day. After the evening service, they enjoy food and wine, and they sing and dance far into the night.

Education. Greek law requires children to go to school from the age of 6 through 15. Elementary school lasts through the sixth grade and is followed by a six-year high school program. All public education in Greece is free.

Greece has a strong educational tradition. Nearly all of the country's adult population can read and write. For Greece's literacy rate, see **Literacy** (table: Literacy rates). Enrollment in higher education programs increased greatly in the last half of the 1900's.

Greece has 16 universities and colleges. The largest are the University of Athens and the Aristotelian University of Thessaloniki. There are also a number of schools for archaeology and for the fine arts. In addition, there are numerous technical and professional schools.

Arts. The most famous artist born in Greece was probably Domenikos Theotokopoulos. He became known as *El Greco* (the Greek) in Spain, where he did most of his painting during the late 1500's and early 1600's. Important Greek writers of the 1800's and 1900's included the poets George Drosines, Kostes Palamas, and Dionysios Solomos. Others were Nikos Kazantzakis, a novelist, and Alexander Papadiamantis, known for his short stories. Two Greek poets have won the Nobel Prize for literature. George Seferis won the prize in 1963, and Odysseus Elytis received the award in 1979. Important Greek musicians of the 1900's included the composers Manos Hadjidakis, Nikos Skalkottas, and Mikis Theodorakis; the conductor Dimitri Mitropoulos; and the opera singer Maria Callas.

Many Greeks are skilled weavers of colorful rugs or articles of clothing. Embroidery is another important handicraft in Greece. Greek silversmiths hammer silver into heavy necklaces and other beautiful jewelry. Traditional Greek folk dances are held at local festivals and other celebrations. The people dance to folk music that features clarinets and *bouzouki* (a stringed instrument that resembles a mandolin). Festivals of ancient Greek dramas are held regularly in bowllike outdoor theaters that were built before the time of Christ. See **Europe** (picture: Ancient Greek drama).

The land

Much of the land of Greece is composed of limestone, either bare or covered with thorny, woody shrub vegetation called *maquis.* Soils in the uplands, which cover about 70 per cent of the country, are poor and stony. However, several large coastal and interior areas have rich soils.

Mountains divide Greece into many land regions. High peaks cut off valleys and plains from one another. The Pindus Mountains, for example, form a barrier between the east and west sections of the mainland. These heavily forested mountains rise over 8,000 feet (2,400 meters) above sea level. Water also shapes the land regions of Greece. Long arms of the sea reach into the coasts, forming many peninsulas. Greece's hundreds of islands together make up about 20 per cent of the country.

Greece has nine main geographic regions. They are: (1) Thrace, (2) Macedonia, (3) Thessaly, (4) Epirus, (5) Central Greece and Euboea, (6) the Peloponnesus, (7) the Ionian Islands, (8) the Aegean Islands, and (9) Crete.

Thrace lies in the extreme northeastern section of Greece, west of Turkey and south of Bulgaria. The region is dominated by the massive, barren Rhodope Mountains near the Bulgarian border and a narrow plain along the coast. An oriental variety of tobacco is grown in the region. Thrace is the home of Greece's largest group of Turkish-speaking Muslims.

Macedonia extends westward from the region of Thrace. It includes portions of the Pindus and southern Balkan mountains, as well as several fertile valleys. Macedonia ranks as the most productive agricultural region of Greece, boasting two rich agricultural plains—Thessaloniki and Serrai. Major crops include corn, cotton, fruits, rice, tobacco, and wheat. Thessaloniki, the region's largest city, is second only to Athens in size and industrial production. It is also a major port. Ptolemais, in the Pindus Mountains of western Macedonia, is the site of the country's principal lignite mines. The self-governing religious community of Mount Athos lies on the easternmost prong of the Khalkidhiki Peninsula in eastern Macedonia. There, about 2,000 monks live in 20 monasteries.

Thessaly, which lies south of Macedonia, is a large plain nearly surrounded by tall mountains. The moun-

Physical features

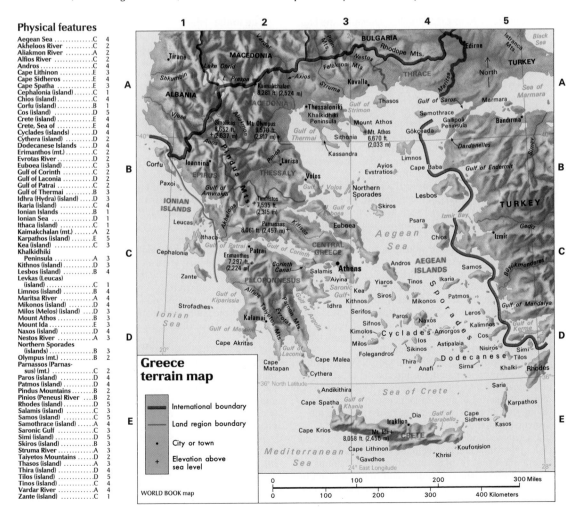

Greece terrain map

International boundary
Land region boundary
• City or town
+ Elevation above sea level

WORLD BOOK map

© Prato, Bruce Coleman Ltd.

The Pindus Mountains separate the east and west sections of the Greek mainland. Forests cover the mountains, which rise more than 8,000 feet (2,400 meters) above sea level.

© H. Luetticke, Zefa

Crete is the largest of the Greek islands. It lies in the Mediterranean Sea, southeast of the mainland of Greece. Steep mountains make up most of the island's southern coast.

tains include 9,570-foot (2,917-meter) Olympus, the highest peak in Greece. Thessaly has long been an important grain-growing area, and wheat is still a major crop. Thessaly also grows more cotton than any other region. Other crops include olives and vegetables. The port city of Volos is the commercial center of the region.

Epirus is a small, sparsely populated region that lies in the northwestern part of the country between Albania and the Gulf of Amvrakia. Its mountainous terrain makes travel difficult. Ioannina, which lies in a major valley, is the largest city in Epirus. Crops grown in the region include citrus fruits, grapes, and rice. Sheep graze in the mountains, and wool is an important product.

Central Greece and Euboea, located south of Epirus and Thessaly, is a region of mountains and hills, small valleys, and many islands. It makes up only about one-fifth of Greece but has nearly half the total population. The Greater Athens area is the nation's leading communications, financial, industrial, and transportation center. It includes the port city of Piraeus and many coastal industrial cities and tourist attractions. In addition to the famous ancient ruins in Athens itself, there are those of Eleusis and other nearby historic sites. The region produces cotton, figs, grains, and olives. Marble and lead are important mineral products. Bauxite is mined at Mount Parnassos, and a large aluminum factory operates on the Gulf of Corinth.

The Peloponnesus is a large peninsula with small valleys and rugged mountains and coastlines. The Corinth Canal cuts through the isthmus that connects the region with the rest of the mainland, making it almost an island. Maquis and scattered pine forest make up the principal plant life. Crops, principally citrus fruits, grapes, olives, and vegetables, grow on less than 20 per cent of the land area, mainly in the coastal plains. The Peloponnesus is one of the most historically famous parts of Greece. Ancient temples and ruins stand at Corinth, Epidaurus, Mycenae, Navplion, Olympia, and other historic sites.

The Ionian Islands lie in the Ionian Sea, west of the Greek mainland. The largest and most heavily populated ones are Cephalonia, Corfu, Leucas, and Zante. One tourist attraction is the island of Ithaca, home of Ulysses in the epic poem *The Odyssey.* Crops grown in the Ionian Islands include citrus fruits, grapes, olives, and vegetables. Sheep and goats graze on the mountains.

The Aegean Islands lie in the Aegean Sea between the Greek mainland and Turkey. These islands are rocky, and few people live there. The northern islands include Chios, Lesbos, Limnos, Samothrace, Thasos, and the Northern Sporades group. To the south are the Cyclades group and the Dodecanese Islands. Major tourist attractions in the Aegean Islands are Rhodes, Delos, Tinos, Paros, Mikonos, and Siros. Another attraction is the island of Thira, which some historians believe is the lost continent of Atlantis.

Crete, in the Mediterranean Sea, is the largest Greek island. It consists mainly of hills and mountains with some fertile valleys. A narrow plain extends along the northern coast, which contains the largest cities and some light manufacturing. Along the southern coast, mountains slope steeply to the sea. The major tourist attraction is the famous ruins of Knossos, the center of the ancient Minoan civilization.

Climate

Greece has a so-called Mediterranean climate, with mild, wet winters and hot, dry summers. However, the climate varies sharply between the mountainous interior and coastal regions. Temperatures average about 40 °F (4 °C) in winter and above 75 °F (24 °C) in summer in coastal locations.

In much of Greece, about three-fourths of the total rainfall occurs in winter. Snow is rare in the lowlands but falls in the high mountains. During the summer, skies are nearly cloudless, and cool sea breezes blow along the coasts every day.

Westerly winds are responsible for most of Greece's

Average January temperatures
In winter, the islands and the coastal regions have milder temperatures than the mountainous interior regions.

Average July temperatures
The islands and the coastal regions have hot summers. The temperatures are cooler in the inland mountains.

Average yearly precipitation
Greece's precipitation is heaviest in winter and lightest in summer. It decreases from northwest to southeast.

WORLD BOOK maps

Degrees Fahrenheit	Degrees Celsius
Above 46	Above 8
39 to 46	4 to 8
32 to 39	0 to 4
Below 32	Below 0

Mediterranean Sea

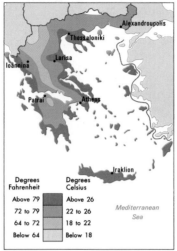

Degrees Fahrenheit	Degrees Celsius
Above 79	Above 26
72 to 79	22 to 26
64 to 72	18 to 22
Below 64	Below 18

Mediterranean Sea

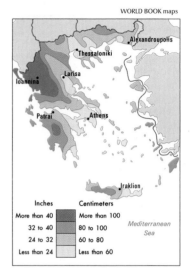

Inches	Centimeters
More than 40	More than 100
32 to 40	80 to 100
24 to 32	60 to 80
Less than 24	Less than 60

Mediterranean Sea

Average monthly weather

	Athens					Alexandroupolis			
	Temperatures			Days of rain or snow		Temperatures			Days of rain or snow
	F° High Low		C° High Low			F° High Low		C° High Low	
Jan.	54	42	12	6	7	50	36	10	2	9
Feb.	55	43	13	6	6	50	35	10	2	6
Mar.	60	46	16	8	5	54	38	12	3	7
Apr.	67	52	19	11	3	65	48	18	9	4
May	77	60	25	16	3	73	55	23	13	5
June	85	67	29	19	2	81	62	27	17	6
July	90	72	32	22	1	89	67	32	19	2
Aug.	90	72	32	22	1	89	67	32	19	1
Sept.	83	66	28	19	2	76	61	24	16	2
Oct.	74	60	23	16	4	69	52	21	11	5
Nov.	64	52	18	11	6	62	47	17	8	8
Dec.	57	46	14	8	7	53	41	12	5	12

rain and snow. These warm, moist winds cool as they rise along the west-facing mountain slopes. As they cool, they drop moisture in the form of rain and snow. Because of this pattern, most of the western mountain slopes are wetter and greener than the eastern slopes.

The *precipitation* (rain, snow, and other forms of moisture) in Greece decreases from the northwest to the southeast. It ranges from more than 60 inches (150 centimeters) a year in northern areas of the Pindus Mountains to less than 15 inches (38 centimeters) on the island of Kea in the Cyclades. The rain usually falls in heavy but brief showers.

Nearly all of Greece's rivers dry up in summer because of the lack of rain. As a result, fresh water must be stored during the winter for use in summer.

Economy

The economy of Greece was almost destroyed during World War II (1939-1945) and during the Greek civil war

(1946-1949). Although still weak by Western European standards, the Greek economy has expanded greatly since the 1950's. The economic expansion has resulted largely from government programs, economic aid from the United States, and trade with the Middle East and with members of the European Union. The European Union is an organization of European nations that cooperate with one another in economic and other matters (see **European Union**).

Service industries, taken together, account for more than 60 percent of Greece's gross domestic product (GDP)—the total value of goods and services produced within a country in a year. Service industries employ more than 50 percent of the country's workers. Community, social, and personal services produce a larger portion of the GDP than any other industry. This industry includes such economic activities as education and health care. Other important service activities include banking, government services, trade, and transportation. Tourism benefits many of Greece's service industries.

Manufacturing accounts for about a fifth of the nation's GDP and employs about a fifth of all Greek workers. Leading industrial products include beverages, cement, chemicals, cigarettes, clothing, fertilizers, footwear, processed foods, and textiles. Greece also produces fabricated metals, *petrochemicals* (chemicals made from petroleum or natural gas), paper, pharmaceuticals, and rubber products. Industrial activity is heavily concentrated in Athens and Thessaloniki.

Agriculture contributes less than 15 percent to Greece's GDP and employs roughly 20 percent of the work force. Greece has dry summers and little fertile soil, and about four-fifths of the land is mountainous. Most Greek farms are small and fragmented. They average 8 acres (3.2 hectares) in size. Crops grow on about 40 percent of the total land area. Another 40 percent of the land consists of pastures or meadows.

Wheat is Greece's main crop. Other major crops in-

Production and workers by economic activities

Economic activities	Percent of GDP produced	Employed workers	
		Number of people	Percent of total
Community, social, & personal services	19	816,000	21
Wholesale and retail trade	14	849,000	22
Agriculture, forestry, & fishing	14	782,000	21
Manufacturing	14	578,000	15
Government	11	*	*
Finance, insurance, real estate, & business services	11	241,000	6
Transportation & communication	7	248,000	7
Construction	6	252,000	7
Utilities	3	42,000	1
Mining	1	16,000	†
Total	100	3,824,000	100

*Included in Community, social, and personal services.
†Less than one-half of one percent.
Figures are for 1995.
Sources: International Labour Office; International Monetary Fund.

Greece's gross domestic product

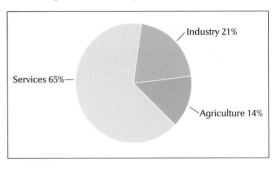

Industry 21%

Services 65%—

Agriculture 14%

Greece's gross domestic product (GDP) was $76,909,000,000 in 1995. The GDP is the total value of goods and services produced within a country in a year. *Services* include community, social, and personal services; finance, insurance, real estate, and business services; government; transportation and communication; utilities; and wholesale and retail trade. *Industry* includes construction, manufacturing, and mining. *Agriculture* includes agriculture, forestry, and fishing.

clude corn and other grains, cotton, olives, oranges, peaches, potatoes, sugar beets, tobacco, and tomatoes. Greece is among the world's leading producers of olives and raisins.

The most important livestock raised in Greece is poultry. Greek farmers also raise sheep, goats, hogs, and cattle. Greece imports much of its livestock, meat, and dairy products from other countries.

Tourism benefits many of Greece's industries. Many tourist hotels and other facilities have been built since the 1950's, and tourism has increased rapidly. Athens, one of the world's most historic cities, attracts more than

90 percent of the tourists who come to Greece. The Acropolis, the center of ancient Athens, is the most famous attraction. The Acropolis includes the beautiful ruins of the Parthenon and several other ancient temples standing on this rocky hilltop. See **Acropolis; Parthenon.**

The Peloponnesus has the most varied ruins of ancient Greece. It includes such historic areas as Corinth, Epidaurus, Mistra, Mycenae, Olympia, and Sparta. In northern Greece are Thessaloniki and Ioannina, centers of the old Byzantine Empire. Other popular tourist areas include the religious community of Mount Athos—

Economy of Greece

This map shows the economic uses of land in Greece. It also indicates the country's main farm products, its chief mineral deposits, and its most important fishing products. Major manufacturing centers are shown in red.

- ▨ Intensively cultivated land
- ▢ Other cultivated land
- ▨ Mostly grazing land
- ▨ Forest land
- ▢ Fishing
- ● Manufacturing center
- ● Mineral deposit

WORLD BOOK map

© Eberhard E. Otto, FPG

Tourism plays an important part in the economy of Greece. In the photograph above, vacationers enjoy the scenic beauty and sunny climate on the island of Mikonos.

though women are not allowed there—and the islands of Corfu, Crete, Mikonos, Rhodes, Thasos, and Thira.

Mining. Greece has varied but limited mineral deposits. Low-quality brown coal called *lignite* is the major mineral product. About 90 percent of it is used to generate electric power. The largest lignite deposits are in the Ptolemais basin of the Pindus Mountains, the island of Euboea, and the central Peloponnesus. Other important minerals include bauxite, the ore from which aluminum is made; and chromite, from which stainless steel is made. Greece also produces barite, iron ore from pyrite, lead, magnesite, and nickel. Greece has large deposits of marble and clays. The country has only one important petroleum deposit, near the island of Thasos in the Aegean Sea.

Foreign trade. Greece's most important exports are cement and cement products, clothing, metal products, olive oil, petroleum products, prepared fruits, and textiles. Major imports consist of chemicals, machinery, basic manufactured goods, meat, petroleum and petroleum products, and transportation equipment.

The value of imported products is more than double that of the country's exports. The difference is made up by income from shipping and tourism, and by money sent home by Greeks who live or work elsewhere.

Germany is Greece's main trading partner. Other leading trading partners include Britain, France, Italy, and the United States. About half of Greece's trade is with other EC member nations.

Energy sources. In 1961, about 45 percent of the dwellings in Greece had no electricity. Since then, power production has increased enormously. By 1990, only a few remote areas were still without electricity. Plants that burn lignite or petroleum produce most of Greece's electric power. Greece also has several hydroelectric plants, most of which are on the Akheloos River and other rivers in the Pindus Mountains.

Greece has only limited deposits of petroleum and natural gas. Consequently, it imports most of its crude

petroleum and natural gas. But Greece is exploring methods of electricity production involving solar, geothermal, and wind power in order to reduce its dependence on imported petroleum.

Transportation. The mountains of Greece make transportation difficult, and most overland routes go through valleys and natural breaks in the mountains. The principal highway and rail routes connect Athens and Thessaloniki, the country's two largest cities. Most of the roads and highways have hard surfaces. Greece has about 1 automobile for every 7 people. The railroad system, owned by the government, links Greece's major cities and provides international connections.

The Greek merchant fleet ranks among the largest in the world. It consists of about 1,800 ships of at least 100 gross tons each. Piraeus, near Athens, is Greece's leading port, followed by Thessaloniki. A fleet of small ships provides transportation among the islands. None of the rivers can be traveled because they flow too swiftly during the wet season and dry up in summer.

Greece has more than 30 commercial airports, the largest of which is located in Athens. Olympic Airways, the national airline, flies within Greece and to most major international cities.

Communication. Greece has more than 100 daily and weekly newspapers. The largest daily newspaper, the *Ta Nea* of Athens, sells over 155,000 copies daily.

The government owns the telephone and telegraph system, the radio broadcasting system, and the television networks. Greece has an average of 1 radio for every 2 people and 1 television set for every 5 people. Motion pictures are a popular form of entertainment in Greece, and more than 140 are produced in the country each year.

History

The recorded history of Greece dates from about 3000 B.C. For Greece's history before A.D. 1453, see **Greece, Ancient; Rome, Ancient; Byzantine Empire.**

Ottoman rule began to spread throughout the Greek lands during the 1300's. These lands were once part of the Byzantine Empire, which had broken up into small states. In 1453, the Ottomans captured the Byzantine capital, Constantinople (now Istanbul, Turkey), and made it the capital of the Ottoman Empire. They had won almost all the Greek lands by then. The Ottomans were Muslims, but allowed religious freedom to the Greeks, who were Christians. They also let the Greeks have much local self-government.

A Greek *national revival* developed during the 1700's, toward the end of Ottoman rule. The Greeks' desire for independence was strengthened by greater prosperity and education. The Greek merchant class increased in size and wealth. The Greeks expanded their manufacturing and trading operations, and developed a large merchant fleet. They built a large number of new schools, and many Greeks studied in more advanced countries. The people became deeply interested in their ancient past and their folk culture. They also began to share in the scientific learning of the West. In 1814, Greek merchants in Odessa, Ukraine (then a part of the Russian Empire), formed the *Philike Hetairia* (Friendly Society). This group organized a movement against the Ottomans that led to a Greek revolt.

Independence. The Greek War of Independence began in 1821. Greek fighters swept down from the mountains and defeated the Ottomans in the Peloponnesus, in Rumely in central Greece, and on many islands in the Aegean Sea. The Greeks held out against repeated Ottoman attacks. In 1825, Egyptian forces allied with the Ottoman Empire invaded the Peloponnesus, and an Ottoman army moved into Greece from the north. Together, they overran the regions that had been freed by the Greeks. But the Ottomans and Egyptians could not defeat the Greeks nor end the revolution.

In 1827, Britain, France, and Russia agreed to use force if necessary to end the fighting and make Greece a self-governing part of the Ottoman Empire. But the Ottomans refused to give up control of Greece. On Oct. 20, 1827, a combined fleet of the three European powers destroyed the Ottoman and Egyptian fleet in the Battle of Navarino off the Peloponnesus. Russia declared war on the Ottoman Empire in 1828, and the Ottomans left Greece to fight the Russians. The Egyptians withdrew in 1829, and Greece became independent.

In an agreement called the London Protocol of 1830, Britain, France, and Russia recognized Greece's independence and pledged to protect it. In 1832, they named a Bavarian prince, Otto, to be the first king of Greece.

Oil painting on canvas (1827); Musée des Beaux-Arts, Bordeaux, France

The defeat of the Greeks at Missolonghi in 1826, during their War of Independence, stirred sympathy in Europe for Greece. The French artist Eugène Delacroix painted *Greece Expiring on the Ruins of Missolonghi* to express his horror at the siege.

They also established Greece's borders.

The new Greek kingdom had fewer than 800,000 people and covered less than half of present-day Greece. About 3 million Greeks lived in what remained Ottoman territory, and 200,000 Greeks lived in the British-controlled Ionian Islands. Greece's expansion to include all these territories became known as the *Megali Idea* (Great Idea) and was the nation's supreme goal.

Otto I, also called Otho I, was chosen in 1832 to become king of Greece. The country had no constitution, and the king, assisted by a few Bavarian advisers, had unlimited power. Neither the people nor individual Greek leaders had any real influence in the government. Great political discontent developed. The country also had serious financial difficulties. In 1843, a peaceful revolution expelled Otto's Bavarian advisers and forced him to accept a constitution that established Greece as a constitutional monarchy in 1844. In 1853, the Crimean War began between Russia and the Ottoman Empire. Otto supported Greek attempts to fight the Ottomans and free the Greeks under them. But the British and French, who helped the Ottoman Empire fight Russia, landed in Greece to stop these attempts. A revolt in 1862 forced Otto to give up the throne. He was replaced in 1863 by a Danish prince, who became George I.

George I gave Greece a much more democratic government than that of Otto. In 1864, a new constitution limited royal power and gave much power to an elected Parliament. Also in 1864, Britain turned over the Ionian Islands to Greece. In exchange, George pledged to discourage Greek revolts in Ottoman territory.

During the 1880's and 1890's, Greece made great progress. Roads and railroads were built and the merchant fleet was expanded. In addition, the educational system and other social services were improved.

In 1881, Greece acquired the region of Thessaly and the district of Arta in southern Epirus from the Ottoman Empire. The transfer had been suggested by the great European powers at the Congress of Berlin in 1878. In 1897, during a revolt in Ottoman-held Crete, war broke out between Greece and the Ottoman Empire. The European powers arranged peace after severe Greek defeats, and set up self-government for Crete in 1898 under a Greek high commissioner.

A group of young Greek army officers called the Military League organized a peaceful revolt in 1909. The league was protesting against political confusion and economic difficulties that had developed in Greece. The league called on Eleutherios Venizelos, a Cretan leader, to be its political adviser. The Parliament agreed to the league's demands for changes in the constitution, and Venizelos became prime minister in 1910. He carried out sweeping reforms in the Greek economy, armed forces, and civil service. Venizelos served as prime minister during much of the period until 1933.

Venizelos helped organize the Balkan alliance of Greece with Bulgaria, Montenegro, and Serbia. This alliance led to the two Balkan Wars of 1912 and 1913. In the first war, the four Balkan countries defeated the Ottoman Empire and took most of its European territory. In the second war, Bulgaria, dissatisfied with its gains, attacked its allies but was defeated. As a result of the Balkan Wars, Greece gained the island of Crete, southern Epirus, part of Macedonia, and many Aegean Islands.

King George was shot by an assassin in 1913. His son Constantine I succeeded him.

World War I began in 1914. Venizelos urged that Greece fight with the Allies against Germany and its partners. But King Constantine, whose wife was a sister of Kaiser Wilhelm II of Germany, kept Greece neutral. Venizelos started a revolutionary movement. It was supported by the Allies, who had established a military base at Thessaloniki. In 1917, Constantine was forced to give the throne to his son, Alexander I. Greece entered the war on the side of the Allies on July 2, 1917.

Thousands of Greek troops joined the British, French, and Serbians at their Thessaloniki base. In September 1918, the Greeks and other Allied forces moved north. They defeated the Bulgarians, who signed an armistice at Thessaloniki. The entire war ended on November 11.

The peace treaties that followed World War I gave Greece most of the territories it had long sought. From the Ottoman Empire, Greece got eastern Thrace; certain islands in the Aegean Sea; and temporary control of the Smyrna (now Izmir) region in Asia Minor. The Greeks gained western Thrace from Bulgaria.

King Alexander died in 1920, and Constantine I returned to the throne. In 1921, Constantine renewed the war against the Ottoman Empire by sending Greek forces into Asia Minor. The Ottomans dealt the Greeks a crushing defeat in 1922, and a military revolt forced Constantine from the throne. Another of his sons, George II, replaced him. A revolution ended the Ottoman Empire in 1922. It became the Republic of Turkey the next year.

In 1923, under the Treaty of Lausanne, Greece returned the Turkish territories it had gained after World War I. The treaty also provided for ending the tensions produced by Turkish rule over Greeks. It required over 1,250,000 Greeks in Turkey to move to Greece and

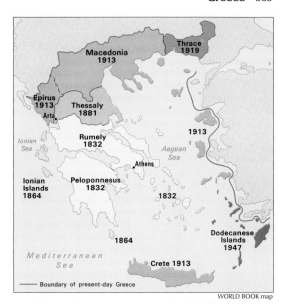

WORLD BOOK map

Expansion of Greece—1832 to 1947. The Greek kingdom formed in 1832 covered less than half of present-day Greece. The country reached its current boundaries in 1947. The dates on the map indicate when each new territory was added.

400,000 Turks in Greece to move to Turkey. After the Greek migration, the only Greeks under foreign rule were in northern Epirus in Albania, British-held Cyprus, and the Italian-held Dodecanese Islands.

Between world wars. Another military revolt forced George II from the Greek throne late in 1923. The next year, Greece declared itself a republic. The republic lasted until 1935, and this period was one of great political confusion and economic weakness. The people were divided between the *republicans,* who supported the republic, and the *royalists,* who wanted a king. Also, Greece's economic resources could not keep up with its population, which had been swollen by the refugees from Turkey and by a high birth rate. The worldwide economic depression of the 1930's further weakened the Greek economy and the government.

The royalists returned to power in the elections of 1933. Two unsuccessful republican revolts took place, in 1933 and 1935. The government recalled George II to the throne later in 1935. The 1936 elections left the royalists and republicans almost evenly matched in parliament. The balance of power rested with the Communists, who held 15 of the 300 seats. As a result, George permitted General John Metaxas to establish a military dictatorship. On Aug. 4, 1936, the king dissolved parliament without fixing a date for new elections and suspended the main provisions of the Constitution. Metaxas remained dictator until his death in 1941.

World War II began in 1939, and Greece declared its neutrality. But on Oct. 28, 1940, Italy attacked Greece. Metaxas had refused to permit Italian troops to build military bases in Greece. The Greek forces were heavily outnumbered, but they pushed the Italians back deep into Albania. Germany came to the aid of Italy. On April 6, 1941, German forces poured into Greece and quickly defeated the Greeks.

Important dates in modern Greece

1453 Constantinople, the Byzantine capital, fell to the Ottoman Empire, which had conquered most Greek lands.

1821-1829 The Ottoman Empire was defeated in the Greek War of Independence, and Greece was formed.

1844 Greece became a constitutional monarchy.

1864 A more democratic constitution was established in Greece under George I.

1909-1910 A military revolt led to major reforms.

1912-1913 Greece gained much land in the Balkan Wars.

1917-1918 Greece fought on the side of the Allies during World War I.

1922 The Ottomans crushed Greek forces in Asia Minor.

1924 Greece became a republic.

1935 Constitutional monarchy was restored in Greece.

1941-1944 Axis forces occupied Greece during World War II.

1946-1949 Communist-led rebels were defeated in Greece.

1967-1973 A military government led by George Papadopoulos controlled Greece.

1974 Greece held its first parliamentary election in more than 10 years, and a civilian government was formed.

1975 Greek voters approved a new constitution, ending the monarchy and making Greece a republic.

1981 Greece joined the European Community, an economic organization that evolved into the European Union.

2001 Greece adopted the euro, the basic unit of currency of most members of the European Union.

The Germans and their allies occupied Greece during the war. The Greeks suffered starvation, mass executions, and other tragedies, and the country's economy was almost destroyed. But the Greeks organized one of the best underground movements in all Europe. The largest and most effective of the several secret Greek resistance groups was the Communist-led National Liberation Front, known as EAM. Its military arm was the National Popular Liberation Army, or ELAS.

The Germans began to withdraw from Greece in September 1944, and British forces landed in October. The British found EAM in control of most of Greece. Civil war broke out in Athens in December, and the British fought ELAS until early in 1945, when ELAS stopped fighting and agreed to break up its forces. The war in Europe ended in May 1945. Greece became one of the original members of the United Nations later that year.

Elections were held in March 1946 and a royalist government was formed. In September, a referendum was held that favored having a king, and George II returned to the throne. By the end of 1946, Communist-led rebels had begun to revolt against the government. The United Kingdom had supported the government by giving Greece economic support and military aid against the rebels, but it could no longer afford to do so. Under the Truman Doctrine, announced in March 1947, the United States took over the British support of Greece. A long, bitter civil war followed. By October 1949, the rebels were defeated, but only after the United States provided the government with massive military aid.

King George died in 1947 and was succeeded by his brother, Paul I. Greece acquired the Dodecanese Islands under a 1947 peace treaty with Italy.

The 1950's brought economic recovery and political stability. Greece joined the North Atlantic Treaty Organization (NATO) in 1952. In 1953, Greece allowed the United States to set up military bases on its territory.

During the 1950's, a serious dispute developed between Greece and Turkey over Cyprus, a British island colony off Turkey. Greeks made up about 80 percent of the island's population, and the rest were Turks. The Greeks of Cyprus demanded union with Greece and organized a revolutionary movement. The Greek government supported this demand, but the United Kingdom—supported by the Turkish government—and Turkish Cypriots opposed it. After severe tensions, an agreement between Greece, Turkey, and the United Kingdom

led to independence for Cyprus in 1960. See **Cyprus** (History).

In 1952, Greek women gained the right to vote and to hold political office. Field Marshal Alexander Papagos, head of the Greek Rally party, became prime minister that year. He held office until his death in 1955. Constantine Caramanlis, head of the National Radical Union party, succeeded him. Under Caramanlis, Greece's economy expanded rapidly with continuing U.S. aid. The government improved finances, controlled rising prices, and encouraged the expansion of agriculture and industry. Caramanlis resigned in 1963.

The revolt of 1967. George Papandreou of the Center Union party became prime minister of Greece in November 1963. Earlier, he had charged that the elections of 1961 had been rigged. He had also suggested that the army, with support from the monarchy, stood in the way of democracy. King Paul died in 1964, and his son came to the throne as Constantine II. Constantine clashed with Papandreou over the king's political powers and control of the armed forces. The king manipulated Papandreou into resigning in 1965. Political confusion developed, and the government remained shaky. In an effort to achieve a stable government, Parliament was dissolved on April 14, 1967, and new elections were called for May 28. But these elections never took place.

On April 21, 1967, Greek army units equipped with tanks and armored cars seized the royal palace, government offices and leaders, and radio stations. Three army officers then set up a military dictatorship. This *junta* consisted of Colonel George Papadopoulos, its leader; Brigadier General Stylianos Pattakos; and Colonel Nicholas Makarezos. The junta prohibited all political activity, and made mass arrests. It replaced the leader of the Greek Orthodox Church, imposed harsh controls on newspapers, and dissolved hundreds of private organizations of which it disapproved.

Constantine remained head of state, though powerless. On Dec. 13, 1967, he tried to overthrow the junta. He failed, and he and his family then fled to Italy. The junta named a *regent* to substitute for the king.

Papadopoulos named himself prime minister and minister of defense. He pardoned many political prisoners, but kept about 2,000 others, mostly Communists, in prison. He loosened some controls on the press. To win popularity, he canceled bank debts of the peasants. In 1968, the junta had a new constitution drawn up. The

Bettmann

The revolt of 1967. Greek army officers seized control of the government on April 21, 1967. Tanks and armored cars surrounded the Parliament Building, *shown here,* and other government offices. Greece remained under military rule until the reestablishment of civilian government in 1974.

constitution provided for a stable government, but at the expense of democracy. It increased the prime minister's power and suspended freedom of the press, parliamentary elections, and various individual rights.

The restoration of democracy. In May 1973, a group of naval officers led an unsuccessful mutiny aboard a Greek destroyer. The government said the mutiny was part of an attempted coup supported by King Constantine. In June, Papadopoulos announced the end of the monarchy and proclaimed Greece a republic. He became president in August and began to prepare the country for parliamentary elections. On Nov. 25, 1973, a group of military officers who opposed Papadopoulos's liberalizing policies overthrew the government. The group's leader, Lieutenant General Phaidon Gizikis, became president.

The conflict between Greece and Turkey over Cyprus was renewed in 1974, when Greek officers led Cypriot troops in overthrowing the government of Cyprus. Turkey claimed that Greece had violated the independence of Cyprus, and Turkish troops invaded the island. After several days of fighting, a cease-fire was signed to prevent full-scale war between Greece and Turkey.

The crisis in Cyprus and economic recession paralyzed Greece's military government. Shortly after the cease-fire was signed, the government collapsed. Military leaders invited Constantine Caramanlis, who had opposed Greece's military government, to become prime minister again. On July 24, 1974, Caramanlis was sworn in as prime minister of a civilian government.

In November 1974, Greece held its first free elections in more than 10 years. Caramanlis's New Democracy Party won the elections by a wide margin. In December, Greek voters chose to make the country a republic rather than a monarchy. Parliament adopted a new constitution in 1975. Civilian control over the military was gradually established. Papadopoulos, Pattakos, and Makarezos were found guilty of treason for their roles in the 1967 revolt. They were sentenced to life in prison. The New Democracy Party retained its majority in 1977.

In 1980, Caramanlis resigned as prime minister, and George Rallis succeeded him. In 1981, Greece joined the European Community. In 1993, the European Community was incorporated into the European Union (EU), which works for both economic and political cooperation among its member nations.

In October 1981, the Panhellenic Socialist Movement (PASOK) party won control of Parliament and became Greece's first socialist government. As head of the party, Andreas Papandreou—son of former Prime Minister George Papandreou—became prime minister. The government increased social benefits and personal incomes. In June 1985, PASOK won elections again, and Papandreou began a second term as prime minister.

PASOK was defeated in June 1989. A coalition government was formed, but it collapsed in early 1990. New elections were held in April, and the New Democracy Party won control of parliament. Constantine Mitsotakis became prime minister. PASOK won elections in October 1993. Papandreou again became prime minister.

Recent developments. In January 1996, Papandreou resigned because of ill health, and Costas Simitis replaced him. In October, PASOK won elections, and Simitis remained prime minister. In April 2000, voters chose Simitis as prime minister by a narrow margin.

After making economic reforms, Greece was allowed to begin using the euro in 2001. Most EU nations use the euro as a common currency. John J. Baxevanis

Related articles in *World Book* include:

Biographies

Callas, Maria	Kazantzakis, Nikos
Caramanlis, Constantine	Mitropoulos, Dimitri
Constantine I	Otto I
Constantine II	Paul I
George I (king of Greece)	Philip, Prince
George II (king of Greece)	Venizelos, Eleutherios
Greco, El	

Cities

Athens	Piraeus	Thessaloniki

Physical features

Aegean Sea	Macedonia (re-	Peloponnesus
Arcadia	gion)	Rhodes
Corinth Canal	Messenia	Salamis
Crete	Milos	Samothrace
Ionian Islands	Mount Olympus	Thessaly
Ionian Sea	Olympia	Thrace
Lesbos	Parnassus	

Other related articles

Acropolis	European Union	Turkey (History)
Balkans	Greek literature	

Outline

I. **Government**
   A. National government   D. Courts
   B. Local government   E. Armed forces
   C. Politics
II. **People**
   A. Population   B. Ancestry   C. Language
III. **Way of life**
   A. City life   D. Food and   F. Religion
   B. Rural life   drink   G. Education
   C. Clothing   E. Recreation H. Arts
IV. **The land**
   A. Thrace   F. The Peloponnesus
   B. Macedonia   G. The Ionian Islands
   C. Thessaly   H. The Aegean Islands
   D. Epirus   I. Crete
   E. Central Greece
      and Euboea
V. **Climate**
VI. **Economy**
   A. Service industries   F. Foreign trade
   B. Manufacturing   G. Energy sources
   C. Agriculture   H. Transportation
   D. Tourism   I. Communication
   E. Mining
VII. **History**

Questions

What meat is the most popular in Greece?
What are some of the chief tourist attractions in Greece?
What was the revolt of 1967?
Why is transportation difficult in Greece?
How did the Treaty of Lausanne affect Greeks in Turkey?
What was the *Megali Idea* (Great Idea)?
What European powers first recognized Greek independence?
Of what three crops is Greece a leading producer?
How was Greece brought into World War II? When?
When did Greek women gain the right to vote?

Additional resources

Clogg, Richard. *A Concise History of Greece.* Cambridge, 1992.
Veremis, Thanos M., and Dragoumis, Mark. *Historical Dictionary of Greece.* Scarecrow, 1995.

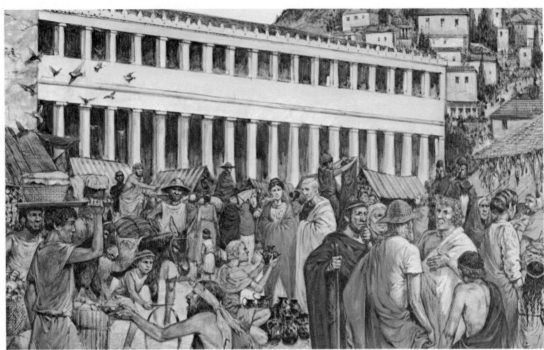

WORLD BOOK illustration by Richard Hook, Linden Artists Ltd.

A bustling market place called the *agora* was the center of activity in ancient Greek cities. In the agora of Athens, *above*, merchants sold their wares, citizens debated issues, and friends exchanged gossip. The long, columned building held shops and served as a meeting place.

Ancient Greece

Greece, Ancient, was the birthplace of Western civilization about 2,500 years ago. The magnificent achievements of the ancient Greeks in government, science, philosophy, and the arts still influence our lives.

Greek civilization developed chiefly in small *city-states.* A city-state consisted of a city or town and the surrounding villages and farmland. The Greek city-states were fiercely independent and often quarreled among themselves. But their small size and constant rivalry had certain advantages. Citizens of a city-state were strongly patriotic, and many citizens took part in public affairs. The most advanced city-states established the world's first democratic governments. The best-known city-states were Athens and Sparta.

The ancient Greek city-states never became united into a nation. However, a common language, religion, and culture bound the people together. The Greeks called themselves Hellenes and their land Hellas. They thought of themselves as different from all other peoples, whom they called *barbarians.*

The ancient Greeks prized their freedom and way of life. This way of life stressed the importance of the individual and encouraged creative thought. Greek thinkers laid the foundations of science and philosophy by seeking logical explanations for what happened in the world

---

Ronald P. Legon, the contributor of this article, is Provost and Professor of History at the University of Baltimore.

---

around them. Greek writers created new forms of expression, which explored human personalities and emotions. Greek civilization reached its height in Athens during the mid-400's B.C., a period of outstanding achievement known as the Golden Age.

This article provides an overview of the people, achievements, government, and history of ancient Greece. Many separate *World Book* articles, listed at the end of this article, have detailed information.

The Greek world

The territory of ancient Greece consisted chiefly of a mountainous peninsula that jutted into the Mediterranean Sea, nearby islands, and the west coast of Asia Minor (now part of Turkey). The peninsula made up mainland Greece. It separated two arms of the Mediterranean—the Aegean Sea and the Ionian Sea. A thin strip of land linked the southern part of the mainland, called the Peloponnesus, to the northern part of the mainland.

The land. Rocky land covered much of ancient Greece. The most fertile land lay in the small valleys and along the coast. In those areas, the Greeks established their city-states. The city or town of each city-state served as a center of trade, government, and religion. The Greeks usually fortified a hill, called an *acropolis,* within or near the city for defense. In addition, walls surrounded some cities to protect them from invaders. At the center of each city was the *agora*—an open area that served as a market place and meeting place.

Ancient Greece had a warm, dry climate. Summers were hot, and winter temperatures seldom dropped below freezing. Annual rainfall on the mainland ranged from as much as 50 inches (130 centimeters) on the west coast to less than 20 inches (50 centimeters) on the east.

Ancient Greece lacked adequate farmland, rainfall, and water for irrigation, and so crop production was limited. The mountains provided huge amounts of limestone and marble for building construction and clay for making bricks and pottery. But Greece had few other mineral deposits. Timber was plentiful at first. However, it became increasingly scarce as the people cut down many trees without replanting the forests.

The shortages of food and natural resources forced the ancient Greeks to depend on overseas trade for needed goods. The poor conditions at home also led many Greeks to found overseas colonies and trading posts. In this way, the Greek world expanded along the shores of the Mediterranean Sea and the Black Sea and came to include southern Italy and the island of Sicily.

The people. Greek civilization began to develop about 2000 B.C. At that time, people from somewhere to the north arrived in Greece and established small farming villages. The people of each community in time developed their own customs and dialect. The two main groups of Greek peoples were the Dorians and Ionians.

By the 700's B.C., the Greek world consisted of many small, independent city-states. Within each city-state, the Greeks distinguished between citizens and noncitizens. Only citizens could own land and take part in government. Citizens were divided into social classes based on ancestry and wealth. In general, the upper class made up about 5 to 10 per cent of a city-state's citizens; the middle class, 20 to 30 per cent; and the poor, 60 to 70 per cent. Noncitizens consisted of women, slaves, and serfs. Unlike slaves, serfs were not considered personal property. As a result of trade, many city-states also had a large noncitizen population made up of Greeks from other city-states and of foreigners.

Life of the people

Family life. The husband headed the household in ancient Greece and was responsible for its members. The wife ran the household and raised the children. In prosperous families, the wife supervised slaves, who looked after the children and did most of the work. Women also spun thread and wove cloth, even in wealthy families. A woman was controlled by her father before she married and by her husband after marriage.

Greek parents usually arranged their children's marriage. Most girls married in their midteens, but many men married around age 30. Few families had more than two or three children. The Greeks considered it a misfortune to have many children because of the expense of raising them. Daughters were especially unwelcome because the family had to provide them with a *dowry*—a gift of money or property—when they married.

Education. In general, only the children of citizens received an education in ancient Greece. Very few girls attended school, but some others learned to read at home. Most children also learned a few practical skills from their parents or from slaves. City-states differed in the kind of education they valued.

In Athens, teachers operated separate schools for general studies, music, and physical education. The general schools taught reading, writing, and arithmetic. At music school, students learned to sing and to play the flutelike *aulos* or the small, harplike *lyre*. The physical education activities included running, jumping, and wrestling. Older boys learned to handle such weapons as the spear and sword.

Education in Sparta differed greatly from education in Athens. The Spartans wanted to build a tough, warlike people, and considered reading and writing much less important than military training. At the age of 7, boys were sent to military camps, where they learned to accept severe discipline and to endure harsh conditions. Even girls engaged in physical competition, which was shocking to most Greeks outside Sparta.

Higher education in ancient Greece consisted of the study of law, medicine, philosophy, or *rhetoric* (public speaking). In the 300's B.C., the Greek philosopher Plato founded a school in Athens known as the Academy. Some scholars consider it to be the world's first university. Plato's most brilliant pupil, Aristotle, later founded a similar school in Athens, the Lyceum.

Food, clothing, and shelter. The Greek diet was based on such grains as wheat and barley, which were used to make bread, cakes, and porridge. The Greeks also ate a variety of fruits and vegetables. Their chief sources of protein were eggs, poultry, and fish. The Greeks used olive oil in place of butter, and they sweetened food with honey.

Greek men and women wore a belted garment of linen or wool called a *chiton* (pronounced *KY tuhn*). Most men's chitons hung to the knees. A woman's chiton fell to the ankles. In cold weather, Greeks draped a cloak called a *himation* (*hih MAT ee ahn*) over their shoulders and arms. Sandals were the chief footwear.

Greece's mild climate enabled the people to carry on many activities outdoors, and so most houses were small and simple. Most poor families lived in one- or two-room houses built of sun-dried bricks with floors of hard-packed earth. Wealthy Greeks lived in larger, more comfortable houses built around a courtyard. The houses had separate rooms for cooking, eating, and sleeping. Stones or tiles covered the floors.

Religion. The Greeks believed that certain *deities* (gods and goddesses) watched over them and directed daily events. Families tried to please household deities with offerings and ceremonies. Each city-state honored one or more deities as protectors of the community and held annual festivals in their honor.

The Greeks believed that their deities could foretell the future. People flocked to shrines called *oracles* to consult priests and priestesses. Deities supposedly spoke through the priests and priestesses to answer questions and reveal the future. The most important oracle was at Delphi. Sick people visited shrines dedicated to Asclepius, the god of healing, in hope of being cured.

Greek deities greatly resembled human beings, except for their immortality and superhuman powers. For example, they showed such emotions as love, jealousy, and anger. The chief deities lived on Mount Olympus and were known as Olympians. Zeus and his wife, Hera, ruled over Olympus. Other Olympians included Aphrodite, goddess of love; Apollo, god of music and light; Ares, god of war; and Athena, goddess of wisdom.

Recreation. Greek men enjoyed talking with friends in the agora or at drinking parties, called *symposiums,* in their homes. Greek men also liked sports, and they exercised and swam at public sports facilities. Greek women were permitted little entertainment outside the home, except for religious festivals. Children had dolls, balls, tops, and other toys. They also played blindman's buff and various dice and board games.

Large crowds gathered for religious festivals in ancient Greece. At these festivals, athletes competed in such events as wrestling, boxing, foot and chariot races, jumping, and javelin throwing. Religious festivals also included feasts, colorful processions, and performances of plays. Several religious festivals brought together people from throughout the Greek world. The Olympic Games, the most famous of these festivals, were held every four years in honor of Zeus. Even wars halted during the Olympics. Victory in the games was the highest honor an athlete could achieve.

Work of the people

Farming. More than half the people of ancient Greece lived by farming or herding. Most farmers worked their land alone or with the help of a few slaves. The entire family helped out during planting and harvesting. Farmers raised pigs, grew wheat and barley, and tended olive groves and vineyards. Sheep and goats grazed on poorer land. The Greeks produced a surplus of olive oil, wine, and wool, which they exported.

Manufacturing. The ancient Greeks manufactured all products by hand. Many craftsmen worked alone. There were also factories with 20 to more than 100 workers, many of them slaves. These workers specialized in the different skills needed to make such goods as pottery, armor, and clothing. Individual city-states became known for certain products. For example, Athens was famous for its decorated pottery, Megara for woolen garments, and Corinth for jewelry and metal goods.

Trade. Greek merchants sold surplus goods abroad in exchange for slaves and such products as grain, timber, and metals. The Greeks' major trading partners included Egypt; Sicily; and Scythia, a country near the Black Sea. In each city-state, inspectors made sure that merchants used proper weights and measures, charged fair prices, paid taxes, and observed restrictions on the import and export of certain goods.

Transportation and communication. The rugged terrain made travel difficult on the Greek mainland. Runners carried most messages. Few roads were good enough for travel on horseback. Wagons or pack ani-

The Greek world Greek civilization arose along the shores of the Aegean and Ionian seas. Ancient Greece consisted chiefly of a peninsula that separated the two seas, nearby islands, and the coast of Asia Minor (now part of Turkey). The map shows important cities, regions, and historic sites of ancient Greece.

WORLD BOOK map

WORLD BOOK illustration by Richard Hook, Linden Artists Ltd.

Greek cargo ships sailed among the Greek islands and to overseas colonies and foreign lands. The ancient Greeks traded such products as wine, olive oil, and pottery for grain, timber, metals, and slaves from abroad. In this illustration, goods are being loaded for transport overseas.

mals hauled goods short distances. Sea travel was far more important than land travel, in spite of the dangers of piracy and shipwreck. Merchant ships sailed along the mainland coast, among the islands, and overseas.

Philosophy, science, and the arts

Philosophy originated in ancient Greece during the 500's B.C. The word *philosophy* comes from two Greek words meaning *love of wisdom.* Many of the questions asked by Greek philosophers would today be considered subjects of scientific inquiry. The earliest philosophers speculated about the underlying substance of the universe and how the universe operated. Later philosophers investigated the nature of knowledge and reality and sought to define such notions as good and evil.

Socrates, Plato, and Aristotle are considered the most important Greek philosophers. Socrates taught by carefully questioning his listeners to expose the weaknesses of their ideas and arguments. Plato explored such subjects as beauty, justice, and good government. Aristotle summed up the achievements of Greek philosophy and science. His authority on many topics remained unquestioned for more than 1,000 years.

Most people in ancient Greece were suspicious of philosophers and their theories. They continued to believe in superstitions and in myths. In 399 B.C., an Athenian jury sentenced Socrates to death for showing disrespect for the gods.

Science. Greek scientists, like Greek philosophers, believed in an orderly universe, which operated according to laws that people could discover. They based many of their theories on logic and mathematics. They also made careful observations of nature and, at times, conducted experiments. But Greek scientists rarely tried to solve practical problems, and so their discoveries had little influence on technology and everyday life.

The ancient Greeks pioneered in medicine, physics, biology, and mathematics. Some of their conclusions anticipated findings of modern science. In the 400's B.C., Democritus said all things consisted of *atoms,* tiny bits of matter that cannot be divided. In the 200's B.C., Aristarchus of Samos first stated that the earth revolved around the sun. But most Greek thinkers argued that the sun, stars, and planets moved around a stationary earth.

The arts. Greek architects, sculptors, and painters made important contributions to the arts. They strove to achieve an ideal of beauty based on harmonious proportions. The most influential architectural works were temples. A Greek temple consisted of an arrangement of columns around a long, inner chamber. The Greeks developed three influential styles for columns—the simple Doric, the graceful Ionic, and the ornate Corinthian. The best-known temples were built on the Acropolis in Athens during the 400's B.C.

Greek sculptors portrayed figures of gods, goddesses, and human beings. Over the centuries, their works became increasingly lifelike and showed figures in more active poses. The most famous Greek sculptors were Phidias, Praxiteles, Lysippus, and Myron.

Few Greek paintings have survived. Our knowledge of Greek painting comes mainly from paintings on pottery, Greek writings, and copies made by the ancient Romans. The pottery paintings and Roman copies portray scenes from mythology and daily life.

Music often accompanied plays and poetry recitals in ancient Greece, and musicians performed at festivals and private parties. Greek music relied chiefly on melody and rhythm. Harmony was unknown to the Greeks.

Greece in the Golden Age

Ancient Greece made lasting contributions to Western civilization. Greek ideas about the arts, government, philosophy, mathematics, and athletics still influence our lives. Many of the most glorious Greek achievements occurred from 477 to 431 B.C., a period called the Golden Age.

The government of Athens was headed by Pericles, *left*, for most of the Golden Age. Athens, then at the height of its power and prosperity, had the most advanced democracy in Greece. An assembly of all male citizens, *below*, passed the laws.

A statue of Athena, patron goddess of Athens, stood in the temple. It was made of gold and ivory.

A band of sculpture decorated the temple. It showed a procession held yearly in Athena's honor.

Detail of a relief sculpture (477-432 B.C.) from the Parthenon; British Museum, London (Art Resource)

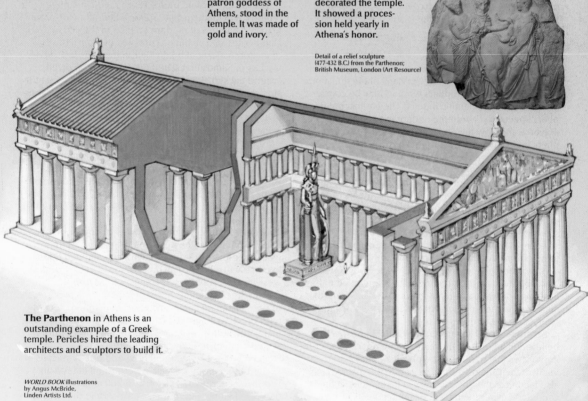

The Parthenon in Athens is an outstanding example of a Greek temple. Pericles hired the leading architects and sculptors to build it.

WORLD BOOK illustrations by Angus McBride, Linden Artists Ltd.

Drama, which was born in Greece, flourished during the Golden Age. Performances of tragedies and comedies took place at religious festivals.

Greek scientists developed the reasoning needed to demonstrate important principles of mathematics.

Socrates advanced Greek philosophy during the Golden Age. Socrates taught by carefully questioning his listeners.

The Olympic Games were held every four years at Olympia in honor of Zeus, king of the gods. Athletes from throughout the Greek world competed in such events as the discus throw, the javelin throw, and the four-horse chariot race. An Olympic victor received a crown of laurel leaves.

Detail of a marble copy of a lost sculpture by Phidias; National Museum, Athens

Athena was the goddess of wisdom and warfare. The Athenians believed she protected their city.

Detail of a marble sculpture (465-457 B.C.); Olympia Museum, Olympia, Greece

Apollo, the god of the sun and of poetry, represented the ideal young man to the ancient Greeks.

Detail of a relief sculpture (380-350 B.C.); National Museum, Athens (Ronald Sheridan)

Medicine was raised to a science by the Greeks. But many people still sought magical cures from the god of healing, Asclepius, shown here treating a patient.

Ancient Greek writers introduced many important literary forms, including lyric and epic poetry, tragic and comic drama, and history. For detailed information, see the article **Greek literature.**

Government

The city-state took shape in ancient Greece by the 700's B.C. Most citizens of a city-state claimed a common ancestry, spoke the same Greek dialect, and followed the same customs and religious practices. A city-state gave its members a sense of belonging because they were like one large family.

A small group of wealthy men governed most city-states of ancient Greece. This form of government, in which a few powerful people rule, is called an *oligarchy.* During the 500's B.C., some city-states began to move toward democracy. They granted all citizens the right to vote on government policies, hold political office, and serve on a jury. However, many poor citizens could not afford the time from making a living to participate in democratic government. In addition, women and slaves had no political rights, even in the democracies.

Athens became the most successful democracy of ancient Greece during the 400's B.C. Every male Athenian citizen had the right to serve permanently in an assembly, which passed laws and determined government policies. The assembly also elected Athenian generals. Each year, the citizens drew lots to select a council of 500 men. This council ran the day-to-day business of government and prepared the bills that the assembly debated and voted on. Jurors were also chosen by lot.

Some wealthy Athenians disliked their system of government. They felt that the poor dominated the government and took advantage of the rich. Most Athenians, however, cherished their democracy.

Sparta was the most powerful oligarchy in ancient Greece. Citizens made up only about 10 per cent of the population. Most people were serfs who farmed the land. Two kings, who inherited their thrones, headed the army. Sparta was governed by 5 officials, called *ephors,* and the *gerousia,* a council made up of 28 elders and the kings. Citizens elected ephors to one-year terms and members of the gerousia to life terms. Sparta had a citizen assembly. But citizens could not propose issues for debate in the assembly.

Military forces. Among the Greek city-states, only Sparta had a standing army. Most city-states trained young men in the art of warfare and required all able-bodied male citizens to take up arms in time of war. Athens had the largest navy, which included hundreds of large warships powered by nearly 200 oarsmen.

A battle formation known as a *phalanx* dominated Greek warfare from the 600's to the 300's B.C. To form a phalanx, armed foot soldiers lined up shoulder to shoulder eight rows deep. On the battlefield, two opposing phalanxes marched toward each other. Combat with spears and swords followed. The battle was won when one side encircled the other or broke through its center.

History

Beginnings. The first major civilization in the region of Greece arose on Crete, an island in the Aegean Sea, about 3000 B.C. It is known as the Minoan culture after King Minos, the legendary ruler of Crete. The Minoans were expert sailors, and they grew wealthy from trade. The remains of luxurious palaces provide evidence of the Minoans' prosperity and building skills. The Minoans had a system of writing. Scholars do not know what language they spoke, except that it was not Greek.

The development of Greek civilization began about 2000 B.C., when small farming villages were set up by people who came to Greece from somewhere to the north. By about 1600 B.C., they had built fortified towns, each centered on a palace, in the major valleys. The culture that developed on the mainland is called Mycenaean after the large and powerful town of Mycenae in the Peloponnesus, the southern part of the mainland.

The Minoans dominated the Aegean world until about 1450 B.C., when the Mycenaeans took control of the region. The Mycenaeans adopted features of the Minoan culture. For example, they adapted the Minoan writing system to Greek. Historians believe Mycenae won a war against Troy, in Asia Minor (now Turkey), in the mid-1200's B.C. This war inspired many major works of classical literature (see **Trojan War**).

Mycenae and most other settlements in the Peloponnesus were destroyed shortly after 1200 B.C. Historians do not know why Mycenae fell. Soon afterward, the Dorians from northern Greece moved into the region. Many Mycenaeans fled to Asia Minor. Greece entered a period known as the Dark Age, which lasted until about 800 B.C. During this time, the people again lived in isolated villages. Knowledge of writing was lost. Memories of past glories were kept alive in songs and oral poetry. The Greeks began to write again after 800 B.C. Their alphabet was based on that of the Phoenicians. Some of their oral poetry was then composed into two great epics, the *Iliad* and the *Odyssey,* which are attributed to the poet Homer.

The development of the Greek city-state began during the Dark Age. At times, neighboring city-states joined together to form a larger state. However, most city-states tried to keep their independence at any cost. At first, kings ruled the city-states, with advice from wealthy nobles. But by about 750 B.C., the nobles in most city-states had overthrown the kings and become rulers. The nobility owned the best land and totally controlled the government.

Meanwhile, ancient Greece faced the problem of too many people and too little farmland. As a result, neighboring city-states often fought over borderlands. Some city-states grew at the expense of others. For example, Sparta became powerful by conquering neighboring peoples. Many of the conquered peoples had to work the land for their Spartan masters.

The land shortage forced numerous Greeks to leave their city-states. From the 700's to the 500's B.C., Greek colonists founded new city-states along the shores of the Mediterranean and Black seas. The largest settlements developed in southern Italy and Sicily, which became known as Magna Graecia (Great Greece).

Most Greek farmers worked small plots and had to borrow money to survive between harvests. In times of poor harvests, farmers could not repay their loans. They then lost their land and were forced into slavery. Other groups were also discontent. For example, merchants and manufacturers wanted a greater voice in government. But the nobility refused to share any power.

New forms of government. The growing unrest brought *tyrants* to power in many Greek city-states as a result of revolutions. The Greeks used the term *tyrant* to describe a leader who seized total power by force. Many tyrants achieved some of the goals of their followers. For example, they distributed farmland to the landless and put people to work on large public building projects. But eventually tyrants grew more concerned with keeping their power than with serving the people.

Most tyrants were soon replaced by an oligarchy in which a few wealthy citizens, rather than the nobility, ran the government. However, a number of city-states moved toward democratic government. In 594 B.C., Athenians gave a statesman named Solon authority to reform the laws. Solon ended the practice of enslaving debtors. He divided citizens into classes by wealth and defined the rights and duties of each class. He also drew up a code of law. Shortly after Solon left office, civil war broke out. In 560 B.C., a tyrant seized power.

In 508 B.C., another Athenian statesman, Cleisthenes, proposed a constitution that made Athens a democracy. Cleisthenes extended voting rights in the assembly to all free adult men. He created a council of 500 members, which was open to any citizen. His reforms thus gave every citizen a chance to serve in the government.

The Persian wars. During the 500's B.C., the Persian Empire expanded rapidly and conquered the Greek city-states in Asia Minor. From 499 to 494 B.C., these city-states rebelled against their Persian rulers. King Darius I of Persia crushed the revolt and sent his army to punish Athens, which had aided the rebels. The Athenian army was outnumbered by the Persians, but it defeated the Persian army at the Battle of Marathon in 490 B.C.

In 480 B.C., King Xerxes I, the son of Darius, led a massive Persian invasion of Greece. Many of the Greek city-states united under Sparta's leadership to fight the invaders. The Persians overwhelmed a tiny Greek force at Thermopylae, north of Athens, and went on to take Athens. The Greek navy followed a plan of the Athenian statesman Themistocles and withdrew to the Bay of Salamis. There, it thoroughly defeated the Persians and sank about half their fleet. Xerxes returned to Persia with many of his troops. The Greeks defeated the remaining Persian forces in 479 B.C.

The Greeks regarded their victory over the Persians as their finest hour. It showed what they could do when they set aside their differences and united.

The rivalry between Athens and Sparta. The cooperation achieved by the Greek city-states during the Persian wars did not last long. In 477 B.C., Athens organized an alliance called the Delian League. It consisted mainly of city-states in Asia Minor and on Aegean islands. Sparta led the Peloponnesian League, an alliance of city-states in the Peloponnesus. Athens was the strongest naval power in ancient Greece, and Sparta was the strongest land-based power. The two rivals struggled for dominance of the Greek world during the middle and late 400's B.C.

During the 400's B.C., Athens reached its height of power and prosperity and was the center of culture in the Greek world. Pericles was the leading Athenian statesman from 461 to 429 B.C. His career spanned most of the Golden Age, a period that began in 477 B.C. and that became famous for its remarkable literary and artis-

Highlights in the history of ancient Greece

The Minoan culture arose on the island of Crete.		The first recorded Olympic Games took place.		During the Golden Age, Greece produced its greatest art.
About 3000 B.C.	1600-1200 B.C.	776 B.C.	490 and 479 B.C.	477-431 B.C.
	The Mycenaean culture prospered on the Greek mainland.		The Greeks twice defeated invading Persian armies.	

Detail of a fresco (1500's-1400's B.C.); Knossos, Crete (Ronald Sheridan)

The Minoan culture was the first major civilization in the Greek world. The Minoans produced skilled works of art, such as this wallpainting.

Detail of a relief sculpture (200's-100's B.C.) by Archelaos of Priene; British Museum, London (Ronald Sheridan)

Homer, *seated*, is traditionally considered the author of the great Greek epics the *Iliad* and the *Odyssey*. The poems were probably written in the 700's B.C.

WORLD BOOK map

Rival alliances were organized by Athens and Sparta during the 400's B.C. The rivalry erupted in the Peloponnesian War, which Sparta won.

tic accomplishments. During the Golden Age, the Greek dramatists Aeschylus, Sophocles, and Euripides wrote many of their masterpieces. The leading Greek architects and sculptors built the Parthenon on the Acropolis.

The Golden Age ended with the outbreak of the Peloponnesian War in 431 B.C. This ruinous war between Athens and Sparta lasted until 404 B.C. and left Athens exhausted. In 430 B.C., a severe plague struck Athens. It killed about a third of the people, including Pericles. Athens lacked able leaders during the rest of the war and finally surrendered.

Sparta dominated the Greek world only a short time. Fighting among the city-states resumed, and Thebes defeated Sparta in 371 B.C. The quality of life declined as a result of the continuing warfare. Economic conditions worsened, and violent clashes between rich and poor became frequent. People grew less public-spirited and more self-centered. The city-states lost their vitality.

Macedonia, a country north of Greece, was becoming stronger as Greece grew weaker. In 353 B.C., Philip II, king of Macedonia, set out to conquer Greece. Greek independence ended in 338 B.C., when Macedonia defeated the Greeks in the Battle of Chaeronea. Philip planned to lead a Greek and Macedonian army against Persia. But he was killed by a Macedonian in 336 B.C.

The Hellenistic Age. Alexander the Great, Philip's son, succeeded his father at the age of 20. In 334 B.C., Alexander carried out Philip's plan to invade Persia. In a brilliant campaign, Alexander conquered the entire Persian Empire in less than 10 years. His empire extended from Greece to India. Alexander's conquests furthered the spread of Greek ideas and the Greek way of life to

Egypt and the Near East. Alexander died in 323 B.C. His generals divided his empire into successor states, with Greece remaining under Macedonian control.

The period of Greek history following Alexander's death is known as the Hellenistic Age. The period lasted until 146 B.C. in Greece, when the Romans took control of Greece. During that time, Greek culture continued to influence the lands Alexander had conquered, and Eastern ideas reached Greece. Greece suffered from frequent warfare and widespread destruction during the 200's B.C. The city-states formed two associations to fight for independence. But Macedonian kings kept control of Greece, and the two associations fought each other.

Roman rule. Through conquests, Rome had become one of the most powerful countries in the western Mediterranean by the 200's B.C. The Romans then began to expand in the east. In the 140's B.C., they took control of Greece and Macedonia. Under Roman rule, the Greek city-states had no important military or political role. But trade, agriculture, industry, and intellectual activities flourished. The Romans borrowed the art, religion, philosophy, and way of life of the ancient Greeks, and they spread Greek culture throughout their empire.

The Roman Empire was divided in A.D. 395, and Greece became part of the East Roman Empire. The West Roman Empire collapsed in A.D. 476. The East Roman Empire survived as the Byzantine Empire until 1453, when it fell to the Turks. Greek was the official language of the Byzantine Empire, and Greek culture formed the basis of Byzantine institutions.

The Greek heritage. The ancient Greeks laid the foundations of Western civilization. Modern democra-

---

Sparta defeated Athens in the Peloponnesian War.

Alexander the Great, ruler of Greece and Macedonia, conquered the Persian Empire.

Greece was conquered by the Romans.

| 431-404 B.C. | 338 B.C. | 334-326 B.C. | 323 B.C. | 146 B.C. |

Philip II of Macedonia conquered the Greeks.

Alexander the Great died, and the Hellenistic Age began.

WORLD BOOK map

Fighting among Greek city-states continued after the Peloponnesian War. Sparta's domination ended in 371 B.C. Afterward, Thebes briefly held power.

Detail of a mosaic (before A.D. 79) from Pompeii, Italy; National Museum of Naples (SCALA/Art Resource)

Alexander the Great conquered most of the territory from Egypt to India by 326 B.C. He built Greek cities and introduced Greek culture wherever he ruled.

Detail of a relief sculpture (146 B.C.) from Delphi; École Française d'Athènes, Athens

Conquest by Roman armies made Greece a province of the Roman Empire. The Romans preserved many of the achievements of Greek culture.

cies owe a debt to Greek beliefs in government by the people, trial by jury, and equality under the law. The ancient Greeks pioneered in many fields that rely on systematic thought, including biology, geometry, history, philosophy, and physics. They introduced and perfected such important literary forms as epic and lyric poetry, history, tragedy, and comedy. In their pursuit of order and proportion, the Greeks created an ideal of beauty that strongly influenced Western art.

Learning about ancient Greece

The writings of the ancient Greeks provide much of our information about the Greek world. For example, Thucydides wrote about a major event in Greek history in his brilliant *History of the Peloponnesian War.* Aristotle's writings summarized and analyzed much of the knowledge of his time. Greek poets and playwrights expressed the attitudes and beliefs of the ancient Greeks.

The remains of Greek settlements and shrines also add to our knowledge of ancient Greece. Archaeologists study buildings and such objects as pottery, tools, and weapons to learn about trade and colonization, technology, art, and everyday life in ancient Greece.

In the 1870's, German archaeologist Heinrich Schliemann conducted the first major excavation of the buried city of Troy. Before then many people doubted that Troy, made famous in the *Iliad* and the *Odyssey,* had existed. Schliemann also made major discoveries at Mycenae. In the early 1900's, Sir Arthur Evans, a British archaeologist, located the palace at Knossos on Crete. He thus established the existence of Minoan civilization. These discoveries spurred further excavations.   Ronald P. Legon

Related articles in *World Book* include:

Biographies

For a list of Greek writers, see the *Related articles* at the end of **Greek literature.** See also the following:

Alcibiades	Democritus	Leonidas I	Pyrrho of Elis
Alexander the	Diogenes	Lycurgus	Pyrrhus
Great	Dionysius the	Lysander	Pythagoras
Anaxagoras	Elder	Lysippus	Pytheas
Apelles	Draco	Miltiades	Socrates
Archimedes	Empedocles	Olympias	Solon
Archon	Epictetus	Parmenides	Strabo
Aristarchus	Epicurus	Pelopidas	Thales
Aristides	Eratosthenes	Pericles	Themistocles
Carneades	Euclid	Phidias	Thespis
Cimon	Heraclitus	Philip II	Zeno of Citium
Cleisthenes	Hipparchus	Pisistratus	Zeno of Elea
Damocles	Hippocrates	Praxiteles	

Cities

Athens	Delphi	Knossos	Sparta
Corinth	Epidaurus	Mycenae	Thebes

Contributions to civilization

Acropolis	Geography	Parthenon
Architecture	Geology (The an-	Philosophy
Astronomy	cient Greeks)	Physics
Classical music	Geometry	Poetry
Column	Greek language	Science
Dance	Greek literature	Sculpture
Drama	Logic	Seven Wonders of
Education (History)	Mathematics	the Ancient
Exploration (The	Mythology	World
Greeks)	Painting	

Government

Areopagus	Athens (History)

Ballot (Older customs)
Citizenship (History)
City-state
Democracy
Law (The influence of ancient Greece)
Sparta

History

Achaeans	Ionians	Peloponnesian
Aegean civilization	Marathon	War
Aeolians	Olympia	Salamis
Dorians	Olympiad	Thermopylae
Hellenistic Age	Olympic Games	Troy

Other related articles

Aesop's fables	Macedonia (historical region)
Arcadia	Messenia
Barbarian	Mount Olympus
Boeotia	Oracle
Bronze (picture: Bronze hel-	Parnassus
met, Greece)	Reincarnation
Clothing (Ancient times; pic-	Ship (Phoenician and Greek
tures)	ships)
Communication (picture: Wax	Thessaly
tablets)	Thrace
Doll (picture)	Venus de Milo
Lyre	Winged Victory

Outline

I. **The Greek world**
  A. The land
  B. The people
II. **Life of the people**
  A. Family life   C. Food, clothing,   D. Religion
  B. Education   and shelter   E. Recreation
III. **Work of the people**
  A. Farming
  B. Manufacturing
  C. Trade
  D. Transportation and communication
IV. **Philosophy, science, and the arts**
  A. Philosophy
  B. Science
  C. The arts
V. **Government**
  A. The city-state
  B. Athens
  C. Sparta
  D. Military forces
VI. **History**
VII. **Learning about ancient Greece**

Questions

What was a Greek city-state and what were some of its features?
How did Cleisthenes reform the Athenian government?
How did education in Sparta differ from education in Athens?
What was the Golden Age?
Why did many ancient Greeks settle in colonies overseas?
In which areas of knowledge did the ancient Greeks pioneer?
What form of government did most Greek city-states have?
Why did most ancient Greeks live in small, simple houses?
Which two empires helped to spread Greek culture?
What event did the ancient Greeks regard as their finest hour and why?

Additional resources

Archibald, Zofia. *Discovering the World of the Ancient Greeks.* Facts on File, 1991.
Garland, Robert. *The Greek Way of Life.* Cornell Univ. Pr., 1989.
Martin, Thomas R. *Ancient Greece.* Yale, 1996.
Nardo, Don. *Ancient Greece.* Lucent Bks., 1994.
Powell, Anton. *Ancient Greece.* Facts on File, 1989. Younger readers.
Sacks, David. *Encyclopedia of the Ancient Greek World.* Facts on File, 1995.

Greek cross. See Cross.

Greek fire was a chemical mixture that burned furiously. It burned even in water. The formula for Greek fire is uncertain, but it probably contained liquid petroleum thickened with resin and sulfur. It was first used in warfare in the A.D. 600's. During medieval times, warriors used tubes and arrows to shoot Greek fire. They also hurled pots and bottles filled with the mixture. In Europe during the 1200's, warriors began to use gunpowder instead of Greek fire. Gunpowder was a more effective means of damaging a distant target.

James E. Kennedy

Greek games. See Olympic Games.

Greek gods. See Mythology.

Greek language is one of the oldest surviving branches of the Indo-European family of languages. It is related to Latin, Hittite, Old Slavic, Celtic, and the Germanic languages.

The *classical* (ancient) Greek language was highly *inflected*—that is, word forms changed to show changes in meaning. Thus, its vocabulary could express a variety of grammatical relationships. A fully inflected classical Greek verb may have more than 500 forms. Changes in the form of a verb can show changes in time, manner, kind of action, or the person acting. In addition, new words could be formed easily, especially through the use of suffixes and prefixes to create compound words.

Greek has interest for students of English because many of our words are borrowed from Greek, often through Latin or one of the Romance languages. Scientific words from Greek include *astronaut, ecology, geography,* and *psychiatry.* Words of Greek origin used in the arts include *architect, criticism, music,* and *poetry.*

Alphabet. Most of the alphabets of modern Europe are modeled on the Greek, which was in turn adapted from the alphabet of the Phoenicians sometime between the 1100's and 700's B.C. There were two main forms of the ancient Greek alphabet, the *western* and the *eastern.* From the western comes the Roman alphabet in which this encyclopedia is printed. The eastern alphabet has 24 letters. This alphabet was used in classical Greek and is still used today, though the letters are pronounced differently in modern Greek. It was the ancestor of the Cyrillic alphabet, which is used in the Russian, Bulgarian, and Serbian languages (see **Russian language**).

Greek writing at first went from right to left. Later, one line was written from right to left, the next line from left to right in a form called *boustrophedon,* "turning like

oxen in plowing." After about 500 B.C., all lines were written from left to right.

Development of ancient Greek. The geography of Greece greatly influenced the development of its language. Mountains and deep bays isolated one group and region from another. Because of this isolation, the Greeks used many different dialects before writing was introduced. But the dialects never differed so much that the Greeks of one region could not understand those of another. The dialects of historic times fall into four main divisions—Ionic, Aeolic, Arcado-Cyprian, and Doric. Attic, the language of Athens, was related to Ionic. It became the most important language for Greek literature.

Scholars do not know when people first began to write in Greek. But in 1953, an amateur British cryptographer proved that one form of Greek writing dates back to at least 1400 B.C. Michael G. F. Ventris deciphered some inscriptions written in the *Linear B* syllables. They

Some common words in ancient Greek

Greek	English spelling	Pronunciation	Meaning
ἄνθρωπος	anthrōpos	*AHN throh pos*	man
βιβλίον	biblion	*bihb LEE ohn*	book
γῆ	gē	*gay*	earth
γράμμα	gramma	*GRAHM mah*	letter
δένδρον	dendron	*DEHN drohn*	tree
ἡμέρα	hēmera	*hay MEH rah*	day
κόσμος	cosmos	*KOHS mohs*	world
λόγος	logos	*LOH gohs*	word
μέγας	megas	*MEH gahs*	large
μήν	mēn	*mayn*	month
μήτηρ	mētēr	*MAY tayr*	mother
μικρός	mikros	*mee KROHS*	small
μόνος	monos	*MOH nohs*	single
οἰκία	oikia	*oy KEE ah*	house
πατήρ	patēr	*pah TAYR*	father
πολύς	polys	*poh LOOS*	many, much
φίλος	philos	*FEE lohs*	friend

showed that Mycenaean Greek was spoken and written in Knossos (in Crete) and Mycenae and Pylos on the mainland (see **Ventris, Michael G. F.**).

The oldest Greek literary texts are the *Iliad* and the *Odyssey,* two epic poems attributed to Homer. Homer's dialect consisted primarily of Ionic and Aeolic, with some words and forms from Arcado-Cyprian and Attic, and even words from languages other than Greek. Later writers of epic also used Homer's dialect. Greek prose developed in Ionia. As a result, the language of prose writers—such as Plato and Aristotle in philosophy, Thucydides in history, and Galen in medicine—was chiefly Ionic or Attic-Ionic. Attic became the standard of classical Greek.

After the conquests of Alexander the Great in the 300's B.C., people in the eastern Mediterranean spoke and wrote a simplified Attic known as *koinē* (common dialect). The New Testament is written in koinē. Greek in this form remained the common language of cultured people of all nations until sometime after the 300's A.D.

Development of modern Greek. Modern Greek began to take shape about A.D. 900. It was the language of the Byzantine Empire, and it remained in use in

Greek alphabet			English sound	Greek alphabet			English sound
A	α	alpha	*arm*	N	ν	nu	*now*
B	β	beta	*but*	Ξ	ξ	xi	*ax*
Γ	γ	gamma	*get*	O	o	omicron	*for*
Δ	δ	delta	*do*	Π	π	pi	*pie*
E	ε	epsilon	*held*	P	ρ	rho	*ran*
Z	ζ	zeta	*adze*	Σ	σ,ς	sigma	*sat*
H	η	eta	*they*	T	τ	tau	*tar*
Θ	θ	theta	*thin*	Y	υ	upsilon	*rude*
I	ι	iota	*machine*	Φ	φ	phi	*fill*
K	κ	kappa	*kite*	X	χ	chi	*elkhorn*
Λ	λ	lambda	*lamb*	Ψ	ψ	psi	*keeps*
M	μ	mu	*man*	Ω	ω	omega	*hold*

English sounds approximately represent those of ancient Greek.

Greece after the Turks conquered the Byzantines in 1453. Today, about 12,000,000 people speak Greek. When printed, modern Greek closely resembles the koinē. A reader of modern Greek can read the ancient language about as well as we do Chaucer. Modern Greek differs from ancient in pronunciation and structure. The spoken language today is called *demotic*. *Katharevousa*, the literary language of the 1800's, was used for official documents and in universities until the mid-1970's. It has largely been replaced by demotic.

Luci Berkowitz

See also **Alphabet** and the articles on each letter of the English alphabet.

Greek-letter society. See Fraternity; Sorority.

Greek literature is the oldest and most influential national literature in the Western world. Ancient Greek literature became the model for all later literature in the West, starting with Latin literature. Greek writers introduced many significant types of literature, including lyric and epic poetry, tragic and comic drama, philosophical essays and dialogues, critical and biographical history, and literary letters.

Early Greek literature

Epic poetry was the first important form of Greek literature. Epics are long narrative poems. Most tell about the heroic deeds of divine beings or mortals. The greatest Greek poet was Homer, who composed two famous epic poems, the *Iliad* and the *Odyssey,* during the 700's B.C. The *Iliad* tells of the Trojan War, which probably took place about 1250 B.C. The *Odyssey* relates the adventures of the Greek hero Odysseus as he returns home after the fall of Troy. The epics developed from a long tradition of oral poetry that covered about 500 years. The poems were based on stories recited by professional singers who accompanied themselves with a stringed instrument called the lyre. The *Iliad* and the *Odyssey* emphasized ideals of honor and bravery and had enormous influence on Greek culture and education as well as Greek literature.

Hesiod, the founder of the *didactic* (instructional) epic, was the first major Greek poet after Homer. Hesiod wrote during the 600's B.C. In his poem *Theogony,* Hesiod became the first writer to organize Greek mythology into a comprehensive philosophical system. Hesiod's other great poem, *Works and Days,* describes the life of Greek peasants, highlighting their hard work, thriftiness, and good judgment. The poem points out that Homer's aristocratic ideal of valor in battle is not the only kind of heroism possible. Hesiod, himself a farmer, also praised the heroism of the farmer's long silent struggle with the earth and the elements.

Lyric poetry. After about 650 B.C. shorter forms of poetry called *lyrics* began to replace the epic. Lyric poetry was originally sung to the music of the lyre. Most lyric poems described personal feelings instead of the acts of heroism portrayed in epic poetry.

One type of lyric poetry is called *melic poetry.* Melic poems are highly emotional and avoid didactic or satirical elements. Unlike elegiac and iambic poetry, melic poetry was composed for a single voice. Usually the poet sang the poems before close friends. Sappho, a poet who lived about 600 B.C., was the most famous melic poet. No Greek love poetry has ever matched the passion and tragic feeling of Sappho's verse.

Other lyric poets composed *choral lyrics.* These were sung by groups and accompanied by music and dancing. The *epinikion,* a serious choral ode written to honor the victor of athletic games, was a popular poetic form. The victory odes of Pindar are masterpieces of choral poetry. Other important writers of choral lyrics were Alcman, Stesichorus, and Simonides of Ceos.

Elegiac poetry was related to lyric poetry. Elegiac poems consisted of couplets that alternated a line of *hexameter* with a line of *pentameter.* Hexameter lines have six *feet,* or rhythmic units, and pentameter lines have five feet. Among the best-known elegiac poets are Callinus, Tyrtaeus, Mimnermus, and Theognis. *Iambic poetry* is also similar to lyric poetry. Iambic poems are written in *iambs,* which are metrical feet consisting of a short syllable followed by a long one. Much iambic poetry expressed the poet's feelings of anger, or was satiric. The three most famous iambic poets are Archilochus, Semonides of Amorgos, and Hipponax.

The Golden Age

During the late 500's B.C., Athens became the center of Greek culture, a position it held for almost 200 years. During the height of this period, from 461 to 431 B.C., the arts—especially literature—flourished. These 30 years are often called the *Golden Age.*

Drama, particularly tragedy, became the most important literary form during the Golden Age. Aeschylus, Sophocles, and Euripides were the three greatest tragic playwrights. The plays of Aeschylus are noted for their seriousness, their majestic language, and their complexity of thought. Sophocles is most famous for his characterization, graceful language, and sense of calm and proportion. Euripides was called the "philosopher of the stage." His plays explore the psychological world of human emotions and passions.

Comedy was also prominent on the Athenian stage during the 400's B.C. Aristophanes, who wrote plays in the style called *Old Comedy,* was a great writer of bawdy and satiric comic plays. His plays reflect the spirit of Athens at that time, with the Athenians' sense of freedom, vitality, and high spirits, and their ability to laugh at themselves.

After Athens was defeated in the Peloponnesian War in 404 B.C., there was less freedom of speech. Old Comedy, with its elements of political and social satire, was no longer permitted by government leaders. Comedy revived in Athens in the late 300's B.C., but in a style called *New Comedy.* This style focused on the individual and the problems people confront in everyday life. Menander was the most popular writer of such plays.

Historical literature. By the end of the 400's B.C. prose had surpassed poetry and verse drama in Greek literature. Historical writings were especially popular. Herodotus, "Father of History," traveled throughout the civilized world during the mid-400's B.C. and recorded the manners and customs of nations older than Greece. His central theme was the conflict between East and West. Thucydides, writing a few years later, was the first scientific historian. He wrote a stirring account of the Peloponnesian War. In recording the events of his day, Thucydides tried to explain the effects of politics on historical events.

Philosophical literature. About 450 B.C., a group of philosophers called Sophists became prominent. Sophists were scholars and teachers of theories of knowledge. Their great literary invention was *rhetoric,* the art of composing and delivering persuasive speeches. The Sophist movement contributed to the rise of prose, especially oration, over poetry in Athens. Such famous writers of orations as Isocrates and Demosthenes were important political figures.

A new literary form was developed by the pupils of Socrates, after the philosopher's death in 399 B.C. This form, called the *Socratic method* or *dialectic,* was based on Socrates' question and answer method of arriving at some important truth. Although Socrates left no writings, his ideas are preserved in writings of other Greeks, especially Plato. Other groups of philosophers, such as the *Epicureans,* the *Stoics,* and the *Peripatetics,* reflected the concerns of Plato's writings. Aristotle also wrote important works, including *Poetics,* a masterpiece of literary criticism.

The Hellenistic Age

During the 300's B.C., the great Macedonian king Alexander the Great conquered and ruled all of ancient Greece as well as most of the rest of the civilized world of his day. As Alexander's empire grew, Greek ideas and culture spread throughout the East. The period following Alexander's death in 323 B.C. is called the Hellenistic Age. At this time, Athens lost its dominant role as the center of Greek culture, and the city of Alexandria in Egypt became the new capital of Greek civilization.

Theocritus, an important poet writing in the 200's B.C., is credited with inventing *pastoral poetry.* Pastoral poems convey an appreciation for nature and country life. Theocritus' poems reflect the discontent of those living in the increasingly over-populated cities of the Hellenistic era. The chief literary figure of this period was Callimachus, a scholar, poet, and critic, who wrote short, highly polished poems. Many poets followed the example of Callimachus and produced powerful poetry within the narrow limits of brief, witty poems called *epigrams.* Not all poets approved of the trend to short poems, however. Apollonius of Rhodes favored traditional long epic poetry and wrote the long romantic epic the *Argonautica* in the 200's B.C.

The Greco-Roman Age

The period following the Hellenistic Age is known as the Greco-Roman Age because of the Roman conquest of Greece in 146 B.C. During the Roman rule, prose again became the most prominent literary form. The biographer and essayist Plutarch is most famous for his biographies contrasting Greek and Roman leaders in *Parallel Lives of Illustrious Greeks and Romans.* Later, Lucian of Samosata wrote amusing commentaries that satirized the popular philosophical schools of his day.

Renewed interest in the art of oratory and rhetoric resulted in the *Second Sophistic Movement* in the A.D. 100's. During this period, Epictetus, a former slave, became the spokesman of the Stoic school of thought. His philosophy emphasizes acceptance and endurance.

Many new and varied types of writings appeared during the A.D. 100's. The travel writer Pausanias wrote an important description of ancient Greece that remains a valuable source of Greek history and religion. A Greek physician named Galen produced medical writings, discussing anatomy, physiology, and psychology. Ptolemy, an astronomer, mathematician, and geographer, also wrote influential scientific works. Another important work of the period is the *Sophists' Banquet,* written by Athenaeus of Naucratis. Athenaeus pretends to record a dinner table discussion between 29 famous wise men. The work contains quotations from many literary works which would otherwise be unknown. Longus wrote an influential pastoral romance, *Daphnis and Chloë,* during the A.D. 100's or 200's. Critics regard this romance masterpiece as an important forerunner of the novel.

The most important writer of the 200's was Plotinus, founder of the *Neoplatonic school* of philosophy. His work was the last great creation of ancient philosophy.

Medieval literature

Greece was part of the Byzantine Empire from A.D. 395 until the empire fell to the Turks in 1453. Constantinople (now Istanbul), the Byzantine capital, became the center of Greek culture and literature for 1,000 years. The Byzantine arts reflect the combination of Greek learning and literary tradition with the teachings of Christianity. Christian religious poetry became the most prominent Greek literature of the Middle Ages.

Romanos the Melode, who lived in the 500's, was the greatest Greek poet of the Middle Ages. He was the chief composer of *kontakia* (singular *kontakion*), which were long metrical hymns that were especially popular during the 500's and 600's. The *kanon,* another type of religious poetry, was introduced during the early 700's by Saint John Damascene, a famous theologian.

Modern Greek literature

From the fall of Constantinople to the Turks in 1453 until the Greek War of Independence in 1821, a more personal poetry flourished in the Frankish-occupied lands. *Erotocritos,* the masterpiece of Cretan literature, was written by Vitzentzos Cornaros in the early 1600's. The poem has more than 10,000 rhyming verses. In Turkish-occupied territories, folk songs and folk tales were almost the only Greek literature produced for 400 years.

The first great modern Greek poet, Dionysios Solomos, wrote during the early 1800's. Solomos adopted *demotic* Greek, the vivid language of the common people, for his poems. Before his poetry, only the official scholarly form of Greek, called *katharevousa,* was used in literature. The Demotic Movement of the 1880's, led by one of Greece's great poets, Costis Palamas, urged the return of art and literature to themes of daily life.

Before World War I, Greek prose was limited largely to short stories describing provincial life and customs. After the war, the psychological and sociological novel became the leading prose form. Nikos Kazantzakis wrote powerful novels dealing with such themes as the conflict between human passion and spiritual ideals.

Modern Greek poetry earned international respect in the 1900's. Constantine Cavafy's narrative and lyric poems received high praise during the mid-1900's, after the poet's death, when they were first translated. In 1963, George Seferis, a lyric poet, became the first Greek to receive the Nobel Prize for literature. Another Greek poet, Odysseus Elytis, won the Nobel Prize for literature in 1979. Poet Yannis Ritsos had perhaps the greatest influence outside of Greece. He wrote over 100 books of poetry before his death in 1990.   Kostas Myrsiades

Related articles in *World Book* include:

Biographies

Aeschylus	Galen	Longinus	Ptolemy
Anacreon	Herodotus	Menander	Sappho
Aristophanes	Hesiod	Pindar	Sophocles
Aristotle	Homer	Plato	Theocritus
Demosthenes	Kazantzakis,	Plotinus	Thucydides
Epictetus	Nikos	Plutarch	Xenophon
Euripides			

Other related articles

Aesop's fables	Hellenistic Age	Oratory
Drama (Greek	Iliad	Peripatetic philos-
drama)	Mythology	ophy
Epigram	Neoplatonism	Philosophy
Greece (Arts)	Novel	Sophists
Greece, Ancient	Odyssey	Stoic philosophy

Additional resources

Easterling, P. E., and Knox, B. M., eds. *The Cambridge History of Classical Literature, Vol. I: Greek Literature.* 1985. Reprint. Cambridge, 1989.
Romilly, Jacqueline de. *A Short History of Greek Literature.* Rev. ed. 1985. Reprint. Univ. of Chicago Pr., 1996.

Greek mythology. See Mythology.

Greek Orthodox Archdiocese of North and South America has under its jurisdiction more than 500 Greek Orthodox Church communities in Canada, the United States, and Central and South America. The archdiocese functions under the ecclesiastical authority of the Ecumenical Patriarchate of Constantinople in Turkey.

The *primate* (leader) of the archdiocese is an archbishop. He is assisted by bishops who administer each of the archdiocese's 10 districts. District headquarters are located in New York City; Chicago; Boston; San Francisco; Atlanta, Georgia; Pittsburgh, Pennsylvania; Detroit; Denver; Toronto, Canada; and Buenos Aires, Argentina.

The archdiocese operates the Hellenic College/Holy Cross School of Theology in Brookline, Massachusetts, and St. Basil's Academy in Garrison, New York. It was established in 1922 and has about 1,950,000 members. Executive offices are in New York City.   Critically reviewed by the Greek Orthodox Archdiocese of North and South America

See also Eastern Orthodox Churches.

Greek Orthodox Church. See Eastern Orthodox Churches.

Greeley, Horace (1811-1872), a prominent American newspaper publisher, founded and edited the *New York Tribune.* He was a leader in the antislavery movement, and his editorials played an important part in molding public opinion, especially during the 20 years before the American Civil War. Greeley's editorials against the spread of slavery into new territory increased the antislavery sentiment of the North. He also fought vigorously in his columns for the protective tariff and for anti-liquor legislation.

His publications. In 1834, Greeley founded *The New-Yorker,* a weekly literary paper. In 1840, he began publication of *The Log Cabin,* a weekly campaign paper supporting William Henry Harrison, the Whig candidate for president. The next year he founded the *New York Tribune,* a penny daily, and combined *The Log Cabin* and *The New-Yorker* into the *New York Weekly Tribune.* The

weekly edition had more readers than any other American publication of the period.

Chicago Historical Society
Horace Greeley

Greeley's writings and remarks were widely quoted. The phrase "Go West, young man" became a byword after he popularized it. It was first used by an Indiana newspaperman, John Soule, in 1851. Soon afterward, Greeley published the phrase in the *New York Tribune* as advice to the unemployed of New York City.

His Civil War role. Greeley was one of the first editors to join the Republican Party. He was a delegate to its second national convention, and helped Abraham Lincoln obtain the nomination for president. Although he supported Lincoln throughout the Civil War, he urged settling the conflict by compromise. In 1864, he met with several agents of the Confederacy in Canada to discuss peace terms, but the conference failed. In addition, Greeley urged giving pardons to all members of the Confederacy after the war. Greeley endured criticism for his views and continued to use the *New York Tribune* to promote stimulating ideas. He rejected the sensational journalistic style then gaining popularity.

His political role. Greeley supported the administration of President Ulysses S. Grant for two years, but then began to disagree with Grant's policies and to oppose him openly. The Liberal Republicans and the Democrats nominated Greeley to run for president against Grant, but Grant won decisively in the 1872 election. Greeley died less than a month later. See **Grant, Ulysses S.** (Election of 1872).

Greeley was born in Amherst, New Hampshire. He was an apprentice in a Vermont newspaper office when he was 15. He later moved to New York City, where, in 1833, he helped found the *Morning Post,* the first two-cent daily paper. It ran for only three weeks. In 1870, he founded a cooperative community, Union Colony, in Colorado, later called Greeley, Colorado. He wrote several books, including *Glances at Europe* (1851), *An Overland Journey to San Francisco in the Summer of 1859* (1860), *The American Conflict* (1866), *Recollections of a Busy Life* (1868), and *What I Know of Farming* (1871).

Michael Emery

See also **Liberal Republican Party.**

Green, Henry (1905-1973), was the pen name of Henry Vincent Yorke, an English novelist. Green's novels are known for their careful and intelligent plots. Many of his novels have one-word titles that reveal the main idea of their actions. Although little of importance seems to happen, Green conveyed his characters' emotions. Green was one of the few major authors of his time to portray relatively happy, satisfied characters.

In *Loving* (1945), Green brings an Irish castle to life, contrasting the romantic affairs of the servants with those of their masters. *Party Going* (1939) is a farewell to prewar society, when young people were more carefree. Green's other works include *Blindness* (1926), *Living* (1929), *Caught* (1943), *Back* (1946), *Concluding* (1948),

Nothing (1950), and *Doting* (1952). Green was born near Tewkesbury.   Michael Seidel

Green, Paul Eliot (1894-1981), was an American playwright. His works include folk plays and outdoor pageants with American historical themes. The pageants, called *symphonic dramas,* include music and dancing. Green's most popular symphonic dramas include *The Lost Colony* (1937), the story of the colonists on Roanoke Island; and *The Common Glory* (1947), a dramatization of Thomas Jefferson's struggle for democracy and Virginia's contribution to the American Revolution.

Green's folk plays include *In Abraham's Bosom* (1926), a tragedy about a black American's struggle for dignity; *The House of Connelly* (1931), a story of a plantation family's decline; and *Hymn to the Rising Sun* (1936), a play about the death of a black man on a chain gang. *In Abraham's Bosom* won the 1927 Pulitzer Prize for drama.

Paul Eliot Green was born near Lillington, North Carolina. He taught dramatic art at the University of North Carolina. His plays show the influence of Frederick Koch, whose Carolina Playmakers led the development of American regional drama.   Frederick C. Wilkins

Green, Theodore Francis (1867-1966), was a Democratic United States senator from Rhode Island. He served in the Senate from 1937 until he retired in 1961 at the age of 93. Green strongly supported the policies of Presidents Franklin D. Roosevelt and Harry S. Truman. He was chairman of the Senate Foreign Relations Committee from 1957 to 1959. Green entered politics as a member of the Rhode Island House of Representatives in 1907. He was elected governor of Rhode Island in 1932, and reelected in 1934. Led by Green, Democrats gained full control of the state government in 1935. They had not held control since before the Civil War. Green was born in Providence, Rhode Island.   William J. Eaton

Green, William (1873-1952), succeeded Samuel Gompers as president of the American Federation of Labor (AFL) in 1924, and held the position until his death. As president of the AFL, Green worked for laws to help workers and unions. During World War II, he helped work out the labor movement's "no-strike" pledge.

Green was born in Coshocton, Ohio, where he became a coal miner. He was elected secretary-treasurer of the United Mine Workers of America in 1913. He also served two years in the Ohio Senate. He helped pass the mine safety and workers' compensation laws in Ohio.

Jack Barbash

Green Bay, Wisconsin (pop. 102,313; met. area pop. 226,778), is one of the most important trade and shipping centers in the state. The city is located in northeastern Wisconsin. It lies at the mouth of the Fox River at the southern point of a body of water called Green Bay (see **Wisconsin** [political map]).

The city of Green Bay is the cultural, educational, industrial, and medical center of the region. Factories in Green Bay manufacture canned goods, cheese, paper and paper products, and paper-converting machinery. In addition, the city is the home of the National Railroad Museum, the National Football League's Green Bay Packers, and the University of Wisconsin-Green Bay.

Green Bay, founded in 1764, was Wisconsin's first permanent settlement. It has a mayor-council government and is the seat of Brown County. For the monthly weather, see **Wisconsin** (Climate).   Michael E. Blecha

Green Berets. See Army, United States (Special Forces); Guerrilla warfare.

Green Mountain Boys were soldiers from Vermont who fought for the American Colonies in the Revolutionary War (1775-1783). Led by Ethan Allen, the soldiers captured Crown Point and helped take Fort Ticonderoga. Later, under the leadership of Colonel Seth Warner, they helped win the Battle of Bennington.

Ethan Allen organized the Green Mountain Boys some years before the Revolution. They raided New York settlements in protest against the claims of New York to the territory of Vermont, which had been under the control of New Hampshire. The Green Mountain Boys whipped New Yorkers, burned their cabins, and stole their cattle. They also beat New York officials. In 1777, Vermont settlers declared their territory an independent republic, which they called New Connecticut. Later that year, the republic was renamed Vermont. Vermont became the 14th state in 1791.   Richard D. Brown

See also **Allen, Ethan; Fort Ticonderoga; Vermont** (Land disputes); **Warner, Seth.**

Green Mountain State. See Vermont.

Green Mountains form part of the Appalachian system. They are one of the oldest mountain ranges in North America. The Green Mountains received their name from the forests of evergreens which covered the mountains when the first settlers came.

The mountains extend north and south, through central Vermont. They make up part of the mountain chain that continues south through Massachusetts and Connecticut. In these two states, the mountains are known as the Berkshire Hills and the Hoosac Mountains. The northern end of the chain reaches Quebec. Water and ice have worn down the peaks so that in some places they are low hills. The highest peak is Mount Mansfield (4,393 feet, or 1,339 meters).

Ash, beech, birch, fir, hemlock, maple, pine, and spruce trees almost cover the mountains. Many tourists visit the area. The mountains receive heavy snow in winter, and they have many ski resorts.   Andrew R. Bodman

See also **Vermont** (physical map; picture).

Green party is any of a number of political parties that are most widely known for promoting environmental issues. Other issues advanced by Green parties include the rights of women and opposition to capitalism, modernism, the building of nuclear power plants, and the testing and production of nuclear weapons.

Green parties operate primarily in industrialized countries. Germany and other Western European nations have some of the strongest Green parties. In 1983, before the German unification, West Germany's Green Party became the first Green party in Europe to win seats in a national legislature. Other countries with Green parties include Australia, Austria, Finland, France, New Zealand, Spain, and Sweden.

The United States has numerous Green parties, many of which belong to the Association of State Green Parties. In 1996 and 2000, Ralph Nader, a prominent lawyer and consumer advocate, represented these groups as the Green Party candidate for president of the United States. Nader won only a small percentage of the votes in either election, but his candidacy brought increased attention to the causes of Green parties in the United States (see **Nader, Ralph**).

Most existing Green parties were founded in the 1980's. But Green parties draw on the traditions of anarchist, socialist, and other left-wing movements that developed in Europe during the 1800's. Because of their diverse objectives, Green parties have had difficulty joining together to challenge better-established parties. As a result, they have sometimes formed alliances with other kinds of parties, such as the Social Democratic Party in Germany.   Kim R. Holmes

Green Revolution. See Food supply (Making farmland more productive).

Greenaway, Kate (1846-1901), was an English illustrator of children's books. She painted in water colors, and became known for the quaint charm of her pictures, her delicate portrayal of flowers and gardens, and her children in old-fashioned dress. She often wrote verses to go with her drawings. Her books include *Under the Window* (1878), her first book; *The Language of Flowers* (1884); *Marigold Garden* (1885); and *A—Apple Pie* (1886).

Catherine Greenaway was born in London, the daughter of an engraver. She became known for her Christmas cards, valentines, and magazine sketches before she began illustrating books.   Marilyn Fain Apseloff

See also **Literature for children** (picture: Mother Goose); **Valentine's Day** (picture).

Greenback is a popular name for United States notes, a kind of paper money. The United States government first issued paper currency in 1861 to finance its Civil War operations. The first bills were redeemable in coins. But after 1862, the notes were only promises by the United States to pay. The reverse side of the bills was printed in green. Because the notes had no metal money behind them as security, people said they were backed only by green ink. In time, the notes became known as *greenbacks*. At one time when people held little confidence in the government, greenbacks were worth only 35 cents in coin for each dollar.

Burton H. Hobson

See also **Money** (The rebirth of paper money).

Greenback Party was an American political party that was active between 1876 and 1884. Its name referred to the *greenbacks,* or paper notes, that had been issued during the Civil War and afterward. Farm prices rose higher than ever before during this period.

After the panic of 1873, prices dropped, mortgages were foreclosed, and the amount of money in circulation dropped greatly. The Greenbackers believed that the issuance of large amounts of paper money would bring prosperity, especially to the farmer, by raising prices and making debts easier to pay. Many farmers of the West and South joined the party, or promoted its policies in the Republican and Democratic parties.

The Greenback Party was founded at a meeting in Indianapolis, Indiana, in 1874. It was originally called the Independent National Party. The first party convention, held in 1876, nominated Peter Cooper for President. The party received few votes. In 1878 it succeeded in electing 14 members of Congress. Some of these people formed a group in the House of Representatives called the *Greenback bloc.* In 1880 the Greenback Party broadened its platform, supporting an income tax, an eight-hour day, votes for women, and other progressive measures. It nominated James B. Weaver, leader of the bloc in Congress, as its candidate for President. The

party made a poor showing in the election and lost some of its seats in Congress. By 1888, the Greenback Party lacked the strength to nominate its own candidate for President.   Donald R. McCoy

See also **Cooper, Peter.**

Greenbottle, a fly. See **Blow fly; Fly** (picture).

Greenbrier is the name for several types of climbing vines that have prickly green stems. Greenbriers are also known as *horse briers* and *catbriers.* These plants have shiny leaves and clusters of small, yellowish-green flowers. They also produce bluish-black or reddish berries. Greenbriers grow in thickets throughout the eastern half of the United States. Greenbriers can spread rapidly, and the plants often are considered weeds.

Scientific classification. Greenbriers belong to the lily family, Liliaceae. The most common species is *Smilax rotundifolia.*

Ronald L. Jones

Greene, Graham (1904-1991), an English author, won fame for both serious novels and for lighter books he called "entertainments." His entertainments include the detective story *This Gun for Hire* (1936) and the adventure mystery *The Third Man* (1950).

Greene's serious novels are set in varied and remote places and deal with troubled individuals. Many of his characters are mentally disturbed, suffering a religious crisis, or engaged in criminal activities. To Greene, these people are both victims and "heroes" of our day because they struggle to achieve a kind of inner harmony. Greene implied that although his heroes are detestable in other ways they at least avoid the common fault of false self-satisfaction. For example, in *The Heart of the Matter* (1948), the main character abandons his church, his wife, and society, and commits suicide. However, by suffering and by confronting himself, he at least gains some understanding. Greene's other serious novels include *Brighton Rock* (1938), *The Power and the Glory* (1940), *The End of the Affair* (1951), *A Burnt-Out Case* (1961), *The Honorary Consul* (1973), and *The Human Factor* (1978).

Greene was born in Berkhampstead, near London. He worked on the editorial staff of *The Times* (London) from 1926 to 1930. He became a Roman Catholic in 1926. Much of his serious writing deals with moral problems of Catholics. He wrote two autobiographies, *A Sort of Life* (1971) and *Ways of Escape* (1981).   Michael Seidel

Greene, Nathanael (1742-1786), an American Revolutionary War general, is noted for his campaigns against the British in North and South Carolina between 1780 and 1782. Many historians rank him second only to Washington as a military leader.

Greene was born to a Quaker family at Potowomut (Warwick), Rhode Island. Because he was interested in military affairs, the Quaker church, which is opposed to war, expelled him. He served in the Rhode Island legislature from 1770 to 1772, and in 1775. In October 1774, when trouble with Britain threatened, he organized a militia company called the Kentish Guards. Because he had a stiff knee, his men would not let him act as an officer, and he served in the ranks. After the battle of Lexington, the Kentish Guards set out to aid the patriots at Boston. The governor of Rhode Island was loyal to the British and recalled them. But Greene and three other men went to Boston. He became a brigadier general in the Continental Army and took part in the siege of

Boston. In 1776, he became a major general, and then commanded the army of occupation in Boston.

Greene fought in the battles of Trenton, Brandywine, and Germantown, and he was with Washington at Valley Forge. In 1778, he became quartermaster general. But he resigned in 1780 because of what he considered an unfair investigation by politicians of his department.

In December 1780, Greene replaced General Horatio Gates, whose army had been badly beaten at Camden, South Carolina. The British suffered heavy losses in fighting against Greene's forces at the Battle of Guilford Court House in North Carolina in March 1781. Greene pushed the British back into Charleston and Savannah by the end of 1781. Georgia later gave him a plantation near Savannah. Rhode Island placed a statue of him in the U.S. Capitol in 1870.　　Paul David Nelson

Greene, Robert (1558?-1592), was an English writer. He was one of the most colorful and important members of a group of university-trained writers called the *University Wits*. The Wits, attempting to make their living by popular literature, made major contributions to the development of Elizabethan drama, fiction, poetry, satire, and journalism.

Greene's first publications were prose romances. Perhaps the best are *Pandosto* (1588), which became a source for Shakespeare's *A Winter's Tale,* and *Menaphon* (1589). His best-known play is *Friar Bacon and Friar Bungay* (about 1589), a comedy that skillfully blends themes of love, magic, and extreme patriotism.

Greene was born in Norwich and received degrees from Oxford and Cambridge. He deserted his wife and child and led a dissolute life in London. His most vivid journalism exploits his own immoral life and observes the London of his day. The best-known example is the pamphlet *Greene's Groatsworth of Wit Bought with a Million of Repentance* (1592). It contains a famous attack on Shakespeare (see **Shakespeare, William** [Early career in London]).　　Stephen Orgel

Greenfield Village is a collection of about 100 historic buildings in Dearborn, Michigan. Henry Ford, who established the Ford Motor Company, collected and restored many of the buildings. The buildings include inventor Thomas A. Edison's laboratory and the courthouse where Abraham Lincoln first practiced law. The village also has craft shops and re-creations of early industries in the United States. Next to Greenfield Village is the Henry Ford Museum. This museum has exhibits in agriculture, communications, and many other fields. See also **Michigan** (Places to visit; picture).

Critically reviewed by the Henry Ford Museum

Greenhouse is a building in which people can grow plants the year around. Its roofs and walls are made of glass or plastic. A greenhouse is a form of *controlled environment agriculture* because the temperature, light, moisture, soil, and other conditions essential for plant growth can be regulated. Greenhouses are sometimes called *hothouses*. Europeans call them *glasshouses*.

Flowers, shrubs, and other types of plants are raised in greenhouses. Such vegetables as cucumbers, lettuce, and tomatoes are grown in these structures and sold out of their normal growing seasons to consumers. Many commercial growers operate *greenhouse ranges*. Greenhouse ranges consist of two or more greenhouses. Some gardeners who raise flowers and other

J. A. Nearing Co., Inc.

A greenhouse enables people to grow plants the year around. The structure protects plants from bad weather and provides the heat, light, and moisture essential for their growth.

plants as a hobby own only a small greenhouse.

The greenhouse roof is slanted to admit a maximum of sunlight. A greenhouse is a solar collector—that is, it traps the sun's heat, and the heat passes back through the roof and walls very slowly. This process resembles the way that the atmosphere helps keep the earth warm by trapping heat from the sun. In fact, scientists use the term *greenhouse effect* for the earth's heating process.

In cold weather, a furnace provides additional heat for a greenhouse. It sends steam, hot water, or hot air through pipes to warm the building. A few greenhouses have special solar collector devices that absorb the sun's heat energy and transfer it to water in a storage tank beneath the greenhouse floor. The stored hot water heats the greenhouse on cold nights.　　William H. Carlson

See also **Cold frame; Hotbed; Industry** (picture: Agriculture).

Greenhouse effect is a warming of the lower atmosphere and surface of a planet by a complex process involving sunlight, gases, and particles in the atmosphere. On the earth, the greenhouse effect began long before human beings existed. However, recent human activity may have added to the effect. The amounts of heat-trapping atmospheric gases, called *greenhouse gases,* have greatly increased since the mid-1800's, when modern industry became widespread. Since the late 1800's, the temperature of the earth's surface has also risen. The greenhouse effect is so named because the atmosphere acts much like the glass roof and walls of a greenhouse, trapping heat from the sun.

The natural greenhouse effect. The atmosphere reflects toward space about 30 percent of the energy in incoming sunlight. The atmosphere absorbs about another 30 percent, and the remaining 40 percent or so reaches the earth's surface.

The earth's surface reflects about 15 percent of the solar energy that reaches it back toward space. The remaining energy heats the lands and seas. The warmed lands and seas then send most of the heat back into the atmosphere, chiefly as *infrared rays* and in evaporated water. Infrared rays are much like light waves but are invisible to the human eye.

When the rays from the lands and seas strike certain substances in the atmosphere, such as greenhouse gases and particles, those substances absorb the rays. As a result, the gases and particles are heated. They then are cooled by sending out infrared rays of their own. Some of the rays go into space. The remainder radiate back toward the earth's surface, adding to the warming of the surface layer of air. Without the natural greenhouse effect, the average temperature of the earth's surface would be about 59 Fahrenheit degrees (33 Celsius degrees) colder than it is now.

The chief greenhouse gases are made up of atoms of carbon (C), hydrogen (H), and oxygen (O). These gases are water vapor (H_2O), carbon dioxide (CO_2), methane (CH_4), and ozone (O_3). The greenhouse particles include cloud droplets, soot, and dust.

Increases in greenhouse gases. Since the early to mid-1800's, the amount of CO_2 in the atmosphere has increased by about 25 percent and the CH_4 concentration has risen by about 150 percent. Most of the increase has been due to human activities—chiefly the burning of *fossil fuels* (coal, oil, and natural gas) and the clearing of land. Fossil fuels contain carbon, and burning them creates CO_2. Trees and other plants absorb the gas through the process of photosynthesis. As land is cleared and forests are cut down, CO_2 levels rise.

The average temperature of the earth's surface has increased by about 0.9 to 1.6 Fahrenheit degrees (0.5 to 0.9 Celsius degree) since the late 1800's. Scientists have not yet proved that an increase in atmospheric CO_2 has raised the surface temperature. But in the likely event that this relationship does exist, the eventual results could be severe. Many scientists estimate that by about 2050, the amount of CO_2 in the atmosphere will have doubled from the preindustrial level. If this increase were to add to the natural greenhouse effect, the earth's surface temperature might rise 2.5 to 10.4 Fahrenheit degrees (1.4 to 5.8 Celsius degrees) by 2100.

The increase in surface temperature, which is called *global warming,* could alter the ecology of many parts of the earth. For example, global warming could change rainfall patterns, melt enough polar ice to raise the sea level, increase the severity of tropical storms, and lead to shifts in plant and animal populations. Ocean currents and wind patterns could change, making some areas cooler than they are now. One remote possibility is that a warming of northern regions will result in more winter snowfall, causing some ice sheets to advance.

Studying the greenhouse effect. Researchers use high-speed computers to study how CO_2 concentration may affect surface temperature. The computers manipulate *mathematical models,* sets of equations that describe relationships between changeable factors. Scientists do not have enough data to prove that variations in CO_2 and other human-caused changes to atmospheric composition cause shifts in surface temperature. They may need until the 2010's to gather enough data. But certain models suggest that the 2010's may be too late to avoid some damage from global warming.

Scientists have also examined evidence from the distant past to determine whether changes in CO_2 concentration cause temperature changes. Cores of ice drilled from great depths in Greenland and Antarctica provide a record for the past 160,000 years. During those years,

the climate warmed and cooled several times. Researchers analyzed the gases and other substances that were trapped in the ice when it formed. During the cooler periods, the atmosphere contained about 30 percent less CO_2 and 50 percent less methane than during the warmer periods.   Stephen H. Schneider

See also **Global warming; National park** (Changes in the environment).

Greenland is the largest island in the world. It is a province of Denmark, though it is part of North America and lies about 1,300 miles (2,090 kilometers) away in the North Atlantic Ocean. At one point, the island is only 10 miles (16 kilometers) from Canada. Its official name is *Kalaallit Nunaat* in the Greenlandic language and *Gronland* in Danish. Both names mean *Greenland.*

Australia, which is larger than Greenland, is surrounded by water—like an island. But geographers class Australia as a continent because of its great size.

Greenland is about 50 times as large as Denmark, but Denmark has about 95 times as many people. Most of Greenland's people are descended from both Inuit (sometimes called Eskimos) and Danes. The population is small because the island has an extremely cold climate and few natural resources. Most of Greenland lies north of the Arctic Circle, and thick ice covers about 80 percent of it. Cape Morris Jesup, the northernmost land in the world, is only about 440 miles (708 kilometers) from the North Pole. The southwestern coast, where almost all Greenlanders live, is the warmest region. But even there, July temperatures average only 50 °F (10 °C). Godthåb, the capital, is in this region.

Viking explorers named the island Greenland to attract settlers. But during Greenland's short summer, only coastal areas are green. Fishing is the major industry. The location of Greenland gives the island special importance. Scientists there can forecast storms on the North Atlantic. United States military bases there form a major part of the North American defense system.

Government. Greenland is a Danish possession with the constitutional right of *home rule* (local self-government). The Danish government is responsible for Greenland's foreign affairs and defense, and the laws of Denmark's constitution are effective in Greenland. But Greenland's provincial government is responsible for internal affairs of the province. For example, it makes tax laws and operates a public school system.

Greenland's provincial government is headed by a parliament and a ruling council. The parliament has from 23 to 27 members, who are elected by the people. The ruling council, which is the executive branch of the

Facts in brief

Capital: Godthåb.
Official languages: Danish and Greenlandic.
Area: 836,330 mi² (2,166,086 km²). *Greatest distances*—north-south, 1,660 mi (2,670 km); east-west, 750 mi (1,210 km). *Coast-line*—8,650 mi (13,920 km).
Elevation: *Highest*—Mount Gunnbjørn, 12,139 ft (3,700 m). *Lowest*—sea level along the coast.
Population: *Estimated 2002 population*—56,000; density, 6 per 100 mi² (2 per 100 km³); distribution, 81 percent urban, 19 percent rural. *1976 census*—49,630.
Chief products: *Agriculture*—sheep, vegetables. *Fishing*—cod, halibut, shrimp. *Hunting*—seals.

Shostal

Greenland's largest shipyard is in Holsteinsborg, a busy town on the country's western coast. Holsteinsborg is also an important fishing center.

Danish Tourist Board

Sheepherding is Greenland's chief agricultural activity. Because of the cold climate, farming takes place only along the southwestern coast.

government, has from 3 to 5 members. Its members are elected by the parliament. Greenland's voters elect two representatives to the Danish parliament. Regional councils are elected to handle local administrative affairs. Greenland has 19 local courts. Appeals of legal decisions are heard in the Provincial Court in Godthåb.

People. About 80 percent of the people of Greenland were born there. Most of the others are Danes who

came to work in such activities as communication, education, government, or trade. Greenlanders have chiefly Inuit (Eskimo) ancestry, but most of them also have Danish ancestors. The people speak Greenlandic, a form of the Inuit language, and many also speak Danish. Most Greenlanders belong to the Evangelical Lutheran Church, the official church of Denmark.

Relatively few Greenlanders have entirely Inuit an-

Greenland

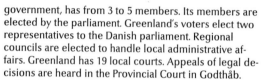

⊛ Capital

• Other Town

▲ MOUNTAIN

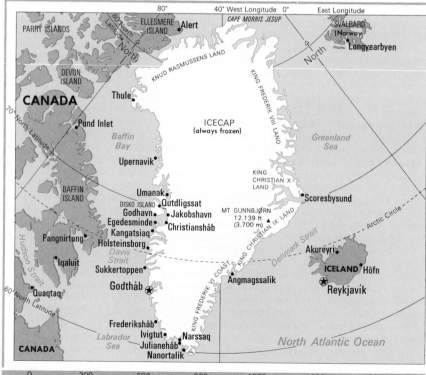

WORLD BOOK maps

cestry. Most of these people follow their old way of life in settlements in the far northwest. They hunt seals and other animals. The Inuit eat the animals' meat, and use the blubber for fuel and the skins for making clothes, kayaks, and summer tents. They build their winter houses of stone and earth. See **Inuit**.

Since the early 1900's, most Greenlanders have given up the old Inuit way of life. The wandering hunters now support themselves and their families through commercial fishing, and motorboats have largely replaced kayaks. Seal meat is still an important food, but Greenlanders also eat fish, mutton, potatoes, vegetables, and canned foods. Houses in the towns and villages are made of wood. European clothing is common, and is sold in local stores. On special occasions, women still wear their traditional costumes.

Greenland's families average six members. At home, a family spends most of its time in one room. To save coal, this room is kept warmer than the others. Many settlements are cut off from other areas in winter, and the families in a settlement visit each other frequently.

About three-fourths of the people live in towns. The largest town is Godthåb, the capital of Greenland. Other large towns, in order of size, include Holsteinsborg, Jakobshavn, Egedesminde, and Julianehåb.

Children from the age of 7 to 14 must go to school, and almost all the people can read and write. Greenland has more than 120 elementary schools, and Godthåb has a high school. Many Greenlanders receive job training in Denmark, but few attend Danish universities. Greenland has a teacher-training school in Godthåb.

The land. Greenland is a low inland plateau surrounded by coastal mountains. A sheet of permanent ice covers the plateau. It covers 672,000 square miles (1,740,500 square kilometers), or about four-fifths of the island. The icecap averages over 1 mile (1.6 kilometers) thick, and a thickness of over 2 miles (3.2 kilometers) has been measured. The highest point in Greenland, 12,139-foot (3,700-meter) Mount Gunnbjørn, rises east of the icecap. Thousands of small islands lie offshore.

Hundreds of long, narrow inlets of the sea called *fiords* cut through the coast between the mountains. Glaciers from the icecap flow down the coastal valleys and form giant icebergs that break off in the fiords.

Climate of Greenland is very cold, but it has been gradually growing warmer since the early 1900's. The coldest region is the center of the icecap. There, temperatures average -53 °F (-47 °C) in February and 12 °F (-11 °C) in July. The lowest temperature ever recorded in North America was -87 °F (-66 °C), in Greenland, in 1954. Along the southwestern coast, the warmest region, temperatures average 18 °F (-8 °C) in February and 50 °F (10 °C) in July. Greenland has little rain or snow, most of it in the south.

Most of the island has long periods when the sun shines 24 hours a day during the summer, and not at all in winter. These periods of *midnight sun* and of continuous darkness lengthen toward the north above the Arctic Circle (see **Midnight sun**).

Economy. Until the early 1900's, Greenland's economy was based on seal hunting. The coastal seas gradually became warmer, and the seal herds migrated to the north. Great numbers of fish came with the warmer waters, and the Danish government promoted a change-

over from seal hunting to fishing. Seals are still hunted in the north, along with arctic hares, foxes, polar bears, and reindeer.

The catching and processing of fish employ more than a third of Greenland's people. Cod is the leading catch, and halibut, salmon, shrimp, and wolf fish are also important. A large part of the total catch of fish and shellfish is canned, frozen, or salted for export.

Greenland's bitter climate makes farming impossible except in some southwestern coastal areas. Agriculture there is limited chiefly to sheep raising. Hay, potatoes, and vegetables are grown during the short summer. Low trees grow there, but the island has no forests.

Greenland has some deposits of coal, graphite, lead, uranium, and zinc. But most of the deposits are of such poor quality that mining would not be profitable. As a result, little mining takes place in Greenland.

History. Norwegian Vikings are believed to have sighted what is now Greenland about A.D. 875. Eric the Red, a Viking, sailed there about 982. He brought the first group of settlers from Iceland about 985. His son, Leif Ericson, led what was probably the first voyage of Europeans to the mainland of America about 1000.

The Greenland colony grew to more than 3,000 people. The people voted in 1261 to join Norway, and Greenland became united with that country. Norway united with Denmark in 1380, and Greenland came under Danish rule. The Greenland settlers died out during the 1400's, probably because of attacks by Inuit from the north and a worsening of the harsh climate.

The colonization of Greenland began again after Hans Egede, a Norwegian missionary, established a mission and trading center near what is now Godthåb in 1721. The union between Denmark and Norway ended in 1814, and Greenland remained with Denmark.

Many Danish scientific expeditions studied Greenland during the 1800's and early 1900's. They discovered much about its geography and resources. In 1933, the Permanent Court of International Justice (World Court) upheld Denmark's claim to all Greenland. Norway had disputed this claim.

In 1940, during World War II, German troops conquered and occupied Denmark. The United States agreed in 1941 to take over the defense of Greenland. The Germans set up weather stations on the island, but the stations were destroyed by American and Danish forces. The United States built and operated several military bases and weather stations in Greenland.

In 1951, a U.S.-Danish agreement placed Greenland's defense under the North Atlantic Treaty Organization (NATO). The United States expanded its air base at Thule during the 1950's. In 1961, the world's most powerful radar station was built there to warn of a surprise missile attack on North America.

In 1953, the new Danish constitution changed Greenland from a colony to a province. It gave Greenland equal rights with the rest of the Danish kingdom. Denmark gave the people of Greenland the right to elect a legislature called the Provincial Council. But the council had little real power. Laws that affected Greenland continued to be made by the Danish government.

In 1966, the Bank of Greenland was established. It was the first bank founded on the island. Also in 1966, Denmark began a $600 million program to expand and modernize Greenland's fishing industry, education system, and housing. In addition, Denmark started to train Greenlanders to take over local administrative and technical jobs held by Danes.

In the 1970's, many Greenlanders began objecting to Denmark's control over their governmental affairs. In 1979, Denmark granted Greenland *home rule.* Under home rule, Greenland established a new provincial government that controls internal affairs of the province.

In 1973, Greenland became part of the European Community when Denmark joined the organization. The European Community was an economic association of European countries. In 1982, a majority of Greenland's citizens voted to quit the European Community. They wanted the province to have more control of its economy. Greenland withdrew from the European Community in 1985.   M. Donald Hancock

Related articles in *World Book* include:

Arctic	Eric the Red	Godthåb	Inuit
Baffin Island	Ericson, Leif	Iceberg	Kayak
Cape York	Fiord	Icecap	Vikings
Denmark			

Greenough, *GREE noh,* **Horatio** (1805-1852), was the first American sculptor to gain international fame. He was also the first to study and work in Italy, setting a fashion among American artists that lasted for 50 years. Greenough's best-known work is a monumental statue of George Washington (1840). The work was ridiculed in its time because it portrayed Washington as a Greek god, bare-chested, and sitting on a throne. Greenough also created busts of Americans and wrote about art and aesthetics. He was born in Boston. See also **Sculpture** (American sculpture; picture).   George Gurney

Greenpeace is an international environmental organization. It works to change government and industrial policies that threaten the world's environment or natural resources. Greenpeace calls attention to the environmental dangers of such actions as whaling, air and water pollution, offshore oil drilling, nuclear weapons testing, and dumping of hazardous wastes. Local chapters of Greenpeace have been set up in many major cities.

Members of Greenpeace use direct and nonviolent methods of protest. They go to the place where an activity is occurring that the group considers harmful. Without using force, they try to stop the activity. For example, to protest whaling, Greenpeace members in boats position themselves between whales and whaling ships.

Greenpeace was founded in 1969 by a group of Canadian environmentalists. It gained international attention for its efforts to save whales and for its opposition to the killing of baby harp seals off the coast of Newfoundland. In 1985, Greenpeace members planned to use their ship *Rainbow Warrior* to protest French nuclear tests in the South Pacific. But an explosion sank the ship in the harbor of Auckland, New Zealand, and a Greenpeace photographer was killed. French government officials admitted responsibility for the sinking.   Joseph M. Petulla

Greensboro, *GREENZ BUR oh* or *GREENZ BUR ruh* (pop. 223,891), is one of the largest cities in North Carolina. Greensboro is a commercial, industrial, and educational center. It lies in the north-central part of the state. For location, see **North Carolina** (political map). Greensboro, Winston-Salem, and High Point form a metropolitan area with a population of 1,251,509.

Greensboro is a manufacturing and petroleum marketing center. Its industries include insurance and the manufacture of brick and clay products, chemicals, electronic equipment, furniture, pharmaceuticals, textiles and apparel, and tobacco products. Greensboro has two branches of the University of North Carolina—North Carolina Agricultural and Technical State University and the University of North Carolina at Greensboro. It is also the home of Bennett, Greensboro, and Guilford colleges.

Greensboro was established in 1808 as the seat of Guilford County. It was named for American Revolutionary War officer Nathanael Greene. In 1781, Greene led troops against the British in the Battle of Guilford Courthouse, north of what is now Greensboro. The city has a council-manager form of government.   Jerry L. Surratt

Greenspan, Alan (1926-   ), became chairman of the Board of Governors of the Federal Reserve System (FRS) in 1987. The FRS, commonly called the Fed, is an independent federal agency that directs the United States banking system and helps manage the nation's economy. Greenspan was appointed chairman by President Ronald Reagan. He was reappointed by President George H. W. Bush in 1991 and by President Bill Clinton in 1996 and 2000.

Greenspan is a conservative economist and an advocate of *laissez faire,* a theory that government should not interfere in most economic affairs. Many people gave Greenspan much credit for a long period of economic expansion that occurred in the United States in the 1990's. In the early 2000's, the Fed lowered interest rates in response to signs of an economic slowdown. But some people claimed the Fed failed to act fast enough.

Greenspan was born in New York City. He earned master's and doctor's degrees in economics from New York University. From 1974 to 1977, he was chairman of the Council of Economic Advisers under President Gerald Ford.   Carol S. Greenwald

Greenway, John Campbell (1872-1926), an American mining engineer and soldier, led in the development of mining and transportation in Arizona. He went to Arizona in 1910 and became an executive in a mining company, a lead company, and a railroad. Greenway served as a Rough Rider during the Spanish-American War and as a lieutenant colonel in World War I (see **Rough Riders**). Arizona placed his statue in Statuary Hall in the United States Capitol in Washington, D.C. He was born in Huntsville, Alabama.   B. R. Burg

Greenwich Meridian, *GREHN ihj muh RIHD ee uhn,* is a north-south line that passes through Greenwich, a borough of London, on a map of the earth. This meridian is often called the *prime meridian.* It has been designated 0° longitude, and all other meridians of longitude are numbered east or west of it. See **Longitude.**

The Greenwich Meridian is also the starting point for the world's time zones. There are 24 time zones, each with a width of 15° longitude. The Greenwich Meridian lies in the middle of a time zone. Moving east of Greenwich, the time becomes one hour later with each time zone entered. Moving to the west, the time becomes one hour earlier with each zone. See **Time.**

In 1884, an international conference decided that the meridian which passed through Britain's Royal Greenwich Observatory would be the world's prime meridian. The observatory had played a key role in early navigation and in the development of timekeeping methods needed for navigation. In the mid-1900's, the Royal Greenwich Observatory was moved from Greenwich to Herstmonceux Castle in Sussex to avoid the lights of London. It was moved to Cambridge in 1990 and closed in 1998. But the original Greenwich site is still the location of the prime meridian.   Donald B. Sullivan

Greenwich Observatory, Royal, *GREHN ihch, GREHN ihj* or *GRIHN ihj,* was founded in 1675 by Charles II of England. It was established to locate celestial bodies more accurately and thereby improve navigation at sea. The observatory was originally in Greenwich (now a borough of London). From 1948 to 1957, it was moved to Herstmonceux, near Eastbourne. It was moved to Cambridge in 1990 and closed in 1998. The Greenwich meridian passes through the original observatory site, where a science museum opened in 1993 (see **Greenwich meridian**). Until 1971, the director of the Royal Greenwich Observatory held the title of *Astronomer Royal.* One director, Edmond Halley, was the first person to predict successfully the return of a comet—the reappearance in 1758 of the comet that now bears his name.

Greer, Germaine (1939-   ), is an Australian writer and intellectual. She won international recognition as an outspoken and often controversial feminist writer and social critic following the publication of her first book, *The Female Eunuch* (1970). The book calls upon women to liberate themselves from traditional social roles and from control by men. Greer was born in Melbourne and educated at the universities of Melbourne and Sydney, and at Cambridge University, where she gained her doctorate. Her later works include *Sex and Destiny* (1984); *Daddy, We Hardly Knew You* (1989), a book about her unsatisfactory relationship with her father; and *The Whole Woman* (1999).   Cynthia Fuchs Epstein

Greeting cards mark special occasions or provide friendly greetings to persons receiving them. Valentines were first commercially produced about 1800. The first Christmas card was made in London in 1843. The British artist John C. Horsley created it for Henry Cole, a government official. A London company published and sold about 1,000 copies of the card. Since that time, the sending of greeting cards has become a social custom. See also **Christmas; Valentine's Day.**   Sharron G. Uhler

Gregg, John Robert (1867-1948), invented the Gregg system of shorthand, in which lines and curves represent letters and syllables. Perfected in 1888, the Gregg system is used throughout the world and has been adapted to 11 languages. Gregg founded a school in Chicago to teach his system and other business subjects. He directed a firm that published his books and other texts on business. He also edited two business magazines. Gregg was born in Ireland. He came to America in 1893. See also **Shorthand.**   Glenn Smith

Gregoire, Paul Cardinal (1911-1993), *gray GWAHR,* was appointed a cardinal of the Roman Catholic Church by Pope John Paul II in 1988. Gregoire had been appointed archbishop of Montreal by Pope Paul VI in 1968, serving until he resigned in 1990.

Gregoire was born in Verdun, Quebec. He was ordained a priest in 1937. He held several positions at the University of Montreal from 1950 to 1961, including student chaplain and professor of the philosophy of education. In 1961, he became auxiliary bishop of Montreal.

He was a member of the Sacred Congregation for the Clergy from 1978 until 1983, when he joined the Sacred Congregation for Catholic Education.   Kenneth Guentert

Gregorian calendar, *gruh GAWR ee uhn,* is the calendar that is used in almost all the world today. All modern business uses its dates. Pope Gregory XIII established it in 1582 to correct the Julian calendar, which Julius Caesar put into effect in 46 B.C. The Julian calendar year was 11 minutes and 14 seconds longer than the solar year. By A.D. 1580, this difference had accumulated to 10 days. Pope Gregory dropped 10 days from October to make the calendar year correspond more closely to the solar year. He also decreed that each fourth year would be a *leap year,* when February would have an extra day. Years marking the century would not be leap years unless divisible by 400. For example, 1600 and 2000 were leap years, but 1700, 1800, and 1900 were not. At present, the average Gregorian year is about 26 seconds longer than the solar year. See also **Calendar.**

James Jespersen

Gregory I, Saint (540?-604), was elected pope in 590. He was responsible for important reorganizations of almost all branches of the papal government. He also reformed the management of the many papal estates in Italy, Sicily, southern Gaul (now mainly France), and northern Africa. Gregory was anxious to protect the rights of the popes, and he defended his *primacy* (position of first importance) against the claims of the patriarch of Constantinople. Gregory wrote a book describing the qualities necessary to be an ideal bishop.

Gregory was born in Rome into an aristocratic family. Two of his ancestors, Saint Felix III and Saint Agapitus I, were popes. By 572 or 573, he had risen to become *prefect* (governor) of the city of Rome. About 574, he became a monk. He distributed his family's great wealth and made his own home in Rome a monastery dedicated to Saint Andrew. He also founded six monasteries on family estates in Sicily. About 578, Pope Benedict I named him one of Rome's seven regional deacons, an important papal administrative office. From about 579 to 585, Gregory was an ambassador to the Byzantine imperial court in Constantinople. Gregory left a body of writings, including over 850 letters.   Thomas F. X. Noble

See also **Pope** (The early Middle Ages; picture).

Gregory VII, Saint (1020?-1085), was elected pope in 1073. He renewed the papal decrees that forbade marriage of the clergy and *simony* (selling of church offices). He also began a reform program that prohibited *lay investiture,* by which laymen granted churchmen the symbols of their offices. The right to perform this ceremony gave laymen control over who received church offices.

The prohibition of lay investiture brought Gregory into conflict with Emperor Henry IV. For centuries, the Holy Roman emperors had appointed priests, abbots, and bishops. Gregory claimed that only the church had this right. After disputes over several church appointments, Henry called a council of bishops and declared the pope deposed. In response, Gregory excommunicated Henry and released his subjects from obedience to him. Because many of the German princes supported the pope, Henry submitted to Gregory at the castle of Canossa in 1077. But the dispute flared up again. In 1080, Gregory again excommunicated Henry and declared him deposed. No pope had ever tried to depose an emperor. That year, Henry and a council of German bishops elected an antipope, Clement III. Henry had him crowned pope in 1084 after the emperor captured Rome. Gregory died in exile in 1085.

Gregory was born in Tuscany, Italy. His given name was Hildebrand.   Kenneth Pennington

See also **Henry IV** (Holy Roman emperor); **Pope** (The peak of papal power).

Gregory IX (about 1155-1241) was elected pope in 1227. His most important accomplishment was publishing the first complete and authoritative collection of papal decrees in 1234. This collection remained the fundamental law of the Roman Catholic Church until a revised code was issued in 1917.

Gregory was born in Anagni, Italy. His given name was Ugolino. His uncle, Pope Innocent III, promoted him to the rank of cardinal in 1198. Gregory was the cardinal protector of the Franciscans, and he furthered the growth of the order before and after he became pope.

Gregory came into frequent conflict with Holy Roman Emperor Frederick II. Frederick had promised repeatedly to lead a crusade to the Holy Land. After he broke his promise again in 1227, Gregory excommunicated him. The next year, in spite of being excommunicated, Frederick led a successful crusade. Gregory concluded a peace treaty with Frederick in 1230. The pope renewed his excommunication in 1239 as part of the battle between the papacy and the empire for control of Italy.

Kenneth Pennington

Gregory X (1210-1276) was elected pope in 1271, after the office had been vacant for almost three years. He issued an important reform decree that regulated papal elections to avoid long vacancies in the future. See **Pope** (The election of a pope [Early days]).

Gregory was born in Piacenza, Italy. His given and family name was Tedaldo Visconti. A deeply religious man of great intellect, he studied theology in Paris. Gregory was in the Holy Land when he learned of his election as pope. He soon called for a general council at Lyons. He hoped that the council would revive the crusading movement and liberate Jerusalem from the Muslims. He also invited delegates from the Byzantine emperor to the council. Gregory hoped to reunite the Greek and Roman churches, which formally split in 1054. He encouraged the German princes to elect a new Holy Roman emperor because the throne had been vacant since 1250. In 1273, the princes elected Rudolf of Habsburg.   Kenneth Pennington

Gregory XIII (1502-1585) was elected pope in 1572 and devoted his reign to Catholic reform. As pope, he gave priority to improving the education of Catholic clergy. Through his efforts, the church set up many seminaries for the training of parish priests. He greatly enlarged the Roman College in Rome, which later became known as the Gregorian University in his honor. These actions helped stop the Protestant advance in Germany and made Poland a Catholic country.

In 1575, Gregory gave approval to the Oratorians religious order, founded by Saint Philip Neri. Gregory encouraged missionary work by the Jesuit order in China, India, Japan, and Brazil. His most famous act was replacing the outmoded Julian calendar with the more accurate Gregorian calendar in 1582.

Gregory was born in Bologna, Italy. His given and family name was Ugo Buoncompagni. Pope Pius IV named him a cardinal in 1565.   Charles L. Stinger

See also **Calendar** (The Gregorian calendar).

Gregory, Dick (1932-   ), is a black American entertainer who gained fame for his satirical views on American racial attitudes. He later became an author, civil rights leader, and business executive.

Gregory was born in St. Louis, Missouri. He began his professional career in 1958 as a master of ceremonies at several Chicago nightclubs. Gregory wrote several books of racial humor, including *From the Back of the Bus* (1964), *nigger* (1964), and *Write Me In* (1968). Also during the 1960's, Gregory became active in civil rights. He believed that the Federal Bureau of Investigation played a role in the assassination of civil rights leader Martin Luther King, Jr., in 1968. Gregory's personal study into the matter resulted in his book *Code Name "Zorro"* (1978). A congressional investigation disagreed with his theory. Gregory was an outspoken critic of American involvement in the Vietnam War (1957-1975). In the 1980's, he became a successful businessman in the area of health and nutrition.   Hanes Walton, Jr.

Gregory, Lady (1852-1932), an Irish playwright and folklorist, helped launch the renaissance in Irish drama associated with Dublin's Abbey Theatre. She excelled in writing lively dialogue and creating simple, strong dramatic situations. Her best-known plays include *The Rising of the Moon, Spreading the News,* and *The Workhouse Ward* (all 1904-1908).

Isabella Augusta Persse was born in County Galway and married Sir William Gregory in 1881. She wrote most of her plays in "Kiltartan," the peasant dialect of her home district. She collected Irish folklore and poetry, pioneered in the use of peasant dialect, and invented the folk history play. Her retelling of the Celtic heroic myths in *Cuchulain of Muirthemne* (1902) and *Gods and Fighting Men* (1904) inspired many Irish writers, especially William Butler Yeats. *Seventy Years,* an autobiography, was published in 1976, after her death.   Edward Hirsch

Gremlin, *GREHM luhn,* is a small imaginary creature that supposedly causes mechanical problems in airplanes. Gremlins may have been originated by British pilots during World War I (1914-1918). They became most famous during World War II (1939-1945). Since then, the term *gremlin* has come to mean a source of trouble in many fields besides aviation.   Alan Dundes

Grenada, *grih NAY duh,* is an island nation in the West Indies. It lies in the Caribbean Sea, about 90 miles (140 kilometers) north of Venezuela. The island of Grenada makes up most of the country. The country also includes several tiny islands near the main island. In addition, it includes Carriacou—which lies about 17 miles (27 kilometers) northeast of the main island—and several other small islands of the Grenadine chain.

Grenada has a population of about 95,000 and a land area of 133 square miles (344 square kilometers). Its tropical climate and beautiful scenery and beaches attract many tourists. The nation is a leading producer of nutmeg and other spices. St. George's is the capital and largest city of Grenada. The East Caribbean dollar is the basic unit of currency. For a picture of the Grenadian flag, see **Flag** (Flags of the Americas). Grenada was a dependency of Britain from the late 1700's until 1974, when it gained independence.

Grenada

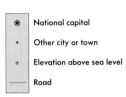

* ⊛ National capital
* • Other city or town
* + Elevation above sea level
* —— Road

Carriacou lies about 17 miles (27 kilometers) northeast of Grenada.

WORLD BOOK maps

People. About 95 percent of Grenada's people are of African or mixed African and European ancestry. Descendants of East Indians or of Europeans make up the rest of the population. The majority of Grenadians speak English, the nation's official language, or a *dialect* (local form) of English. A French-African *patois* (mixture of languages) is also commonly spoken. More than half the population are Roman Catholics. Other religious groups include Anglicans, Methodists, and Seventh-day Adventists.

Children between the ages of 6 and 14 must attend school. Grenada's government provides most of the funding for the country's many public and technical schools. Grenada is home to a branch of the University of the West Indies.

Land and climate. The mountainous, thickly forested countryside of the main island of Grenada has many gorges and waterfalls. Grand Etang, a lake in the crater of a volcano, lies near the center of the island.

Temperatures in Grenada seldom fall below 65 °F (18 °C) in winter or rise above 90 °F (32 °C) in summer. The coast of the mainland receives up to 60 inches (150 centimeters) of rainfall each year. The mountain regions receive up to 200 inches (510 centimeters). The dry season in Grenada extends from January until May.

Economy of Grenada is based chiefly on agriculture and tourism. The nation has few factories. The standard of living remains low because most Grenadians either cannot find work or must work for low wages. The is-

land's chief exports include bananas, cocoa, nutmeg, and a spice called *mace*. Other products include coconut, cotton, limes, and sugar cane. Grenada needs many products made in other countries, and so it imports more than it exports. St. George's is the chief port, but the country also has several smaller ports.

Britain, Canada, and the United States rank as Grenada's leading trade partners. In 1974, Grenada sought to increase trade with its neighbors by joining the Caribbean Community and Common Market (CARICOM), an economic union of nations.

Grenada has about 600 miles (970 kilometers) of roads, most of which are surfaced. The nation has two airports and bus service but no railroads. Five newspapers and a radio station serve the island.

History and government. Arawak Indians were the first people to live in what is now Grenada. During the 1300's, Carib Indians from South America took over the main island. In 1498, Christopher Columbus became the first European explorer to land there. He named it *Concepcion,* but other Europeans later called it Grenada. The Caribs defeated early European efforts to colonize Grenada. In 1650, the French claimed Grenada and later slaughtered many of the Indians. Some Caribs killed themselves rather than submit to French rule.

Control of Grenada shifted between France and Britain several times before the island became a British colony in 1783. Through the years, European planters brought many African slaves to work on plantations there. After the British ended slavery in 1833, East Indians came to work in Grenada.

In the mid-1900's, the British gave Grenada some control over its own affairs. In the early 1970's, Prime Minister Eric M. Gairy led a movement for independence. Political unrest developed because some groups opposed independence and accused Gairy of becoming a dictator. Grenada gained independence in 1974. The new country became a constitutional monarchy and joined the Commonwealth of Nations. A prime minister headed the government. A governor general, a symbolic official, was appointed by the British monarch.

Gairy served as prime minister of Grenada until 1979, when rebels led by Maurice Bishop overthrew his government. The rebels set up a new government and named Bishop prime minister. Bishop, a Marxist, estab-

Shostal
St. George's, the scenic capital of Grenada, lies among thickly forested hills on the island's southwest coast.

lished close ties with Cuba and adopted a number of leftist policies. But some other rebels denounced him for not adopting a complete Marxist system. In 1983, rebels took over the government and killed Bishop.

Other Caribbean nations feared Grenada would be used as a base by Cuba and the Soviet Union to support terrorism and leftist revolutions in Latin America. Soon after Bishop was killed, several Caribbean nations asked the United States to help restore order in Grenada.

On Oct. 25, 1983, U.S. troops invaded Grenada. U.S. President Ronald Reagan said the action was necessary to protect the lives of Americans in Grenada, including nearly 600 students at St. George's University School of Medicine. Troops from six Caribbean nations also took part in the invasion. The nations were Antigua and Barbuda, Barbados, Dominica, Jamaica, St. Lucia, and St. Vincent and the Grenadines. The multinational force quickly took major objectives, including an airport being constructed at Point Salines with Cuban assistance. After several days, the multinational force took complete control of Grenada. By December 15, all U.S. troops had been pulled out of the country. About 250 noncombat U.S. military personnel remained in Grenada until 1985 to maintain law and order.

After the fighting ended, Sir Paul Godwin Scoon, governor general of Grenada, took temporary control of the government. He appointed a nine-member advisory council to help him rule the country. In 1984, Grenada's democratically elected government was restored. A prime minister again headed the government. The government ended the leftist policies that the Marxist government had adopted. Gerald R. Showalter

See also **Grenadines; Saint George's; West Indies**.

Grenade is a small explosive bomb that may be thrown, or may be fired from a rifle. *Fragmentation* grenades contain a coil of notched square wire that shatters when the grenades explode. *Chemical* grenades are filled with gas, smoke, or white phosphorus, which burns with a hot, smoky fire. *Illuminating* grenades are used at night to light up land areas.

Grenades were used in the 1400's. In the 1600's and 1700's, specially trained soldiers called *grenadiers* used them. Today, grenades are a common weapon of all infantry soldiers. Frances M. Lussier

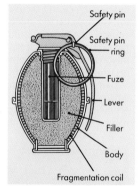

Safety pin
Safety pin ring
Fuze
Lever
Filler
Body
Fragmentation coil

A grenade explodes seconds after the ring is pulled and the lever is released.

See also **Bomb; Fragmentation**.

Grenadines, *GREHN uh DEENZ,* make up a chain of over 100 small and mostly uninhabited islands in the West Indies. The Grenadines stretch for about 60 miles (97 kilometers) across the Caribbean Sea between the islands of St. Vincent and Grenada. For location, see **West Indies** (map). They have a population of about 10,000 and a total land area of about 32 square miles (83 square kilometers). Carriacou, which covers 13 square miles (34 square kilometers), is the largest island of the group.

The Grenadines from Carriacou southward and the island of Grenada form the nation of Grenada. The Grenadines from Union Island northward and the island of St. Vincent make up the nation of St. Vincent and the Grenadines. See **Grenada; Saint Vincent and the Grenadines**.

The Grenadines were settled by the French in the 1600's but came under British control in 1763. The southern islands and Grenada gained independence in 1974. The northern islands and St. Vincent did so in 1979. Gerald R. Showalter

Grenfell, Sir Wilfred Thomason (1865-1940), a British medical missionary, became known as Grenfell of Labrador. He helped establish hospitals, orphanages, nursing stations, schools, and cooperative stores in the cold, bleak regions near the Arctic Circle.

Grenfell was born in Cheshire, England. He studied medicine at Oxford University and at the London Hospital. During the late 1880's, he entered the medical service of the Royal National Mission to Deep Sea Fishermen, and sailed on fishing cruises from the Bay of Biscay to Iceland. In 1892, Grenfell was sent with hospital supplies to explore health conditions in Labrador and Newfoundland. He found much illness, especially beriberi and tuberculosis, and hardly anyone to give medical care. The following year, he established the first hospital of the Labrador Medical Mission at Battle Harbour. He also organized a program that enabled medical students and other volunteers to work in this remote region. Grenfell worked in the area until 1935, when ill health forced his retirement. Kenneth R. Manning

Grenoble, *gruh NOH buhl* (pop. 153,973; met. area pop. 400,141), is a manufacturing city in southeastern France. It is the capital of the Isère *department* (administrative district). Grenoble lies along the Isère River in a valley of the French Alps (see **France** [political map]).

The beauty of the nearby Alps, skiing areas there, and numerous medieval buildings in Grenoble attract many tourists to the city. Grenoble's landmarks include the University of Grenoble, the Cathedral of Notre Dame, and the Church of St. André. Grenoble is the chief manufacturing center of its region. Its products include cement, chemicals, metals, plastics, processed foods, textiles, and turbines. The city is a major producer of hydroelectric power. It also has many scientific laboratories and ranks as one of France's leading centers of scientific research.

The Gauls, an ancient European people, had founded a village on the site of what is now Grenoble by 400 B.C. From the 1100's to the 1300's, the city was the capital of the independent state of Dauphine. Grenoble served as the site of the 1968 Winter Olympics. Mark Kesselman

Grenville, Sir Richard (1542-1591), an English naval commander, led Sir Walter Raleigh's first colonizing expedition to America. He helped establish the first English colony there, on Roanoke Island, in 1585. Grenville sailed back to England later that year. In 1586, he returned to the colony with supplies, but it had been abandoned shortly before he arrived (see **Lost Colony**).

Grenville commanded a squadron against the Spanish Armada in 1588 (see **Spanish Armada**). In 1591, he took part in an expedition under Lord Thomas Howard to intercept a Spanish treasure fleet near the Azores Islands.

A large Spanish fleet surprised the expedition off the island of Flores. Howard withdrew with the majority of the English ships. But Grenville, then vice admiral, was killed when his ship, the *Revenge,* could not break through the Spanish fleet.

Grenville was born near Bideford, Devonshire. He was knighted in 1577. Richard L. Greaves

Gresham's law is an economic principle dealing with the circulation of money. The law states that "bad money tends to drive out good money." It was named after Sir Thomas Gresham, an English treasury official of the 1500's, though other people had noted the same principle earlier. Gresham's law applies, for example, where coins have equal face value but hold different amounts of metal or metal of unequal worth. People will spend the lighter or cheaper coins (the "bad money") before the heavier or more precious ones (the "good money").

Gresham's law often came into play in the past, when coins were made of gold, silver, or other precious metals. Dishonest people shaved slivers of valuable metal from the edges of coins before spending them. People who received the lighter coins passed them on quickly and saved any heavier ones they got.

Gold and silver were legal money in the United States during the late 1700's and much of the 1800's. Under this system, the value of gold coins in relation to silver ones was fixed by law. But the market price of gold and silver rose and fell in relation to demand for and availability of the metals. Gold coins usually were worth more than their face value, and silver coins usually worth less. As a result, people hoarded, melted down, or exported gold coins. Thus, gold disappeared from circulation.

In a related way, U.S. dimes and quarters minted in 1965 or later drove earlier dimes and quarters out of circulation. This occurred because the pre-1965 coins were made from more valuable metals. Richard C. Wiles

Gretzky, Wayne (1961-   ), became the greatest scorer in the history of the National Hockey League (NHL). During his 20-year career, Gretzky scored 2,857 points on 894 goals and 1,963 assists, all NHL records. Gretzky led the NHL in scoring 10 times and was named the league's most valuable player 9 times. In the 1981-1982 season, Gretzky became the first player to score 200 points in one season. His 92 goals that year set another NHL record. In the 1985-1986 season, he scored 163 assists, another record. His 215 points that season set a scoring record. Gretzky also holds several playoff scoring records, including most points during a single year (47), set in 1985.

Gretzky was born in Brantford, Ontario. A center, he began his professional career with the Indianapolis Racers of the World Hockey Association (WHA) in 1978. He joined the Edmonton Oilers of the WHA later in 1978. After the 1978-1979 season, the WHA disbanded and the Oilers joined the NHL.

In 1980—at age 19— Gretzky became the youngest player to receive

AP/Wide World

Wayne Gretzky

the Hart Memorial Trophy as the most valuable player in the NHL. In 1988, Gretzky was traded to the Los Angeles Kings. Los Angeles traded him to the St. Louis Blues in 1996. After the end of the 1995-1996 season, Gretzky signed with the New York Rangers as a free agent. He retired after the 1998-1999 regular season. Larry Wigge

Grey, Earl (1851-1917), a British diplomat, served as governor general of Canada from 1904 to 1911. Under his administration, Alberta and Saskatchewan became provinces in 1905. Grey used his warm personal charm to promote unity and understanding among English- and French-speaking Canadians. He was very popular and became one of the few governors general of the era to complete a full term. In 1909, he donated the Grey Cup, a trophy that today goes to the annual champion of the Canadian Football League. See **Grey Cup.**

Albert Henry George Grey was born in London. In 1880, he was elected to the British Parliament. A Liberal, Grey served until 1886. In 1894, he succeeded his uncle to become the fourth Earl Grey. Jacques Monet

Grey, Lady Jane (1537-1554), became known as "the nine-day queen" of England. She was the great-granddaughter of King Henry VII of England, and daughter of Henry Grey, Duke of Suffolk. At the age of 15, she married Lord Guildford Dudley, son of the Duke of Northumberland. The Duke of Northumberland persuaded King Edward VI to give Lady Jane the right to succeed him as ruler. Edward feared that if the crown should descend to his half sister Mary, who was a Roman Catholic, England would no longer be a Protestant nation. Edward died on July 6, 1553. His death was kept secret for several days, and Lady Jane was proclaimed queen on July 10. But on July 19, Mary's claims to the throne were recognized. Lady Jane, who had not wanted the crown, was imprisoned in the Tower of London and charged with high treason. Later, Mary suspected Jane was involved in an uprising against her led by Sir Thomas Wyatt, an English soldier. Mary had Jane and her husband beheaded on Feb. 12, 1554. Lady Jane Grey was born in Bradgate, near Leicester. Richard L. Greaves

See also **Mary I.**

Grey, Zane (1872-1939), ranks as one of the most popular authors in American literature of novels about the Wild West. Grey wrote more than 50 novels.

In Grey's books, the heroes and heroines overcome the challenges of the West. They learn to tame and use nature, and they fight to protect loved ones. The characters achieve maturity in the process. Grey has been criticized for creating unrealistic characters and predictable plots. But his best novels reflect careful research and provide authentic details about Western life.

In 1907, Grey traveled through the West with a retired buffalo hunter. The trip inspired Grey to begin writing Westerns. His first success was *The Heritage of the Desert* (1910). Some critics have judged his next book, *Riders of the Purple Sage* (1912), to be the best Western ever written. In his last best seller, *Forlorn River* (1927), Grey created his most memorable hero, Jim (Nevada) Lacy. Grey was born in Zanesville, Ohio. Arthur R. Huseboe

Grey Cup is a Canadian professional football trophy. It goes to the winner of the annual play-off game between the champions of the two divisions of the Canadian Football League (CFL). Earl Grey, a Canadian governor general, donated the cup in 1909 for "the amateur rugby

Grey Cup winners

Year	Team	Year	Team
1909	University of Toronto	1957	Hamilton
1910	University of Toronto	1958	Winnipeg
1911	University of Toronto	1959	Winnipeg
1912	Hamilton	1960	Ottawa
1913	Hamilton	1961	Winnipeg
1914	Toronto	1962	Winnipeg
1915	Hamilton	1963	Hamilton
1916-1919	No Games—World War I	1964	British Columbia
1920	University of Toronto	1965	Hamilton
1921	Toronto	1966	Saskatchewan
1922	Queen's University	1967	Hamilton
1923	Queen's University	1968	Ottawa
1924	Queen's University	1969	Ottawa
1925	Ottawa	1970	Montreal
1926	Ottawa	1971	Calgary
1927	Toronto Balmy Beach	1972	Hamilton
1928	Hamilton	1973	Ottawa
1929	Hamilton	1974	Montreal
1930	Toronto Balmy Beach	1975	Edmonton
1931	Montreal	1976	Ottawa
1932	Hamilton	1977	Montreal
1933	Toronto	1978	Edmonton
1934	Sarnia	1979	Edmonton
1935	Winnipeg	1980	Edmonton
1936	Sarnia	1981	Edmonton
1937	Toronto	1982	Edmonton
1938	Toronto	1983	Toronto
1939	Winnipeg	1984	Winnipeg
1940	Ottawa	1985	British Columbia
1941	Winnipeg	1986	Hamilton
1942	Toronto	1987	Edmonton
1943	Hamilton	1988	Winnipeg
1944	Montreal	1989	Saskatchewan
1945	Toronto	1990	Winnipeg
1946	Toronto	1991	Toronto
1947	Toronto	1992	Calgary
1948	Calgary	1993	Edmonton
1949	Montreal	1994	British Columbia
1950	Toronto	1995	Baltimore
1951	Ottawa	1996	Toronto
1952	Toronto	1997	Toronto
1953	Hamilton	1998	Calgary
1954	Edmonton	1999	Hamilton
1955	Edmonton	2000	British Columbia
1956	Edmonton		

football championship of Canada." Any amateur, college, or semiprofessional team registered with the Canadian Rugby Union could compete. But since 1954, only professional football teams have played for the Grey Cup. The CFL gained permanent possession of the cup in 1966.   William F. Reed

See also **Football** (Canadian football); **Grey, Earl.**

Grey Owl (1888-1938) was the Indian name of Archibald Stansfeld Belaney, an adopted Ojibwa who gained fame as a wildlife writer and lecturer. Grey Owl's books and lectures were popular during the 1930's, particularly in England, and stirred interest in conservation. Grey Owl wrote mainly about beavers. *Tales of an Empty Cabin* (1936) is considered one of his best books.

Belaney was born in Hastings, England. He moved to Canada at the age of 18 and became a guide in northern Ontario. In 1907, he joined a band of Ojibwa Indians, who later adopted him and gave him the name Grey Owl. He became a trapper, but he eventually abandoned the profession, which he came to view as a violent trade that was destroying animal species. He began writing as a career in 1929. Grey Owl's identity as an Englishman rather than an Indian was not generally known until after his death.   Rosemary Sullivan

Greyhound is one of the fastest of all dogs. It originated more than 5,000 years ago in Egypt, where it was used to hunt gazelles. Greyhounds also were once used to hunt game in North America, especially on the Kansas plains. The dogs hunted mainly by sight and chased down the game animal. Today, greyhounds compete in track racing, in which they chase a mechanical lure on an oval track. See **Dog racing** (with picture).

A greyhound is a strong and elegant animal. It has a streamlined body, a long head, an arched flank, a slender waist, and strong, powerful legs. It has a short coat that may be gray, white, black, yellowish-brown, reddish, or bluish-gray, or a mixture of colors. The animal weighs 60 to 70 pounds (27 to 30 kilograms).

Greyhounds used in track racing are registered with the National Greyhound Association in Abilene, Kansas. Greyhounds bred for show are registered with the American Kennel Club in New York City.

Critically reviewed by the Greyhound Club of America

See also **Dog** (picture: Hounds).

Grieg, *greeg,* **Edvard** (1843-1907), was a Norwegian composer. He wrote much of his music in the style of Norwegian folk songs and folk dances. Grieg's works include songs, music for chorus and orchestra, and numbers for small instrumental groups. Many of his compositions feature expressive melodies and original rhythms and harmonies.

Grieg's most famous music includes such compositions for piano as the 10-volume *Lyric Pieces.* This work includes a number of well-known pieces—"Album-Leaf" (1867), "To Spring" (1886), and "Wedding Day at Troldhaugen" (1896). Grieg was also noted for his *Concerto in A Minor* (1869) for piano and orchestra. The *Peer Gynt* suite (1876), Grieg's most famous orchestral work, includes "Morning," "Anitra's Dance," and "In the Hall of the Mountain King." This suite was arranged from the music that Grieg wrote for Henrik Ibsen's play *Peer Gynt.*

Edvard Hagerup Grieg was born in Bergen, Norway, and became a skillful pianist as a boy. At the age of 15, he enrolled at the Conservatory in Leipzig, Germany. He graduated in 1862 and traveled to Copenhagen, Denmark, in 1863. There he met the young Norwegian composer Rikard Nordraak. Grieg and Nordraak hoped to establish a Norwegian school of composition, but Nordraak died in 1866.

After Nordraak's death, Grieg returned to Norway. In 1867, he founded the Norwegian Academy of Music in Christiania (now Oslo), the capital of Norway. That year, Grieg married his cousin, Nina Hagerup. He wrote many songs for her, including "I Love Thee" (1864). Grieg lived in Christiania from 1866 to 1874 and became famous as a composer and conductor.   R. M. Longyear

Griffey, Ken, Jr. (1969-   ), ranks among the most exciting players in baseball. As a batter, Griffey combines power with the ability to hit for a high average. His speed has made him one of the finest outfielders in baseball. He won nine consecutive Gold Glove awards from 1991 to 1999 for his defensive play. Griffey played with the Seattle Mariners of the American League from 1989 until he was traded in 2000 to the Cincinnati Reds of the National League. He led the American League in home runs in 1994 with 40; in 1997 and 1998, hitting 56 home runs both years; and in 1999, hitting 48. In 1997, Griffey also led the major leagues in runs batted in with

147, and led the American League in runs scored with 125. He was named the league's Most Valuable Player that year. Griffey bats and throws left-handed.

George Kenneth Griffey, Jr., was born in Donora, Pennsylvania. His father, Ken Griffey, Sr., played in the major leagues from 1973 to 1991. They were the first father and son to play in the major leagues at the same time. Seattle selected the younger Griffey as the first player in the 1987 free agent draft. He played in the minor leagues for two seasons before becoming a regular with Seattle in 1989. Dave Nightingale

Griffin was a strange creature of Greek mythology, with the head and wings of an eagle and the body of a lion. In Scythia, a country northeast of Greece, the griffins guarded a great store of gold from the Arimaspians, who were constantly trying to steal it. Mary R. Lefkowitz

Griffith, Arthur (1872-1922), an Irish journalist and politician, was a leader in Ireland's fight for independence from Britain. In 1905, he founded the *Sinn Féin* (we ourselves) society, which played a prominent role in the Irish independence movement. Griffith believed Ireland would gain independence only through *passive resistance* (nonviolent opposition). In 1916, however, he supported the Easter Rebellion, a weeklong armed revolt that sought to establish an independent Ireland. A full-scale guerrilla war followed from 1919 through 1921. In this conflict, the rebels forced Britain to grant *dominion home rule* to most of Ireland. Under this arrangement, 26 counties became the *Irish Free State* within the British Commonwealth. Griffith served briefly as the new state's provisional leader before his death in 1922. He was born in Dublin. Thomas E. Hachey

See also **Ireland** (The Easter Rising); **Sinn Féin**.

Griffith, D. W. (1875-1948), was a pioneer American motion-picture director and producer. Between 1908 and 1912, he developed basic strategies that helped turn filmmaking into a popular narrative art. His principal contributions included his skillful methods of *editing* (linking scenes within a film). His major period as a filmmaker extended from 1913 to 1924.

David Wark Griffith was born near Crestwood, Kentucky. He acted in stage plays and managed stage companies before entering the motion-picture industry in 1908. Griffith's most famous film was the historical spectacle *The Birth of a Nation* (1915), which deals with the American Civil War and the rise of the Ku Klux Klan. His next film, *Intolerance* (1916), was a lengthy epic covering four historical periods. It offered more spectacle, but was less successful with audiences than *The Birth of a Nation.* His other major silent films include *Broken Blossoms* (1919), *Way Down East* (1920), and *Orphans of the Storm* (1921). Griffith directed two sound films, *Abraham Lincoln* (1930) and *The Struggle* (1931). Robert Sklar

See also **Motion picture** (D. W. Griffith).

Grimes, Martha (1931-   ), is an American author famous for detective novels with an English background. Her novels feature Inspector Richard Jury of Scotland Yard and aristocratic amateur detective Melrose Plant.

The first Richard Jury novel was *The Man with a Load of Mischief* (1981). Later novels in the series include *The Old Fox Deceiv'd* (1982), *The Anodyne Necklace* (1983), *The Dirty Duck* (1984), *Jerusalem Inn* (1984), *Help the Poor Struggler* (1985), *The Deer Leap* (1985), *I Am the Only Running Footman* (1986), *The Five Bells and Blade-*

bone (1987), *The Old Silent* (1989), *The Old Contemptibles* (1991), and *The Lamorna Wink* (1999). Grimes's first book with an American background was *The End of the Pier* (1992). It concerns a small-town police chief's search for a mass killer. She also wrote another suspense novel with an American background, *Biting the Moon* (1999). In addition, Grimes wrote *Send Bygraves* (1989), a satire of the classical detective novel. She was born in Pittsburgh, Pennsylvania. Jon L. Breen

Grimké, *GRIHM kee,* was the family name of two sisters who became abolitionists and pioneers in the women's rights movement in the United States. Sarah and Angelina Grimké were born in Charleston, South Carolina. Their father, John F. Grimké, was a chief judge of South Carolina. Their mother, Mary Smith Grimké, came from a leading family in South Carolina politics.

The Grimké sisters became active in the abolitionist movement during the mid-1830's. They gave antislavery lectures in several Northeastern states and were among the first women to lecture in public in the United States.

Bettmann Archive   Historical Pictures Service

Sarah Grimké   **Angelina Grimké**

Their speeches and writings against slavery attracted considerable attention, especially because the sisters were refined, wealthy women from the South.

The Grimké sisters began fighting for women's rights after many people criticized their role in the abolitionist movement as shocking behavior for women. Their vigorous defense of women's rights helped cause a split among abolitionists. The Grimké sisters argued that the fight for women's rights and the fight for abolition both supported human rights. But other abolitionists considered the women's rights issue unrelated to abolitionism. They feared that the antislavery movement would be weakened by any connection between the two groups.

Sarah Moore Grimké (1792-1873) left Charleston in 1821 because of her strong antislavery beliefs and moved to Philadelphia. She joined the abolitionist movement in 1836, a year after Angelina did so. Later in 1836, Sarah published an antislavery pamphlet called *Epistle to the Clergy of the Southern States.* Her *Letters on the Equality of the Sexes and the Condition of Woman* (1838) was one of the first essays by an American on women's equality. See **Feminism**.

Angelina Emily Grimké (1805-1879) joined Sarah in Philadelphia in 1829 and became a lecturer for the American Anti-Slavery Society. In the pamphlet *Appeal to the Christian Women of the South* (1836), Angelina urged women to fight slavery. In 1838, she married the abolitionist Theodore Weld and retired from public life.

Sarah also retired and moved in with the Welds. The Grimké sisters continued to work occasionally for both the abolitionist and women's rights movements.

Keith E. Melder

Grimm is the family name of two German brothers, **Jakob Ludwig Grimm** (1785-1863) and **Wilhelm Karl Grimm** (1786-1859). They are scholars known for their collection of German fairy tales and for their work in establishing the *German Dictionary.* Jakob Grimm is also known for his great work, the *German Grammar.*

The Grimms were influenced by the German romantic movement (see **Romanticism**). Their chief area of research was German *antiquity* (olden times). Living in a time of cultural, political, and social change, they hoped that their studies might awaken national pride and purpose.

Jakob studied the historical development of literature, law, and language. His work is basic to the study of historical *linguistics* (the science of language). In his chief work, the *German Grammar* (1819-1837), he compared different Germanic and other European languages and stages of language development. One of the main results was the set of sound correspondences called *Grimm's Law.* The law is basic to the later development of comparative linguistics (see **Linguistics** [Comparative and historical linguistics]). Wilhelm was most directly responsible for editing the *Fairy Tales* (1812, 1815). He also wrote valuable introductions to medieval literature, which he edited.

The work of the brothers on the *German Dictionary* was a pioneer effort that has served as a model for later *lexicographers* (dictionary writers). The Grimms worked on it from 1838 until their deaths. It was finally completed by scholars in the mid-1900's.

The Grimms were born in Hanau. They studied law at the University of Marburg and came into contact there and at Heidelberg with some of the leading romanticists. They held several positions as librarians and professors in the 1820's and 1830's. In 1840, they became members of the Academy of Sciences in Berlin and received professorships at the University of Berlin. Jakob also served in several diplomatic positions during his life and was a member of the Parliament of Frankfurt in 1848. The brothers remained in Berlin until their deaths and lived and worked together nearly all their lives.

James M. McGlathery

Grimmelshausen, Hans Jakob Christoffel von (1622?-1676), was a German author. His novel *Simplicius Simplicissimus* (1668) is one of the major works of German literature. In it, he described the adventures of a youth caught in the Thirty Years' War (1618-1648). The youth finally gains peace of soul as a hermit.

Grimmelshausen was born in Gelnhausen. As a youth, he apparently lost his parents in the Thirty Years' War and was taken from his home as a prisoner. These experiences seem to have been the beginning of a colorful series of adventures which he wove into his many prose works. James F. Poag

See also **German literature** (Baroque literature).

Grimm's Fairy Tales is a famous collection of German folk tales. Most of them were collected by two brothers, Jakob and Wilhelm Grimm. The most famous tales include "Hansel and Gretel," "Little Red Riding Hood," "Snow-White," "Rumpelstiltskin," "Sleeping Beauty," "Cinderella," and "Rapunzel." As the Grimms knew, some of their stories had been previously published, especially in Italy and France.

Between 1807 and 1814, the Grimms collected the tales mainly from friends and acquaintances who lived in and around Kassel, Germany. The brothers published the tales to preserve work they believed was created by the people. They regarded the tales as an expression of the spirit of the German people, and they worried that fewer and fewer people could tell the tales accurately.

The Grimms tried to retell the stories faithfully, but made changes to suit public taste or their ideas about how to tell the tales most effectively. The brothers gathered many tales themselves, including those stories told to them by a woman who came to town to sell produce.

The first volume (1812) contained 86 tales. The second (1815) contained 70. Jakob spent much time helping Wilhelm collect tales for the first volume, but the second volume and later editions were largely Wilhelm's work. By the last edition of 1857, there were 210 tales. The Grimms collected most of the last stories, as well as some from the first edition, from printed sources.

In collecting the tales, the Grimms were influenced by the romantic movement in German literature (see **Romanticism**). German romanticism expressed itself in many ways, but it dealt primarily with German history and mythology, nature, fantasy, and the supernatural. All these elements appear in the Grimms' fairy tales.

James M. McGlathery

Additional resources

Kamenetsky, Christa. *The Brothers Grimm and Their Critics: Folktales and the Quest for Meaning.* Ohio Univ. Pr., 1992.
Wenzel, David, and Wheeler, Doug. *Fairy Tales of the Brothers Grimm.* NBM, 1995. Younger readers.
Zipes, Jack D., ed. *The Complete Fairy Tales of the Brothers Grimm.* 1987. Reprint. Bantam, 1992.

Grinding and polishing are two important manufacturing processes. Grinding uses abrasives to remove material, and polishing uses them to smooth surfaces.

Granger Collection

Jakob and Wilhelm Grimm collected fairy stories.

Grinding probably ranks as the earliest of all manufacturing processes. Its use goes back to prehistoric times, when ancient people shaped stone tools by rubbing them against hard, rough stones or other kinds of abrasive materials.

Grinding

Grinding tools. Most grinding is done by abrasive wheels that rotate at high speed, or by power-driven cloth or paper belts coated with an abrasive.

Grinding wheels are available in many sizes and with a wide range of abrasive grains from coarse to fine. Manufacturers use *coarse* wheels for rough grinding, *medium* wheels for general sharpening and grinding, and *fine* wheels for finished grinding on products that must have an extremely smooth surface.

The most common abrasives are silicon carbide, used for grinding hard, brittle materials such as cast iron; and aluminum oxide, a tougher abrasive used for tool steel and wrought iron. Various cementing materials bond the abrasive grains together into a wheel. In most wheels, the bonding material is clay. The clay is mixed with the abrasive grains and heated so that it becomes glasslike. Water and high temperatures do not affect it. Other bonding materials include common water glass (sodium silicate), plastic resins, and rubber.

Grinding belts use the same abrasives as wheels, as well as such natural abrasives as crushed garnet and flint. Belts grind metals, glass, and ceramics.

Grinding methods. The chief grinding methods include (1) offhand grinding, (2) surface grinding, (3) cylindrical grinding, and (4) abrasive wheel cutting.

Offhand grinding is the simplest method of grinding. The worker holds the material against the rotating wheel or belt. If the work is too large to be held conveniently, the worker may use a small motor-driven grinder and leave the material stationary. Manufacturers use offhand grinding chiefly to sharpen such hand tools as chisels, knives, and drills, and to remove roughness and projections from metal castings.

Surface grinding produces a smooth, accurate flat surface on machine parts, tools, and dies. Surface grinding machines may have the axis of the wheel either horizontal or vertical to the surface of the work. In the *horizontal* type of surface grinder, the work is attached to a table that moves back and forth at a right angle to the axis of the wheel. The *vertical* type uses a cup-shaped wheel. This type often has a large, rotating table to which the work is attached. The table rotates slowly so that the finished work may be removed and the new work attached in a single continuous operation.

Cylindrical grinding is used to finish accurately the outer surface of shafts, pistons, and other cylindrical machine parts. This is called *external* grinding. Manufacturers also use *internal* cylindrical grinding to finish such parts as the insides of automobile cylinders. Cylindrical grinding can be done on a lathe or on a special grinding machine, usually one with a grinding wheel.

Abrasive wheel cutting uses a narrow grinding wheel, usually bonded with rubber. The wheel rotates at a high speed. A cooling liquid keeps the work and the tool from overheating. Abrasive wheels do fast, smooth work in cutting steel shafts and bars.

Polishing

Polishing, also called *buffing*, is usually done with wheels made of cloth, felt, or leather coated with a fine abrasive such as a fine grade of silicon carbide or aluminum oxide. For finer work, wheels coated with *jewelers' rouge,* a fine ferric-oxide powder, or *tripoli,* a type of silica, may be used.

In some polishing, manufacturers use abrasive belts or a special polishing wheel made of soft rubber with abrasive grains molded in it. The rubber wears away just fast enough to prevent the wheel from becoming clogged or glazed on the surface. Most polishing on irregularly shaped pieces is done by hand. For big jobs, such as finishing stainless-steel sheets, manufacturers use large, high-speed machines.   Mihir K. Das

See also **Machine tool** (Abrasive processes); **Whetstone.**

John Lei, Stock, Boston

Polishing machines, such as the one shown above, have an abrasive belt that buffs jewelry, silverware, and other objects.

Jim Pickerell

Grinding machines perform such operations as shaping and sharpening. This worker uses a machine with a rotating wheel.

Gris, *grees,* **Juan,** *hwahn* (1887-1927), a Spanish-born painter, made important contributions to the modern style of painting called *cubism.* The objects in his paintings and collages are more clearly defined and richly colored than those in the works of the earlier cubists Pablo Picasso and Georges Braque. His attention to the object in his compositions and more typically Spanish hues link his work to the Spanish still-life tradition. Gris once called his work "flat, colored architecture." His version of cubism became known as *synthetic cubism.* For an example of his work, see **Cubism.**

Gris was born in Madrid. His real name was José Victoriano González. He began drawing in 1904 and in 1906 he moved to Paris, where he met Picasso and Braque. Gris was greatly influenced by their styles. The writer Gertrude Stein was among the first to praise his work, and she later helped support him.   Pamela A. Ivinski

Grisham, John (1955-   ), is a popular American author known for his suspense novels with lawyer heroes. Grisham gained fame with his second novel, *The Firm* (1991). The story concerns an ethical lawyer who battles a dangerous conspiracy, at the risk of the lawyer's life. Grisham dealt with the same theme in his next two novels, *The Pelican Brief* (1992) and *The Client* (1993). He followed these works with the best-selling legal thrillers *The Chamber* (1994), *The Rainmaker* (1995), *The Runaway Jury* (1996), and *The Partner* (1997).

Grisham was born in Jonesboro, Arkansas, and received a law degree from the University of Mississippi in 1981. He practiced law in Mississippi from 1981 to 1990. He also served in the Mississippi House of Representatives from 1984 to 1990. Grisham has drawn on his own experiences in his fiction. His first novel, *A Time to Kill* (1989), deals with the trial of a black man accused of killing two white men who raped his 10-year-old daughter. Grisham wrote the novel after he witnessed a girl testifying in a rape trial.   Jon L. Breen

Grison, *GRY suhn* or *GRIHZ uhn,* is the name of two species of furry, weasellike animals that live in Central and South America. The *greater grison* is grayish or grayish-brown and measures about $27\frac{1}{2}$ inches (70 centimeters) long. The *little grison* is smaller and has yellowish or brownish fur. Both species have black underparts.

Gary Milburn, Tom Stack & Assoc.

The little grison has a whitish stripe that runs across its forehead and down its neck. It lives in forests and open areas.

A whitish stripe runs across the forehead and down the neck on both sides.

Grisons live in forests and open country. They build dens under tree roots or rocks, in hollow logs, or in burrows of other animals. Grisons eat mice and other rodents, and insects, snakes, and birds. Females give birth to two to four young in the year.   Charles A. Long

Scientific classification. Grisons belong to the weasel family, Mustelidae. The greater grison is *Galictis vittata.* The little grison is *M. cuja.*

Grissom, Virgil Ivan (1926-1967), was one of the first United States astronauts, and the first American to make more than one space flight. Grissom and astronauts Edward H. White II and Roger Chaffee were killed on Jan. 27, 1967, when fire swept through their Apollo command module during a test on the launch pad at Cape

Kennedy (now Cape Canaveral), Florida.

Grissom made his first space flight on July 21, 1961. His Mercury spacecraft rocketed 118 miles (190 kilometers) into space from Cape Canaveral and landed 303 miles (488 kilometers) away in the Atlantic Ocean. The spacecraft filled with water and sank after its explosive hatch blew open accidentally. But Grissom escaped and was rescued by a helicopter.

In 1965, Grissom and astronaut John W. Young made the first two-man Gemini flight. On this flight, he became the first space pilot to change his craft's orbit, a feat he accomplished by firing the craft's thrusters. In 1966, he became command pilot of the first three-man Apollo flight. He died in a test for this flight.

Grissom, whose nickname was Gus, was born in Mitchell, Indiana. He graduated from Purdue University. He flew 100 combat missions during the Korean War, and received the Distinguished Flying Cross and Air Medal with cluster. In the late 1950's, he became a test pilot in the U.S. Air Force.   James R. Hansen

See also **Space exploration** (picture: The first seven U.S. astronauts).

Grizzly bear is a large, powerful bear of western North America. Grizzly bears live primarily in Alaska and western Canada. In addition, small numbers of grizzlies are found in Idaho, Montana, Washington, and Wyo-

Rick McIntyre, Tom Stack & Assoc.

A massive grizzly bear rises up on its hind legs. Grizzlies may grow to a length of 8 feet (2.4 meters). Grizzly bears live in parts of western North America.

ming. Grizzlies belong to a species of bears called *big brown bears.* A hump on the shoulders of big brown bears distinguishes them from other bears. Several other subspecies of big brown bears, including Kodiak bears, are sometimes called grizzlies.

Adult grizzly bears measure from 6 to 8 feet (1.8 to 2.4 meters) long. Most adult males weigh 400 to 500 pounds (180 to 230 kilograms). Most adult females weigh 350 to 400 pounds (160 to 180 kilograms). Grizzly bears have thick, woolly underfur that ranges in color from light tan to almost black. Grizzlies also have coarse white- or silver-tipped outer hairs, giving them a *grizzled* (grayish) appearance. Grizzlies are sometimes called *silvertips.*

Habits. Grizzly bears feed primarily on land animals, fish, berries, grasses, leaves, and roots. During the summer and fall, a grizzly may eat 80 to 90 pounds (35 to 40 kilograms) of food per day.

During the winter, grizzly bears live in dens. Some grizzlies den in caves or other natural shelters. Others build beds under branches or dig holes in the ground. In the den, the female normally gives birth to one or two cubs. The cubs stay with the mother $1\frac{1}{2}$ to $3\frac{1}{2}$ years, learning feeding and survival methods. Grizzlies fiercely protect themselves, their young, and their food.

Grizzly bears and people. Most grizzly bears try to avoid contacts with people. But grizzlies sometimes damage cabins and campsites or prey on livestock. On rare occasions, they may attack people, and some people have been killed by grizzlies.

Through the years, people have destroyed much of the grizzly bear's natural habitat by clearing land for settlements and other purposes. Today, the grizzly is a subject of controversy. Many people regard the grizzly as a symbol of the wild. They feel that the bear and its habitat should be protected. However, concern over the animal's habitat obstructs housing, agricultural, and industrial development in some areas. The United States government classifies the grizzly as a threatened species in every state except Alaska.

Scientific classification. Grizzly bears belong to the family Ursidae. They are *Ursus arctos horribilis.*   Charles J. Jonkel

See also **Bear** (Kinds of bears; picture).

Grofé, *groh FAY,* **Ferde,** *FUR dee* (1892-1972), was an American composer and arranger. Most of his compositions are orchestral works that portray the natural beauty of the United States or scenes from American life. Grofé's best-known work is *The Grand Canyon Suite* (1931), especially the third section, "On the Trail." Grofé's other compositions include *The Hudson River Suite* (1956), *Niagara Falls Suite* (1960), and *World's Fair Suite* (1963). In some works, Grofé experimented with nonmusical sounds to create added realism. For example, *Symphony in Steel* (1934) includes the sounds of a locomotive bell and a pneumatic drill.

Ferdinand Rudolph von Grofé was born in New York City. From 1917 to 1933, he was the chief arranger for Paul Whiteman's band. Grofé arranged George Gershwin's *Rhapsody in Blue* (1924), which Whiteman had commissioned for the band. Grofé's arrangement contributed greatly to the success of the work. Grofé arranged music to fit the talents of various musicians in the Whiteman band. These performers included such jazz musicians as the cornetist Bix Beiderbecke and the saxophonist Frankie Trumbauer.   Richard Jackson

Gromyko, *groh MEE koh,* **Andrei Andreyevich** (1909-1989), was an important official of the Soviet Union for many years. He served as the country's foreign minister from 1957 to 1985. In 1985, he was replaced as foreign minister and appointed chairman of the Presidium of the Supreme Soviet, which was then a largely ceremonial post. In 1973, Gromyko had become a member of the Politburo, the policymaking body of the Soviet Communist Party. He retired from his posts in 1988.

Gromyko, the son of peasant parents, was born near Minsk. He joined the Soviet diplomatic service in 1939. He was Soviet ambassador to the United States from 1943 to 1946. In 1944, he headed the Soviet delegation to the Dumbarton Oaks Conference in Washington, D.C., that helped create the United Nations (UN). Starting in 1946, he was chief Soviet delegate at the UN and at many international conferences. He became known for his bitter opposition to the Western powers. From June 1952 to May 1953 he served as ambassador to Great Britain. He was deputy foreign minister from 1947 to 1952 and from 1953 to 1957.

As foreign minister, Gromyko went with Premier Nikita S. Khrushchev to the United States in 1959. In 1961, Gromyko took part in a meeting between Khrushchev and President John F. Kennedy in Vienna, Austria. Gromyko headed the Soviet negotiating team that arranged a partial nuclear test ban treaty with Great Britain and the United States in Moscow in 1963.   Melvin Croan

Gropius, *GROH pee uhs,* **Walter** (1883-1969), was a German architect. He had great influence on modern architecture not only as an architect but also as an educator. Gropius is perhaps best known as the founder of the famous Bauhaus school of design in Germany.

Gropius was born in Berlin. From 1908 to 1910, he was the chief assistant to the German architect Peter Behrens. Gropius collaborated with Adolf Meyer in designing the factory for the Fagus Works in Alfeld in 1910 and 1911, and a model factory for an exhibition in Cologne in 1914. Both simple cubic structures were built largely of glass and steel, materials often symbolizing the qualities of modern industrial civilization.

In 1919, Gropius founded the Bauhaus in Weimar. He hired outstanding painters, sculptors, architects, and designers for the faculty. They included Wassily Kandinsky, Paul Klee, László Moholy-Nagy, and Oskar Schlemmer. Gropius designed the new buildings for the school when it moved to Dessau in 1925. These buildings were noted for their asymmetrical organization of cubic shapes and use of the transparent and reflective qualities of glass. In recalling the character of the factory, Gropius sought to give the efficiency and seriousness of industrial production to artistic practice. See **Bauhaus**.

In 1928, Gropius resigned as Bauhaus director and returned to private practice in Berlin. He fled to England in 1934 after the Nazis took power in Germany. He settled in the United States in 1937 and was chairman of the Department of Architecture at Harvard University from 1938 to 1952. Through this position, Gropius spread the theories of modern European architecture throughout the United States.

Gropius believed in designing buildings by collaborating with other architects and designers. In 1946, he and several of his former students formed The Architects Collaborative (TAC). As its first major project, the

A **Gropius building** designed in the International Style houses the offices of The Architects Collaborative (TAC) in Cambridge, Mass. Gropius helped form TAC in 1946. He believed that architecture should be a collaboration among architects, designers, and other specialists.

© Nick Wheeler

group designed the Graduate Center at Harvard in 1948. TAC also designed the Pan Am Building (now MetLife Building) in New York City in 1958, the United States Embassy in Athens in 1959, the Kennedy Federal Building in Boston in 1961, and the Rosenthal China Factory in Selb, Germany, in 1965.   Nicholas Adams

See also **Furniture** (The Bauhaus).

Gros Ventre Indians make up two tribes of Plains Indians. These tribes are the Atsina, or Gros Ventre of the Prairie (pronounced *groh VAHNT*); and the Hidatsa, also called Minitari or Gros Ventre of the Missouri (pronounced *groh VAHN*). The name *Gros Ventre* is a French term meaning *big belly.* White explorers gave the Indians this name because the explorers did not understand the sign-language gesture for these people. The gesture was a movement of both hands in front of the stomach.

The Atsina are a branch of the Arapaho Indians. The Atsina once lived in tepees and hunted buffalo on the northern Great Plains. In the early 1800's, they helped the Blackfeet Indians drive American beaver trappers from the upper Missouri Valley. In the 1830's, the Atsina established friendly relations with American traders and, later, with the U.S. government. Today, the Atsina live on Fort Belknap Reservation in Montana. Some Atsina raise cattle, grain, and hay. Others work for government agencies or private businesses.

The Hidatsa, who were related to the Crow Indians, lived near the Mandan Indians on the Missouri River in what is now North Dakota. Their customs resembled Mandan customs (see **Mandan Indians**). The Hidatsa, with the Mandan and Arikara, now live on Fort Berthold Reservation in North Dakota.   Loretta Fowler

Grosbeak, *GROHS beek,* is any one of several handsome songbirds that have thick, powerful bills. The word *gros* is a French term meaning *large.* Grosbeaks use their beaks to crack seeds, a main source of food. There are about 25 species. These birds measure about 6 to 10 inches (15 to 25 centimeters) long.

The *rose-breasted grosbeak* breeds in the eastern part of the United States and in southern Canada and winters in Central and South America. The male is black and white with a rose-red patch on its breast. The *evening grosbeak* of central North America travels in flocks and often eats sunflower seeds from bird feeders in the winter. The male has a yellow body and black and white wings. The *pine grosbeak* lives in the northern and western parts of the United States and in Canada, north-

ern Europe, and Asia. The male has rose-red feathers.

Scientific classification. Some grosbeaks belong to the subfamily Cardinalinae of the emberizid family, Emberizidae. Others are in the subfamily Carduelinae of the finch family, Fringillidae. The scientific name for the rose-breasted grosbeak is *Pheucticus ludovicianus.*   Martha Hatch Balph

See also **Bird** (picture: Birds' eggs); **Finch.**

Groseilliers, *GROH zeh YAY,* **Sieur des** (1618?-1696?), was a French explorer and fur trader. Historians believe he and his brother-in-law, Pierre Esprit Radisson, probably were the first whites to explore north and west of the Great Lakes.

Groseilliers was born in Charly-sur-Marne, France, near Meaux. His given and family name was Médard Chouart. Groseilliers came to Canada about 1641. From 1654 to 1656, he explored and traded for furs in what are now Michigan and Ontario. Later, he and Radisson explored that region and present-day Manitoba, Minnesota, Quebec, and Wisconsin.

In the early 1660's, French authorities arrested Groseilliers for fur trading without a license. Angered by this treatment, Groseilliers and Radisson went to England in 1665 and told King Charles II about the fur riches of Canada. In 1668, Groseilliers led an English fur-trading expedition to Hudson Bay in Canada. This trip resulted in the establishment of the Hudson's Bay Company in 1670.   P. B. Waite

See also **Hudson's Bay Company; Radisson, Pierre E.**

WORLD BOOK illustration by John Dawson

The male rose-breasted grosbeak, *above,* has a rose-red patch on its breast. Rose-breasted grosbeaks nest in the United States and Canada and winter in Central and South America.

Gross domestic product (GDP) is the value of all goods and services produced in a country during a given period. It is one of the most widely used measures of a nation's total economic performance in a single year.

Measuring the GDP. One way to determine the GDP is to add up the sum of spending on four kinds of goods and services in any year.

(1) *Personal consumption expenditures* include private spending on durable goods, such as automobiles and appliances; nondurable goods, such as food and clothing; and services, such as haircuts and motion-picture tickets. In the United States, these expenditures make up about two-thirds of the GDP each year.

(2) *Private investment expenditures* include spending by business companies for new buildings, machinery, and tools. They also include spending for goods to be stored for future sale. These expenditures average about 20 percent of the annual GDP of the United States.

(3) *Government purchases of goods and services* include spending for new highways, missiles, and the wages of teachers, firefighters, and government employees. Such spending amounts to about 20 percent of the United States GDP each year.

(4) *Net exports* represent the value of domestically produced goods and services sold abroad, less the value of goods and services purchased from abroad during the same period. Currently, the value of U.S. exports is exceeded by that of U.S. imports. Net exports thus show a negative percentage in the U.S. GDP. The negative percentage accounts for percentages in the other three major parts of the U.S. GDP totaling more than 100 percent.

Real GDP. A nation may produce the same amount of goods and services this year as it did last year. Yet this year's GDP may be 5 percent higher than last year's. Such a situation would occur if prices of goods and services had risen by an average of 5 percent. To adjust for such price changes, economists measure the GDP in *constant dollars.* They determine what each year's GDP would be if dollars were worth as much during the current year as in a certain previous year, called the *base year.* In other words, they calculate the value of each year's production in terms of the base year's prices. When GDP measured in current dollars is divided by GDP in constant dollars, the result is an index of inflation called the *GDP deflator.*

Interpreting the GDP. GDP figures, though only estimates, are useful. Business people, economists, and government officials study them to help determine how fast the economy is growing and which parts of it are doing best. The figures also show how the economic performance of one country compares with that of other nations.

The United States has long had the highest GDP of any country, but it no longer has the highest GDP *per capita* (for each person). The GDP per capita can be determined by dividing the total GDP by the nation's population. In addition, the United States no longer has the fastest-growing GDP. The GDP in constant dollars has doubled about once every 20 years since 1900. But this growth has been uneven. A severe decline occurred during the early 1930's, and a sharp rise took place during World War II (1939-1945). The GDP has risen almost every year since 1950, but the growth rate has varied.

Canada's GDP has followed a similar path. The Canadian GDP in constant dollars was over 10 times as high in the late 1990's as in 1927. Today, the gross domestic product of Canada ranks among the world's highest.

GDP figures do not tell everything about a nation's economy. For example, they tell little about the well-being of individuals and families. Even the GDP per capita does not tell who uses various goods and services. It cannot show, for example, how much of the GDP goes

Gross domestic product in the United States

Gross domestic product (GDP) is the value of goods and services produced in a given period. In the table and graph below, current dollars show the value of the GDP in the year indicated, while constant dollars show the value adjusted for inflation.

Year	Current dollars	Constant dollars (1996)	Per capita (constant dollars)
1929	$ 103,700,000,000	$ 822,200,000,000	$ 6,697
1930	91,300,000,000	751,500,000,000	6,121
1935	73,300,000,000	728,300,000,000	5,725
1940	101,300,000,000	980,700,000,000	7,448
1945	223,000,000,000	1,693,300,000,000	11,994
1950	294,300,000,000	1,686,600,000,000	11,192
1955	415,200,000,000	2,099,500,000,000	12,723
1960	527,400,000,000	2,376,700,000,000	13,254
1965	720,100,000,000	3,028,500,000,000	15,833
1970	1,039,700,000,000	3,578,000,000,000	17,605
1975	1,635,200,000,000	4,084,400,000,000	19,007
1980	2,795,600,000,000	4,900,900,000,000	21,633
1985	4,213,000,000,000	5,717,100,000,000	24,012
1990	5,803,200,000,000	6,707,900,000,000	26,871
1992	6,318,900,000,000	6,880,000,000,000	26,876
1994	7,054,300,000,000	7,347,700,000,000	28,007
1996	7,813,200,000,000	7,813,200,000,000	29,077
1998	8,790,200,000,000	8,515,200,000,000	30,959
2000	9,963,100,000,000	8,867,000,000,000	33,112

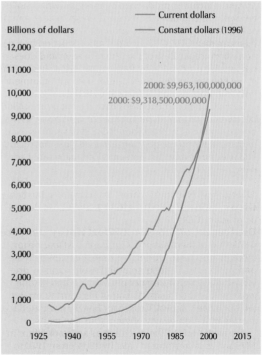

Billions of dollars

—— Current dollars
—— Constant dollars (1996)

2000: $9,963,100,000,000
2000: $9,318,500,000,000

Sources: U.S. Bureau of Economic Analysis and *World Book* estimates.

Leading countries in total gross domestic product

Total value of goods and services produced in a year*

United States	●●●●●●●●●●●●●	$9,299,200,000,000
Japan	●●●●●◖	$4,348,800,000,000
Germany	●●◖	$2,112,000,000,000
United Kingdom	●◖	$1,442,800,000,000
France	●◖	$1,378,800,000,000
Italy	●◖	$1,171,000,000,000
China	●◖	$ 991,200,000,000
Canada	◖	$ 644,800,000,000
Spain	◖	$ 595,600,000,000
Brazil	◖	$ 529,400,000,000

*In U.S. dollars.
Figures are for 1999.
Source: International Monetary Fund.

Leading countries in per capita gross domestic product

Value of goods and services produced per person in a year*

Luxembourg	●●●●●●●●●●●●●	$45,852
Switzerland	●●●●●●●●●	$34,834
Norway	●●●●●●●●●	$34,689
Japan	●●●●●●●●◐	$34,461
Denmark	●●●●●●●●◖	$33,503
United States	●●●●●●●●◖	$33,450
Iceland	●●●●●●●●◖	$31,538
Sweden	●●●●●●●	$26,719
Germany	●●●●●●◖	$25,856
Ireland	●●●●●●◖	$25,700

*In U.S. dollars.
Figures are for 1999.
Sources: *World Book* estimates based on data from the International Monetary Fund and the United Nations.

to the poorest 20 percent of the population and how much goes to the wealthiest 20 percent. Nor does the GDP per capita tell anything about the quality of a country's goods and services.

GDP excludes production by facilities that are owned by a nation's citizens if the facilities are in another country, and it includes production by foreign-owned facilities within the country. Some economists believe another figure, the *gross national product* (GNP), is a better measure than GDP. GNP includes all production by a nation's firms regardless of the firms' location and does not include production by foreign-owned facilities within the country. In 1991, the U.S. Commerce Department switched from using GNP data to GDP data.

Some Communist countries have used a figure called *net material product* (NMP) instead of GDP. NMP shows the total value of goods produced and of services used in manufacturing the goods in a year. It does not include financial, governmental, personal, and many other services.   Paul Taubman

See also **Inflation** (Measuring inflation); **National debt** (Debt policy); **National income; Standard of living** (table).

Gross national product (GNP). See Gross domestic product (GDP).

Grosvenor, *GROHV nuhr,* **Gilbert Hovey,** *HUHV ee* (1875-1966), edited *National Geographic Magazine* for more than 50 years. During this time, he helped create popular interest in geography and exploration by presenting lively articles on people, wildlife, and natural wonders in exotic lands. As part of his effort to expand the magazine's appeal, Grosvenor heavily illustrated the articles with high-quality photographs and maps.

Grosvenor joined the magazine as assistant editor in 1899 and rose to editor in chief by 1903. From 1920 to 1954, he served as president of the National Geographic Society, and then was chairman of its board of directors. He was born in Istanbul, Turkey.   Lee B. Jolliffe

See also **National Geographic Society**.

Grosz, *grohs,* **George** (1893-1959), a German painter, became famous in the 1920's for his biting satires of the military and wealthy classes, and for drawings criticizing the moral collapse of society after World War I (1914-1918). For a time in the 1930's, his paintings became less gloomy, but he usually painted works on social evil and war. In 1933, disturbed by the trend toward fascism, Grosz moved from Germany to New York City. He became a United States citizen in 1938. Grosz was born in Berlin.   Deborah Emont Scott

Grotius, *GROH shee uhs,* **Hugo** (1583-1645), a Dutch lawyer, theologian, statesman, and poet, is considered the founder of international law. He wrote *On the Law of War and Peace*. Born Huig de Groot in Delft, he graduated from the University of Leiden at 15. He became chief magistrate of Rotterdam in 1613. Grotius was condemned to life imprisonment in 1619 for opposing strict Calvinism. His wife helped him escape. From 1635 to 1645, he served as Swedish ambassador to France.

Daniel J. Dykstra

See also **International law** (In early days); **Peace** (From the 1400's to the 1700's).

Ground, in electricity, is an electrical conductor that is connected to the earth to complete a circuit. In electrical equipment, such as household appliances, the ground conducts electric current that may build up in the appliance because of a "leak" or a short circuit. If the appliance were not grounded, the high voltage it acquires might kill someone. In some electrical equipment, the metal frame serves as a ground. Many appliance plugs have two flat prongs and one round one. The round prong serves as a ground connection.   Lucille B. Garmon

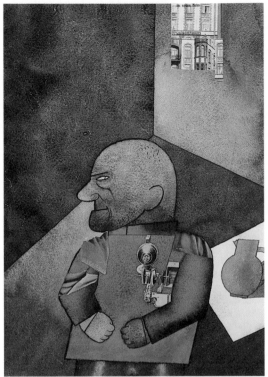

Water color and collage (1920); Collection, The Museum of Modern Art, New York City, gift of A. Conger Goodyear

George Grosz painted satirical pictures of German life in the 1920's and 1930's. *The Engineer Heartfield, above,* is his satire on the inhuman, machinelike qualities he saw in Germans.

Ground hog. See Woodchuck.

Ground-Hog Day is an American tradition that supposedly predicts when spring will arrive. According to legend, the ground hog, also called the *woodchuck,* awakens from its winter sleep on February 2 and emerges from its burrow. If the sun is shining that day and the ground hog sees its shadow, it will be scared back into its den, and there will be six more weeks of winter. But if it is cloudy and the ground hog does not see its shadow, it will come out, and spring will arrive soon.

For hundreds of years, European farmers had similar traditions that involved bears, badgers, and other animals. Germans who settled in Pennsylvania brought the custom to America. The ground hog, which is plentiful in the Eastern and Midwestern United States, became linked with the custom. Today, Ground-Hog Day is treated largely as a joke. But the custom is partly based on ancient and traditional weather signs. People have long looked to the awakening of hibernating animals as one of the first signs of spring.   Jack Santino

Ground pine. See Club moss.

Ground sloth is a huge, extinct animal of the sloth family. The largest ground sloth was about 20 feet (6 meters) long, and as large as an elephant. It had huge bones, heavy back legs, and a strong tail. This indicates that the ground sloth could stand on its hind legs to reach high branches and leaves. It ate only plants. Unlike present-day sloths, it did not climb trees.

Painting by Charles R. Knight; Field Museum of Natural History

Hairy ground sloths lived about 1 million years ago. These huge animals, as large as present-day elephants, roamed over what is now North and South America.

The front feet of the ground sloth had long claws placed so that the animal must have walked on its knuckles, with only the outer edge of the foot resting on the ground. The ancestors of the ground sloths lived in trees and used their hooked claws to hang from the branches.

Ground sloths originally lived in South America. But during the Ice Age, these animals also lived in what is now the United States, along with prehistoric people.

Scientific classification. The giant ground sloth belonged to the ground sloth family, Megatheriidae. It made up the genus *Megatherium.*   Keith Stewart Thomson

See also **Sloth.**

Ground squirrel is any member of the squirrel family that burrows underground to build its nest. Ground squirrels live in deserts, meadows, mountains, prairies, and other areas. There are about 30 kinds of ground squirrels in North America, the best known of which include chipmunks, marmots, prairie dogs, and wood-

Karl Maslowski, Photo Researchers, Inc.

The thirteen-lined ground squirrel is a common species of ground squirrel that lives throughout the Midwestern States.

chucks. Other common ground squirrels include the golden-mantled ground squirrel, Richardson's ground squirrel, and the thirteen-lined ground squirrel.

North American ground squirrels vary in length from about 7 to 27 inches (18 to 69 centimeters), including the tail. Their fur is black, brown, gray, red, or white, and some species have spots or stripes.

Ground squirrels are active only during the day. They eat a variety of grasses, seeds, and insects. Badgers, coyotes, eagles, and hawks are their main enemies. Most kinds of ground squirrels hibernate during the fall and winter. A female ground squirrel may give birth to 4 to 12 young every spring.

Scientific classification. Ground squirrels belong to the squirrel family, Sciuridae.   Clark E. Adams

See also **Chipmunk; Marmot; Prairie dog; Squirrel; Woodchuck.**

Ground water is water beneath the surface of the earth. It is the source of water for wells and many springs. Ground water provides about 20 per cent of the fresh water used in the United States. Most rural areas and some cities depend heavily on ground water.

Ground water accumulates chiefly from rain and melted snow that filters through the soil. It also collects from water that seeps into the ground from lakes and ponds. The water settles into the pores and cracks of underground rocks and into the spaces between grains of sand and pieces of gravel. A layer or bed of such porous materials that yields useful amounts of ground water is called an *aquifer.* Wells are drilled down to aquifers to draw ground water to the surface.

The level of ground water, called the *water table,* drops when more water is withdrawn than can be replaced naturally. Many regions of the world are using up the ground water faster than aquifers are being *recharged* (replenished). In some areas, the ground water supply may have to be recharged with water from another area. For example, water can be returned to the earth through special recharge wells, ponds, or ditches that allow surplus water to seep into the ground. Lowering of the water table causes special problems in coastal areas, because salt water from the ocean enters reservoirs of ground water. In some areas, when the water table drops, the land surface cracks and sinks. This action can cause great damage to buildings, roads, pipelines, and other structures.

Pollution of ground water is a serious problem, especially near cities and industrial sites. Pollutants that seep into the ground result from contaminated surface water, leaks from sewer pipes and septic tanks, and chemical spills. Ground water may also be polluted by seepage from landfills, buried radioactive wastes, and the misuse of agricultural chemicals.   Gilbert L. Bertoldi

See also **Artesian well; Hydrology; Spring; Well.**

Groundnut. See Peanut.

Group dynamics includes the forces that work on any group of people and determine what it does. The group may be a club, a business organization, an army, or even an entire nation.

Before 1900, scientists knew little about the forces at work in groups of people. Then sociologists, and later psychologists, anthropologists, political scientists, and educators began using the tools of science to probe the mysteries of group life. Beginning in the 1930's, group dynamics became a recognized field of study in the social sciences. Several universities have established research groups to study group dynamics.

A large body of knowledge has been built up about group dynamics. This knowledge has shed light on such aspects of group life as the nature and requirements of leadership, the different roles of members of a group, friendship or attraction in groups, and the process of making decisions in a group. The research also has provided information on communications and relationships among members in a group, and the hidden forces that influence what people do in groups. This basic research has led to new ideas about what brings about high morale and effective action in groups.

Attempts have been made to translate the findings of basic research in group dynamics into practical principles and techniques. This *applied* group dynamics has led to the development of new training programs for group members and leaders. One such program involves people living together for a few days to several weeks. The people observe their own behavior and gain new insights about how their actions affect others.

Much of the money used to finance research in group dynamics comes from industry, government, and national voluntary organizations. These organizations are using applied group dynamics in improving leadership and group operation.   Kenneth J. Gergen

See also **Social psychology; Collective behavior; Morale; Role playing.**

Group of Seven was a school of Canadian landscape painters. Members of the group sought to develop a distinctively Canadian style of painting through an expressive response to the landscape of northern Canada. The group's style featured brilliant colors and free brushstrokes. The original members of the group were Franklin Carmichael, Lawren Harris, A. Y. Jackson, Franz Johnston, Arthur Lismer, J. E. H. MacDonald, and Frederick H. Varley. All lived in Toronto, Ont.

The group's origin dated back to the period from 1911 to 1913. In those years, the seven artists plus Tom Thomson, who died in 1917, began sketching and painting together. The Group of Seven was formally estab-

Fraser's Lodge (1915), an oil painting on wood; Ernest E. Poole Estate

The work of Tom Thomson influenced several members of the Group of Seven. These Canadian painters were inspired by Thomson's use of vivid colors and thick brushstrokes.

The Elements by J. E. H. Mac-Donald shows a storm forming over Georgian Bay in Ontario. Like other members of the Group of Seven, MacDonald painted dramatic scenes of the Canadian wilderness, emphasizing brilliant colors and bold patterns.

Oil painting on wood (1916); Art Gallery of Ontario, gift of Dr. Lorne Pierce, 1958, in memory of Edith Chown Pierce

lished at its first exhibition in 1920. Despite initial opposition from art critics, the group became a dominant force in Canadian art in the 1920's and 1930's.

The group's influence continued as careers of the artists and the membership changed. Varley began to emphasize portraits instead of landscapes, and Harris turned to an abstract style. Johnston left the group in 1922, and A. J. Casson was added in 1926. MacDonald died in 1932. To broaden its geographical base, the group admitted Edwin Holgate of Montreal, about 1930 and L. L. FitzGerald of Winnipeg, Man., in 1932. The group held its last exhibition in 1931. In 1933, it dissolved in favor of a successor organization, the Canadian Group of Painters.   David Burnett

See also **Canada** (The Arts [picture]); **Jackson, Alexander Young; MacDonald, J. E. H.; Thomson, Tom.**
Group therapy. See Psychotherapy.
Grouper is a type of ocean fish that lives in warm and temperate seas, mostly around rocky shores and coral reefs. All groupers have large mouths. They feed on fish and marine animals and swallow them whole. In color, groupers resemble the corals and algae among which they live. They can change their colors quickly. All groupers are born as females and later change into males. Some groupers, including the *Nassau grouper* and the *black grouper,* live along the southern Atlantic Coast of the United States. The *red grouper* lives along the Atlantic Coast from Massachusetts to Brazil.

Groupers are valued as food. However, the flesh of some large groupers is poisoned with a substance that may cause a serious illness called *ciguatera.*

Scientific classification. Groupers belong to the sea bass family, Serranidae. The red grouper is classified as *Epinephelas morio* and the Nassau grouper is *E. striatus.* The black grouper is classified as *Mycteroperca bonaci.*   William J. Richards

See also **Fish** (picture: Fish of coral reefs); **Jewfish.**

Grouse is a type of bird that lives in the Northern Hemisphere. It is somewhat like domestic fowl. People often use the names *grouse, quail,* and *partridge* incorrectly. In the South, the *ruffed grouse* is often called a pheasant. New Englanders call it a partridge. The *spruce grouse* is called the *swamp partridge* or *spruce partridge.* In other places, partridges and pheasants are often called grouse. Several grouse are called quail.

General appearance. A grouse has dull feathers, and grows to about the size of a large chicken. Like a fowl, it has four toes, with the hind one raised above the ground. Feathers hide its nostrils. These birds usually live in high or northern places. Feathers cover the legs of most species to keep them from freezing.

Habits. During the mating season, the males court the hens with a kind of dance and fight each other

WORLD BOOK illustration by John F. Eggert

The red grouper lives along the coast of the Atlantic Ocean. This fish can change its color to match the rocks and coral reefs in its surroundings. Like other groupers, it has a large mouth.

WORLD BOOK illustration by John Rignall, Linden Artists Ltd.

The spruce grouse has dull-colored feathers and somewhat resembles domestic fowl. It is a popular game bird.

fiercely. Grouse build their nests on the ground in places that are well-hidden. The hens usually lay 10 to 15 eggs. The eggs are buff-colored with brown dots. The chicks leave the nest almost as soon as they hatch. When danger threatens, the mother gives a sharp call that warns the chicks. The chicks then become still. The color of their feathers helps them blend into the background and hide from enemies. A flock of grouse is called a *covey.*

Grouse eat insects and berries in summer. In autumn, they may visit grain fields for the seeds, and in winter they live on catkins, leaves, and buds. Their food habits usually do not harm growing things. In Europe and North America, grouse increase in number and grow scarce over 9- to 11-year periods. Hunters consider grouse good game birds because they show intelligence in escaping when hunted.

Many species of grouse live in North America. The ruffed grouse lives from Alaska south to Georgia. The spruce grouse lives from New England west to Alaska. Some grouse, including the spruce grouse and the *blue grouse,* are called *fool hens* by hunters. These birds are very curious. Sometimes they become so interested that they stand around watching the hunters and can be shot very easily.   Donald F. Bruning

Scientific classification. Grouse make up the grouse subfamily, Tetraoninae, in the family Phasianidae. The scientific name for the ruffed grouse is *Bonasa umbellus.* The spruce grouse is *Dendragapus canadensis,* and the blue grouse is *D. obscurus.*

Related articles in *World Book* include:

Partridge	Ptarmigan	Ruffed grouse
Prairie-chicken	Quail	Sandgrouse

Grove, Frederick Philip (1879-1948), was a Canadian novelist noted for his realistic descriptions of prairie life combined with romantic fatalism. In several prairie novels, Grove dealt with people's struggle against nature and with the gap between generations and between the sexes. These books include *Settlers of the Marsh* (1925), *Our Daily Bread* (1928), *The Yoke of Life* (1930), and *Fruits of the Earth* (1933).

Grove is also known for two collections of nature sketches—*Over Prairie Trails* (1922) and *The Turn of the Year* (1923). His last novel, *The Master of the Mill* (1944), is a study of a capitalist dynasty in Ontario.

Grove was born in Randomno, Prussia, to German parents. His given and family name was Felix Paul Greve. He grew up in Germany and came to North America in 1909. He became a schoolteacher in Manitoba in 1912 and taught there until 1923. Grove's fictionalized autobiography, *In Search of Myself* (1946), won the 1946 Governor General's Award for nonfiction.   Laurie R. Ricou

Growth is an increase in the number or size of a living thing's cells. All living things grow. A seed can grow into a plant. The giant redwood grows from a seed $\frac{1}{16}$ inch (1.6 millimeters) in diameter to become a tree often more than 300 feet (91 meters) tall. A microscope must be used to see a whale egg, but a full-grown whale may be up to 100 feet (30 meters) long and weigh about 160,000 pounds (72,600 kilograms). All living things do not grow to the same extent. As a result, species differ in size. Adult guinea pigs are only five times heavier than baby guinea pigs. But adult elephants are usually 40 times heavier than baby elephants.

How growth takes place

In living things. Every living organism consists of cells. Each individual begins life as a single cell. The cell takes in materials and converts them into the building blocks that it needs to grow. Thus, the single cell grows from within. This cell can multiply and divide to form other cells. The process of building, multiplying, and dividing is growth. It continues until the organism is fully developed.

As the cells grow, they also change in character. Some grow into the tissues that form skin. Others grow into muscle tissues. Still others form body organs, such as the heart, lungs, and liver. This growth and organization of the cells into specific structures is called *differentiation.* The process of differentiation follows definite rules. The seed of a redwood always grows into a redwood tree, not into a pansy or an oak tree. A dog's tail always grows at the base of the spine, not between the ears. The process is controlled by the cell's hereditary traits. Heredity influences certain chemical and physical processes in the cell to make it grow into an organism having the traits of its parents. See **Heredity.**

Other kinds of regulators are also produced by the cells. As growth proceeds, certain cells develop that produce specific substances that influence and regulate the further development of the organism. These substances are called *hormones* and are found both in plants and in animals. See **Hormone.**

In nonliving things. Some substances that are not alive also exhibit a kind of growth. Objects like rocks can increase in size if they are in a proper environment. But nonliving things do not consist of cells and therefore do not grow from within. The growth of a rock or mineral is *growth by accretion.* For example, water dripping from a cave ceiling leaves behind tiny mineral particles. These particles cling together until, after hundreds of years, they form great "icicles" of stone called *stalactites.*

Human growth

Early development. In its earliest stage of development, the human organism is called an *embryo.* The embryo develops slowly. When the embryo is about 2 months old, it is only about $1\frac{1}{2}$ inches (3.8 centimeters) long, but it has the form of a human being. All the parts of the body are well formed. However, the head is quite large compared with the trunk and limbs. At this time, the fully developed embryo becomes known as a *fetus*.

At 7 months, the fetus weighs about 2 pounds (0.9 kilogram) and is about 15 inches (38 centimeters) long. Two months later, or just before birth, the fetus usually weighs about 6 to 8 pounds (2.7 to 3.6 kilograms) and may be from 19 to 21 inches (48 to 53 centimeters) long. Thus, by the time babies are born, they are growing at an extremely rapid rate.

Growth rate. The rate of growth depends on the balance between the rate of *synthesis* (formation) and the rate of breakdown of body materials. The rapid rate of growth during the first part of a baby's life occurs because the rate of synthesis in the baby's body far exceeds the rate of breakdown. Boys and girls grow most rapidly during the first two years of their lives. Then, their growth rate becomes gradually slower until they reach adolescence.

For about two years during their adolescent period, boys and girls suddenly grow rapidly. This is what some people call the "adolescent spurt" in height growth. Although all adolescents develop this spurt in height, the age at which it begins and the length of time it continues vary with the individual.

Adolescent boys usually exhibit this spurt of growth between the ages of 12 and 14 years. Their gain in height often ranges from 4 to 12 inches (10 to 30 centimeters). But the fastest rate of growth in boys may take place any time between the ages of 12 and 17.

The adolescent growth spurt in girls usually begins about 2 years earlier than in boys, and their maximum growth rate is somewhat less than that of boys. Women are generally smaller than men, chiefly because of this difference in the adolescent growth spurt. Until that period is reached, the average heights of boys and girls are almost the same.

Comparative rates of growth. Some children are fast growers, and others are slow growers. Some individuals have large, heavy bones and weigh more than individuals with small, light bones. Thus, height-weight-age tables are not necessarily a good indication of what a child should weigh.

Studies indicate that people have increased in size over the course of time. Suits of armor worn by knights of the Middle Ages are too small for an average man today. From 1876 to 1976, the average height of 18-year-old males in the United States increased by about 4 inches (10 centimeters). However, statistics indicate that Americans probably have reached their maximum growth potential, and that the trend of increasing height has ended in the United States.

Skeletal age. Because children grow and develop at different rates, scientists often assign developmental ages rather than *chronological*, or calendar, ages to growing children. Doctors often evaluate growth on the basis of the growth of the bones of the skeleton. If children are developing slowly, they could actually be 6 years old, but their bone structure might only have reached that of a 5-year-old. The skeletal age of people who mature late could run below their actual age until they become adults. Certain diseases may slow down bone growth. Doctors are able to determine the extent of such *retardation*, or slowing down, by determining their skeletal age.

Average normal growth for boys and girls

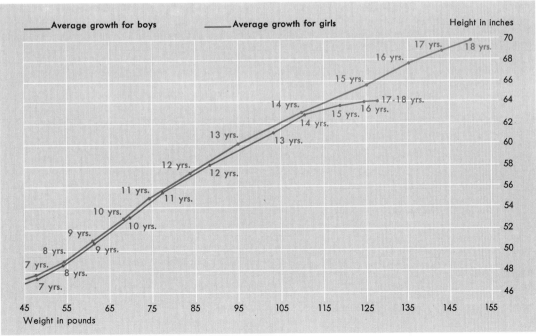

Source: National Center for Health Statistics

When people stop growing. Most healthy human beings stop growing some time between the ages of 18 and 30. But their weight may continue to increase until they are well into their 40's. Some time after people stop growing in height, they actually begin to shrink. This decrease in height is exceedingly slow and usually does not become noticeable until a person reaches old age. It is caused by a thinning of the pads of cartilage that grow between the bones of the vertebral column, or backbone. The curves in the vertebral column in elderly people also tend to become greater. This results in the bent appearance of many old people, as well as a further reduction in height.

Factors affecting human growth. Tall parents usually have tall children, and short parents have short children. Therefore, the tendency to be tall or short seems to be largely hereditary. However, tallness appears to be *recessive.* This means that short parents may have tall children. When one parent is tall and the other short, the children may be tall or short or even midway between. This occurs because the hereditary pattern is complex, and other factors are often involved.

Hormones produced by glands in the body modify growth. Secretions from the pancreas, thyroid gland, and pituitary gland particularly affect growth (see **Gland**). These secretions—*insulin, thyroxin, and growth hormone*—greatly influence cell size and cell number. Too little of any of these hormones can slow growth. In hormone-deficient patients, treatment with the particular hormone increases growth.

Foods are also a factor in growth. Certain foods but not others contain materials essential for growth. To promote proper growth, a person should eat a balanced diet that contains proteins, minerals, and vitamins, as well as sugars, fats, and starches. See **Nutrition.**

Other factors can affect growth. Exercise may promote muscle growth and inactivity may slow it. Communicable diseases or infections interrupt growth. Stress and emotional disturbances can also interfere with it.

Influence of growth. During spurts of growth, children use energy in the process of growth itself. They need additional food and rest. It is more difficult to study, to pay attention, and to withstand strain during this time. Children should not worry if they seem to be growing much more slowly or rapidly than their friends. They should realize that everyone grows at a different rate.　　Julie M. Fagan

Related articles in *World Book* include:

Adolescent	Child (The stages of child-
Aging	hood; Individual differ-
Baby (Growth and develop-	ences)
ment)	Gibberellin
Cell (Cell division)	Life cycle
	Regeneration

Additional resources

Fosket, Donald E. *Plant Growth and Development.* Academic Pr., 1994.
Tanner, James M. *Foetus into Man.* Rev. ed. Harvard Univ. Pr., 1990.
Ulijaszek, Stanley J., and others, eds. *The Cambridge Encyclopedia of Human Growth and Development.* Cambridge, 1998.

Growth fund. See Mutual fund.

Grub is the name given to the *larva* (immature form) of certain insects. Grubs are soft, thick creatures that look like tiny worms or caterpillars. Most grubs are white or pale-colored. Many grubs live in wood, soil, or the flesh of animals. Insects whose larvae are called grubs include various bees, beetles, flies, and wasps.
James E. Lloyd

Gruening, *GREE nihng,* **Ernest** (1887-1974), was a leader in Alaska's drive for statehood. Gruening served as territorial governor of Alaska from 1939 to 1953. In 1954, he wrote *The State of Alaska,* which criticized the federal government's neglect of Alaska. In 1956, Alaskans made him an unofficial "United States Senator" to work in Washington, D.C., for statehood. Gruening, a Democrat, was elected to the United States Senate in 1958, the year Congress voted to admit Alaska as a state. He served in the Senate until 1969.

Gruening was born in New York City, and graduated from Harvard University. He worked for many years as a newspaper reporter and as an editor. Gruening became President Franklin D. Roosevelt's adviser on Latin-American affairs in 1933. He moved to Alaska in 1939. During the 1960's, Gruening strongly criticized the involvement of the United States in the Vietnam War.
Claus-M. Naske

Grumman, *GRUHM muhn,* **Leroy** (1895-1982), an American industrialist, founded and became chairman of the board of the Grumman Aircraft Corporation (now part of the Northrop Grumman Corporation) in 1929. He became honorary chairman of the board in 1966.

The company produces military and commercial aircraft. It began by producing the first fighter plane with retractable landing gear. Later, the company and its affiliates produced boats, canoes, and truck and trailer bodies. Grumman was born in Huntington, New York.
Robert B. Hotz

Grünewald, *GROO nuh VAHLT,* **Matthias,** *mah TEE ahs* (1470's-1528), was a German painter of dramatic religious scenes. Grünewald's name and work were nearly forgotten after his death until art historians rediscovered him in the late 1890's. German expressionist artists of the early 1900's were attracted to his powerful and sometimes shocking use of form and color to create emotional impact.

Grünewald primarily painted altarpieces. All of his work reveals a highly individual style and deep religious feeling. He created his greatest altarpiece for the hospital chapel at a monastery in Isenheim, in what is now northeastern France, from 1512 to 1515. The work contains scenes from the lives of Jesus Christ and Saint Anthony.

Grünewald used fiery reds and yellows and radiant blues to communicate a sense of triumph in his *Resurrection.* In the *Crucifixion,* one of several works he painted on this theme, Grünewald painted brightly lit figures with tragic expressions and set them against a dark, empty background to produce a feeling of intense suffering.

Grünewald was born in Würzburg, Germany. From about 1508 to 1525, he served as court painter for two archbishops of Mainz. Grünewald's given and family name was Mathis Gothart-Nithart, but an art historian mistakenly gave him the name Grünewald during the late 1600's.
Jane Campbell Hutchison

Grunion, *GRUHN yuhn,* is a small, silvery fish that lives along the coast of southern California and northwestern Mexico. Grunions lay their eggs on sandy beaches from late February to early September. This must be done on nights of the highest tide. Many people gather on the beaches at this time of year and catch the fish. Grunion eggs hatch two weeks after they are laid, during the next series of high tides. A related fish, the *gulf grunion,* is found only in the northern part of the Gulf of

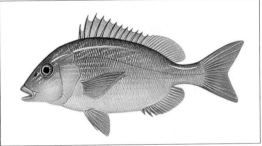

WORLD BOOK illustration by Colin Newman, Linden Artists Ltd.

One species of American grunt is the pigfish, *above.*

WORLD BOOK illustration by Colin Newman, Linden Artists Ltd.

The grunion is a small, silvery fish that lives along the coast of southern California and northwestern Mexico.

California. The gulf grunion lays its eggs during the day as well as at night. See also **Biological clock** (Other rhythms).

Scientific classification. The grunion belongs to the silverside family, Atherinidae. Its scientific name is *Leuresthes tenuis.* The gulf grunion is *L. sardina.*   Tomio Iwamoto

Grunt is an ocean fish that makes grunting sounds when taken from the water. Grunts make up a large family. Many are valuable as food. One of the most important food fishes of the American species is the *pigfish,* which lives along the Atlantic and Gulf coasts of the United States. It grows a foot (30 centimeters) long or

more, and is light blue above and silvery below, with blue and brown side marks.

Scientific classification. Grunts are in the family Haemulidae. The scientific name for the pigfish is *Orthopristis chrysoptera.*   William J. Richards

See also **Fish** (pictures: Fish of coral reefs).

Gu Kaizhi, *goo ky jur* (A.D. 345?-406?), also spelled *Ku K'ai-chih,* was the first Chinese painter recognized as a great master. He is the only painter of his time represented today by a possible original work as well as by copies. His specialty was figure painting. His skill in catching the spirit as well as the look of his subjects amazed his contemporaries. Gu Kaizhi's works illustrate moral stories and Buddhist and Taoist tales. His most famous work is a scroll, *Admonitions of the Instructress in the Palace.*   Elizabeth deS. Swinton

Guacamole. See Avocado.

Guacharo. See Oilbird.

Guadalajara, *GWAHD uh luh HAHR uh* (pop. 1,650,205; met. area pop. 2,846,720), is the second largest city in Mexico. Only Mexico City has more people. Guadalajara is the capital of the state of Jalisco. The city lies in a rich farming region (see **Mexico** [political map]).

The tree-shaded public squares and parks of this beautiful old city date back to Mexico's days as a Spanish colony. Guadalajara is an important manufacturing center. It has won fame for its fine pottery and blown glass. Other products include textiles, hosiery, flour, steel, and alcoholic beverages. Several buildings have murals by José Clemente Orozco, a famous painter. The city was founded in 1531 by Nuño de Guzmán, a Spanish conquistador. It was named for the city in Spain where Guzmán was born.   Roderic A. Camp

Guadalcanal Island, *GWAHD uhl kuh NAL,* lies in the Coral Sea, east of the southern tip of New Guinea. It is the largest island of the nation of Solomon Islands. Honiara, the nation's capital and largest city, is on Guadalcanal. Guadalcanal covers 2,500 square miles (6,475 square kilometers). Most of the 71,000 people are Melanesians. The island's chief exports include coconuts, gold, palm oil, and timber.

Japanese troops occupied Guadalcanal early in World War II. It was the scene of heavy fighting in 1942 and 1943 when United States forces landed and forced the Japanese to evacuate the island.   Geoffrey M. White

See also **Pacific Islands** (Melanesians); **Solomon Islands; World War II** (The South Pacific).

Guadalupe Day, *GWAH duh LOOP,* commemorates the day that the Virgin Mary is believed to have ap-

Oil painting on linden wood (about 1510); National Gallery of Art, Washington, D.C., Samuel H. Kress Collection

Grünewald's *The Small Crucifixion* illustrates the artist's use of brightly lit dramatic figures against a dark, empty background to create a feeling of intense suffering.

peared to Juan Diego, a poor Indian. According to legend, on Dec. 9, 1531, Juan was hurrying over Tepeyac Hill, in what is now Mexico City, when a vision appeared to him. A lady told him to ask the bishop to build a shrine where she stood. But the bishop did not believe Juan until the vision appeared again, on December 12, and produced a sign. During this appearance, the lady called herself Holy Mary of Guadalupe. Our Lady of Guadalupe became the patron saint of Mexico. Roman Catholics throughout Mexico and in parts of the Southwestern United States celebrate the feast of Our Lady of Guadalupe on December 12. David G. Truemper

Guadalupe Hidalgo, *gwahth ah LOO pay ee THAHL goh* or *GWAHD uhl OOP hih DAHL goh,* **Treaty of,** officially ended the Mexican War (1846-1848). The United States and Mexico signed the treaty on Feb. 2, 1848, after conducting negotiations at Villa de Guadalupe Hidalgo, now part of Mexico City. Under the treaty, Mexico *ceded* (surrendered) land that now makes up California, Nevada, and Utah, most of Arizona, and parts of Colorado, New Mexico, and Wyoming. This land became known as the Mexican Cession. The United States agreed to pay Mexico $15 million for the land and to pay all past claims held by American citizens against Mexico up to a total of $3,250,000. The treaty guaranteed Mexicans in the ceded territory the protection of their property and freedom of religion. Also under the treaty, Mexico gave up all claims to Texas. See also **Hispanic Americans** (Conflict); **Mexican War.** W. Dirk Raat

Guadalupe Mountains National Park, *gwahth ah LOO pay* or *GWAHD uhl OOP,* in western Texas, contains one of the most significant fossil reefs in the world. Guadalupe Peak (8,749 feet, or 2,667 meters), Texas's highest point, stands in the park. Congress authorized the park in 1966. It was opened to the public in 1972. See **National Park System** (table: National parks).

Critically reviewed by the National Park Service

Guadeloupe, *GWAHD uhl OOP,* is a group of islands in the West Indies. It forms an overseas *department* (administrative district) of France. It consists of two main islands separated by a narrow sea channel, a small island group called Îles des Saintes, and five small islands. It covers about 687 square miles (1,780 square kilometers). The larger of the main islands is called Guadeloupe, or Basse-Terre, and the other is Grande-Terre. The small islands are Marie-Galante, Désirade, St.-Barthélemy, the northern part of St. Martin, and Petite-Terre. The town of Basse-Terre is the capital. See **Basse-Terre.**

Guadeloupe has a population of about 467,000. Most of the people are of mixed black and white ancestry. A group of descendants of the original Norman and Breton settlers lives in the Îles des Saintes group. French is the official language, but many people speak a mixture of African words and French called *patois.* Guadeloupe has a hot, humid climate from June to December. But steady winds tend to moderate the heat. The islands have cooler, drier weather from January to May.

Most people in Guadeloupe are employed in service industries. But agriculture is the chief source of income for the islands. Leading farm products include bananas, cocoa, coffee, and sugar cane. Rum is distilled and exported. Guadeloupe's chief port and largest town is Pointe-à-Pitre on Grande-Terre Island.

A general council of elected members governs Gua-

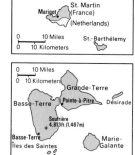

WORLD BOOK maps

Guadeloupe is a French possession in the West Indies.

deloupe. Deputies represent the group in the French National Assembly. The Carib Indians occupied Guadeloupe when the first French settlers arrived in 1635. Since then, Guadeloupe has remained a French possession, except for temporary British occupations between 1759 and 1813. In 1989, Hurricane Hugo killed six people on Basse-Terre and Grande-Terre. Gerald R. Showalter

Guam, *gwahm,* is a territory of the United States in the Mariana Islands. It serves as a vital U.S. air and naval base in the Pacific Ocean. Hågatña is Guam's capital.

Guam lies at the south end of the Marianas, about 1,300 miles (2,100 kilometers) east of the Philippines. About 30 miles (48 kilometers) long and 4 to 10 miles (6.4 to 16 kilometers) wide, Guam covers 209 square miles (541 square kilometers). It has a population of 173,000.

Land and climate. Coral reefs lie off the coast of Guam. A limestone plateau rises on the northern part of the island. Many forests in the north have been cleared for farms and airfields. The southern half of Guam has a range of mountains of volcanic origin. Several rivers originate in the mountains and run to the coast. Earthquakes occasionally strike the island. The War in the Pacific National Historical Park is on Guam. It honors the U.S. troops who fought in the Pacific in World War II (1939-1945).

Guam has warm weather most of the year. Average temperatures range from 68 to 90 °F (20 to 32 °C). But typhoons frequently hit the island, and rainfall averages 90 inches (230 centimeters) a year. The rainy season generally lasts from May to November.

People. About 40 percent of the Guamanian people are *Chamorros.* Chamorros are descendants of the island's original inhabitants and other Micronesian islanders, and of Filipinos and Spaniards. Other Guamanians are descended from American, Italian, French, British, Japanese, Chinese, and Mexican settlers. About one-sixth of the people on Guam are U.S. military personnel and their dependents. English and Chamorro are the official languages of Guam. English is the most widely used language. The University of Guam, in Mangilao, is the only university. Tamuning is the largest town.

Economy. Tourism and related industries produce the largest part of Guam's income. Each year, more than 500,000 tourists, mostly Japanese, visit Guam. The U.S. military is the second largest source of income. It maintains Andersen Air Force Base and a number of naval facilities on the island. Military facilities provide many jobs for Guamanians. Agriculture and fishing are minor eco-

Guam

——	Boundary
——	Road
★	Capital
•	Town
+	Elevation above sea level

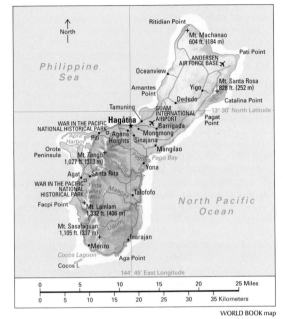

WORLD BOOK map

nomic activities. Farmers grow coconuts, sweet potatoes, and taro. Tuna is the most important fish. Apra Harbor is Guam's chief port.

History and government. Chamorros were the first inhabitants of Guam. They came from Southeast Asia, perhaps as early as 3000 B.C. Through the years, many

Chamorros and other settlers in Guam intermarried. The descendants of these people are still called Chamorros.

The Portuguese explorer Ferdinand Magellan led the first European expedition to Guam. His group arrived there in 1521. Spain made the island a possession in 1565. But the Spanish did not take actual control over Guam until 1668. Spain ceded Guam to the United States in 1898 after the Spanish-American War. Guam was placed under the administration of the U.S. Navy. Japan attacked Guam on Dec. 8, 1941, during World War II. It captured the island on December 10. United States forces landed on Guam on July 21, 1944, but they did not completely recapture the island until Aug. 10, 1944.

After World War II ended in 1945, the U.S. military took over about one-third of Guam's land. In 1954, the U.S. Air Force established Andersen Air Force Base in Guam.

The United States made Guam a territory on Aug. 1, 1950, and transferred its supervision from the Navy to the Department of the Interior. The people became United States citizens. Guam voters elect a one-house Legislature. They elect a governor and lieutenant governor for four-year terms. Before 1970, governors were appointed by the U.S. president. Since 1972, Guam voters have elected a delegate to the U.S. House of Representatives. The delegate may vote in House committees, but not on the House floor.   Donald H. Rubinstein

See also **Flag** (picture: Flags of the U.S. states and territories); **Hagåtña.**

Guan, *gwahn,* is the name of a group of tropical American game birds. Guans measure from 22 to 36 inches (56 to 91 centimeters) long and weigh up to 4 pounds (1.8 kilograms). Their feathers are greenish-black mixed with white and brown. Guans have long tails, and most species have a crest on the head. They eat fruits and seeds.

Bertin W. Anderson

Scientific classification. Guans belong to the family Cracidae. They make up four genera—*Penelope, Aburria, Chamaepetes,* and *Oreophasis.*

Guanaco, *gwuh NAH koh,* is an animal that looks like a small camel without a hump. The guanaco and its rela-

Superstock

Hagåtña, Guam's capital, lies on the west coast of the island. Dense, tropical vegetation grows near Hagåtña and covers much of the rest of Guam.

© M. A. Chappell, Animals Animals
The guanaco is a wool-bearing animal of South America.

tive, the vicuña, are wild, wool-bearing animals of South America. A guanaco stands $3\frac{1}{2}$ to 4 feet (107 to 122 centimeters) high at the shoulder. It is cinnamon-brown in color with white undersides and a gray to black face.

Guanacos live in groups in the dry foothills of the Andes Mountains in Peru, Chile, and Argentina, and on the Patagonian plateau in Argentina. They live at elevations from sea level to 14,000 feet (4,300 meters) above sea level. After a *gestation period* (pregnancy) of $11\frac{1}{2}$ months, the female guanaco bears one baby, called a *chulengo*. The llama and alpaca of South America may be descended from the guanaco.

Scientific classification. The guanaco belongs to the camel family, Camelidae. It is *Lama guanicoe*.　　William L. Franklin

See also **Alpaca; Llama; Vicuña.**

Guangzhou, *gwahng joh* (pop. 3,918,010), is the largest city in southern China and a major center of international trade. It is also an industrial center and one of China's principal ports. Guangzhou is sometimes called *Yangcheng* (city of goats) by the Chinese. Foreigners have known it as *Canton* (pronounced *kan TAHN*), and its people as *Cantonese*. The city lies at the head of the Zhu Jiang (Pearl River) Delta. It is about 75 miles (121 kilometers) northwest of Hong Kong and the South China Sea. For location, see **China** (political map).

The city is the capital of Guangdong Province. Guangzhou is one of China's most modern cities. Many of its people live in three- or four-story concrete apartment buildings. Until 1960, thousands of Cantonese lived on boats anchored in the Zhu Jiang. Since then, the government has moved these people into apartments.

The city has a sports stadium and several public parks and museums. It also has many national monuments, including the Peasant Movement Training Institute. In 1925 and 1926, Chairman Mao Zedong of the Chinese Communist Party taught Communist beliefs to party workers at the institute. Another monument marks the burial site of the people who died in the Guangzhou Uprising of 1927. That year, the Communists failed in an attempt to take over the city's government. Jinan University and Zhongshan University are in Guangzhou.

Economy of Guangzhou is based largely on trade, and the city has an ideal location as a trade center. Tributaries of four rivers—the Zhu Jiang, the North, the East, and the West—connect Guangzhou and Guangxi Autonomous Region. Just east of Guangzhou is the deepwater port of Huangpu (also called Whampoa), which serves oceangoing ships. A railroad links Guangzhou to Hong Kong and to the industrial center of Wuhan, about 600 miles (966 kilometers) north of Guangzhou.

China's largest foreign trade fair takes place twice annually in Guangzhou. This event, called the Export Commodities Fair, is held for a month each spring and fall. It attracts thousands of foreign merchants.

Products manufactured in Guangzhou include paper, sewing machines, and textiles. Shipbuilding and sugar refining are also important industries in the city.

Guangzhou has long been a center of handicraft industries. The city's craftworkers are famous for their ivory and jade carvings, lacquerware, and porcelain.

History. Guangzhou was founded about 214 B.C. by Shi Huangdi, the emperor of China's Qin dynasty. During the time of the Roman Empire, from about 27 B.C. to A.D. 476, Roman merchants went to Guangzhou for silks, spices, and tea. Arab and Persian traders visited the city during the A.D. 600's. Portuguese merchants first went to Guangzhou in 1516. By the early 1800's, British, Dutch, French, and Portuguese traders controlled most of the trade between Guangzhou and the West. From 1759 to 1842, Guangzhou was the only Chinese port open to foreign trade. See **China** (Clash with the Western powers).

Many leaders of the 1911 revolution came from Guangzhou. This revolt led to the establishment of the Chinese republic in 1912. One of the leaders was Sun Yat-sen, who helped form the Nationalist Party that year and became its first leader. The party had its headquarters in Guangzhou from 1917 to 1926. The Japanese occupied Guangzhou from 1938 until World War II ended in 1945. In 1949, Chiang Kai-shek, head of the Nationalist Party since the mid-1920's, moved his government from Nanjing to Guangzhou. The Chinese Communists took over China later in 1949, and the Chinese Nationalists fled from Guangzhou to Taiwan.　　Parris H. Chang

Kurt Scholz, Shostal
Guangzhou is a major port of China and one of the country's most modern cities. The city's downtown area, shown above, lies along the Zhu Jiang. Guangzhou is also an important Chinese center of industry and of trade with other nations.

Guano, *GWAH noh,* is the waste matter of sea birds and bats. It makes a valuable fertilizer because it is rich in nitrate and phosphate. Large colonies of birds such as cormorants, gannets, guanays, pelicans, penguins, and petrels leave immense deposits of this material.

The islands off the coast of Peru have long been the chief source of supply. Deposits on the Chincha Islands

Joe Barnell, Shostal

Sea birds leave deposits of guano, a waste matter that is valuable as fertilizer.

at one time covered the surface to a depth of more than 100 feet (30 meters). Other valuable deposits lie on the Galapagos Islands of Ecuador. Deposits have been found in other parts of Latin America, on the Pacific Islands, and in the Grand Canyon Bat Cave in Arizona. See **Peru** (Mining). Taylor J. Johnston

Guantánamo, *gwahn TAH nuh мон* (pop. 203,371), is a city in southern Cuba. It lies about 10 miles (16 kilometers) inland from Guantánamo Bay, the site of a United States naval base. For location, see **Cuba** (political map). Guantánamo is a major sugar-refining center. It also serves as a processing and trading center for cacao, coffee, and corn from southern Cuba.

In 1903, Cuba leased Guantánamo Bay to the United States for $2,000 a year. The two nations signed a treaty giving the United States the right to establish a naval base on the bay. This treaty was renewed in 1934. It can be canceled only by mutual agreement or by voluntary U.S. withdrawal. In 1962, the Cuban leader Fidel Castro accused the United States of territorial interference. He demanded that the United States give up the naval base immediately. President John F. Kennedy refused and sent Marines to protect the base. Since then, Castro has not cashed the annual checks that the United States has sent for payment of the lease. Castro has continued to maintain that the U.S. presence at Guantánamo Bay is illegal. During the 1990's, thousands of refugees fleeing from Haiti and Cuba were temporarily housed at the U.S. base at Guantánamo Bay. Ivan A. Schulman

Guar, *gwahr,* is a hardy, drought-resistant legume grown for its seeds, as forage, and as a green manure crop to improve the soil. The plant, first found in India,

was brought to the United States in the early 1900's. It is grown mostly in the Southwest. One bushy variety grows about 4 feet (1.2 meters) high. The special seed-producing type grows higher. The seeds develop in pods and contain the chemical compound *mannogalactan,* used in manufacturing paper and textiles, processing minerals, and treating waste water.

Scientific classification. Guar is in the pea family, Fabaceae or Leguminosae. Its scientific name is *Cyamopsis tetragonoloba.*
Daniel F. Austin

Guaraní Indians. See **Tupí-Guaraní Indians.**

Guaranty, *GAR uhn tee,* is an agreement whereby one person promises to pay another's debt if the latter fails to pay. The *guarantor* is the one who promises to pay. The person in whose interest the promise is made is the *principal,* and the *guarantee* or *beneficiary* is the person who accepts the promise. In the United States, most states require that such agreements be in writing. A guaranty differs from a *warranty,* which refers to the condition of goods or title to land. If sellers guarantee their products will work, they are really giving a warranty. John Krahmer

Guardian, in law, is a person appointed by a court to care for another person called a *ward,* or for another person's property, or both. A guardian may be appointed for *minors* (people under legal age), spendthrifts, insane people, or people unable to take care of themselves. The courts also have the power to remove guardians.

A guardian usually has control of the person, as well as management of the property of a ward. The guardian must maintain and educate the ward from the income of the ward's estate. The guardian cannot reap any benefits from the estate. The guardian must have a court order before buying or selling real estate for the ward's account. The guardian must file an inventory and render all financial accounts before the court.

Parents generally act as guardians of their own minor children. In English common law, the father was the sole guardian. But this rule has been changed in virtually all parts of the United States and the Commonwealth of Nations. Because parents become guardians without appointment by a court, they are called *guardians by nature* to distinguish them from *guardians by law.* In most states, a child without parents is allowed to choose his or her own guardian at the age of 14, but the court may reject the child's choice. A *guardian ad litem* is a guardian appointed by a court for the purpose of a single lawsuit. Aidan R. Gough

See also **Parent; Receiver; Ward.**

Guarneri, *gwahr NAIR ee,* is the name of a famous family of violinmakers who lived in Cremona, Italy. The first member of the family to win fame for his violins was Andrea (1626-1698). He was a fellow student of Stradivari in the workshop of Nicolo Amati, but was not an outstanding craftsman. Andrea's business was carried on after his death by his sons Pietro (1655-1728) and Giuseppe (1666-1739?). Andrea's nephew, Giuseppe Antonio (1687-1745), called "del Gesù," became the most celebrated member of the family. His violins were known for their original design and rich, powerful tone. Guarneri's best models compare well with the best of Stradivari. See also **Amati family; Stradivari, Antonio.**

Dorothy DeLay

Max & Bea Hunn, FPG

Donna Tomasello Falk

Urban and rural Guatemala contrast greatly, as shown here. The National Palace, a government center, stands in downtown Guatemala City. A rural village lies along a river.

Guatemala

Guatemala, GWAH *tuh MAH luh,* has more people than any other Central American country. Most of Guatemala's people live in the rugged mountains in the central part of the country. There, on a high plateau, lies Guatemala City, the capital and industrial center of Guatemala, and the largest city in Central America.

Almost half the people are Indians whose way of life differs greatly from that of other Guatemalans. Their ancestors, the Maya Indians, built a highly developed civilization hundreds of years before Christopher Columbus landed in America. Today, the Indians live in peasant or farm communities apart from the main life of the country. Most speak Indian languages and wear Indian clothing. Most of the other Guatemalans—called *Ladinos*—are of mixed Indian and Spanish ancestry. They speak Spanish and follow a Guatemalan form of Spanish-American customs. The Ladinos include peasants and laborers as well as the people in cities and towns who control the government and economy.

The main sources of Guatemala's income are exported farm products, especially coffee. Guatemala has close economic and political ties with the United States. The United States is Guatemala's chief trading partner and imports much Guatemalan coffee. Most of Guatemala's coffee is grown along the southern edge of the broad central mountainous region. A large, thinly populated plain with thick rain forests lies north of the

mountains. South of the mountains, farmers grow such crops as corn, cotton, and sugar cane and raise beef cattle on a grassy lowland between the mountains and the Pacific Ocean.

Government

National government. Guatemala has a democratic form of government. The people elect a president to head the government for a term of four years. A vice president elected by the people also serves a four-year term. The president and vice president can serve only one term each. The president appoints a Cabinet of ministers who carry out the operations of the government. An 80-member Congress makes the laws of Guate-

Facts in brief

Capital: Guatemala City.
Official language: Spanish.
Area: 42,042 mi² (108,889 km²). *Greatest distances*—north-south, 283 mi (455 km); east-west, 261 mi (420 km). *Coastlines*—Pacific, 152 mi (245 km); Caribbean, 53 mi (85 km).
Elevation: *Highest*—Volcán Tajumulco, 13,845 ft (4,220 m) above sea level. *Lowest*—sea level along the coasts.
Population: *Estimated 2002 population*—11,980,000; density, 285 per mi² (110 per km²); distribution, 61 percent rural, 39 percent urban. *1994 census*—8,322,051.
Chief products: *Agriculture*—bananas, beans, beef cattle, cardamom, coffee, corn, cotton, sugar cane. *Manufacturing*—clothing and textiles, handicrafts, processed foods and beverages.
Money: *Basic unit*—quetzal. One hundred centavos equal one quetzal.

Gary S. Elbow, the contributor of this article, is Professor of Geography at Texas Tech University.

mala. Members of Congress are elected by the people to four-year terms, which can be renewed.

Guatemala has several political parties. The two major parties are the National Advancement Party and the Guatemalan Republican Front.

Local government. Guatemala is divided into 22 departments for purposes of local government. The departments are divided into a total of about 330 *municipios* (cities or townships). A governor, appointed by the president, heads each department, except for the capital department. A mayor and a council, both elected by the people, head the capital department. An elected mayor and council also head each municipio.

Courts. The Supreme Court of Justice is Guatemala's highest court. The president appoints its members and the members of some other high courts in the country. The Supreme Court of Justice appoints the judges of the lower courts.

Armed forces. Guatemala has an army of about 31,400 men. The army includes a small air force and naval force. Men between the ages of 18 and 50 are required to serve from 2 to $2\frac{1}{2}$ years.

People

The people of Guatemala may be divided into two main groups—Indians and people of mixed Spanish and Indian ancestry. But in Guatemala, being called an Indian or a non-Indian does not depend entirely on a person's ancestry. It is chiefly a matter of how people live and of how they think of themselves. For example, a Guatemalan is considered an Indian if he or she speaks an Indian language, wears Indian clothing, and lives in a community where the people follow the Indian ways of life. The Indians think of themselves more as part of their community than of their country. They pay little attention to affairs outside the community. Indians make up about 45 percent of the people of Guatemala. Most of them are extremely poor and uneducated.

About 55 percent of Guatemala's people follow Spanish-American customs and traditions. These people are called *Ladinos.* They speak Spanish, the official language of Guatemala. Indians, even ones of unmixed ancestry, may become Ladinos if they drop their Indian ways of life and join a Ladino community. Many Ladinos are poor farmworkers who are no better off than the Indians. Others control the government and the economy of the country. Ladinos are thought of chiefly in terms of their income and social class, not on the basis of how much Indian or Spanish ancestry they have.

The Indians live in small country settlements or in towns. Most of the Ladinos live in cities or towns. The number of Ladinos is increasing much faster than that of the Indians. This is largely because the Ladinos have greater opportunities for medical care in the cities and towns, which are chiefly Ladino. As a result, they have a lower death rate than the Indians. There has also been a gradual shift among the Indians toward Ladino ways of life.

Indians. Almost all the Indians of Guatemala speak one of the many Maya Indian languages. Many of the men and some women also speak Spanish. There is hardly any social or political unity among Indian communities, even those of a single language group. An Indian is known by his or her community. There are no or-

ganized tribes. They began to dissolve during the period of the Spanish conquest.

Almost every Indian community in Guatemala has its own colorful style of clothing. The Indians often travel far from home to trade in local markets or to find work. As a result, Indians wearing a wide variety of clothing styles can be seen in many parts of central and western Guatemala.

About 70 percent of all Guatemalans are Roman Catholics, and about 30 percent are Protestants. The Indians also follow many religious practices from their pre-Christian past. They worship local gods and spirits along with God, Jesus Christ, the Virgin Mary, and their local patron saint. Such natural features as hills represent various Indian gods, and the Indians pray to them, especially during planting and harvesting times.

Ladinos. In farm areas with few Indians, especially in the eastern and southern regions, Ladinos make up the laboring class as well as the middle and upper classes. The tools and homes of Ladino peasants are crude and simple, much like those of the Indians. The tools include an ax, digging stick, hoe, and machete. Some farmers with flat, fertile land have oxen and plows. Most farm Ladinos live in one- or two-room houses of adobe or

Guatemala's state flag, used by the government, was adopted in 1871. The national flag of Guatemala does not include the coat of arms.

Guatemala's coat of arms includes a quetzal, the national bird of Guatemala, and a scroll bearing the date when independence was declared.

WORLD BOOK map

Guatemala is bordered by Mexico, Belize, the Caribbean Sea, Honduras, El Salvador, and the Pacific Ocean.

© Robert Frerck, Odyssey Productions

A Roman Catholic church decorated for Holy Week draws Guatemalan worshipers. A carpet of flowers is in the center of the church. Most of Guatemala's people are Roman Catholics.

Emil Muench, Östman

Inactive volcanoes rise near the town of Sololá and beautiful Lake Atitlán. The lake bed is believed to be an ancient valley that was dammed by volcanic ash.

pole walls, with roofs made of palm leaves, straw, or tiles.

In Indian areas, the Ladinos live in towns. They control much local commerce and politics, and most of them feel superior to the Indians. The few wealthy Ladinos have a high standard of living similar to that of wealthy people in other Western countries. The customs and clothing of Ladinos do not vary much by region, but by wealth and occupation.

Recreation. In Guatemala's Ladino cities and towns, the people enjoy such sports as basketball, bicycling, and soccer. For Ladino and Indian peasants, religious feast days provide the main sources of recreation. These holidays include religious processions, fireworks, and Guatemala's famous marimba music (see **Marimba**). In Indian communities, the people also perform dances that represent events from history or legends.

Education. Guatemalan law requires children to go to school from the age of 7 through 13. About 55 percent of the children attend primary school, but only about 15 percent go to high school. School attendance is much higher in the cities than in rural areas. Guatemala does not have enough schools for all its children, and some rural areas have no schools at all. Few of the country's teachers speak the Indian languages. As a result, many of the rural Indians cannot read and write. However, most of the urban Ladinos can read and write, and the country as a whole has more literate than illiterate people. For Guatemala's literacy rate, see **Literacy** (table: Literacy rates).

Guatemala has five universities. The University of San Carlos, in Guatemala City, is the oldest and largest. It was founded in 1676. Between 5 and 10 percent of the people of college age go to a university.

Population. Approximately one-eighth of Guatemala's people live in Guatemala City, the nation's capital and largest city. Guatemala City has about 12 times as many people as the second largest city, Quezaltenango. Antigua was the capital of Guatemala during most of the Spanish colonial period.

The land

Guatemala has three main land regions: (1) the Northern Plain, (2) the Highlands, and (3) the Pacific Lowland.

The Northern Plain is the most thinly populated and least developed part of Guatemala. Tropical rain forests of hardwood trees cover most of the plain, and there are some grasslands. Some chicle, a gummy substance used in making chewing gum, is taken from the trees. Many ancient Mayan ruins, of which Tikal is perhaps the most famous, are in the forests. The country's largest lake, 228-square-mile (591-square-kilometer) Lake Izabal, lies near the Caribbean Sea.

The Highlands are a chain of mountains extending across Guatemala in an east-west direction. They are highest in the west. There, Volcán Tajumulco—the highest mountain in Central America—rises 13,845 feet (4,220 meters) above sea level. The region has many volcanoes, some of which are active. Earthquakes sometimes occur in the Highlands. Guatemala's longest river, the 250-mile (402-kilometer) Motagua, rises in the Highlands and flows to the Caribbean Sea.

Most Guatemalans live in the Highlands, and most of the coffee- and corn-growing farmland is there. A majority of Indians live in crowded communities in the western Highlands. Most people in the eastern Highlands are Ladinos. Guatemala City lies 4,850 feet (1,478 meters) above sea level in the middle of the region.

The Pacific Lowland consists largely of farmlands. Many forest-lined streams that rise in the Highlands flow through the lowland to the Pacific Ocean. The lowland has been thinly populated, but its farmlands have been developed since the late 1940's. The Pacific Lowland has sugar cane and cotton plantations, cattle ranches, and farms.

Climate

Guatemala has a tropical climate. Temperatures vary greatly from area to area because of differences in altitude. The plains and lowlands have an average yearly temperature of about 80 °F (27 °C), with little seasonal change. Mountain valleys 4,000 to 6,000 feet (1,200 to 1,800 meters) high are usually comfortably mild. They have a yearly average temperature of 60 °F to 70 °F (16 °C to 21 °C). The higher valleys sometimes have frost, and average 40 °F (4 °C).

The Pacific Lowland and western Highlands receive from 30 to 60 inches (76 to 150 centimeters) of rain a year, and the eastern Highlands get 20 to 30 inches (51 to 76 centimeters). The rainy season in Guatemala generally lasts from May to November, and daily showers fall during most of this period. Most of the Northern Plain receives from 80 to 150 inches (200 to 381 centimeters)

of rain annually. There, rain falls throughout most of the year. The edge of a hurricane sometimes hits Guatemala, causing some damage to the country's banana and coffee crops.

Economy

Guatemala is a developing country. Its major natural resource is fertile soil, and farming is the leading goods-producing industry. Thick forests cover almost half the land. Most of the forests consist of cedrela, mahogany,

Guatemala map index

Guatemala

WORLD BOOK map

International boundary
Road
Railroad
National capital
Department capital
Other city or town
Elevation above sea level
Ruin

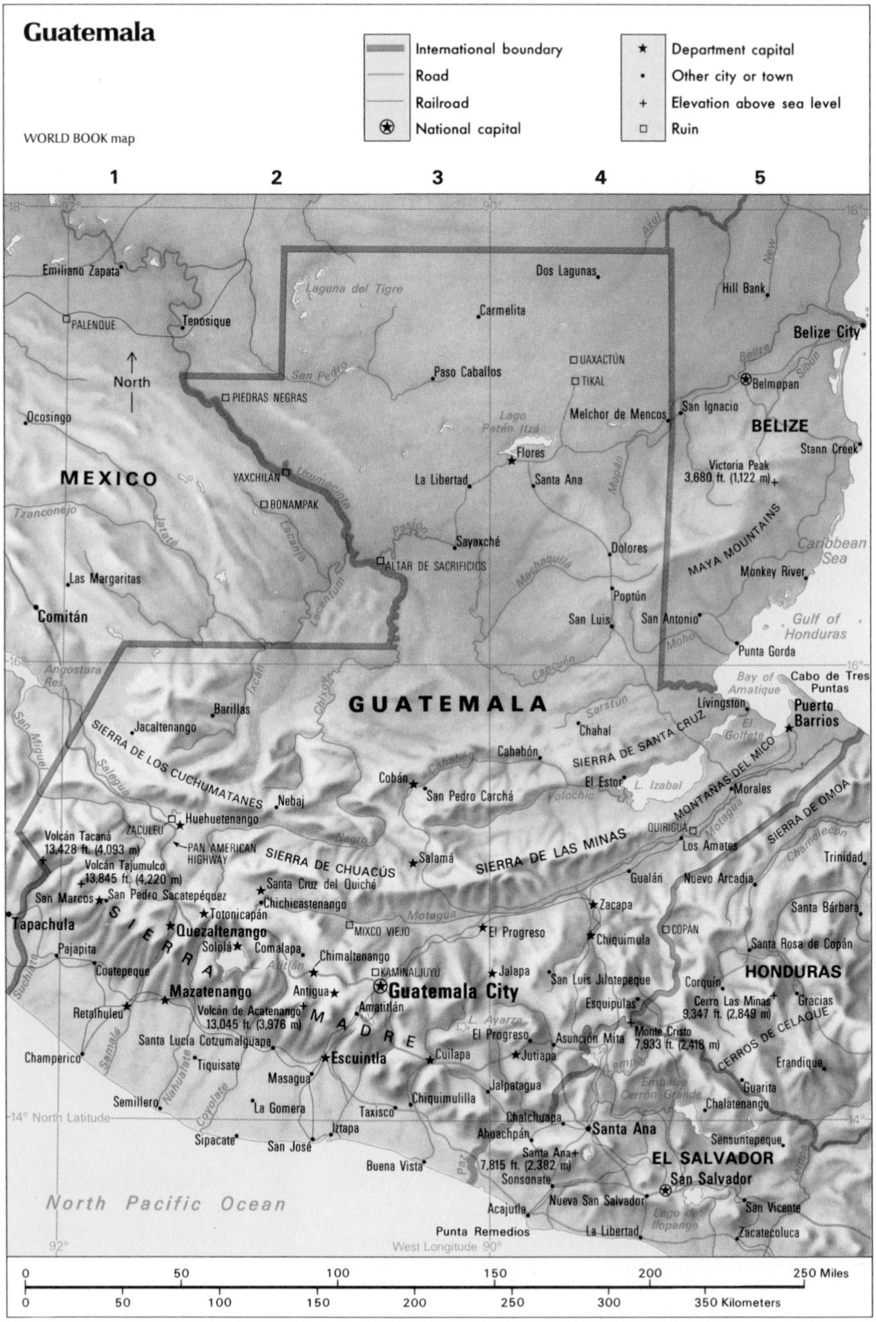

and other hardwood trees. Guatemala has deposits of petroleum, antimony, lead, nickel, zinc, and other minerals. The country's many mountain streams are a source of inexpensive hydroelectric power. Guatemala has several hydroelectric plants, the first of which opened in 1970.

Guatemala is a member of two economic unions. They are the Central American Common Market, a union of five nations, and the Association of Caribbean States, a union of 25 nations. These organizations work to establish closer economic ties between member nations. Guatemala's leading trading partners include the United States, El Salvador, and Mexico.

Agriculture provides about 25 percent of Guatemala's *gross domestic product* (GDP)—the annual value of goods and services produced in the country. The nation's economy depends heavily on the export of farm products. The chief exports are coffee, bananas, sugar, and a spice called *cardamom.*

Coffee makes up about 30 percent of the total value of exports. The best coffee-growing land extends along the southern edge of the Highlands region. Some workers live permanently on the coffee plantations. In addition, many Indians from the western Highlands come every year to help harvest the coffee crop. They do not have enough land of their own to support themselves. The southern edge of the Highlands region is also the chief cardamom-growing region. Bananas are grown mainly near Guatemala's Caribbean coast. Farmers in the Pacific Lowland region grow sugar cane, rubber-yielding trees, cotton, and corn. Corn is the basic food of most Guatemalans and the chief crop grown for use within the country. Other important food crops include beans, rice, and wheat. Farmers raise livestock, especially beef cattle, throughout Guatemala. The major cattle ranches are in the Pacific Lowland.

Service industries are those economic activities that provide services rather than producing goods. Such activities account for about 60 percent of Guatemala's GDP. Wholesale and retail trade form the most important category of services in Guatemala in terms of the GDP. Much of the country's trade is based on the distribution of agricultural products. Other important service industry categories include finance and real estate, transportation and communication, and government. Services are most important in the large cities, especially Guatemala City.

Manufacturing accounts for about 15 percent of Guatemala's GDP. The industry is growing, but it has not kept up with the heavy movement of people to Guatemala City and other cities. As a result, the cities have a serious unemployment problem. The people's low income, along with limited power sources and poor transportation, prevent faster industrial growth.

Most of Guatemala's manufactured products are consumer goods, such as processed foods and beverages, cigarettes, clothing, and textiles. Cement is also a valuable product. Much small manufacturing activity centers around Indian handicrafts, including blankets, pottery, and wood products.

Transportation. Two major highways cross Guatemala from Mexico to El Salvador, and another connects the Pacific and Caribbean coasts. Less than 3 percent of Guatemalans own an automobile. Many people travel by bus. Railroads link Guatemala City with both coasts.

Guatemala City has an international airport. The major seaport, Puerto Barrios, is on the Caribbean Sea.

Communication. Guatemala has about 5 daily newspapers, most of which are privately owned. The government-operated postal, telegraph, and telephone systems provide service only to the cities and towns. Guatemala has an average of about 1 television set for every 20 people and about 1 radio for every 15 people.

History

Indian period. Historians know little about the people who lived in what is now Guatemala before farming developed there. The earliest well-known society, at Las Charcas in the Highlands region, dates from the 1000's B.C. The people of this community grew corn, made pottery, and wove mats and ropes.

Much of the famous Maya Indian civilization thrived in Guatemala between A.D. 250 and 900. The Maya recorded important dates on tall, carved blocks of stone called *stelae,* and used a kind of picture writing. They built many large cities, mainly in the Northern Plain region. These cities included beautiful palaces, pyramids, and temples—all made of limestone. The Maya apparently abandoned these cities during the 900's, for reasons that are not clear. When the Spaniards arrived, most of the Maya were living in the Highlands region. See **Maya.**

Colonial period. In 1523, a Spanish expedition led by Pedro de Alvarado set out from New Spain, the Spanish colony in Mexico, and invaded Guatemala. Alvarado defeated all the major Guatemalan Indian groups, and established Spanish rule in the country.

In 1570, Spain set up the Audiencia of Guatemala, a high court of judges and administrators, in what is now

Jane Latta, Keystone

Coffee beans dry in the sun on plantations in the Highlands region. Workers turn the beans to dry them evenly.

Antigua. The Spaniards found little gold or silver in Guatemala but stayed on as plantation owners with Indian labor. In 1776, the Audiencia was moved to Guatemala City after an earthquake destroyed Antigua.

Independence. On Sept. 15, 1821, Guatemala and other Central American states declared their independence. They later became part of the Mexican empire, but they broke away in 1823 and formed the United Provinces of Central America. This union generally followed liberal economic and political policies. For example, the member states established various civil rights and ended the special privileges of powerful landowners.

The union began to fall apart under various pressures, including efforts by the conservative nobles to get their old privileges back. In 1839, Guatemala left the union. A conservative general, Rafael Carrera, then ruled as dictator-president for most of the period until 1865.

The liberals returned to power in 1871. They ended the special privileges that Carrera had restored, but the people still did not have political freedom. A number of liberal dictator-presidents ruled until 1944. They promoted economic development, especially coffee growing. Foreigners were encouraged to immigrate to Guatemala to develop the land. Germans became especially active in coffee production. In 1906, the United Fruit Company (now Chiquita Brands International), a U.S. firm, began developing banana plantations in Guatemala.

The mid-1900's. In 1944, a 10-year period of social and economic revolution began after protests forced dictator Jorge Ubico to resign. A new constitution, adopted in 1945, provided political liberties that the people of Guatemala had never known. Under President Juan José Arévalo, the government promoted education and health measures, and encouraged the rapid growth of labor unions. A free press developed, along with various political parties.

Colonel Jacobo Arbenz Guzmán became president in 1951. The next year, the government began to take over much privately owned land and distribute it among landless peasants. This program included large areas owned by the United Fruit Company, by then the largest landowner in Guatemala.

The United States government, which had begun to fear Communist influences in the Arbenz administration, supported a revolt against him. In June 1954, the rebels attacked from their base in Honduras. The Guatemalan Army refused to support Arbenz, and he resigned. A temporary military government was set up.

Guatemala's fifth constitution was adopted in 1956, but political confusion continued. The army seized the government again in 1963, and a sixth constitution went into effect in 1966. Elections were held that year, and civilian government was restored under President Julio César Méndez Montenegro. But the country remained troubled. Secret political extremist groups—both rightist and leftist—made terror raids. Guatemalan political leaders, the U.S. ambassador, and others were killed.

In 1976, a major earthquake struck Guatemala. It caused about 23,000 deaths and about $700 million worth of property damage.

Civil conflict. In the late 1970's, violence became widespread in Guatemala. Various groups of leftists fought government forces. The antigovernment groups included Indians and other rural people who have little economic and political power. Warfare between rebels and government forces caused many Indians in the west and north to flee deeper into the mountains, to Mexico, or to the United States. In 1996, the opposition groups and the government signed a peace agreement ending the conflict. After the agreement was signed, about 40,000 refugees returned to Guatemala.

Political developments. Guatemala held four presidential elections between 1970 and 1982. Military officers won each time. But many people claimed the elections were fraudulent. General Angel Anibal Guevara won the 1982 presidential election, held early in March. But later that month, before Guevara took office, a group of military leaders took control of the government and established a three-member military junta. General Efraín Ríos Montt, the junta's leader, suspended the Constitution, abolished the Congress, and banned political party activities. In June, Ríos Montt removed the other junta members from power and declared himself Guatemala's only leader. In 1983, military leaders overthrew Ríos Montt.

In 1985, the people elected Marco Vinicio Cerezo Arévalo, a civilian, president of Guatemala. A new constitution was written, the Congress was reestablished, and political party activities were allowed once again. The new civilian government took office in 1986. Guatemala's military leaders tried several times to overthrow the civilian government, but their attempts were unsuccessful.

A new civilian president, Jorge Serrano Elias, was elected in 1991. In May 1993, Serrano dissolved Congress and announced he would rule by presidential order. Large numbers of Guatemalans protested his actions. Guatemala's military removed Serrano from office in June. Congress then elected Ramiro de León Carpio president. In 1996, the voters elected Alvaro Arzú Irigoyen president. In 1999, Alfonso Portillo Cabrera won election as president.   Gary S. Elbow

Related articles in *World Book* include:

Outline

I. **Government**
   A. National government   C. Courts
   B. Local government   D. Armed forces
II. **People**
   A. Indians   C. Recreation   E. Population
   B. Ladinos   D. Education
III. **The land**
   A. The Northern Plain   C. The Pacific Lowland
   B. The Highlands
IV. **Climate**
V. **Economy**
   A. Agriculture
   B. Service industries
   C. Manufacturing
   D. Transportation
   E. Communication
VI. **History**

Questions

What is the major source of Guatemala's income?
What is the chief crop grown for the people's use?
What was the United Provinces of Central America?

What percentage of the Guatemalans are Indians?
Who are the Ladinos?
How did Guatemala come under Spanish control?
What is the chief religion in Guatemala?
In what region do most Guatemalans live?

Guatemala City, *GWAH tuh MAH luh,* is the capital and largest city of Guatemala. The city lies on a plateau in south-central Guatemala that is about 5,000 feet (1,500 meters) above sea level. For location, see **Guatemala** (map).

Guatemala City's downtown is in the northeast section of the city. It has broad avenues lined with modern hotels, office buildings, and shopping centers. The National Palace, the center of Guatemala's government, faces a park in the heart of the downtown area. Minerva Park, in a residential area north of downtown, is known for its huge relief map of Guatemala. The concrete map, made to scale, covers about $\frac{2}{3}$ acre (0.25 hectare). Aurora Park, in the southern part of the city, is the site of several museums, a zoo, and a race track. Aurora International Airport is located just east of the park. Guatemala City has four universities, including the University of San Carlos, which was founded in the 1600's.

Guatemala City is growing rapidly. The country's 1981 census reported that the city had 754,243 people. But, according to estimates, the population had grown to more than 1 million by 1995. The city faces problems of overcrowding and poverty. Many poor people have settled in ravines on the outskirts of the city.

Guatemala City is the country's chief manufacturing center. Its products include beverages, processed foods, and textiles. Retail trade and government also employ many people. The Central American Common Market has its headquarters in the city.

Guatemala City was founded in 1776 as the capital of the Spanish colony of Guatemala. In 1917 and 1918, earthquakes almost completely destroyed Guatemala City, and the city had to be rebuilt. An earthquake that struck Guatemala in 1976 caused thousands of deaths and widespread damage to the outlying areas of Guatemala City.   Neale J. Pearson

Guava is a tropical fruit. Guavas are round, oval, or pear-shaped and weigh from about 1 ounce (28 grams) to more than 1 pound (450 grams). They have yellow or light green skin and white, yellow, or pink flesh. The fruit has many gritty seeds and is an excellent source of vitamin C and various minerals.

Some guava varieties taste sweet, and others have a sour taste. Sweet varieties may be eaten fresh. They taste best when fully ripe but not soft. Both the flesh and the seeds may be eaten. People often serve sliced sweet guavas with cream for dessert. Most sour guavas are made into jams, jellies, or juices or are used to flavor cakes, pies, or ice cream.

Guavas grow on evergreen trees 5 to 30 feet (1.5 to 9 meters) tall. The trees have shiny smooth bark and drooping branches.

Guavas originated in what are now Colombia and Peru. Today, farmers grow guavas in India, Taiwan, Thailand, the Philippines, Australia, Brazil, and other tropical countries. In the United States, farmers raise guavas in California, Florida, and Hawaii.   Philip J. Ito

Scientific classification. Guavas make up the genus *Psidium* in the myrtle family, Myrtaceae.

Guayaquil, *GWAH yah KEEL* (pop. 1,764,170), is the largest city and chief seaport in Ecuador. It lies on the Guayas River, about 40 miles (64 kilometers) from the Pacific Ocean (see **Ecuador** [political map]). Oceangoing ships reach Guayaquil's deep-water port by way of the Gulf of Guayaquil and the Estero Salado ship channel, which is 36 miles (58 kilometers) long.

Guayaquil was founded by Spaniards in 1538. Pirates looted the city several times during the 1600's. Today, Guayaquil is a busy commercial center. It has breweries, a cement plant, flour mills, ironworks, sawmills, small shipyards, and textile mills.   Murdo J. MacLeod

Guayule, *gwah YOO lee,* or *wy OO lee,* is a rubber-producing shrub that is native to the desert of southwestern Texas and north-central Mexico. The guayule plant grows to between 1 and 3 feet (30 to 90 centimeters) tall. Its branches have silver leaves shaped like spearheads. Tiny white flowers grow in small clusters on the stems.

The Aztec Indians played games with rubber balls made from guayule. They chewed guayule bark to get rubber from the plant. In the 1880's and 1890's, businesses became interested in guayule as a source of rubber. By 1910, several factories in the United States and Germany were producing rubber from wild guayule. The rubber industry soon switched almost entirely to the tropical hevea rubber tree as its source of natural rubber. During World War II (1939-1945), Japanese occupation of the Far East endangered the U.S. rubber supply from the hevea tree. Guayule rubber production was revived in California to help maintain a secure source of rubber.   Margaret R. Bolick

Scientific classification. Guayule belongs to the composite family, Compositae. Its scientific name is *Parthenium argentatum.*

See also **Rubber.**

Guelder-rose. See Snowball.

Guelphs and Ghibellines, *gwehlfs, GIHB uh lihnz,* were two political groups in Italy during the late Middle Ages. *Guelph* is the Italian form of the German family name *Welf.* It was the Welf family that held the duchies

WORLD BOOK illustration by Kate Lloyd Jones, Linden Artists Ltd.

Guavas develop from small, white flowers on certain shrubs and trees of the myrtle family. Guavas have many hard seeds.

of Bavaria and Saxony in the 1100's. Ghibelline is said to have come from *Waiblingen,* the name of an estate of the Hohenstaufen family.

The contest of these two families for the throne of Germany began the strife between the two Italian parties. The Ghibellines favored the imperial cause, and the Guelphs supported the pope, who opposed the authority of the German emperor in Italy.

The Hohenstaufens died out in the mid-1200's and the names lost their original meaning. By tradition, certain towns were Guelph and others Ghibelline. If the ruling authorities in any town took one name, the opposition usually took the other.   Jonathan W. Zophy

Guenevere. See Arthur, King; Round Table; Lancelot, Sir.

Guenon, *guh NAWN,* is any of a group of monkeys that live throughout Africa south of the Sahara. Guenons have a long tail, a roundish head, and a short face. Adult guenons weigh from 3 to 15 pounds (1.4 to 7 kilograms). The females are slightly smaller than the males. The hair on the face and body of these monkeys grows in various patterns of colors, especially black, white, and red. Some adult guenons have long, white facial hair that resembles a beard and mustache.

There are more than 20 species of guenons. They inhabit a wide variety of forested environments, including swamps, tropical rain forests, and wooded, grassy plains. Almost all guenons live in trees. A type of guenon called the *vervet* is probably the most common species of monkey in Africa.

Guenons eat many kinds of food. They feed mainly on fruit, leaves, buds, and seeds. They also eat insects. Occasionally, they prey on young birds and other small animals. Guenons have small pouches in their cheeks that allow them to hold extra food.

Guenons live in groups that consist of a number of adult males and females and their young. Some groups have a male leader, but he does not have strong control.

Scientific classification. Guenons belong to the Old World monkey family, Cercopithecidae. They are included in four genera: *Cercopithecus, Miopithecus, Allenopithecus,* and *Erythrocebus.*   Randall L. Susman

See also **Monkey** (diagram: The skeleton of a guenon monkey; picture: De Brazza's guenon).

Guernsey. See Cattle (Dairy cattle; picture).

Guernsey, *GURN zee,* is the westernmost of the Channel Islands in the English Channel. For location, see **Channel Islands** (map). Guernsey has a population of about 56,000. A large part of the island's 24-square-mile (63-square-kilometer) area is covered with small farms, hedged fields, and narrow, winding lanes. Greenhouses are used to grow tomatoes and many varieties of flowers. Tan-and-white Guernsey cattle on the island produce rich milk. Banking and the production of knitted garments are also important industries. St. Peter Port is the chief town.   D. Ian Scargill

Guerrilla warfare, *guh RIHL uh,* is warfare by roving bands of fighters who torment the enemy with ambushes, sudden raids, and other small-scale attacks. Guerrillas may be organized, but they usually fight in small bands. They most often operate behind enemy lines and use hit-and-run tactics and sabotage to surprise and torment the enemy. They take advantage of natural features of the terrain—such as forests, hills, lakes, and rivers—to conceal and launch attacks. When waged in cities, such operations are usually called "urban terrorism." They feature bombings, kidnappings, and other violent actions. Guerrillas are sometimes called *underground* or *resistance fighters,* or *partisans.* Guerrilla tactics are usually used by groups with limited resources against an enemy with vastly superior power and strength. The word *guerrilla* means *little war* in Spanish and was first used during the Napoleonic Peninsular War (1808-1814).

Since ancient times, people have waged guerrilla warfare against invading armies. Guerrilla tactics deprived the enemy of food and shelter, destroyed lines of communication and supply, and helped organize resistance among the people.

In modern times, many peoples have used guerrilla warfare to fight and try to overthrow an existing government. Guerrilla warfare against a government occurs most frequently in rural areas of chiefly agricultural nations. The people of such nations often feel that the government does not act in their best interest. In turn, the people have little loyalty to, or contact with, the government. In outlying areas, the people may even have a different culture and speak a different language than the nation's rulers. They do not cooperate with the government and generally oppose it. Their guerrilla activities may range from ordinary banditry and theft to raids by disciplined, well-trained forces. Members of many guerrilla bands are civilians, such as farmers or laborers, who act secretly as guerrillas. After making an attack, they disappear into the civilian population.

Because of the importance of guerrilla warfare, the United States Army has formed units of specially trained troops who are experts in guerrilla tactics. These Special Forces soldiers are often called *Green Berets* because of the caps they wear. See **Army, United States** (Special units).

The vervet is the most common type of guenon.

Randall L. Susman, State University of New York at Stony Brook

In guerrilla warfare, bands of fighters often take advantage of hills and other natural features in staging surprise attacks against enemy armies. Afghan guerrillas, like the one shown here, fought Soviet soldiers after the Soviet invasion of Afghanistan in late 1979 and early 1980.

P. Manoukian, Sygma

Modern guerrilla techniques were perfected by Mao Zedong, leader of the Chinese Communists, during his long—and finally successful—fight against the Chinese Nationalists from 1927 to 1949. In modern guerrilla warfare, small groups of revolutionaries try to gain the sympathy and support of—and control over—the people of the countryside. They gain recruits and build up supplies of food and other necessities. Guerrillas may take years to gain popular support.

The guerrillas use ambush, sabotage, assassination, and other terrorist attacks to torment government forces. They design these tactics to weaken the people's confidence in the government and to persuade them to believe that the government cannot defend either itself or the people. At this stage, guerrillas deliberately avoid combat except under conditions and against targets that they select. A guerrilla band could easily be wiped out in open battle by a superior government force using infantry, artillery, and warplanes. The guerrillas sometimes become strong enough to "liberate" some areas of the country, provoke a civil war, and overcome the government troops in battle.

The guerrillas' strength comes mainly from their ability to control the people. Guerrillas use many methods to appeal to the people and gain their sympathy and support. They provoke political, racial, and social troubles so that the government acts against the people. The guerrillas hope that such action will set more and more people against the government.

Most guerrilla propaganda includes promises to take land from the rich and give it to the poor. Such promises help stir up a nation's peasants against the ruling class. Peasant support is sometimes sought by appeals to nationalism, especially in countries where a foreign nation has much influence. Guerrillas also try to take advantage of the hopes and ambitions of the peasants for improving their way of life. If all peaceful methods fail, guerrillas use threats and force to gain support.

To defeat guerrillas, a government must win back the people's support. For example, the people may be pacified with political and social reform. They may be given such necessities as food, clothing, shelter, and medicine. The people must also be protected from the guerrillas and trained to defend themselves.

History. Guerrilla tactics against enemy armies date back to ancient times. Fierce Scottish Highland tribes launched guerrilla attacks against the Roman armies that occupied Great Britain during the first century after Christ. During the Thirty Years' War (1618-1648), bands of armed peasants in some European countries attacked soldiers who had wandered from their camps. American Indians used guerrilla tactics against enemy tribes and, later, against the white settlers. During the Revolutionary War in America (1775-1783), General Francis Marion used guerrilla tactics against the British. In the American Civil War (1861-1865), Confederate guerrillas made cavalry raids on Union forces.

During World War I (1914-1918), guerrilla warfare did not occur in Europe mainly because armies fought from trenches along fixed battlefronts. But in the Middle East, Arabs used guerrilla tactics when they revolted and won independence from the Ottoman Empire.

During World War II (1939-1945), citizens of several European countries, including France and Yugoslavia, formed underground guerrilla groups that fought the Nazi invaders. In Burma and the Philippines, guerrillas operated against invading Japanese forces.

After World War II, people of many countries waged guerrilla warfare against their governments. Some fought the colonial governments of European powers. In China, Mao Zedong led the Communists to victory over the Nationalists in 1949 after a 22-year struggle. In 1954, France lost its Indochinese colonies to Communist forces following eight years of fighting against guerrillas. France lost Algeria in 1962 after guerrillas in Algeria revolted and gained independence.

In the Western Hemisphere, the Cuban leader Fidel Castro began an attempt in 1953 to overthrow the country's government. Castro's small force of revolutionaries was almost wiped out at first. But Castro used guerrilla methods skillfully and he gradually gained recruits from the population. Using strong appeals and propaganda, Castro also encouraged soldiers to desert from the Cuban Army. By 1959, the guerrillas had become strong enough to defeat the army and Castro took over as dictator of Cuba. Several years after the Cuban revolution, one of Castro's top aides, Ché Guevara, went to South America to head a similar revolt. Guevara was killed in

1967 while leading a force against Bolivian government troops. See **Guevara, Ché.**

Many other guerrilla revolts have failed. In the Philippines, the Communist Huks turned against their government after the Japanese occupation ended in 1945. To overcome them, the government undertook a campaign that included land reform, rewards for Huks who surrendered, and attacks on guerrilla hideouts. By 1954, the Huks had been defeated.

The British conducted a successful antiguerrilla campaign in Malaya after Communist revolutionaries tried to take over that nation in 1948. British troops attacked the guerrillas, and the government improved economic, political, and social conditions. The revolutionaries had used these conditions to gain the people's support. By 1957, when Malaya became an independent nation, the guerrillas had been defeated.

After 1960, guerrilla fighters battled government troops in many parts of the world. In Northern Ireland, the Irish Republican Army (IRA) used guerrilla tactics against British government forces and installations. Arab guerrillas raided Israel from neighboring Egypt, Jordan, and Syria. Communist guerrillas in the Philippines battled government troops there. In Southeast Asia, the Viet Cong used guerrilla tactics in the Vietnam War (1957-1975).

During the 1960's and 1970's, various urban guerrilla bands in the United States, Latin America, and Western Europe staged kidnappings, bombings of public buildings, assassinations, and other terrorist acts. But none of these groups seized power.

In Rhodesia, now called Zimbabwe, black guerrillas fought government troops during most of the 1970's in an attempt to overthrow the white-ruled government. In 1979, blacks gained control of the government. That same year, Afghan guerrillas began fighting both the government of Afghanistan and Soviet troops supporting the government. The Soviet troops withdrew in 1988 and 1989. The guerrillas overthrew the Afghan government in 1992, but continued to fight among themselves afterward.   Stephen Goode

See also **Partisans; Spain** (French conquest); **Terrorism; Underground.**

Additional resources

Asprey, Robert B. *War in the Shadows: Guerrillas in History.* Rev. ed. Morrow, 1994.
Chaliand, Gérard, ed. *Guerrilla Stategies: An Historical Anthology from the Long March to Afghanistan.* Univ. of Calif. Pr., 1982.
Clutterbuck, Richard. *Terrorism and Guerrilla Warfare.* Routledge, 1990.

Guest, Edgar Albert (1881-1959), an English-born American poet, wrote about friendship, family affection, the home, and similar subjects. One of his famous lines is "It takes a heap o' living to make a house a home." Guest was born in Birmingham, England, and came to the United States as a boy. He attended public schools in Detroit and began to work for the *Detroit Free Press* in 1895. His poetry was published in many collections, including *A Heap o' Living* (1916) and *Life's Highway* (1933).
          Bonnie Costello

Guevara, *gay VAH rah,* **Ché,** *chay* (1928-1967), was one of the most powerful members of the Cuban government under Fidel Castro. He served as minister of industry from 1961 to 1965 and directed much of the govern-

ment's economic planning. Guevara was killed while leading a guerrilla band trying to overthrow the government of Bolivia.

Guevara was born in Rosario, Argentina. His real name was Ernesto Guevara, but most people called him by his nickname, Ché. Guevara received an M.D. degree from the University of Buenos Aires. Guevara became a revolutionary be-

United Press Int.

Ché Guevara

cause he believed that armed struggle was the only way to improve social conditions and eliminate poverty.

In 1954, Guevara held a minor post in the government of Guatemala. After the overthrow of the Guatemalan government that year, he fled to Mexico. While in Mexico, Guevara met Castro and joined his movement to overthrow the government of Cuba. Guevara served as a physician and military commander in Castro's guerrilla forces in Cuba during the late 1950's. After Castro took control of Cuba in 1959, he appointed Guevara as president of the National Bank of Cuba. In 1965, Guevara went to Africa, where he led a group of Cuban soldiers in support of a revolt in the Congo. He later became the leader of a band of guerrillas in Bolivia. He became a hero to many people who regarded him as an idealist.
          Louis A. Pérez, Jr.

Guggenheim, *GOO guhn HYM,* **Meyer,** *MY uhr* (1828?-1905), was a Swiss-born industrialist who made a fortune in the United States in the mining and smelting business. Members of Guggenheim's family gave much of their wealth to charitable and educational organizations.

Guggenheim was born in Lengnau, in the canton of Aargau, Switzerland. He came to the United States in 1848 and worked first as a door-to-door peddler in Philadelphia. Guggenheim greatly increased his wealth by importing and selling Swiss lace. In 1881, he bought a share in two mines in Leadville, Colorado. Guggenheim later bought the share of a partner and gained the controlling interest in the mines. Soon afterward, rich quantities of silver and lead were discovered in the mines. Guggenheim recognized that smelting offered even greater profits. He built a smelter in Pueblo, Colorado, in 1888, and another one in Monterrey, Mexico, in 1891. Eventually, Guggenheim's mining and smelting operations extended to South America and Africa.

In 1899, many Colorado smelting companies combined to form the American Smelting and Refining Company. Guggenheim refused to join because he knew he would not run the company. In 1901, however, American Smelting and Refining began to collapse, and Guggenheim bought control of it. His son Daniel became chairman of the board.

Several of Guggenheim's sons became noted for their philanthropy. Daniel set up the Daniel and Florence Guggenheim Foundation to promote the "well-being of mankind." He also founded the School of Aeronautics at New York University. Murry established the Murry and Leonie Guggenheim Foundation, which set up free dental clinics. Simon founded the John Simon Guggenheim Memorial Foundation to offer grants for study. Solomon R. Guggenheim founded the Guggenheim Museum in New York City.　　　Peter d'A. Jones

Guggenheim Museum, *GOO guhn HYM,* houses an important collection of paintings, sculptures, and other works of art created in the late 1800's and 1900's. The museum is located in New York City in a unique circular building designed by Frank Lloyd Wright. The museum has a continuous program of exhibitions taken from its permanent collections and from public and private collections throughout the world. Solomon R. Guggenheim founded the museum in 1937 to promote nonobjective art and education in art. The museum is operated by the Solomon R. Guggenheim Foundation. See also **Guggenheim, Meyer; New York** (picture).

Critically reviewed by the Solomon R. Guggenheim Museum

Guiana, *gee AH nuh,* is a name for regions on the northeast coast of South America. See **French Guiana; Guyana; Suriname.**

Guidance, in education, is the process of helping students make the best possible decisions about their lives. It is used at all educational levels from grade school through college. Guidance helps students understand themselves by focusing attention on their interests, abilities, and needs in relation to their home, school, and community. Guidance also helps students develop decision-making abilities that they can use to plan their education, choose an occupation, and solve personal problems. To make wise decisions, students must have full and accurate information about themselves and their world. The major goals of guidance are to help students identify and obtain information they need and use it effectively to make the best decisions possible.

Many people contribute to the guidance of students. Some schools have specially trained counselors who lead the guidance program. Parents, teachers, and community representatives also contribute to the process.

There are a wide variety of guidance techniques. For example, counselors often conduct workshops that help students improve their communication skills, decision-making abilities, temperament, or job search skills. Other techniques include testing students for skills and in-

terests and providing vocational information and planning. Many schools use computers, simulations, and audio-visual devices to convey guidance information to students.

Most guidance programs are made up of three major areas: *educational, vocational or career,* and *personal-social.* These areas overlap, and a decision made about one almost always affects the other two.

Educational guidance usually starts with helping students learn which courses the school offers. Guidance also involves helping students decide what courses to take or what curriculum to follow. This decision is often difficult for junior high school or high school students. It is difficult because the pattern of courses students choose and their success with them create some future opportunities but eliminate others. Most students must decide whether to choose a curriculum or pattern of courses that will permit them to attend college or some other form of higher education, or to go directly to work. Such choices often involve decisions about personal values and financial resources.

The choice of courses also depends on other factors. Some students do not have the abilities or interests that will enable them to succeed in every course a school has to offer. Each course makes different demands on the student. Educational guidance uses a combination of counseling, testing, and other techniques to help students make educational decisions and solve problems.

Vocational or career guidance is closely related to educational guidance and uses many of the same methods. But vocational or career guidance is concerned mainly with the student's choice of a future career. It helps a student understand how jobs or occupations differ, what job opportunities are emerging, and which jobs best fit the student's abilities, values, and interests. Vocational or career guidance also makes the student aware of the types of education and training needed to be successful in a chosen career. It also helps the student understand the relationships between work, family roles, and leisure. In addition, vocational or career guidance is concerned with helping students learn good interviewing skills and positive work habits.

Personal-social guidance is often related to educational and vocational guidance, but may emphasize areas that they do not. For example, personal-social guidance stresses interpersonal skills more than educational or vocational guidance do. Personal-social guidance may be designed to help students deal with a variety of problems. These problems include effective communication with other family members, mental health problems, anxieties about tests, and management of stress. Techniques used in personal-social guidance may include individual and group counseling and referrals to community agencies.　　　Edwin L. Herr

Additional resources

Elkind, David. *Parenting Your Teenager in the Nineties.* Modern Learning, 1993.
Robbins, Wendy H. *The Portable College Adviser: A Guide for High School Students.* Watts, 1996.
Unger, Harlow G. *But What if I Don't Want to Go to College? A Guide to Success Through Alternative Education.* Facts on File, 1992.
VGM's Careers Encyclopedia. 3rd ed. NTC Pub. Group, 1991.

Guide dog. See **Dog guide.**

© David R. Frazier

A guidance counselor helps a student gather information that may be important to the youth's future.

U.S. Army

U.S. Navy

U.S. Air Force

Many kinds of U.S. missiles, including those shown above, stand ready for battle. The Poseidon, *left,* blasts off from an underwater submarine. Ground troops launch the Dragon, *upper right,* against tanks. An underground location called a *silo* holds a giant Minuteman, *lower right.*

Guided missile

Guided missile is a bomblike flying weapon that is steered to its target. Some guided missiles steer themselves. They contain a computer and other special equipment that guides them. Some of these guided missiles can even chase and destroy a moving target, such as an airplane or missile. Others fly under human control, though they carry no pilot. They follow directions that are radioed to them from controllers who may be far away.

Most guided missiles look like rockets. Some have stubby, airplanelike wings. Most actually consist of a rocket with one or more explosive sections called *warheads.* A jet engine, rather than a rocket motor, powers a few kinds of missiles. Still others are winged bombs with no engine. An airplane drops such *glide bombs.*

Guided missiles have a wide range of sizes. A small rocket about 4 feet (1.2 meters) long can be launched on the battlefield at a tank or an airplane. A giant missile about 60 feet (18 meters) tall can reach one-third of the way around the world. Such a missile, with a nuclear warhead, can destroy an entire city. No nation has ever launched a nuclear missile against an enemy.

Paul Zarchan, the contributor of this article, is staff engineer at C. S. Draper Laboratory in Cambridge, Mass., and author of Tactical and Strategic Missile Guidance.

The Persian Gulf War of 1991 marked the first time that precision-guided missiles played an important role in warfare. A coalition led by the United States launched several kinds of guided missiles against Iraq. These missiles were much more accurate than those used by Iraq. For details, see **Persian Gulf War.**

Parts of a guided missile

A guided missile consists basically of a warhead attached to a tubelike body. A rocket or a jet engine may power the missile. Special equipment in the missile guides it to its target. This section of the article deals with (1) the warhead, (2) the engine, and (3) guidance and control equipment. It also describes equipment needed to launch a guided missile.

The warhead may contain a high explosive, such as TNT, or a nuclear device. High-explosive warheads work in various ways. Some damage their target mainly by creating a tremendous blast of air pressure. Others explode and shoot out many metal *fragments* (pieces) in all directions. The flying fragments then strike and damage the target.

A nuclear warhead may contain an atomic or hydrogen explosive device. Some nuclear missiles contain several warheads. A nation would launch such a missile against a group of closely spaced targets. When the missile neared the target area, the warheads would separate and each would proceed toward its own target. Such warheads are called Multiple Independently Targetable Reentry Vehicles (MIRV's).

Every missile has a *fuzing system* that causes the warhead to explode at the proper time. This system first puts the warhead in a "ready" condition so that it will explode when triggered. At the proper time, the fuzing system triggers the main explosion by setting off a small charge. This action may occur automatically after the missile has come near its target. In some cases, human controllers trigger the explosion.

The engine. A rocket engine powers most guided missiles. This engine works by burning chemicals. The burning produces gases that have a very high pressure. The high pressure forces the gases backward out of the engine. At the same time, the pressure pushes the engine—and the missile—forward.

The chemicals burned in a rocket engine are called *propellants.* Most guided missiles use solid propellants shaped in the form of a hollow rod called a *grain.* Some missile engines use liquid propellants, which are carried in special tanks inside the body of the missile.

Rocket propellants include two types, the fuel and the oxidizer. The *fuel* provides the basic burning substance. The *oxidizer* supplies the oxygen needed to make the fuel burn. In solid-propellant rockets, the fuel and oxidizer are both in solid form and are combined in the grain. Once the grain has been set on fire, the two propellants unite and continue to burn. In missiles that use liquid propellants, the propellants must be pumped or forced in some other way into the engine's *combustion chamber.* There, the propellants unite and burn.

A jet engine powers some guided missiles. A jet engine uses fuel as does a rocket. However, a jet engine gets its oxygen from the atmosphere, taking in air as it flies. Because a jet engine requires oxygen, jet-powered missiles cannot operate in space, where there is almost no air. Rockets carry their own oxidizer, and so they can work in space. See **Rocket; Jet propulsion.**

Guidance and control systems work together to keep a missile on course. The guidance system may include a computer and other special instruments. These instruments "remember" the course planned for the missile and send electronic steering "instructions" to the control system. The control system includes movable devices that control the missile's flight, such as fins, vanes, and wings. These devices use the instructions from the guidance system to turn the missile in the desired direction. For more details on guidance systems, see the section of this article on *Kinds of guidance systems.*

Launching equipment guides a missile while it is being launched. Some missiles are launched from a tube. Others take off from a launcher that has tracks or rails, along which the missile runs. Launching equipment set up in a permanent location makes up a missile *site.* An underground site is called a *silo.* Some silo-based missiles are launched from their underground position. Others first rise to the ground on an elevator.

On the battlefield, special trucks move missiles to desired launching locations then serve as launchers. Launchers can be attached to the wings or body of an airplane or set up on a ship. Missile submarines use compressed air to push the missile up to the surface, where the rocket engine takes over.

Kinds of guided missiles

Guided missiles can be classified in various ways, depending on such characteristics as how far they fly and what targets they attack. For example, one important group of missiles—ballistic missiles—get their name from the way they fly. They follow an arching, *ballistic* path like that followed by a ball thrown through the air.

Parts of a rocket-powered missile   Most guided missiles are powered by a rocket engine. These diagrams show the main parts of two kinds of rocket-powered missiles. One kind uses liquid *propellants,* which consist of a fuel and an *oxidizer* (substance needed to make the fuel burn). The other kind uses a solid propellant.

WORLD BOOK diagram by Mas Nakagawa

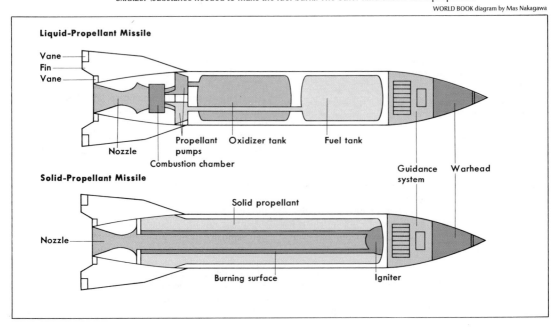

Liquid-Propellant Missile

Vane
Fin
Vane

Nozzle   Propellant pumps   Oxidizer tank   Fuel tank
Combustion chamber

Guidance system   Warhead

Solid-Propellant Missile

Solid propellant

Nozzle

Burning surface   Igniter

General Dynamics

A surface-to-air missile blasts away from a U.S. Navy patrol gunboat. The missile shown above, called the Standard, is classified as a ship-to-air missile by the Navy.

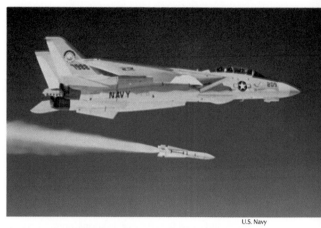

U.S. Navy

An air-to-air missile drops from a U.S. fighter and roars toward its target. This missile, called the Phoenix, can strike enemy aircraft up to 126 miles (203 kilometers) away.

All other missiles can be described as *nonballistic.* Guided missiles also may be grouped into four other types, depending on where their flight begins and ends. These types are: (1) surface-to-surface, (2) surface-to-air, (3) air-to-air, and (4) air-to-surface.

Ballistic missiles. The flight of a ballistic missile has two parts. During the first part, the missile's rocket engine blasts the missile onto its planned course and gives it the desired speed. After a short time, the engine shuts off. The missile then coasts through the second part of the flight until it drops down on its target. A ballistic missile is guided only during the first part of its flight.

Ballistic missiles travel great distances. They need to carry large amounts of propellants to reach the proper speed and altitude for a long flight. In fact, nearly 90 per cent of the weight of a ballistic missile may be propellants. As a result, ballistic missiles are the largest of all missiles.

An *intercontinental ballistic missile* (ICBM) may strike a target from about 3,400 to 9,200 miles (5,500 to 15,000 kilometers) away after soaring as high as 700 miles (1,100 kilometers). An *intermediate-range ballistic missile* (IRBM) flies shorter distances—from about 1,700 to 3,400 miles (2,700 to 5,500 kilometers). An ICBM or IRBM launched from a submarine may be called a *submarine launched ballistic missile* (SLBM). A *medium-range ballistic missile* (MRBM) can reach from about 700 to 1,700 miles (1,100 to 2,700 kilometers). A *short-range ballistic missile* (SRBM) can reach up to approximately 700 miles (1,100 kilometers). The Pershing 1a missile and the Scud missile used by Iraq during the Persian Gulf War are SRBM's.

An ICBM with a nuclear warhead can destroy an entire city. Such long-range missiles are important in military *strategy* (overall planning). As a result, they are called *strategic missiles.*

A MIRV attack and a defense against it

Several warheads from a single missile can attack different targets. Such warheads are called Multiple Independently Targetable Reentry Vehicles (MIRV's). Antiballistic missiles (ABM's) might defend against the attack. The United States currently has no such defense.

WORLD BOOK diagrams by Mas Nakagawa

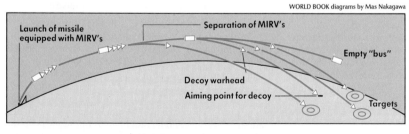

A MIRV attack might consist of three warheads directed to three different targets, plus a *decoy,* or dummy, warhead. The purpose of the decoy is to attract a defending missile that might otherwise destroy a real warhead.

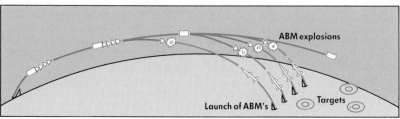

An ABM defense against a MIRV attack would require as many missiles as there are attacking warheads. In the maneuver shown, four ABM's have exploded, each destroying one of the warheads, including the decoy.

Nonballistic missiles. Most guided missiles are nonballistic. Some fly their entire course under power from their engine and under the control of their guidance system. They are usually fired at *tactical* (battlefield) targets, including planes, ships, or fixed targets. However, certain types of nonballistic missiles can serve as strategic weapons. For example, *cruise missiles* equipped with either nuclear or conventional warheads can destroy industrial centers and military installations. These jet-powered missiles can fly at extremely low altitudes to escape radar detection. They can be launched from the ground, from large aircraft, and from submarines.

Nonballistic missiles are often named for their special characteristics. Most of those described in the following sections are nonballistic missiles.

Surface-to-surface missiles (SSM's) are launched from the ground or the sea against surface targets. SSM's include a wide variety of weapons, some carrying nuclear warheads. The largest SSM's are the intercontinental ballistic missiles. Small, short-range surface-to-surface missiles can support battlefield operations by knocking out such targets as enemy supply dumps. Such SSM's travel up to 400 miles (640 kilometers). The smallest battlefield support missiles can be fired by one soldier at nearby troops or tanks.

Antisubmarine missiles are an important kind of SSM. These missiles fly through the air, plunge into the water above an enemy submarine, and then dive down to destroy the sub. Antisubmarine SSM's may be fired from surface ships or from submarines.

Surface-to-air missiles (SAM's) are fired from the ground or from ships at airplanes or missiles. The Redeye, a surface-to-air missile used by the U.S. Army, is small enough for one soldier to carry and launch. The U.S. Army's Patriot missile, on the other hand, weighs about 2,000 pounds (910 kilograms).

Missiles designed to be launched against approaching missiles are called *antimissile missiles.* A special type, called an *antiballistic missile* (ABM), guards against ballistic missiles. The Patriot missile is an ABM.

Air-to-air missiles (AAM's) are launched from fighter airplanes or helicopters against enemy aircraft. In the U.S. Air Force, such missiles are called *air interceptor missiles* (AIM's). Most of them are small, short-range weapons. The Air Force Sidewinder missile, for example, has a range of about 12 miles (19 kilometers).

Air-to-surface missiles (ASM's) are launched from aircraft at targets on the ground or at ships. During the Persian Gulf War, allied forces destroyed Iraqi radar-controlled missile sites with air-to-surface *H*igh Speed *A*nti-*R*adiation *M*issiles (HARM's). These missiles find the enemy radar beam and destroy the transmitter.

Kinds of guidance systems

One or more kinds of guidance systems may steer a missile to its target. For example, one kind may control a missile during the early part of its flight, and another kind may take over for the final attack. The four main kinds of missile guidance systems are: (1) preset, (2) command, (3) beam-riding, and (4) homing.

Preset guidance makes a missile follow a course that is mapped out before the missile is launched. The guidance system is set to direct the missile to its target. Some preset systems turn the missile's control vanes ac-cording to a set pattern and turn off the missile engine at a planned time. Others measure the accuracy of the flight and make corrections as necessary.

The preset guidance system of the U.S. Navy's Tomahawk cruise missile is so accurate that the missile could fly through the goal posts at both ends of a football field after flying hundreds of miles. The missile obtains this accuracy through *terrain contour mapping* (TERCOM). The missile takes pictures of the terrain at regular intervals during its journey and compares them with images stored on its on-board computer. The missile can then correct its course at a specific point or landmark.

Command guidance enables the missile launching crew to steer the missile. There are several ways to send *command* (steering) signals to the missile. In a *wire-command* system, electronic signals go to the missile over long wires that remain attached to the missile in flight. A missile with this kind of guidance is the U.S. Army's Tube-launched, Optically tracked, Wire command-link guided (TOW) antitank missile. Other systems transmit commands by radar or radio waves or by a laser beam. The Patriot ABM has a radar-controlled guidance system.

Beam-riding guidance leads a missile to its target by means of radar or a laser beam. The main use of this kind of system is to destroy airplanes. First, an aiming station in the launching area directs a narrow radar beam at the enemy aircraft. Then, the missile is launched. The missile, controlled by a computer inside it, "rides" the beam to the target.

Homing guidance enables a missile to hit a target by following some form of energy coming from the target. For example, the target may give off heat, or it may reflect radar signals. The missile follows the heat or radar signals "home" to the target.

Guidance systems that home on heat include the one in the U.S. Army's Redeye missile. This weapon follows the trail of hot gases produced by the target aircraft's jet engines. Homing systems that use radar are of two types. In one type, equipment in the missile itself sends out radar signals that are reflected by the target. In the other type, the radar signals come from an aircraft, a ground station, or a ship, instead of from the missile.

The flight of an advanced missile

Highly advanced guided missiles use computer-controlled radar and reflected radar signals to home in on enemy aircraft and missiles. The U.S. Army's Patriot is an example of such a missile. The Patriot system includes a ground-based *phased-array radar* transmitter and receiver, a ground control station, and a radar antenna mounted inside the missile. A phased-array radar shifts its beam electronically, rather than by rotating an antenna as conventional radars do. A phased-array radar can shift the beam instantly.

In the Patriot system, the radar first detects the target. The system then verifies that the target is a threat. Next, a computer in the control station predicts the path that the target will take. It also determines the best time to launch the missile.

At launch, the missile takes off in the general direction of the target. The radar continues to track the incoming target and begins to track the Patriot. The missile rapidly builds up speed.

How missiles are guided

Four main kinds of guidance systems steer missiles to their target. These diagrams show the guidance systems in simplified form.

WORLD BOOK diagrams by Mas Nakagawa

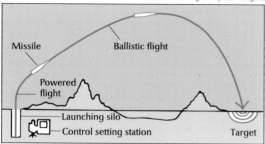

Preset guidance system gives a ballistic missile the proper speed, height, and direction to reach the target. The system operates only during the powered part of the missile's flight.

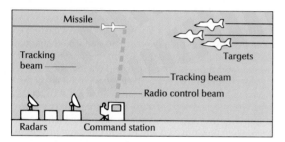

Command guidance system enables human operators to control a missile. This drawing shows a missile being guided by radio control. Separate radar sets track the missile and its target.

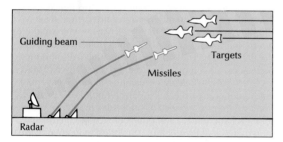

Beam-riding guidance system involves an electronic beam, such as radar, that remains pointed at the target. Equipment in the missile keeps the missile traveling along the beam.

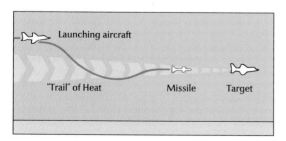

Homing guidance system detects a "trail" of heat or some other radiation coming from the target. The missile, controlled by the guidance system, follows the trail to the target.

During the next phase of flight, the control station transmits electronic guidance commands to the missile to keep the missile on course. When the missile gets within a certain distance from the target, the missile's *seeker,* an on-board radar antenna, picks up radar waves reflected from the target. These waves provide information about the direction to the target.

Because the missile's seeker is closer to the target than the ground-based radar is, the seeker receives more precise information than the radar does. The seeker transmits this information to the control station. A computer in the station combines the data from the seeker and the radar to calculate guidance commands. The station then transmits the commands to the missile. This process continues until the missile comes very close to the target. A fuzing mechanism on the missile then triggers the warhead.

History

Early development. The Chinese used unguided rockets as fireworks perhaps as early as the 1200's. By the 1300's, such rockets were used widely in Asia and Europe. During the early 1800's, William Congreve, a British Army officer, developed unguided, rocket-powered missiles that could carry explosives. These missiles were used widely in wars fought in Asia, Europe, and North and South America.

The military use of rocket missiles dropped off during the late 1800's. By that time, artillery weapons had become so accurate that they were more effective than were rocket missiles. During World War I (1914-1918), France made limited use of unguided rockets to shoot down war balloons.

The first guided missiles. The United States experimented with pilotless airplanes during World War I. These early types of guided missiles carried explosives and were guided by preset controls. In 1924, the United States Navy developed a similar missile-plane guided by radio control. Neither of these planes was used in combat.

During World War II (1939-1945), Germany developed the first guided missiles used in combat. By the early 1940's, Germany had produced two terrifying weapons—first the V-1, then the V-2. These missiles caused great destruction and loss of life in European cities.

The V-1 was about 25 feet (7.6 meters) long and carried about a ton of explosives. It had preset guidance and flew about 360 miles (580 kilometers) per hour. The V-1 used a jet engine.

The V-2, twice as long as the V-1, flew under rocket power. Like the V-1, the V-2 had preset guidance. But the V-2 traveled more than 3,300 miles (5,300 kilometers) per hour, a speed faster than the speed of sound. People in target cities could not hear the V-2 coming.

The United States made limited use of guided missiles during World War II. One U.S. missile, the Azon, was a radio-controlled bomb that could be steered after being dropped from a plane. The U.S. Navy used a missile called the Bat. This air-to-ship glide bomb used a radar homing guidance system.

Postwar developments. After the war, the United States and the Soviet Union began a missile development race, each trying to produce more powerful guided missiles than the other. In the late 1950's, each

NASA, Marshall Space Flight Center

Germany launched V-2 missiles against European cities near the end of World War II. These missiles stood about as tall as a five-story building and flew faster than the speed of sound.

C. Beam-riding guidance
D. Homing guidance
IV. **The flight of an advanced missile**
V. **History**

Questions

What is a missile *silo?*
What two German missiles caused great destruction during World War II?
What is the purpose of a missile's fuzing system?
How does an ICBM differ from an IRBM?
What type of guidance system depends on heat or some other energy coming from a target?
What propellants are needed in a rocket-powered missile?
What is the difference between *strategic* and *tactical* missiles?
What kind of guided missile flies without an engine?
How is a missile launched from an underwater submarine?
Why are ballistic missiles the largest of all missiles?

Additional resources

Levine, Alan J. *The Missile and Space Race.* Praeger, 1994.
Pitt, Matthew. *The Tomahawk Cruise Missile.* Children's Pr., 2000. Younger readers.
Zarchan, Paul. *Tactical and Strategic Missile Guidance.* 3rd ed. Am. Inst. of Aeronautics and Astronautics, 1997.

nation test-launched its first intercontinental ballistic missiles and worked to create submarine-launched missiles. During the 1960's, the United States and the Soviet Union developed antiballistic missiles. By the late 1960's, the total number of missiles and nuclear warheads had grown alarmingly large. The two nations then began negotiations to end the missile race.

The United States and the Soviet Union reached a number of agreements. The first pacts called for limits on the production of certain missiles. Beginning in the late 1980's, the two nations agreed to sharp reductions in their missile arsenals. The future of these agreements became uncertain when the Soviet Union broke up in December 1991. However, in 1992, Russia and other independent states that had been part of the Soviet Union also agreed to the sharp reductions. For additional details, see **Arms control** (History of arms control).

Paul Zarchan

Related articles in *World Book* include:

Outline

I. **Parts of a guided missile**
  A. The warhead
  B. The engine
  C. Guidance and control systems
  D. Launching equipment
II. **Kinds of guided missiles**
  A. Ballistic missiles
  B. Nonballistic missiles
  C. Surface-to-surface missiles
  D. Surface-to-air missiles
  E. Air-to-air missiles
  F. Air-to-surface missiles
III. **Kinds of guidance systems**
  A. Preset guidance   B. Command guidance

Guild, *gihld,* in the Middle Ages, was an association of people with a common interest. People formed charitable, religious, and social guilds. But the most important were associations of merchants and craftworkers.

Merchant guilds. Trade declined after the fall of the Roman Empire in A.D. 476 but revived in the A.D. 1000's and 1100's. The revival of trade made merchants more important. They organized guilds to protect their members when they traveled and to gain common privileges and greater profits. Guild members could buy large quantities of goods cheaply, and they could control the market for selling. They allowed no one to sell who was not a member. They set prices and standards of quality for their goods, and agreed on wages for their workers. They also helped members with charity, funeral ceremonies, and prayers for the dead. Most merchant guilds were found in towns. By 1200, such guilds were powerful in town government. The guilds built halls and marketplaces, and contributed to church and town projects.

Craft guilds. Bakers, goldsmiths, tailors, weavers, and other craftworkers also formed guilds. To protect their members, they established rules much like those of merchant guilds. Craft guilds controlled the quality and quantity of production. They tried to keep individual members from getting too much business so none would take business away from other members.

Craftworkers who knew a trade well and had their own shops were called *masters.* A craftworker who knew most of a craft, or who could not afford a shop, was a *journeyman.* He worked at a daily wage for a master. A boy or young man who was learning a craft was called an *apprentice.* He usually received housing and meals from the master who was teaching him. It took an apprentice from two to seven years to become a journeyman. A journeyman who wanted to become a master had to show evidence of great skill. He had to pass an examination or make a product in his craft that would be judged a *masterpiece* by the other masters who belonged to his guild.

Guilds in later years. By the 1300's, guilds were losing their protective and democratic sides. Masters tried to keep journeymen on wages. Guild membership passed from fathers to sons, making it harder for new members to join. Merchants controlled both the production and the sale of goods. Their power in town government allowed them to impose their own rules.

During the 1300's and 1400's, the craft guilds of the large industries became associations of hired workers. These workers often struggled with their masters for higher wages and better working conditions. Strikes often became civil wars within the towns, and the conflict spilled over into town politics. The craft guilds were rarely strong enough to win their fights, but there are many similarities between these medieval guilds and modern trade unions.

Medieval guilds were no longer economically or politically important by 1600. But many lasted into modern times in the form of ceremonial and fraternal organizations.   Joel T. Rosenthal

See also **Apprentice; Education** (Christian education in the Middle Ages); **Labor movement** (Origins of the labor movement).

Guilder, *GIHL duhr,* is a monetary unit of the Netherlands and the Netherlands Antilles. It is scheduled to be replaced by the euro, a new European Union currency, by early 2002. The name *guilder* also applies to several German and Dutch coins no longer in use. Other names for the guilder are *gulden* and *florin.*   Burton H. Hobson

Guilford Courthouse, Battle of. See **Revolutionary War in America** (Cowpens and Guilford Courthouse; table: Major battles).

Guillemot, *GIHL uh maht,* is a sea bird in the auk family. The *black guillemot,* or *sea pigeon,* lives on both coasts of the North Atlantic. It is about 13 inches (33 centimeters) long, and it has a slender, pointed bill and bright red legs and feet. Its feathers are black with white wing patches in summer. It is mostly white in winter. The *pigeon guillemot,* or *sea pigeon,* lives on the Pacific coast of North America.   George L. Hunt, Jr.

WORLD BOOK illustration by Trevor Boyer, Linden Artists Ltd.
The black guillemot lives on North Atlantic coasts.

Scientific classification. Guillemots belong to the auk family, Alcidae. The black guillemot is *Cepphus grylle,* and the pigeon guillemot is *C. columba.*

Guillotine, *GIHL uh teen,* was a beheading machine. It became the official instrument of execution in France in 1792, during the French Revolution. The device was

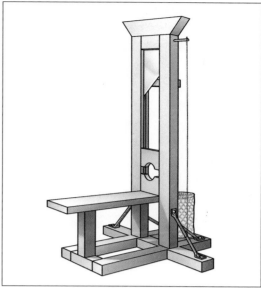

WORLD BOOK illustration by Oxford Illustrators Limited
The guillotine was first proposed as a device for beheading people by Joseph Guillotin, a French doctor, in 1792.

named for Joseph Ignace Guillotin (1738-1814), a member of the Revolutionary assembly. He regarded the device as a quick and merciful type of execution.

A guillotine had two posts joined by a crossbeam at the top. A heavy steel knife with a slanting edge fit in grooves in the posts. A cord held the knife in place. When the executioner cut the cord, the knife dropped and cut off the victim's head.

Ancient Persians are said to have had a similar machine. The Italians and the Scots also had beheading machines. It was not until 1981, when France abolished capital punishment, that the use of the guillotine ended.   Franklin E. Zimring

Guinea, *GIHN ee,* is a region on the west coast of Africa. Its exact boundaries have never been clearly defined. But it is commonly thought of as the area extending along the Atlantic Ocean between Gambia on the north and Gabon on the south. The Niger River divides it into Upper Guinea and Lower Guinea. For location, see **Africa** (political map).

The name Guinea came into use in the 1400's. The name may have come from a Berber word meaning the *land of the blacks.* Early European traders named different parts of the Upper Guinea coast for their colonial trade. These included the Grain Coast, which included present-day Liberia; the Ivory Coast (Côte d'Ivoire); the Gold Coast, which is now part of Ghana; and the Slave Coast, which included present-day Benin and Nigeria.

Three independent countries in the region use the name *Guinea* today. They are Equatorial Guinea, Guinea-Bissau, and the Republic of Guinea. Equatorial Guinea was a Spanish colony called Spanish Guinea, and, later, Spanish Equatorial Region. Guinea-Bissau was an overseas territory of Portugal called Portuguese Guinea. The Republic of Guinea was formerly the colony of French Guinea.   Hartmut S. Walter

See also **Equatorial Guinea; Guinea; Guinea-Bissau.**

A market in Conakry offers household items for sale. Conakry is Guinea's capital and largest city. Some Guineans, especially those who live in Conakry and other towns, wear Western-style clothing. However, most Guineans still wear traditional clothing.

J. C. Francolon, Gamma/Liaison

Guinea, *GIHN ee,* is a country on the west coast of Africa. It lies on the huge bulge of Africa that juts westward toward the Atlantic Ocean. Guinea is a land of coastal swamps, crusty plateaus, grassy plains, and forested hills. The country's official name is République de Guinée (Republic of Guinea). Conakry is the capital and largest city.

Guinea has much potential for economic growth because of its abundant natural resources. Its economy is based on agriculture and mining. Guinea has large deposits of *bauxite,* a mineral from which aluminum is made. Guinea was a colony of France from the late 1800's until 1958, when it became an independent nation.

Government. Guinea's government is based on a constitution that was adopted in 1990 and went into effect in 1991. The new constitution established Guinea as a republic.

The president of Guinea is the head of state and the head of government. The president is elected by the people to a five-year term. The president appoints a cabinet, which helps administer the government. Guinea has a one-house legislative body called the National Assembly. The Assembly has 114 members, who are elected to five-year terms by the people.

Guinea is divided into four regions, each headed by a resident minister appointed by the president. The regions are further divided into 33 government units that are called *prefectures.*

People. The people of Guinea are called *Guineans.* Almost all the people are black Africans. About 75 percent of them belong to one of three main ethnic groups. The largest of these groups is the Fulani, or Peul. Most of the Fulani live in a central plateau region called the Fouta Djallon. The Malinke, the second largest group, occupy much of northeastern Guinea, especially the towns of Kankan, Kouroussa, and Siguiri. The Sosso, the third largest group, live along the coast of Guinea. Smaller black ethnic groups make up most of the rest of the population of Guinea.

French is the official language of Guinea. But most of the people speak one of the country's eight African languages. About 85 percent of the people of Guinea are Muslims. Only about 1 percent are Christians, most of

them Roman Catholics. Other Guineans follow traditional African religions.

Most Guineans live in rural areas. A majority of the rural people are farmers who raise crops to feed their families and for export. In the cities and towns, people work in business, manufacturing, or for service industries, including the government.

Most rural housing consists of round buildings made of sun-dried mud bricks, with a thatched roof. In the cities and towns, most people live in one-story rectangular houses made of mud bricks or wood. Few homes in Guinea have electric service or indoor plumbing. Conakry has a serious housing shortage.

Many Guineans, especially those living in cities and towns, wear Western-style clothing. However, most people still wear traditional clothes. For men, the traditional garment is a loose robe called a *boubou.* Women wear a blouse with a skirt made from a piece of colored cloth tied around the waist.

Corn, millet, and rice are main foods of Guineans. The grain is cooked into meal and served with a spicy sauce, or pounded to form a porridge. The porridge is served with sour milk. Bananas are also an important food. Some meals include cassava and other vegetables and

Facts in brief

Capital: Conakry.
Official language: French.
Area: 94,926 mi² (245,857 km²). *Greatest distances*—east-west, 450 mi (725 km); north-south, 350 mi (565 km). *Coastline*—190 mi (305 km).
Elevation: *Highest*—Mount Nimba, 5,748 ft (1,752 m) above sea level. *Lowest*—sea level.
Population: *Estimated 2002 population*—7,794,000; density, 82 per mi² (32 per km²); distribution, 74 percent rural, 26 percent urban. *1983 census*—4,533,240.
Chief products: *Agriculture*—bananas, cassava, coffee, corn, palm products, peanuts, plantains, rice, sweet potatoes. *Manufacturing*—alumina, food products, textiles. *Mining*—bauxite, diamonds, gold.
National anthem: "Liberté" ("Liberty").
Flag: The flag has three vertical stripes: red (for the spirit of sacrifice), gold (for sun and wealth), and green (for the forests). See **Flag** (picture: Flags of Africa).
Money: *Basic unit*—franc.

such fruits as mangoes, oranges, papayas, pineapples, or plantains. Beef, fish, lamb, and poultry are also popular foods. In addition, most Guineans enjoy homemade ginger drinks.

The government operates free public schools and requires all children between the ages of 7 and 19 to attend. However, many Guineans prefer to send their children to private Muslim schools. There is a shortage of teachers and classrooms. The country has universities in Conakry and Kankan. Most adult Guineans cannot read or write. For Guinea's literacy rate, see **Literacy** (table: Literacy rates).

Guineans have a rich popular culture, which they express through music, oral folk tales, and drama. History, also an important part of Guinean culture, is recited by storytellers called *griots*. Guinean craftworkers make woven baskets, metal jewelry, and leather products.

Land and climate. Guinea has four main land regions: (1) Lower Guinea, a swampy coastal strip; (2) Fouta Djallon, or Middle Guinea, a central plateau of hard, crusty soil; (3) Upper Guinea, a northern *savanna* (grassland with scattered trees); and (4) the Forest Region, an area of forests and hills in the southeast. This region includes the country's highest point, Mount Nimba, which rises to 5,748 feet (1,752 meters) above sea level. Guinea has many rivers, including the sources of the Niger, the Sénégal, and the Gambie (Gambia) rivers.

Clumps of mangrove trees grow along the mouths of Guinea's rivers. The wildlife in Guinea includes such animals as antelope, buffaloes, crocodiles, elephants, hippopotamuses, leopards, lions, monkeys, and snakes.

Guinea has a tropical climate. Average temperatures

M. P. Revelen, Gamma/Liaison

A village in southern Guinea has huts with thatched roofs. A majority of Guinea's people live in rural areas. Most of the country's rural people are farmers.

in Lower Guinea along the coast range from 73 to 84 °F (23 to 29 °C). Lower Guinea receives about 110 inches (279 centimeters) of rain each year. The Fouta Djallon region is cooler than the coast, and it receives from 60 to 100 inches of rain (152 to 254 centimeters) a year. Upper Guinea is drier than the coast, with a rainfall of about 60 inches (152 centimeters) a year. The Forest Region is humid and cool, and receives from about 75 to 100 inches (190 to 254 centimeters) of rain each year.

Economy. Although underdeveloped, Guinea has many valuable natural resources that could turn it into a prosperous nation. It has about one-third of the world's reserves of bauxite. Other important mineral deposits include iron ore, diamonds, gold, and uranium.

About 80 percent of Guinea's people work in agriculture. They grow bananas, cassava, coffee, corn, peanuts, pineapples, plantains, rice, sweet potatoes, and other crops. Farmers in the plains and highlands raise livestock. Mining, manufacturing, and construction employ about 10 percent of all Guinean workers. Factories in Guinea manufacture food products, textiles, and *alumina* (a processed form of bauxite).

Bauxite, alumina, and diamonds rank as Guinea's main exports. Together, they account for more than 95 percent of the country's export income. Guinea also exports such agricultural goods as bananas, coffee, palm products, and pineapples. Leading imports include building materials, food, machinery, petroleum products, transportation equipment, and consumer goods. Guinea's main trade partners include Canada, Japan, the United States, and various European countries.

Inadequate transportation systems hamper economic development in Guinea. The country's roads are in poor condition, and most of them are unpaved. Most of the country's railroad tracks need repair. Conakry has an international airport, and smaller airports operate at Kankan, Labé, and other cities. Conakry and Kamsar serve as international shipping ports.

The government of Guinea controls the country's newspapers and radio and television services. The

Guinea

- International boundary
- Road
- Railroad
- ⊛ National capital
- • Other city or town
- + Elevation above sea level

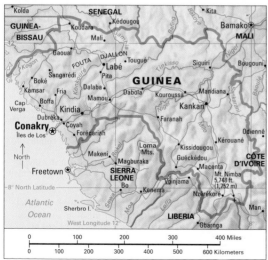

WORLD BOOK maps

M. P. Revelen, Gamma/Liaison

Mining bauxite is one of Guinea's chief industries. Bauxite is a mineral used to make aluminum. Guinea has about a third of the world's reserves of bauxite.

country's largest general-interest newspaper is published several times a week. Many people own radios, but few have television sets. Television reception is limited to Conakry and a few other cities.

History. Stone tools found in several places throughout what is now Guinea indicate that people have lived in the area since prehistoric times. People from the Sahara region had probably migrated to Guinea by about 2000 B.C. Early inhabitants hunted and gathered wild fruit. By about 1000 B.C., people had begun to raise livestock and grow crops, and agricultural societies largely replaced hunting communities.

Parts of Guinea fell under the control or influence of several empires from the A.D. 1000's to 1500's. The gold-producing region of Upper Guinea came under the influence of the Ghana Empire in the 1000's. The Mali Empire, founded by the Malinke people, was the most powerful state in Guinea from the 1200's to the 1500's. Fulani from the north moved to Guinea from the 1300's to about 1700. Muslim Fulani and Malinke fought a *jihad* (holy war) against non-Muslim Fulani and Malinke in the early 1700's, and they then gained control of the Fouta Djallon.

Portuguese explorers were the first Europeans to reach Guinea, beginning in the mid-1400's. By the 1600's, traders from other European nations also had entered West Africa. France began to control parts of Guinea in the mid-1800's. The French gained territory through treaties and through conquest. In 1891, Guinea became a French colony called French Guinea. Samory Touré, a powerful Malinke leader, resisted French rule, but was defeated and captured in 1898.

After World War II ended in 1945, political parties and labor unions became active in Guinea. The Democratic Party of Guinea (*Parti Démocratique de Guinée,* or PDG) was formed in 1947. Sékou Touré became its head in 1952. The PDG won control of the legislature in 1957. On Sept. 28, 1958, the people of Guinea voted for complete independence from France. Guinea officially became independent on October 2, with Touré as its first president. Guinea's first constitution took effect on November 12. In December, a law made the PDG Guinea's only political party.

The government under Touré and the PDG took nearly complete control of Guinea's economy in an effort to create a socialist state. The government also hoped to encourage unity among the peoples of the new nation and strengthen Guinea's ties with other African countries and socialist nations. But there were many problems. Guinea failed to develop its plentiful natural resources, and most of the country's people remained poor. Throughout the 1960's and early 1970's, Touré's government crushed all opposition to his policies and imprisoned many citizens without cause.

Touré died on March 26, 1984. In early April, military leaders took control of the government. They suspended the constitution and abolished the PDG. Colonel Lansana Conté, the leader of the ruling military committee, became president. His government abandoned Touré's socialist economic policies and adopted free enterprise policies. It also strengthened economic ties with France and other countries. In 1990, Guinean voters approved a new Constitution that provided for a transition to civilian rule and multiparty democracy. In 1993, Guinean voters elected Conté as president in multiparty elections. Conté's party, the Party of Unity and Progress, won the majority of seats in elections for the civilian legislature in 1995. The voters reelected Conté as president in 1998. Lansiné Kaba

See also **Conakry; Mali Empire; Touré, Sékou.**

Guinea, *GIHN ee,* was an old English coin, equal to 21 shillings. It was first coined in 1663 out of gold from the Guinea coast in West Africa and took its name from that region. It was the chief English gold coin until 1813, when the *sovereign,* equal to 20 shillings, took its place.
  Burton H. Hobson

Guinea-Bissau, *GIHN ee bih SOW,* is a small, independent country on the bulge of Africa's west coast. It includes the offshore Bijagós (or Bissagos) Islands. Bissau is the capital, chief port, and largest city (see **Bissau**).

Most of the people of Guinea-Bissau are farmers. The leading crops include peanuts and rice, which thrive in the country's tropical climate. Guinea-Bissau was Portuguese Guinea, an overseas province of Portugal, until

Facts in brief

Capital: Bissau.
Official language: Portuguese.
Official name: Republic of Guinea-Bissau.
Area: 13,948 mi² (36,125 km²). *Greatest distances*—north-south, 120 mi (193 km); east-west, 200 mi (322 km). *Coastline*—247 mi (398 km).
Elevation: *Highest*—in the south-central part of the country, 403 ft (123 m) above sea level. *Lowest*—sea level.
Population: *Estimated 2002 population*—1,264,000; density, 91 per mi² (35 per km²); distribution, 78 percent rural, 22 percent urban. *1991 census*—983,367.
Chief products: Palm kernels, peanuts, rice.
Flag: A black star is centered on a red vertical stripe to the left of two horizontal stripes. The top horizontal stripe is yellow, and the bottom one is green. See **Flag** (picture: Flags of Africa).
Money: *Basic unit*—franc. One hundred centimes equal one franc.

Guinea-Bissau

International boundary
Road
⊛ National capital
• Other city or town
+ Elevation above sea level

WORLD BOOK maps

1974. That same year, the province won its independence after an 11-year war against Portuguese rule.

Government. A president heads the government of Guinea-Bissau. The president is elected by the people to a five-year term. The National People's Assembly is the country's legislature. The people elect the Assembly's 102 members to terms lasting no more than four years.

In 1991, the Assembly approved constitutional amendments that made Guinea-Bissau a multiparty democracy. Until then, the only political party had been the African Party for the Independence of Guinea and Cape Verde. This party is usually known by the initials PAIGC, the abbreviation of its name in Portuguese. Other important parties include the Social Renewal Party and the Guinea-Bissau Resistance.

People. Black Africans make up about 85 percent of Guinea-Bissau's people. Most of the rest consist of *mestizos* (people of mixed black African and Portuguese ancestry). The black Africans belong to about 20 ethnic groups. The largest groups, in order of size, are the Balante; the Fulani; the Manjako; and the Malinke, or Mandingo (see **Fulani; Mandingo**).

Most of the people in Guinea-Bissau live in rural areas and make a bare living farming. Many of them live in straw houses with thatched roofs. Most of the people practice *animism,* the belief that everything in nature has a spirit. Many others are Muslims. The official language of Guinea-Bissau is Portuguese. But most of the people more often speak *crioulo,* which is a local language that combines other local African languages and Portuguese.

While under Portuguese rule, the people of Guinea-Bissau received little education. When the country won its freedom, only about 5 percent of the people could read and write. During the war for independence, rebel leaders began many schools and adult education programs in areas under their control. After the war, the new government turned several former Portuguese military buildings into schools.

Land and climate. Guinea-Bissau's coastal area consists of rain forests and thick swamps. Mangrove trees grow in the water along the shore. The land slopes upward from the coast, and *savannas* (grasslands with scattered trees) cover most of the inland regions. Many rivers flow through the country. The chief rivers include the Cacheu, the Corubal, and the Geba.

Guinea-Bissau has a tropical climate with a dry and a wet season. During the dry season, which lasts from December to May, temperatures average 74 °F (23 °C). During the wet season, which lasts from June to November, temperatures average 83 °F (28 °C). The heaviest rains fall in July and August. The yearly rainfall averages 95 inches (241 centimeters) along the coast and 55 inches (140 centimeters) inland.

Economy. Guinea-Bissau's agriculture, industry, and mineral resources are underdeveloped. More than half of all workers are farmers. The chief crops include beans, coconuts, corn, palm kernels, peanuts, and rice.

Guinea-Bissau's few industries employ only a small percentage of the nation's workers. Building construc-

G. Ricatto, Shostal

Bissau, the capital of Guinea-Bissau, is a quiet port town on the Geba River. This picture shows a department store on Amilcar Cabral Avenue. The street was named after a Guinean who led the country during its war for independence from Portugal.

A. Dejean, Sygma

Guinea-Bissauans celebrated their independence from Portugal in September 1974. Rebel forces in the former colony had fought for freedom from Portuguese rule for over 10 years.

tion and food processing are the chief industries.

Peanuts, cashew nuts, and shrimp rank as the country's main exports. Other exports include coconuts and palm kernels, both of which grow on the Bijagós Islands and along the coast. Leading imports include fuels and textiles. Guinea-Bissau trades chiefly with Portugal.

Since the war, the government has tried to increase farm production to meet the country's food needs. The government has planned projects to cultivate unused land and to modernize farming methods. The government has also sought to develop the nation's mineral resources with the mining of bauxite, copper, phosphates, zinc, and other minerals. But because of political instability and a shortage of trained workers, the government has had little initial success in carrying out these plans.

Guinea-Bissau has few paved roads. Rivers serve as a chief means of transportation. The Cacheu, Corubal, and Geba rivers are deep enough for some oceangoing ships to travel about 80 miles (130 kilometers) upstream. The nation has several small airfields.

History. Many black African groups lived in what is now Guinea-Bissau before Portuguese explorers arrived in 1446. From the 1600's to the 1800's, the Portuguese used the area as a slave trading base. The area became a Portuguese colony called Portuguese Guinea in 1879. It became an overseas province of Portugal in 1951.

During the 1950's and 1960's, an independence movement swept across Africa. In 1956, African nationalist leaders in Portuguese Guinea founded the African Party for the Independence of Guinea and Cape Verde (PAIGC). The party sought independence for both Portuguese Guinea and Cape Verde. Cape Verde was a Portuguese-ruled island group about 475 miles (764 kilometers) northwest of Portuguese Guinea. Amilcar Cabral headed the party from 1956 to 1973, when he was assassinated. During the early 1960's, the PAIGC trained many Portuguese Guinean farmers in guerrilla warfare.

The war for independence began in 1963. By 1968, the PAIGC controlled about two-thirds of the province. The people in these areas elected the first National Popular Assembly in 1972. The next year, the assembly declared the province to be an independent nation called Guinea-

Bissau. Luis Cabral, a PAIGC leader and a brother of Amilcar Cabral, became the new nation's first president. The war ended in 1974, when Portugal recognized Guinea-Bissau's independence. Cape Verde became independent in 1975. The PAIGC, under General Secretary Aristides Pereira, began work to rebuild and develop the country. The party also worked to unite Guinea-Bissau and Cape Verde under one government.

In 1980, military leaders overthrew the civilian government. They abolished the national assembly and formed a ruling military council. The military government forcefully opposed the unification of Guinea-Bissau and Cape Verde. In 1984, it adopted a constitution that set up a new national assembly. The Assembly elected a new president, Brigadier General João Bernardo Vieira.

The PAIGC was Guinea-Bissau's only political party until 1991. That year, the Assembly legalized the formation of other parties. Vieira won multiparty elections held in 1994 and remained president. In May 1999, rebel forces removed Vieira from office. Malan Bacai Sanha, who had been head of the Assembly, then became acting president. In parliamentary elections held in November, the Social Renewal Party won the most seats in the Assembly. In January 2000, Guinea-Bissau's voters elected Kumba Yala, the head of the Social Renewal Party, as the country's president.   John A. Marcum

See also **Bissau; Cape Verde.**

Guinea pig, *GIHN ee,* is the name of a group of furry South American mammals. There are about 20 species of guinea pigs. Scientists have used these animals in experiments that have led to the development of many drugs. Guinea pigs also have been used in research in the fields of behavior, heredity, and nutrition. Many people keep guinea pigs as pets because the animals seldom bite and are easy to care for.

Guinea pigs are not really pigs. They are rodents, as are beavers, rats, and squirrels. Guinea pigs measure from 10 to 14 inches (25 to 36 centimeters) long and weigh about 2 pounds (0.9 kilogram). They have a large head, small ears, and short legs. Most guinea pigs that live in their natural surroundings have long, coarse, brown or gray fur. Guinea pigs bred by animal raisers may have long or short fur of varying texture. The animals may be colored black, brown, red, or white, or a

Grant Heilman

A guinea pig has a large head, small ears, and short legs. Domestic guinea pigs, such as this one, are bred as pets or for use in biological and medical experiments.

combination of colors. In some countries, guinea pigs are popular as show animals.

Most kinds of wild guinea pigs live in groups of from 5 to 10 animals. They make their home on grassy plains and the edges of forests and in marshes and rocky areas. Guinea pigs dig burrows in soil or among rocks and stay there during the day. They sometimes take over burrows abandoned by other animals. They are active mostly at night, when they feed on plants. They are timid and utter loud whistlelike screams when frightened.

After mating, a female carries her young in her body for about 70 days. Most wild females have from one to four young. In captivity, as many as eight babies may be born. The young weigh about 3 ounces (85 grams) at birth. The mother cares for them for about three weeks. Domestic guinea pigs may live up to eight years.

Guinea pigs have been hunted for food for hundreds of years. The Inca Indians of Peru had domesticated them when Spanish explorers arrived in the 1500's. Dutch traders later brought guinea pigs to Europe.

Pet guinea pigs should be kept in a well-ventilated cage. Their diet should contain commercial food pellets and hay, supplemented with fruits and vegetables. Owners must make certain the guinea pigs get enough vitamin C in their diet, or they will become sick. Food and clean water should always be available for them. Guinea pigs' front teeth continue to grow all their lives. For this reason, guinea pigs should have a nonpoisonous piece of wood to gnaw on in order to wear down the tips of their teeth. The animals are healthiest in places with a temperature above 65 °F (18 °C). They are sensitive to dampness and rapid temperature change.   Clyde Jones

Scientific classification. Guinea pigs are in the family Caviidae and the genus *Cavia.* Most pet guinea pigs are *C. porcellus.*

See also **Cavy.**

Additional resources

Hansen, Elvig. *Guinea Pigs.* Carolrhoda, 1992. Younger readers.
Kelsey-Wood, Dennis. *Guinea Pigs Today.* T. F. H., 1997. Younger readers.

Guineafowl, *GIHN ee FOWL,* is a close relative of the pheasant. Guineafowl have dark gray feathers with small white spots. The neck and head are bare, and a bony ridge, or *casque,* covers the top of the head. Wild guineafowl live in Africa. People in many parts of the world also keep domesticated guineafowl. Their continual harsh cries make them unpopular, though they serve as good "watchdogs." People consider the flesh of guineafowl a delicacy and also eat the eggs. See also **Pheasant; Poultry.**   Bertin W. Anderson

Scientific classification. Guineafowl belong to the subfamily Numidinae of the family Phasianidae.

Guinness, *GIHN ihs,* **Alec** (1914-2000), was a famous English stage and motion-picture actor. He was a member of the great generation of British actors that included Laurence Olivier, Ralph Richardson, Michael Redgrave, and John Gielgud. Guinness won the 1957 Academy Award as best actor for his performance in *The Bridge on the River Kwai.* He was born in London, and made his stage debut in 1934. He appeared in many classical roles with the Old Vic Theatre from 1936 to 1939. Guinness made his motion-picture debut in 1947 in *Great Expectations.* He gained fame for playing eight roles in *Kind Hearts and Coronets* (1949).

Guinness's other major films include *The Lavender Hill Mob* (1951), *The Man in the White Suit* (1951), *The Horse's Mouth* (1959), *Tunes of Glory* (1960), *Lawrence of Arabia* (1962), *Dr. Zhivago* (1965), *Star Wars* (1977), and *A Passage to India* (1984). He also wrote an autobiography, *Blessings in Disguise* (1986). He was knighted in 1959.   Rachel Gallagher

© 1957 Columbia Pictures Corp.
Alec Guinness

Guitar is a popular stringed instrument. A guitar can be used to accompany singers, as a solo instrument, or as part of a band or orchestra. Guitarists can play chords by strumming the strings, or they can play one note at a time by plucking a single string.

For centuries, musicians have played *acoustical* guitars, which produce sound from the vibrations of the strings. In the 1930's, electric guitars began to be produced commercially. An electric guitar has an electromagnetic device that picks up the string vibrations and translates them into electrical impulses. An amplifier modifies the impulses. Loudspeakers change impulses back into sound. An electric guitar produces a greater range of sounds than an acoustical guitar.

Most guitars are made of light wood. They have curved sides and a flat or arched top and back. Guitar strings are made of bronze, nylon, or steel. Most guitars have 6 strings, but some have 4 or 12. The strings are fastened to the *bridge,* a small piece of wood on top of the instrument. They extend along the *finger board* and are tied to tuning keys at the *head.* Narrow metal strips called *frets* lie on the finger board below the strings. Each fret marks the position of a specific tone. Guitarists press the strings against the frets with the fingers of one hand. They strum or pluck the strings with the other

WORLD BOOK illustration by John Rignall, Linden Artists Ltd.
The guineafowl has dark, spotted feathers and a bony ridge called a *casque* on the head. The bird is related to the pheasant.

Craig Kersten

An acoustical guitar produces sounds when a musician plucks or strums its six strings. Acoustical guitars are used as solo instruments in classical music and in folk music. They also provide accompaniment for dances, country music, and the blues.

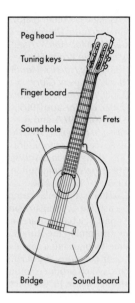

Peg head
Tuning keys
Finger board
Sound hole
Frets
Bridge   Sound board

Pamella McReynolds

An electric guitar produces sounds by electronic amplification. An electric cord connects the guitar to an amplifier and a speaker. Controls on the guitar regulate the sound. Electric guitars are popular instruments for rock music and jazz.

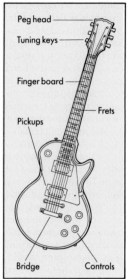

Peg head
Tuning keys
Finger board
Pickups
Frets
Bridge   Controls

WORLD BOOK illustrations by
Oxford Illustrators Limited

hand or with a *plectrum*, which guitarists sometimes call a *pick.*

Historians believe guitarlike instruments were known in ancient Egypt. The Moors, who invaded Spain in A.D. 711, are credited for bringing the guitar from northern Africa to Europe. Antonio de Torres Jurado, a Spanish guitar maker, developed the modern guitar in the late 1800's. Francisco Tárrega, a Spanish guitarist and composer, originated modern guitar-playing methods at about that time.　　Valerie Woodring Goertzen

See also **Christian, Charlie; Hendrix, Jimi; Jazz** (The guitar); **Segovia, Andrés.**

Gulden. See Guilder.

Gulf is a large body of salt water that is partially enclosed by land. Gulfs open onto oceans, and they share many of their characteristics. For example, many gulfs are as deep as oceans. Because of similarities of this kind, such gulfs as the Gulf of Bothnia and the Gulf of Mexico are often called *marginal seas.*

Gulfs are formed by movements of the earth's crust along the borders of continents. In some cases, a sinking of the crust causes an area to drop below sea level. In other cases, *faulting* occurs—that is, the crust fractures, and the land on the seaward side of the break shifts downward. In both cases, seawater floods the sunken area.

The way in which a gulf is formed determines its shape. The Gulf of Mexico, for example, occupies a circular basin that was formed by the settling of a layer of sand and other sediments about $7\frac{1}{2}$ miles (12 kilometers) thick. During the course of about 150 million years, the weight of the sediments caused the land to sink, producing the basin. In contrast, a long, narrow inlet, such as the Gulf of California, was produced by faulting.

Anthony J. Lewis

Gulf Cooperation Council is an organization of Arab states that work together in such matters as military defense and economic policy. Its six members are Bahrain, Kuwait, Oman, Qatar, Saudi Arabia, and the United Arab Emirates. The council formed in 1981. In

1990, it condemned Iraq's invasion of Kuwait and demanded complete, unconditional withdrawal of Iraqi troops from Kuwait. Member countries of the council sided with the United States and its allies in the 1991 Persian Gulf War, in which Iraq was defeated.

David A. Deese

See also **Persian Gulf War.**

Gulf Intracoastal Waterway is a water route along the Gulf of Mexico from Carrabelle, Florida, to Brownsville, Texas. This $80-million inland waterway was completed in 1949. It is 12 feet (3.7 meters) deep and 125 feet

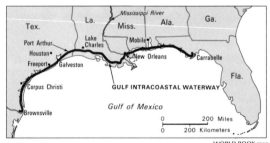

WORLD BOOK map

The Gulf Intracoastal Waterway runs along the Gulf of Mexico from Carrabelle, Florida, to Brownsville, Texas. It is 1,065 miles (1,714 kilometers) long.

(38 meters) wide at its bottom. Freight barges and pleasure boats travel 1,065 miles (1,714 kilometers) along the Gulf Coast, safe from the dangers of the open sea. Petroleum and petroleum products are the chief goods carried by the freight barges. Barges from the East and Midwest move down the Mississippi River to the waterway.　　John Edwin Coffman

See also **Texas** (Transportation).

Gulf of California is an arm of the Pacific Ocean that lies between the Lower California peninsula and mainland Mexico. The Gulf of California was once known as the Sea of Cortés, because the Spanish adventurer Hernando Cortés first explored it in 1536. The gulf was also called the Vermilion Sea. Many kinds of fish, including big-game sailfish, can be found in the Gulf of California.

Oyster beds lie along the gulf's eastern shore. The western shore has pearl and sponge fisheries. The gulf is about 700 miles (1,100 kilometers) long, from 30 to 150 miles (48 to 241 kilometers) wide, and from 600 to 6,000 feet (180 to 1,800 meters) deep. The Colorado River is the largest stream that flows into the gulf. Its largest islands are Ángel de la Guarda and Tiburón.   James D. Riley

Location of the Gulf of California

WORLD BOOK map

Gulf of Finland. See Baltic Sea.

Gulf of Mexico is a great curved arm of the Atlantic Ocean. It is almost surrounded by the United States and Mexico. The gulf forms a huge ocean basin that covers nearly 700,000 square miles (1,800,000 square kilometers). It is 800 miles (1,300 kilometers) long (north to south) and 1,100 miles (1,770 kilometers) wide. The Yucatán Channel connects it with the Caribbean Sea, and the Straits of Florida join it to the Atlantic Ocean. Warm waters flowing through the Straits of Florida form the Gulf Stream, a major Atlantic current (see **Gulf Stream**).

The low, level coastline is about 3,000 miles (4,800 kilometers) long. It has hundreds of *estuaries* (inlets) and many salty marshes bordered by barrier islands. The coast has few good harbors. The best are the gulf ports of Veracruz, Mexico; Galveston, Texas; Mobile, Alabama; Pensacola and Tampa, Florida; and Havana, Cuba.

The water of the gulf is deepest (12,700 feet, or 3,871 meters) near the coast of Mexico. Most of the gulf ranges in depth from about 500 feet (150 meters) to

Location of the Gulf of Mexico

WORLD BOOK map

more than 10,000 feet (3,000 meters). Along a continental shelf, the gulf has many shallow places with gently sloping beds, formed by the silt poured in by rivers.

The Mississippi is the largest river that empties into the gulf. Others are the Rio Grande, and the Grijalva and Usumacinta in southern Mexico. Many small islands lie off the Florida and Yucatán coasts.   Daniel D. Arreola

See also **Mississippi River**.

Gulf of Saint Lawrence is a deep arm of the Atlantic Ocean and the largest gulf on the North American coast, except for the Gulf of Mexico. The gulf is partly bordered by Newfoundland on the east, and by Nova Scotia and New Brunswick on the south. It washes the eastern shores of Quebec. For location, see **Canada** (political map). The gulf is the outlet of the St. Lawrence River and the Great Lakes, which are the chief trade highways for eastern Canada and the northern United States.

Since the opening of the deepened St. Lawrence Seaway in 1959, large oceangoing vessels can sail from the Gulf of St. Lawrence to the ends of the Great Lakes. The seaway makes the gulf the gateway to the transatlantic trade of the North American interior. The gulf enters the Atlantic by two channels. The larger channel, Cabot Strait, extends for over 60 miles (97 kilometers) between Cape Breton and Newfoundland. The Strait of Belle Isle lies between Labrador and Newfoundland.

Telegraph cables cross the Gulf of St. Lawrence, and many steamers sail between Quebec and the Atlantic Provinces. The tides are low, but the changing currents, dense fogs, and floating ice often make shipping dangerous. Prince Edward Island is in the south end of the gulf. Anticosti Island is near the mouth of the St. Lawrence River. Smaller islands lie in the southern part of the gulf and along the northern shore.

Both the Gulf of St. Lawrence and the St. Lawrence River were discovered by Jacques Cartier. On his second trip, on Aug. 10, 1535, he entered a bay on the gulf's north coast. It was the feast day of Saint Lawrence, and he called the bay the *Baye St. Laurens.* This name was gradually applied to the gulf and river.   Simon M. Evans

See also **Saint Lawrence River; Saint Lawrence Seaway.**

Gulf States are the states that border on the Gulf of Mexico. They are Florida, Alabama, Mississippi, Louisiana, and Texas.

Gulf Stream is an important ocean current. It forms the northwestern edge of a large, clockwise system of currents in the North Atlantic Ocean. The Gulf Stream has a major effect on climate, transportation by sea, and the circulation of nutrients and wastes in the ocean.

The Gulf Stream was named by the United States statesman and scientist Benjamin Franklin. He thought it started in the Gulf of Mexico, but it forms in the western Caribbean Sea and flows through the Gulf of Mexico and the Straits of Florida. It moves north along the U.S. east coast to Cape Hatteras in North Carolina, where it turns northeast. Part of the current later recirculates, forming a countercurrent. Other major ocean currents in the North Atlantic system include the North Equatorial Current, North Atlantic Current, and Canary Current.

Effects of the Gulf Stream. The Gulf Stream, warmed by the hot Caribbean sun, ranges from 11 to 18 Fahrenheit degrees (6 to 10 Celsius degrees) warmer than the surrounding water. In winter, the temperature of the current east of Cape Hatteras is warmer than the air temperature, and the water warms the air. The westerly winds that blow toward Europe are thus warmed as they cross the Gulf Stream. The British Isles and Norway have milder winters than other regions of the same latitude because this warm air from the Gulf Stream blows over their coasts.

The swift flow of the Gulf Stream plays an important role in sea transportation. For example, navigators of ships traveling from the Panama Canal to New York City have learned to travel with the Gulf Stream and get a boost from its current.

Another important effect of the Gulf Stream is its circulation of water along the east coast of the United States. Cities and industries dump wastes into the ocean in that area, and the flow of the current helps scatter and dilute the pollutants. The current, which reaches the ocean bottom, also brings nutrients from the ocean floor to the surface. This promotes the growth of aquatic organisms that live near the surface. These organisms, in turn, are eaten by various kinds of fish.

The path of the Gulf Stream, unlike that of a river, varies somewhat from day to day. The current originates in the western Caribbean Sea as the result of westward-blowing trade winds (see **Trade wind**). It then flows into the Gulf of Mexico, where it forms a large loop that may reach the mouth of the Mississippi River. As the Gulf Stream moves through the Straits of Florida, the current reaches a surface speed of about 5 knots (nautical miles per hour). Its volume of flow in this area is about 1,100 million cubic feet (30 million cubic meters) of water per second. This volume is over 50 times as great as the total flow of all the world's rivers.

The Gulf Stream travels north along the Florida and Carolina coasts until it heads northeast at Cape Hatteras. Its path becomes twisted as large swirls of warm water break off, and colder water from the north sweeps southward across its route. A portion of the Gulf Stream forms a countercurrent that flows south and then west. This countercurrent rejoins the Gulf Stream on its sea-

ward side along the Florida and Carolina coasts, adding to the volume and strength of the current.

The main part of the Gulf Stream continues northeast until it breaks up into swirling currents called *eddies* east of the Grand Banks, off the coast of Newfoundland. Some eddies drift toward the British Isles and Norway and form the North Atlantic Current. An even larger portion of the Gulf Stream flows south and east. The water becomes part of countercurrents that flow westward, or it joins the Canary Current.

Scientists use orbiting space satellites to follow the flow of the Gulf Stream. These satellites map the temperature and color of the current's surface patterns. Gulf Stream water is extremely clear, which makes it appear bluer than the surrounding water.   Pearn Niiler

Gulf War. See Persian Gulf War.

Gulf War syndrome is a puzzling pattern of symptoms reported by some veterans of the Persian Gulf War of 1991. These symptoms include fatigue, headaches, rashes, digestive disorders, and muscle and joint pain. Veterans also report stress, depression, insomnia, and trouble remembering or concentrating. Members of the armed forces of the United Kingdom, the United States, and other nations have reported symptoms. Although affected veterans describe similar ailments, their health problems do not match the pattern of any previously known illness. Experts have proposed several theories to explain Gulf War syndrome.

One theory is that small doses of chemical weapons may have caused Gulf War syndrome. Iraq stored large quantities of nerve gas and other deadly chemicals in weapons stockpiles. After the fighting ended, the United States and its allies bombed some storage sites to destroy Iraq's weapon reserves. This bombing may have released clouds of chemicals that drifted long distances, exposing troops to tiny amounts of deadly gases. Researchers are studying whether such low doses of chemical weapons can cause health problems.

Another theory is that a combination of insecticides and a drug called *pyridostigmine bromide* played a role in Gulf War syndrome. United States troops were given pyridostigmine bromide (pronounced *PIHR uh doh STIHG meen BROH myd,* often shortened to PB) experimentally in an effort to protect them against nerve gas. At the same time, soldiers used large quantities of pesticides and insect repellents to control desert pests. PB protects against nerve gas by inactivating an enzyme that also breaks down the chemicals in pesticides. As a result, some experts think that PB allowed pesticides to build up to damaging levels in the soldiers' bodies.

In addition, troops were vaccinated against many diseases and were exposed to blowing sand, heavy smoke from burning oil wells, and other environmental hazards. Some experts believe the syndrome is chiefly a stress reaction resulting from the harsh environment, physical hardship, and constant threat of attack.

Affected veterans are frustrated by the delay in understanding Gulf War syndrome and by certain government actions regarding it. For example, the United States Department of Defense denied until 1996 that American troops might have been exposed to any chemical weapons. Researchers are gathering additional data about the health of Gulf War veterans, and more studies are planned. But experts caution that Gulf War syn-

WORLD BOOK map

The Gulf Stream originates in the western Caribbean Sea. It passes through the Gulf of Mexico and the Straits of Florida, and then flows northeast along the North American coast. At the Grand Banks, the Gulf Stream breaks up into several currents.

drome may never be conclusively explained.

M. Donald Whorton

See also **Chemical-biological-radiological warfare; Persian Gulf War.**

Gulick, *GOO lihk,* **Luther Halsey,** *HAWL sih* (1865-1918), an American physical education teacher, encouraged James Naismith to start the game of basketball. In 1910, Gulick helped found the Boy Scouts of America and, with his wife, Charlotte Vetter Gulick, organized the Camp Fire Girls (now called Camp Fire Boys and Girls). He also established physical training at the International YMCA Training School (now Springfield College) and reorganized physical education in the New York schools. Gulick was born in Honolulu, Hawaii.

Glenn Smith

See also **Camp Fire Boys and Girls** (History); **Naismith, James.**

Gull is a type of long-winged bird about the size of a pigeon or larger. Gulls are often seen swooping over most large bodies of water. Most gulls make their home near the ocean, but they also live on the Great Lakes and other inland waters. Gulls are close relatives of another kind of sea bird, the tern.

The adults of many species of gulls are pearl-gray above and white below. The feathers of some species also show some black, brown, or gray. The colors change with the season and with the age of the birds. Young birds look grayish or brownish. Some become white the second year, while others may not grow their adult feathers until they are 4 years old. Most gulls have broader wings, squarer tails, and larger, stockier bodies

WORLD BOOK illustration by John Rignall, Linden Artists Ltd.

Gulls of North America include, *from top to bottom,* the ring-billed gull, the herring gull, and the great black-backed gull. These birds live along coasts and inland waters.

than terns. Gulls look less graceful in flight than terns, but they can swim better. Gulls often rest by floating on the water.

American gulls. Many species of American gulls are migratory. They fly to warm regions in the winter and fly back north to breed in the summer. They build their nests on the rocky ledges of islands or in marshes. Large colonies may be seen where their breeding places have not been disturbed. The female gull lays one to four grayish or greenish-brown spotted eggs. Soft fluffy feathers, called *down,* cover the birds when they hatch.

Gulls eat fish and other water animals, insects, rotten meat, and the eggs and young of other birds. When they live around harbors and shore waters, they are useful scavengers. They devour any kind of food or garbage that floats. Gulls are familiar to steamship passengers because great flocks follow ships for hours at a time. If food is thrown overboard, the birds swoop down eagerly to the water and pick it from the surface with their strong hooked bills. Inland gulls destroy many insects.

Their homes. In North America, the *ring-billed gull* spends the winter on the coasts and nests from the Mississippi Valley to as far west as the state of Washington. The *kittiwake* makes its home in Arctic America. The *great black-backed gull* is another bird of the Atlantic Coast. *Franklin's gull* of the upper Mississippi Valley is a bird of the plains and marshy lakes. The *laughing gull* lives from the Atlantic and Gulf coasts to the West Indies. The *California gull* winters on the Pacific Coast and nests on inland lakes. The *herring gull* is the large white bird often seen at Atlantic ports. The herring gull is also seen on inland waters. George L. Hunt, Jr.

Scientific classification. Gulls belong to the gull family, Laridae. The scientific name for the ring-billed gull is *Larus delawarensis.* The herring gull is *L. argentatus.* The great black-backed gull is *L. marinus.*

See also **Bird** (table: State birds; pictures: Birds of inland waters and marshes; Birds of the seacoasts); **Jaeger; Kittiwake; Tern.**

Gullet. See Esophagus.

Gulliver's Travels is a great satire in English literature, and a favorite children's story. It was published in London in 1726 under the name of Lemuel Gulliver, supposedly a ship's surgeon and later a captain. In reality, Jonathan Swift, the witty dean of St. Patrick's Cathedral in Dublin, wrote the book.

Swift wanted to make fun of people in high office. But the tale was so fascinating that even the people Swift attacked failed to realize its meaning at first. Nearly 80 years later, a Glasgow painter published a simplified children's version of the first two parts. This version became a juvenile classic. Many adults enjoy reading the original story in its entirety.

In the book, Dr. Gulliver describes his fantastic adventures in distant lands. The story begins with a shipwreck. Gulliver, the only survivor, swims ashore. He finds himself in Lilliput *(LIHL uh puht),* where the people are only 6 inches (15 centimeters) high. But the Lilliputians *(LIHL uh PYOO shuhnz)* take themselves very seriously. In writing the emperor's description of his country, Swift makes fun of his own land, and of all people who take themselves too seriously.

Gulliver's second voyage takes him to Brobdingnag *(BRAHB dihng nag).* The people there are tremendous giants but better tempered than the Lilliputians. Gulliver becomes the pet of a little girl 9 years old, "and not above 40 foot high, being little for her age." He has terrifying experiences. The third part of the book describes Gulliver's voyage to several strange lands. The fourth part tells of the Houyhnhnms *(hoo IHN uhmz* or *HWIHN uhmz),* the wise, talking horses. The Houyhnhnms domesticate herds of wild Yahoos, which are beasts that resemble human beings.   Michael Seidel

See also **Satire; Swift, Jonathan.**

Gum is any of many sticky substances that have a number of uses in industry. Most gums are obtained from plants. Manufacturers prepare gum for use by dissolving it in water or other liquids. This process forms a mixture generally called *mucilage.* This mixture is used to glue or thicken products or to preserve their form.

The ancient Egyptians used gum as an adhesive coating for the linen in which they wrapped mummies. Today, gum is a popular glue for stamps and labels. It also binds the color into paint and cosmetics. Gum has many uses in foods. It keeps whipping cream fluffy and beer foamy by holding in the air bubbles. Gum also thickens and adds smoothness to ice cream, pudding, baked goods, and drugs. It also preserves the shape of candy by preventing sugar crystals from bunching together. Gum is used in paper production to keep wood fibers separated. A gumlike substance called *chicle* is used as a base for chewing gum.

The best-known natural gum is *gum arabic,* which comes from acacia trees in Africa. Workers make slashes in the bark and collect the lumps of sap that form four to six weeks later. Some gums are processed from the seeds of certain plants, including flax, guar, locust, psyllium, and quince. Other sources of natural gum include brown and red seaweeds. Gum is also manufactured artificially. Some types of gum are made from chemicals. Manufacturers also change such natural substances as cellulose and starch into gum by means of chemical processes.   James Nelson Rieck

See also **Chewing gum; Chicle; Gum arabic; Mucilage.**

Gum arabic is a gum that dissolves easily in water. It is used chiefly in making perfumes, medicine, candies, and mucilage. Gum arabic is sometimes called *gum acacia.* It is obtained from the sap of the *Acacia senegal,* a tree that grows in Sudan in Africa. When used for mucilage on labels and envelope flaps, the gum is mixed with glycerin and sugar. This prevents the gum from becoming stiff enough to crack and fall from the paper. Gum arabic adds luster and stiffening to textiles. See also **Gum; Lithography; Mucilage.**   Susan M. Gaud

Gum tree is the name of many trees that produce gum or a gumlike substance. One type, the *sapodilla,* produces a gummy latex called *chicle*—an ingredient in chewing gum. This forest tree grows in Central America and is widely cultivated. The sapodilla must grow for more than 20 years before it can be tapped. Its clustered leaves are long and have pointed ends. The tree also produces small flowers and delicious fruit. Many other tropical trees produce gums, some of which are edible.

Several kinds of North American trees are also called gum trees. These kinds of trees include sweet gum, tupelo, and black gum. In addition, some Australian eucalyptus trees are known as gum trees.   Alwyn H. Gentry

Related articles in *World Book* include:

Acacia	Eucalyptus	Sapodilla	Tupelo
Chicle	Gum	Sweet gum	

Gumbo. See Okra.

Gums. See Teeth (Periodontal diseases).

Gun is a weapon that fires a bullet, a shell, or some other missile. Most guns fire by the force of a gas created by the rapid burning of gunpowder.

Guns are classified according to size. Hand-carried guns, called *small arms,* include pistols, rifles, and shotguns. Portable, automatic weapons that can fire from 400 to 1,600 rounds of ammunition per minute are called *machine guns.* Large guns are called *cannon* or *artillery.* They may be stationary, as on ships, or mounted on wheels or on self-propelled carriers.

Gun size is expressed in terms of *caliber,* the inside diameter of the gun's barrel, measured in inches, hundredths of an inch, or in millimeters or centimeters. A .45-caliber revolver has a barrel with an inside diameter of $\frac{45}{100}$ of an inch (11 millimeters). A 75-millimeter cannon has a barrel with an inside diameter of 75 millimeters. Most guns have spiral grooves called *rifling* on the inside of the barrel. The rifling gives a spiraling motion to a bullet or shell. This motion helps prevent the bullet from wobbling, and helps provide accuracy and range.

No one knows who invented the gun. But most historians believe the first guns may have been cannonlike weapons used by Arabs in North Africa during the 1300's. These and other early guns consisted of a brass or iron tube with a small hole at the closed end for igniting the gunpowder.   Ronald A. Ogan

Related articles in *World Book.* For information on various firearms, such as pistols, rifles, and shotguns, see the separate articles listed at the end of the **Firearm** article. See also:

Ammunition	Bazooka	Machine	Mortar
Artillery	Cannon	gun	Warship

Gun control is an effort to fight violent crime by strengthening laws on the ownership of firearms. The use of a gun in a crime is more likely to result in a person's death than is the use of most other kinds of weapons, including knives. Many people own guns for the protection of their home, for use in hunting or target shooting, or for other legitimate reasons. Gun control laws aim to reduce the criminal use of guns as much as possible and, at the same time, to interfere as little as possible with other gun use.

Approaches to gun control. The federal government and all U.S. states have some gun control laws. These laws use two main approaches to reducing gun violence. The first involves keeping *high-risk people* from obtaining firearms. The second prohibits *high-risk guns* from being acquired by anyone but the police.

High-risk people are those whom authorities consider most likely to misuse firearms. They include alcoholics, drug addicts, mentally unbalanced people, and people with serious criminal records. Federal and state laws prohibit these people from owning guns. The laws also prohibit sales of firearms to minors.

In the United States and other countries, laws have been adopted to give law enforcement officials a chance to make sure the buyer is not a high-risk person. For example, some U.S. states require a person who wishes to own a gun to first get a license. In 1993, Congress passed the "Brady bill," which made gun buyers go through a waiting period of five working days between the time they purchased a *handgun* (revolver or pistol) and the time they took possession of it. In 1998, new federal legislation replaced the waiting period with a requirement that gun buyers undergo background checks prior to purchasing a handgun, rifle, or shotgun. Under Canadian law, first-time gun buyers must wait 28 days to buy a gun. Moreover, in 1995, Canada's Parliament voted to require all gun owners to obtain a license by 2001 and to register their guns by 2003.

High-risk firearms are those considered more likely to be misused than ordinary firearms. Since 1934, for example, U.S. federal law has placed special restrictions on machine guns—which can fire many bullets with a single pull of the trigger—and *sawed-off* (short-barreled) shotguns. A law passed by Congress in 1994 bans the sale of certain *semiautomatic guns,* often called *assault weapons.* These kinds of guns require a separate pull of the trigger to fire each bullet but can quickly fire many bullets.

Some communities severely restrict ownership of handguns by ordinary citizens. In these areas, only citizens who can prove a special need and obtain special permission can own such a weapon. Backers of such laws argue that handguns are involved in many accidental shootings and have little value in household self-defense. Until the 1990's, most states prohibited ordinary citizens from carrying concealed guns. Since 1987, however, many states have adopted laws that allow their citizens to obtain licenses to carry concealed guns.

In the late 1990's, several local governments in the United States began to sue gun manufacturers for the effects of violence committed with guns. In 2000, the gun-manufacturing company Smith & Wesson agreed to adopt a number of restrictions on the distribution and design of its guns, including safety locks on handguns to make them more child-resistant. In return, many of the lawsuits against that company were dropped. Other gun manufacturers and many opponents of gun control condemned the agreement.

Opposition to gun control. People opposed to gun control argue that taking guns from law-abiding citizens does not prevent the possession of guns by criminals. People who oppose licensing, waiting periods, and background checks argue that legitimate gun owners must pay the cost of the procedures, bear their inconvenience, or both. Opponents of laws forbidding concealed weapons argue that criminals are less likely to commit crimes if they think their victims may be armed.

Some U.S. citizens argue that gun control laws violate their right to own guns. Many of these people claim this right is guaranteed by the Second Amendment to the Constitution. The amendment reads: "A well-regulated militia, being necessary to the security of a free state, the right of the people to keep and bear arms shall not be infringed." However, in 1939, the Supreme Court of the United States ruled that the amendment does not prohibit most gun control laws. Franklin E. Zimring

See also **Handgun** (Gun control); **National Rifle Association of America; Second Amendment.**

Additional resources

Gottfried, Ted. *Gun Control.* Millbrook, 1993.
Zimring, Franklin E., and Hawkins, Gordon. *Citizen's Guide to Gun Control.* 1987. Reprint. Macmillan, 1992.

Guncotton is an explosive. It is obtained when cotton or purified wood cellulose is soaked in a mixture of sulfuric and nitric acids. By 1846, C. F. Schönbein, a German chemist, had discovered the process for making guncotton. After the cotton is soaked in the acid mixture, it is drained and washed. Then, it is boiled in water to remove the acid and impurities. The cotton is ground to a pulp and drained. It is pressed into small slabs, or blocks, while damp. It may be dried in air, either after boiling, or after it has been made into blocks.

When ignited, dried guncotton burns rapidly. A blow from a hammer will cause it to explode. Wet guncotton is much safer to handle. It will not burn or explode unless another explosive sets it off. Ordinary guncotton burns too fast to be used as an explosive in firearms. When it is *colloided* (gelatinized) in nitroglycerin or other solvents, its burning rate can be controlled. Colloided guncotton is a major ingredient of smokeless gunpowder and is used in certain rocket propellants.

Guncotton is a kind of *cellulose nitrate,* a chemical that is also known as *nitrocellulose.* It is the most highly nitrated form of nitrocellulose. James E. Kennedy

Gunpowder is an explosive material that burns rapidly to form high-pressure gas. Expansion of this gas inside the barrel of a gun can accelerate a bullet to great speed. Gunpowder is therefore used as a *propellant* in a variety of ammunition. It is also used in explosives for blasting operations, in fireworks, and in fuses.

Kinds of gunpowder. The first important substance used as gunpowder in guns and cannons was *black powder.* Black powder consists of a mixture of saltpeter (potassium nitrate), charcoal, and sulfur. These ingredients are pressed together and then broken into small pieces. In some cases, graphite is added. Grains of black powder range from fine powder to pellets.

Variations of the basic formula for black powder have been used for special purposes. *Sulfurless gunpowder* contains saltpeter and charcoal but no sulfur. It is not as powerful as regular black powder, but it causes less *corrosion* (gradual wearing away) of the gun barrel. For black powder used in fireworks and blasting, saltpeter sometimes is replaced by less expensive sodium nitrate. Smokeless gunpowders include nitrocellulose, and sometimes nitrate salts and additives. These ingredients largely eliminate the smoke that is produced by ordinary black powder. In some smokeless powders, called *colloided powders,* the nitrocellulose is dissolved in nitroglycerin.

History. People in Asia were probably the first to learn of the explosive properties of saltpeter and sulfur. Their knowledge moved westward, probably through contact with the Arabs, and eventually reached Europe in the 1200's. Gunpowder affected the social system of Europe in the 1300's and 1400's. The existing system, called *feudalism,* relied in part on stone castles to defend the estates of lords and nobles. The castles could not stand against assaults by heavy cannonballs fired by gunpowder (see **Feudalism** [The decline of feudalism]).

Smokeless gunpowder was developed in the 1800's. An early kind of smokeless powder was *guncotton,* an invention of the mid-1840's. It exploded powerfully but was dangerous to manufacture. A more useful powder was invented in 1864. About 1887, the Swedish chemist Alfred Nobel created the first colloided powder. Today, smokeless powder is more commonly used in ammunition than is black powder.   James E. Kennedy

Related articles in *World Book* include:

Ammunition	Explosive	Rifle	Shrapnel
Charcoal	Greek fire	Saltpeter	Sulfur
Cordite	Guncotton		

Gunpowder Plot was a plan to blow up the English Houses of Parliament on Nov. 5, 1605, when King James I and a council of government officials were to be present. A group led by Robert Catesby and including Guy Fawkes originated the plan (see **Fawkes, Guy**). This group resented the hostile attitude of the English government toward Roman Catholicism. But the plot was discovered and all 12 conspirators were killed. Afterward, public hostility toward Catholics grew in England and remained strong for more than a century.

The English hold a festival every November 5, when they burn Guy Fawkes in effigy. In memory of the plot, the vaults beneath the Houses of Parliament are searched before each new session.   Richard L. Greaves

Guppy is a small tropical fish. It rivals the goldfish as the world's most popular aquarium pet. Guppies have beautiful, featherlike tails and fins. Many male guppies have several bright colors in a pattern on their body, and they often look like small jewels. Adult males are about 1 inch (2.5 centimeters) long. Female guppies grow about twice as long and are mostly gray.

Guppies are native to the warm, freshwater streams of Venezuela and adjacent Caribbean islands. In their natural habitat, they feed mainly on such small animals as worms, shellfish, and insect *larvae* (young). Groups of these fish have been released in many lakes and ponds throughout the world to control mosquitoes.

Guppies are closely related to swordtails, mollies, and mosquito fish. All these fishes are called *live-bearers* because they give birth to live, fully formed young. Most other fishes reproduce by laying eggs. Guppies reproduce as frequently as every four to six weeks. The male guppy uses a special fin on its underside to place *semen* (fertilizing fluid) inside the female. The female produces from 30 to 50 young at a time. Newborn guppies are so tiny that they are barely visible. They measure only about $\frac{1}{8}$ inch (3 millimeters) long.

A hardy fish, guppies are an excellent choice for a beginner's home aquarium. They can be kept in fishbowls

E. R. Degginger
Guppies are small tropical fish. The male guppy, *shown at the top,* is more colorful than the female, *below.*

or other small containers. Make sure the water temperature is at least 68 °F (20 °C). Adult guppies sometimes feed on young guppies. For this reason, baby guppies should be separated from the larger fish until they grow big enough to live among them safely.

Guppys are named after R. J. L. Guppy, a British scientist who worked in Trinidad. He introduced the fish to aquariums in England during the 1800's.
     Leighton R. Taylor, Jr.

Scientific classification. The guppy belongs to the family of live-bearing fishes, Poeciliidae. It is *Poecilia reticulata.*

Gupta dynasty, *GUHP tuh* or *GUP tuh,* was a series of rulers of one family who reigned in what is now northern India and Bangladesh from about A.D. 320 to about 500. During the Gupta period, India's literature, sculpture, and other arts reached high levels of accomplishment. Textile manufacturing and trade, particularly with Southeast Asia and China, both flourished.

Rise and fall of the dynasty. The Gupta family of rulers gained control of Magadha, a small kingdom in the Ganges Valley. Chandragupta I, who reigned from about 320 to about 335, established the dynasty's prestige and expanded its territory through marriage and war. Samudragupta, who ruled from about 335 to about 375, and his successor, Chandragupta II, who governed until about 415, seized much additional territory in the Ganges and Indus valleys. They also forced many rulers along India's coastlines to submit to their power.

After 450, Huns from central Asia increasingly attacked the empire. Skandagupta, who ruled from about 454 to 467, defeated many Hun invaders and put down revolts by regional rulers. The Huns finally pierced the Gupta defenses about 500 and eventually conquered much of northern India. But small kingdoms, whose rulers claimed descent from the Gupta dynasty, lasted in eastern India until the mid-500's.

Though the Guptas called themselves emperors, their empire was loosely organized. They directly controlled the Ganges Valley, but outlying areas and regional rulers had much independence as long as they paid tribute to the Guptas. Even in the Ganges Valley, villages and cities chose their local officials and managed their own affairs.

Cultural life under the Guptas received support from the prosperous upper classes of the cities, especially the capital city, Pataliputra. Most Gupta rulers were Hindus, but Hinduism, Buddhism, and Jainism all flourished in the empire. Under the Guptas, Hinduism developed many of the social and religious forms found today. For example, the image of a Hindu god or goddess became important as an object of worship. Images were offered food, bathed, and sung to.

During the Gupta period, music and dance developed the complex forms that are the basis of classical Indian music and dance. The detailed, yet restrained, Hindu and Buddhist sculpture of the Gupta period became the model for much of later Indian art. Some excellent examples decorate the Buddhist *stupa* (dome-shaped monument) at Sarnath. Gupta wallpaintings included scenes of Indian life and events in Buddha's life. Most of the paintings that remain are in caves, such as those at Ajanta.

Sanskrit, India's classical language, flowered during the Gupta era. Court and popular playwrights wrote both dramas and comedies, and all classes of people at-

Gupta art explored both Hindu and Buddhist religious themes. This relief sculpture carved about A.D. 425 decorates an exterior wall of the Dashavatara Temple at Deogarh, India. It portrays the Hindu god Vishnu sleeping on the coils of a giant serpent.

Dr. Suresh Vasant, ACSAA, University of Michigan, Ann Arbor

tended the theater. The famous poet and dramatist Kalidasa wrote about love among human beings, gods, and goddesses. Many of his works taught moral lessons.

Hindu schools and Buddhist monasteries taught astronomy, grammar, mathematics, medicine, philosophy, and religion. The Buddhist monastery at Nalanda held large libraries and attracted students of many religions from as far as China and Java. Gupta mathematicians invented the decimal system and the Hindu-Arabic numerals that most of the world uses today.

Indian culture and religious practices of the Gupta period spread to other regions. Many kings in Southeast Asia adopted the Sanskrit language and Hindu ceremonies for use in their courts.   Michael H. Fisher

See also **India** (History).

Gurnard, *GUR nuhrd,* is the name of certain marine fishes that live in all warm seas. Gurnards are most common off the Atlantic coast of Europe and Africa. A gurnard has a large, angular head, a tapering body, and large *pectoral fins* (shoulder fins). The lower three rays of the pectoral fins move separately like fingers.

The *flying gurnard* has immense, winglike pectoral fins that reach almost to the tail. The fish can glide through the water for several yards or meters without moving its fins. Contrary to popular belief, it does not leap above the water like a flyingfish. Flying gurnards live on or near coral reefs off both the eastern and western coasts of the Atlantic. They are often seen near coral reefs by snorkelers or divers.   William J. Richards

Scientific classification. Most gurnards belong to the sea robin family, Triglidae. The flying gurnard belongs to the flying gurnard family, Dactylopteridae. Its scientific name is *Dactylopterus volitans.*

Guru. See **Buddhism** (The Mantrayana); **Religion** (Hinduism).

Gustav I Vasa, *GUS tahv, VAH suh* (1496-1560), was the first king of independent Sweden. He was the son of a nobleman of the Vasa family, Erik Johansson. At 18, he fought for Sweden in its struggle for independence from Denmark. After being held as a hostage, he escaped to Sweden, raised a peasant army, and ousted the Danes. In 1523, Gustav was elected king. He provided

good government and established the Lutheran faith as the state religion.   Odd S. Lovoll

See also **Sweden** (The beginnings of modern Sweden).

Gustavus Adolphus, *guh STAY vuhs* or *guh STAH vuhs, uh DAHL fuhs* (1594-1632), was king of Sweden from 1611 to 1632. He came to the throne as Gustavus II Adolphus, also called Gustav II Adolf, when Sweden was at war with Denmark, Poland, and Russia. After winning these wars, he led an army into Germany in 1630 to save the Protestants there from Roman Catholic domination. In 1631, he defeated the Catholics at the Battle of Breitenfeld. In 1632, his troops overwhelmed those of Bohemian general Albrecht von Wallenstein at Lützen. But Gustavus died on the battlefield. His victory saved Protestantism in Germany, and won German territory for Sweden.   Odd S. Lovoll

See also **Oxenstierna, Axel Gustafsson; Sweden** (picture: King Gustavus Adolphus); **Thirty Years' War.**

Guston, *GUHS tuhn,* **Philip** (1913-1980), was an American painter. About 1947, he abandoned the use of explicit human figures. Instead, he painted shimmering abstractions produced by floating strokes of bright colors. Guston applied the strokes freely, in the manner associated with the Abstract Expressionist movement. See **Abstract expressionism.**

Guston's work in the 1950's develops mysterious relationships among ambiguous forms that seem to move in unconfined spaces. His later works are dominated by thickly painted strokes of blacks, grays, and silver-whites that suggest a somber, powerful feeling. In his final years, Guston developed a unique style, painting tragic satires and social criticism in a frank, sometimes cartoonlike manner. Guston was born in Montreal, Canada, and grew up in Los Angeles.   Dore Ashton

Gutenberg, *GOOT uhn BURG,* **Johannes,** *yoh HAHN uhs* (1395?-1468?), invented processes that made printing from movable type practical for the first time. His printing method used a supply of letters that were uniformly cast on equal metal bodies. Gutenberg and others used his invention to produce books in Mainz, Germany, during the mid-1400's.

Studio Popp

A replica of Gutenberg's printing press is displayed in the inventor's original workshop in Mainz, Germany.

United Press Int.

Johannes Gutenberg

Gutenberg was born in Mainz, a member of the aristocratic Gensfleisch family. He used his mother's name. He may have learned the necessary skills in metalwork from an uncle who was master of the mint. At that time, Mainz was a center for many goldsmiths and jewelers. As an aristocrat, Gutenberg did not have to serve a regular apprenticeship.

Because of his family's involvement in local political squabbles, Gutenberg spent a number of years in exile in Strasbourg. He carried on experiments there to develop a method for printing books that would replace handwritten copying. Gutenberg produced types that could be *ranged* in even lines of composition. Then, they could be locked firmly together under the pressure of *quoins* (wedges) to make up a *form* (unit). A number of pages containing thousands of types could easily be put on and taken off the press. After printing, the types could be separated and used again to set up other pages. Gutenberg adapted the ink for his press from materials known to early Flemish painters.

Long before Gutenberg's time, the Chinese and Koreans had been printing text and pictures cut on wood blocks. They had even invented movable type made of porcelain and metal. But their languages required so many different characters for printing that the method was difficult for them and fell into disuse. The idea was lost until Gutenberg applied it successfully to the alphabet. Others were struggling to solve the problem. At least one Dutch printer was well along the road to successful typography. But Gutenberg and his associates, Johannes Fust and Peter Schöffer, perfected it. Their magnificent Bible, known as the *Mazarin Bible* and *Gutenberg Bible,* shows that these pioneer printers had mastered every technical detail.   Frank J. Romano

See also **Bible** (picture); **Book** (The development of printed books); **Communication** (The rise of printing); **Printing** (History).

Additional resources

Burch, Joann J. *Fine Print: A Story About Johann Gutenberg.* Carolrhoda, 1991. Younger readers.
Fisher, Leonard E. *Gutenberg.* Macmillan, 1993. Younger readers.
Ing, Janet. *Johann Gutenberg and His Bible.* Typophiles, 1988.
Kapr, Albert. *Johann Gutenberg.* Scolar, 1996.

Guthrie, *GUHTH ree,* **A. B., Jr.** (1901-1991), was an American author known for his novels about the Oregon Trail and frontier life in the Rocky Mountains. Guthrie's books are noted for their historical accuracy, their lyrical descriptions of nature, and their vivid character portrayals. His novel *The Way West* (1949) won the 1950 Pulitzer Prize for fiction. The book portrays a wagon train traveling from Missouri to Oregon in 1846.

Guthrie's first major novel, *The Big Sky* (1947), describes the lives of trappers and American Indians during the 1830's and 1840's. His other novels include *These Thousand Hills* (1956), *Arfive* (1970), *The Last Valley* (1975), and *Fair Land, Fair Land* (1983). In addition, Guthrie wrote three detective stories, *Wild Pitch* (1973), *The Genuine Article* (1977), and *No Second Wind* (1980), which are set in the modern West. His short stories were published in the collection *The Big It* (1960). Guthrie wrote the script for the Western motion picture *Shane* (1953). His autobiography is *The Blue Hen's Chick* (1965).

Alfred Bertram Guthrie, Jr., was born in Bedford, Indiana, and grew up in Montana. He worked as a journalist in Kentucky from 1926 to 1947.   Arthur R. Huseboe

Guthrie, *GUHTH ree,* **Tyrone** (1900-1971), was an English director and producer who specialized in inventive productions of plays by William Shakespeare and other classics. He often experimented with stage techniques, such as using modern costumes for classic plays, to make the works more accessible. He also stressed the psychology of the characters and guided performers toward more realistic acting.

William Tyrone Guthrie was born in Tunbridge Wells, England. He directed the Old Vic Theatre in London from 1933 to 1945. He helped create the Stratford Festival that began in 1953 in Ontario. In 1963, he established the Tyrone Guthrie Theater in Minneapolis, Minnesota, one of the first nonprofit regional repertory companies in the United States. In 1961, Queen Elizabeth II knighted Guthrie for his services to the theater, and he became known as Sir Tyrone Guthrie.   Gerald M. Berkowitz

Guthrie, *GUHTH ree,* **Woody** (1912-1967), was an American folk singer and composer. His songs and vocal style influenced a number of younger professional folk singers, including Bob Dylan and Jack Elliot. Guthrie wrote more than 1,000 songs in traditional style, including the well-known "This Land Is Your Land."

Woodrow Wilson Guthrie was born in Okemah, Oklahoma. He began to travel at about the age of 16, and he spent much

Robin Carson,
courtesy Marjorie Mazia Guthrie

Woody Guthrie

of his life roaming the United States. Guthrie composed songs about migrant workers and about ordinary people who became victims of the Great Depression. His songs also described the beauty of the American land. Guthrie had many personal misfortunes, but his music expressed a hopeful view of life. During his last 13 years, he suffered from Huntington's disease, a nerve disorder that caused his death. Guthrie wrote an autobiography, *Bound for Glory* (1943). His son Arlo (1947-   ) also became a professional folk music performer and song writer.   Valerie Woodring Goertzen

Gutiérrez, *goo TYEHR rehs,* **José Angel,** *hoh SAY AHN hayl* (1944-   ), is a leader of the Chicano movement, a Mexican American civil rights campaign. In 1970, he founded a political party, *La Raza Unida* (People Together). Raza Unida nominated Mexican Americans for public office in the Midwest and Southwest. According to Gutiérrez, the Democratic and Republican parties ignored the needs of Mexican Americans.

In 1970, running as a Raza Unida candidate, Gutiérrez was elected president of the school board of Crystal City, Texas. As president, he ordered that all elementary school classes be taught in both English and Spanish. Raza Unida later sponsored successful city council and school board candidates in other parts of Texas and in Arizona, California, Colorado, and New Mexico. In 1974, Gutiérrez won election as a county judge in Zavala County, Texas.

Rafael Torres

José Angel Gutiérrez

Gutiérrez was born in Crystal City. He graduated from Texas A&I University and earned a Ph.D. degree at the University of Texas.

Gutta-percha, *GUHT uh PUR chuh,* is a milky juice obtained chiefly from the *Palaquium gutta* trees of Malaysia. It is used as insulation for electric wire. It is also used to make containers for acids, surgical bandages, castings, soles for shoes, machine belts, and temporary tooth fillings.

To obtain gutta-percha, workers cut the bark of the tree and catch the juice in cups as it flows slowly out. The juice is then boiled in open kettles. The boiled juice cools, hardens, and is cut into blocks, which range from white to a dark gray in color. It is so soft that it can be dented, and it does not break easily. When it is heated, it can be stretched. Gutta-percha without stabilizers cannot be exposed to light or air for long periods, or it will oxidize and become brittle.   Jim L Bowyer

See also **Latex.**

Guy of Warwick, *WAWR ihk,* was the legendary hero of an English romance. Guy was in love with Felice, daughter of the Earl of Warwick. But she at first refused to marry him. After he had rescued a German princess, killed a dragon, and defeated the Muslims, Sir Guy married Felice. But he left on a crusade, and when he returned he lived as a hermit. Finally, he sent his wife a ring she recognized, and they were reunited.

Ellen J. Stekert

Guyana, *gy AN uh,* is a country on the northeast coast of South America. It is a tropical land with large sugar plantations and small rice farms. Guyana has valuable mineral resources, dense forests, and wild mountain country. Much of the land is difficult to reach, and some areas have never been explored. *Guyana* is an *Amerindian* (American Indian) word meaning *Land of Waters.* The country's official name is the Cooperative Republic of Guyana. Guyana is made up of people from several national and ethnic groups. East Indians and blacks form the largest groups.

Guyana was one of the first areas in the Western Hemisphere to be settled by Europeans. Christopher Columbus sailed along its coast in 1498. In 1581, the Dutch founded a settlement in what is now Guyana and claimed the area. Sir Walter Raleigh searched there in 1595 for El Dorado, the legendary city of gold. In 1831, the United Kingdom created the colony of British Guiana there. It became the independent nation of Guyana in 1966. Georgetown is the capital and largest city.

Government. Guyana is a republic, with a president and a 65-member National Assembly. The political party that wins the most votes in an election gains the most seats in the Assembly, and that party's leader becomes president. Fifty-three seats are filled by the popular vote and 12 by regional and local representatives. The National Assembly makes the country's laws, but the president has the power to veto laws. The president appoints a prime minister and a Cabinet.

People. About half of Guyana's people are East Indians whose ancestors were brought from India to work on plantations. Most live in rural areas. Some work on sugar plantations. Others live on small farms where they grow rice and vegetables. Gradually, the East Indians have been moving to cities and towns where many of them work as merchants, doctors, and lawyers.

About 40 percent of the people of Guyana are blacks whose ancestors were brought from Africa as slaves. Most of them live in cities and towns. They work as teachers, police officers, government employees, and as skilled workers in the sugar grinding mills and bauxite mines. The rest of the people are Amerindians, Europeans, or Chinese. Some of the Amerindians make their

Facts in brief

Capital: Georgetown.
Official language: English.
Area: 83,000 mi² (214,969 km²). *Greatest distances*—north-south, 495 mi (797 km); east-west, 290 mi (467 km). *Coastline*—270 mi (435 km).
Population: *Estimated 2002 population*—872,000; density, 11 per mi² (4 per km²); distribution, 64 percent rural, 36 percent urban. *1993 census*—701,704.
Chief products: *Agriculture*—sugar cane, rice. *Manufacturing and processing*—sugar, rice, timber, coconuts. *Mining*—bauxite, diamonds, gold.
Flag: The flag is green (representing agriculture and forests) with a red triangle (zeal in nation building) and a golden yellow arrowhead (minerals). The triangle has a black border (endurance) and the arrowhead has a white border (water resources). See **Flag** (picture: Flags of the Americas).
National anthem: "Guyana National Anthem."
Money: *Basic unit*—Guyana dollar. One hundred cents equal one dollar.

Guyana

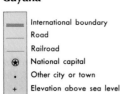

▰▰▰	International boundary
	Road
	Railroad
⊛	National capital
•	Other city or town
+	Elevation above sea level

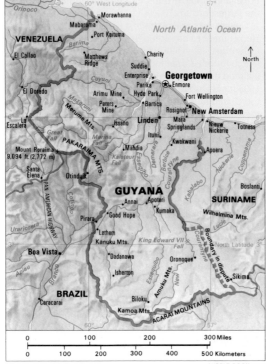

WORLD BOOK maps

living by hunting. Others farm or cut and sell timber. Some Amerindians live in remote forest areas in much the same way as their ancestors lived. Most Europeans and Chinese are business people.

English is Guyana's official language and is spoken by most of the people. Many of the people speak a broken form of English called Creole. Hindi and Urdu are widely used by Guyana's East Indians.

Tension between the East Indians and blacks caused political difficulty in the 1950's and early 1960's. Most East Indians support the People's Progressive Party. The People's National Congress is supported by most blacks. The United Force and the Working People's Alliance are supported by people of several ethnic groups.

Almost all of Guyana's adults can read and write. Guyanese children between the ages of 6 and 14 must attend school. Most education is free for children between the ages of 5 and 16. The government operates most of the schools. The University of Guyana, located in Georgetown, is the only university in Guyana.

Land. Guyana is divided into three main regions: the *coastal plain, inland forest,* and *highland.*

The coastal plain, a strip of land along the Atlantic

Ocean, is from 2 to 30 miles (3.2 to 48 kilometers) wide. Most of it lies about 4 feet (1.2 meters) below sea level at high tide. Sea walls, dikes, and drainage canals keep out the sea and protect the people and their crops from floods. About 95 percent of the people live on the plain. Farms cover much of it, and the main crops—sugar cane and rice—are grown and processed there.

The inland forest covers a plateau south of the coastal plain. The inland forest region covers about 85 percent of Guyana and has about a thousand types of timber.

The highland consists of mountains and *savannas* (grasslands with scattered trees). The mountainous parts of the highland are in the south and southwest. These areas are generally isolated from the rest of the country and are difficult to reach. Most of the Amerindians live there. The main savanna area covers about 6,000 square miles (16,000 square kilometers) in the southwest. A smaller savanna lies in the northeast. Farmers run some small farms and raise cattle in the savannas.

The four main rivers, the Essequibo, the Demerara, the Berbice, and the Courantyne, flow north into the Atlantic. Guyana has several spectacular waterfalls. Great Fall drops 1,600 feet (488 meters) on the Kamarang River. The nearby Great Falls drops 840 feet (256 meters) on the Mazaruni River. Kaieteur Fall on the Potaro River drops 741 feet (226 meters).

The coastal plain has a hot, humid climate that averages 80 °F (27 °C) and about 90 inches (230 centimeters) of rain a year. More rain falls in the forest area, and temperatures are higher in the forest and highland.

Economy. Agriculture and mining are the major economic activities of the country. Guyana has rich soil, valuable forests, and large deposits of minerals.

Sugar cane is Guyana's most important crop and an important export. Most sugar cane is raised on large plantations. On smaller farms on the coastal plain, many people raise rice—the second most important crop. Citrus fruits, cocoa, coconuts, coffee, and *plantains* (bananalike fruit) also rank as major crops.

Guyana produces large amounts of *bauxite,* the ore used in making aluminum. Bauxite is one of the country's leading exports. The country also has diamond, manganese, and gold mines.

Forests cover about 85 percent of the land in Guyana. The wood of the greenheart tree, the most important kind found there, is used to build wharves.

Guyana's main roads run through the coastal plain region. There are about 80 miles (130 kilometers) of railroads. Only ferryboats and small vessels can travel on most of the rivers beyond the coastal plain. Oceangoing ships can sail up the Demerara River about 65 miles (105 kilometers).

History. When European explorers came to Guyana in the late 1500's and early 1600's, they found Arawak, Carib, and Warrau Indians living in the area. The Dutch founded a settlement in what is now Guyana in 1581 and claimed the area. Later, Britain and France also claimed it. In 1814, Britain gained control, and in 1831, it formed the colony of British Guiana.

Early settlers started sugar plantations and brought in black slaves to work on them. Slavery was *abolished* (made illegal) by 1838, and many of the blacks stopped working on the plantations. The planters then brought in laborers from India to work on the plantations.

Carol Lee

Georgetown is Guyana's capital and largest city. It lies on the Atlantic Coast and is the country's chief port.

During the 1940's, the British increased their efforts to prepare British Guiana for self-government. More of the people were allowed to vote, and they elected more members of the legislature.

A new constitution was adopted in 1953, and elections were held in April 1953. The People's Progressive Party (PPP), led by Cheddi B. Jagan, won most of the seats in the legislature. But the British suspended the Constitution and removed the Jagan administration from office in October 1953. They said Jagan's policies threatened to make British Guiana a Communist state. Jagan's party returned to office by winning the 1957 and 1961 elections.

British Guiana seemed to be nearing independence in 1961. A new constitution gave the colony control of its national affairs, though the United Kingdom still controlled its defense and its relations with other nations. But violence between East Indians and blacks broke out in 1962. After more outbreaks during the next two years, the United Kingdom declared that another election would have to be held before British Guiana could become independent. In 1964, the People's National Congress (PNC) and the United Force, the two parties that made up the opposition to Jagan's government, won a majority of seats in the legislature and formed a coalition government.

British Guiana became the independent nation of Guyana on May 26, 1966. Forbes Burnham, a black lawyer and head of the PNC, became Guyana's first prime minister and most powerful leader.

Guyana's development during the late 1960's was marked by few outbreaks of racial violence. Its economy expanded, and it worked for economic cooperation among Caribbean nations. During the 1970's, the government took control of bauxite mines and other industries owned by foreign companies. The government also took over the major Guyanese industries.

Also during the 1970's, a number of religious groups called *cults* moved to Guyana from other countries. They included the People's Temple, a cult from the United States led by Jim Jones, a Protestant clergyman. The People's Temple established a settlement in northern Guyana that became known as Jonestown. In 1978, Jones ordered the members of his cult to commit suicide. Over 900 members, including Jones, then died. Most took

poison. Some were murdered by other members.

Burnham served as Guyana's prime minister until 1980. In 1980, he led a movement that greatly increased the power of the presidency and made it the top government office. He served as president until his death in 1985. In 1992 elections, the PPP won the most seats in the legislature and party leader Jagan became president. Jagan died in March 1997. Later that year, his widow, Janet Jagan, was elected president. She resigned in 1999 because of poor health and was succeeded as president by Prime Minister Bharrat Jagdeo. Jagdeo and the PPP remained in power after elections in 2001.

In 1988, the government introduced economic reforms. Since then, many state-owned companies have been sold to private owners. Anthony P. Maingot

See also **Georgetown.**

Gwinnett, *gwih NEHT,* **Button** (1735?-1777), a Georgia signer of the Declaration of Independence, served in the Georgia Assembly in 1769 and in the Continental Congress in 1776 and 1777. He was acting governor of Georgia for a brief period in 1777.

Gwinnett was born in Gloucestershire, England. He settled in Charleston, South Carolina, in 1765 and then moved to Savannah, Georgia. Later, he purchased St. Catherine's Island, off Georgia, and became a plantation owner. Gwinnett made enemies because many older Georgians regarded him as a latecomer. He was killed in a duel with General Lachlan McIntosh. Their duel resulted from their rivalry for the post of brigadier general of troops raised in Georgia. Gary D. Hermalyn

Gwyn, *gwihn,* **Nell** (1650-1687), was a popular English actress and a mistress of King Charles II of England. She first appeared on stage at the age of 15 in John Dryden's *The Indian Emperor* (1665) at the Theatre Royal (later the Drury Lane Theatre) in London. Gwyn was not a talented actress, but she was charming and lively. In 1667, she performed in men's clothes as Florimel in Dryden's *Secret Love* and scored a hit. She soon came to the attention of King Charles II and became his mistress. She probably made her last stage appearance about 1670.

Eleanor Gwyn may have been born in Hereford or London. Before she began acting, she worked as an orange seller at the Theatre Royal. J. P. Wearing

Gymnasium is a room or building for physical training, athletic competitions, and games. In addition, many schools use their gymnasiums for such special events as performances, concerts, social dances, and graduation ceremonies. In some European countries, *gymnasium* is the name for a type of secondary school. The word *gymnasium* comes from a Greek word meaning to *exercise naked.* In ancient Greece, the word was used to mean public places set aside for athletic sports. To have freedom of bodily movement, Greek boys and young men wore no clothes when taking part in games. The first gymnasium on a campus in the United States opened in 1860 at Amherst College. William R. Ruskin

See also **Education** (Ancient Greek education; The Renaissance); **Gymnastics; Physical education; Physical fitness.**

Gymnastics is a competitive sport for both men and women in which participants demonstrate body control over a wide range of acrobatic exercises and other movements. Gymnastics activities may use either heavy or light equipment and a variety of mats. Gymnastics

Some men's events

Dave Black

The pommel horse event is performed on a piece of equipment called a *horse*. The gymnast uses his hands to support his weight and performs various leg movements without stopping.

Dave Black

The rings is an event held on two rings suspended from cables. The gymnast tries to keep the rings motionless while he executes a number of maneuvers with his body.

Dave Black

The parallel bars event takes place on two long bars. While supporting himself with his hands, the gymnast carries out acrobatic movements that require great strength.

can also be a recreational or educational activity.

Two or more teams compete in a gymnastics meet, which takes place in a gymnasium. Judges watch each gymnast's performance, called a *routine,* and decide what score he or she has earned. Gymnasts must develop balance, endurance, flexibility, and strength. A serious gymnast will devote many hours to practice.

Friedrich Jahn, a German schoolteacher, built the first modern gymnastics equipment in the early 1800's. Gymnastics has been a part of the Olympic Games since the modern Olympics began in 1896. Worldwide television coverage of the Olympics has helped gymnastics grow remarkably as a spectator sport.

Men's events

A men's gymnastics meet consists of six events that are held in a set order. These events, in order of performance, are the (1) floor exercise, (2) pommel horse, (3) rings, (4) horse vault, (5) parallel bars, and (6) horizontal bar. Men who compete in all six events are called *all-around gymnasts.* Those who enter fewer than six events are called *specialists.*

The floor exercise is performed on a mat that measures about 40 feet (12 meters) square. The gymnast performs a continuous series of movements that require balance, flexibility, and strength. These movements include handsprings, leaps, somersaults in the air, and tumbling. The floor exercise must be completed in not less than 50 seconds and not more than 70 seconds.

The pommel horse, or *side horse,* is named for the padded piece of equipment on which this event is held. The horse measures about 5 feet 4 inches (1.63 meters) long and about 14 inches (36 centimeters) wide. It has two handles on top called *pommels* which are about 4 feet 2 inches (1.27 meters) from the floor. The gymnast uses the pommels to support his weight entirely with his hands. He swings his legs in circles around the sides and top of the horse without stopping. He also performs a movement called the *scissors,* beginning with one leg on each side of the horse. He switches the positions of his legs as he swings them from side to side. He must frequently support himself with only one hand while raising the other hand to swing his legs past.

The rings. This event is performed on two rings suspended from cables about 8 feet 4 inches (2.54 meters) above the floor. The gymnast leaps up and grasps the rings and then tries to keep them motionless while performing various movements. These include handstands and complete circular swings. The athlete supports his body in various *strength positions,* which require exceptional power. In a movement called the *cross,* for example, he supports himself in an upright position with his arms extended sideways. The event also includes *holding positions,* which require him to remain motionless for three seconds.

The horse vault is performed on a piece of equipment that resembles the pommel horse but has no pommels. In this event, the gymnast vaults across the length of the horse. He approaches the horse at a run and jumps up and forward from a low springboard. He places one or both hands on the horse for support as he goes over. He may twist around in the air, do a somersault, or perform any one of several movements. In some competitions, the gymnast vaults twice and his final score comes from an average of his two vaults. In other competitions, the gymnast vaults once.

The parallel bars. In this event, the gymnast performs on two long bars about 5 feet 5 inches (1.65 meters) high and slightly more than shoulder width apart. He supports himself on the bars with his hands while performing handstands, swings, twists, and other acrobatic movements. The gymnast may perform several *holding positions* on the parallel bars. In each one, he must remain motionless for one or two seconds. In addition, he performs various *strength movements* that require great arm power and must be done slowly.

The horizontal bar event takes place on a somewhat flexible bar fastened about 8 feet 4 inches (2.54 meters) above the floor between two supports. The gymnast holds the bar with one or both hands and swings around it repeatedly. He performs several acrobatic movements without coming to a full stop. During this routine, he must reverse his position, which involves a change of grip on the bar. He also must perform maneuvers that require him to release his grip and regain it again while in the air. Many gymnasts finish this event with a spectacular *dismount* from the bar. They swing rapidly around the bar, let go, and twist or somersault in the air before landing on their feet.

All-around competition for men consists of all six events. In college and international meets, an all-around competitor must perform a *compulsory routine* in each event. This routine involves a set sequence of movements. The compulsory routine will be dropped from international competition after the 1996 Olympic Games. The gymnast then performs an *optional* routine in each of the six events, doing whatever movements he chooses.

Women's events

A women's gymnastics meet has four events. In order of performance, they are (1) vault, (2) uneven parallel bars, (3) balance beam, and (4) floor exercise. Most women gymnasts enter all these events.

The vault is performed on the same equipment used in men's vaulting. But women gymnasts vault across the horse's width rather than its length. The gymnast vaults twice. Depending on the rules being used, the score is the average of the two vaults or the higher scorer.

The uneven parallel bars. In this event, gymnasts compete on two parallel bars. The upper bar is 7 feet 9 inches (2.36 meters) high and the lower bar's height is 5 feet 2 inches (1.57 meters). The athlete swings around one bar at a time, performing maneuvers that require great flexibility and agility. She switches rapidly back and forth from one bar to another, trying to keep in constant motion.

The balance beam involves a long beam 4 inches (10 centimeters) wide. Competitors perform jumps, leaps, running steps, and turns on it and try to use its full length. The best performers also do back handsprings and somersaults. The routine must last from 70 to 90 seconds.

The floor exercise is performed on a mat that resembles the one used in the men's floor exercise. Women gymnasts perform this event with a musical accompaniment. Each contestant designs her routine to match the tempo and mood of the music she has se-

Some women's events

Dave Black

The vault consists of leaping across the width of the horse. After a running start, the gymnast jumps from a springboard, bracing her hands on the horse as she goes over.

Dave Black

The uneven parallel bars event is performed on two bars. The competitor swings back and forth from bar to bar and executes difficult maneuvers while in constant motion.

Dave Black

The balance beam is performed on a long beam. The gymnast tries to use the full length of the beam while she performs acrobatic movements, jumps, leaps, running steps, and turns.

lected. The contestant must take from 70 to 90 seconds to demonstrate her skill in acrobatics, dancing, and tumbling.

All-around competition for women includes all four events. In national and international meets, every competitor performs a compulsory routine in each event and then an optional routine in each.

Rhythmic gymnastics is a separate type of gymnastic competition. Rhythmic gymnastics involves body movements and dance combined with the handling of small equipment—a rope, a hoop, a ball, clubs, and a long ribbon. The exercise is performed to music on a mat similar to the one used in floor exercise competition. Routines must cover the entire mat and include jumps, leaps, balances, and flexibility movements.

There are two categories of competition, individual and group. The group event involves five gymnasts who perform simultaneously. The group exercise requires a minimum number of formations and exchanges of equipment. Individual routines must last from 60 to 90 seconds. Group routines must last from 2 minutes to 2 minutes 30 seconds.

Gymnastics competition

Judging. At major competitions, four to six judges sit at each piece of equipment. Each judge arrives at a score independently. The high and low scores are dropped. The average of the remaining scores becomes the participant's final score. A judges' conference is called when the scores fail to fall within a range set by the rules. The gymnast's all-around score is compiled by adding each event's score together. The highest total determines the all-around winner of the competition.

Women start with a score of 9.40 and men start with 9.00. Judges make deductions for flaws in execution and for any missing requirements in the composition of the exercise. A judge may award a bonus of up to 0.6 for women and 1.0 for men. A perfect score is 10.

Gymnastics skills are divided into five levels of difficulty. The skills range from "A" as the easiest to "E" as the most difficult. Each routine must have a minimum number of elements from the levels, depending on the competition.

There are two panels of judges for each rhythmic gymnastics routine. One panel judges the composition and the other judges the execution. The basic score is 9.60. For exceptional performances, judges may award a bonus score of up to 0.40 points for seniors and 0.20 points for juniors. Senior competitors can receive a maximum score of 10.00 and juniors a maximum of 9.80. The base score of a group exercise is 19.20 and the maximum, including the bonus, is 20.00.

Organization. USA Gymnastics governs gymnastics in the United States. This organization is a member of the International Gymnastics Federation. The federation governs international gymnastics. In the United States, many states hold a championship competition for high school athletes. The National Collegiate Athletic Association (NCAA) has both men's and women's championships.

USA Gymnastics conducts programs for men and women that determine the members of United States teams for international competition. Such competition includes the Olympic Games, the Pan American Games, the World Games, and the World University Games.

Critically reviewed by USA Gymnastics

See also **Olympic Games** (table; pictures); **Comaneci, Nadia.**

Additional resources

Goodbody, John. *The Illustrated History of Gymnastics.* Beaufort Bks., 1983.
Gutman, Dan. *Gymnastics.* Viking, 1996. Younger readers.
Jensen, Julie. *Beginning Gymnastics.* Lerner, 1995. Younger readers.
O'Quinn, Garland Jr. *Teaching Developmental Gymnastics: Skills to Take Through Life.* Univ. of Tex. Pr., 1990.

Gymnosperm, *JIHM nuh spurm,* is the name of one of two large groups of seed plants. The plants have naked, or uncovered, seeds. The term *gymnosperm* comes from two Greek words meaning *naked* and *seed.* The other group, called the *angiosperms,* consists of plants whose seeds have a protective *ovary* (seed case).

Gymnosperms are woody perennials, which are among the largest and oldest living plants. There are about 800 species of gymnosperms. About 600 are conifers such as the pines, firs, spruces, and balsams.

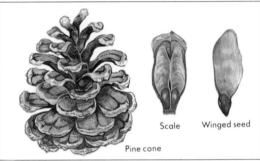

Scale   Winged seed

Pine cone

WORLD BOOK illustration by Lorraine Epstein

A gymnosperm is a plant that has exposed seeds. The pine tree, which bears seeds upon cone scales, is a gymnosperm.

These cone-bearing trees make up the largest *division* (group) of gymnosperms. The tropical and subtropical *cycads,* also gymnosperms, are among the most primitive living seed plants (see **Cycad**). The *ginkgo,* also called the *maidenhair tree,* is another primitive gymnosperm (see **Ginkgo**).

Many of the gymnosperms are evergreen with a wide variety in the structure of the leaves. They do not bear flowers. Tiny male cones produce the pollen, which is usually spread by the wind. The naked, or exposed, seeds are borne between the scales of the female cones and drop when they become ripe. Gymnosperms provide the source of many valuable products such as tar, turpentine, rosin, and timber.   Bruce H. Tiffney

Scientific classification. Gymnosperms belong to the divisions Coniferophyta, Cycadophyta, Ginkgophyta, and Gnetophyta.

See also **Angiosperm; Conifer; Seed.**

Gynecology. See Obstetrics and gynecology.

Györ, *juhr* (pop. 130,941), is a major commercial and industrial city in northwestern Hungary. It lies where the Rába River and a branch of the Danube River meet. For location, see **Hungary** (political map).

Györ serves as a commercial center for the surrounding region, which is linked to the city by railroads and highways. The city's chief manufactured products are machines and textiles. Györ has a cathedral that dates from the 1100's and several houses built in the baroque style of architecture. Roman soldiers established a camp on the site of what is now Györ in about A.D. 50. During the Middle Ages, the community gained importance because of its strategic location on the route between Vienna, Austria, and what is now Budapest, Hungary. It became a commercial, intellectual, and religious center for western Hungary. Györ's industrial development began during the mid-1800's and has been especially rapid since World War II ended in 1945.   Vojtech Mastny

Gypsies, also spelled *Gipsies,* are a group of wandering people whose ancestors originally lived in India. Today, Gypsies live in almost every part of the world. Some have settled down, but many are still nomads.

No one knows how many Gypsies there are, because they are organized into small groups and usually avoid contact with official census agencies. Estimates of the Gypsy population throughout the world range from 1 million to more than 6 million. The largest numbers of Gypsies live in eastern Europe. There are many groups of Gypsies, including the *Calé* of Spain, the *Manouches* of France, and the *Sinte* of Germany. The best-known Gypsy groups in the United States belong to the *Rom* tribes. The Rom are the largest group of Gypsies and live in nearly every part of the world.

Culture. A Rom family consists of a husband and wife, their unmarried children, their married sons, and the sons' wives and children. In many cases, a group of related families forms a band that lives together and cooperates in economic matters. The highest authority is the *kris,* a system of rules of conduct based on Rom religious and philosophical beliefs.

Most Gypsies speak the language of the people among whom they live. However, many also speak their own native language, often called *Romany,* which belongs to the Indo-Iranian group of languages. Romany varies from place to place.

Gypsies have long been noted as musicians and dancers. They have borrowed from and added to the music and dance of other peoples. Large numbers of Gypsies

follow traditional Gypsy occupations, such as fortune-telling, metalworking, horse trading, and animal doctoring. However, many have other vocations.

History. The Gypsies left India about A.D. 1000 and began to wander westward through the Middle East. They first arrived in western Europe during the early 1400's, claiming to have come from a country called *Little Egypt.* The word *Gypsy* is a shortened form of *Egyptian.*

The Europeans welcomed the Gypsies at first. But they soon turned against the Gypsies as the newcomers wandered through Europe, telling fortunes and begging. The Gypsies stayed in Europe despite growing prejudice against them. After Europeans began to colonize the Americas, some Gypsies settled there.

During World War II (1939-1945), the Nazis murdered thousands of European Gypsies. Today, more and more Gypsies are settling down, but they preserve their unique culture.   Vojtech Mastny

See also **Cave dwellers; Flamenco.**

Gypsum, *JIHP suhm* (chemical formula, $CaSO_4 \cdot 2H_2O$), is a white to yellowish-white mineral used to make plaster of Paris. Large beds of gypsum formed when sea water evaporated, leaving dissolved calcium and sulfate to form deposits of gypsum. Gypsum is so soft that it can be scratched with the fingernail. Sometimes it forms transparent crystals called *selenite* or fibrous crystals called *satin spar.*

The chemical formula of gypsum shows that it is a *hydrate* of calcium sulfate. A hydrate contains water. When gypsum is heated, it loses three-fourths of its water. This process, called *calcination,* changes the gypsum to the fine white powder called *plaster of Paris.* The plaster hardens after it is mixed with water and exposed to the air. Plaster of Paris is used to make all types of casts.

Heating gypsum at high temperatures will drive off all the water. Calcined gypsum in this form is used in the building industry for base-coat plaster, plasterboard, lath, and wallboard. It is also used as a filler in such products as candy and paint.

Ground gypsum (*land plaster*) is sometimes used as a fertilizer for soils that need calcium. It is not used much today, because ground limestone and prepared fertiliz-

Filip Horvat, Picture Group

A gypsy wedding dance is performed by friends and relatives following a wedding ceremony. Gypsies are well known for their musical skills, and many of them become professional singers and dancers.

ers contain more calcium. Raw gypsum is used to keep portland cement from hardening too quickly. It is also used to make paint, filters, insulation, and wall plaster.

Most of the "hard" water that is found in springs and wells contains dissolved gypsum. When the water is boiled or evaporated, some of the gypsum forms a white crust.

Gypsum is found throughout the world. The United States produces and uses more gypsum than any other country. The leading gypsum-producing states are California, Iowa, New York, Texas, and Oklahoma. Canada, France, Japan, and Iran are the leading sources outside the United States. The name *plaster of Paris* comes from gypsum deposits in the Paris Basin, France. Large sand dunes composed of gypsum are found in New Mexico and Arizona. The sand dunes at White Sands National Monument, near Alamogordo, N. Mex., are composed of gypsum.   Kenneth J. De Nault

See also **Alabaster; Hardness; Mineral** (picture); **Plaster of Paris; White Sands National Monument.**

Gypsy moth is an insect that is destructive to forest, shade, and fruit trees. Gypsy moth caterpillars eat the leaves of both broadleaf and needleleaf trees. During large outbreaks, the caterpillars can completely strip a tree of its leaves. A single stripping can kill a needleleaf tree, and a broadleaf tree may die after being stripped of leaves over a period of several consecutive years. Gypsy moth caterpillars are particularly destructive to oak trees.

About 1869, gypsy moths from France were accidentally introduced into the forests of Massachusetts. Since then, these European gypsy moths have spread as far north as southern Canada, as far south as North Carolina, and westward into Ohio and Michigan. They have been found as far west as California and Oregon.

The caterpillars of European gypsy moths hatch in spring. They are brown to black with tufts of hairs. Older caterpillars have five pairs of blue spots and six pairs of red spots on their backs. The caterpillars reach their full size of $1\frac{1}{2}$ to $2\frac{1}{2}$ inches (3.8 to 6.4 centimeters) by midsummer. They then enter the *pupal stage.* After 10 to 17 days in a hard, brown pupal shell, the insects emerge as adult moths. The brownish male moths are strong fliers. The much-larger, cream-white females cannot fly. The moths do not feed. After mating, the females lay amber-colored clusters of fewer than 100 to more than 1,000 eggs. The moths die soon after mating.

In 1991, gypsy moths from Asia were mistakenly introduced into Oregon, Washington, and British Columbia. They also were brought into North Carolina in 1993. Asian gypsy moths are similar in appearance to European moths. But unlike the female European gypsy moth, the female Asian gypsy moth can fly. It may lay eggs more than 20 miles (32 kilometers) from where it lived as a caterpillar.

Natural enemies of gypsy moths include predatory and parasitic insects, disease-causing microbes, fungi, and insect-eating birds and mammals. To help control the moths in North America, scientists have introduced various predatory and parasitic insects from Europe and Asia. A fungus native to Japan has helped control gypsy moth caterpillars in parts of the Northeast. This fungus, called *Entomophaga maimaiga,* feeds on the tissues of the caterpillar.

Gypsy moths can be destroyed by coating the egg clusters with a pesticide or by collecting and sealing the eggs in cans. Caterpillars can be collected by banding tree trunks with coarse cloth or with a sticky substance called *tanglefoot.* Spraying trees with insecticides in the spring kills gypsy moths, but it can harm the environment. Gypsy moths can also be killed by spraying trees with *Bacillus thuringiensis,* which is a naturally occurring bacterium.

Scientific classification. Gypsy moths belong to the family Lymantriidae. Their scientific name is *Lymantria dispar.*

John F. Anderson

See also **Tussock moth.**

Gyrocompass is a mechanical device that determines direction. It is used in navigating all major commercial and naval ships, and some aircraft and land vehicles. A gyrocompass is more accurate than a magnetic compass, which relies on the earth's magnetic field to indicate *magnetic north.* A gyrocompass points to *true north,* or *geographic north.* It is not affected by magnetic forces or by the rolling and pitching of the vehicle.

An instrument called a *gyroscope* enables a gyrocompass to indicate direction. A gyroscope consists of a *rotor* (wheel) that is mounted on movable frames. When the rotor spins at high speed, the axle on which it turns continues to point to the same direction, regardless of how the frames are moved. The axle is called the *spin axis.* In a gyrocompass, the spin axis is automatically positioned parallel to the earth's axis. The rotor is powered by an electric motor and enclosed in a case that hangs like a pendulum. The information about the direction

WORLD BOOK illustration by John F. Eggert

The gypsy moth is a destructive forest pest. During its caterpillar stage, *above,* the insect eats tree leaves. The adult female moth, *below,* and the adult male moth do not feed.

WORLD BOOK illustration by Oxford Illustrators Limited

appears on an indicator on the gyrocompass.

A gyroscope turns over slowly as the earth rotates. This turning, called *precession,* can cause the spin axis to change direction. To offset errors caused by precession, a gyrocompass has an intricate system of weights and balances. Changes in the latitude or speed of a vehicle also can affect the spin axis, and so the gyrocompass must be adjusted as such changes occur.

A gyrocompass must be protected from vibrations and jolts. Some units float in a container filled with oil to cushion them. On most ships, the gyrocompass is mounted in a compartment below deck. Compass information is transmitted from the gyrocompass to the bridge and equipment. For example, the information may be transmitted to devices that aim guns and guide missiles on warships.

The gyrocompass was invented in 1908 by Hermann Anschütz-Kämpfe, a German engineer. Elmer A. Sperry, an American inventor, also developed a gyrocompass, which was demonstrated successfully in 1911 on the United States battleship *Delaware.*   Richard R. Hobbs

See also **Gyroscope; Sperry, Elmer A.**

Gyropilot. See Automatic pilot.

Gyroscope, *JY ruh skohp,* also called a *gyro,* is a device that uses rotation to produce a stable direction in space. A basic gyroscope consists of a spinning wheel or ball, called the *rotor,* and a support system. Once the rotor is set in motion, the gyroscope resists any attempt to change its direction of rotation. Because of this property, gyroscopes are widely used in flight and navigation instruments. For example, a gyroscope is used to provide heading or course information that is unaffected by air turbulence or heavy seas.

Another gyroscopic instrument, the *turn and slip indicator* or *turn-and-bank indicator,* helps pilots maintain the desired course of their aircraft. Automatic pilots using gyros can steer a ship or plane closer to a course than a human pilot can. Gyroscopic devices are also

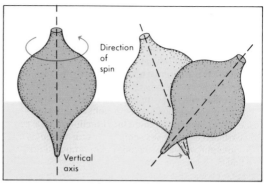

WORLD BOOK illustration by J. Harlan Hunt

Gyroscopic inertia is the tendency of a spinning body to resist change in the direction of its axis. Inertia keeps the axis of a spinning top, *above,* straight up until the top slows.

necessary for guiding torpedoes, missiles, satellites, and space vehicles.

Gyroscopic properties

Gyroscopes are useful for detecting changes in direction because of the properties of spinning bodies. All spinning bodies demonstrate (1) gyroscopic inertia and (2) precession.

Gyroscopic inertia is the tendency of a spinning body to resist any attempt to change the direction of its *axis of rotation.* For example, the earth spins around its axis, an imaginary line that connects the North and South poles. Because of gyroscopic inertia, the north axis of the earth continues to point to the North Star as the earth moves in its orbit around the sun.

Gyroscopic inertia enables the axis of a spinning gyroscope always to point in the same direction, no matter how the support of the gyroscope moves about. The *magnitude* (strength) of the inertia depends on the distribution of the weight of the rotor and the speed of its spin. Gyroscopes with most of their weight at the rotor's rim have the greatest amount of inertia. Thus, a bicycle wheel makes a good gyroscope, but a pencil spinning on its point does not. In addition, the faster the rotor spins, the more gyroscopic inertia it possesses.

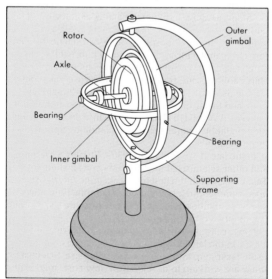

WORLD BOOK illustration by J. Harlan Hunt

A two-degree-of-freedom gyroscope has its rotor and axle mounted on two pivoting rings, called *gimbals,* that enable the axle to maintain its direction when the gyro's support moves.

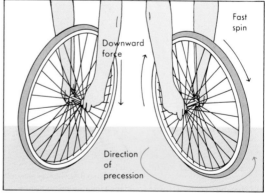

WORLD BOOK illustration by J. Harlan Hunt

Precession is the tendency of a spinning body to move at right angles to the direction of an applied force. A bicycle wheel precesses when a force is exerted on one side of its axle, *above.*

Precession is the tendency of a spinning body to move at right angles to the direction of any force that tries to change its direction of rotation. You can use precession to guide a rolling hoop. When you roll the hoop, it will not fall down if you push from the side against the top. In this case, the hoop merely turns a corner. The hoop *precesses,* or turns at right angles to the force that you have applied against it. Similarly, a spinning gyroscope will move at right angles to any force that attempts to change the direction of its axis. The earth itself precesses slightly. This turn occurs because the pull of gravity by the sun and moon tends to tip it over.

Kinds of gyroscopes

Mechanical gyroscopes commonly consist of a rotor and axle supported by a fixed frame and base. In a *single-degree-of-freedom gyroscope,* the rotor and axle are mounted on a ring, called a *gimbal,* that pivots inside the gyroscope's frame. The gyro can then rotate freely around an imaginary line running perpendicular to the rotor's axle. To allow the gyroscope to rotate in a second direction, the gimbal can be mounted on bearings inside another gimbal. A frame and base support both gimbals, and the gyroscope's axle is then free to point in the same direction no matter how the frame is held. Gyroscopes with two gimbals are called *two-degree-of-freedom gyros.*

Gyroscope rotors are driven by an electric motor or high-speed jets of air. Rotors used in aircraft instruments may be smaller than 2 inches (5 centimeters) across and rotate 30,000 times a minute. On the other hand, three gyroscope rotors, each 13 feet (4 meters) across, were built in 1933 for the gyrostabilizers in the ocean liner *Conte Di Savoia.* Each weighed 110 short tons (100 metric tons) and rotated 800 times a minute.

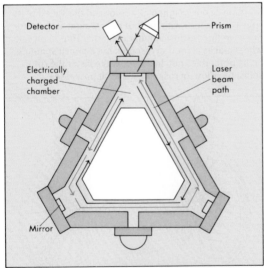

Detector — Prism

Electrically charged chamber

Laser beam path

Mirror

WORLD BOOK illustration by J. Harlan Hunt

A laser gyroscope provides guidance without using a spinning rotor. Two laser beams travel in opposite directions around a path in the gyro. When the gyro tilts due to a change in direction, a detector records the resulting change in the beams' relationship.

The bearings on which a gyroscope rotates must be made with great accuracy, so that they will have as little friction as possible. Friction causes the rotor's axis to drift away from the proper direction. The best mechanical gyroscopes use ball bearings that are almost perfectly smooth and round. These gyroscopes are assembled in special windowless *clean rooms* because even a speck of dust can affect a gyroscope's performance. Rotors can also be cushioned to minimize friction by floating the rotor in liquid or supporting the bearings with a thin layer of pressurized gas.

Electrically suspended gyroscopes are among the most accurate gyroscopes made. The rotor in these gyroscopes is a light ball of the metal beryllium. The ball is suspended in a vacuum by electric forces and then sent spinning by magnetic forces.

Laser gyroscopes provide directional information without using a spinning rotor. In a laser gyroscope, two laser beams are sent in opposite directions around a triangular or rectangular path known as a *ring.* Initially, the light waves of the lasers are all in step with one another. However, if the gyro is tilted—as when an airplane turns—one of the beams will have to travel farther than the other to complete the ring. The beams will thus be out of step after traveling around the path. Computers then analyze how much the beams are out of step and compute the plane's change in direction.

History

The first gyroscope that resembled modern mechanical gyroscopes was made by G. C. Bohnenberger, a German inventor, in 1810. In 1852, Jean Foucault, a French physicist, built a gyroscope to demonstrate that the earth rotates on its axis. Foucault named the instrument from two Greek words—*gyros,* meaning *circle* or *ring,* and *skopein,* meaning *to view*—because the gyroscope had enabled him to view the revolution of the earth.

The first gyroscopically controlled torpedoes were developed during the 1890's. The gyrocompass was invented in 1908 by Hermann Anschütz-Kämpfe, a German engineer.

In 1911, Elmer A. Sperry, an American scientist, inventor, and manufacturer, developed an improved gyrocompass for ships. Sperry also produced gyroscopic ship stabilizers and some of the first gyroscopic flight instruments. The rate-of-turn indicator, the directional gyro, and the artificial horizon were used in aircraft during World War II (1939-1945). These instruments permitted safe flight at night and precise landing approaches through clouds.

In the late 1940's and early 1950's, Charles S. Draper and other scientists at the Massachusetts Institute of Technology built the first highly accurate *inertial guidance systems.* Such systems use a combination of gyroscopes and other guidance devices to keep a vehicle on its course (see **Inertial guidance**).

Electrically suspended gyroscopes date from the 1950's. In the late 1970's, an inertial guidance system using laser gyros was chosen for airline use. Scientists today are working to develop new, low-cost, solid-state laser gyros that send light through special transparent *optical fibers.*   W. N. Hubin

See also **Automatic pilot; Foucault, Jean B. L.; Sperry, Elmer A.**